U0864208

国家重点基础研究发展计划项目(973)资助

Disaster Information Catalog of Global Earthquakes

全球地震灾害信息目录

9999B. C. ～ 2010A. D.

宋治平　张国民　刘　杰　尹继尧　薛　艳　宋先月　编著

地震出版社

图书在版编目(CIP)数据

全球地震灾害信息目录/宋治平等编著．—北京：地震出版社，2011.9

ISBN 978-7-5028-3925-3

Ⅰ．①全… Ⅱ．①宋… Ⅲ．①地震灾害—资料—世界—专题目录 Ⅳ．①Z88：P316.1

中国版本图书馆 CIP 数据核字(2011)第 191153 号

地震版 XM2108

全球地震灾害信息目录

宋治平 张国民 刘 杰 尹继尧 薛 艳 宋先月 编著

责任编辑：王 伟

责任校对：庞亚萍

出版发行：地 震 出 版 社

北京民族学院南路 9 号 邮编：100081

发行部：68423031 68467993 传真：88421706

门市部：68467991 传真：68467991

总编室：68462709 68423029 传真：68455221

专业部：68467982 68721991

网址：http://www.dzpress.com.cn

经销：全国各地新华书店

印刷：北京鑫丰华彩印有限公司

版（印）次：2011 年 9 月第一版 2011 年 9 月第一次印刷

开本：880×1230 1/16

字数：1579 千字

印张：32.5

书号：ISBN 978-7-5028-3925-3/p（4597）

定价：120.00 元

版权所有 翻印必究

（图书出现印装问题，本社负责调换）

序

在自然界的各种灾害中，地震是对人类生存安全危害最大的灾种，根据20世纪全球资料统计，地震所造成的人员死亡占了所有自然灾害人员死亡总数的一半以上。我国是全球地震灾害最为严重的国家之一，1976年的唐山大地震是20世纪最大的地震劫难。进入新世纪以来，地震灾害肆虐。2001年1月26日印度古吉拉特邦地震2万余人死亡；2003年12月26日伊朗巴姆地震4万多人死亡；2004年12月26日12月26日印尼苏门答腊大地震大海啸，夺去了20多万人的生命；2005年10月8日南亚巴基斯坦地震，死亡人数近9万；2008年5月12日我国汶川大地震，死亡和失踪人数超过8万；2010年1月12日海地太子港地震20多万人遇难。今年3月11日的日本大地震大海啸造成近3万人死亡与失踪。地震不仅对人类生存安全造成巨大灾害，而且对人类文明的进步和经济社会的发展构成严重的威胁，2011年日本9.0级大地震大海啸造成核电站核泄漏使国际社会震惊。

地震灾害关系社会安全，因而对地震灾害的研究已成为自然灾害研究中的热点之一。就是在这一大背景下，结合国家重点基础研究（973）计划项目“汶川地震发生机理及其大区动力学环境研究”中第四课题的第五专题关于全球地震构造格局和地震活动性研究的需要，在前人研究的基础上，编辑了《全球地震灾害信息目录（9999B. C. ~2010A. D.)》。在编辑本书工作中所用前人关于全球地震灾害信息资料主要包括：1992年Paula等收集出版的《全球重大灾害性地震目录（2150B. C. ~1991A. D.)》，该书于1995年由罗伟等译成中文并由地震出版社出版。在Paula等的工作之后，美国地质调查局（USGS）的国家地震信息中心（NEIC）自1992年起延续编制全球重大灾害性地震目录，并发布在USGS网站。包括Paula等汇编的资料，USGS收集了自公元前2150年至公元2011年6月全球重大灾害性地震信息共5700多条，地震信息包括时间、地点、震级、震源深度、烈度、死亡人数（或死亡级别）、经济损失数目（或经济损失级别）、受伤人数（或受伤级别）、房屋毁坏数目（或房屋毁坏级别）、房屋受损数目（或房屋受损级别）以及海啸等信息。

在Paula等人和USGS工作的基础上，本书着重做了两方面工作，一是进一步扩展灾害性地震信息资料，汇集了相关项目（如GSHAP项目等）以及日本、中国、意大利、美国、菲律宾、朝鲜和韩国等相关研究的资料，将地震灾害信息目录尽可能往前追溯，使地震灾害信息由USGS网站（含Paula等的资料）5700多条拓展到13000多条。二是增加相关条目中的地震信息，重点是确定和补充震级参数。在USGS网站的5700多条地震信息中，震级参数的缺失占有相当的比例，在公元前2150年至公元1899年的地震信息中，无震级参数的地震事件占69.2%，在公元1900~2009年的地震信息中，无震级参数的占14.4%。因此，确定无震级地震事件的震级参数是本书研究工作的重点。专题组在研究中建立了地震灾害信息的优势震级概念，根据地震发生的不同构造区域和自然区域、不同年代、不同灾害类型、不同震源深度等因素，通过分类统计研究，建立了在不同条件下的地震灾害信息的优势震级参数并给出震级误差范围。在此基础上，确定了无震级地震事件的震级参数4400多条。

全书主要包括三部分。第一部分是全球地震灾害信息目录，即公元前9999年至公元2011年6月的地震灾害信息目录。第二部分是全球巨大地震灾害信息目录，即全球地震灾害中死亡人数超过一万人或经济损失超过$ 100 million（即1亿美元）的灾害信息目录，是从第一部分中提取的缩影本，可称之为地震巨灾目录。第三部分是全球无震级地震事件的震级确定方法与灾害信息目录修订。

需要说明的是本书所汇编的全球地震灾害信息目录，对于不同时期、不同国家和地区、乃至同一地区的不同人文期，其资料的完整性、可靠性和灾害参数的准确程度等方面差异都相当大。就国家与地区而言，中国、日本、美国、俄罗斯和欧洲的地中海地区，地震灾害的研究程度较高，其灾害信息资料的完整性和可靠性亦相对较高。就时代而言，总体上，公元1900年以来的近代地震灾害信息资料基本完整和可靠。1900年以前，由于历史记录的局限性，越往前震灾信息资料的完整性越差，其可靠程度亦越低。公元前2000年（或公元前3000年）之前的地震事件，往往是由地震考古（即古地震）方法获取的，因而所给的信息参数的不确定性很大，希望读者在使用时充分注意这一点。

然而本书作为地震灾害研究的基础资料，仍不失为一个迄今在地震灾害信息方面内容丰富、资料齐全、编辑系统的好材料，希望其在防震减灾研究工作中发挥应有的作用。

马宗晋

2011年8月

Preface

Among various kinds of natural disasters, the disaster of earthquakes is the one that threatens the safety of human existence the most. Global statistics in the twentieth century show that the number of deaths caused by earthquakes accounted for more than half of the total number of deaths caused by all natural disasters. China is one of the countries with the most serious earthquake disasters in the world; the 1976 Tangshan earthquake was the largest earthquake catastrophe in the twentieth century. Since the beginning of the new century (21st century), earthquake disasters have caused terrible havoc. The Gujarat, India, earthquake on January 26,2001 caused more than 20,000 deaths; the Bam, Iran, earthquake on December 26,2003 killed more than 40,000 people; the Sumatra, Indonesia, earthquake - tsunami on December 26,2004 killed more than 200 thousand people; in the Pakistan, South Asia, earthquake on October 8,2005, the death toll amounted to nearly 90,000; in the Wenchuan, China, earthquake on May 12,2008, the number of killed and missing people was more than 80,000; and the Port - Au - Prince, Haiti, earthquake on January 12,2010 killed more than 200 thousand people. In this year, the Japan great earthquake and great tsunami on March 11 made nearly 30,000 people dead or missing. Earthquakes not only cause severe catastrophe for the safety of human existence, but also make serious threat against the progress of human civilization and the development of economical society. The nuclear leakage caused by the Japan M9. 0 great earthquake and great tsunami in 2011 shocked the international community.

The earthquake disaster is related to social safety; hence the study on earthquake disaster has become one of the hot topics in natural disasters research. Just against such a grand background, the *Disaster Information Catalog of Global Earthquakes* (*9999 B. C. – 2010 A. D.*) was compiled on the basis of previous studies; the purpose is to meet the need of the research on the global seismotectonic pattern and seismic activity, which is the fifth special subject of the fourth project in the National Key Basic Research (973) Program of China, "Research on the Genetic Mechanism of the Wenchuan Earthquake and Its Regional Dynamic Environment". The global earthquake information and materials of predecessors used in compiling this book mainly come from *Catalog of Significant Earthquakes* 2150 *B. C.* – 1991 *A. D.* compiled by Paula K. Dunbar, Patricia A. Lockridge, and Lowell S. Whiteside (Dept. of Commerce, National Oceanic and Atmospheric Administration, September 1992), which was translated into Chinese by Luo Wei et al. and published by Seismological Press, Beijing, in 1996. After the work of Paula et al., the National Earthquake Information Center (NEIC) of the United States Geological Survey (USGS) have compiled the catalog of global major disastrous earthquakes and released it on the USGS Website since 1992. With the information compiled by Paula et al. included, the USGS collected a total of more than 5, 700 pieces of information of major disastrous earthquakes in the world with in the time span from 2150 B. C. to June 2011 A. D.; the contents include the time, location, magnitude, focal depth and intensity of earthquake, number of deaths (or mortality level), amount of economic loss (or economic loss level), number of injuries (or injury level), number of destroyed houses (or the level of house destruction), number of damaged houses (or house damage level), tsunami, and other information.

Based on the work of Paula et al. and USGS, this book was focused on two aspects. First, the earthquake disaster information was further extended. For this purpose, the materials of relevant projects (such as GSHAP project and so on) and related studies in Japan, China, Italy, USA, Philippines, North and South Korea and so on were collected so as to trace back the earthquake disaster information catalog as far as possible. As a result, the information was extended from more than 5,700 pieces released by the USGS earthquake website (including the data from Paula et al.) to more than 13,000 pieces. The second was to increase the earthquake information in relevant items; the focus was to determine and add the magnitude parameters. In the 5,700 pieces of earthquake information from the USGS Website, events with their magnitude parameters lacking were of a considerable proportion. In the earthquake information from 2150 B. C. to 1899 A. D., 69.2% of the earthquake events did not have magnitude parameters; in the earthquakes information from 1900 A. D. to 2009 A. D., 14.4% of the events did not have magnitude parameters. Therefore, to determine the magnitude parameter of seismic events without magnitude information was the focus of research in the book. In the study of the research group, the concept of predominating magnitude of earthquake disaster information was put forward; with reference to the differences in structural and natural area, in time, in disaster type, in focal depth, and in other factors, sorted statistical studies were made; the predominating magnitude parameters for earthquake disaster information under different conditions were established; and their error range of magnitude was given. Based on the above, the magnitude parameters of more than 4,400 earthquake events with their magnitudes missing were determined.

The book includes three parts. The first part is the global earthquake disaster information catalog, that is, the disaster information catalog of earthquakes in the time span from 9999 B. C. to June 2011. The second part is the disaster information catalog of global huge earthquakes, which is the disaster information catalog of global earthquakes which caused a death toll of more than one million people or economic loss of more than 100 million US dollars. It is an abridged version of the first part and can be called the huge disaster catalog. The third part gives the method of determining the magnitude of events with the magnitude lacking and the revision of involved earthquake disaster information catalog.

What should be indicated is that the completeness and reliability of materials, the precision of disaster parameters, and so on, of the global earthquake disaster information catalog compiled in this book bear relatively large differences; they are quite different in different periods, different countries and regions, as well as in different cultural periods of the same area. In regard to the countries and regions, the level of earthquake disaster research is somewhat higher in China, Japan, the United States, Russia and Europe's Mediterranean region; and the completeness and reliability of disaster information data there are relatively higher too.

In general, when the time of earthquake occurrence is concerned, the information of earthquakes after 1900 A. D. is complete and reliable in essence. Before 1900 A. D., the earlier the earthquake is, the worse the completeness and the lower the reliability of earthquake information would be, due to the limitations of historical records. The seismic events before 2000 B. C. (or 3000 B. C.) are often disclosed by seismic archaeology (i. e., ancient earthquakes) method; therefore, the uncertainty of information parameters so obtained is quite large. It is hoped that the readers pay full attention to this when they use the book.

However, as the basic material for earthquake disaster research, this book is still a well compiled material source with rich contents of earthquake disaster information and complete data so far. The authors hope that the book can play its due role in the research on earthquake prevention and disaster reduction.

Zongjin Ma

Aug 2011

目 录

编辑说明

该目录包括自公元前9999年至公元2011年6月全球地震造成的灾害信息目录。这些地震事件的灾害信息是从官方网站、正式出版的书籍和文献(包括全球各国和地区地震目录以及多学科资料等)以及单个地震灾害信息报告中收集、编辑而成,并且在研究地震灾害信息与地震震级的关系基础上,利用灾害信息确定了无震级地震事件的震级。本书中给出如下参数:

1 地震参数

地震的基本参数包括发震时间、震中位置、震源深度、地震震级。由于不同时期的地震事件其参数的确定方法有很大的差别,因此其内涵(所定参数的误差与不确定性)也有很大差别。1900年后的地震事件参数主要是由地震台网测定的,其参数相对完整和准确。从1900年之前一直追溯到公元前2000~3000年间的地震事件,通常是从历史记载地震信息资料中确定的,被称为历史地震,其参数的不完整性和不确定性都较大。而公元前2000年或3000年之前的地震事件,往往是通过地震考古即通常所说的古地震方法确定其参数的,如发震时间是应用地质测年的方法确定的,其误差可达数百年,因此对于早期的地震事件,其参数具有很大的不确定性,望读者在使用时注意。

1.1 日期和时间

世界标准时间(UTC)的年、月、日、时、分、秒。

1.2 震中

纬度(°)(Latitude,北纬为正,南纬为负),经度(°)(Longitude,东经为正,西经为负)。1900年之前的地震事件没有仪器记录,因此给出的震中位置是根据遭受地震破坏情况确定的城市的经度和纬度。1900年之后的地震震中一般是通过仪器测定的震中经度和纬度。以震中经度和纬度在Google Earth上修订地震震中参考地名(中文或英文)。

1.3 震源深度(Depth)

震源深度(H)单位为公里(km)。震源深度小于70km的地震为浅源地震;震源深度在70~299km的地震为中源地震;震源深度大于等于300km的地震为深源地震。

1.4 震级(Magnitude)

在地震目录编辑和修订过程中,从多种渠道得到的同一条地震事件的震级,首先考虑Engdahl给出的震级,其次考虑各地区收集的震级的最大震级,同时给出相应的震级标度(Scale)。对于无震级地震事件的震级则由本书确定。以下为本书涉及到的震级标度。

矩震级(M_W):由标量矩(M_0)计算得到,$M_W = \frac{2}{3}\lg M_0 - 10.7$ (Hanks and Kanamori, 1979)。

面波震级(M_S):对于仪器记录地震而言,深度通常小于50km在震中距20°~160°记录到的周期18~22s的面波最大地面振幅计算而得。而对于无仪器记录的地震,震级标度为M_S的震级一般均是通过统计计算而得。

体波震级(m_b):根据震中距大于或等于5°记录到周期为0.1~3s的地震体波最大地面振幅计算而得。

宽频带体波震级(m_B):由Gutenberg和Richter(1956)定义的,根据震中距大于或等于5°记录到的周期为5~10s地震体波的最大地面振幅计算而得。

日本气象厅震级(M_j):对于仪器记录地震而言,应用最大地面位移或最大地面速度计算而得。而对于无仪器记录的地震,由日本气象厅给出的震级其标度也用M_j表示。

能量震级(M_e):根据宽频带P波能量谱密度得到的地震辐射能量(E_S)计算而得,$M_e = \frac{2}{3}\lg E_S - 2.9$(Choy and Boatwright,1995)。

地方性震级或近震震级(M_L):震中距在100~1000km范围内的地震,根据体波计算而到。

Lg波震级(M_{Lg}):应用Lg地震波(短周期面波)周期为1s的垂直分量计算而得。

持续时间震级(M_d,Duration Magnitudes):根据地震波持续时间和尾波长度计算而得。

断层面积震级(M_{fa},Felt Area Magnitudes):由断层面积计算而得,大约等效于m_b值。通常应用于无地震仪器时代发生的地震。

震源机制震级(M):利用震源机制计算而得。

未知震级(M_{uk}):计算方法不明或不能确定(Unknown)出版来源的震级。一般该震级是通过统计计算而得,该震级标度以“M_{uk}”表示,有些文献用“UK”表示。

灾害信息确定的震级(M_k):对于无震级的地震事件,我们在对有震级的地震事件灾害信息的优势震级研究基础上,利用无震级地震事件的灾害信息确定了其震级。为了表示这类无震级的地震事件的震级由本书确定(Known),因此该类地震的震级标度表示为M_k,在地震目录中“资料来源”以“Song”标注。

2　地震灾害信息

2.1　地震烈度(I)

对于发生在陆地的地震,其烈度值一般是震中烈度;如果地震发生海域,则其烈度值为距离陆地最近的最大烈度记录值,这一类烈度值并不代表震中烈度。

本书收集的地震烈度值统一为“修订的麦卡利烈度”(MMI,Modified Mercalli Intensity)(Harry等,1931;Paula等,1992;罗伟等编译,1996),该烈度表中的不同烈度值用罗马数字Ⅰ~Ⅻ表示,而本书用阿拉伯数字1~12表示。不同烈度对应的灾害简要描述如下:

Ⅰ(1):除个别情况,一般没有人感觉到。

Ⅱ(2):有少数处于休息状态,特别是在楼上的人有感,轻微的悬挂物体可能晃动。

Ⅲ(3):室内的人明显有感,特别是在楼上的人,但许多人不以为是地震,站在汽车上的人感到轻微震动,震感如同卡车过路,并持续一段时间。

Ⅳ(4):白天室内很多人有感,室外也有少数人有感,晚上则有些人被惊醒,碗碟和门窗都突然震动,墙壁嘎吱作响,犹如重型卡车驶过楼旁。站在汽车上的人明显地感到震动。

Ⅴ(5):几乎每个人都有感,很多人被惊醒,有些碗碟和窗户等被震碎,少量墙壁上出现裂缝,不稳定的物体翻倒,有的树木和电线杆等高的物体明显摆动,摆式钟可能停摆。

Ⅵ(6):所有的人都有感,很多人惊恐外逃,有的笨重家具被移动位置,少数墙壁倒塌,烟囱被震裂,破坏轻微。

Ⅶ(7):所有的人都跑出户外,较坚固的建筑物没有明显破坏,而普通房屋有较轻微或中等破坏,结构差的房屋则破坏很明显,部分烟囱倒塌,驾驶汽车行进的人也能感觉到。

Ⅷ(8):特殊设计的建筑物有轻微破坏;普通坚固建筑物有明显的破坏甚至部分倒塌;差的房屋破坏严

重,面板墙脱离框架结构,烟囱、工厂排气管、柱、碑、院墙等倒塌,重型家具翻倒。少量沙土和泥浆喷出地表,井水变浑,汽车驾驶人员受到干扰。

Ⅸ(9):特殊设计的建筑物有明显的破坏;框架结构的墙体歪斜;大部分坚固的建筑物被破坏,一部分甚至倒塌。建筑物与地基相对位移,地表有明显裂缝,地下管道断裂。

Ⅹ(10):某些优质木结构建筑物被破坏;大部分砖石结构和框架结构工程被摧毁;铁轨弯曲,有明显的河岸塌方和崖坎倾斜,沿河岸沙土与泥浆外溢。

Ⅺ(11):只剩下极少量的砖石建筑,桥梁被摧毁,地面广泛裂开,地下管道完全失效,疏松地带发生地陷和塌落,铁轨严重弯曲。

Ⅻ(12):建筑物破坏殆尽,可见到地面波动,视线与水平线畸变,物体被抛向空中。

2.2 人员伤、亡数量与级别

(1)死亡人数和死亡级别(*Dd*,Description of Deaths):

当不同文献给出不同的死亡人数时,则列出信度最高的文献给出的死亡人数。在历史文献中,死亡人数用某些字符描述时,如 Some(一些),Few(少数),Many(许多)等,则按照 Paula 等(1992)定义的四个死亡级别(表1)进行分级。为了区别死亡人数特别严重(超过1万人)的地震,本书增加了死亡人数超过1万人的死亡级别 *Dd*=5。

(2)受伤人数和受伤级别的定义与死亡人数和死亡级别为同一标准(表1)。

表1 死亡(或受伤)人数(*Num*)和死亡(或受伤)级别(*Dd*)定义

死亡(或受伤)级别 *Dd*	文字描述	死亡(或受伤)人数(Paula 等定义)	死亡(或受伤)人数(本书定义)
1	少数(Few)	1~50 人	1~50 人
2	一些(Some)	51~100 人	51~100 人
3	许多(Many)	101~1000 人	101~1000 人
4	非常多(Very Many)	≥1001 人	1001~9999 人
5			≥10000 人

2.3 经济损失数量和经济损失级别(*De*,Description of Economy)

基于文献给出的经济损失数量,根据地震事件发生时的货币兑换关系(如中国货币与美元的兑换关系"人民币(¥)对美元($)汇率"(表2)等)将各国货币换成美元,再将当时的美元值换算成1990年的美元值,并以百万美元($ 1 million)为单位的数量列入,即为经济损失数量。值得注意的是1990年前的经济损失数量均按照"美元消费价格指数(Consumer Price Index)"(表3)换算为1990年的美元值,但是1991年之后的经济损失数量为地震发生时的美元值,如果需要换算,可以参照表3进行换算。

如1976年7月27日(UTC)唐山7.8级地震经济损失总计为100亿元人民币(见《中国震例(1976~1980)》),由表2可得1976年1 $ =1.8803¥,即经济损失为53.183亿美元,由表3查得1976年的1 $相当于1990年的2.297 $,因此该经济损失相当于1990年的122.321亿美元,也就是说,在该书中查得唐山7.8级地震经济损失总计为12232.1百万美元。

如2008年5月12日(UTC)中国四川省汶川8级地震的直接经济损失为8451亿元人民币,由表2可得2008年4月10日的1 $ =7.0¥,即经济损失为1207.286亿美元,因此在本书中可以查得该次地震的经济损失为120728.6百万美元。如果转换为1990年的美元,由表3查得,2008年1 $相当于1990年0.61 $,因此该次地震的经济损失相当于1990年的73644.4百万美元。

如果没有经济损失数量评估的地震,按照表4中的文字描述确定经济损失等级。

Paula 等(1992)定义经济损失级别为四个级别(表4),为了区别经济损失特别严重(超过1亿美元,即≥$ 100 million)的地震,本书增加经济损失数量超过1亿美元的级别 *De*=5。

表2　人民币(¥)对美元($)汇率

(http://www.douban.com/group/topic/14371415)

时间	1 $ = ? ¥	时间	1 $ = ? ¥	时间	1 $ = ? ¥	时间	1 $ = ? ¥
1949年	2.3	1968年	2.4618	1987年	3.7221	2006年1月4日	8.0702
1950年	2.75	1969年	2.4618	1988年	3.7221	2006年9月28日	7.9
1951年	2.238	1970年	2.4618	1989年	3.7659	2006年12月29日	7.8074
1952年	2.617	1971年	2.2673	1990年	4.7838	2007年1月11日	7.8
1953年	2.617	1972年	2.2401	1991年	5.3227	2007年3月8日	7.73
1954年	2.617	1973年	2.0202	1992年	5.5149	2007年5月8日	7.7
1955年	2.4618	1974年	1.8397	1993年	5.7619	2007年7月3日	7.6
1956年	2.4618	1975年	1.9663	1994年	8.6187	2007年10月24日	7.5
1957年	2.4618	1976年	1.8803	1995年	8.3507	2007年11月23日	7.4
1958年	2.4618	1977年	1.73	1996年	8.3142	2007年12月12日	7.3
1959年	2.4618	1978年	1.5771	1997年	8.2898	2008年4月10日	7.0
1960年	2.4618	1979年	1.4962	1998年	8.2791	2009年1月1日	6.8967
1961年	2.4618	1980年	1.5303	1999年	8.2796	2009年8月1日	6.8364
1962年	2.4618	1981年	1.7051	2000年	8.2784	2009年12月1日	6.8282
1963年	2.4618	1982年	1.8926	2001年	8.277	2010年1月1日	6.8262
1964年	2.4618	1983年	1.9757	2002年	8.277	2011年1月1日	6.6215
1965年	2.4618	1984年	2.327	2003年	8.2774		
1966年	2.4618	1985年	2.9367	2004年	8.278		
1967年	2.4618	1986年	3.4528	2005年	8.1013		

注:1949~2005年为年平均汇率;2006年后为汇率变化较大的时间点。

表3　美元消费价格指数(Consumer Price Index)(1990=1)

(http://data.bls.gov/cgi-bin/cpicalc.pl)

时间	CPI	时间	CPI	时间	CPI	时间	CPI	时间	CPI	时间	CPI
1800	7.677	1836	11.865	1872	10.876	1908	14.502	1944	7.426	1980	1.586
1801	7.831	1837	11.516	1873	10.876	1909	14.502	1945	7.261	1981	1.438
1802	9.106	1838	12.236	1874	11.516	1910	13.984	1946	6.703	1982	1.354
1803	8.701	1839	12.236	1875	11.865	1911	13.984	1947	5.861	1983	1.312
1804	8.701	1840	13.052	1876	12.236	1912	13.502	1948	5.432	1984	1.258
1805	8.701	1841	12.63	1877	12.236	1913	13.202	1949	5.492	1985	1.215
1806	8.331	1842	13.502	1878	13.502	1914	13.07	1950	5.423	1986	1.193
1807	8.899	1843	13.984	1879	13.984	1915	12.941	1951	5.027	1987	1.151
1808	8.157	1844	13.984	1880	13.502	1916	11.911	1952	4.932	1988	1.105
1809	8.331	1845	13.984	1881	13.502	1917	10.211	1953	4.895	1989	1.054
1810	8.331	1846	14.502	1882	13.502	1918	8.656	1954	4.859	1990	1
1811	7.831	1847	13.984	1883	13.984	1919	7.555	1955	4.877	1991	0.96

续表

时间	CPI	时间	CPI	时间	CPI	时间	CPI	时间	CPI	时间	CPI
1812	7. 677	1848	15. 059	1884	14. 502	1920	6. 535	1956	4. 805	1992	0. 93
1813	6. 751	1849	15. 662	1885	14. 502	1921	7. 302	1957	4. 651	1993	0. 90
1814	6. 215	1850	15. 662	1886	14. 502	1922	7. 78	1958	4. 522	1994	0. 88
1815	7. 119	1851	15. 662	1887	14. 502	1923	7. 643	1959	4. 491	1995	0. 86
1816	7. 677	1852	15. 662	1888	14. 502	1924	7. 643	1960	4. 416	1996	0. 83
1817	8. 157	1853	15. 662	1889	14. 502	1925	7. 469	1961	4. 371	1997	0. 81
1818	8. 512	1854	14. 502	1890	14. 502	1926	7. 384	1962	4. 328	1998	0. 80
1819	8. 512	1855	13. 984	1891	14. 502	1927	7. 511	1963	4. 271	1999	0. 78
1820	9. 323	1856	14. 502	1892	14. 502	1928	7. 643	1964	4. 216	2000	0. 76
1821	9. 789	1857	13. 984	1893	14. 502	1929	7. 643	1965	4. 149	2001	0. 74
1822	9. 789	1858	15. 059	1894	15. 059	1930	7. 826	1966	4. 034	2002	0. 73
1823	10. 88	1859	14. 502	1895	15. 662	1931	8. 599	1967	3. 913	2003	0. 71
1824	11. 87	1860	14. 502	1896	15. 662	1932	9. 54	1968	3. 756	2004	0. 69
1825	11. 52	1861	14. 502	1897	15. 662	1933	10. 054	1969	3. 561	2005	0. 67
1826	11. 52	1862	13. 052	1898	15. 662	1934	9. 754	1970	3. 369	2006	0. 65
1827	11. 52	1863	10. 582	1899	15. 662	1935	9. 54	1971	3. 227	2007	0. 63
1828	11. 87	1864	8. 331	1900	15. 662	1936	9. 403	1972	3. 127	2008	0. 61
1829	12. 24	1865	8. 512	1901	15. 662	1937	9. 076	1973	2. 944	2009	0. 61
1830	12. 24	1866	8. 899	1902	15. 059	1938	9. 27	1974	2. 651	2010	0. 60
1831	12. 24	1867	9. 323	1903	14. 502	1939	9. 403	1975	2. 429	2011	0. 58
1832	13. 05	1868	9. 789	1904	14. 502	1940	9. 336	1976	2. 297		
1833	13. 05	1869	9. 789	1905	14. 502	1941	8. 891	1977	2. 157		
1834	13. 05	1870	10. 304	1906	14. 502	1942	8. 018	1978	2. 005		
1835	12. 63	1871	10. 876	1907	13. 984	1943	7. 555	1979	1. 8		

注:CPI 表示为以 1990 年美元作为标准的当年的消费价格指数或购买力。

表 4　经济损失数量(*Num*)和经济损失级别(*De*)定义

经济损失级别 *De*	文字描述	经济损失数量(Paula 等定义)	经济损失数量(本书定义)
1	有限(Limited);轻微(Slight);较少(Minor);轻(Light)	< $ 1 million	< $ 1 million
2	中等(Moderate)	$ 1 ~ 4. 9 million	$ 1 ~ 4. 9 million
3	严重(Severe);较大(Major);广泛(Extensive);重(Heavy)	$ 5 ~ 24 million	$ 5 ~ 24 million
4	非常严重(Extreme);灾难性(Catastrophic)	≥ $ 25 million	$ 25 ~ 99 million
5			≥ $ 100 million

2.4 房屋毁坏(受损)数量和级别(*Dh*, Description of Houses)

房屋破坏情况分为毁坏(Destroyed)和受损(Damaged)两种信息,单位为间(栋)。

当文献中给出了房屋毁坏(受损)数量,直接可列出房屋毁坏(受损)数量(*Num*)和级别(*Dh*)的具体数值。如果历史文献中,描述房屋毁坏(或受损)情况只有定性描述,如Some代表一些,Few代表少数,Many代表许多。则按照表5中的定性描述确定房屋毁坏(受损)级别(*Dh*)。

Paula等(1992)定义房屋毁坏(受损)级别为四个级别(表5),为了区别房屋破坏特别严重(超过1万间)的地震,本书增加房屋毁坏(受损)数量超过1万间的级别 $Dh=5$。

表5 房屋毁坏(受损)数量(*Num*)和级别(*Dh*)定义

房屋毁坏(受损)级别(*Dh*)	文字描述	毁坏(受损)数量(*Num*)(Paula等定义)	毁坏(受损)数量(*Num*)(本书定义)
1	少数(Few)	1~50间	1~50间
2	一些(Some)	51~100间	51~100间
3	许多(Many)	101~1000间	101~1000间
4	非常多(Very Many)	≥1001间	1001~9999间
5			≥10000间

3 地震(火山)海啸灾害信息

通过美国国家海洋和大气管理局(NOAA, National Oceanic and Atmospheric Administration)网站(http://www.nesdis.noaa.gov/)收集全球海啸灾害信息,挑选出地震(包括既有火山又有地震)造成的海啸灾害信息。

3.1 海啸源(Tsunami Source)

本书收集了两大类的海啸,其一是地震造成的海啸;其二是地震(伴有火山)造成的海啸。根据海啸源是地震的可信程度,将地震造成的海啸共分为5种情况(表6)。在本书地震目录中海啸源用“源”或“Sr”表示。

表6 海啸源类别分类与描述

海啸源(Tsunami Source)	英文描述	中文描述
1	very doubtful tsunami	非常怀疑是地震造成的海啸
2	questionable tsunami	怀疑是地震造成的海啸
3	probable tsunami	可能是地震造成的海啸
4	definite tsunami	确定是地震造成的海啸
5	Volcano and Earthquake	地震(伴有火山)共同造成的海啸

3.2 海啸最大浪高(Maximum Water Height)

在本书中收集了海啸形成的最大浪高或海啸造成的水位高度最大值,用 W_h 表示,单位为米。

3.3 海啸级别(Tsunami Magnitude)

本书中收集了两种海啸级别(简称为啸级),其一是根据Iida等(1967)定义的海啸级别 $m = \log_2 h$,其

中 h 为最大浪高，单位为米，海啸级别范围为 -5~10。在地震灾害信息目录中，根据该方法计算的海啸级别（即啸级 I）用“级 I”或“mI”表示。

其二是根据 Soloviev 等（1974）定义的海啸级别 $m = \log_2(2^{1/2} * h)$，其中 h 为最大浪高，单位为米，海啸级别范围为 -5~10。在地震灾害信息目录中，根据该方法计算的海啸级别（即啸级 S）用“级 S”或“mS”表示。

由两种定义可得，两种海啸级别的关系为：$mS = 0.5 + mI$。在本书中“资料来源”均用“NOAA”表示。

4 资料来源

全球历史地震及灾害信息收集来源于多种渠道，表 7 列出不同地区地震目录的资料来源及标注符号。

表 7 全球历史地震与灾害性地震资料收集来源及标注

地　区	标注符号	资料来源（网址及出版物）
非洲地区地震目录	GSHAP	http://www.seismo.ethz.ch/gshap/earift/
美国地震目录	USGS	http://neic.usgs.gov/neis/epic/epic_global.html
美国加州地震目录	CGS	http://www.conservation.ca.gov/CGS/rghm/quakes/Pages/eq_chron.aspx
南美洲地震目录	GSHAP	http://www.seismo.ethz.ch/gshap/ceresis/
阿富汗地震目录	Afghan	http://sgsingapore.com/earthquake-afghanistan
北欧地区地震目录	GSHAP	http://www.seismo.ethz.ch/gshap/ceresis/
伊朗地震目录	Iran	http://www.iiees.ac.ir/english/bank/irancat.txt
意大利地震目录	Italy	http://emidius.mi.ingv.it/CPTI04/
中欧地区地震目录	GSHAP	http://www.seismo.ethz.ch/gshap/cirpan/
冰岛地区地震目录	Iceland	http://hraun.vedur.is/ja/ymislegt/storskjalf.html
土耳其地震目录	Turkey	http://www.seismo.ethz.ch/gshap/turkey/
东亚地区地震目录	GSHAP	http://www.seismo.ethz.ch/gshap/eastasia/final-cata.txt
印度及邻区地震目录	GSHAP	http://www.seismo.ethz.ch/gshap/ict/indcat.txt
印度地震目录	India	http://www.imd.ernet.in/section/seismo/static/signif.htm
中国历史强震目录	China	国家地震局震害防御司编，《中国历史强震目录（公元前 23 世纪~公元 1911 年）》，北京：地震出版社，1995 顾功叙等编，《中国地震目录（公元前 1831~公元 1969 年）》，北京：科学出版社，1983
中国近代强震目录	Wang S.	汪素云等编，《中国近代地震目录》（公元 1912~1990 年）》，北京：中国科学技术出版社，1999
中国历史有感地震目录（-618~1949）	Diao S.	刁守中等编，《中国历史有感地震目录》，北京：地震出版社，2008
中国历史有感地震目录（1950~1969）	Jin X.	金学申研究成果，金学申提供的未出版的内部资料
世界地震目录	Shi Z.	时振梁等编，《世界地震目录：1900~1980 年（$M \geqslant 6$）》，北京：地图出版社，1986
中国地震台网（CSN）地震目录	CSN	http://www.csndmc.ac.cn/newweb/catalog_direct_link.htm

续表

地　区	标注符号	资料来源（网址及出版物）
国际地震中心（ISC）地震目录	ISC	http://www.csndmc.ac.cn/newweb/catalog_direct_link.htm
美国国家地震信息中心（NEIC）地震目录	NEIC	http://www.csndmc.ac.cn/newweb/catalog_direct_link.htm
世纪地震目录	Engdahl	http://earthquake.usgs.gov/research/data/centennial.php#cat22
全球重大灾害性地震目录	*	http://neic.usgs.gov/neis/epic/epic_global.html 或 http://earthquake.usgs.gov/earthquakes/eqarchives/epic/
	* *	Paula K. Dunbar, Patricia A. Lockridge, and Lowell S. Whiteside. Catalog of significant earthquakes 2150 B.C. – 1991 A.D. U.S. Dept. of Commerce, National Oceanic and Atmospheric Administration. September 1992 罗伟等编译,《全球重大灾害性地震目录(2150B.C. ~1991A.D.)》,北京:地震出版社,1996
全球地震灾害评估计划	GSHAP	http://www.seismo.ethz.ch/GSHAP/index.html
菲律宾地震目录	Nakamura	http://www.cseas.kyoto-u.ac.jp/seas/15/4/150406.pdf
菲律宾地震目录（1599~1909）	Maso	http://www.gutenberg.org/files/18556/18556-h/18556-h.htm
菲律宾地震目录	Bautista	http://www.sciencedirect.com/science/article/pii/S0040195199002723。 Bautista, M. L. P. and K. Oike, Estimation of the magnitudes and epicenters of Philippine historical earthquakes, Tectonophys, 317, 137-169, 2000
朝鲜半岛地震目录	Korea	李裕澈编译,《朝鲜·韩国地震目录(公元27~1985年)》,北京:地震出版社,2001
日本地震目录	Usami	http://repository.dl.itc.u-tokyo.ac.jp/dspace/bitstream/2261/12734/1/ji0543001.pdf
	Japan	卢振恒编,《日本破坏地震概观》,北京:地震出版社,1991,159-334
澳大利亚地震目录	Australia	http://www.seismicity.see.uwa.edu.au/welcome/seismicity_in_australia#impotEQ
中国地震灾害信息	Dis	http://www.china-disaster.cn/ 参考资料还包括: 谢毓寿、蔡美彪主编,《中国地震历史资料汇编(第五卷)》,北京:科学出版社,1983 《中国地震年鉴》编纂委员会,《中国地震年鉴(1949~1981)》,北京:地震出版社,1990 高建国,《地震损失简表》,北京:地震出版社,1990 郭增建,陈鑫连主编,《地震对策》,北京:地震出版社,1986 张肇诚,罗兰格,李海华等编,《中国震例(1966~1975)》,北京:地震出版社,1988 张肇诚,罗兰格,李海华等编,《中国震例(1976~1980)》,北京:地震出版社,1990 张肇诚,罗兰格,李海华等编,《中国震例(1981~1985)》,北京:地震出版社,1990 张肇诚,郑大林,徐京华等编,《中国震例(1986~1988)》,北京:地震出版社,1999 张肇诚,郑大林,徐京华等编,《中国震例(1989~1991)》,北京:地震出版社,2000 陈棋福,郑大林,车时等编,《中国震例(1992~1994)》,北京:地震出版社,2002 陈棋福,郑大林,刘桂萍等编,《中国震例(1995~1996)》,北京:地震出版社,2002 陈棋福,郑大林,高荣胜等编,《中国震例(1997~1999)》,北京:地震出版社,2003 陈棋福,郑大林,车时等编,《中国震例(2000~2002)》,北京:地震出版社,2008

续表

地　区	标注符号	资料来源（网址及出版物）
全球地震（火山）海啸信息	NOAA	从美国国家海洋和大气管理局（NOAA，National Oceanic and Atmospheric Administration）网站收集全球海啸灾害信息（http://www.nesdis.noaa.gov/）
全球地震目录	USGS	http://earthquake.usgs.gov/earthquakes/eqarchives/epic/

5 目录标题说明

（1）时间（Date）：世界标准时间（UTC）的年（Year），月（Mo），日（Dy），时（Hr），分（Mn），秒（Sec）。

（2）海啸（Tsunami）：源（即海啸源）（Sr），浪高（*Wh*），级 I（*mI*），级 S（*mS*）。

（3）资料来源（Information）。

（4）震中（Earthquake Epicenter）：地名（Name）（英文（English）和中文（Chinese）），纬度（°）（Latitude），经度（°）（Longitude）。

（5）深度（Depth），震级（Mag），标度即震级标度（Scale），烈度（MMI）。

（6）死亡人数（Deaths）包括数量（以"Num"表示，单位人）和级别（简称"级"，以"*Dd*"表示）。

（7）受伤人数（Injuries）包括数量（以"Num"表示，单位人）和级别（简称"级"，以"*Dd*"表示）。

（8）经济损失（Damage Millions Dollars，以"Damage"表示），包括数量（单位为百万美元，以"$ Mill"表示）和级别（简称"级"，以"*De*"表示）。

（9）房屋毁坏（Houses Destroyed，以"Destroyed"表示），包括数量（以"Num"表示，单位为间）和级别（简称"级"，以"*Dh*"表示）。

（10）房屋受损（Houses Damaged，以"Damaged"表示），包括数量（以"Num"表示，单位为间）和级别（简称"级"，以"*Dh*"表示）。

Editorial Comments

The *Disaster Information Catalog of Global Earthquakes* includes the information catalog of disasters caused by earthquakes in the world in the time span from 9999 B. C. to June 2011 A. D. The disaster information of these earthquakes was collected and compiled by consulting multiple Websites, a variety of formally published books and documents (including earthquake catalog and multi – disciplinary information of countries and regions all over the world, etc.), as well as individual reports of earthquake disaster information. Besides, on the basis of studying the relation between the earthquake disaster information and earthquake magnitude and by use of the disaster information, the magnitude of seismic event with the magnitude lacking was determined. The parameters given in the book are stated as follows.

1 Earthquake Parameters

The basic parameters of earthquakes include the time of origin, epicenter location, focal depth, and magnitude. Because the seismic events occurred in different periods of time, the methods used to determine the parameters are quite different; therefore the connotations (the error and uncertainty) of the determined parameters also differ greatly. The parameters of earthquake events after 1900 A. D. are mainly determined by the seismic network, so the parameters are complete and precise in a relative sense. The seismic events before 1900 A. D. but after 2000 B. C. or 3000 B. C. are often identified by earthquake information recorded in history; they are called historical earthquakes. Their parameters are more incomplete and uncertain. The parameters of seismic events before 2000 B. C. or 3000 B. C. were often determined by seismic archeology or the so – called ancient earthquake method; for example, the occurrence time was determined by the geological dating method, with an error of one hundred years or more. Therefore, the parameters of the early seismic events bear quite large uncertainty. It is hoped that the readers pay due attention when using this book.

1. 1 Date and Time

Year, month, day, hour, minute, second in the Coordinated Universal Time (abbreviated to UTC).

1. 2 Epicenter

Latitude (north latitude is taken as positive, and south latitude as negative), longitude (east longitude is taken as positive, and west longitude as negative). For the seismic events before 1900A. D. , there are no instrumental records. So the earthquake epicenter position is given as the latitude and longitude of a city determined on the basis of destruction analysis. For the seismic events after 1900A. D. , the earthquake epicenter is usually given as the longitude and latitude of epicenter measured by instruments. The reference name (Chinese or English) of the epicenter has been revised on Google Earth in accordance with the longitude and latitude of epicenter.

1. 3 Focal Depth (Depth)

The focal depth (H) is measured in kilometers (km). Earthquakes with H less than 70km are called shallow earthquakes; those with H of 70km to 299km are called intermediate earthquakes; and those with H greater than or equal to 300km are called deep focus earthquakes.

1.4 Earthquake Magnitude

During the compilation and revision of the earthquake catalog, for the same event, there were usually a number of magnitude values obtained from various sources. Among them, the value given by Engdahl was considered first, and then the largest magnitude values collected from relevant regions. Meanwhile, the corresponding magnitude scale (Scale) was given. The magnitude of earthquake events having no magnitude records was determined by the book. The magnitude scales involved in the book are as follows.

Moment magnitude (Mw): it is calculated from the scalar moment (M_0) by the formula

$$M_W = \frac{2}{3}\lg M_0 - 10.7$$ (Hanks and Kanamori, 1979).

Surface wave magnitude (M_S): For instrumentally recorded earthquakes, it is calculated from the maximum ground surface amplitude of S – wave within a period range of 18 – 22s recorded in the epicentral distance range of 20° – 160°; the depth is usually less than 50km. For earthquakes that have no instrumental records, the magnitude of magnitude scale Ms is generally calculated by statistics.

Body wave magnitude (m_b): It is calculated from the maximum ground surface amplitude of P – wave within a period range of 0.1 – 3s recorded at the epicentral distance equal to or greater than 5°.

Broadband body wave magnitude (m_B): It was defined by Gutenberg and Richter (1956). It is calculated from the maximum ground surface amplitude of P – wave within a period range of 5 – 10s recorded at the epicentral distance equal to or greater than 5°.

Magnitude from Japan Meteorological Agency (M_j): It is used for earthquakes that have instrumental records, and is calculated from the maximum ground surface displacement or the maximum ground surface velocity. For earthquakes that have no instrumental records, the magnitude given by the Japan Meteorological Agency is also in M_j scale.

Energy magnitude (M_e):. It is calculated from the seismic radiation energy (E_S) given by the broadband P – wave energy spectrum density. The formula is $M_e = \frac{2}{3}\lg E_S - 2.9$ (Choy and Boatwright, 1995).

Local magnitude or near shock magnitude (M_L): It is used for earthquakes whose epicentral distance is within the range of 100 to 1,000 kilometers, and is calculated from the body wave.

Lg wave magnitude (M_{Lg}): It is calculated from the vertical component of Lg seismic wave (short – period surface wave) with a period of 1s.

Duration magnitude (M_d): It is calculated from the seismic wave duration and tail wave length.

Fault area magnitude (M_{fa}): It is calculated from the fault area, approximately equivalent to the mb value, and is often used for earthquakes in the age when seismic instruments did not appear.

Focal mechanism magnitude (M): It is calculated by use of the focal mechanism.

Unknown magnitude (M_{uk}): The magnitude is calculated by unknown method or is from uncertain publication source. Such magnitude is generally calculated by statistics; the magnitude scale is denoted by "M_{uk}", or "UK" in some of the literature.

Magnitude determined from the disaster information (M_k): This kind of magnitude is used for seismic events with no magnitude records. The predominant magnitude corresponding to definite disaster information has been obtained by studying the disaster information of earthquake events with known magnitudes. Based on the results of such study, the magnitude of seismic events with no magnitude records can be determined from the disaster information. In order to show that the magnitude is determined (Known) by the method proposed in this book, the magnitude scale of this type of earthquakes is expressed as M_k, and the "data source" given in the Catalog is labeled "Song".

2 Earthquake Disaster Information

2.1 Earthquake Intensity (I)

For earthquakes that occur on land, the intensity value is usually the epicenter intensity. For earthquakes that occur in the sea area, the intensity value is the maximum value recorded at the place which is nearest to the land; intensity values of this type do not represent the epicenter intensity.

All the seismic intensity values collected in this book are given as the "Modified Mercalli Intensity" (MMI) (Harry, et al., 1931; Paula, et al., 1992; Luo Wei, et al. (eds.), 1996). In the Modified Mercalli Intensity Table, the twelve intensity values are expressed with Roman numerals I – XII; in this book, they are expressed with Arabic numerals 1 to 12. Different intensity values correspond to the disasters described as follows (http://earthquake.usgs.gov/earthquakes/eqarchives/epic/):

I (1): Not felt except by a very few under especially favorable circumstances.

II(2): Felt only by a few persons at rest, especially on upper floors of buildings. Delicately suspended objects may swing.

III(3): Felt quite noticeably indoors, especially on upper floors of buildings, but many people do not recognize it as an earthquake. Standing motor cars may rock slightly. Vibration like passing truck. Duration estimated.

IV(4): During the day felt indoors by many, outdoors by few. At night some awakened. Dishes, windows, and doors disturbed; walls make creaking sound. Sensation like heavy truck striking building. Standing motorcars rock noticeably.

V(5): Felt by nearly everyone; many awakened. Some dishes, windows, etc., broken; a few instances of cracked plaster; unstable objects overturned. Disturbance of trees, poles, and other tall objects sometimes noticed. Pendulum clocks may stop.

VI(6): Felt by all; many frightened and run outdoors. Some heavy furniture moved; a few instances of fallen plaster or damaged chimneys. Damage slight.

VII(7): Everybody runs outdoors. Damage negligible in buildings of good design and construction slight to moderate in well built ordinary structures; considerable in poorly built or badly designed structures. Some chimneys broken. Noticed by persons driving motor cars.

VIII(8): Damage slight in specially designed structures; considerable in ordinary substantial buildings, with partial collapse; great in poorly built structures. Panel walls thrown out of frame structures. Fall of chimneys, factory stacks, columns, monuments, walls. Heavy furniture overturned. Sand and mud ejected in small amounts. Changes in well water. Persons driving motor cars disturbed.

IX(9): Damage considerable in specially designed structures; well – designed frame structures thrown out of plumb; great in substantial buildings, with partial collapse. Buildings shifted off foundations. Ground cracked conspicuously. Underground pipes broken.

X(10): Some well – built wooden structures destroyed; most masonry and frame structures destroyed with foundations; ground badly cracked. Rails bent. Landslides considerable from river banks and steep slopes. Shifted sand and mud. Water splashed over banks.

XI(11): Few, if any (masonry), structures remain standing. Bridges destroyed. Broad fissures in ground. Underground pipelines completely out of service. Earth slumps and land slips in soft ground. Rails bent greatly.

XII(12): Damage total. Waves seen on ground surfaces. Lines of sight and level distorted. Objects thrown upward into the air.

2.2 Number and Level of Deaths and Injuries

(1) Number of deaths and death level (Dd, Description of Deaths)

When different references gave different numbers of deaths, the number given by the most reliable reference was listed. When the number of deaths in the historical literature was described in terms of some words, such as Some, Few, Many, and so on, the four levels of mortality (Table 1) defined by Paula et al. (1992) were adopted. In order to distinguish the earthquakes that caused particularly serious deaths (over 10,000 people) from others, a deaths level Dd = 5 used to describe more than 10 thousand deaths was added in the book.

(2) The number of injuries and injury level were defined with the same standard as the number of deaths and death level (Table 1).

Table 1 Definition of the number of death (or injured) (Num) and death (or injured) level (Dd)

Death (or injured) level (Dd)	Written description	Number of death (or injured) (Defined by Paula et al., 1992)	Number of death (or injured) (Defined in this book)
1	Few	1 - 50 (people)	1 - 50 (people)
2	Some	51 - 100 (people)	51 - 100 (people)
3	Many	101 - 1000 (people)	101 - 1000 (people)
4	Very many	≥1001 (people)	1000 - 9999 (people)
5			≥10000 (people)

2.3 The Quantity of Economic Losses and Economic Loss Level (De, Description of Economy)

The quantity of economic losses is determined from that given in the literature. It is first converted from the currency of the stricken country into U. S. dollars according to the currency exchange table (for example, the RMB Yuan (¥) to U. S. dollar ($) exchange rate table (Table 2), etc.) at the time when the seismic event occurred. Then the amount of U. S. dollar is further converted into the U. S. dollar value in 1990, and finally the quantity of economic losses in million of U. S. dollars ($ 1 million) is filled in.

Here the July 27, 1976 (UTC) M_S7.8 earthquake in Tangshan, China, can be taken as an example. It caused an economic loss of 10,000 million Yuan (RMB) in total (see *Earthquake Cases in China* (1976 ~ 1980)). It can be seen from Table 2 that 1U. S. dollar = 1.8803 Yuan (RMB) in 1976, so the economic losses were 5,318.3 million U. S. dollars at that time. Table 3 shows that 1 U. S. dollar in 1976 equals 2.297 U. S. dollars in 1990. Therefore, the economic losses equal 12,232,100,000 U. S. dollars in 1990, that is, the economic losses of the Tangshan M_S7.8 earthquake are 12,232.1 million U. S. dollars in total in this book.

Another example is the May 12, 2008 (UTC) earthquake with M_S8.0 in Wenchuan, Sichuan, China. It caused direct economic losses of 845,100 million Yuan (RMB). Table 2 shows that 1 U. S. dollar = 7.0 Yuan (RMB) on April 10, 2008; so the economic losses were 120,728.6 million U. S. dollars at that time. If the amount of U. S. dollars in 2008 is converted into U. S. dollars in 1990 from Table 3, which shows that 1 U. S. dollar on April 10, 2008 is equal to 0.61 U. S. dollar in 1990, so economic losses of the Wenchuan earthquake is equal to 73644.4 million U. S. dollars in 1990.

If there is no quantitative assessment of earthquake economic losses, the level of economic losses can be determined according to the descriptions in Table 4.

In the definition given by Paula et al. (1992), the economic damage was classified into four levels (Table 4). In order to distinguish earthquakes that caused particularly serious economic losses (more than 100 million U. S. dollars, that is, ≥ 100 million U. S. dollars) from others, the level De = 5 for economic losses over 100 million U. S. dollars was added in the book.

Table 2 Exchange rate of RMB Yuan (¥) vs. U. S. dollar ($)
(http://www.douban.com/group/topic/14371415)

Time	1 $ = ? ¥	Time	1 $ = ? ¥	Time	1 $ = ? ¥	Time	1 $ = ? ¥
1949	2.3	1968	2.4618	1987	3.7221	2006 - 1 - 4	8.0702
1950	2.75	1969	2.4618	1988	3.7221	2006 - 9 - 28	7.9

续表

Time	1 $ = ? ¥	Time	1 $ = ? ¥	Time	1 $ = ? ¥	Time	1 $ = ? ¥
1951	2.238	1970	2.4618	1989	3.7659	2006 - 12 - 29	7.8074
1952	2.617	1971	2.2673	1990	4.7838	2007 - 1 - 11	7.8
1953	2.617	1972	2.2401	1991	5.3227	2007 - 3 - 8	7.73
1954	2.617	1973	2.0202	1992	5.5149	2007 - 5 - 8	7.7
1955	2.4618	1974	1.8397	1993	5.7619	2007 - 7 - 3	7.6
1956	2.4618	1975	1.9663	1994	8.6187	2007 - 10 - 24	7.5
1957	2.4618	1976	1.8803	1995	8.3507	2007 - 11 - 23	7.4
1958	2.4618	1977	1.73	1996	8.3142	2007 - 12 - 12	7.3
1959	2.4618	1978	1.5771	1997	8.2898	2008 - 4 - 10	7.0
1960	2.4618	1979	1.4962	1998	8.2791	2009 - 1 - 1	6.8967
1961	2.4618	1980	1.5303	1999	8.2796	2009 - 8 - 1	6.8364
1962	2.4618	1981	1.7051	2000	8.2784	2009 - 12 - 1	6.8282
1963	2.4618	1982	1.8926	2001	8.277	2010 - 1 - 1	6.8262
1964	2.4618	1983	1.9757	2002	8.277	2011 - 1 - 1	6.6215
1965	2.4618	1984	2.327	2003	8.2774		
1966	2.4618	1985	2.9367	2004	8.278		
1967	2.4618	1986	3.4528	2005	8.1013		

Notes: For the period from 1949 to 2005, the annual average exchange rates are given; for the period after 2006, the time points where the exchange rate changed more and the corresponding exchange rate are given.

Table 3 Consumer Price Index (CPI) of U. S. dollar in 1800 - 2011 (the CPI in 1990 is taken as 1)

(http://data.bls.gov/cgi-bin/cpicalc.pl)

Time	CPI	Time	CPI	Time	CPI	Time	CPI	Time	CPI	Time	CPI
1800	7.677	1836	11.865	1872	10.876	1908	14.502	1944	7.426	1980	1.586
1801	7.831	1837	11.516	1873	10.876	1909	14.502	1945	7.261	1981	1.438
1802	9.106	1838	12.236	1874	11.516	1910	13.984	1946	6.703	1982	1.354
1803	8.701	1839	12.236	1875	11.865	1911	13.984	1947	5.861	1983	1.312
1804	8.701	1840	13.052	1876	12.236	1912	13.502	1948	5.432	1984	1.258
1805	8.701	1841	12.63	1877	12.236	1913	13.202	1949	5.492	1985	1.215
1806	8.331	1842	13.502	1878	13.502	1914	13.07	1950	5.423	1986	1.193
1807	8.899	1843	13.984	1879	13.984	1915	12.941	1951	5.027	1987	1.151
1808	8.157	1844	13.984	1880	13.502	1916	11.911	1952	4.932	1988	1.105
1809	8.331	1845	13.984	1881	13.502	1917	10.211	1953	4.895	1989	1.054
1810	8.331	1846	14.502	1882	13.502	1918	8.656	1954	4.859	1990	1
1811	7.831	1847	13.984	1883	13.984	1919	7.555	1955	4.877	1991	0.96
1812	7.677	1848	15.059	1884	14.502	1920	6.535	1956	4.805	1992	0.93
1813	6.751	1849	15.662	1885	14.502	1921	7.302	1957	4.651	1993	0.90

续表

Time	CPI	Time	CPI	Time	CPI	Time	CPI	Time	CPI	Time	CPI
1814	6. 215	1850	15. 662	1886	14. 502	1922	7. 78	1958	4. 522	1994	0. 88
1815	7. 119	1851	15. 662	1887	14. 502	1923	7. 643	1959	4. 491	1995	0. 86
1816	7. 677	1852	15. 662	1888	14. 502	1924	7. 643	1960	4. 416	1996	0. 83
1817	8. 157	1853	15. 662	1889	14. 502	1925	7. 469	1961	4. 371	1997	0. 81
1818	8. 512	1854	14. 502	1890	14. 502	1926	7. 384	1962	4. 328	1998	0. 80
1819	8. 512	1855	13. 984	1891	14. 502	1927	7. 511	1963	4. 271	1999	0. 78
1820	9. 323	1856	14. 502	1892	14. 502	1928	7. 643	1964	4. 216	2000	0. 76
1821	9. 789	1857	13. 984	1893	14. 502	1929	7. 643	1965	4. 149	2001	0. 74
1822	9. 789	1858	15. 059	1894	15. 059	1930	7. 826	1966	4. 034	2002	0. 73
1823	10. 88	1859	14. 502	1895	15. 662	1931	8. 599	1967	3. 913	2003	0. 71
1824	11. 87	1860	14. 502	1896	15. 662	1932	9. 54	1968	3. 756	2004	0. 69
1825	11. 52	1861	14. 502	1897	15. 662	1933	10. 054	1969	3. 561	2005	0. 67
1826	11. 52	1862	13. 052	1898	15. 662	1934	9. 754	1970	3. 369	2006	0. 65
1827	11. 52	1863	10. 582	1899	15. 662	1935	9. 54	1971	3. 227	2007	0. 63
1828	11. 87	1864	8. 331	1900	15. 662	1936	9. 403	1972	3. 127	2008	0. 61
1829	12. 24	1865	8. 512	1901	15. 662	1937	9. 076	1973	2. 944	2009	0. 61
1830	12. 24	1866	8. 899	1902	15. 059	1938	9. 27	1974	2. 651	2010	0. 60
1831	12. 24	1867	9. 323	1903	14. 502	1939	9. 403	1975	2. 429	2011	0. 58
1832	13. 05	1868	9. 789	1904	14. 502	1940	9. 336	1976	2. 297		
1833	13. 05	1869	9. 789	1905	14. 502	1941	8. 891	1977	2. 157		
1834	13. 05	1870	10. 304	1906	14. 502	1942	8. 018	1978	2. 005		
1835	12. 63	1871	10. 876	1907	13. 984	1943	7. 555	1979	1. 8		

Note: CPI is the consumer price index or purchasing power expressed with the U. S. dollar in 1990 as a standard.

Table 4 Definitions of Economic losses amount (Num) and economic losses level (De)

The level of economic losses (De)	Description	Economic losses amount (definited by Paula et al., 1992)	Economic losses amount (definited by this book)
1	Limited; Slight; Minor; Light	$ 1 million	$ 1 million
2	Moderate	$ 1 – 4. 9 million	$ 1 – 4. 9 million
3	Severe; Major; Extensive; Heavy	$ 5 – 24 million	$ 5 – 24 million
4	Very heavy; Catastrophic	≥ $ 25 million	$ 25 – 99 million
5			≥ $ 100 million

2. 4 The Amount and Level of Houses Destroyed (Damaged) (Dh, Description)

Two kinds of information are given for the destroyed (Destroyed) and damaged (Damaged) houses, expressed in the unit of room (building).

When the number of houses destroyed (damaged) is given in the literature, the number (Num) and level (Dh) of destroyed (damaged) houses can be given directly as the specific values. If there are only qualitative descriptions, such as Some, Few, Many, etc., about the situation of destroyed (or damaged) houses in the historical literature, the houses destruction (or damage) level (Dh) is determined based on the qualitative descriptions in Table 5.

Paula et al. (1992) classified the destruction (damage) of houses into four levels (Table 5). In order to distinguish earthquakes that caused particularly serious destruction of houses (over 10,000 rooms) from others, the level of house destruction (damage) Dh = 5 was added in this book, in which the number of destroyed (damaged) rooms is more than 10,000.

Table 5 Definitions of the number (Num) and level (Dh) of destroyed (damaged) houses

Houses destruction (damage) level (Dh)	Description	Number of destroyed (damaged) houses (defined by Paula et al., 1992)	Number of destroyed (damaged) houses (definite in this book)
1	Few	1 – 50 (room)	1 – 50 (room)
2	Some	51 – 100 (room)	51 – 100 (room)
3	Many	101 – 1000 (room)	101 – 1000 (room)
4	Very Many	1001 (room)	1000 – 9999 (room)
5			10000 (room)

3 Earthquake (Volcano) Tsunami Disaster Information

From the NOAA (National Oceanic and Atmospheric Administration) website (http://www.nesdis.noaa.gov/) of the United States, the information of global earthquake – caused tsunami disaster (including those caused by both volcano and earthquake) was collected.

3.1 Tsunami Source

This book collected two categories of tsunami; one of them is caused by earthquakes, while the other is caused by the united effect of tsunami and earthquake. According to the credibility of whether the tsunami source is earthquake or not, there are four possibilities; so the earthquake – induced tsunami is divided into five cases (Table 6). In the earthquake disaster information catalog of this book, the tsunami source is expressed as "source" or "Sr".

Table 6 Classification and description of the tsunami source category

Tsunami Source	Description in Chinese
1	Strongly suspected as earthquake – caused tsunami
2	Suspected as earthquake – caused tsunami
3	Probably earthquake – caused tsunami
4	Definitely earthquake – caused tsunami
5	Tsunami caused by earthquake with volcano

3.2 Maximum Wave Height of Tsunami

In this book, the maximum wave height formed in tsunami or the maximum water level caused by tsunami, expressed as W_h and measured in meter, was collected.

3.3 Tsunami Magnitude

Two types of tsunami level were collected in this book. The first is the tsunami level $m = \log_2 h$ based on the definition given by Iida et al. (1967), where h is the maximum wave height measured in meter, and the tsunami level m ranges from −5 to 10. In the earthquake disaster information catalog of this book, tsunami levels calculated by the method mentioned above are expressed as "level I" or "mI".

The second is the tsunami level $m = \log_2(\sqrt{2} * h)$ defined by Soloviev et al. (1974), where h is the maximum wave height in meter, and the tsunami level ranges from −5 to 10. In the earthquake disaster information catalog, the tsunami level calculated by the method mentioned above (i. e., tsunami level S) is expressed as "level S" or "mS".

It can be known from the two definitions that the relation between the two types of tsunami level is $mS = 0.5 + mI$. In the book, the "Data Source" is uniquely expressed as NOAA.

4 Data Source

The global information of historical earthquakes and earthquake disasters was collected from a variety of channels. Table 7 shows the data sources of earthquake catalog for different parts of the world and the labels used for the data sources.

Table 7 Data sources of the global information of historical earthquakes and earthquake disasters and labels used for the sources

Area	Label	Data source (Website and Publication)
African Earthquake Catalog	GSHAP	http://www.seismo.ethz.ch/gshap/earift/
Earthquake Catalog of U. S. A.	USGS	http://neic.usgs.gov/neis/epic/epic_global.html
Earthquake Catalog of California, USA	CGS	http://www.conservation.ca.gov/CGS/rghm/quakes/Pages/eq_chron.aspx
South American Earthquake Catalog	GSHAP	http://www.seismo.ethz.ch/gshap/ceresis/
Afghanistan Earthquake Catalog	Afghan	http://sgsingapore.com/earthquake-afghanistan
Earthquake Catalog of Northern Europe Region	GSHAP	http://www.seismo.ethz.ch/gshap/ceresis/
Iran Earthquake Catalog	Iran	http://www.iiees.ac.ir/english/bank/irancat.txt
Italian Earthquake Catalog	Italy	http://emidius.mi.ingv.it/CPTI04/
Central Europe Earthquake Catalog	GSHAP	http://www.seismo.ethz.ch/gshap/cirpan/
Iceland Earthquake Catalog	Iceland	http://hraun.vedur.is/ja/ymislegt/storskjalf.html
Turkey Earthquake Catalog	Turkey	http://www.seismo.ethz.ch/gshap/turkey/
East Asia Earthquake Catalog	GSHAP	http://www.seismo.ethz.ch/gshap/eastasia/final-cata.txt
Earthquake Catalog of India and Adjacent Areas	GSHAP	http://www.seismo.ethz.ch/gshap/ict/indcat.txt
India Earthquake Catalog	India	http://www.imd.ernet.in/section/seismo/static/signif.htm
Historical Strong Earthquake Catalog of China	China	Department of Earthquake Disaster Prevention (ed.), China Seismological Bureau, 1995. *Historical Strong Earthquake Catalog of China* (2300 *B. C.* – 1911 *A. C.*), Seismological Press, Beijing. Gu Gongxu et al. (eds.), 1983. *China Earthquake Catalog* (1831 *B. C.* – 1969 *A. D.*), Science Press, Beijing.

续表

Area	Label	Data source(Website and Publication)
Recent Strong Earthquake Catalog of China	Wang S.	Wang Suyun et al. (eds.), 1999. *Recent Strong Earthquake Catalog of China* (1912 – 1990), Science and Technology Press of China, Beijing.
Historical Felt Earthquake Catalog of China (618 B.C. – 1949)	Diao S.	Diao Shouzhong et al. (eds.), 2008. *Historical Felt Earthquake Catalog of China* (618 *B. C.* – 1949), Seismological Press, Beijing.
Historical Felt Earthquake Catalog of China (1950 – 1969)	Jin X.	Research Result of Jin Xueshen, unpublished internal information offered by Jin Xueshen
World Earthquake Catalog	Shi Z.	Shi Zhenliang et al. (eds.), *World Earthquake Catalog*: 1900 – 1980 ($M \geqslant 6.0$), Sinomap Press, Beijing, China, 1986.
Earthquake Catalog of China Seismic Networks	CSN	http://www.csndmc.ac.cn/newweb/catalog_direct_link.htm
Earthquake Catalog of International Seismological Center (ISC)	ISC	http://www.csndmc.ac.cn/newweb/catalog_direct_link.htm
Earthquake Catalog of the National Earthquake Information Center (NEIC)	NEIC	http://www.csndmc.ac.cn/newweb/catalog_direct_link.htm
Century Earthquake Catalog	Engdahl	http://earthquake.usgs.gov/research/data/centennial.php#cat22
Catalog of Significant Earthquakes	*	http://neic.usgs.gov/neis/epic/epic_global.html or http://earthquake.usgs.gov/earthquakes/eqarchives/epic/
	* *	Paula K. Dunbar, Patricia A. Lockridge, and Lowell S. Whiteside, September 1992. *Catalog of Significant Earthquakes* 2150 *B. C.* – 1991 *A. D.*, U. S. Dept. of Commerce, National Oceanic and Atmospheric Administration. Luo Wei et al. (eds.), 1996. *Catalog of Significant Earthquakes* (2150 *B. C.* – 1991 *A. D.*), Seismological Press, Beijing.
The Global Seismic Hazard Assessment Program (GSHAP)	GSHAP	http://www.seismo.ethz.ch/GSHAP/index.html
Philippines Earthquake Catalog	Nakamura	http://www.cseas.kyoto-u.ac.jp/seas/15/4/150406.pdf
Philippines Earthquake Catalog (1599 – 1909)	Maso	http://www.gutenberg.org/files/18556/18556-h/18556-h.htm
Philippines Earthquake Catalog	Bautista	http://www.sciencedirect.com/science/article/pii/S0040195199002723 Bautista, M. L. P. and K. Oike, 2000. Estimation of the magnitudes and epicenters of Philippine historical earthquakes, Tectonophys., 317: 137 – 169.
Korean Peninsula Earthquake Catalog	Korea	Li Yuche et al. (eds.), 2001. *North Korea & South Korea Earthquake Catalog* (*A. D.* 27 – 1985), Seismological Press, Beijing.

续表

Area	Label	Data source(Website and Publication)
Japan Earthquake Catalog	Usami	http://repository. dl. itc. u-tokyo. ac. jp/dspace/bitstream/2261/12734/1/ji0543001. pdf
	Japan	Lu Zhenheng (ed.), 1991. *Overview of the Destructive Earthquakes in Japan*, Seismological Press, Beijing, pp. 159 – 334.
Australian Earthquake Catalog	Australia	http://www. seismicity. see. uwa. edu. au/welcome/seismicity_in_australia#impotEQ
China Earthquake Disaster Information	Dis	http://www. china – disaster. cn/ Reference materials include: Xie Yushou and Cai Meibiao (eds), 1983. *Compilation of Historical Earthquake Data of China*, *Vol.* 5, Science Press, Beijing. Editorial Board of China Earthquake Yearbook, 1990. *China Earthquake Yearbook* (1949 ~ 1981), Seismological Press, Beijing. Gao Jianguo, 1990. *Summary of Earthquake Losses*, Seismological Press, Beijing. Guo Zengjian and Chen Xinlian (eds.), 1986. *Earthquake Countermeasures*, Seismological Press, Beijing. Zhang Zhaocheng, Luo Lange, Li Haihua et al. (eds.), 1988. *Earthquake Cases in China* (1966 ~ 1975), Seismological Press, Beijing. Zhang Zhaocheng, Luo Lange, Li Haihua et al. (eds.), 1990. *Earthquake Cases in China* (1976 ~ 1980), Seismological Press, Beijing. Zhang Zhaocheng, Luo Lan' ge, Li Haihua et al. (eds.), 1990. *Earthquake Cases in China* (1981 ~ 1985), Seismological Press, Beijing. Zhang Zhaocheng, Zheng Dalin, Xu Jinghua et al. (eds.), 1999. *Earthquake Cases in China* (1986 ~ 1988), Seismological Press, Beijing. Zhang Zhaocheng, Zheng Dalin, Xu Jinghua et al. (eds.), 2000. *Earthquake Cases in China* (1989 ~ 1991), Seismological Press, Beijing. Chen Qifu, Zheng Dalin, Che Shi et al. (eds.), 2002. *Earthquake Cases in China* (1992 ~ 1994), Seismological Press, Beijing. Chen Qifu, Zheng Dalin, Liu Guiping et al. (eds.), 2002. *Earthquake Cases in China* (1995 ~ 1996), Seismological Press, Beijing. Chen Qifu, Zheng Dalin, Gao Rongsheng et al. (eds.), 2003. *Earthquake Cases in China* (1997 ~ 1999), Seismological Press, Beijing. Chen Qifu, Zheng Dalin, Che Shi et al. (eds.), 2008. *Earthquake Cases in China* (2000 ~ 2002), Seismological Press, Beijing.
Global Earthquake (Volcanic) Tsunami Information	NOAA	Information on global tsunami disaster collected by the U. S. National Oceanic and Atmospheric Administration (NOAA) Website. (http://www. nesdis. noaa. gov/)
Global Earthquake Catalog	USGS	http://earthquake. usgs. gov/earthquakes/eqarchives/epic/

5 Description of Headings in the Catalog

1. Time: year (Year), month (Mo), day (Dy), hour (Hr), minute (Mn), second (Sec) in Universal Time (UTC).

2. Tsunami (Tsunami): source (that is, the tsunami source) (Sr), wave height (Wh), class I (mI), class S (mS).

3. Data source (Information).

4. The epicenter (Earthquake Epicenter): names (Name) (English and Chinese), latitude (Latitude), longitude (Longitude).

5. Depth (Depth), magnitude (Mag), magnitude scale (Scale), intensity (MMI).

6. Deaths (Deaths), including number of deaths (expressed as "Num", in unit of people) and death level (referred to as "class", expressed as "Dd").

7. Injured (Injured) including the number (expressed as "Num", in unit of people) and level (referred to as "class", expressed as "Dd") of injured.

8. Economic losses (Losses in Millions of Dollars, expressed as "Losses"), including the amount (in millions of U. S. dollars, expressed by "$ Mill") and level (referred to as "class", expressed as "De").

9. Houses destroyed (Houses Destroyed, expressed as "Destroyed"), including the number (expressed as "Num", in unit of room) and level (referred to as "class", expressed with "Dh").

10. Houses damaged (Houses Damaged, expressed as "Damaged"), including the number (expressed as "Num", in unit of room) and level (referred to as "class", expressed as "Dh").

第一部分

全球地震灾害信息目录

全球公元前9999年至公元2011年6月地震灾害信息目录

时间 年 Year	月 Mo	日 Dy	时 Hr	分 Mn	秒 Sec	海啸 Tsunami 源 Sr	浪高 Wh	级 I mI	级 S mS	资料来源 Information	震中 Earthquake Epicenter 地名(英文) Name(English)	地名(中文) Name(Chinese)	纬度(°) Latitude	经度(°) Longitude	深度 Depth	震级 Mag	标度 Scale	烈度 MMI	死亡人数 Deaths 数量/人 Num	级别 Dd	受伤人数 Injuries 数量/人 Num	级别 Dd	经济损失 Damage 数量/$ Mill $ Mill	级别 De	房屋毁坏 Houses Destroyed 数量/间 Num	级别 Dh	房屋受损 Houses Damaged 数量/间 Num	级别 Dh
-9999										GSHAP	Armenia: Gyumri, Spitak	亚美尼亚:久姆里,斯皮塔克	40.9	44.2	16	7	Mfa	9.5										
-7670										GSHAP	Russia: Irkutsk, Slyudyanka	俄罗斯:伊尔库茨克州斯柳江卡	51.84	103.25	15	7.2	Mfa	10										
-5600										GSHAP	Russia: Irkutsk, Slyudyanka	俄罗斯:伊尔库茨克州斯柳江卡	51.82	103.35	15	7.6	Mfa	10										
-5435										GSHAP	Russia: Buryatiya, Kyren	俄罗斯:布里亚特州克廖恩	51.69	103.01	15	6.6	Mfa	9										
-4890										GSHAP	Russia: Buryatiya, Kyren	俄罗斯:布里亚特州克廖恩	51.91	102.36	15	7.1	Mfa	10										
-3830										GSHAP	Russia: Buryatiya, Kyren	俄罗斯:布里亚特州克廖恩	51.69	103.01	15	6.6	Mfa	9										
-3170										GSHAP	Russia: Buryatiya, Kyren	俄罗斯:布里亚特州克廖恩	51.91	102.36	15	7.1	Mfa	10										
-2700										GSHAP	Russia: Irkutsk, Slyudyanka	俄罗斯:伊尔库茨克州斯柳江卡	51.8	103.4	15	7.4	Mfa	10										
-2500										GSHAP	Armenia: Gyumri, Spitak	亚美尼亚:久姆里,斯皮塔克	40.9	44.2	15	6.5	Mfa	9										
-2300										China	China: Shanxi, Yongji	中国:山西永济	34.9	110.4		5.5	Ms	7										
-2210										GSHAP	Russia: Buryatiya, Kyren	俄罗斯:布里亚特州克廖恩	51.91	102.36	15	7.1	Mfa	10										
-2150										*	Jordan: Al - Karak	约旦:卡拉克	31.1	35.5		7.3	Muk							3				
-2000						2			6	* NOAA, Song	Syria: Ugarit	叙利亚:乌加里特	35.683	35.8		7	Mk	10		3				4				
-2000										*	Turkmenistan: Asgabat	土库曼斯坦:阿什哈巴德	38	58.2	18	7.1	Ms	10	1	1				1		1		
-1890										* * Song	Greece: Crete Island	希腊:克里特岛	35.5	25.5		7	Mk	10										
-1770										GSHAP	Russia: Buryatiya, Kyren	俄罗斯:布里亚特州克廖恩	51.91	102.36	15	7.1	Ms	10										
-1767										China	China: Henan, Songxian	中国:河南嵩县	34.2	112		6	Ms	8										
-1650						5			10	* * NOAA, Song	Greece: Thera Island (Santorini)	希腊:锡拉岛(圣托里尼岛)	36.404	25.396		7	Mk			3				3				
-1590										GSHAP	Russia: Buryatiya, Kyren	俄罗斯:布里亚特州克廖恩	51.91	102.36	15	7.1	Ms	10										
-1566										* Song	Israel: Hebron	以色列:希布伦	31.5	35.3		7.3	Mk	10						3				
-1450										* Song	Greece: Crete Island	希腊:克里特岛	35.5	25.5		7	Mk	10										
-1414										GSHAP	Russia: Lake Baykal	俄罗斯:贝加尔湖	51.92	106.15	15	6.5	Ms	9										
-1410						5			6	* NOAA, Song	Greece: Thirasia	希腊:锡拉夏岛	36.5	25.5		7.1	Mk	12		3				3				
-1365						3			7	* GSHAP, NOAA	Turkey: Hatay; Syria: Aleppo	土耳其:哈塔伊;叙利亚:阿勒颇	35.683	35.8	25	7.3	Ms	9						3				
-1300						2			5	NOAA	Greece: Ionian Islands Coasts	希腊:伊奥尼亚群岛海域	37.8	21.2		6	Ms											

时间						海啸				资料来源	震中				深度	震级	标度	烈度	死亡人数		受伤人数		经济损失		房屋毁坏		房屋受损	
年	月	日	时	分	秒	源	浪高	级I	级S		地名(英文)	地名(中文)	纬度(°)	经度(°)					数量/人	级别	数量/人	级别	数量/$ Mill	级别	数量/间	级别	数量/间	级别
Date						Tsunami				Information	Earthquake Epicenter				Depth	Mag	Scale	MMI	Deaths		Injuries		Damage		Houses Destroyed		Houses Damaged	
Year	Mo	Dy	Hr	Mn	Sec	Sr	Wh	mI	mS		Name(English)	Name(Chinese)	Latitude	Longitude					Num	Dd	Num	Dd	$ Mill	De	Num	Dh	Num	Dh
-1250										*	Israel:Jerusalem	以色列:耶路撒冷	32	35.5		6.5	Muk							3				
-1250										GSHAP	Georgia:Zugdidi	格鲁吉亚:祖格迪迪	42.7	42.2	15	6.9	Ms	9.5										
-1235										GSHAP	Russia:Lake Baykal	俄罗斯:贝加尔湖	51.92	106.15	15	6.5	Ms	9										
-1084										GSHAP	Russia:Lake Baykal	俄罗斯:贝加尔湖	51.92	106.15	15	6.5	Ms	9										
-1050										*	Jordan:Timna Copper Mines	约旦:提姆纳	29.6	35		6.2	Muk							3				
-1039										GSHAP	Russia:Lake Baykal	俄罗斯:贝加尔湖	51.92	106.15	15	6.5	Ms	9										
-976										GSHAP	Russia:Lake Baykal	俄罗斯:贝加尔湖	51.92	106.15	15	6.5	Ms	9										
-800										GSHAP	Black Sea	黑海	44.7	37.3	15	6.5	Ms	9										
-780										China	China:Shaanxi,Qishan	中国:陕西岐山	34.5	107.8		7	Ms	9										
-759						3			4	* NOAA,Song	Israel:Zefat (Safed)	以色列:采法特(萨法德)	33	35.5		7.1	Mk	11						3				
-750										GSHAP	Russia:Chita,Burpala	俄罗斯:赤塔州布尔帕拉	56.52	119.46	15	6.4	Ms	8.5										
-750										GSHAP	Russia: Buryatiya, Kurort Baunt	俄罗斯:布里亚特州库罗尔特巴温特	55.11	112.75	15	6.6	Ms	9										
-699										GSHAP	Russia:Lake Baykal	俄罗斯:贝加尔湖	51.92	106.14	15	6.5	Ms	9										
-646										China	China:Shanxi,Hongtong	中国:山西洪洞	36.3	111.7		5	Ms	6										
-600										GSHAP	Iraq:As Sulaymaniyah	伊拉克:苏莱曼尼亚	35	45	12	6.5	Ms	9										
-600										* * Song	Aegean Sea	爱琴海	38.5	22.5		7	Mk	10										
-590						2			6	* NOAA,Song	Lebanon:Sour (Tyre)	黎巴嫩:苏尔	33.2	35.1		6.7	Mk	6										
-550										* GSHAP	Aegean Sea	爱琴海	37.4	24.9		6	Ms	10										
-525						2			2.5	* NOAA,Song	Lebanon:Sour (Tyre), Sayda (Saida)	黎巴嫩:苏尔,塞达	33.2	35.1		6.7	Mk											
-519	8	8								China	China:Henan,Luoyang	中国:河南洛阳	34.7	112.5		5.5	Ms	7										
-480	12	29				1				* GSHAP,NOAA	Greece:Megara	希腊:墨伽拉	37.9	23.3		6.3	Ms											
-479						2			3	* NOAA,GSHAP	Aegean Sea	爱琴海	40.2	23.5		7	Ms	10		3								
-464										* * Song	Greece:Skoura	希腊:斯库拉	37	22.5		7	Mk	10										
-432										* Song	Greece:Lakonia	希腊:拉科尼亚	37	22.5		5.5	Mk							1		1		
-426	6					3			4	* NOAA,GSHAP	Greece:Lamia	希腊:拉米亚	38.9	22.7		7	Ms	10	2500	4				3		3		
-400										*	Iran:Tehran,Vārāmīn	伊朗:德黑兰,瓦拉明	35.5	51.8		7.6	Ms							3				
-373						2			5	* NOAA	Greece:Patrai	希腊:帕特雷	38	22		7.3	Ms	11		3				3		3		
-368										* * Song	Greece:Crete Island	希腊:克里特岛	35	25	100	7	Mk	10										
-364										* Song	Greece:Crete Island	希腊:克里特岛	35	25	100	5.4	Mk							1				
-350										GSHAP	Iran:Tehran,Vārāmīn	伊朗:德黑兰,瓦拉明	35.5	51.8	16	7.6	Ms	10.5										
-342										GSHAP	Turkey:Kesan,S.	土耳其:凯尚南部	40.4	26.6	14	6.1	Ms	8.5										
-331										GSHAP	Syria:Aleppo	叙利亚:阿勒颇	36.1	36.1	20	6.6	Ms	8.5										
-330						1				* GSHAP,NOAA	Aegean Sea	爱琴海	40	25	15	7	Ms	11										
-326	11					2				* NOAA,Song	India:Anjar	印度:安贾尔	23	71		7	Mk											
-282										* Song	Greece:Delphi	希腊:德尔斐	38.5	22.5		5.5	Mk							1				

时间 年 Year	月 Mo	日 Dy	时 Hr	分 Mn	秒 Sec	海啸 Tsunami 源 Sr	浪高 Wh	级 I mI	级 S mS	资料来源 Information	震中 Earthquake Epicenter 地名(英文) Name(English)	地名(中文) Name(Chinese)	纬度(°) Latitude	经度(°) Longitude	深度 Depth	震级 Mag	标度 Scale	烈度 MMI	死亡人数 Deaths 数量/人 Num	级别 Dd	受伤人数 Injuries 数量/人 Num	级别 Dd	经济损失 Damage 数量/$ Mill	级别 De	房屋毁坏 Houses Destroyed 数量/间 Num	级别 Dh	房屋受损 Houses Damaged 数量/间 Num	级别 Dh
-282										* GSHAP	Turkey:Kesan,S.	土耳其:凯尚南部	40.6	26.6	14	6.1	Ms	10										
-280										China	China:Shaanxi,Xianyang,NE.	中国:陕西咸阳东北	34.4	108.8		5.5	Ms	7										
-267										* * Song	Greece:Crete Island	希腊:克里特岛	35	25		7	Mk	10										
-255										* * Song	Greece:Crete Island	希腊:克里特岛	35	25		7	Mk	10										
-250										*	Kyrgyzstan:Bishkek	吉尔吉斯斯坦:比什凯克	42.7	77.5	20	6.7	Ms	9						3				
-231										China	China:Hebei,Pingyin,SE.	中国:河北平阴东南	39.8	114.2		6.5	Ms	8										
-230										China	China:Shanxi,Yongji	中国:山西永济	34.9	110.4		5.5	Ms	7										
-227						2			3	* GSHAP,NOAA	Turkey:Bodrum	土耳其:博得卢姆	36.5	27.8	100	7.5	Ms	10						1		1		
-226						1				GSHAP,NOAA	Greece:Lamia	希腊:拉米亚	38.8	22.7		6.5	Ms											
-223	10					2				* NOAA,Song	Greece:Itea Gulf	希腊:伊泰阿海湾	38.4	22.4		6.6	Mk											
-221										* Song	Egypt:Siwa Oasis	埃及:西瓦绿洲	29.2	25.5		5.9	Mk	7						2				
-220										* *	Greece:Dodecanese Islands	希腊:多德卡尼斯群岛	36.5	28.2	100	7.2	Ms	10										
-218						4				* Song	Steait of Gibraltar,Coast W.	直布罗陀海峡西部海域	36.2	-7.17		7	Mk											
-217	6									* Italy	Italy:Toscana	意大利:托斯卡纳	43.25	11.25		6.56	Ms							3				
-210						4				* Song	Steait of Gibraltar,Coast W.	直布罗陀海峡西部海域	36	-10.5		7	Mk											
-198						5				* GSHAP, NOAA	Greece:Thera Island (Santorini)	希腊:锡拉岛(圣托里尼岛)	36.4	25.4		6	Ms											
-197						5				GSHAP,NOAA	Greece:Limnos	希腊:利姆诺斯岛	40	25.4		7	Ms											
-193	2									* China	China:Gansu,Lintao	中国:甘肃临洮	35.4	103.9		6.5	Ms	8						2	400	3		
-186	2	22								* China	China:Gansu,Wudu,NE.	中国:甘肃武都东北	33.8	105.6		7	Ms	8	760	3								
-184										GSHAP	Syria:Aleppo	叙利亚:阿勒颇	36.2	36.3	15	6.1	Ms	8										
-183										* * Song	Greece:Dodecanese Islands	希腊:多德卡尼斯群岛	36	28	100	7	Mk	10										
-177										* Song	France:Montpellier	法国:蒙彼利埃	43.5	3.9	100	5.5	Mk							2		2		
-176										China	China:Henan,Songxian	中国:河南嵩县	34.2	112		6	Ms	8										
-150										GSHAP	Russia:Krasnodar,Krymsk	俄罗斯:克拉斯诺达尔区克雷姆斯克	44.6	38.1	14	6.1	Ms	8.5										
-150										GSHAP	Russia: Buryatiya, Severo-muysk	俄罗斯:布里亚特州谢韦罗穆伊斯克城	56.17	113.8	15	7	Ms	9										
-143	6	7								China	China:Hubei,Zhushan,SW.	中国:湖北竹山西南	32.1	110.1		5	Ms	6										
-138						2			3	NOAA	Israel:Haifa,Coast W.	以色列:海法西部海域	32.9	34.7		7	Ms											
-92	2	28								GSHAP	Mediterranean Sea	地中海	35	35	20	7	Ms	9										
-91	10	10								China	China:Shaanxi,Xi-an	中国:陕西西安	34.3	108.9		5.5	Ms	7										
-70	6	1								* China	China:Shandong,Zhucheng,NW.	中国:山东诸城西北	36.3	119.2		7	Ms	9	6000	4								
-69										GSHAP	Turkey:Hatay; Syria:Aleppo	土耳其:哈塔伊;叙利亚:阿勒颇	36	36.2	30	7.4	Ms	9										

年 Year	月 Mo	日 Dy	时 Hr	分 Mn	秒 Sec	源 Sr	浪高 Wh	级I mI	级S mS	资料来源 Information	地名(英文) Name(English)	地名(中文) Name(Chinese)	纬度(°) Latitude	经度(°) Longitude	深度 Depth	震级 Mag	标度 Scale	烈度 MMI	死亡人数 Deaths 数量/人 Num	死亡人数 Deaths 级别 Dd	受伤人数 Injuries 数量/人 Num	受伤人数 Injuries 级别 Dd	经济损失 Damage 数量/$ Mill	经济损失 Damage 级别 De	房屋毁坏 Houses Destroyed 数量/间 Num	房屋毁坏 Houses Destroyed 级别 Dh	房屋受损 Houses Damaged 数量/间 Num	房屋受损 Houses Damaged 级别 Dh
-63	10									* GSHAP	Sea of Azov	亚速海	45.6	36.2	20	6.4	Ms	8						3				
-60						1				* NOAA	Portugal: Coast SW.	葡萄牙:西南海域	36	-10		6.7	Ms	9										
-58						1				* GSHAP, NOAA	Albania: Durres	阿尔巴尼亚:都拉斯	41.5	19.4		6.6	Ms											
-57						2			3	NOAA	Albania: Durres	阿尔巴尼亚:都拉斯	41.5	19.4		6.6	Ms											
-50						4				* Song	Georgia: Sukhumi	格鲁吉亚:苏呼米	43	41		5.5	Ms	8						2				
-50										* Song	Bulgaria: Shabla	保加利亚:沙布拉	43.5	28.5		5.9	Mk							2				
-47	4	17								* China	China: Gansu, Longxi	中国:甘肃陇西	34.9	104.7		6.75	Ms	9		3				2		3		
-35	7	9								China	China: Shaanxi, Xi-an	中国:陕西西安	34.3	109		5.75	Ms	7										
-33										* Song	Egypt: Yamit	埃及:耶米特	31.2	34.2		7.7	Mk	9	30000	5								
-31	9	2								*	Israel: Jerusalem	以色列:耶路撒冷	32	35.5		7	Muk							3				
-27										* Song	Egypt: Luxor	埃及:卢克索	25.7	32.7		6.3	Mk							3				
-26	3	26								* China	China: Sichuan, Yibin	中国:四川宜宾	28.8	104.6		5.5	Ms	7	13	1				2				
-26						4				* Song	Cyprus: Salamis	塞浦路斯:萨拉米斯	35	33		6.7	Mk	9										
-23						1			3	* * NOAA, Song	Greece: Patrai	希腊:帕特雷	38.25	22.25		6.7	Mk	9										
-15										* Song	Cyprus: Salamis	塞浦路斯:萨拉米斯	35.2	34		7.1	Mk							4				
10										*	Turkmenistan: Asgabat	土库曼斯坦:阿什哈巴德	38	58.3	18	7.1	Muk	10						3				
11										* Song	Turkey: Mandelia	土耳其:曼德拉	37.8	27.4		7.3	Mk	10										
17										* Song	Turkey: Izmir, Efes, Aydin	土耳其:伊兹密尔,艾菲斯,艾登	37.85	27.3		7.3	Mk	10						3				
19	2									China	China: Jilin, Ji-an	中国:吉林集安	41.1	126.2		5	Ms	6										
23										* GSHAP	Greece: Patrai	希腊:帕特雷	38.2	22.2		6.3	Ms	10										
25										* Song	Pakistan: Sargodha	巴基斯坦:萨戈达	33	72		6.3	Mk							3				
27	11									* Korea	South Korea: Kwangju	韩国:光州市	35.9	126.5		6.3	Muk	8						3				
29										* Song	Turkey: Iznik, Izmit	土耳其:伊兹尼克,伊兹米特	40.5	28.9		7.3	Mk	10						3				
30										GSHAP	Turkey: Bursa	土耳其:布尔萨	40.5	29.5	15	6.5	Ms	9										
33										* Song	Egypt: Yamit	埃及:耶米特	31.2	34.2		5.9	Mk							2				
37										GSHAP	Syria: Hamah (Hama)	叙利亚:哈马	35.7	36.3	20	6.7	Ms	8.5										
46	10	21								* China	China: Henan, Nanyang	中国:河南南阳	33	112.5		6.5	Ms	8		2				2		2		
46						1			3	GSHAP, NOAA	Greece: Thera Island (Santorini)	希腊:锡拉岛(圣托里尼岛)	36.4	25.4		6.5	Ms											
50										* Song	Afghan: Kondoz	阿富汗:昆都士	37	68.5		6.3	Mk							3				
50						2				* NOAA	Georgia: Sukhumi	格鲁吉亚:苏呼米	42.9	41	30	5.5	Ms	8						2				
52										* Song	Greece: Philippi, Drama, Kavala	希腊:腓立比,兹拉马,卡瓦拉	41	24.3		6.3	Mk							3				
52										* Song	Turkey: Hatay	土耳其:哈塔伊	36.1	36.1		6.5	Mk	9						3				
53										GSHAP	Syria: Idlib	叙利亚:伊德利卜	36.2	36.5	30	7.4	Ms	9										
55										* Song	Greece: Crete Island	希腊:克里特岛	35	25		7	Mk	10										
57										* Song	Albania: Durres	阿尔巴尼亚:都拉斯	41.2	19.3		6.2	Mk	10										

年 Year	月 Mo	日 Dy	时 Hr	分 Mn	秒 Sec	海啸 Tsunami 源 Sr	海啸 Tsunami 浪高 Wh	海啸 Tsunami 级I mI	海啸 Tsunami 级S mS	资料来源 Information	震中 Earthquake Epicenter 地名(英文) Name(English)	震中 Earthquake Epicenter 地名(中文) Name(Chinese)	纬度(°) Latitude	经度(°) Longitude	深度 Depth	震级 Mag	标度 Scale	烈度 MMI	死亡人数 Deaths 数量/人 Num	死亡人数 Deaths 级别 Dd	受伤人数 Injuries 数量/人 Num	受伤人数 Injuries 级别 Dd	经济损失 Damage 数量/$ Mill	经济损失 Damage 级别 De	房屋毁坏 Houses Destroyed 数量/间 Num	房屋毁坏 Houses Destroyed 级别 Dh	房屋受损 Houses Damaged 数量/间 Num	房屋受损 Houses Damaged 级别 Dh
60										* Turkey	Turkey:Pamukkale, Denizli	土耳其:帕木卡雷,丹兹利	37.9	29.2		7	Ms	9						3				
62						5			3	* NOAA	Greece:Thera Island (Santorini)	希腊:锡拉岛(圣托里尼岛)	36.404	25.396		6.7	Ms											
62						1				* GSHAP	Greece:Crete Island	希腊:克里特岛	34.8	25		7	Ms	9										
63	10									* *	Ukraine:Kerch	乌克兰:刻赤	45.2	36.6	20	6.4	Ms							3				
63										* Song	Italy:Pompei	意大利:庞培	40.7	14.5		6	Mk	10										
66						4				* * NOAA	Greece:Crete Island	希腊:克里特岛	35.5	25.5		6.9	Ms	10										
76						1				GSHAP	Cyprus:Gazimagusa	塞浦路斯:法马古斯塔	35	34	20	6.8	Ms	10										
76										*	Cyprus: Paphos	塞浦路斯:帕福斯	34.8	32		7	Mk	10						3		3		
77	6	20				1			4	* * NOAA	Greece:Argolida	希腊:阿尔戈利斯	37.9	22.9		6.3	Ms	10										
79	8	25	7			5			4	* Italy,NOAA	Italy:Torre Del Greco	意大利:托雷德尔格雷科	40.8	14.38		5.77	Ms	10	3500	4								
79	11	23								* * Song	Italy:Naples (Napoli)	意大利:拿坡里(那不勒斯)	40.8	14.4	5	6	Mk	10										
82										GSHAP	Syria:Aleppo	叙利亚:阿勒颇	36.1	36.2	16	6.5	Ms	8.5										
89	7									* Korea	South Korea:Kwangju	韩国:光州市	35.9	126.5		7	Muk	9		3				2				
92										GSHAP	Turkey:Kesan,S.	土耳其:凯尚南部	40.5	26.6	25	6.5	Ms	9										
93										* Song	Turkey:Hellespont	土耳其:达达尼尔海峡	40.6	26.7		6.3	Mk			3				3				
100	12									* Korea	South Korea:Kyongju	韩国:庆州	35.8	129.2		6.3	Ms	8		3				2		3		
105										* Song	Turkey:Ayvalik; Greece:Khios	土耳其:艾伐利克;希腊:俄斯	39.5	27		7.3	Mk	10										
115	12	13				2				* NOAA	Turkey:Hatay	土耳其:哈塔伊	36.1	36.1		7.5	Ms	11	260000	5				4				
117	11	10								GSHAP	Turkey:Manyas	土耳其:马尼亚斯	40.4	28	14	6.1	Ms	8.5										
120	11	10				3			2	GSHAP,NOAA	Turkey:Istanbul	土耳其:伊斯坦布尔	40.7	29.1		7.2	Ms											
123										*	South Korea:Kyongju	韩国:庆州	35.8	129.2		6.3	Ms	8						1		2		
128	2	22								* China	China:Gansu,Gangu	中国:甘肃甘谷	34.7	105.4		6.5	Ms	8		2				2		2		
138	2	28								* China	China:Gansu,Lintao,NW.	中国:甘肃临洮西北	35.8	103.5		6.75	Ms	9		3				3		3		
142						3			4	* GSHAP,NOAA	Greece:Rhodes Island	希腊:罗德岛	36.7	28		7.6	Ms											
143	10									* China	China:Gansu,Longxi	中国:甘肃陇西	35	104		7	Ms	9		1				1				
144	2	15								Japan,Song	Japan:Niigata	日本:新潟	37.7	139.4		6.1	Mk											1
144	10	25								China	China:Shanxi,Xinzhou	中国:山西忻州	38.6	112.6		5.5	Ms	7										
155										* Song	Greece:Dodecanese Islands	希腊:多德卡尼斯群岛	36.5	28.5	100	7	Mk	10										
161										GSHAP	Syria:Dayr Az – Zawr	叙利亚:代尔祖尔	34.7	40.7	18	6	Ms	8										
170	5	3								GSHAP	Turkey:Iznik,Izmit	土耳其:伊兹尼克,伊兹米特	40.3	28.7	15	6.5	Ms	9										
170										* Song	Aegean Sea	爱琴海	39	24.5		6.3	Mk							3				
173	6	28				3		1	1	* NOAA,Song	China:Bohai Sea	中国:渤海	37.5	120		7	Mk											
177										* Song	Turkey:Izmir;Aegean Islands	土耳其:伊兹密尔;爱琴群岛	38.6	26.65		5.9	Mk	7		3				2				

年 Year	月 Mo	日 Dy	时 Hr	分 Mn	秒 Sec	海啸 Tsunami 源 Sr	浪高 Wh	级 I mI	级 S mS	资料来源 Information	震中 Earthquake Epicenter 地名(英文) Name(English)	地名(中文) Name(Chinese)	纬度(°) Latitude	经度(°) Longitude	深度 Depth	震级 Mag	标度 Scale	烈度 MMI	死亡人数 Deaths 数量/人 Num	级别 Dd	受伤人数 Injuries 数量/人 Num	级别 Dd	经济损失 Damage 数量/$ Mill	级别 De	房屋毁坏 Houses Destroyed 数量/间 Num	级别 Dh	房屋受损 Houses Damaged 数量/间 Num	级别 Dh
177						2			6	NOAA,Song	Italy:Sicilia Island	意大利:西西里岛	38	15		6.7	Mk	9						3				
180	9									* China	China:Gansu,Gaotai,W.	中国:甘肃高台西	39.4	99.5		7.5	Ms	10										
200										GSHAP	Russia:Irkutsk,Slyudyanka	俄罗斯:伊尔库茨克州斯柳江卡	51.83	103.31	15	7.4	Ms	10										
242										GSHAP	Turkey:Osmaniye	土耳其:奥斯曼尼耶	37.3	36.5	45	7.5	Ms	8.5										
243										*	Italy:Verona,Benaco	意大利:维罗那,贝纳科	45.3	11		5.3	Muk							4				
251	7	9								* Song	Greece:Crete Island	希腊:克里特岛	35.5	25.5		7	Mk	10										
253	7	9								* Song	Turkey:Izmir	土耳其:伊兹密尔	39.1	27.2		7.3	Mk	10										
258						2			4	NOAA,Song	Italy:Tyrrhenian Sea	意大利:第勒尼安海	42	12.5		6.7	Mk											
262						1			4	* NOAA,Song	Libya:Albayda	利比亚:贝达	32.8	21.9		6.7	Mk							2				
294	7									* China	China:Anhui,Shouxian	中国:安徽寿县	32.6	116.8		5.5	Ms	7		1								
294	9									* China	China:Beijing,Yanqing,E.	中国:北京延庆东	40.5	116		6	Ms	8	101	3								
304	9									Korea	South Korea:Kyongju	韩国:庆州	35.8	129.2		5	Ms	7										
304	10									* Korea	South Korea:Kyongju	韩国:庆州	35.5	129.1		6.3	Muk	8		3				2				
306										* Song	Lebanon:Sur (Tyre), Sayda (Saida)	黎巴嫩:苏尔,塞达	33.2	35.1		6.5	Mk	9						3				
315	2									China	China:Shanxi,Linfen	中国:山西临汾	36.1	111.5		5	Ms	6										
315						1			3	NOAA,Song	Israel:Hebron;Dead Sea	以色列:希布伦;死海	31.5	35.5		6.7	Mk											
318	5	26								China	China:Qinghai,Xining	中国:青海西宁	36.6	101.8		4.75	Ms	6										
319	6	18								* China	China:Gansu,Tianshui,S.	中国:甘肃天水南	34.3	105.3		5	Ms	6		2								
324	8	6								* Song	Italy:Campania	意大利:坎佩尼亚	40.5	14.5		6	Mk	10										
330										GSHAP	Cyprus:Gazimagusa	塞浦路斯:法马古斯塔	35	34	14	6.3	Ms	8.5										
330						1				NOAA	Greece:Aegean Islands	希腊:爱琴群岛	40	25		7	Ms											
334										* GSHAP	Albania:Durres	阿尔巴尼亚:都拉斯	41.2	19.3		6.1	Ms	10										
334										GSHAP	Syria:Aleppo	叙利亚:阿勒颇	36.1	36.2	16	7	Ms	9.5										
337										GSHAP	Cyprus:Nicosia,W.	塞浦路斯:尼科西亚西部	35	33	20	7	Ms	9										
340										* Song	Turkey:Hatay	土耳其:哈塔伊	36.1	36.1		6.5	Mk	9						3				
341										* Song	Turkey:Hatay	土耳其:哈塔伊	36.2	36.1		5.5	Mk	7										
342										* Song	Albania:Durres	阿尔巴尼亚:都拉斯	41.2	19.3		6.2	Mk	10						2				
342										* Song	Turkey:Hatay	土耳其:哈塔伊	36.2	36.1		7.7	Mk		40000	5				4				
344	4	11								* Song	Italy:Campania	意大利:坎佩尼亚	40.5	14.5		6	Mk	10										
344	12									* China	China:Henan,Weihui	中国:河南卫辉	35.4	114.3		6	Ms	8	101	3								
344						3				* NOAA,Song	Turkey:Umurbey	土耳其:乌穆尔贝伊	40.3	26.5		7.2	Mk	9						4				
346						1				GSHAP,NOAA	Albania:Durres	阿尔巴尼亚:都拉斯	41.4	19.4		6.8	Ms											
348						2			3	* NOAA,Song	Lebanon:Bayrut (Beirut)	黎巴嫩:贝鲁特	33.9	35.5		6.8	Mk	9						3				
350	10									* Song	Turkey:Izmit	土耳其:伊兹米特	41	30		7.3	Mk	10										
355										* Song	Turkey:Izmit,Nicomedia	土耳其:伊兹米特,尼可米迪亚	40.7	29.7		6.5	Mk	9						3				

年 Year	月 Mo	日 Dy	时 Hr	分 Mn	秒 Sec	海啸 Tsunami 源 Sr	浪高 Wh	级 I mI	级 S mS	资料来源 Information	震中 Earthquake Epicenter 地名(英文) Name(English)	地名(中文) Name(Chinese)	纬度(°) Latitude	经度(°) Longitude	深度 Depth	震级 Mag	标度 Scale	烈度 MMI	死亡人数 Deaths 数量/人 Num	级别 Dd	受伤人数 Injuries 数量/人 Num	级别 Dd	经济损失 Damage 数量/$ Mill	级别 De	房屋毁坏 Houses Destroyed 数量/间 Num	级别 Dh	房屋受损 Houses Damaged 数量/间 Num	级别 Dh
358	8	24								* Song	Turkey: Iznik, Izmit	土耳其:伊兹尼克,伊兹米特	40.8	29.9		6.3	Mk							3				
361										* Song	Macedonia: Prilep	马其顿:普里莱普	41.6	21.5		7.1	Mk	12						4				
362	5	24				2			3	* NOAA	Jordan: Al – Karak	约旦:卡拉克	31.3	35.6		6.4	Ms							3				
362	5	27								China	China: Gansu, Wuwei, W.	中国:甘肃武威西部	37.9	102.6		4.75	Ms	6										
362	12	2								* Song	Turkey: Gebze	土耳其:盖布泽	41	29.5		7.3	Mk	10										
365	7	21				4			4	* Turkey, NOAA	Greece: Crete, Knossos	希腊:克里特岛,克诺撒斯	35	23	70	8.3	Ms	11	5700	4				4		3		3
366	3									China	China: Gansu, Wuwei, W.	中国:甘肃武威西部	37.9	102.6		5	Ms	6										
367	10	11								* Song	Turkey: Iznik, Nicaea	土耳其:伊兹尼克,尼西亚	40.7	29.7		6.3	Mk		1000	3				3				
367										GSHAP	Mediterranean Sea	地中海	35	30	150	8.3	Ms	9.5										
368	10	11								* Song	Greece: Nikea	希腊:尼基亚	39.5	22.5		6.3	Mk							3				
368	10	11				2				* GSHAP, NOAA	Turkey: Bursa	土耳其:布尔萨	40.5	29.6		6.4	Ms							3				
368						4				* GSHAP	Turkey: Marmara Sea	土耳其:马尔马拉海	40.5	29.6		6.8	Ms							2				
369										* Song	Italy: Benevento	意大利:贝内文托	41.1	14.8		6	Mk	10										
372	8									China	China: Qinghai, Xining	中国:青海西宁	36.6	101.8		5	Ms	6										
374	8	9								China	China: Gansu, Wuwei, W.	中国:甘肃武威西部	37.9	102.6		4.75	Ms	6										
382						1				* NOAA, Song	Portugal: Coast SW.	葡萄牙:西南海域	37	-10		7	Mk											
394										* GSHAP	Syria: Idlib	叙利亚:伊德利卜	35.8	36.3	32	7.1	Ms	9						3				
396										* Song	Turkey: Hatay	土耳其:哈塔伊	36.1	36.1		6.5	Mk	9						3				
407	4	1				2			4	* NOAA	Turkey: Balikesir, N.	土耳其:巴勒克西尔北部	40.2	28		6.6	Ms	8						1				
408										China	China: Gansu, Zhangye	中国:甘肃张掖	39	100.5		4.75	Ms	6										
408										China	China: Shandong, Linzi	中国:山东临淄	36.8	118.3		5	Ms	6										
412										* Song	Tunisia: Rafraf	突尼斯:赖夫拉夫	37.067	10.067		7.3	Mk	10										
416										China	China: Gansu, Tianshui	中国:甘肃天水	34.5	105.6		5	Ms	6										
419										China	China: Liaoning, Chaoyang	中国:辽宁朝阳	41.6	120.4		5.5	Ms	7										
419										* Song	Egypt: Yamit	埃及:耶米特	31.2	34.2		6.3	Mk							3				
425										* Song	Israel: Ramla	以色列:拉姆拉	31.9	34.9		7.3	Mk	10						3				
426						3			4	* NOAA, Song	Greece: Lamia	希腊:拉米亚	38.8	22.8		6.7	Mk	10										
427										*	Azerbaijan: Gəncə	阿塞拜疆:占贾	40.5	46.5	12	6.7	Muk	10						3				
438										* Song	Greece: Crete Island	希腊:克里特岛	35.5	25.5		7	Mk	10										
440	10	26								* GSHAP	Turkey: Istanbul	土耳其:伊斯坦布尔	41	29	15	5.8	Ms	7						3				
447	1	26				3			4	** NOAA, GSHAP	Turkey: Marmara Sea	土耳其:马尔马拉海	40.9	28.5		7.3	Ms											
447										* * Song	Israel: Hebron	以色列:希布伦	31.5	35.1		6.5	Mk	9						3				
447										GSHAP	Turkey: Manyas	土耳其:马尼亚斯	40.5	28	40	8	Ms	9.5										
448	9	6								* Song	Greece: Crete Island	希腊:克里特岛	35	25		7	Mk	10										
457										* Song	Turkey: Hatay	土耳其:哈塔伊	36.1	36.1		7.3	Mk	10						4				
458	3									GSHAP, Korea	South Korea: Kyongju	韩国:庆州	35.9	129.3		5.5	Ms	7										

时间 年 Year	月 Mo	日 Dy	时 Hr	分 Mn	秒 Sec	海啸 源 Sr	浪高 Wh	级I mI	级S mS	资料来源 Information	震中 地名(英文) Name(English)	地名(中文) Name(Chinese)	纬度(°) Latitude	经度(°) Longitude	深度 Depth	震级 Mag	标度 Scale	烈度 MMI	死亡人数 数量/人 Num	级别 Dd	受伤人数 数量/人 Num	级别 Dd	经济损失 数量/$ Mill	级别 De	房屋毁坏 数量/间 Num	级别 Dh	房屋受损 数量/间 Num	级别 Dh
458	9									* GSHAP	Turkey:Hatay	土耳其:哈塔伊	36.2	36.4	20	7.7	Ms	10	80000	5				3				
460	7	22								* Song	Thailand:Mae Chan	泰国:湄占	20.3	100		8.5	Mk	12		3				3				
462	8	17								China	China:Shandong,Yanzhou,S.	中国:山东兖州南	34.8	117		6.5	Ms	8										
464										GSHAP	Turkey:Marmara Sea	土耳其:马尔马拉海	40.4	27.8	16	7.3	Ms	10										
470										* Song	France:Vienne,Vivarais	法国:维也纳,维瓦赖	44.4	4.3		6.3	Mk							3				
477	9	25				3				* GSHAP	Turkey:Istanbul	土耳其:伊斯坦布尔	40.9	28.8	16	7	Ms	10		3				3				
478	9	25								* NOAA,Song	Turkey:Istanbul	土耳其:伊斯坦布尔	41	29		6.1	Mk	8										
494										* Song	Lebanon:Tarabulus (Tripolis)	黎巴嫩:塔拉布卢斯(黎波里)	34.3	35.5		7.3	Mk	10						3				
495	4	1								China	China:Shandong,Rushan,SE.	中国:山东乳山东南	36.8	121.6		5.5	Ms	7										
499	8	5								* China	China:Jiangsu,Nanjing	中国:江苏南京	32.1	118.8		4.75	Ms	6						2		3		
500										*	Kazakhstan:Almaty	哈萨克斯坦:阿拉木图	42.7	76.5	20	6.7	Muk	8						3				
500										GSHAP	Turkey:Hatay	土耳其:哈塔伊	36.3	36.2	35	7.3	Ms	9										
501										*	North Korea:Pyongyang	朝鲜:平壤	39	125.3		6.3	Muk	8		3				2				
506	9	1								China	China:Gansu,Wuwei,W.	中国:甘肃武威西部	37.9	102.6		4.75	Ms	6										
510	6									* Korea	South Korea:Kyongju	韩国:庆州	35.5	129.1		6.3	Muk	8		3				2				
512	5	23								* China	China:Shanxi,Yuanping	中国:山西原平	38.9	112.8		7.5	Ms	10	5130	4	2720	4		4				
518										* GSHAP	Macedonia:Skopje, Stamer	马其顿:斯科普里,斯坦莫	42	21.4		7	Ms	12						4				
521										* GSHAP	Albania:Durres	阿尔巴尼亚:都拉斯	41.2	19.6		6.3	Ms							3				
521										GSHAP	Turkey:Osmaniye	土耳其:奥斯曼尼耶	37	36.5	40	7.4	Ms	8.5										
522										* Song	Albania:Durres	阿尔巴尼亚:都拉斯	41.2	19.3		6.2	Mk	10										
522										* Song	Syria:Aleppo	叙利亚:阿勒颇	36.2	36.1		7.3	Mk	10						3				
525	5	29								* GSHAP	Turkey:Antakya, Samandag	土耳其:哈塔伊,沙满列	36.25	36.1	40	7.9	Ms	9.5	250000	5				4				
527										* Song	Greece:Jannina (Epirus)	希腊:伊庇鲁斯	40.1	20.8		7	Mk	10										
528	11	29								*	Turkey:Hatay	土耳其:哈塔伊	36.25	36.1		7.1	Ms	10	4870	4				4				
533	11	29								* Song	Syria:Halab (Aleppo)	叙利亚:阿勒颇	36.1	37.1		7.7	Mk		130000	5								
535	1	5								GSHAP	Syria:Aleppo	叙利亚:阿勒颇	36.2	36.3	15	6.3	Ms	8.5										
542	9	6				3			4	* NOAA	Turkey:Balikesir,N.	土耳其:巴勒克西尔北部	40.3	27.8		6.8	Ms	10						3				
543	9	6				2				GSHAP,NOAA	Turkey:Marmara Sea	土耳其:马尔马拉海	40.39	27.8		7	Ms											
550										GSHAP	Turkey:Marmara Sea	土耳其:马尔马拉海	40.9	28.5	25	7.2	Ms	9.5										
551	7	7				2			4	* NOAA	Greece:Patrai	希腊:帕特雷	38.4	22.3		7.1	Ms	11	4000	4								
551	7	9				2			3	* NOAA	Lebanon:Bayrut (Beirut)	黎巴嫩:贝鲁特	33.9	35.5		7.8	Ms	10						3				
552	5					3				NOAA	Greece:Itea Gulf	希腊:伊泰阿海湾	38.4	22.4		7.2	Ms											
552	7	9								* Song	Syria:Halab (Aleppo)	叙利亚:阿勒颇(阿勒颇)	36.1	37.1		7.3	Mk	10						3				

年 Year	月 Mo	日 Dy	时 Hr	分 Mn	秒 Sec	源 Sr	浪高 Wh	级 I mI	级 S mS	资料来源 Information	地名(英文) Name(English)	地名(中文) Name(Chinese)	纬度(°) Latitude	经度(°) Longitude	深度 Depth	震级 Mag	标度 Scale	烈度 MMI	死亡人数 Deaths 数量/人 Num	死亡人数 Deaths 级别 Dd	受伤人数 Injuries 数量/人 Num	受伤人数 Injuries 级别 Dd	经济损失 Damage 数量/$ Mill	经济损失 Damage 级别 De	房屋毁坏 Houses Destroyed 数量/间 Num	房屋毁坏 Houses Destroyed 级别 Dh	房屋受损 Houses Damaged 数量/间 Num	房屋受损 Houses Damaged 级别 Dh
553	7	9								* Song	Lebanon: Bayrut (Beirut)	黎巴嫩:贝鲁特	33.9	35.5		7.3	Mk	10						3				
554	8	15				3			4	* NOAA	Greece: Dodecanese Islands	希腊:多德卡尼斯群岛	36.5	27.5		7	Ms	11										
555	8	15								* GSHAP	Turkey: Istanbul	土耳其:伊斯坦布尔	41.04	28.98		7	Mk	10										
557	7	9								* Song	Turkey: Hatay	土耳其:哈塔伊	36.1	36.1		7.3	Mk	10										
557	10	14				3	2	1	3	* NOAA	Turkey: Marmara Sea	土耳其:马尔马拉海	40.9	27.6		7	Ms											
558	12	14				2				* NOAA	Turkey: Marmara Sea	土耳其:马尔马拉海	40.9	28.8		7	Ms	9										
558	12	25								* Song	Italy: Ancona	意大利:安科纳	43.6	13.5		6	Mk	10										
558						4			6	NOAA	Turkey: Mumcular	土耳其:蒙朱拉尔	37.1	27.7		7	Ms											
565										* Song	Turkey: Hatay	土耳其:哈塔伊	36.2	36.1		7.7	Mk		30000	5								
567										* GSHAP	Slovenia: Novo Mesto	斯洛文尼亚:新梅斯托	45.6	15.3	16	6	Ms	10										
574										China	China: Gansu, Wuwei, W.	中国:甘肃武威西部	37.9	102.6		5.5	Ms	7										
579										* Song	Turkey: Hatay	土耳其:哈塔伊	36	36		6.3	Mk							3				
581	7	9								* Song	Turkey: Hatay	土耳其:哈塔伊	36.1	36.1		6.5	Mk	9						3				
587	9	30								* Song	Turkey: Hatay	土耳其:哈塔伊	36.1	36.1		7.7	Mk	9	60000	5				4				
599	5	28								Japan, Usami	Japan: Nara	日本:奈良	34.6	135.7		7	Ms	8								1		
600	12	16								China	China: Gansu, Tianshui	中国:甘肃天水	34.5	106.5		6	Ms	7	1001	4				2		3		
614										* Song	Italy: Ariano Irpino	意大利:阿维利诺	41	15		6	Mk		1000	3				3				
624	8	18								China	China: Sichuan, Xichang	中国:四川西昌	27.9	102.2		6	Ms	8										
634										GSHAP	Syria: Aleppo	叙利亚:阿勒颇	36.3	36.8	15	6.3	Ms	8.5										
634										* Song	Iran: Tabriz	伊朗:大不里士	38	46.2		6.3	Mk							3				
638	2	14								China	China: Sichuan, Songpan, NW.	中国:四川松潘西北	32.8	103.4		5.75	Ms	7										
649	9	15								* China	China: Shanxi, Linfen	中国:山西临汾	36.1	111.5		6.75	Ms	9	50	1				2		2		
650										GSHAP	Russia: Dagestan, Izberbash	俄罗斯:达吉斯坦共和国伊兹别尔巴什	42.6	47.7	20	6.1	Ms	8										
662	4	26								* Song	Iran: Semnan, Damghan	伊朗:塞姆南,达木罕	35.3	54		7.7	Mk		40000	5				3				
664	9	12								*	South Korea: Kyongju	韩国:庆州	35.5	129.1		6.3	Muk	8						3				
668	3									Korea	North Korea: Pyongyang	朝鲜:平壤	39	125.8		5.3	Ms	7										
678										* Song	Iraq: Laqlaq	伊拉克:莱格莱格	35	43.5		6.3	Mk	7						3				
678										GSHAP	Turkey: Diyarbakir	土耳其:迪亚巴克尔	38.2	39.5	20	7.6	Ms	10										
679	1									Japan, Usami	Japan: Shimabara	日本:长崎岛原	32.7	130.4		6.7	Ms	8								3		
684	11	29				4	3	1.6	1	* Usami, NOAA	Japan: Shikoku, Near Coast	日本:四国近海	32.5	134		8.4	Muk	10		3				3		3		
688										* Song	Turkey: Izmir	土耳其:伊兹密尔	38.4	27.2		7	Mk	9	2000	4				3				
692	3									China	China: Shandong, Huimin, SE.	中国:山东惠民东南	37.4	117.7		5	Ms	6										
701	5	12				4		2	2	* NOAA	Japan Sea	日本海	35.7	135.4		7	Ms	9						3				
704	8	2				4		2	2	* NOAA	Japan: Shingu, Near Coast	日本:和歌山新宫近海	33.8	136.7		7	Ms											
712	2	19								China	China: Shanxi, Qixian	中国:山西祁县	37.3	112.2		5.5	Ms	7										
713	3	20								* GSHAP	Syria: Idlib	叙利亚:伊德利卜	35.7	36.3	30	7.4	Ms	9						3				

年 Year	月 Mo	日 Dy	时 Hr	分 Mn	秒 Sec	海啸 Tsunami 源 Sr	浪高 Wh	级 I mI	级 S mS	资料来源 Information	震中 Earthquake Epicenter 地名(英文) Name(English)	地名(中文) Name(Chinese)	纬度(°) Latitude	经度(°) Longitude	深度 Depth	震级 Mag	标度 Scale	烈度 MMI	死亡人数 Deaths 数量/人 Num	级别 Dd	受伤人数 Injuries 数量/人 Num	级别 Dd	经济损失 Damage 数量/$ Mill	级别 De	房屋毁坏 Houses Destroyed 数量/间 Num	级别 Dh	房屋受损 Houses Damaged 数量/间 Num	级别 Dh
713										* * Song	Turkey:Hatay	土耳其:哈塔伊	36. 2	36. 1		5. 5	Mk	7										
715	7	4								Japan, Usami	Japan:Tenryu	日本:静冈滨松天龙区	35. 1	137. 9		6. 4	Ms	7								1		
715	7	5								Japan	Japan:Aichi	日本:爱知	34. 7	137. 4		6. 7	Ms	8							47	1		
715										* Turkey	Turkey:Iznik	土耳其:伊兹尼克	40. 4	28. 9		7	Ms	9						2				
716	8	25								* Song	Turkey:Hatay	土耳其:哈塔伊	36	36		5. 9	Mk							2				
734	3	23								* China	China:Gansu, Tianshui	中国:甘肃天水	34. 6	105. 6		7	Ms	9	101	3				2		3		
734	5	18								Japan, Usami	Japan:Nara, Kinki	日本:奈良,近畿	34. 3	136. 1		7	Ms	9								3		
735	6	21								* Iran	Armenia:Gavar (Kamo)	亚美尼亚:卡莫	39. 7	45. 5	16	6. 5	Ms	8						2				
735	7	21								GSHAP	Armenia:Gavar (Kamo)	亚美尼亚:卡莫	39. 7	45. 6	16	6. 5	Ms	9										
740	10	26				3			3	* GSHAP, NOAA	Turkey:Istanbul	土耳其:伊斯坦布尔	41	28. 8	25	7. 3	Ms	9						3				
742										* Song	Syria:Ar Raqqah	叙利亚:拉卡	35	38		6. 3	Mk			3				3				
743										*	Caspian Sea	里海	42. 1	48. 2	20	5. 5	Ms	7						1				
743										* Iran	Iran:Garmsar	伊朗:加姆萨尔	35. 3	52. 1		7. 2	Ms	9						3				
744	6	30				4		2	2	* Japan, NOAA	Japan:Sagami Bay	日本:相模湾	35. 1	139. 5		6. 4	Ms		1560	4				3	470	3		
745	6	5								* Usami	Japan:Toyonaka	日本:大阪丰中	34. 8	135. 5		7. 9	Ms	11								3		
745	6	9				3		1	1	* NOAA	Japan:Osaka	日本:大阪	34. 6	135. 3		6. 5	Ms	10		3								
746	1	18				2			3	* NOAA	Israel:Jerusalem	以色列:耶路撒冷	32	35. 5		7	Muk	11						3				
748	8	31								* Song	Syria:Dimashq (Damascus)	叙利亚:大马士革	33. 5	36. 3		5. 9	Mk							2				
749	1	25								* Song	Iraq:Jazirah, NE. of Tharthar River	伊拉克:贾兹拉,塞尔萨尔河东北	35	43. 5		7. 3	Mk	10						3				
756	11	27								GSHAP	China:Gansu, Sunan, NW.	中国:甘肃肃南西北	39. 2	99. 5	20	6	Ms	7										
756	12	1								China	China:Gansu, Sunan, NW.	中国:甘肃肃南西北	39. 2	99. 5		6	Ms	8										
758										* Song	Egypt:Yamit	埃及:耶米特	31. 2	34. 2		5. 9	Mk	7						2				
762	6	9								Japan, Usami	Japan:Gifu	日本:岐阜	35. 6	137. 3		7. 4	Ms	10										
762										* * Song	Iran:Qeshm Island	伊朗:格什姆岛	26. 6	56. 2		6. 3	Mk							3				
763										* GSHAP	Iran:Birjand	伊朗:比尔詹德	33. 3	59. 3	16	7. 6	Ms	10. 5										
765										* *	Iran:Razavi Khorasan	伊朗:呼罗珊	35. 2	60. 4	25	7. 5	Ms	10										
766	7	20				5		1. 5	1. 5	* NOAA	Japan:Kagoshima	日本:鹿岛	31. 6	130. 7		6. 5	Muk			3								
768	9									GSHAP, Korea	South Korea:Kyongju	韩国:庆州	35. 8	129. 2		5. 3	Ms	7										
771	7	13								Japan, Song	Japan Sea	日本海	35. 9	132. 2		6. 5	Mk			1								
775										GSHAP	Syria:Aleppo	叙利亚:阿勒颇	36. 5	36. 7	30	6. 7	Ms	8										
777										* China	China:Hebei, Ningjin, NE.	中国:河北宁晋东北	37. 8	115. 2		6	Ms	8	200	3				2		3		
778										*	Italy:Treviso	意大利:特雷维索	45. 4	12. 2		5. 6	Muk		48	1				2				
779	4									* Korea	South Korea:Kyongju	韩国:庆州	35. 5	129. 1		6. 3	Muk	8	100	2				2				
788	3	12								* China	China:Hubei, Fangxian, NW.	中国:湖北房县西北	32. 4	109. 9		6. 5	Ms	8						2		3		
791										GSHAP	Syria:Idlib	叙利亚:伊德利卜	36. 2	36. 7	30	6. 8	Ms	8										
792	2									GSHAP	Slovenia:Ljubljana	斯洛文尼亚:卢布尔雅那	46	14. 5	18	6	Ms	8										

时间 年 Date Year	月 Mo	日 Dy	时 Hr	分 Mn	秒 Sec	海啸 Tsunami 源 Sr	浪高 Wh	级I mI	级S mS	资料来源 Information	震中 Earthquake Epicenter 地名(英文) Name(English)	地名(中文) Name(Chinese)	纬度(°) Latitude	经度(°) Longitude	深度 Depth	震级 Mag	标度 Scale	烈度 MMI	死亡人数 Deaths 数量/人 Num	级别 Dd	受伤人数 Injuries 数量/人 Num	级别 Dd	经济损失 Damage 数量/$ Mill	级别 De	房屋毁坏 Houses Destroyed 数量/间 Num	级别 Dh	房屋受损 Houses Damaged 数量/间 Num	级别 Dh
792	4	30				1			3	* NOAA, Song	Italy: Verona	意大利:维罗那	45.5	11		7	Mk			3				3				
793	5	31								China	China: Shaanxi, Huaxian	中国:陕西华县	34.5	109.7		6	Ms	8										
796	4	7								* Song	Greece: Crete Island	希腊:克里特岛	35	25	100	7	Mk	10										
799	9	18				2	2	1	1	NOAA, Japan, Usami, Song	Japan Trench	日本海沟	34.2	142		7	Ms											
800										GSHAP	Syria: Ar Raqqah	叙利亚:拉卡	35.7	38.7	12	6.5	Ms	9										
800						1				NOAA, Song	Greece: Ionian Sea	希腊:伊奥尼亚海	36.2	23.2		6.6	Mk											
801	4	30	1							* Italy	Italy: Roma (Rome)	意大利:罗马	41.9	12.48		5.37	Ms	10						4				
802	5	31								* Song	Italy: Padova	意大利:帕多瓦	45.4	11.9		6	Mk	10										
803	12	19				2			3	* NOAA, Song	Turkey: Gulf of Iskenderun	土耳其:伊斯肯德伦湾	36.95	35.6		6.7	Mk							1				
811										* Song	England: Scotland: St Andrews	英国:苏格兰:圣安德鲁	56.3	-2.8		7	Mk		1400	4				3		3		3
814	4	6								* China	China: Sichuan, Xichang	中国:四川西昌	27.9	102.2		7	Ms	9	101	3				1				
815										GSHAP	Turkey: Istanbul	土耳其:伊斯坦布尔	41	28.5	25	7.6	Ms	10										
818	1	27								* * Song	Afghan: Balkh, Fariab	阿富汗:巴尔赫,法里亚布	36.5	66.5		6.3	Mk							3				
818	5	15								*	Afghan: Kazahkstan	阿富汗:朱兹詹	36.8	66.2	50	7.5	Ms	8		3				3				
818	7	9								* * Song	Iran: Mashhad	伊朗:马什哈德	36	60		6.3	Mk							3				
818	8					4		2	1	* Usami, NOAA	Japan: Odawara	日本:神奈川小田原	35.2	139.3		7.9	Ms	11		3						1		
827	8	11								Japan, Usami	Japan: Kyoto	日本:京都	34.9	135.6		6.7	Ms	8								3		
830	2	3								Japan, Usami	Japan: Akita	日本:秋田	39.8	140.1		7.4	Ms	10	15		100	2				1		
835	1	5								* GSHAP	Turkey: Hatay	土耳其:哈塔伊	36	36	14	6.1	Mk	9						3				
835	4	15								China	China: Shaanxi, Xi-an	中国:陕西西安	34.3	108.9		4.75	Ms	6										
836	2	29								China	China: Shaanxi, Xi-an	中国:陕西西安	34.3	108.9		4.75	Ms	6										
838	11	23								* Song	Uzbekistan: Fergana	乌兹别克斯坦:费尔干纳	40.4	71.3		7.7	Mk		15000	5				4				
838										GSHAP	Uzbekistan: Fergana	乌兹别克斯坦:费尔干纳	40.4	71.8	10	5.3	Ms	7.5										
840	7									GSHAP	Iran: Razavi Khorasan	伊朗:呼罗珊	35.2	60.4	15	6.5	Ms	8.5										
841	3	13								Japan, Usami	Japan: Nagano	日本:长野	36.6	137.8		6.7	Ms	8								2		
841	6									Japan, Usami	Japan: Shizuoka	日本:静冈	35.1	138.9		7	Ms	9		1						1		
842	10	24				1				* NOAA, Song	England: Guernsey Islands	英国:根西岛	49.5	-2.5		7	Mk							1				
844	9	18								* Song	Syria: Dimashq (Damascus)	叙利亚:大马士革	33.5	36.3		7.7	Mk	8	50000	5				4				
845	9	6								* Song	Iraq: Al-Mawsil (Mosul)	伊拉克:勿斯离(摩苏尔)	36.2	43.1		7.7	Mk		50000	5								
846										* Song	Turkey: Hatay; Syria: Aleppo	土耳其:哈塔伊;叙利亚:阿勒颇	36.1	36.1		6.3	Mk	8						3				
847	6									* Italy	Italy: Molise	意大利:莫利塞	41.48	14.27		6	Ms	10		1				3				

时间 Date 年 Year	月 Mo	日 Dy	时 Hr	分 Mn	秒 Sec	海啸 Tsunami 源 Sr	浪高 Wh	级 I mI	级 S mS	资料来源 Information	震中 Earthquake Epicenter 地名(英文) Name(English)	地名(中文) Name(Chinese)	纬度(°) Latitude	经度(°) Longitude	深度 Depth	震级 Mag	标度 Scale	烈度 MMI	死亡人数 Deaths 数量/人 Num	级别 Dd	受伤人数 Injuries 数量/人 Num	级别 Dd	经济损失 Damage 数量/$ Mill $ Mill	级别 De	房屋毁坏 Houses Destroyed 数量/间 Num	级别 Dh	房屋受损 Houses Damaged 数量/间 Num	级别 Dh
847	11	24								* Song	Syria:Dimashq (Damascus)	叙利亚:大马士革	33.5	36.3		5.9	Mk							2				
847										* Song	Iraq:Al – Mawsil(Mosul)	伊拉克:勿斯离(摩苏尔)	36.21	42.08		7.7	Mk	10	70000	5				3				
849	10	24								China	China:Inner Mongolia, Baotou	中国:内蒙包头	40.8	109.8		7	Ms		1001	4								
850	7	15								* Song	Iran:Tehran, Mahmudabad	伊朗:德黑兰,马哈茂达巴德	35.3	51.2		7.7	Mk		45000	5				3				
850	11	27				4	4	2	2	* Usami, NOAA	Japan:Yamagata	日本:山形	39	139.9		7	Ms	9		3				2		1		
851										*	Armenia:Yerevan(Erivan)	亚美尼亚:耶烈万(叶里温)	40	44.6	10	5.2	Ms	8	12000	5				3				
853										* Song	Italy:Boiano	意大利:波亚诺	41.5	14.5		6	Mk	10										
854	6	2								* Song	Tunisia:Kairouan, Tunis	突尼斯:凯鲁万,突尼斯	35.7	10.1		7.3	Mk	10						2				
854										* Song	France:Cambrai, Tournai, Mayence	法国:坎布雷,图尔奈,马恩斯	50.1	3.1		6.1	Mk	8						2				
854										* Song	Armenia:Yerevan(Erivan)	亚美尼亚:耶烈万(叶里温)	40	45		7	Mk		2000	4				3				
855	5	22								* Iran	Iran:Tehran, Mahmudabad	伊朗:德黑兰,马哈茂达巴德	35.3	51.2		7.1	Ms							4				
855	6	26				4				Japan, NOAA, Song	Japan:Nara, Kii	日本:奈良,纪伊	34.7	135.8		7	Mk											
855										GSHAP	Iran:Tehran	伊朗:德黑兰	35.6	51.5	10	6.1	Ms	9										
856	1									*	Armenia:Yerevan(Erivan)	亚美尼亚:耶烈万(叶里温)	40	44.6	10	5.3	Muk	8						3				
856	12	3								* Song	Iran:Razavi Khorasan	伊朗:呼罗珊	35	58		6.3	Mk							3				
856	12	3								* Song	Tunisia:Tunis	突尼斯:突尼斯	36.8	10.2		7.7	Mk	10	45000	5				4				
856	12	22								* Iran	Iran:Semnan, Dāmghān	伊朗:塞姆南,达姆甘	35.9	54		7.9	Ms	10	200000	5				4		4		
856	12									* Song	Greece:Korinthos, Patrai (Patras)	希腊:科林斯,帕特雷	37.9	22.9		7.7	Mk		45000	5								
856										Japan, Usami	Japan:Kyoto	日本:京都	35.1	135.8		6.4	Ms	7								1		
857	4	4								Japan, Usami	Japan:Odate	日本:秋田大馆	40.3	140.6		7	Ms	9								1		
857	4									* Song	Egypt:Al – Qahirah (Cairo)	埃及:开罗	30	31.1		5.9	Mk							2		2		2
858	1									*	Armenia:Yerevan	亚美尼亚:叶里温	40	44.6	10	5.2	Muk		12000	5				3				
858	4	19								* GSHAP, Iran	Iran:Tabriz	伊朗:大不里士	38	46.2	6	6	Mk	9.5		3				3				
859	4	8				2			3	* GSHAP, NOAA	Turkey:Hatay; Syria:Aleppo	土耳其:哈塔伊;叙利亚:阿勒颇	36	36		8	Ms	11		3				3				
860	5	23								* Song	Iraq:Baghdad	伊拉克:巴格达	33	44.5		6.1	Mk	8						2				
863	1									China	China:Shanxi, Yicheng	中国:山西翼城	35.6	111.7		5.5	Ms	7		4								
863	2	24								* Song	Iran:Tehran, Mahmudabad	伊朗:德黑兰,马哈茂达巴德	35.3	51.2		6.3	Mk			3				3				

年 Year	月 Mo	日 Dy	时 Hr	分 Mn	秒 Sec	源 Sr	浪高 Wh	级 I mI	级 S mS	资料来源 Information	地名(英文) Name(English)	地名(中文) Name(Chinese)	纬度(°) Latitude	经度(°) Longitude	深度 Depth	震级 Mag	标度 Scale	烈度 MMI	死亡人数 数量/人 Deaths Num	死亡人数 级别 Deaths Dd	受伤人数 数量/人 Injuries Num	受伤人数 级别 Injuries Dd	经济损失 数量/$ Mill Damage $ Mill	经济损失 级别 Damage De	房屋毁坏 数量/间 Houses Destroyed Num	房屋毁坏 级别 Houses Destroyed Dh	房屋受损 数量/间 Houses Damaged Num	房屋受损 级别 Houses Damaged Dh
863	4									*	Armenia:Yerevan,S.	亚美尼亚:叶里温南部	40	44.6	10	4.9	Muk			3				2				
863	7	10				4		2	2	* Usami,NOAA	Japan:Niigata	日本:新潟	37.1	138		7	Ms	9		3				2		1		
863										* Song	Iran:Tabriz	伊朗:大不里士	38	46.2		6.3	Mk			3				3				
864	1	15								* Song	Iran:Tehran,Mahmudabad	伊朗:德黑兰,马哈茂达巴德	35.3	51.2		5.9	Mk							2				
866	1									China	China:Shanxi,Linfen,S.	中国:山西临汾	35.9	111.4		5.5	Ms	7										
867	1	9								* Song	Turkey:Istanbul	土耳其:伊斯坦布尔	41	29		7.3	Mk	10										
867	2	18								China	China:Shanxi,Linfen,S.	中国:山西临汾	35.9	111.4		5.5	Ms	7										
868	8	3								Japan,Usami	Japan:Takasago	日本:兵库高砂	34.8	134.8		7.1	Ms	9								3		
869	7	13				4		4	4	* Usami,NOAA	Japan Trench	日本海沟	38.5	143.8		8.6	Ms	11	1000	3				4		3		
870	1	23								Japan,Song	Japan:Sagami Bay	日本:相模湾	35.1	139.5		6.3	Mk									1		
871	11	18								*	Iran:Kermānshāh	伊朗:克尔曼沙赫	33.2	47.2		6.8	Ms	7	20000	5				4		4		
872	6	22								* * GSHAP	Iran:Lorestan,W.	伊朗:洛雷斯坦西部	33	47	30	7.8	Ms	9.5	3000	4				3				
874										GSHAP	Iran:Gorgan	伊朗:戈尔甘	37.2	55.2	10	6	Ms	9										
876	7	18								* China	China:Ningxia,Qingtongxia,S.	中国:宁夏青铜峡南	37.8	105.9		6.5	Ms	8		3				2		2		
878	11	1								Japan,Usami	Japan:Atsugi	日本:神奈川厚木	35.5	139.3		7.4	Ms	9		3						3		
879	3									China	China:Shaanxi,Lantian	中国:陕西蓝田	34.2	109.3		4.75	Ms	6										
880	2									China	China:Shaanxi,Qishan	中国:陕西岐山	34.5	107.6		4.75	Ms	6										
880	11	23								Japan,Usami	Japan:Izumo	日本:岛根出云	35.4	132.8		7.4	Ms	8								3		
881	1	13								Japan,Usami	Japan:Kyoto	日本:京都	35.1	135.8		6.4	Ms	7								3		
881	5	27								* Song	Morocco:Marrakech	摩洛哥:马拉喀什	30	-6		7.3	Mk	10										
885	11	27								* Song	Egypt:Al – Qahirah (Cairo)	埃及:开罗	30	31.1		7.3	Mk	10	1000	3				3		3		3
886										China	China:Yunnan,Dali	中国:云南大理	25.7	100.2		5.5	Ms	7										
887	8	2				3	4	2	2	* Japan,Usami,NOAA	Japan:Sado Island	日本:佐渡岛	37.5	138.1		6.5	Ms	9	2000	4								
887	8	26	6			4	10	3	3	* Japan,Usami,NOAA	Japan:Wakayama,Near Coast	日本:和歌山近海	33	135.3		8.6	Ms	11		3				3		3		
887	8	26								Japan,Usami	Japan:Shinano	日本:长野信浓町	36.6	138.1		7.4	Ms	10		3								
890	7	10								Japan,Usami	Japan:Kyoto	日本:京都	35.1	135.8		6.2	Ms	7										
891										*	Iran:Ardabil	伊朗:阿尔达比勒	38.3	48.3	20	6.3	Muk	9						3				
893	12	24								* Song	Armenia:Yerevan(Erivan)	亚美尼亚:耶烈万(叶里温)	40	44.6	10	7.7	Mk	10	180000	5				4		4		
894	1	6								GSHAP	Iran:Tabriz	伊朗:大不里士	37.7	47.5	28	7.7	Ms	10										
894										*	Italy:Verona	意大利:维罗那	45.3	11		5.3	Muk			2				2				
896	2									GSHAP	Greece:Edhessa, Kilkis	希腊:埃泽萨,基尔基斯	40.5	22.2		6	Ms	8.5										
896	9	4								* Song	Macedonia(Fyrom):Stip	马其顿:斯提普	41.7	22.9		6.3	Mk	10										
896										* Song	Italy:Roma (Rome)	意大利:罗马	41.9	12.6		6	Mk			3				3				

时间						海啸				资料来源	震中				深度	震级	标度	烈度	死亡人数		受伤人数		经济损失		房屋毁坏		房屋受损	
年	月	日	时	分	秒	源	浪高	级I	级S		地名(英文)	地名(中文)	纬度(°)	经度(°)					数量/人	级别	数量/人	级别	数量/$ Mill	级别	数量/间	级别	数量/间	级别
Date						Tsunami				Information	Earthquake Epicenter				Depth	Mag	Scale	MMI	Deaths		Injuries		Damage		Houses Destroyed		Houses Damaged	
Year	Mo	Dy	Hr	Mn	Sec	Sr	Wh	mI	mS		Name(English)	Name(Chinese)	Latitude	Longitude					Num	Dd	Num	Dd	$ Mill	De	Num	Dh	Num	Dh
898										＊Song	Iran:Tehran, Mahmudabad	伊朗:德黑兰,马哈茂达巴德	35. 3	51. 2		6. 3	Mk							3				
900										GSHAP	Russia:Khabarovsk, Talakan	俄罗斯:哈巴罗夫斯克区塔拉坎	49. 61	134. 07	15	6. 5	Ms	9										
900										GSHAP	Russia:Khabarovsk, Komsomolsk – On – Amur	俄罗斯:哈巴罗夫斯克区阿穆尔河畔共青城	50. 85	134. 15	15	6. 3	Ms	9										
900										GSHAP	Russia:Buryatiya, Severomuysk	俄罗斯:布里亚特州谢韦罗穆伊斯克城	55. 75	115. 25	15	6. 8	Ms	9										
900										GSHAP	Russia:Buryatiya, Ust′– Paramok	俄罗斯:布里亚特州乌斯季帕拉莫克	56. 63	115. 43	15	6. 9	Ms	9										
900										GSHAP	Russia:Buryatiya, Severomuysk	俄罗斯:布里亚特州谢韦罗穆伊斯克城	55. 76	113. 43	15	7	Ms	9										
900						1				NOAA, Song	India:Nagapattinam	印度:纳加帕蒂南	10. 46	79. 53		7. 7	Mk			3				3		2		
902	6									GSHAP	Iraq:Mandali, Jalula, Baghdad	伊拉克:曼代利,杰卢拉,巴格达	33. 5	45	16	6. 5	Ms	8. 5										
906	4									GSHAP	Azerbaijan:Naxcivan	阿塞拜疆:纳希切万	39. 7	45	14	6. 1	Ms	8. 5										
910	9	9								＊Song	Iraq:Kufah, Baghdad	伊拉克:库法,巴格达	33. 2	44. 2		5. 9	Mk							2				
912	4									＊Song	Iran:Kermanshah	伊朗:克尔曼沙赫	34. 6	47. 8		6. 3	Mk							3				
914	4									GSHAP	Uzbekistan:Bukhara	乌兹别克斯坦:布哈拉	40	64	13	6. 1	Ms	8										
922						4	2	1	1	＊Usami, NOAA	Japan:Shingu, Near Coast	日本:和歌山新宫近海	33. 8	136. 7		7	Ms	9						1				
927	8									China	China:Henan, Zhengzhou	中国:河南郑州	34. 8	113. 6		4. 75	Ms	6	2	1								
929										China	China:Zhejiang, Hangzhou	中国:浙江杭州	30. 3	120. 2		5	Ms	6								2		
934	7	16	3							Japan, Usami	Japan:Kyoto	日本:京都	35. 1	135. 8		6. 2	Ms	7										
938	5	22	11							Japan, Usami	Japan:Kyoto, Kii	日本:京都,纪伊	34. 8	135. 8		6. 9	Ms	8	4							3		
942	6									＊	Uzbekistan:Bukhara	乌兹别克斯坦:布哈拉	39. 7	64. 5	20	6. 7	Muk	9						3				
942	9	15								＊Song	Iran:Tehran	伊朗:德黑兰	36	51. 7		6. 2	Mk			3								
943	8	20								＊Iran	Turkmenistan:Asgabat	土库曼斯坦:阿什哈巴德	38	58. 3		7. 6	Ms		5000	4				3				
951	9									＊GSHAP	Syria:Halab (Aleppo)	叙利亚:阿勒颇	36. 3	36. 8	16	6. 8	Ms	9						3				
953	8	20								＊	Turkmenistan:Asgabat	土库曼斯坦:阿什哈巴德	38	58. 3	18	7. 1	Muk	10						3				
953	11									China	China:Hebei, Daming	中国:河北大名	36. 3	115. 2		4. 75	Ms	6										
956	4	15								＊Iran	Iran:Hamadan	伊朗:哈马丹	34. 9	48. 4		5. 3	Ms			3				2				
957	4	4				1			3	＊NOAA, Song	Iran:Persian Gulf	伊朗:波斯湾	35. 7	51. 4		6. 7	Mk											
957	4									＊Song	Iraq:Diyala	伊拉克:迪亚拉	34. 3	45. 2		6. 3	Mk	7						3				
958	2	23								＊	Iran:Tehran	伊朗:德黑兰	36. 2	51. 1		6. 5	Ms							3				
958	2	23								＊	Iran:Tehran	伊朗:德黑兰	36	51. 1		7. 7	Ms			3				3				
958	2									＊＊Song	Afghan:Taloqan	阿富汗:塔卢坎	36. 7	69. 6		6	Mk			2								
958	3									＊Song	Iraq:Halwan, Jalula	伊拉克:哈勒万,杰卢拉	33. 2	44. 2		6. 3	Mk							3				
958	4									GSHAP	Iran:Kermanshah	伊朗:克尔曼沙赫	34	46	16	6. 8	Ms	9										

时间 Date 年 Year	月 Mo	日 Dy	时 Hr	分 Mn	秒 Sec	海啸 Tsunami 源 Sr	浪高 Wh	级I mI	级S mS	资料来源 Information	震中 Earthquake Epicenter 地名(英文) Name(English)	地名(中文) Name(Chinese)	纬度(°) Latitude	经度(°) Longitude	深度 Depth	震级 Mag	标度 Scale	烈度 MMI	死亡人数 Deaths 数量/人 Num	级别 Dd	受伤人数 Injuries 数量/人 Num	级别 Dd	经济损失 Damage 数量/$ Mill	级别 De	房屋毁坏 Houses Destroyed 数量/间 Num	级别 Dh	房屋受损 Houses Damaged 数量/间 Num	级别 Dh
958										* * Song	Iran:Esfahan	伊朗:伊斯法罕	33.6	51.3		6.3	Mk							3				
963	7	22				3			5	* NOAA,Song	Italy:Sicilia Island	意大利:西西里岛	38	15		7.1	Mk	11		4								
972	10	12								* GSHAP	Syria:Aleppo	叙利亚:阿勒颇	36	36.3	16	6.8	Ms	9						2				
975	10	26				2			3	GSHAP,NOAA	Turkey:Istanbul	土耳其:伊斯坦布尔	41	29	15	5.8	Ms											
976	7	22	7							Japan,Usami	Japan:Yamashiro,Oumi	日本:山城,近江	34.9	135.8		6.7	Ms	8	50						30	1		
977	8	19								* Song	Iran:Kangan,Akhtar	伊朗:坎根,阿赫塔尔	27.4	52.2		6.3	Mk							3				
978	6	17								*	Iran:Kangan	伊朗:坎根	27.7	52.3		5.3	Ms	7	2000	4				3		3		
985	2	10								* Song	Italy:Benevento	意大利:贝内文托	41.1	14.8		5.5	Mk							2				
986	5	13								* Song	Irag:Mosul	伊拉克:摩苏尔	36.2	43.1		6.3	Mk	8		3				3				
986	10	26				3			4	NOAA	Turkey:Marmara Sea	土耳其:马尔马拉海	40.8	29.2		7.5	Ms											
986	11									GSHAP	Iran:Zanjān	伊朗:赞詹	36.2	48.1	14	6.1	Ms	9										
990										* Song	Italy:Benevento	意大利:贝内文托	41.1	14.8		6	Mk	10										
991	4	5				1				* NOAA,Song	Syria:Dimashq (Damascus)	叙利亚:大马士革	33.5	36.3		6.7	Mk	9						2				
999	10									* China	China:Jiangsu,Changzhou	中国:江苏常州	31.8	119.9		5.5	Ms	7						1				
1000	1	23								China	China:Hebei,Xingtai	中国:河北邢台	37.1	114.5		5	Ms	7										
1000	1									* GSHAP	Slovenia:Kranj	斯洛文尼亚:叶塞尼采	46.5	14	40	6.9	Ms	8						3				
1001										*	Italy:Verona	意大利:维罗那	45.3	11		6	Muk			3				2				
1002	11	10								GSHAP	Turkey:Hatay	土耳其:哈塔伊	36.5	36.5	18	6.8	Ms	9										
1003										* Song	Turkey:Kars, Digor	土耳其:卡尔斯,季戈尔	40.5	43.3	20	6.2	Mk	7		3				2				
1003										* Song	France:Burgundy	法国:布尔戈尼	47	6		6.3	Mk							3				
1007	9	17								* Song	Iraq:Dinavar,Baghdad	伊拉克:迪娜,巴格达	33.2	44.2		7.7	Mk	8	16000	5				3				
1008	4	11				2				* NOAA,Song	Iran:Persian Gulf	伊朗:波斯湾	27.665	52.348		7.7	Mk		16000	5				4				
1008	4	27								GSHAP	Iran:Kermanshah	伊朗:克尔曼沙赫	34.6	47.7	9	7	Ms	10.5										
1010	3	9								* GSHAP	Turkey:Gebze	土耳其:盖布泽	41	29.5		7.4	Mk	10										
1011	8									China	China:Hebei,Zhengding	中国:河北正定	38.2	114.6		4.75	Ms	6										
1013										* Song	Iceland:Sudurland	冰岛:苏杜尔兰德	64	−21		7.3	Mk	10	11	1								
1021	5	12	10							* Song	Switzerland:Reinach	瑞士:赖纳赫	47.5	7.6		6.5	Mk	9						3				
1022	4									*	China:Shanxi,Huairen	中国:山西怀仁	39.8	113.1		6.5	Ms	8						1		1		
1026	6	16				3	10	3.3	3	* NOAA	Japan:Masuda	日本:岛根益田	34.8	131.8		7.5	Ms		1000	3				3	3000	4		
1033	12	10								* Song	Israel:Jerusalem	以色列:耶路撒冷	32	35		7.7	Mk	10	70000	5				3		3		
1034	2	17								* Song	Israel:Acre	以色列:阿卡	33	35		5.5	Mk							1				
1035	4					3			4	* NOAA,Song	Syria:Akko	叙利亚:阿克	33	35		6.7	Mk							1				
1035	9									* Song	Israel:Jerusalem	以色列:耶路撒冷	32	35		5.5	Mk							1				
1036	7	17								* Korea	South Korea:Kyongju	韩国:庆州	35.8	129.2		6.5	Ms	9						2				
1038	1	15								* China	China:Shanxi,Dingxiang	中国:山西定襄	38.4	112.9		7.25	Ms	10	32300	5				4				
1038	1	30								Japan,Usami	Japan:Wakayama	日本:和歌山	34.3	135.6		6.7	Ms	8								3		
1039	2	2				2				* GSHAP,NOAA	Turkey:Izmir	土耳其:伊兹密尔	38.4	27.3		6.8	Ms			3				2		2		2
1040										* Song	Tunisia:Al – Qayrawan	突尼斯:凯鲁万	35.7	10		6.5	Mk	11						3				

时间 年 Date Year	月 Mo	日 Dy	时 Hr	分 Mn	秒 Sec	海啸 Tsunami 源 Sr	浪高 Wh	级 I mI	级 S mS	资料来源 Information	震中 Earthquake Epicenter 地名(英文) Name(English)	地名(中文) Name(Chinese)	纬度(°) Latitude	经度(°) Longitude	深度 Depth	震级 Mag	标度 Scale	烈度 MMI	死亡人数 Deaths 数量/人 Num	级别 Dd	受伤人数 Injuries 数量/人 Num	级别 Dd	经济损失 Damage 数量/$ Mill $ Mill	级别 De	房屋毁坏 Houses Destroyed 数量/间 Num	级别 Dh	房屋受损 Houses Damaged 数量/间 Num	级别 Dh
1041	8	25								Japan, Usami	Japan:Kyoto	日本:京都	35.1	135.8		6.4	Ms	7								1		
1042	1	21								Japan, Song	Japan:Gujo	日本:岐阜郡上	35.7	139.5		6.3	Mk									1		
1042	8	21								* Song	Iran:Tabriz	伊朗:大不里士	38	46.2		7.7	Mk		40000	5				4				
1042	11	4	13	30						*	Iran:Tabriz	伊朗:大不里士	38.1	46.3	15	7.6	Muk	9	50000	5				4				
1045										* Turkey	Turkey:Erzurum, Erzincan	土耳其:埃尔佐鲁姆,埃尔津占	39.7	39.5		7	Ms	9						2				
1046	7	8								GSHAP	Turkey:Elazig	土耳其:埃拉泽	39	40	30	7.8	Ms	9.5										
1046										* GSHAP	Turkey:Kars	土耳其:卡尔斯	40.5	43.5	15	6.3	Ms	8.5		3				3				
1048										* Song	England:Royston	英国:罗伊斯顿	52	0		6.2	Mk			3								
1052	3									*	Iran:Neyshabur	伊朗:内沙布尔	36	58.8	10	6.2	Ms							3				
1052	6	2								GSHAP	Iran:Sabzevar	伊朗:萨卜泽瓦尔	36.2	57.7	16	7	Ms	10.5										
1052										* Iran	Iran:Ahwaz, W.	伊朗:阿瓦士西部	31.5	50		6.8	Ms	9						3				
1053	9	23								GSHAP	Iraq:Diyala	伊拉克:迪亚拉	34.5	45.5	16	6.4	Ms	9.5										
1053										GSHAP	Syria:Aleppo	叙利亚:阿勒颇	36.2	36.2	12	6.2	Ms	8.5										
1057	3	30								* China	China:Beijing, Daxing	中国:北京大兴	39.7	116.3		6.75	Ms	9	25000	5				4				
1058	2	28								* * Song	Iraq:Al – Mawsil (Mosul)	伊拉克:匆斯离(摩苏尔)	36.2	43.1		6.3	Mk			3				3				
1058	10									* * Song	Iran:Zanjān	伊朗:赞詹	36	48.1		6.5	Mk	9		3				3				
1058	12	2								* * Song	Iraq:Al – Mawsil (Mosul)	伊拉克:匆斯离(摩苏尔)	36.2	43.1		6.5	Mk	9		3								
1058	12	8	15							* Iran	Iraq:Chay Khanah	伊拉克:恰伊哈奈	34.3	44.7		6.4	Ms	9		3				3				
1058	12	8	18							GSHAP	Iraq:Makhmur	伊拉克:迈赫穆尔	35.8	43.6	25	7.2	Ms	9										
1063	7									* Song	Lebanon:Tarabulus (Tripolis)	黎巴嫩:塔拉布卢斯(黎波里)	34.3	35.5		6.3	Mk	8		3				3				
1063	9	23								* GSHAP	Turkey:Istanbul, Trakya	土耳其:伊斯坦布尔,拉基亚	40.9	28.3	15	7.5	Ms	9										
1064										* Song	Turkey:Iznik, Nicaea	土耳其:伊兹尼克,尼西亚	40.7	29.7		6.3	Mk							3				
1065	1	21								* Song	Italy:Sicily, Catania, Messina	意大利:西西里岛,墨西拿,米拉佐	38.1	15.1		6	Mk	10	975	3				3				
1065	9	23				3				NOAA, Song	Turkey:Marmara Sea	土耳其:马尔马拉海	41	28.1		6.6	Mk											
1065	12	3								* Song	Iran:Razavi Khorasan	伊朗:呼罗珊	35	58		6.3	Mk			3				3				
1066	3	31								* Song	Iran:Razavi Khorasan	伊朗:呼罗珊	34	58		6.3	Mk			3				3				
1067	4	20								* *	Jordan:Aqaba	约旦:亚喀巴	29.5	35		6.5	Ms		25000	5				3				
1067	11	12								* China	China:Guangdong, Chaozhou	中国:广东潮州	23.6	116.5		6.75	Ms	9		3				4				
1068	3	18				3			4	* NOAA, Song	Israel:Ramla	以色列:拉姆拉	31.92	34.85		7.2	Mk	9	25000	5				4		4		
1068	8	20								* China	China:Hebei, Hejian	中国:河北河间	38.5	116.5		6.5	Ms	8		3				3		3		
1069	1	24								China	China:Hebei, Cangzhou, SE.	中国:河北沧州东南	38.2	117		5	Ms	6										

年 Year	月 Mo	日 Dy	时 Hr	分 Mn	秒 Sec	源 Sr	浪高 Wh	级 I mI	级 S mS	资料来源 Information	地名(英文) Name(English)	地名(中文) Name(Chinese)	纬度(°) Latitude	经度(°) Longitude	深度 Depth	震级 Mag	标度 Scale	烈度 MMI	死亡人数 Deaths 数量/人 Num	级别 Dd	受伤人数 Injuries 数量/人 Num	级别 Dd	经济损失 Damage 数量/$ Mill	级别 De	房屋毁坏 Houses Destroyed 数量/间 Num	级别 Dh	房屋受损 Houses Damaged 数量/间 Num	级别 Dh
1070	2	25								* Song	Egypt: Al – Qahirah (Cairo); Israel: Jerusalem	埃及:开罗;以色列:耶路撒冷	30	31. 1		5. 9	Mk							2				
1072										* Song	Yemen: Sanaa	也门:萨纳	14. 2	43. 3		6. 1	Mk	8	50	1				2		2		2
1076	12									China	China: Beijing	中国:北京	39. 9	116. 4		5	Ms	6								2		
1076										* Song	Syria: Tudmur (Palmyra)	叙利亚:帕尔米拉	35	38		6. 3	Mk	8		3				3				
1082	12	6								* Song	Turkey: Iznik, Izmit	土耳其:伊兹尼克,伊兹米特	40. 5	28. 5		7. 3	Mk	10										
1085	4	29								* Song	Turkey: Erzurum	土耳其:埃尔佐鲁姆	39. 9	41. 1		6. 2	Mk			3								
1085	4	29								* Song	Iran: Ahwaz	伊朗:阿瓦士	31	49		6. 3	Mk			3				3				
1086	4	18								* Song	Iraq: Mesopotamia, Jazirah	伊拉克:美索不达米亚,贾兹拉	34	44		6. 1	Mk	8						2				
1086										* Song	Italy: Siracusa (Syracuse)	意大利:锡拉库萨(锡拉丘兹)	37	15. 3		6	Mk		1000	3				3				
1088	4	22								*	Turkey: Damal	土耳其:达马尔	41. 4	43. 2	10	5. 3	Muk			3				3				
1088	4	23								GSHAP	Georgia: Akhalkalaki	格鲁吉亚:阿卡卡拉吉	41. 4	43. 3	15	6	Ms	9										
1088	6	10				4		1	1. 5	* NOAA	Japan: Aomori, Near Coast	日本:青森近海	40. 5	143		7	Ms											
1089										* Song	Syria: Tudmur (Palmyra)	叙利亚:帕尔米拉	34. 3	38. 2		6. 3	Mk	8						3				
1091	9	17								GSHAP	Syria: Aleppo	叙利亚:阿勒颇	35. 9	36. 3	30	7. 4	Ms	9										
1091	9	28	7							Japan, Usami	Japan: Yamashiro, Daiwa	日本:山城,大和	34. 3	135. 8		6. 2	Ms	7								1		
1091										GSHAP	Romania: Nereju	罗马尼亚:内雷茹	45. 7	26. 6	150	6. 4	Ms	7										
1091										* Song	Turkey: Hatay	土耳其:哈塔伊	36. 1	36. 1		6. 5	Mk	9						3				
1092	7	6								GSHAP	Hungary: Miskolc	匈牙利:米什科尔茨	48	21	10	5. 6	Ms	8										
1092	12									China	China: Gansu, Wuwei, W.	中国:甘肃武威西部	37. 9	102. 6		4. 75	Ms	6										
1093	3	19	5							Japan, Usami	Japan: Kyoto	日本:京都	35. 1	135. 8		6. 4	Ms	7										
1096	12	17				4	7	2. 5	2	* Usami, NOAA	Japan: Shizuoka, Near Coast	日本:静冈近海	34	137. 5		8. 4	Ms	10	400	3				2	400	3		
1099	2	22				4		2. 5		* Usami, NOAA	Japan: Wakayama, Near Coast	日本:和歌山近海	33	135. 5		8. 4	Ms	11						1				
1099	9	20								Japan, Usami	Japan: Osaka	日本:大阪	34. 7	135. 4		6. 4	Ms	7								1		
1100										GSHAP	Georgia: Tkvarcheli	格鲁吉亚:特克瓦谢利	43. 1	42. 2	14	6. 9	Ms	9. 5										
1100										GSHAP	Russia: Karachaevo – Cherkess, Pkhiya	俄罗斯:卡拉恰伊 – 切尔克斯州普希亚村镇	43. 4	41	15	7. 2	Ms	10										
1101										*	Iran: Neyshabur	伊朗:内沙布尔	36	59	10	6. 5	Muk	10	60000	5				3				
1102	1	22								* China	China: Shanxi, Jinyuan	中国:山西晋源	37. 7	112. 4		6. 5	Ms	8		3				3				
1102	2	28								*	Afghan: Gerat	阿富汗:杰拉特	35	62. 1	15	6. 1	Ms	8						2				
1106										* Song	Turkey: Hatay	土耳其:哈塔伊	36. 1	36. 1		6. 1	Mk	8						1		1		1
1107	2	12	3							GSHAP	Romania: Nereju	罗马尼亚:内雷茹	45. 7	26. 6	150	6. 9	Ms	7										
1107	9									GSHAP	Iran: Kermanshah	伊朗:克尔曼沙赫	34. 6	47. 4	11	6. 5	Ms	9. 5										
1109										* Song	Turkey: Hatay	土耳其:哈塔伊	36. 1	36. 1		8	Mk	11						3		3		3
1111										China	China: Yunnan, Dali	中国:云南大理	25. 7	100. 2		5. 5	Ms	7										

时间						海啸				资料来源	震中				深度	震级	标度	烈度	死亡人数		受伤人数		经济损失		房屋毁坏		房屋受损	
年	月	日	时	分	秒	源	浪高	级 I	级 S		地名(英文)	地名(中文)	纬度(°)	经度(°)					数量/人	级别	数量/人	级别	数量/$ Mill	级别	数量/间	级别	数量/间	级别
Date						Tsunami				Information	Earthquake Epicenter				Depth	Mag	Scale	MMI	Deaths		Injuries		Damage		Houses Destroyed		Houses Damaged	
Year	Mo	Dy	Hr	Mn	Sec	Sr	Wh	mI	mS		Name(English)	Name(Chinese)	Latitude	Longitude					Num	Dd	Num	Dd	$ Mill	De	Num	Dh	Num	Dh
1111										* Turkey	Turkey:Van,N.	土耳其:凡城北部	38.5	43.4		7	Ms	9						3				
1112	6	20				2			4	* NOAA,Song	Tyrrhenian Sea	第勒尼安海(伊特鲁里亚海)	40	14		6.7	Mk	9										
1114	3	12				2			3	* NOAA	Turkey:Besni	土耳其:贝斯尼	37.5	38.5		7	Ms											
1114	6	7								* Song	Turkey:Urfa	土耳其:乌尔法	37	38.9		6.3	Mk			3				3				
1114	8	10								GSHAP	Turkey:Besni	土耳其:贝斯尼	37.5	38	30	8	Ms	10										
1114										* Song	Turkey:Hatay	土耳其:哈塔伊	36.1	36.1		5.9	Mk							2				
1114										* Song	Turkey:Urfa	土耳其:乌尔法	37	38.9		6.5	Mk	9						2				
1115										* Song	Turkey:Antioch; Syria:Aleppo	土耳其:安提俄克; 叙利亚:阿勒颇	36.1	36.1		6.3	Mk							3				
1115										* Song	Iran:Hengam Island	伊朗:亨加姆岛	26.4	55.5		6.3	Mk							3				
1115										* Song	Turkey:Harran,Kufa,Samsat	土耳其:哈兰,库法,桑沙特	36.8	39		7.3	Mk	10						3				
1117	1	3	21	30						* Italy	Italy:Verona	意大利:维罗那	45.33	11.2		6.49	Ms	11										
1117	3	1								* Song	Italy:Venezia (Venice) To Emilia	意大利:威尼斯,艾米利亚	44.8	11.3		6	Mk	10		3				3				
1117										GSHAP	Iraq:Baghdad	伊拉克:巴格达	33.5	44.5	24	6.8	Ms	8.5										
1118										* Song	England:Birmingham	英国:伯明翰	52.5	-2.1		7.1	Mk			3				4				
1119	2									China	China:Jilin,Songyuan	中国:吉林松原	44.9	124.8		6.75	Ms	9										
1119	12	10								*	Iran:Qazvin	伊朗:加兹温	36.2	50		6.5	Muk							3				
1122	10									GSHAP	Romania:Nereju	罗马尼亚:内雷茹	45.7	26.6	150	6.1	Ms	6.5										
1122										GSHAP	Azerbaijan:Gəncə	阿塞拜疆:占贾	40.3	46.3	24	6.1	Ms	7.5										
1125	9	6								* China	China:Gansu,Lanzhou	中国:甘肃兰州	36.1	103.7		7	Ms	9						3		3		
1125	10	11								* Italy	Italy:Benevento	意大利:贝内文托	41.6	15		5.71	Ms	10										
1126	8	8								GSHAP	Romania:Nereju	罗马尼亚:内雷茹	45.7	26.6	150	6.8	Ms	7										
1127										GSHAP	Iran:Mazanderan	伊朗:马赞德兰	36.3	53.6	14	6.8	Ms	9.5										
1130	2	12								* Song	Iraq:Al-Mawsil, Jabal,Jazirah	伊拉克:勿斯离, 直布罗,贾兹拉	36.2	43.1		6.3	Mk							3				
1130	2	27								GSHAP	Iraq:Diyala	伊拉克:迪亚拉	33.8	45.5	27	7	Ms	8.5										
1130	2	28								* Iran	Iraq:Tursaq	伊拉克:图尔萨格	33.6	45.7		6.8	Ms	7						2				
1132										GSHAP	Turkey:Kars	土耳其:卡尔斯	40.5	43.5	18	6	Ms	8										
1135	7	25								GSHAP	Iran:Kordestan,W.	伊朗:库尔德斯坦西部	36.1	45.9	24	6.1	Ms	7.5										
1135	8	13								GSHAP	Iran:Kordestan,W.	伊朗:库尔德斯坦西部	36.1	45.9	30	6.4	Ms	7.5										
1136										GSHAP	Iraq:Al-Mawsil (Mosul)	伊拉克:勿斯离(摩苏尔)	36	43.5	20	7	Ms	9										
1137	9	19								* Song	Iran:Zanjān	伊朗:赞詹	36	48.1		7.1	Mk	9		3				4				
1137	9	19								GSHAP	Syria:Aleppo	叙利亚:阿勒颇	36	36.4	25	7.3	Ms	9										
1137										* Song	Iraq:Al Anbar	伊拉克:安巴尔	32	42.3		6.2	Mk			3								
1137										* Song	Italy:Sicily,Catania	意大利:西西里岛,卡塔尼亚	37.3	15.1		6.8	Mk		15000	5								

时间						海啸				资料来源	震中				深度	震级	标度	烈度	死亡人数		受伤人数		经济损失		房屋毁坏		房屋受损	
年	月	日	时	分	秒	源	浪高	级I	级S		地名(英文)	地名(中文)	纬度(°)	经度(°)					数量/人	级别	数量/人	级别	数量/$ Mill	级别	数量/间	级别	数量/间	级别
Date						Tsunami				Information	Earthquake Epicenter				Depth	Mag	Scale	MMI	Deaths		Injuries		Damage		Houses Destroyed		Houses Damaged	
Year	Mo	Dy	Hr	Mn	Sec	Sr	Wh	mI	mS		Name(English)	Name(Chinese)	Latitude	Longitude					Num	Dd	Num	Dd	$ Mill	De	Num	Dh	Num	Dh
1138	8	22								China	China:Hebei,Yixian	中国:河北易县	39.3	115.5		5.5	Ms	7	13	1								
1139	9	30								* GSHAP	Azerbaijan:Gəncə	阿塞拜疆:占贾	40.3	46.3	16	7.3	Ms	11	230000	5				4				
1143	4									* China	China:Ningxia,Yinchuan	中国:宁夏银川	38.5	106.3		6.5	Ms	8	10000	5				3		3		
1144	8	16								China	China:Hebei,Hejian	中国:河北河间	38.5	116		6	Ms	8										
1149	5	11								* Song	Iraq:Baghdad	伊拉克:巴格达	33.2	44.4		6.2	Mk			3								
1149										GSHAP	Syria:Aleppo	叙利亚:阿勒颇	35.9	36.4	30	6.6	Ms	8										
1149										GSHAP	Iraq:Diyala	伊拉克:迪亚拉	34	45.5	25	7.4	Ms	10										
1150	4	1	12							GSHAP,Iran	Iran:Kermanshah	伊朗:克尔曼沙赫	34	46	18	7.4	Ms	10										
1151	9	28								GSHAP	Syria:Hamah (Hama)	叙利亚:哈马	35.2	36.5	12	6.1	Ms	8.5										
1151										GSHAP	Turkey:Kars	土耳其:卡尔斯	40.6	43.1	10	4.5	Ms	7										
1151										* Song	Portugal:Lisbon	葡萄牙:里斯本	38.7	-9.1		6.2	Mk		1000	3				1				
1151										*	Syria:Busra	叙利亚:布斯拉	32.6	36.7		6.2	Muk	9						3				
1153										* GSHAP	Greece:Thesprotia,N.	希腊:塞斯普罗蒂亚北部	39.8	20.1		6	Ms	10										
1155	1	18								* Song	Italy:Scopa	意大利:斯科帕	45.8	8.1		6	Mk			3								
1155										* Song	Syria:Dimashq (Damascus)	叙利亚:大马士革	34.5	36.5		7	Mk		2000	4				3		3		
1156	5	18								GSHAP	Syria:Aleppo	叙利亚:阿勒颇	36.5	36.6	30	7.3	Ms	9										
1156	10	26								* Song	Syria:Halab (Aleppo),Dimashq	叙利亚:阿勒颇,大马士革	38.4	38.3		5.5	Mk	7										
1157	2	13								* Song	Syria:Halab (Aleppo)	叙利亚:阿勒颇	36.3	37.3		7.1	Mk		8000	4				4				
1157	7	15								GSHAP	Syria:Hamah (Hama)	叙利亚:哈马	35.4	36.5	30	6.1	Ms	7										
1157	8	12								GSHAP	Syria:Hamah (Hama)	叙利亚:哈马	35.2	36.3	20	7.2	Ms	9.5										
1158										* Song	Syria:Malatya,Dimashq	叙利亚:马拉蒂亚,大马士革	34.5	36.5		7.7	Mk		20000	5				4		4		
1160										*	Israel:Jerusalem	以色列:耶路撒冷	32	35.5		6.1	Muk							3				
1161	11	9								China	China:Shaanxi,Zhouzhi	中国:陕西周至	34.2	108.2		5	Ms	6										
1164										* Song	Iceland:Grimsnes	冰岛:格里姆斯内斯	64.3	-20		7.3	Mk	10	19	1								
1169	1	31								China	China:Sichuan,Beichuan,N.	中国:四川北川北	31.9	104.4		5	Ms	6										
1169	2	4				5			4	* Italy,NOAA	Italy:Sicily,Siracusa (Syracuse)	意大利:西西里岛,锡拉库萨	37.32	15.03		7	Ms	11	16000	5				4				
1169										* Song	Syria:Halab (Aleppo),Dimashq	叙利亚:阿勒颇,大马士革	36.3	37.3		7.7	Mk	10	80000	5				3				
1170	4	1								GSHAP	Romania:Nereju	罗马尼亚:内雷茹	45.7	26.6	150	7	Ms	8										
1170	7	17								GSHAP	Syria:Hamah (Hama)	叙利亚:哈马	35	36.4	40	7.7	Ms	9										
1171										* Song	Lebanon:Tarabulus (Trippoles)	黎巴嫩:泰拉布鲁斯	34.4	35.8		6.3	Mk							3				
1172						3				* NOAA,Song	Italy:Sicilia Island	意大利:西西里岛	38	15		6.8	Mk			3								
1175	7	22								* Song	Iran:Tehran,Mahmudabad	伊朗:德黑兰,马哈茂达巴德	35.3	51.2		6.3	Mk			3				3				

时间 Date						海啸 Tsunami				资料来源	震中 Earthquake Epicenter				深度	震级	标度	烈度	死亡人数 Deaths		受伤人数 Injuries		经济损失 Damage		房屋毁坏 Houses Destroyed		房屋受损 Houses Damaged	
年	月	日	时	分	秒	源	浪高	级 I	级 S	Information	地名（英文）	地名（中文）	纬度（°）	经度（°）	Depth	Mag	Scale	MMI	数量/人	级别	数量/人	级别	数量/$ Mill	级别	数量/间	级别	数量/间	级别
Year	Mo	Dy	Hr	Mn	Sec	Sr	Wh	mI	mS		Name（English）	Name（Chinese）	Latitude	Longitude					Num	Dd	Num	Dd	$ Mill	De	Num	Dh	Num	Dh
1175										*	Afghan：Jowzjan，NW.	阿富汗：朱兹詹西北	37.5	65.5	15	7.1	Muk	10										
1177	5									* GSHAP	Iran：Qazvin	伊朗：加兹温	35.7	50.7	20	7.2	Ms	9.5						3				
1177										GSHAP	Iraq：Baghdad	伊拉克：巴格达	33.5	44.3	10	6	Ms	8.5										
1179	4	29								GSHAP	Iraq：Arbil	伊拉克：阿尔贝拉	36.5	44.2	16	6.8	Ms	9.5										
1179										* Song	Turkey：Antioch；Syria：Damascus	土耳其：安提俄克；叙利亚：大马士革	36.1	36.1		6.3	Mk							3				
1180										* Song	Italy：Ariano	意大利：诺伊皮诺	41.1	15.1		6	Mk	10										
1182										*	Syria：Busra	叙利亚：布斯拉	32.6	36.7		6.7	Muk	10						3				
1182										* Song	Iceland：Southland	冰岛：绍斯兰	64	−21		7.3	Mk	10	11	1								
1183										* GSHAP	Syria：Aleppo	叙利亚：阿勒颇	36	36.3	12	6.3	Ms	9	20000	5				3				
1184	5	24								* Italy	Italy：Cosenza	意大利：科森扎	39.43	16.25		6	Ms	10						3				
1185	6	15								China	China：Fujian，Zhangzhou	中国：福建漳州	24.3	118		6.5	Ms			1						2		
1185	8	13	3							Japan，Usami	Japan：Takashima	日本：滋贺高岛	35.3	136.1		7.4	Ms	10		3						3		
1192										GSHAP	Azerbaijan：Samaxi	阿塞拜疆：沙马基区	40.6	48.6	5	4.5	Ms	7.5										
1196	2	13	7							GSHAP	Romania：Nereju	罗马尼亚：内雷茹	45.7	26.6	150	7.3	Ms	8										
1200	5	4								GSHAP	Austria：Murau	奥地利：穆劳	47.1	14.2	20	6.2	Ms	8										
1201	4	25	14							* GSHAP	Slovenia：Styria	斯洛文尼亚：斯特利亚	46.4	15.3		5.4	Ms	8						3				
1202	5	20				4			5	* NOAA	Syria：Dimashq（Damascus）	叙利亚：大马士革	33.5	36		7.6	Ms	11	1100000	5				4		4		
1208	7	16								*	Iran：Neyshabur	伊朗：内沙布尔	36.1	58.5		6.5	Muk							3				
1208										*	Turkmenistan：Dashoguz	土库曼斯坦：达沙古兹	42	60	10	6.1	Muk	9	2000	4				3				
1208										* GSHAP	Iran：Sabzevar	伊朗：萨卜泽瓦尔	36.3	57.6		6.5	Ms	9						3				
1208										GSHAP	Turkey：Ahlat	土耳其：阿赫拉特	38.7	42.5	35	6.7	Ms	7.5										
1209	12	13								* China	China：Shanxi，Fushan	中国：山西浮山	36	111.8		6.5	Ms	9	3000	4				3		3		
1209										*	Iran：Neyshabur	伊朗：内沙布尔	36	58.8	10	7.6	Muk	9						3				
1211	6	15								* Song	Egypt：Al－Qahirah（Cairo）	埃及：开罗	30.5	31.3		6.2	Mk			3								
1213	1	31								Japan，Usami，Song	Japan：Kamakura	日本：神奈川镰仓	35.3	139.5		6.8	Mk			1						3		
1213	6	18	3							Japan，Usami	Japan：Kamakura	日本：神奈川镰仓	35.3	139.5		6.4	Ms	7								1		
1216	3	24								China	China：Sichuan，Leibo，NE.	中国：四川雷波东北	28.4	103.8		7	Ms	9										
1216	7	2								China	China：Sichuan，Hanyuan，N.	中国：四川汉源北	29.6	102.6		5	Ms	6										
1219	6	9								* China	China：Ningxia，Guyuan，S.	中国：宁夏固原南	35.6	106.2		6.5	Ms	9	10000	5				4				
1220	1	11								GSHAP	Turkey：Erzurum	土耳其：埃尔佐鲁姆	40.7	42.4	10	4.5	Ms	7										
1222	5					3			4	* NOAA	Mediterranean Sea	地中海	34.5	33		6.6	Ms											
1222	12	25	11							* Italy	Italy：Brescia	意大利：布雷西亚	45.48	10.68		6.05	Ms	10	12000	5				4		4		
1223										* Song	Italy：Siponto	意大利：曼夫雷多尼亚	41.6	15.9		6	Mk	10										
1226	10	29								Korea	North Korea：Kaesong	朝鲜：开城	38	126.5		5.3	Ms	7										
1226	11	18	6							GSHAP	Iraq：As Sulaymaniyah	伊拉克：苏莱曼尼亚	35.3	46	15	6.5	Ms	9										
1227	4	1	11							Japan，Usami	Japan：Kamakura	日本：神奈川镰仓	35.3	139.5		6.2	Ms	7								1		
1227	7									* China	China：Ningxia，Yinchuan	中国：宁夏银川	38.5	106.3		5.5	Ms	7						1		1		1

年 Year	月 Mo	日 Dy	时 Hr	分 Mn	秒 Sec	源 Sr	浪高 Wh	级I mI	级S mS	资料来源 Information	地名(英文) Name(English)	地名(中文) Name(Chinese)	纬度(°) Latitude	经度(°) Longitude	深度 Depth	震级 Mag	标度 Scale	烈度 MMI	死亡人数 Deaths 数量/人 Num	死亡人数 Deaths 级别 Dd	受伤人数 Injuries 数量/人 Num	受伤人数 Injuries 级别 Dd	经济损失 Damage 数量/$ Mill	经济损失 Damage 级别 De	房屋毁坏 Houses Destroyed 数量/间 Num	房屋毁坏 Houses Destroyed 级别 Dh	房屋受损 Houses Damaged 数量/间 Num	房屋受损 Houses Damaged 级别 Dh
1227										GSHAP	Iraq:Makhmur	伊拉克:迈赫穆尔	35.8	43	16	6.9	Ms	9										
1227										*Song	France:Lambesc	法国:兰巴塞克	43.6	5.3		8	Mk	11	5000	4				4				
1230	3	15								Japan,Song	Japan:Kamakura	日本:神奈川镰仓	35.3	139.5		6.3	Mk									1		
1230	5	10	7							GSHAP	Romania:Nereju	罗马尼亚:内雷茹	45.7	26.6	150	7.1	Ms	8.5										
1231	3	11				2			3	GSHAP,NOAA	Turkey:Istanbul	土耳其:伊斯坦布尔	41	28.6		6.9	Ms											
1231	6	1								*Italy	Italy:Germano,S.	意大利:热尔马诺南部	41.48	13.83		5.35	Ms			2								
1233	3	24								Japan,Song	Japan:Wakayama	日本:和歌山	34.3	135.6		6.5	Mk			1						1		
1233										*	Italy:Venezia (Venice)	意大利:威尼斯	45.3	12.2		5.6	Muk							3				
1237	3									*Song	Albania:Durres	阿尔巴尼亚:都拉斯	41.3	19.5		6.2	Mk	10										
1237	8	24								*Song	Iran:Razavi Khorasan	伊朗:呼罗珊	34.2	58.4		6.3	Mk							3				
1237										*Song	Albania:Durres	阿尔巴尼亚:都拉斯	41.2	19.3		6.2	Mk	10										
1240	3	23	21							Japan,Usami	Japan:Kamakura	日本:神奈川镰仓	35.3	139.5		6.4	Ms	7								1		
1241	5	22				4	2	1	1	*Usami,NOAA	Japan:Kamakura	日本:神奈川镰仓	35.2	139.4		7	Ms	9								1		
1245	8	26	19							Japan,Usami	Japan:Kyoto	日本:京都	35.1	135.8		6.2	Ms	7								1		
1248										*Song	Italy:Sabaudia	意大利:撒波迪亚岛	41	13		6.6	Mk		9000	4				4				
1257	10	9	11			4		1	1	*Usami,NOAA	Japan:Sagami Bay	日本:相模湾	35.2	139.5		7	Ms	9						1		3		
1257	10	9				4		2	2	*NOAA	Japan Trench	日本海沟	39	144		7.5	Ms											
1258	2	7	13							GSHAP	Romania:Nereju	罗马尼亚:内雷茹	45.7	26.6	150	6.9	Ms	8										
1259										*Song	Italy:Trapani	意大利:特拉帕尼	38	12.5		6	Mk	10										
1260	7	23								Korea	South Korea:Incheon	韩国:仁川	37.7	126.5		5.5	Ms	7										
1261										GSHAP	Georgia:Akhalkalaki	格鲁吉亚:阿卡卡垃吉	41.4	43.2	10	5.3	Ms	8										
1262										GSHAP	Iraq:Al – Mawsil (Mosul)	伊拉克:勿斯离(摩苏尔)	36.1	43	10	6	Ms	8.5										
1264										China	China:Xizang (Tibet), Doilungdeqen	中国:西藏堆龙德庆	29.7	90.6		6	Ms	8										
1265	8	11				3			3	GSHAP,NOAA	Turkey:Marmara Sea	土耳其:马尔马拉海	40.7	27.4		6.6	Ms											
1267										*	Iran:Neyshabur	伊朗:内沙布尔	36	58.8	10	5.8	Muk	9						3				
1268	9	10								*GSHAP	Turkey:Seyhan	土耳其:杰伊汗	37.5	35.5	12	6.2	Ms	9	50000	5								
1270	3					3			3	NOAA,Song	Albania:Durres	阿尔巴尼亚:普克区	41.3	19.5		6.7	Mk											
1272	7	29								*Song	Iran:Tabriz	伊朗:大不里士	38	46.2		6.2	Mk		250	3				2				
1273	9					2			3	*NOAA	Albania:Tirana	阿尔巴尼亚:地拉那	41.3	19.7		6.5	Ms	9										
1273										*Italy	Italy:Potenza	意大利:波坦察	40.63	15.8		5.84	Ms	10										
1275	4	14								*	Georgia:Gori	格鲁吉亚:哥里	42.1	44.2	28	6.7	Muk			3				3				
1275	6	27								GSHAP	Turkey:Siirt	土耳其:锡尔特	38	42	20	6.8	Ms	8.5										
1276										GSHAP	Romania:Craiova	罗马尼亚:克拉奥华	44.3	23.8	13	6	Ms	8										
1276										*Song	Morocco:El Araish (Larache)	摩洛哥:拉腊什	35.1	-6.1		6.3	Mk			3				3				
1277	7	20								*	Italy:Verona	意大利:维罗那	45.3	11		5.1	Muk			2				2				
1279	4	30	18							*Italy,GSHAP	Italy:Romagna	意大利:弗里	43.093	12.872		6.33	Ms	11		3								
1279	4	30	23							*Italy,GSHAP	Italy:Forli	意大利:罗马尼阿	44.125	11.919		5.55	Ms	10						3				

年 Year	月 Mo	日 Dy	时 Hr	分 Mn	秒 Sec	海啸 Tsunami 源 Sr	浪高 Wh	级 I mI	级 S mS	资料来源 Information	震中 Earthquake Epicenter 地名(英文) Name(English)	地名(中文) Name(Chinese)	纬度(°) Latitude	经度(°) Longitude	深度 Depth	震级 Mag	标度 Scale	烈度 MMI	死亡人数 Deaths 数量/人 Num	级别 Dd	受伤人数 Injuries 数量/人 Num	级别 Dd	经济损失 Damage 数量/$ Mill	级别 De	房屋毁坏 Houses Destroyed 数量/间 Num	级别 Dh	房屋受损 Houses Damaged 数量/间 Num	级别 Dh
1280	5	3								* GSHAP	Iran:Neyshabur	伊朗:内沙布尔	36.1	58.5	10	5.8	Ms	8.5						3				
1280	6	6								* GSHAP	Croatia:Zadar	克罗地亚:扎达尔	44.1	15.2		5.7	Ms	10										
1280	11	3								* GSHAP	Croatia:Zadar	克罗地亚:扎达尔	44.1	15.2		5.7	Ms	10										
1281										*	Iran:Neyshabur	伊朗:内沙布尔	36.1	58.8	10	5.8	Muk	9						3				
1283	4	17	9							* * GSHAP	Georgia:Borzhomi	格鲁吉亚:博尔若米	41.7	43.2	14	6.3	Ms	9						3				
1283										*	Georgia:Borzhomi	格鲁吉亚:博尔若米	41.7	43.2	14	6.3	Muk	9						3				
1284										* Song	Syria:Dimashq (Damascus)	叙利亚:大马士革	33.3	36.2		7.3	Mk	10										
1286										* Song	France:Vannes	法国:瓦纳	47.4	2.5		5.9	Mk							2				
1287										GSHAP	Syria:Hamah (Hama)	叙利亚:哈马	35.5	36.2	24	7.2	Ms	8.5										
1289	7	29								* China	China:Shanxi,Taigu	中国:山西太谷	37.5	112.5		4.75	Ms	6		1								
1289	11	25								* Song	France:Strasbourg	法国:施特拉斯堡	48.6	7.8		5.9	Mk	7						2				
1290	10	4								* China	China:Inner Mongolia, Ningcheng,W.	中国:内蒙古宁城西	41.6	119.3		6.75	Ms	9	100000	5				4				
1291	1	4								* Song	Iran:Fars,Shiraz	伊朗:法尔斯,设拉子	29.4	52.3		5.9	Mk							2				
1291	9	1								* China	China:Shanxi,Linfen	中国:山西临汾	36.1	111.5		6.5	Ms	8	150	3				3				
1292	2	4	2							GSHAP	Black Sea	黑海	44.7	35.1	15	4.5	Ms	5.5										
1293	1	11								* Song	Israel:Jerusalem	以色列:耶路撒冷	32	34.9		6.3	Mk							3				
1293	5	26	21			4		1	1	* Japan,NOAA	Japan:Kamakura	日本:神奈川镰仓	35.2	139.4		7.1	Ms		23024	5				3		3		
1295	4	5								* Song	Switzerland:Chur	瑞士:库尔	46.9	9.5		6.3	Mk	8		3				3				
1295	9	3								* Italy	Switzerland:Chur	瑞士:库尔	46.9	9.5		5.79	Ms	8		2				3				
1298	11	30								* GSHAP	Italy:Terni	意大利:特尔尼	42.5	12.83		6.1	Ms	10										
1298	12	1								* * Italy	Italy:Rieti	意大利:列蒂	42.55	12.83		5.93	Ms	10										
1299	6	4								Japan,Song	Japan:Osaka,Kinai	日本:大阪畿内	32	132		8	Mk		10000	5								
1300	9	30								* GSHAP	Croatia:Zadar	克罗地亚:扎达尔	44.1	15.2		5.7	Ms	10										
1300										* Song	Italy:Rieti	意大利:列蒂	42.4	12.9		6	Mk							3				
1300										*	Iran:Shāhrūd	伊朗:沙赫鲁德	36.8	56		6.5	Muk							3				
1301										* Iran	Iran:Mazanderan	伊朗:马赞德兰	36.1	53.2		6.7	Ms							3				
1303	8	8				3			4	* NOAA,GSHAP	Mediterranean Sea	地中海	36.1	29		8	Ms	9		3				3		3		3
1303	9	25								* China	China:Shanxi,Hongtong	中国:山西洪洞	36.3	111.7		8	Ms	11		4				4	100000	5	100000	5
1303	12					3				* * NOAA,Song	Mediterranean Sea	地中海	34	26		7	Mk			3				3		3		3
1304	2									China	China:Shanxi,Linfen	中国:山西临汾	36.1	111.5		5	Ms	6										
1304	9	11								China	China:Shanxi,Taigu	中国:山西太谷	37.4	112.6		4.75	Ms	6										
1304	11	7								*	Iran:Tabriz	伊朗:大不里士	38.5	45.5		6.7	Ms	8						2				
1304	11	8								GSHAP	Iran:Tabriz	伊朗:大不里士	38.2	46.3	15	4.9	Ms	7										
1305	5	11								* China	China:Shanxi,Huairen	中国:山西怀仁	39.8	113.1		6.5	Ms	9	2000	4				3	5800	4		
1306	9	20								* China	China:Ningxia,Guyuan,S.	中国:宁夏固原南	35.9	106.1		6.5	Ms	9	5000	4				3		3		
1306										* Song	Iran:Qeshm Island	伊朗:格什姆岛	26.6	56.2		6.3	Mk							3				
1306										* Song	Greece:Crete Island	希腊:克里特岛	35.5	25.5		7	Mk	10										
1307										China	China:Shaanxi,Qishan	中国:陕西岐山	34.5	107.6		5	Ms	6										

时间						海啸				资料来源	震中				深度	震级	标度	烈度	死亡人数		受伤人数		经济损失		房屋毁坏		房屋受损	
年	月	日	时	分	秒	源	浪高	级I	级S		地名(英文)	地名(中文)	纬度(°)	经度(°)					数量/人	级别	数量/人	级别	数量/$ Mill	级别	数量/间	级别	数量/间	级别
Date						Tsunami				Information	Earthquake Epicenter				Depth	Mag	Scale	MMI	Deaths		Injuries		Damage		Houses Destroyed		Houses Damaged	
Year	Mo	Dy	Hr	Mn	Sec	Sr	Wh	mI	mS		Name(English)	Name(Chinese)	Latitude	Longitude					Num	Dd	Num	Dd	$ Mill	De	Num	Dh	Num	Dh
1310										* Iran	Iraq: As – Sulaymaniyah	伊拉克:苏莱曼尼亚	35.5	45.5		5.5	Ms	8		3								
1310										* Song	Iraq: Sulaimaniya, Baghdad	伊拉克:苏莱曼尼亚,巴格达	33.2	44.2		5.9	Mk	7						2				
1310										* Song	Iran: Hengam Island	伊朗:亨加姆岛	26.4	55.5		6.3	Mk							3				
1310										GSHAP	Russia: Buryatiya, Kyren	俄罗斯:布里亚特州克廖恩	51.69	103.01	15	6.6	Ms	9										
1311	4	24								China	China: Ningxia, Yinchuan	中国:宁夏银川	38.5	106.3		4.75	Ms	6										
1314	10	13								* China	China: Hebei, Shexian	中国:河北涉县	36.6	113.8		6	Ms	8	340	3				2		2		
1316	1	5								GSHAP	Iran: Lorestan	伊朗:洛雷斯坦	33.5	49.4	7	6	Ms	9.5										
1316										China	China: Shanxi, Puxian	中国:山西蒲县	36.4	111.1		5.5	Ms	7										
1317	2	22								Japan, Song	Japan: Kyoto	日本:京都	35.1	135.8		6.3	Mk									1		
1317	2	23	19							Japan, Usami	Japan: Kyoto	日本:京都	35.1	135.8		6.7	Ms	8	5							3		
1318	2	21								China	China: Liaoning, Zhangwu	中国:辽宁彰武	42.6	122.1		5	Ms	6										
1319										* Iran	Iran: Maku	伊朗:马库	39.1	44.5		5.9	Ms	7	75	2				3		3		
1319										* Song	Italy: Montecassino	意大利:蒙特卡西诺	41.5	13.8		6	Mk	10										
1319										* GSHAP	Turkey: Igdir	土耳其:厄德尔	39.8	44.2	30	7.4	Ms	9						3				
1320	12	9								* Song	Portugal: Cabo De San Vicente, SW.	葡萄牙:德聖維森特西南	36	–10.7		7.3	Mk	10										
1321						2			3	NOAA, Song	Italy: Gulf of Venice	意大利:威尼斯海湾	45.4	12.3		6.7	Mk											
1323	1	7								China	China: Hebei, Xuanhua	中国:河北宣化	40.6	115.1		5	Ms	6										
1323										* Italy	Croatia: Rijeka	克罗地亚:里耶卡	45.2	14.7		6	Ms	10										
1325	12	5	13							Japan, Usami	Japan: Tsuruga	日本:福井敦贺	35.6	136.1		6.7	Ms	8								1		
1327	1	1								GSHAP	Romania: Nereju	罗马尼亚:内雷茹	45.7	26.6	150	7	Ms	8										
1327	9									* China	China: Sichuan, Tianquan	中国:四川天全	30.1	102.7		6	Ms	6		1								
1328	12	1								* Italy, GSHAP	Italy: Norcia	意大利:诺尔恰	42.8	13		6.3	Ms	10	5000	4				3				
1329	6	28				2			3	NOAA, Song	Italy: Sicilia Island	意大利:西西里岛	37.8	15		6.7	Mk											
1331	8	15				4		0		* Japan, Usami, NOAA	Japan: Tokushima	日本:德岛	33.7	135.2		7	Ms	9										
1332	2	12				2			3	* NOAA	Turkey: Balikesir, N.	土耳其:巴勒克西尔北部	40	28		6.8	Ms											
1336	3	9								China	China: Hubei, Huangmei	中国:湖北黄梅	30.2	116		4.75	Ms	6										
1336	5	9								* Song	Iran: Qeshm Island	伊朗:格什姆岛	26.6	56.2		6.3	Mk							3				
1336	10	21	1	30						*	Iran: Razavi Khorasan	伊朗:呼罗珊	34.7	59.7		7.6	Muk		20000	5				3				
1337	9	16								* China	China: Hebei, Huailai	中国:河北怀来	40.4	115.7		6.5	Ms	8				1		1				
1338	8	10								China	China: Hebei, Zhuolu	中国:河北涿鹿	40.4	115.2		5	Ms	6								1		
1339										* Song	Lebanon: Tarabulus (Tripolis)	黎巴嫩:塔拉布卢斯(黎波里)	34.3	35.5		6.1	Mk	8	60	2				2				
1341	4									China	China: Shanxi, Taiyuan	中国:山西太原	37.9	112.4		4.75	Ms	6										
1341	10	31				3		2.5	2.5	* Japan, NOAA	Japan: Aomori, Near Coast of W.	日本:青森西部近海	41	139.5		7	Ms		2600	4								

年 Year	月 Mo	日 Dy	时 Hr	分 Mn	秒 Sec	源 Sr	浪高 Wh	级 I mI	级 S mS	资料来源 Information	地名(英文) Name(English)	地名(中文) Name(Chinese)	纬度(°) Latitude	经度(°) Longitude	深度 Depth	震级 Mag	标度 Scale	烈度 MMI	死亡人数 Deaths 数量/人 Num	死亡人数 Deaths 级别 Dd	受伤人数 Injuries 数量/人 Num	受伤人数 Injuries 级别 Dd	经济损失 Damage 数量/$ Mill	经济损失 Damage 级别 De	房屋毁坏 Houses Destroyed 数量/间 Num	房屋毁坏 Houses Destroyed 级别 Dh	房屋受损 Houses Damaged 数量/间 Num	房屋受损 Houses Damaged 级别 Dh
1342	4	23								China	China:Henan,Tongxu	中国:河南通许	34.5	114.5		4.75	Ms	6								1		
1342	5	13								China	China:Shanxi,Jinyuan	中国:山西晋源	37.7	112.5		5.5	Ms	7										
1343	1	1								* Song	Syria:Dimashq (Damascus)	叙利亚:大马士革	33.3	36.2		7	Mk	9	5700	4				3				
1343	6	30								* GSHAP	Croatia:Zadar	克罗地亚:扎达尔	44	15		5.7	Ms	10										
1343	10	18	19			3			4	GSHAP,NOAA	Turkey:Manyas, Bursa	土耳其:马尼亚斯,布尔萨	40.8	28.3		7.5	Ms											
1343	10	20	14			2			4	NOAA,Song	Turkey:Marmara Sea	土耳其:马尔马拉海	41	28.1		6.7	Mk											
1343	11	25				2			4	NOAA,Song	Italy:Bay of Napli	意大利:那不勒斯湾	40.8	14.4		6.7	Mk											
1343										GSHAP	Turkey:Gaziantep	土耳其:加济安泰普	37.3	37.4	30	7.5	Ms	9										
1344	2	12				4			5	* NOAA	Turkey:Marmara Sea	土耳其:马尔马拉海	40.8	28.8		6.9	Ms											
1344	5	15								* Iran	Iran:Esfahan	伊朗:伊斯法罕	32.9	52.3		5.7	Ms		20	1				1				
1344	10									GSHAP	Turkey:Manyas	土耳其:马尼亚斯	40.9	28	16	7	Ms	9.5										
1344										* Song	Portugal:Lisbon	葡萄牙:里斯本	38	-9		6.3	Mk							3				
1345	9	12								* GSHAP,Italy	Italy:Firenze (Florence)	意大利:佛罗伦萨	43.777	11.249		5.6	Ms			3				3				
1346	4									China	China:Shandong,Gaoqing,SE.	中国:山东高青东南	37.1	117.9		4.75	Ms	6										
1346	11	24	23							* Song	Switzerland:Reinach	瑞士:赖纳赫	47.5	7.6		6.3	Mk	8						3				
1348	1	25	23			2			3	* Italy,GSHAP,NOAA	Austria:Villach	奥地利:菲拉赫	46.6	13.85		6.66	Ms	11	5000	4				4				
1349	9	9								* Song	Italy:L'Aquila	意大利:拉奎拉	42.2	13.2		6	Mk	10	1000	3				3				
1350	7	6	7							Japan,Usami	Japan:Kyoto	日本:京都	35	135.8		6.2	Ms		5	1						1		
1350										*	Georgia:Kotais	格鲁吉亚:库塔伊西	43	43	20	6.5	Muk	9						3				
1351	5	7								* China	China:Shanxi,Jinyuan	中国:山西晋源	37.7	112.5		5.5	Ms	7		3								
1352	4	26								* China	China:Gansu,Huining,SE.	中国:甘肃会宁东南	35.6	105.3		7	Ms	9						2		2		
1352	12	25								* Italy	Italy:Sansepolcro	意大利:圣塞波尔克罗	43.465	12.127		6	Ms	11	2000	4				3				
1353	3	1								* * GSHAP	Turkey:Hellespont	土耳其:达达尼尔海峡	40.8	27		7.3	Ms	11										
1354	5	2								China	China:Shanxi,Jiexiu	中国:山西介休	37	111.9		4.75	Ms	6										
1354										* Song	Syria:Hamah (Hama)	叙利亚:哈马	35.1	36.4		5.9	Mk	7	24	1				2				
1356	8	24								* Song	Portugal:Cabo De San Vicente,SW.	葡萄牙:德圣维森特西南	36.8	-9		7.3	Mk	10						3				
1356	10	18	21	30						* Song	Switzerland:Basel	瑞士:巴塞尔	47.4	7.6		7.3	Mk	10	300	3				4				
1358										* GSHAP	Yemen:Zabid,Adan	也门:札比德,艾顿	14.1	43.2		5.5	Ms	8	61	2				2				
1360	11	23				4	6	2	2	* Japan,Usami,NOAA	Japan:Shingu,Near Coast	日本:和歌山新宫近海	33.4	136.2		7	Ms	9		3								
1360										* Song	Iran:Qeshm Island	伊朗:格什姆岛	26.8	55.9		6.3	Mk							3				
1360										Japan,Song	Japan:Chiba	日本:千叶	35.2	140		6.3	Mk									1		
1361	7	17								* Italy	Italy:Basilicata To Pouilles	意大利:巴西利卡塔	41.23	15.45		6.06	Ms	10	4000	4				3				
1361	7	31	21							Japan,Usami,Song	Japan:Gujo	日本:岐阜郡上	35.7	137.6		6.3	Mk									1		

年	月	日	时	分	秒	源	浪高	级I	级S	资料来源	地名(英文)	地名(中文)	纬度(°)	经度(°)	深度	震级	标度	烈度	死亡人数 数量/人	死亡人数 级别	受伤人数 数量/人	受伤人数 级别	经济损失 数量/$ Mill	经济损失 级别	房屋毁坏 数量/间	房屋毁坏 级别	房屋受损 数量/间	房屋受损 级别
Date						Tsunami				Information	Earthquake Epicenter				Depth	Mag	Scale	MMI	Deaths		Injuries		Damage		Houses Destroyed		Houses Damaged	
Year	Mo	Dy	Hr	Mn	Sec	Sr	Wh	mI	mS		Name(English)	Name(Chinese)	Latitude	Longitude					Num	Dd	Num	Dd	$ Mill	De	Num	Dh	Num	Dh
1361	8	2	19			4		3	3	* Japan, Usami, NOAA	Japan: Tokushima, Near Coast	日本:德岛近海	33	135	4	8.4	Ms		660	3				3	1700	4		
1361										*	China: Jiangxi, Jing – an	中国:江西靖安	28.8	115.3		5	Ms	6		3								
1365	1	2				3				* NOAA, Song	Algeria: Algiers	阿尔及利亚:阿尔及尔	36.8	3		7	Mk			3				3		3		3
1366	8	15								China	China: Shanxi, Yangqu	中国:山西阳曲	38	112.7		5.75	Ms	7		1								
1367										China	China: Shanxi, Taiyuan	中国:山西太原	37.9	112.5		5.5	Ms	7	10000	5								
1367										* Song	Iran: Rudbar, Rasht	伊朗:鲁德巴,拉什特	37.3	49.7		6.3	Mk							3				
1368	7	16								* China	China: Shanxi, Fangshan, SE.	中国:山西方山东南	37.8	111.5		5.25	Ms	7		2				3				
1369	9	7								Japan, Usami	Japan: Kyoto	日本:京都	35.1	135.8		6.1	Ms	7										
1372	8	16								*	China: Jiangsu, Nanjing	中国:江苏南京	32	118.8		4.8	Ms	6	16	1								
1372	9	25								China	China: Guangdong, Guangzhou	中国:广东广州	23.1	113.3		4.75	Ms	6										
1374	2	2								* Song	Spain: Ribagorza	西班牙:里巴哥札山	42.1	–0.3		7.3	Mk	10		3								
1375										* Italy	Switzerland: Engelberg	瑞士:恩格尔贝格	46.9	8.4		5.57	Ms	8		3				3				
1377										* Song	Yemen: Adan	也门:艾顿	12.4	45.1		5.9	Mk							2				
1378	5	8								China	China: Ningxia, Yinchuan	中国:宁夏银川	38.5	106.3		5.75	Ms	7										
1380										* GSHAP	Albania: Elbasan	阿尔巴尼亚:爱尔巴桑	41.1	20.1		6	Ms	10										
1382	3	17								* Song	Iran: Tehran, Mahmudabad	伊朗:德黑兰,马哈茂达巴德	35.3	51.2		6.3	Mk							3				
1383	8	6								* Song	Greece: Kalloni	希腊:卡洛尼	39.2	26.2		7	Mk	10										
1384	8									* Song	Greece: Lesbos, Aegean Sea	希腊:莱斯沃斯,爱琴海	39	26		6.2	Mk	7	500	3								
1385	8	1								*	South Korea: Incheon	韩国:仁川	37.6	126.3		6.3	Muk	8						2				
1386	1	1								* GSHAP, Song	Bosnia: Zenica	波斯尼亚:泽尼察	44.2	17.7		5.7	Mk	10										
1387	3	5								* GSHAP	Croatia: Zadar	克罗地亚:扎达尔	44.1	15.2		5.7	Ms	10										
1387	9	5								* Song	Yemen: Adan	也门:艾顿	12.4	45.1		6.3	Mk			3				3				
1389	1	20								*	Iran: Neyshabur	伊朗:内沙布尔	36.2	58.5	10	5.8	Muk	9		3				3				
1389	1	30								* Song	Iran: Neyshabur	伊朗:内沙布尔	36.1	58.5		6.3	Mk							3				
1389	2									*	Iran: Neyshabur	伊朗:内沙布尔	36.2	58.8		7.6	Muk							3				
1389	3	20				2			3	* GSHAP, NOAA	Turkey: Karaburun	土耳其:卡拉布伦	38.5	26.5		6.8	Ms	10										
1390	5									*	Uzbekistan: Buhoro	乌兹别克斯坦:布哈拉	39.8	64.4	20	6.1	Ms	8		1				2				
1390	12	5	24							* GSHAP	Croatia: Zadar	克罗地亚:扎达尔	44.1	15.2		5.7	Mk	10										
1391	3	23								* Song	Switzerland: Porrentruy	瑞士:波朗特吕	47.4	7.2		6.3	Mk	8						3				
1391	11	20	3							Japan, Song	Japan: Kyoto	日本:京都	35.1	135.8		6.5	Mk			1						1		
1399	11	6	20							* GSHAP	Croatia: Zadar	克罗地亚:扎达尔	44.1	15.2		5.7	Ms	10										
1400										* Iran	Iran: Lar	伊朗:拉尔	27.7	54.3		5.3	Ms							2				
1400										* Song	Iran: Zanjān	伊朗:赞詹	36.5	49		5.9	Mk							2				
1400										GSHAP	Russia: Irkutsk, Slyudyanka	俄罗斯:伊尔库茨克州斯柳江卡	51.72	103.68	15	6	Ms	8.5										
1402	6					2			5	GSHAP, NOAA	Greece: Patrai	希腊:帕特雷	38.11	22.41		7	Ms											

时间 Date						海啸 Tsunami				资料来源	震中 Earthquake Epicenter				深度	震级	标度	烈度	死亡人数 Deaths		受伤人数 Injuries		经济损失 Damage		房屋毁坏 Houses Destroyed		房屋受损 Houses Damaged	
年	月	日	时	分	秒	源	浪高	级 I	级 S		地名(英文)	地名(中文)	纬度(°)	经度(°)					数量/人	级别	数量/人	级别	数量/$ Mill	级别	数量/间	级别	数量/间	级别
Year	Mo	Dy	Hr	Mn	Sec	Sr	Wh	mI	mS	Information	Name(English)	Name(Chinese)	Latitude	Longitude	Depth	Mag	Scale	MMI	Num	Dd	Num	Dd	$ Mill	De	Num	Dh	Num	Dh
1402						2				＊NOAA, Song	Syria: Tudmur (Palmyra)	叙利亚:帕尔米拉	35	37		6.8	Mk							3				
1403	11	16				2			3	＊NOAA, Song	Syria: Ar Raqqah	叙利亚:拉卡	35	37		6.7	Mk											
1403	12					4	2	1	1	＊NOAA	Japan: Shingu, Near Coast	日本:和歌山新宫近海	33.7	136.5		7	Ms											
1404	2	13								＊GSHAP	Syria: Halab (Aleppo)	叙利亚:阿勒颇(阿勒颇)	36.1	37.1	36	7	Ms	9						3				
1405	1	29								＊	Iran: Neyshabur	伊朗:内沙布尔	36	58.8	15	6.7	Muk	9		3				4				
1406	10	16								＊Usami	Japan: Shizuoka, Near Coast	日本:静冈近海	34.4	138.4		6.2	Ms							1		1		
1407	4	9								＊Song	Turkey: Hatay	土耳其:哈塔伊	36	36		6.2	Mk			3								
1407	4	29								GSHAP	Syria: Hamah (Hama)	叙利亚:哈马	35.7	36.3	16	7	Ms	9.5										
1407										China	China: Hubei, Zhongxiang	中国:湖北钟祥	31.2	112.6		5.5	Ms	7										
1408	1	21	9			4	2	1	1	＊Japan, Usami, NOAA	Japan: Mie, Near Coast	日本:三重近海	33.8	136.9		7	Ms	9										
1408	12	20				2				＊NOAA, Song	Turkey: Antioch; Syria: Aleppo	土耳其:安提俄克; 叙利亚:阿勒颇	36.2	36.1		7	Mk	10		3				3				
1411	10	8								China	China: Xizang (Tibet), Damxung, SW.	中国:西藏当雄西南	30.1	90.5		8	Ms	11		4								
1414	8	3								＊Song	Italy: Sansepolcro	意大利:圣塞波尔克罗	43.5	12.1		6	Mk	10	200	3				2				
1416	5	23								GSHAP, Korea	South Korea: Uiseong	韩国:义城郡	36.6	128.7		5	Ms	7										
1417										＊Song	Italy: Ariano Irpino	意大利:阿维利诺	41	15		6	Mk							3				
1418	4	7								＊Song	Croatia: Sibenik	克罗地亚:希贝尼克	43.9	15.6		6.3	Mk	10						3				
1419	3	15				1				＊GSHAP	Turkey: Tosya	土耳其:托斯亚	41	34	25	7.5	Ms	9.5										
1419	5	25				3				＊＊NOAA, GSHAP	Turkey: Marmara Sea	土耳其:马尔马拉海	40.9	28.9		6.6	Ms											
1420	9	7				1	2	1	1	Japan, NOAA, Song	Japan: Hitachiota	日本:茨城常陆太田	36.6	140.5		7	Mk											
1423	11	22	23							Japan, Usami	Japan: Akita	日本:秋田	39.2	140.1		6.7	Ms	8		3						3		
1425	3	16								China	China: Anhui, Liuan	中国:安徽六安	31.7	116.5		5.75	Ms	7								2		
1425	11	23	1							Japan, Usami	Japan: Kyoto	日本:京都	35	135.8		6	Ms									1		
1426										＊Song	Yemen: Zabid, Bahrain	也门:札比德,巴林	14.1	43.2		8	Mk	11	60	2				3				
1427	5	15								＊Song	Spain: Olot, Barcelona	西班牙:奥罗特,巴塞罗纳	41.7	2.2		8	Mk	11		3				3				
1428	2	2								＊Song	France: Prats De Mollo, Arles – Sur – Tech	法国:普拉德莫洛,阿尔勒	43.4	4.4		6.5	Mk	9	600	3				2				
1430	4	24								＊Song	Spain: Granada	西班牙:格拉纳达	37.2	–3.6		8	Mk	11						3				
1433	11	6				4	2	1	1	＊Usami, NOAA	Japan: Oshima	日本:东京大岛	34.9	139.5		7.1	Ms	9		3				3		1		
1433	11	7								Japan, Usami	Japan: Fukushima	日本:福岛	37.7	139.8		6.7	Ms	8								3		
1437	11	28				1				NOAA, Song	Turkey: Canakkale	土耳其:恰纳卡莱	40	26.1		6.6	Mk											
1440	11	4								＊China	China: Gansu, Yongdeng	中国:甘肃永登	36.7	103.3		6.25	Ms	8	200	3				2		2		
1440	12	25								China	China: Gansu, Yongdeng	中国:甘肃永登	36.3	103.4		5.5	Ms	7										

年 Year	月 Mo	日 Dy	时 Hr	分 Mn	秒 Sec	源 Sr	浪高 Wh	级 I mI	级 S mS	资料来源 Information	地名(英文) Name(English)	地名(中文) Name(Chinese)	纬度(°) Latitude	经度(°) Longitude	深度 Depth	震级 Mag	标度 Scale	烈度 MMI	死亡人数 Deaths 数量/人 Num	死亡人数 Deaths 级别 Dd	受伤人数 Injuries 数量/人 Num	受伤人数 Injuries 级别 Dd	经济损失 Damage 数量/$ Mill	经济损失 Damage 级别 De	房屋毁坏 Houses Destroyed 数量/间 Num	房屋毁坏 Houses Destroyed 级别 Dh	房屋受损 Houses Damaged 数量/间 Num	房屋受损 Houses Damaged 级别 Dh
1440										* Iran	Iran:Hormozgan	伊朗:荷姆兹甘	28.3	53.1		7.1	Muk							3				
1441										* Song	Iran:Tabriz	伊朗:大不里士	38	46.2		6.3	Mk							3				
1441										* Turkey	Turkey:Van,Nemrut	土耳其:凡城,尼姆鲁特	38.3	43.2		6.4	Ms							3				
1443	6	5								* GSHAP	Slovakia:Banska Stiavnica	斯洛伐克:班斯卡什佳夫尼察	48.5	19.1	36	6.4	Ms	10	30	1								
1444	5	26								China	China:Yunnan,Nanhua,NW.	中国:云南南华西北	25.3	101.1		4.75	Ms	6										
1444	11									* Song	Bulgaria:Varna	保加利亚:瓦尔纳	43.2	27.9		6.3	Mk							3		3		3
1444										* Song	Turkey:Nemrut Mtns	土耳其:尼姆鲁特山	38.7	42.2		7.7	Mk		30000	5								
1445	12	21								* China	China:Fujian,Zhangzhou	中国:福建漳州	24.5	117.6		6.25	Ms	8		3				3		3		
1445										China	China:Guangdong,Sihui	中国:广东四会	23.4	112.6		4.75	Ms	6										
1446	4	8								China	China:Yunnan,Jianshui	中国:云南建水	23.6	102.8		5.5	Ms	7										
1446	10	10	4							GSHAP	Romania:Nereju	罗马尼亚:内雷茹	45.7	26.6	150	7.6	Ms	9										
1447	11	4								* Song	Italy:Roma (Rome)	意大利:罗马	41.9	12.6		6	Mk			3				3				
1447										China	China:Xizang (Tibet),Sagya	中国:西藏萨迦	29	88		5.5	Ms	7										
1448	9	19				3		2	2	* NOAA	Japan:Sado Island	日本:佐渡岛	37.5	138.2		7	Ms							2				
1448	10	9								China	China:Shaanxi,Yulin	中国:陕西榆林	38.3	109.7		5.5	Ms	7										
1449	5	12	23							Japan,Usami	Japan:Yamashiro,Daiwa	日本:山城,大和	35	135.6	0	6.4	Ms			3						1		
1450										GSHAP	Black Sea	黑海	44.3	34.3	20	6.5	Ms	8.5										
1451	1	1								* GSHAP,Song	Croatia:Dubrovnik	克罗地亚:杜布罗夫尼克	42.6	18		5.7	Mk	10										
1454	9	14	23							* Song	Switzerland:Reinach	瑞士:赖纳赫	47.5	7.6		6	Mk			2								
1454	9	15	1							* Song	Switzerland:Reinach	瑞士:赖纳赫	47.5	7.6		6	Mk			2								
1455	1	24								* Korea	South Korea:Kwangju	韩国:光州市	35.9	126.5		6.8	Muk	9		3				2				
1455	12	5								* Song	Italy:Napoli (Naples)	意大利:那不勒斯(拿坡里)	40.4	14.1		6.8	Mk		40000	5								
1456	2	14								Japan,Usami,Song	Japan:Hakone	日本:神奈川箱根	35.2	139		6.4	Mk	8								1		
1456	6	16								* GSHAP	Kosovo:Prizren	科索沃:普里兹伦	42.2	20.7		5.7	Ms	10										
1456	7	12								China	China:Hebei,Huailai,NE.	中国:河北怀来东北	40.4	115.7		5	Ms	6										
1456	11	29								* Song	Turkey:Erzincan	土耳其:埃尔津占	39.8	39.5		6.3	Mk							3				
1456	12	5	4	30		2			4	* Italy,NOAA	Italy:Benevento,Campobasso	意大利:贝内文托,坎布巴索	41.15	14.867		6.96	Ms	11	30000	5				4				
1457										* Song	Egypt:Yamit	埃及:耶米特	31.2	34.2		7.7	Mk		32000	5								
1458	11	12								* Song	Egypt:Yamit	埃及:耶米特	31.2	34.2		6.1	Mk	8	100	2				2		3		
1458										* Turkey	Turkey:Erzincan	土耳其:埃尔津占	39.9	40.4		7.5	Ms	10	32000	5				3				
1459	5	20								* GSHAP	Croatia:Varazdin	克罗地亚:瓦拉日丁	46.3	16.3	13	6	Ms	10										
1461	11	27	0	15						* Song	Italy:L'Aquila (Aquila)	意大利:拉奎拉	42.3	13.4		6	Mk	10										

时间						海啸				资料来源	震中				深度	震级	标度	烈度	死亡人数		受伤人数		经济损失		房屋毁坏		房屋受损	
年	月	日	时	分	秒	源	浪高	级I	级S		地名(英文)	地名(中文)	纬度(°)	经度(°)					数量/人	级别	数量/人	级别	数量/$ Mill	级别	数量/间	级别	数量/间	级别
Date						Tsunami				Information	Earthquake Epicenter				Depth	Mag	Scale	MMI	Deaths		Injuries		Damage		Houses Destroyed		Houses Damaged	
Year	Mo	Dy	Hr	Mn	Sec	Sr	Wh	mI	mS		Name(English)	Name(Chinese)	Latitude	Longitude					Num	Dd	Num	Dd	$ Mill	De	Num	Dh	Num	Dh
1461	11	28	2	15						* Song	Italy:L'Aquila	意大利:拉奎拉	42.3	13.5		6	Mk	10										
1463										* Song	Yemen:Zabid	也门:札比德	14.1	43.2		6.5	Mk	9	10	1					50	1	50	1
1464										* Song	Spain:Sevilla (Seville)	西班牙:塞维利亚	37.3	-5.6		6.5	Mk	9						3				
1466	5	29								Japan, Song	Japan:Kyoto, Daiwa	日本:京都,大和	34.8	135.7		6.3	Mk									1		
1467	1	28								China	China:Sichuan, Yanyuan	中国:四川盐源	27.5	101.6		6.5	Ms	8								3		
1467	6	18								China	China:Shanxi, Pinglu	中国:山西平鲁	39.6	112.3		5.5	Ms	7										
1469	4									* GSHAP	Greece:Nisia Ionioy	希腊:伊奥尼亚群岛	38.5	20.5		7.2	Ms	10										
1469	11	13								China	China:Hubei, Zhongxiang	中国:湖北钟祥	31.2	112.6		5.5	Ms	7										
1471	8	29	8							GSHAP	Romania:Nereju	罗马尼亚:内雷茹	45.7	26.6	150	6.8	Ms	8.5										
1471										* Song	Croatia:Dubrovnik	克罗地亚:杜布罗夫尼克	42.6	18.1		6.3	Mk	10										
1471										*	Peru:Arequipa	秘鲁:阿雷基帕	-16.3	-71	25	8	Muk	9										
1474	11	5								China	China:Yunnan, Heqing	中国:云南鹤庆	26.6	100.2		5.5	Ms	7										
1474	12	20								China	China:Ningxia, Wuzhong	中国:宁夏吴忠	37.9	106.3		5.5	Ms	7										
1475										*	Kyrgyzstan:Tokmok	吉尔吉斯斯坦:托克马克	42.6	75.2	5	6.4	Muk	9						2				
1477	3	28								China	China:Gansu, Lintao	中国:甘肃临洮	35.2	104.2		5.5	Ms	7										
1477	5	22								China	China:Ningxia, Yinchuan, W.	中国:宁夏银川西	38.5	106.3		6.5	Ms	8										
1478	8	26								* China	China:Sichuan, Yanyuan	中国:四川盐源	27.5	101.6		6	Ms	8		3				2		2		
1479	10	20								* GSHAP	Croatia:Split, SE.	克罗地亚:斯普利特东南	43	17.6		5.7	Ms	10										
1480	9	22								China	China:Sichuan, Yuexi	中国:四川越西	28.6	102.5		5.5	Ms	7										
1481	3									GSHAP	Turkey:Erzincan	土耳其:埃尔津占	39.9	40.4	17	7.7	Ms	10.5										
1481	5	3				2	1.8	1.8	3	* NOAA	Greece:Dodecanese Islands	希腊:多德卡尼斯群岛	36	28		7.1	Ms	10	30000	5				4				
1481	7	24								* China	China:Yunnan, Jianchuan	中国:云南剑川	26.5	99.9		6.25	Ms	8		3				3		3		
1481	9	10								* Song	Italy:Rodi Garganico	意大利:城镇如罗迪城	42	15.9		6	Mk							3				
1481	12	18								*	Greece: Rhodes	希腊:罗得	36	28		6	Mk			3				3				
1482	2	15	15							* GSHAP	Croatia:Dubrovnik	克罗地亚:杜布罗夫尼克	42.6	18.1		5.7	Ms	10										
1482										*	Gulf of Oman	阿曼湾	26.1	56.9		6.5	Muk							3				
1482										*	Turkey:Erzincan, Erzurum	土耳其:埃尔津占,埃尔佐鲁姆	39.9	40.4		7.5	Muk	10	30000	5				3				
1483	10	18								* Song	Greece:Dodecanese Islands	希腊:多德卡尼斯群岛	36.2	27.5		7	Mk	10										
1484	2	7								* China	China:Beijing, Yanqing	中国:北京延庆	40.5	116.1		6.75	Ms	9		2				2		2		
1484	8	27								* Song	Iran:Zanjān	伊朗:赞詹	37	49		6.3	Mk			3				3				
1485	1	26								China	China:Shanxi, Yongji	中国:山西永济	34.8	110.3		5.5	Ms	7										
1485	3	15								China	China:Shandong, Feixian	中国:山东费县	35.3	117.9		5.5	Ms	7										
1485	6	5								China	China:Hebei, Zunhua	中国:河北遵化	40.2	117.9		5	Ms	6										
1485	8	14								* Iran, GSHAP	Iran:Qazvin	伊朗:加兹温	36.7	50.5	20	7.2	Muk	9.5						3				

时间 Date						海啸 Tsunami				资料来源 Information	震中 Earthquake Epicenter				深度 Depth	震级 Mag	标度 Scale	烈度 MMI	死亡人数 Deaths		受伤人数 Injuries		经济损失 Damage		房屋毁坏 Houses Destroyed		房屋受损 Houses Damaged	
年 Year	月 Mo	日 Dy	时 Hr	分 Mn	秒 Sec	源 Sr	浪高 Wh	级 I mI	级 S mS		地名(英文) Name(English)	地名(中文) Name(Chinese)	纬度(°) Latitude	经度(°) Longitude					数量/人 Num	级别 Dd	数量/人 Num	级别 Dd	数量/$ Mill $ Mill	级别 De	数量/间 Num	级别 Dh	数量/间 Num	级别 Dh
1487	8	19								* China	China:Shaanxi,Xianyang,NE.	中国:陕西咸阳东北	34.4	108.9		6.25	Ms	8	1900	4				3		3		
1488	9	25								* China	China:Sichuan,Maoxian	中国:四川茂县	31.7	103.9		5.5	Ms	7		2				1	37	1		
1488										China	China:Yunnan,Dayao	中国:云南大姚	25.7	101.3		5	Ms	6										
1489	1	15								China	China:Sichuan,Xichang	中国:四川西昌	27.8	102.3		6.75	Ms	9										
1489						2			3	* NOAA,Song	Mediterranean Sea	地中海	35.5	29.5		6.7	Mk											
1490	2	20								*	Uzbekistan:Samarkand	乌兹别克斯坦:撒马尔罕	39.4	67.1	15	5.8	Muk	8						3				
1490	11	1								* Song	Greece:Dodecanese Islands	希腊:多德卡尼斯群岛	36.5	27		7	Mk	10										
1490										GSHAP	Russia:Khabarovsk, Komsomolsk – On – Amur	俄罗斯:哈巴罗夫斯克区阿穆尔河畔共青城	50.85	134.15	30	6.5	Ms	8.5										
1491	4	25								GSHAP	Cyprus:Nicosia	塞浦路斯:尼科西亚	35.2	33.2	15	6.9	Ms	9.5										
1491	10									* Song	Greece:Kos	希腊:科斯	36.9	27		7	Mk		5000	4				3				
1493	1	10								* Iran	Iran:Birjand	伊朗:比尔詹德	33	59.8		7	Muk							3				
1493	8	18								* Turkey	Greece:Kos Island	希腊:科斯岛	36.8	27		6.8	Ms	9										
1494	4	2								* China	China:Yunnan,Qujing	中国:云南曲靖	25.5	103.8		5.5	Ms	7	3	1				2	200	3		
1494	6	13								* Song	France:Near S. Coast	法国:南部近海	43.8	7		7.3	Mk	10										
1494	6	19	3							Japan,Usami	Japan:Nara	日本:奈良	34.6	135.7		6.4	Ms	8								1		
1494	6	23								* Song	France:Lantosque,Roquebilliere	法国:朗托斯克,罗克比列尔	43.4	7.1		6.1	Mk	8						2				
1494	7	1				3			2	* NOAA	Greece:Crete Island	希腊:克里特岛	35.5	25.5		7.2	Ms							2		2		2
1494										GSHAP	Uzbekistan:Namangan	乌兹别克斯坦:納曼干	41	71.6	6	5.1	Ms	8										
1495	4	19								* China	China:Ningxia,Zhongning	中国:宁夏中宁	37.6	105.6		6.5	Ms	8			12	1		2	50	1		
1495	9	12				4	5	2	2	* Japan,NOAA	Japan:Kanagawa	日本:神奈川	35.1	139.5		7.1	Ms		200	3				1		1		
1496	1	23	17							* GSHAP	Croatia:Split	克罗地亚:斯普利特	43.5	16.1		5.7	Ms	10										
1497	2	26								China	China:Shanxi,Tunliu	中国:山西屯留	36.3	112.9		5	Ms	6										
1498	7	9				2		0		* Japan,NOAA	Japan:Shizuoka,Near Coast	日本:静冈近海	34.4	137.7		6.4	Ms			1				1		1		
1498	8	2				2				* NOAA,Song	Venezuela:Maturín	委内瑞拉:马图林	9.9	-62.3		7	Mk											
1498	9	20				4		2		* NOAA	Japan:Wakayama,Near Coast	日本:和歌山近海	33.5	135.2		7.5	Ms							1				
1498	9	20				4	10	3	4	* Japan,Usami,NOAA	Japan:Shizuoka,Near Coast	日本:静冈近海	34	138.1		8.6	Ms	11	26000	5				4	5000	4		
1498	11	23								China	China:Yunnan,Eryuan	中国:云南洱源	26.1	99.9		5	Ms	6										
1498										GSHAP, Iran	Iran:Gorgan	伊朗:戈尔甘	37.2	55.2	15	6.5	Ms	9.5										
1499	7	26								China	China:Yunnan,Weishan	中国:云南巍山	25.2	100.3		5.5	Ms	7										
1500	1	13								* China	China:Yunnan,Yiliang	中国:云南宜良	24.9	103.1		7	Ms	9	10000	5								
1500										GSHAP	Russia:Chita,Geologicheskiy	俄罗斯:赤塔州格奥洛吉切斯基	56.98	119.57	15	5.9	Ms	8.5										

年 Year	月 Mo	日 Dy	时 Hr	分 Mn	秒 Sec	海啸 源 Sr	海啸 浪高 Wh	海啸 级 I mI	海啸 级 S mS	资料来源 Information	震中 地名(英文) Earthquake Epicenter Name(English)	震中 地名(中文) Name(Chinese)	纬度(°) Latitude	经度(°) Longitude	深度 Depth	震级 Mag	标度 Scale	烈度 MMI	死亡人数 Deaths 数量/人 Num	死亡人数 级别 Dd	受伤人数 Injuries 数量/人 Num	受伤人数 级别 Dd	经济损失 Damage 数量/$ Mill	经济损失 级别 De	房屋毁坏 Houses Destroyed 数量/间 Num	房屋毁坏 级别 Dh	房屋受损 Houses Damaged 数量/间 Num	房屋受损 级别 Dh
1500										GSHAP	Russia:Khabarovsk, Komsomolsk – On – Amur	俄罗斯:哈巴罗夫斯克区阿穆尔河畔共青城	50.53	134.22	15	6.1	Ms	8.5										
1500										GSHAP	Russia:Buryatiya, Arshan	俄罗斯:布里亚特州阿尔尚	54.74	110.74	15	6.2	Ms	8.5										
1500										GSHAP	Russia:Buryatiya, Barguzin	俄罗斯:布里亚特州巴尔古津	53.67	109.69	15	6.3	Ms	8.5										
1500										GSHAP	Russia:Buryatiya, Gusinoye Ozero	俄罗斯:布里亚特州古西诺耶奥泽罗	51.13	106.25	15	6.3	Ms	8.5										
1500										GSHAP	Russia:Buryatiya, Barguzin	俄罗斯:布里亚特州巴尔古津	54.17	110.14	15	6.4	Ms	8.5										
1500										GSHAP	Russia:Lake Baykal	俄罗斯:贝加尔湖	54.43	108.51	15	6.6	Ms	9										
1500										GSHAP	Russia:Buryatiya, Taksimo	俄罗斯:布里亚特州塔克西莫村镇	56.42	114.95	15	6.8	Ms	9										
1500										GSHAP	Russia:Buryatiya, Kichera	俄罗斯:布里亚特州基切拉镇	56.09	110.62	15	6.9	Ms	9										
1500						2				* NOAA, Song	Hawaiian Islands	夏威夷群岛	19	−155.5		7	Mk			2								
1500										GSHAP	Russia:Lake Baykal	俄罗斯:贝加尔湖	54.1	108.25	15	7	Ms	9										
1500										GSHAP	Russia:Buryatiya, Yanchukan	俄罗斯:布里亚特州扬丘坎镇	56.12	113.03	15	7	Ms	9										
1501	1	29								* China	China:Shaanxi, Dali, E.	中国:陕西大荔东	34.8	110.1		7	Ms	9	400	3				4	5400	4		
1501	6	11								China	China:Yunnan, Jianchuan	中国:云南剑川	26.5	99.9		5.75	Ms	7										
1501										* Song	Greece:Crete Island	希腊:克里特岛	35.5	25		7	Mk	10										
1502	1	28								Japan, Usami	Japan:Joetsu	日本:新潟上越	37.2	138.2		6.9	Ms	8		3						3		
1502	3	26	13							* GSHAP	Croatia:Bedekovcina	克罗地亚:贝代科夫契纳	45.8	16.1	10	6	Ms	10										
1502	10	27								* China	China:Henan, Puyang	中国:河南濮阳	35.7	115.3		6.5	Ms	8	50	1				2				
1502										China	China:Jiangsu, Yancheng	中国:江苏盐城	33.4	120.1		4.75	Ms	6										
1502										* Song	Dominica:Santo Domingo	多米尼加:多米尼加	18.3	−69.5		6.3	Mk							3				
1503										GSHAP	Turkey:Hakkari	土耳其:哈卡里	37.4	43.8	28	7.3	Ms	9										
1504	3									* Song	Switzerland:Scuol	瑞士:施库尔	46.8	10.2		6.3	Mk	8		2				3				
1504	4	5	9			1				* NOAA, Song	Spain:Carmona	西班牙:卡尔莫纳	37.3	−5.4		7.9	Mk	10	100	2				2				
1504	12	7	24							* GSHAP	Croatia:Dubrovnik	克罗地亚:杜布罗夫尼克	42.6	18.1		5.7	Ms	10										
1505	1	1								* GSHAP, Song	Slovenia:Kapele	斯洛文尼亚:卡佩尔	45.9	14.2		5.7	Mk	10						3				
1505	7	6								* Afghan	Afghan:Kabul	阿富汗:喀布尔	34.7	69.2		7.3	Ms	12		3				3				
1505	7	20								China	China:Ningxia, Qingtongxia, S.	中国:宁夏青铜峡南	37.8	105.9		5.25	Ms	7										
1505	10	19				4			1	* * China, NOAA	China:South Yellow Sea	中国:南黄海	32.5	123		6.5	Ms											
1505	10	26								* China	China:Shanxi, Linyi	中国:山西临猗	35.2	110.9		5.25	Ms	6		2								
1506	3	29								China	China:Shaanxi, Heyang	中国:陕西合阳	35.3	110.1		5.5	Ms	7										
1506	5	7								China	China:Yunnan, Xundian	中国:云南寻甸	25.4	103.3		5.5	Ms	7										

时间						海啸				资料来源	震中				深度	震级	标度	烈度	死亡人数		受伤人数		经济损失		房屋毁坏		房屋受损	
年	月	日	时	分	秒	源	浪高	级I	级S		地名(英文)	地名(中文)	纬度(°)	经度(°)					数量/人	级别	数量/人	级别	数量/$ Mill	级别	数量/间	级别	数量/间	级别
Date						Tsunami				Information	Earthquake Epicenter				Depth	Mag	Scale	MMI	Deaths		Injuries		Damage		Houses Destroyed		Houses Damaged	
Year	Mo	Dy	Hr	Mn	Sec	Sr	Wh	mI	mS		Name(English)	Name(Chinese)	Latitude	Longitude					Num	Dd	Num	Dd	$ Mill	De	Num	Dh	Num	Dh
1506	9	7								China	China:Shandong,Jimo,E.	中国:山东即墨东	36.3	120.7		4.75	Ms	6										
1507	11	14								*China	China:Yunnan,Anning,SE.	中国:云南安宁东南	24.8	102.6		5.25	Ms	6		2								
1508	5	29				2			3	*NOAA	Greece:Crete,Iraklion	希腊:克里特岛,伊拉克利翁	35.2	25.1	100	7.1	Ms	10	300	3				2				
1509	2	25								*Song	Italy:Reggio Calabria	意大利:卡拉布里亚雷焦	38.1	15.7		6	Mk	10										
1509	9	14	0	15						*Song	Slovenia:Bled	斯洛文尼亚:布莱德	46.2	14.1		6.3	Mk	8						3		3		
1509	9	14				3			3	*NOAA,GSHAP	Turkey:Istanbul	土耳其:伊斯坦布尔	40.7	29.3		7.7	Ms	11	13000	5				4	1700	4		
1509	10	1								China	China:Guangdong,Huazhou	中国:广东化州	21.6	110.6		4.75	Ms	6										
1509	11	16								*GSHAP	Turkey:Edirne	土耳其:埃迪尔内	41.7	26.6	40	7.4	Mk	8.5						2				
1509										China	China:Hunan,Yiyang	中国:湖南益阳	28.6	112.4		4.75	Ms	6										
1510	6	10								*Song	Germany:Bavaria,Nordlingen	德国:巴伐利亚,诺德林根	48.8	10.5		7	Mk		2000	4								
1510	9	21				4	2	1	1	*Usami,NOAA	Japan:Osaka	日本:大阪	34.6	135.4		6.7	Ms	8		1				1		1		
1510										*Song	Slovenia:Ljubljana	斯洛文尼亚:卢布尔雅那	46.1	14.5		6.3	Mk	10										
1511	3	6								**GSHAP	Slovenia:Ljubljana	斯洛文尼亚:卢布尔雅那	46.1	14.5		5.7	Ms	10										
1511	3	26	14	30		2			3	*NOAA,GSHAP	Slovenia:Idrija,Skofja Loka	斯洛文尼亚:伊德里亚,什科菲亚洛卡	46.1	14	7	6.9	Ms	10	6000	4				4				
1511	5	22								China	China:Yunnan,Chuxiong	中国:云南楚雄	25	101.6		5.5	Ms	7										
1511	8	8								*GSHAP	Italy:Cividale Del Fruili	意大利:弗留利地区奇维达莱	46.1	13.4		5.7	Ms		3000	4								
1511	11	27								*China	China:Yunnan,Jianchuan	中国:云南剑川	26.6	100		5.75	Ms	7		2								
1511	12	2								Japan,Song	Japan:Mobara	日本:千叶茂原	35.4	140.3		6.3	Mk									1		
1512	10	18								*China	China:Yunnan,Tengchong	中国:云南腾冲	25	98.5		6.75	Ms	9						3		3		
1512	10					1			1.5	Japan,NOAA,Song	Japan:Tokushima	日本:德岛	33.9	134.8		7.9	Mk		3700	4								
1512										*Song	Switzerland:Biasca	瑞士:比亚斯卡	46.4	9		6.3	Mk	7		3				3				
1513										GSHAP	Turkey:Kahramanmaras	土耳其:卡赫拉曼马什拉	37.5	36.5	14	7.4	Ms	9.5										
1513										*	Peru:Mollendo,Near Coast	秘鲁:莫延多近海	-17.2	-72.3	30	8.7	Muk	8										
1514	4	16								*GSHAP	Greece:Zakynthos	希腊:扎金索斯岛	37.8	21		6.5	Ms	10										
1514	8	14								GSHAP	Croatia:Senj	克罗地亚:塞尼	45.1	14.8	16	6	Ms	8										
1514	9	14								*China	China:Yunnan,Baoshan	中国:云南保山	25.1	99.2		5.5	Ms	7		3								
1514										China	China:Yunnan,Lanping	中国:云南兰坪	26.3	99.4		5	Ms	6										
1515	6	27								*China	China:Yunnan,Yongsheng,NW.	中国:云南永胜西北	26.7	100.7		7.75	Ms	10	1001	4				3		3		
1515	10	23								*China	China:Yunnan,Dali	中国:云南大理	25.7	100.2		6	Ms	8	200	3				3		3		

时间						海啸				资料来源	震中				深度	震级	标度	烈度	死亡人数		受伤人数		经济损失		房屋毁坏		房屋受损	
年	月	日	时	分	秒	源	浪高	级 I	级 S		地名(英文)	地名(中文)	纬度(°)	经度(°)					数量/人	级别	数量/人	级别	数量/$ Mill	级别	数量/间	级别	数量/间	级别
Date						Tsunami				Information	Earthquake Epicenter				Depth	Mag	Scale	MMI	Deaths		Injuries		Damage		Houses Destroyed		Houses Damaged	
Year	Mo	Dy	Hr	Mn	Sec	Sr	Wh	mI	mS		Name(English)	Name(Chinese)	Latitude	Longitude					Num	Dd	Num	Dd	$ Mill	De	Num	Dh	Num	Dh
1516	5	6	10							* GSHAP	Croatia:Dubrovnik	克罗地亚:杜布罗夫尼克	42.6	18.1		5.7	Ms	10										
1516	7	28								* GSHAP	Croatia:Dubrovnik	克罗地亚:杜布罗夫尼克	42.6	18.1		5.7	Ms	10										
1516	11	24	12							* Song	Romania:Nereju	罗马尼亚:内雷茹	45.7	26.6	100	7	Mk	10										
1516	11	24								GSHAP	Romania:Nereju	罗马尼亚:内雷茹	45.7	26.6	150	6.7	Ms	8										
1517	7	18								Japan, Usami	Japan:Niigata	日本:新潟	37.7	139.4		6.4	Ms	7								3		
1517	7	22								* China	China:Yunnan, Tonghai, W.	中国:云南通海西	24.1	102.6		5.75	Ms	7		2				1		1		
1518	7	2								*	North Korea:Ongjin	朝鲜:瓮津	38	125		6.7	Muk	9						2				
1518	7	12								China	China:Yunnan, Lufeng	中国:云南禄丰	25.4	101.8		4.75	Ms	6										
1518	11	9								* Song	Spain:Vera	西班牙:薇拉	37.2	−1.5		8	Mk	11		3				4				
1520	4	4	7			4	2	1	1	* Usami, NOAA	Japan:Shingu, Near Coast	日本:和歌山新宫近海	33.6	136.3		7	Ms	9								1		
1520	4	5								* China	China:Yunnan, Weishan	中国:云南巍山	25.2	100.3		5.5	Ms	7		3				1				
1520	8	28								China	China:Yunnan, Jingdong	中国:云南景东	24.4	100.8		5.75	Ms	7										
1520										* Song	Chile:Near Coast of S.	智利:南部近海	−40	−74		7.3	Mk	10										
1522	2	7								China	China:Henan, Yanling	中国:河南鄢陵	34.2	114.1		5.75	Ms	7										
1522	9	21								* Song	Spain:Almeria	西班牙:阿尔梅利亚	36.5	−2.3		8	Mk	11		3				3				
1522	10	22				1				* * NOAA, Song	Azores:Vila Franca	亚速尔群岛:维拉弗兰卡	37.4	−25.3		7.9	Mk	10										
1522										China	China:Yunnan, Eryuan	中国:云南洱源	26.1	99.9		5	Ms	6										
1522										* * Song	Iran:Tabriz	伊朗:大不里士	38	46.2		7.7	Mk		70000	5				3				
1523	6	9								GSHAP	Romania:Nereju	罗马尼亚:内雷茹	45.7	26.6	150	7	Ms	8.5										
1523	8	24								China	China:Zhejiang, Zhenhai	中国:浙江镇海	30	121.7		4.75	Ms	6										
1523	11	19								GSHAP	Romania:Campulung	罗马尼亚:肯普隆格	45.6	25	30	6.8	Ms	8										
1523										* Song	Mexico:Veracruz	墨西哥:韦拉克鲁斯	19.2	−96.4		6.3	Mk							3				
1524	2	14								China	China:Henan, Yanling	中国:河南鄢陵	34	114.1		6	Ms	7										
1524	4	15								China	China:Hainan, Qionghai	中国:海南琼海	19.3	110.5		5	Ms	6										
1524						2				NOAA, Song	Pakistan:Karachi	巴基斯坦:卡拉奇	24.87	67.05		7	Mk											
1525	9	20								Japan, Song	Japan:Kamakura	日本:神奈川镰仓	35.3	139.5		6.9	Mk	9										
1526	5	31								China	China:Guizhou, Qinglong	中国:贵州晴隆	25.8	105.2		5	Ms	6										
1526	6	9								China	China:Guizhou, Qinglong	中国:贵州晴隆	25.8	105.2		5	Ms	6										
1527										China	China:Hebei, Fengrui	中国:河北丰润	39.8	118.1		5.5	Ms	7										
1527										* Song	Iran:Tabriz	伊朗:大不里士	38	46.2		6.3	Mk							3				
1528	6									China	China:Hebei, Luancheng	中国:河北栾城	37.9	114.6		5	Ms	6										
1530	7	22								* GSHAP	Croatia:Dubrovnik	克罗地亚:杜布罗夫尼克	42.6	18.1		5.7	Ms	10										
1530	9	1	14	30		4	7.3	2.6		* NOAA	Venezuela:Cumana	委内瑞拉:库马纳	10.5	−64.2	10	8	Mw	10						2		3		
1530	9	11	15							* * Song	Venezuela:Cumana	委内瑞拉:库马纳	10.5	−64.2		6.3	Mk			3				3				
1531	1	26				1				* NOAA, Song	Portugal:Lisbon	葡萄牙:里斯本	38.7	−9.1		8	Mk	10	30000	5				3	1500	4		
1531	1									*	China:Jiangsu, Chizhou	中国:江苏池州	30.7	117.5		4.8	Ms	6						1				
1532	7	12								Japan, Song	Japan:Kyoto, Oumi	日本:京都,近江	34.8	135.8		6.5	Mk			1								

年 Year	月 Mo	日 Dy	时 Hr	分 Mn	秒 Sec	海啸 Tsunami 源 Sr	浪高 Wh	级 I mI	级 S mS	资料来源 Information	震中 Earthquake Epicenter 地名(英文) Name(English)	地名(中文) Name(Chinese)	纬度(°) Latitude	经度(°) Longitude	深度 Depth	震级 Mag	标度 Scale	烈度 MMI	死亡人数 Deaths 数量/人 Num	级别 Dd	受伤人数 Injuries 数量/人 Num	级别 Dd	经济损失 Damage 数量/$ Mill	级别 De	房屋毁坏 Houses Destroyed 数量/间 Num	级别 Dh	房屋受损 Houses Damaged 数量/间 Num	级别 Dh
1533	2	22								China	China:Yunnan,Luliang,NW.	中国:云南陆良西北	25.2	103.6		5.5	Ms	7								1		
1533	2									GSHAP,Song	Peru:Lima,Near Coast	秘鲁:利马近海	-12.3	-77.3		5	Mk	6										
1533										Japan,Song	Japan:Iyo,Saijo	日本:伊予西条	33.7	132.4		6.3	Mk									1		
1534						2			3	NOAA,Song	Egypt:Dumyat,Coast N.	埃及:达米埃塔北部海岸	31.6	31.7		6.7	Mk											
1535	1									China	China:Anhui,Chizhou	中国:安徽池州	30.7	117.5		4.75	Ms	6										
1535	5									* China	China:Fujian,Changting	中国:福建长汀	25.8	116.4		4.75	Ms	6		3				1				
1536	3	29								* China	China:Sichuan,Xichang,N.	中国:四川西昌北	28.1	102.2		7.5	Ms	10	3	1				3		3		
1536	11	1								China	China:Beijing,Tongzhou	中国:北京通州	39.8	116.8		6	Ms	8		1						3		
1537	5	23								China	China:Anhui,Lingbi	中国:安徽灵璧	33.6	117.6		5.5	Ms	7										
1537	6	10								GSHAP	Syria:Hamah (Hama)	叙利亚:哈马	35.8	36.3	20	6.4	Ms	8										
1537						1				* NOAA,Song	Mexico:Mexico City	墨西哥:墨西哥城	19.2	-99.1		7.7	Mk							3				
1538	9	27				2			4	* Italy,NOAA	Italy:Pozzuoli	意大利:波佐利	40.822	14.123		5.37	Ms	11						3				
1538	10									China	China:Fujian, Xiamen,Near Coast	中国:福建厦门近海	24.7	118.5		4.75	Ms	6										
1538										China	China:Hebei,Shenxian	中国:河北深县	38	115.6		5	Ms	6										
1538										* Song	Mexico:Mexico City	墨西哥:墨西哥城	19.2	-99.1		6.3	Mk							3				
1539	8	18								* China	China:Yunnan,Jianshui	中国:云南建水	23.6	102.8		5.5	Ms	7		2								
1539	11	24				2				* NOAA,Song	Honduras:Jano	洪都拉斯:哈诺	15	-86.5		7	Mk							1		1		
1541	4									GSHAP	Ecuador:Quito	厄瓜多尔:基多	-0.14	-78.27		6.3	Ms	8										
1541	12	25				2				* NOAA,Song	Venezuela:Cubagua Island	委内瑞拉:库巴瓜岛	10.8	-64.2		7	Mk							1				
1542	3	17								* Song	Mexico:Mexico City	墨西哥:墨西哥城	19.2	-99.1		6.3	Mk							3				
1542	6	1								China	China:Hunan,Ningxiang	中国:湖南宁乡	28.4	112.4		4.75	Ms	6										
1542	6	13	1							* Italy	Italy:Scarperia	意大利:斯卡尔佩里亚	44	11.38		5.91	Ms	10	113	3				3			1740	4
1542	8	21								China	China:Shanxi,Baode	中国:山西保德	39	111.1		5	Ms	6										
1542	11	29								China	China:Gansu,Wushan	中国:甘肃武山	34.7	104.9		5.5	Ms	7										
1542	12	10	17	30						* Italy	Italy:Siracusa, Militello	意大利:锡拉库萨,波比米里特洛	37.22	14.95		6.62	Mw	10						3				
1542	12									China	China:GansuHuixian,N.	中国:甘肃徽县北部	34.2	106		5	Ms	6										
1543	9	1				4				* * NOAA,Song	Venezuela:Isla Cubagua	委内瑞拉:库巴瓜岛	10.6	-64.1		7.7	Mk			3				3				
1543										GSHAP	Romania:Nereju	罗马尼亚:内雷茹	45.7	26.6	150	6.3	Ms	7										
1543										Japan,Usami,Song	Japan:Hiroshima	日本:广岛	34.4	132.45		6.8	Mk			1						3		
1543										* Song	Chile:Arica,Near Coast	智利:阿里卡近海	-19	-70.5		7.3	Mk	10		1								
1544	1									GSHAP	Turkey:Kahramanmaras	土耳其:卡赫拉曼马什拉	38	37	10	6.7	Ms	10										
1545	2	7				2				* Japan,Song,NOAA	Japan:Higashiizu	日本:静冈东伊豆	34.8	139		7	Mk							1				
1545	7	9	8	30						GSHAP	Romania:Nereju	罗马尼亚:内雷茹	45.7	26.6	150	6.9	Ms	8.5										

时间 年 Year	月 Mo	日 Dy	时 Hr	分 Mn	秒 Sec	海啸 Tsunami 源 Sr	浪高 Wh	级 I mI	级 S mS	资料来源 Information	震中 Earthquake Epicenter 地名(英文) Name(English)	地名(中文) Name(Chinese)	纬度(°) Latitude	经度(°) Longitude	深度 Depth	震级 Mag	标度 Scale	烈度 MMI	死亡人数 Deaths 数量/人 Num	级别 Dd	受伤人数 Injuries 数量/人 Num	级别 Dd	经济损失 Damage 数量/$ Mill $ Mill	级别 De	房屋毁坏 Houses Destroyed 数量/间 Num	级别 Dh	房屋受损 Houses Damaged 数量/间 Num	级别 Dh
1546	1	14				3			3	* NOAA	Israel:Jerusalem	以色列:耶路撒冷	32	35.5		7	Muk	11		3				3				
1546	9	29								China	China:Jiangsu,Pizhou	中国:江苏邳州	34.5	117.7		5.5	Ms	7	3	1								
1547	5	17	13	14						* Song	Azores:Fregues	亚速尔群岛:望德堂区	38.7	-27.3		7.3	Mk	10										
1548	9	22								China	China:Bohai Sea	中国:渤海	38	121		7	Ms									3		
1548										China	China:Gansu,Zhangye	中国:甘肃张掖	38.9	100.4		5	Ms	6										
1549	1	30								* Song	Iran:Razavi Khorasan	伊朗:呼罗珊	33.5	59.1		7	Mk		3000	4				3				
1549	2	15	24							Iran,GSHAP	Iran:Birjand	伊朗:比尔詹德	33.7	60	13	6.7	Ms	9.5										
1549	4									China	China:Shanxi,Jiexiu	中国:山西介休	37	111.9		5.5	Ms	7								3		
1550	1	20								* GSHAP	Iran:Tabriz	伊朗:大不里士	38	46.1	14	7.3	Ms	9.5		3				3				
1550	8	25								* Song	Italy:Vallo Di Diano	意大利:瓦洛迪狄安诺	40.7	15.1		6	Mk	10										
1551	1	28								* Song	Portugal:Lisbon	葡萄牙:里斯本	38.7	-9.1		7	Mk	9	2000	4				3	200	3		
1551	3	26								GSHAP	Slovenia:Idrija	斯洛文尼亚:伊德里亚	46.2	14	16	6	Ms	8										
1551										*	China:Guizhou,Qinglong	中国:贵州晴隆	25.8	105.2		5	Ms	6		3								
1552	7	2	10	30						*	Peru:Arequipa	秘鲁:阿雷基帕	-16.6	-71.3	30	7.6	Muk	9										
1552	8	21	2	30						GSHAP	Romania:Nereju	罗马尼亚:内雷茹	45.7	26.6	150	6.4	Ms	7										
1552										Japan,Usami,Song	Japan:Wakayama	日本:和歌山	34.3	135.6		6.3	Mk									1		
1553	2	20								Korea	South Korea:Seongju	韩国:庆尚北道	35.9	128.3		5.5	Ms	7										
1553	3	2								*	South Korea:Kyongsang - Do	韩国:忠清道	35.8	128.8		6.3	Muk	8						3				
1553	10	11								Japan,Song	Japan:Kamakura	日本:神奈川镰仓	35.3	139.5		6.3	Mk									1		
1553										GSHAP,Song	Peru:Lima	秘鲁:利马	-12.08	-77		4.5	Mk	5										
1555	9	14								Japan,Usami	Japan:Fukushima	日本:福岛	37.7	139.8		6.7	Ms									1		
1555	11	15								* GSHAP	Peru:Lima,Near Coast	秘鲁:利马近海	-11.9	-77.6	30	8.4	Muk	7										
1555										* Song	Bulgaria:Pernik	保加利亚:佩尔尼克	42.8	22.8		7.1	Mk	12						4				
1556	1	24								* GSHAP,Italy	Austria:Steiermark	奥地利:施蒂利亚州	47	15		6.6	Ms							3				
1556	2	2								* China	China:Shaanxi,Huaxian	中国:陕西华县	34.5	109.7		8.25	Ms	11	830000	5				4				
1556	3	10								* Song	Turkey:Istanbul	土耳其:伊斯坦布尔	41	29		5	Mk	5										
1556	5	10								* GSHAP	Turkey:Istanbul	土耳其:伊斯坦布尔	41	29		7	Ms							2				
1556	12	13								China	China:Gansu,Shandan	中国:甘肃山丹	38.8	101.1		5	Ms	6										
1558	6									China	China:Shanxi,Jiaocheng	中国:山西交城	37.5	112.2		5	Ms	6										
1558	6									China	China:Guangdong,Fengkai	中国:广东封开	23.4	111.5		5.5	Ms	7										
1558	12	1								China	China:Shaanxi,Huaxian	中国:陕西华县	34.5	109.7		5.5	Ms	7								3		
1560	1	22								GSHAP	Ecuador:Quito	厄瓜多尔:基多	-0.22	-78.5		4.3	Ms	5										
1560	4									* China	China:Yunnan,Yiliang	中国:云南宜良	24.9	103.1		5.5	Ms	7		4				3		3		
1560										* China	China:Yunnan,Tonghai,N.	中国:云南通海北	24.2	102.7		5.5	Ms	7	100	2				2		2		
1561	3	3								China	China:Gansu,Shandan	中国:甘肃山丹	38.8	101.1		5.5	Ms	7										
1561	7	31								* Song	Italy:Tito,Buccino	意大利:蒂托,布奇诺	40.8	15.3		6	Mk	10	600	3				2				
1561	8	4								* China	China:Ningxia,Zhongning,E.	中国:宁夏中宁东	37.5	106.2		7.25	Ms	10	1001	4				4				

时间 Date						海啸 Tsunami				资料来源 Information	震中 Earthquake Epicenter				深度 Depth	震级 Mag	标度 Scale	烈度 MMI	死亡人数 Deaths		受伤人数 Injuries		经济损失 Damage		房屋毁坏 Houses Destroyed		房屋受损 Houses Damaged	
年 Year	月 Mo	日 Dy	时 Hr	分 Mn	秒 Sec	源 Sr	浪高 Wh	级 I mI	级 S mS		地名(英文) Name(English)	地名(中文) Name(Chinese)	纬度(°) Latitude	经度(°) Longitude					数量/人 Num	级别 Dd	数量/人 Num	级别 Dd	数量/$ Mill $ Mill	级别 De	数量/间 Num	级别 Dh	数量/间 Num	级别 Dh
1561	8	19	14	30						* Italy	Italy: Vallo Di Diano	意大利:瓦洛迪狄安诺	40.52	15.48		6.36	Ms	10										
1562	2	24								China	China: Ningxia, Yinchuan	中国:宁夏银川	38.5	106.3		5.5	Ms	7										
1562	6									China	China: Hebei, Luanxian, S.	中国:河北滦县南	39.6	118.7		5	Ms	6										
1562	7	25				1				Japan, NOAA, Song	Japan: Taketa	日本:大分竹田	33	131.3		7	Mk											
1562	10	20				3			4	NOAA, Song	Italy: Reggio Di Calabria	意大利:雷焦卡拉布里亚	40.5	15.5		6.7	Mk											
1562	10	28	10			4	16	4	3.5	* NOAA	Chile: Carahue	智利:卡拉韦	-38.7	-73.15		8.3	Ms	11		3				3				
1562										China	China: Jiangxi, Ruijin	中国:江西瑞金	25.8	116		4.75	Ms	6										
1563	6	13	12							* Turkey	Montenegro: Herceg Novi	蒙特尼哥罗(黑山):新海尔采格	42.4	18.8		7	Ms	10										
1563	10									China	China: Shanxi, Wuxiang	中国:山西武乡	36.8	112.9		5	Ms	6										
1564	4	20								* Song	Dominica: Concepcion, De La Vega	多米尼加:康塞普西翁,德拉维加	19.1	-70.3		6.3	Mk							3				
1564	7	20	18			4			4	* Italy, NOAA	France: La Bollene – Vesubie, La Penne	法国:博莱纳–维苏威火山,拉佩纳	44	7.2		5.79	Ms	10	900	3				4				
1565	8									* Song	Guatemala: Ciudad Vieja	危地马拉:别哈城	14.6	-90.7		5.9	Mk							2		2		
1566	5									*	Guatemala: Ciudad Vieja	危地马拉:别哈城	14.6	-90.7		6.3	Mk							3		3		
1566										* Song	Iran: Lar	伊朗:拉尔	27.7	54.3		6.3	Mk							3				
1566										*	Colombia: Timbiqui	哥伦比亚:廷比基	3	-77.3		7.8	Muk	7										
1567	3									GSHAP, Song	Peru: Lima	秘鲁:利马	-12.08	-77.2		4.5	Mk	5										
1567										China	China: Hebei, Changli	中国:河北昌黎	39.7	119.2		4.75	Ms	6										
1567										China	China: Yunnan, Yunlong	中国:云南云龙	25.8	99.2		5	Ms	6										
1568	1									China	China: Shaanxi, Lantian	中国:陕西蓝田	34.2	109.3		5.5	Ms	7										
1568	4	4								GSHAP	Peru: Ica	秘鲁:伊卡	-14.38	-75.72	80	6.6	Ms	9										
1568	4	11								China	China: Shaanxi, Lintong	中国:陕西临潼	34.4	109.2		5.5	Ms	7										
1568	4	11								China	China: Ningxia, Yinchuan	中国:宁夏银川	38.5	106.3		5.75	Ms	7										
1568	4	22								China	China: Shaanxi, Hanzhong	中国:陕西汉中	33.1	107		5	Ms	6										
1568	4	23								China	China: Shaanxi, Hanzhong	中国:陕西汉中	33.1	107		5	Ms	6										
1568	5	5								* China	China: Bohai Sea	中国:渤海	39	119		6	Ms							3				
1568	5	25								* China	China: Shaanxi, Xi – an, NE.	中国:陕西西安东北	34.4	109		6.75	Ms	9	200	3				2				
1568	12	27								* Song	Mexico: Cocula, Jalisco	墨西哥:科库拉,哈利斯科	20.2	-103.5		6.3	Mk		60	2				3				
1568										China	China: Gansu, Qingyang	中国:甘肃庆阳	36	107.9		5.5	Ms	7										
1568										USGS, Song	US: Connecticut, East Haddam	美国:康涅狄格州东哈德姆	41.5	-72.5		5.5	Mk	6										
1569										China	China: Shaanxi, Ankang	中国:陕西安康	32.7	109		5	Ms	6										
1569										China	China: Shaanxi, Tongguan	中国:陕西潼关	34.6	110.3		5	Ms	6										
1570	2	8	13			4	4	2	3	* NOAA	Chile: Old Concepcion	智利:老康塞普西翁	-36.8	-73		8.8	Ms	11		3				3		3		
1570	11	17								* Italy	Italy: Ferrara, Bologna	意大利:费拉拉,波洛尼亚	44.82	11.63		5.48	Ms	9	125	3								

时间 Date						海啸 Tsunami				资料来源 Information	震中 Earthquake Epicenter				深度 Depth	震级 Mag	标度 Scale	烈度 MMI	死亡人数 Deaths		受伤人数 Injuries		经济损失 Damage		房屋毁坏 Houses Destroyed		房屋受损 Houses Damaged	
年 Year	月 Mo	日 Dy	时 Hr	分 Mn	秒 Sec	源 Sr	浪高 Wh	级 I mI	级 S mS		地名(英文) Name(English)	地名(中文) Name(Chinese)	纬度(°) Latitude	经度(°) Longitude					数量/人 Num	级别 Dd	数量/人 Num	级别 Dd	数量/$ Mill $ Mill	级别 De	数量/间 Num	级别 Dh	数量/间 Num	级别 Dh
1570						1				NOAA,Song	Greece:Amorgos	希腊:阿莫尔戈斯	36.9	26		6.6	Mk											
1571	5	10								GSHAP	Romania:Nehoiu	罗马尼亚:内霍尤	45.5	26.6	100	6	Ms	6.5										
1571	5	20				2	2	1	1.5	* NOAA,Song	Japan:Chita	日本:爱知知多市	35	136.8		7	Mk											
1571	7	17	18	2		3			3	NOAA,Song	Turkey:Marmara Sea	土耳其:马尔马拉海	41	28.1		6.7	Mk											
1571	9	19								* China	China:Yunnan,Tonghai	中国:云南通海	24.1	102.8		6.25	Ms	8		2				3	1000	3		
1572	5									GSHAP	Aegean Sea	爱琴海	40.2	24.5	30	6.6	Ms	8										
1572										China	China:Yunnan,Xuanwei	中国:云南宣威	26.2	104.1		5	Ms	6										
1573	1	20								* China	China:Gansu,Minxian	中国:甘肃岷县	34.4	104		6.75	Ms	9		3				3		3		
1573										* Song	Mexico:Colima	墨西哥:科利马	19.2	-104		6.3	Mk							3				
1573										GSHAP	Iraq:As Sulaymaniyah	伊拉克:苏莱曼尼亚	35.4	45	20	6.9	Ms	9										
1574	5	3								* Italy	Switzerland:Geneve	瑞士:日内瓦	46.2	6.2		5.17	Ms	7						3				
1574	8	14								* Italy	Croatia:Senj	克罗地亚:塞尼	45.1	14.8		5.57	Ms	10										
1574										China	China:Zhejiang,Qingyuan	中国:浙江庆元	27.6	119.1		5.5	Ms	7										
1574										* Song	Iran:Kashan	伊朗:卡尚	34	51.4		7	Mk		1200	4				3				
1575	9	8								*	Ecuador:Quito	厄瓜多尔:基多	-0.2	-78.6		7.8	Muk			3								
1575	12	16	18	30		4		2	2.5	* NOAA	Chile:Valdivia	智利:巴尔迪维亚	-39.8	-73.2		8.5	Muk	10	1221	4				3				
1576	5	23								* Song	El Salvador:San Marcos	萨尔瓦多:圣马科斯	13.5	-89.3		7.1	Mk			3				4				
1576										China	China:Yunnan,Yunlong	中国:云南云龙	25.8	99.2		5	Ms	6										
1577	2	27								China	China:Jiangxi,Dingnan	中国:江西定南	24.8	115		4.75	Ms	6										
1577	3	23								* China	China:Yunnan,Tengchong	中国:云南腾冲	25	98.5		6.75	Ms	9	170	3				2				
1577										GSHAP	Syria:Hamah (Hama)	叙利亚:哈马	35.5	36.5	25	6.6	Ms	8.5										
1578	6	17								* Song	Peru:Lima,Near Coast	秘鲁:利马近海	-12.5	-77		5.9	Mk							2				
1578	12	31								* China	China:Yunnan,Baoshan	中国:云南保山	25.1	99.2		5.25	Ms	6	10	1				1				
1579	2	25	1							Japan,Usami	Japan:Settsu	日本:大阪摄津	34.7	135.5		6.2	Ms									1		
1579										* Song	Morocco:Melilla	摩洛哥:梅利利亚	35.3	-2.97		6.3	Mk							3				
1580	4	6				3				* NOAA	England:Dover	英国:多佛尔	51.019	1.309	33	6.2	ML			2				2				
1580	9	15								China	China:Shanxi,Pinglu	中国:山西平鲁	39.5	112.3		5.75	Ms	7										
1581	5	28								China	China:Hebei,Yuxian	中国:河北蔚县	39.8	114.5		5.75	Ms	7										
1581	7									China	China:Gansu,Wenxian	中国:甘肃文县	32.9	104.6		5.5	Ms	7										
1581										*	Peru:Yanaoca	秘鲁:亚纳奥卡	-14.1	-71.5	15	6.4	Muk	10		3				1				
1581										*	Peru:Lima,Near Coast	秘鲁:利马近海	-12.4	-77.7	30	7.6	Ms	6										
1582	1	22	16	30		1				* NOAA	Peru:Arequipa	秘鲁:阿雷基帕	-16.6	-71.6	30	8.2	Ms	10		3		3		3		4		
1582	3									China	China:Shanxi,Datong	中国:山西大同	40.1	113.2		5	Ms	6										
1582	5									* Italy	Italy:Pozzuoli	意大利:波佐利	40.822	14.123		5.37	Ms							2				
1582	8	7								GSHAP,Song	Chile:Santiago	智利:圣地亚哥	-33.4	-70.6		6	Mk	8										
1582	8	15								*	Peru:Lima,Near Coast	秘鲁:利马近海	-12.2	-77.6	30	7.8	Muk	7										
1582										China	China:Gansu,Qingyang	中国:甘肃庆阳	35.7	107.3		5	Ms	6										
1583	5	17								China	China:Shanxi,Guangling	中国:山西广灵	39.7	114		5.5	Ms	7										
1583	9									China	China:Shanxi,Jingle	中国:山西静乐	38.4	111.9		4.75	Ms	6										
1584	3	1	11							* Italy	Switzerland:Monthey	瑞士:蒙泰	46.2	7		5.17	Ms	7	100	2				3				

年 Year	月 Mo	日 Dy	时 Hr	分 Mn	秒 Sec	海啸 Tsunami 源 Sr	浪高 Wh	级 I mI	级 S mS	资料来源 Information	震中 Earthquake Epicenter 地名(英文) Name(English)	地名(中文) Name(Chinese)	纬度(°) Latitude	经度(°) Longitude	深度 Depth	震级 Mag	标度 Scale	烈度 MMI	死亡人数 Deaths 数量/人 Num	级别 Dd	受伤人数 Injuries 数量/人 Num	级别 Dd	经济损失 Damage 数量/$ Mill	级别 De	房屋毁坏 Houses Destroyed 数量/间 Num	级别 Dh	房屋受损 Houses Damaged 数量/间 Num	级别 Dh
1584	3	3								* Song	Switzerland:Monthey	瑞士:蒙泰	46.2	7		6.3	Mk	5		3				3				
1584	3	4								* Song	Switzerland:Monthey	瑞士:蒙泰	46.3	7		6.3	Mk	5		3				3				
1584	3	17								*	Peru:Lima,Near Coast	秘鲁:利马近海	-11.8	-77.8	30	8.4	Muk	7						1				1
1585	3	6								China	China:Anhui,Chaohu,S.	中国:安徽巢县南	31.2	117.7		5.75	Ms	7										
1585	6	11				2	2	1	1	Japan,NOAA,Song	Japan:Iwate	日本:岩手	39.2	141.2		7	Mk											
1585	7									GSHAP	Aegean Sea	爱琴海	40.1	24.3	28	6.6	Ms	8										
1586	1	15								Japan,Song	Japan:Fukui	日本:福井	36.2	136.2		6.3	Mk									1		
1586	1	18				4	6	2	1	* Usami,NOAA	Japan:Ise Bay	日本:伊势湾	35	136.8		8.2	Ms	11	8000	4				3	10000	5		
1586	4	2								* China	China:Yunnan,Weishan	中国:云南巍山	25.2	100.3		5.75	Ms	7	20	1				1		1		
1586	5	26								China	China:Beijing	中国:北京	39.9	116.3		5	Ms	6										
1586	6	11				2			1	* * NOAA,Song	Japan:Chita	日本:爱知知多市	35	136.8		7	Mk											
1586	7	10	0	30		4	26	4.6	3.5	* NOAA	Peru:Lima,Near Coast	秘鲁:利马近海	-12.3	-77.7	60	8.5	Muk	10	22	1				3				
1586										*	Guatemala:Ciudad Vieja	危地马拉:别哈城	14.553	-90.735		5.9	Mk							2		2		
1587	4	10								China	China:Henan,Xiuqu,N.	中国:河南修武北	35.3	113.5		6	Ms	8										
1587	7	9				1				* NOAA	Peru:Sechura	秘鲁:塞丘拉	-5.3	-80.5		6.2	Ms	9		3				2				
1587	8	31								* Song	Ecuador:Quito	厄瓜多尔:基多	-0.2	-78.5		6.5	Mk	9		3								
1587	9	3								* *	Ecuador:Quito	厄瓜多尔:基多	-0.2	-78.5		7.5	Ms			1				2				
1587	9	4	1							* *	Ecuador:Quito	厄瓜多尔:基多	-0.2	-78.5		7.7	Ms	10										
1587	10	4								China	China:Shanxi,Linyi	中国:山西临猗	35.2	110.8		5	Ms	6										
1587	11									* Song	Portugal:Loule	葡萄牙:洛莱	37.1	-8		7.3	Mk	10	170	3				1		1		1
1588	7	2								China	China:Shandong,Dongying,NW.	中国:山东东营西北	37.5	118.5		5	Ms	6										
1588	7									China	China:Shanxi,Xinzhou	中国:山西忻州	38.4	112.8		5	Ms	6										
1588	8	9								* China	China:Yunnan,Jianshui,Qujiang	中国:云南建水曲江	24	102.8		7	Ms	9		2								
1588	11	20								* Song	Iran:Fars,Shiraz	伊朗:法尔斯,设拉子	29.4	52.3		5.9	Mk							2				
1589	3	21				4	2	1	1	* Usami,NOAA	Japan:Shizuoka	日本:静冈	34.8	138.2		6.7	Ms	8		3				3		1		
1589										China	China:Shanxi,Jinyuan	中国:山西晋源	37.7	112.5		4.75	Ms	6										
1589										* Song	Spain:Montilla	西班牙:梦提拉	37.9	-4.8		7.3	Mk	10										
1590	3	31				4				Japan,NOAA,Song	Japan:Atsugi	日本:神奈川厚木	35.5	139.3		7	Mk									1		
1590	7	7								* China	China:Gansu,Lintao	中国:甘肃临洮	35.5	103.9		5.5	Ms	7		3				3				
1590	7	25								* Song	Croatia:Senj	克罗地亚:塞尼	45	14.9		6.3	Mk	10						3				
1590	7									China	China:Gansu,Ledu	中国:甘肃乐都	36.5	102.7		5	Ms	6										
1590	8	7								* Song	Ecuador:Napo	厄瓜多尔:纳波	-0.5	-78.2		5.9	Mk							2				
1590	8	10	19							GSHAP	Romania:Sibiu	罗马尼亚:锡比乌	45.7	24.5	30	6.8	Ms	8										
1590	9	5								* GSHAP	Croatia:Zagreb	克罗地亚:萨格勒布	45.9	16.3	10	6	Ms	10		3				3				
1590	9	15								*	Austria:Loosdorf	奥地利:洛斯多夫	48.3	15.5		6.6	Muk	10		3				3				
1590						2			1.5	* GSHAP,NOAA	Peru:Camana,Near Coast	秘鲁:卡马纳近海	-17.2	-72.9	40	7.7	Muk	7		3				1		1		

年 Year	月 Mo	日 Dy	时 Hr	分 Mn	秒 Sec	源 Sr	浪高 Wh	级 I mI	级 S mS	资料来源 Information	地名(英文) Name(English)	地名(中文) Name(Chinese)	纬度(°) Latitude	经度(°) Longitude	深度 Depth	震级 Mag	标度 Scale	烈度 MMI	死亡人数 Deaths 数量/人 Num	死亡人数 Deaths 级别 Dd	受伤人数 Injuries 数量/人 Num	受伤人数 Injuries 级别 Dd	经济损失 Damage 数量/$ Mill	经济损失 Damage 级别 De	房屋毁坏 Houses Destroyed 数量/间 Num	房屋毁坏 Houses Destroyed 级别 Dh	房屋受损 Houses Damaged 数量/间 Num	房屋受损 Houses Damaged 级别 Dh
1591	7	26				1				* NOAA, Song	Azores: Sao Miguel (San Miguel)	亚速尔群岛:圣米格尔	37.5	-25.3		7.9	Mk	10										
1591	11	21								China	China: Gansu, Shandan	中国:甘肃山丹	38.8	101.1		5	Ms	6										
1591										China	China: Shaanxi, Yanchang	中国:陕西延长	36.6	110		5	Ms	6		3								
1592	1									China	China: Yunnan, Tengchong	中国:云南腾冲	25	98.5		5.75	Ms	7		3								
1592	10	8	1							Japan, Usami	Japan: Chiba	日本:千叶	35.8	140		6.7	Ms							1				
1593	4	8								* Song	France: Chinon	法国:希农	47.1	0.1		6.1	Mk	8						2				
1593										GSHAP	Iran: Tabriz	伊朗:大不里士	37.8	47.5	12	6.1	Ms	9										
1594	10	26								China	China: Liaoning, Kaiyuan, N.	中国:辽宁开原北	42.6	124		4.75	Ms	6										
1594	12	18								* Song	Peru: Ica	秘鲁:伊卡	-14	-76		6.5	Mk	9	40	1				2				
1594						2			5	NOAA, Song	Italy: Bay of Napli	意大利:那不勒斯湾	40.8	14.4		6.7	Mk											
1595	4	21	10							GSHAP	Romania: Nereju	罗马尼亚:内雷茹	45.7	26.6	150	6.9	Ms	8										
1595										Japan, Song	Japan: Iyo	日本:爱媛伊予市	33.7	132.4		6.3	Mk									1		
1596	4	16								GSHAP	Romania: Nereju	罗马尼亚:内雷茹	45.7	26.6	150	6.3	Ms	6.5										
1596	9	4	6							Japan, Usami	Japan: Kyoto, Kinai	日本:京都,畿内	34.8	135.7		6.9	Ms	9	700							3		
1596	9	4	15			4	5	2	2	* Japan, Usami, NOAA	Japan: Oita	日本:大分	33.3	131.7		7.25	Ms	9	1100	4				4		3		
1596	10									China	China: Fujian, Quanzhou	中国:福建泉州	25	118.7		4.75	Ms	6										
1596										China	China: Liaoning, Kaiyuan, N.	中国:辽宁开原北	42.6	124		5.5	Ms	7										
1597	2	14								China	China: Sichuan, Beichuan	中国:四川北川	31.9	104.4		5.5	Ms	7										
1597	7	28								* Song	Portugal: Monte Santo, Lisbon	葡萄牙:孟地圣托,里斯本	38.8	-9.4		6.5	Mk	9						1		1		1
1597	9	10				3	2	1	1	* Japan, Usami, NOAA	Japan: Oita	日本:大分	33.3	131.6		6.4	Ms		40	1					70	2		
1597	10	7								Korea	North Korea: Samsu	朝鲜:三水	41.3	128		5	Ms	7										
1598	6	25	22							GSHAP, Song	Peru: Zana	秘鲁:萨尼亚	-6.9	-79.6		4.5	Mk	5										
1598	7	22								* Song	Portugal: Monte Santo, Lisbon	葡萄牙:孟地圣托,里斯本	38.8	-9.4		5.5	Mk							1				
1598	11	22	3	30						GSHAP	Romania: Nereju	罗马尼亚:内雷茹	45.7	26.6	150	6.3	Ms	7										
1599	3	4								GSHAP	Romania: Nereju	罗马尼亚:内雷茹	45.7	26.6	150	6	Ms	6.5										
1599	6	21	2							*	Philippines: Manila	菲律宾:马尼拉	14.6	121		6.1	Mk	8						2				
1599	6	25	3	20						* * Maso, Song	Philippines: Manila	菲律宾:马尼拉	14.6	121		6.5	Mk	9						2				
1599	9									China	China: Guangxi, Lingchuaan	中国:广西灵川	25.5	110.4		4.75	Ms	6										
1599	10	16								China	China: Yunnan, Songming	中国:云南嵩明	25.3	103		5	Ms	6										
1599										China	China: Shaanxi, Huangling	中国:陕西黄陵	35.6	109.2		4.75	Ms	6										
1600	1	2								* * Maso, Song	Philippines: Manila	菲律宾:马尼拉	14.6	121		6.1	Mk	8										
1600	2	14	2							GSHAP, Song	Peru: Moquegua	秘鲁:莫克瓜	-16.7	-70.8	6	4.5	Mk	5										
1600	2	19	2							GSHAP, Song	Peru: Moquegua	秘鲁:莫克瓜	-16.7	-70.8	6	4.5	Mk	5										

年 Year	月 Mo	日 Dy	时 Hr	分 Mn	秒 Sec	源 Sr	浪高 Wh	级I mI	级S mS	资料来源 Information	地名(英文) Name(English)	地名(中文) Name(Chinese)	纬度(°) Latitude	经度(°) Longitude	深度 Depth	震级 Mag	标度 Scale	烈度 MMI	死亡人数 Deaths 数量/人 Num	死亡人数 级别 Dd	受伤人数 Injuries 数量/人 Num	受伤人数 级别 Dd	经济损失 Damage 数量/$ Mill	经济损失 级别 De	房屋毁坏 Houses Destroyed 数量/间 Num	房屋毁坏 级别 Dh	房屋受损 Houses Damaged 数量/间 Num	房屋受损 级别 Dh
1600	2	19	10							*	Peru:Huaynaputina Volcano	秘鲁:纳普蒂纳火山	-16.8	-70.9	20	7.9	Ms	11						2				
1600	2	19	22							GSHAP,Song	Peru:Moquegua	秘鲁:莫克瓜	-16.7	-70.8	6	4.5	Mk	5										
1600	2	20	2							GSHAP,Song	Peru:Moquegua	秘鲁:莫克瓜	-16.7	-70.8		4.5	Mk	5										
1600	2	28	20							*	Peru:Moquegua	秘鲁:莫克瓜	-16.6	-70.8	20	8.1	Muk	10						1				
1600	3	26								China	China:Fujian,Zhaoan	中国:福建诏安	23.8	117.2		5.5	Ms	7										
1600	9	29								*China	China:Guangdong, Nan-ao,Near Coast	中国:广东南澳近海	23.5	117.2		7	Ms	9		3		2		3		3		
1600	11									*Song	Philippines:Manila	菲律宾:马尼拉	14.6	121		5.9	Mk	6						2				
1600										GSHAP	Russia:Irkutsk,Slyudyanka	俄罗斯:伊尔库茨克州斯柳江卡	51.72	103.68	15	6	Ms	8.5										
1600										GSHAP	Russia:Buryatiya,Kichera	俄罗斯:布里亚特州基切拉镇	56.02	110.09	15	6.9	Ms	9										
1600										China, GSHAP	China:Xinjiang,Kashi,N.	中国:新疆喀什北部	40	76	30	6	Ms	8										
1601	1	16	16							*Song	Philippines:Manila	菲律宾:马尼拉	14.6	121		6.1	Mk	8		1				2				
1601	9	8	1							*Song	Switzerland:Engelberg	瑞士:恩格尔贝格	46.8	8.5		6.5	Mk	9		3				3				
1601						2				NOAA,Song	Greece:Crete Island	希腊:克里特岛	35.5	25.5		6.6	Mk											
1602	2	8				4		1	1	*NOAA	Japan:Boso,Near Coast	日本:房总半岛近海	35.1	140.5		7.2	Ms			3								
1602	6									China	China:Guizhou,Qinglong	中国:贵州晴隆	25.8	105.2		5	Ms	6										
1602	10	23								China	China:Yunnan,Eryuan	中国:云南洱源	26.1	99.9		5	Ms	6										
1603	5	30								China	China:Hubei,Zhongxiang	中国:湖北钟祥	31.2	112.6		5	Ms	6										
1603										*Song	Mexico:Oaxaca,Mixteca	墨西哥:瓦哈卡,加的	17	-96.3		6.3	Mk							3		3		
1603						2	2	1	1.5	NOAA,Song	Japan:Mie,Near Coast	日本:三重近海	33.8	136.9		7	Mk											
1604	3									*Song	Mexico:Oaxaca	墨西哥:瓦哈卡	17	-96.3		6.3	Mk							3				
1604	10	25								China	China:Gansu,Lixian	中国:甘肃礼县	34.2	105.1		6	Ms	8								3		
1604	11	24	18	30		4	16	4	3.5	*NOAA	Peru:Tacna	秘鲁:塔克纳	-17.88	-70.94	30	8.5	Ms	11	174	3				3		3		
1604	12	29				1				*China,NOAA	China:Taiwan Strait	中国:台湾海峡	24.7	119		7.5	Ms					1		3		3		
1604	12									*Song	Chile:Coquimbo	智利:科金博	-29.9	-71.3		7.3	Mk	10										
1604						1				*GSHAP,NOAA	Greece:Crete Island	希腊:克里特岛	35.5	25.5		7	Ms	10										
1605	2	3				4	10	3	3	*Japan,NOAA	Japan:Tokushima,Near Coast	日本:德岛近海	33	134.9		7.9	Ms	11	5000	4				3	700	3		3
1605	7	13								*China	China:Hainan,Haikou	中国:海南海口	20	110.5		7.5	Ms	10	2000	4				4		4		
1605	12	24	15	30						GSHAP	Romania:Nereju	罗马尼亚:内雷茹	45.7	26.6	150	6	Ms	6.5										
1606	1	13	1	30						GSHAP	Romania:Nereju	罗马尼亚:内雷茹	45.7	26.6	150	6.6	Ms	7.5										
1606	1	23				5				Japan,NOAA	Japan:South Honshu Ridge	日本:本州南部海岭	32	140		6.7	Ms											
1606	3	23	20							GSHAP,Song	Peru:Chiclayo,Near Coast	秘鲁:奇克拉约近海	-7	-80.3	40	5	Mk	6										
1606	10	25	13							GSHAP	Peru:Lima,Near Coast	秘鲁:利马近海	-11.8	-77.8	60	6.8	Ms	9										
1606	11	30								*China	China:Yunnan,Jianshui	中国:云南建水	23.6	102.8		6.75	Ms	9	2000	4				4		4		
1607	10	2								China	China:Shaanxi,Xi-an	中国:陕西西安	34.3	108.9		5	Ms	6										
1607										China	China:Taiwan Strait	中国:台湾海峡	24.8	119		5.25	Ms	7										
1608	1	8								*Song	Mexico:Oaxaca	墨西哥:瓦哈卡	17	-96.3		6.3	Mk							3				

时间 Date						海啸 Tsunami				资料来源 Information	震中 Earthquake Epicenter				深度 Depth	震级 Mag	标度 Scale	烈度 MMI	死亡人数 Deaths		受伤人数 Injuries		经济损失 Damage		房屋毁坏 Houses Destroyed		房屋受损 Houses Damaged	
年 Year	月 Mo	日 Dy	时 Hr	分 Mn	秒 Sec	源 Sr	浪高 Wh	级I mI	级S mS		地名(英文) Name(English)	地名(中文) Name(Chinese)	纬度(°) Latitude	经度(°) Longitude					数量/人 Num	级别 Dd	数量/人 Num	级别 Dd	数量/$ Mill $ Mill	级别 De	数量/间 Num	级别 Dh	数量/间 Num	级别 Dh
1608	4	20				3				* NOAA	Iran:Qazvin	伊朗:加兹温	36.4	50.5		7.6	Ms							3		3		
1608	5	14								* GSHAP	Montenegro:Herceg Novi	蒙特尼哥罗(黑山):新海尔采格	42.4	18.7		5.7	Ms	10										
1608	7	25								* GSHAP	Montenegro:Cetinje	蒙特尼哥罗(黑山):采蒂涅	42.4	18.7		6.3	Ms	10						3				
1608	9	15	11							* GSHAP	Croatia:Dubrovnik,SE.	克罗地亚:杜布罗夫尼克东南	42.4	18.5		5.7	Ms	11						3				
1608	9	23								China	China:Ningxia,Qingtongxia,S.	中国:宁夏青铜峡南	37.7	105.8		5.5	Ms	7										
1608	12	3								Bautista,Maso	Philippines:Samar Island	菲律宾:萨马岛	11.1	124.8		5	Muk	7										
1609	4					2			4	GSHAP,NOAA	Greece:Dodecanese Islands	希腊:多德卡尼斯群岛	36.4	28.4		7.2	Ms											
1609	7	12								* China	China:Gansu,Jiuquan,SE.	中国:甘肃酒泉东南	39.2	99		7.25	Ms	10	840	3				3		3		
1609	7	20								* Italy	Italy:Nicastro	意大利:尼可斯特洛	38.968	16.353		5.57	Ms							3				
1609	10	20	1							*	Peru:Lima,Near Coast	秘鲁:利马近海	-11.9	-77.4	40	8.6	Muk	9										
1610	2	3	19	30						*	Venezuela:La Grita,Merida	委内瑞拉:拉格里塔,梅里达	8.3	-71.8		7.9	Muk	10	60	2				3				
1610	2	3								China	China:Sichuan,Gaoxian	中国:四川高县	28.5	104.5		5.5	Ms	7										
1610	3	13								China	China:Sichuan,Pingwu,E.	中国:四川平武东	32.4	104.6		5.5	Ms	7								3		
1610	11	29								* Song	France:Leymen	法国:莱芒	47.5	7.5		6.3	Mk	8						3				
1610	11									* Song	Philippines:Cauayan	菲律宾:卡瓦延	17	122		6.5	Mk	9						3				
1611	4									China	China:Yunnan,Ruili	中国:云南瑞丽	24	97.8		4.75	Ms	6										
1611	9	9								* China	China:Guangdong,Maoming,Near Coast	中国:广东茂名近海	21.4	111.2		6	Ms	7	2	1				1		2		
1611	9	25								* Song	Mexico:Mexico City	墨西哥:墨西哥城	19.5	-99.1		6.3	Mk							3				
1611	9	27								* Japan,Usami	Japan:Fukushima	日本:福岛	37.5	140		6.9	Ms	10	3700	4					20000	5		
1611	12	2	1			4	25	4.6	4	* Japan,Usami,NOAA	Japan Trench	日本海沟	39	144.5		8.1	Ms	11	5783	4				4				
1611	12	9								* Song	Iran:Mashhad	伊朗:马什哈德	35.1	58.9		6.3	Mk	8						3				
1612	3	13								China	China:Yunnan,Kaiyuan	中国:云南开远	23.6	103.2		5	Ms	6										
1612	5	16								* Song	Greece:Leukas (Ionian Islands)	希腊:琉卡斯(伊奥尼亚群岛)	38.8	20.8		7	Mk	10										
1612	6	3								China	China:Yunnan,Xundian	中国:云南寻甸	25.4	103.3		5.5	Ms	7										
1612	11	8				2			4	* NOAA	Greece:Crete Island	希腊:克里特岛	35.5	25.5		6.7	Ms											
1613	7	16								*	South Korea:Suwon	韩国:水原	37.2	127		6.3	Muk	8						2				
1613	8	25				2			4	* Italy,NOAA	Italy:Sicilia Island	意大利:西西里岛	38.12	14.78		5.57	Ms	10										
1613	10	2								* * Song	Greece:Leukas (Ionian Islands)	希腊:琉卡斯(伊奥尼亚群岛)	38.8	20.8		7	Mk	10										
1613										* Song	Greece:Crete,Iraklion	希腊:克里特岛,伊拉克利翁	35.3	25.1		6.2	Mk			3								
1614	5	4	17							* Song	Azores:Praia	亚速尔群岛:普拉亚	38.4	-27		8	Mk	11										
1614	5	24								* Song	Azores:Terceira	亚速尔群岛:特塞拉岛	38.4	-24.1		7.3	Mk	10										

时间 Date						海啸 Tsunami				资料来源 Information	震中 Earthquake Epicenter				深度 Depth	震级 Mag	标度 Scale	烈度 MMI	死亡人数 Deaths		受伤人数 Injuries		经济损失 Damage		房屋毁坏 Houses Destroyed		房屋受损 Houses Damaged	
年 Year	月 Mo	日 Dy	时 Hr	分 Mn	秒 Sec	源 Sr	浪高 Wh	级I mI	级S mS		地名(英文) Name(English)	地名(中文) Name(Chinese)	纬度(°) Latitude	经度(°) Longitude					数量/人 Num	级别 Dd	数量/人 Num	级别 Dd	数量/$ Mill $ Mill	级别 De	数量/间 Num	级别 Dh	数量/间 Num	级别 Dh
1614	10	23								* China	China: Shanxi, Pingyaao	中国:山西平遥	37.2	112.1		6.5	Ms	8		1				3		3		
1614	11	26				4	6	2	1	* Japan, Usami, NOAA	Japan: Niigata	日本:新潟	37.5	138		7.7	Ms	10		3				3		1		
1615	3	1								China	China: Jiangsu, Nantong	中国:江苏南通	32	120.9		5	Ms	6										
1615	6	5								* GSHAP	Black Sea	黑海	44.9	35.5	16	6	Ms	8										
1615	6	26								* Japan, Usami	Japan: Tokyo	日本:东京	35.7	139.7		6.4	Muk	7		3				2		1		
1615	7	20								China	China: Ningxia, Pingluo, SW.	中国:宁夏平罗西南	38.8	106.3		5.5	Ms	7										
1615	8	24								China	China: Yunnan, Chuxiong	中国:云南楚雄	25	101.6		5.25	Ms	6										
1615	9	8								* Song	Dominica: Santo Domingo	多米尼加:圣多明哥	18.5	-70		6.3	Mk							3				
1615	9	16	23	30		4	4	2	1.5	* Chile, NOAA	Chile: Arica	智利:阿里卡	-18.5	-70.35		8.8	Ms	10						2				
1615										GSHAP	Georgia: Zugdidi	格鲁吉亚:祖格迪迪	42.4	41.7	5	4.9	Ms	8										
1616	2	10								China	China: Ningxia, Qingtongxia, SW.	中国:宁夏青铜峡西南	37.7	105.9		5.75	Ms	7										
1616	2									GSHAP	Colombia: Zipaquirá	哥伦比亚:锡帕基拉	5	-74		7	Ms	9										
1616	3									* Song	Switzerland: Engelberg	瑞士:恩格尔贝格	46.8	8.4		6.3	Mk	8						3				
1616	8	27								* GSHAP	Turkey: Kilis	土耳其:基利斯	36.8	37	20	6.9	Ms	9						3				
1616	9	9				4	2	1	1	* Japan, Usami, NOAA	Japan: Miyagi, Near Coast	日本:宫城近海	38.1	142		7	Ms	9		3				2		1		
1616	10	10								China	China: Hebei, Chicheng, SE.	中国:河北赤城东南	40.7	116.1		5	Ms	6										
1616	12	6				2	2	1	1	* NOAA	Japan Trench	日本海沟	39	144.5		7.5	Ms		200	3								
1618	5	20								* China	China: Shanxi, Jiexiu	中国:山西介休	37	111.9		6	Ms	8		3				3		3		
1618	5	26								* Song	India: Bombay	印度:孟买	18.9	72.9		7	Mk	9	2000	4				3				
1618	6	18								* Song	France: Duranus, Coaraze	法国:迪拉尼,科沙拉兹	43.6	7.3		6.1	Mk	8						2				
1618	8	25								* Song	Italy: Piuro	意大利:皮乌罗	46.3	9.5		6.3	Mk	7		3				3				
1618	9	30								Japan, Usami, Song	Japan: Kyoto	日本:京都	35.1	135.8		6.3	Mk									1		
1618	11	16								China	China: Hebei, Yuxian	中国:河北蔚县	39.8	114.5		6.5	Ms	8								3		
1618	12	19								* Song	Iran: Razavi Khorasan	伊朗:呼罗珊	35	58		6.3	Mk		800	3				3				
1618										China	China: Yunnan, Yunlong	中国:云南云龙	25.8	99.2		5.25	Ms	6										
1618										China	China: Hainan, Chengmai	中国:海南澄迈	20	110.1		5.5	Ms	7										
1619	2	13								* Song	Mexico: Oaxaca	墨西哥:瓦哈卡	17	-96.3		6.3	Mk							3				
1619	2	14	16	30						*	Peru: Trujillo, Piura	秘鲁:特鲁希略,皮乌拉	-7.941	-79.038	40	8.6	Ms	9	350	3				3				
1619	5	1				4				* Japan, Usami, NOAA	Japan: Yatsushiro	日本:熊本	32.5	130.6		6.4	Ms									1		
1619	11	30	16							* Bautista	Philippines: Aparri	菲律宾:阿帕里	18.5	121.6		8	Ms	10		3				3				
1619										* Song	Germany: Frankfurt	德国:法兰克福	52.3	14.6		6.3	Mk			3				3				
1620	10	19								China	China: Shandong, Zouping, NW.	中国:山东邹平西北	37.1	117.5		5	Ms	6										

年 Year	月 Mo	日 Dy	时 Hr	分 Mn	秒 Sec	源 Sr	浪高 Wh	级 I mI	级 S mS	资料来源 Information	地名(英文) Name(English)	地名(中文) Name(Chinese)	纬度(°) Latitude	经度(°) Longitude	深度 Depth	震级 Mag	标度 Scale	烈度 MMI	死亡人数 Deaths 数量/人 Num	死亡人数 Deaths 级别 Dd	受伤人数 Injuries 数量/人 Num	受伤人数 Injuries 级别 Dd	经济损失 Damage 数量/$ Mill	经济损失 Damage 级别 De	房屋毁坏 Houses Destroyed 数量/间 Num	房屋毁坏 Houses Destroyed 级别 Dh	房屋受损 Houses Damaged 数量/间 Num	房屋受损 Houses Damaged 级别 Dh
1620	11	8	12	30						GSHAP	Romania: Blaj	罗马尼亚:布拉日	46.2	23.9	30	6.5	Ms	8										
1620	12	1								GSHAP	Romania: Nereju	罗马尼亚:内雷茹	45.7	26.6		6.6	Ms	7.5										
1620	12									China	China: Yunnan, Malong	中国:云南马龙	25.5	103.5		5.25	Ms	7										
1620										*	Uzbekistan: Akhsy	乌兹别克斯坦:阿赫苏	40.9	71.4	6	5.8	Muk	9		3				3				
1620										* Song	Philippines: Panay, Iloilo, Capiz	菲律宾:班乃,伊洛伊洛,卡皮斯	10.8	122.5		6.5	Mk	9						3				
1621	3									* China	China: Hebei, Yongqing, NE.	中国:河北永清东北	39.5	116.7		5.5	Ms	7		1				1		1		
1621	5	2								* Song	Panama: Panama City	巴拿马:巴拿马城	8.6	-79.3		5.9	Mk							2				
1621	11									China	China: Jiangsu, Wujiang, S.	中国:江苏吴江南	31	120.6		4.75	Ms	6										
1622	3	18								China	China: Shandong, Yuncheng, S.	中国:山东郓城南	35.5	116		6	Ms	8								3		
1622	5	5				2				* GSHAP, NOAA	Greece: Zante	希腊:赞特	37.5	21		6.6	Ms	10										
1622	5	6								* Song	Mexico: Zacatecas	墨西哥:萨卡特卡斯	23	-103		6.3	Mk							3				
1622	7	25								* Song	Switzerland: Scuol	瑞士:施库尔	46.8	10.3		6	Mk	6		2				1				
1622	8	3								* Italy	Switzerland: Scuol	瑞士:施库尔	46.8	10.3		5.17	Ms	7		2								
1622	10	25								* China	China: Ningxia, Haiyuan, N.	中国:宁夏固原北	36.5	106.3		7	Ms	10	12000	5				4	11800	5		
1622	10	26								China	China: Gansu, Lintao	中国:甘肃临洮	35.4	103.9		5.5	Ms	7										
1622										GSHAP	Russia: Dagestan, Derbent, W.	俄罗斯:达吉斯坦共和国杰尔宾特西部	42.1	47.6	15	5.1	Ms	6.5										
1623	5	4								China	China: Yunnan, Xiangyun, NW.	中国:云南祥云西北	25.5	100.4		6.25	Ms	8							500	3		
1623	6	23								China	China: Sichuan, Songpan, E.	中国:四川松潘东	32.6	104.1		5.5	Ms	7										
1623	12	26								China	China: Henan, Nanle	中国:河南南乐	36.1	115.2		4.75	Ms	6										
1624	2	10								China	China: Jiangsu, Yangzhou	中国:江苏扬州	32.3	119.4		6	Ms	8								3		
1624	3	18	19	45						* * Italy	Italy: Argenta, Naso	意大利:阿金塔	44.65	11.85		5.43	Ms	10	25	1				3				
1624	3	19	20			2			3	* Italy, NOAA	Italy: Argenta	意大利:阿金塔	44.6	11.8		5.43	Ms	10										
1624	3	26								China	China: Yunnan, Jianchuan	中国:云南剑川	26.5	99.9		5.75	Ms	7										
1624	3									China	China: Shanxi, Xinzhou	中国:山西忻州	38.4	112.7		5	Ms	6								3		
1624	4	17								China	China: Hebei, Luanxian	中国:河北滦县	39.5	118.8		6.5	Ms	8								3		
1624	7	4								China	China: Gansu, Jingning	中国:甘肃静宁	35.4	105.9		6	Ms	8								3		
1624	7	19								China	China: Hebei, Baoding	中国:河北保定	38.9	115.5		5.5	Ms	7		3						3		
1624	7									China	China: Yunnan, Lijiang	中国:云南丽江	26.9	100.2		5	Ms	6										
1624	9	1								China	China: Shanghai, Pudong Xinqu	中国:上海浦东新区	31.2	121.5		4.75	Ms	6										
1624	10									China	China: Shaanxi, Xiangxian	中国:陕西洋县	33.2	107.5		5.5	Ms	7										
1624										* Song	Morocco: Fes (Fez), Meknes	摩洛哥:菲斯,梅克内斯	34	-4.6		6.3	Mk							3				
1625	1	21								Japan, Usami, Song	Japan: Hiroshima	日本:广岛	34.4	132.45		6.3	Mk									1		
1625	4									China	China: Hebei, Cangzhou	中国:河北沧州	38.3	116.9		5	Ms	6										

时间 Date 年 Year	月 Mo	日 Dy	时 Hr	分 Mn	秒 Sec	海啸 Tsunami 源 Sr	浪高 Wh	级 I mI	级 S mS	资料来源 Information	震中 Earthquake Epicenter 地名(英文) Name(English)	地名(中文) Name(Chinese)	纬度(°) Latitude	经度(°) Longitude	深度 Depth	震级 Mag	标度 Scale	烈度 MMI	死亡人数 Deaths 数量/人 Num	级别 Dd	受伤人数 Injuries 数量/人 Num	级别 Dd	经济损失 Damage 数量/$ Mill	级别 De	房屋毁坏 Houses Destroyed 数量/间 Num	级别 Dh	房屋受损 Houses Damaged 数量/间 Num	级别 Dh
1625	6	18								* Song	Greece: Leukas (Ionian Islands)	希腊:琉卡斯(伊奥尼亚群岛)	38.8	20.8		7	Mk	10										
1625	7	21								Japan, Usami, Song	Japan: Kumamoto	日本:熊本	32.8	130.6		6.5	Mk		50	1								
1625										GSHAP	Syria: Hamah (Hama)	叙利亚:哈马	35.2	36.4	20	6.1	Ms	7.5										
1625						4				Japan, Song	Japan: Ishigaki – Jima	日本:石垣岛	24.3	124.2		7	Mk			1						1		
1626	4	4	12	45						* Italy	Italy: Girifalco	意大利:吉里法尔科	38.82	16.42		6.08	Ms	10						3		3		
1626	5	4								GSHAP	Russia: White Sea	俄罗斯:白海	66	35.5	20	6.3	Ms	8										
1626	5	30								China	China: Tianjin, Jixian	中国:天津蓟县	40	117.4		5.5	Ms	7										
1626	6	22								GSHAP	Finland: Oulu	芬兰:奥卢	64.7	26.7	30	4.7	Ms	5										
1626	6	28								* China	China: Shanxi, Lingqiu	中国:山西灵丘	39.4	114.2		7	Ms	9	5200	4				4		4		
1626	7	3								* * Song	Adriatic Sea	亚得里亚海	44	14		6	Mk	10										
1626	7	30								* Italy	Italy: Napoli (Naples)	意大利:那不勒斯	41.73	15.35		6.73	Ms		70000	5				3				
1626	10	8								China	China: Hunan, Huitong	中国:湖南会同	26.9	109.7		5	Ms	6										
1627	2	6								* China	China: Ningxia, Zhongning	中国:宁夏中宁	37.5	105.5		6	Ms	8		2				1		1		
1627	3	8								Japan, Song	Japan: Tokyo, Adachi	日本:东京足立	35.8	139.8		6.5	Mk			1								
1627	3	27								Japan, Song	Japan: Koginsasi	日本:津轻	40.7	140.6		6.3	Mk									1		
1627	3									China	China: Shanxi, Pingding	中国:山西平定	37.8	113.6		5.5	Ms	7								3		
1627	6	26	11							* Song	Ecuador: Quito	厄瓜多尔:基多	-0.2	-78.5		6.1	Mk	8						2				
1627	7	30	10	50		4			5	* NOAA	Italy: Lesina	意大利:莱西那	41.7	15.3		6.7	Ms	10	5000	4				3				
1627	9	14				3		2	3.5	* Nakamura, Maso, NOAA	Philippines: Aparri	菲律宾:阿帕里	18	121.5		8	Ms	10						3		3		3
1627	10	22								Japan	Japan: Nagano	日本:长野	36.6	138.2		6	Ms			1					80	2		
1627										USGS, Song	US: Massachusetts, Peabody	美国:马萨诸塞州皮博迪	42.6	-70.8		5.5	Mk	6										
1628	3	31								China, Diao S.	China: Hunan, Taoyuan, NW.	中国:湖南桃源西北	29	111.4		4.75	Ms	6										
1628	5	15								GSHAP	Ecuador: Quito	厄瓜多尔:基多	-0.22	-78.5		4.3	Ms	5										
1628	6	17	18							* Italy	Slovenia: Brezice	斯洛文尼亚:布雷日采	46	15.5	7	5.57	Muk	8						2				
1628	8	10	3							Japan, Usami	Japan: Tokyo, Adachi	日本:东京足立	35.8	139.8		6.1	Ms									1		
1628	10	7								* China	China: Hebei, Huaian, W.	中国:河北怀安西	40.6	114.2		6.5	Ms	8	63	2				3		3		
1628										* Song	Philippines: Camalig	菲律宾:卡马利格	13.2	123.7		6.5	Mk	9						3		3		3
1629	2	27				2			3	* NOAA	Greece: Crete Island	希腊:克里特岛	35.5	25		7	Ms											
1629	3	7	9			2			3	* NOAA	Greece: Crete Island	希腊:克里特岛	35.5	25	70	7	Ms											
1629	3	9	9			1				GSHAP, NOAA	Greece: Crete Island	希腊:克里特岛	35	23.7		7.3	Ms											
1629	3									China	China: Gansu, Lanzhou	中国:甘肃兰州	36.1	103.7		5.5	Ms	7								3		
1629	8	1				4	16	4	4.5	* NOAA, Song	Indonesia: Banda Sea	印度尼西亚:班达海	-4.6	129.9		7.9	Mk							2		2		
1629										GSHAP, Song	Venezuela: Cumana	委内瑞拉:库马纳	10.47	-64.17		6	Mk	7										
1629										* Song	Germany: Mecklenburg	德国:梅克伦堡	53.6	12.3		6.2	Mk			3								
1630	1	16								* China	China: Sichuan, Songpan, E.	中国:四川松潘东	32.6	104.1		6.5	Ms	8		2				1				

年 Year	月 Mo	日 Dy	时 Hr	分 Mn	秒 Sec	海啸 Tsunami 源 Sr	浪高 Wh	级I mI	级S mS	资料来源 Information	震中 Earthquake Epicenter 地名(英文) Name(English)	地名(中文) Name(Chinese)	纬度(°) Latitude	经度(°) Longitude	深度 Depth	震级 Mag	标度 Scale	烈度 MMI	死亡人数 Deaths 数量/人 Num	级别 Dd	受伤人数 Injuries 数量/人 Num	级别 Dd	经济损失 Damage 数量/$ Mill	级别 De	房屋毁坏 Houses Destroyed 数量/间 Num	级别 Dh	房屋受损 Houses Damaged 数量/间 Num	级别 Dh
1630	2	4								China	China:Jiangsu,Jurong	中国:江苏句容	32	119.2		4.75	Ms	6										
1630	3	9	9	1		4			3	NOAA	Aegean Sea	爱琴海	36	24		6.8	Ms											
1630	6									China	China:Hubei,Tianmen	中国:湖北天门	30.7	113.5		5	Ms	6								3		
1630	7	22								* Song	Greece:Levkas,Cephalonia	希腊:莱夫卡斯,凯法隆尼亚	38.3	20.5		6.3	Mk	9		3				3				
1630	8	1	15							Japan,Usami	Japan:Tokyo,Adachi	日本:东京足立	35.8	139.8		6.7	Ms									1		
1630	10	14								China	China:Hubei,Xiantao	中国:湖北仙桃	30.2	113.2		5	Ms	6		1								
1630	11	27	16	30						*	Peru:Lima,Near Coast	秘鲁:利马近海	-12.2	-77.5	30	8.1	Muk	7		1				1				
1630						1				* NOAA,Song	Indonesia:Banda Sea	印度尼西亚:班达海	-4.6	129.9		7	Mk											
1631	2	10								*	Ethiopia:Afar	埃塞俄比亚:阿法尔区	11.2	41.7		5.7	Muk	9						2				
1631	7	21								* China	China:Gansu,Lintao	中国:甘肃临洮	35.2	104.3		5.5	Ms	7		1				1				
1631	7									* China	China:Gansu,Qingyang	中国:甘肃庆阳	35.5	107.9		5	Ms	6		1								
1631	8	14								* China	China:Hunan,Changde	中国:湖南常德	29.2	111.7		6.75	Ms	8		4				4		4		
1631	9									China	China:Guizhou,Qinglong	中国:贵州晴隆	25.8	105.2		4.75	Ms	6										
1631	12	17				5			5	* Italy,NOAA	Italy:Vesuvio	意大利:维苏威	40.833	14.417		5.17	Ms		4000	4				4		4		
1631										China	China:GansuHuixian,S.	中国:甘肃徽县南	33.7	106.1		5.5	Ms	7										
1632	1	1								* GSHAP	Croatia:Dubrovnik,SE.	克罗地亚:杜布罗夫尼克东南	42.4	18.4		6.6	Ms	10										
1632										China	China:Hubei,Zhuxi	中国:湖北竹溪	32.4	109.7		5	Ms	6										
1633	3	1				4	2	1	1	* Japan,Usami,NOAA	Japan:Odawara	日本:神奈川小田原	35.2	139.2		7.1	Ms	9	150	3				2		3		
1633	5	14				2	2	1	1.5	* NOAA,Song	Chile:Ancud	智利:安库德	-41.8	-74		7	Mk							2		2		
1633	11	5				2			3	* GSHAP,NOAA	Greece:Zakinthos (Zante)	希腊:扎金索斯岛(桑特岛)	37.5	20.3		7	Ms	10		3				3				
1633										China	China:Shanxi,Fenyang	中国:山西汾阳	37.3	111.8		4.75	Ms	6										
1633										* Song	Iran:Tabriz	伊朗:大不里士	38	46.2		5.9	Mk							2				
1633										* Song	Chile:Santiago	智利:圣地亚哥	-33.4	-70.7		6.3	Mk							3				
1634	1	14								* China	China:Gansu,Xihe	中国:甘肃西和	34	105.2		6	Ms	8	30	1				3		3		
1634	3	30								* China	China:Hubei,Luotian	中国:湖北罗田	30.7	115.4		5.5	Ms	7						1				
1634	12									* China	China:Gansu,Lingtai	中国:甘肃灵台	35.1	107.6		5.5	Ms	7				3		1				
1634	12									China	China:Gansu,Wenxian	中国:甘肃文县	33.2	104.8		5.5	Ms	7		3						3		
1635	3	12	4							Japan,Usami	Japan:Tokyo,Adachi	日本:东京足立	35.8	139.8		6.1	Ms									1		
1635	10	26								China	China:Shaanxi,Xiangxian	中国:陕西洋县	33.2	107.5		5.5	Ms	7								3		
1636	9	30								* Song	Greece:Cephalonia	希腊:凯法隆尼亚	38	20.6		7	Mk	10	520	3								
1636	10	12	18	30		2			3	NOAA	Greece:Ionian Sea	希腊:伊奥尼亚海	38.1	20.3		7.2	Ms											
1636	12	3								Japan,Song	Japan:Niigata	日本:新潟	37.7	139.4		6.3	Mk									1		
1636	12	18	14							*	Ghana:Takoradi,	加纳:塔科拉迪	5.1	-2.2		5.7	Muk	9		3				3				
1636	12	21	4							* Bautista	Philippines:Mindanao,Illana Bay	菲律宾:棉兰老岛,伊拉纳湾	7.4	123.6		6.5	Ms	9						2				
1636										China	China:Shaanxi,Zhidan	中国:陕西志丹	36.8	108.8		5	Ms	6										

年 Year	月 Mo	日 Dy	时 Hr	分 Mn	秒 Sec	海啸 Tsunami 源 Sr	浪高 Wh	级 I mI	级 S mS	资料来源 Information	震中 Earthquake Epicenter 地名(英文) Name(English)	地名(中文) Name(Chinese)	纬度(°) Latitude	经度(°) Longitude	深度 Depth	震级 Mag	标度 Scale	烈度 MMI	死亡人数 Deaths 数量/人 Num	级别 Dd	受伤人数 Injuries 数量/人 Num	级别 Dd	经济损失 Damage 数量/$ Mill $ Mill	级别 De	房屋毁坏 Houses Destroyed 数量/间 Num	级别 Dh	房屋受损 Houses Damaged 数量/间 Num	级别 Dh
1636										China	China:Shaanxi,Hanzhong	中国:陕西汉中	33.1	107		5.5	Ms	7		3						3		
1637	2	1	1	30						GSHAP	Romania:Nereju	罗马尼亚:内雷茹	45.7	26.6	150	6.6	Ms	7.5										
1638	1									China	China:Ningxia,Haiyuan	中国:宁夏海原	36.6	105.5		5.5	Ms	7										
1638	3	27	15			2			5	* Italy,NOAA	Italy:Calabria,Cosenza	意大利:卡拉布里亚,科森扎	39.3	16.2		7	Ms	11	19000	5				4				
1638	6	8	9	45						* Italy	Italy:Cerenzia	意大利:切伦齐亚	39.28	16.82		6.6	Ms	9	52·	2				2		2		
1638	6	11	7							USGS,Song	Canada:Québec	加拿大:魁北克	46.5	-72.5		6.6	Mk	9										
1639	5	4								* Song	Iran:Qazvin	伊朗:加兹温	36.2	50		7.7	Mk		12000	5				3				
1639	7	28	18	30						* Song	Croatia:Dubrovnik	克罗地亚:杜布罗夫尼克	42.5	18.1		6.3	Mk	10										
1639	10	8	1	30						* Italy	Italy:Amatrice	意大利:阿马特里切	42.636	13.252		6.26	Ms	10						3				
1639	11	25								Japan	Japan:Fukui	日本:福井	35.9	136.2		6.1	Ms		380	3					1500	4		
1639	12									* Song	Chile:Coquimbo	智利:科金博	-30	-71.4		7.3	Mk	10										
1639										GSHAP	Iran:Qazvin	伊朗:加兹温	36.6	50	14	6.1	Ms	8.5										
1640	2	27								* GSHAP	Iran:Tabriz	伊朗:大不里士	38.2	46.3	15	6.1	Muk	7						2				
1640	2									* Song	Ecuador:Chimborazo,N.	厄瓜多尔:钦博腊索山北部	-1.7	-78.6		7	Mk		5000	4				3				
1640	4	4				1				* NOAA,Song	Germany:Roer Valley	德国:洛尔峡谷	50.8	5.7		7	Mk											
1640	4									China	China:Henan,Luoyang	中国:河南洛阳	34.7	112.5		4.75	Ms	6										
1640	6	19								* Song	Italy:Badolato	意大利:巴多拉托	38.57	16.53		6	Mk	9	300	3				2				
1640	7	31	1			5	6	2	1	* Japan,NOAA	Japan:Uchiura Bay	日本:内浦湾	42.07	140.68		6.5	Ms		700	3				1	20	1		
1640	9	16				2		1	1	NOAA,Song	China:Guangdong,Shantou,Near Coast	中国:广东汕头海域	23	117		7	Mk											
1640	9									China	China:Hubei,Huanggang	中国:湖北黄冈	30.5	114.9		5	Ms	6										
1640	11	23								Japan,Usami	Japan:Fukui	日本:福井	36.2	136.2		6.7	Ms	8		1						1		
1640										China	China:Ningxia,Zhongning	中国:宁夏中宁	37.5	105.6		5	Ms	6		1								
1640										* Italy	Slovenia:Brezice	斯洛文尼亚:布雷日采	45.9	15.5		6	Ms	10										
1641	1	4								* Maso,Song	Philippines:Aparri	菲律宾:阿帕里	18.2	121.7		7.3	Mk	10						3				
1641	2	5								* Iran	Iran:Tabriz	伊朗:大不里士	37.9	46.1		6.8	Ms	9	30000	5				3				
1641	5									* * GSHAP	Bulgaria:Kyustendil	保加利亚:丘斯滕迪尔	42.3	22.7	10	6	Ms	10										
1641	6	11	12	45						* Song	Venezuela:Caracas	委内瑞拉:加拉加斯	10.9	-66.7		6.3	Mk	9						3				
1641	11	26								* China	China:Guangdong,Jieyang,E.	中国:广东揭阳东	23.5	116.5		5.75	Ms	7		1				1		1		
1641	12	21				1				NOAA,Song	Portugal:Azores	葡萄牙:亚速尔群岛	38.4	-28.1		7	Mk											
1641										China	China:Gansu,Gangu,S.	中国:甘肃甘谷南	34.5	105.5		5	Ms	6										
1641										* Song	Venezuela:Caracas	委内瑞拉:加拉加斯	11	-67		6.3	Mk			3				3				
1642	6	30								* China	China:Shanxi,Yuncheng	中国:山西运城	35	110.9		6	Ms	8		2				1		1		
1642	9	4				4	2	1	1	* NOAA	Japan:Isumi	日本:千叶夷隅	35.2	140.6		6.7	Ms											
1642	10	4								China	China:Anhui,Xiaoxian	中国:安徽萧县	34.2	116.9		4.75	Ms	6										
1642	11	20								China	China:Jiangsu,Xuyi	中国:江苏盱眙	33.1	118.5		5	Ms	6										

年 Year	月 Mo	日 Dy	时 Hr	分 Mn	秒 Sec	海啸 Tsunami 源 Sr	浪高 Wh	级 I mI	级 S mS	资料来源 Information	震中 Earthquake Epicenter 地名(英文) Name(English)	地名(中文) Name(Chinese)	纬度(°) Latitude	经度(°) Longitude	深度 Depth	震级 Mag	标度 Scale	烈度 MMI	死亡人数 Deaths 数量/人 Num	级别 Dd	受伤人数 Injuries 数量/人 Num	级别 Dd	经济损失 Damage 数量/$ Mill $ Mill	级别 De	房屋毁坏 Houses Destroyed 数量/间 Num	级别 Dh	房屋受损 Houses Damaged 数量/间 Num	级别 Dh
1642										* China	China: Xizang (Tibet), Lhorong, NW.	中国:西藏洛隆西北	30.8	95.6		7	Ms	9										
1643	4	24	1	30						GSHAP	Colombia: Tunja	哥伦比亚:通哈	5.5	-73.3		3	Ms	5										
1643	7	24				3		1	1	* Korea, NOAA	South Korea: Kyongju	韩国:庆州	35.5	129.3		6.3	Ms											
1643	9	6	10							GSHAP, Song	Chile: Santiago	智利:圣地亚哥	-33.4	-70.6		6	Mk	8										
1643	12	6								Japan, Usami	Japan: Tokyo, Adachi	日本:东京足立	35.8	139.8		6.2	Ms									1		
1643	12									China	China: Yunnan, Yaoan, NW.	中国:云南姚安西北	25.7	101.1		5.5	Ms	7								3		
1644	1	16	8	30						*	Venezuela: Merida, Tariba	委内瑞拉:梅里达,打拉	7.5	-72.5		7	Muk	10		3				3				
1644	2	8								China	China: Anhui, Fengyang	中国:安徽凤阳	32.9	117.5		5.5	Ms	7										
1644	2	15	9	20						* Italy	Italy: Alpi Marittime	意大利:阿尔卑斯山山脉	43.98	7.32		5.88	Mk	8	150	3				2				
1644	3	16	10							* Song	Venezuela: San Cristobal	委内瑞拉:圣克里斯托瓦尔	7.6	-73		6.3	Mk	8		3				3				
1644	4	7								Japan, Usami	Japan: Nikko	日本:栃木日光	36.7	139.7		5.9	Ms									1		
1644	5									China	China: Yunnan, Wuding	中国:云南武定	25.5	102.4		5	Ms	6										
1644	7	30								China	China: Taiwan, Tainan	中国:台湾台南	23	120.1		5.25	Ms	7										
1644	10	18				4	2	1	1	* Japan, Usami, NOAA	Japan: Akita	日本:秋田	39.4	140.1		6.9	Ms	7	117	3				2	28	1		
1645	2	19								*	Ecuador: Chimborazo, N.	厄瓜多尔:钦博腊索山北部	-1.7	-78.6		7.5	Muk			3								
1645	3	15								GSHAP	Ecuador: Chimborazo, N.	厄瓜多尔:钦博腊索山北部	-1.68	-78.55		7	Ms	9										
1645	11	3								Japan, Song	Japan: Odawara	日本:神奈川小田原	35.3	139.1		6.3	Mk									1		
1645	11	30	12	30		2				* Nakamura, NOAA, Bautista	Philippines: Quezon City	菲律宾:奎松市	14.4	121		8	Ms	10	3000	4	2500	4		4				
1645	12	5	15			2				* NOAA, Song	Philippines: Quezon City	菲律宾:奎松市	14.4	121		7.7	Mk	8						3				
1646	2	17								* Song	Turkey: Van	土耳其:凡城	38.3	43.2		6.3	Mk							3				
1646	3									Maso, Song	Philippines: Quezon City	菲律宾:奎松市	14.4	121		5	Mk	6										
1646	4	3	8							GSHAP	Colombia: Sogamoso	哥伦比亚:索加莫索	5.7	-73		6.3	Ms	8										
1646	4	5	20			2			3	Italy, NOAA	Italy: Livorno	意大利:里窝那	43.55	10.321		5.17	Ms											
1646	4	5				2			4	* NOAA, Turkey	Turkey: Marmaraereglisi	土耳其:马尔马拉埃雷利西	41	28		5.8	Ms											
1646	5	31	1	30						* Italy	Italy: Gargano	意大利:加尔加诺	41.87	15.93		6.19	Ms	10										
1646	6	9								* Japan, Usami	Japan: Fukushima, Near Coast	日本:福岛近海	37.7	141.7		7.6	Muk	10						3				
1646	12	7								Japan	Japan: Tokyo, Adachi	日本:东京足立	35.8	139.8		6.5	Ms									1		
1647	5	7				3	2.8	1.5	2	* NOAA, Song	Peru: Ica	秘鲁:伊卡	-14.2	-75.7		7.5	Mk		14	1				2				
1647	5	13	15	30						GSHAP, Song	Peru: Chincha Alta, Near Coast	秘鲁:上钦查近海	-14	-76.5	40	6	Mk	7										
1647	5	14	2	30						* Chile	Chile: Santiago	智利:圣地亚哥	-33.4	-70.6		8.5	Ms	11	2000	4				4		3		

年 Year	月 Mo	日 Dy	时 Hr	分 Mn	秒 Sec	海啸 Tsunami 源 Sr	浪高 Wh	级 I mI	级 S mS	资料来源 Information	震中 Earthquake Epicenter 地名(英文) Name(English)	地名(中文) Name(Chinese)	纬度(°) Latitude	经度(°) Longitude	深度 Depth	震级 Mag	标度 Scale	烈度 MMI	死亡人数 Deaths 数量/人 Num	级别 Dd	受伤人数 Injuries 数量/人 Num	级别 Dd	经济损失 Damage 数量/$ Mill	级别 De	房屋毁坏 Houses Destroyed 数量/间 Num	级别 Dh	房屋受损 Houses Damaged 数量/间 Num	级别 Dh
1647	6	16								* Japan, Usami	Japan: Joso	日本:茨城常总	36	140		6.4	Muk	7		2								
1647	9	3								Japan, Usami, Song	Japan: Tokyo, Adachi	日本:东京足立	35.8	139.8		6.3	Mk									1		
1648	3	31								* Iran	Turkey: Van	土耳其:凡城	38.3	43.5		6.5	Ms		2000	4				3				
1648	6	13								Japan, Usami	Japan: Sagami Bay	日本:相模湾	35.1	139.3		7.1	Ms	8								3		
1648										* Song	Nicaragua: Leon	尼加拉瓜:里昂	12.5	−86.8		5.9	Mk							2				
1648										* Song	Croatia: Senj	克罗地亚:塞尼	45	14.9		6.3	Mk	10										
1648										* Maso, Song	Philippines: San Rafael	菲律宾:圣拉斐尔	15	121		6.3	Mk	8						3				
1649	1					2			5	Italy, NOAA	Italy: Messina Straits	意大利:梅西纳海峡	38.187	15.549		5.03	Ms											
1649	3	2	8							GSHAP, Song	Peru: Lima	秘鲁:利马	−12.08	−77		4.5	Mk	5										
1649	3	17								Japan, Usami	Japan: Iyo, Aki	日本:伊予,安艺	33.7	132.4		7.1	Ms	9								1		
1649	7	29	16							* Japan, Usami	Japan: Ichihara	日本:千叶市原	35.5	140		7.1	Ms	9	200	3					700	3	700	3
1649	9	1	4							Japan, Usami	Japan: Yokohama	日本:神奈川横滨	35.5	139.6		6.4	Ms	8		1					150	3	140	3
1649	12	9				3		1	1	* NOAA	South Korea: Yeonggwang, Coast	韩国:灵光郡海域	35.5	126		6.5	Ms							2				
1650	1	4								* Song	Iran: Tabriz	伊朗:大不里士	38	46.2		6.3	Mk			3				3				
1650	3	31	19							*	Peru: Cuzco; Bolivia: Sicasica	秘鲁:库斯科;玻利维亚:西卡西卡	−13.5	−72	30	8.1	Muk	10						1				
1650	4	19								GSHAP	Romania: Nereju	罗马尼亚:内雷茹	45.7	26.6	100	6.4	Ms	7										
1650	4	23	20							Japan, Usami	Japan: Yokohama	日本:神奈川横滨	35.5	139.6		6.6	Ms									1		
1650	5	30								Japan, Song	Japan: Fukui	日本:福井	36.2	136.2		6.3	Mk									1		
1650	9	29	15			5	30	5.6	6	NOAA	Greece: Thera Island (Santorini)	希腊:锡拉岛(圣托里尼岛)	36.404	25.396		6.3	Ms											
1650	11	10	16							GSHAP	Bolivia: Sucre	玻利维亚:苏克雷	−19.04	−65.32		6.4	Ms	8										
1650	12	13				1		2	2.5	Japan, NOAA, Song	Japan: Fukui	日本:福井	35.9	136.2		7.5	Mk		21	1				2	500	3		
1650										GSHAP	Iran: Tabriz	伊朗:大不里士	38.2	46.3	15	4.9	Ms	7										
1651	1	17								China	China: Fujian, Ninghua	中国:福建宁化	26.2	116.6		5.5	Ms	6										
1651	12	4								GSHAP	Ecuador: Quito	厄瓜多尔:基多	−0.22	−78.5		4.3	Ms	5										
1651						1			1.5	NOAA, Song	Japan: Aomori, Near Coast	日本:青森近海	40.9	142.1		7	Mk											
1652	3	23								China	China: Anhui, Heshan, NE.	中国:安徽霍山东北	31.5	116.5		6	Ms	7										
1652	6	8								*	Russia: Dagestan, Derbent, W.	俄罗斯:达吉斯坦共和国杰尔宾特西部	42.1	47.7	10	5.8	Muk	9						2				
1652	7	13								* China	China: Yunnan, Midu, S.	中国:云南弥渡南	25.2	100.6		7	Ms	9	3000	4				4		4		
1653	2	23								*	Turkey: Izmir, Alasehir	土耳其:伊兹密尔,阿拉谢希尔	38.2	28.2		7.5	Muk	10	2500	4				3				
1653	5	1								Maso, Song	Philippines: Manila	菲律宾:马尼拉	14.6	121		5	Mk	6										
1653	6					4			1	* NOAA, Song	Sulu Sea, SW.	苏禄海西南	6.4	119.1		7	Mk											
1653	7	9								GSHAP	Ecuador: Guayaquil	厄瓜多尔:瓜亚基尔	−2.2	−79.9		5	Ms	6										

时间 年 Date Year	月 Mo	日 Dy	时 Hr	分 Mn	秒 Sec	海啸 Tsunami 源 Sr	浪高 Wh	级 I mI	级 S mS	资料来源 Information	震中 Earthquake Epicenter 地名(英文) Name(English)	地名(中文) Name(Chinese)	纬度(°) Latitude	经度(°) Longitude	深度 Depth	震级 Mag	标度 Scale	烈度 MMI	死亡人数 Deaths 数量/人 Num	级别 Dd	受伤人数 Injuries 数量/人 Num	级别 Dd	经济损失 Damage 数量/$ Mill	级别 De	房屋毁坏 Houses Destroyed 数量/间 Num	级别 Dh	房屋受损 Houses Damaged 数量/间 Num	级别 Dh
1653	9	11								China	China:Guangdong,Lianjiang	中国:广东廉江	21.7	110.2		4.75	Ms	6										
1654	7	21								* China	China:Gansu,Tianshui,S.	中国:甘肃天水南	34.3	105.5		8	Ms	11	10400	5				4		4		
1654	7	23								* Italy	Italy:Alvito,Bellomonte	意大利:阿莱维图,蒙吉贝洛	41.63	13.68		6.17	Ms	10	600	3				3				
1654	9	15								China	China:Shandong,Shenxian	中国:山东莘县	36.1	115.6		5.5	Ms	7										
1654	10	20								* Song	Spain:Menorca	西班牙:梅诺卡岛	40.1	3.6		6.5	Mk	9		3				1				
1654										* Song	Peru:Lima	秘鲁:利马	-12.1	-76.6		7.7	Mk		11000	5								
1655	1									* Song	Greece:Crete Island	希腊:克里特岛	35	25		7	Mk	10										
1655	4	17								China	China:Yunnan,Yuxi	中国:云南玉溪	24.4	102.6		5	Ms	6								3		
1655	11	13	19	38		1				* GSHAP,NOAA	Peru:Lima,Near Coast	秘鲁:利马近海	-12.3	-77.6	30	7.7	Ms	10						2		3		
1655	12	15								GSHAP	Ecuador:Quito	厄瓜多尔:基多	-0.22	-78.5		5	Ms	6										
1655										China	China:Taiwan,Tainan	中国:台湾台南	23	120.2		6	Ms	8										
1656	1	1								GSHAP	Ecuador:Quito	厄瓜多尔:基多	-0.22	-78.5		4.3	Ms	5										
1656	3									China	China:Guangdong,Jiangmen	中国:广东江门	22.6	112.8		4.75	Ms	6										
1656	4	16								Japan,Song	Japan:Hachinohe	日本:青森八户	40.6	141.6		6.3	Mk									1		
1656										* Song	Lebanon:Tarabulus (Trippoles)	黎巴嫩:泰拉布鲁斯	34.3	35.5		6.5	Mk	9						3				
1656										* Song	Peru:Lima,Near Coast	秘鲁:利马近海	-12.5	-77		7.7	Mk		11000	5				2				
1657	1	3								Japan,Usami,Song	Japan:Nagasaki	日本:长崎	32.7	129.9		6.3	Mk									1		
1657	2	15								* Song	France:Sainte Maure	法国:圣摩尔	47.1	0.6		6.1	Mk	8		1				2				
1657	3	15	23	30		3	8	3	2.5	* NOAA	Chile:Concepcion, Chillan	智利:康塞普西翁,奇廉	-36.8	-73.03		8	Muk	11	40	1				3		3		
1657	4	21								* China	China:Sichuan,Wenchuan	中国:四川汶川	31.3	103.5		6.5	Ms	8		3				3		3		
1657	7	9				4				* Song	Chile:Santiago	智利:圣地亚哥	-33.5	-70.7		7	Mk							1				
1657	12					2			1	* NOAA,Song	Indonesia:Maluku Islands	印度尼西亚:摩鹿加群岛	-3	128		7	Mk											
1657										* Song	Peru:Lima	秘鲁:利马	-12.4	-76.8		7.7	Mk		11000	5								
1658	2	3								* China	China:Hebei,Laishui	中国:河北涞水	39.4	115.7		6	Ms	8		3				2		2		
1658	2	14								*	Peru:Trujillo,Near Coast	秘鲁:特鲁希略近海	-8.2	-80.1	40	7.7	Ms	7		3				3				
1658	5	5								Japan,Usami	Japan:Nikko	日本:枥木日光	36.7	139.7		6.2	Ms									1		
1658	8	1								* Song	Greece:Cephalonia	希腊:凯法隆尼亚	38	21		7	Mk	10										
1658	8	20	9							* Bautista	Philippines:Luzon,Manila	菲律宾:吕宋岛马尼拉	14.4	120.6		5.7	Ms	9		2				2				
1659	2	17	17	2		1				GSHAP,NOAA	Turkey:Marmara Sea	土耳其:马尔马拉海	41	27.8		7.4	Ms											
1659	4	21								* Japan,Usami	Japan:Fukushima	日本:福岛	37.5	140		6.7	Ms	8	39	1	100	2		2	489	3		
1659	9	30								* Song	El Salvador:San Vicente	萨尔瓦多:圣维森特	13.7	-88.7		7.1	Mk			3				4				
1659	11	5	17							* Italy	Italy:Umbriatico,Panaija	意大利:温布里亚蒂科	38.7	16.25		6.5	Ms		2035	4				4		4		
1659	11	9				5	1.5		1	* Song,NOAA	Indonesia:Banda Sea	印度尼西亚:班达海	-6.92	129.125		7	Mk											

年 Year	月 Mo	日 Dy	时 Hr	分 Mn	秒 Sec	海啸 Tsunami 源 Sr	浪高 Wh	级 I mI	级 S mS	资料来源 Information	震中 Earthquake Epicenter 地名(英文) Name(English)	地名(中文) Name(Chinese)	纬度(°) Latitude	经度(°) Longitude	深度 Depth	震级 Mag	标度 Scale	烈度 MMI	死亡人数 Deaths 数量/人 Num	级别 Dd	受伤人数 Injuries 数量/人 Num	级别 Dd	经济损失 Damage 数量/$ Mill $ Mill	级别 De	房屋毁坏 Houses Destroyed 数量/间 Num	级别 Dh	房屋受损 Houses Damaged 数量/间 Num	级别 Dh
1659	11	10	0	30						* * Song	Italy:Soriano	意大利:索里亚诺	38.7	16.3		6	Mk	10										
1660	3									* GSHAP	Greece:Achaia	希腊:阿凯亚	38.3	22.4		6.4	Ms	10	2	1				1		1		
1660	6	21								* Song	France:Bagneres De Bigorre,Lourdes,Bordeaux	法国:德比戈尔,洛德斯,波尔多	43.1	0.2		6.5	Mk	9		3				2				
1660	10	27	14							*	Ecuador:Quito	厄瓜多尔:基多	-0.2	-78.5		7.7	Muk	7										
1660	12									GSHAP	Ecuador:Quito	厄瓜多尔:基多	-0.5	-78.4		5	Ms	6										
1660										Italiani	Italy:Modena	意大利:摩德纳	44.647	10.925		4.63	Ms	6						1				
1660										* Song	Morocco:Melilla	摩洛哥:梅利利亚	35.3	-2.97		5.9	Mk							2				
1660										* Song	Italy:Tuscany	意大利:托斯卡纳区	43.6	12.3		6.2	Mk							4				
1660										GSHAP	Turkey:Erzurum	土耳其:埃尔佐鲁姆	40	41.3	15	6.5	Ms	9										
1660										* Song	Greece:Cephalonia	希腊:凯法隆尼亚	38	21		7	Mk	10										
1661	1	8				2			1.5	* NOAA	China:Taiwan,Tainan	中国:台湾台南	23	120.1		6.4	Ms							1	31	1		
1661	2	15								* China	China:Taiwan,Tainan	中国:台湾台南	23	120.2		6.5	Ms	8		3				1	23	1		
1661	3	12								* * Italy	Italy:Montecchio	意大利:蒙特基奥	45.73	10.07		5.17	Ms	6						1				
1661	3	22	13	30						* Italy	Italy:Predappio	意大利:普雷达皮奥	44.02	11.9		5.83	Ms	10		3				3				
1661	3	22				3			3	* NOAA,Song	Italy:Firenze (Florence)	意大利:佛罗伦萨	43.5	11.2		7.1	Mk	11		3				3				
1661	12	10								Japan,Usami	Japan:Tosa,Kochi	日本:土佐,高知	33.5	133.4		6.1	Ms									1		
1661	12									GSHAP	Ecuador:Quito	厄瓜多尔:基多	-0.22	-78.5		4.3	Ms	5										
1661										GSHAP	Iraq:As Sulaymaniyah	伊拉克:苏莱曼尼亚	35.6	45.7	10	6	Ms	8.5										
1662	1	1								* GSHAP	Ecuador:Quito	厄瓜多尔:基多	-0.2	-78.4		5.9	Ms	6						2				
1662	3									GSHAP	Ecuador:Quito	厄瓜多尔:基多	-0.22	-78.5		5.7	Ms	7										
1662	6	7								* Song	Mexico:Oaxaca	墨西哥:瓦哈卡	17	-96.3		6.3	Mk							3				
1662	6	16	3							* Japan,Usami	Japan:Fukui	日本:福井	35.5	136		7.6	Ms	10	1100	4				3	4000	4		
1662	10	11								China	China:Henan,Xiangcheng	中国:河南项城	33.2	114.8		5.5	Ms	7							200	3		
1662	10	20				4				Japan,NOAA,Song	Ryukyu Islands	琉球群岛	26.4	127.7		7	Mk											
1662	10	30	14			4	1	2	2.5	* Japan,Usami,NOAA	Japan:Miyazaki,Near Coast	日本:宫崎近海	31.7	132		7.6	Ms	10	220	3				2	3591	4	510	3
1662										China	China:Jiangsu,Yancheng	中国:江苏盐城	33.4	120.1		4.75	Ms	6								1		
1662										* Song	Greece:Crete Island	希腊:克里特岛	35	25		7	Mk	10										
1663	2	5	22	30						* USGS,Song	Canada:St Lawrence Valley	加拿大:圣劳伦斯河峡谷	47.6	-70.1		7.6	Ms	10						1				
1663	4									China	China:Yunnan,Eryuan	中国:云南洱源	26.1	99.9		5.25	Ms	6										
1663										* Song	Nicaragua:Momotomba,Granada	尼加拉瓜:莫莫通博,格拉纳达	12.4	-86.6		6.3	Mk							3				
1664	1	4	11							Japan,Usami	Japan:Kyoto,Yamashiro	日本:京都,山城	34.8	135.8		5.9	Ms									1		
1664	4	1								China	China:Beijing,Tongzhou	中国:北京通州	39.9	116.7		4.75	Ms	6										
1664	5	12	9	15						* GSHAP	Peru:Ica,Pisco	秘鲁:伊卡,皮斯科	-14.1	-75.8	15	7.5	Ms	10	400	3				3				
1664	8	3								Japan,Usami	Japan:Wakayama	日本:和歌山	34.3	135.6		6.6	Ms									1		
1664	8	12								*	South Korea:Chonju	韩国:全州	35.5	127.1		6.3	Muk	8	50	1								

时间						海啸				资料来源	震中				深度	震级	标度	烈度	死亡人数		受伤人数		经济损失		房屋毁坏		房屋受损	
年	月	日	时	分	秒	源	浪高	级 I	级 S		地名(英文)	地名(中文)	纬度(°)	经度(°)					数量/人	级别	数量/人	级别	数量/$ Mill	级别	数量/间	级别	数量/间	级别
Date						Tsunami				Information	Earthquake Epicenter				Depth	Mag	Scale	MMI	Deaths		Injuries		Damage		Houses Destroyed		Houses Damaged	
Year	Mo	Dy	Hr	Mn	Sec	Sr	Wh	mI	mS		Name(English)	Name(Chinese)	Latitude	Longitude					Num	Dd	Num	Dd	$ Mill	De	Num	Dh	Num	Dh
1664										＊China	China:Shanxi,Yuanping	中国:山西原平	38.7	112.7		5.5	Ms	7		3								
1664						5	2	1	1	Japan, Usami, NOAA,Song	Ryukyu Islands	琉球群岛	27.8	128.2		7	Mk			2				1		1		
1664										＊Song	Iran:Tabriz	伊朗:大不里士	38	46.2		7	Mk		1500	4				3		3		
1665	1									＊Song	Greece:Crete Island	希腊:克里特岛	35	25		7	Mk	10										
1665	4	16								China	China:Beijing,Tongzhou	中国:北京通州	39.9	116.6		6.5	Ms	8								4		
1665	6	15								＊Iran,GSHAP	Iran:Tehran,Damāvand	伊朗:德黑兰,达马万德	35.7	52.1	11	6.5	Ms	9.5		3				3				
1665	6	19								＊Song	Philippines:Manila	菲律宾:马尼拉	14.6	121		6.1	Mk	8	19	1				2				
1665	6	25	9							Japan,Usami	Japan:Kyoto	日本:京都	35.1	135.8		6.1	Ms									1		
1665	9	19								China	China:Guangdong,Luoding	中国:广东罗定	22.7	111.6		5	Ms	6										
1665										China	China:Gansu,Wuwei,W.	中国:甘肃武威西部	37.9	102.6		5	Ms	6										
1666	2	1								＊Japan,Usami	Japan:Niigata	日本:新潟	37	138		6.4	Ms	8	1500	4					700	3		
1666	2									GSHAP	Romania:Nereju	罗马尼亚:内雷茹	45.7	26.6	150	6	Ms	6.5										
1666	5	31				3	2	1	1	＊Japan,NOAA	Japan:Chita	日本:爱知知多市	35	136.8		6.4	Ms			2				1				
1666	9	22								GSHAP	Iraq:Duhok	伊拉克:杜胡克	37	43	15	6.6	Ms	9										
1666	11									＊Song	Iraq:Al－Mawsil(Mosul)	伊拉克:毋斯离(摩苏尔)	36	42.5		6.3	Mk							3				
1666										GSHAP,Iran	Iran:Khuzestan	伊朗:胡齐斯坦	32.1	50.5	11	6.5	Ms	9.5										
1667	2	3								＊Song	Iran:Rasht	伊朗:拉什特	37.2	50		6.3	Mk							3				
1667	4	6	6			2			4	＊NOAA	Croatia:Dubrovnik	克罗地亚:杜布罗夫尼克	42.6	18.1		7.7	Ms	12	5000	4				4		4		
1667	4	16	8							＊＊Song	Croatia:Dubrovnik	克罗地亚:杜布罗夫尼克	42.6	18.1		6.3	Mk	10										
1667	7	30								＊Song	Mexico:Puebla	墨西哥:普埃布拉	18.8	－98		6.3	Mk							3				
1667	8	22	1							Japan,Usami	Japan:Hachinohe	日本:青森八户	40.6	141.6		6.4	Ms									1		
1667	11	18								＊Song	Iran:Bojnurd	伊朗:博季努尔德	37.2	57.5		7.7	Mk		12000	5				3				
1667	11	30				2			2	＊NOAA	Turkey:Izmir	土耳其:伊兹密尔	38.4	27.1		6.6	Ms	6										
1667	12	17								＊GSHAP	Azerbaijan:Samaxi	阿塞拜疆:沙马基区	40.6	48.6	12	6.9	Ms	10	80000	5				4		4		
1667										＊Song	Jamaica:Montego Bay	牙买加:蒙特歌湾	18.3	－77.5		5.9	Mk							2				
1667						4	2	1	1	＊NOAA	Japan:Miyako－Jima	日本:宫古岛	25	125.5		6.7	Ms											
1668	1	4								＊GSHAP	Georgia:Kakhetiya	格鲁吉亚:卡赫季州	42	45.4	12	4.9	Ms	7.5						3				
1668	1	14								GSHAP	Azerbaijan:Qebele	阿塞拜疆:盖贝莱区	41	48	40	7.8	Ms	10										
1668	5	2								＊Song	India:Samawani (Samaji)	印度:萨马瓦尼	24	68	10	6.3	Mk							3				
1668	6	14								Japan,Song	Japan:Toyama	日本:富山	36.7	137.1		6.3	Mk									1		
1668	7	10				3			2	＊NOAA	Turkey:Izmir	土耳其:伊兹密尔	38.4	26.9		6.6	Ms	10	17500	5				3				
1668	7	25				3				＊China,NOAA	China:Shandong,Tancheng	中国:山东郯城	34.8	118.5		8.5	Ms	12	42578	5				4		4		
1668	7	31				2		1	1.5	＊Korea,NOAA	North Korea:Sinuiju	朝鲜:新义州	39.7	124.7		5.3	Ms			1				1		1		
1668	8	10								GSHAP	Ecuador:Ibarra	厄瓜多尔:伊瓦拉	0.3	－78.2		5	Ms	6										
1668	8	17								GSHAP	Turkey:Ladik	土耳其:拉迪克	41	36	40	8	Ms	9.5										

年 Year	月 Mo	日 Dy	时 Hr	分 Mn	秒 Sec	海啸 Tsunami 源 Sr	浪高 Wh	级 I mI	级 S mS	资料来源 Information	震中 Earthquake Epicenter 地名(英文) Name(English)	地名(中文) Name(Chinese)	纬度(°) Latitude	经度(°) Longitude	深度 Depth	震级 Mag	标度 Scale	烈度 MMI	死亡人数 Deaths 数量/人 Num	级别 Dd	受伤人数 Injuries 数量/人 Num	级别 Dd	经济损失 Damage 数量/$ Mill $ Mill	级别 De	房屋毁坏 Houses Destroyed 数量/间 Num	级别 Dh	房屋受损 Houses Damaged 数量/间 Num	级别 Dh
1668	8	28	8							Japan, Usami	Japan: Narashino	日本:千叶习志野	35.7	140		5.9	Ms									1		
1668										GSHAP	Russia: Dagestan, Kizlyar	俄罗斯:达吉斯坦共和国基兹利亚尔	44	47	40	6.6	Ms	8										
1669	1	4								*	Azerbaijan: Samaxi	阿塞拜疆:沙马基区	40.6	48.6	5	5.7	Muk	9	7000	4				3				
1669	3	11	11							* Song	Italy: Nicolosi	意大利:尼柯洛西	37.6	15		7.3	Mk	10										
1669	6	4								* Song	Pakistan: Rawalpindi	巴基斯坦:拉瓦尔品第	33.4	73.3		8	Mk	11										
1669	6	29								Japan, Usami	Japan: Nagoya	日本:爱知名古屋	35.2	136.9		5.9	Ms									1		
1670	6	22								Japan	Japan: Niigata	日本:新潟	37.7	139.4		6.4	Ms		13						503	3		
1670	7	17	2							* Italy	Austria: Innsbruck, Schwaz	奥地利:因斯布鲁克,施瓦茨	47.2	11.4		6.57	Ms	9						3				
1670	7	21	3							Japan, Usami	Japan: Kanagawa	日本:神奈川	35.4	139.2		6.4	Ms								100	2		
1670	7									China	China: Yunnan, Lufeng	中国:云南禄丰	25.2	102.2		5.5	Ms	7										
1670	8	1								GSHAP	Turkey: Siirt	土耳其:锡尔特	38	42	20	6.6	Ms	8.5										
1670	8	3								GSHAP	Ukraine: L'Viv	乌克兰:利沃夫	49.9	23.6	8	4.5	Ms	6										
1670	8	19				3		1	1.5	* NOAA	China: South Yellow Sea	中国:南黄海	33	122.5		6.8	Ms			3								
1670	10	30								* GSHAP	South Korea: Kwangju, Sunchang	韩国:光州市,淳昌郡	35.9	126.5		6.3	Muk	8						2				
1670	12	17				4	2	1	1	* NOAA	Japan: Chiba, Near Coast	日本:千叶近海	35.5	141		6.4	Ms											
1670	12									China	China: Shandong, Feixian	中国:山东费县	35.3	118		5	Ms	6										
1670										* Song	Iran: Jahrom, S.	伊朗:贾赫罗姆南部	27.5	53.6		6.3	Mk							3				
1671	1	1								* GSHAP	Azerbaijan: Samaxi	阿塞拜疆:沙马基区	40.6	48.6	5	5.2	Ms	9		3				2				
1671	2	1								GSHAP	Azerbaijan: Samaxi	阿塞拜疆:沙马基区	40.6	48.6	3	4.8	Ms	8										
1671	7	6								Japan, Song	Japan: Tokyo	日本:东京	35.7	139.8		6.5	Mk			1						1		
1671	9									China	China: Shandong, Feixian	中国:山东费县	35.3	118		5	Ms	6										
1671										Japan, Song	Japan: Iwate, Hanamaki	日本:岩手花卷	39.4	141.1		6.3	Mk									1		
1672	2	14				3				GSHAP, NOAA	Greece: Lesbos	希腊:莱斯沃斯	39.9	26		7	Ms											
1672	4	14	15	15		3			3	* Italy, GSHAP, NOAA	Italy: Rimini	意大利:里米尼	43.93	12.58		5.6	Ms	10	1500	4				3				
1672	4					1				* GSHAP, NOAA	Aegean Sea	爱琴海	40	26	14	6.5	Ms	8.5										
1672	7	28								Japan, Song	Japan: Aomori	日本:青森	40.65	140.3		6.3	Mk									1		
1672						1			1	* NOAA, Song	Greece: Thirasia	希腊:锡拉夏岛	36.5	25.5		6.7	Mk	10										
1673	3	29								China	China: Anhui, Hefei	中国:安徽合肥	31.8	117.3		5	Ms	6										
1673	5	9								* Song	Dominica: Santo Domingo	多米尼加:多米尼加	18.3	-69.5		6.3	Mk		5	1				3				
1673	5	20				4				* Song	Indonesia: Maluku Utara	印度尼西亚:北马鲁古	1.375	127.52		7	Mk							1				
1673	6	15								* Song	Iran: Mashhad	伊朗:马什哈德	36.2	59.4		7	Mk		5600	4				3				
1673	7	12				4				* Song	Indonesia: Maluku Islands	印度尼西亚:摩鹿加群岛	-3	128		7	Mk							1				
1673	7	13								Japan, Song	Japan: Tokyo	日本:东京	35.7	139.8		6.5	Mk			1								
1673	7	30								* Iran	Iran: Neyshabur	伊朗:内沙布尔	36.3	59.3		6.6	Muk	7						2				
1673	8	1								*	Iran: Mashhad	伊朗:马什哈德	35.5	59	10	6.2	Muk	9						3				

时间 Date						海啸 Tsunami				资料来源 Information	震中 Earthquake Epicenter				深度 Depth	震级 Mag	标度 Scale	烈度 MMI	死亡人数 Deaths		受伤人数 Injuries		经济损失 Damage		房屋毁坏 Houses Destroyed		房屋受损 Houses Damaged	
年 Year	月 Mo	日 Dy	时 Hr	分 Mn	秒 Sec	源 Sr	浪高 Wh	级 I mI	级 S mS		地名(英文) Name(English)	地名(中文) Name(Chinese)	纬度(°) Latitude	经度(°) Longitude					数量/人 Num	级别 Dd	数量/人 Num	级别 Dd	数量/$ Mill $ Mill	级别 De	数量/间 Num	级别 Dh	数量/间 Num	级别 Dh
1673	8	12				5		1	1	* Song, NOAA	Indonesia: Maluku Utara	印度尼西亚:北马鲁古	1.375	127.52		7	Mk							1				
1673	12	8	8	30						GSHAP, Song	Venezuela: Trujillo	委内瑞拉:特鲁希略	9.33	-70.64		5	Mk	6										
1674	1	1								* GSHAP	Greece: Thesprotia	希腊:塞斯普罗蒂亚	39.5	20		6.5	Ms	10										
1674	1	16	20							GSHAP, Song	Venezuela: Trujillo	委内瑞拉:特鲁希略	9.33	-70.64		6	Mk	7										
1674	2	17	11	30		4	10	2	1.5	* NOAA	Indonesia: Maluku Islands	印度尼西亚:摩鹿加群岛	-3.7	128.2		6.8	Ms		2329	4	35	1		4		3		
1674	4									China	China: Yunnan, Luxi	中国:云南泸西	24.5	103.8		5	Ms	6										
1674	5	6				3		1	1	* NOAA	Indonesia: Maluku Islands	印度尼西亚:摩鹿加群岛	-3.7	128.2		6	Ms											
1674	8	29								*	Ecuador: Chimborazo, Bolivar	厄瓜多尔:钦博拉索山,玻利瓦	-1.7	-79		7.7	Muk	10						3				
1675	3					2			1	* Bautista, NOAA	Philippines: Mindoro Island	菲律宾:民都洛岛	13.2	121.35		6	Ms	8										
1675	6									China	China: Shanxi, Yuncheng, S.	中国:山西运城南	34.8	111.1		5	Ms	6										
1675	8	3								China	China: Shandong, Yanzhou	中国:山东兖州	35.6	116.8		5	Ms	6										
1675										China	China: Henan, Taikang	中国:河南太康	34.1	114.8		5.5	Ms	7										
1676	6	11								China	China: Jiangsu, Yangzhou	中国:江苏扬州	32.4	119.4		4.75	Ms	6										
1676	7	12								* Usami, Japan	Japan: Shimane	日本:岛根	34.5	132		6.6	Ms	8	7	1					133	3		
1676	11					1	2		1	Japan, NOAA, Song	Japan: Hitachiota	日本:茨城常陆太田	36.6	140.5		7	Mk			1				1		1		
1676						1			1	NOAA, Song	Portugal: Azores	葡萄牙:亚速尔群岛	38.733	-27.066		7	Mk											
1677	4	13	10			4	6	2.6	2	* Usami, Japan, NOAA	Japan Trench	日本海沟	40	144		8.1	Ms	9		1				1		1		
1677	9									* China	China: Gansu, Wudu	中国:甘肃武都	33.4	104.9		5.5	Ms	7		3				1				
1677	11	4	8			4	8	3	3	* Usami, Japan, NOAA	Japan: Chiba, Near Coast	日本:千叶近海	35	141.5		7.4	Ms	10	500	3				2	1000	3		
1677	12	7	11	30		2		1	1	* Bautista, NOAA	Philippines: Luzon, Coast SW.	菲律宾:吕宋岛西南海域	14.5	119.5		7.3	Ms		2	1				2				
1677										China	China: Shanxi, Pingding	中国:山西平定	37.7	113.7		5	Ms	7										
1677										GSHAP	Iran: Mashhad	伊朗:马什哈德	36.3	59.6	10	5.8	Ms	8.5										
1677										* Song	Jamaica: Port Royal	牙买加:罗亚尔港	17.6	-76.5		5.9	Mk							2				
1678	1	5	6	30						GSHAP	Ecuador: Quito	厄瓜多尔:基多	-0.22	-78.5		4.3	Ms	5										
1678	2	3								* Iran	Iran: Rudbar, Rasht	伊朗:鲁德巴,拉什特	37.2	50		6.5	Ms							3				
1678	2	11	14							* Song	Cuba: Santiago De Cuba	古巴:圣地亚哥	20	-75.5		6.3	Mk							3				
1678	2	23								* Afghan	Iran: Razavi Khorasan	伊朗:呼罗珊	34.3	58.6	8	6.5	Ms							3				
1678	5	26								China	China: Zhejiang, Haiyan	中国:浙江海盐	30.5	121		4.75	Ms	6										
1678	6	18	1	45		4		2	2.5	* GSHAP, NOAA	Peru: Caraz	秘鲁:卡拉斯	-9	-78	40	8.4	Ms	9		3				3		3		
1678	6									China	China: Hebei, Xuanhua, NW.	中国:河北宣化西北	40.7	115.3		5	Ms	6										
1678	10	2	8							* Usami, Japan	Japan: Miyagi, Near Coast	日本:宫城近海	38.6	142		7.4	Muk	9	1	1				2	20	1		

年 Year	月 Mo	日 Dy	时 Hr	分 Mn	秒 Sec	海啸 Tsunami 源 Sr	浪高 Wh	级 I mI	级 S mS	资料来源 Information	震中 Earthquake Epicenter 地名(英文) Name(English)	地名(中文) Name(Chinese)	纬度(°) Latitude	经度(°) Longitude	深度 Depth	震级 Mag	标度 Scale	烈度 MMI	死亡人数 Deaths 数量/人 Num	级别 Dd	受伤人数 Injuries 数量/人 Num	级别 Dd	经济损失 Damage 数量/$ Mill	级别 De	房屋毁坏 Houses Destroyed 数量/间 Num	级别 Dh	房屋受损 Houses Damaged 数量/间 Num	级别 Dh
1679	6	4								* Iran	Armenia: Yerevan	亚美尼亚:叶里温	40.2	44.6	15	6.2	Muk		7600	4				4				
1679	8	9	1							GSHAP	Romania: Nereju	罗马尼亚:内雷茹	45.7	26.6		7.3	Ms	8										
1679	9	2								* China	China: Hebei, Shanhe – Pinggu	中国:河北三河平谷	40	117		8	Ms	11	13162	5				4		4		
1679	9	21								* Song	Yemen: Mocha	也门:穆哈	13.3	43.3		5.5	Mk							1				
1679	10									China	China: Shanxi, Qingxu	中国:山西清徐	37.6	112.5		5.5	Ms	7										
1679	12	26								* China	China: Jiangsu, Liyang	中国:江苏溧阳	31.4	119.5		5.25	Ms	7		1				1		1		
1680	8	29				4				Japan, NOAA, Song	Japan: Iwata	日本:静冈磐田	34.7	137.85		7	Mk		94	2								
1680	9	9								* China	China: Yunnan, Chuxiong	中国:云南楚雄	25	101.6		6.75	Ms	9	2700	4				3		3		
1680	10	9	7	30		4			3	* NOAA, Song	Spain: Málaga, Off Coast of S.	西班牙:马拉加南部近海	36.5	-4.4		7.7	Mk	9	70	2				3				
1681	1	10				1				GSHAP, NOAA	Greece: Crete Island	希腊:克里特岛	35.4	25.2		6.3	Ms											
1681	3	10				3				* NOAA	Chile: Arica, Near Coast	智利:阿里卡近海	-18.5	-70.4		7.5	Muk	10										
1681	6	12				1				* NOAA, GSHAP	South Korea: Gangneung	韩国:江陵	38	129		7	Ms											
1681	6	26				1				Korea, NOAA	South Korea: Samcheok	韩国:江原道	37.51	129.3		7.3	Ms	10										
1681	8	18								GSHAP	Romania: Nereju	罗马尼亚:内雷茹	45.7	26.6	150	6.7	Ms	8										
1681	12	11				3				NOAA, Song	Indonesia: Southern Sumatra	印度尼西亚:苏门答腊南部	-3.484	100.114		7	Mk											
1681										China	China: Shaanxi, Luochuan	中国:陕西洛川	35.8	109.4		5	Ms	6										
1682	3	19								GSHAP, Korea	South Korea: Okcheon	韩国:沃川郡	37.4	127.4		5.5	Ms	6										
1682	5	12								* Song	France: Remiremont, Fougerolles	法国:勒米尔蒙,富日罗勒	48	6.5		6.5	Mk	9						2				
1682	8					3			3	NOAA, Song	Italy: Bay of Napli	意大利:那不勒斯湾	40.8	14.4		6.7	Mk											
1682	11	14								Japan, Song	Japan: Tsugarau	日本:津轻	40.85	140.45		6.6	Mk							1				
1682	12	13								Japan, Song	Japan: Tsugarau	日本:津轻	40.85	140.45		6.6	Mk							1		1		
1682										* Song	Cuba: Santiago De Cuba	古巴:圣地亚哥	20	-75.5		5.9	Mk							2				
1682										* Song	Mexico: Oaxaca, Mexico City	墨西哥:瓦哈卡,墨西哥城	17	-96.3		6.3	Mk							3				
1683	6	16	23							Usami, Japan	Japan: Utsunomiya	日本:宇都宫市	36.7	139.6		6.4	Ms	7						1				
1683	6	18	2							Usami, Japan	Japan: Utsunomiya	日本:宇都宫市	36.75	139.65		7.3	Ms	8						1				
1683	8	24								Maso, Song	Philippines: Manila	菲律宾:马尼拉	14.6	121		5.5	Mk	7										
1683	10	10								China	China: Guangdong, Fushan	中国:广东佛山	23.1	113		5	Ms	6										
1683	10	20								Usami, Japan	Japan: Utsunomiya	日本:宇都宫市	36.8	139.7		6.8	Ms	7						1				
1683	11	22								* China	China: Shanxi, Yuanping	中国:山西原平	38.7	112.7		7	Ms	9	1001	4				4		4		
1683	11	27								* Song	Iran: Lar	伊朗:拉尔	27.7	54.3		6.3	Mk							3				
1683										* Song	Armenia: Yerevan (Erivan)	亚美尼亚:耶烈万(叶里温)	40.1	44.3		6.3	Mk							3				
1683										Japan, Song	Japan: Satsumasendai	日本:鹿岛萨摩川内	31.8	130.3		6.3	Mk									1		
1684	5	5	0	30						GSHAP, Song	Venezuela: Cumana	委内瑞拉:库马纳	10.47	-64.17		6	Mk	7										

年 Year	月 Mo	日 Dy	时 Hr	分 Mn	秒 Sec	海啸 Tsunami 源 Sr	浪高 Wh	级 I mI	级 S mS	资料来源 Information	震中 Earthquake Epicenter 地名(英文) Name(English)	地名(中文) Name(Chinese)	纬度(°) Latitude	经度(°) Longitude	深度 Depth	震级 Mag	标度 Scale	烈度 MMI	死亡人数 Deaths 数量/人 Num	级别 Dd	受伤人数 Injuries 数量/人 Num	级别 Dd	经济损失 Damage 数量/$ Mill $ Mill	级别 De	房屋毁坏 Houses Destroyed 数量/间 Num	级别 Dh	房屋受损 Houses Damaged 数量/间 Num	级别 Dh
1684										* Song	Dominica:Santo Domingo,Azua	多米尼加:多米尼加,阿苏阿	19	-71		6.3	Mk							3				
1685	11	22	23							GSHAP	Turkey:Solhan	土耳其:索尔汉	39	41	24	6.7	Ms	8.5										
1685	11	22								Japan,Song	Japan:Tokyo	日本:东京	35.7	139.8		6.3	Mk									1		
1685										Japan,Usami,Song	Japan:Handa	日本:爱知半田市	34.9	136.9		6.5	Mk			1						1		
1686	1	4								Japan,Usami,Song	Japan:Yamaguchi	日本:山口	34	132.3		6.8	Mk	8		1						3		
1686	5	12								China	China:Taiwan,Chiayi	中国:台湾嘉义	23.5	120.4		5.5	Ms	7										
1686	5									Japan,Song	Japan:Miyako-Jima	日本:宫古岛	25	125.5		6.3	Mk									1		
1686	10	2	22							Usami,Japan	Japan:Aichi	日本:爱知	34.45	137.4		7	Ms	8		1								
1686										China	China:Ningxia,Tongxin,NE.	中国:宁夏同心东北	37.1	106.5		5.5	Ms	7										
1687	1	28								GSHAP,Song	Peru:Acoria	秘鲁:阿科里亚	-12.582	-74.552	20	6	Mk	7										
1687	2	19	13							* Song	Jamaica:Montego Bay	牙买加:蒙特歌湾	18.3	-77.5		5.9	Mk							2				
1687	2									Maso,Song	Philippines:Mariveles	菲律宾:马里韦莱斯	14.4	120.6		5	Mk	6										
1687	4	1	5							GSHAP,Song	Peru:Lima,Near Coast	秘鲁:利马近海	-12.3	-77.2		5	Mk	6										
1687	4									* Afghan	Iran:Mashhad	伊朗:马什哈德	36.2	59.4		5	Ms							3				
1687	7	12	7			4				* Chile,NOAA	Chile:San Felipe	智利:圣费利佩	-32.8	-70.7		7.5	Ms	8		1				1		1		
1687	10	20	9	15						GSHAP	Peru:Lima,Near Coast	秘鲁:利马近海	-11.35	-78.2	70	6.4	Ms	6										
1687	10	20	10	30		4	8	3	3.5	* NOAA,GSHAP	Peru:Chincha Alta,Near Coast	秘鲁:上钦查近海	-13.5	-76.5	30	8.5	Ms	10	5000	4				3				
1687	11	22								*	Ecuador:Ambato	厄瓜多尔:安巴托	-1.3	-78.6		7.3	Muk	8						2				
1687										GSHAP, Iran	Iran:Mazanderan	伊朗:马赞德兰	36.3	52.6	15	6.5	Ms	9										
1688	1									* Song	Italy:Pisticci	意大利:皮斯提西	40.2	16.3		6.6	Mk	10	2000	4				3				
1688	2	19								* Song	Jamaica:Port Royal	牙买加:罗亚尔港	17.917	-76.867		5.9	Mk							2				
1688	3	1				1				* NOAA,Song	Jamaica:Port Royal	牙买加:罗亚尔港	17.6	-76.5		7	Mk											
1688	4	11	11							* Italy	Italy:Cotignola,Bagnacavallo	意大利:科蒂尼奥拉,巴尼亚卡瓦洛	44.39	11.942		5.88	Ms	10		3				3				
1688	5									* Song	Pakistan:Delta of The Indus	巴基斯坦:印度河的三角洲	24	68		6.3	Mk							3				
1688	6	5	13	15						* Italy	Italy:Benevento	意大利:贝内文托	41.28	14.57		6.72	Ms	11	3311	4				3		3		
1688	6	16								* China	China:Yunnan,Jianchuan	中国:云南剑川	26.5	99.9		6.25	Ms	8	190	3				2		3		
1688	7	5								* Song	Turkey:Izmir	土耳其:伊兹密尔	38.3	27.1		7.7	Mk		15000	5								
1688	7	10	11	45		2			2	* NOAA	Turkey:Izmir	土耳其:伊兹密尔	38.4	26.9		7	Ms	10	16000	5				3		3		3
1688	7	12								GSHAP,Song	Chile:Santiago	智利:圣地亚哥	-33.4	-70.6		6	Mk	8										
1688	10	10	21	30						GSHAP,Song	Peru:Lima	秘鲁:利马	-12.08	-77		5	Mk	6										
1688	11	28								Japan,Song	Japan:Akita	日本:秋田	39.7	140.1		6.3	Mk									1		
1688										*	Russia:Novosibirsk,Tersk	俄罗斯:新西伯利亚州捷尔斯克村	43.7	44.7	15	5.3	Ms	7						2				

时间 Date						海啸 Tsunami				资料来源	震中 Earthquake Epicenter				深度	震级	标度	烈度	死亡人数 Deaths		受伤人数 Injuries		经济损失 Damage		房屋毁坏 Houses Destroyed		房屋受损 Houses Damaged	
年	月	日	时	分	秒	源	浪高	级 I	级 S	Information	地名(英文)	地名(中文)	纬度(°)	经度(°)					数量/人	级别	数量/人	级别	数量/$ Mill	级别	数量/间	级别	数量/间	级别
Year	Mo	Dy	Hr	Mn	Sec	Sr	Wh	mI	mS		Name(English)	Name(Chinese)	Latitude	Longitude	Depth	Mag	Scale	MMI	Num	Dd	Num	Dd	$ Mill	De	Num	Dh	Num	Dh
1689	3									*	Ecuador:Tixan	厄瓜多尔:蒂克桑	-2.2	-78.9	5	6.8	Muk	10										
1689	12	22								* Italy	Germany:Schongau	德国:熊高	47.7	10.9		5.57	Ms	9	19	1								
1689						2	2	1	1.5	NOAA,Song	Japan:Aomori,Near Coast	日本:青森近海	40.9	142.1		7	Mk											
1690	2	3				5			3	NOAA	Italy:Bay of Napli	意大利:那不勒斯湾	40.8	14.4		7.7	Ms											
1690	4	16				4				* NOAA	Antigua And Barbuda:St Kitts	安提瓜和巴布达:圣基茨	17.5	-61.5		7.5	Mk	9		2				3				
1690	7	9								GSHAP,Song	Chile:Santiago	智利:圣地亚哥	-33.4	-70.6		6	Mk	8										
1690	11	20	19	30						GSHAP,Song	Peru:Lima,Near Coast	秘鲁:利马近海	-12.55	-77	40	5	Mk	6										
1690	12	4	15	45						* Italy	Austria:Kaernten	奥地利:克恩顿州	46.633	13.872		6	Ms	10	20	1				3				
1691	5									China	China:Fujian,Xiamen,Near Coast	中国:福建厦门近海	24.6	118.5		4.75	Ms	6										
1691	7	26				1				NOAA,Song	Portugal:Azores	葡萄牙:亚速尔群岛	38.5	-28		7	Mk											
1691	11	10								Japan,Song	Japan:Nagasaki	日本:长崎	32.7	129.9		6.6	Mk							1				
1691										Usami	Japan:Kaga	日本:石川加贺	36.3	136.3		6.2	Ms	8								1		
1691										* Song	Dominica:Azua	多米尼加:阿苏阿	18.3	-70.4		6.3	Mk							3				
1692	6	7				4	1.8			* NOAA	Jamaica:Port Royal	牙买加:罗亚尔港	17.8	-76.7	10	7.7	Ms		3000	4				3				
1692	9	12								China	China:Yunnan,Luxi	中国:云南泸西	24.5	103.8		5.5	Ms	7										
1692	9	13	11							*	Argentina:Salta	阿根廷:萨尔塔	-25.4	-64.8		7	Muk	9						3				
1692										* Song	Armenia:Yerevan(Erivan)	亚美尼亚:耶烈万(叶里温)	40.1	44.3		6.3	Mk							3				
1693	1	11	13	30		5			4	* Italy,NOAA	Italy:Sicily, Calabria, Catania	意大利:西西里岛, 卡拉布里亚,卡塔尼亚	37.13	15.02		7.41	Ms	11	93000	5				4	972	3		
1693	4	25								China	China:Guangdong,Haifeng	中国:广东海丰	23	115.3		4.75	Ms	6										
1693										* Song	Cuba:Havana	古巴:哈瓦那	23.1	-82.4		5.9	Mk							2				
1693										GSHAP	Iraq:Ninawa	伊拉克:尼尼微	36.5	41.9	15	6.7	Ms	9										
1694	5									China	China:Taiwan,Taipei	中国:台湾台北	25	121.5		5.5	Ms	7										
1694	6	18	21							* Usami,Japan	Japan:Akita	日本:秋田	40	139.5		7	Ms	9	394	3				3	2760	4		
1694	9	8	10	45		2			3	* Italy,NOAA	Italy:Calitri	意大利:卡利特里	40.88	15.35		6.87	Ms	10	4057	4				3				
1694	11	21								GSHAP,Song	Peru:Lima	秘鲁:利马	-12.08	-77.2		4.5	Mk	5										
1694	12	12								Usami,Japan	Japan:Tango	日本:丹後	33.2	138.7		6.1	Ms									1		
1695	2	25	5	30						* Italy	Italy:Asolo	意大利:阿索洛	45.8	11.95		6.61	Muk	10						4				
1695	5	11	24							Iran,GSHAP	Iran:Sabzevar	伊朗:萨卜泽瓦尔	36.8	57	15	7	Ms	9.5										
1695	5	18								* China	China:Shanxi,Linfen	中国:山西临汾	36	111.5		7.75	Ms	10	20000	5				4		4		
1695	6	11	2	30						* Italy,GSHAP	Italy:Bagnoregio	意大利:巴尼奥雷焦	42.612	12.11		5.77	Ms	10	31	1				2				
1696	4	14								* Iran	Turkey:Caldiran	土耳其:恰尔德兰	39.1	43.9		7	Ms							2				
1696	6	1								Usami,Japan,Song	Japan:South Honshu Ridge	日本:本州南部海岭	31.448	140.036		6.6	Mk							1				
1696	7	7								China	China:Yunnan,Kunming	中国:云南昆明	25	102.8		5.75	Ms	7										
1696	7	14	9							GSHAP	Peru:Lima,Near Coast	秘鲁:利马近海	-12.8	-77.7	20	6.7	Ms	6										
1696	9	4								* GSHAP	Greece:Zakynthos	希腊:扎金索斯岛	37.8	21		6.5	Mk	10										

时间 年 Year	月 Mo	日 Dy	时 Hr	分 Mn	秒 Sec	海啸 Tsunami 源 Sr	浪高 Wh	级 I mI	级 S mS	资料来源 Information	震中 Earthquake Epicenter 地名(英文) Name(English)	地名(中文) Name(Chinese)	纬度(°) Latitude	经度(°) Longitude	深度 Depth	震级 Mag	标度 Scale	烈度 MMI	死亡人数 Deaths 数量/人 Num	级别 Dd	受伤人数 Injuries 数量/人 Num	级别 Dd	经济损失 Damage 数量/$ Mill $ Mill	级别 De	房屋毁坏 Houses Destroyed 数量/间 Num	级别 Dh	房屋受损 Houses Damaged 数量/间 Num	级别 Dh
1696	11	25				1		1	2	Japan, NOAA, Song	Japan: Ishinomaki	日本:宫城石卷	38.4	141.3		7.5	Mk			1				1				
1696										GSHAP	Colombia: Narino	哥伦比亚:纳里尼奥	1.2	-77.2		6.3	Ms	8										
1697	2	25								*	Mexico: Mexico City, Acapulco	墨西哥:墨西哥城,阿卡普尔科	16.7	-99.2		7.8	Muk							3				
1697	9	29	13	30						GSHAP	Peru: Lima, Near Coast	秘鲁:利马近海	-12.3	-77.4	30	7.3	Ms	6										
1697	11	25	3							Usami, Japan	Japan: Kanagawa	日本:神奈川	35.5	139.6		6.9	Ms	8								1		
1698	5	14	10			2			3	NOAA, Song	Italy: Bay of Naples	意大利:那不勒斯湾	40.7	14.15		6.7	Mk											
1698	6	20	6							* GSHAP	Ecuador: Chimborazo, N.	厄瓜多尔:钦博腊索山北部	-1.7	-78.6		7.7	Muk	10		3								
1698	6	28	11							GSHAP	Ecuador: Napo	厄瓜多尔:纳波	-1	-78.3		5.7	Ms	7										
1698	7	19								* Song	Ecuador: Ambato	厄瓜多尔:安巴托	-1.3	-78.7		6.3	Mk		1000	3				3				
1698	10	24								Japan	Japan: Oita	日本:大分	33.1	131.5		6	Ms									1		
1698	10	31	6							Usami, Japan, Song	Japan: Miyazaki, Near Coast	日本:宫崎近海	32.034	131.837		6.3	Mk									1		
1698	12	22				4				* Japan, NOAA	Japan: Osaka	日本:大阪	33.3	131.7		6	Ms											
1698										China	China: Liaoning, Yixian	中国:辽宁义县	41.5	121.2		5	Ms	6										
1699	1					2			4	NOAA, Song	Italy: Catania	意大利:卡塔尼亚	37.15	15.1		6.7	Mk											
1699	2	11								* GSHAP, Italy	Slovenia: Novo Mesto	斯洛文尼亚:新梅斯托	45.6	15.3	14	6.1	Muk	8.5		2				3				
1699	7	14	9							*	Peru: Lima, Near Coast	秘鲁:利马近海	-11.8	-77.5	40	7.8	Muk	7						3				
1699										China	China: Gansu, Gaotai, NW.	中国:甘肃高台西北	39.8	99.5		4.75	Ms	6										
1699										* Maso, Song	Philippines: Mariveles	菲律宾:马里韦莱斯	14.4	120.6		6.3	Mk	7						3				
1699						4				Japan, NOAA, Song	Japan: Nagasaki	日本:长崎	32.7	129.7		7	Mk							1				
1700	1	26				4				NOAA	US: Near Coast of W. Oregon	美国:俄勒冈州西部近海	45	-125		9	Ms			1				3				
1700	1	27				4				Japan, Song	Japan: Kumano	日本:三重熊野	34	136		7	Mk											
1700	4	1				2		2.5	2	Japan, NOAA, Song	Japan: Nagasaki	日本:长崎	32.7	129.7		7.5	Mk		1000	3				2	300	3		
1700	4	16				2	6			* Japan, NOAA	Japan: Tsushima	日本:长崎对马	34.3	129.3		7	Ms		1000	3				3		3		
1700	4	29								GSHAP, Korea	South Korea: Jinju	韩国:金州	35.1	128.1		5.3	Ms	7										
1700	8	2	21							GSHAP	Peru: Cuzco	秘鲁:库斯科	-13.9	-72.1	10	4.1	Ms	5										
1700	9	12				4			1	* NOAA	South Korea: Boryeong	韩国:保宁市	36.5	126.5		6.5	Ms											
1701	6	12								GSHAP	Romania: Nereju	罗马尼亚:内雷茹	45.7	26.6	150	7.1	Ms	8										
1701	11	9								* Song	Haiti: Leogane, Petit Goave	海地:利欧干,佩蒂特,高维	18.3	-72.4		5.9	Mk							2				
1701	12	21								* Song	Mexico: Oaxaca	墨西哥:瓦哈卡	16.5	-97		6.3	Mk							3				
1701										China	China: Yunnan, Fumin	中国:云南富民	25.2	102.5		5.5	Ms	7										
1702	3	14								* Italy	Italy: Benevento	意大利:贝内文托	41.12	14.98		6.32	Ms	10	150	3				2				

时间						海啸				资料来源	震中				深度	震级	标度	烈度	死亡人数		受伤人数		经济损失		房屋毁坏		房屋受损	
年	月	日	时	分	秒	源	浪高	级 I	级 S		地名(英文)	地名(中文)	纬度(°)	经度(°)					数量/人	级别	数量/人	级别	数量/$ Mill	级别	数量/间	级别	数量/间	级别
Date						Tsunami				Information	Earthquake Epicenter				Depth	Mag	Scale	MMI	Deaths		Injuries		Damage		Houses Destroyed		Houses Damaged	
Year	Mo	Dy	Hr	Mn	Sec	Sr	Wh	mI	mS		Name(English)	Name(Chinese)	Latitude	Longitude					Num	Dd	Num	Dd	$ Mill	De	Num	Dh	Num	Dh
1702	9									* Song	Martinique Island	马提尼克岛(拉丁美洲)	14.4	-61		5.9	Mk							2				
1703	1	14	18							* Italy,GSHAP	Italy:Norcia,L'Aquila	意大利:诺尔恰,拉奎拉	42.68	13.12		6.81	Ms	11	40000	5				4				
1703	1	16	14							* * GSHAP	Italy:Norcia,Montereale	意大利:诺尔恰,蒙特利勒	42.5	13.2		5.1	Ms	11										
1703	2	2	1			2			3	* Italy,GSHAP,NOAA	Italy:L'Aquila (Aquila)	意大利:拉奎拉(阿奎拉)	42.3	13.4		6.65	Ms	11	5000	4				3				
1703	3									GSHAP	Ecuador:Cotopaxi	厄瓜多尔:科托帕希	-0.9	-78.65		5.7	Ms	7										
1703	5	17								* Song	Iran:Qeshm Island	伊朗:格什姆岛	26.6	56.2		6.3	Mk							3				
1703	6	22								Japan,Song	Japan:Saga	日本:佐贺	33.3	130.2		6.6	Mk							1				
1703	7	1				2			3	NOAA,Song	Ligurian Sea	利古里亚海	44.2	8.8		6.7	Mk											
1703	12	30	17			4	11	4	3	* Usami,NOAA	Japan:Chiba	日本:千叶	35	140		8.2	Ms	11	5233	4				4	20162	5		
1703	12	31								Japan	Japan:Oita	日本:大分	33.3	131.4		6.5	Ms			1					800	3		
1703										China	China:Xizang (Tibet),Shannan	中国:西藏山南	29	91.6		5	Ms	6										
1703										GSHAP,Song	Venezuela:Caracas	委内瑞拉:加拉加斯	10.5	-66.92		5	Mk	6										
1703										* Iran	Iran:Hengam Island	伊朗:亨加姆岛	26.6	54.9		6.8	Ms							3				
1704	1					2	2	1	1	Japan,NOAA,Song	Japan:Tokyo	日本:东京	35.65	139.7		7	Mk											
1704	5	27	3							* Usami	Japan:Aomori,Near Coast	日本:青森近海	41	139.5		6.8	Ms	9	98	2				3	1500	4		
1704	9	18								* China	China:Hebei,Botou	中国:河北泊头	38.1	116.7		5.5	Ms	7		3				2		2		
1704	9	28								* China	China:Shaanxi,Longxian	中国:陕西陇县	34.9	107		6	Ms	8		4				3		3		
1704	11	11								* Song	Greece:Leukas (Ionian Islands)	希腊:琉卡斯(伊奥尼亚群岛)	38.8	20.8		7	Mk	10										
1704										GSHAP	Bulgaria:Sofia	保加利亚:索菲亚	42.8	24	14	6.1	Ms	8.5										
1704						2	2	1	1	Japan,NOAA,Song	Japan:Kumano	日本:三重熊野	34	136		7	Mk							1	30	1		
1705	1	27								GSHAP	Turkey:Mus	土耳其:穆什	38.7	41.7	13	6.7	Ms	9.5										
1705	5	24								Japan,Song	Japan:Oita	日本:大分	33	131.2		6.5	Mk		36	1								
1705	11	26				1	8	3	3	* NOAA,Song	Chile:Arica	智利:阿里卡	-18.6	-70.2		7.7	Mk							2				
1706	1	19								Japan	Japan:Syonai	日本:山形县汤殿山	38.6	139.9		5.8	Ms									1		
1706	4	20								* Iceland	Iceland:Selfoss	冰岛:塞尔福斯	64	-21.2		6	Ms	10						3				
1706	6	6								Japan,Song	Japan:Kumamoto	日本:熊本	32.8	130.7		6.5	Mk			1						1		
1706	10	21	13							Usami	Japan:Tokyo Bay	日本:东京湾	35.6	139.8		6.6	Ms									1		
1706	11	3	14							* Italy,GSHAP	Italy:Abruzzi	意大利:阿布鲁佐	42.08	14.08		6.6	Ms	10	1000	3				3				
1706										Usami,Japan,Song	Japan:South Honshu Ridge	日本:本州南部海岭	31.448	140.036		6.5	Mk			1						1		
1707	7	7				4				Japan,NOAA,Song	Japan:Ise Bay	日本:伊势湾	35	136.8		7	Mk											

时间						海啸				资料来源	震中				深度	震级	标度	烈度	死亡人数		受伤人数		经济损失		房屋毁坏		房屋受损	
年	月	日	时	分	秒	源	浪高	级I	级S		地名(英文)	地名(中文)	纬度(°)	经度(°)					数量/人	级别	数量/人	级别	数量/$ Mill	级别	数量/间	级别	数量/间	级别
Date						Tsunami				Information	Earthquake Epicenter				Depth	Mag	Scale	MMI	Deaths		Injuries		Damage		Houses Destroyed		Houses Damaged	
Year	Mo	Dy	Hr	Mn	Sec	Sr	Wh	mI	mS		Name(English)	Name(Chinese)	Latitude	Longitude					Num	Dd	Num	Dd	$ Mill	De	Num	Dh	Num	Dh
1707	7	20	17			3			3	NOAA, Song	Italy: Bay of Napli	意大利:那不勒斯湾	40.8	14.4		6.7	Mk											
1707	9	17	16	48						*	Peru: Cuzco	秘鲁:库斯科	-13	-72	10	5.8	Muk	10	160	3								
1707	9	18	13							GSHAP	Peru: Cuzco	秘鲁:库斯科	-13.9	-72.1	10	4.3	Ms	5										
1707	9	27								Japan, Song	Japan: Nagano	日本:长野	36.6	138.2		6.7	Mk								80	2		
1707	10	28	5			5	26	3.5	4	* Usami, Japan, NOAA	Japan: Tokushima, Near Coast	日本:德岛近海	33.2	134.8		8.4	Muk	11	30000	5				4	29000	5		
1707										* Song	El Salvador: San Vicente	萨尔瓦多:圣维森特	13.7	-88.7		7.1	Mk			3				4				
1707										* Song	Turkey: Kars	土耳其:卡尔斯	40.4	43		6.3	Mk	7		3				3				
1708	2	13				4	2	1	1	* Japan, NOAA	Japan: Shima	日本:三重志摩	34.3	137		6.8	Ms									1		
1708	8	14								* Song	France: Manosque	法国:马诺斯克	43.8	5.8		6.5	Mk	9						2				
1708	10	26								China	China: Hebei, Yongnian, SE.	中国:河北永年东南	36.7	114.7		5.5	Ms	7								4		
1708	11	28				4		2	2	* NOAA, Song	Indonesia: Maluku Islands	印度尼西亚:摩鹿加群岛	-3	128		7.5	Mk											
1709	4	15								GSHAP, Song	Peru: Lima	秘鲁:利马	-12	-77		4.5	Mk	5										
1709	4	20								GSHAP, Song	Peru: Lima	秘鲁:利马	-12	-77		4.5	Mk	5										
1709	5	26	7							GSHAP, Song	Peru: Lima, Near Coast	秘鲁:利马近海	-12.7	-77.4		4.5	Mk	5										
1709	5	26	15							GSHAP, Song	Peru: Lima, Near Coast	秘鲁:利马近海	-12.2	-77.8		4.5	Mk	5										
1709	6	3								GSHAP, Song	Peru: Lima	秘鲁:利马	-12	-77		4.5	Mk	5										
1709	7	9	12							GSHAP, Song	Peru: Lima, Near Coast	秘鲁:利马近海	-11.2	-78.7		4.5	Mk	5										
1709	10	14								* China	China: Ningxia, Zhongwei	中国:宁夏中卫	37.4	105.3		7.5	Ms	10	2032	4				4		4		
1709	10	21	9							GSHAP, Song	Peru: Lima	秘鲁:利马	-12	-77		4.5	Mk	5										
1709	12	20	10							GSHAP	Peru: Lima, Near Coast	秘鲁:利马近海	-12.3	-77.3	60	6.3	Ms	6										
1709	12	23	15							GSHAP, Song	Peru: Lima	秘鲁:利马	-12	-77		5	Mk	6										
1709	12	30	10							GSHAP, Song	Peru: Lima	秘鲁:利马	-12	-77		4.5	Mk	5										
1710	3	6				4		1	1.5	* NOAA, Song	Indonesia: Banda Sea	印度尼西亚:班达海	-4.3	129.6		7	Mk											
1710	4	16								* China	China: Hunan, Xinhua	中国:湖南新化	27.8	111.3		5.5	Ms	7						2		3		
1710	8	28								Japan, Song	Japan: Fukushima	日本:福岛	37.7	139.8		6.3	Mk									1		
1710	9	13	9							Usami, Japan	Japan: Fukushima, Near Coast	日本:福岛近海	37	141.5		6.4	Ms									1		
1710	9	15								Japan, Song	Japan: Fukushima	日本:福岛	37.3	139.8		6.3	Mk									1		
1710	10	3	4							Usami, Japan	Japan: Tottori	日本:鸟取	35.4	133.7		6.6	Ms	8	75	3					1092	4		
1710	11	21								Japan, Song	Japan: Yamaguchi	日本:山口	34.2	131.7		6.5	Mk		3	1	15	1			289	3		
1711	3	19	14							* Usami	Japan: Tottori	日本:鸟取	35.5	133.7		6.6	Ms	8	4	1				2	500	3		
1711	8	16								* Song	Mexico: Colima, Mexico City	墨西哥:科利马,墨西哥城	19.1	-103.4		6.3	Mk							3				
1711	9	5				4		1	1.5	* NOAA	Indonesia: Banda Sea	印度尼西亚:班达海	-4	129		7	Ms											
1711	9	16								* Song	Mexico: Colima	墨西哥:科利马	19.1	-103.5		5.8	Mk			1								
1711	10	6								* Song	France: Moncontour, Loudun	法国:蒙孔图尔,卢丹	47	0.1		6.3	Mk	8						3				
1711	10	11	0	30						GSHAP	Romania: Nereju	罗马尼亚:内雷茹	45.7	26.6	150	6.4	Ms	7										

时间 年 Date Year	月 Mo	日 Dy	时 Hr	分 Mn	秒 Sec	海啸 源 Tsunami Sr	浪高 Wh	级 I mI	级 S mS	资料来源 Information	震中 地名(英文) Earthquake Epicenter Name(English)	地名(中文) Name(Chinese)	纬度(°) Latitude	经度(°) Longitude	深度 Depth	震级 Mag	标度 Scale	烈度 MMI	死亡人数 数量/人 Deaths Num	级别 Dd	受伤人数 数量/人 Injuries Num	级别 Dd	经济损失 数量/$ Mill Damage $ Mill	级别 De	房屋毁坏 数量/间 Houses Destroyed Num	级别 Dh	房屋受损 数量/间 Houses Damaged Num	级别 Dh
1711	10	22								China	China:Taiwan,Tainan,Coast of W.	中国:台湾台南西部海域	23.2	120		6.5	Ms	8								3		
1711	12	20	5			4	2	1	1	* Usami,NOAA	Japan:Kagawa	日本:香川	34.3	134		6.7	Ms	8	1000	3				3	1713	4		
1712	5	28								Japan	Japan:Hachinohe	日本:青森八户	40.5	141.5		5.5	Ms									1		
1713	2	26								* China	China:Yunnan,Xundian	中国:云南寻甸	25.6	103.3		6.75	Ms	9	2100	4				4		4		
1713	5	8								GSHAP,Song	Peru:Lima	秘鲁:利马	-12	-77		4.5	Mk	5										
1713	9	4								* China	China:Sichuan,Maoxian,Diexi	中国:四川茂县叠溪	32	103.7		7	Ms	9		3				1		1		
1714	4	28	12							* Usami	Japan:Nagano	日本:长野	36.5	138		6.4	Ms	7	100	2				1	900	3		
1714	5	5								* Song	Mexico:Oaxaca	墨西哥:瓦哈卡	17	-96.3		6.3	Mk							3				
1714	7	27								* GSHAP	Greece:Patrai	希腊:帕特雷	38.2	21.8		6.3	Ms	10										
1714	8	28								* GSHAP	Greece:Nisia Ionioy	希腊:伊奥尼亚群岛	38	20.5		6.4	Ms	10										
1714										GSHAP	Afghan:Qonduz	阿富汗:昆都士	36.5	69	20	6.4	Ms	8										
1714						4				Japan,Song	Japan:Ishigaki - Jima	日本:石垣岛	24.3	124.2		7	Mk			1						1		
1715	2	1								Usami,Japan	Japan:Tarui	日本:岐阜垂井	35.4	136.6		6.2	Ms									1		
1715	3	8								* Iran	Turkey:Gürpinar	土耳其:居尔珀纳尔	38.4	43.9		6.6	Ms			3				3		3		3
1715	8	23				3				* NOAA	Chile:Arica	智利:阿里卡	-18.5	-70.3	80	7.5	Ms	7		1				1		1		
1715	10	11								China	China:Taiwan,Chiayi	中国:台湾嘉义	23.5	120.4		5.5	Ms	7								3		
1715	12	29				4				* NOAA	Japan:Oita	日本:大分	33.3	131.7		6.6	Ms											
1715										* Song	Turkey:Van	土耳其:凡城	38.3	43.2		5.9	Mk							2				
1716	2	3								* Song	Algeria:Algiers	阿尔及利亚:阿尔及尔	36.8	3		5.5	Mk							1				
1716	2	6								*	Peru:Torata	秘鲁:塔克纳	-17.2	-71.2	40	8.8	Muk	9		3				1				
1716	2	11	1							*	Peru:North Ica	秘鲁:伊卡北部	-13.7	-76	50	8.6	Muk	10										
1716	2	16								* Song	Mexico:Baja California	墨西哥:下加利福尼亚	29	-114		6.3	Mk							3				
1716	5									* Song	Algeria:Algiers	阿尔及利亚:阿尔及尔	36.8	3		7.7	Mk		20000	5				4				
1716	9	24				5				* Maso,Song,NOAA	Philippines: Taal, Manila,Rizal	菲律宾:塔尔,马尼拉,黎萨	13.6	121.1		7.7	Mk	7						3		3		
1716						4				Japan,NOAA,Song	Japan:Iwate	日本:岩手	39.2	141.2		7	Mk											
1716										* GSHAP	China:Xinjiang,Aksu	中国:新疆阿克苏	41.2	80.3	30	7.5	Ms	9						3				
1717	5	13								* Usami	Japan:Iwate,Near Coast	日本:岩手近海	39	142.7		7.6	Muk	10								1		
1717	7	28								* GSHAP	Croatia:Zadar	克罗地亚:扎达尔	44.1	15.2		5.7	Ms	10										
1717										* Song	Puerto Rico:Arecibo	波多黎各:阿雷西波	18.3	-66.4		6.3	Mk							3				
1718	2	26								Usami	Japan:Aomori,Hachinohe	日本:青森,八户	40.7	142		6.2	Ms									1		
1718	6	19								* China	China:Gansu,Tongwei,S.	中国:甘肃通渭南	35	105.2		7.5	Ms	10	73000	5				4		4		
1718	8	3	11							GSHAP,Song	Peru:Cusco	秘鲁:库斯科	-13.55	-71.52		5	Mk	6										
1718	8	22	4							Usami,Japan	Japan:Iida	日本:长野饭田	35.3	137.9		6.4	Ms	8	50						350	3		
1718	9	20	11							GSHAP,Song	Peru:Cusco	秘鲁:库斯科	-13.55	-71.52		4.5	Mk	5										
1718	9	20	15							GSHAP,Song	Peru:Cusco	秘鲁:库斯科	-13.55	-71.52		4.5	Mk	5										
1718	9	30								Japan	Japan:Narashino	日本:千叶习志野	35.7	140		7	Ms							2				

年 Year	月 Mo	日 Dy	时 Hr	分 Mn	秒 Sec	海啸 Tsunami 源 Sr	浪高 Wh	级 I mI	级 S mS	资料来源 Information	震中 Earthquake Epicenter 地名(英文) Name(English)	地名(中文) Name(Chinese)	纬度(°) Latitude	经度(°) Longitude	深度 Depth	震级 Mag	标度 Scale	烈度 MMI	死亡人数 Deaths 数量/人 Num	级别 Dd	受伤人数 Injuries 数量/人 Num	级别 Dd	经济损失 Damage 数量/$ Mill $ Mill	级别 De	房屋毁坏 Houses Destroyed 数量/间 Num	级别 Dh	房屋受损 Houses Damaged 数量/间 Num	级别 Dh
1718	10	5								Usami, Japan	Japan: Iiyama	日本:长野饭山	36.9	138.4		6.2	Ms											1
1718	12	10								GSHAP	Cyprus: Nicosia	塞浦路斯:尼科西亚	35.2	33.2	13	6	Ms	8.5										
1719	3									GSHAP	Syria: Aleppo	叙利亚:阿勒颇	36.5	36.9	20	6.4	Ms	8										
1719	4	14	1							GSHAP, Song	Peru: Cusco	秘鲁:库斯科	-13.55	-71.52		4.5	Mk	5										
1719	5	25	12							* GSHAP	Turkey: Gebze	土耳其:盖布泽	40.8	29.4	14	6.1	Ms	10										
1719	6	17								GSHAP, Song	Peru: Huancavelica	秘鲁:万卡韦利卡	-13.2	-74.4	20	5	Mk	6										
1719	11	22	10							GSHAP, Song	Peru: Cusco	秘鲁:库斯科	-13.55	-71.52		4.5	Mk	5										
1719										* Song	El Salvador: San Vicente	萨尔瓦多:圣维森特	13.7	-88.7		7.1	Mk			3				4				
1719										* Song	Morocco: Marrakech	摩洛哥:马拉客什	31.4	-8		6.3	Mk							3				
1720	4	22	3							GSHAP, Song	Peru: Cusco	秘鲁:库斯科	-13.55	-71.52		5	Mk	6										
1720	7	12								* China	China: Hebei, Shacheng	中国:河北沙城	40.4	115.5		6.75	Ms	9		3				2		2		
1720	7	15								* India	India: Delhi	印度:德里	29	77.5		7.5	Ms			3				2				
1720	8	12								* Song	Azores: Sao Miguel (San Miguel)	亚速尔群岛:圣米格尔	38.218	-26.635		7.3	Mk	10										
1720	10	31								* China	China: Taiwan, Tainan	中国:台湾台南	23.1	120.3		6.75	Ms	9		3				1		1		
1720	12	8								* Song	North Atlantic Ocean, Azores Islands	北大西洋:亚速尔群岛	38.2	-26.6		7.3	Mk	10										
1720	12	20	4	30						* Italy	Switzerland: Teufen	瑞士:托伊芬	47.4	9.5		5.57	Ms	8						3				
1721	1	5								*	China: Taiwan, Tainan	中国:台湾台南	23	120.3		6	Ms	8		3				3		3		
1721	1	12								* Italy, GSHAP	Croatia: Rijeka	克罗地亚:里耶卡	45.3	14.4		6	Ms	10										
1721	1	14	11							* Bautista	Philippines: Aparri	菲律宾:阿帕里	18.65	121.7		6.9	Ms							2				
1721	3	24				1				NOAA, Song	Spain: Balearic Islands	西班牙:巴利阿里群岛	39.5	2.85		6.6	Mk											
1721	4	26	3							* GSHAP	Iran: Tabriz	伊朗:大不里士	37.9	46.7	15	7.7	Ms		40000	5				4		4		
1721	9					1				* China, NOAA	China: Taiwan, Tainan	中国:台湾台南	23	120.2		6	Ms	8	2000	4				4		4		
1722	2									China	China: Yunnan, Eshan	中国:云南峨山	24.2	102.4		5	Ms	6										
1722	5	22								* Song	Greece: Athens	希腊:雅典	38	23.4		6.3	Mk	9		3				3				
1722	8	15								GSHAP	Russia: Dagestan, Derbent	俄罗斯:达吉斯坦共和国的杰尔宾特	42	48.1	20	4.6	Ms	5.5										
1722	9	24				4				Usami, NOAA, Song	Japan: Gifu	日本:岐阜	35.5	137		7	Mk			1						1		
1722	10					1				* NOAA, Song	Indonesia: Jakarta	印度尼西亚:雅加达	-6.174	106.829		7	Mk											
1722	12	27	16	30		1				* NOAA, Song	Portugal: Tavira, Algarve	葡萄牙:塔维拉,阿尔加维	37.2	-7.6		7.9	Mk	10		3				2	27	1		
1722										China	China: Sichuan, Batang	中国:四川巴塘	30	99.1		6	Ms	8										
1723	2	21	3			2			3	* NOAA	Greece: Nisia Ionioy	希腊:伊奥尼亚群岛	38.5	20.5		7	Ms	10										
1723	3	28				2			3	NOAA, Song	Italy: Bay of Napli	意大利:那不勒斯湾	40.8	14.4		6.7	Mk											
1723	11	11	3							GSHAP, Song	Peru: Cuzco	秘鲁:库斯科	-13.5	-72		4.5	Mk	5										
1723	12	18								Usami, Japan	Japan: Fukuoka, W.	日本:福冈西部	33.2	130.4		6.2	Ms		2	1	25	1				1		
1724	3	24								GSHAP, Song	Chile: Santiago	智利:圣地亚哥	-33.4	-70.6		6	Mk	8										
1724	11									GSHAP	Colombia: Chita	哥伦比亚:奇塔	6.19	-72.48		7.7	Ms	10										

时间 年 Year	月 Mo	日 Dy	时 Hr	分 Mn	秒 Sec	海啸 Tsunami 源 Sr	浪高 Wh	级 I mI	级 S mS	资料来源 Information	震中 Earthquake Epicenter 地名(英文) Name(English)	地名(中文) Name(Chinese)	纬度(°) Latitude	经度(°) Longitude	深度 Depth	震级 Mag	标度 Scale	烈度 MMI	死亡人数 Deaths 数量/人 Num	级别 Dd	受伤人数 Injuries 数量/人 Num	级别 Dd	经济损失 Damage 数量/$ Mill $ Mill	级别 De	房屋毁坏 Houses Destroyed 数量/间 Num	级别 Dh	房屋受损 Houses Damaged 数量/间 Num	级别 Dh
1724										China	China:Hebei,Huailai	中国:河北怀来	40.5	115.3		5	Ms	6										
1725	1	7	4	25						* GSHAP	Peru:Trujillo,Ancash	秘鲁:特鲁希略,安卡什	-9	-79	60	7.7	Ms	9	1500	4				3		3		
1725	1	8	13							*	Peru:Moquegua	秘鲁:莫克瓜	-16.4	-70.8	3	7.6	Ms	7						1				1
1725	1	8								* China	China:Yunnan,Yiliang	中国:云南宜良	25.1	103.1		6.75	Ms	9	614	3	184	3		3		3		
1725	2	1	11							*	Russia:Chita,Novaya Chara	俄罗斯:赤塔州诺瓦亚恰拉村镇	56.5	118.5	50	8.2	Muk	11										
1725	2	4	6							GSHAP,Song	Peru:Lima	秘鲁:利马	-12	-77		4.5	Mk	5										
1725	2									GSHAP	Ecuador:Cotopaxi	厄瓜多尔:科托帕希	-0.8	-78.9		4.3	Ms	5										
1725	3	27				2	2	1	1.5	* NOAA,Song	Peru:Camana	秘鲁:卡马纳	-16.6	-72.7	50	7.1	Mk	7						2				
1725	5	29	5			4				Usami	Japan:Utsunomiya	日本:宇都宫市	36.75	139.6		6.6	Ms	7										1
1725	6	17								Usami,Japan	Japan:Kaga	日本:石川加贺	36.4	136.4		5.9	Ms											1
1725	7	1	3							GSHAP,Song	Peru:Lima	秘鲁:利马	-12	-77		4.5	Mk	5										
1725	8	1								* China	China:Sichuan,Garze	中国:四川甘孜	30	101.9		7	Ms	9		4				2				
1725	8	14	4							Usami,Japan	Japan:Ina	日本:长野伊那	35.8	138.1		6.1	Ms		4	1	8	1			1000	3		
1725	10	31								Japan,Song	Japan:Nagasaki	日本:长崎	32.7	129.7		6.1	Mk											1
1725	11	8								Usami,Japan	Japan:Saikai	日本:长崎西海	33	129.8		6.2	Ms											1
1725										GSHAP	Russia:Buryatiya,Tonnel'nyy	俄罗斯:布里亚特州通涅利内城	56.27	113.45	15	6.6	Ms	9										
1726	4	1				4	2	1	1	* NOAA	Japan:Fukui,Near Coast	日本:福井近海	36.3	136		6.6	Ms											
1726	4	15								GSHAP	Turkey:Hatay	土耳其:哈塔伊	36.3	36.6	15	6.1	Ms	8										
1726	4	20								Japan,Song	Japan:Fukui	日本:福井	35.9	136.2		7	Mk		170	3					150	3		
1726	9	1	4	5		2			3	* Italy,NOAA	Italy:Sicily,Palermo	意大利:西西里岛,巴勒莫	38.12	13.35		5.61	Ms	9	6000	4				3	1614	4		
1726						2				NOAA,Song	Venezuela:Araya	委内瑞拉:阿拉亚	10.633	-64.3		7	Mk											
1727	3	10								* Song	Mexico:Mexico City,Oaxaca	墨西哥:墨西哥城,瓦哈卡	19.2	-99.1		6.3	Mk							3				
1727	6	20								* Korea	North Korea:Yonghung	朝鲜:永兴	39.5	127.3		6	Muk	8						2				
1727	7	4				2			3	Italy,NOAA	Italy:Sicilia Island	意大利:西西里岛	37.5	13		5.17	Ms											
1727	11	7								* Song	Martinique Island	马提尼克岛(拉丁美洲)	14.4	-61		5.9	Mk							2				
1727	11	10	3	40						USGS,Song	US:Massachusetts,Newburyport	美国:马萨诸塞州纽伯里波特	42.8	-70.8		5.7	Mk	7										
1727	11	18								* Song	Iran:Tabriz	伊朗:大不里士	38	46.2		7.7	Mk	8	77000	5				4				
1728	3	7								Japan,Song	Japan:Hachinohe	日本:青森八户	40.5	141.5		6.1	Mk											1
1728	10									GSHAP	Ecuador:Napo	厄瓜多尔:纳波	-0.5	-78.2		5	Ms	6										
1728	11	28								* Maso,Song	Philippines:Luzon,Manila	菲律宾:吕宋岛马尼拉	14.4	121		6.5	Mk	9						2				
1729	3	8	2							Usami,Japan,Song	Japan:Mie,Near Coast	日本:三重近海	33.513	137.835		6.3	Mk									1		
1729	8	1	4							* Usami,Japan	Japan:Noto	日本:能登岛	37.5	137		6.9	Ms	8	5	1				2	835	3		

时间						海啸				资料来源	震中				深度	震级	标度	烈度	死亡人数		受伤人数		经济损失		房屋毁坏		房屋受损	
年	月	日	时	分	秒	源	浪高	级 I	级 S		地名(英文)	地名(中文)	纬度(°)	经度(°)					数量/人	级别	数量/人	级别	数量/$ Mill	级别	数量/间	级别	数量/间	级别
Date						Tsunami				Information	Earthquake Epicenter				Depth	Mag	Scale	MMI	Deaths		Injuries		Damage		Houses Destroyed		Houses Damaged	
Year	Mo	Dy	Hr	Mn	Sec	Sr	Wh	mI	mS		Name(English)	Name(Chinese)	Latitude	Longitude					Num	Dd	Num	Dd	$ Mill	De	Num	Dh	Num	Dh
1729	8	10								China	China:Yunnan,Dali	中国:云南大理	25.6	100.2		5.25	Ms	6							31	1		
1730	3	12								Japan,Song	Japan:Tsushima	日本:长崎对马	34.4	129.3		6.1	Mk											1
1730	3	23				2			2	NOAA,Song	Italy:Torre Annunziata	意大利:托雷安农齐亚塔	40.7	14.45		6.7	Mk											
1730	3	28								* Song	Italy:Massa,Carrara	意大利:马萨,卡拉拉	44	10.1		6	Mk	9		3								
1730	5	12	3	15						* Italy	Italy:Norcia	意大利:诺尔恰	42.752	13.117		5.85	Ms	10	200	3				3				
1730	5	23	16							GSHAP,Song	Peru:Cuzco	秘鲁:库斯科	-13.5	-72		4.5	Mk	5										
1730	6	13								* Song	Azores:Luz	亚速尔群岛:路姿	38.5	-28		8	Mk	11										
1730	7	8	8	45		4	16	4	3.5	* NOAA	Chile:Valparaiso	智利:瓦尔帕莱索	-32.5	-71.5		8.7	Ms	11	5	1				3		3		
1730	9	9	20							GSHAP,Song	Peru:Cuzco	秘鲁:库斯科	-13.5	-72		4.5	Mk	5										
1730	9	30								* China	China:Beijing,NW.	中国:北京西北	40	116.2		6.5	Ms	8	658	3				4	26000	5		
1730	12	30								* * Song	Japan:Hokkaido	日本:北海道	43.3	142.5		7.7	Mk		137000	5								
1730										China	China:Shandong,Zouping	中国:山东邹平	36.9	117.9		5	Ms	6										
1730										GSHAP	Romania:Nereju	罗马尼亚:内雷茹	45.7	26.6	100	5.8	Ms	6										
1730										* Bautista,Maso	Philippines:Tayabas,Laguna	菲律宾:塔亚巴斯,拉古娜	14.1	121.4		6.9	Ms	9						2				
1731	3	20	2	30		2			4	* Italy,NOAA	Italy:Foggia	意大利:福贾	41.27	15.75		6.34	Ms	10	3600	4								
1731	10	7								Usami,Japan	Japan:Miyagi	日本:宫城	37.9	140.6		6.6	Ms	8	1						300	3		
1731	11	13								Japan,Song	Japan:Tsuruga	日本:福井敦贺	35.6	136.1		6.8	Mk									3		
1731	11	15								* Song	Mexico:Zacatecas	墨西哥:萨卡特卡斯	23	-102		6.3	Mk		1	1				3				
1731	11									China	China:Jiangsu,Kunshan,S.	中国:江苏昆山南	31.3	121		5	Ms	6										
1731										* Song	Morocco: Santa Cruz (Agadir)	摩洛哥:圣克鲁斯(阿加迪尔)	30.3	-9.4		6.3	Mk							3				
1732	1	24								GSHAP,Song	Peru:Lima	秘鲁:利马	-12	-77		4.5	Mk	5										
1732	1	29								China	China:Sichuan,Xichang,SE.	中国:四川西昌东南	27.7	102.4		6.75	Ms	9								3		
1732	2	25				4	3	1.6	2	* NOAA,Song	Mexico:Guerrero,Acapulco,E.	墨西哥:格雷罗州阿卡普尔科东部	17	-99		7.7	Mk							3		3		
1732	9	7	6							* Iceland	Iceland:Asolfsstadhir	冰岛:奥索尔斯塔济	64	-20.1	8	6.7	Ms							3		3		
1732	9	16	16							USGS,Song	Canada:Quebec,Montréal	加拿大:魁北克省蒙特利尔	45.5	-73.6		6.6	Mk	9										
1732	11	29	6	30						* Italy	Italy:Ariano Irpino,Arianese	意大利:阿维利诺,伊尔皮纳	41.08	15.05		6.61	Ms	10	1940	4				3		3		
1732	11									China	China:Yunnan,Shiping	中国:云南石屏	23.7	102.5		5	Ms	6										
1732	11					2			2	GSHAP,NOAA	Greece:Thesprotia	希腊:塞斯普罗蒂亚	39.5	20.1		6.5	Ms											
1732	12	2	6							GSHAP,Song	Peru:Lima,Near Coast	秘鲁:利马近海	-11.8	-77.6	50	5	Mk	6										
1732	12	4				3	2	1	1	* NOAA	Japan:Kimitsu,Near Coast	日本:千叶近海	35.2	140.8		6.5	Ms											
1732	12	21								Usami,Japan	Japan:Hakodate	日本:北海道函馆	41.8	140.7		6.2	Ms											1
1732						1	2	1	1	Japan,NOAA,Song	Japan:South Honshu Ridge	日本:本州南部海岭	32	140		7	Mk							1				
1733	8	2								* China	China:Yunnan,Dongchuan	中国:云南东川	26.3	103.1		7.75	Ms	10		2				2		2		

年 Year	月 Mo	日 Dy	时 Hr	分 Mn	秒 Sec	海啸 Tsunami 源 Sr	浪高 Wh	级 I mI	级 S mS	资料来源 Information	震中 Earthquake Epicenter 地名(英文) Name(English)	地名(中文) Name(Chinese)	纬度(°) Latitude	经度(°) Longitude	深度 Depth	震级 Mag	标度 Scale	烈度 MMI	死亡人数 Deaths 数量/人 Num	级别 Dd	受伤人数 Injuries 数量/人 Num	级别 Dd	经济损失 Damage 数量/$ Mill	级别 De	房屋毁坏 Houses Destroyed 数量/间 Num	级别 Dh	房屋受损 Houses Damaged 数量/间 Num	级别 Dh
1733	9	18	4							Usami, Japan	Japan: Aki	日本:广岛安艺郡	34.4	132.6		6.6	Ms	8								2		
1733	11	29								* Song	Eritrea: Asmara	厄立特里亚:阿斯马拉	15.7	39		6	Mk			2								
1734	3	21								* * Iceland	Iceland: Selfoss	冰岛:塞尔福斯	63.9	-20.8	8	6.8	Ms							3		3		
1734	3									China	China: Sichuan, Pujiang	中国:四川蒲江	30.2	103.5		5	Ms	6										
1734	5	28								GSHAP, Song	Peru: Lima	秘鲁:利马	-12	-77		5	Mk	6										
1734	6	10								GSHAP	Romania: Nereju	罗马尼亚:内雷茹	45.7	26.6	20	5	Ms	6										
1734										* Song	England: Birmingham	英国:伯明翰	52.5	-2.1		6.3	Mk							3	105	3		
1735	2	2	18							* Song	Colombia: Cauca	哥伦比亚:考卡	2.6	-76.5		6.3	Mk							3				
1735	2	27				2			1.5	* NOAA, Song	Philippines: San Jose	菲律宾:圣琼斯	16	121		7	Mk			3				2		2		
1735	4	6	1							Usami, Japan	Japan: Utsunomiya	日本:宇都宫市	36.75	139.6		5.9	Ms											1
1735	5	30								Japan, Song	Japan: Tokyo	日本:东京	35.7	139.8		6.1	Mk											1
1735	8	20								Japan, Song	Japan: Shima	日本:三重志摩	34.3	137		6.1	Mk											1
1735	12									GSHAP	Cyprus: Gazimagusa	塞浦路斯:法马古斯塔	35	34	24	6.5	Ms	8										
1735										GSHAP	Russia: Dagestan, Chirkey	俄罗斯:达吉斯坦共和国奇尔克伊	43	47	20	4.9	Ms	6										
1736	1	30								* China	China: Taiwan, Tainan	中国:台湾台南	23.1	120.3		6.25	Ms	8	260	3	100	2		2	500	3		
1736	2	2	14							* Song	Colombia: Cauca	哥伦比亚:考卡	2.5	-76.5		6.3	Mk	8						3				
1736	3	3	1	30						GSHAP, Song	Peru: Cuzco	秘鲁:库斯科	-13.5	-72		4.5	Mk	5										
1736	4	30								Usami	Japan: Miyagi	日本:宫城	38.3	140.8		6.2	Ms											1
1736	5	16	15	30						GSHAP, Song	Peru: Cuzco	秘鲁:库斯科	-13.5	-72		4.5	Mk	5										
1736	12	5								* GSHAP	Ecuador: Cotopaxi	厄瓜多尔:科托帕希	-0.9	-78.6		6.3	Ms	8						2				
1736										China	China: Sichuan, Dawu, SE.	中国:四川道孚东南	30.6	101.5		5.5	Ms	7										
1737	5	1	11	45						GSHAP, Song	Peru: Cusco	秘鲁:库斯科	-13.56	-71.96		4.5	Mk	5										
1737	9	30								China	China: Henan, Fenggou	中国:河南封丘	35.1	114.4		5.5	Ms	7										
1737	10	11				4				* GSHAP	Myanmar: Sagaing	缅甸:实皆	24.4	95.2		7.5	Ms		300000	5								
1737	10	16	16			4	64	4.5		* NOAA	Kuril Islands	千岛群岛	50	157	50	7.5	Ms	9	3	1				1		3		
1737	11	4	8							* GSHAP	Russia: Kamchatka, Near East Coast	俄罗斯:堪察加东部近海	55.5	163	20	7.8	Muk	10										
1737	12	17	15	30		4				* GSHAP	Kuril Islands	千岛群岛	50	157	40	7.5	Muk	10										
1737	12	19	3	45						USGS, Song	US: New Jersey, High Bridge	美国:新泽西州海伊布里奇	40.8	-74		5.7	Mk	7										
1737	12	24				4				* NOAA	Chile: Valdivia	智利:瓦尔迪维亚	-39.8	-73.2		8	Muk	11		2				2		2		
1737										GSHAP, Song	Venezuela: Lara	委内瑞拉:拉腊	10.05	-69.3		6	Mk	7										
1738	1	3								Japan	Japan: Niigata	日本:新潟	37	138.7		5.5	Ms											1
1738	5	19								* China	China: Sichuan, Jiuzhaigou	中国:四川九寨沟	33.3	104.2		5.75	Ms	7		2				2		2		
1738	6	11	10	30						GSHAP	Romania: Nereju	罗马尼亚:内雷茹	45.7	26.6	150	7.5	Ms	8.5										
1738	12	23								* China	China: Qinghai, Yushu	中国:青海玉树	33.3	96.6		6.5	Ms	8	336	3								
1738	12	26	1							GSHAP, Song	Russia: Kamchatka Peninsula	俄罗斯:堪察加半岛	55	157.5	350	7.5	Mk	6										

时间						海啸				资料来源	震中				深度	震级	标度	烈度	死亡人数		受伤人数		经济损失		房屋毁坏		房屋受损	
年	月	日	时	分	秒	源	浪高	级 I	级 S		地名(英文)	地名(中文)	纬度(°)	经度(°)					数量/人	级别	数量/人	级别	数量/$ Mill	级别	数量/间	级别	数量/间	级别
Date						Tsunami				Information	Earthquake Epicenter				Depth	Mag	Scale	MMI	Deaths		Injuries		Damage		Houses Destroyed		Houses Damaged	
Year	Mo	Dy	Hr	Mn	Sec	Sr	Wh	mI	mS		Name(English)	Name(Chinese)	Latitude	Longitude					Num	Dd	Num	Dd	$ Mill	De	Num	Dh	Num	Dh
1738										GSHAP	Russia:Dagestan,Chirkey	俄罗斯:达吉斯坦共和国奇尔克伊	43	47	20	4.9	Ms	6										
1738						3			3	* NOAA	Greece:Milos Island	希腊:米洛斯岛	36.8	24.4		6.5	Ms											
1739	1	3								* China	China:Ningxia,Pingluo	中国:宁夏平罗	38.8	106.5		8	Ms	10	50000	5				4		4		
1739	2	4								* GSHAP	Serbia:Jagodina	塞尔维亚:雅戈丁那	44	21.3	14	6.1	Ms	10										
1739	2	23								China	China:Ningxia,Yinchuan	中国:宁夏银川	38.5	106.3		5.5	Ms	7										
1739	3	24								* Song	Peru:Apurimac	秘鲁:阿普里马克	-14.1	-73.2		6.3	Mk	7		3				3				
1739	4	10								GSHAP	Ecuador:Morona Santiago,N.	厄瓜多尔:莫罗纳－圣地亚哥北部	-1.9	-78.3		4.3	Ms	5										
1739	7	14								* Song	Mexico:Colima	墨西哥:科利马	19.2	-104		6.3	Mk							3				
1739	7									* Song	Azores:Flores	亚速尔群岛:弗洛勒斯岛	39.3	-31.1		7.3	Mk	10										
1739	8	16								* Usami	Japan:Aomori,Near Coast	日本:青森近海	40.7	142.3		7.1	Muk	9						2		1		
1739	10	31								Japan,Song	Japan:Sado	日本:佐渡	38	138.4		6.1	Mk											1
1740	4	5	20							GSHAP	Romania:Nereju	罗马尼亚:内雷茹	45.7	26.6	100	5.5	Ms	6.5										
1740	5	22								China	China:Ningxia,Yinchuan	中国:宁夏银川	38.5	106.3		4.75	Ms	6										
1740	7	20								Japan,Song	Japan:Nara	日本:奈良	34.6	135.7		6.1	Mk											1
1740	8	2	8	30						GSHAP,Song	Peru:Lima	秘鲁:利马	-12	-77		4.5	Mk	5										
1740	8	25								* Song	Mexico:Oaxaca,Mexico City	墨西哥:瓦哈卡,墨西哥城	17	-96.3		6.3	Mk							3				
1740	8	27	14							GSHAP	Ecuador:Quito	厄瓜多尔:基多	-0.22	-78.5		4.3	Ms	5										
1740	11	12								* GSHAP	Serbia:Novi Sad	塞尔维亚:诺威萨	45.1	19.8		5.7	Ms	10										
1740	12	19	21							GSHAP	Russia:Kamchatka Peninsula	俄罗斯:堪察加半岛	55.1	157.4	5	4.5	Ms	7										
1741	1	31	1	15		3			4	GSHAP,NOAA	Mediterranean Sea	地中海	36.2	28.5		7.3	Ms											
1741	4	24								* Italy	Italy:Fabriano	意大利:法布里安诺	43.425	13.004		6.08	Ms	10						3				
1741	4	27	9							GSHAP,Song	Peru:Lima	秘鲁:利马	-12	-77		5	Mk	6										
1741	4	29	9							GSHAP,Song	Peru:Andahuaylas	秘鲁:安达韦拉斯	-13.65	-73.45		5	Mk	6										
1741	6	23								* Song	Greece:Nisia Ionioy	希腊:伊奥尼亚群岛	38.5	20.5		7	Mk	10										
1741	8	28				5	9	3.2	2.5	Usami,Japan,NOAA	Japan:Hokkaido	日本:北海道	41.6	139.4		6.9	Ms		1475	4				4	873	3		
1741	11	14								China	China:Yunnan,Shiping	中国:云南石屏	23.7	102.5		5	Ms	6										
1741										China	China:Sichuan,Dawu,SE.	中国:四川道孚东南	30.6	101.5		5	Ms	6										
1742	1	16				4			3	NOAA,Song	Italy:Livorno	意大利:里窝那	43.5	10.2		6.7	Mk											
1742	2	14	2							* Song	Greece:Zakynthos	希腊:扎金索斯岛	37.8	21		7	Mk	10										
1742	2	17	14							GSHAP,Song	Russia:Ostrov Beringa	俄罗斯:白令岛	54.5	167	20	6.2	Mk	8										
1742	2	20				3				GSHAP,NOAA	Greece:Elliniko	希腊:埃利尼科	38.1	22.5		6	Ms											
1742	3	23				4				* Song	Chile:Concepción	智利:康塞普西翁	-36.8	-73		7	Mk											
1742	3	25	2							GSHAP,Song	Peru:Cuzco	秘鲁:库斯科	-13.6	-72		5	Mk	6										
1742	5	9	14	45						GSHAP,Song	Peru:Lima	秘鲁:利马	-12	-77		5	Mk	6										

时间						海啸				资料来源	震中				深度	震级	标度	烈度	死亡人数		受伤人数		经济损失		房屋毁坏		房屋受损	
年	月	日	时	分	秒	源	浪高	级I	级S		地名(英文)	地名(中文)	纬度(°)	经度(°)					数量/人	级别	数量/人	级别	数量/$ Mill	级别	数量/间	级别	数量/间	级别
Date						Tsunami				Information	Earthquake Epicenter				Depth	Mag	Scale	MMI	Deaths		Injuries		Damage		Houses Destroyed		Houses Damaged	
Year	Mo	Dy	Hr	Mn	Sec	Sr	Wh	mI	mS		Name(English)	Name(Chinese)	Latitude	Longitude					Num	Dd	Num	Dd	$ Mill	De	Num	Dh	Num	Dh
1742	5	27	22	35						GSHAP, Song	Peru: Lima	秘鲁:利马	-12	-77		5	Mk	6										
1742	6	12	10	45						GSHAP, Song	Peru: Lima	秘鲁:利马	-12	-77		4.5	Mk	5										
1742	6	15								GSHAP	Ecuador: Cotopaxi, NE.	厄瓜多尔:科托帕希东北	-0.7	-78.4		4.3	Ms	5										
1742	6	27	5	30						* GSHAP	Russia: Ust Orda Buryatia, Bokhan	俄罗斯:布里亚特特区,博汉村镇	53.3	104	40	7.7	Muk	10										
1742	8	5								GSHAP	Georgia: Kakhetiya	格鲁吉亚:卡赫季州	42.1	45.2	15	6.7	Ms	9										
1742	8	24	14	30						GSHAP, Song	Peru: Cuzco	秘鲁:库斯科	-13.6	-72		4.5	Mk	5										
1742	9	14								* Song	Greece: Zakynthos	希腊:扎金索斯岛	37.8	21		7	Mk	10										
1742	10	15	2							GSHAP, Song	Peru: Lima	秘鲁:利马	-12	-77		4.5	Mk	5										
1742	11	18				3		1	1.5	* NOAA, GSHAP	Kuril Islands	千岛群岛	50.5	157	40	7.5	Muk	8										
1742	12	9	18							GSHAP	Ecuador: Cotopaxi, NE.	厄瓜多尔:科托帕希东北	-0.7	-78.4		4.3	Ms	5										
1742	12	27	17							GSHAP, Song	Peru: Cuzco	秘鲁:库斯科	-13.6	-72		4.5	Mk	5										
1742										China	China: Hubei, Fangxian	中国:湖北房县	32.1	110.8		5	Ms	6										
1742										China	China: Sichuan, Dawu, SE.	中国:四川道孚东南	30.6	101.5		5	Ms	6										
1742										GSHAP	Russia: Dagestan, Makhachkala	俄罗斯:达吉斯坦共和国马哈奇卡拉	43.1	46.7	15	5.2	Ms	7										
1743	1	12	9							* Bautista	Philippines: Tayabas	菲律宾:塔亚巴斯	14	121.6		6.6	Ms	10	5	1				2				
1743	2	20	23	30		1				* NOAA, Italy	Greece: Ionian Sea	希腊:伊奥尼亚海	39	20.3		6.9	Ms											
1743	3	22	8							GSHAP, Song	Peru: Cuzco	秘鲁:库斯科	-13.5	-72		4.5	Mk	5										
1743	4	12	18	30						GSHAP, Song	Peru: Lima	秘鲁:利马	-12	-77		4.5	Mk	5										
1743	4	19	6							GSHAP, Song	Peru: Cuzco	秘鲁:库斯科	-13.5	-72		4.5	Mk	5										
1743	5	9	18	15						GSHAP, Song	Peru: Cuzco	秘鲁:库斯科	-13.5	-72		5	Mk	6										
1743	6	30								China	China: Anhui, Jingxian	中国:安徽泾县	30.7	118.4		5	Ms	7										
1743	8	7	1							Usami, , Song	Japan: Aomori, Hachinohe	日本:青森,八户	40.7	142		6.7	Mk									2		
1743	8	12	1							* * Maso, Song	Philippines: Calamba	菲律宾:卡兰巴	14.2	121		6.5	Mk	9										
1743	9									* Song	Philippines: Leyte Island	菲律宾:莱特岛	11.2	124.3		6.3	Mk							3				
1743	10	18	15	45						* Song	Colombia: Villavicencio	哥伦比亚:比亚维森西奥	4.5	-73.8		6.3	Mk							3				
1743	10	18	21							GSHAP	Colombia: Villavicencio	哥伦比亚:比亚维森西奥	4.5	-73.8		4.5	Ms	5										
1743	10	18								GSHAP	Colombia: Villavicencio	哥伦比亚:比亚维森西奥	4.5	-73.8		4.5	Ms	5										
1743	11	22								Japan, Song	Japan: Hachinohe	日本:青森八户	40.7	142		6.1	Mk											1
1744	6	14	15	15						USGS, Song	US: Massachusetts, Peabody	美国:马萨诸塞州皮博迪	42.6	-70.9		5.5	Mk	6										
1744	6	25	5	30						GSHAP, Song	Peru: Apurimac	秘鲁:阿普里马克	-14.2	-73.3	80	4.5	Mk	5										
1744	11	14	11	30						GSHAP, Song	Peru: Cuzco	秘鲁:库斯科	-13.5	-72	10	6	Mk	7										
1744	11	19	11	30						GSHAP, Song	Peru: Cuzco	秘鲁:库斯科	-13.77	-72.1	20	5	Mk	6										
1744										GSHAP	Ecuador: Tungurahua	厄瓜多尔:东谷拉瓦	-1.5	-78.6		5.7	Ms	7										

年 Year	月 Mo	日 Dy	时 Hr	分 Mn	秒 Sec	海啸 源 Tsunami Sr	浪高 Wh	级 I mI	级 S mS	资料来源 Information	震中 地名(英文) Earthquake Epicenter Name(English)	地名(中文) Name(Chinese)	纬度(°) Latitude	经度(°) Longitude	深度 Depth	震级 Mag	标度 Scale	烈度 MMI	死亡人数 数量/人 Deaths Num	级别 Dd	受伤人数 数量/人 Injuries Num	级别 Dd	经济损失 数量/$ Mill Damage $ Mill	级别 De	房屋毁坏 数量/间 Houses Destroyed Num	级别 Dh	房屋受损 数量/间 Houses Damaged Num	级别 Dh
1744						2			1	* NOAA, Song	Philippines: San Jose	菲律宾:圣琼斯	16	121		7	Mk											
1745										GSHAP	Ecuador: Tungurahua	厄瓜多尔:东谷拉瓦	-1.4	-78.4		5.7	Ms	7										
1746	2	9	13							GSHAP, Song	Peru: Cuzco	秘鲁:库斯科	-13.5	-72		5	Mk	6										
1746	2	11								GSHAP, Song	Peru: Cusco	秘鲁:库斯科	-14	-71.7	20	6	Mk	7										
1746	3	19	4							GSHAP, Song	Peru: Cusco	秘鲁:库斯科	-13.85	-71.9		4.5	Mk	5										
1746	4	28	6	30						GSHAP, Song	Peru: Cuzco	秘鲁:库斯科	-13.5	-72		4.5	Mk	5										
1746	5	14	10							Usami	Japan: Tokyo	日本:东京	35.65	139.8		6.9	Ms	9										1
1746	7	29								China	China: Beijing, Changping	中国:北京昌平	40.2	116.2		5	Ms	6										
1746	10	8	11							GSHAP, Song	Peru: Cuzco	秘鲁:库斯科	-13.5	-72		4.5	Mk	5										
1746	10	29	3	30		4	24	4.6	3.5	* NOAA	Peru: Lima, Callao	秘鲁:利马,卡亚俄	-12	-77	30	8	Ms	11	5941	4				4	2975	4		
1747	1	8	14							GSHAP, Song	Peru: Cusco	秘鲁:库斯科	-13.6	-71.9		5	Mk	6										
1747	1	15	20	30						GSHAP, Song	Peru: Cusco	秘鲁:库斯科	-13.6	-71.9		4.5	Mk	5										
1747	2	4								* GSHAP, Song	Peru: Puno, N.	秘鲁:普诺北部	-13.9	-70.3	20	6.5	Mk	9		3				3				
1747	3	14	18	30						GSHAP, Song	Peru: Chimbote, NE.	秘鲁:钦博特东北	-8.58	-78.1	20	6	Mk	7										
1747	3	19								GSHAP, Song	Peru: Cusco	秘鲁:库斯科	-13.5	-71.6	80	6	Mk	7										
1747	3									China	China: Sichuan, Luhuo	中国:四川炉霍	31.4	100.7		6.75	Ms	8										
1747	3					2		1	1.5	Japan, NOAA, Song	Japan: South Honshu Ridge	日本:本州南部海岭	32	140		7	Mk											
1747	7					1				NOAA, Song	Philippines: Samar Island, N.	菲律宾:萨马岛北部	12.77	124.05		7	Mk											
1748	1	20								GSHAP, Song	Peru: Puno, N.	秘鲁:普诺北部	-13.5	-70.3		4.5	Mk	5										
1748	1	27								Japan, Song	Japan: Fukui	日本:福井	36	136.2		7	Mk		615	3								
1748	2	23								China	China: Sichuan, Wenchuan	中国:四川汶川	31.3	103.5		5.5	Ms	7										
1748	3	6								* China	China: Sichuan, Garze, NW.	中国:四川甘孜西北	30.2	101.5		5.75	Ms	7	15	1				1	14	1		
1748	3	23								* Song	Spain: Valencia	西班牙:巴伦西亚	39.5	-0.4		7.3	Mk	10		3				2				
1748	5	2								* China	China: Sichuan, Songpan, N.	中国:四川松潘北	32.8	103.7		6.5	Ms	7						2				
1748	5	25				4	10		3	* NOAA	Greece: Achaia	希腊:阿凯亚	38.25	22.25		6.8	Ms	9						2		2		
1748	6	18								Japan, Song	Japan: Shimane	日本:岛根	35.47	133.05		6.1	Mk											3
1748	8	30								* China	China: Sichuan, Garze, NW.	中国:四川甘孜西北	30.4	101.6		6.5	Ms	8	5					1	72	2		
1748	10	12								China	China: Sichuan, Xiaojin	中国:四川小金	31	102.4		5.5	Ms	6										
1748	11	21								* China	China: Ningxia, Guyuan, N.	中国:宁夏固原北	36.4	106.1		5.5	Ms	7	40	1				2	130	3		
1749	1	20								GSHAP	Ecuador: Loja	厄瓜多尔:洛哈	-4	-79.2		6.3	Ms	8										
1749	2	28								China	China: Guangdong, Yunfu	中国:广东云浮	22.9	112		5	Ms	6										
1749	3	25								* Song	Spain: Valencia	西班牙:巴伦西亚	39.5	-0.4		7	Mk		5000	4								
1749	5	25	1							Usami, Japan	Japan: Ehime	日本:爱媛	33.2	132.6		7	Ms	9								3		
1749	8	12	9			5				* Maso, NOAA, Song	Philippines: Taal Volcano	菲律宾:塔尔火山	13.6	121.1		7.7	Mk	9						3		3		
1749										* Song	Mexico: Colima, Guadalajara	墨西哥:科利马,瓜达拉哈拉	20.4	-103.2		6.3	Mk							3		3		
1750	5	24								* Song	France: Tarbes, Lourdes	法国:塔碧斯,洛德斯	43.1	0.2		6.5	Mk	9		3				3				

时间						海啸				资料来源	震中				深度	震级	标度	烈度	死亡人数		受伤人数		经济损失		房屋毁坏		房屋受损	
年	月	日	时	分	秒	源	浪高	级 I	级 S		地名(英文)	地名(中文)	纬度(°)	经度(°)					数量/人	级别	数量/人	级别	数量/$ Mill	级别	数量/间	级别	数量/间	级别
Date						Tsunami				Information	Earthquake Epicenter				Depth	Mag	Scale	MMI	Deaths		Injuries		Damage		Houses Destroyed		Houses Damaged	
Year	Mo	Dy	Hr	Mn	Sec	Sr	Wh	mI	mS		Name(English)	Name(Chinese)	Latitude	Longitude					Num	Dd	Num	Dd	$ Mill	De	Num	Dh	Num	Dh
1750	6	7								* Song	Greece:Morea,Cerigo	希腊:摩里亚,察里哥	36.2	23		7	Mk	10	2000	4								
1750	9	15								* China	China:Yunnan,Chengjiang	中国:云南澄江	24.7	102.9		6.25	Ms	8	37	1				2		2		
1750	10					4				* GSHAP	Bulgaria:Asenovgrad	保加利亚:阿塞诺夫格勒	42.1	24.8	20	7.2	Ms	10						3		3		3
1750	12	17								* Italy	Croatia:Rijeka	克罗地亚:里耶卡	45.391	14.411		5.37	Ms	9										
1750	12	17				2			3	* Italy,NOAA	Croatia:Rijeka	克罗地亚:里耶卡	45.2	14.2		6.3	Ms	11		3				3		3		
1750										* Song	Mexico:Colima,Guadalajara	墨西哥:科利马,瓜达拉哈拉	20.4	-103.2		6.3	Mk							3		3		
1750										China	China:Sichuan,Dawu,SE.	中国:四川道孚东南	30.6	101.5		5	Ms	6										
1750										GSHAP	Georgia:Tkvarcheli	格鲁吉亚:特克瓦谢利	43	42.8	15	6.9	Ms	9.5										
1750										GSHAP	Georgia:Tkvarcheli	格鲁吉亚:特克瓦谢利	43	42.6	15	6.8	Ms	9.5										
1750						1				* NOAA,Song	Venezuela:Cumana	委内瑞拉:库马纳	10.5	-64.2		7	Mk											
1750										GSHAP	Georgia:Zugdidi	格鲁吉亚:祖格迪迪	42.9	41.9	16	7	Ms	9.5										
1750						1			4	* NOAA,Song	Myanmar:Thandwe,Near Coast	缅甸:丹兑近海	18.5	93.4		7.9	Mk											
1751	3	26	4							Usami,Japan	Japan:Nose	日本:大阪能势町	35	135.4		6.4	Ms											1
1751	3	26								China,Diao S.	China:Guangxi,Tianyang	中国:广西田阳	23.7	106.9		4.75	Ms	6										
1751	4	25								* Song	Colombia:Cauca	哥伦比亚:考卡	2.5	-76.5		6.3	Mk	7						3				
1751	5	20				4	2	1	1	* Usami,NOAA	Japan:Joetsu	日本:新潟上越	37.2	138.1		6.6	Ms	9	2100	4				3	5800	4		
1751	5	25	5	30		4	3.5	1.8	3.5	* NOAA	Chile:Concepcion, Chillan	智利:康塞普西翁,奇廉	-36.83	-71.63		8.5	Ms	11	65	2				3		3		
1751	5	25								* China	China:Yunnan,Jianchuan	中国:云南剑川	26.5	99.9		6.75	Ms	9	900	3				4	15712	5		
1751	6	7								* Song	Turkey:Izmir, Efes, Aydin	土耳其:伊兹密尔,艾菲斯,艾登	37.8	27		7.3	Mk	10										
1751	7	24				1				NOAA,Song	Japan:Miyagi	日本:宫城	38.9	142.2		7	Mk											
1751	7	26	19	30						* Italy	Italy:Gualdo,Nocera	意大利:瓜尔多,诺切拉	43.222	12.73		6.3	Ms	10										
1751	7									China	China:Xizang (Tibet),Damxung	中国:西藏当雄	30.2	91.5		4.75	Ms	6										
1751	8	18								* Song	Dominica:Concepcion, De La Vega	多米尼加:康塞普西翁,德拉维加	19	-70		6.3	Mk							3				
1751	9	15				4				* Song	Haiti:Port - Au - Prince	海地:太子港	18.5	-72.3		7.1	Mk							2				
1751	10	18	19			2				* NOAA	Dominica:Azua De Compostela	多米尼加:波斯特拉的阿苏阿	18.5	-70.7	33	7.3	Ms							3				
1751	11	21	9	45		2			3	* NOAA,Song	Italy:Genova, Near Coast of S.	意大利:热那亚南部近海	43.8	9		6.7	Mk	7						1				
1751	11	21	12	50		4				* Song	Haiti:Port - Au - Prince	海地:太子港	18.5	-72.3		7.7	Mk							3				
1752	4	28				1				* NOAA,Song	Portugal:Buarcos, Aveiro	葡萄牙:布阿尔库什,阿维罗	40.4	-8.7		7	Mk											
1752	6	21				2			3	* GSHAP, NOAA	Syria:Hamah (Hama)	叙利亚:哈马	35	36		7	Ms	9	20000	5								
1752	6									* GSHAP	Greece:Zakynthos	希腊:扎金索斯岛	37.8	21		6.2	Ms	10										

时间 年 Year	月 Mo	日 Dy	时 Hr	分 Mn	秒 Sec	海啸 Tsunami 源 Sr	浪高 Wh	级 I mI	级 S mS	资料来源 Information	震中 Earthquake Epicenter 地名(英文) Name(English)	地名(中文) Name(Chinese)	纬度(°) Latitude	经度(°) Longitude	深度 Depth	震级 Mag	标度 Scale	烈度 MMI	死亡人数 Deaths 数量/人 Num	级别 Dd	受伤人数 Injuries 数量/人 Num	级别 Dd	经济损失 Damage 数量/$ Mill	级别 De	房屋毁坏 Houses Destroyed 数量/间 Num	级别 Dh	房屋受损 Houses Damaged 数量/间 Num	级别 Dh
1752	7	29								GSHAP	Greece: Didymoteicho	希腊:季季莫蒂霍	41.41	26.61		7.5	Ms	9										
1752										China	China: Xizang (Tibet), Zanda	中国:西藏札达	31.4	79.9		6.5	Ms	8						4				
1752										* Song	Egypt: Yamit	埃及:耶米特	31.2	34.2		7.7	Mk	8	20000	5								
1753	2	10	16							Usami, Song	Japan: Tokyo	日本:东京	35.65	139.8		6.1	Mk											
1754	4					3			0.5	NOAA	China: Taiwan Strait	中国:台湾海峡	25.3	121.4		6	Ms											1
1754	5	15	21			5				* Maso, Song	Philippines: Taal Volcano	菲律宾:塔尔火山	13.6	121.1		8	Mk	10	12	1				4		4		
1754	5									China	China: Shanxi, Jinyuan	中国:山西晋源	37.7	112.5		5	Ms	6										
1754	6									China	China: Yunnan, Chuxiong	中国:云南楚雄	25	101.6		5	Ms	6										
1754	8	18				4				* NOAA	Indonesia: Maluku Islands	印度尼西亚:摩鹿加群岛	-3.5	128.5		6.5	Ms											
1754	9	1				4	4	2	2	* NOAA	Mexico: Acapulco	墨西哥:阿卡普尔科	16.7	-99.2		7.8	Muk							3		3		
1754	9	2	21	30		2				* GSHAP, NOAA	Egypt: Al – Qahirah (Cairo)	埃及:开罗	30.8	31		7.2	Ms		40000	5				3				
1754	9	7				3		1	1	* NOAA, Song	Indonesia: Maluku Islands	印度尼西亚:摩鹿加群岛	-3.567	128.548		7	Mk											
1754	9	16	16	3		2				NOAA, Song	Turkey: Marmara Sea	土耳其:马尔马拉海	41	28.1		6.6	Mk											
1754	9	22								Japan, Song	Japan: Hachinohe	日本:青森八户	40.7	142		6.3	Mk											
1754										China	China: Taiwan, Hsinchu	中国:台湾新竹	24.8	121		5	Ms	6								1		
1755	1	27								* China	China: Yunnan, Yimen	中国:云南易门	24.7	102.2		6.5	Ms	8	270	3	80	2		3	4040	4		
1755	2	8								* China	China: Yunnan, Jianshui	中国:云南建水	23.7	102.8		6	Ms	8	70	2	20	1		2	700	3		
1755	2	26								* GSHAP	Serbia: Vranje	塞尔维亚:弗拉涅	42.5	21.9		5.7	Ms	10										
1755	3	29								Usami	Japan Trench	日本海沟	40.5	143.5		6.2	Ms											
1755	4	21	5							Usami	Japan: Utsunomiya	日本:宇都宫市	36.75	139.6		6.2	Ms											1
1755	4	26								*	Ecuador: Quito	厄瓜多尔:基多	-0.2	-78.5		7	Muk	9		3				3				1
1755	6	7								* Iran	Iran: Kashan	伊朗:卡尚	34	51.4		5.9	Ms		40000	5				3				
1755	11	1	8	50		4	30	3.6		* NOAA	Steait Of Gibraltar, W.	直布罗陀海峡西部	36	-11		8.5	Ms	11	60000	5				4				
1755	11	1								GSHAP, Song	Peru: Lima	秘鲁:利马	-12	-77		4.5	Mk	5										
1755	11	16	15	30		2				NOAA, Song	Spain: Coruna	西班牙:拉科鲁尼亚	43.37	8.4		6.6	Mk											
1755	11	18	9	11	35	1				* NOAA	US: Massachusetts, Gloucester, Near Coast	美国:马萨诸塞州格洛斯特近海	42.7	-70.3		7	ML	8						2				
1755	11	19								* Song	Morocco: Meknes, Fes	摩洛哥:梅克内斯,菲斯	34.08	-5		7.3	Mk	10	3000	4				3				
1755	12	9	13	30						* Italy	Switzerland: Naters	瑞士:纳特尔斯	46.3	8		5.9	Ms	8						3				
1755	12	21	9			2				NOAA, Song	Portugal: Coast SW.	葡萄牙:西南海域	37	-10		7	Mk											
1755										GSHAP	Colombia: Tamara	哥伦比亚:塔马拉	5.8	-72.31		5.7	Ms	7										
1756	2	27				2	1.8	0.8	1.5	NOAA, Song	England: Bristol Channel	英国:布里斯托海峡	51.208	-4.122		6.7	Mk											
1756	3	29				1				* NOAA, Song	Portugal: Lisbon	葡萄牙:里斯本	38.7	-9		7	Mk											
1756	10	22	15	30		1			4	GSHAP, NOAA	Greece: Argos	希腊:阿尔戈斯	37.7	22.8		7	Ms											
1756	11	19	23	12						GSHAP, Song	Peru: Lima	秘鲁:利马	-12	-77		4.5	Mk	5										
1756	12	4	4	45						GSHAP, Song	Peru: Lima	秘鲁:利马	-12	-77		4.5	Mk	5										

年	月	日	时	分	秒	源	浪高	级 I	级 S	资料来源	震中 地名(英文)	地名(中文)	纬度(°)	经度(°)	深度	震级	标度	烈度	死亡人数 数量/人	级别	受伤人数 数量/人	级别	经济损失 数量/$ Mill	级别	房屋毁坏 数量/间	级别	房屋受损 数量/间	级别
Date						Tsunami				Information	Earthquake Epicenter				Depth	Mag	Scale	MMI	Deaths		Injuries		Damage		Houses Destroyed		Houses Damaged	
Year	Mo	Dy	Hr	Mn	Sec	Sr	Wh	mI	mS		Name(English)	Name(Chinese)	Latitude	Longitude					Num	Dd	Num	Dd	$ Mill	De	Num	Dh	Num	Dh
1756	12	8	12							GSHAP, Song	Peru: Lima	秘鲁:利马	-12	-77		4.5	Mk	5										
1756										GSHAP	Georgia: TBilisi	格鲁吉亚:第比利斯	41.9	45.3	10	4.7	Ms	7										
1756										GSHAP	Russia: Kamchatka Peninsula	俄罗斯:堪察加半岛	56	163	20	6.7	Ms	9										
1757	2	22								*	Ecuador: Pichincha, S.	厄瓜多尔:皮钦查南部	-0.6	-78.4		7	Muk	9	1000	3				3				
1757	4	15								* Song	Morocco: Sale, Cape Cantin	摩洛哥:塞拉,坎汀海角	34	-6.8		7	Mk		3000	4				3				
1757	5	9	6							GSHAP, Song	Peru: Lima	秘鲁:利马	-12	-77		4.5	Mk	5										
1757	5	20								GSHAP, Song	Peru: Lima	秘鲁:利马	-12	-77		4.5	Mk	5										
1757	6	3	2	30						GSHAP, Song	Peru: Lima	秘鲁:利马	-12	-77		4.5	Mk	5										
1757	6	13								China	China: Yunnan, Yingjiang	中国:云南腾冲	24.9	98.4		5.5	Ms	7										
1757	7	4								* Song	Croatia: Pozega	克罗地亚:波热加	45.8	17.4		6.3	Mk	10										
1757	7	9	23	45		5				* NOAA, Song	Azores: Sao Jorge	亚速尔群岛:苏乔治丘陵	38.65	-28.08		8	Mk	11	1053	4				3		4		
1757	7	14								* Song	Italy: Calabria, Cosenza	意大利:卡拉布里亚,科森扎	39.3	16.2		5.5	Mk							2				
1757	7	15				1				* NOAA, Song	England: St. Mary, Scilly Islands	英国:圣马里,锡利群岛	49.92	-6.32		7	Mk											
1757	7	30								GSHAP. Korea	South Korea: Cheongyang	韩国:青阳郡	36.6	126.8		5	Ms	7										
1757	8	6								* Song	Italy: Siracusa (Syracuse)	意大利:锡拉库萨(锡拉丘兹)	37	15		6.6	Mk	10	10000	5				3				
1757	8	24				2	0.5		-05	* NOAA	Indonesia: Jakarta	印度尼西亚:雅加达	-6	107		7.5	Ms											
1758	1									* Song	Tunisia: Tunis	突尼斯:突尼斯	36.8	10.2		7.3	Mk	10	3000	4				3		3		3
1758	5					1				GSHAP, NOAA	Greece: Lamia	希腊:拉米亚	38.9	22.9		6.6	Ms											
1758	6	13								* Song	Azores: Luz	亚速尔群岛:路姿	37	-26		8	Mk	11										
1758	12	6								GSHAP	Norway: Karasjok	挪威:卡拉绍克	69.5	25.5	25	4.8	Ms	5										
1758	12	31	21	30						GSHAP	Finland: Inari	芬兰:伊纳里	68.8	26.4	30	4.7	Ms	5										
1759	3	30	13	30						* Song	Italy: Pinerolo	意大利:皮奈罗洛	44.9	7.3		6	Mk	10										
1759	4	27	4							GSHAP, Song	Peru: Lima	秘鲁:利马	-12	-77		4.5	Mk	5										
1759	6	2	1							* Song	Greece: Nisia Ionioy	希腊:伊奥尼亚群岛	38	20.5		7	Mk	10										
1759	6	26								* Song	Greece: Serres	希腊:塞雷	41	24		6.3	Mk							3				
1759	6	29								GSHAP	Bulgaria: Asenovgrad	保加利亚:阿塞诺夫格勒	42.1	24.8	14	6.1	Ms	8.5										
1759	6	29								* Song	Mexico: Jorullo	墨西哥:霍鲁约	19.5	-102.3		6.3	Mk							3				
1759	9	3	4	15						GSHAP, Song	Peru: Chimbote, Near Coast	秘鲁:钦博特近海	-8.6	-79.8	50	6	Mk	7										
1759	10	30				2	8	1.3	4	* NOAA	Israel: Zefat (Safed)	以色列:采法特(萨法德)	33	35.5		6.4	Ms							2				
1759	11	25								* Song	Lebanon: Sur (Tyre)	黎巴嫩:苏尔	33.3	35.7		7.7	Mk		30000	5								
1759										GSHAP	Colombia: Quibdo	哥伦比亚:乔科的基沃多	5.7	-76.6		5	Ms	6										
1760	1	21				2				NOAA, Song	Denmark: Ringkobing	丹麦:灵克宾	56.2	8		7	Mk											

时间						海啸				资料来源	震中				深度	震级	标度	烈度	死亡人数		受伤人数		经济损失		房屋毁坏		房屋受损	
年	月	日	时	分	秒	源	浪高	级 I	级 S		地名(英文)	地名(中文)	纬度(°)	经度(°)					数量/人	级别	数量/人	级别	数量/$ Mill	级别	数量/间	级别	数量/间	级别
Date						Tsunami				Information	Earthquake Epicenter				Depth	Mag	Scale	MMI	Deaths		Injuries		Damage		Houses Destroyed		Houses Damaged	
Year	Mo	Dy	Hr	Mn	Sec	Sr	Wh	mI	mS		Name(English)	Name(Chinese)	Latitude	Longitude					Num	Dd	Num	Dd	$ Mill	De	Num	Dh	Num	Dh
1760	5	14	16							Usami, , Song	Japan: South Honshu Ridge	日本:本州南部海岭	31.448	140.036		6.3	Mk											
1760	6	16	16			1			3	NOAA, Song	Italy: Bay of Napli	意大利:那不勒斯湾	40.8	14.4		6.7	Mk									1		
1760	7	11								* Song	Cuba: Santiago De Cuba	古巴:圣地亚哥	20	-75.5		6.2	Mk			3				2				
1761	3	12	7	15						USGS, Song	US: Massachusetts, Gloucester, Near Coast	美国:马萨诸塞州格洛斯特近海	42.7	-70.3		5	Mk	5										
1761	3	30	23	1		4	2.4	1.3		* NOAA	Steait Of Gibraltar, W.	直布罗陀海峡西部	34.5	-13		8.5	Ms	9										
1761	5	23								* China	China: Yunnan, Yuxi, N.	中国:云南玉溪北	24.4	102.6		6.25	Ms	8	120	3	120	3		3	1900	4		
1761	8	14				1				NOAA, Song	England: Jersey Island	英国:泽西岛	49.465	-2.585		7	Mk											
1761	11	3								* China	China: Yunnan, Yuxi	中国:云南玉溪	24.4	102.6		5.75	Ms	7	50	1	30	1		2	960	3		
1761	12	9	17	20						* GSHAP	Russia: Tuva, Mugur – Aksy, SW.	俄罗斯:唐努图瓦州穆古尔阿克瑟西南	50	90	30	8.3	Muk	10.5										
1761	12	12	18							GSHAP	Kazakhstan: Zyryanovsk	哈萨克斯坦:济良诺夫斯克	50.5	83	20	5	Ms	6										
1762	3	29	2							Usami, Japan	Japan: Niigata	日本:新潟	37.8	139		5.9	Ms	8										1
1762	4	2				4	1.8	0.8	1	* NOAA, Song	India: Chittagong, Dacca	印度:吉大港,达卡	22	92		8	Mk	11	200	3				3				
1762	9	27				1	3	1.6	1.5	NOAA, Song	England: Dover Straits	英国:多佛尔海峡	51.5	0.1		6.7	Mk											
1762	10	31	5			4	2	1	1	* Usami, Japan, NOAA	Japan Sea	日本海	38.1	138.7		6.6	Ms	9	26	1					26	1		
1763	1	29	9			4	5	2.3	2	* Usami, NOAA	Japan: Aomori, Near Coast	日本:青森近海	40.5	143.5		8	Muk	10	3					2		3		
1763	3	11				4	2	1	1	* Usami, Japan, NOAA	Japan: Aomori, Near Coast	日本:青森近海	41	142.5		7.75	Ms	10								1		
1763	3	15				4	2	1	1	* Usami, Japan, NOAA	Japan: Aomori, Hachinohe	日本:青森,八户	40.7	142		7.1	Muk	9		3				3		1		
1763	6	28	5	28						*	Hungary: Komarom	匈牙利:科马罗姆	47.7	18.2		6.2	Muk	9	83	2				1				
1763	9	12				3	9		3.5	* NOAA, Song	Indonesia: Banda Sea	印度尼西亚:班达海	-4.5	130		7.7	Mk		7	1				2		3		
1763	9	18				1	3	1.6	1.5	NOAA, Song	England: Poole	英国:普尔	50.6	-2.466		6.7	Mk											
1763	12	30								* China	China: Yunnan, Jiangchuan	中国:云南江川	24.2	102.8		6.5	Ms	8	1000	3				4	4500	4		
1764	7	15	5	30						GSHAP	Ecuador: Quito	厄瓜多尔:基多	-0.22	-78.5		4.3	Ms	5										
1764	10	29								Japan, Song	Japan: Ise Bay	日本:伊势湾	35	136.8		6.1	Mk											
1764	12	26	10			2				* NOAA, Song	Portugal: Lisbon	葡萄牙:里斯本	38.7	-9.2		7	Mk											1
1764										GSHAP	Russia: Dagestan, Tpig	俄罗斯:达吉斯坦共和国特皮格	41.7	47.5	20	5.1	Ms	6										
1765	2	9								* China	China: Xinjiang, Jinghe	中国:新疆精河	44.7	82.9		6.5	Ms	8	1	1					147	3		
1765	3	15								China	China: Liaoning, Shenyang	中国:辽宁沈阳	41.8	123.4		5.5	Ms	7										
1765	3	21								GSHAP	Aegean Sea	爱琴海	40.2	24.7	36	6.6	Ms	7.5										
1765	5	1								China	China: Gansu, Lintao	中国:甘肃临洮	35.3	103.9		5.5	Ms	7	6	1					242	3		
1765	9	2								* China	China: Gansu, Gangu, N.	中国:甘肃甘谷西北	34.8	105		6.5	Ms	9	2068	4				4	74748	5		
1765										China	China: Sichuan, Dawu, SE.	中国:四川道孚东南	30.6	101.5		5	Ms	6										
1765										* Song	El Salvador: San Salvador	萨尔瓦多:圣萨尔瓦多	13.7	-89.2		5.9	Mk							2				
1766	1	22	21							GSHAP	Ecuador: Ibarra	厄瓜多尔:伊瓦拉	0.44	-77.97		4.3	Ms	5										

时间						海啸				资料来源	震中				深度	震级	标度	烈度	死亡人数		受伤人数		经济损失		房屋毁坏		房屋受损	
年	月	日	时	分	秒	源	浪高	级 I	级 S		地名(英文)	地名(中文)	纬度(°)	经度(°)					数量/人	级别	数量/人	级别	数量/$ Mill	级别	数量/间	级别	数量/间	级别
Date						Tsunami				Information	Earthquake Epicenter				Depth	Mag	Scale	MMI	Deaths		Injuries		Damage		Houses Destroyed		Houses Damaged	
Year	Mo	Dy	Hr	Mn	Sec	Sr	Wh	mI	mS		Name(English)	Name(Chinese)	Latitude	Longitude					Num	Dd	Num	Dd	$ Mill	De	Num	Dh	Num	Dh
1766	2	2								USGS, Song	US: Massachusetts, Boston, Near Coast	美国:马萨诸塞州波士顿近海	42	-68		5.5	Mk	6										
1766	3	8	9			4	2	-01	1	* Usami, Japan, NOAA	Japan: Aomori, Near Coast	日本:青森近海	40.9	141.7		6.9	Ms	9	1700	4				3	8200	4	8200	4
1766	5	22	5	30		2			2	* NOAA	Turkey: Istanbul	土耳其:伊斯坦布尔	41	29		6.5	Ms	10										
1766	6	9								* Song	Iran: Lar	伊朗:拉尔	27.7	54.3		6.3	Mk							3				
1766	6	12	4	45						*	Cuba: Santiago De Cuba	古巴:圣地亚哥	19.9	-76.1	25	6.8	Ms		40	1	700	3		3				
1766	7	9	21							* Song	Colombia: Buga, Cali, Popayan	哥伦比亚:布加,卡利,波帕扬	3.7	-76.3		6.5	Mk	9						3				
1766	7	11	5	6						* Song	Greece: Nisia Ionioy	希腊:伊奥尼亚群岛	38	20.5		7	Mk	10										
1766	8	25								* Song	Martinique Island: Saint – Pierre	马提尼克岛:圣彼得	14.4	-61.1		5.9	Mk							2				
1766	10	21	9			1				* NOAA	Venezuela: Cumana	委内瑞拉:库马纳	10.47	-64.17		7.5	Ms	9						3				
1766	12	7	10	45						Maso, Song	Philippines: Calamba	菲律宾:卡兰巴	14.2	121		5.5	Mk	7										
1766										* Song	Guatemala: Chiquimula, Quetzaltepeque	危地马拉:奇基穆拉,奎札特佩奎	14.5	-89.3		5.9	Mk							2				
1767	2	8	1	5						Maso, Song	Philippines: Calamba	菲律宾:卡兰巴	14.2	121		5.5	Mk	7										
1767	2	12	22							GSHAP	Russia: Dagestan, Kizlyar	俄罗斯:达吉斯坦共和国基兹利亚尔	43.9	46.7	15	4.6	Ms	6										
1767	4	24	6			3				* NOAA, Song	Martinique Island	马提尼克岛(拉丁美洲)	14.4	-61		7	Mk											
1767	5	4								Usami, Japan, Song	Japan: Miyagi, Near Coast	日本:宫城近海	38.6	142		6.3	Mk								21	1		
1767	7	11	4							* Song	Greece: Nisia Ionioy	希腊:伊奥尼亚群岛	38.2	20.2		7	Mk	10										
1767	7	14								* Italy	Italy: Crati	意大利:克拉提	39.38	16.28		5.83	Ms	10	40	1				3				
1767	8	1	23							GSHAP	Brasil: Serra	巴西:塞拉	-20.31	-40.33		3.1	Ms	5										
1767	9	5				1	1.5	0.6	1.5	NOAA, Song	Ireland: Clare, Near Coast	爱尔兰:克莱尔郡近海	53	-10		7	Mk											
1767	10	22								Japan	Japan: Tokyo	日本:东京	35.7	139.8		6	Ms								15	1		1
1767	11	13	7	25						* Maso, Song	Philippines: Calamba	菲律宾:卡兰巴	14.2	121		5.9	Mk	7						2				
1767	11	22				2				* NOAA, Song	China: South China Sea	中国:南海	18	108		7	Mk											
1767						1				NOAA, Song	Guam	关岛(西太平洋)	14	143.3		7	Mk											
1768	3	12								GSHAP	Russia: Kamchatka Peninsula	俄罗斯:堪察加半岛	56	163	20	4.9	Ms	6										
1768	4	3	2	30						GSHAP	Ecuador: Cotopaxi, NE.	厄瓜多尔:科托帕希东北	-0.7	-78.4		5	Ms	6										
1768	6	22				3			1	* NOAA	Papua New Guinea: East New Britain, E.	巴布亚新几内亚:东新不列颠东部	-5	152.5		7.5	Ms											
1768	7	19								Japan	Japan: Kanagawa	日本:神奈川	35.5	139.1		5	Ms											1
1768	7	22	2			4	1.2	0.3	1	* NOAA, Japan, Usami,	Ryukyu Islands	琉球群岛	26.2	127.5		6.5	Ms							2	9	1		

年 Year	月 Mo	日 Dy	时 Hr	分 Mn	秒 Sec	海啸 Tsunami 源 Sr	浪高 Wh	级 I mI	级 S mS	资料来源 Information	震中 Earthquake Epicenter 地名(英文) Name(English)	地名(中文) Name(Chinese)	纬度(°) Latitude	经度(°) Longitude	深度 Depth	震级 Mag	标度 Scale	烈度 MMI	死亡人数 Deaths 数量/人 Num	级别 Dd	受伤人数 Injuries 数量/人 Num	级别 Dd	经济损失 Damage 数量/$ Mill $ Mill	级别 De	房屋毁坏 Houses Destroyed 数量/间 Num	级别 Dh	房屋受损 Houses Damaged 数量/间 Num	级别 Dh
1768	9	8								Usami, Japan	Japan: Hachinohe	日本:青森八户	40.7	142		5.9	Ms											1
1768	10	19	23							* Italy	Italy: Santa Sofia	意大利:圣安娜索非亚	43.93	11.87		5.84	Ms	10	120	3				3				
1768	11	28								* GSHAP	Croatia: Zadar	克罗地亚:扎达尔	44.1	15.2		5.7	Ms	10										
1769	5	1								* Song	Iraq: Baghdad	伊拉克:巴格达	33	44.5		6.3	Mk	7						3	2000	4		
1769	5	7								* Song	Iran: Shiraz	伊朗:设拉子	29.4	52.3		5.9	Mk							2				
1769	6	12	23							Japan	Japan: Aomori	日本:青森	40.85	139.95		5.9	Ms											1
1769	7	22								Usami	Japan: Hachinohe	日本:青森八户	40.7	142		5.9	Ms									3		1
1769	7	28								USGS	US: California, Los Angeles	美国:加利福尼亚州洛杉矶	33.9	-117.8		6	Ms	8										
1769	8	29	5			4	2	1	1	* Usami, NOAA	Japan: Miyazzaki, Near Coast	日本:宫崎近海	32.3	132		7.4	Ms	9	2						1000	3		
1769	10	1								* Song	Greece: Leukas (Ionian Islands)	希腊:琉卡斯 (伊奥尼亚群岛)	38.8	20.8		7	Mk	10										
1769	10	24	13							*	Russia: Lake Baykal	俄罗斯:贝加尔湖	51.8	105.5	40	7.3	Muk	10										
1769						3				NOAA	Greece: Corinth Gulf	希腊:科林斯海湾	38.4	22.2		6.5	Ms											
1769										* Song	Switzerland: Chur	瑞士:库尔	46.9	9.5		6.3	Mk	5						3				
1770	1									* Song	Greece: Lefkada	希腊:莱夫卡斯	38.717	20.65		6.2	Mk			3				2	700	3		
1770	5	26	21							* Usami, Japan	Japan: Miyagi, Near Coast	日本:宫城近海	38.6	142		7.4	Muk	10		3								
1770	6	3	19	15		4				* NOAA, Song	Haiti: Port - Au - Prince	海地:太子港	18.5	-73.4	10	7.7	Mk		200	3				3				
1770	9	26								* China	China: Yunnan, Fengqing, N.	中国:云南凤庆北	24.9	99.9		5.5	Ms	7						1	80	2		
1770	11	23								Japan, Song	Japan: Kumano	日本:三重熊野	34	136		6.1	Mk											1
1770	12					1				* Maso, Song, NOAA	Philippines: Calamba	菲律宾:卡兰巴	14.2	121		7.3	Mk	8						2		3		
1770										China	China: Xizang (Tibet), Shannan	中国:西藏山南	29.3	91.5		5.75	Ms	7										
1770										* Song	Iran: Hormozgan	伊朗:荷姆兹甘	27.1	54.2		6.3	Mk							3				
1770										GSHAP	Kyrgyzstan: Bishkek	吉尔吉斯斯坦:比什凯克	42.8	74.1	15	6	Ms	8										
1770						3			0.5	NOAA	Indonesia: Sumatra, Coast of SW.	印度尼西亚:苏门答腊西南海域	-5	102		7	Ms							3		3		
1771	2	1	12							* Bautista, Maso	Philippines: Manila	菲律宾:马尼拉	14.55	121.15		5	Ms	8						3				
1771	3	1	2							GSHAP	Russia: Altai Krai, Chagan - Uzun, N.	俄罗斯:阿尔泰边疆区恰甘乌尊北部	51	89	30	6	Ms	6.5										
1771	4	24				4	85	6.4	6	* Usami, Japan, NOAA	Ryukyu Islands	琉球群岛	24	124.3		7.4	Ms	10	13486	5				4	3237	4		
1771	9	3	13							* Song	Jamaica: Port Royal, Kingston	牙买加:罗亚尔港,金斯敦	17.6	-76.5		5.9	Mk							2				
1772	2	18	17							GSHAP	Russia: Murmansk, Murmansk	俄罗斯:摩尔曼斯克州摩尔曼斯克	68.7	33.3	20	5	Ms	6										
1772	3	1								China	China: Hebei, Lingshou	中国:河北灵寿	38.3	114.4		5	Ms	6										

时间						海啸				资料来源	震中				深度	震级	标度	烈度	死亡人数		受伤人数		经济损失		房屋毁坏		房屋受损	
年	月	日	时	分	秒	源	浪高	级 I	级 S		地名(英文)	地名(中文)	纬度(°)	经度(°)					数量/人	级别	数量/人	级别	数量/$ Mill	级别	数量/间	级别	数量/间	级别
Date						Tsunami				Information	Earthquake Epicenter				Depth	Mag	Scale	MMI	Deaths		Injuries		Damage		Houses Destroyed		Houses Damaged	
Year	Mo	Dy	Hr	Mn	Sec	Sr	Wh	mI	mS		Name(English)	Name(Chinese)	Latitude	Longitude					Num	Dd	Num	Dd	$ Mill	De	Num	Dh	Num	Dh
1772	5	12								* Song	Greece:Thesprotia	希腊:塞斯普罗蒂亚	39.5	20		7	Mk	10										
1772	6	3								* Usami	Japan:Iwate,Near Coast	日本:岩手近海	39.3	142.7		7.4	Muk	10		2						1		
1772	6									* Song	France:Valence	法国:瓦朗斯	44.4	4.8		6.1	Mk	8						2				
1772	11	24	7	45		3				GSHAP,NOAA	Turkey:Izmir	土耳其:伊兹密尔	38.8	26.7		6.4	Ms											
1772	12	4	21	55						GSHAP	Mongolia:Suhbaatar	蒙古:苏赫巴托尔	50.6	106.2	18	6	Ms	7.5										
1773	5	6				2	9		3.5	* NOAA,Song	Morocco:Tangiers	摩洛哥:丹吉尔	35.8	-5.83		7.7	Mk							2				
1773	6	3								* Song	Guatemala:Santiago	危地马拉:圣地亚哥	14.6	-91.2		7	Mk		8000	4				4		4		4
1773	6	29								GSHAP,Song	Chile:Copiapo	智利:科皮亚波	-27.35	-70.35		6	Mk	8										
1773	7	29								* Song	Guatemala:Santiago	危地马拉:圣地亚哥	14.6	-91.2		6	Mk		100	2				2		2		2
1774	1	22	13							Usami,Japan,Song	Japan:Tango	日本:丹後	33.2	138.7		6.1	Mk											1
1774	2	21	19	11						USGS	US:Virginia,Petersburg	美国:弗吉尼亚州彼得斯堡	37.2	-77.4		4.5	Ms	6										
1774	7	24				1			3	NOAA,Song	Italy:Livorno	意大利:里窝那	43.5	10.2		6.7	Mk											
1774	8									* * Song	French Guiana:Cayenne	法属圭亚那:卡宴	4.6	-52.2		6.3	Mk							3				
1774	9	10	15	25						* Italy	Switzerland:Altdorf	瑞士:阿尔特多夫	46.9	8.7		5.57	Ms	8		2				3				
1774										* Song	Canada:Newfoundland	加拿大:纽芬兰(岛)	47	-55		6.2	Mk		300	3								
1775	2	11				3				* NOAA,Song	Cuba:Santiago De Cuba	古巴:圣地亚哥	19.9	-76		7.7	Mk							3				
1775	3	17								GSHAP,Song	Chile:Valparaiso	智利:瓦尔帕莱索	-33.05	-71.63		6	Mk	8										
1775	3					2				* NOAA,Song	Haiti:Hinche	海地:安什	19	-72.4		7	Mk											
1775	4	18				3			0	* NOAA,Song	Indonesia:Banda Sea	印度尼西亚:班达海	-4	129		7	Mk							1				
1775	10	13	10							* GSHAP	Croatia:Bedekovcina	克罗地亚:贝代科夫契纳	46	15.9		6.3	Ms	10						3				
1775	10	22				1				NOAA,Song	France:Island of Corsica	法国:科西嘉岛	42	8.5		6.6	Mk											
1775	10					2	2	1	1.5	NOAA,Song	Japan:Boso,Near Coast	日本:房总半岛近海	35.1	140.5		7.5	Mk			3						2		
1775	12	18				2				* NOAA,Song	Haiti:Hinche	海地:安什	19	-72.4		7	Mk											
1775	12									* Song	Venezuela:Trujillo	委内瑞拉:特鲁希略	9.2	-70.3		6.1	Mk	8						2				
1775										China	China:Liaoning,Tieling	中国:辽宁铁岭	42.3	123.9		5.5	Ms	7								3		
1775										GSHAP	Russia:Lake Baykal	俄罗斯:贝加尔湖	53.13	106.85	15	6.5	Ms	9										
1775										GSHAP	Russia:Buryatiya,Sorok	俄罗斯:布里亚特州索罗克	52.35	100.4	15	6.5	Ms	9										
1775										GSHAP	Russia:Chita,Kodar	俄罗斯:赤塔州科达尔村	56.61	117.22	15	6.5	Ms	9										
1776	1	1	14							USGS,Song	US:Ohio,Ringgold	美国:俄亥俄州灵戈尔德	39.6	-81.9		5.5	Mk	6										
1776	1	3								GSHAP	Ecuador:Tungurahua	厄瓜多尔:东谷拉瓦	-1.47	-78.44		4.3	Ms	5										
1776	1	18								GSHAP	Romania:Nehoiu	罗马尼亚:内霍尤	45.5	26.6	150	6.4	Ms	7										
1776	1	30								* Song	Dominica:Puerto Rico,W.	多米尼加:波多黎各西部	19	-70.4		6.3	Mk							3				
1776	2	6	19	30						GSHAP	Russia:Sakha,Churan	俄罗斯:萨哈共和国丘兰	61.2	137.4	20	5	Ms	6										

时间 Date						海啸 Tsunami				资料来源 Information	震中 Earthquake Epicenter				深度 Depth	震级 Mag	标度 Scale	烈度 MMI	死亡人数 Deaths		受伤人数 Injuries		经济损失 Damage		房屋毁坏 Houses Destroyed		房屋受损 Houses Damaged	
年	月	日	时	分	秒	源	浪高	级 I	级 S		地名(英文)	地名(中文)	纬度(°)	经度(°)					数量/人	级别	数量/人	级别	数量/$ Mill	级别	数量/间	级别	数量/间	级别
Year	Mo	Dy	Hr	Mn	Sec	Sr	Wh	mI	mS		Name(English)	Name(Chinese)	Latitude	Longitude					Num	Dd	Num	Dd	$ Mill	De	Num	Dh	Num	Dh
1776	4	21								* Song	Mexico: Guerrero, Morelos, Oaxaca	墨西哥:格雷罗,莫雷洛斯,瓦哈卡	16.7	-99.2		6.3	Mk							3				
1776	12									* China	China: Taiwan, Chiayi	中国:台湾嘉义	23.5	120.5		6	Ms	7		3				2		2		
1777	1	26	8							GSHAP, Song	Peru: Lima, Near Coast	秘鲁:利马近海	-11.8	-77.4	50	5	Mk	6										
1777	1	26	21							GSHAP, Song	Peru: Lima	秘鲁:利马	-12	-77		5	Mk	6										
1777	11	14				1				NOAA, Song	Sweden: Sundsvall	瑞典:松兹瓦尔	62.366	17.333		7	Mk											
1777										* Song	Morocco: Tangier, Sale	摩洛哥:丹吉尔,塞拉	35.5	-5.4		6.3	Mk							3				
1777										* Song	Mexico: Jalisco	墨西哥:哈利斯科	20.3	-103.7		6.3	Mk							3				
1778	1	30								* Song	Iran: Esfahan	伊朗:伊斯法罕	33.6	51.3		7.7	Mk		30000	5				3				
1778	2	13	21							Usami, Japan	Japan: Hiroshima	日本:广岛	34.6	132.7		6.6	Ms	8								1		
1778	3	4				1				NOAA, Song	Baltic Sea	波罗的海	58.5	20		7	Mk											
1778	6	16	18	30		3			3	* NOAA, Song	Turkey: Izmir	土耳其:伊兹密尔	38.5	27		6.7	Mk	10										
1778	7					1		1	0	* * NOAA, Song	Japan: Sagami Bay	日本:相模湾	35.1	139.5		7	Mk											
1778	11	25								Japan	Japan: Kumano	日本:三重熊野	34	136		6	Ms									1		
1778	12	15								* Iran	Iran: Kashan	伊朗:卡尚	34	51.3		6.2	Ms							3				
1778	12	23	5	45						GSHAP	Slovak: Humenne	斯洛伐克:胡门内	48.9	21.8	8	5.4	Ms	8										
1779	3									China	China: Inner Mongolia, Hure Qi	中国:内蒙古库伦	42.7	121.8		5.75	Ms	7		3						3		
1779	4	6	13	15						GSHAP	Slovak: Humenne	斯洛伐克:胡门内	48.9	21.8	7	4.6	Ms	7										
1779	8	1	13	9						GSHAP	Russia: Lake Baykal	俄罗斯:贝加尔湖	51.7	104.5	15	6.6	Ms	9										
1779	12	17								Japan, Song	Japan: Sado	日本:佐渡	38	138.4		6.1	Mk											1
1779	12	27								*	Iran: Tabriz	伊朗:大不里士	38	46.7		6.5	Muk	7	10000	5				3				
1780	1	8	19	30						*	Iran: Tabriz	伊朗:大不里士	38	46.2	20	7.7	Muk	9	200000	5				4		4		
1780	2	6								USGS, Song	US: Florida, Pensacola	美国:佛罗里达州彭萨科拉	30.4	-87.2		5.5	Mk	6										
1780	4	11				4				Japan, NOAA, Song	Japan: Sakurajima	日本:樱岛	31.6	130.7		7	Mk		15	1								
1780	5	31				4				Usami	Kuril Islands	千岛群岛	45.3	151.2		7	Ms	9	4									
1780	6	18				1				NOAA, Song	Japan: Hokkaido	日本:北海道	41.8	142.7		7	Mk		12	1								
1780	6	29				4	12	3.6	3	* NOAA	Kuril Islands	千岛群岛	45.3	151.2	40	7.5	Muk		12	1								
1780	7	20								Japan	Japan: Sakata	日本:山形酒田	38.9	139.9		6.5	Ms		2	1								1
1780	9	9				4	2	1	1	Japan, NOAA, Song	Japan: Sakurajima	日本:樱岛	31.6	130.7		7	Mk											3
1780	9	21	14							* GSHAP	Montenegro: Herceg Novi	蒙特尼哥罗(黑山):新海尔采格	42.5	18.7		5.7	Ms	10						3				
1780	10	3				4	3			* Song	Jamaica: Savanna La Mar	牙买加:滨海萨凡纳	18.2	-78.1		7.5	Mk		300	3								
1780	10	28								* GSHAP	Greece: Crete Island	希腊:克里特岛	35	25.8		7	Mk	10										
1780	10	31				5	2	1	1	Japan, NOAA, Song	Japan: Sakurajima	日本:樱岛	31.6	130.7		7	Mk		8	1								

年 Year	月 Mo	日 Dy	时 Hr	分 Mn	秒 Sec	海啸 源 Sr	海啸 浪高 Wh	海啸 级I mI	海啸 级S mS	资料来源 Information	震中 地名(英文) Name(English)	震中 地名(中文) Name(Chinese)	纬度(°) Latitude	经度(°) Longitude	深度 Depth	震级 Mag	标度 Scale	烈度 MMI	死亡人数 数量/人 Deaths Num	死亡人数 级别 Dd	受伤人数 数量/人 Injuries Num	受伤人数 级别 Dd	经济损失 数量/$ Mill Damage $ Mill	经济损失 级别 De	房屋毁坏 数量/间 Houses Destroyed Num	房屋毁坏 级别 Dh	房屋受损 数量/间 Houses Damaged Num	房屋受损 级别 Dh
1780										GSHAP	Russia:Sakha,SW.	俄罗斯:萨哈共和国西南	58.5	121	20	5.7	Ms	7										
1780										GSHAP	Iran:Mashhad	伊朗:马什哈德	36	60	30	6.5	Ms	7.5										
1781	6	3	10	10						* Italy,GSHAP	Italy:Cagli	意大利:卡利	43.594	12.506		6.23	Ms	10						3				
1781	8	1				2				* NOAA,Song	Jamaica:Montego Bay	牙买加:蒙特歌湾	18.1	-77.3		7.1	Mk							2				
1781	10	3								China	China:Yunnan,Dayao,NW.	中国:云南大姚西北	25.9	101.1		5.25	Ms	7										
1781										* GSHAP	Iran:Kordestan	伊朗:库尔德斯坦	36.2	46	14	7	Ms	10	80	2				2				
1782	4	30								China	China:Hunan,Shuangpai	中国:湖南双牌	25.8	111.8		5	Ms	6										
1782	5	22	16							GSHAP	Argentina:Mendoza	阿根廷:门多萨	-33	-69.2	30	7	Ms	8										
1782	5	22				2			2.5	* NOAA	China:South China Sea	中国:南海	18	108		7	Ms											
1782	8	22	16			4	2	1	1	* Usami,Japan,NOAA	Japan:Miura	日本:神奈川三浦	35.1	139.7		7.3	Ms	8		3				3	1000	3		
1782	9	21								Usami,Japan	Japan: Hachinohe	日本:青森八户	40.7	142		6.1	Ms											1
1783	1	13								GSHAP	Turkey:Igdir	土耳其:厄德尔	39.7	44.3	12	4.6	Ms	7										
1783	1	17	10							GSHAP	Kazakhstan:Semey	哈萨克斯坦:塞米伊	50.7	81.2	27	5.9	Ms	7										
1783	2	5	8			2			3	* NOAA,Song	Italy:Crotone	意大利:克罗托内	38.9	17.1		6.7	Mk											
1783	2	5	12			4			4	* Italy,NOAA	Italy:Sicily,Messina	意大利:西西里岛,墨西拿	38.3	15.97	13	6.91	Ms	11	30000	5				4		4		
1783	2	6	1	6		4	16			* Italy,NOAA	Italy:Villa San Giovanni	意大利:圣乔瓦尼镇	38.22	15.63		5.94	Ms	8	1500	4				2		2		
1783	2	7	13	10		1				* Italy,NOAA	Italy:Vibo Valentia	意大利:维博瓦伦蒂亚	38.58	16.2		6.59	Ms	11						3		3		
1783	2	7	15							* Song	Italy:Vibo Valentia	意大利:维博瓦伦蒂亚	38.2	15.55		5.7	Mk	9						3		3		
1783	3	1	1	40		3			3	* Italy,NOAA	Italy:Monteleone	意大利:蒙特莱奥内	38.77	16.3		5.92	Ms	9						3		3		
1783	3	5								Japan,Song	Japan:Tokyo	日本:东京	35.7	139.8		6.1	Mk											1
1783	3	20								* Song	Turkey:Amaxiki	土耳其:阿马西克	38.7	30.7		7.3	Mk	10	26	1								
1783	3	28	1	15		3				* Italy,NOAA	Italy:Monteleone	意大利:蒙特莱奥内	38.78	16.47		6.94	Ms	10	1141	4				3		3		
1783	4	19								Maso,Song	Celebes Sea	西里伯斯海	7.3	123.75		5	Mk	6										
1783	7	20								GSHAP	Syria:Hamah (Hama)	叙利亚:哈马	35.6	36.4	45	6.5	Ms	7										
1783	7	29								* Song	Italy:Gerace	意大利:杰拉切	38.3	16.3		6	Mk							3		3		3
1783	11	30	3	50						USGS	US:New Jersey,Oak Ridge	美国:新泽西州橡树岭	41	-74.5		5.3	Ms	6										
1783										China	China:Yunnan,Zhanyi	中国:云南沾益	25.6	103.8		5.25	Ms	7										
1783										* Song	Dominica:Santiago	多米尼加:圣地亚哥	19.3	-70.4		5.9	Mk							2				
1784	1	7				4			5	* NOAA	Italy:Messina	意大利:墨西拿	38.2	15.5		4.1	Ms	6						1		3		
1784	1	9	2			2			3	NOAA	Italy:Messina Straits	意大利:墨西拿海峡	38.167	15.633		4.1	Ms											
1784	1	19				2			3	* NOAA	Italy:Messina Straits	意大利:墨西拿海峡	38.167	15.633		4.1	Ms	6										
1784	1	23	21							GSHAP	Romania:Sighetu Marmatiei	罗马尼亚:锡盖图-马尔马切伊	47.9	23.9	10	4.7	Ms	6.5										
1784	3	28				1	3.7		2	* NOAA,Song	Mexico:Guerrero,Acapulco	墨西哥:格雷罗,阿卡普尔科	16.5	-99.5		7.7	Mk			3				3				
1784	4	2								* Song	Mexico:Oaxaca	墨西哥:瓦哈卡	17	-96.3		6.3	Mk							3				
1784	5	13	10							GSHAP,Song	Peru:Arequipa	秘鲁:阿雷基帕	-16.4	-71.5		4.5	Mk	5										

年 Year	月 Mo	日 Dy	时 Hr	分 Mn	秒 Sec	海啸 Tsunami 源 Sr	浪高 Wh	级 I mI	级 S mS	资料来源 Information	震中 Earthquake Epicenter 地名(英文) Name(English)	地名(中文) Name(Chinese)	纬度(°) Latitude	经度(°) Longitude	深度 Depth	震级 Mag	标度 Scale	烈度 MMI	死亡人数 Deaths 数量/人 Num	级别 Dd	受伤人数 Injuries 数量/人 Num	级别 Dd	经济损失 Damage 数量/$ Mill $ Mill	级别 De	房屋毁坏 Houses Destroyed 数量/间 Num	级别 Dh	房屋受损 Houses Damaged 数量/间 Num	级别 Dh
1784	5	13	12	35		2				* GSHAP, NOAA	Peru: Arequipa, Camana	秘鲁:阿雷基帕,卡马那	-16.5	-72	70	8.4	Ms	10	383	3				3		3		
1784	5	14	7	30						GSHAP, Song	Peru: Arequipa	秘鲁:阿雷基帕	-16.2	-72.1		5	Mk	6										
1784	5	16	5	30						GSHAP, Song	Peru: Arequipa	秘鲁:阿雷基帕	-16.2	-72.1		5	Mk	6										
1784	5	16	7							GSHAP, Song	Peru: Arequipa	秘鲁:阿雷基帕	-16.5	-72		4.5	Mk	5										
1784	5	16	8	15						GSHAP, Song	Peru: Arequipa	秘鲁:阿雷基帕	-16.2	-72.1		5	Mk	6										
1784	5	16	16	43						GSHAP, Song	Peru: Arequipa	秘鲁:阿雷基帕	-16.2	-72.1		5	Mk	6										
1784	5	16	17	40						GSHAP, Song	Peru: Arequipa	秘鲁:阿雷基帕	-16.2	-72.1		4.5	Mk	5										
1784	5	17	7							GSHAP, Song	Peru: Arequipa	秘鲁:阿雷基帕	-16.2	-72.1		5	Mk	6										
1784	5	17	19	56						GSHAP, Song	Peru: Arequipa	秘鲁:阿雷基帕	-16.2	-72.1		5	Mk	6										
1784	5	18	7							GSHAP, Song	Peru: Arequipa	秘鲁:阿雷基帕	-16.2	-72.1		4.5	Mk	5										
1784	5	18	9	30						GSHAP, Song	Peru: Arequipa	秘鲁:阿雷基帕	-16.2	-72.1		4.5	Mk	5										
1784	5	18	9	50						GSHAP, Song	Peru: Arequipa	秘鲁:阿雷基帕	-16.2	-72.1		5	Mk	6										
1784	5	18	16	30						GSHAP, Song	Peru: Arequipa	秘鲁:阿雷基帕	-16.2	-72.1		5	Mk	6										
1784	5	20	1	30						GSHAP, Song	Peru: Arequipa	秘鲁:阿雷基帕	-16.2	-72.1		4.5	Mk	5										
1784	5	20	7							GSHAP, Song	Peru: Arequipa	秘鲁:阿雷基帕	-16.2	-72.1		4.5	Mk	5										
1784	5	20	8	15						GSHAP, Song	Peru: Arequipa	秘鲁:阿雷基帕	-16.2	-72.1		4.5	Mk	5										
1784	5	20	8							GSHAP, Song	Peru: Arequipa	秘鲁:阿雷基帕	-16.2	-72.1		4.5	Mk	5										
1784	5	21	1	46						GSHAP, Song	Peru: Arequipa	秘鲁:阿雷基帕	-16.2	-72.1		5	Mk	6										
1784	5	21	7							GSHAP, Song	Peru: Arequipa	秘鲁:阿雷基帕	-16.2	-72.1		4.5	Mk	5										
1784	5	22	16	58						GSHAP, Song	Peru: Arequipa	秘鲁:阿雷基帕	-16.2	-72.1		4.5	Mk	5										
1784	5	23	7	15						GSHAP, Song	Peru: Arequipa	秘鲁:阿雷基帕	-16.2	-72.1		4.5	Mk	5										
1784	5	27								GSHAP, Song	Peru: Arequipa	秘鲁:阿雷基帕	-16.2	-72.1		4.5	Mk	5										
1784	5	29	6	15						GSHAP, Song	Peru: Arequipa	秘鲁:阿雷基帕	-16.2	-72.1		4.5	Mk	5										
1784	5	29	9	33						GSHAP, Song	Peru: Arequipa	秘鲁:阿雷基帕	-16.2	-72.1		4.5	Mk	5										
1784	5	30	10	35						GSHAP, Song	Peru: Arequipa	秘鲁:阿雷基帕	-16.2	-72.1		5	Mk	6										
1784	5	30	19	5						GSHAP, Song	Peru: Arequipa	秘鲁:阿雷基帕	-16.2	-72.1		4.5	Mk	5										
1784	5	31	15							GSHAP, Song	Peru: Arequipa	秘鲁:阿雷基帕	-16.2	-72.1		4.5	Mk	5										
1784	6	2	8	50						GSHAP, Song	Peru: Arequipa	秘鲁:阿雷基帕	-16.2	-72.1		4.5	Mk	5										
1784	6	2	23	56						GSHAP, Song	Peru: Arequipa	秘鲁:阿雷基帕	-16.2	-72.1		4.5	Mk	5										
1784	6	6	22	36						GSHAP, Song	Peru: Arequipa	秘鲁:阿雷基帕	-16.2	-72.1		5	Mk	6										
1784	6	10	1							GSHAP, Song	Peru: Arequipa	秘鲁:阿雷基帕	-16.2	-72.1		4.5	Mk	5										
1784	6	10	5	48						GSHAP, Song	Peru: Arequipa	秘鲁:阿雷基帕	-16.2	-72.1		4.5	Mk	5										
1784	6	10	21	58						GSHAP, Song	Peru: Arequipa	秘鲁:阿雷基帕	-16.2	-72.1		4.5	Mk	5										
1784	6	19	1	30						GSHAP, Song	Peru: Arequipa	秘鲁:阿雷基帕	-16.2	-72.1		4.5	Mk	5										
1784	6	20	4							GSHAP, Song	Peru: Arequipa	秘鲁:阿雷基帕	-16.2	-72.1		5	Mk	6										
1784	6	30	0	45						GSHAP, Song	Peru: Arequipa	秘鲁:阿雷基帕	-16.2	-72.1		4.5	Mk	5										
1784	7	1	20	30						GSHAP, Song	Peru: Arequipa	秘鲁:阿雷基帕	-16.2	-72.1		4.5	Mk	5										
1784	7	8	8							GSHAP, Song	Peru: Arequipa	秘鲁:阿雷基帕	-16.2	-72.1		5	Mk	6										
1784	7	14	21	30						GSHAP, Song	Peru: Arequipa	秘鲁:阿雷基帕	-16.2	-72.1		4.5	Mk	5										

年 Year	月 Mo	日 Dy	时 Hr	分 Mn	秒 Sec	源 Sr	浪高 Wh	级 I mI	级 S mS	资料来源 Information	地名(英文) Name(English)	地名(中文) Name(Chinese)	纬度(°) Latitude	经度(°) Longitude	深度 Depth	震级 Mag	标度 Scale	烈度 MMI	死亡人数 Deaths 数量/人 Num	死亡人数 Deaths 级别 Dd	受伤人数 Injuries 数量/人 Num	受伤人数 Injuries 级别 Dd	经济损失 Damage 数量/$ Mill	经济损失 Damage 级别 De	房屋毁坏 Houses Destroyed 数量/间 Num	房屋毁坏 Houses Destroyed 级别 Dh	房屋受损 Houses Damaged 数量/间 Num	房屋受损 Houses Damaged 级别 Dh
1784	7	18	14	55						GSHAP, Song	Peru: Arequipa	秘鲁:阿雷基帕	-16.2	-72.1		5	Mk	6										
1784	7	22	20	30						GSHAP, Song	Peru: Arequipa	秘鲁:阿雷基帕	-16.2	-72.1		5	Mk	6										
1784	7	23	8							GSHAP, Song	Peru: Arequipa	秘鲁:阿雷基帕	-16.2	-72.1		5	Mk	6										
1784	7	23								* Song	Turkey: Erzurum, Erzincan	土耳其:埃尔佐鲁姆,埃尔津占	39.7	39.5		7	Mk		5000	4				3				
1784	7	29	10	45						GSHAP, Song	Peru: Arequipa	秘鲁:阿雷基帕	-16.2	-72.1		5	Mk	6										
1784	7	29	14	10						* Song	Haiti: Petit Goave, Leogane	海地:佩蒂特高维,利欧干	18.5	-72.3		6.3	Mk							3				
1784	7	30	6	30						GSHAP, Song	Peru: Arequipa	秘鲁:阿雷基帕	-16.2	-72.1		4.5	Mk	5										
1784	8	2	0	30						GSHAP, Song	Peru: Arequipa	秘鲁:阿雷基帕	-16.2	-72.1		5	Mk	6										
1784	8	3	8							GSHAP, Song	Peru: Arequipa	秘鲁:阿雷基帕	-16.2	-72.1		4.5	Mk	5										
1784	8	12	12	15						GSHAP, Song	Peru: Arequipa	秘鲁:阿雷基帕	-16.2	-72.1		4.5	Mk	5										
1784	8	13	12	30						GSHAP, Song	Peru: Arequipa	秘鲁:阿雷基帕	-16.2	-72.1		4.5	Mk	5										
1784	8	14								* Iceland	Iceland: Selfoss	冰岛:塞尔福斯	64	-20.5	10	7.1	Ms							3				
1784	8	15								* Song	Spain: L'Arnes Syssel	西班牙:拉内斯,西塞尔	40.9	0.3		6.5	Mk	9						2				
1784	8	29								Usami, Japan	Japan: Tokyo Bay	日本:东京湾	35.6	139.8		6.1	Ms											1
1784	12	2	13							GSHAP, Song	Peru: Arequipa	秘鲁:阿雷基帕	-16.2	-72.1		5	Mk	6										
1785	1	30								* Song	Greece: Patrai	希腊:帕特累	38.2	21.7		6.1	Mk	9	38	1				2				
1785	2	23	1	2						GSHAP, Turkey	Russia: Chechnia, Grozny	俄罗斯:车臣共和国格罗兹尼	43.1	46.3	16	5.5	Ms	6.5										
1785	2	23								GSHAP	Caspian Sea	里海	44.5	47	60	6	Ms	5.5										
1785	4	18								* China	China: Gansu, Jiayuguan	中国:甘肃嘉峪关	39.9	98		6.5	Ms	8	36	1				2		2		
1785	7	12	12	45						* GSHAP	Colombia: Bogota, Soacha	哥伦比亚:波哥达,索阿查	4.6	-74		7	Ms	9	14	1				3				
1785	7	14	9	45						* * GSHAP	Colombia: Santa Fe	哥伦比亚:圣达菲	4.5	-74.6		5.9	Ms							2				
1785	12									GSHAP	Georgia: Poti	格鲁吉亚:波季	41.8	42	7	4.5	Ms	7.5										
1785	12									China	China: Sichuan, Dawu, SE.	中国:四川道孚东南	30.6	101.5		5.75	Ms	7										
1785										*	Mexico: Guerrero, Acapulco, E.	墨西哥:格雷罗州阿卡普尔科东部	16.7	-99.2		7.8	Muk							3				
1785										China	China: Yunnan, Tengchong	中国:云南腾冲	25	98.5		5.25	Ms	7										
1786	2	5								* GSHAP	Greece: Corfu (Kerkira)	希腊:科孚岛	39.7	19.8		7	Ms		120	3				3				
1786	3	9								* Italy	Italy: Sicily, Melazzo	意大利:西西里岛,米拉佐	38.1	15.02		6.02	Ms	10										
1786	3	23								Usami, Japan	Japan: Hakone	日本:神奈川箱根	35.2	139.1		5.5	Ms									1		
1786	5	10	15							GSHAP	Ecuador: Chimborazo, N.	厄瓜多尔:钦博腊索山北部	-1.7	-78.8		6.3	Ms	8										
1786	6	1								* China	China: Sichuan, Garze, S.	中国:四川甘孜南	29.9	102		7.75	Ms	9	435	3				3		3		
1786	6	10								China	China: Sichuan, Luding, S.	中国:四川泸定南	29.4	102.2		7	Ms							2				
1786	6	13								GSHAP	Ecuador: Chimborazo, N.	厄瓜多尔:钦博腊索山北部	-1.67	-78.7		4.3	Ms	5										

时间						海啸				资料来源	震中				深度	震级	标度	烈度	死亡人数		受伤人数		经济损失		房屋毁坏		房屋受损	
年	月	日	时	分	秒	源	浪高	级I	级S		地名(英文)	地名(中文)	纬度(°)	经度(°)					数量/人	级别	数量/人	级别	数量/$ Mill	级别	数量/间	级别	数量/间	级别
Date						Tsunami				Information	Earthquake Epicenter				Depth	Mag	Scale	MMI	Deaths		Injuries		Damage		Houses Destroyed		Houses Damaged	
Year	Mo	Dy	Hr	Mn	Sec	Sr	Wh	mI	mS		Name(English)	Name(Chinese)	Latitude	Longitude					Num	Dd	Num	Dd	$ Mill	De	Num	Dh	Num	Dh
1786	6	18								* GSHAP	China: Xinjiang, Ili	中国:新疆伊犁	44	80.8		6.5	Ms	8						2		3		
1786	6	23	2	30						GSHAP	Ecuador: Chimborazo, N.	厄瓜多尔:钦博腊索山北部	-1.7	-78.7		4.3	Ms	5										
1786	9	5								GSHAP, Song	Ecuador: Chimborazo, N.	厄瓜多尔:钦博腊索山北部	-1.7	-78.7		4.5	Mk	5										
1786	10									GSHAP	Iran: Tabriz	伊朗:大不里士	38.3	45.6	9	6.3	Ms	9.5										
1786										* Song	Venezuela: Merida	委内瑞拉:梅里达	8.5	-71.2		6.1	Mk	8						2				
1787	1	18								GSHAP	Romania: Nereju	罗马尼亚:内雷茹	45.7	26.6	150	6.4	Ms	7										
1787	3	22	15							GSHAP, Song	Peru: Arequipa	秘鲁:阿雷基帕	-16.2	-72.1		4.5	Mk	5										
1787	3	23	11							GSHAP, Song	Peru: Arequipa	秘鲁:阿雷基帕	-16.2	-72.1		4.5	Mk	5										
1787	3	23	17							GSHAP, Song	Peru: Arequipa	秘鲁:阿雷基帕	-16.2	-72.1		4.5	Mk	5										
1787	3	28	17	30		4	4	2	2.5	* NOAA	Mexico: San Marcos, Oaxaca	墨西哥:圣马科斯,瓦哈卡	16.5	-98.5		8.3	Ms		11	1				3				
1787	4	3	15	30		2	4	2	1	* NOAA	Mexico: San Marcos, Oaxaca	墨西哥:圣马科斯,瓦哈卡	15.5	-97		7.3	Ms							2				
1787	5	2								* Song	Puerto Rico: Arecibo, Mayaguez	波多黎各:阿雷西波,马亚盖斯	18.3	-66.4		5.9	Mk							2				
1787	5	10								* Song	Puerto Rico: Ponce, San Juan	波多黎各:蓬塞,圣胡安	18	-66.4		5.9	Mk							2				
1787	5	13	6							* Maso, Song	Philippines: Panay, Capiz, Iloilo	菲律宾:班乃,卡皮斯,伊洛伊洛	10.8	122.5		7.3	Mk	10		3				2				
1787	6	11	14	45						GSHAP	Ecuador: Guayaquil	厄瓜多尔:瓜亚基尔	-2.2	-79.9		5	Ms	6										
1787	7	12	22	45						* Bautista, Maso	Philippines: Panay, Iloilo	菲律宾:班乃,伊洛伊洛	11.05	122.25		7.4	Ms	10		3				3				
1787	10	27				1				* NOAA, Song	Jamaica: Montego Bay	牙买加:蒙特歌湾	18.3	-77.5		7	Mk											
1787	12	13								China	China: Sichuan, Dujiangyan	中国:四川都江堰	31	103.6		4.75	Ms	6										
1787										* * Song	Iran: Tabrīz	伊朗:大不里士	38	46.2		6.3	Mk							3				
1788	7	8				1				NOAA, Song	England: Douglas, Near Coast	英国:道格拉斯,近海	53.8	-4.9		7	Mk											
1788	7	21				4	30	3	3	* NOAA	Alaska: Kodiak Island	阿拉斯加:科迪亚克岛	57	-153		8	Ms			3				1		1		
1788	7	22								USGS, Song	Aleutian Islands	阿留申群岛	56	-157		5.7	Mk	7										
1788	8	6				4	30	3.3	4	* NOAA	Aleutian Islands	阿留申群岛	55	-161		8	Ms			3				1				
1788	10	12								* Song	Saint Lucia: Castries	圣卢西亚:卡斯特里	14	-61		6.5	Mk	9	900	3				3				
1788										*	Benin: Abomey	贝宁:阿波美	7.6	1.7		5.6	Muk	8						2				
1789	5	9	15			2			1	* * Usami, Japan, NOAA	Japan: Shikoku, Near Coast	日本:四国近海	32.9	134.5		7.4	Ms	10										
1789	5	29								GSHAP	Turkey: Elazig	土耳其:埃拉泽	39	40	40	7	Ms	8										
1789	6	7								* China	China: Yunnan, Huaning	中国:云南华宁	24.2	102.9		7	Ms	9		3		3		3		3		
1789	9	30	4	15						* Italy	Italy: Citta Di Castello, Sansepolcro	意大利:卡斯得洛城,圣塞波尔克罗	43.505	12.208		5.8	Ms	10	500	3				3				

年 Year	月 Mo	日 Dy	时 Hr	分 Mn	秒 Sec	源 Sr	浪高 Wh	级I mI	级S mS	资料来源 Information	地名(英文) Name(English)	地名(中文) Name(Chinese)	纬度(°) Latitude	经度(°) Longitude	深度 Depth	震级 Mag	标度 Scale	烈度 MMI	死亡人数 数量/人 Deaths Num	死亡人数 级别 Deaths Dd	受伤人数 数量/人 Injuries Num	受伤人数 级别 Injuries Dd	经济损失 数量/$ Mill Damage $ Mill	经济损失 级别 Damage De	房屋毁坏 数量/间 Houses Destroyed Num	房屋毁坏 级别 Houses Destroyed Dh	房屋受损 数量/间 Houses Damaged Num	房屋受损 级别 Houses Damaged Dh
1789	11	7								* China	China:Shaanxi,Tongguan	中国:陕西潼关	34.6	110.3		5	Ms	6		2				1		1		
1790	4	5								GSHAP	Russia:Kamchatka, Near East Coast	俄罗斯:堪察加东部近海	53	160	20	4.9	Ms	6										
1790	4	6	19	29						GSHAP	Romania:Nereju	罗马尼亚:内雷茹	45.7	26.6	150	6.9	Ms	8										
1790	10	9	1	15		3			4	* NOAA,Song	Algeria:Oran	阿尔及利亚:奥兰	35.7	-0.6		7	Mk	10	3000	4				3		3		
1790	12	2	1							*	Russia:Kamchatka, Near East Coast	俄罗斯:堪察加东部近海	54	162	20	7.5	Muk	10										
1791	1	1								Usami,Japan	Japan:Tokyo	日本:东京	35.65	139.8		6.5	Ms											1
1791	2	11								China	China:Hebei,Shenxian,W.	中国:河北深县西	38	115		5.5	Ms	6										
1791	4	8								* China	China:Fujian,Dongshan	中国:福建东山	23.8	117.5		5.5	Ms	7						2		3		
1791	4	14	7			1				* NOAA	Russia:Kamchatka Peninsula	俄罗斯:堪察加半岛	56	163		6.8	Ms											
1791	4	15	7			1				* GSHAP, NOAA	Russia:Kamchatka Peninsula	俄罗斯:堪察加半岛	56	163	20	6.8	Ms	9										
1791	5	12	21			2	11	2	2.5	Japan,NOAA, Song	Japan:Shimabara	日本:长崎岛原	32.8	130.3		7.5	Mk							1				1
1791	5	16	13							USGS,Song	US:Connecticut,East Haddam	美国:康涅狄格州东哈德姆	41.5	-72.5		5.7	Mk	7										
1791	7	4	10	30						GSHAP,Song	Peru:Lima,Near Coast	秘鲁:利马近海	-11.8	-77.4	50	5	Mk	6										
1791	7	23								Japan	Japan:Matsumoto	日本:长野松本	36.2	138		6.75	Ms								550	3		
1791	9	13				3		1	1	* Japan,NOAA	Japan:Sakai	日本:大阪堺市	34.5	135.4		6.5	Muk			2								
1791	10	12	17							* Italy	Italy:Tropea – Vibo Valentia	意大利:特罗佩阿–维博瓦伦蒂亚	38.7	16.1		6	Ms	9	15	1				2				
1791	10	15	1	17						GSHAP,Song	Peru:Perene	秘鲁:佩雷内	-10.8	-75.6	30	5	Mk	6										
1791	10	22								* Song	Greece:Zakinthos (Zante)	希腊:扎金索斯岛(桑特岛)	37.5	20.3		7	Mk	10	22	1				3				
1791	11	2	21			2			3	* NOAA, GSHAP	Mediterranean Sea	地中海	35.8	21		7	Ms	10						2				
1791										* Song	Morocco:Melilla	摩洛哥:梅利利亚	35.3	-2.97		5.9	Mk							2				
1791										* Song	Iran:Tabriz	伊朗:大不里士	38	46.2		5.9	Mk							2				
1791										* Song	Guatemala:Mazatenango	危地马拉:马萨特南戈	14.6	-91.5		6.3	Mk							3				
1791										China	China:Xizang (Tibet),Banbar	中国:西藏边坝	30.8	95		6.75	Ms	9										
1792	4	13								GSHAP	Colombia:Urrao	哥伦比亚:乌劳	6.2	-76.5		5.7	Ms	7										
1792	4									China	China:Jiangxi,Anfu,W.	中国:江西安福西	27.4	114.6		4.75	Ms	6										
1792	5	21	9			5	55	3.5	3	* Usami,Japan, NOAA	Japan:Nagasaki	日本:长崎	32.8	130.3		6.4	Ms		15030	5		3		3	6200	4		
1792	6	13	6			4		1	2	* Usami,Japan, NOAA	Japan:W. Hokkaido Island	日本:北海道岛西部海域	43.5	140.6		6.9	Muk		5	1				1				
1792	7	12	2	50						GSHAP,Song	Peru:Huancavelica	秘鲁:万卡韦利卡	-13.1	-75		5	Mk	6										
1792	8	7								GSHAP,Song	Chile:Arica	智利:阿里卡	-18.5	-70.35		6	Mk	8										

时间 年 Date Year	月 Mo	日 Dy	时 Hr	分 Mn	秒 Sec	海啸 源 Tsunami Sr	浪高 Wh	级 I mI	级 S mS	资料来源 Information	震中 地名(英文) Earthquake Epicenter Name(English)	地名(中文) Name(Chinese)	纬度(°) Latitude	经度(°) Longitude	深度 Depth	震级 Mag	标度 Scale	烈度 MMI	死亡人数 数量/人 Deaths Num	级别 Dd	受伤人数 数量/人 Injuries Num	级别 Dd	经济损失 数量/$ Mill Damage $ Mill	级别 De	房屋毁坏 数量/间 Houses Destroyed Num	级别 Dh	房屋受损 数量/间 Houses Damaged Num	级别 Dh
1792	8	9				2	10			* China, NOAA	China: Taiwan, Chiayi	中国:台湾嘉义	23.6	120.6		7	Ms	9	252	3	432	3		3	14889	5		
1792	8	16								Japan, Song	Japan: Tokyo	日本:东京	35.7	139.8		6.5	Mk		20	1								
1792	8	22	18			1			2	* NOAA	Russia: Kamchatka, Near East Coast	俄罗斯:堪察加东部近海	54	162	40	8.4	Muk	11										
1792	9	7								* China	China: Sichuan, Dawu, SE.	中国:四川道孚东南	30.8	101.2		6.75	Ms	8	205	3				2		3		
1792	11	30								China	China: Sichuan, Dawu, SE.	中国:四川道孚东南	30.6	101.5		5.5	Ms	7							202	3		
1792						1			1	* USGS, NOAA	Alaska: Kodiak Island	阿拉斯加:科迪亚克岛	57	-152		5.7	Ms	7						1		1		
1793	1	13								Usami, Japan	Japan: Yamaguchi	日本:山口	34.1	131.5		6.9	Ms									1		
1793	2	8	4			4	3.6	1	1	* Usami, NOAA	Japan: Aomori	日本:青森	40.85	139.95		6.9	Muk	9	12	1				1	175	3		
1793	2	17				4	4.5	2.2	2	* Usami, NOAA	Japan Trench	日本海沟	38.5	144		8.3	Ms	11	732	3				3	1060	4		
1793	2									Japan, Song	Japan: Iwate	日本:岩手	39.2	141.2		6.3	Mk									1		1
1793	4	12								* Song	Haiti: Santo Domingo (St Domingue)	海地:多米尼加(圣多明哥)	19	-72.3		5.9	Mk							2				
1793	4	17								Japan, Song	Japan: Aomori, Near Coast	日本:青森近海	40.7	142.3		6.1	Mk											1
1793	5	15								* China	China: Sichuan, Dawu, SE.	中国:四川道孚东南	30.6	101.5		6	Ms	8	200	3	30	1		2		3		
1793	7									* Song	Azores: Flores	亚速尔群岛:弗洛勒斯岛	39.3	-31.1		7.3	Mk	10										
1793	12	8	7	30						GSHAP	Black Sea	黑海	44.8	33.2	30	5.5	Ms	6										
1793	12	8	18							GSHAP	Romania: Nereju	罗马尼亚:内雷茹	45.7	26.6	100	6.4	Ms	6.5										
1794	3	14								* Song	Iran: Kashan	伊朗:卡尚	34	51.4		5.9	Mk							2				
1794	3	26								GSHAP, Song	Peru: Cusco	秘鲁:库斯科	-12	-72		4.5	Mk	5										
1794	6	11	3			3				GSHAP, NOAA	Greece: Achaia	希腊:阿凯亚	38.3	22.4		6.7	Ms											
1794	9	7								GSHAP, Song	Peru: Lima, Near Coast	秘鲁:利马近海	-12.2	-77.4	40	4.5	Mk	5										
1794	9	10								* Song	Venezuela: Cumana	委内瑞拉:库马纳	10.5	-64.2		5.9	Mk							2				
1794	11	15								Japan, Song	Japan: Tokyo	日本:东京	35.7	139.8		6.3	Mk									1		
1795	5	20	22							*	Guinea: Conakry	几内亚:科纳克里	9.3	-13.4		5.2	Muk	5						2				
1795	5	23								* Song	Mexico: Oaxaca	墨西哥:瓦哈卡	17	-96.3		6.3	Mk							3				
1795	8	5								China	China: Hebei, Luanxian	中国:河北滦县	39.7	118.7		5.5	Ms	7										
1796	1	3								Japan	Japan: Tottori	日本:鸟取	35.7	134.3		6	Ms									1		1
1796	2	15								* Song	Colombia: N Santander, Pamplona	哥伦比亚:北桑坦德,潘普洛纳	7.4	-72.7		5.9	Mk	6						2				
1796	2	26								* Song	Syria: Al - Ladhiqiyah (Latakia)	叙利亚:拉塔基亚	35.2	35.8		7	Mk	9	1500	4				3				
1796	3	18								* Italy	Italy: Isola D'Ischia	意大利:伊斯基亚岛	40.75	13.92		5.17	Ms		7	1				2				
1796	3	30	10	45						*	Chile: Copiapo, Vallenar	智利:科皮亚波,巴耶纳尔	-27.35	-70.35		7.7	Muk	11		1				2		3		
1796	3									China	China: Shandong, Zhucheng	中国:山东诸城	36	119.4		5	Ms	6										
1796	11	5	6			4				* Bautista, Maso	Philippines: Luzon, Pangasinan	菲律宾:吕宋岛雅丝兰	16.1	120.5		6.9	Ms	9						3				

年 Year	月 Mo	日 Dy	时 Hr	分 Mn	秒 Sec	源 Sr	浪高 Wh	级 I mI	级 S mS	资料来源 Information	地名(英文) Name(English)	地名(中文) Name(Chinese)	纬度(°) Latitude	经度(°) Longitude	深度 Depth	震级 Mag	标度 Scale	烈度 MMI	死亡人数 Deaths 数量/人 Num	死亡人数 Deaths 级别 Dd	受伤人数 Injuries 数量/人 Num	受伤人数 Injuries 级别 Dd	经济损失 Damage 数量/$ Mill	经济损失 Damage 级别 De	房屋毁坏 Houses Destroyed 数量/间 Num	房屋毁坏 Houses Destroyed 级别 Dh	房屋受损 Houses Damaged 数量/间 Num	房屋受损 Houses Damaged 级别 Dh
1797	2	4	12	30						* GSHAP	Ecuador: Chimborazo, N.	厄瓜多尔:钦博腊索山北部	-1.7	-78.7		8.3	Muk	11	40000	5				4				
1797	2	6	21							GSHAP	Ecuador: Tungurahua	厄瓜多尔:东谷拉瓦	-1.43	-78.55		4.3	Ms	5										
1797	2	9	0	30						GSHAP	Ecuador: Tungurahua	厄瓜多尔:东谷拉瓦	-1.43	-78.55		5	Ms	6										
1797	2	10				4			3	* NOAA, Song	Indonesia: Southern Sumatra	印度尼西亚:苏门答腊南部	-1	100		7.7	Mk		300	3				2		3		
1797	3	18	20	25						GSHAP	Ecuador: Carchi, E.	厄瓜多尔:卡尔奇东部	0.4	-77.8		4.3	Ms	5										
1797	3									Maso, Song	Philippines: Manila	菲律宾:马尼拉	14.6	121		5.5	Mk	7										
1797	8	5								China	China: Hebei, Leting	中国:河北乐亭	39.4	118.9		5	Ms	6										
1797	11	21				4				Japan, NOAA, Song	Japan: Sakurajima	日本:樱岛	31.6	130.7		7	Mk											
1797	12	4								* Song	Venezuela: Cumana, Cariaco	委内瑞拉:库马纳,卡利亚科	10.5	-64.2		7.7	Mk		16000	5								
1797	12	14	23	30						GSHAP, Song	Venezuela: Isla Cubagua	委内瑞拉:库巴瓜岛	10.6	-64.1		6.5	Mk	9										
1797										China	China: Taiwan, Tainan	中国:台湾台南	23	120.2		5	Ms	6										
1798	2	2								* Song	El Salvador: San Vicente	萨尔瓦多:圣维森特	13.7	-88.7		7.1	Mk			3				4				
1798	2	12								GSHAP	Colombia: El Bajito	哥伦比亚:埃尔巴希托	1.9	-78.7		4	Ms	5										
1798	2	22				2				* NOAA, Song	Costa Rica: Limón	哥斯达黎加:利蒙	10.2	-82.9		7	Mk											
1798	5	23	4	30						GSHAP	Russia: Perm, Lysva	俄罗斯:彼尔姆州雷西瓦	58	58	15	4.5	Ms	6										
1798	5	26								* Italy	Italy: Firenze (Florence)	意大利:佛罗伦萨	43.342	11.416		5.17	Ms	10						3				
1798	6									* Song	Greece: Morea, Cerigo	希腊:摩里亚,察里哥	36.2	23		7	Mk	10										
1798	8	24								* Song	Chile: Copiapo	智利:科皮亚波	-27.35	-70.35		5.9	Mk							2		2		
1799	1	21	21							GSHAP, Song	Peru: Lima, Near Coast	秘鲁:利马近海	-12.2	-77.4	40	5	Mk	6										
1799	1	25								* Song	France: Machecoul, Bouin	法国:马什库勒,布安	46.9	-2		6.1	Mk	8						2				
1799	6	29	7			4	2	1	1	* Usami, NOAA	Japan: Kanazawa	日本:石川金泽	36.6	136.6		6.4	Ms	8	15						5000	4		
1799	7	29	20							* Italy	Italy: Camerino	意大利:卡梅利诺	43.147	13.123		5.93	Ms	10	60	2				3				
1799	8	27								* China	China: Yunnan, Shiping, NW.	中国:云南石屏西北	23.8	102.4		7	Ms	9	2000	4				4	15236	5		
1799	9	16	16	22						GSHAP	Russia: Krasnodar, Krymsk	俄罗斯:克拉斯诺达尔区克雷姆斯克	45.2	38.2	30	5.1	Ms	5.5										
1799	9									*	Colombia: Bucaramanga	哥伦比亚:布卡拉曼加	7.5	-73.5		5	Ms	7						3				
1799	10	7	4	50						GSHAP, Song	Peru: Cusco	秘鲁:库斯科	-12	-72		4.5	Mk	5										
1799	11	4	20	42						GSHAP, Song	Venezuela: Cumana	委内瑞拉:库马纳	10.47	-64.17		5	Mk	6										
1799										* Song	Indonesia: Sumatra, Palembang	印度尼西亚:苏门答腊,巨港	-2.983	104.75		5.9	Mk							2				
1799										*	Uzbekistan: Uzgut	乌兹别克斯坦:乌尔古特	39.4	67.2	10	6	Muk	9						3				
1799						2			1	* NOAA, Song	Peru: Chimbote, Off Coast	秘鲁:钦博特沿海	-10	-84		7.7	Mk							3				
1800	2	4								GSHAP	Colombia: Mapiripan	哥伦比亚:梅塔的马皮里潘	3.5	-73		5	Ms	7										

时间						海啸				资料来源	震中				深度	震级	标度	烈度	死亡人数		受伤人数		经济损失		房屋毁坏		房屋受损	
年	月	日	时	分	秒	源	浪高	级I	级S		地名(英文)	地名(中文)	纬度(°)	经度(°)					数量/人	级别	数量/人	级别	数量/$ Mill	级别	数量/间	级别	数量/间	级别
Date						Tsunami				Information	Earthquake Epicenter				Depth	Mag	Scale	MMI	Deaths		Injuries		Damage		Houses Destroyed		Houses Damaged	
Year	Mo	Dy	Hr	Mn	Sec	Sr	Wh	mI	mS		Name(English)	Name(Chinese)	Latitude	Longitude					Num	Dd	Num	Dd	$ Mill	De	Num	Dh	Num	Dh
1800	2	27	9							GSHAP,Song	Peru:Lima	秘鲁:利马	-12	-77		5	Mk	6										
1800	3	8								* Song	Mexico:Mexico City,Oaxaca	墨西哥:墨西哥城,瓦哈卡	19.2	-99.1		6.3	Mk							3				
1800	5	10	15	30						GSHAP,Song	Peru:Lima	秘鲁:利马	-12	-77		4.5	Mk	5										
1800	6	2	20	17		2				NOAA,Song	Portugal:Azores	葡萄牙:亚速尔群岛	38.5	-28		7	Mk											
1800	10	11								CGS,USGS	US:California,San Juan Bautista	美国:加利福尼亚州圣胡安包蒂斯塔	36.8	-121.5		5.5	Ms	7										
1800	11	22	21	30						USGS	US:California,San Diego	美国:加利福尼亚州圣地亚哥	33	-117.3		6.5	Ms	7										
1800	12	18								GSHAP,Song	Peru:Lima	秘鲁:利马	-12	-77		4.5	Mk	5										
1800	12	25								USGS,Song	US:Massachusetts,Taunton	美国:马萨诸塞州汤顿	41.9	-71.1		5.5	Mk	6										
1800										GSHAP	Russia:Lake Baykal	俄罗斯:贝加尔湖	55.05	108.91	15	6.3	Ms	8.5										
1800										*	Iran:Mazanderan	伊朗:马赞德兰	36.2	53.3		6.5	Muk							3				
1800										GSHAP	Russia:Buryatiya,Mol To	俄罗斯:布里亚特州莫利托村	52.8	100	15	6.9	Ms	9										
1801	1	1								GSHAP,Song	Chile:Coquimbo	智利:科金博	-29.95	-71.25		6	Mk	8										
1801	5	5								* Song	Mexico:Oaxaca	墨西哥:瓦哈卡	17	-96.3		6.3	Mk		7	1				3				
1801	5	14	21	30						* Song	Switzerland:Altdorf	瑞士:阿尔特多夫	46.9	8.6		6	Mk	4		2								
1801	5	26								Usami	Japan:Kimitsu	日本:千叶君津	35.3	140		6.5	Ms									1		1
1801	11	26	19							Japan,Song	Japan:Inabe	日本:三重员弁	35.2	136.5		6.1	Mk											1
1802	1	3	6	30						GSHAP,Italy	Croatia:Rijeka	克罗地亚:里耶卡	45.4	14.4	12	6.1	Ms	7.5										
1802	1	4	7			2			3	NOAA,Song	Croatia:Rijeka	克罗地亚:里耶卡	45.3	14.4		6.7	Mk											
1802	3	19				2				* NOAA,Song	Antigua And Barbuda:St Kitts	安提瓜和巴布达:圣基茨	17.2	-62.4		7	Mk											
1802	5	12	9	30						* Italy	Italy:Soncino	意大利:松奇诺	45.42	9.85		5.67	Ms	9						2				
1802	5	20	20	30						GSHAP,Song	Venezuela:El Tocuyo	委内瑞拉:托丘约	10.48	-68.03		5	Mk	6										
1802	8	15				3				* NOAA,Song	Venezuela:Cumana	委内瑞拉:库马纳	10.5	-64.2		7	Mk							1				
1802	8					3		1	1.5	* NOAA,Song	Indonesia:Banda Sea	印度尼西亚:班达海	-4	129		7	Mk											
1802	10	26	10	55						* GSHAP	Romania:Nereju	罗马尼亚:内雷茹	45.7	26.6	150	7.7	Muk	10						2				
1802	11	7	10	45		3			2	* NOAA,Song	Algeria:Kolea,Blida, Algiers	阿尔及利亚:布利达,阿尔及尔	36.5	2.9		7	Mk			3				3	1100	4	1100	4
1802	11	15								Japan,Song	Japan:Inabe	日本:三重员弁	35.2	136.5		6.1	Mk											1
1802	11	18								Japan	Japan:Inabe	日本:三重员弁	35.2	136.5		7	Ms									1		1
1802	12	9	5			4		0		* Usami,NOAA	Japan:Sado Island	日本:佐渡岛	37.7	138.3		6.6	Ms	9	37	1				3	1500	4		
1802	12	28				4				* * NOAA,Song	Japan:Sado Island	日本:佐渡岛	38	138		7.1	Mk		20	1				2				
1802										GSHAP	Ecuador:Cotopaxi	厄瓜多尔:科托帕希	-0.93	-78.61		5	Ms	6										
1803	2	2								* China	China:Yunnan,Binchuan	中国:云南宾川	25.7	100.5		6.25	Ms	8	200	3				2		2		
1803	5	25								CGS,USGS	US:California,Poway	美国:加利福尼亚州波韦	32.8	-117.1		5.5	Ms	6										

年 Year	月 Mo	日 Dy	时 Hr	分 Mn	秒 Sec	海啸 Tsunami 源 Sr	浪高 Wh	级 I mI	级 S mS	资料来源 Information	震中 Earthquake Epicenter 地名(英文) Name(English)	地名(中文) Name(Chinese)	纬度(°) Latitude	经度(°) Longitude	深度 Depth	震级 Mag	标度 Scale	烈度 MMI	死亡人数 Deaths 数量/人 Num	级别 Dd	受伤人数 Injuries 数量/人 Num	级别 Dd	经济损失 Damage 数量/$ Mill	级别 De	房屋毁坏 Houses Destroyed 数量/间 Num	级别 Dh	房屋受损 Houses Damaged 数量/间 Num	级别 Dh
1803	9	1	1	30						* India, GSHAP	India: Treasury Mahon	印度:库马翁	31	79		8.1	Ms							3				
1803										GSHAP	Ecuador: Chimborazo, N.	厄瓜多尔:钦博腊索山北部	-1.67	-78.64		5	Ms	6										
1804	1	8				1				* NOAA, Song	Greece: Achaia, Patrai (Patras)	希腊:阿凯亚,帕特累	38.3	21.8		6.7	Mk	9		2								
1804	1	13	17	45		4			2	NOAA, Song	Spain: Alboran Sea	西班牙:阿尔沃兰海	36.833	-1.167		6.7	Mk											
1804	4	22								GSHAP, Song	Peru: Cuzco	秘鲁:库斯科	-13.5	-72		5	Mk	6										
1804	5	5	17							GSHAP	Russia: Lake Baykal	俄罗斯:贝加尔湖	52	105.5	15	6	Ms	8										
1804	6	8	1			2			3	* NOAA, GSHAP	Greece: Patrai	希腊:帕特累	38.2	21.8		6.7	Ms	10		2				3				
1804	7	10	13			4	1	0.5	1	* Usami, NOAA	Japan: Sakata	日本:山形酒田	39.05	139.95		7.3	Ms	9	450	3		4		4	10810	5		
1804	7	20								Japan, Song	Japan: Hiroshima	日本:广岛	34.6	132.7		6.4	Mk	8										
1804	7	31	22			2			3	NOAA, Song	Italy: Bay of Naples	意大利:那不勒斯湾	40.7	14.15		6.7	Mk											
1804	8	20	20	10						USGS	US: Illinois, Chicago	美国:伊利诺斯州芝加哥	42	-87.8		4.4	Ms	6										
1804	8	25	7							* Song	Spain: Dalias	西班牙:达利亚斯	36.9	-2.4		7.3	Mk	10	162	3				2				
1804	12									China	China: Jiangxi, Xunwu	中国:江西寻乌	24.9	115.6		5.25	Ms	7								3		
1805	1	9	12	30						GSHAP, Song	Peru: Lima	秘鲁:利马	-12	-77		4.5	Mk	5										
1805	1	10	10							GSHAP, Song	Peru: Lima	秘鲁:利马	-12	-77		4.5	Mk	5										
1805	1	27	13							* Song	Venezuela: Cumana	委内瑞拉:库马纳	10.5	-64.2		6.1	Mk	8						2				
1805	1	28	2							GSHAP, Song	Peru: Lima	秘鲁:利马	-12	-77		4.5	Mk	5										
1805	2	21	21	30						GSHAP, Song	Peru: Lima	秘鲁:利马	-12	-77		4.5	Mk	5										
1805	3	1	10							GSHAP, Song	Peru: Lima	秘鲁:利马	-12	-77		4.5	Mk	5										
1805	6	11								GSHAP	Russia: Kamchatka, Near East Coast	俄罗斯:堪察加东部近海	53	160	30	6.6	Ms	8										
1805	6	16	8	15						* GSHAP	Colombia: Caparrapi	哥伦比亚:卡帕拉皮	5.3	-74.6		7	Ms	9	200	3				3				
1805	6	25								China	China: Hebei, Xingtai	中国:河北邢台	37.1	114.5		5	Ms	6										
1805	7	1	10							GSHAP, Song	Peru: Lima	秘鲁:利马	-12	-77		4.5	Mk	5										
1805	7	26	20	57		2			2	* Italy, NOAA	Italy: Molise, Napoli	意大利:莫利塞,那不勒斯	41.5	14.47		6.57	Ms	11	5600	4				4				
1805	8	5								China	China: Hebei, Changli	中国:河北昌黎	39.7	119.2		5.5	Ms	7							235	3		
1805	9	27								China	China: Sichuan, Luding	中国:四川泸定	29.9	102.2		4.75	Ms	6										
1805	11	8	1							GSHAP, Song	Peru: Lima	秘鲁:利马	-12	-77		4.5	Mk	5										
1805	11	10	1	30						GSHAP, Song	Peru: Lima	秘鲁:利马	-12	-77		4.5	Mk	5										
1805	12	14	21	30						GSHAP, Song	Peru: Lima	秘鲁:利马	-12	-77		4.5	Mk	5										
1805										* Song	Iran: Tehran, Damāvand	伊朗:德黑兰,达马万德	36.3	52.4		5.9	Mk							2				
1806	1	11								China	China: Jiangxi, Huichang, S.	中国:江西会昌南	25.3	115.7		6	Ms	8										
1806	3	25	8			2				* NOAA, Song	US: California, Santa Barbara	美国:加利福尼亚州圣巴巴拉	34.4	-119.7		7.2	Mk	6						1				
1806	3	25								*	Mexico: Jalisco, Oaxaca	墨西哥:哈利斯科,瓦哈卡	18.9	-103.8		7.5	Ms			3								

年 Year	月 Mo	日 Dy	时 Hr	分 Mn	秒 Sec	源 Sr	浪高 Wh	级 I mI	级 S mS	资料来源 Information	地名(英文) Name(English)	地名(中文) Name(Chinese)	纬度(°) Latitude	经度(°) Longitude	深度 Depth	震级 Mag	标度 Scale	烈度 MMI	死亡人数 Deaths 数量/人 Num	死亡人数 Deaths 级别 Dd	受伤人数 Injuries 数量/人 Num	受伤人数 Injuries 级别 Dd	经济损失 Damage 数量/$ Mill	经济损失 Damage 级别 De	房屋毁坏 Houses Destroyed 数量/间 Num	房屋毁坏 Houses Destroyed 级别 Dh	房屋受损 Houses Damaged 数量/间 Num	房屋受损 Houses Damaged 级别 Dh
1806	6	11								China	China:Xizang (Tibet), Cona, NW.	中国:西藏错那西北	28. 2	91. 8		7. 5	Ms	10	101	3								
1806	7	18								China	China:Guangxi, Rong – an, SE.	中国:广西融安东南	25. 1	109. 4		4. 75	Ms	6										
1806	8	26	13	20		2			2	* Italy, NOAA	Italy:Albano	意大利:阿尔巴诺	41. 72	12. 73		5. 47	Ms	8										
1806	12	1	23			3	1		0. 5	* NOAA	Peru:Lima, Near Coast	秘鲁:利马近海	– 12	– 78	30	7. 5	Muk	8						1				
1806	12	30	18	45						GSHAP, Song	Peru:Lima, Near Coast	秘鲁:利马近海	– 12	– 78		4. 5	Mk	5										
1806										GSHAP	Russia:Lake Baykal	俄罗斯:贝加尔湖	52. 16	106. 25	15	6. 5	Ms	9										
1807	2	17	17							GSHAP	Colombia:Tame	哥伦比亚:塔梅	6. 5	– 71. 7		5. 7	Ms	7										
1807	2	23								GSHAP, Song	Peru:Paccha	秘鲁:帕克查	– 11. 8	– 75. 5		4. 5	Mk	5										
1807	2	25	12							GSHAP	Russia:Kamchatka, Near East Coast	俄罗斯:堪察加东部近海	55. 5	163	10	6	Ms	8. 5										
1807	9	15	17							GSHAP	Russia:Mari El, Yurino	俄罗斯:马里埃尔共和国尤里诺	56. 2	46. 5	5	5	Ms	7										
1807										GSHAP	Kazakhstan:Almaty	哈萨克斯坦:阿拉木图	43. 1	76. 9	20	6. 7	Ms	8. 5										
1808	4	2	16	43		3			2	Italy, NOAA	Italy:Pinerolo	意大利:皮奈罗洛	44. 83	7. 25		5. 67	Ms											
1808	4									* Song	Morocco:Melilla	摩洛哥:梅利利亚	35. 3	– 2. 97		5. 9	Mk							2				
1808	6	21								CGS, USGS	US:California, San Francisco	美国:加利福尼亚州旧金山	37. 8	– 122. 6		6	Ms	8										
1808	6	26	18							GSHAP	Iran:Semnan	伊朗:塞姆南	35. 3	54. 5	12	6. 6	Ms	9. 5										
1808	8	8	11							GSHAP	Brasil:Caraúbas	巴西:卡拉乌巴斯	– 5. 7	– 37. 7	15	4. 8	Ms	6										
1808	8	8				4	1. 5	0. 5	0. 5	* NOAA	Japan:Tokushima, E. Awa	日本:德岛, 阿波东部	33. 9	134. 8		6. 5	Ms											
1808	8	16								China	China:Xizang (Tibet), Lhunze	中国:西藏隆子	28. 4	92. 3		5. 5	Ms	7										
1808	10	9								* Song	Iran:Mazanderan	伊朗:马赞德兰	36. 3	53. 3		6. 3	Mk							3				
1808	12	4				1				Japan, NOAA, Song	Japan:Wakayama	日本:和歌山	34. 3	135. 6		7	Mk											
1808	12	16								* Iran	Iran:Qazvin	伊朗:加兹温	36. 4	50. 3		5. 9	Ms							3				
1808										GSHAP, Song	Peru:Lima	秘鲁:利马	– 12	– 77		5	Mk	6										
1808										* Song	Ecuador:Quito	厄瓜多尔:基多	– 0. 2	– 78. 3		5. 5	Mk							1				
1808										Japan, Song	Japan:Satsumasendai	日本:鹿岛萨摩川内	31. 8	130. 3		6. 4	Mk	8										
1809	3	9	23	30						GSHAP	Russia:Kirov, Kirovo – Chepetsk	俄罗斯:基洛夫州基洛夫切佩茨克	58. 5	50	10	5	Ms	6										
1809	7	3				2			3	NOAA, Song	Italy:Pinerolo	意大利:皮奈罗洛	44. 8	7. 2		6. 7	Mk											
1809	11	17	21	40						GSHAP	Poland:Presov	斯洛伐克:普雷绍夫	49	21. 25	10	5	Ms	7										
1809	11	18	19							GSHAP	Russia:Kamchatka, Near East Coast	俄罗斯:堪察加东部近海	52	159	30	6. 8	Ms	8. 5										
1809	12	4				1				* NOAA, Song	South Africa:Cape of Good Hope	南非:好望角	– 33. 88	18. 45		7	Mk											
1809	12	7								* Iran, GSHAP	Iran:Mazanderan	伊朗:马赞德兰	36. 3	52. 5	11	6. 5	Ms	9. 5						3				

年 Year	月 Mo	日 Dy	时 Hr	分 Mn	秒 Sec	海啸 Tsunami 源 Sr	浪高 Wh	级 I mI	级 S mS	资料来源 Information	地名(英文) Name(English)	地名(中文) Name(Chinese)	纬度(°) Latitude	经度(°) Longitude	深度 Depth	震级 Mag	标度 Scale	烈度 MMI	死亡人数 Deaths 数量/人 Num	级别 Dd	受伤人数 Injuries 数量/人 Num	级别 Dd	经济损失 Damage 数量/$ Mill	级别 De	房屋毁坏 Houses Destroyed 数量/间 Num	级别 Dh	房屋受损 Houses Damaged 数量/间 Num	级别 Dh
1809						1				NOAA, Song	Guam	关岛(西太平洋)	14	143.3		7	Mk											
1810	1	7	14							GSHAP, Song	Peru: Lima	秘鲁:利马	-12	-77		4.5	Mk	5										
1810	1	11	22							GSHAP, Song	Peru: Lima	秘鲁:利马	-12	-77		4.5	Mk	5										
1810	2	16								* Song	Greece: Crete, Iraklion	希腊:克里特岛,伊拉克利翁	35.5	25	100	7	Mk	10	2000	4				3		3		3
1810	2	19								Korea, GSHAP	North Korea: Nanam	朝鲜:罗南	41.8	129.8		6.5	Ms	9										
1810	3	20								* Song	Canary Islands: Tenerife	加那利群岛:特纳利夫岛	28.2	-16.6		6.5	Mk	9		3								
1810	5	15	10							GSHAP, Song	Peru: Lima	秘鲁:利马	-12	-77		4.5	Mk	5										
1810	6	15	10	30						GSHAP, Song	Peru: Lima	秘鲁:利马	-12	-77		4.5	Mk	5										
1810	9	25	6			4	1	1	-1	* Usami, NOAA	Japan: Akita	日本:秋田	39.9	139.9		6.6	Ms	8	59	2				3	1804	4		
1810	10									* Song	Cuba: Havana, Santiago De Cuba	古巴:哈瓦那,圣地亚哥	23.8	-82.2		5.9	Mk							2				
1810	11	10	2	15						USGS, Song	US: New Hampshire, Hampton	美国:新汉普郡州汉普顿	43	-70.8		5.5	Mk	6										
1810	11	15	4	45						GSHAP, Song	Chile: Arica	智利:阿里卡	-18.5	-70.2		4.5	Mk	5										
1810	11	17	10							GSHAP, Song	Peru: Lima	秘鲁:利马	-12	-77		4.5	Mk	5										
1810	11	26	22	30						GSHAP, Song	Peru: Lima	秘鲁:利马	-12	-77		4.5	Mk	5										
1810	12	27	1	35						GSHAP, Song	Peru: Arequipa	秘鲁:阿雷基帕	-16.4	-71.6		4.5	Mk	5										
1810	12	28	3							GSHAP, Song	Peru: Arequipa	秘鲁:阿雷基帕	-16.4	-71.6		4.5	Mk	5										
1810										GSHAP, Iran	Iran: Bojnurd	伊朗:博季努尔德	38	57	11	6.5	Ms	9.5										
1811	1	1	5							*	Georgia: TBilisi	格鲁吉亚:第比利斯	41.8	45.2	7	4.2	Muk	7						2				
1811	1	1	23							GSHAP	Brasil: Porto Alegre	巴西:阿雷格里港	-30.04	-51.3		4.3	Ms	5										
1811	1	14	17	30						GSHAP, Song	Peru: Arequipa	秘鲁:阿雷基帕	-16.4	-71.6		5	Mk	6										
1811	1	25	8							GSHAP, Song	Peru: Arequipa	秘鲁:阿雷基帕	-16.4	-71.6		4.5	Mk	5										
1811	1	27								Japan, Song	Japan: Miyake Jima	日本:三宅岛	33.941	139.513		6.4	Mk	8										
1811	1	30	8							GSHAP, Song	Peru: Arequipa	秘鲁:阿雷基帕	-16.4	-71.6		4.5	Mk	5										
1811	2	3	3							GSHAP, Song	Peru: Arequipa	秘鲁:阿雷基帕	-16.4	-71.6		4.5	Mk	5										
1811	3	9	11							GSHAP, Song	Peru: Lima	秘鲁:利马	-12	-77		4.5	Mk	5										
1811	3	18								* China	China: Taiwan, Miaoli, Coast of W.	中国:台湾苗栗西部海域	24.8	120.8		6.75	Ms		21	1	21	1		2				
1811	4	14	7							GSHAP, Song	Peru: Lima	秘鲁:利马	-12	-77		4.5	Mk	5										
1811	4	20	19	30						GSHAP, Song	Peru: Lima	秘鲁:利马	-12	-77		4.5	Mk	5										
1811	4	21	2	30						GSHAP, Song	Peru: Lima	秘鲁:利马	-12	-77		4.5	Mk	5										
1811	6	4	18	50						GSHAP, Song	Peru: Lima	秘鲁:利马	-12	-77		5	Mk	6										
1811	6	7	19							GSHAP, Song	Peru: Lima	秘鲁:利马	-12	-77		4.5	Mk	5										
1811	6	8	2	45						GSHAP, Song	Peru: Sayán	秘鲁:萨扬	-11.4	-77		5	Mk	6										
1811	7	2								GSHAP, Song	Peru: Lima	秘鲁:利马	-12	-77		4.5	Mk	5										
1811	7	6	13	15						GSHAP, Song	Peru: Lima	秘鲁:利马	-12	-77		4.5	Mk	5										
1811	7	11	12	13						GSHAP, Song	Peru: Lima	秘鲁:利马	-12	-77		4.5	Mk	5										

年 Year	月 Mo	日 Dy	时 Hr	分 Mn	秒 Sec	源 Sr	浪高 Wh	级I mI	级S mS	资料来源 Information	地名(英文) Name(English)	地名(中文) Name(Chinese)	纬度(°) Latitude	经度(°) Longitude	深度 Depth	震级 Mag	标度 Scale	烈度 MMI	死亡人数 Deaths 数量/人 Num	级别 Dd	受伤人数 Injuries 数量/人 Num	级别 Dd	经济损失 Damage 数量/$ Mill	级别 De	房屋毁坏 Houses Destroyed 数量/间 Num	级别 Dh	房屋受损 Houses Damaged 数量/间 Num	级别 Dh
1811	7	14	11	37						GSHAP, Song	Peru: Lima	秘鲁:利马	-12	-77		5	Mk	6										
1811	7	23	21	45						GSHAP, Song	Peru: Lima	秘鲁:利马	-12	-77		4.5	Mk	5										
1811	7	26	1	30						GSHAP, Song	Peru: Lima	秘鲁:利马	-12	-77		5	Mk	6										
1811	7	30	7	45						GSHAP, Song	Peru: Lima	秘鲁:利马	-12	-77		5	Mk	6										
1811	8	3	16	30						GSHAP, Song	Peru: Lima	秘鲁:利马	-12	-77		5	Mk	6										
1811	8	16	2	35						GSHAP, Song	Peru: Lima	秘鲁:利马	-12	-77		4.5	Mk	5										
1811	8	18								GSHAP, Song	Peru: Lima	秘鲁:利马	-12	-77		5	Mk	6										
1811	8	23								GSHAP, Song	Peru: Lima	秘鲁:利马	-12	-77		4.5	Mk	5										
1811	8	25	9	35						GSHAP, Song	Peru: Lima	秘鲁:利马	-12	-77		4.5	Mk	5										
1811	8	26								GSHAP, Song	Peru: Lima	秘鲁:利马	-12	-77		4.5	Mk	5										
1811	8	29	8	45						GSHAP, Song	Peru: Lima	秘鲁:利马	-12	-77		4.5	Mk	5										
1811	9	1								GSHAP, Song	Peru: Lima	秘鲁:利马	-12	-77		4.5	Mk	5										
1811	9	2	10	30						GSHAP, Song	Peru: Lima	秘鲁:利马	-12	-77		4.5	Mk	5										
1811	9	27	15							GSHAP, Song	Peru: Lima	秘鲁:利马	-12	-77		4.5	Mk	5										
1811	9	27								* China	China: Sichuan, Luhuo, NW.	中国:四川炉霍西北	31.7	100.3		6.75	Ms	9	480	3				2	598	3		
1811	10	5								* Bautista, Maso	Philippines: Camarines	菲律宾:馬利納	13.55	123.1		6.7	Ms	9						2				
1811	10	23	2							GSHAP, Song	Peru: Lima	秘鲁:利马	-12	-77		5	Mk	6										
1811	10	28	15	30						GSHAP, Song	Peru: Lima	秘鲁:利马	-12	-77		4.5	Mk	5										
1811	10	28	22	30						GSHAP	Brasil: Olinda	巴西:奥林达	-8.08	-34.87		3.8	Ms	5										
1811	11	19	14	15		2	4	2	2	* NOAA, Song	Chile: Valparaiso	智利:瓦尔帕莱索	-33.08	-71.67		7.5	Mk											
1811	11	25	4	45						GSHAP, Song	Peru: Lima	秘鲁:利马	-12	-77		4.5	Mk	5										
1811	12	2	9	30						GSHAP, Song	Peru: Lima	秘鲁:利马	-12	-77		4.5	Mk	5										
1811	12	6	16	30						GSHAP, Song	Peru: Lima	秘鲁:利马	-12	-77		4.5	Mk	5										
1811	12	16	8	15						* NOAA	US: Arkansas, Lepanto	美国:阿肯色州勒班陀	35.6	-90.4		8.5	Ms	11		1				3				
1811	12	16	14	15						* NOAA	US: Arkansas, Lepanto	美国:阿肯色州勒班陀	35.6	-90.4		8	Ms	10										
1811	12	21	15							GSHAP, Song	Peru: Lima	秘鲁:利马	-12	-77		5	Mk	6										
1811	12	23	4	45						GSHAP, Song	Peru: Lima	秘鲁:利马	-12	-77		5	Mk	6										
1811	12	30								GSHAP, Song	Peru: Lima	秘鲁:利马	-12	-77		5	Mk	6										
1811										China	China: Sichuan, Dawu, SE.	中国:四川道孚东南	30.6	101.5		5.75	Ms	7										
1812	1	3	16	45						GSHAP, Song	Peru: Arequipa	秘鲁:阿雷基帕	-16.8	-71.8	25	5	Mk	6										
1812	1	23	15							* NOAA	US: Missouri, New Madrid	美国:密苏里州新马德里	36.3	-89.6		8.4	Ms	11						3				
1812	2	7	9	45						* NOAA	US: Missouri, New Madrid	美国:密苏里州新马德里	36.5	-89.6		8.8	Ms	10						3				
1812	3	5	12	30						GSHAP	Romania: Nereju	罗马尼亚:内雷茹	45.7	26.6	150	6.4	Ms	7										
1812	3	8								* China	China: Xinjiang, Nilka, E.	中国:新疆尼勒克东	43.7	83.5		8	Ms	11		4								
1812	3	22								* Italy	Italy: Roma (Rome)	意大利:罗马	41.895	12.482		5.03	Ms	8						2				
1812	3	23								* Song	France: Beaumont, Pierrevert	法国:博蒙特,皮耶维尔丘	43.7	5.7		6.5	Mk	9						2				
1812	3	26	20	7		2				* NOAA	Venezuela: La Guaira	委内瑞拉:拉瓜伊拉	10.6	-66.9	33	7.7	Muk	10	26000	5				3				

时间						海啸				资料来源	震中				深度	震级	标度	烈度	死亡人数		受伤人数		经济损失		房屋毁坏		房屋受损	
年	月	日	时	分	秒	源	浪高	级 I	级 S		地名(英文)	地名(中文)	纬度(°)	经度(°)					数量/人	级别	数量/人	级别	数量/$ Mill	级别	数量/间	级别	数量/间	级别
Date						Tsunami				Information	Earthquake Epicenter				Depth	Mag	Scale	MMI	Deaths		Injuries		Damage		Houses Destroyed		Houses Damaged	
Year	Mo	Dy	Hr	Mn	Sec	Sr	Wh	mI	mS		Name(English)	Name(Chinese)	Latitude	Longitude					Num	Dd	Num	Dd	$ Mill	De	Num	Dh	Num	Dh
1812	4	2								China	China:Henan,Ruicheng	中国:河南芮城	34.6	110.6		5.5	Ms	7										
1812	4	21	10							Usami,Japan	Japan:Yamaguchi	日本:山口	33.8	132.5		6.9	Ms	9								1		
1812	5	29	4	30						GSHAP	Colombia:Cauca	哥伦比亚:考卡	2.5	-76.5		4.5	Ms	5										
1812	6	23				2				* NOAA,Song	France:Prats De Mollo, Arles-Sur-Tech	法国:普拉德莫洛,阿尔勒	43.3	5.366		6.6	Mk											
1812	9	18	1							GSHAP,Song	Peru:Arequipa	秘鲁:阿雷基帕	-16.4	-71.6		4.5	Mk	5										
1812	11	9	22							USGS,Song	US:Missouri,New Madrid	美国:密苏里州新马德里	36.5	-89.6		5.5	Mk	6										
1812	11	11	10	50		2				* NOAA,Song	Jamaica:Kingston	牙买加:金斯敦	18	-76.5		7.1	Mk							2				
1812	12	4								GSHAP,Song	Peru:Arequipa	秘鲁:阿雷基帕	-16.4	-71.6		4.5	Mk	5										
1812	12	7	6							* Usami,Japan	Japan:Yokohama	日本:神奈川横滨	35.4	139.6		6.6	Muk	8		3						1		
1812	12	8	15							*	US:California, San Juan Capistrano	美国:加利福尼亚州圣胡安卡皮斯特拉诺	34.37	-117.65		6.9	ML	8	40	1				2				
1812	12	21	19			4	3.4	1.8	1.5	* CGS,USGS,NOAA	US:California,Oxnard	美国:加利福尼亚州奥克斯纳德	34.2	-119.9		7.7	Muk	8	1	1				2				
1812	12	28	10	30						GSHAP,Song	Peru:Arequipa	秘鲁:阿雷基帕	-16.4	-71.6		4.5	Mk	5										
1813	3	30	9	30						* Song	Peru:Ica	秘鲁:伊卡	-14.1	-75.4		5.9	Mk		32	1				2				
1813	5	17				2			2	NOAA,Song	Tyrrhenian Sea	第勒尼安海(伊特鲁里亚海)	40	14		6.7	Mk											
1813	10	17								China	China:Zhejiang,Wenzhou	中国:浙江温州	28	120.7		4.75	Ms	6										
1813										China	China:Shanxi,Linfen,S.	中国:山西临汾	36	111.4		5.25	Ms	7								3		
1813										* Song	Iran:Fars,Shiraz	伊朗:法尔斯,设拉子	29.6	52.6		5.9	Mk							2				
1814	1	10								China	China:Henan,Xinmi	中国:河南新密	34.6	113.5		5	Ms	6										
1814	2	1	10							GSHAP,Song	Peru:Paita	秘鲁:派塔	-5	-81	40	5	Mk	6										
1814	2	2								* Maso,Song	Philippines:Sorsogon	菲律宾:索索贡	13.1	123.9		6.3	Mk	7						3				
1814	2	4								* China	China:Henan,Hebi	中国:河南鹤壁	35.8	114.4		5.5	Ms	7	4	1		3		1		2		
1814	5	22								* Song	France:Gan,Oloron,Benejacq	法国:冈,奥洛龙,塔碧斯	43.2	0.4		5.9	Mk	7						2				
1814	9	2	20							GSHAP	Russia:Buryatiya,Kyren	俄罗斯:布里亚特州克廖恩	51.8	102.4	15	6.4	Ms	8.5										
1814	11	19	4	15						GSHAP	Colombia:Bogota	哥伦比亚:波哥达	4.6	-74		4.5	Ms	5										
1814	11	20	5							GSHAP	Colombia:Cauca	哥伦比亚:考卡	2.5	-76.5		4.5	Ms	5										
1814	11	22	8							Usami,Japan	Japan:Tosa	日本:高知土佐	33.5	133.4		6.2	Ms											1
1814	11	24								* China	China:Yunnan,Shiping	中国:云南石屏	23.7	102.5		6	Ms	8	900	3				3	900	3		
1814	12	16	23							GSHAP	Russia:Buryatiya,Tankhoy	俄罗斯:布里亚特州坦霍伊	51.5	105	15	6.4	Ms	8.5										
1814						2		1	1	* NOAA,Song	Indonesia:Timor Island	印度尼西亚:帝汶岛	-9.6	124.7		7	Mk							3				
1815	3	1	14							Usami	Japan:Kaga	日本:石川加贺	36.4	136.5		6.2	Ms											1
1815	4	11				2				* NOAA,Song	Indonesia:Ambon Island	印度尼西亚:安汶岛	-3.7	128.2		7	Mk							1		1		
1815	4	18	14	20						GSHAP,Song	Peru:Lima	秘鲁:利马	-12	-77		4.5	Mk	5										

年 Year	月 Mo	日 Dy	时 Hr	分 Mn	秒 Sec	海啸 Tsunami 源 Sr	浪高 Wh	级 I mI	级 S mS	资料来源 Information	震中 Earthquake Epicenter 地名(英文) Name(English)	地名(中文) Name(Chinese)	纬度(°) Latitude	经度(°) Longitude	深度 Depth	震级 Mag	标度 Scale	烈度 MMI	死亡人数 Deaths 数量/人 Num	级别 Dd	受伤人数 Injuries 数量/人 Num	级别 Dd	经济损失 Damage 数量/$ Mill $ Mill	级别 De	房屋毁坏 Houses Destroyed 数量/间 Num	级别 Dh	房屋受损 Houses Damaged 数量/间 Num	级别 Dh
1815	5	3								* Song	Mexico:Oaxaca,Tamazulapan	墨西哥:瓦哈卡,塔马卒拉潘	17	-96.3		6.3	Mk							3				
1815	6									GSHAP	Brasil:Salvador	巴西:萨尔瓦多	-12.76	-38.49		4	Ms	6										
1815	7									China	China:Taiwan,Yilan	中国:台湾宜兰	24.8	121.8		5	Ms	6										
1815	8	5								China	China:Tianjin	中国:天津	39.1	117.2		5	Ms	6										
1815	10	13								* China	China:Taiwan,Taoyuan	中国:台湾桃园	25	121.3		6.75	Ms	8	111	3				3		3		
1815	10	23								* China	China:Shanxi,Pinglu	中国:山西平陆	34.8	111.2		6.75	Ms	9	13000	5				4	20000	5		
1815	11	22				3		1	1.5	* NOAA	Indonesia:Bali Island	印度尼西亚:巴厘岛	-8	115.2	122	7	Ms		11453	5								
1815	11	26								China	China:Shanxi,Pinglu	中国:山西平陆	34.8	111.2		4.75	Ms	6										
1815	12	29	2							GSHAP,Song	Peru:Arequipa	秘鲁:阿雷基帕	-16.4	-71.6		4.5	Mk	5										
1815	12									* Song,Turkey	Greece:Crete Island	希腊:克里特岛	35	25.75		6.3	Mk	9						3		3		3
1815										* Song,Turkey	Greece: Ionian Islands, Levkas	希腊:伊奥尼亚群岛,莱夫卡斯	38.8	20.5		5.8	Mk	8		1								
1816	1	20	17							GSHAP,Song	Chile:Concepcion	智利:康塞普西翁	-36.83	-73.03		6	Mk	8										
1816	2	1	12	45						GSHAP,Song	Peru:Arequipa	秘鲁:阿雷基帕	-16.4	-71.6		4.5	Mk	5										
1816	3									China	China:Taiwan,Yilan	中国:台湾宜兰	24.8	121.8		5.75	Ms	7										
1816	5	1				2			0	* NOAA,Song	Malaysia:Penang Island	马来西亚:潘昂岛	5.383	100.25		7	Mk											
1816	7	8	10	30						GSHAP,Song	Peru:Arequipa	秘鲁:阿雷基帕	-16.4	-71.6		4.5	Mk	5										
1816	7	22	15	30						*	Guatemala:Huehuetenango	危地马拉:韦韦特南戈	15.5	-91.5	33	7.5	Muk	9	23	1				3		3		
1816	9									China	China:Taiwan,Yilan	中国:台湾宜兰	24.8	121.8		5.5	Ms	7										
1816	10	2	0	30						GSHAP,Song	Peru:Arequipa	秘鲁:阿雷基帕	-16.4	-71.6		4.5	Mk	5										
1816	11	29	2							GSHAP	Colombia:Neiva	哥伦比亚:内瓦	3	-75.4		4.5	Ms	7										
1816	11	29	19							GSHAP	Colombia:Neiva	哥伦比亚:内瓦	3	-75.4		4.5	Ms	5										
1816	12	8								* China	China:Sichuan,Luhuo	中国:四川炉霍	31.4	100.7		7.5	Ms	10	2854	4				3	1104	4		
1817	1	1				1				NOAA,Song	Greece:Ionian Sea	希腊:伊奥尼亚海	38.25	22.25		6.6	Mk											
1817	1	8	9							USGS	US:South Carolina,Charleston	美国:卡罗莱纳州查尔斯顿	32.9	-80		5	Ms	5										
1817	1	8				4	0.3			* Song	US:New Jersey,Cherry Hill	美国:新泽西州切里希尔	39.95	-75.1		7	Mk											
1817	1	14	3	30		2			3	NOAA,Song	Italy:Sicilia Island	意大利:西西里岛	37.5	13		6.7	Mk											
1817	3	11	20	10						*	France:Chamonix Valley	法国:夏蒙尼峡谷	45.9	6.8		8	Muk		4	1				3				
1817	8	23	8			2	5		3	* NOAA	Greece:Achaia	希腊:阿凯亚	38.25	22.25		6.8	Ms	10										
1817	9	18								GSHAP	Colombia:Cauca	哥伦比亚:考卡	2.5	-76.5		5.7	Ms	7										
1817	10	5	16	45						USGS,Song	US:Massachusetts,Medford	美国:马萨诸塞州梅德福	42.5	-71.2		5.5	Mk	6										
1817										GSHAP	Uzbekistan:Samarkand	乌兹别克斯坦:撒马尔罕	39.4	67.1	10	5.3	Ms	8										
1818	1					1				NOAA,Song	Greece:Athens	希腊:雅典	38	23.6		6.6	Mk											
1818	2	20	18	10		3			3	* Italy,NOAA	Italy:Acireale, Catania	意大利:阿瑟瑞尔,卡塔尼亚	37.6	15.13		6	Ms	10	72	2				3		3		

年 Year	月 Mo	日 Dy	时 Hr	分 Mn	秒 Sec	海啸 Tsunami 源 Sr	浪高 Wh	级 I mI	级 S mS	资料来源 Information	震中 Earthquake Epicenter 地名(英文) Name(English)	地名(中文) Name(Chinese)	纬度(°) Latitude	经度(°) Longitude	深度 Depth	震级 Mag	标度 Scale	烈度 MMI	死亡人数 Deaths 数量/人 Num	级别 Dd	受伤人数 Injuries 数量/人 Num	级别 Dd	经济损失 Damage 数量/$ Mill $ Mill	级别 De	房屋毁坏 Houses Destroyed 数量/间 Num	级别 Dh	房屋受损 Houses Damaged 数量/间 Num	级别 Dh
1818	2	23	18	10		3			3	* Italy, NOAA	Italy: Imperia, Near Coast	意大利：因佩里亚近海岸	43. 92	8. 034		5. 55	Ms	10						3		3		
1818	3	18				3			1. 5	* NOAA	Indonesia: Bengkulu	印度尼西亚：明古鲁	-3. 767	102. 267		7	Ms							1				
1818	4	23								* GSHAP	Bulgaria: Breznik	保加利亚：布雷兹尼克	42. 8	23. 3		6. 5	Ms	10										
1818	5	31								* Song	Mexico: Mexico City	墨西哥：墨西哥城	19. 2	-99. 1		6. 3	Mk							3				
1818	9	5								Japan, Song	Japan: Tokyo	日本：东京	35. 7	139. 8		6. 4	Mk	8										
1818	9	8	9	37						* Italy	Italy: Sicilia Island	意大利：西西里岛	37. 82	14. 08		5. 31	Ms	10	100	2				3		3		
1818	11	8				2	3. 5		2	* NOAA	Indonesia: Bali Sea	印度尼西亚：巴厘海	-7	117	600	8. 5	Ms							2		3		
1818	12	8	4	5						GSHAP, Song	Peru: Arequipa	秘鲁：阿雷基帕	-16. 4	-71. 6		4. 5	Mk	5										
1818	12	9	18	52		2			3	Italy, NOAA	Italy: Langhirano	意大利：兰吉拉诺	44. 668	10. 286		5. 57	Ms											
1818										Maso, Song	Philippines: Mansalay	菲律宾：曼萨莱	12. 51	121. 31		5. 5	Mk	7										
1819	1	8	22	30		2			3	Italy, NOAA	Italy: Albenga, , Near Coast	意大利：阿尔本加近海	44. 05	8. 2		5. 34	Ms											
1819	1	29	19							GSHAP	Georgia: Tbilisi	格鲁吉亚：第比利斯	41. 7	44. 8	20	4. 5	Ms	6										
1819	2	5	9							GSHAP	Colombia: Cauca	哥伦比亚：考卡	2. 5	-76. 5		4. 4	Ms	5										
1819	2	9	3	45						GSHAP, Song	Peru: Arequipa	秘鲁：阿雷基帕	-16. 4	-71. 6		4. 5	Mk	5										
1819	2	24								* China	China: Qinghai, Ledu	中国：青海化隆	36. 1	102. 3		5. 75	Ms	7	126	3	58	2		2	108	3	108	3
1819	2	28								GSHAP	Georgia: Tbilisi	格鲁吉亚：第比利斯	41. 7	44. 8	20	4. 5	Ms	6										
1819	3									* Song	Algeria: Mascara	阿尔及利亚：马斯卡拉	35. 07	0. 02		7. 3	Mk	10		3				3		3		
1819	4	3	14							*	Chile: Copiapo	智利：科皮亚波	-27. 4	-70. 3		8	Muk							2		2		
1819	4	4	20							*	Chile: Copiapo	智利：科皮亚波	-27. 4	-70. 3		8	Muk			3				3		3		
1819	4	12	3	10						GSHAP, Song	Peru: Arequipa	秘鲁：阿雷基帕	-16. 4	-71. 6		5	Mk	6										
1819	4	12	3			4	4	2	2	* NOAA	Chile: Copiapo, Near Coast	智利：科皮亚波近海	-27	-71. 5		8. 5	Mfa	10		1				3		3		
1819	5	26	17							* Italy	Italy: Tarquinia	意大利：塔尔奎尼亚	42. 252	11. 757		5. 17	Ms	9		3				3				
1819	6	16	23	30		3				* NOAA, GSHAP, India	India: Rann of Kutch, Ahmadabad	印度：库奇的兰恩，艾哈迈德巴德	23	71		8. 3	Ms	11	2000	4				4	1547	4		
1819	8	2	5							Usami, Japan	Japan: Hikone	日本：滋贺彦根	35. 2	136. 3		7. 4	Ms	8	70		300	3			600	3		
1819	8	31				3				* NOAA	Norway: Rana	挪威：摩城	66. 416	12. 85		5. 8	Ms	7										
1819	9	14								China	China: Guizhou, Guiding	中国：贵州贵定	26. 5	107. 2		5. 75	Ms	7										
1820	3	1				5			0. 5	* Song, NOAA	Alaska: Unimak Island	阿拉斯加：乌尼马克岛	53. 6	-166. 4		7	Mk											
1820	3	17								* Song	Greece: Ionian Islands, Levkas	希腊：伊奥尼亚群岛，莱夫卡斯	38. 8	20. 5		6. 1	Mk	9						2				
1820	3	18	8	45						GSHAP, Song	Peru: Arequipa	秘鲁：阿雷基帕	-16. 4	-71. 6		4. 5	Mk	5										
1820	5	4				4	4	1	1. 5	* NOAA	Mexico: Guerrero, Oaxaca, Puebla	墨西哥：格雷罗，瓦哈卡，普埃布拉	17. 2	-99. 6		7. 6	Ms							3				
1820	5	5	14	59						GSHAP, Song	Peru: Arequipa	秘鲁：阿雷基帕	-16. 4	-71. 6		4. 5	Mk	5										
1820	6	3	13	45						GSHAP, Song	Peru: Arequipa	秘鲁：阿雷基帕	-16. 4	-71. 6		4. 5	Mk	5										
1820	7	8								GSHAP	Colombia: Jambalo	哥伦比亚：考卡的汉巴洛	3	-76. 5		4. 5	Ms	7										
1820	7	23				2			3	NOAA, Song	Italy: Genova, Near Coast of S.	意大利：热那亚南部近海	43. 8	9		6. 7	Mk											

时间						海啸				资料来源	震中				深度	震级	标度	烈度	死亡人数		受伤人数		经济损失		房屋毁坏		房屋受损	
年	月	日	时	分	秒	源	浪高	级 I	级 S		地名(英文)	地名(中文)	纬度(°)	经度(°)					数量/人	级别	数量/人	级别	数量/$ Mill	级别	数量/间	级别	数量/间	级别
Date						Tsunami				Information	Earthquake Epicenter				Depth	Mag	Scale	MMI	Deaths		Injuries		Damage		Houses Destroyed		Houses Damaged	
Year	Mo	Dy	Hr	Mn	Sec	Sr	Wh	mI	mS		Name(English)	Name(Chinese)	Latitude	Longitude					Num	Dd	Num	Dd	$ Mill	De	Num	Dh	Num	Dh
1820	8	4								* China	China:Henan,Xuchang,NE.	中国:河南许昌东北	34.1	113.9		6	Ms	8	430	3	590	3		4	26040	5		
1820	9	29	0	5						GSHAP,Song	Peru:Arequipa	秘鲁:阿雷基帕	-16.4	-71.6		4.5	Mk	5										
1820	10	9								* Song	Iran:Fars,Shiraz	伊朗:法尔斯,设拉子	29.6	52.5		6.3	Mk			3				3				
1820	10	28								GSHAP	Russia:Kamchatka, Near East Coast	俄罗斯:堪察加东部近海	53	162	30	5.2	Ms	5.5										
1820	10									China	China:Henan,Sanmenxia	中国:河南三门峡	34.8	111.2		5	Ms	6										
1820	12	29	3	30		3			3	* NOAA	Greece:Ionian Islands,Zante	希腊:伊奥尼亚群岛,赞特	37.8	21.2		6.9	Ms	10	8	1				1				
1820	12	29				4	25	4	5	* NOAA,Song	Indonesia:Sulawesi,Makasar	印度尼西亚:苏拉威西岛,望加锡	-5.1	119.4		7.9	Mk		500	3				2		3		
1820										* Song	Venezuela:Cumana	委内瑞拉:库马纳	10.5	-64.2		5.9	Mk							2				
1820										* Song	Iran:Mazanderan	伊朗:马赞德兰	36.5	53.5		5.9	Mk							2				
1820						2				* NOAA	Congo:Loango	刚果:洛安戈	-4.5	11.6		6.2	Mfa	5		3				1				
1820										Japan,Song	Japan:Tokyo	日本:东京	35.65	139.7		6.4	Mk	8										
1821	1	4	0	15						GSHAP,Song	Peru:Arequipa	秘鲁:阿雷基帕	-16.4	-71.6		4.5	Mk	5										
1821	1	6	17	15		4				* NOAA	Greece:Zamte	希腊:赞特	37.8	21.2		6.5	Ms	10		3				2				
1821	1	8	3	10						GSHAP,Song	Peru:Arequipa	秘鲁:阿雷基帕	-16.4	-71.6		4.5	Mk	5										
1821	2	10								GSHAP	Romania:Nereju	罗马尼亚:内雷茹	45.7	26.6	100	6	Ms	6.5										
1821	2	21	4							GSHAP	Latvia:Aizkraukle	拉脱维亚:艾兹克劳克莱	56.6	25.3	13	4.5	Ms	7										
1821	3	16	12							GSHAP,Song	Peru:Arequipa	秘鲁:阿雷基帕	-16.4	-71.6		4.5	Mk	5										
1821	4	8								* Song	Morocco:Melilla	摩洛哥:梅利利亚	35.3	-2.97		6.3	Mk							3				
1821	4	10				2				NOAA,Song	Costa Rica:Limón	哥斯达黎加:利蒙	10.1	-83.3		7	Mk											
1821	5	26	2	45						GSHAP,Song	Peru:Arequipa	秘鲁:阿雷基帕	-16.4	-71.6		4.5	Mk	5										
1821	5					2				NOAA,Song	St. Helena Island:Jamestown	圣赫勒拿岛:詹姆斯敦	-15.95	-5.7		7	Mk		3	1				1				
1821	6	29	2	10						GSHAP,Song	Peru:Moquegua	秘鲁:莫克瓜	-16.9	-71.2		4.5	Mk	5										
1821	7	1	4							GSHAP,Song	Peru:Arequipa	秘鲁:阿雷基帕	-16.4	-71.6		4.5	Mk	5										
1821	7	10	13							* Song	Peru:Camana, Ocona	秘鲁:卡马那,奥科尼亚	-16.107	-72.967		6.3	Mk	8	162	3				3				
1821	7	10	18	10						GSHAP,Song	Peru:Arequipa	秘鲁:阿雷基帕	-16.4	-71.6		4.5	Mk	5										
1821	7	17	7							GSHAP,Song	Peru:Arequipa	秘鲁:阿雷基帕	-16.4	-71.6		4.5	Mk	5										
1821	7	17	9	45						GSHAP,Song	Peru:Arequipa	秘鲁:阿雷基帕	-16.4	-71.6		4.5	Mk	5										
1821	7	19	7							GSHAP,Song	Peru:Arequipa	秘鲁:阿雷基帕	-16.4	-71.6		4.5	Mk	5										
1821	7	24	3	30						GSHAP,Song	Peru:Arequipa	秘鲁:阿雷基帕	-16.4	-71.6		4.5	Mk	5										
1821	7	30	1	25						GSHAP,Song	Peru:Arequipa	秘鲁:阿雷基帕	-16.4	-71.6		4.5	Mk	5										
1821	8	2	4	45						GSHAP,Song	Peru:Arequipa	秘鲁:阿雷基帕	-16.4	-71.6		4.5	Mk	5										
1821	8	3	6	40						GSHAP,Song	Peru:Arequipa	秘鲁:阿雷基帕	-16.4	-71.6		4.5	Mk	5										
1821	8	5	3	45						GSHAP,Song	Peru:Arequipa	秘鲁:阿雷基帕	-16.4	-71.6		4.5	Mk	5										
1821	9	1	1	2						GSHAP,Song	Peru:Arequipa	秘鲁:阿雷基帕	-16.4	-71.6		4.5	Mk	5										

年 Year	月 Mo	日 Dy	时 Hr	分 Mn	秒 Sec	源 Sr	浪高 Wh	级 I mI	级 S mS	资料来源 Information	地名(英文) Name(English)	地名(中文) Name(Chinese)	纬度(°) Latitude	经度(°) Longitude	深度 Depth	震级 Mag	标度 Scale	烈度 MMI	死亡人数 Deaths 数量/人 Num	死亡人数 Deaths 级别 Dd	受伤人数 Injuries 数量/人 Num	受伤人数 Injuries 级别 Dd	经济损失 Damage 数量/$ Mill	经济损失 Damage 级别 De	房屋毁坏 Houses Destroyed 数量/间 Num	房屋毁坏 Houses Destroyed 级别 Dh	房屋受损 Houses Damaged 数量/间 Num	房屋受损 Houses Damaged 级别 Dh
1821	9	12	3							Usami, Japan	Japan: Aomori	日本:青森	40.5	141.4		5.9	Ms		1	1								
1821	9	24	0	2						GSHAP, Song	Peru: Arequipa	秘鲁:阿雷基帕	-16.4	-71.6		4.5	Mk	5								1		1
1821	11	7	1	25						GSHAP, Song	Peru: Arequipa	秘鲁:阿雷基帕	-16.4	-71.6		4.5	Mk	5										
1821	11	17	13	30						* GSHAP	Romania: Nereju	罗马尼亚:内雷茹	45.7	26.6		6.7	Ms	8										
1821	12	13								Usami	Japan: Fukushima	日本:福岛	37.4	139.5		6.1	Ms	8		3					130	3	300	3
1821										GSHAP	Uzbekistan: Bukhara	乌兹别克斯坦:布哈拉	39.5	64	20	6.4	Ms	8										
1822	2	8	2	15						GSHAP, Song	Peru: Arequipa	秘鲁:阿雷基帕	-16.4	-71.6		4.5	Mk	5										
1822	2	15	10	59						GSHAP, Song	Peru: Arequipa	秘鲁:阿雷基帕	-16.4	-71.6		4.5	Mk	5										
1822	2	19	5	13						GSHAP, Song	Peru: Arequipa	秘鲁:阿雷基帕	-16.4	-71.6		4.5	Mk	5										
1822	3	12								GSHAP, Song	Peru: Arequipa	秘鲁:阿雷基帕	-16.4	-71.6		4.5	Mk	5										
1822	3	18	2							GSHAP, Song	Peru: Arequipa	秘鲁:阿雷基帕	-16.4	-71.6		4.5	Mk	5										
1822	3	18	7	30						GSHAP, Song	Peru: Arequipa	秘鲁:阿雷基帕	-16.4	-71.6		4.5	Mk	5										
1822	3	20				1				NOAA, Song	Lebanon: Bayrut (Beirut)	黎巴嫩:贝鲁特	33.9	35.5		6.6	Mk											
1822	4	10				1				NOAA, Song	Italy: Sicilia Island	意大利:西西里岛	37.45	14.25		6.6	Mk											
1822	4	24								* China	China: Gansu, Wenxian	中国:甘肃文县	33	104.6		5.5	Ms	7	23	1	20	1		1	70	2		
1822	5	7				2				* NOAA, Song	Costa Rica: Limón	哥斯达黎加:利蒙	10.1	-83.3		7.1	Mk							2				
1822	5	26	11	15						GSHAP, Song	Peru: Arequipa	秘鲁:阿雷基帕	-16.4	-71.6		4.5	Mk	5										
1822	5	27	4	40						GSHAP, Song	Peru: Arequipa	秘鲁:阿雷基帕	-16.4	-71.6		4.5	Mk	5										
1822	8	13	20			2			3	* GSHAP, NOAA	Turkey: Hatay; Syria: Aleppo	土耳其:哈塔伊;叙利亚:阿勒颇	36	36	17	7.4	Ms	11	8000	4				4				
1822	8	17	0	45						GSHAP, Song	Peru: Arequipa	秘鲁:阿雷基帕	-16.4	-71.6		4.5	Mk	5										
1822	9	5								* Song	Turkey: Hatay; Syria: Aleppo	土耳其:哈塔伊;叙利亚:阿勒颇	36	36		7.7	Mk	11	20000	5				4				
1822	9									GSHAP	Uzbekistan: Fergana	乌兹别克斯坦:费尔干纳	40.3	71.5	12	6.2	Ms	8.5										
1822	10	1	2							GSHAP, Song	Peru: Arequipa	秘鲁:阿雷基帕	-16.4	-71.6		4.5	Mk	5										
1822	10	9	0	55						GSHAP, Song	Peru: Arequipa	秘鲁:阿雷基帕	-16.4	-71.6		4.5	Mk	5										
1822	10	14	4	10						GSHAP, Song	Peru: Arequipa	秘鲁:阿雷基帕	-16.4	-71.6		4.5	Mk	5										
1822	10	21	8	45						GSHAP, Song	Peru: Arequipa	秘鲁:阿雷基帕	-16.4	-71.6		4.5	Mk	5										
1822	11	5								GSHAP, Song	Chile: Copiapo	智利:科皮亚波	-27.35	-70.35		6	Mk	8										
1822	11	20	2	30		4	3.5	1.8	2	* NOAA	Chile: Valparaiso, Quillota, Concon	智利:瓦尔帕莱索,基洛塔,康孔	-33	-71.63		8.5	Ms	11		3				4		3		
1822	11	23	2	30						GSHAP, Song	Chile: Valparaiso	智利:瓦尔帕莱索	-33.05	-71.63		6	Mk	8										
1822	11	25	12	15						* Song	Chile: Valparaiso	智利:瓦尔帕莱索	-33.05	-71.63		7.3	Mk	10						1				
1822	12	1								* Song	Venezuela: Blanquilla Island	委内瑞拉:布兰基亚岛	12.1	-64.1		5.9	Mk							2				
1823	1	14								Japan	Japan: Shimane	日本:岛根	35.1	132.6		6	Ms	8									10	1
1823	1	26	1	30						GSHAP, Song	Peru: Arequipa	秘鲁:阿雷基帕	-16.4	-71.6		4.5	Mk	5										
1823	1	26	6	26						GSHAP, Song	Peru: Arequipa	秘鲁:阿雷基帕	-16.4	-71.6		4.5	Mk	5										

时间						海啸				资料来源	震中				深度	震级	标度	烈度	死亡人数		受伤人数		经济损失		房屋毁坏		房屋受损	
年	月	日	时	分	秒	源	浪高	级 I	级 S		地名(英文)	地名(中文)	纬度(°)	经度(°)					数量/人	级别	数量/人	级别	数量/$ Mill	级别	数量/间	级别	数量/间	级别
Date						Tsunami				Information	Earthquake Epicenter				Depth	Mag	Scale	MMI	Deaths		Injuries		Damage		Houses Destroyed		Houses Damaged	
Year	Mo	Dy	Hr	Mn	Sec	Sr	Wh	mI	mS		Name(English)	Name(Chinese)	Latitude	Longitude					Num	Dd	Num	Dd	$ Mill	De	Num	Dh	Num	Dh
1823	3	5	16	37		2			5	* Italy, NOAA	Italy: Naso, Sicily	意大利:纳苏,西西里岛	38	14. 1		5. 87	Ms	10	22	1				3				
1823	3	7	6	10						GSHAP, Song	Peru: Arequipa	秘鲁:阿雷基帕	-16. 4	-71. 6		4. 5	Mk	5										
1823	3	15	4	40						GSHAP, Song	Peru: Arequipa	秘鲁:阿雷基帕	-16. 4	-71. 6		4. 5	Mk	5										
1823	3	18	4	20						GSHAP, Song	Peru: Arequipa	秘鲁:阿雷基帕	-16. 4	-71. 6		4. 5	Mk	5										
1823	5	18	2	20						GSHAP, Song	Peru: Arequipa	秘鲁:阿雷基帕	-16. 4	-71. 6		4. 5	Mk	5										
1823	5	30				4	2. 7			* Song	US: New York, Buffalo	美国:纽约州水牛城	42. 7	-79		7	Mk											
1823	6	8								USGS, Song	Hawaiian Islands	夏威夷群岛	19. 25	-155		6. 6	Mk	9										
1823	6	13	6	45						GSHAP, Song	Peru: Arequipa	秘鲁:阿雷基帕	-16. 4	-71. 6		4. 5	Mk	5										
1823	6	19								* Song	Greece: Thesprotia, N.	希腊:塞斯普罗蒂亚北部	39. 75	20. 75		6. 3	Mk	9						3		3		
1823	8	20				2			4	NOAA, Song	Croatia: Split	克罗地亚:斯普利特	43. 4	16. 7		6. 7	Mk											
1823	8									China	China: Shaanxi, Zhenba, N.	中国:陕西镇巴北	32. 7	107. 9		5. 5	Ms	7										
1823	8									* Song	Venezuela: Cariaco, Island of Margarita	委内瑞拉:卡利亚科,玛格丽特岛	10. 5	-63. 8		6. 1	Mk	8						2				
1823	9	7								* Song	Iran: Mazanderan	伊朗:马赞德兰	36. 3	53. 3		6. 3	Mk			3				3				
1823	9	8	2	30						GSHAP, Song	Peru: Arequipa	秘鲁:阿雷基帕	-16. 4	-71. 6		4. 5	Mk	5										
1823	9	9				2	0. 3		-15	* NOAA	Indonesia: Java Island	印度尼西亚:爪哇岛	-6. 5	108. 5	150	6. 8	Ms											
1823	9	29								Japan	Japan: Mt. Iwate	日本:岩手山	40	141. 1		5. 9	Ms	8	70						10	1		
1823	10	23								Usami	Japan: Mt. Iwate	日本:岩手山	40	141. 1		5. 9	Ms			1						1		
1823	10									* Song	Bosnia and Herzegovina: Trebinje	波斯尼亚和黑塞哥维那:特雷比涅	42. 7	18. 2		6. 2	Mk			3				2				
1823	11	30	7	45						GSHAP, Song	Peru: Arequipa	秘鲁:阿雷基帕	-16. 4	-71. 6		4. 5	Mk	5										
1823	11	30				4				* NOAA, Song	Martinique Island: Saint - Pierre	马提尼克岛:圣彼得	14. 4	-61. 1		7	Mk											
1823	12	12	15	14						GSHAP, Song	Peru: Arequipa	秘鲁:阿雷基帕	-16. 4	-71. 6		4. 5	Mk	5										
1823										* Song	Iran: Fars, Shiraz	伊朗:法尔斯,设拉子	29. 6	52. 5		5. 9	Mk							2				
1824	1	28	23	30						GSHAP, Song	Peru: Arequipa	秘鲁:阿雷基帕	-16. 4	-71. 6		4. 5	Mk	5										
1824	1									Maso, Song	Philippines: Manila	菲律宾:马尼拉	14. 51	121. 11		5. 5	Mk	7										
1824	3	31	21							GSHAP	Kazakhstan: Zyryanovsk	哈萨克斯坦:济良诺夫斯克	50. 6	83. 4	20	5. 2	Ms	6										
1824	4	10								* Song	Jamaica: Kingston	牙买加:金斯敦	18	-76. 5		5. 9	Mk							2				
1824	5	24	7	45						GSHAP, Song	Peru: Arequipa	秘鲁:阿雷基帕	-16. 4	-71. 6		4. 5	Mk	5										
1824	6	2								* Song	Iran: Shiraz	伊朗:设拉子	29. 7	51. 6		7. 1	Mk			4				4		4		
1824	6	5								GSHAP, Song	Peru: Arequipa	秘鲁:阿雷基帕	-16. 4	-71. 6		4. 5	Mk	5										
1824	6	25								* Iran	Iran: Fars, Shiraz	伊朗:法尔斯,设拉子	29. 8	52. 4		6. 4	Ms	8		3				3		2		3
1824	8	12	7	22						GSHAP, Song	Peru: Arequipa	秘鲁:阿雷基帕	-16. 4	-71. 6		4. 5	Mk	5										
1824	8	29	6							GSHAP, Song	Chile: Santiago	智利:圣地亚哥	-33. 4	-70. 6		6	Mk	8										
1824	9	6	10							GSHAP, Song	Peru: Arequipa	秘鲁:阿雷基帕	-16. 4	-71. 6		4. 5	Mk	5										
1824	9	8	13	40						GSHAP, Song	Peru: Arequipa	秘鲁:阿雷基帕	-16. 4	-71. 6		4. 5	Mk	5										

时间 Date 年 Year	月 Mo	日 Dy	时 Hr	分 Mn	秒 Sec	海啸 Tsunami 源 Sr	浪高 Wh	级 I mI	级 S mS	资料来源 Information	震中 Earthquake Epicenter 地名(英文) Name(English)	地名(中文) Name(Chinese)	纬度(°) Latitude	经度(°) Longitude	深度 Depth	震级 Mag	标度 Scale	烈度 MMI	死亡人数 Deaths 数量/人 Num	级别 Dd	受伤人数 Injuries 数量/人 Num	级别 Dd	经济损失 Damage 数量/$ Mill $ Mill	级别 De	房屋毁坏 Houses Destroyed 数量/间 Num	级别 Dh	房屋受损 Houses Damaged 数量/间 Num	级别 Dh
1824	9	13				1				* Song	Montserrat:Plymouth	蒙特塞拉特:普利茅斯	16.7	-62.2		7	Mk											
1824	9	29	6	30						* Maso,Song	Philippines:Tayabas	菲律宾:塔亚巴斯	13.7	121.7		6.5	Mk	9						2				
1824	10	26				1			1	* Bautista, Maso, NOAA	Philippines:Mauban	菲律宾:毛班	14.2	121.9		7.4	Ms	9		3				2				
1824	10	31	23							GSHAP,Song	Peru:Arequipa	秘鲁:阿雷基帕	-16.4	-71.6		4.5	Mk	5										
1824	11	1	2							GSHAP,Song	Peru:Arequipa	秘鲁:阿雷基帕	-16.4	-71.6		4.5	Mk	5										
1824	11	22	0	35						GSHAP,Song	Peru:Arequipa	秘鲁:阿雷基帕	-16.4	-71.6		4.5	Mk	5										
1824	11	30				2				* NOAA,Song	Martinique Island: Saint-Pierre	马提尼克岛:圣彼得	14.4	-61		7	Mk											
1824	12	2	4	45						GSHAP,Song	Peru:Arequipa	秘鲁:阿雷基帕	-16.4	-71.6		4.5	Mk	5										
1824	12	18	4							GSHAP	Colombia:Falan	哥伦比亚:托利马的法兰	5.2	-74.9		4.5	Ms	6										
1824										GSHAP	Brasil:Salgueiro	巴西:萨尔盖鲁	-7.59	-39.28		3.1	Ms	5										
1824										GSHAP	Brasil:Campo Grande	巴西:大坎普	-21.98	-44.88		4	Ms	5										
1825	1	1								GSHAP	Colombia:Ibagué	哥伦比亚:托利马的伊瓦格	4.5	-75.2		4	Ms	6										
1825	1	19	11	45		2			3	* NOAA	Greece:Ionian Islands,Leukas	希腊:伊奥尼亚群岛,琉卡斯	38.75	20.75		6.8	Ms	11	58	2				3		3		
1825	2	26				1				* NOAA	Colombia:Santa Marta	哥伦比亚:圣玛尔塔	11.1	-74.1		6.3	Ms							2				
1825	3	2	7							* Song	Algeria:Blida, Algiers	阿尔及利亚:布利达,阿尔及尔	36.4	2.8		7.3	Mk	10	7000	4				4		4		4
1825	4					2				* Maso,NOAA	Mariana Islands	马里亚纳群岛	14	143.3		6.1	Ms	8						2		3		
1825	7	31	9							GSHAP,Song	Peru:Arequipa	秘鲁:阿雷基帕	-16.4	-71.6		4.5	Mk	5										
1825	9	21	1	45		2				* NOAA,Song	Trinidad & Tobago: Port of Spain	特立尼达和多巴哥:西班牙港	10.4	-61.3		7.1	Mk							2				
1825	10	3								GSHAP,Song	Peru:Arequipa	秘鲁:阿雷基帕	-16.4	-71.6		4.5	Mk	5										
1825	10									China	China:Fujian,Yongtai	中国:福建永泰	25.9	119		4.75	Ms	6										
1825	10									* Song	Iran:Fars,Shiraz	伊朗:法尔斯,设拉子	29.4	52.3		5.9	Mk	7						2		1		
1825	11	7	23	33						GSHAP	Russia:Kamchatka Peninsula	俄罗斯:堪察加半岛	53	161	30	6.4	Ms	8										
1825	11	29	2	45						GSHAP,Song	Peru:Arequipa	秘鲁:阿雷基帕	-16.4	-71.6		4.5	Mk	5										
1825	12	24	20	30						GSHAP,Song	Chile:Santiago	智利:圣地亚哥	-33.4	-70.6		6	Mk	8										
1825	12	25	21	8						* Song	Spain:Arenas Del Rey	西班牙:阿雷纳斯-德尔雷伊	36.9	-4		7.3	Mk	10										
1825										* GSHAP,Iran	Iran:Mazanderan	伊朗:马赞德兰	36.1	52.6	13	6.7	Ms	9.5		3				3		3		
1826	2	12	7	15						GSHAP,Song	Peru:Arequipa	秘鲁:阿雷基帕	-16.4	-71.6		4.5	Mk	5										
1826	3	18	0	20		2			3	NOAA,Song	Italy:Senigallia	意大利:塞尼加利亚	43.8	13		6.7	Mk											
1826	4	7	5	40						GSHAP,Song	Peru:Arequipa	秘鲁:阿雷基帕	-16.4	-71.6		4.5	Mk	5										
1826	6	18	3	40						*	Colombia:Bogota	哥伦比亚:波哥达	4.6	-73.9	10	8.2	Ms	9						3				
1826	6	21	10							GSHAP	Colombia:La Calera	哥伦比亚:昆地那马加的拉卡利拉	4.8	-73.9		4.5	Ms	6										

年 Year	月 Mo	日 Dy	时 Hr	分 Mn	秒 Sec	海啸 Tsunami 源 Sr	浪高 Wh	级 I mI	级 S mS	资料来源 Information	震中 Earthquake Epicenter 地名(英文) Name(English)	地名(中文) Name(Chinese)	纬度(°) Latitude	经度(°) Longitude	深度 Depth	震级 Mag	标度 Scale	烈度 MMI	死亡人数 Deaths 数量/人 Num	级别 Dd	受伤人数 Injuries 数量/人 Num	级别 Dd	经济损失 Damage 数量/$ Mill $ Mill	级别 De	房屋毁坏 Houses Destroyed 数量/间 Num	级别 Dh	房屋受损 Houses Damaged 数量/间 Num	级别 Dh
1826	6	22	9	45						GSHAP	Colombia:La Calera	哥伦比亚:昆地那马加的拉卡利拉	4.8	-73.9		4.5	Ms	5										
1826	7	7								GSHAP	Colombia:La Calera	哥伦比亚:昆地那马加的拉卡利拉	4.8	-73.9		4.5	Ms	5										
1826	7	14	5							GSHAP,Song	Peru:Arequipa	秘鲁:阿雷基帕	-16.4	-71.6		4.5	Mk	5										
1826	7	16	1							GSHAP	Colombia:Bogota	哥伦比亚:波哥达	4.6	-74		4	Ms	5										
1826	8	28	2							Usami,Japan	Japan:Hida	日本:岐阜飞驒	36.2	137.3		6.2	Ms	8								1		
1826	8	30	4							GSHAP,Song	Peru:Arequipa	秘鲁:阿雷基帕	-16.4	-71.6		4.5	Mk	5										
1826	8	30	5							GSHAP,Song	Peru:Arequipa	秘鲁:阿雷基帕	-16.4	-71.6		4.5	Mk	5										
1826	9	8	5							GSHAP,Song	Peru:Arequipa	秘鲁:阿雷基帕	-16.4	-71.6		4.5	Mk	5										
1826	9	11	4							GSHAP,Song	Peru:Arequipa	秘鲁:阿雷基帕	-16.4	-71.6		4.5	Mk	5										
1826	9	18	8							* Song	Cuba:Santiago De Cuba	古巴:圣地亚哥	20	-75.5		5.9	Mk							2				
1826	11	5	4	15						GSHAP,Song	Peru:Arequipa	秘鲁:阿雷基帕	-16.4	-71.6		4.5	Mk	5										
1826			.			2				* NOAA	New Zealand:South Island,Anchor Island	新西兰:南岛,安克岛	-45.8	166.5		8	Ms											
1827	2	3	14	45						GSHAP,Song	Peru:Arequipa	秘鲁:阿雷基帕	-16.4	-71.6		4.5	Mk	5										
1827	3	23								* China	China:Shanxi,Yuncheng,S.	中国:山西运城南	34.9	111.1		5.5	Ms	7	84	2		2		1	55	2		
1827	4	22								China	China:Henan,Sanmenxia	中国:河南三门峡	34.6	111.3		4.75	Ms	6										
1827	5	1	3							GSHAP	Colombia:Bogota	哥伦比亚:波哥达	4.6	-74		4	Ms	5										
1827	5									GSHAP	Russia:Irkutsk,Kirensk	俄罗斯:伊尔库茨克州基廉斯克	58	108.5	15	6.5	Ms	8										
1827	6	24								GSHAP,Song	Venezuela:El Palmar	委内瑞拉:埃尔帕尔马	8.15	-71.96		6	Mk	7										
1827	6									* Song	Turkey:Erbaa	土耳其:埃尔巴	40.7	36.6		7.3	Mk	10						2				
1827	7	5	11	30						USGS	US:Indiana,Evansville	美国:印第安纳州埃文斯维尔	38	-87.5		4.8	Ms	6										
1827	7	17	4	55						GSHAP,Song	Peru:Arequipa	秘鲁:阿雷基帕	-16.4	-71.6		4.5	Mk	5										
1827	8	1	9							GSHAP,Song	Peru:Arequipa	秘鲁:阿雷基帕	-16.4	-71.6		4.5	Mk	5										
1827	8	7	4	30						USGS	US:Indiana,Evansville	美国:印第安纳州埃文斯维尔	38	-88		4.8	Ms	5										
1827	8	7	7							USGS	US:Indiana,Evansville	美国:印第安纳州埃文斯维尔	38	-88		4.7	Ms	5										
1827	8	9				5			1.5	* NOAA,Song	Russia:Kamchatka Peninsula	俄罗斯:堪察加半岛	53	158.5		7	Mk							1				
1827	8	26								Japan,Song	Japan:Nikko	日本:枥木日光	36.7	139.7		6.1	Mk											1
1827	9	24	4							CGS,USGS	US:California,Oxnard	美国:加利福尼亚州奥克斯纳德	34	-119		6	Ms	6										
1827	9	26								* Song	Pakistan:Punjab	巴基斯坦:旁遮普	31	75.3		6.3	Mk		1000	3				3				
1827	10	10	9	25						GSHAP	Colombia:Supía	哥伦比亚:卡尔达斯的苏皮亚	5.4	-75.5		4	Ms	5										
1827	10	20	9							GSHAP	Armenia:Dilijan	亚美尼亚:迪利然	40.7	44.9	18	6.4	Ms	8.5										

时间						海啸				资料来源	震中				深度	震级	标度	烈度	死亡人数		受伤人数		经济损失		房屋毁坏		房屋受损	
年	月	日	时	分	秒	源	浪高	级I	级S		地名(英文)	地名(中文)	纬度(°)	经度(°)					数量/人	级别	数量/人	级别	数量/$ Mill	级别	数量/间	级别	数量/间	级别
Date						Tsunami				Information	Earthquake Epicenter				Depth	Mag	Scale	MMI	Deaths		Injuries		Damage		Houses Destroyed		Houses Damaged	
Year	Mo	Dy	Hr	Mn	Sec	Sr	Wh	mI	mS		Name(English)	Name(Chinese)	Latitude	Longitude					Num	Dd	Num	Dd	$ Mill	De	Num	Dh	Num	Dh
1827	10	21								GSHAP	Russia:Stavropol,Krasnoye	俄罗斯:斯塔夫罗波尔区克拉斯诺耶	45	42.5	15	4.6	Ms	6.5										
1827	11	16	22	45						*	Colombia:Bogota, Neiva, Popayan	哥伦比亚:波哥达,内瓦,波帕扬	1.8	-76.4		7	Ms	11	250	3				3				
1827	11	17	4	10						GSHAP	Colombia:Huila	哥伦比亚:乌伊拉	1.8	-76.4		4.5	Ms	5										
1827	11	17	16	45						GSHAP	Colombia:Huila	哥伦比亚:乌伊拉	1.8	-76.4		4.5	Ms	5										
1827	11	30	6	45						* Song	Martinique Island	马提尼克岛(拉丁美洲)	14.4	-61		5.9	Mk							2				
1828	1	26	4							GSHAP,Song	Peru:Arequipa	秘鲁:阿雷基帕	-16.4	-71.6		4.5	Mk	5										
1828	2	2	13	15						* Italy	Italy:Island of Ischia	意大利:伊斯基亚岛	40.75	13.9		5.57	Ms	10	28	1				1		1		
1828	2	21	4	20						GSHAP,Song	Peru:Arequipa	秘鲁:阿雷基帕	-16.4	-71.6		4.5	Mk	5										
1828	3	10	3							USGS	US:Virginia,Rocky Mt.	美国:弗吉尼亚州落基山城	37	-80		4.6	Ms	5										
1828	3	16								GSHAP,Song	Peru:Arequipa	秘鲁:阿雷基帕	-16.4	-71.6		5	Mk	6										
1828	3	30	12	35		4				*	Peru:Lima,Near Coast	秘鲁:利马近海	-12.1	-77.8	50	8.3	Muk	7	30	1		3		2				2
1828	4	6	2	5						GSHAP,Song	Peru:Arequipa	秘鲁:阿雷基帕	-16.4	-71.6		4.5	Mk	5										
1828	4	8	12							GSHAP,Song	Peru:Arequipa	秘鲁:阿雷基帕	-16.4	-71.6		4.5	Mk	5										
1828	5	26	13			4				* Usami,Japan,NOAA	Japan:Nagasaki	日本:长崎	32.6	129.9		6.4	Ms	8								1		
1828	6	6								* Song	India:Kashmir	印度:克什米尔	34.2	74.5		6.3	Mk		1000	3				3				
1828	8	9	16							*	Azerbaijan:Samaxi	阿塞拜疆:沙马基区	40.7	48.4	10	5.7	Muk	8						3				
1828	9	27	1	30						GSHAP,Song	Peru:Arequipa	秘鲁:阿雷基帕	-16.4	-71.6		4.5	Mk	5										
1828	10	9	13	11		2			3	NOAA,Song	Italy:Genova,Near Coast of S.	意大利:热那亚南部近海	43.8	9		6.7	Mk											
1828	10	25	3							GSHAP,Song	Peru:Arequipa	秘鲁:阿雷基帕	-16.4	-71.6		4.5	Mk	5										
1828	11	9	9	18		1			0.5	* Nakamura,NOAA	Philippines:Calamba	菲律宾:卡兰巴	14.2	121		7.5	Ms	8						2				
1828	11	22	4	55						GSHAP,Song	Peru:Arequipa	秘鲁:阿雷基帕	-16.4	-71.6		4.5	Mk	5										
1828	12	17	22			4				* Usami,Japan	Japan:Fukushima	日本:福岛	37.5	139.5		6.9	Ms	9	1443	4				4	11750	5	7276	4
1828	12	29				4				* Song	Indonesia:Sulawesi	印度尼西亚:苏拉威西岛	-2	121		7.7	Mk	9		3				3				
1829	1	28	22	30						GSHAP,Song	Peru:Arequipa	秘鲁:阿雷基帕	-16.4	-71.6		4.5	Mk	5										
1829	3	7	22							* GSHAP	Russia:Irkutsk,Baykalsk	俄罗斯:伊尔库茨克州贝加尔斯克	51.4	104.1	40	7.5	Muk	10										
1829	3	8	3	50						GSHAP,Song	Peru:Arequipa	秘鲁:阿雷基帕	-16.4	-71.6		4.5	Mk	5										
1829	3	21	18	30						* Song	Spain:Torrevieja, Murcia	西班牙:特拉维哈,穆尔西亚	38.1	-0.7		7.3	Mk	10	2000	4				3		4		4
1829	4	21								GSHAP	Kazakhstan:Zyryanovsk	哈萨克斯坦:济良诺夫斯克	50.1	83.9	24	5.2	Ms	6										
1829	4	23	16			2			2	* NOAA	Greece:Xanthi - Drama	希腊:克桑西 - 兹拉马	41.2	24.5		7.3	Ms	10										
1829	4									China	China:Shanxi,Lvliang	中国:山西吕梁	37.5	111.2		5.5	Ms	7										

时间 Date						海啸 Tsunami				资料来源 Information	震中 Earthquake Epicenter				深度 Depth	震级 Mag	标度 Scale	烈度 MMI	死亡人数 Deaths		受伤人数 Injuries		经济损失 Damage		房屋毁坏 Houses Destroyed		房屋受损 Houses Damaged	
年 Year	月 Mo	日 Dy	时 Hr	分 Mn	秒 Sec	源 Sr	浪高 Wh	级 I mI	级 S mS		地名(英文) Name(English)	地名(中文) Name(Chinese)	纬度(°) Latitude	经度(°) Longitude					数量/人 Num	级别 Dd	数量/人 Num	级别 Dd	数量/$ Mill $ Mill	级别 De	数量/间 Num	级别 Dh	数量/间 Num	级别 Dh
1829	5	5	9							* GSHAP	Greece:Xanthi – Drama	希腊:克桑西－兹拉马	41.2	24.5		7.3	Ms	9		2				2				
1829	5	13	17							GSHAP	Russia:Kamchatka Peninsula	俄罗斯:堪察加半岛	53	161	30	6.4	Ms	8.5										
1829	6	25								Japan,Song	Japan:Aki, Saeki	日本:安艺郡佐伯郡	34.4	132.5		6.4	Mk	8										
1829	7	1	19	30						GSHAP	Romania:Bihor,N.	罗马尼亚:比霍尔北部	47.5	22.2	35	6.2	Ms	7										
1829	8	18								China	China:Henan,Ruicheng	中国:河南芮城	34.6	110.6		4.75	Ms	6										
1829	8	31	23	30						GSHAP	Russia:Arkhangelsk,Kizema	俄罗斯:阿尔汉格尔斯克州基泽马	61	44.5	10	4.5	Ms	6										
1829	9	26	14	30		4				*	Chile:Valparaiso	智利:瓦尔帕莱索	-33.1	-71.6		7	Muk	11		1								
1829	9									USGS,Song	US:California,Pacifica	美国:加利福尼亚州帕西菲卡	37.5	-122.5		5.7	Mk	7										
1829	10	1	16	3						GSHAP,Song	Chile:El Quisco	智利:埃尔基斯科	-33.4	-71.6		6	Mk	8										
1829	11	18								* China	China:Anhui,Wuhe	中国:安徽五河	33.2	117.9		5.5	Ms	7		3				3		3		
1829	11	19								* China	China:Shandong,Linqu	中国:山东临朐	36.6	118.5		6.25	Ms	8	200	3				2		2		
1829	11	26	1	40						* GSHAP	Romania:Bucharest	罗马尼亚:布加勒斯特	44.2	26.1		5.9	Ms	10						3				
1829	12	1	3							GSHAP	Russia:Novosibirsk,Suzun	俄罗斯:新西伯利亚州苏尊	53.8	82.4	14	5.5	Ms	7										
1829	12	9	9	30						GSHAP	Colombia:Manizales	哥伦比亚:卡尔达斯的马尼萨莱斯	5	-75.5		5	Ms	6										
1830	1	18	9	15		4				* Bautista,Maso	Philippines:Mauban	菲律宾:毛班	14.3	121.85		6.3	Ms	9		3				2				
1830	1									* Song	Mexico:Oaxaca	墨西哥:瓦哈卡	17	-96.3		6.3	Mk							3				
1830	3	9	11	22						*	Russia:Dagestan,Makhachkala	俄罗斯:达吉斯坦共和国马哈奇卡拉	43	47	16	6.3	Muk	9	410	3				2				
1830	3	27								GSHAP	Iran:Tehran,Damāvand	伊朗:德黑兰,达马万德	35.7	52.5	18	7.1	Ms	9.5										
1830	4	3								*	Iran:Dāmghān	伊朗:达姆甘	36.4	54.3		6.5	Muk							3				
1830	5	5	7	20						GSHAP,Song	Peru:Arequipa	秘鲁:阿雷基帕	-16.4	-71.6		4.5	Mk	5										
1830	5	9								* Song	Iran:Tehran,Damāvand	伊朗:德黑兰,达马万德	35.7	52.1		6.3	Mk		500	3				3				
1830	6	12								* China	China:Hebei,Cixian	中国:河北磁县	36.4	114.3		7.5	Ms	10	7477	4		4		4	200000	5		
1830	6	24								China	China:Hebei,Longyao,SW.	中国:河北隆尧西南	37.3	114.7		5.5	Ms	7										
1830	6	25	20	45						GSHAP	Russia:Dagestan,Chirkey	俄罗斯:达吉斯坦共和国奇尔克伊	43	47	15	4.8	Ms	6.5										
1830	6	26								China	China:Hebei,Cixian	中国:河北磁县	36.4	114.3		5.75	Ms	7								3		
1830	8	19	6							* Usami,Japan	Japan:Kyoto	日本:京都	35	136		6.4	Ms	8	285	3	1300	4				4		
1830	9	13								China	China:Sichuan,Dechang,S.	中国:四川德昌南	27.2	102.2		4.75	Ms	6										
1830	9	16				2			1	NOAA,Song	Philippines:Bayawan	菲律宾:巴亚万	9.3	122.7		7	Mk											
1830	12	4	5							GSHAP	Black Sea	黑海	44.9	37.3	12	4.8	Ms	6.5										
1830										CGS,USGS	US:California,San Luis Obispo	美国:加利福尼亚州圣路易斯－奥比斯保	35.35	-120.65		6	Ms	7										
1831	2	29	0	45						GSHAP,Song	Peru:Arequipa	秘鲁:阿雷基帕	-16.4	-71.6		4.5	Mk	5										

时间						海啸				资料来源	震中				深度	震级	标度	烈度	死亡人数		受伤人数		经济损失		房屋毁坏		房屋受损	
年	月	日	时	分	秒	源	浪高	级 I	级 S		地名(英文)	地名(中文)	纬度(°)	经度(°)					数量/人	级别	数量/人	级别	数量/$ Mill	级别	数量/间	级别	数量/间	级别
Date						Tsunami				Information	Earthquake Epicenter				Depth	Mag	Scale	MMI	Deaths		Injuries		Damage		Houses Destroyed		Houses Damaged	
Year	Mo	Dy	Hr	Mn	Sec	Sr	Wh	mI	mS		Name(English)	Name(Chinese)	Latitude	Longitude					Num	Dd	Num	Dd	$ Mill	De	Num	Dh	Num	Dh
1831	3	26								Japan	Japan:Tokyo	日本:东京	35.7	139.8		5.5	Ms											
1831	3	28								Japan,Song	Japan:Iwate	日本:岩手	39.2	141.2		6.1	Mk											1
1831	4	3								*Song	Greece:Samos Island	希腊:萨摩斯岛	37.8	27		6	Mk	7		2								1
1831	5	17	21	5						GSHAP	Colombia:Cauca	哥伦比亚:考卡	2.5	-76.5		4.5	Ms	5										
1831	5	26	10	25		2			3	*Italy,NOAA	Italy:Sanremo,Near Coast	意大利:圣雷默近海	43.85	7.85		5.54	Ms	9	4	1				3				
1831	6	22	21	30						GSHAP	Russia:Altayskiy Kray,Gornyak	俄罗斯:阿尔泰边疆区戈尔尼亚克	51.5	82.6	32	4.9	Ms	5										
1831	7	2				2			1	NOAA,Song	Italy:Marsala,Near Coast of S.	意大利:马尔萨拉南部近海	37.05	12.3		6.7	Mk											
1831	8	3	3							GSHAP	Romania:Nereju	罗马尼亚:内雷茹	45.7	26.6	100	5.8	Ms	6										
1831	8	11								*Song	Barbados Island:Bridgetown	巴巴多斯岛:布里奇顿	13	-59.3		7	Mk		3000	4				3				
1831	9	11								*Song	Italy:Reggio Calabria	意大利:卡拉布里亚雷焦	38.1	15.7		5.7	Mk	9						3				
1831	9	28								*China	China:Anhui,Fengtai,NE.	中国:安徽凤台东北	32.8	116.8		6.25	Ms	8					3	2				
1831	10	9	2	15						*Chile	Peru:Tacna,Arica	秘鲁:塔克纳,阿里卡	-18.5	-71		7.8	Ms	10	33	1				1		1		
1831	11	13	16							Usami,Japan	Japan:Fukuoka,W.	日本:福冈西部	33.2	130.2		6.1	Ms	8		2				1				
1831	11	13								Japan,Song	Japan:Fukushima	日本:福岛	37.7	140.4		6.1	Mk									4		
1831	12	3	23	40		1				*NOAA	Grenada:St Georges	格林纳达:圣乔治	12.4	-61.5		7	Ms											1
1831	12	24	16	45						GSHAP,Song	Chile:Concepcion	智利:康塞普西翁	-36.83	-73.03		6	Mk	8										
1831										China	China:Shandong,Xintai	中国:山东新泰	35.9	117.8		4.75	Ms	6										
1832	1	13	13							*Italy	Italy:Foligno	意大利:福利尼奥	42.967	12.659		5.8	Ms	10	22	1				2				
1832	1	21	15							GSHAP,Song	Chile:Quellon	智利:克永	-43	-73		6	Mk	8										
1832	1	22								*Afghan,GSHAP	Afghan:Badakhshan	阿富汗:巴达赫尚	36.5	71	180	7.4	Ms	9		3				3				
1832	1									China	China:Fujian,Pinghe,W.	中国:福建平和西	24.3	117		5	Ms	6										
1832	2	17	1	45						GSHAP	Romania:Nereju	罗马尼亚:内雷茹	45.7	26.6	100	5.7	Ms	6										
1832	3	8	18	15		2			3	*Italy,NOAA	Italy:Cutro	意大利:卡特罗	39.07	16.9		6.48	Ms	10	234	3								
1832	3	15								Japan	Japan:Hachinohe	日本:青森八户	40.5	141.5		6.5	Ms											
1832	4	12								GSHAP	Russia:Buryatiya,Pokrovka	俄罗斯:布里亚特州波克罗夫卡	51	105.5	15	6.3	Ms	8										1
1832	6	5	10							GSHAP	Colombia:Cauca	哥伦比亚:考卡	2.5	-76.5		4	Ms	5										
1832	8	3								GSHAP	Azerbaijan:Samaxi	阿塞拜疆:沙马基区	40.6	48.6	20	5.4	Ms	6.5										
1832	8									China	China:Gansu,Yumen	中国:甘肃玉门	39.9	96.8		5.5	Ms	7										
1833	1	19				2			4	*NOAA,GSHAP	Albania:Vlore, Sazan	阿尔巴尼亚:发罗拉,萨森岛	40.2	19.3		6.5	Ms	10										
1833	3	10				3		1	0.5	*NOAA,Song	Mexico:Near Coast of Guerrero	墨西哥:格雷罗近海	16.6	-99.6		7	Mk											
1833	4	25	14	30						*Song	Chile:Vallenar	智利:巴耶纳尔	-28.5	-71.3		7.3	Mk	10										
1833	5	1	8							GSHAP	Colombia:Cauca	哥伦比亚:考卡	2.5	-76.5		4	Ms	5										
1833	5	27	4							Usami,Japan	Japan:Motosu	日本:岐阜本巢	35.5	136.6		6.4	Ms	8	30	1						1		

时间 Date 年 Year	月 Mo	日 Dy	时 Hr	分 Mn	秒 Sec	海啸 Tsunami 源 Sr	浪高 Wh	级 I mI	级 S mS	资料来源 Information	震中 Earthquake Epicenter 地名(英文) Name(English)	地名(中文) Name(Chinese)	纬度(°) Latitude	经度(°) Longitude	深度 Depth	震级 Mag	标度 Scale	烈度 MMI	死亡人数 Deaths 数量/人 Num	级别 Dd	受伤人数 Injuries 数量/人 Num	级别 Dd	经济损失 Damage 数量/$ Mill $ Mill	级别 De	房屋毁坏 Houses Destroyed 数量/间 Num	级别 Dh	房屋受损 Houses Damaged 数量/间 Num	级别 Dh
1833	6	30	2							GSHAP, Song	Peru: Arequipa	秘鲁:阿雷基帕	-16.4	-71.6		4.5	Mk	5										
1833	8	26								* China, India	Nepal: Kathmandu, N.	尼泊尔:加德满都北部	28.3	85.5		8	Ms	10	414	3				3		3		3
1833	8	27	11							USGS	US: Virginia, Goochland	美国:弗吉尼亚州古奇兰	37.7	-78		4.5	Ms	5										
1833	9	6								* China	China: Yunnan, Songming	中国:云南嵩明	25	103		8	Ms	11	6700	4				4	87620	5		
1833	9	18	10	31						* Song	Peru: Arequipa, Tacna	秘鲁:阿雷基帕,塔克纳	-17.6	-70.8		5.9	Mk		18	1				2				
1833	9	18	10	31						* Chile	Chile: Arica, Near Coast	智利:阿里卡近海	-18.5	-70.4	60	7.8	Ms	10	18	1				2				
1833	11	7								Japan	Japan: Nagano	日本:长野	36.6	137.8		6.25	Ms											1
1833	11	24				4			2.5	* NOAA	Indonesia: Southern Sumatra	印度尼西亚:苏门答腊南部	-3.5	102.2	75	8.3	Ms	9		1				2		1		1
1833	12	7	6			4	9	2.5	2.5	* Usami, Japan, NOAA	Japan Sea	日本海	38.9	139.15		7.4	Ms	9	129	3	24	1		3	1140	4	1790	4
1833	12	13								China	China: Taiwan, Yilan	中国:台湾宜兰	24.8	121.8		5	Ms	6										
1833										GSHAP	Iran: Qūchān	伊朗:古昌	37.3	58.1	14	6.2	Ms	8.5										
1834	1	20	12							*	Colombia: Putumayo, Pasto	哥伦比亚:普图马约,帕斯托	1.2	-77	5	7	Muk	11	80	2				3				
1834	2	9	1			4		2	1	* Usami, NOAA	Japan: W. Hokkaido Island	日本:北海道西部	43.3	141.4		6.4	Ms	8						1	73	2		
1834	2	10	22	15						GSHAP, Song	Peru: Arequipa	秘鲁:阿雷基帕	-16.4	-71.6		4.5	Mk	5										
1834	2	14								* Italy	Italy: Borgo Val Di Taro	意大利:塔罗谷镇	44.449	9.859		5.64	Ms	10	60	2			0.17	1				
1834	2	20	4	30						USGS, Song	Hawaiian Islands	夏威夷群岛	19.25	-155		5.5	Mk	6										
1834	2	20	17	51						GSHAP	Black Sea	黑海	44.8	36.9	20	5.5	Ms	6.5										
1834	3	1	13							* GSHAP	Colombia: Narino	哥伦比亚:纳里尼奥	1.4	-77.1		5	Ms	6						1				
1834	3	14				3		1		* NOAA	Mexico: Guerrero, Acapulco, E.	墨西哥:格雷罗州阿卡普尔科东部	17	-100		7	Ms											
1834	4	11								* China	China: Yunnan, Yiliang	中国:云南宜良	25	103		5	Ms	6		1				1				
1834	5	6	20							GSHAP	Romania: Nereju	罗马尼亚:内雷茹	45.7	26.6	100	5.3	Ms	5.5										
1834	5	22	7							* Song	Colombia: Santa Marta, Cartagena	哥伦比亚:圣玛尔塔,卡塔赫纳	11	-74.2		5.9	Mk							2				
1834	5	23								GSHAP	Colombia: Soledad, Near Coast	哥伦比亚:索莱达近海	12	-75		4	Ms	5										
1834	5	23								*	Jordan: Al - Karak; Israel: Nabulus	约旦:卡拉克;以色列:纳布卢斯	31.3	35.6		6.3	Muk	9						2				
1834	5	24								GSHAP	Colombia: Soledad, Near Coast	哥伦比亚:索莱达近海	12	-75		5	Ms	7										
1834	5	25								GSHAP	Colombia: Soledad, Near Coast	哥伦比亚:索莱达近海	12	-75		4	Ms	5										
1834	5	31								GSHAP, Song	Peru: Arequipa	秘鲁:阿雷基帕	-16.4	-71.6		4.5	Mk	5										
1834	5					4				Maso, Song	Guam	关岛(西太平洋)	14	143.3		7.3	Mk	8										
1834	6	8	9	30						GSHAP	Colombia: Antioquia	哥伦比亚:安提奥基亚	7.4	-74.9		4.5	Ms	5										

时间						海啸				资料来源	震中				深度	震级	标度	烈度	死亡人数		受伤人数		经济损失		房屋毁坏		房屋受损	
年	月	日	时	分	秒	源	浪高	级I	级S		地名(英文)	地名(中文)	纬度(°)	经度(°)					数量/人	级别	数量/人	级别	数量/$ Mill	级别	数量/间	级别	数量/间	级别
Date						Tsunami				Information	Earthquake Epicenter				Depth	Mag	Scale	MMI	Deaths		Injuries		Damage		Houses Destroyed		Houses Damaged	
Year	Mo	Dy	Hr	Mn	Sec	Sr	Wh	mI	mS		Name(English)	Name(Chinese)	Latitude	Longitude					Num	Dd	Num	Dd	$ Mill	De	Num	Dh	Num	Dh
1834	6	17								* China	China:Xizang (Tibet), Tingri, SW.	中国:西藏日喀则定日西南	28	86.3		6.25	Ms	8		3						1		
1834	8	12	15	30						* Song	Venezuela:Merida	委内瑞拉:梅里达	8.8	-70.9		6	Mk			2								
1834	9	22	1	15						GSHAP, Song	Peru:Arequipa	秘鲁:阿雷基帕	-16.4	-71.6		4.5	Mk	5										
1834	10	10								* Song	Indonesia:Java, Buitenzorg	印度尼西亚:爪哇岛,波格尔	-6.9	107		5.9	Mk							2				
1834	10	15	6	30						*	Romania:Carei	罗马尼亚:卡雷	47.6	22.3	32	6.8	Muk	8						3				
1834	12									* China	China:Qinghai, Yushu	中国:青海玉树	33	97		5.5	Ms	7	88	2								
1834										GSHAP	Turkey:Igdir	土耳其:伊迪尔	39.7	43.7	14	6	Ms	8.5										
1835	1	23	7							GSHAP	Colombia:Near Coast	哥伦比亚:近海	1.8	-79		5	Ms	6										
1835	2	20	16	22		4	24	4	3	* Chile, NOAA	Chile:Concepcion	智利:康塞普西翁	-36.8	-73		8.5	Mfa	11	500	3	510	3		4		3		
1835	3	12								Japan	Japan:Shimane	日本:岛根	35.1	132.6		5.5	Ms	8										1
1835	4	18	17	25						* Italy	Switzerland:Interlaken	瑞士:因特拉肯	46.7	7.8		4.83	Ms	6						3				
1835	4	21	20	30						GSHAP	Romania:Nereju	罗马尼亚:内雷茹	45.7	26.6	100	6.2	Ms	6										
1835	6	6								China	China:Shandong, Pingyin	中国:山东平阴	36.3	116.4		5	Ms	6										
1835	6	14	13							GSHAP	Mongolia:Suhbaatar	蒙古:苏赫巴托尔	50.5	105.5	15	6.2	Ms	8										
1835	7	12				2			2	NOAA, Song	Greece:Ionian Islands	希腊:伊奥尼亚群岛	39.5	20		6.7	Mk											
1835	7	20	5	6		4	5	2.3	2	* Japan, NOAA	Japan:Miyagi, Near Coast	日本:宫城近海	37.9	141.9		7.6	Muk	7								3		
1835	8	19				2				Japan, NOAA, Song	Japan:Iwate	日本:岩手	38.9	141.1		7	Mk											1
1835	8	23	15							* Turkey	Turkey:Kayseri	土耳其:凯瑟利	38.5	35.5		5.8	Ms	10	300	3				2				
1835	9	6								Japan, Song	Japan:Sukagawa	日本:福岛须贺川	37.3	140.4		6.1	Mk											1
1835	10	12	23							* Italy	Italy:Cosenza	意大利:科森扎	39.33	16.3		5.91	Ms	11	100	2				2				
1835	11	1								* Song	Indonesia:Banda Sea, N.	印度尼西亚:班达海北部	-3.4	128.1		6.5	Mk	9						2				
1835	11	3								Japan, Song	Japan:Nikko	日本:栃木日光	36.7	139.7		6.3	Mk									1		
1836	1	5								Maso, Song	Philippines:Mindoro Island	菲律宾:民都洛岛	13.4	121.11		5.5	Mk	7										
1836	1	21				1				NOAA, Song	Australia:Tasman Sea	澳大利亚:塔斯曼海	-43.3	148.9		7	Mk											
1836	2	4	3	15						GSHAP	Colombia:Bogota	哥伦比亚:波哥达	4.6	-74		4	Ms	5										
1836	3	5				2			0.5	* NOAA, Song	Indonesia:Mataram	印度尼西亚:马塔兰	-8.5	116		7	Mk											
1836	3	8								Japan, Song	Japan:Iwate, Near Coast	日本:岩手近海	39	143		6.8	Mk									3		
1836	3	31								Japan	Japan:Shizuoka, Near Coast	日本:静冈近海	34.4	139.2		6	Ms									1		
1836	4	14								USGS, Song	Alaska:St George Island	阿拉斯加:圣乔治	57	-170		5.7	Mk	7										
1836	4	22								Japan, Song	Japan:Miyako - Jima	日本:宫古岛	25	125.5		6.1	Mk											1
1836	4	24	23	15		3			4	* Italy, NOAA	Italy:Rossano, Crosia, Craco	意大利:罗珊诺,克罗西亚,克拉科	39.57	16.73		6.16	Ms	11	589	3				3				
1836	4	26	22	30						GSHAP, Song	Chile:Concepcion	智利:康塞普西翁	-36.83	-73.03		6	Mk	8										
1836	6	3				3		1	1	NOAA, Song	Chile:Iquique, N.	智利:伊基克北部	-19.6	-70.2		7	Mk											

年 Year	月 Mo	日 Dy	时 Hr	分 Mn	秒 Sec	海啸 Tsunami 源 Sr	浪高 Wh	级 I mI	级 S mS	资料来源 Information	震中 Earthquake Epicenter 地名(英文) Name(English)	地名(中文) Name(Chinese)	纬度(°) Latitude	经度(°) Longitude	深度 Depth	震级 Mag	标度 Scale	烈度 MMI	死亡人数 Deaths 数量/人 Num	级别 Dd	受伤人数 Injuries 数量/人 Num	级别 Dd	经济损失 Damage 数量/$ Mill	级别 De	房屋毁坏 Houses Destroyed 数量/间 Num	级别 Dh	房屋受损 Houses Damaged 数量/间 Num	级别 Dh
1836	6	10	15	30						* Song	US: California, Concord	美国:加利福尼亚州康科德市	38	-122		7.3	Mk	10										
1836	7	3				2	2	1	1	* NOAA	Chile: Tocopilla, Near Coast	智利:托科皮亚近海	-22.5	-70.3		7.5	Ms											
1836	8	7								Japan, Song	Japan: Narashino	日本:千叶习志野	35.7	140		6.1	Mk											1
1836	8									USGS, Song	Alaska: St George Island	阿拉斯加:圣乔治	57	-170		5.5	Mk	6										
1836	9	5								Japan	Japan: Iwate	日本:岩手	38.9	141.1		5.9	Ms									2		
1836	11	20	7							* Italy	Italy: Basilicata	意大利:巴西利卡塔	40.15	15.78		5.83	Ms	11	21	1				2				
1836	11	28				2			0.5	* NOAA	Flores Sea	弗洛勒斯海	-8.3	118.7		7.5	Ms											
1837	1	1	1			3			4	* NOAA	Israel: Zefat (Safed)	以色列:采法特(萨法德)	33	35.5		6.4	Ms	11	5700	4				4		4		
1837	4	11	17							* Italy	Italy: Carrara	意大利:卡拉拉	44.174	10.181		5.65	Ms	9	5	1				2				
1837	8	2				4				* Song	British Virgin Islands: Road Town	英属维尔京群岛:罗德城	18.2	-64.5		7.7	Mk							3				
1837	9	10	18							* Song	Venezuela: Santa Teresa Del Tuy	委内瑞拉:圣安娜 圣特雷萨	10.3	-66.6		5.9	Mk			1				2				
1837	9	29				5			0.5	* NOAA	Indonesia: North of Sumatera	印度尼西亚:苏门答腊北部	5.5	96		7.3	Ms							2				
1837	9									* China	China: Gansu, Minxian, NW.	中国:甘肃岷县西北	34.6	103.7		6	Ms	8	37	1				2	941	3		
1837	11	7	12	51		4	6	3	3	* NOAA	Chile: Castro	智利:卡斯特罗	-42.5	-74		8.5	Mfa	10	16	1				2		3		
1837	11	22								*	Mexico: Tomatlan	墨西哥:托马特兰	20	-105		7.5	Ms							3		3		
1837	11	28								* Song	Indonesia: Sumbawa, Bima	印度尼西亚:松巴哇,比玛	-8.3	118.4		6.5	Mk	9						2				
1838	1	23	18	36						* GSHAP	Romania: Nereju	罗马尼亚:内雷茹	45.7	26.6	150	7.3	Muk	9						2				
1838	5	7				2	0.7	-05		* NOAA, Song	Chile: Concepcion	智利:康塞普西翁	-36.7	-73.1		7	Mk											
1838	6	9	14	45						USGS	US: Illinois, Centralia	美国:伊利诺斯州森特勒利亚	38.5	-89		5.2	Ms	7										
1838	6									* CGS, USGS	US: California, San Francisco, San Jose	美国:加利福尼亚州 旧金山,圣何塞	37.6	-122.4		7.4	Ms	8						1				
1838	8	10	19	30		2			3	Italy, NOAA	Croatia: Rijeka	克罗地亚:里耶卡	45.3	14.6		5.03	Ms											
1838	12	12	23	30						USGS, Song	Hawaiian Islands	夏威夷群岛	19.25	-155		5.5	Mk	6										
1838										* Song	Myanmar: Ava (Innwa)	缅甸:英瓦	21.8	96		6.3	Mk							3				
1838										* Song	Israel: Jerusalem	以色列:耶路撒冷	32	34.5		7	Mk		3000	4				3				
1839	1	11	9	55						*	Martinique Island: Saint-Pierre	马提尼克岛:圣彼得	14.4	-61.1	33	7.8	Muk	9	390	3				3				
1839	2	7								* China	China: Yunnan, Eryuan	中国:云南洱源	26.1	99.9		6.25	Ms	8	100	2				2	600	3		
1839	2	23								* China	China: Yunnan, Eryuan	中国:云南洱源	26.1	99.9		6.25	Ms	8	129	3	18	1		2	1667	4		
1839	3	22								* Song	El Salvador: San Salvador	萨尔瓦多:圣萨尔瓦多	13.8	-89.2		7.1	Mk			3				4				
1839	3	23								* Song	Myanmar: Ava, Amarapura	缅甸:阿瓦,阿马拉普拉	21.8	96		8	Mk	11	400	3				3		3		3

时间						海啸				资料来源	震中				深度	震级	标度	烈度	死亡人数		受伤人数		经济损失		房屋毁坏		房屋受损	
年	月	日	时	分	秒	源	浪高	级 I	级 S		地名(英文)	地名(中文)	纬度(°)	经度(°)					数量/人	级别	数量/人	级别	数量/$ Mill	级别	数量/间	级别	数量/间	级别
Date						Tsunami				Information	Earthquake Epicenter				Depth	Mag	Scale	MMI	Deaths		Injuries		Damage		Houses Destroyed		Houses Damaged	
Year	Mo	Dy	Hr	Mn	Sec	Sr	Wh	mI	mS		Name(English)	Name(Chinese)	Latitude	Longitude					Num	Dd	Num	Dd	$ Mill	De	Num	Dh	Num	Dh
1839	3					1				* NOAA, Song	Hawaiian Islands	夏威夷群岛	19	-155.5		7	Mk											
1839	4	12								* Song	Venezuela: Cumana	委内瑞拉:库马纳	10.5	-64.2		5.9	Mk			1				2				
1839	5	1	4			1		1	1	* Usami, Japan, NOAA	Japan: Hokkaido	日本:北海道	42.5	145		7.3	Ms							1		1		
1839	6	28								* China	China: Taiwan, Chiayi	中国:台湾嘉义	23.5	120.4		6.5	Ms	8	117	3	534	3		3	6600	4		
1839	7	5	0	30						GSHAP, Song	Peru: Perene	秘鲁:佩雷内	-11	-75	20	6	Mk	7										
1839	8	16	17	30						* Song	France: Annecy	法国:阿讷西	45.9	6.1		6	Mk	7		2				1				
1840	1	4				2			0	* NOAA	Indonesia: Java, Purworejo	印度尼西亚:爪哇,普沃勒佐	-7.4	110	150	7	Ms	9						3		3		
1840	1	16								USGS, Song	US: California, Carmel, Near Coast	美国:加利福尼亚州卡梅尔近海	36.5	-122.1		5.5	Mk	6										
1840	1	28	8			1				* NOAA, GSHAP, Song	Peru: Lima, Near Coast	秘鲁:利马近海	-12.3	-77.3	40	7	Mk	5										
1840	2	2								USGS, Song	Hawaiian Islands	夏威夷群岛	19.25	-155		5	Mk	5										
1840	2	14				5			0.5	* NOAA, Song	Indonesia: Molucca Sea	印度尼西亚:马鲁古海	1	126.25		7	Mk											
1840	3	22	0	30		1		1	1	* Bautista, Maso, NOAA	Philippines: Sorsogon, Masbate Is.	菲律宾:索索贡,马斯巴特岛	12.9	123.9		6.8	Ms	9	17	1	200	3		3		3		
1840	4									USGS, Song	Alaska Peninsula, S.	阿拉斯加半岛南部	60.5	-152		5.5	Mk	6										
1840	5	13	16	30						GSHAP, Song	Peru: Lima	秘鲁:利马	-12	-77		4.5	Mk	5										
1840	7	2	16							* Iran	Turkey: Caldiran	土耳其:恰尔德兰	39.5	43.9		7.4	Ms	9	1049	4				4		4		
1840	7	6								GSHAP	Turkey: Aralik	土耳其:阿拉勒克	39.7	44.4	12	4.7	Ms	7										
1840	7	26								GSHAP	Turkey: Aralik	土耳其:阿拉勒克	39.7	44.4	14	5	Ms	7										
1840	7	27	16							GSHAP	Azerbaijan: Naxcivan	阿塞拜疆:纳希切万	39.5	45.1	10	4.8	Ms	7.5										
1840	8	14	7							GSHAP	Turkey: Igdir	土耳其:伊迪尔	40	44	22	4.7	Ms	6										
1840	8	27	12	5						* Italy	Slovenia: Ljubljana	斯洛文尼亚:卢布尔雅那	46.2	14.7	8	5.37	Muk	7						2				
1840	9	18	22	30						GSHAP	Colombia: El Bajito	哥伦比亚:埃尔巴希托	1.8	-78.8		5	Ms	6										
1840	10	9								GSHAP	Ecuador: Tungurahua	厄瓜多尔:东谷拉瓦	-1.35	-78.5		5.7	Ms	7										
1840	10	30	9	29						* GSHAP	Greece: Zakinthos (Zante)	希腊:扎金索斯岛(桑特岛)	38	21		6.5	Mk	10	12	1				3				
1840	11	11				1				*	US: New Jersey, Sewell	美国:新泽西州苏埃尔	39.8	-75.2		5.2	ML											
1840	11									China	China: Taiwan, Chiayi	中国:台湾嘉义	23.6	120.5		5.5	Ms	7										
1840	12	11	6	15						GSHAP	Colombia: Bogota	哥伦比亚:波哥达	4.6	-74		4.5	Ms	5										
1840										* * Song	Fiji Islands: Kandavu	斐济群岛:坎达武	-19	178		6.3	Mk	8		3				3				
1841	4	8	10	15						USGS, Song	Hawaiian Islands	夏威夷群岛	19.25	-155		5.5	Mk	6										
1841	4	22	4							Usami	Japan: Shizuoka	日本:静冈	35	138.5		6.4	Ms	7										1
1841	5	17	21	30		4	15	3.9	3	* NOAA	Russia: Kamchatka Peninsula	俄罗斯:堪察加半岛	52	158	30	8.4	Mfa	11						2				
1841	6	15	5	30						* Song	Azores: Praia Da Vitoria	亚速尔群岛:维多利亚:普拉亚	38.4	-25.3		7.3	Mk	10										

年 Year	月 Mo	日 Dy	时 Hr	分 Mn	秒 Sec	海啸 源 Sr	海啸 浪高 Wh	海啸 级 I mI	海啸 级 S mS	资料来源 Information	地名(英文) Name(English)	地名(中文) Name(Chinese)	纬度(°) Latitude	经度(°) Longitude	深度 Depth	震级 Mag	标度 Scale	烈度 MMI	死亡人数 数量/人 Num	死亡人数 级别 Dd	受伤人数 数量/人 Num	受伤人数 级别 Dd	经济损失 数量/$ Mill	经济损失 级别 De	房屋毁坏 数量/间 Num	房屋毁坏 级别 Dh	房屋受损 数量/间 Num	房屋受损 级别 Dh
1841	7	3	22	7						CGS, USGS	US: California, San Juan Bautista	美国:加利福尼亚州圣胡安包蒂斯塔	36.8	-121.5		6.2	Ms	6										
1841	9	2	12	15						* Song	Costa Rica: Cartago, San Jose	哥斯达黎加:卡塔哥,圣何塞	10	-84		6.2	Mk			3				2				
1841	9	22	16							GSHAP	Iran: Maku	伊朗:马库	39.4	44.4	20	4.9	Ms	6.5										
1841	11	3								Japan	Japan: Uwajima	日本:爱媛宇和岛市	33.2	132.4		6	Ms											1
1841	11	10								Japan, Song	Japan Sea	日本海	35.9	132.2		6.8	Mk									3		
1841	11	26				3	3	1.5	2	* NOAA, Song	Indonesia: Banda Sea	印度尼西亚:班达海	-5	130		7.5	Mk											
1841	12	9								Japan, Song	Japan: Shinano	日本:长野信浓町	36.8	138.2		6.3	Mk									1		
1841	12	16				3	1.5	1	1.5	* NOAA	Indonesia: Banda Sea	印度尼西亚:班达海	-4	127.5		6	Ms	8						2				
1841	12	25	6	54						GSHAP	Black Sea	黑海	44.8	37.4	12	4.5	Ms	6										
1841	12	28	5	50						USGS	US: Kentucky, Hickman	美国:肯塔基州希克曼	36.6	-89.2		4.6	Ms	5										
1842	1	2								*	Azerbaijan: Baki	阿塞拜疆:巴库	40.5	50	3	4.3	Muk	8						2				
1842	1	28	9	45						GSHAP	Colombia: Bogota	哥伦比亚:波哥达	4.6	-74		4.5	Ms	5										
1842	2	19								* Afghan	Afghan: Jalalabad	阿富汗:贾拉拉巴德	34.4	70.5		7.5	Ms		500	3				3				
1842	4	17								Usami, Japan, Song	Japan: South Honshu Ridge	日本:本州南部海岭	31.448	140.036		6.1	Mk											1
1842	4	18	8	30						* GSHAP, Song	Greece: Peninsula of Maina (Laconia)	希腊:马伊纳半岛	36.5	22.3	100	6.1	Mk	9		2								
1842	5	7	21			4	5	4.2		* NOAA	Haiti: Cap - Haitien	海地:海地角	19.75	-72.2		8.1	Ms		5000	4				4				
1842	6	11								* China	China: Xinjiang, Barkol	中国:新疆巴里坤	43.5	93.1		7	Ms	9		2		3		3	5460	4		
1842	11	1				2				* NOAA, Song	Canada: Ottawa, S.	加拿大:渥太华南部	44	-76.5		7	Mk											
1842	11	11	21	38		1				* GSHAP, NOAA	Bangladesh: Dhaka, N.	孟加拉:达卡北部	25	90		6.8	Ms							1				
1842	12	8								* Song	Ethiopia: Ankober	埃塞俄比亚:安可贝	9.6	39.8		6.5	Mk	9		3				3				
1843	1	5	2	45						USGS	US: Arkansas, Marked Tree	美国:阿肯色州马克德特里	35.5	-90.5		6	Ms	7										
1843	1	5				4			2	* NOAA	Indonesia: Off West Coast of N. Sumatera	印度尼西亚:北苏门答腊西部海域	1.5	98	70	7.3	Ms							3		3		2
1843	1	6				4				NOAA, Song	Indonesia: Off West Coast of N. Sumatera	印度尼西亚:北苏门答腊西部海域	1.5	98		7	Mk											
1843	2	1								* Song	Iran: Orumiyeh	伊朗:乌尔米耶	38.3	44.6		5.9	Mk							2				
1843	2	7				1			0	* NOAA	Indonesia: Java Island	印度尼西亚:爪哇岛	-7.2	114		6	Ms											
1843	2	8	14	50		4	1.2	0.3		* NOAA	Montserrat: Plymouth	蒙特塞拉特:普利茅斯	16.5	-62.2	33	8.3	Muk	9	5000	4				4				
1843	2	17	5							USGS	US: Arkansas, Marked Tree	美国:阿肯色州马克德特里	35.5	-90.5		4.8	Ms	5										
1843	3	9	2							Usami, Japan	Japan: Odawara	日本:神奈川小田原	35.25	139.2		6.3	Ms	8										1
1843	4	1								* GSHAP	India: Deccan	印度:德干高原	19	77		5.8	Mk							2				
1843	4	18								* Iran	Iran: Salmas, N.	伊朗:萨勒马斯北部	38.7	44.9		5.9	Ms	7	1000	3				3				
1843	4	24	21			4	4.5	2.2	2.5	* Usami, NOAA	Japan Trench	日本海沟	41.8	144.8		8.4	Ms	10	46	1				2	75	2		
1843	7	4								Japan	Japan: Akita	日本:秋田	39.5	140.7		6	Ms											1

时间						海啸				资料来源	震中				深度	震级	标度	烈度	死亡人数		受伤人数		经济损失		房屋毁坏		房屋受损	
年	月	日	时	分	秒	源	浪高	级 I	级 S		地名(英文)	地名(中文)	纬度(°)	经度(°)					数量/人	级别	数量/人	级别	数量/$ Mill	级别	数量/间	级别	数量/间	级别
Date						Tsunami				Information	Earthquake Epicenter				Depth	Mag	Scale	MMI	Deaths		Injuries		Damage		Houses Destroyed		Houses Damaged	
Year	Mo	Dy	Hr	Mn	Sec	Sr	Wh	mI	mS		Name(English)	Name(Chinese)	Latitude	Longitude					Num	Dd	Num	Dd	$ Mill	De	Num	Dh	Num	Dh
1843	7	8				1				*	New Zealand: North Island, Wanganui	新西兰:北岛,旺加努伊	-39.9	175	33	7.5	Muk											
1843	9	10								GSHAP	Romania: Nereju	罗马尼亚:内雷茹	45.7	26.6	100	5.5	Ms	6										
1843	9	14	10	30		2			4	NOAA	Croatia: Dubrovnik	克罗地亚:杜布罗夫尼克	42.6	18.1		6.5	Ms											
1843	9	27								Japan, Song	Japan: Tokyo	日本:东京	35.7	139.8		6.1	Mk											1
1843	10	2	9	5						GSHAP	Romania: Nereju	罗马尼亚:内雷茹	45.7	26.6	100	5.4	Ms	5.5										
1843	10	18				2			4	* GSHAP, NOAA	Greece: Chalki (Dodecanese)	希腊:秋奇(萨摩斯岛)	36.3	27.5		6.5	Ms	9		2								
1843	12	16								Japan, Song	Japan: Tokyo	日本:东京	35.7	139.8		6.1	Mk											1
1843	12	17	1							USGS, Song	Gulf of Alaska, SE.	阿拉斯加湾东南	57	-136		5.5	Mk	6										
1843	12	17	22	15						* Song	Chile: Coquimbo	智利:科金博	-29.9	-71.3		7.3	Mk	10										
1843	12	26	23	30						GSHAP	Russia: Kamchatka Peninsula	俄罗斯:堪察加半岛	54	159	30	5.6	Ms	8										
1844	1	22								* * Song	Iran: Tabriz	伊朗:大不里士	37.6	47.3		5.9	Mk							2				
1844	2	19	5							USGS, Song	Hawaiian Islands	夏威夷群岛	19.25	-155		5	Mk	5										
1844	3	3	18	25		2			3	NOAA, Song	Croatia: Split	克罗地亚:斯普利特	43.4	16.7		6.7	Mk											
1844	3	12								GSHAP	Russia: Dagestan, Makhachkala	俄罗斯:达吉斯坦共和国马哈奇卡拉	42.5	46.7	15	5.3	Ms	7										
1844	3	22	10	13		2			2	NOAA, Song	Croatia: Split	克罗地亚:斯普利特	43.4	16.7		6.7	Mk											
1844	4	13	10							USGS, Song	Gulf of Alaska	阿拉斯加湾	57	-152		5.5	Mk	6										
1844	4	16	13	20						* Song	Puerto Rico: San Juan; St Thomas	波多黎各:圣胡安;圣托马斯	18.3	-66.8		6.1	Mk	8						2				
1844	4	23								* * Song	Iran: Tabriz	伊朗:大不里士	37.3	47.4		6.3	Mk							3				
1844	5	12								* Turkey	Turkey: Osmancik	土耳其:奥斯曼哲克	41	35		5.8	Mk	9	200	3		3		3		3	200	3
1844	5	12								* Iran	Iran: Esfahan	伊朗:伊斯法罕	33.6	51.4		6.4	Ms		1500	4		3		3		3	1500	4
1844	5	13	19							* GSHAP	Iran: Tabriz	伊朗:大不里士	37.4	48	15	6.9	Ms	9.5		4		4		4		4		4
1844	6	10				1				* NOAA, Song	Marquesas Islands	马克萨斯群岛[南太平洋]	-9	-140		7	Mk											
1844	8	8								Usami, Japan, Song	Japan: Taketa	日本:大分竹田	33	131.3		6.3	Mk									1		
1844	8	30	7	10						* Song	St Vincent & Grenadines: Kingstown	圣文森特和格林纳丁斯:金斯敦	13.1	-61.1		5.9	Mk							2				
1844	8									* Song	Nicaragua: San Juan Del Norte	尼加拉瓜:北圣胡安	11	-84		5.9	Mk							2				
1844	9	18	23							GSHAP	Argentina: Salta	阿根廷:萨尔塔	-24.8	-64.7	30	6.5	Ms	7										
1844	10	19	1	30						* Song	Argentina: Salta, Jujuy	阿根廷:萨尔塔,胡胡伊	-25	-66		6.3	Mk	8						3				
1844	11	28	13							USGS	US: Tennessee, Knoxville	美国:田纳西州诺克斯维尔	36	-84		4.2	Ms	6										

时间						海啸				资料来源	震中				深度	震级	标度	烈度	死亡人数		受伤人数		经济损失		房屋毁坏		房屋受损	
年	月	日	时	分	秒	源	浪高	级 I	级 S		地名(英文)	地名(中文)	纬度(°)	经度(°)					数量/人	级别	数量/人	级别	数量/$ Mill	级别	数量/间	级别	数量/间	级别
Date						Tsunami				Information	Earthquake Epicenter				Depth	Mag	Scale	MMI	Deaths		Injuries		Damage		Houses Destroyed		Houses Damaged	
Year	Mo	Dy	Hr	Mn	Sec	Sr	Wh	mI	mS		Name(English)	Name(Chinese)	Latitude	Longitude					Num	Dd	Num	Dd	$ Mill	De	Num	Dh	Num	Dh
1844	12	26								GSHAP	Russia: Stavropol, Mineralnye Vody	俄罗斯：斯塔夫罗波尔区矿水城	44. 1	43	10	5	Ms	7										
1844										GSHAP	Kazakhstan: Semey	哈萨克斯坦：塞米伊	49. 5	81. 5	20	4. 8	Ms	5. 5										
1844										Japan, Song	Japan: Tokyo	日本：东京	35. 7	139. 8		6. 1	Mk											1
1845	1	14								GSHAP	Bolivia: Santa Cruz de la Sierra	玻利维亚：圣克鲁斯	-17. 78	-63. 17		5. 2	Ms	6										
1845	2	8	7	30		5			0	* NOAA	Indonesia: Menado, Tikala	印度尼西亚：万鸦老，托拉雅	-1. 3	124. 5		7	Ms	9	118	3				3		3		
1845	2	12								* Song	Ethiopia: Amhara	埃塞俄比亚：阿姆哈拉区	12. 3	39		6	Mk			2								
1845	2	19	12							GSHAP	Colombia: Ibagué	哥伦比亚：托利马的伊瓦格	4. 5	-75. 4		4	Ms	5										
1845	2	19	12							* GSHAP, Song	Colombia: Magdalena, Near Coast	哥伦比亚：马格达莱纳近海	11. 1	-74. 5		6. 2	Mk	8		3								
1845	2									* China	China: Taiwan, Changhua	中国：台湾彰化	24. 1	120. 5		6. 25	Ms	8	380	3		3		3	4000	4		
1845	3	9								* Song	Mexico: Oaxaca	墨西哥：瓦哈卡	17	-96. 3		6. 3	Mk							3				
1845	4	7				4			1. 5	* NOAA	Mexico: Mexico City	墨西哥：墨西哥城	19. 2	-99. 1		8	Ms							3				
1845	5	24	1							GSHAP	Georgia: Borzhomi	格鲁吉亚：博尔若米	41. 6	43. 5	12	4. 6	Ms	7										2
1845	5									GSHAP, Song	Peru: Arequipa	秘鲁：阿雷基帕	-16. 6	-71. 6	25	5	Mk	6										
1845	6	4	2	15						* Song	Chile: Arica, Near Coast	智利：阿里卡近海	-18. 5	-70. 4		7. 3	Mk	10										
1845	6	4	3	45						GSHAP, Song	Peru: Arequipa	秘鲁：阿雷基帕	-16. 6	-71. 6	30	5	Mk	6										
1845	6	18				1				NOAA, Song	Italy: Sicilia Island	意大利：西西里岛	36. 4	13. 44		6. 6	Mk											
1845	6	19				3				* NOAA	India: Bhuj, NW.	印度：普杰西北	23. 583	68. 367		6. 3	Ms	8										
1845	7	5				2			0. 5	* NOAA, Song	New Zealand: North Island, Wanganui	新西兰：北岛，旺加努伊	-39. 93	175. 05		7	Mk											
1845	8	16	16	38		1			3	NOAA, Song	Croatia: Split	克罗地亚：斯普利特	43. 4	16. 7		6. 7	Mk											
1845	9	21	21							GSHAP	Russia: Kamchatka Peninsula	俄罗斯：堪察加半岛	53	160. 5	20	5. 9	Ms	7. 5										
1845	10	11	2							* GSHAP	Greece: Kalloni	希腊：卡洛尼	39. 1	26. 2		6. 7	Mk	10										
1845	10	19	19							GSHAP	Argentina: Chivilcoy	阿根廷：奇维尔科伊	-35. 1	-59. 8	30	5	Ms	5										
1845	10	26	23	15						USGS, Song	US: Connecticut, Fairfield	美国：康涅狄格州费尔菲尔德	41. 2	-73. 3		5. 5	Mk	6										
1845	11									China	China: Yunnan, Dengchuan	中国：云南邓川	26	100. 1		5. 5	Ms	7										
1845	12	21	20	40						* Italy	Slovenia: Ljubljana	斯洛文尼亚：卢布尔雅那	46. 1	14. 5	7	4. 9	Muk	7						2				
1846	1	25				4			0. 5	* NOAA	Indonesia: East of Sangihe Islands	印度尼西亚：桑义赫群岛东部	2	126. 5		7. 2	Ms											
1846	2	14								* Song	Indonesia: Maluku Utara, Coast of W.	印度尼西亚：北马鲁古西部海域	0. 5	127. 3		6. 3	Mk			3				3				
1846	3	13	11							GSHAP, Song	Chile: Copiapo	智利：科皮亚波	-27. 35	-70. 35		6	Mk	8										
1846	3					4	2	1	1	* NOAA	Japan: Iwate, Near Coast	日本：岩手近海	39. 5	142. 5		6. 9	Ms											

时间 年 Year	月 Mo	日 Dy	时 Hr	分 Mn	秒 Sec	海啸 Tsunami 源 Sr	浪高 Wh	级 I mI	级 S mS	资料来源 Information	震中 Earthquake Epicenter 地名(英文) Name(English)	地名(中文) Name(Chinese)	纬度(°) Latitude	经度(°) Longitude	深度 Depth	震级 Mag	标度 Scale	烈度 MMI	死亡人数 Deaths 数量/人 Num	级别 Dd	受伤人数 Injuries 数量/人 Num	级别 Dd	经济损失 Damage 数量/$ Mill	级别 De	房屋毁坏 Houses Destroyed 数量/间 Num	级别 Dh	房屋受损 Houses Damaged 数量/间 Num	级别 Dh
1846	6	10	18							*	Greece: Kalamata	希腊:卡拉玛达	37	22		7	Mk	10	30	2			0.8	1				
1846	6	28	1	15						*	Peru:Pisco,Near Coast	秘鲁:皮斯科近海	-14	-76.8	50	7.8	Muk	6										
1846	7	25	17	30		2			3	NOAA,Song	Turkey:Izmir	土耳其:伊兹密尔	38.4	27.3		6.7	Mk											
1846	8	7								*Song	Italy:Siracusa (Syracuse)	意大利:锡拉库萨(锡拉丘兹)	37	15.3		6.5	Mk	11						2				
1846	8	14	12	35		3			3	*NOAA	Italy:Orciano, Luciana	意大利:奥尔恰诺,卢西亚娜	43.4	10.6	5	6.1	Ms	10	56	2				3				
1846	8	26	17	23		3			4	NOAA,Song	Italy:Livorno	意大利:来航	43.5	10.5		6.7	Mk											
1846	9	12				3				NOAA,Song	Italy:Livorno	意大利:来航	43.5	10.5		6.6	Mk											
1846	9	19				3				NOAA,Song	Italy:Livorno	意大利:来航	43.5	10.5		6.6	Mk											
1846	10	4	22	15		3				NOAA,Song	Italy:Livorno	意大利:来航	43.5	10.5		6.6	Mk											
1846	10	14	11	15		3				NOAA,Song	Italy:Livorno	意大利:来航	43.5	10.5		6.6	Mk											
1846	10	19				3				NOAA,Song	Italy:Livorno	意大利:来航	43.5	10.5		6.6	Mk											
1846	10	24				3				NOAA,Song	Italy:Livorno	意大利:来航	43.5	10.5		6.6	Mk											
1846	10	28				3				NOAA,Song	Italy:Livorno	意大利:来航	43.5	10.5		6.6	Mk											
1846	10	30	21							GSHAP	Kazakhstan:Kokpekty	哈萨克斯坦:科克佩克特	48.5	81.8	40	5.4	Ms	5.5										
1846	11	29	0	55		3				NOAA,Song	Italy:Livorno	意大利:来航	43.5	10.5		6.6	Mk											
1846	12	3				2			3	NOAA,Song	Italy:Tuscany Coast	意大利:托斯卡纳沿海	43.3	10.7		6.7	Mk											
1846						2			3	NOAA,Song	Turkey:Izmir	土耳其:伊兹密尔	38.4	26.9		6.7	Mk											
1847	1	19	14	50						GSHAP,Song	Chile:Copiapo	智利:科皮亚波	-27.35	-70.35		6	Mk	8										
1847	3	8	15							*Song	Chile:Valparaiso	智利:瓦尔帕莱索	-32.5	-71.3		7.3	Mk	10										
1847	4	15				3				NOAA,Song	Italy:Livorno	意大利:里窝那	43.5	10.2		6.6	Mk											
1847	4	16	16							USGS,Song	Aleutian Islands	阿留申群岛	55	-158		5.5	Mk	6										
1847	4	16				3				NOAA,Song	Italy:Livorno	意大利:里窝那	43.5	10.2		6.6	Mk											
1847	4	17				3				NOAA,Song	Italy:Livorno	意大利:里窝那	43.5	10.2		6.6	Mk											
1847	4	27	8							GSHAP	Russia:Sverdlovsk, Baranchinskiy	俄罗斯:斯威尔德洛夫斯克州巴兰钦斯基	58.4	59.5	15	4.8	Ms	6										
1847	5	8	13							*Usami	Japan:Naganoi	日本:长野	37	138		7.4	Ms	10	12000	5				4	34000	5		
1847	5	13	3							Japan	Japan:Naganoi	日本:长野	37.2	138.3		6.5	Ms		200	3					2000	4		
1847	5	23				2	2	1	1.5	*NOAA,Song	Peru:Lima,Near Coast	秘鲁:利马近海	-12.1	-77.1		7	Mk							1				
1847	5	24				2			1.5	**NOAA,Song	Peru:Lima,Near Coast	秘鲁:利马近海	-12	-78		7	Mk											
1847	8	7								*Song	Egypt:Al-Fayyum, Cairo	埃及:法尤姆,开罗	29.5	30.5		8	Mk	11	185	3		4		4	4072	4	4072	4
1847	8	8	15							USGS,Song	US:Massachusetts,Harwich	美国:马萨诸塞州哈威奇	41.7	-70.1		5.5	Mk	6										
1847	8	26				2			2	NOAA,Song	Italy:Livorno	意大利:里窝那	43.5	10.2		6.7	Mk											
1847	8	27				2				Japan,NOAA,Song	Japan:Miyagi,Near Coast	日本:宫城近海	38.6	142		7.5	Mk		335	3								
1847	10	8	11	30		4				*	Chile:Coquimbo	智利:科金博	-31.61	-71.18		7.3	Ms	8		1								
1847	10	19				2				**NOAA,Song	Chile:Coquimbo	智利:科金博	-29.9	-71.4		7	Mk											

时间						海啸				资料来源	震中				深度	震级	标度	烈度	死亡人数		受伤人数		经济损失		房屋毁坏		房屋受损	
年	月	日	时	分	秒	源	浪高	级 I	级 S		地名(英文)	地名(中文)	纬度(°)	经度(°)					数量/人	级别	数量/人	级别	数量/$ Mill	级别	数量/间	级别	数量/间	级别
Date						Tsunami				Information	Earthquake Epicenter				Depth	Mag	Scale	MMI	Deaths		Injuries		Damage		Houses Destroyed		Houses Damaged	
Year	Mo	Dy	Hr	Mn	Sec	Sr	Wh	mI	mS		Name(English)	Name(Chinese)	Latitude	Longitude					Num	Dd	Num	Dd	$ Mill	De	Num	Dh	Num	Dh
1847	10	31				3				* NOAA, Song	India: Andaman – Nicobar Islands	印度:安达曼 – 尼科巴群岛	7.333	93.667		7	Mk											
1847	10									* Song	Mexico: Oaxaca	墨西哥:瓦哈卡	17	−96.3		6.3	Mk							3				
1847	11	16								* Song	Indonesia: Java, Cirebon (Cheribon)	印度尼西亚:爪哇,井里汶	−6.9	108.3		5.9	Mk							2				
1847	12	19	6							* Song	Portugal: Lisbon	葡萄牙:里斯本	38.7	−9.2		7.3	Mk	10						2		2		2
1847										USGS, Song	Gulf of Alaska, SE.	阿拉斯加湾东南	57	−136		5.7	Mk	7										
1847										GSHAP, Song	Peru: Apurimac	秘鲁:阿普里马克	−13.7	−73.1	20	6.5	Mk	9										
1848	1	10								Usami	Japan: Fukuoka, W.	日本:福冈西部	33.2	130.4		5.9	Ms											
1848	1	11								* Italy	Italy: Sicilia Island	意大利:西西里岛	37.367	15.154		5.48	Ms	11								3		
1848	1	12	18							Usami	Japan: Koginsasi	日本:津轻	40.7	140.6		5.9	Ms							2				
1848	1	25								Japan, Song	Japan: Kumamoto	日本:熊本	32.9	130.7		6.1	Mk									3		
1848	2	20	17							GSHAP	Azerbaijan: Naxcivan	阿塞拜疆:纳希切万	39.2	45.3	10	4.8	Ms	5.5										1
1848	2	22								GSHAP	Russia: Novosibirsk, Tersk	俄罗斯:新西伯利亚州捷尔斯克村	43.7	44.7	15	4.8	Ms	6.5										
1848	2									* Song	Morocco: Melilla	摩洛哥:梅利利亚	35.3	−2.97		5.9	Mk							2				
1848	3	30	10	45						USGS, Song	Gulf of Alaska, SE.	阿拉斯加湾东南	57	−136		5.5	Mk	6										
1848	5	31								* Song	Mexico: Oaxaca, Guerrero	墨西哥:瓦哈卡,格雷罗	17	−96.3		6.3	Mk							3				
1848	6	9								Japan, Song	Japan: Tokyo	日本:东京	35.7	139.8		6.1	Mk											1
1848	6	30	10			1				USGS, NOAA, Song	Aleutian Islands	阿留申群岛	55	−155		7	Mk	6										
1848	7	9	14	45						USGS, Song	Hawaiian Islands	夏威夷群岛	19.25	−155		5	Mk	5										
1848	7	12				2				* NOAA, Song	French Polynesia: Tahiti Is.	法属波利尼西亚:塔希提岛	−17.9	−149.9		7	Mk							1				
1848	9	24	20							GSHAP	Azerbaijan: Samaxi	阿塞拜疆:沙马基区	40.6	48.6	7	4.6	Ms	7										
1848	10	15	13	40		3	0.3	−1	0.5	* NOAA	New Zealand: Cook Strait	新西兰:库克海峡	−41.3	174.5		7.8	Ms							1				
1848	12	3								* China	China: Taiwan, Changhua	中国:台湾彰化	24.1	120.5		6.75	Ms	9	1001	4		4		4	20300	5		
1848										Japan, Song	Japan: Fukui	日本:福井	35.9	136.2		6.5	Mk	7		2						1		
1849	1	24	6	56		3	6.1	1	2	* NOAA	Guam	关岛(西太平洋)	14	143.3		7.5	Muk	9	1	1		2		3		3		
1849	1	29	4	53						GSHAP	Russia: Tyumen, Ishim	俄罗斯:秋明州伊希姆	56.1	69.3	10	5	Ms	6.5										
1849	2	26	9	30						*	Colombia: Pamplona	哥伦比亚:潘普洛纳	7.3	−72.3	13	6	Muk	9	40	1				2				
1849	5	3	10							* Song	Venezuela: Maracaibo	委内瑞拉:马拉开波湾	10.7	−71.6		6.2	Mk			3				2				
1849	5	3	17	5						GSHAP, Song	Venezuela: Maracaibo	委内瑞拉:马拉开波湾	10.7	−71.6		5	Mk	6										
1849	7	1	17	30						GSHAP	Russia: Sakha, Churan	俄罗斯:萨哈共和国丘兰	61.2	137.4	20	5	Ms	6										
1849	9	29	9			4				* NOAA, Song	Russia: Kamchatka, Near East Coast	俄罗斯:堪察加东部近海	56	167		7	Mk							1		1		
1849	10	28	9			4				* NOAA	Russia: Komandorsky Islands	俄罗斯:科曼多尔群岛	55	166	20	7.5	Muk	10										
1849	12	17	10	10		4	5	2.3	2.3	* NOAA	Chile: Coquimbo	智利:科金博	−29.95	−71.37		7.5	Ms	8						1				

时间 Date						海啸 Tsunami				资料来源 Information	震中 Earthquake Epicenter				深度 Depth	震级 Mag	标度 Scale	烈度 MMI	死亡人数 Deaths		受伤人数 Injuries		经济损失 Damage		房屋毁坏 Houses Destroyed		房屋受损 Houses Damaged	
年 Year	月 Mo	日 Dy	时 Hr	分 Mn	秒 Sec	源 Sr	浪高 Wh	级 I mI	级 S mS		地名(英文) Name(English)	地名(中文) Name(Chinese)	纬度(°) Latitude	经度(°) Longitude					数量/人 Num	级别 Dd	数量/人 Num	级别 Dd	数量/$ Mill $ Mill	级别 De	数量/间 Num	级别 Dh	数量/间 Num	级别 Dh
1849										China	China:Guangdong,Puning	中国:广东普宁	23.4	116.2		4.75	Ms	6										
1850	1	18	18	30						GSHAP	Russia:Sakha,SW.	俄罗斯:萨哈共和国西南	58.5	121	20	6.1	Ms	7.5										
1850	4	5	2	5						USGS	US:Kentucky,Barlow	美国:肯塔基州巴洛	37	-88		4.9	Ms	5										
1850	4	29								* Song	Croatia:Dubrovnik	克罗地亚:杜布罗夫尼克	42.8	17.7		6.3	Mk	11										
1850	7	20				2	2	1	1	Japan,NOAA,Song	Japan:Iwate	日本:岩手	39.2	141.2		7	Mk			1								
1850	9	12								* China	China:Sichuan,Xichang,SE.	中国:四川西昌东南	27.7	102.4		7.5	Ms	10	20650	5				4				
1850	10	20				2				NOAA,Song	Italy:Livorno	意大利:里窝那	43.5	10.2		6.6	Mk											
1850										* China	China:Gansu,Wushan	中国:甘肃武山	34.7	104.9		5	Ms	6		2				1		1		
1850										GSHAP	Turkey:Igdir	土耳其:伊迪尔	39.9	43.3	20	6.2	Ms	8										
1851	1	1								* Italy	Switzerland:Naters	瑞士:纳特尔斯	46.3	8		4.83	Ms	6		2								
1851	1	20								* Song	Albania:Elbasan	阿尔巴尼亚:爱尔巴桑	41.2	20.2		5.8	Mk	9						2				
1851	2	2	10							* Song	Colombia:Cartagena	哥伦比亚:卡塔赫纳	10.4	-75.4		6.2	Mk			3				2				
1851	2	7								* * Song	Colombia:Cartagena	哥伦比亚:卡塔赫纳	10.5	-75.7		6.3	Mk	6		3				3				
1851	2	28	15			3	0.9	-0.1	3	* GSHAP,NOAA	Mediterranean Sea	地中海	36.5	29		7.2	Ms	10						2				
1851	4	2	10	48		4				*	Chile:Valparaiso	智利:瓦尔帕莱索	-33.32	-71.42		7.1	Ms	8		1				3		3		
1851	4	2	11	27						* Song	Chile:Valparaiso	智利:瓦尔帕莱索	-33	-71.5		5.9	Mk			1				2				
1851	4	3				3			3	NOAA,Song	Mediterranean Sea	地中海	35.5	29.5		6.7	Mk											
1851	4	9								GSHAP	Azerbaijan:Agcabedi	阿塞拜疆:阿格贾贝迪区	40	47.3	20	6.2	Ms	8										
1851	4	19	14	30						* Song	Pakistan:Gwadar	巴基斯坦:瓜达尔	25.1	62.3		5.9	Mk							2		3		3
1851	5	4				3	1.5	3.9	1.5	NOAA,Song	Indonesia:Java Island	印度尼西亚:爪哇岛	-6.05	105.92		7	Mk											
1851	5	15	16	10		1				* NOAA,Song	US:California,San Francisco	美国:加利福尼亚州旧金山	37.8	-122.4		7.2	Mk	6										
1851	5	16	13							* Song	Guadeloupe:Sainte - Anne	瓜德罗普岛:圣安娜	16.2	-61.4		5.9	Mk							2				
1851	5	23				2			2	NOAA,Song	Greece:Dodekanisa	希腊:十二群岛	36	27.5		6.7	Mk											
1851	5	26	18	14		4	3	1.6	2	* NOAA	Chile:Valparaiso	智利:科皮亚波	-27.35	-70.35		7.2	Ms	10						2		3		
1851	6									* GSHAP,Afghan	Iran:Qūchān	伊朗:古昌	36.8	58.4	15	6.9	Ms	9.5						2				
1851	7	5	12							GSHAP	Bolivia:Potosi	玻利维亚:波托西	-19.75	-65.58		5.8	Ms	7										
1851	7	28	18	33		1			2	NOAA	Italy:Pisa	意大利:比萨	43.75	10.3		4.1	Ms											
1851	8	14	13	22						* Italy	Italy:Melfi	意大利:梅尔菲	41	15.7		6.5	Ms	11	671	3				3		3		
1851	10	12	6			2	0.7	-0.1	3	* GSHAP,NOAA	Albania:Vlore(Valona),Berat	阿尔巴尼亚:发罗拉,培拉特	40.6	19.9		6.8	Ms	11	2000	4				4		4		
1851	10	17								* Song	Albania:Berat	阿尔巴尼亚:培拉特	40.4	19.6		6.2	Mk	10	400	3				3		3		
1851	11	12	1	30						GSHAP,Song	Peru:Lima	秘鲁:利马	-12	-77		4.5	Mk	5										
1851	11	13	2	51		1				* NOAA,Song	US:California,Red Bluff	美国:加利福尼亚州雷德布拉夫	40	-122		7	Mk											
1851	11	27	20							GSHAP	Russia:Magadan,Sredniy	俄罗斯:马加丹州斯列德尼	59.5	153.3	25	6.5	Ms	8										

年 Year	月 Mo	日 Dy	时 Hr	分 Mn	秒 Sec	海啸 Tsunami 源 Sr	浪高 Wh	级 I mI	级 S mS	资料来源 Information	震中 Earthquake Epicenter 地名(英文) Name(English)	地名(中文) Name(Chinese)	纬度(°) Latitude	经度(°) Longitude	深度 Depth	震级 Mag	标度 Scale	烈度 MMI	死亡人数 Deaths 数量/人 Num	级别 Dd	受伤人数 Injuries 数量/人 Num	级别 Dd	经济损失 Damage 数量/$ Mill $ Mill	级别 De	房屋毁坏 Houses Destroyed 数量/间 Num	级别 Dh	房屋受损 Houses Damaged 数量/间 Num	级别 Dh
1851	12	7								GSHAP	Russia:Kamchatka Peninsula	俄罗斯:堪察加半岛	53	160.5	20	5.9	Ms	7.5										
1851	12	30								Japan,Song	Japan:Koginsasi	日本:津轻	40.7	140.6		6.1	Mk											1
1852	1	24	3	45						* Afghan	Pakistan:Sibbi	巴基斯坦:锡比	29.3	68.8		6.7	Mk		350	3				3		3		3
1852	1	24								* Song	Mexico:Oaxaca	墨西哥:瓦哈卡	17	-96.3		6.3	Mk							3				
1852	1	26								Japan	Japan:Shinano	日本:长野信浓町	36.8	138.2		5.9	Ms									1		
1852	2	22								*	Iran:Qūchān	伊朗:古昌	37.1	58.4	10	5.8	Muk	9	2000	4				3				
1852	4	16	22	16						* Song	Azores:Sao Miguel (San Miguel)	亚速尔群岛:圣米格尔	37.5	-25.3		7.3	Mk	10										
1852	4	29	18							USGS	US:Virginia,Mouth of Wilson	美国:弗吉尼亚州毛斯奥夫威尔逊	36.6	-81.6		4.8	Ms	6										
1852	5	12	2			2			3	NOAA,Song	Mediterranean Sea	地中海	35.5	29.5		6.7	Mk											
1852	5	26								* China	China:Ningxia,Zhongwei,SW.	中国:宁夏中卫西南	37.4	105.1		6	Ms	8	300	3	400	3		3	20000	5		
1852	6	26	7	15		2				NOAA,Song	Italy:Livorno	意大利:里窝那	43.5	10.2		6.6	Mk											
1852	7	17				2				* NOAA,Song	Cuba:Santiago De Cuba	古巴:圣地亚哥	20	-75.8		7.1	Mk							2				
1852	7	24								* GSHAP	Turkey:Erzurum	土耳其:埃尔佐鲁姆	39.9	41.3	12	7.3	Muk	8.5	17	1				1				
1852	9	8	22	30		3			3	NOAA,Song	Mediterranean Sea	地中海	35.5	29.5		6.7	Mk											
1852	9	16	10	30		3			1.5	* Bautista,Maso,Nakamura,NOAA	Philippines:Luzon,Manila	菲律宾:吕宋岛马尼拉	14.3	120.05		7.6	Ms	9	3	1				3		3		3
1852	9	25								Bautista,Maso,Song	Philippines:Libmanan,SE.	菲律宾:利马南东南	13.35	123.3		5	Mk	6										
1852	10	8								Japan,Song	Japan:Aki	日本:广岛安艺郡	34.4	132.6		6.1	Mk											1
1852	11	2	23	35						USGS	US:Virginia,Buckingham	美国:弗吉尼亚州白金汉	37.6	-78.6		4.3	Ms	6										
1852	11	10				2				NOAA,Song	Italy:Livorno	意大利:里窝那	43.5	10.2		6.6	Mk											
1852	11	11				1			0	* NOAA	Indonesia:Northern Sumatra	印度尼西亚:苏门答腊北部	1.7	98.8		6.8	Ms											
1852	11	25	7	9		1				* NOAA,Song	US:California,Concord	美国:加利福尼亚州康科德市	38	-122		7	Mk											
1852	11	26				4	15	3	4	* NOAA,Song	Indonesia:Banda Sea,E.	印度尼西亚:班达海东部	-4.6	129.9		7.9	Mk	9	60	2				2		2		
1852	11	27				1				* NOAA,Song	Peru:Lima	秘鲁:利马	-12	-77.1		7	Mk											
1852	11	29				4	3		1	*	Mexico:Mexicali	墨西哥:墨西卡利	32.5	-115.5		7	Ms	9										
1852	12	4				4				* NOAA	Mexico:Guerrero,Acapulco,E.	墨西哥:格雷罗州阿卡普尔科东部	17	-100		7	Ms		1	1		4		3		3		
1852	12	17								USGS,Song	US:California,San Simeon	美国:加利福尼亚州圣西米恩	35.5	-121		5.5	Mk	6										
1852	12	21	10							* Song	Azores:Fayal Island	亚速尔群岛:法亚尔岛	38.3	-28.4		7.3	Mk	10										
1852	12	24	14							* Bautista,Maso	Philippines:Batangas	菲律宾:八打雁	13.85	120.9		5.1	Ms	9						2				
1852	12	24				1			2	NOAA	Indonesia:Banda Sea	印度尼西亚:班达海	-5	130.5		7	Ms											

时间						海啸				资料来源	震中				深度	震级	标度	烈度	死亡人数		受伤人数		经济损失		房屋毁坏		房屋受损	
年	月	日	时	分	秒	源	浪高	级 I	级 S		地名(英文)	地名(中文)	纬度(°)	经度(°)					数量/人	级别	数量/人	级别	数量/$ Mill	级别	数量/间	级别	数量/间	级别
Date						Tsunami				Information	Earthquake Epicenter				Depth	Mag	Scale	MMI	Deaths		Injuries		Damage		Houses Destroyed		Houses Damaged	
Year	Mo	Dy	Hr	Mn	Sec	Sr	Wh	mI	mS		Name(English)	Name(Chinese)	Latitude	Longitude					Num	Dd	Num	Dd	$ Mill	De	Num	Dh	Num	Dh
1852	12									Japan, Song	Japan: Shimane	日本:岛根	35.3	133.2		6.3	Mk								3	1		
1852										Japan, Song	Japan: Sakai	日本:福井坂井	36.1	136.2		6.1	Mk											1
1853	1	26								Usami, Japan	Japan: Nagano	日本:长野	36.5	138.1		6.5	Ms	8							48	1		
1853	2	1	21							* Song	US: California, San Simeon	美国:加利福尼亚州圣西米恩	35.5	-121		6.1	Mk	8						2				
1853	2	8								China	China: Hunan, Jianghua, S.	中国:湖南江华南	24.9	111.7		4.75	Ms	6										
1853	3	11	1							* Usami, Japan	Japan: Kanagawa	日本:神奈川	35.5	139.5		6.5	Ms	8	79	2				3	1032	4		
1853	3	12	7	30						USGS, Song	US: New York, Glenfield	美国:纽约州格伦菲尔德	43.7	-75.5		5.5	Mk	6										
1853	4	8	17	50		2				NOAA, Song	Italy: Tyrrhenian Sea	意大利:第勒尼安海	40.821	14.426		6.6	Mk											
1853	4	9								* Italy	Italy: Caposele, Calabritto, Lioni	意大利:卡拉布里托,利奥尼	40.82	15.22		5.9	Ms	9	12	1				2				
1853	4	22								* Song	Iran: Fars, Shiraz	伊朗:法尔斯,设拉子	29.6	52.5		7.7	Mk	9	13000	5				4		4		
1853	5	2	14	20						USGS	US: West Virginia, Brandywine	美国:西弗吉尼亚州布兰迪万	38.5	-79.5		4.6	Ms	5										
1853	5	18	20							* Song	Italy: Caposele, Calabritto, Lioni	意大利:卡拉布里托,利奥尼	40.8	15.2		6.5	Mk	12										
1853	5	20								USGS, Song	US: South Carolina, Lexington	美国:南卡罗来纳州列克星敦	34	-81.2		5.5	Mk	6										
1853	7	15				3	5			* NOAA	Venezuela: Cumana	委内瑞拉:库马纳	10.5	-64.2	14	6.7	Muk	9	1000	3								
1853	8	18	8	30		3			3	* GSHAP, NOAA	Greece: Erythres	希腊:埃里斯雷	38.25	23.5		6.6	Ms	9	17	1				2				
1853	10	23								CGS, USGS	US: California, Eureka	美国:加利福尼亚州尤里卡	40.8	-124.2		5.5	Ms	6										
1853	11									China	China: Xinjiang, Kashi	中国:新疆喀什	39	76.2		5.5	Ms	7										
1853	11					1		2	2	* NOAA, Song	Kuril Islands	千岛群岛	47	154		7.5	Mk											
1853	12	11	16	15		2	1		3	NOAA, Song	Adriatic Sea	亚得里亚海	41.9	17.3		6.7	Mk											
1853	12	24				1				* NOAA, Song	Tonga Islands, S.	汤加群岛南部	-24	-175.8		7	Mk											
1853										* Maso, Song	Philippines: Camarines	菲律宾:馬利納	13.6	123		6.1	Mk	8						2		2		
1854	1	2								* Song	Mexico: Durango	墨西哥:杜兰戈	24	-104.4		6.3	Mk							3				
1854	1	4				2				* NOAA	Indonesia: Maluku Islands	印度尼西亚:摩鹿加群岛	-3.5	128.6		6	Ms											
1854	1	13								* Song	Mexico: Tlapujahua	墨西哥:特拉尔普胡瓦	19.8	-100.2		6.3	Mk							3				
1854	1	14	23	10						GSHAP, Song	Chile: Coquimbo	智利:科金博	-29.95	-71.35		6	Mk	8										
1854	1	27	18	10		3	2.4		1.5	* NOAA, Song	Gulf of Alaska	阿拉斯加湾	57	-152		7	Mk											
1854	1	28	18							USGS, Song	Alaska: Kodiak Island	阿拉斯加:科迪亚克岛	57	-152		5	Mk	5										
1854	2	8								GSHAP	Russia: Kamchatka Peninsula	俄罗斯:堪察加半岛	52.5	159.5	30	6	Ms	7										
1854	2	12								* Italy	Italy: Cosenza	意大利:科森扎	43.064	12.582		5.37	Ms	10	468	3				3				
1854	2	12								* Italy	Italy: Cosenza	意大利:科森扎	39.3	16.3		6.15	Ms	10	232	3				3				
1854	3	21								GSHAP	Iran: Neyshabur	伊朗:内沙布尔	36.5	58.3	10	5.1	Ms	7										
1854	3	31	5							* * Song	Italy: Cosenza	意大利:科森扎	39.3	16.3		6.5	Mk	12										

时间						海啸				资料来源	震中				深度	震级	标度	烈度	死亡人数		受伤人数		经济损失		房屋毁坏		房屋受损	
年	月	日	时	分	秒	源	浪高	级 I	级 S		地名(英文)	地名(中文)	纬度(°)	经度(°)					数量/人	级别	数量/人	级别	数量/$ Mill	级别	数量/间	级别	数量/间	级别
Date						Tsunami				Information	Earthquake Epicenter				Depth	Mag	Scale	MMI	Deaths		Injuries		Damage		Houses Destroyed		Houses Damaged	
Year	Mo	Dy	Hr	Mn	Sec	Sr	Wh	mI	mS		Name(English)	Name(Chinese)	Latitude	Longitude					Num	Dd	Num	Dd	$ Mill	De	Num	Dh	Num	Dh
1854	4	14								* Song	El Salvador: San Salvador	萨尔瓦多:圣萨尔瓦多	13.8	−89.2		7.1	Mk		1000	3				4				
1854	5	5								* Song	Mexico: Veracruz, Oaxaca	墨西哥:韦拉克鲁斯,瓦哈卡	17	−96.3		6.3	Mk							3				
1854	5	31	12	59		2			1	* NOAA, Song	US: California, Poway	美国:加利福尼亚州波韦	33	−117		7	Mk											
1854	6	16	17							* Song	Italy: Faentino	意大利:法恩扎	44.3	11.8		6.5	Mk	12										
1854	7	8	16							* Usami, Japan	Japan: Shiga	日本:滋贺	35	136		7.6	Ms	9	1352	4				3	5000	4		
1854	7	20	1	45						* Song	France: Pau	法国:波城	43	−0.1		5.9	Mk	9						2				
1854	7	26	20							Japan, Song	Japan: Miyagi, Near Coast	日本:宫城近海	38.6	142		6.3	Mk									1		
1854	7	30	2	30						* GSHAP	Greece: Igoumenitsa	希腊:伊古迈尼察	39.6	20.1		6.5	Ms	10		3				3		3		
1854	7	30								GSHAP	Russia: Kamchatka, Near East Coast	俄罗斯:堪察加东部近海	52	159	20	6.9	Ms	9										
1854	8	4				2			1.5	* NOAA	Costa Rica: Pavones	哥斯达黎加:帕沃内斯	8.5	−83		7.2	Ms											
1854	8	7				2			1.5	* NOAA	Costa Rica: Pavones	哥斯达黎加:帕沃内斯	8.5	−83		7.2	Ms							3				
1854	8	25								Japan, Song	Japan: Hachinohe	日本:青森八户	40.5	141.5		6.8	Mk											
1854	8	28								Japan	Japan: Aomori	日本:青森	40.6	141.6		6.5	Ms	8								3		
1854	9	22								*	Iran: Tabriz	伊朗:大不里士	38.06	45.03		4.5	Ms	6								1		
1854	9	27				3			0.5	* NOAA, Song	Indonesia: Molucca Sea	印度尼西亚:马鲁古海	1	126.25		7	Mk							2		2		
1854	9									* * Song	Iran: Tabriz	伊朗:大不里士	38	46.2		6.3	Mk											
1854	10	11								Japan, Song	Japan: Iseshi	日本:三重伊勢	34.5	136.7		6.5	Mk		70	2				3		1		
1854	10	22	3	45		2				* NOAA, Song	US: California, Concord	美国:加利福尼亚州康科德市	38	−122		7	Mk											
1854	11	18	13							GSHAP	Russia: Kamchatka Peninsula	俄罗斯:堪察加半岛	52.5	159.5	40	6.5	Ms	8										
1854	12	23								GSHAP	Ecuador: Ibarra	厄瓜多尔:伊瓦拉	0.36	−78.1		5	Ms	6										
1854	12	23				4	21	4	3	* Usami, NOAA, Japan	Japan: Shizuoka, Near Coast	日本:静冈近海	34	137.9		8.3	Mfa		300	3				3	600	3		
1854	12	24	8			4	28	4	3	* Usami, NOAA, Japan	Japan: Tokushima, Near Coast	日本:德岛近海	33.1	135		8.4	Mfa		3000	4				4	30000	5		
1854	12	24								* China	China: Chongqing, Nanchuan, SW.	中国:重庆南川西南	29.1	107		5.5	Ms	7		3				2		2		
1854	12	26	1							Usami, Japan	Japan: Oita	日本:大分	33.4	132.1		7	Ms	9							100	2		
1854	12	29	1	45		2				Italy, NOAA	Italy: Ventimiglia, Near Coast	意大利:文蒂米利亚近海	43.82	7.55		5.77	Ms											
1855	1	1								Japan	Japan: Morioka	日本:岩手盛冈	39.7	141.1		7.5	Ms											1
1855	1	23	9			3	9	3.2	3	* NOAA	New Zealand: Wellington, Waiouru	新西兰:惠灵顿,怀乌鲁	−41	175	33	8	Ms							3		3		
1855	1	25	6							CGS, USGS	US: California, Sierraville	美国:加利福尼亚州谢拉维尔	39.5	−120.3		6	Ms	6										

年 Year	月 Mo	日 Dy	时 Hr	分 Mn	秒 Sec	海啸 Tsunami 源 Sr	浪高 Wh	级 I mI	级 S mS	资料来源 Information	震中 Earthquake Epicenter 地名(英文) Name(English)	地名(中文) Name(Chinese)	纬度(°) Latitude	经度(°) Longitude	深度 Depth	震级 Mag	标度 Scale	烈度 MMI	死亡人数 Deaths 数量/人 Num	级别 Dd	受伤人数 Injuries 数量/人 Num	级别 Dd	经济损失 Damage 数量/$ Mill	级别 De	房屋毁坏 Houses Destroyed 数量/间 Num	级别 Dh	房屋受损 Houses Damaged 数量/间 Num	级别 Dh
1855	2	1								* Song	Mexico:Oaxaca	墨西哥:瓦哈卡	17	-96.3		6.3	Mk							3				
1855	2	7	4	30						USGS,Song	US:New York,Saugerties	美国:纽约州索格蒂斯	42	-74		5.5	Mk	6										
1855	2	13				2			3	NOAA,Song	Mediterranean Sea	地中海	35.5	29.5		6.7	Mk											
1855	2	17				2	10	1.6	3	NOAA,Song	Portugal:Azores	葡萄牙:亚速尔群岛	38.5	-28		7.7	Mk											
1855	2	20	8	30						GSHAP	Russia: Dagestan, Derbent, W.	俄罗斯:达吉斯坦共和国杰尔宾特西部	42	47.5	50	4.6	Ms	5.5										
1855	2	28	1							* GSHAP	Turkey:Tayabas	土耳其:塔亚巴斯	40.2	29.1		6.7	Muk	10	1900	4				3				
1855	3	8								* Song	Mexico:Oaxaca	墨西哥:瓦哈卡	17	-96.3		6.3	Mk							3				
1855	3	15								Japan,Song	Japan:Tenryu	日本:静冈滨松天龙区	35.1	137.9		6.1	Mk											1
1855	3	18	5							Usami,Japan	Japan:Gifu	日本:岐阜	36.2	136.9		6.75	Ms	7	12	1					2	1		
1855	3	20	0	30		1				* NOAA	US:California,Pine Hills	美国:加利福尼亚州派恩高地	40.75	-124.2		6	Ms	5										
1855	3	22								* Maso,Song	Philippines:San Jose	菲律宾:圣琼斯	16	121		6.1	Mk	8						2				
1855	4	11	17	40						* Song	Turkey:Bursa	土耳其:布尔萨	40.2	29.1		7.3	Mk	10	400	3				2				
1855	4	14				3				NOAA,Song	Indonesia:Flores Island	印度尼西亚:弗洛勒斯岛	-9	121		7	Mk							1				
1855	4	20	5							USGS,Song	US:New Mexico,Socorro	美国:新墨西哥州索科罗	34	-107		5.5	Mk	6										
1855	4	29								*	Turkey:Bursa	土耳其:布尔萨	40.2	29.1		6.7	Muk		1300	4				3				
1855	5	18	14			2			3	NOAA,Song	France:Nice	法国:尼斯	43.7	7.25		6.7	Mk											
1855	7	3								* GSHAP	Albania:Shkoder, Zadrime	阿尔巴尼亚:斯库台,扎德里马	42	19.5		6.5	Ms	10						2				
1855	7	8	10	30						GSHAP	Colombia:Bogota	哥伦比亚:波哥达	4.6	-74		4.5	Ms	5										
1855	7	11	4	15		3				* NOAA	US:California,Whittier	美国:加利福尼亚州惠提尔	34.1	-118.1		6	Ms	8						2				
1855	7	14								* Song	Indonesia:Maluku Utara	印度尼西亚:北马鲁古	-0.5	127.2		6.5	Mk	9	34	1				2				
1855	7	19	21	30						GSHAP,Song	Peru:Lima	秘鲁:利马	-12	-77		4.5	Mk	5										
1855	7	25	9							GSHAP	Brasil:Minas Gerais	巴西:米纳斯吉拉斯	-19.95	-43.46		4.3	Ms	5										
1855	7	25	12							* Italy	Switzerland:Haut - Valais	瑞士:上瓦莱州	46.217	7.85		8.5	Muk	11	1	1				3				
1855	7	26	9	15						* Song	Switzerland:Eisten	瑞士:埃斯滕	46.2	7.9		6.3	Mk	8						3				
1855	7	28	10							* Song	Switzerland:Visp	瑞士:菲斯普	46.3	7.8		6.3	Mk	7						3				
1855	8	6								Japan,Song	Japan:Oita	日本:大分	33.1	131.5		6.1	Mk											1
1855	8	11	9	15		4				* Song	Chile:Valparaiso	智利:瓦尔帕莱索	-33	-71.7		7	Mk											
1855	8	16								Japan,Song	Japan:Yonago	日本:鸟取米子	35.4	133.3		6.4	Mk	8										1
1855	8	22	12							* Song	Algeria:Djidjelli	阿尔及利亚:吉杰勒	37.1	5.7		7.3	Mk	10						2				
1855	8	27	11							USGS	US:California,San Rafael	美国:加利福尼亚州圣拉斐尔	38.1	-122.5		5.5	Ms	6										
1855	9	13								Japan	Japan:Miyagi	日本:宫城	38.1	142		7.5	Ms	8										1
1855	9	25				1				* NOAA,Song	Honduras:Trujillo	洪都拉斯:特鲁希略	15.91	-85.96		7	Mk											
1855	9									* China	China:Chongqing,Pengshui	中国:重庆彭水	29.3	108.1		4.75	Ms	6						1				
1855	10	29								GSHAP	Black Sea	黑海	44.3	34.3	20	5.5	Ms	6.5										

年 Year	月 Mo	日 Dy	时 Hr	分 Mn	秒 Sec	海啸 源 Sr	浪高 Wh	级 I mI	级 S mS	资料来源 Information	地名(英文) Name(English)	地名(中文) Name(Chinese)	纬度(°) Latitude	经度(°) Longitude	深度 Depth	震级 Mag	标度 Scale	烈度 MMI	死亡人数 Deaths 数量/人 Num	级别 Dd	受伤人数 Injuries 数量/人 Num	级别 Dd	经济损失 Damage 数量/$ Mill	级别 De	房屋毁坏 Houses Destroyed 数量/间 Num	级别 Dh	房屋受损 Houses Damaged 数量/间 Num	级别 Dh
1855	11	6	3	30						* Song	Switzerland:Eisten	瑞士:埃斯滕	46.2	7.9		6.3	Mk	6						3				
1855	11	7				4	3	1		* NOAA,Japan	Japan:Toba,Near Coast	日本:三重鸟羽近海	34.5	137.6		7.5	Ms	8	2					1		1		
1855	11	11	13			4				* Usami,NOAA	Japan:Tokyo	日本:东京	35.65	139.8		7	Ms	9	6757	4				4	50000	5		
1855	11	16								Japan,Song	Japan:Matsuyama	日本:爱媛县松山	33.8	132.7		6.4	Mk	8							20	1		
1855	12	3				1				*	Japan: Tokushima,Coast of S.	日本:德岛南部海域	32.5	134.5		7	Ms											
1855	12	10								Japan,Song	Japan:Oita	日本:大分	33.1	131.5		6.8	Mk									3		
1855	12	11								* China	China:Liaoning,Jinzhou	中国:辽宁金州	39.2	121.6		5.5	Ms	7	7	1				2	560	3		
1855	12	12	20	30						* Italy	France:Rougon	法国:鲁贡	43.85	6.417		5.57	Ms	8						2				
1855	12									China	China:Zhejiang,Fuyang	中国:浙江富阳	30.1	120		4.75	Ms	6										
1855										Japan,Song	Japan:Owase	日本:三重尾鹫	34.1	136.2		6.1	Mk											1
1856	1	2	18	15						CGS,USGS	US:California,Pacifica	美国:加利福尼亚州帕西菲卡	37.5	-122.5		5.7	Ms	6										
1856	1	12	10	20						* Song	Portugal:Tavira, Algarve	葡萄牙:塔维拉,阿尔加维	37.1	-8		7.3	Mk	10						2	100	2		
1856	2	2								* Song	Mexico:Oaxaca	墨西哥:瓦哈卡	17	-96.3		6.3	Mk							3				
1856	2	10								GSHAP	Ecuador:Azuay	厄瓜多尔:阿苏艾	-2.9	-79		5.7	Ms	7										
1856	2	15	13	25		3	0.6		-1	* CGS, USGS, NOAA	US:California,San Mateo	美国:加利福尼亚州圣马特奥	37.5	-122.3		5.9	Ms	7						1				
1856	3	2				5		1	1	* Song,NOAA	Indonesia:Sangihe Islands	印度尼西亚:桑义赫群岛	3.67	125.5		7.9	Mk		2806	4				2		3		
1856	3					2	1		1	NOAA,Song	New Zealand: South Island,Ashburton	新西兰:南岛,阿什伯顿	-44	172		7	Mk											
1856	4	10								China	China:Liaoning,Jinzhou	中国:辽宁金州	39.1	121.7		5.25	Ms	7										
1856	6	5								* Italy	Italy:Pieve Santo Stefano	意大利:皮耶韦-圣斯特凡诺	43.67	12.041		5.03	Ms	9						2				
1856	6	10								* China	China:HubeiXianfeng,W.	中国:湖北咸丰西	29.7	108.8		6.25	Ms	8	300	3				2				
1856	6	11	12	30						GSHAP,Song	Peru:Lima	秘鲁:利马	-12	-77		4.5	Mk	5										
1856	7	23	14							GSHAP	Azerbaijan:Samaxi	阿塞拜疆:沙马基区	40.6	48.6	5	4.7	Ms	7.5										
1856	7	25				2				* NOAA,Song	Indonesia:Java Island	印度尼西亚:爪哇岛	-8.5	116		7	Mk											
1856	8	9				4	5			* NOAA	Honduras:Omoa	洪都拉斯:奥莫亚	15.75	-88.17		7.5	Ms							3				
1856	8	21	21	45		4			4	* NOAA,Song	Algeria:Djidjelli	阿尔及利亚:吉杰勒	37.1	5.7		6.7	Mk	9										
1856	8	22	11	40		3	5		4	* NOAA,Song	Algeria:Djidjelli	阿尔及利亚:吉杰勒	37.1	5.7		6.7	Mk	9	3	1								
1856	8	23	4	30		4	6	2.6	2	* Usami, Japan, NOAA	Japan Trench	日本海沟	40.5	143.5		7.8	Ms	11	60	2				2	100	2		
1856	9	21	7	30						CGS,USGS	US:California,Poway	美国:加利福尼亚州波韦	33	-117		5.5	Ms	6										
1856	10	12	0	45		2			3	* NOAA, Turkey	Greece:Crete Island	希腊:克里特岛	35.5	26	100	8.3	Ms	11	538	3				3	8000	4	8000	4
1856	11	4								Usami,Japan	Japan:Tokyo,Adachi	日本:东京足立	35.8	139.8		6.6	Ms	7			23	1				1		
1856	11	13				3			3	* NOAA	Greece:Chios	希腊:希俄斯岛	38.25	26.25		6.6	Ms	9		2				2		3		
1856	12	8	18	55						GSHAP,Song	Peru:Lima	秘鲁:利马	-12	-77		4.5	Mk	5										

年 Year	月 Mo	日 Dy	时 Hr	分 Mn	秒 Sec	源 Sr	浪高 Wh	级 I mI	级 S mS	资料来源 Information	地名(英文) Name(English)	地名(中文) Name(Chinese)	纬度(°) Latitude	经度(°) Longitude	深度 Depth	震级 Mag	标度 Scale	烈度 MMI	死亡人数 Deaths 数量/人 Num	死亡人数 Deaths 级别 Dd	受伤人数 Injuries 数量/人 Num	受伤人数 Injuries 级别 Dd	经济损失 Damage 数量/$ Mill	经济损失 Damage 级别 De	房屋毁坏 Houses Destroyed 数量/间 Num	房屋毁坏 Houses Destroyed 级别 Dh	房屋受损 Houses Damaged 数量/间 Num	房屋受损 Houses Damaged 级别 Dh
1856	12	9								Japan, Song	Japan: Masuda	日本:岛根益田	34.7	131.8		6.3	Mk									1		
1857	1	6	19							* Song	Sudan: Gondokoro	苏丹:冈多科罗	4.9	31.7		5	Mk							1				
1857	1	9	10	13						*	US: California, Bakersfield	美国:加利福尼亚州贝克斯菲尔德	35	−119		8.3	Muk	7						3				
1857	1	29								China	China: Guangxi, Beiliu	中国:广西北流	22.7	110.3		4.75	Ms	6										
1857	4	9								* Song	Iran: Orumiyeh	伊朗:乌尔米耶	37.4	45.3		6.3	Mk							3				
1857	4	9								*	Turkey: Bitlis	土耳其:比特利斯	38.4	42.1		6.7	Ms	9		3				3		3		
1857	4	17				4			1.5	* NOAA	Papua New Guinea: Umboi Island	巴布亚新几内亚:温博伊岛	−5.5	147		8	Ms			2				2		2		
1857	4	25								GSHAP	Iran: Neyshabur	伊朗:内沙布尔	36.5	58.3	10	5.1	Ms	7										
1857	5	13				4	3.4	1.6	2	* NOAA	Indonesia: Bali Sea	印度尼西亚:巴厘海	−8	115.5	50	7	Ms		36	1				2				
1857	5	18	11							GSHAP	Latvia: Ventspils	拉脱维亚:文茨皮尔斯	57.7	22.2	10	4.5	Ms	7										
1857	5	23	9			2				* NOAA, Song	Algeria: Sea of Alboran	阿尔及利亚:阿尔沃兰海	36.5	1.3		6.6	Mk											
1857	7	8								Japan	Japan: Yamaguchi	日本:山口	34.4	131.4		6	Ms									1		
1857	7	13	22			4	2			* Usami, NOAA	Japan: Yaizu	日本:静冈烧津	34.8	138.3		6.4	Ms	7	8							1		
1857	7	30	11	30						USGS, Song	Hawaiian Islands	夏威夷群岛	19.25	−155		5	Mk	5										
1857	8	20	12							GSHAP, Song	Peru: Sechura	秘鲁:塞丘拉	−5.3	−80.54	40	6.5	Mk	9										
1857	9	3	3	5						CGS, USGS	US: California, Truckee	美国:加利福尼亚州特拉基	39.3	−120		6.3	Ms	5										
1857	9	8	21							USGS, Song	Alaska: Kodiak Island	阿拉斯加:科迪亚克岛	58	−152		5	Mk	5										
1857	9	16								* Song	Italy: Calabria, Montemurro	意大利: 卡拉布里亚,蒙特穆罗	39.4	16.4		6.8	Mk		10000	5				3				
1857	9	17	22			1				* NOAA, Song	Turkey: Bursa	土耳其:布尔萨	40.2	29		6.6	Mk											
1857	10	8	10							USGS	US: Illinois, Carlyle	美国:伊利诺斯州卡莱尔	38.7	−89.2		4.9	Ms	7										
1857	10	11	23							Usami	Japan: Matsuyama	日本:爱媛县松山	33.9	132.7		6.9	Ms	8	8						3	1		
1857	10	23	20	15						USGS	US: New York, Lockport	美国:纽约州洛克波特市	43.2	−78.6		4.3	Ms	6										
1857	10	27								* Song	Iran: Tabriz	伊朗:大不里士	38.3	45.4		6.3	Mk	7						3				
1857	11	7	15	21						GSHAP, Song	Chile: Copiapo	智利:科皮亚波	−27.35	−70.35		6	Mk	8										
1857	11	17				3			1.5	* NOAA, Song	Indonesia: Sulawesi Utara	印度尼西亚:北苏拉威西	1	125		7	Mk											
1857	11	18				3				* NOAA, Song	Indonesia: Sulawesi Utara	印度尼西亚:北苏拉威西	1	125		7	Mk											
1857	12	12	8							GSHAP	Finland: Keitele	芬兰:凯泰莱	63.2	26.4	20	4.7	Ms	5										
1857	12	16	21	18						* Italy	Italy: Campania, Montemurro	意大利:坎佩尼亚,蒙特穆罗	40.3	16		6.96	Muk	10	13488	5				4				
1857	12	23	18	30						USGS, Song	US: Maine, Lewiston	美国:缅因州刘易斯顿	44.1	−70.2		5.5	Mk	6										

时间						海啸				资料来源	震中				深度	震级	标度	烈度	死亡人数		受伤人数		经济损失		房屋毁坏		房屋受损	
年	月	日	时	分	秒	源	浪高	级 I	级 S		地名(英文)	地名(中文)	纬度(°)	经度(°)					数量/人	级别	数量/人	级别	数量/$ Mill	级别	数量/间	级别	数量/间	级别
Date						Tsunami				Information	Earthquake Epicenter				Depth	Mag	Scale	MMI	Deaths		Injuries		Damage		Houses Destroyed		Houses Damaged	
Year	Mo	Dy	Hr	Mn	Sec	Sr	Wh	mI	mS		Name(English)	Name(Chinese)	Latitude	Longitude					Num	Dd	Num	Dd	$ Mill	De	Num	Dh	Num	Dh
1857	12	24	7	50						GSHAP	Kazakhstan:Zyryanovsk,S.	哈萨克斯坦:济良诺夫斯克南部	48. 3	83. 4	24	6. 4	Ms	7. 5										
1858	1	13								Japan,Song	Japan:Aomori	日本:青森	40. 6	141. 6		6. 1	Mk											1
1858	1	15								* Song	Slovakia:Zilina	斯洛伐克:日利纳	49. 2	18. 8		6. 5	Mk	9					0. 05	1				
1858	1	22								*	Russia:Komandorsky Islands	俄罗斯:科曼多尔群岛	55	166	20	7. 5	Muk	10										
1858	1	31				2				NOAA,Song	Australia:Tasman Sea	澳大利亚:塔斯曼海	-43. 3	148. 9		7	Mk											
1858	2	3	1							Japan,Song	Japan:Kumamoto	日本:熊本	32. 8	130. 8		6. 1	Mk											3
1858	2	21	7	30		1				* NOAA	Greece:Korinthos	希腊:科林斯	38	23		6. 5	Ms	10	19	1				3				
1858	3	9								Japan	Japan:Saitama	日本:埼玉	35. 9	139. 7		5. 9	Ms											1
1858	4	1								Japan,Song	Japan:Naganoi	日本:长野	37. 2	138. 3		6. 1	Mk											1
1858	4	8	16							* Usami	Japan:Toyama	日本:富山	36. 5	137. 2		6. 8	Ms	10	380	3				2	2000	4		
1858	4	8	19							Usami	Japan:Fukui	日本:福井	36. 2	136. 3		6. 9	Ms	9							200	3		
1858	4	10	12	30						GSHAP,Song	Chile:Coquimbo	智利:科金博	-29. 9	-71. 25		6	Mk	8										
1858	4	22	23							Usami,Japan	Japan:Nagano	日本:长野	36. 6	138. 2		5. 9	Ms	8		1						1	300	3
1858	4	24	11	15		2	2	1	1	* NOAA	Chile:Coquimbo	智利:科金博	-30	-71. 4		6. 5	Ms	8		1								
1858	5	2								* Song	Mexico:Oaxaca	墨西哥:瓦哈卡	17	-96. 3		6. 3	Mk							3				
1858	5	11	6	45						GSHAP,Song	Peru:Lima	秘鲁:利马	-12	-77		4. 5	Mk	5										
1858	5	11								Japan,Song	Japan:Hachinohe	日本:青森八户	40. 5	141. 5		6. 1	Mk											1
1858	5	17								Japan,Song	Japan:Shinano	日本:长野信浓町	36. 8	138. 2		6. 3	Mk								4	1		
1858	6	5				2	2. 4		1. 5	NOAA,Song	England:Dover Straits	英国:多佛尔海峡	51. 03	1. 61		6. 7	Mk											
1858	6	11	6	15						GSHAP	Russia:Krasnoyarsk	俄罗斯:克拉斯诺亚尔斯克	56	93	10	4. 7	Ms	6. 5										
1858	6	19								* Song	Mexico:Mexico City	墨西哥:墨西哥城	19. 2	-99. 1		6. 3	Mk							3				
1858	7	8								Japan	Japan:Hachinohe	日本:青森八户	40. 8	142		7. 5	Ms									1		
1858	7	11	22	45						GSHAP,Song	Peru:Lima	秘鲁:利马	-12	-77		4. 5	Mk	5										
1858	8	24								Japan,Song	Japan:Kumano	日本:三重熊野	34	136		6. 1	Mk											1
1858	8	24								* Song	Myanmar:Thayetmyo, Prome	缅甸:德耶,勃郎	19	95		6. 3	Mk							3				
1858	9	15				2			0. 5	NOAA,Song	New Zealand:South Island,Ashburton	新西兰:南岛,阿什伯顿	-44	172		7	Mk											
1858	9	20								* Song	Albania:Delvine	阿尔巴尼亚:德维纳区	40	20		6. 2	Mk	10	12	1				3	1556	4		
1858	9	21								USGS	US:Tennessee,Woodland Mills	美国:田纳西州伍德兰米尔斯	36. 5	-89. 2		4. 2	Ms	6										
1858	9	28	23							Japan	Japan:Aomori	日本:青森	40. 6	141. 6		6. 6	Ms									1		
1858	9	30								* GSHAP	Bulgaria:Breznik	保加利亚:布雷兹尼克	42. 8	23. 2		6. 6	Ms	10										
1858	9					2			0. 5	* NOAA,Song	Ryukyu Islands	琉球群岛	26. 2	127. 5		7	Mk											
1858	10	10	9	30						* GSHAP	Albania:Vlore, Kanina	阿尔巴尼亚:发罗拉,卡妮娜	40	20. 1		6. 3	Mk	10						2				
1858	11	11	6	15						* Song	Portugal:Setubal	葡萄牙:塞图巴尔	38. 2	-9		7. 3	Mk	10	6	1				3	605	3		

时间 Date						海啸 Tsunami				资料来源 Information	震中 Earthquake Epicenter				深度 Depth	震级 Mag	标度 Scale	烈度 MMI	死亡人数 Deaths		受伤人数 Injuries		经济损失 Damage		房屋毁坏 Houses Destroyed		房屋受损 Houses Damaged	
年 Year	月 Mo	日 Dy	时 Hr	分 Mn	秒 Sec	源 Sr	浪高 Wh	级I mI	级S mS		地名(英文) Name(English)	地名(中文) Name(Chinese)	纬度(°) Latitude	经度(°) Longitude					数量/人 Num	级别 Dd	数量/人 Num	级别 Dd	数量/$ Mill $ Mill	级别 De	数量/间 Num	级别 Dh	数量/间 Num	级别 Dh
1858	11	26	8	35						* Song	US:California,San Francisco	美国:加利福尼亚州旧金山	37.5	-122		6.5	Mk	9						3				
1858	12	13				3			1.5	* NOAA,Song	Indonesia:Molucca Sea	印度尼西亚:马鲁古海	1	126		7.7	Mk			3				3		3		
1858	12	16	2	30						USGS,Song	US:California,Los Angeles	美国:加利福尼亚州洛杉矶	34	-117.5		5.5	Mk	6										
1858	12	16	10							USGS	US:California,Los Angeles	美国:加利福尼亚州洛杉矶	34	-117.5		6	Ms	8										
1858										Maso,Song	Philippines:Mindanao Island	菲律宾:棉兰老岛	7.2	124.11		5	Mk	6										
1859	1	5	9							Usami,Japan	Japan:Masuda	日本:岛根益田	34.7	131.8		5.9	Ms	7							20	1		
1859	1	11								Japan,Song	Japan:Saitama	日本:埼玉	35.9	139.7		6.1	Mk											1
1859	3	22	13	30						* Song	Ecuador:Quito	厄瓜多尔:基多	-0.3	-78.5		6.3	Mk	8		1				3				
1859	4	10	10	30						GSHAP,Song	Peru:Lima	秘鲁:利马	-12	-77		4.5	Mk	5										
1859	4	12	9	55						* Song	Italy:Radda	意大利:拉达	43.4	11.3		6.5	Mk	12										
1859	6	2	8							*	Turkey:Erzurum	土耳其:埃尔佐鲁姆	39.9	41.3		6.1	Muk		15000	5				3				
1859	6	11	13							*	Azerbaijan:Samaxi	阿塞拜疆:沙马基区	40.7	48.5	10	5.9	Muk	9	100	2				2				
1859	6	28				4	10	3.2	3	* NOAA	Indonesia:Molucca Sea	印度尼西亚:马鲁古海	1	126.5		7	Ms											
1859	7	17								GSHAP	Turkey:Erzurum	土耳其:埃尔佐鲁姆	39.9	41.3	14	6	Ms	8.5										
1859	7	20				3				* NOAA,Song	Indonesia:Banda Sea	印度尼西亚:班达海	-5.5	130.5		7	Mk											
1859	7	29				4		1	1.5	* NOAA	Molukka Sea	马鲁古海	0	125.5		7.2	Ms											
1859	8	21	11	55		3			3	* Turkey,NOAA	Aegean Sea	爱琴海	40.2	25.8		6.9	Ms	9						3				
1859	8	22	17	15						* Italy	Italy:Norcia	意大利:诺尔恰	42.825	13.097		5.7	Ms	11	100	2				2				
1859	8	25				4		1	1.5	* NOAA	Honduras:Choluteca	洪都拉斯:乔卢特卡	13	-87.5		6.2	Ms							1				
1859	9	19								China	China:Liaoning,Yingkou	中国:辽宁营口	40.7	122.2		5.25	Ms	7										
1859	9	24				2	4.6	2.2	1.5	* NOAA,Song	US:California,San Mateo	美国:加利福尼亚州圣马特奥	37.6	-122.3		7	Mk							1				
1859	9	25				2		1	0.5	* NOAA	Indonesia:Banda Sea	印度尼西亚:班达海	-5.5	130.5		6.7	Ms											
1859	10	4	1							Usami	Japan:Masuda	日本:岛根益田	34.7	131.9		5.9	Ms	7								1		
1859	10	5	15			4	6	2.5	2.5	* NOAA	Chile:Copiapo	智利:科皮亚波	-27.35	-70.35		7.6	Ms	10	10	1			0.93	1	339	3		
1859	10	5	20	16						USGS,Song	US:California,San Francisco	美国:加利福尼亚州旧金山	37.8	-122.4		5.5	Mk	6										
1859	10	20				1			2	NOAA,Song	Greece:Pireaus	希腊:皮埃里亚	37.9	23.6		6.7	Mk											
1859	10	20				2			1	* NOAA,Song	Indonesia:Java Ridge	印度尼西亚:爪哇海岭	-9	111		7	Mk		2	1								
1859	11	17								Japan,Song	Japan:Tochigi	日本:枥木枥木	36.6	139.9		6.1	Mk											1
1859	11	21	12	50						USGS,Song	Hawaiian Islands	夏威夷群岛	20	-156		5	Mk	5										
1859	11	22				2				* NOAA,Song	Australia:Tasman Sea	澳大利亚:塔斯曼海	-40.85	145.32		7	Mk											
1859	12	9	2			4		1	1.5	* NOAA	El Salvador:Sonsonate	萨尔瓦多:松萨卡特	13.7	-89.8		7	Ms							3		3		
1859	12	17				2				* NOAA,Song	Indonesia:Molucca Sea	印度尼西亚:马鲁古海	1	126.5		7	Mk											
1859	12	25				3			1	NOAA,Song	Indonesia:Maluku Utara	印度尼西亚:北马鲁古	1.375	127.52		7	Mk											
1859										Usami	Japan:Saitama	日本:埼玉	35.9	139.7		5.9	Ms	7										

时间						海啸				资料来源	震中				深度	震级	标度	烈度	死亡人数		受伤人数		经济损失		房屋毁坏		房屋受损	
年	月	日	时	分	秒	源	浪高	级 I	级 S		地名(英文)	地名(中文)	纬度(°)	经度(°)					数量/人	级别	数量/人	级别	数量/$ Mill	级别	数量/间	级别	数量/间	级别
Date						Tsunami				Information	Earthquake Epicenter				Depth	Mag	Scale	MMI	Deaths		Injuries		Damage		Houses Destroyed		Houses Damaged	
Year	Mo	Dy	Hr	Mn	Sec	Sr	Wh	mI	mS		Name(English)	Name(Chinese)	Latitude	Longitude					Num	Dd	Num	Dd	$ Mill	De	Num	Dh	Num	Dh
1860	1	6				2			2	NOAA,Song	Spain:Alboran Sea	西班牙:阿尔沃兰海	36.833	-1.167		6.7	Mk											
1860	3	15	19							CGS,USGS	US:Nevada,Patrick	美国:内华达州帕特里克	39.5	-119.5		6.5	Ms	6										
1860	3	17				1				NOAA,Song	Mexico:Acapulco	墨西哥:阿卡普尔科	17.171	-99.651		7	Mk											
1860	4	8	11			4				* NOAA	Haiti:Anse - A - Veau	海地:昂萨沃,太子港	18.52	-73.35		7.5	Ms							2				
1860	4	10								* GSHAP	Albania:Gjirokaster	阿尔巴尼亚:吉诺卡斯特	40	20.1		6.5	Ms	11										
1860	4	18	13	30						GSHAP,Song	Peru:Arequipa	秘鲁:阿雷基帕	-16.4	-71.6		4.5	Mk	5										
1860	4	22	7							GSHAP,Song	Peru:Lima,Near Coast	秘鲁:利马近海	-12.3	-77.3	40	5	Mk	6										
1860	4	22	19							GSHAP,Song	Peru:Lima,Near Coast	秘鲁:利马近海	-12.1	-77		5	Mk	6										
1860	4	23				3	0.7	-05		* NOAA,Song	Peru:Lima	秘鲁:利马	-12	-77.1		7	Mk	6						3				
1860	4	24	11							GSHAP,Song	Peru:Lima	秘鲁:利马	-12	-77		5	Mk	6										
1860	5	13	18	30						GSHAP	Iran:Parsabad	伊朗:法尔萨巴德	39.4	47.8	35	5.2	Ms	5.5										
1860	7	19	2	30						USGS,Song	Hawaiian Islands	夏威夷群岛	19.25	-155		5	Mk	5										
1860	7	27								Japan,Song	Japan:Aomori	日本:青森	40.6	141.6		6.3	Mk									1		
1860	8					1				* NOAA,Song	Molukka Sea,N.	马鲁古海北部	4	127		7	Mk											
1860	9	20	23	30						GSHAP,Song	Chile:Arica	智利:阿里卡	-18.5	-70.35		6	Mk	8										
1860	10	6				3				* NOAA,Song	Molukka Sea	马鲁古海	-1.4	128.5		7	Mk											
1860	11	13								CGS,USGS	US:California,Eureka	美国:加利福尼亚州尤里卡	40.8	-124.2		5.5	Ms	7										
1860	12	1				2	3.6	1.8	2	NOAA,Song	Hawaiian Islands	夏威夷群岛	20	-156		7.5	Mk											
1860										USGS,Song	US:Minnesota,Long Prairie	美国:明尼苏达州朗普雷里	46	-94.8		5.5	Mk	6										
1860										Japan,Song	Japan:Otsuki	日本:山梨大月	35.6	139		6.1	Mk											1
1861	2	16				4	7		3	* NOAA	Indonesia:Lagundi,Simuk	印度尼西亚:拉贡迪,锡穆克	-1	97.9	70	8.5	Ms	9	1001	4				2				
1861	2	22								GSHAP	Russia:Ostrov Beringa	俄罗斯:白令岛	55	167	20	6.2	Ms	8.5										
1861	3	9				4			2	* NOAA	Indonesia:Northern Sumatra	印度尼西亚:苏门答腊北部	0	98	20	7	Ms		900	3				3	96	2		
1861	3	21	0	16		4				* NOAA,Song	Argentina:Mendoza	阿根廷:门多萨	-32.8	-68.8		8	Mk		14000	5				4		4		4
1861	3	21								Japan	Japan:Nishio	日本:爱知西尾市	34.8	137.1		6	Ms									1		1
1861	4	3	23							GSHAP,Song	Peru:Chincha Alta,Near Coast	秘鲁:上钦查近海	-13.6	-76.35		4.5	Mk	5										
1861	4	13	5	30						GSHAP,Song	Peru:Chincha Alta,Near Coast	秘鲁:上钦查近海	-13.6	-76.35		5	Mk	6										
1861	4	13	22	30						* Song	Peru:Andahuaylas	秘鲁:安达韦拉斯	-13.8	-73.4	20	7.3	Mk	10										
1861	4	26				4			1.5	* NOAA	Indonesia:Sumatera,Nias Island	印度尼西亚:苏门答腊,尼亚斯岛	1	97.5		7	Ms											
1861	4	27	20	15						* Song	Jamaica:Montego Bay	牙买加:蒙特哥贝	18.5	-77.9		5.9	Mk							2				
1861	5	7	3							GSHAP,Song	Peru:Lima	秘鲁:利马	-12.08	-77		5	Mk	6										
1861	5	7								* Song	Eritrea:Dankalia	厄立特里亚:丹卡利亚	13.74	41.55		6.3	Mk		106	3				3		3		

年 Year	月 Mo	日 Dy	时 Hr	分 Mn	秒 Sec	海啸 Tsunami 源 Sr	浪高 Wh	级 I mI	级 S mS	资料来源 Information	震中 Earthquake Epicenter 地名(英文) Name(English)	地名(中文) Name(Chinese)	纬度(°) Latitude	经度(°) Longitude	深度 Depth	震级 Mag	标度 Scale	烈度 MMI	死亡人数 Deaths 数量/人 Num	级别 Dd	受伤人数 Injuries 数量/人 Num	级别 Dd	经济损失 Damage 数量/$ Mill	级别 De	房屋毁坏 Houses Destroyed 数量/间 Num	级别 Dh	房屋受损 Houses Damaged 数量/间 Num	级别 Dh
1861	5	9	1	53						* Italy	Italy: Citta Della Pieve	意大利:皮耶韦城	46	12		5.03	Ms	11	1	1				2				
1861	5	10	5							GSHAP, Song	Peru: Lima	秘鲁:利马	-12.08	-77		5	Mk	6										
1861	6	2	7							USGS, Song	Hawaiian Islands	夏威夷群岛	19.25	-155		5	Mk	5										
1861	6	5				2		1	1	NOAA, Song	Indonesia: Java Island	印度尼西亚:爪哇岛	-6.3	107.3		7	Mk							1				
1861	6	17				3			0.5	* NOAA	Indonesia: Sumatera, Nias Island	印度尼西亚:苏门答腊,尼亚斯岛	1	97.5		6.8	Ms											
1861	7	4	0	11						* Song	US: California, Contra Costa	美国:加利福尼亚州康特拉科斯塔	37.5	-122		8	Mk	11						3				
1861	7	19								* China	China: Liaoning, Jinzhou	中国:辽宁金州	39.1	121.7		6	Ms	8	2	1	8	1		2	780	3		
1861	7	31	4							GSHAP	Brasil: Sao Paulo	巴西:圣保罗	-22.6	-45.2		4.4	Ms	5										
1861	7									China	China: Yunnan, Huaning	中国:云南华宁	24.2	102.9		4.75	Ms	6										
1861	8	30	1							GSHAP, Song	Chile: Santiago	智利:圣地亚哥	-33.6	-70.58		6	Mk	8										
1861	8	31	10	22						USGS	US: North Carolina, North Wilkesboro	美国:北卡罗来纳州北威尔克斯伯勒	36.1	-81.1		5	Ms	6										
1861	9	25				3			1.5	* NOAA	Indonesia: Southern Sumatra	印度尼西亚:苏门答腊南部	-1.5	100		6.5	Ms							1		1		
1861	10	20	17	30		4	4	2	2	* Usami, NOAA	Japan: Miyagi	日本:宫城	38.5	142		7.4	Ms	9		1				2	70	2		
1861	11	5								GSHAP	Russia: Kabardino – Balkaria, Nalchik	俄罗斯:卡尔梅克州纳尔奇克	43.7	43.2	25	4.5	Ms	5.5										
1861	11	14								GSHAP, Song	Peru: Arequipa	秘鲁:阿雷基帕	-16.4	-71.56		4.5	Mk	5										
1861	12	5	22	20						USGS, Song	Hawaiian Islands	夏威夷群岛	21	-157		5.5	Mk	6										
1861	12	15	4	15						GSHAP, Song	Peru: Tacna	秘鲁:塔克纳	-18	-70.4		5	Mk	6										
1861	12	26	5			4	2.1	1.1	4	* NOAA	Greece: Achaie, Tripolis	希腊:阿哈亚群岛,特里波利斯	38.2	22.2		7.5	Muk	10	17	1			0.04	1				
1862	1	1	8	45		3			2	NOAA, Song	Greece: Ionian Sea	希腊:伊奥尼亚海	38.25	22.25		6.7	Mk							1		1		
1862	1	12	7	19						*	Russia: Lake Baykal	俄罗斯:贝加尔湖	52.3	106.7	40	7.5	Muk	10										
1862	2	4								GSHAP, Song	Peru: Arequipa	秘鲁:阿雷基帕	-16.4	-71.56		4.5	Mk	5										
1862	2									China	China: Yunnan, Dali	中国:云南大理	25.9	100.1		5.5	Ms	7										
1862	3	4	9	30		1			0.5	* Bautista, Maso, Nakamura, NOAA	Philippines: Looc	菲律宾:洛克	13.75	120.4		6.1	Ms	7										
1862	3	14	1	30						* Song	Greece: Argostoli (Kephallenia)	希腊:阿尔戈斯托利	38.3	20.5		7	Mk	10						2				
1862	3	18				2				NOAA, Song	France: Nice	法国:尼斯	43.7	7.25		6.6	Mk											
1862	5	4	4							* Song	Albania: Vlore, Kanina	阿尔巴尼亚:发罗拉,卡妮娜	40.3	19.3		6.2	Mk	10										
1862	5	27	20			4	1.2	0.3		* CGS, USGS, NOAA	US: California, San Diego	美国:加利福尼亚州圣地亚哥	32.7	-117.2		6.2	Ms	7										
1862	5	28	18	25						GSHAP, Song	Peru: Lima	秘鲁:利马	-12.08	-77		5	Mk	6										
1862	6	7								* China	China: Taiwan, Tainan	中国:台湾台南	23.3	120.2		6.75	Ms	9	2000	4				3		3		
1862	6	30	23	48		4				Maso, Song	Guam	关岛(西太平洋)	14	143.3		7.3	Mk	7										

时间 年 Year	月 Mo	日 Dy	时 Hr	分 Mn	秒 Sec	海啸 Tsunami 源 Sr	浪高 Wh	级 I mI	级 S mS	资料来源 Information	震中 Earthquake Epicenter 地名(英文) Name(English)	地名(中文) Name(Chinese)	纬度(°) Latitude	经度(°) Longitude	深度 Depth	震级 Mag	标度 Scale	烈度 MMI	死亡人数 Deaths 数量/人 Num	级别 Dd	受伤人数 Injuries 数量/人 Num	级别 Dd	经济损失 Damage 数量/$ Mill $ Mill	级别 De	房屋毁坏 Houses Destroyed 数量/间 Num	级别 Dh	房屋受损 Houses Damaged 数量/间 Num	级别 Dh
1862	7	10	8	15		2				* NOAA	Ghana: Accra, Christiansborg	加纳:阿克拉,克里斯蒂安堡	7	0.4		6.5	Mfa	9	3	1				3		3		
1862	7	10	18	10						GSHAP, Song	Peru: Lima	秘鲁:利马	-12.08	-77		5	Mk	6										
1862	7	13	8							Bautista, Maso	Philippines: San Jose, Coast E.	菲律宾:圣琼斯东部海域	15.65	121.5		5.8	Muk	7										
1862	7	27	17							GSHAP	Mongolia: North of Ulaanbaatar	蒙古:乌兰巴托北部	48.5	106.5	15	6	Ms	8										
1862	8	13								* Song	Iran: Mashhad	伊朗:马什哈德	35	59		5.9	Mk							2				
1862	8	14	7	15						GSHAP, Song	Peru: Arequipa	秘鲁:阿雷基帕	-16.4	-71.55		5	Mk	6										
1862	8	16	7	15						GSHAP, Song	Peru: Arequipa	秘鲁:阿雷基帕	-16.4	-71.55		4.5	Mk	5										
1862	9	8	19							Bautista, Maso	Philippines: Vigan	菲律宾:美岸	17.9	120.5		6.2	Muk	8										
1862	10	16	1	10						GSHAP	Romania: Nereju	罗马尼亚:内雷茹	45.7	26.6	150	6.4	Ms	7										
1862	10	16								*	Turkey: Suhut	土耳其:舒胡特	38.8	30.5		6.1	Muk		800	3				2				
1862	10	29	16							Maso, Bautista, Song	Philippines: Calamba	菲律宾:卡兰巴	14.1	121.2		5	Mk	6										
1862	12	20	1	15						* Song	Nicaragua: Chinandega	尼加拉瓜:奇南德加	12.7	-87		6.3	Mk							3				
1862	12	26								* China	China: Shanxi, Quwo	中国:山西曲沃	35.6	111.5		5.5	Ms	7		2				2		3		
1863	1	2								* Song	Iran: Ardabil	伊朗:阿尔达比勒	38.1	48.2		6.1	Mk	8						2				
1863	3	16				1			0	* NOAA, Song	Indonesia: Java Island	印度尼西亚:爪哇岛	-6.133	106.75		7	Mk											
1863	3	22	21	30		1				NOAA, Song	Greece: Rhodes	希腊:罗德港	36.5	28		6.6	Mk											
1863	4	22	20	30						* GSHAP	Greece: Rhodes, Kos	希腊:罗德岛,科斯	36.5	28	90	7.8	Ms	11		1				3	2500	4		
1863	6	3	11	20		3		1	1	* Bautista, Maso, NOAA	Philippines: Manila, Rizal	菲律宾:马尼拉,黎萨	14.55	120.9		6.5	Ms	10	400	3	2000	4		4	1172	4		
1863	6	9								* Maso, Song	Philippines: Mariveles	菲律宾:马里韦莱斯	14.6	120.5		5.5	Mk	7						2				
1863	6	9								* Song	France: Beynes, Mezel	法国:贝纳,梅泽勒	44	6.2		6.1	Mk	8						2				
1863	6	29	12	15						GSHAP, Song	Peru: Arequipa	秘鲁:阿雷基帕	-16.4	-71.56		5	Mk	6										
1863	6									* China	China: Yunnan, Dengchuan, S.	中国:云南邓川南	25.8	100.1		5.5	Ms	7		3				3		3		
1863	7	6	19			4				Maso, Song	Guam	关岛(西太平洋)	14	143.3		7.2	Mk	6										
1863	7	18	17							GSHAP	Russia: Dagestan, Chirkey, NE.	俄罗斯:达吉斯坦共和国奇尔克伊东北	43	47.1	16	5	Ms	6.5										
1863	7	31								* Song	Indonesia: Jav, Banyumas	印度尼西亚:爪哇,班尤马	-7.5	109.2		5.9	Mk							2				
1863	8	16								* Song	Greece: Chios	希腊:希俄斯岛	38.25	26.25		6.3	Mk	8						3		3		
1863	8	17				2			1	* NOAA	Vanuatu Islands	瓦努阿图群岛	-19	168.5		7.5	Ms											
1863	8	30								China	China: Jiangxi, Xiushui, W.	中国:江西修水西	29.1	114.1		5	Ms	6										
1863	9	20				3				* NOAA	Japan: Hokkaido	日本:北海道	44.6	141.5		6.4	Ms											
1863	9	25								* China	China: Xinjiang, Urumqi	中国:新疆乌鲁木齐	43.8	87.6		5.5	Ms	7	9	1	10	1						
1863	10	21								GSHAP, Song	Peru: Trujillo, Near Coast	秘鲁:特鲁希略近海	-8.2	-79.1		5	Mk	6										
1863	10	25	16	45						GSHAP, Song	Peru: Trujillo, Near Coast	秘鲁:特鲁希略近海	-8.2	-79.1		5	Mk	6										

年 Year	月 Mo	日 Dy	时 Hr	分 Mn	秒 Sec	源 Sr	浪高 Wh	级 I mI	级 S mS	资料来源 Information	地名(英文) Name(English)	地名(中文) Name(Chinese)	纬度(°) Latitude	经度(°) Longitude	深度 Depth	震级 Mag	标度 Scale	烈度 MMI	死亡人数 Deaths 数量/人 Num	死亡人数 Deaths 级别 Dd	受伤人数 Injuries 数量/人 Num	受伤人数 Injuries 级别 Dd	经济损失 Damage 数量/$ Mill	经济损失 Damage 级别 De	房屋毁坏 Houses Destroyed 数量/间 Num	房屋毁坏 Houses Destroyed 级别 Dh	房屋受损 Houses Damaged 数量/间 Num	房屋受损 Houses Damaged 级别 Dh
1863	11	6	10							* GSHAP	Turkey:Yalova	土耳其:亚洛瓦	40.5	29.1		6.7	Ms	10	2	1				1				1
1863	11	29	10	30						GSHAP,Song	Peru:Lima	秘鲁:利马	-12.08	-77		5	Mk	6										
1863	12	4	12	15						GSHAP,Song	Peru:Lima	秘鲁:利马	-12.08	-77		4.5	Mk	5										
1863	12	19	22	38						USGS	US:California,Redwood City	美国:加利福尼亚州红木城	37.5	-122.2		4.8	Ms	5										
1863	12									* Iran	Iran:Ardabil	伊朗:阿尔达比勒	38.2	48.6		6.1	Ms		500	3				3				
1863										* GSHAP	Turkey:Suhut	土耳其:舒胡特	38.5	30.6	10	6.3	Ms	10	800	3				3				
1863						1				NOAA,Song	Canada:Newfoundland	加拿大:纽芬兰(岛)	47	-55		7	Mk											
1864	1	3	9							Bautista,Maso	Philippines:Mindanao Island	菲律宾:棉兰老岛	6	124.1		6.9	Muk	6										
1864	1	3								* Song	Iran:Ardabil	伊朗:阿尔达比勒	38.2	48.3		6.3	Mk	9	500	3				3		3		
1864	1	12	6	9						GSHAP,Song	Chile:Copiapo	智利:科皮亚波	-27.35	-70.35		6	Mk	8										
1864	1	17								* GSHAP	Iran:Kerman	伊朗:克尔曼	30.6	57	6	6	Ms	9.5		3				3				
1864	2	15	15	18						* * Song	Italy:Vergato	意大利:韦尔加托	44.3	11.1		6.5	Mk	12										
1864	2	18	10							* * Song	Italy:Vergato	意大利:韦尔加托	44.3	11.1		6.5	Mk	12										
1864	2	26	13	47						CGS,USGS	US:California,Morgan Hill	美国:加利福尼亚州摩根希尔	37.2	-121.6		6.1	Ms	6										
1864	3	5	16	49						CGS,USGS	US:California,Fremont	美国:加利福尼亚州弗里蒙特	37.5528	-121.855		6	Ms	6										
1864	3	5	16							Usami	Japan:Hyogo	日本:兵库	35	134.8		6.4	Ms									1		
1864	3	29								Japan,Song	Japan:Iwate	日本:岩手	39.2	141.2		6.1	Mk											1
1864	5	19				1				* NOAA,Song	Haiti:Jacmel	海地:雅克梅勒	18.1	-72.3		7.1	Mk							2				
1864	5	21	2	1						CGS,USGS	US:California,Fremont	美国:加利福尼亚州弗里蒙特	37.6	-121.9		5.8	Ms	6										
1864	5	23				3	3	3.6	1.5	* NOAA	Indonesia:Manokwari	印度尼西亚:马诺夸里	-1	135		7.8	Ms	7	250	3				3		3		
1864	6	14								GSHAP	Aegean Sea	爱琴海	40.3	25.1	40	7	Ms	8										
1864	6	27	22	30		3				* NOAA,Song	Canada:Newfoundland	加拿大:纽芬兰(岛)	46.5	-53.7		7	Mk											
1864	6	28	7	35						GSHAP,Song	Peru:Lima	秘鲁:利马	-12.08	-77		5	Mk	6										
1864	7	22	6	40						USGS	US:California,Fremont	美国:加利福尼亚州弗里蒙特	37.6	-122		4.7	Ms	5										
1864	7	26	9	50						GSHAP,Song	Peru:Lima	秘鲁:利马	-12.08	-77		5	Mk	6										
1864	7	26	10	3						GSHAP,Song	Peru:Lima	秘鲁:利马	-12.08	-77		4.5	Mk	5										
1864	8	9	14	45						GSHAP	Ukraine:Odesa	乌克兰:敖德萨	46	30	28	4.7	Ms	5										
1864	8	18	13	18						USGS	US:California,Nevada City	美国:加利福尼亚州内华达城	39.3	-121		4.5	Ms	5										
1864	10	3								* Song	Mexico:Puebla,Veracruz	墨西哥:普埃布拉,韦拉克鲁斯	18.6	-97.5		6.3	Mk		20	1				3				
1864	10	31	22	45						GSHAP,Song	Peru:Lima	秘鲁:利马	-12.08	-77		5	Mk	6										
1864	11	23	14	30						GSHAP	Brasil:Sao Luís	巴西:圣路易斯	-2.53	-44.3		3.1	Ms	5										
1864	12	2								*	Iraq:Tursaq	伊拉克:图尔萨格	33.38	45.98		6.4	Ms	8	100	2				2	100	2		
1864	12	20								* * Song	Iraq:Wasit	伊拉克:瓦西特	33	46		6	Mk		100	2				2				

年 Year	月 Mo	日 Dy	时 Hr	分 Mn	秒 Sec	海啸 Tsunami 源 Sr	浪高 Wh	级 I mI	级 S mS	资料来源 Information	震中 Earthquake Epicenter 地名(英文) Name(English)	地名(中文) Name(Chinese)	纬度(°) Latitude	经度(°) Longitude	深度 Depth	震级 Mag	标度 Scale	烈度 MMI	死亡人数 Deaths 数量/人 Num	级别 Dd	受伤人数 Injuries 数量/人 Num	级别 Dd	经济损失 Damage 数量/$ Mill $ Mill	级别 De	房屋毁坏 Houses Destroyed 数量/间 Num	级别 Dh	房屋受损 Houses Damaged 数量/间 Num	级别 Dh
1864	12	25								* * Song	Iraq: Baghdad, Al – Basrah (Basra)	伊拉克：巴格达，巴士拉	33.2	44.4		5.9	Mk							2				
1865	1	8				3	2	1	1.5	* NOAA, Song	Peru: Lima	秘鲁：利马	−12	−77.1		7	Mk		5	1				1		1		
1865	1	31	5							GSHAP, Song	Peru: Lima	秘鲁：利马	−12.08	−77		4.5	Mk	5										
1865	2	8								* Song	Iraq: Qalat Sukkar	伊拉克：苏凯尔堡	32.2	46		5.9	Mk	7						2		2		
1865	3	7	14							* Song	US: California, Pope Valley	美国：加利福尼亚州波普瓦利	38.5	−122.5		6.1	Mk	8						2				
1865	3	8	14	30						USGS	US: California, Santa Rosa	美国：加利福尼亚州圣罗莎	38.4	−122.6		4.7	Ms	7										
1865	3	22	0	53						GSHAP	Kazakhstan: Talas, SE.	哈萨克斯坦：塔拉兹东南	42.7	73.2	15	6.4	Ms	8.5										
1865	4	27								GSHAP	Black Sea	黑海	44.5	29.5	20	6.4	Ms	8										
1865	5	1	11	50						GSHAP	Russia: Krasnodar, Ust – Labinsk	俄罗斯：克拉斯诺达尔区乌斯季拉宾斯克	45.2	39.5	20	4.5	Ms	5										
1865	5	24	11	21						CGS, USGS	US: California, Los Gatos	美国：加利福尼亚州洛斯加托斯	37.1	−121.8		5.9	Ms	6										
1865	5	29	11							GSHAP, Song	Peru: Lima	秘鲁：利马	−12.08	−77		4.5	Mk	5										
1865	6									* Iran	Iran: Fars, Shiraz	伊朗：法尔斯，设拉子	29.6	53.1		6	Ms	7						3		3		
1865	7	16	3			1				NOAA, Song	Aleutian Islands	阿留申群岛	54	−167		7	Mk											
1865	7	16								* Song	Indonesia: Java, Ambarawa	印度尼西亚：爪哇，安巴拉瓦	−7	110.3		5.9	Mk							2				
1865	7	19	1							* Italy	Italy: Etna	意大利：埃特纳	37.7	15.15		5.03	Ms	10	60	2				1				
1865	7	23	21	30						* GSHAP	Greece: Molyvos (Lesbos)	希腊：莫利沃斯(莱斯沃斯)	39.4	26.2		6.6	Ms	10		2								
1865	8	17	15							USGS	US: Missouri, New Madrid	美国：密苏里州新马德里	36	−89.5		5	Ms	7										
1865	8	28	10	50						GSHAP	Russia: Chechnia, Grozny, S.	俄罗斯：车臣共和国格罗兹尼北部	42.6	46.1	16	4.8	Ms	6										
1865	10	1	17	15						* Song	US: California, North Coast	美国：加利福尼亚州北部近海	41	−124.5		6.5	Mk	9						2				
1865	10	5	15	45						GSHAP, Song	Peru: Lima	秘鲁：利马	−12.08	−77		4.5	Mk	5										
1865	10	8	20	46		3			0.5	* CGS, USGS, NOAA	US: California, San Jose	美国：加利福尼亚州圣荷西	37.2	−121.9		6.6	Ms	8					0.5	1		2		
1865	10	19	14	30		2				* Nakamura, Bautista, NOAA	Philippines: Tiwi	菲律宾：维岛	13.6	123.6		6.5	Ms							2				
1865	11	18				4	1.3		3	* NOAA	Tonga Islands	汤加群岛	−21.6	−175.6		8	Ms							1	20	1		
1865	11	22	20							Maso, Song	Philippines: Tanay	菲律宾：塔奈	14.4	121.21		5	Mk	6										
1865	11	28				1			1	* * NOAA, GSHAP, Song	Peru: Lima	秘鲁：利马	−12.08	−77		7.2	Mk	6										
1865	12	14	8	30						GSHAP, Song	Peru: Lima	秘鲁：利马	−12.08	−77		5	Mk	6										
1865	12	15	21	15						GSHAP, Song	Venezuela: Caracas	委内瑞拉：加拉加斯	10.64	−66.92		5	Mk	6										

年 Year	月 Mo	日 Dy	时 Hr	分 Mn	秒 Sec	海啸 Tsunami 源 Sr	浪高 Wh	级I mI	级S mS	资料来源 Information	地名(英文) Name(English)	地名(中文) Name(Chinese)	纬度(°) Latitude	经度(°) Longitude	深度 Depth	震级 Mag	标度 Scale	烈度 MMI	死亡人数 Deaths 数量/人 Num	级别 Dd	受伤人数 Injuries 数量/人 Num	级别 Dd	经济损失 Damage 数量/$ Mill	级别 De	房屋毁坏 Houses Destroyed 数量/间 Num	级别 Dh	房屋受损 Houses Damaged 数量/间 Num	级别 Dh
1865										* * Iran	Iran:Hormozgan	伊朗:荷姆兹甘	27.2	53.1		5.6	Ms							3				
1866	1	2	9			2			4	* NOAA, GSHAP	Albania:Narta, Vlore	阿尔巴尼亚:娜塔,发罗拉	40.4	19.5		6.6	Ms	10	60	2								
1866	1	2								* Song	Mexico:Puebla,Veracruz	墨西哥:普埃布拉,韦拉克鲁斯	18.8	-98		6.3	Mk							3				
1866	1	6				3			3	NOAA,Song	Albania:Durres	阿尔巴尼亚:都拉斯	41.4	19.4		6.7	Mk											
1866	1	19				2				NOAA	Greece:Aegean Islands	希腊:爱琴群岛	38	25		6.8	Ms											
1866	1	31	24			5				GSHAP,NOAA	Greece:Thera Island (Santorini)	希腊:锡拉岛(圣托里尼岛)	36.4	25.4		6.1	Ms											
1866	2	2				2			3	GSHAP,NOAA	Greece:Chios	希腊:希俄斯岛	38.4	26		6.4	Ms											
1866	2	3	19	30						GSHAP,Song	Peru:Lima	秘鲁:利马	-12.08	-77		5	Mk	6										
1866	2	6				3	8.6		4	* GSHAP, NOAA	Greece:Ionian Sea, Amalias	希腊:伊奥尼亚海,亚美雅斯	36	23		6.8	Ms											
1866	3	2	15	30		3			3	* NOAA	Albania:Narta, Vlore	阿尔巴尼亚:娜塔,发罗拉	40.4	19.5		6.3	Ms	10	20	1				1				
1866	3	6				3			4	NOAA	Greece:Thera Island (Santorini)	希腊:锡拉岛(圣托里尼岛)	36.404	25.396		6	Ms											
1866	3	8	4	30						GSHAP	Russia:Lake Baykal	俄罗斯:贝加尔湖	51.7	104.5	15	6	Ms	8										
1866	3	13				2			3	NOAA	Albania:Durres	阿尔巴尼亚:都拉斯	41.4	19.4		5.5	Ms											
1866	3	26	20	12						CGS,USGS	US:California,Morgan Hill	美国:加利福尼亚州摩根希尔	37	-121.7		5.8	Ms	7										
1866	5	23								* GSHAP	Nepal:Kazahkstan	尼泊尔:加德满都	27.7	85.3		7.6	Ms							2		2		2
1866	6	20	14							GSHAP	Turkey:Diyarbakir	土耳其:迪亚巴克尔	38.5	41	23	6.8	Ms	8.5										
1866	6	22								GSHAP,Song	Chile:Copiapo	智利:科皮亚波	-27.35	-70.35		6	Mk	8										
1866	6	24	5			4				Maso,Song	Guam	关岛(西太平洋)	14	143.3		7.2	Mk	6										
1866	7	15	6	30						CGS,USGS	US:California,Tracy	美国:加利福尼亚州特雷西	37.7	-121.5		6	Ms	5										
1866	8	9				1			-1	NOAA,Song	Australia:Sydney Harbor	澳大利亚:悉尼港口	-33.8	151.3		7	Mk											
1866	8	15				1			-1	NOAA,Song	Australia:Sydney Harbor	澳大利亚:悉尼港口	-33.8	151.3		7	Mk											
1866	9	5	13			2				* NOAA,Song	Alaska:Kodiak Island	阿拉斯加:科迪亚克岛	58	-152		7	Mk											
1866	9	6								GSHAP	Russia:Kamchatka Peninsula	俄罗斯:堪察加半岛	52.5	159.5	30	7	Ms	9										
1866	9	21								China	China:Zhejiang,Jingning	中国:浙江景宁	28	119.6		4.75	Ms	6										
1866	10					1				NOAA,Song	Greece:Mitilini	希腊:米蒂利尼	39	26.5		6.6	Mk											
1866	11	4	10	25						GSHAP	Moldova:Balti,N.	摩尔多瓦:巴蒂北部	48.1	28.1	10	4.7	Ms	6.5										
1866	11	23	14	20						GSHAP,Song	Peru:Lima	秘鲁:利马	-12.08	-77		4.5	Mk	5										
1866	12	4								*	Albania:Himara	阿尔巴尼亚:希马拉	40.1	20.1		6.7	Muk							2				
1866	12	28	19							* Maso, Song, Bautista	Philippines:Laoag	菲律宾:拉瓦格	18.2	120.6		5.5	Mk	8						2				
1867	1	2	6	13						* Song	Algeria:Blida	阿尔及利亚:卜利达	36.4	2.7		7.3	Mk	10	70	2	100	2		2		3		
1867	1	5	1	45						Maso,Song	Philippines:Kalibo	菲律宾:卡利博	11.81	122.31		5	Mk	6										

时间 年 Year	月 Mo	日 Dy	时 Hr	分 Mn	秒 Sec	海啸 源 Sr	浪高 Wh	级 I mI	级 S mS	资料来源 Information	震中 地名(英文) Name(English)	地名(中文) Name(Chinese)	纬度(°) Latitude	经度(°) Longitude	深度 Depth	震级 Mag	标度 Scale	烈度 MMI	死亡人数 Deaths 数量/人 Num	级别 Dd	受伤人数 Injuries 数量/人 Num	级别 Dd	经济损失 Damage 数量/$ Mill	级别 De	房屋毁坏 Houses Destroyed 数量/间 Num	级别 Dh	房屋受损 Houses Damaged 数量/间 Num	级别 Dh
1867	1	27								* GSHAP	Greece:Jannina (Epirus)	希腊:伊庇鲁斯	39.8	20.8		6.2	Ms	10										
1867	2	4	3			3			2	* NOAA	Greece:Nisia Ionioy	希腊:伊奥尼亚群岛	38.4	20.2	100	7.9	Muk	10	200	3				3				
1867	2	15								GSHAP,Song	Peru:Lima	秘鲁:利马	-12.08	-77		5	Mk	6										
1867	3	7	14			4				*	Greece:Mitilini	希腊:米蒂利尼	39.2	26.4		7	Ms		500	3				3				
1867	3	17	10	45						* Song	British Virgin Islands:Spanish Town	英属维尔京群岛:斯帕尼什陶恩	18.4	-64.3		6.1	Mk	8						2				
1867	3	26	5							Maso,Song	Philippines:Tabuk	菲律宾:塔布克	17.5	121.21		5	Mk	6										
1867	4	10				2			2	NOAA,Song	Greece:Lixouri	希腊:利克苏里翁	38.2	20.4		6.7	Mk											
1867	4	14								* Song	Iraq:Mandali,Jalula,Baghdad	伊拉克:曼代利,杰卢拉,巴格达	33.5	44.9		6.3	Mk							3				
1867	4	20	0	31						GSHAP,Song	Venezuela:Merida	委内瑞拉:梅里达	8.33	-71.75		5	Mk	6										
1867	4	24	20	22						USGS	UA:Kansas,Topeka	美国:堪萨斯州托皮卡	39.2	-96.3		5.1	Ms	7										
1867	5	7	10			4			3	NOAA,Song	Norway:Stavanger	挪威:斯塔万格	58.667	6.167		7.7	Mk											
1867	6	10								* Song	Indonesia:Java,Yogyakarta	印度尼西亚:爪哇,约尔卡塔	-7.8	110.5		6.5	Mk	9	5	1				3				
1867	7	20	9							USGS,Song	Alaska Peninsula,S.	阿拉斯加半岛南部	62	-161		5	Mk	5										
1867	8	5				1			-1	NOAA,Song	Australia:Sydney Harbor	澳大利亚:悉尼港口	-33.8	151.3		7	Mk											
1867	8	31	17	30						GSHAP,Song	Peru:Lima	秘鲁:利马	-12.08	-77		5	Mk	6										
1867	9	20	3	15		4	6		4	* NOAA,GSHAP	Greece:Peninsula of Maina (Laconia)	希腊:马伊纳半岛	36.5	22.25		7.1	Ms	9		2								
1867	9									China	China:Zhejiang,Haining,SW.	中国:浙江海宁西南	30.4	120.5		4.75	Ms	6										
1867	9					1				* NOAA	Venezuela:Isla De Margarita	委内瑞拉:玛格丽特岛	10.9	-64.1		7.5	Ms											
1867	10	4				2				NOAA,Song	Greece:Ionian Sea	希腊:伊奥尼亚海	38.25	22.25		6.6	Mk											
1867	11	18	18	45		4	10	2.3		* NOAA	Virgin Islands:Charlotte Amalie	维尔京群岛:夏洛特阿马利亚	18.1	-65.1	33	7.5	Muk	10	30	1				4				
1867	11	19	21			1				NOAA,Song	Turkey:Izmir	土耳其:伊兹密尔	38.5	27		6.6	Mk											
1867	12	1	11	10						* Song	British Virgin Islands:Spanish Town	英属维尔京群岛:斯帕尼什陶恩	18.4	-64.3		6.1	Mk	8						2				
1867	12	18	8							USGS	US:New York,De Kalb	美国:纽约州迪卡尔布	44.7	-75.2		4.3	Ms	6										
1867	12	18				4		2	2	* China,NOAA	China:Taiwan,Keelung,Coast of NE.	中国:台湾基隆东北海域	25.3	121.8		7	Ms		200	3				2		2		
1867	12	26	18	30						Bautista,Maso	Philippines:Samar Island	菲律宾:萨马岛	11.95	125.65		5.5	Muk	6										
1868	1	20								* GSHAP	Iran:Shāhrūd	伊朗:沙赫鲁德	36.3	56.3	12	5.1	Ms	7						3				
1868	2	18	17							GSHAP	Georgia:Akhalkalaki	格鲁吉亚:阿卡卡垃吉	41.2	43.8	15	4.5	Ms	6.5										
1868	2	25	11	10						GSHAP	Turkey:Ardahan	土耳其:阿尔达汉	41	43	25	6.2	Ms	8										
1868	3	17	11	37		3	1.5	-07	1	* NOAA,Song	Virgin Islands:Charlotte Amalie	维尔京群岛:夏洛特阿马利亚	18.1	-65.1		7	Mk											

年 Year	月 Mo	日 Dy	时 Hr	分 Mn	秒 Sec	海啸 Tsunami 源 Sr	浪高 Wh	级I mI	级S mS	资料来源 Information	震中 Earthquake Epicenter 地名(英文) Name(English)	地名(中文) Name(Chinese)	纬度(°) Latitude	经度(°) Longitude	深度 Depth	震级 Mag	标度 Scale	烈度 MMI	死亡人数 Deaths 数量/人 Num	级别 Dd	受伤人数 Injuries 数量/人 Num	级别 Dd	经济损失 Damage 数量/$ Mill	级别 De	房屋毁坏 Houses Destroyed 数量/间 Num	级别 Dh	房屋受损 Houses Damaged 数量/间 Num	级别 Dh
1868	3	21	15	22						GSHAP	Russia:Chechnia,Grozny,N.	俄罗斯:车臣共和国格罗兹尼北部	43.4	45.7	12	4.6	Ms	6.5										
1868	3	29	0	15						USGS	Hawaiian Islands	夏威夷群岛	19	-155.5		7	Ms	8										
1868	4	3	2	25		5	14	4.3	3.4	* NOAA	Hawaiian Islands	夏威夷群岛	19	-155.5		7.9	Mfa	10	78	2				2		3		
1868	4	3	21	15						*	Uzbekistan:Tashkent	乌兹别克斯坦:塔什干	41.2	69.6	18	6.5	Muk	8						3				
1868	4	4	1							Bautista,Maso	Philippines:Masbate Island	菲律宾:马斯巴特岛	11.3	124.55		5.4	Muk	6										
1868	4	4	10	57						USGS,Song	Hawaiian Islands	夏威夷群岛	20.5	-156.5		5.7	Mk	7										
1868	4	7								* Song	Mexico:Guanajuato	墨西哥:瓜纳华多	21	-101		6.3	Mk							3				
1868	4	9								Japan,Song	Japan:Gunma	日本:群马	36.4	139		6.4	Mk	8										
1868	4	23	3	30						* GSHAP	Turkey:Erzurum	土耳其:埃尔佐鲁姆	40	41.7		6.7	Muk	8						2				
1868	5	15				2	6.1		2.5	* NOAA,Song	Aleutian Islands	阿留申群岛	55	-161		7.5	Mk											
1868	5	17	18							GSHAP	Ecuador:Ambato	厄瓜多尔:安巴托	-1.33	-78.45		7.3	Ms	8										
1868	5	20								GSHAP,Song	Peru:Torata	秘鲁:塔克纳	-17.6	-71.2		5	Mk	6										
1868	5	21								GSHAP,Song	Peru:Torata	秘鲁:塔克纳	-17.6	-71.2		4.5	Mk	5										
1868	5	22								GSHAP,Song	Peru:Torata	秘鲁:塔克纳	-17.6	-71.2		5	Mk	6										
1868	5	22								* Song	Mexico:San Jose De Iturbide	墨西哥:图尔比德的圣何塞	21.2	-100.5		6.3	Mk							3				
1868	5	22				3				NOAA,Song	Italy:Lake Garda	意大利:加尔达湖	45.7	10.7		6.6	Mk											
1868	5	25	10	30						USGS,Song	Hawaiian Islands	夏威夷群岛	19	-155.5		5	Mk	5										
1868	5	25				2				* NOAA,Song	Mexico:Acapulco	墨西哥:阿卡普尔科	17	-100		7	Mk											
1868	5	30	5	10						CGS,USGS	US:Nevada,Reno	美国:内华达州雷诺	39.3	-119.7		6	Ms	7										
1868	6	10								GSHAP,Song	Peru:Torata	秘鲁:塔克纳	-17.6	-71.2		5	Mk	6										
1868	6	29	0	11						Bautista,Maso	Philippines:Panay Island	菲律宾:班乃岛	10.45	122.25		5.5	Muk	6										
1868	7	25	9	10						USGS,Song	Hawaiian Islands	夏威夷群岛	19	-155.5		5	Mk	5										
1868	8	1								GSHAP	Iran:Semnan	伊朗:塞姆南	34.9	52.5	30	6.4	Ms	7.5										
1868	8	12				3				* NOAA,Song	Mexico:Jalisco	墨西哥:哈利斯科	20	-105		7	Mk											
1868	8	13	21	23						GSHAP,Song	Peru:Arequipa	秘鲁:阿雷基帕	-16.4	-71.56		7	Mk	10										
1868	8	13	21	30		4	18	4.2	3.5	* GSHAP,NOAA	Chile:Arica,Near Coast	智利:阿里卡近海	-18.6	-71	25	8.5	Ms	11	25000	5			300	5				
1868	8	13	21	46						GSHAP,Song	Peru:Tacna,Near Coast	秘鲁:塔克纳近海	-18.29	-70.59		5	Mk	6										
1868	8	13	22	15						GSHAP,Song	Chile:Arica	智利:阿里卡	-18.45	-70.2		5	Mk	6										
1868	8	13	23	30						GSHAP,Song	Peru:Lima	秘鲁:利马	-12.01	-77.02		4.5	Mk	5										
1868	8	13				2				* NOAA	Venezuela:Rio Caribe	委内瑞拉:里约卡利宾	10.7	-63.1		7	Mk											
1868	8	15	19	30						*	Ecuador:Concepcion	厄瓜多尔:康塞普西翁	0.81	-77.72		8	Ms	8		1				3		3		
1868	8	15								GSHAP	Colombia:Narino	哥伦比亚:纳里尼奥	0.8	-77.7		4.5	Ms	5										
1868	8	16	6	30						*	Ecuador:Imbabura	厄瓜多尔:因巴布拉	0.31	-78.18	20	7.7	Ms	10	70000	5				4		4		
1868	8	16								GSHAP,Song	Peru:Torata	秘鲁:塔克纳	-17.1	-70.9		4.5	Mk	5										
1868	8	19				4	4	2	2	NOAA,Song	India:Andaman Islands	印度:安达曼群岛	11.67	92.73		7.5	Mk											
1868	8	26								GSHAP	Ecuador:Ibarra	厄瓜多尔:伊瓦拉	0.22	-78.26		4	Ms	5										

时间						海啸				资料来源	震中				深度	震级	标度	烈度	死亡人数		受伤人数		经济损失		房屋毁坏		房屋受损	
年	月	日	时	分	秒	源	浪高	级 I	级 S		地名(英文)	地名(中文)	纬度(°)	经度(°)					数量/人	级别	数量/人	级别	数量/$ Mill	级别	数量/间	级别	数量/间	级别
Date						Tsunami				Information	Earthquake Epicenter				Depth	Mag	Scale	MMI	Deaths		Injuries		Damage		Houses Destroyed		Houses Damaged	
Year	Mo	Dy	Hr	Mn	Sec	Sr	Wh	mI	mS		Name(English)	Name(Chinese)	Latitude	Longitude					Num	Dd	Num	Dd	$ Mill	De	Num	Dh	Num	Dh
1868	8	29	8							GSHAP	Kyrgyzstan:Bishkek	吉尔吉斯斯坦:比什凯克	42.7	75.9	20	6.4	Ms	8										
1868	9	4	16							USGS,Song	US:California,Badger,E.	美国:加利福尼亚州巴杰东部	36.6	-118.4		5.5	Mk	6										
1868	9	5	2			5				*NOAA,Song	Italy:Acireale, Catania	意大利:阿瑟瑞尔,卡塔尼亚	37.6	15.133		6.6	Mk											
1868	9	14				2	1		0.5	*NOAA,Song	Chile:Concepcion,Near Coast	智利:康塞普西翁近海	-36.7	-73.2		7	Mk											
1868	9	17	16	55						CGS,USGS	US:California,Delano	美国:加利福尼亚州德拉诺	38.6	-119.7		5.6	Ms	5										
1868	10	2	7	30		2	6.1	3.2	2.5	*NOAA,Song	Philippines:Aroroy	菲律宾:阿罗罗伊	12.3	123.1		7.5	Mk											
1868	10	2				2	1		0.5	*NOAA,Song	Peru:Mollendo,Near Coast	秘鲁:莫延多近海	-17	-72.5		7	Mk							1				
1868	10	12	5	20						GSHAP,Song	Chile:Copiapo	智利:科皮亚波	-27.35	-70.35		6	Mk	8										
1868	10	16				3	1		0.5	*NOAA,Song	Chile:Valparaiso	智利:瓦尔帕莱索	-33.1	-71.7		7	Mk											
1868	10	18	17							*	Georgia:Akhalkalaki	格鲁吉亚:阿卡卡垃吉	41.2	43.8	15	4.5	Muk	7						2				
1868	10	21	15	53		3	4.5	2.2	0.5	*CGS, USGS, NOAA	US:California,Hayward, San Francisco	美国:加利福尼亚州海沃德,旧金山	37.7	-122.1		7	Ms	9	30	1			0.35	1		3		
1868	10	30								*China	China:Anhui,Dingyuan,S.	中国:安徽定远南	32.4	117.8		5.5	Ms	7		2								
1868	11	13	6	50						GSHAP	Romania:Nereju	罗马尼亚:内雷茹	45.7	26.6	100	5.8	Ms	6										
1868	11	17	8	30						USGS,Song	Hawaiian Islands	夏威夷群岛	19	-155.5		5	Mk	5										
1868	11	27	20	30						GSHAP	Romania:Nereju	罗马尼亚:内雷茹	45.7	26.6	150	6.4	Ms	7										
1868	12	31	2	15						*Song	Colombia:Simacota, Barichara De Cabrera	哥伦比亚:锡马科塔,巴里查拉	7	-73		6.1	Mk	8						2				
1868										China	China:Gansu,Tianshui	中国:甘肃天水	34.6	105.7		4.75	Ms	6										
1868										Japan,Song	Japan:Miyako-Jima	日本:宫古岛	25	125.5		6.1	Mk											1
1868										Japan,Song	Japan:Shizuoka	日本:静冈	35.1	138.9		6.1	Mk											1
1869	1	10								*India	India:Assam: Cachar,Silchar	印度:阿萨姆邦:察查,锡尔杰尔	24.5	92.5		7.5	Ms		2	1				3				
1869	1	27				3	0.7	-0.5		*NOAA,Song	Chile:Tome	智利:托梅	-36.6	-72.9		7	Mk											
1869	1	28	18							GSHAP,Song	Peru:Lima	秘鲁:利马	-12.08	-77		4.5	Mk	5										
1869	2	6				2	0.7	-0.5		*NOAA,Song	Chile:Valdivia	智利:瓦尔迪维亚	-39.9	-73.4		7	Mk											
1869	2	14	0	30						GSHAP	Colombia:Bolivar	哥伦比亚:波利瓦尔	9	-74		5.5	Ms	7										
1869	2	17	4							*Song	Venezuela:San Cristobal, Tachira (Lobatera)	委内瑞拉:圣克里斯托瓦尔,塔希提	7.5	-72.1		5.9	Mk			1				2				
1869	2	19	10	30						USGS,Song	Hawaiian Islands	夏威夷群岛	19	-155.5		5	Mk	5										
1869	2	22	12	10						USGS,Song	Hawaiian Islands	夏威夷群岛	19	-155.5		5	Mk	5										
1869	3	6	11	30						*Song	Colombia:Cachira	哥伦比亚:北桑坦德的卡奇拉	7.7	-73.3		5.9	Mk							2				
1869	3	18								Japan,Song	Japan:Hiroshima	日本:广岛	34.4	132.45		6.1	Mk											3
1869	3	20	9							GSHAP	Colombia:Terraimbe	哥伦比亚:特赖恩贝	1.7	-78.1		4	Ms	5										

时间 Date						海啸 Tsunami				资料来源 Information	震中 Earthquake Epicenter				深度 Depth	震级 Mag	标度 Scale	烈度 MMI	死亡人数 Deaths		受伤人数 Injuries		经济损失 Damage		房屋毁坏 Houses Destroyed		房屋受损 Houses Damaged	
年 Year	月 Mo	日 Dy	时 Hr	分 Mn	秒 Sec	源 Sr	浪高 Wh	级 I mI	级 S mS		地名(英文) Name(English)	地名(中文) Name(Chinese)	纬度(°) Latitude	经度(°) Longitude					数量/人 Num	级别 Dd	数量/人 Num	级别 Dd	数量/$ Mill $ Mill	级别 De	数量/间 Num	级别 Dh	数量/间 Num	级别 Dh
1869	3	25	0	30						GSHAP	Kyrgyzstan:Suluktu	吉尔吉斯斯坦:苏柳克塔	39.8	69.5	30	5.5	Ms	6										
1869	4	18	13							USGS,Song	US:New Mexico,Socorro	美国:新墨西哥州索科罗	34	-107		5.7	Mk	7										
1869	4	20								USGS,Song	US:New Mexico,Socorro	美国:新墨西哥州索科罗	34	-107		5.5	Mk	6										
1869	4	22				1			1	*NOAA,Song	Peru:Arequipa	秘鲁:阿雷基帕	-16	-73.5		7	Mk							3				3
1869	4	30	2	56						GSHAP,Song	Chile:Talca	智利:塔尔卡	-35.43	-71.67		6	Mk	8										
1869	6	25				2				*NOAA,Song	Chile:Iquique,N.	智利:伊基克北部	-19.6	-70.2		7	Mk											
1869	7	7								*GSHAP	Nepal:Kazahkstan	尼泊尔:加德满都	27.7	85.3		7.4	Ms			3				4		4		4
1869	7	11								China	China:Guangxi,Ningming	中国:广西宁明	22.2	107.3		4.75	Ms	6										
1869	7	22	15							GSHAP,Song	Peru:Arequipa	秘鲁:阿雷基帕	-16.4	-71.56		5	Mk	6										
1869	7	24				3	8.2	3.2	3	*NOAA,Song	Hawaiian Islands	夏威夷群岛	20	-155		7.7	Mk											
1869	7	27	16	30						GSHAP,Song	Peru:Perene	秘鲁:佩雷内	-11.3	-75.7		5	Mk	6										
1869	7	29	2							GSHAP,Song	Peru:Sechura	秘鲁:塞丘拉	-5.3	-80.6		5	Mk	6										
1869	8	9				3	3	1.6	2	*NOAA,Song	Chile:Coquimbo	智利:科金博	-30	-71.4		7.5	Mk											
1869	8	11				1			-1	NOAA,Song	Australia:Sydney Harbor	澳大利亚:悉尼港口	-33.8	151.3		7	Mk											
1869	8	14								*GSHAP	Albania:Vlore, Kanina	阿尔巴尼亚:发罗拉,卡妮娜	40.3	19.3		6	Ms	10										
1869	8	15	14	30						USGS,Song	Hawaiian Islands	夏威夷群岛	19	-155.5		5	Mk	5										
1869	8	15								**Song	Ecuador:Ibarra	厄瓜多尔:伊瓦拉	0.3	-78.1		5.8	Mk		32	1								
1869	8	16	7			2				*Bautista,Maso,Nakamura,NOAA	Philippines:Masbate Island	菲律宾:马斯巴特岛	12.4	123.85		7	Ms	9						4				
1869	8	16	8	30						GSHAP,Song	Chile:Arica	智利:阿里卡	-18.5	-70.35		6	Mk	8										
1869	8	19				2				*NOAA	Peru:Arequipa	秘鲁:阿雷基帕	-16	-73.5		6.5	Ms							1				
1869	8	21	16	40		1				*NOAA	Chile:Tarapaca,S.	智利:塔拉帕卡南部	-21	-70		6.8	Ms											
1869	8	24	18	45		3	2		1.5	*GSHAP, NOAA, Chile	Peru:Ilo,Near Coast	秘鲁:伊洛近海	-17.5	-72	30	7.5	Ms	8						1				
1869	8	24	20							GSHAP,Song	Peru:Tacna	秘鲁:塔克纳	-18.1	-69.9		5	Mk	6										
1869	9	2	12							GSHAP	Turkey:Kars	土耳其:卡尔斯	40.7	43	6	5	Ms	8										
1869	9	9				2				NOAA,Song	Turkey:Izmir	土耳其:伊兹密尔	38.5	27		6.6	Mk											
1869	10	1	3	15						*Bautista, Maso	Philippines:Luzon,Manila	菲律宾:吕宋岛马尼拉	14.25	120.45		6.6	Ms	8						2				
1869	10	2	7	15						GSHAP,Song	Peru:Lima	秘鲁:利马	-12.08	-77		4.5	Mk	5										
1869	10	8	9	30						CGS,USGS	US:California,Ukiah	美国:加利福尼亚州尤凯亚	39.1	-123.1		5.6	Ms	7										
1869	10	11	11	10		3			3	*NOAA	Ukraine:Crimea,Sudak	乌克兰:克里米亚,苏达克	44.8	34.9	18	5.6	Ms	7										
1869	10	23	8	30						Bautista,Maso	Philippines:Mauban	菲律宾:毛班	14.05	121.8		5.6	Muk	7										
1869	11	4	0	30						GSHAP,Song	Peru:Arequipa	秘鲁:阿雷基帕	-16.6	-71.65	30	5	Mk	6										
1869	11	16	11	45						*Song	Algeria:Biskra	阿尔及利亚:比斯卡拉	34.9	5.9		7.3	Mk	10	40	1				2		3		
1869	12	1	16							*	Turkey:Bodrum	土耳其:博德鲁姆	37	28		7.5	Ms	10						3		3		

年 Year	月 Mo	日 Dy	时 Hr	分 Mn	秒 Sec	海啸 Tsunami 源 Sr	浪高 Wh	级 I mI	级 S mS	资料来源 Information	震中 Earthquake Epicenter 地名(英文) Name(English)	地名(中文) Name(Chinese)	纬度(°) Latitude	经度(°) Longitude	深度 Depth	震级 Mag	标度 Scale	烈度 MMI	死亡人数 Deaths 数量/人 Num	级别 Dd	受伤人数 Injuries 数量/人 Num	级别 Dd	经济损失 Damage 数量/$ Mill $ Mill	级别 De	房屋毁坏 Houses Destroyed 数量/间 Num	级别 Dh	房屋受损 Houses Damaged 数量/间 Num	级别 Dh
1869	12	9	12	43						＊＊Song	Italy:Mileto	意大利:米莱托	38.7	16.1		6.5	Mk	12										
1869	12	15	22							GSHAP,Song	Peru:Arequipa	秘鲁:阿雷基帕	-16.4	-71.56		4.5	Mk	5										
1869	12	19	3							GSHAP	Azerbaijan:Sirvan	阿塞拜疆:希尔万	39.9	48.3	33	5.2	Ms	5.5										
1869	12	21	4							USGS	US: California, Baltimore Town	美国:加利福尼亚州巴尔的摩陶恩	39.5	-120.6		4.8	Ms	5										
1869	12	27	10							CGS,USGS	US:Nevada,Johnson Lane	美国:内华达州约翰逊巷	39.1	-119.8		6.2	Ms	7										
1869	12	28	3			3			2	＊NOAA,GSHAP	Greece:Leukas (Ionian Islands)	希腊:琉卡斯(伊奥尼亚群岛)	38.8	20.8		6.9	Ms	11	15	1				3				
1869										GSHAP	Iran:Qūchān	伊朗:古昌	37.1	58.4	10	5	Ms	7										
1870	2	3	15							GSHAP,Song	Ecuador:Quito	厄瓜多尔:基多	-0.18	-78.44		4.5	Mk	5										
1870	2	8								USGS,Song	US:Maine,Jonesport,Near Coast	美国:缅因州琼斯波特近海	44.1	-67.1		5.5	Mk	6										
1870	2	17	20	12						CGS,USGS	US:California,San Jose	美国:加利福尼亚州圣荷西	37.1	-122		5.9	Ms	7										
1870	3	1	19	57						GSHAP,Italy	Croatia:Rijeka	克罗地亚:里耶卡	45.4	14.4	18	6.6	Ms	8										
1870	3	1	19							Maso,Song	Philippines:Mindanao Island	菲律宾:棉兰老岛	11.6	126.31		5	Mk	6										
1870	3	22	7							USGS,Song	Hawaiian Islands	夏威夷群岛	19	-155.5		5	Mk	5										
1870	3	27	16							GSHAP,Song	Peru:Cuzco	秘鲁:库斯科	-13.55	-72		4.5	Mk	5										
1870	3	28	17	40						GSHAP,Song	Peru:Cuzco	秘鲁:库斯科	-13.55	-72		5	Mk	6										
1870	3	28	18	37						GSHAP,Song	Peru:Arequipa	秘鲁:阿雷基帕	-16.4	-71.56		4.5	Mk	5										
1870	4	2	19	48						CGS,USGS	US:California,Richmond	美国:加利福尼亚州里奇蒙	37.9	-122.3		5.8	Ms	6										
1870	4	5	2	52						GSHAP	Colombia:Bogota	哥伦比亚:波哥达	4.6	-74		4.5	Ms	5										
1870	4	6	11							GSHAP,Song	Peru:Tacna	秘鲁:塔克纳	-18.1	-69.9		5	Mk	6										
1870	4	11								＊China	China:Sichuan,Batang	中国:四川巴塘	30	99.1		7.25	Ms	10	2300	4				4		4		
1870	4	12	20							GSHAP,Song	Peru:Casma	秘鲁:卡斯马	-9.4	-78.2		4.5	Mk	5										
1870	4	22	13	20						＊Song	Chile:Calama	智利:卡拉马	-22.5	-68.9		7.3	Mk	10										
1870	5	11	23	30		2				＊NOAA	Mexico:Oaxaca	墨西哥:瓦哈卡	17	-96.3		7.9	Ms		24	1	20	1		3		3		
1870	5	12								Japan	Japan:Kanagawa	日本:神奈川	35.3	139.1		6.5	Ms									1		
1870	5	13	7	27		4				Maso,Song	Guam	关岛(西太平洋)	14	143.3		7.2	Mk	6										
1870	5	23	15	30						Bautista,Maso	Philippines:Laoag	菲律宾:佬沃	18.2	120.85		6.1	Muk	7										
1870	6	18								＊Song	Nicaragua:Leon	尼加拉瓜:里昂	12.4	-86.6		5.9	Mk							2				
1870	6	24				3				NOAA,Song	Mediterranean Sea	地中海	32.2	29.6		6.6	Mk											
1870	6	26	15							＊Song	Venezuela:Acarigua	委内瑞拉:阿卡里瓜	9.5	-69.5		5.9	Mk		3	1				2				
1870	7	5								China	China:Yunnan,Xinping	中国:云南新平	24.1	102		5.25	Ms	7										
1870	7	7	9	36						GSHAP	Russia:Krasnodar,Sochi	俄罗斯:克拉斯诺达尔区索契	43.6	39.9	10	4.8	Ms	7										
1870	7	8	7	20						GSHAP	Russia:Krasnodar,Sochi	俄罗斯:克拉斯诺达尔区索契	43.6	39.9	13	5.3	Ms	7.5										

时间 年 Year	月 Mo	日 Dy	时 Hr	分 Mn	秒 Sec	海啸 Tsunami 源 Sr	浪高 Wh	级 I mI	级 S mS	资料来源 Information	震中 Earthquake Epicenter 地名(英文) Name(English)	地名(中文) Name(Chinese)	纬度(°) Latitude	经度(°) Longitude	深度 Depth	震级 Mag	标度 Scale	烈度 MMI	死亡人数 Deaths 数量/人 Num	级别 Dd	受伤人数 Injuries 数量/人 Num	级别 Dd	经济损失 Damage 数量/$ Mill $ Mill	级别 De	房屋毁坏 Houses Destroyed 数量/间 Num	级别 Dh	房屋受损 Houses Damaged 数量/间 Num	级别 Dh
1870	7	10	18	30						GSHAP, Song	Peru: Cuzco	秘鲁:库斯科	-14.5	-72		5	Mk	6										
1870	7	29				2			3	NOAA, Song	Adriatic Sea	亚得里亚海	44	14.5		6.7	Mk											
1870	8	1	2	40		2				* NOAA	Greece: Delphi	希腊:德尔斐	38.5	22.5		7	Ms	10		2								
1870	8	6				3				* NOAA, Song	Greece: Crete Island	希腊:克里特岛	35.2	25.1		6.6	Mk											
1870	8	7	14	43						USGS	Hawaiian Islands	夏威夷群岛	20.5	-157		6	Ms	5										
1870	8	12				1			-1	* NOAA, Song	Australia: Tasman Sea	澳大利亚:塔斯曼海	-37.8	161.4		7	Mk											
1870	9	30	23							*	Greece: Patrai	希腊:帕特雷	38.5	22.5		7.5	Muk		100	2				3				
1870	10	4	16	55						* Italy	Italy: Cosenza	意大利:科森扎	39.22	16.33		6.16	Ms	10	136	3				2				
1870	10	21	18							GSHAP, Song	Peru: Arequipa	秘鲁:阿雷基帕	-16.4	-71.56		5	Mk	6										
1870	10	28	9	45		3				* NOAA, Song	Italy: Tyrrhenian Sea	意大利:第勒尼安海	39.28	16.28		6.6	Mk											
1870	11	2	3	30		2				* NOAA, Song	Italy: Calabria	意大利:卡拉布里亚	38.3	15.9		6.6	Mk											
1870	11	4	7							* Bautista, Maso	Philippines: Mindanao, Davao, Blanco	菲律宾:棉兰老岛,达沃,兰科	7	127.1		6.8	Ms	7	4	1				2				
1870	11	6	5							GSHAP, Song	Peru: Arequipa	秘鲁:阿雷基帕	-16.5	-71.56		5	Mk	6										
1870	11	25	6	15						GSHAP, Song	Peru: Arequipa	秘鲁:阿雷基帕	-16.5	-71.65		4.5	Mk	5										
1870	11	26	10	15						GSHAP, Song	Peru: Arequipa	秘鲁:阿雷基帕	-16.5	-71.56		5	Mk	6										
1870	12	28	21	37						GSHAP, Song	Peru: Lima	秘鲁:利马	-12.08	-77		4.5	Mk	5										
1870										China	China: Taiwan, Pingtung	中国:台湾屏东	22.4	120.6		5.75	Ms	7										
1870										GSHAP	Mongolia: Dalandzadgad	蒙古:达兰扎得嘎德	43.3	104.2	15	6	Ms	8										
1871	1	17				1			4	* NOAA, Song	Ligurian Sea	利古里亚海	43.7	8.1		6.7	Mk											
1871	2	5				1			1	* NOAA, Song	Peru: Ica	秘鲁:伊卡	-14.2	-75.7		7	Mk											
1871	2	20	8	41		1				* USGS, NOAA	Hawaiian Islands	夏威夷群岛	20.7	-157	15	7	Muk	8										
1871	2	20	20			1				* Bautista, Maso, NOAA	Philippines: Camiguin Island	菲律宾:卡蜜桂茵岛	9.1	124.7		5	Ms	9						2				
1871	2	23	6	30						GSHAP	Bolivia: Cochabamba	玻利维亚:科恰班巴	-16.94	-65.38		5.2	Ms	6										
1871	3	2	21	5						* CGS, USGS	US: California, Petrolia	美国:加利福尼亚州彼得罗利亚	40.4	-124.2		6.3	Ms	7						1				
1871	3	3	23	17						GSHAP	Russia: Lake Baykal	俄罗斯:贝加尔湖	52	106	18	6.3	Ms	8.5										
1871	3	17								GSHAP	Turkey: Catak	土耳其:恰塔克	38	43	32	6.8	Ms	8										
1871	3	25	14	56		3	1		0.5	* NOAA, GSHAP	Chile: Talca	智利:塔尔卡	-35	-72.5		7.5	Ms	8						3		3		
1871	6	18				2				* NOAA, Song	US: New York, Rockaway Beach	美国:纽约州罗卡韦滩	40.5	-73.9		7	Mk											
1871	6	27	21	30						Maso, Song	Philippines: Mindanao Island	菲律宾:棉兰老岛	7.11	125.61		5	Mk	6										
1871	6									China	China: Xizang (Tibet), Cona, W.	中国:西藏错那西部	28	91.5		7.5	Ms	10		2						4		
1871	7	5	21	6						CGS, USGS	US: California, Owens Valley	美国:加利福尼亚州欧文斯谷	36.4	-118		5.5	Ms	6										
1871	7	11	13							Bautista, Maso	Philippines: Manabo	菲律宾:马纳博	17.05	120.45		5.2	Muk	6										
1871	8	20				2	1	-1	0.5	* NOAA, Song	Peru: Valparaíso	秘鲁:瓦尔帕莱索	-33.1	-71.7		7	Mk											

年 Year	月 Mo	日 Dy	时 Hr	分 Mn	秒 Sec	海啸 Tsunami 源 Sr	浪高 Wh	级 I mI	级 S mS	资料来源 Information	地名(英文) Name(English)	地名(中文) Name(Chinese)	纬度(°) Latitude	经度(°) Longitude	深度 Depth	震级 Mag	标度 Scale	烈度 MMI	死亡人数 Deaths 数量/人 Num	级别 Dd	受伤人数 Injuries 数量/人 Num	级别 Dd	经济损失 Damage 数量/$ Mill	级别 De	房屋毁坏 Houses Destroyed 数量/间 Num	级别 Dh	房屋受损 Houses Damaged 数量/间 Num	级别 Dh
1871	8	21								* Song	British Virgin Islands: Road Town	英属维尔京群岛:罗德城	18.2	-64.6		6	Mk			2				2	100	2		
1871	8	21				2	2	1	1	* NOAA	Peru: Lima	秘鲁:利马	-12	-76.6		7	Ms											
1871	8	25				1				* NOAA, Song	Indonesia: Molucca Sea	印度尼西亚:马鲁古海	1	126.25		7	Mk											
1871	9	13	10	45						USGS, Song	Hawaiian Islands	夏威夷群岛	19.25	-155		5.7	Mk	7										
1871	10	4	12	30						Maso, Song	Philippines: Davao Gulf	菲律宾:达沃湾	7.01	125.71		5.5	Mk	7										
1871	10	5	9			4				*	Chile: Iquique	智利:伊基克	-20.2	-70.2		7.3	Muk	10		1				3	101	3		
1871	10	9	14	40						USGS, Song	US: Delaware, Wilmington	美国:特拉华州威尔明顿	39.7	-75.5		5.7	Mk	7										
1871	10									USGS, Song	US: Colorado, Maybell	美国:科罗拉多州梅贝尔	40.5	-108.5		5.5	Mk	6										
1871	11	2	1	20						GSHAP	Romania: Galati	罗马尼亚:加拉茨	45.8	27.5	20	5	Ms	6										
1871	11	5	0	45						Bautista, Maso	Philippine Trench	菲律宾海沟	8.9	126.9		7.3	Muk	7										
1871	11	29	8	30						Bautista, Maso	Philippines: Culasi	菲律宾:库拉西	7.4	121.6		5.9	Muk	7										
1871	12	8	9	30						* Bautista, Maso	Philippines: Mindanao, Cotabato	菲律宾:棉兰老岛,哥打巴托	7.3	123.75		7	Ms	9						2				
1871	12	8	23	30						Maso, Song	Philippines: Mindanao, Cotabato	菲律宾:棉兰老岛,哥打巴托	7.3	123.75		6.1	Mk	8										
1871	12	19	11							Bautista, Maso	Philippine Trench	菲律宾海沟	8.5	126.9		7.2	Muk	7										
1871	12	23								* GSHAP, Afghan	Iran: Qūchān	伊朗:古昌	37.3	58.3	15	7.2	Muk	7.5	2000	4				3				
1871	12	28				2			0.5	* NOAA, Song	Chile: Puerto Montt	智利:蒙特港	-41.5	-73		7	Mk											
1872	1	6								*	Iran: Qūchān	伊朗:古昌	37.3	58.3	15	6.3	Muk	7	4000	4				3				
1872	1	10				1			0	* NOAA	Peru: Arequipa	秘鲁:阿雷基帕	-16.4	-71.5		6.5	Ms											
1872	1	26	12	30		3			1.5	* Nakamura, Maso, Bautista, NOAA	Philippines: Santa Cruz, Near Coast of W.	菲律宾:圣克鲁斯西部近海	15.8	119.45		6.8	Ms	7						1				
1872	1	27	8	30						Maso, Song	Philippines: Santa Cruz, Near Coast of W.	菲律宾:圣克鲁斯西部近海	15.8	119.45		5	Mk	6										
1872	1	27				4				Japan, NOAA, Song	Japan: Fukushima	日本:福岛	37.3	139.8		7	Mk		1	1								
1872	1	28	7							*	Azerbaijan: Shemakha (Semacha)	阿塞拜疆:舍马罕	40.6	48.7	7	5.7	Ms	10						3				
1872	1	29	11							GSHAP	Azerbaijan: Shemakha (Semacha)	阿塞拜疆:舍马罕	40.6	48.9	12	4.8	Ms	6.5										
1872	2	11	20							* GSHAP	Greece: Thesprotia, N.	希腊:塞斯普罗蒂亚北部	39.8	20.3		6.1	Ms	10		2				3				
1872	2	28	7							* *	Azerbaijan: Samaxi	阿塞拜疆:沙马基区	40.6	48.6	7	5.7	Ms		118	3				4				
1872	3	14	8	20		4	3	1.6	1	* Usami, NOAA	Japan: Hamada	日本:岛根滨田	34.9	132		7.4	Ms	9	804	3				4	5796	4		
1872	3	16								Japan, Song	Japan: Fukuoka	日本:福冈	33.4	130.6		6.8	Mk									3		
1872	3	23	21	41						USGS	US: Nevada, Imlay, SE.	美国:内华达州伊姆莱东南	40	-117.5		5.5	Ms	6										

时间 年	月	日	时	分	秒	海啸 源	浪高	级 I	级 S	资料来源	震中 地名(英文)	地名(中文)	纬度(°)	经度(°)	深度	震级	标度	烈度	死亡人数 数量/人	级别	受伤人数 数量/人	级别	经济损失 数量/$ Mill	级别	房屋毁坏 数量/间	级别	房屋受损 数量/间	级别
Date Year	Mo	Dy	Hr	Mn	Sec	Tsunami Sr	Wh	mI	mS	Information	Earthquake Epicenter Name(English)	Name(Chinese)	Latitude	Longitude	Depth	Mag	Scale	MMI	Deaths Num	Dd	Injuries Num	Dd	Damage $ Mill	De	Houses Destroyed Num	Dh	Houses Damaged Num	Dh
1872	3	26	10	30		4				* CGS	US:California, Owens Valley	美国:加利福尼亚州欧文斯谷	36.7	−118.1		7.8	Mw	10	27	1	56	2	0.25	1	52	2		
1872	3	26	14	6						CGS, USGS	US:California, Blackrock	美国:加利福尼亚州布莱克罗克	36.9	−118.2		6.8	Ms	5										
1872	3	27								* Song	Mexico:Oaxaca, Mexico City	墨西哥:瓦哈卡,墨西哥城	17	−96.3		6.3	Mk							3				
1872	3	28	13							USGS	US:California, Sierraville	美国:加利福尼亚州谢拉维尔	39.5	−120.4		4.9	Ms	6										
1872	4	3	12	15						CGS, USGS	US:California, Aberdeen	美国:加利福尼亚州阿伯丁	37	−118.2		6.3	Ms	5										
1872	4	3	16	30						GSHAP	Black Sea	黑海	44.9	35.4	10	4.8	Ms	6.5										
1872	4	3								*	Turkey:Hatay; Syria:Aleppo	土耳其:哈塔伊;叙利亚:阿勒颇	36.2	36.2		7.5	Ms	10	1800	4				3		3		3
1872	4	11	19							CGS, USGS	US:California, Chalfant Valley	美国:加利福尼亚州夏芬谷	37.5	−118.5		6.8	Ms	9										
1872	4	14	23							*	Ghana:Accra	加纳:阿克拉	5.5	−0.4		4.9	Muk	7						2				
1872	4	18	12							USGS, Song	US:California, Lone Pine	美国:加利福尼亚州隆派恩	36.5	−117.8		5.5	Mk	6										
1872	4	22	3							USGS, Song	Hawaiian Islands	夏威夷群岛	19.25	−155.5		5	Mk	5										
1872	5	3	1							CGS, USGS	US:California, Holtville, E.	美国:加利福尼亚州霍尔特维尔东部	33	−115		5.8	Ms	6										
1872	5	17	21							USGS, Song	US:California, Owens Valley	美国:加利福尼亚州欧文斯谷	36.6	−118.1		5.5	Mk	6										
1872	6									* Iran	Iran: Hamadan	伊朗:哈马丹	34.7	47.7		6.1	Ms							3				
1872	7	22	14	50						Maso, Song	Philippines:Libmanan	菲律宾:利马南	13.6	123.21		5	Mk	6										
1872	8	23	18	6		4	1.3	1.6	0.5	* NOAA, Song	Aleutian Islands	阿留申群岛	52.2	−168.5		7	Mk											
1872	8	24	13							Maso, Song	Philippines:Mansalay	菲律宾:曼萨莱	12.6	121.4		5	Mk	6										
1872	9	5	19							Bautista, Maso	Philippines:Laoang	菲律宾:拉旺	12.9	124.7		6.2	Muk	6										
1872	9	10	12	20						Maso, Song	Philippines:Laoang	菲律宾:拉旺	12.9	124.7		5	Mk	6										
1872	9	16								* Song	Iran:Kermanshah	伊朗:克尔曼沙赫	34.8	47.6		6.3	Mk							3				
1872	11	18				2	0.5			* NOAA, Song	US:New Hampshire, Concord	美国:新汉普郡州康科德	43.2	−71.53		7.5	Mk											
1872	12	10	23	30						USGS	US:Montana, Sheridan	美国:蒙大纳州谢立丹	46.4	−112.5		5	Ms	6										
1872	12	15	5	40						USGS	US:Washington, Manson	美国:华盛顿州曼森	47.9	−120.3		7	Ms	9										
1872	12	26	13	40						*	Ukraine:Carpathians, Khust	乌克兰:喀尔巴阡山脉,库斯特	48.4	23.3	5	4.3	Muk	7						2				
1872	12	29	3	48						* Bautista, Maso	Philippines:Mariveles	菲律宾:马里韦莱斯	14.4	120.35		6.4	Ms	8						2				
1872						4				* NOAA, Song	Iceland:Hella	冰岛:海德拉	64	−19.683		7	Mk											
1873	1	16	15	45						Bautista, Maso	Philippines:Cabanatuan, SE.	菲律宾:甲万那端东南	15.05	121.5		5.6	Muk	6										
1873	1	20								* * Song	Italy:Marino	意大利:马里诺	41.8	12.7		6.5	Mk	12										

时间 年 Date Year	月 Mo	日 Dy	时 Hr	分 Mn	秒 Sec	海啸 源 Tsunami Sr	浪高 Wh	级 I mI	级 S mS	资料来源 Information	震中 地名(英文) Earthquake Epicenter Name(English)	地名(中文) Name(Chinese)	纬度(°) Latitude	经度(°) Longitude	深度 Depth	震级 Mag	标度 Scale	烈度 MMI	死亡人数 数量/人 Deaths Num	级别 Dd	受伤人数 数量/人 Injuries Num	级别 Dd	经济损失 数量/$ Mill Damage $ Mill	级别 De	房屋毁坏 数量/间 Houses Destroyed Num	级别 Dh	房屋受损 数量/间 Houses Damaged Num	级别 Dh
1873	1	31	23	15						* Song	Greece:Samos Island	希腊:萨摩斯岛	37.8	27		6.1	Mk	9		2								
1873	2	21	2							GSHAP	Russia:Murmansk,Murmansk	俄罗斯:摩尔曼斯克州摩尔曼斯克	68.7	33.3	20	5	Ms	6										
1873	3	4								* Song	El Salvador:San Vicente	萨尔瓦多:圣维森特	13.7	-88.7		7.1	Mk		800	3				4		3		
1873	3	18	5							Maso,Song	Philippines:Mindanao Island	菲律宾:棉兰老岛	11.01	126		6.1	Mk	8										
1873	3	30	17	58						Bautista,Maso	Philippines:Laoag	菲律宾:佬沃	18.1	120.55		5	Muk	7										
1873	4	11								* Song	El Salvador:Salvador,San Vicente	萨尔瓦多:萨尔瓦多,圣维森特	13.6	-89		6.2	Mk		300	3								
1873	6	11	15	15						Bautista,Maso	Philippines:Mindoro Island	菲律宾:民都洛岛	13.2	121.2		4.8	Muk	6										
1873	6	29	3	58						* Italy,GSHAP	Italy:Belluno	意大利:贝卢诺	46.1	12.3		6	Ms	10	55	2				2				
1873	7	7	6	26		4				* Song	Chile:Petorca	智利:佩托尔卡	-32.3	-71.16		7.7	Mk			1				3		3		
1873	7	12	6	6						* Italy	Italy:Alvito	意大利:阿尔维托	41.68	13.78		5.4	Ms	10						3		3		
1873	7	19								* Song	France:Chateauneuf – Du – Rhone,Donzere	法国:罗纳新堡,栋泽尔	44.5	4.7		6.1	Mk	8						2				
1873	7	23	0	25						* * Song	Italy:Sora	意大利:索拉	41.7	13.7		6.5	Mk	12										
1873	7	28								Japan,Song	Japan:Kumamoto	日本:熊本	32.8	130.8		6.6	Mk							1				
1873	10	13				1				* NOAA,Song	Panama:Panama City	巴拿马:巴拿马城	8.96	-79.53		7	Mk											
1873	10	25	22	38		4				* GSHAP,Song	Greece:Megara	希腊:墨伽拉	38	23.3		6.6	Mk	8						2		2		
1873	11	14	9	30						Bautista,Maso	Philippines:Lopez	菲律宾:洛佩斯	13.6	122.25		6.5	Muk	8										
1873	11	19				2	2.8	1.5	2	* NOAA,Song	Chile:Antofagasta,C.	智利:安托法加斯塔中部	-23.6	-70.4		7.5	Mk											
1873	11	23	5	9		3	3.1			* CGS,USGS,NOAA	US:California,Smith River	美国:加利福尼亚州史密斯里弗	42	-124		6.9	Ms	8						1				
1873										China	China:Taiwan,Tainan	中国:台湾台南	23	120.2		5.5	Ms	7										
1873						3		1	2	* NOAA	Papua New Guinea:Madang	巴布亚新几内亚:马当	-5.5	146		8	Ms											
1874	1	16	20							Bautista,Maso	Philippines:Aroroy	菲律宾:阿罗罗伊	12.5	123.5		5.3	Muk	6										
1874	1	18	15							GSHAP	Kyrgyzstan:Issyk – Kul,N.	吉尔吉斯斯坦:伊塞克湖州北部	42.9	77.4	20	5.9	Ms	7										
1874	2	6	13	35						* Song	Venezuela:La Guaira (La Guaayra)	委内瑞拉:拉瓜伊拉	10.4	-66.6		5.9	Mk							2				
1874	2	6	14	5						GSHAP,Song	Venezuela:Caracas	委内瑞拉:加拉加斯	10.64	-66.92		5	Mk	6										
1874	2	28								Usami,Japan	Japan:Hokkaido	日本:北海道	43.9	141.6		6.4	Ms	8								1		
1874	3	11				2				* NOAA,Song	Virgin Islands:Charlotte Amalie	维尔京群岛:夏洛特阿马利亚	18.1	-65.1		7	Mk											
1874	3	16								* Song	Mexico:Morelos,Guerrero	墨西哥:莫雷洛斯,格雷罗	18.2	-100.2		6.3	Mk							3				
1874	4	13	22	20						Bautista,Maso	Philippines:Laoag	菲律宾:佬沃	18.1	120.45		5.1	Muk	6										

时间 Date 年 Year	月 Mo	日 Dy	时 Hr	分 Mn	秒 Sec	海啸 Tsunami 源 Sr	浪高 Wh	级 I mI	级 S mS	资料来源 Information	震中 Earthquake Epicenter 地名(英文) Name(English)	地名(中文) Name(Chinese)	纬度(°) Latitude	经度(°) Longitude	深度 Depth	震级 Mag	标度 Scale	烈度 MMI	死亡人数 Deaths 数量/人 Num	级别 Dd	受伤人数 Injuries 数量/人 Num	级别 Dd	经济损失 Damage 数量/$ Mill	级别 De	房屋毁坏 Houses Destroyed 数量/间 Num	级别 Dh	房屋受损 Houses Damaged 数量/间 Num	级别 Dh
1874	5	3	7							* GSHAP	Turkey: Malatya	土耳其:马拉蒂亚	38.8	38.8	14	7.1	Muk	10						2				
1874	5	15	22	15						USGS, Song	Hawaiian Islands	夏威夷群岛	19.25	-155		5	Mk	5										
1874	5					1				* NOAA, Song	Indonesia: Molucca Sea	印度尼西亚:马鲁古海	1	126.25		7	Mk											
1874	5					2				* NOAA, Song	Bangladesh: Satkhira	孟加拉:萨德基拉	22	89		7.9	Mk		2000	4								
1874	7	8	2	32						Bautista, Maso	Philippines: Santiago, SE.	菲律宾:圣地亚哥东南	16.1	122.25		6.1	Muk	6										
1874	7									China	China: Guangdong, Haifeng	中国:广东海丰	23	115.3		4.75	Ms	6										
1874	8	3								* Song	Philippines: Suyo	菲律宾:苏约	17	120.6		5.9	Mk							2				
1874	8	18	2	30						*	Venezuela: Pilar	委内瑞拉:比拉尔	10.5	-63.1	16	5.9	Muk	7						2				
1874	8	23	22	50						GSHAP	Russia: Vladikavkaz	俄罗斯:符拉迪克奥克兹	43.2	44.8	6	4.5	Ms	7										
1874	8	24	22	15						* Bautista, Maso	Philippines: Mindanao, Zamboanga	菲律宾:棉兰老岛,三宝颜	7.2	121.5		6.4	Ms	8						2				
1874	9	3	3	2						* Song	Guatemala: Antigua, Chimaltenango	危地马拉:安地瓜,奇马尔特南戈	14.5	-90.7		6.2	Mk		300	3								
1874	9	21	1	30						GSHAP	Kazakhstan: Gerasimovka	哈萨克斯坦:格拉西莫夫卡	45.6	80.6	15	4.5	Ms	5										
1874	10	14	23							GSHAP	Russia: Karachaevo - Cherkess, Kurdzhinovo	俄罗斯:卡拉恰伊 - 切尔克斯州库尔吉诺沃	44.1	41.3	12	4.7	Ms	6.5										
1874	10	16	2	9						Bautista, Maso	Philippines: San Fernando, E.	菲律宾:圣费尔南多东部	15.4	121.4		5.9	Muk	7										
1874	10	18								* Afghan	Afghan: Charikar	阿富汗:恰里卡尔	35	69		7	Ms			3				3				
1874	10	30	12	30						GSHAP	Brasil: Sao Paulo	巴西:圣保罗	-23.5	-47.5		3.6	Ms	5										
1874	12	29	16	30						USGS, Song	Hawaiian Islands	夏威夷群岛	19.25	-155		5	Mk	5										
1875	1	24	12							CGS, USGS	US: California, Milford	美国:加利福尼亚州米尔福德	40.2	-120.5		6.2	Ms	6										
1875	2	24				3				* NOAA, Song	Mexico: Jalisco	墨西哥:哈利斯科	20	-105		7	Mk											
1875	3	3	22	48						GSHAP	Turkey: Elazig	土耳其:埃拉泽	38.5	39.5	35	6.7	Ms	7.5										
1875	3	8	17	22						Bautista, Maso	Philippines: Manabo	菲律宾:马纳博	17	120.5		5.6	Muk	7										
1875	3	18	18	0	51	4			4	NOAA, Song	Italy: Adriatic Sea	意大利:亚得里亚海	44.2	12.4		6.7	Mk											
1875	3	28				4	4	2	2.5	* NOAA, Song	New Caledonia: Loyalty Islands, Lifou Island	新喀里多尼亚:罗亚尔特群岛,利富岛	-21	167		7.7	Mk			3				3		3		
1875	4	2	2							USGS, Song	US: Nevada, Eureka	美国:内华达州尤里卡	39.5	-115.8		5.5	Mk	6										
1875	4	24								* Song	Greece: Kyparissia (Messinia)	希腊:麦锡尼	37.3	21.8		6	Mk	7		2								
1875	5	3								* GSHAP	Turkey: Evciler, Dinar	土耳其:艾布西雷尔,第纳尔	38.1	30.2		7.3	Ms	10	1300	4				3	1000	3	1000	3
1875	5	10				2			0.5	* NOAA	Vanuatu Islands	瓦努阿图群岛	-18.5	168		7	Ms											
1875	5	11								* GSHAP	Turkey: Usak	土耳其:乌沙克	38.7	29.4	40	7	Muk	8	.	2								
1875	5	18	16	25						*	Colombia: Cucuta, San Cayetano	哥伦比亚:库库塔,圣卡耶塔诺	7.9	-72.5	20	7.5	Muk	10	10000	5				3				
1875	5	19	3	30						* Bautista, Maso	Philippines: Camarines	菲律宾:馬利納	13.6	123.05		6.1	Ms	8						2				

年 Year	月 Mo	日 Dy	时 Hr	分 Mn	秒 Sec	海啸 Tsunami 源 Sr	浪高 Wh	级 I mI	级 S mS	资料来源 Information	震中 Earthquake Epicenter 地名(英文) Name(English)	地名(中文) Name(Chinese)	纬度(°) Latitude	经度(°) Longitude	深度 Depth	震级 Mag	标度 Scale	烈度 MMI	死亡人数 Deaths 数量/人 Num	级别 Dd	受伤人数 Injuries 数量/人 Num	级别 Dd	经济损失 Damage 数量/$ Mill $ Mill	级别 De	房屋毁坏 Houses Destroyed 数量/间 Num	级别 Dh	房屋受损 Houses Damaged 数量/间 Num	级别 Dh
1875	6	8								China	China:Guangxi,Leye,N.	中国:广西乐业北部	25	106.4		6.5	Ms			3						3		
1875	6	18	12	43						USGS	US:Ohio,Urbana	美国:俄亥俄州厄巴纳	40.2	-84		4.7	Ms	7										
1875	7	7								* Song	Turkey:Soke, Aydin	土耳其:瑟凯,艾登	37.7	27		7.3	Mk	10						2	150	3		
1875	7	25	4	28						*	Ukraine:Crimea, Kherson	乌克兰:克里米亚,赫尔松	44.5	33.4	9	5.2	Muk	8						2				
1875	8	7	16							GSHAP	Azerbaijan:Shemakha (Semacha)	阿塞拜疆:萨马基	40.7	48.7	8	5.4	Ms	8										
1875	8	8	11							GSHAP	Black Sea	黑海	45	35.5	12	4.9	Ms	6.5										
1875	8	17	15	45						GSHAP	Ukraine:L'Viv	乌克兰:利沃夫	50.3	24.2	19	5.3	Ms	6										
1875	9	30	12	30						CGS,USGS	US:California,Pine Hills	美国:加利福尼亚州派恩高地	40.7	-124		5.9	Ms	7										
1875	10	15	15							* Song	Philippines:Benguet, La Trinidad	菲律宾:本格特,特立尼达拉	16.3	120.3		5.9	Mk							2				
1875	10	25								* Song	Indonesia:Java Island,Kuningan	印度尼西亚:爪哇岛,库宁	-6.9	108.3		6.1	Mk	8	7	1				2				
1875	10									* Song	Turkey:Canakkale	土耳其:恰纳卡莱	40.2	26.4		7.3	Mk	10										
1875	11	1	10							GSHAP	Turkey:Mus	土耳其:穆什	38.8	41.4	14	6.1	Ms	8.5										
1875	11	2	2	55						USGS	US:Georgia,Lincolnton	美国:佐治亚州林肯顿	33.8	-82.5		4.3	Ms	6										
1875	11	2								*	Eritrea: Kelun	厄立特里亚:克伦	16	38.5		6.2	Muk			2				3				
1875	11	23	22							USGS,Song	Hawaiian Islands	夏威夷群岛	19.25	-155		5	Mk	5										
1875	12	6	2	30						GSHAP,Song	Peru:Cuzco	秘鲁:库斯科	-13.4	-72.7	20	5	Mk	6										
1875	12	23	4	45						USGS	US:Virginia,Goochland	美国:弗吉尼亚州古奇兰	37.8	-78		4.8	Ms	7										
1875	12									* Song	Puerto Rico:Arecibo	波多黎各:阿雷西波	18.3	-66.4		5.9	Mk							2				
1875										China	China:Liaoning,Kaiyuan,N.	中国:辽宁开原北	42.6	124		4.75	Ms	6										
1875										China	China:Yunnan,Zhaotong	中国:云南昭通	27.3	103.7		5	Ms	6										
1875										GSHAP	Russia:Sakha,SW.	俄罗斯:萨哈共和国西南	57.01	121.28	15	5.9	Ms	8.5										
1875										GSHAP	Russia:Chita,Novaya Chara	俄罗斯:赤塔州诺瓦亚恰拉村镇	56.56	118.29	15	6	Ms	8.5										
1875										GSHAP	Russia:Chita,Chapo - Ologo	俄罗斯:赤塔州恰波奥洛戈镇	57.28	119.3	15	6.5	Ms	9										
1875										GSHAP	Russia:Buryatiya,Yanchukan	俄罗斯:布里亚特州扬丘坎镇	56.17	112.59	15	6.7	Ms	9										
1875						2				NOAA,Song	East Caroline Basin	东加罗林海盆	0	150		7	Mk											
1876	2	11	21							GSHAP,Song	Chile:Illapel	智利:伊亚佩尔	-31.62	-71.18		6	Mk	8										
1876	3	22								USGS,Song	US:Utah, Huntington	美国:犹他州亨廷顿	39.5	-111.6		5.5	Mk	6										
1876	4	7	8	30						GSHAP	Caspian Sea	里海	40.1	53.1	15	5.2	Ms	7										
1876	5	13	6							* Song	Turkey:Suhut	土耳其:舒胡特	38.8	30.5		7.3	Mk	10										

年 Year	月 Mo	日 Dy	时 Hr	分 Mn	秒 Sec	海啸 Tsunami 源 Sr	浪高 Wh	级 I mI	级 S mS	资料来源 Information	震中 Earthquake Epicenter 地名(英文) Name(English)	地名(中文) Name(Chinese)	纬度(°) Latitude	经度(°) Longitude	深度 Depth	震级 Mag	标度 Scale	烈度 MMI	死亡人数 Deaths 数量/人 Num	级别 Dd	受伤人数 Injuries 数量/人 Num	级别 Dd	经济损失 Damage 数量/$ Mill	级别 De	房屋毁坏 Houses Destroyed 数量/间 Num	级别 Dh	房屋受损 Houses Damaged 数量/间 Num	级别 Dh
1876	5	14	1							GSHAP	Russia:Dagestan, Makhachkala	俄罗斯:达吉斯坦共和国马哈奇卡拉	42.7	47	15	4.8	Ms	6										
1876	5	28				3	0.3		-1	*NOAA	Indonesia:Ceram Sea	印度尼西亚:塞兰海	-3	127.2	50	6.8	Ms							1				3
1876	5	29	18	55						USGS	US:California, Santa Rosa	美国:加利福尼亚州圣罗莎	38.4	-122.9		4.2	Ms	6										
1876	8	5								*China	China:Yunnan, Yongping	中国:云南永平	25.5	99.5		6	Ms	8			60	2		2		3		
1876	9	25	6	15						USGS	US:Illinois, Mt Carmel	美国:伊利诺斯州芒特卡梅尔	38.5	-87.8		4.8	Ms	7										
1876	9									China	China:Yunnan, Dali	中国:云南大理	25.7	100.2		5	Ms	6										
1876	10	26	14							GSHAP, Song	Chile:Antofagasta, N.	智利:安托法加斯塔北部	-22.07	-69.63		6	Mk	8										
1876										**India	India:Andaman Islands	印度:安达曼群岛	12	92.8		8.5	Ms		215000	5			0.25	1				
1877	5	8	4	8						GSHAP, Song	Peru:Arequipa	秘鲁:阿雷基帕	-16.4	-71.56		4.5	Mk	5										
1877	5	10	0	59		4	24	4.4	3.5	*Chile, NOAA	Chile:Huara	智利:瓦拉	-19.6	-70.2	40	8.5	Muk	11	2541	4				3		3		
1877	5	10	1	28						GSHAP, Song	Peru:Tacna, Near Coast	秘鲁:塔克纳近海	-18.33	-71.183	40	6	Mk	7										
1877	5	14				2				*NOAA, Song	Peru:Lima	秘鲁:利马	-12.07	-77.15		7	Mk											
1877	5	15				2				*NOAA, Song	Chile:Arica	智利:阿里卡	-18.5	-70.3		7	Mk											
1877	5	15				2				*NOAA, Song	Peru:Lima	秘鲁:利马	-12.07	-77.15		7	Mk											
1877	5	31	14	50						USGS	Hawaiian Islands	夏威夷群岛	19.25	-155		6.2	Ms	6										
1877	6	2	15	6						Bautista, Maso	Philippines:Tarlac	菲律宾:打拉	15.55	120.45		5.8	Muk	6										
1877	6	15				1				*NOAA, Song	Chile:Tarapaca, S.	智利:塔拉帕卡南部	-20.9	-70.1		7	Mk											
1877	6	23	23							Maso, Song	Philippines:Mindoro Island	菲律宾:民都洛岛	13.81	121		5.5	Mk	7										
1877	7	4	17	7						Bautista, Maso	Philippines:Basud	菲律宾:巴苏德	14.1	123.1		6.6	Muk	7										
1877	7	23	8	20						Bautista, Maso	Philippines:Samar Island	菲律宾:萨马岛	11.1	124.65		5.5	Muk	7										
1877	7	27	3	40						GSHAP, Song	Chile:Coquimbo	智利:科金博	-29.95	-71.35		6	Mk	8										
1877	8	10	12	20						GSHAP, Song	Peru:Arequipa	秘鲁:阿雷基帕	-16.4	-71.56		4.5	Mk	5										
1877	8	13	17	50						GSHAP	Russia:Sakha, Polyarnik	俄罗斯:萨哈共和国波利亚尔尼克	65.8	137	20	5	Ms	6										
1877	8	23				3	1		0.5	*NOAA, Song	Chile:Iquique	智利:伊基克	-20.2	-70.1		7	Mk											
1877	9	2				1			0.5	**NOAA, Song	Chile:Ancud	智利:安库德	-41.8	-74		7	Mk											
1877	9	8	5	5						GSHAP, Song	Peru:Lima	秘鲁:利马	-12.08	-77		4.5	Mk	5										
1877	10	4	2	50						GSHAP, Song	Peru:Lima	秘鲁:利马	-12.08	-77		4.5	Mk	5										
1877	10	9				1			0.5	*NOAA, Song	Peru:Ica	秘鲁:伊卡	-14.2	-75.7		7	Mk											
1877	10	12	21	53						USGS, Song	US:Oregon, Portland	美国:俄勒冈州波特兰	45.75	-122.5		5.7	Mk	7										
1877	10									China	China:Yunnan, Yuanmou, N.	中国:云南元谋北	26	101.9		5	Ms	6										
1877	11	4	6	56						USGS	US:New York, Lake Clear	美国:纽约州莱克克利尔	44.5	-74		4.9	Ms	7										
1877	11	15	17	45						USGS	US:Nebraska, Seward	美国:奈伯拉斯卡州西沃德	41	-97		5.1	Ms	7										

时间						海啸				资料来源	震中				深度	震级	标度	烈度	死亡人数		受伤人数		经济损失		房屋毁坏		房屋受损	
年	月	日	时	分	秒	源	浪高	级 I	级 S		地名(英文)	地名(中文)	纬度(°)	经度(°)					数量/人	级别	数量/人	级别	数量/$ Mill	级别	数量/间	级别	数量/间	级别
Date						Tsunami				Information	Earthquake Epicenter				Depth	Mag	Scale	MMI	Deaths		Injuries		Damage		Houses Destroyed		Houses Damaged	
Year	Mo	Dy	Hr	Mn	Sec	Sr	Wh	mI	mS		Name(English)	Name(Chinese)	Latitude	Longitude					Num	Dd	Num	Dd	$ Mill	De	Num	Dh	Num	Dh
1877	11	26	21	30						GSHAP, Song	Peru: Lima	秘鲁:利马	-12.08	-77		4.5	Mk	5										
1877	11	26								GSHAP, Song	Peru: Tarapoto	秘鲁:塔拉波托	-6	-77.6	20	5	Mk	6										
1878	1	10				5	12	3.6	3	* NOAA	Vanuatu Islands	瓦努阿图群岛	-19	168.5		7.5	Ms							1				
1878	1	20				3	3.6	1.6	2	* NOAA, Song	Alaska: Unimak Island	阿拉斯加:乌尼马克岛	53.6	-166.4		7.5	Mk											
1878	1	23	12	5		1				* NOAA	Chile: Huara, Near Coast	智利:瓦拉近海	-19.92	-70.335	40	7.9	Ms	8		1				3		3		
1878	1	23								GSHAP, Song	Chile: Iquique, Off Coast	智利:伊基克沿海	-20.05	-77	40	6	Mk	7										
1878	1	27				3			1.5	NOAA, Song	Peru: Lima	秘鲁:利马	-12	-77		7	Mk		5	1								
1878	1	28				1			1.5	NOAA, Song	Chile: Iquique, N.	智利:伊基克北部	-19.6	-70.2		7	Mk											
1878	2	3				1				NOAA, Song	Chile: Iquique, N.	智利:伊基克北部	-19.6	-70.2		7	Mk											
1878	2	4				1				* NOAA, Song	Peru: Lima	秘鲁:利马	-12	-77		7	Mk											
1878	2	4				5	4	2	2	* NOAA, Song	Papua New Guinea: East New Britain	巴布亚新几内亚:东新不列颠	-4.25	152.25		7.5	Mk		1	1								
1878	2	5	16	20						USGS, Song	US: New York, Bronx	美国:纽约州布朗克斯	40.8	-73.9		5.5	Mk	6										
1878	2	9	19	30						* Song	Colombia: Manizales	哥伦比亚:马尼萨莱斯	5.1	-75.5		6.3	Mk	6						3				
1878	2	11				3		1	1.5	* NOAA	Vanuatu Islands	瓦努阿图群岛	-19	168.5		8	Ms											
1878	2	14				2		-05	0	* NOAA, Song	Chile: Concepcion	智利:康塞普西翁	-36.8	-73		7	Mk											
1878	3	12	10							USGS	US: Kentucky, Arlington	美国:肯塔基州阿灵顿	36.8	-89.1		4.2	Ms	6										
1878	3	12				2		-05	0	* NOAA, Song	Chile: Iquique	智利:伊基克	-20.2	-70.1		7	Mk											
1878	3	16	3							GSHAP, Song	Peru: Lima, Near Coast	秘鲁:利马近海	-12.4	-77		4.5	Mk	5										
1878	3	22								* Song	Mexico: Jalisco	墨西哥:哈利斯科	20.3	-103.4		6.3	Mk							3				
1878	3	28	17							GSHAP	China: Xinjiang, Qoqek	中国:新疆塔城	46.7	82.8	15	4.7	Ms	6										
1878	4	4	21	56						GSHAP, Song	Peru: Lima	秘鲁:利马	-12.08	-77		4.5	Mk	5										
1878	4	5	18	35						GSHAP, Song	Peru: Arequipa	秘鲁:阿雷基帕	-16.4	-71.56		5	Mk	6										
1878	4	12	0	41						*	Venezuela: Cua, Charallave, San Diego	委内瑞拉:库阿,加拉加斯	10.3	-66.8	13	5.9	Ms	9	400	3				3				
1878	4	12				2			0.5	* NOAA, Song	Chile: Iquique	智利:伊基克	-20.2	-70.1		7	Mk											
1878	4	15				1				NOAA, Song	Turkey: Marmara Sea	土耳其:马尔马拉海	40.5	28.7		6.6	Mk											
1878	4	19	7			3				* NOAA	Turkey: Istanbul	土耳其:伊斯坦布尔	40.8	29		6.7	Muk	10	40	1				2				
1878	4	29	0	30						* Song	Venezuela: Ocumare Del Tuy	委内瑞拉:奥库马雷	10.7	-66.5		5.9	Mk							2				
1878	5	4								GSHAP, Turkey	Russia: Dagestan, Makhachkala	俄罗斯:达吉斯坦共和国马哈奇卡拉	41.6	48.1	20	5.7	Ms	7										
1878	5	9	4	25						CGS, USGS	US: California, North Coast	美国:加利福尼亚州北部近海	40.4	-125.2		7	Ms	7										
1878	5	16	1	36						GSHAP, Song	Peru: Tacna	秘鲁:塔克纳	-18	-70.24		4.5	Mk	5										
1878	5	21								*	US: California, Victorville	美国:加利福尼亚州维克托维尔	34.1	-117.3		4.3	Muk							3				
1878	6	2								GSHAP, Song	Peru: Arequipa	秘鲁:阿雷基帕	-16.4	-71.56		4.5	Mk	5										
1878	6	12	7	20						USGS, Song	US: California, Long Beach	美国:加利福尼亚州长滩	34	-118		5.5	Mk	6										

年 Year	月 Mo	日 Dy	时 Hr	分 Mn	秒 Sec	海啸 Tsunami 源 Sr	浪高 Wh	级 I mI	级 S mS	资料来源 Information	震中 Earthquake Epicenter 地名(英文) Name(English)	地名(中文) Name(Chinese)	纬度(°) Latitude	经度(°) Longitude	深度 Depth	震级 Mag	标度 Scale	烈度 MMI	死亡人数 Deaths 数量/人 Num	级别 Dd	受伤人数 Injuries 数量/人 Num	级别 Dd	经济损失 Damage 数量/$ Mill	级别 De	房屋毁坏 Houses Destroyed 数量/间 Num	级别 Dh	房屋受损 Houses Damaged 数量/间 Num	级别 Dh
1878	6	12				2		-0.5	0	* NOAA, Song	Chile: Antofagasta, C.	智利:安托法加斯塔中部	-23.7	-70.4		7	Mk											
1878	6	14								USGS, Song	US: New Mexcico, Cimarron	美国:新墨西哥州锡马龙	36.5	-104.9		5.5	Mk	6										
1878	6	30				2				NOAA, Song	Chile: Iquique, N.	智利:伊基克北部	-19.6	-70.2		7	Mk											
1878	8	7								* China	China: Yunnan, Ninglang	中国:云南宁蒗	27.3	100.9		5.5	Ms	7	70	2				3		3		
1878	8	13	4	14						Bautista, Maso	Philippines: Olongapo, Near Coast of W.	菲律宾:奥隆阿波西部近海	14.6	119.8		6.2	Muk	6										
1878	8	29				5		1	1.5	* NOAA, USGS, Song	Alaska: Unimak Island	阿拉斯加:乌尼马克岛	53.6	-166.4		7.3	Mk	7										
1878	8					1				* NOAA, Song	Vanuatu Islands	瓦努阿图群岛	-19	168.5		7	Mk											
1878	9	16	4	15						* Bautista, Maso	Philippines: Samal	菲律宾:萨马尔	6.95	125.75		6.5	Ms	7						2				
1878	9	30				1			0.5	NOAA, Song	Chile: Calama, N.	智利:卡拉马北部	-21.7	-69.5		7	Mk											
1878	10	2								* Song	El Salvador: Jucuapa	萨尔瓦多:胡夸帕	13.5	-88.4		6.3	Mk			3				3		3		
1878	10	4	12	30						GSHAP	Colombia: Cauca	哥伦比亚:考卡	2.5	-76.5		5	Ms	7										
1878	10	11				1				NOAA, Song	Russia: Sakhalin Island	俄罗斯:库页岛(萨哈林岛)	47.116	141.798		7	Mk											
1878	11	8	20	30						* GSHAP	Croatia: Varazdin	克罗地亚:瓦拉日丁	46.2	16.8		5.7	Ms	10										
1878	11	19	5	52						USGS	US: Arkansas, Harrisburg	美国:阿肯色州哈里斯堡	35.5	-90.7		4.9	Ms	6										
1878	11	23				2			0.5	NOAA, Song	Chile: Off Coast of C.	智利:中部沿海	-32.5	-72.5		7	Mk											
1878	12	17	23	30						USGS, Song	US: Arizona, Yuma	美国:亚利桑那州尤马	32.7	-114.6		5.5	Mk	6										
1878	12									China	China: Xizang (Tibet), Zayu	中国:西藏察隅	28.5	97.5		6.5	Ms	8										
1879	1	7	23							GSHAP	Russia: Vladikavkaz	俄罗斯:符拉迪克奥克兹	43.1	44.1	15	4.6	Ms	6										
1879	1	13	4	45						USGS, Song	US: Florida, Citra	美国:佛罗里达州锡特拉	29.5	-82		5.5	Mk	6										
1879	2	4	8	8						USGS, Song	US: California, Visalia	美国:加利福尼亚州维塞利亚	36.3	-119.3		5.5	Mk	6										
1879	2	11	6							*	Cote D'Ivoire: Abidjan	科特迪瓦:阿比让	6.5	-3.3		5.7	Muk	8						2				
1879	3	7	23	15						* GSHAP, Song	Venezuela: San Juan De Los Morro	委内瑞拉:圣胡安－德洛斯莫罗斯	9.5	-67.2		5.9	Mk	6						2				
1879	3	22								*	Iran: Tabriz	伊朗:大不里士	37.8	47.9		6.7	Ms	9	2000	4				3		4		
1879	3	27	12							GSHAP	Russia: Krasnoyarsk, S.	俄罗斯:克拉斯罗亚尔斯克南部	52.1	92.5	18	5.6	Ms	7										
1879	4	2								*	Iran: Bojnurd	伊朗:博季努尔德	37.5	57.4	15	6.7	Muk	9	700	3				3				
1879	5	1								GSHAP	Brasil: Cuiabá	巴西:库亚巴	-15.6	-56.1		4.3	Ms	5										
1879	5	16	8							USGS, Song	Hawaiian Islands	夏威夷群岛	19.25	-155		5	Mk	5										
1879	5	18	23							GSHAP	Ukraine: Carpathians, Khust	乌克兰:喀尔巴阡山脉,库斯特	48	23.3	15	4.6	Ms	5.5										

时间						海啸				资料来源	震中				深度	震级	标度	烈度	死亡人数		受伤人数		经济损失		房屋毁坏		房屋受损	
年	月	日	时	分	秒	源	浪高	级I	级S		地名(英文)	地名(中文)	纬度(°)	经度(°)					数量/人	级别	数量/人	级别	数量/$ Mill	级别	数量/间	级别	数量/间	级别
Date						Tsunami				Information	Earthquake Epicenter				Depth	Mag	Scale	MMI	Deaths		Injuries		Damage		Houses Destroyed		Houses Damaged	
Year	Mo	Dy	Hr	Mn	Sec	Sr	Wh	mI	mS		Name(English)	Name(Chinese)	Latitude	Longitude					Num	Dd	Num	Dd	$ Mill	De	Num	Dh	Num	Dh
1879	6	30	15	5						* Bautista, Maso	Philippines: Mindanao, Surigao	菲律宾:老棉兰岛,苏利高	9.35	125.6		6.9	Ms	10						4				
1879	7	1								* China	China: Gansu, Wudu, S.	中国:甘肃武都南	33.2	104.7		8	Ms	11	22000	5		4		4		4		
1879	7	11	18			3				* NOAA	Egypt: Gulf of Suez	埃及:苏伊士海湾	29	33		5.9	Ms											
1879	7	17								* Song	Italy: Sicilia Island	意大利:西西里岛	37.5	15		6	Mk	10	10	1				2				
1879	7	24	20	25						GSHAP	Brasil: Natal	巴西:纳塔耳	-5.77	-35.21		3.4	Ms	5										
1879	8	8				2			0.5	NOAA, Song	Chile: Off Coast of C.	智利:中部沿海	-32.5	-72.5		7	Mk											
1879	8	10	21	7		2				* NOAA, Song	US: California, San Fernando	美国:加利福尼亚州圣费尔南多	34.227	-118.433		7	Mk											
1879	8	28	22							Maso, Song	Philippines: Mindanao Island	菲律宾:棉兰老岛	7.41	124.21		5	Mk	6										
1879	9	28								Maso, Song	Philippines: Mindanao Island	菲律宾:棉兰老岛	7.01	125.5		5	Mk	6										
1879	10	4	3	30						GSHAP, Song	Peru: Arequipa	秘鲁:阿雷基帕	-16.4	-71.56		4.5	Mk	5										
1879	10	9	19	30						GSHAP	Russia: Krasnodar, Krymsk	俄罗斯:克拉斯诺达尔区克雷姆斯克	45.1	37.9	25	6	Ms	7										
1879	10	14	1							Maso, Song	Philippines: Tabuk	菲律宾:塔布克	17.5	121.21		5.5	Mk	7										
1879	10	18	13	28						Bautista, Maso	Philippines: Mindoro Island	菲律宾:民都洛岛	13.8	120.2		5.5	Muk	7										
1879	11	4	19	25						USGS, Song	Hawaiian Islands	夏威夷群岛	19.25	-155		5	Mk	5										
1879	11	23								China	China: Yunnan, Longling	中国:云南龙陵	24.6	98.7		5	Ms	6										
1879	12									China	China: Yunnan, Mile	中国:云南弥勒	24.4	103.4		5.5	Ms	7										
1879	12									* Song	El Salvador: San Salvador, Soyapango	萨尔瓦多:圣萨尔瓦多,索亚潘戈	13.4	-89.1		5.9	Mk							2				
1879										Japan, Song	Japan: Tokyo	日本:东京	35.7	139.8		6.2	Mk	7										
1880	1	23	4							* Song	Cuba: San Cristobal, Candelaria	古巴:圣克里斯托瓦尔,坎德拉里亚	22.4	-83		6.5	Mk	9		2				2				
1880	2	11	20	45						GSHAP, Song	Peru: Lima	秘鲁:利马	-12.08	-77		4.5	Mk	5										
1880	2	21	15	50						Usami	Japan: Yokohama	日本:神奈川横滨	35.4	139.75		5.9	Ms							2		1		
1880	2	27	9	20						Bautista, Maso	Philippines: Tabuk	菲律宾:塔布克	17.05	121.05		5.2	Muk	6										
1880	2	29								China	China: Taiwan, Miaoli	中国:台湾苗栗	24.6	120.8		5.5	Ms	7										
1880	3	28								*	Turkey: Yozgat	土耳其:约兹加特	40.2	35.2		5.5	Ms	9						2	60	2	60	2
1880	4	4								GSHAP	Uzbekistan: Samarqand	乌兹别克斯坦:撒马尔罕	39.4	67.3	15	5.1	Ms	7										
1880	4	26	7	45		1				NOAA, Song	Italy: Sicilia Island	意大利:西西里岛	37.27	14.68		6.6	Mk											
1880	6	22								* China	China: Gansu, Wenxian	中国:甘肃文县	32.9	104.6		5.5	Ms	7	8	1	9	1		2				
1880	6	29								* Song	Turkey: Izmir	土耳其:伊兹密尔	38.6	27.1		7.3	Mk	10						3				
1880	7	14	16	53						* Bautista, Maso	Philippines: Lake Bay	菲律宾:湾状湖	14.9	121.85		6.2	Ms	8						2				
1880	7	17								China	China: Shaanxi, Yongshou	中国:陕西永寿	34.8	108.1		5	Ms	6		3								

年 Year	月 Mo	日 Dy	时 Hr	分 Mn	秒 Sec	源 Sr	浪高 Wh	级 I mI	级 S mS	资料来源 Information	地名(英文) Name(English)	地名(中文) Name(Chinese)	纬度(°) Latitude	经度(°) Longitude	深度 Depth	震级 Mag	标度 Scale	烈度 MMI	死亡人数 Deaths 数量/人 Num	级别 Dd	受伤人数 Injuries 数量/人 Num	级别 Dd	经济损失 Damage 数量/$ Mill	级别 De	房屋毁坏 Houses Destroyed 数量/间 Num	级别 Dh	房屋受损 Houses Damaged 数量/间 Num	级别 Dh
1880	7	18	4	40		4			0	*Nakamura, Maso, Bautista, NOAA	Philippines: Infanta	菲律宾:因凡塔	14.9	121.55	100	7.6	Ms	9	20	1	50	1		3		3		
1880	7	20	7	40						*Bautista, Maso	Philippines: SW. of Lake Bay, Manila	菲律宾:湾状湖西南,马尼拉	14.4	121.7		5.9	Ms	8	20	1				3		3		3
1880	7	22								*	Turkey: Izmir	土耳其:伊兹密尔	38.1	27.8		6.1	Muk			3				1				
1880	7	29	2	40						*	Turkey: Izmir	土耳其:伊兹密尔	38.6	27.1		6.7	Muk	10	30	1				1				
1880	8	15	12	48		1			0.5	*NOAA	Chile: Illapel	智利:伊亚佩尔	-31.6	-71.2		7.7	Muk	10	2	1				3	600	3		
1880	8	22	21	25						USGS, Song	US: Washington, Seattle	美国:华盛顿州西雅图	48	-123		5.5	Mk	6										
1880	8									*Song	Iran: Hormozgan	伊朗:荷姆兹甘	27.1	54.2		6.2	Mk		120	3				2				
1880	9	2				1				NOAA, Song	Greece: Ionian Sea	希腊:伊奥尼亚海	38.25	22.25		6.6	Mk											
1880	9	6								China	China: Hebei, Luanxian	中国:河北滦县	39.7	118.7		5	Ms	6										
1880	9	23	14	30						Maso, Song	Philippines: San Fernando, W.	菲律宾:圣费尔南多西部	15.31	120.11		5	Mk	6										
1880	9	24	1	45						USGS, Song	Hawaiian Islands	夏威夷群岛	19.25	-155		5	Mk	5										
1880	9	25	14	30						USGS, Song	Hawaiian Islands	夏威夷群岛	19.25	-155		5	Mk	5										
1880	9	29	4			3				*NOAA, USGS	Aleutian Islands	阿留申群岛	55.8	-155.6		6.3	Ms	8										
1880	10	16	2	22						GSHAP, Song	Peru: Lima	秘鲁:利马	-12.08	-77		5	Mk	6										
1880	10	26	22	20		3	1.8	5.9		*USGS, NOAA	Gulf of Alaska, SE.	阿拉斯加湾东南	57	-136		6.4	Ms	8										
1880	11	9	6	33						*GSHAP	Croatia: Bedekovcina	克罗地亚:贝代科夫契纳	45.9	16.1		6.2	Ms	10										
1880	12	1	23	30						GSHAP	Kazakhstan: Almaty	哈萨克斯坦:阿拉木图	43.1	76.9	14	5.7	Ms	7.5										
1880	12	8	15	13						GSHAP, Song	Peru: Lima	秘鲁:利马	-12.08	-77		4.5	Mk	5										
1880	12	13	4	40						USGS, Song	US: Washington, Seattle	美国:华盛顿州西雅图	47.5	-122.5		5	Mk	5										
1880	12	18								*Song	Azerbaijan: Samaxi	阿塞拜疆:沙马基区	40.5	48.1		6.1	Mk	8		1								
1880	12	19	23	35						CGS, USGS	US: California, Riverside	美国:加利福尼亚州里弗赛德	34	-117		5.9	Ms	6										
1880	12	25	14	30						GSHAP	Romania: Nereju	罗马尼亚:内雷茹	45.7	26.6	150	6.5	Ms	7										
1880	12	27	20							GSHAP	Turkmenistan: Balkanabat	土库曼斯坦:巴尔坎纳巴德	39.6	54.5	10	4.6	Ms	6.5										
1880										*Song	Iran: Kordestan	伊朗:库尔德斯坦	36.1	46.2		6.3	Mk							3				
1881	1	7	2	25						CGS, USGS	US: California, Red Bluff	美国:加利福尼亚州雷德布拉夫	40	-122		5.6	Ms	5										
1881	2	2	0	11						CGS, USGS	US: California, Bradley	美国:加利福尼亚州布拉德利	36.1	-120.6		6	Ms	7										
1881	2	18								*China	China: Taiwan, Miaoli	中国:台湾苗栗	24.5	120.7		6	Ms	8	11	1				2		2		
1881	3	4	12							*Italy	Italy: Isola D'Ischia	意大利:伊斯基亚岛	40.75	13.917		5.57	Ms	9	126	3			0.2	1				
1881	3	9	1							**Song	Italy: Foligno, Scopoli	意大利:福利尼奥	43	12.8		6.5	Mk	12										
1881	3	16								**Song	Italy: Island of Ischia	意大利:伊斯基亚岛	40.7	13.9		6	Mk		114	3			0.186	1				
1881	4	3	11	30		3			2	*NOAA	Greece: Chios	希腊:希俄斯岛	38.25	26.25		7.3	Ms	11	7866	4				4		4		4
1881	4	10	10							CGS, USGS	US: California, Patterson	美国:加利福尼亚州帕特森	37.4	-121.4		6.3	Ms	6										

年 Year	月 Mo	日 Dy	时 Hr	分 Mn	秒 Sec	海啸 Tsunami 源 Sr	浪高 Wh	级 I mI	级 S mS	资料来源 Information	震中 Earthquake Epicenter 地名(英文) Name(English)	地名(中文) Name(Chinese)	纬度(°) Latitude	经度(°) Longitude	深度 Depth	震级 Mag	标度 Scale	烈度 MMI	死亡人数 Deaths 数量/人 Num	级别 Dd	受伤人数 Injuries 数量/人 Num	级别 Dd	经济损失 Damage 数量/$ Mill	级别 De	房屋毁坏 Houses Destroyed 数量/间 Num	级别 Dh	房屋受损 Houses Damaged 数量/间 Num	级别 Dh
1881	4	11				1				* NOAA, Song	Greece: Chios	希腊:希俄斯岛	38.2	26.2		6.6	Mk							2				
1881	4	22	1							USGS, Song	Hawaiian Islands	夏威夷群岛	21	-157		5	Mk	5										
1881	4	29	3							* Song	Nicaragua: San Juan Del Sur, Chinandega	尼加拉瓜:南圣胡安,奇南德加	11.5	-86.3		5.9	Mk							2				
1881	5	27								USGS	US: Illinois, Ottawa	美国:伊利诺斯州渥太华	41.3	-89.1		4.6	Ms	6										
1881	6	7								* Song	Turkey: Van, Nemrut	土耳其:凡城,尼姆鲁特	38.5	43.3		6	Mk	7	95	2				2				
1881	6	9								* Song	Nicaragua: Santa Cruz	尼加拉瓜:圣克鲁斯	11	-84		5.9	Mk							2				
1881	6									China	China: Sichuan, Yuexi	中国:四川越西	28.6	102.5		5	Ms	6										
1881	7	5	10	35						GSHAP	Russia: Krasnodar, Krymsk	俄罗斯:克拉斯诺达尔区克雷姆斯克	45	38.1	30	5.1	Ms	5.5										
1881	7	9	19	30						GSHAP, Song	Peru: Lima	秘鲁:利马	-12.08	-77		4.5	Mk	5										
1881	7	11	4	35						Bautista, Maso	Sulu Sea	苏禄海	10.45	121.9		6.3	Muk	6										
1881	7	12				2	0.5	1	1	* NOAA	Fiji Islands	斐济群岛	-16	179		7	Ms											
1881	7	14				3	1.4	0.5	1	* NOAA, Song	Chile: Iquique	智利:伊基克	-20.2	-70.1		7	Mk											
1881	7	20								* China	China: Gansu, Lixian, SW.	中国:甘肃礼县西南	33.6	104.6		6.5	Ms	8	480	3				3	4800	4		
1881	7	27	8	10						Bautista, Maso	Philippines: Nueva Vizcaya, Bayombong	菲律宾:新比斯开,巴云邦	16.35	120.9		5.3	Muk	7										
1881	8	1	9	30						GSHAP	Armenia: Zangezur	亚美尼亚:休尼克	39.4	46.2	24	4.6	Ms	6										
1881	8	9	8	30						GSHAP, Song	Peru: Lima	秘鲁:利马	-12.08	-77		4.5	Mk	5										
1881	8	12				1	0.5			* NOAA, Song	Jamaica: Kingston	牙买加:金斯敦	17.97	-76.8		7	Mk											
1881	8	26								* Song	Greece: Chios	希腊:希俄斯	38.4	26.1		7	Mk	10										
1881	8	28								* Song	Iran: Orumiyeh	伊朗:乌尔米耶	38.3	44.6		5.9	Mk	7						2				
1881	9	1	4	10						* Maso, Song, Bautista	Philippines: Nueva Vizcaya, Bayombong	菲律宾:新比斯开,巴云邦	16.45	120.9		6.5	Mk	9						2				
1881	9	13								USGS, Song	Hawaiian Islands	夏威夷群岛	21	-156		5	Mk	5										
1881	9	17	20	55						Maso, Song, Bautista	Philippines: Nueva Vizcaya, Bayombong	菲律宾:新比斯开,巴云邦	16.35	120.95		6.1	Mk	8										
1881	9	18	15	40						Maso, Song, Bautista	Philippines: Nueva Vizcaya, Bayombong	菲律宾:新比斯开,巴云邦	16.4	120.9		6.1	Mk	8										
1881	9	20	1	10						Bautista, Maso	Philippines: Nueva Vizcaya, Bayombong	菲律宾:新比斯开,巴云邦	16.5	120.95		6.1	Muk	8										
1881	9	21	10							GSHAP	Azerbaijan: Naxcivan	阿塞拜疆:纳希切万	39.1	45.4	15	5	Ms	6.5										
1881	9	25	8							* China	China: Taiwan, Taipei	中国:台湾台北	25.1	121.6		5.5	Ms	7		1				2		3		
1881	9	28								*	Turkey: Ilgaz	土耳其:厄尔加兹	40.6	33.6		6.1	Muk		12	1				1				
1881	9	30	2	40						* Bautista	Philippines: Nueva Vizcaya	菲律宾:新比斯开	16.4	121		6	Ms							2				
1881	9	30	15	23						USGS	Hawaiian Islands	夏威夷群岛	19.5	-156		6	Ms	8										
1881	10	25	12	22		1				* Usami, Japan	Kuril Islands	千岛群岛	43.3	147.3		7	Ms											

时间 Date						海啸 Tsunami				资料来源 Information	震中 Earthquake Epicenter				深度 Depth	震级 Mag	标度 Scale	烈度 MMI	死亡人数 Deaths		受伤人数 Injuries		经济损失 Damage		房屋毁坏 Houses Destroyed		房屋受损 Houses Damaged	
年 Year	月 Mo	日 Dy	时 Hr	分 Mn	秒 Sec	源 Sr	浪高 Wh	级 I mI	级 S mS		地名(英文) Name(English)	地名(中文) Name(Chinese)	纬度(°) Latitude	经度(°) Longitude					数量/人 Num	级别 Dd	数量/人 Num	级别 Dd	数量/$ Mill $ Mill	级别 De	数量/间 Num	级别 Dh	数量/间 Num	级别 Dh
1881	10	27				2	0.7	-0.5		* NOAA, Song	Chile: Huara	智利:瓦拉	-19.6	-70.2		7	Mk											
1881	11	24				1				NOAA, Song	Tonga Islands	汤加群岛	-21.38	-175.65		7	Mk											
1881	12	19	12	35						GSHAP, Song	Peru: Lima	秘鲁:利马	-12.08	-77		4.5	Mk	5										
1881	12	31				3	1.2	0.3		* India, NOAA	India: Andaman - Nicobar Islands	印度:安达曼-尼科巴群岛	12	92.4		8	Ms							3				3
1882	1	1								GSHAP	China: Xinjiang, Karakorum Pass, E.	中国:新疆喀喇昆仑山口东	37	79.5	33	7	Ms	9										
1882	1									China	China: Yunnan, Mile	中国:云南弥勒	24.4	103.4		5.75	Ms	7										
1882	1					3				* NOAA, GSHAP	Sri Lanka: Trincomalee	斯里兰卡:亭可马里	8.57	81.23		6.1	Ms											
1882	2	23				2	0.7	-0.5		* NOAA, Song	Chile: Copiapo	智利:科皮亚波	-27.9	-70.1		7	Mk											
1882	3	6	21	45						CGS, USGS	US: California, Tres Pinos, S.	美国:加利福尼亚州特雷斯皮诺斯南部	36.5	-121.1		5.9	Ms	6										
1882	3	15	23	50						GSHAP	Russia: Novosibirsk, Berdsk	俄罗斯:新西伯利亚州别尔茨克	54.7	83.2	20	5.7	Ms	7										
1882	3	18	13	5						GSHAP, Song	Peru: Lima	秘鲁:利马	-12.08	-77		4.5	Mk	5										
1882	4	10	11	30						Maso, Song	Philippines: San Fernando, E.	菲律宾:圣费尔南多东部	15.4	121.21		5	Mk	6										
1882	5	1	6	50						USGS, Song	US: Washington, Olympia	美国:华盛顿州奥林匹亚	47	-123		5.5	Mk	6										
1882	5	31	18	25						GSHAP, Song	Peru: Lima	秘鲁:利马	-12.08	-77		4.5	Mk	5										
1882	6	24	2	2						Japan, Song	Japan: Shikoku	日本:四国	33.3	133.5		6.3	Mk									1		
1882	6	27	13	32						CGS, USGS	US: California, Los Gatos	美国:加利福尼亚州洛斯加托斯	37.1	-121.9		5.8	Ms	7										
1882	7	17	7	51						* Italy	Slovenia: Ljubljana, W.	斯洛文尼亚:卢布尔雅那西部	46	14.2	12	4.8	Muk	7						2				
1882	7	19								* Song	Mexico: Puebla, Huamuxtitlan	墨西哥:普埃布拉,瓦穆斯蒂特兰	17.5	-98.3		6.3	Mk		7	1	10	1		3				
1882	7	28	20	25						* Song	Italy: Island of Ischia	意大利:伊斯基亚岛	40.7	13.9		6.6	Mk	9	2313	4				3				
1882	7	31	11	30						GSHAP, Song	Peru: Lima	秘鲁:利马	-12.08	-77		4.5	Mk	5										
1882	8	16	11							GSHAP, Song	Peru: Lima	秘鲁:利马	-12.08	-77		4.5	Mk	5										
1882	8	18	4	30						GSHAP, Song	Peru: Lima	秘鲁:利马	-12.08	-77		4.5	Mk	5										
1882	8	27	11	30						GSHAP, Song	Peru: Lima	秘鲁:利马	-12.08	-77		5	Mk	6										
1882	9	2								* Song	Italy: Vesuvio	意大利:维苏威	40.9	14.4		5.7	Mk		11	1				1				
1882	9	7	7	50		4	3		1	* NOAA	Panama: San Blas Archipelago	巴拿马:圣布拉群岛	9.5	-78.9	40	8.3	Muk	11		2				3		3		
1882	9	8	8	35						GSHAP, Song	Peru: Lima	秘鲁:利马	-12.08	-77		5	Mk	6										
1882	9	14				2	0.7	-0.5		* NOAA, Song	Chile: Huara	智利:瓦拉	-19.6	-70.2		7	Mk											
1882	9	17	23	15						GSHAP, Song	Peru: Lima	秘鲁:利马	-12.08	-77		5	Mk	6										
1882	9	20	18	40						GSHAP, Song	Peru: Lima	秘鲁:利马	-12.08	-77		5	Mk	6										
1882	9	21	4	10						GSHAP, Song	Peru: Lima	秘鲁:利马	-12.08	-77.08		4.5	Mk	5										

时间 Date						海啸 Tsunami				资料来源 Information	震中 Earthquake Epicenter				深度 Depth	震级 Mag	标度 Scale	烈度 MMI	死亡人数 Deaths		受伤人数 Injuries		经济损失 Damage		房屋毁坏 Houses Destroyed		房屋受损 Houses Damaged	
年 Year	月 Mo	日 Dy	时 Hr	分 Mn	秒 Sec	源 Sr	浪高 Wh	级 I mI	级 S mS		地名(英文) Name(English)	地名(中文) Name(Chinese)	纬度(°) Latitude	经度(°) Longitude					数量/人 Num	级别 Dd	数量/人 Num	级别 Dd	数量/$ Mill $ Mill	级别 De	数量/间 Num	级别 Dh	数量/间 Num	级别 Dh
1882	9	27	10	20						USGS	US:Illinois,Ayers	美国:伊利诺斯州艾尔斯	39	-89.5		4.4	Ms	6										
1882	9	28	20							Japan,Song	Japan:Atami	日本:静冈热海	35.1	139.1		6.3	Mk									1		
1882	10	7	9	20						* * Song	Panama:Punta Robalo	巴拿马:蓬塔罗瓦洛	9	-82		6.1	Mk	8						1				
1882	10	10	8	46						Bautista,Maso	Philippines:Camarines	菲律宾:馬利納	13.9	123.1		5.6	Muk	7										
1882	10	10				3			0.5	* NOAA	Indonesia:Banda Sea	印度尼西亚:班达海	-4.6	129.9		7.5	Ms											
1882	10	22	22	15						USGS	US:Oklahoma,Bennington	美国:俄克拉荷马州本宁顿	34	-96		4.9	Ms	6										
1882	11	8	1	30						USGS	US:Colorado,Drake	美国:科罗拉多州德雷克	40.5	-105.5		6.2	Ms	7										
1882	12	2								* China	China:Hebei,Shenxian	中国:河北深县	38.1	115.5		6	Ms	8	11	1				3		3		
1882	12	6								China	China:Hebei,Shenxian	中国:河北深县	38.1	115.5		5.5	Ms	7										
1882	12	6								Bautista,Maso	Philippines:Masbate Island	菲律宾:马斯巴特岛	11.8	124.15		6	Muk	7										
1882	12	9	10	22						China	China:Taiwan,Yunlin	中国:台湾云林	23.8	120.5		6.75	Ms		11	1					30	1		
1882	12									China	China:Jilin,Huadian	中国:吉林桦甸	43	126.7		4.75	Ms	6										
1883	1	11	7	12						USGS	US:Missouri:Charleston	美国:密苏里州查尔斯顿	37	-89		4.6	Ms	6										
1883	1	27	4	15						GSHAP,Song	Peru:Lima	秘鲁:利马	-12.08	-77		4.5	Mk	5										
1883	2	9	19	28						Bautista,Maso	Philippines:Nueva Vizcaya	菲律宾:新比斯开	16.3	121		5.6	Muk	7										
1883	3	9								* Song	Colombia:Antioquia	哥伦比亚:安提奥基亚	7	-76		5.9	Mk	7						2				
1883	3	12				3		3.4	2	NOAA,Song	Mexico:Acapulco	墨西哥:阿卡普尔科	17.171	-99.651		7.5	Mk											
1883	3	23								GSHAP	Colombia:Riosucio	哥伦比亚:乔科的里奥苏西奥	7.4	-76.9		5.5	Ms	6										
1883	3	24				1			1	NOAA,Song	Kiribati:Malden Island	基里巴斯:莫尔登岛	-5	-155		7	Mk											
1883	3	30	15	45						CGS,USGS	US:California,San Juan Bautista	美国:加利福尼亚州圣胡安包蒂斯塔	36.8	-121.5		6	Ms	7										
1883	4	12	8	36						USGS,Song	US:Illinois,Cairo	美国:伊利诺斯州开罗	37	-89.2		5.5	Mk	6										
1883	5	3								* Iran	Iran:Tabriz	伊朗:大不里士	38.1	46.3		6.2	Ms	7		3				3				
1883	5	26	11	30						GSHAP,Song	Peru:Lima	秘鲁:利马	-12.08	-77		4.5	Mk	5										
1883	6	2	18	30						GSHAP,Song	Peru:Lima	秘鲁:利马	-12.08	-77		4.5	Mk	5										
1883	6	12	14	30						GSHAP,Song	Venezuela:Barinas	委内瑞拉:巴里纳斯	8.62	-70.11		5	Mk	6										
1883	6	23								* China	China:Shanxi,Taiyuan	中国:山西太原	37.9	112.6		5.5	Ms	7						2		3		
1883	6	27				2			3	NOAA,Song	Greece:Ionian Islands	希腊:伊奥尼亚群岛	39.5	20		6.7	Mk											
1883	7	10	10	35						GSHAP,Song	Peru:Lima	秘鲁:利马	-12.08	-77		4.5	Mk	5										
1883	7	23								* * Song	Italy:Lacco Ameno	意大利:拉科阿梅诺	40.5	13.9		6.6	Mk		1990	4				3				
1883	7	28	20	25						* Italy	Italy:Island of Ischia,Casamicciola	意大利:伊斯基亚岛,乔拉	40.75	13.88		5.78	Ms	10	2313	4	374	3		4	2278	4		
1883	8	2	17	25						GSHAP,Song	Peru:Lima	秘鲁:利马	-12.08	-77		5	Mk	6										
1883	9	5	12	30						CGS,USGS	US:California,Ojai,N.	美国:加利福尼亚州奥海镇北部	34.7	-119.2		6.3	Ms	6										
1883	9	7	4	30						GSHAP,Song	Peru:Lima	秘鲁:利马	-12.08	-77		4.5	Mk	5										

年 Year	月 Mo	日 Dy	时 Hr	分 Mn	秒 Sec	海啸 Tsunami 源 Sr	浪高 Wh	级 I mI	级 S mS	资料来源 Information	震中 Earthquake Epicenter 地名(英文) Name(English)	地名(中文) Name(Chinese)	纬度(°) Latitude	经度(°) Longitude	深度 Depth	震级 Mag	标度 Scale	烈度 MMI	死亡人数 Deaths 数量/人 Num	级别 Dd	受伤人数 Injuries 数量/人 Num	级别 Dd	经济损失 Damage 数量/$ Mill	级别 De	房屋毁坏 Houses Destroyed 数量/间 Num	级别 Dh	房屋受损 Houses Damaged 数量/间 Num	级别 Dh
1883	9	9	14	15						* *	Greece:Patrai	希腊:帕特雷	38. 2	22. 1		5. 8	Ms			2				2				
1883	10	1	11	35						GSHAP, Song	Peru:Arequipa	秘鲁:阿雷基帕	-16. 4	-71. 56		5	Mk	6										
1883	10	6	19	4		5	9. 1	3. 2	3	NOAA, Song	Alaska Peninsula, S.	阿拉斯加半岛南部	59. 4	-153. 4		7. 7	Mk			1				1		1		
1883	10	15	13	30						*	Greece:Chios	希腊:希俄斯岛	38. 4	26. 1		7. 3	Ms	10	15000	5				4	3600	4		
1883	10	16	21							* Iran	Iran:Kangan	伊朗:坎根	27. 7	52. 3		5. 8	Ms	7						2				
1883	10									China	China:Xizang (Tibet), Burang	中国:西藏普兰	30. 2	81. 2		7	Ms	9										
1883	11	14	17							GSHAP	Kyrgyzstan:Osh	吉尔吉斯斯坦:奥什	40. 6	72. 8	12	5. 5	Ms	7. 5										
1883	11	19	0	45						GSHAP, Song	Peru:Lima	秘鲁:利马	-12. 08	-77		5	Mk	6										
1883	11	25	11							GSHAP, Song	Venezuela:Coro	委内瑞拉:科罗	11. 42	-69. 68		5	Mk	6										
1883	12	5	15	20						USGS	US:Arkansas, Pocahontas	美国:阿肯色州波卡洪特斯	36. 3	-91. 2		4. 8	Ms	5										
1883	12	18	4							GSHAP, Song	Peru:Lima	秘鲁:利马	-12. 08	-77		5	Mk	6										
1883										* * Song	Iran:Hengam Island	伊朗:亨加姆岛	26. 4	55. 5		6. 3	Mk							3				
1884	1	9	23	22						Bautista, Maso	Philippines:Camarines	菲律宾:馬利納	13. 55	122. 65		5. 2	Muk	7										
1884	1	14				1				* NOAA, Song	Uruguay:Montevideo	乌拉圭:蒙得维的亚	-34. 917	-56. 167		7	Mk			2								
1884	1	28	7	30						CGS, USGS	US:California, Hoopa	美国:加利福尼亚州胡帕	41. 1001	-123. 6		6. 1	Ms	5										
1884	1									* China	China:Taiwan, Chiayi	中国:台湾嘉义	23. 5	120. 4		5. 5	Ms	7						2		3		
1884	1					1				* NOAA, Song	Johnston Island, NW.	约翰斯顿岛西北[太平洋]	16	179		7. 3	Mk	7						1				
1884	2	10								GSHAP	Turkey:Siirt	土耳其:锡尔特	37. 8	42. 4	24	6. 8	Ms	8. 5										
1884	2					2				* * NOAA, Song	Indonesia:Sunda Strait	印度尼西亚:巽他海峡	-6. 102	105. 423		7	Mk											
1884	3	5	6	30						GSHAP, Song	Peru:Lima	秘鲁:利马	-12. 08	-77		5	Mk	6										
1884	3	13	5	7						GSHAP	Kyrgyzstan:Bishkek	吉尔吉斯斯坦:比什凯克	42. 7	78. 2	20	5. 8	Ms	7										
1884	3	26	0	40						CGS, USGS	US:California, Davenport	美国:加利福尼亚州达文波特	37	-122. 25		5. 9	Ms	6										
1884	4	24	5	38						GSHAP, Song	Peru:Lima	秘鲁:利马	-12. 08	-77		5	Mk	6										
1884	5	19								* Song	Iran:Qeshm Island	伊朗:格什姆岛	26. 81	55. 91		6. 3	Mk	8	238	3	500	3		3		3		
1884	5	27	18	45						GSHAP, Song	Peru:Lima	秘鲁:利马	-12. 08	-77		5	Mk	6										
1884	6	5								Bautista, Maso	Philippines:Mindanao Island	菲律宾:棉兰老岛	8. 6	124. 8		5. 1	Muk	6										
1884	6									China	China:Taiwan, Chiayi	中国:台湾嘉义	23. 5	120. 4		5	Ms	6										
1884	7	19	6	14						GSHAP, Song	Peru:Lima	秘鲁:利马	-12. 08	-77		4. 5	Mk	5										
1884	7	20	9	30		4				* NOAA	Eritrea:Massawa	厄立特里亚:马萨瓦	15. 7	39. 6		6. 2	Ms							2		3		
1884	8	10	19	7		2	1. 8			* NOAA	US:New York, Rockaway Beach	美国:纽约州罗卡韦滩	40. 6	-73. 75		5. 5	Mfa	7										

时间						海啸				资料来源	震中				深度	震级	标度	烈度	死亡人数		受伤人数		经济损失		房屋毁坏		房屋受损	
年	月	日	时	分	秒	源	浪高	级 I	级 S		地名(英文)	地名(中文)	纬度(°)	经度(°)					数量/人	级别	数量/人	级别	数量/$ Mill	级别	数量/间	级别	数量/间	级别
Date						Tsunami				Information	Earthquake Epicenter				Depth	Mag	Scale	MMI	Deaths		Injuries		Damage		Houses Destroyed		Houses Damaged	
Year	Mo	Dy	Hr	Mn	Sec	Sr	Wh	mI	mS		Name(English)	Name(Chinese)	Latitude	Longitude					Num	Dd	Num	Dd	$ Mill	De	Num	Dh	Num	Dh
1884	9	19	19	14						USGS	US:Ohio,Lima	美国:俄亥俄州利马	40.7	-84.1		4.8	Ms	6										
1884	10	14	19	21						Japan,Song	Japan:Tokyo	日本:东京	35.7	139.8		6.3	Mk									1		
1884	10	28	20	6						Bautista,Maso	Philippines:Quezon,Coast E.	菲律宾:奎松东部海域	14.95	121.85		5.5	Muk	6										
1884	11	5								GSHAP	Colombia:Cartago	哥伦比亚:卡塔戈	5	-76		6.3	Ms	8										
1884	11	5				1				* NOAA	Panama:Pacora	巴拿马:帕科拉	9.1	-79.4		7.5	Ms	6						2		2		
1884	11	10	8	50						USGS,Song	US:Idaho,Fish Haven	美国:爱达荷州菲什黑文	42	-111.3		5.7	Mk	7										
1884	11	14								* China	China:Yunnan,Pu-er	中国:云南普洱	23.1	101		6.5	Ms	8	17	1	80	2		2		3		
1884	11	22	12	4						GSHAP,Song	Peru:Lima	秘鲁:利马	-12.08	-77		4.5	Mk	5										
1884	11	26	23	10						GSHAP	Bolivia:Sucre	玻利维亚:苏克雷	-19.17	-64.91		5.2	Ms	6										
1884	12	21				1	2.4		1.5	* NOAA,Song	US:Connecticut,New Haven	美国:康涅狄格州纽黑文	41.31	-72.92		7	Mk											
1884	12	23	21							Bautista,Maso	Philippines:Masbate Island	菲律宾:马斯巴特岛	11.4	124.5		5.1	Muk	6										
1884	12	25	21	8						*	Spain:Vega,Alhama,Malaga	西班牙:阿哈马,马拉加	37	-4		6.7	Muk	11	745	3				3				
1884	12									* Song	El Salvador:Usulutan	萨尔瓦多:乌苏卢坦	13.4	-88.5		5.9	Mk							2				
1885	1	12	16							GSHAP	Russia:Lake Baykal	俄罗斯:贝加尔湖	52.5	106.5	25	6.7	Ms	8.5										
1885	1	13	16	29						USGS	Hawaiian Islands	夏威夷群岛	21	-156		6	Ms	6										
1885	1	15								* China	China:Gansu,Tianshui,S.	中国:甘肃天水南	34	105.7		6	Ms	8	80	2				2	1001	4		
1885	1	16	8			3			4	NOAA,Song	France:Nice	法国:尼斯	43.7	7.25		6.7	Mk											
1885	1	31	5	45						CGS,USGS	US:California,Susanville	美国:加利福尼亚州苏珊维尔	40.4	-120.6		6.1	Ms	7										
1885	2	10	6	30						GSHAP,Song	Peru:Lima	秘鲁:利马	-12.08	-77		4.5	Mk	5										
1885	2	11								* Song	Mexico:Jalisco,Guadalajara	墨西哥:哈利斯科,瓜达拉哈拉	20.8	-103.4		6.1	Mk	8						2				
1885	2	22	7	30						* Bautista,Maso	Philippines:Mindanao,Surigao	菲律宾:棉兰老岛,苏利高	7.9	127.1		7.2	Ms	8						3				
1885	3	15	17	40						GSHAP	Russia:Krasnoyarsk,S.	俄罗斯:克拉斯罗亚尔斯克南部	52.8	93.1	15	6.2	Ms	8										
1885	3	28	18	23						* Song	Greece:Kyparissia (Messinia)	希腊:麦锡尼	37	22		6.1	Mk	9		2								
1885	3	31	7	56						CGS,USGS	US:California,Tres Pinos	美国:加利福尼亚州特雷斯皮诺斯	36.7	-121.2		5.7	Ms	7										
1885	4	2	15	25						CGS,USGS	US:California,Tres Pinos,S.	美国:加利福尼亚州特雷斯皮诺斯南部	36.6	-121.1		5.9	Ms	5										
1885	4	7								China	China:Liaoning,Yingkou	中国:辽宁营口	40.7	122.2		5.5	Ms	7										
1885	4	12	4	5						CGS,USGS	US:California,Tres Pinos,S.	美国:加利福尼亚州特雷斯皮诺斯南部	36.2	-120.8		6.5	Ms	7										
1885	4	30				3			0.5	* NOAA	Indonesia:Ceram Sea	印度尼西亚:塞兰海	-2.5	127.5		7.3	Ms											

时间						海啸				资料来源	震中				深度	震级	标度	烈度	死亡人数		受伤人数		经济损失		房屋毁坏		房屋受损	
年	月	日	时	分	秒	源	浪高	级 I	级 S		地名(英文)	地名(中文)	纬度(°)	经度(°)					数量/人	级别	数量/人	级别	数量/$ Mill	级别	数量/间	级别	数量/间	级别
Date						Tsunami				Information	Earthquake Epicenter				Depth	Mag	Scale	MMI	Deaths		Injuries		Damage		Houses Destroyed		Houses Damaged	
Year	Mo	Dy	Hr	Mn	Sec	Sr	Wh	mI	mS		Name(English)	Name(Chinese)	Latitude	Longitude					Num	Dd	Num	Dd	$ Mill	De	Num	Dh	Num	Dh
1885	5	1								*	Russia: Dagestan, Derbent, W.	俄罗斯:达吉斯坦共和国杰尔宾特西部	41.9	47.8	3	4	Muk	7						2				
1885	5	25	20							* GSHAP	Colombia:Cauca	哥伦比亚:考卡	2.5	-76.5		6.3	Ms	8						2				
1885	5	30								* GSHAP	India:Srinagar	印度:斯利那加	33.5	75		7	Ms		3000	4				4		4		4
1885	6	6								* Song	India:Kashmir	印度:克什米尔	34	76		6.3	Mk							3				
1885	7	7								GSHAP	Russia:Khakassia, Abakan	俄罗斯:哈卡斯州阿巴坎	53.5	91.4	16	4.5	Ms	5.5										
1885	7	23	2	45						* Bautista	Philippines:Mindanao, Cavite	菲律宾:棉兰老岛,甲米地	8.85	123.1		7	Ms	10						2				
1885	7	23	14	45						* Maso, Song	Philippines:Mindanao, Dapitan	菲律宾:棉兰老岛,达皮丹	8.6	123.4		6.5	Mk	9						2		2		
1885	7	29				2			0	* NOAA	Indonesia:Banda Aceh	印度尼西亚:班达亚齐	0.2	99.383		6.8	Ms											
1885	8	1	0	10						USGS, Song	US:California, Cloverdale	美国:加利福尼亚州克洛弗代尔	38.8	-123		5.5	Mk	6										
1885	8	2	21	20						*	Kyrgyzstan:Bishkek	吉尔吉斯斯坦:比什凯克	42.7	74.1	15	6.9	Muk	10	54	2				2				
1885	8	3				1				NOAA, Song	Indonesia:Maluku Utara	印度尼西亚:北马鲁古	1.375	127.52		7	Mk											
1885	9	19	20							GSHAP	Kyrgyzstan:Naryn, C.	吉尔吉斯斯坦:纳伦中部	41.7	75.8	14	5	Ms	6.5										
1885	9	29	22							Bautista, Maso	Philippines:Mindanao Island	菲律宾:棉兰老岛	10.1	126.6		6.2	Muk	6										
1885	10	12	4	30						* Song	Nicaragua:Leon, Chinandega	尼加拉瓜:里昂,奇南德加	12.3	-86.8		6.5	Mk	9						3				
1885	11	12				3	1		0.5	* NOAA, Song	Chile:Iquique	智利:伊基克	-20.2	-70.1		7	Mk											
1885	11	19	3	15						Bautista, Maso	Philippines:Baguio	菲律宾:碧瑶市	16.65	120.9		6	Muk	7										
1885	11	19	20	50						GSHAP	Russia:Buryatiya, Tugnuy	俄罗斯:布里亚特州图格努伊镇	51.3	108.1	20	6.2	Ms	8										
1885	11	24								China	China:Guangxi, Longzhou	中国:广西龙州	22.3	106.8		4.75	Ms	6										
1885	12	14				1				* NOAA, Song	Indonesia:North of Sumatera	印度尼西亚:苏门答腊北部	5.5	96		7	Mk											
1885	12	22								* China	China:Yunnan, Qiubei, SW.	中国:云南丘北西南	23.9	103.7		5.25	Ms	6	4	1		2		1		1		
1885										China	China:Xinjiang, Kuytun	中国:新疆奎屯	44.3	85		5.5	Ms	7										
1886	1	13								China	China:Guangdong, Shantou	中国:广东汕头	23.4	116.7		4.75	Ms	6										
1886	1	31				1				* NOAA, Song	Indonesia:North of Sumatera	印度尼西亚:苏门答腊北部	5.5	96		7	Mk											
1886	2	25	21	37						GSHAP, Song	Peru:Lima	秘鲁:利马	-12.08	-77		4.5	Mk	5										
1886	3	5	9	30						GSHAP, Song	Peru:Arequipa	秘鲁:阿雷基帕	-16.4	-71.56		4.5	Mk	5										
1886	3	5	16	15						GSHAP, Song	Peru:Arequipa	秘鲁:阿雷基帕	-16.4	-71.56		5	Mk	6										
1886	4	10	1							Bautista, Maso	Philippines:Panay Island	菲律宾:班乃岛	10.5	122.2		5.4	Muk	6										
1886	4	14	3	20						USGS, Song	US:California, Bishop	美国:加利福尼亚州毕晓普	37.2	-117.7		5.5	Mk	6										

年 Year	月 Mo	日 Dy	时 Hr	分 Mn	秒 Sec	海啸 Tsunami 源 Sr	浪高 Wh	级 I mI	级 S mS	资料来源 Information	震中 Earthquake Epicenter 地名(英文) Name(English)	地名(中文) Name(Chinese)	纬度(°) Latitude	经度(°) Longitude	深度 Depth	震级 Mag	标度 Scale	烈度 MMI	死亡人数 Deaths 数量/人 Num	级别 Dd	受伤人数 Injuries 数量/人 Num	级别 Dd	经济损失 Damage 数量/$ Mill $ Mill	级别 De	房屋毁坏 Houses Destroyed 数量/间 Num	级别 Dh	房屋受损 Houses Damaged 数量/间 Num	级别 Dh
1886	5	9	18	15						GSHAP	Brasil:Rio De Janeiro	巴西:里约热内卢	-22.66	-43.69		4.3	Ms	5										
1886	5	19				1				* NOAA, Song	Philippines:Hinatuan, Laak	菲律宾:希纳图安,圣维森特	8	125.4		7	Mk											
1886	7	22	15	57						Usami, Japan	Japan:Niigata	日本:新潟	37.1	138.5		6.1	Ms	7							2	1		
1886	8	27	21	32		3			3	* NOAA	Greece:Kyparissia (Messinia)	希腊:麦锡尼	37.1	21.5		7.5	Muk	10	600	3				3				
1886	8	28	8	45						USGS, Song	US:South Carolina, Charleston	美国:卡罗莱纳州查尔斯顿	32.9	-80		5.5	Mk	6										
1886	9	1	2	51		4				* USGS, NOAA	US:South Carolina, Charleston	美国:卡罗莱纳州查尔斯顿	32.9	-80		7.7	Mw	10	60	2			5.0	3				
1886	9	6	4	6						USGS, Song	US:South Carolina, Charleston	美国:卡罗莱纳州查尔斯顿	32.9	-80		5.5	Mk	6										
1886	9	17	6	29						USGS, Song	US:South Carolina, Charleston	美国:卡罗莱纳州查尔斯顿	32.9	-80		5.5	Mk	6										
1886	9	21	10	15						USGS, Song	US:South Carolina, Charleston	美国:卡罗莱纳州查尔斯顿	32.9	-80		5.5	Mk	6										
1886	9	27	19	2						USGS, Song	US:South Carolina, Charleston	美国:卡罗莱纳州查尔斯顿	32.9	-80		5.5	Mk	6										
1886	9	29	6	20						* Song	Venezuela:Trujillo	委内瑞拉:特鲁希略	9.3	-70.4		5.9	Mk							2				
1886	10	2	12							GSHAP, Song	Peru:Lima	秘鲁:利马	-12.08	-77		4.5	Mk	5										
1886	10	22	10	20						USGS, Song	US:South Carolina, Charleston	美国:卡罗莱纳州查尔斯顿	32.9	-80		5.5	Mk	6										
1886	10	22	19	45						USGS, Song	US:South Carolina, Charleston	美国:卡罗莱纳州查尔斯顿	32.9	-80		5.7	Mk	7										
1886	11	5	17	20						USGS, Song	US:South Carolina, Charleston	美国:卡罗莱纳州查尔斯顿	32.9	-80		5.5	Mk	6										
1886	11	8								GSHAP	Kazakhstan:Georgiyevka	哈萨克斯坦:格奥尔吉耶夫卡	43	75	28	5.4	Ms	6										
1886	11	29	4	13						GSHAP	Uzbekistan:Tashkent	乌兹别克斯坦:塔什干	41.4	69.5	26	6.7	Ms	8										
1886						1				NOAA, Song	Bangladesh:Satkhira	孟加拉:萨德基拉	22	89		7	Mk											
1887	1	13	20	45						GSHAP	Kazakhstan:Zyryanovsk	哈萨克斯坦:济良诺夫斯克	50.3	82.9	18	5.8	Ms	7										
1887	1	15	9	51						Usami, Japan	Japan:Atsugi	日本:神奈川厚木	35.5	139.3		6.3	Ms	7								1		
1887	1	20	7	30						GSHAP, Song	Peru:Arequipa	秘鲁:阿雷基帕	-16.4	-71.56		4.5	Mk	5										
1887	1	24	9	57						USGS	Hawaiian Islands	夏威夷群岛	19.25	-155.5		6	Ms	8										
1887	2	2	15			1				* Bautista, Maso, NOAA	Philippines:Panay, Iloilo	菲律宾:班乃,伊洛伊洛	11.45	122.05		7.3	Ms	9						2		2		
1887	2	6	22	15						USGS	US:Indiana, Vincennes	美国:印第安纳州温森斯	38.7	-87.5		4.6	Ms	6										
1887	2	8	10							GSHAP, Song	Peru:Lima	秘鲁:利马	-12.08	-77		4.5	Mk	5										
1887	2	15	23	30						GSHAP, Song	Peru:Arequipa	秘鲁:阿雷基帕	-16.4	-71.56		4.5	Mk	5										

时间 Date						海啸 Tsunami				资料来源 Information	震中 Earthquake Epicenter				深度 Depth	震级 Mag	标度 Scale	烈度 MMI	死亡人数 Deaths		受伤人数 Injuries		经济损失 Damage		房屋毁坏 Houses Destroyed		房屋受损 Houses Damaged	
年 Year	月 Mo	日 Dy	时 Hr	分 Mn	秒 Sec	源 Sr	浪高 Wh	级 I mI	级 S mS		地名(英文) Name(English)	地名(中文) Name(Chinese)	纬度(°) Latitude	经度(°) Longitude					数量/人 Num	级别 Dd	数量/人 Num	级别 Dd	数量/$ Mill	级别 De	数量/间 Num	级别 Dh	数量/间 Num	级别 Dh
1887	2	16	4							GSHAP, Song	Peru: Arequipa	秘鲁:阿雷基帕	-16.4	-71.56		4.5	Mk	5										
1887	2	23	5	23		3	2		3	* Italy, NOAA	Italy: Imperia, Near Coast	意大利:因佩里亚近海岸	43.92	8.07		6.29	Ms	10	1000	3				4				
1887	3	17	14	9						USGS, Song	US: South Carolina, Charleston	美国:卡罗莱纳州查尔斯顿	32.9	-80		5.5	Mk	6										
1887	3	24	13	14						* Bautista, Maso	Philippines: Libmanan, SE.	菲律宾:利马南东南	13.45	123.25		5.6	Ms	8						2				
1887	4	8								China	China: Guangdong, Chaozhou	中国:广东潮州	24	116.8		5	Ms	6										
1887	4	16	18	5						GSHAP, Song	Peru: Arequipa	秘鲁:阿雷基帕	-16.4	-71.56		4.5	Mk	5										
1887	5	3				2			1	* USGS, NOAA	Mexico: Agua Prieta	墨西哥:索诺拉的阿瓜普列塔	31	-109	80	8	Ms	10	44	1		3		3		3		
1887	5	29								* Song	Mexico: Guerrero, Morelos	墨西哥:格雷罗,莫雷洛斯	18.2	-100.2		6.3	Mk							3				
1887	6	3	10	48						CGS, USGS	US: Nevada, Carson City	美国:内华达州卡森市	39.2	-119.8		6.5	Ms	8										
1887	6	8	23	35						*	Kazakhstan: Almaty	哈萨克斯坦:阿拉木图	43.1	76.8	20	7.3	Muk	10						2				
1887	6	13	16	17						GSHAP, Song	Peru: Lima	秘鲁:利马	-12.08	-77		4.5	Mk	5										
1887	6	30	17	15						GSHAP, Song	Peru: Lima	秘鲁:利马	-12.08	-77		4.5	Mk	5										
1887	7	16	17	45						GSHAP	Georgia: Poti	格鲁吉亚:波季	42.1	42	14	4.9	Ms	7										
1887	7	22	11	27						Usami, Japan	Japan: Niigata	日本:新潟	37.5	138.9		6.1	Ms									1		
1887	7	25	2	20						GSHAP, Song	Peru: Arequipa	秘鲁:阿雷基帕	-16.4	-71.56		4.5	Mk	5										
1887	7									China	China: Gansu, Jingtai, N.	中国:甘肃景泰北	37.4	103.8		5	Ms	6										
1887	8	2	18	36						USGS	US: Illinois, Golconda	美国:伊利诺斯州戈尔孔达	37.2	-88.5		4.9	Ms	6										
1887	8	15	9	30						GSHAP, Song	Peru: Arequipa	秘鲁:阿雷基帕	-16.4	-71.56		4.5	Mk	5										
1887	8	21	21							GSHAP	Kazakhstan: Almaty	哈萨克斯坦:阿拉木图	43.1	76.8	20	5.7	Ms	7										
1887	8	29								* Song	Mexico: Guerrero, Chilpancingo, W.	墨西哥:格雷罗州奇尔潘辛戈西部	17.7	-100		6.3	Mk							3				
1887	9	5	6	23						Usami, Japan	Japan: Chiba	日本:千叶	35.8	140.5		6.4	Ms	7										
1887	9	23	4							GSHAP	Bolivia: Tarija	玻利维亚:塔里哈	-22.03	-63.7		6.4	Ms	8										
1887	9	23	12			4				* NOAA, Song	Haiti: Mole Saint Nicolas	海地:摩尔圣尼古拉	19.7	-74.4		7.7	Mk							3		3		
1887	9	23	21							GSHAP, Song	Peru: Arequipa	秘鲁:阿雷基帕	-16.4	-71.56		4.5	Mk	5										
1887	10	3	22	53		2			3	* GSHAP, NOAA	Greece: Antikyra	希腊:安迪基拉	38.3	22.8		6.5	Ms	8		2								
1887	10	12	6	20						GSHAP, Song	Peru: Tacna	秘鲁:塔克纳	-18	-70.24		4.5	Mk	5										
1887	11	9	2	15						* Song	Italy: Faentino	意大利:法恩扎	44.2	12		6.5	Mk	12										
1887	11	29	12	30						* Song	Algeria: Relizane	阿尔及利亚:赫利赞	35.58	0.33		7.3	Mk	10	20	1				3	331	3		
1887	12	3	18	55						USGS	US: California, Leggett	美国:加利福尼亚州莱格特	39.3	-123.6		4.9	Ms	7										
1887	12	3								* Italy	Italy: Bisignano	意大利:比西纳诺	39.57	16.22		5.52	Ms							2				
1887	12	5	15	30						USGS, Song	US: Utah, Kanab	美国:犹他州卡纳布	37.1	-112.5		5.5	Mk	6										
1887	12	10								GSHAP	Kazakhstan: Semey	哈萨克斯坦:塞米伊	50.5	80.5	15	5.2	Ms	7										
1887	12	16								* China	China: Yunnan, Shiping	中国:云南石屏	23.7	102.5		7	Ms	9	2000	4	3000	4		3		3		

年 Year	月 Mo	日 Dy	时 Hr	分 Mn	秒 Sec	海啸 Tsunami 源 Sr	浪高 Wh	级 I mI	级 S mS	资料来源 Information	震中 Earthquake Epicenter 地名(英文) Name(English)	地名(中文) Name(Chinese)	纬度(°) Latitude	经度(°) Longitude	深度 Depth	震级 Mag	标度 Scale	烈度 MMI	死亡人数 Deaths 数量/人 Num	级别 Dd	受伤人数 Injuries 数量/人 Num	级别 Dd	经济损失 Damage 数量/$ Mill $ Mill	级别 De	房屋毁坏 Houses Destroyed 数量/间 Num	级别 Dh	房屋受损 Houses Damaged 数量/间 Num	级别 Dh
1887										China	China:Hubei,Shiyan	中国:湖北十堰	32.4	111		4.75	Ms	6								3		
1888	1	10	12	49						* GSHAP	Venezuela:Carupano	委内瑞拉:卡鲁帕诺	10.4	-63.1		6.5	Ms	8						2				
1888	1	26	19	45						Bautista,Maso	Philippine Trench	菲律宾海沟	8.85	126.75		5.8	Muk	6										
1888	1	30	6	35						USGS	US:California, South Lake Tahoe	美国:加利福尼亚州南莱克塔霍	39	-120		4.5	Ms	5										
1888	1	31	19	5						GSHAP	Kazakhstan:Talas,SE.	哈萨克斯坦:塔拉兹东南	42.8	73.3	20	4.8	Ms	5.5										
1888	2	18	10	50						CGS,USGS	US:California,Comptche	美国:加利福尼亚州康普奇	39.2	-123.6		5.5	Ms	5										
1888	2	27	12	35						GSHAP,Song	Peru:Arequipa	秘鲁:阿雷基帕	-16.4	-71.56		4.5	Mk	5										
1888	2	28	2	45						GSHAP,Song	Peru:Lima	秘鲁:利马	-12.08	-77		4.5	Mk	5										
1888	2	29	22	50						USGS	US:California,Two Rock	美国:加利福尼亚州图城罗克	38.3	-122.7		4.2	Ms	6										
1888	3	11								*	China:Qinghai,Ledu	中国:青海乐都	36.5	102.2		5	Ms	6		1		1		1		2		2
1888	3	13				5	15	3.4	3.5	NOAA,Song	Papua New Guinea: Umboi Island	巴布亚新几内亚:温博伊岛	-5.52	148.121		7.7	Mk			3				3				
1888	3	21				1				* NOAA,Song	Philippines:Hinatuan,Laak	菲律宾:希纳图安,圣维森特	8	125.4		7	Mk											
1888	3	25	3							GSHAP,Song	Peru:Arequipa	秘鲁:阿雷基帕	-16.4	-71.56		4.5	Mk	5										
1888	4	14	3	30						USGS	US:California,Alturas	美国:加利福尼亚州阿尔图拉斯	41.5	-120.5		4.6	Ms	6										
1888	4	28	4	40						GSHAP,Song	Peru:Lima	秘鲁:利马	-12.08	-77		4.5	Mk	5										
1888	4	29	1							Usami,Japan	Japan:Utsunomiya	日本:宇都宫市	36.6	140		6.2	Ms	7								1		
1888	4	29	4	48						CGS,USGS	US:California,Sierra City	美国:加利福尼亚州谢拉锡蒂	39.7	-120.7		6.2	Ms	7										
1888	5	25	10							GSHAP,Song	Peru:Arequipa	秘鲁:阿雷基帕	-16.4	-71.56		4.5	Mk	5										
1888	6	5	3	20		1				* GSHAP, NOAA	Argentina:Buenos Aires	阿根廷:布宜诺斯艾利斯	-34.6	-57.9	30	5.5	Ms	6						1				
1888	6	13	2	15						GSHAP,Song	Peru:Arequipa	秘鲁:阿雷基帕	-16.4	-71.56		4.5	Mk	5										
1888	6	13	18	45						GSHAP,Song	Peru:Arequipa	秘鲁:阿雷基帕	-16.4	-71.56		4.5	Mk	5										
1888	6	13								* China	China:Bohai Bay	中国:渤海湾	38.5	119		7.5	Ms			1				3		3		
1888	7	30	8	27		2			3	NOAA,Song	Italy:Pisa	意大利:比萨	43.75	10.3		6.7	Mk											
1888	8	19	6	39						Bautista,Maso	Philippines:Luzon,Coast N.	菲律宾:吕宋岛北部海域	18.7	121.9		5.2	Muk	6										
1888	8	19	11							USGS,Song	US:Arizona,Yuma	美国:亚利桑那州尤马	32.7	-114.6		5.5	Mk	6										
1888	8	20	18	5						USGS,Song	Hawaiian Islands	夏威夷群岛	19.25	-155		5	Mk	5										
1888	8	31	16	10						*	New Zealand:North Island:Cape Reinga	新西兰:北岛:雷恩加角	-34.5	172.7		7.3	Muk	9						3				
1888	9	9	15	15		4				* NOAA	Greece:Achaia	希腊:阿凯亚	38.2	22.1		6.1	Ms	10		2								
1888	9	16	19							GSHAP	Kyrgyzstan:Bishkek	吉尔吉斯斯坦:比什凯克	42.8	74.8	20	5.4	Ms	6.5										

年 Year	月 Mo	日 Dy	时 Hr	分 Mn	秒 Sec	海啸 Tsunami 源 Sr	浪高 Wh	级 I mI	级 S mS	资料来源 Information	震中 Earthquake Epicenter 地名(英文) Name(English)	地名(中文) Name(Chinese)	纬度(°) Latitude	经度(°) Longitude	深度 Depth	震级 Mag	标度 Scale	烈度 MMI	死亡人数 Deaths 数量/人 Num	级别 Dd	受伤人数 Injuries 数量/人 Num	级别 Dd	经济损失 Damage 数量/$ Mill	级别 De	房屋毁坏 Houses Destroyed 数量/间 Num	级别 Dh	房屋受损 Houses Damaged 数量/间 Num	级别 Dh
1888	9	17	11	51						USGS	US:California,Los Gatos	美国:加利福尼亚州洛斯加托斯	37.1	-121.8		4.5	Ms	5										
1888	9	22	5	10						GSHAP,Song	Peru:Lima	秘鲁:利马	-12.08	-77		4.5	Mk	5										
1888	9	22	10							*	Georgia:Akhalkalaki	格鲁吉亚:阿卡卡垃吉	41.3	43.3		6.1	Muk			3				2				
1888	9	23	12	30						GSHAP	Turkey:Ardahan	土耳其:阿尔达汉	40.9	42.8	12	5.1	Ms	7.5										
1888	10	4	6	15						GSHAP	Russia:Jewish,Samara	俄罗斯:犹太州萨马拉	47.8	131.1	10	5	Ms	7										
1888	10	13	6							GSHAP,Song	Peru:Lima	秘鲁:利马	-12.08	-77		4.5	Mk	5										
1888	10	20	3	45						GSHAP,Song	Peru:Lima	秘鲁:利马	-12.08	-77		4.5	Mk	5										
1888	10	20	6	30						GSHAP,Song	Peru:Lima	秘鲁:利马	-12.08	-77		4.5	Mk	5										
1888	11	2	4							GSHAP,Song	Peru:Lima	秘鲁:利马	-12.08	-77		5	Mk	6										
1888	11	2								* China	China:Gansu,Jingtai	中国:甘肃景泰	37.1	104.2		6.25	Ms	8		3				3		3		
1888	11	10	20							GSHAP	China:Xinjiang,Wenquan,S.	中国:新疆温泉南	44.7	80.5	20	6.2	Ms	7.5										
1888	11	14								GSHAP	Kazakhstan:Almaty	哈萨克斯坦:阿拉木图	44.8	78.5	20	5.7	Ms	7										
1888	11	17	17	30						* Song	Venezuela:Guanare	委内瑞拉:瓜纳累	9.2	-69.8		5.9	Mk							2				
1888	11	18	22	28						USGS	US:California,Richmond	美国:加利福尼亚州里奇蒙	37.9	-122.3		4.3	Ms	7										
1888	11	28	6	40						GSHAP	Kyrgyzstan:Lavater	吉尔吉斯斯坦:拉瓦特	40	69.8	20	6.3	Ms	8										
1888	11	29								GSHAP	Kazakhstan:Almaty	哈萨克斯坦:阿拉木图	44.9	75.1	30	6.1	Ms	7										
1888										GSHAP	Iran:Qūchān	伊朗:古昌	37.1	58.4	10	5.4	Ms	8										
1888										* Song	Iran:Lorestan	伊朗:洛雷斯坦	33.3	49.3		6.3	Mk							3				
1889	1	1	2	20						Bautista,Maso	Philippines:Mindanao Island	菲律宾:棉兰老岛	9.35	126.3		6.7	Muk	7										
1889	2	5	8							Bautista,Maso	Philippines:Mindanao Island	菲律宾:棉兰老岛	7.3	123.6		6.6	Muk	8										
1889	2	7	5	20						CGS,USGS	US:California,Landers	美国:加利福尼亚州兰德斯	34.1	-116.7		5.6	Ms	5										
1889	2	17	21	9						Usami,Japan	Japan:Yokohama	日本:神奈川横滨	35.5	139.7		6.2	Ms	7										
1889	2	25	6	8						GSHAP	Kazakhstan:Almaty	哈萨克斯坦:阿拉木图	43.1	76.9	15	5	Ms	6.5										
1889	2	28	5	45						GSHAP	Russia:Krasnodar,Sochi	俄罗斯:克拉斯诺达尔区索契	43.7	39.6	8	4.9	Ms	7										
1889	3	29	5							GSHAP,Song	Peru:Tacna	秘鲁:塔克纳	-18	-70.24		5	Mk	6										
1889	4	2	13	28						GSHAP,Song	Peru:Tacna	秘鲁:塔克纳	-18	-70.24		5	Mk	6										
1889	4	3	7							GSHAP,Song	Peru:Lima	秘鲁:利马	-12.08	-77		5	Mk	6										
1889	4	3	8	10						GSHAP,Song	Peru:Lima	秘鲁:利马	-12.08	-77		5	Mk	6										
1889	4	3	20	30						GSHAP,Song	Peru:Tacna	秘鲁:塔克纳	-18	-70.24		4.5	Mk	5										
1889	4	15	3	28						CGS,USGS	US:California,Hollister	美国:加利福尼亚州霍利斯特	36.95	-121.4		5.5	Ms	6										
1889	5	12	1	42						Usami,Japan	Japan:Gifu	日本:岐阜	35.4	136.8		6.7	Ms	7										
1889	5	19	11	10						CGS,USGS	US:California,Fairfield	美国:加利福尼亚州费尔菲尔德	38.1	-121.8		6	Ms	7										

年 Year	月 Mo	日 Dy	时 Hr	分 Mn	秒 Sec	源 Sr	浪高 Wh	级I mI	级S mS	资料来源 Information	地名(英文) Name(English)	地名(中文) Name(Chinese)	纬度(°) Latitude	经度(°) Longitude	深度 Depth	震级 Mag	标度 Scale	烈度 MMI	死亡人数 数量/人 Deaths Num	死亡人数 级别 Dd	受伤人数 数量/人 Injuries Num	受伤人数 级别 Dd	经济损失 数量/$ Mill Damage $ Mill	经济损失 级别 De	房屋毁坏 数量/间 Houses Destroyed Num	房屋毁坏 级别 Dh	房屋受损 数量/间 Houses Damaged Num	房屋受损 级别 Dh
1889	5	25	18	23		2	0.1		−3	* Nakamura, Maso, NOAA	Philippines: Mindoro, Calapan	菲律宾:民都洛岛,卡拉潘	13.5	121		6.8	Ms	8						2				
1889	6	20	6							CGS, USGS	US: Oregon, Wasco	美国:俄勒冈州沃斯科	40.5	−120.7		6.2	Ms	7										
1889	7	11	22	14						*	Kazakhstan: Almaty	哈萨克斯坦:阿拉木图	43.2	78.7		8.3	Muk	10						2				
1889	7	18	20	30						GSHAP	Kyrgyzstan: Bishkek	吉尔吉斯斯坦:比什凯克	42.8	74.9	20	5.8	Ms	7										
1889	7	19								GSHAP	Caspian Sea	里海	40.1	53.1	15	5.7	Ms	7.5										
1889	7	28	14	45						* Usami, Japan	Japan: Kagoshima	日本:鹿岛	31.5	131		6.3	Ms		20	1				1	320	3		
1889	7	31	12	47						CGS, USGS	US: California, San Francisco	美国:加利福尼亚州旧金山	37.8	−122.2		5.6	Ms	7										
1889	7	31	15							GSHAP	Azerbaijan: Lenkeran, N.	阿塞拜疆:连科兰北部	39	49	20	4.5	Ms	6										
1889	8	16				1			1	NOAA, Song	Indonesia: Java Island	印度尼西亚:爪哇岛	−6.05	105.92		7	Mk											
1889	8	17								* Song	Mexico: Guerrero, Chilpancingo, W.	墨西哥:格雷罗州奇尔潘辛戈西部	17.7	−100		6.3	Mk							3				
1889	8	25	19	13						* Song	Greece: Achaia	希腊:阿凯亚	38.3	22		6	Mk	8		2								
1889	8	28	2	15						CGS, USGS	US: California, Glendora	美国:加利福尼亚州格伦多拉	34.2	−117.9		5.6	Ms	6										
1889	8									China	China: Xinjiang, Tashkurghan	中国:新疆塔什库尔干	37.7	75.2		6	Ms	8										
1889	9	6				5	4	1	2.5	* NOAA	Indonesia: Molucca Sea	印度尼西亚:马鲁古海	1	126.25		8	Ms							2				
1889	9	30	5	20						CGS, USGS	US: California, Caliente	美国:加利福尼亚州卡连特	37.2	−118.7		6	Ms	5										
1889	9	30	16	50						Usami, Japan	Ryukyu Islands	琉球群岛	28	130		6	Ms	7										1
1889	9									China	China: Ningxia, Lingwu	中国:宁夏灵武	38.1	106.3		5.5	Ms	7										
1889	10	1								* Song	Mexico: Morelos	墨西哥:莫雷洛斯	18.8	−99		6.3	Mk							3				
1889	10	6	3	15						Bautista, Maso	Philippine Trench	菲律宾海沟	5.9	127		7.3	Muk	7										
1889	10	25	21	29						*	Greece: Lesbos	希腊:莱斯沃斯	39.2	26		6.9	Muk	11	25	1				2				
1889	10									China	China: Hebei, Daming	中国:河北大名	36.3	115.1		5	Ms	6										
1889	11	21	9							China	China: Taiwan, Tainan	中国:台湾台南	23	120.2		5	Ms	6										
1889	11	22								GSHAP	Kazakhstan: Koktal	哈萨克斯坦:科克塔尔	44.2	80.3	12	5.5	Ms	7.5										
1889	11	23				3			1	* NOAA	Indonesia: Madura Island, Java	印度尼西亚:马都拉岛,爪哇	−7	113.5		6	Ms											
1889	12	8				1				Italy, NOAA	Italy: Apricena	意大利:阿普里切纳	41.83	15.692		5.55	Ms											
1889										*	Cote D'Ivoire: Daloa	科特迪瓦:达洛亚	6.8	−6.7		4.7	Muk	8						2				
1889										GSHAP	China: Xinjiang, Pishan, S.	中国:新疆皮山南	38	77.5	33	7	Ms	9										
1890	1	7	6	43						Usami, Japan	Japan: Nagano	日本:长野	36.5	138		6.2	Ms		1	1				2				
1890	1	7	19	50						GSHAP, Song	Peru: Lima	秘鲁:利马	−12.08	−77		5	Mk	6										
1890	1	13	10	20						GSHAP, Song	Peru: Arequipa	秘鲁:阿雷基帕	−16.4	−71.56		4.5	Mk	5										
1890	1	19	4							GSHAP, Song	Peru: Arequipa	秘鲁:阿雷基帕	−16.4	−71.56		4.5	Mk	5										
1890	1	31	8							GSHAP, Song	Peru: Lima	秘鲁:利马	−12.08	−77		4.5	Mk	5										

时间						海啸				资料来源	震中				深度	震级	标度	烈度	死亡人数		受伤人数		经济损失		房屋毁坏		房屋受损	
年	月	日	时	分	秒	源	浪高	级 I	级 S		地名(英文)	地名(中文)	纬度(°)	经度(°)					数量/人	级别	数量/人	级别	数量/$ Mill	级别	数量/间	级别	数量/间	级别
Date						Tsunami				Information	Earthquake Epicenter				Depth	Mag	Scale	MMI	Deaths		Injuries		Damage		Houses Destroyed		Houses Damaged	
Year	Mo	Dy	Hr	Mn	Sec	Sr	Wh	mI	mS		Name(English)	Name(Chinese)	Latitude	Longitude					Num	Dd	Num	Dd	$ Mill	De	Num	Dh	Num	Dh
1890	2	7	4	30						* Maso, Song	Philippines: Samar, Leyte	菲律宾:萨马岛,莱特	11.2	124.4		6.1	Mk	8						2				
1890	2	9	12	6						CGS, USGS	US: California, Borrego Springs	美国:加利福尼亚州博雷戈斯普林斯	33.4	-116.3		6.8	Ms	6										
1890	2	10	5							GSHAP, Song	Peru: Arequipa	秘鲁:阿雷基帕	-16.4	-71.56		4.5	Mk	5										
1890	2	17								China	China: Qinghai, Haidong	中国:青海海东	36.5	102		5.25	Ms	6										
1890	2	25	17	30						GSHAP	Kazakhstan: Almaty	哈萨克斯坦:阿拉木图	43	78	40	6.4	Ms	7										
1890	2	26	3	30						GSHAP	Azerbaijan: Agcabədi	阿塞拜疆:阿格贾贝迪区	40.6	47.7	22	4.6	Ms	5										
1890	4	13	6	4						Bautista, Maso	Philippines: Luzon, Coast N.	菲律宾:吕宋岛北部海域	18.75	120.25		5.9	Muk	6										
1890	4	16	12	34						Usami, Japan	Japan: Miyake Jima	日本:三宅岛	34.1	139.5		6.8	Ms									1		
1890	4	22								China	China: Yunnan, Jianchuan	中国:云南剑川	26.5	99.9		5.5	Ms	7								3		
1890	4	24	11	36						CGS, USGS	US: California, Watsonville	美国:加利福尼亚州沃森维尔	36.9	-121.6		6.3	Ms	8										
1890	4	24								GSHAP, Song	Chile: Valparaiso	智利:瓦尔帕莱索	-32.75	-70.73		6	Mk	8										
1890	4	30	23							GSHAP	Kazakhstan: Urdzhar, E.	哈萨克斯坦:乌尔贾尔东部	46.6	82.6	20	5	Ms	6										
1890	5	14								GSHAP	Azerbaijan: Gence, N.	阿塞拜疆:占贾北部	41.8	46.7	15	4.5	Ms	6										
1890	6	11	1	54						USGS, Song	US: Arizona, Yuma	美国:亚利桑那州尤马	32.7	-114.6		5.5	Mk	6										
1890	6	28								* * Song	Iran: Mashhad	伊朗:马什哈德	36.2	59.4		6.3	Mk			3				3				
1890	7	11	7	55		3				* NOAA	Iran: Gorgan	伊朗:戈尔甘	36.6	54.6	10	7.2	Ms	10	171	3				3		3		
1890	7	26	9	40						CGS, USGS	US: California, Fortuna	美国:加利福尼亚州福图纳	40.5	-124.2		6.3	Ms	7										
1890	8	7	9	40						USGS, Song	Hawaiian Islands	夏威夷群岛	19.25	-155		5.5	Mk	6										
1890	9	19	15	30						GSHAP, Song	Chile: Copiapo	智利:科皮亚波	-27.35	-70.35		6	Mk	8										
1890	10	6								China	China: Yunnan, Lijiang, N.	中国:云南丽江北	27.3	100.3		5	Ms	6										
1890	10	28	19							GSHAP	Georgia: Tbilisi	格鲁吉亚:第比利斯	41.9	44.6	18	4.9	Ms	6.5										
1890	11	15								GSHAP	Bolivia: Santa Cruz de la Sierra	玻利维亚:圣克鲁斯	-17.78	-63.17		5.2	Ms	6										
1890	11	23								* Song	Indonesia: Sulawesi, Makasar	印度尼西亚:苏拉威西岛,望加锡	-5	120		5.9	Mk	7						2				
1890	11	25	5	30						GSHAP, Song	Peru: Lima	秘鲁:利马	-12.08	-77		4.5	Mk	5										
1890	12	12								* Song	Indonesia: Java, Pati	印度尼西亚:爪哇,帕蒂	-6.4	111		6.1	Mk	8		2				1				
1890	12	20	14							GSHAP, Song	Peru: Lima	秘鲁:利马	-12.08	-77		4.5	Mk	5										
1890										* China	China: Shanxi, Wuxiang	中国:山西武乡	36.9	112.9		5.5	Ms	7						2		3		
1891	1	2	20							CGS, USGS	US: California, Morgan Hill	美国:加利福尼亚州莫干山	37.3	-121.8		5.8	Ms	6										
1891	1	15	3	55		3				* NOAA, Song	Algeria: Bourava, Gouraya	阿尔及利亚:古拉亚	36.5	1.8		6.7	Mk	10	36	1				2	75	2		
1891	3	8	3	40						USGS	US: Washington, Seattle	美国:华盛顿州西雅图	47.5	-121.5		5	Ms	5										
1891	3	27	18	30						GSHAP	Georgia: Gori	格鲁吉亚:哥里	42.1	43.9	22	4.5	Ms	5.5										

时间 Date						海啸 Tsunami				资料来源 Information	震中 Earthquake Epicenter				深度 Depth	震级 Mag	标度 Scale	烈度 MMI	死亡人数 Deaths		受伤人数 Injuries		经济损失 Damage		房屋毁坏 Houses Destroyed		房屋受损 Houses Damaged	
年 Year	月 Mo	日 Dy	时 Hr	分 Mn	秒 Sec	源 Sr	浪高 Wh	级 I mI	级 S mS		地名(英文) Name(English)	地名(中文) Name(Chinese)	纬度(°) Latitude	经度(°) Longitude					数量/人 Num	级别 Dd	数量/人 Num	级别 Dd	数量/$ Mill $ Mill	级别 De	数量/间 Num	级别 Dh	数量/间 Num	级别 Dh
1891	4	3								* Song	Turkey: Van	土耳其:凡城	38.3	43.2		6.3	Mk			3				3				
1891	4	17								* China	China: Shanxi, Jiexiu	中国:山西介休	37.1	111.9		5.75	Ms	7	31	1				1		2		
1891	4	20	13	55						USGS, Song	US: Utah, St George	美国:犹他州圣乔治	37.1	-113.6		5.5	Mk	6										
1891	6	10				1			0.5	NOAA, Song	Indonesia: Maluku Utara	印度尼西亚:北马鲁古	1.375	127.52		7	Mk											
1891	6	20				3				NOAA, Song	Indonesia: Maluku Islands	印度尼西亚:摩鹿加群岛	-3.6	128.7		7	Mk											
1891	6	22	18	40		1				* Song	New Zealand: North Island, Near Coast of E.	新西兰:北岛东部近海	-40.5	177		7	Mk											
1891	6	24	19	42						Bautista, Maso	Philippines: Mindanao Island	菲律宾:棉兰老岛	7.6	126		7.2	Muk	7										
1891	7	27	2	28						USGS	US: Kentucky, Henderson	美国:肯塔基州亨德森	37.9	-87.5		4.1	Ms	6										
1891	7	30				1			1	* NOAA, CGS	Mexico: Mexicali	墨西哥:墨西卡利	32	-115		6.6	Mk											
1891	8	15	11	2						GSHAP	Bolivia: La Paz	玻利维亚:拉巴斯	-15.33	-68.54		5.8	Ms	7										
1891	9	23	5	10						GSHAP, Song	Peru: Lima	秘鲁:利马	-12.08	-77		5	Mk	6										
1891	9	27	4	55						USGS	US: Illinois, Belle Prairie City	美国:伊利诺斯州贝莱普雷里锡蒂	38.25	-88.5		5.2	Ms	7										
1891	10	2								GSHAP, Song	Peru: Lima	秘鲁:利马	-12.08	-77		4.5	Mk	5										
1891	10	5				3			0.5	* NOAA	Indonesia: Timor Island	印度尼西亚:帝汶岛	-9	124	80	7	Ms											
1891	10	12	6	28						CGS, USGS	US: California, Napa	美国:加利福尼亚州那帕	38.3	-122.4		5.9	Ms	8										
1891	10	15	22	6						Usami, Japan	Japan: Oita	日本:大分	33.2	131.8		6.8	Ms	8										1
1891	10	23	16	56						GSHAP	Ecuador: Quito	厄瓜多尔:基多	-0.22	-78.5		4.3	Ms	5										
1891	10	27	21	37						* Usami	Japan: Gifu	日本:岐阜	35.5	137		8.4	Muk		7273	4				4	142177	5		
1891	11	29	23	21		3	2.4	1.3	1.5	* NOAA, Song	US: Washington, Clallam Bay	美国:华盛顿州克拉勒姆贝	48	-123.5		7.2	Mk	6										
1891	11									China	China: Taiwan, Tainan	中国:台湾台南	23	120.2		5	Ms	6										
1891	12	23	20	35						Usami	Japan: Yamanakako	日本:山梨山中湖村	35.4	138.9		6.9	Ms	7										1
1891	12		21							USGS, Song	US: Colorado, Maybell	美国:科罗拉多州梅贝尔	40.5	-108		5.5	Mk	6										
1892	1	26				1				* NOAA, Australia, Song	Australia: Tasman Sea	澳大利亚:塔斯曼海	-40.4	149.5		6.9	Mk											
1892	2	2	8	30						USGS, Song	US: Arizona, Flagstaff	美国:亚利桑那州弗拉格斯塔夫	35.2	-111.6		5.5	Mk	6										
1892	2	4	4	30						USGS	US: Oregon, Portland	美国:俄勒冈州波特兰	45.5	-122.7		5	Ms	5										
1892	2	10								China	China: Sichuan, Nanxi	中国:四川南溪	28.9	105		5	Ms	6										
1892	2	23	17	10						GSHAP, Song	Peru: Lima	秘鲁:利马	-12.08	-77		4.5	Mk	5										
1892	2	24	7	20						* Song	Mexico: Baja California	墨西哥:下加利福尼亚	31.5	-116.5		7.3	Mk	10						3				
1892	3	8								* Bautista, Maso	Philippines: Batan Island, San Domingo	菲律宾:巴丹岛,圣多明哥	20.4	121.45		6.8	Ms	8						2				
1892	3	14	14							GSHAP, Song	Chile: Arica	智利:阿里卡	-18.5	-70.35		6	Mk	8										
1892	3	16	12	58						* Bautista, Maso	Philippines: San Fernando	菲律宾:圣费尔南多	16.4	120.4		6.6	Ms	10	2	1				3				

年 Year	月 Mo	日 Dy	时 Hr	分 Mn	秒 Sec	源 Sr	浪高 Wh	级 I mI	级 S mS	资料来源 Information	地名(英文) Name(English)	地名(中文) Name(Chinese)	纬度(°) Latitude	经度(°) Longitude	深度 Depth	震级 Mag	标度 Scale	烈度 MMI	死亡人数 Deaths 数量/人 Num	级别 Dd	受伤人数 Injuries 数量/人 Num	级别 Dd	经济损失 Damage 数量/$ Mill	级别 De	房屋毁坏 Houses Destroyed 数量/间 Num	级别 Dh	房屋受损 Houses Damaged 数量/间 Num	级别 Dh
1892	3	16	16	34						Maso, Song	Philippines: San Fernando	菲律宾:圣费尔南多	16.4	120.4		5.5	Mk	7										
1892	3									China	China: Qinghai, Ledu	中国:青海乐都	36.5	102.4		4.75	Ms	6										
1892	4	17	22	50						USGS, Song	US: Washington, Olympia	美国:华盛顿州奥林匹亚	47	-123		5.5	Mk	6										
1892	4	19	10	50						* CGS, USGS	US: California, Pope Valley	美国:加利福尼亚州波普瓦利	38.5	-122.5		6.6	Ms	9					0.25	1				
1892	4	21	17	43						* CGS, USGS	US: California, Fairfield	美国:加利福尼亚州费尔菲尔德	38.5	-121.9		6.4	Ms	9						2				
1892	4	22								China	China: Taiwan, Kaohsiung	中国:台湾高雄	22.7	120.2		6	Ms	7		3								
1892	4	30	0	9						CGS, USGS	US: California, Fairfield	美国:加利福尼亚州费尔菲尔德	38.4	-121.8		5.6	Ms	6										
1892	5	16	21	10		4			0.5	* Maso, NOAA	Guam	关岛(西太平洋)	14	143.3		7.5	Ms	8						3		1		
1892	5	17	12	10		3			1	* NOAA, Song	Indonesia: Northern Sumatera	印度尼西亚:苏门答腊北部	2.5	99.5		7.2	Mk	6						2		3		3
1892	5	28	11	15						CGS, USGS	US: California, Borrego Springs	美国:加利福尼亚州博雷戈斯普林斯	33.2	-116.2		6.5	Ms	5										
1892	6	2	22	10						Usami, Japan	Japan: Tokyo	日本:东京	35.7	139.9		6.7	Ms	7							1	1		
1892	6	14	13	25						CGS, USGS	US: California, Victorville	美国:加利福尼亚州维克托维尔	34.2	-117.5		5.5	Ms	5										
1892	7	10	9	52						GSHAP	Russia: Sverdlovsk, Sysert	俄罗斯:斯威尔德洛夫斯克州瑟谢尔季	56.5	60.9	15	4.5	Ms	6										
1892	7	28								China	China: Hainan, Ding - An	中国:海南定安	19.8	110.5		5	Ms	6										
1892	8	9	1							GSHAP	Azerbaijan: Lenkeran	阿塞拜疆:连科兰	38.8	49	15	4.6	Ms	6										
1892	9	6	20	42						Japan	Japan: Fukui	日本:福井	36.1	136.51		6.6	Ms	7										
1892	9	18	20	46						GSHAP	Uzbekistan: Navoiy	乌兹别克斯坦:纳沃伊州	40.7	66.5	28	6.1	Ms	7										
1892	10	14	5	55						GSHAP	Romania: Cernavoda	罗马尼亚:切尔纳沃德	44.5	28	70	6.8	Ms	7										
1892	11	13	12	45						CGS, USGS	US: California, Tres Pinos	美国:加利福尼亚州特雷斯皮诺斯	36.75	-121.4		5.9	Ms	6										
1892	11	15	11	20		1				NOAA, Song	Tyrrhenian Sea	第勒尼安海(伊特鲁里亚海)	40.54	13		6.6	Mk											
1892	11	18				3			-1	* NOAA	Indonesia: Ceram Sea	印度尼西亚:塞兰海	-3	127.8		7	Ms											
1892	11	24	9	45						GSHAP	Caspian Sea	里海	39.9	53.1	15	5.7	Ms	7.5										
1892	12	9	1	42		4				* Usami, Japan, NOAA	Japan: Nanao	日本:石川七尾	37.1	136.7		6.5	Ms		1	1					2	1		
1892	12	10	16	34						Japan	Japan: Nanao	日本:石川七尾	37	136.7		6.5	Ms		1	1	2	1				1		
1892	12	20								* Song	Pakistan: Chaman, Baluchistan	巴基斯坦:洽曼,俾路支	30.5	66.2		6.3	Mk							3				
1893	1	28				1				GSHAP, NOAA	Aegean Sea	爱琴海	40.5	25.6	15	5.8	Ms											
1893	1	31	2	30						*	Greece: Zakynthos	希腊:扎金索斯岛	37.7	20.9		6.4	Ms	11						3				
1893	2	9	16			3	1		3	* NOAA, GSHAP	Greece: Samothraki	希腊:萨莫色雷斯	40.5	25.5		6.8	Muk	10						2				

时间						海啸				资料来源	震中				深度	震级	标度	烈度	死亡人数		受伤人数		经济损失		房屋毁坏		房屋受损	
年	月	日	时	分	秒	源	浪高	级I	级S		地名(英文)	地名(中文)	纬度(°)	经度(°)					数量/人	级别	数量/人	级别	数量/$ Mill	级别	数量/间	级别	数量/间	级别
Date						Tsunami				Information	Earthquake Epicenter				Depth	Mag	Scale	MMI	Deaths		Injuries		Damage		Houses Destroyed		Houses Damaged	
Year	Mo	Dy	Hr	Mn	Sec	Sr	Wh	mI	mS		Name(English)	Name(Chinese)	Latitude	Longitude					Num	Dd	Num	Dd	$ Mill	De	Num	Dh	Num	Dh
1893	2	19				2				* NOAA, Song	Jamaica: Kingston	牙买加:金斯敦	17.97	-76.8		7	Mk											
1893	2	22	21	25						GSHAP, Song	Chile: Coquimbo	智利:科金博	-29.9	-71.25		6	Mk	8										
1893	2	23								China	China: Hebei, Cangzhou	中国:河北沧州	38.3	116.8		5	Ms	6										
1893	3	7	1	3						USGS	US: Oregon, Hermiston	美国:俄勒冈州赫米斯顿	45.9	-119.3		4.7	Ms	6										
1893	3	8	16	39						Bautista, Maso	Philippines: San Fernando	菲律宾:圣费尔南多	16.85	120.2		5.6	Muk	6										
1893	3	31								*	Turkey: Malatya	土耳其:马拉蒂亚	38.3	38.3		6.7	Ms	9	400	3				3				
1893	4	4	19	40						CGS, USGS	US: California, Santa Clarita	美国:加利福尼亚州圣塔克拉利塔	34.3	-118.6		5.8	Ms	8										
1893	4	8	3	20						USGS, Song	US: New Mexico, La Joya	美国:新墨西哥州拉霍亚	34.5	-106.8		5.5	Mk	6										
1893	4	8	13	47						* GSHAP	Serbia: Kragujevac	塞尔维亚:克拉古耶瓦茨	44.3	21		5.7	Mk	10	3	1				3		3		
1893	4	12	5	51						Bautista, Maso	Philippines: Legazpi	菲律宾:黎牙实比	13.1	123.65		5.5	Muk	6										
1893	4	17	5			3				* NOAA	Greece: Zakynthos	希腊:扎金索斯岛	37.7	20.9		6.4	Ms	10		2				3	2000	4		
1893	4									China	China: Yunnan, Luquan	中国:云南禄劝	25.6	102.5		5	Ms	6	3	1								
1893	5	19	0	35						CGS, USGS	US: California, Oxnard	美国:加利福尼亚州奥克斯纳德	34.1	-119.4		5.8	Ms	5										
1893	6	1								* China	China: Qinghai, Xining	中国:青海西宁	36.6	101.8		5.5	Ms	7		3				2	300	3	300	3
1893	6	2	22	30						Bautista, Maso	Philippines: Mindanao Island	菲律宾:棉兰老岛	7.6	123.8		5.9	Muk	7										
1893	6	3	17	27		4	3	1.6	1.5	* Usami, GSHAP, NOAA	Kuril Islands	千岛群岛	43.5	148		7	Ms		1									
1893	6	13				4			1	* NOAA	Japan Trench	日本海沟	42.5	145.5		6.9	Ms											
1893	6	14				2			3	* NOAA, GSHAP	Albania: Himara, Vlore	阿尔巴尼亚:希马拉,发罗拉	40.2	19.7		7.5	Ms	11						3				
1893	6	21	7	30		4				* Bautista, Maso	Philippines: Mindanao, Davao	菲律宾:棉兰老岛,达沃	7.65	126.1		7.3	Ms	10		3				3		3		
1893	6	30	13	30						USGS	US: California, Richmond	美国:加利福尼亚州里奇蒙	38	-122.4		4.6	Ms	5										
1893	6	30	20	8						Maso, Song	Philippines: Mindanao Island	菲律宾:棉兰老岛	8.1	126.21		5.5	Mk	7										
1893	7	2	1	15						GSHAP	Russia: Dagestan, Makhachkala	俄罗斯:达吉斯坦共和国马哈奇卡拉	42.5	46.7	20	4.9	Ms	5.5										
1893	7	31				1				* NOAA	Vanuatu Islands	瓦努阿图群岛	-18	168		6	Ms											
1893	7									GSHAP	Black Sea	黑海	44.3	34.6	22	4.8	Ms	5.5										
1893	8	9	9	15						CGS, USGS	US: California, Santa Rosa	美国:加利福尼亚州圣罗莎	38.4	-122.7		5.6	Ms	7										
1893	8	10	9							* Italy	Italy: Mattinata	意大利:福贾,玛蒂娜妲	41.72	16.08		5.44	Ms	10										
1893	8	17	14	25						GSHAP	Romania: Nereju	罗马尼亚:内雷茹	45.7	26.6	100	6.6	Ms	7.5										

年 Year	月 Mo	日 Dy	时 Hr	分 Mn	秒 Sec	海啸 Tsunami 源 Sr	浪高 Wh	级 I mI	级 S mS	资料来源 Information	震中 Earthquake Epicenter 地名(英文) Name(English)	地名(中文) Name(Chinese)	纬度(°) Latitude	经度(°) Longitude	深度 Depth	震级 Mag	标度 Scale	烈度 MMI	死亡人数 Deaths 数量/人 Num	级别 Dd	受伤人数 Injuries 数量/人 Num	级别 Dd	经济损失 Damage 数量/$ Mill $ Mill	级别 De	房屋毁坏 Houses Destroyed 数量/间 Num	级别 Dh	房屋受损 Houses Damaged 数量/间 Num	级别 Dh
1893	8	27				2				NOAA, Song	Vanuatu Islands	瓦努阿图群岛	-15.5	167.2		7	Mk											
1893	8	29								* China	China: Sichuan, Dawu, SE.	中国:四川道孚东南	30.6	101.5		7	Ms	9	288	3	133	3		3		3		
1893	9	5	22	45						GSHAP	Ecuador: Azuay	厄瓜多尔:阿苏艾	-3.1	-79		5.7	Ms	7										
1893	9	6	17	25						Usami, Japan	Japan: Kagoshima	日本:鹿岛	31.4	130.5		6.4	Ms											2
1893	9	7								USGS, Song	US: New Mexico, La Joya	美国:新墨西哥州拉霍亚	34.5	-106.8		5.7	Mk	7										
1893	9	10	3	42						GSHAP	Romania: Nereju	罗马尼亚:内雷茹	45.7	26.6	100	6.1	Ms	7										
1893	9	11								GSHAP	Colombia: Cauca	哥伦比亚:考卡	2.5	-76.6		5.7	Ms	7										
1893	10	17								China	China: Taiwan, Taipei	中国:台湾台北	25.1	121.5		5	Ms	6										
1893	11	5	3	30						GSHAP	Tadzhikistan: Sabah	塔吉克斯坦:萨巴赫	39.5	69.4	40	5.9	Ms	7										
1893	11	17	15	6						* Iran	Iran: Qūchān	伊朗:古昌	37	58.4		7.1	Ms	10	18000	5				4		4		
1893	11	19								GSHAP	Iran: Qūchān	伊朗:古昌	37.8	58.2	15	4.5	Ms	6										
1893	11	26								China	China: Guangxi, Fusui, N.	中国:广西扶绥北	22.8	107.8		4.75	Ms	6										
1893	12	17								* China	China: Xinjiang, Kuqa, SW.	中国:新疆库车西南	41.7	82.8		6.75	Ms	9	90	2	32	1		3	556	3		
1893	12	23	16	20						Bautista, Maso	Philippines: Masbate Island	菲律宾:马斯巴特岛	12	124.1		5.6	Muk	6										
1893	12	25								* China	China: Xinjiang, Aksu	中国:新疆阿克苏	41.2	80.3		6.5	Ms	8		3		3		2		3		
1894	1	4	13	9						Usami, Japan	Japan: Kagoshima	日本:鹿岛	31.4	130.5		6.3	Ms	8										1
1894	1	10	9	45						Japan	Japan: Mizuho	日本:岐阜瑞穗	35.4	136.7		7.4	Ms											1
1894	1	17								* Song	Iran: Qūchān	伊朗:古昌	37.1	58.3		5.9	Mk							2				
1894	2	9	17	5						* Bautista, Maso	Philippines: Mindanao, Davao Gulf	菲律宾:棉兰老岛,达沃海湾	6.3	125.85		6.7	Ms	8						2				
1894	2	17	21	23						Maso, Song	Philippines: Mindanao Island	菲律宾:棉兰老岛	8.2	126.11		5	Mk	6										
1894	2	20	1	45						GSHAP, Song	Peru: Tacna	秘鲁:塔克纳	-18	-70.24		4.5	Mk	5										
1894	2	26								* Iran	Iran: Fars, Shiraz	伊朗:法尔斯,设拉子	29.5	53.3		5.9	Ms							2				
1894	3	4	6	35						GSHAP	Romania: Nereju	罗马尼亚:内雷茹	45.7	26.6	100	5.8	Ms	6.5										
1894	3	22	10	23		4	4	2	2	* Usami, NOAA	Japan: Hokkaido	日本:北海道	42.5	146	40	8	Ms	9	1	1	2	1		1	14	1	99	2
1894	4	1	22	34						Maso, Song	Philippines: Cabanatuan	菲律宾:甲万那端	15.4	120.9		5	Mk	6										
1894	4	20	16	52						*	Greece: Sterea Ellada	希腊:斯戴里亚艾尔拉达	38.6	23.2		6.7	Ms	10	255	3				3				
1894	4	27	19	42		4	3	1.6	4	* Turkey, NOAA	Greece: Sterea Ellada	希腊:斯戴里亚艾尔拉达	38.7	23.1		7.2	Ms	11		3				3				
1894	4	29	2	45						*	Venezuela: Merida	委内瑞拉:梅里达	8.5	-71.7	20	8.2	Ms	9	400	3								
1894	5	14								GSHAP	Turkey: Adana	土耳其:阿达纳	36.6	35.6	30	6.1	Ms	7										
1894	6	20	5	4						* Usami	Japan: Tokyo	日本:东京	35.7	139.9		7.5	Ms		31	1	157	3		1	90	2		
1894	6	20	8							GSHAP	Azerbaijan: Samaxi	阿塞拜疆:沙马基区	40.4	47.7	17	4.5	Ms	5.5										
1894	6	21	6	30						GSHAP	Azerbaijan: Yevlax	阿塞拜疆:叶夫拉赫	40.7	47.1	15	4.7	Ms	6										
1894	6	28	18	57						* Maso, Song	Philippines: Mindanao, Agusan River Valley	菲律宾:棉兰老岛,阿古桑河流域	8.2	126.1		6.2	Mk	8		3				1				

年 Year	月 Mo	日 Dy	时 Hr	分 Mn	秒 Sec	海啸 源 Sr	海啸 浪高 Wh	海啸 级I mI	海啸 级S mS	资料来源 Information	震中 地名(英文) Name(English)	震中 地名(中文) Name(Chinese)	纬度(°) Latitude	经度(°) Longitude	深度 Depth	震级 Mag	标度 Scale	烈度 MMI	死亡人数 数量/人 Num	死亡人数 级别 Dd	受伤人数 数量/人 Num	受伤人数 级别 Dd	经济损失 数量/$ Mill	经济损失 级别 De	房屋毁坏 数量/间 Num	房屋毁坏 级别 Dh	房屋受损 数量/间 Num	房屋受损 级别 Dh
1894	6	29	21	50						Maso, Song	Philippines: Mindanao, Agusan River Valley	菲律宾:棉兰老岛,阿古桑河流域	8. 2	126. 1		5. 5	Mk	7										
1894	7	10	12	33		2			3	* NOAA, GSHAP	Turkey: Iznik, Izmit	土耳其:伊兹尼克,伊兹米特	40. 6	28. 7		7	Ms	10										
1894	7	18	22	50						USGS, Song	US: Nevada, Wells	美国:内华达州韦尔斯	41. 2	-112		5. 5	Mk	6										
1894	7	26	0	15						*	Greece: Dukat	希腊:杜卡特	37. 75	21. 75		6. 3	Ms							2		2		
1894	7	28								GSHAP	Uzbekistan: Namangan	乌兹别克斯坦:纳曼干	41	71. 2	10	5	Ms	7										
1894	7	30	5	12						CGS, USGS	US: California, Victorville	美国:加利福尼亚州维克托维尔	34. 3	-117. 6		6. 2	Ms	6										
1894	8	8	14	19						Usami, Japan	Japan: Kumamoto	日本:熊本	32. 8	131		6. 8	Ms	8								3		
1894	8	24								China	China: Yunnan, Xuanwei	中国:云南宣威	26. 2	104. 1		5	Ms	6										
1894	8	31	12	20						GSHAP	Romania: Nereju	罗马尼亚:内雷茹	45. 7	26. 6	150	6. 8	Ms	8										
1894	9	30	17	36						CGS, USGS	US: California, North Coast	美国:加利福尼亚州北部近海	40. 3	-124. 5		6. 5	Ms	7										
1894	10	19	14	30						GSHAP	Kazakhstan: Zyryanovsk	哈萨克斯坦:济良诺夫斯克	50. 8	84	26	5. 9	Ms	6. 5										
1894	10	22	8	35		4		-1	-1	* GSHAP, Usami, NOAA	Japan: Yamagata	日本:山形	38. 9	139. 8	40	7. 3	Ms	8	726	3				3	6000	4		
1894	10	23	23	3						CGS, USGS	US: California, Alpine	美国:加利福尼亚州阿尔派恩	32. 8	-116. 8		6. 1	Ms	6										
1894	10	27	19	30						*	Argentina: La Rioja, San Juan	阿根廷:拉里奥哈,圣胡安	-32	-68. 5		7. 5	Ms	9						2				
1894	11	4	16	45						* Song	Venezuela: Carache	委内瑞拉:卡拉切	9. 4	-70. 1		5. 9	Mk							2				
1894	11	16	18	52		2				* Italy, NOAA	Italy: Palmi, Santa Cristina	意大利:帕尔米,圣克里斯蒂娜	38. 28	15. 87		6. 05	Ms	10	101	3				3				
1894	11	18	10	49						USGS, Song	US: Nevada, Dayton	美国:内华达州代顿	39. 2	-119. 5		5. 5	Mk	6										
1894	11	29	10	30						GSHAP	Georgia: Tbilisi	格鲁吉亚:第比利斯	41. 9	44. 6	24	4. 6	Ms	5. 5										
1894	12	6	14	35						GSHAP	Turkmenistan: Turkmenbasy	土库曼斯坦:土库曼巴希	40	53. 2	15	5. 1	Ms	6. 5										
1895	1	17	8	30						*	Iran: Qūchān	伊朗:古昌	37. 1	58. 4		6. 8	Ms		11000	5				4		4		
1895	1	18	13	48						Usami	Japan: Namegata	日本:茨城行方	36. 1	140. 4		7. 2	Ms		6	1					52	2		
1895	1	18								GSHAP	Kazakhstan: Urdzhar, E.	哈萨克斯坦:乌尔贾尔东部	46. 7	82. 7	20	5	Ms	6										
1895	3	6	8	35		4	6	2. 6	2	* NOAA	Solomon Sea, W.	所罗门海西部	-8. 5	151		7. 5	Ms			2				2		2		
1895	3	9				2				* NOAA, Song	US: California, Sonoma	美国:加利福尼亚州索诺马	38. 2	-122. 4		7	Mk											
1895	4	14	20	17	30					* Italy	Slovenia: Ljubljana	斯洛文尼亚:卢布尔雅那	46. 1	14. 5	16	6. 25	Ms	9	7	1				3		3		
1895	5	1	8							GSHAP	Colombia: Huila	哥伦比亚:乌伊拉	2	-75. 9		5	Ms	6										
1895	5	13	22	45						* Bautista, Maso	Philippines: Mindoro, Calapan	菲律宾:民都洛岛,卡拉潘	13. 5	120. 9		5. 4	Ms	7						1				

时间 Date						海啸 Tsunami				资料来源 Information	震中 Earthquake Epicenter				深度 Depth	震级 Mag	标度 Scale	烈度 MMI	死亡人数 Deaths		受伤人数 Injuries		经济损失 Damage		房屋毁坏 Houses Destroyed		房屋受损 Houses Damaged	
年 Year	月 Mo	日 Dy	时 Hr	分 Mn	秒 Sec	源 Sr	浪高 Wh	级 I mI	级 S mS		地名(英文) Name(English)	地名(中文) Name(Chinese)	纬度(°) Latitude	经度(°) Longitude					数量/人 Num	级别 Dd	数量/人 Num	级别 Dd	数量/$ Mill $ Mill	级别 De	数量/间 Num	级别 Dh	数量/间 Num	级别 Dh
1895	5	13	22							* GSHAP	Albania: Himara	阿尔巴尼亚:希马拉	40. 1	19. 4		6. 4	Mk	10		3				2				
1895	5	14	3							*	Greece: Thesprotia	希腊:塞斯普罗蒂亚	39. 5	20. 5		7. 5	Ms	10		2				3				
1895	5	15								*	Albania: Gjirokaster	阿尔巴尼亚:吉诺卡斯特	40	20. 1		6. 4	Ms	10						2				
1895	5	18	19	54						* Italy	Italy: Florence, Martino	意大利:佛罗伦萨,马尔蒂诺	43. 75	11. 25		5. 17	Ms	10						3		3		
1895	5	25				1			0. 5	* NOAA, Song	Japan: Omura	日本:长崎大村	33	130		7	Mk											
1895	6	7	13	56						Maso, Song	Philippines: Mindoro Island	菲律宾:民都洛岛	13. 51	121		5. 5	Mk	7										
1895	6	16	10							* Song	Greece: Thesprotia	希腊:塞斯普罗蒂亚	39. 5	20. 5		7	Mk	10										
1895	7	5								China	China: Xinjiang, Tashkurghan	中国:新疆塔什库尔干	37. 7	75. 1		7	Ms	9										
1895	7	8	21	30		2				* NOAA	Turkmenistan: Balkanabat	土库曼斯坦:巴尔坎纳巴德	39. 5	53. 7	60	8. 2	Ms	10						3		3		
1895	7	11								China	China: Yunnan, Weishan	中国:云南巍山	25. 2	100. 3		5	Ms	6										
1895	8	4	8							GSHAP	China: Xinjiang, Tashkurghan	中国:新疆塔什库尔干	37. 8	75. 2	20	6. 4	Ms	8										
1895	8	6	2							* Song	Albania: Durres	阿尔巴尼亚:都拉斯	41. 2	19. 3		6. 2	Mk	10										
1895	8	8								GSHAP	Russia: Khabarovsk, Nurki, W.	俄罗斯:哈巴罗夫斯克区努尔基村以西	57	133	15	6	Ms	8										
1895	8	30								* China	China: Guangdong, Jieyang	中国:广东揭阳	23. 5	116. 5		6	Ms	8		2	14	1		2		3		
1895	9	1	11	9		3				* NOAA	US: New Jersey, High Bridge	美国:新泽西州海伊布里奇	40. 667	-74. 883		4. 3	Mfa	6										
1895	9	6	19	20						USGS	US: Montana, Butte	美国:蒙大纳州比尤特	46	-112. 5		5	Ms	5										
1895	10	31	11	8						* Song	US: Missouri, Sikeston	美国:密苏里州赛克斯顿	37	-89. 4		6. 1	Mk	8										
1895	11	1				1			3	* Italy, NOAA	Italy: Fiumicino	意大利:菲乌米奇诺	41. 768	12. 44		4. 83	Ms											
1895	11	13	14	30						GSHAP	Tadzhikistan: Garm	塔吉克斯坦:加尔姆	38. 98	70. 41	5	5. 1	Ms	8										
1895	12	9	9	34						USGS, Song	Hawaiian Islands	夏威夷群岛	21	-157		5	Mk	5										
1895	12	18	13	4						GSHAP	Kyrgyzstan: Osh	吉尔吉斯斯坦:奥什	40	73	35	6	Ms	6. 5										
1895	12	25								* Song	Iran: Tehran	伊朗:德黑兰	35. 7	51. 4		5. 9	Mk							2				
1895										* Song	Myanmar: Rangoon	缅甸:仰光	16. 8	96. 2		5. 9	Mk							2				
1896	1	2								* GSHAP	Iran: Ardabil	伊朗:阿尔达比勒	37. 8	48. 3	12	6. 7	Ms	9. 5	300	3				3				
1896	1	4	6	15						USGS, Song	US: Washington, Seattle	美国:华盛顿州西雅图	48. 5	-122. 8		5	Mk	5										
1896	1	5								* Song	Iran: Orumiyeh	伊朗:乌尔米耶	38. 5	45		6. 3	Mk		800	3				3				
1896	1	9	13	17		4			-25	* Usami, NOAA	Japan: Ibaraki, Near Coast	日本:茨城近海	36. 5	141		7. 6	Ms											
1896	1	15	18	40						GSHAP	Kyrgyzstan: Jalalabad	吉尔吉斯斯坦:贾拉拉巴德	41. 5	70. 9	23	6. 6	Ms	8										
1896	1	27	21	1						USGS, Song	US: Nevada, Johnson Lane	美国:内华达州约翰逊巷	39. 1	-119. 8		5. 5	Mk	6										
1896	2	12								China	China: Yunnan, Lijiang	中国:云南丽江	26. 9	100. 2		5. 5	Ms	7										

年 Year	月 Mo	日 Dy	时 Hr	分 Mn	秒 Sec	海啸 Tsunami 源 Sr	浪高 Wh	级 I mI	级 S mS	资料来源 Information	震中 Earthquake Epicenter 地名(英文) Name(English)	地名(中文) Name(Chinese)	纬度(°) Latitude	经度(°) Longitude	深度 Depth	震级 Mag	标度 Scale	烈度 MMI	死亡人数 Deaths 数量/人 Num	级别 Dd	受伤人数 Injuries 数量/人 Num	级别 Dd	经济损失 Damage 数量/$ Mill $ Mill	级别 De	房屋毁坏 Houses Destroyed 数量/间 Num	级别 Dh	房屋受损 Houses Damaged 数量/间 Num	级别 Dh
1896	2	14								* China	China: Sichuan, Zigong	中国:四川自贡	29.3	104.9		5.75	Ms	7	26	1	12	1		2		3		
1896	2	27	7	20						GSHAP	Kyrgyzstan: Issyk – Kul, N.	吉尔吉斯斯坦:伊塞克湖州北部	42.8	77.3	10	4.6	Ms	6.5										
1896	3	2								* Song	Mexico: Colima	墨西哥:科利马	19.2	−104		6.3	Mk							3				
1896	3	4	5	5						* China, GSHAP	China: Xinjiang, Tashkurghan	中国:新疆塔什库尔干	38	76	40	7.1	Ms	8	7	1	4	1		1	42	1		
1896	3	11	23	30						GSHAP	Romania: Nereju	罗马尼亚:内雷茹	45.7	26.6	100	6.3	Ms	6										
1896	3	14	2	30						* GSHAP, Song	Chile: Valparaiso	智利:瓦尔帕莱索	−33	−71		6.1	Mk	8						1				
1896	3									China	China: Sichuan, Shiqu, S.	中国:四川石渠南	32.5	98		7	Ms	9										
1896	4	1	16	41						Usami	Japan: Suzu	日本:石川珠洲	37.5	137.3		5.7	Ms								17	1		
1896	4	2	11	17						USGS	US: Oregon, McMinnville	美国:俄勒冈州麦克明维尔	45.2	−123.2		5	Ms	5										
1896	4	18								* Song	Indonesia: Timor	印度尼西亚:帝汶	−8.3	126		6.2	Mk	8	250	3				2				
1896	5	3	13	45						GSHAP	Ecuador: Portoviejo	厄瓜多尔:波托维耶霍	−0.51	−80.45		7	Ms	9										
1896	5	3								GSHAP	Peru: Piura	秘鲁:皮乌拉	−5.1	−80.45		4.3	Ms	5										
1896	5									USGS, Song	Gulf of Alaska	阿拉斯加湾	61	−146		5.7	Mk	7										
1896	6	1								GSHAP	Kazakhstan: Almaty	哈萨克斯坦:阿拉木图	44.3	78.4	15	5.4	Ms	7										
1896	6	14	14	20						GSHAP, Song	Chile: Arica	智利:阿里卡	−18.5	−70.35		6	Mk	8										
1896	6	15	10	33		4	38	5.2	3.8	* GSHAP, NOAA	Japan Trench	日本海沟	39.5	144		8.4	Muk		31122	5	13247	5		4	11000	5		
1896	6	17	12							GSHAP	Afghan: Balkh	阿富汗:巴尔赫	37	68	15	5.2	Ms	7										
1896	7	6	11	2						GSHAP, Song	Bolivia: La Paz	玻利维亚:拉巴斯	−15.33	−68.54		4.5	Mk	5										
1896	8	1	2	49						Japan	Japan: Fukushima, Off Coast	日本:福岛沿海	37.5	141.5		7.7	Ms											1
1896	8	17	11	30						CGS, USGS	US: California, Seven Pines	美国:加利福尼亚州塞文派因斯	36.7	−118.3		6.3	Ms	6										
1896	8	18								GSHAP	Russia: Krasnodar, Krasnodar	俄罗斯:克拉斯诺达尔区克拉斯诺达尔	45.4	39.2	10	4.7	Ms	6.5										
1896	8	23	6	56						Japan	Japan: Akita	日本:秋田	39.9	140.6		6.5	Ms	7										
1896	8	26								* Iceland	Iceland: Asolfsstadhir	冰岛:奥索尔斯塔济	64	−20.2	5	6.9	Ms							3				
1896	8	31	8	6						* Usami, Japan	Japan: Mt. Iwate	日本:岩手山	40	141		7.2	Ms		209	3				4	6024	4		
1896	9	13	4	58						Maso, Song	Philippines: Calanasan	菲律宾:巴亚格	18.31	121.11		5.5	Mk	7										
1896	9	13	15	30						USGS	Hawaiian Islands	夏威夷群岛	19.25	−155		6	Ms	5										
1896	9	22	5							GSHAP	Georgia: T'Bilisi	格鲁吉亚:第比利斯	41.6	45.2	18	5.2	Ms	7										
1896	9	23	23	20						*	Afghan: Badakhshan	阿富汗:巴达赫尚	37	71	160	7.5	Muk	6										
1896	9	27	16	27						GSHAP	Kyrgyzstan: Osh, SW.	吉尔吉斯斯坦:奥什西南	39.6	73.6	18	5.6	Ms	7										
1896	9	28	21	30						GSHAP, Song	Peru: Arequipa	秘鲁:阿雷基帕	−16.4	−71.56		4.5	Mk	5										
1896	10	1	15	30						GSHAP	Iran: Parsabad	伊朗:法尔萨巴德	39.5	47.6	25	5.2	Ms	6										
1896	10	10				2			0	* NOAA	Indonesia: Southern Sumatra	印度尼西亚:苏门答腊南部	−3.5	102.5		6.8	Ms							1				
1896	10	16	6	15		1			2	* Italy, NOAA	Italy: Badalucco	意大利:巴达卢科	43.909	7.872		4.9	Ms	7										

时间 Date 年 Year	月 Mo	日 Dy	时 Hr	分 Mn	秒 Sec	海啸 Tsunami 源 Sr	浪高 Wh	级I mI	级S mS	资料来源 Information	震中 Earthquake Epicenter 地名(英文) Name(English)	地名(中文) Name(Chinese)	纬度(°) Latitude	经度(°) Longitude	深度 Depth	震级 Mag	标度 Scale	烈度 MMI	死亡人数 Deaths 数量/人 Num	级别 Dd	受伤人数 Injuries 数量/人 Num	级别 Dd	经济损失 Damage 数量/$ Mill $ Mill	级别 De	房屋毁坏 Houses Destroyed 数量/间 Num	级别 Dh	房屋受损 Houses Damaged 数量/间 Num	级别 Dh
1896	10	23	11	35						GSHAP, Song	Peru: Arequipa	秘鲁:阿雷基帕	-16.4	-71.56		4.5	Mk	5										
1896	11	1								* China	China: Xinjiang, Kashi	中国:新疆喀什	39.4	75.8	25	6.5	Ms	8	7	1	5	1		2	73	2		
1896	11	5	2	50		3				NOAA, Song	Greece: Ionian Sea	希腊:伊奥尼亚海	38.25	22.25		6.6	Mk											
1896	11	18	2	6						* Japan	Kuril Islands	千岛群岛	43.5	146	40	8	Mj	9										
1896	11	24	18	50						GSHAP	Romania: Nereju	罗马尼亚:内雷茹	45.7	26.6	100	5.2	Ms	5.5										
1896										* Song	Iran: Kerman	伊朗:克尔曼	30.3	57.1		6.3	Mk							3				
1896						4				NOAA, Song	Iceland: Hella	冰岛:海德拉	64	-19.683		7	Mk											
1897	1	5								China	China: Hubei, Yangxin	中国:湖北阳新	29.9	115.2		5	Ms	6										
1897	1	11	3							* Iran	Iran: Qeshm Island	伊朗:格什姆岛	26.9	56	33	6.4	Ms	8	1600	4				4		4		
1897	1	11								USGS, Song	Gulf of Alaska, SE.	阿拉斯加湾东南	60	-140		5	Mk	5										
1897	1	16	15	49						Usami, Japan	Japan: Chikusei	日本:茨城筑西	36.2	139.9		6.9	Ms											1
1897	1	16	20	36						Usami, Japan	Japan: Naganoi	日本:长野	36.7	138.3		6.3	Ms	7										1
1897	1	17	18	35						Maso, Song	Philippines: Aparri	菲律宾:阿帕里	18	121.5		5	Mk	6										
1897	1	17								* Song	Albania: Gjirokaster	阿尔巴尼亚:吉诺卡斯特	40	20.1		5.8	Mk	9						2				
1897	2	15	21	4						Maso, Song	Philippines: Mindanao Island	菲律宾:棉兰老岛	8.2	126.11		5.5	Mk	7										
1897	2	19	20	50		4	1			* NOAA, GSHAP, Japan	Japan: Miyagi, Near Coast	日本:宫城近海	38.1	141.9	30	7.8	Ms							2		3		
1897	3	14								* China	China: Taiwan, Yilan	中国:台湾宜兰	24.7	121.8		6	Ms	8	56	2	100	2		1	50	1		
1897	3	15				4			1	* NOAA	Flores Sea	弗洛勒斯海	-6.8	120.8		5.5	Ms											
1897	4	8	13	20						Maso, Song	Philippines: Mindanao Island	菲律宾:棉兰老岛	8.2	126.11		6.1	Mk	8										
1897	4	29	14	15						* Song	Guadeloupe: Grand Bourg	瓜德罗普岛:格朗布尔	16.1	-61.3		6.5	Mk	9	4	1				2				
1897	4	30	7	2						Japan	Japan: Naganoi	日本:长野	36.7	138.3		6.3	Ms											1
1897	5	3	17	18						USGS	US: Virginia, Pulaski	美国:弗吉尼亚州普瓦斯基	37.1	-80.7		4.3	Ms	6										
1897	5	10	5	26						*	Australia: Beachport, Robe	澳大利亚:海滩港,金斯敦	-37.3	139.7	14	6.5	Muk	9										
1897	5	13	11	22						*	Philippines: Masbate Island	菲律宾:马斯巴特岛	12	124	33	7.9	Ms	8						3		2		
1897	5	15	14	36						* Song	Tyrrhenian Sea	第勒尼安海(伊特鲁里亚海)	39	12.5		6.5	Mk	12										
1897	5	15	19	4						USGS, Song	US: Nevada, Reno	美国:内华达州雷诺	39.3	-119.7		5	Mk	5										
1897	5	23	12	22						Japan	Japan: Iwate, Near Coast	日本:岩手近海	39.01	142.51		7.5	Ms	7										
1897	5	28	3	16						USGS	US: New York, West Chazy, S.	美国:纽约州西谢齐南部	44.5	-73.5		4.7	Ms	6										
1897	5	31	18	58						USGS	US: Virginia, Eggleston	美国:弗吉尼亚州埃格尔斯顿	37.3	-80.7		5.6	Ms	8										
1897	6	5	12	22						USGS	US: Montana, Helena	美国:蒙大纳州海伦娜	46.6	-112		5	Ms	5										

年 Year	月 Mo	日 Dy	时 Hr	分 Mn	秒 Sec	海啸 Tsunami 源 Sr	浪高 Wh	级 I mI	级 S mS	资料来源 Information	震中 Earthquake Epicenter 地名(英文) Name(English)	地名(中文) Name(Chinese)	纬度(°) Latitude	经度(°) Longitude	深度 Depth	震级 Mag	标度 Scale	烈度 MMI	死亡人数 Deaths 数量/人 Num	级别 Dd	受伤人数 Injuries 数量/人 Num	级别 Dd	经济损失 Damage 数量/$ Mill	级别 De	房屋毁坏 Houses Destroyed 数量/间 Num	级别 Dh	房屋受损 Houses Damaged 数量/间 Num	级别 Dh
1897	6	5								*	Mexico:Oaxaca,Tehuantepec	墨西哥:瓦哈卡,特万特佩克	17	-96.3		7	Muk							3				
1897	6	12	11	6						*	India:Assam	印度:阿萨姆邦	26	91	33	8.7	Ms	10	1542	4				4		4		4
1897	6	20	20	14						CGS,USGS	US:California,Gilroy	美国:加利福尼亚州吉尔罗伊	37	-121.5		6.4	Ms	8										
1897	6	20				3				*NOAA	Mexico:Oaxaca,Salina Cruz	墨西哥:瓦哈卡,萨利纳克鲁斯	16	-95		7	Ms							2		2		
1897	8	5	0	10		4	3	1.5	1	*NOAA	Japan Trench	日本海沟	38	143.7		7.7	Ms							1				
1897	8	15	12	18						*	Philippines:Laoag,Near Coast	菲律宾:佬沃近海	18	120	33	7.9	Ms	8										
1897	8	25	13							GSHAP	Russia:Komi,Puzla	俄罗斯:科米州普兹拉	62.5	55	15	5.3	Ms	7										
1897	8	27	18							GSHAP	Black Sea	黑海	44.8	35.4	20	4.7	Ms	5.5										
1897	9	17	15	10						GSHAP	Uzbekistan:Jazzakh	乌兹别克斯坦:吉扎克	39.8	68.4	25	6.6	Ms	8										
1897	9	17	17	19						GSHAP	Uzbekistan:Jazzakh	乌兹别克斯坦:吉扎克	39.9	68	45	6.7	Ms	7										
1897	9	20	16	25						*GSHAP	Peru:Lima	秘鲁:利马	-11.9	-76.8	70	7.7	Muk	7										
1897	9	20	19	6						*	Philippines:Mindanao,Dapitan	菲律宾:棉兰老岛,达皮丹	6	122	33	8.6	Ms	7						1				
1897	9	21	5	12		4	7	2.6	2.5	*NOAA	Philippines:Mindanao,Zamboanga	菲律宾:棉兰老岛,三宝颜	6	122	33	8.7	Ms	9		3		3		3		2		
1897	9	21	7	14		1				NOAA,Song	New Zealand:Wellington	新西兰:惠灵顿	-41.3	174.8		7	Mk											
1897	10	7	21							Maso,Song	Philippines:Mindanao Island	菲律宾:棉兰老岛	7.11	125.61		5	Mk	6										
1897	10	18	23	48						*	Philippines:Samar Island,E.	菲律宾:萨马岛东部	12	126	33	8.1	Ms	9						2	17	1		
1897	10	19	7	15						*Maso,Song	Philippines:Samar Island,E.	菲律宾:萨马岛东部	12	126		6.1	Mk	8						1				
1897	11	4	9	29						USGS	US:Montana,Dillon	美国:蒙大纳州狄龙	45.3	-112.6		6.4	Ms	6										
1897	11	14	0	59						Maso,Song	Philippines:Aparri	菲律宾:阿帕里	18	121.5		5.5	Mk	7										
1897	11	14	13	30						USGS,Song	US:Wyoming,Casper	美国:怀俄明州卡斯珀	42.9	-106.3		5.5	Mk	6										
1897	12	10	15							GSHAP,Song	Peru:Lima	秘鲁:利马	-12.08	-77		4.5	Mk	5										
1897	12					1				NOAA,Song	Greece:Ionian Islands	希腊:伊奥尼亚群岛	39.5	20		6.6	Mk											
1897										USGS,Song	US:New Mexico,Socorro	美国:新墨西哥州索科罗	34	-107		5.5	Mk	6										
1898	1	15	3	42						*GSHAP	Iran:Semnan,Dāmghān	伊朗:塞姆南,达姆甘	36.5	54.9	12	5.5	Muk	8						2				
1898	1	30	11	15						Maso,Song	Celebes Sea	西里伯斯海	5.8	121		5.5	Mk	7										
1898	2	5	20							USGS	US:Virginia,Wytheville	美国:弗吉尼亚州威斯维尔	37	-81		4.4	Ms	6										
1898	2	25	4							GSHAP	Brasil:Jaragua	巴西:南雅拉瓜	-26.93	-49.06		3.9	Ms	5										
1898	3	31	7	43		1	0.3	2	2	*NOAA	US:California,Sonoma	美国:加利福尼亚州索诺马	38.2	-122.4		6.5	Ms	8						2				
1898	4	3	6	48						Usami	Japan:Yamaguchi	日本:山口	34.6	131.2		6.2	Ms									1		

时间						海啸				资料来源	震中				深度	震级	标度	烈度	死亡人数		受伤人数		经济损失		房屋毁坏		房屋受损	
年	月	日	时	分	秒	源	浪高	级 I	级 S		地名(英文)	地名(中文)	纬度(°)	经度(°)					数量/人	级别	数量/人	级别	数量/$ Mill	级别	数量/间	级别	数量/间	级别
Date						Tsunami				Information	Earthquake Epicenter				Depth	Mag	Scale	MMI	Deaths		Injuries		Damage		Houses Destroyed		Houses Damaged	
Year	Mo	Dy	Hr	Mn	Sec	Sr	Wh	mI	mS		Name(English)	Name(Chinese)	Latitude	Longitude					Num	Dd	Num	Dd	$ Mill	De	Num	Dh	Num	Dh
1898	4	14								* Song	US: California, Manchester, Near Coast	美国:加利福尼亚州曼彻斯特近海	39	-124		7.3	Mk	10						1				
1898	4	17								GSHAP	Ecuador: Portoviejo	厄瓜多尔:波托维耶霍	-0.5	-80.5		5.7	Ms	7										
1898	4	22	23	37		4	0.1		-2	* Usami, NOAA	Japan: Miyagi, Near Coast	日本:宫城近海	38.6	142	60	7.8	Muk							1	1	1		
1898	4	29	13	5						GSHAP, Song	Peru: Lima	秘鲁:利马	-12.08	-77		4.5	Mk	5										
1898	4	29	16	18						*	Nicaragua: Leon, Chinandega	尼加拉瓜:里昂,奇南德加	12	-86	33	7.9	Ms	8						2				
1898	6	2	21	40		3				GSHAP, NOAA	Greece: Argolida	希腊:阿尔戈利斯	37.6	22.5	90	7	Ms											
1898	6	14	15	26						USGS	US: Kentucky, Bell City	美国:肯塔基州贝尔锡蒂	36.5	-88.5		4.5	Ms	5										
1898	6	19	6	40						GSHAP	Russia: Kemerovo, Novokuzneck	俄罗斯:克麦罗沃州新库兹涅茨克	53.8	87.6	22	5.7	Ms	7										
1898	6	21								* China, GSHAP	China: Xinjiang, Artux	中国:新疆阿图什	39.8	76.6	15	6.5	Ms	8	47	1	85	2		2	425	3		
1898	6	27	22	38						* Italy	Italy: Rieti	意大利:列蒂	42.415	12.905		5.48	Ms	10						2				
1898	7	2	4	20						* GSHAP	Croatia: Split	克罗地亚:斯普利特	43.6	16.7		5.5	Ms	10		2				1				
1898	7	20	4	20						GSHAP	Ecuador: Portoviejo	厄瓜多尔:波托维耶霍	-0.4	-80.45		4.3	Ms	5										
1898	7	23	2	17		1				* NOAA, GSHAP	Chile: Limache, Almendral	智利:利马切	-37	-74		6.5	Ms	8	6	1				2		2		
1898	7	29	2							GSHAP	Ecuador: Azuay	厄瓜多尔:阿苏艾	-2.9	-79		4.3	Ms	5										
1898	7	31	5	40						*	Greece: Janina	希腊:伊欧亚尼纳	39.75	20.75		6.2	Ms	10						2				
1898	8	1								USGS, Song	Alaska Peninsula, S.	阿拉斯加半岛南部	61	-150		5.5	Mk	6										
1898	8	12	4	3						Japan	Japan Sea	日本海	35.5	130.2		6.5	Ms				3	1				1		
1898	8									China	China: Yunnan, Zhaotong	中国:云南昭通	27.3	103.7		5	Ms	6										
1898	9	19	20							GSHAP	Ecuador: Babahoyo	厄瓜多尔:巴巴奥约	-1.56	-79.75		4.3	Ms	5										
1898	9	22								* China	China: Shanxi, Daixian	中国:山西代县	39.1	113		5.75	Ms	7	12	1		2		2	570	3		
1898	11	17	15	6						*	Iran: Qūchān	伊朗:古昌	37.2	58.4	11	6.6	Muk	10	18000	5				3				
1898	11	25	20							USGS	US: Virginia, Wytheville	美国:弗吉尼亚州威斯维尔	37	-81		4.5	Ms	5										
1898	12	3	5	50		2			3	* NOAA, Song	Greece: Zakynthos	希腊:扎金索斯岛	37.8	21		6.7	Mk	8										
1898										China	China: Inner Mongolia, Horinger	中国:内蒙古和林格尔	40.4	111.9		4.75	Ms	6										
1899	1	15				3			1.5	* NOAA, Song	Papua New Guinea: New Ireland	巴布亚新几内亚:新爱尔兰	-3	152		7.5	Mk			3				2		3		
1899	1	22	7	56		2			3	* NOAA	Greece: Kyparissia (Messinia)	希腊:麦锡尼	37.25	21.75		6.6	Ms	9		2								
1899	1	24	23	43						*	Mexico: Guerrero - Oaxaca	墨西哥:格雷罗 - 瓦哈卡	17	-98	60	8.4	Muk							3				
1899	1	29				1	1.8		1	* NOAA, Song	Australia: Northern Australia	澳大利亚:北澳	-12.4	130.7		7	Mk											
1899	2	13	9	30						USGS	US: Virginia, Wytheville	美国:弗吉尼亚州威斯维尔	37	-81		4.5	Ms	5										
1899	3	7	0	55						Usami	Japan: Kihoku	日本:三重纪北	34.2	136.2		7	Ms		7	1					67	2		

时间 Date						海啸 Tsunami				资料来源 Information	震中 Earthquake Epicenter				深度 Depth	震级 Mag	标度 Scale	烈度 MMI	死亡人数 Deaths		受伤人数 Injuries		经济损失 Damage		房屋毁坏 Houses Destroyed		房屋受损 Houses Damaged	
年 Year	月 Mo	日 Dy	时 Hr	分 Mn	秒 Sec	源 Sr	浪高 Wh	级I mI	级S mS		地名(英文) Name(English)	地名(中文) Name(Chinese)	纬度(°) Latitude	经度(°) Longitude					数量/人 Num	级别 Dd	数量/人 Num	级别 Dd	数量/$ Mill $ Mill	级别 De	数量/间 Num	级别 Dh	数量/间 Num	级别 Dh
1899	3	23	18							*	Bolivia:Tarija	玻利维亚:塔里哈	-21.97	-63.67	10	6.9	Ms	10										
1899	3	24	4	5						Usami,Japan	Japan:Miyazzaki	日本:宫崎	31.8	131.1		7.2	Ms											1
1899	3	31	14	1						Usami,Japan	Japan:Motosu	日本:岐阜本巢	35.6	136.6		6	Ms	7										
1899	3									China	China:Yunnan,Yingjiang	中国:云南盈江	24.8	98.3		5.5	Ms	7							101	3		
1899	4	2	3	30						USGS,Song	Aleutian Islands	阿留申群岛	55	-161		5	Mk	5										
1899	4	15	10	25						Japan	Japan:Ibaraki,Near Coast	日本:茨城近海	36.3	141		7	Ms	7										
1899	4	16	13	40						USGS	US:California,Off Coast N.	美国:加利福尼亚州北部沿海	41	-126		7	Ms	6										
1899	4	30	2	5						USGS	US:Indiana,Petersburg	美国:印第安纳州彼得斯堡	38.5	-87.4		4.9	Ms	7										
1899	4	30	22	41						CGS,USGS	US:California, San Juan Bautista	美国:加利福尼亚州 圣胡安包蒂斯塔	36.85	-121.6		6	Ms	7										
1899	4									GSHAP	Brasil:Uberlandia	巴西:乌贝兰迪亚	-18.59	-46.52		4	Ms	5										
1899	5	8	3	29						GSHAP,Usami	Kuril Islands	千岛群岛	43	146	40	7.2	Ms	8										
1899	6	2	7	19						CGS,USGS	US:California,San Francisco	美国:加利福尼亚州旧金山	37.7	-122.5		5.6	Ms	7										
1899	7	6	20	10						USGS	US:California,Morgan Hill	美国:加利福尼亚州摩根希尔	37.2	-121.5		5.8	Ms	7										
1899	7	14	6							* Song	Venezuela:Lara	委内瑞拉:拉腊	10.4	-69.2		5.9	Mk							2				
1899	7	22	0	46						CGS,USGS	US:California,San Bernardino	美国:加利福尼亚州 圣贝纳迪诺	34.2	-117.4		5.9	Ms	6										
1899	7	22	20	32						CGS,USGS	US:California,Victorville	美国:加利福尼亚州 维克托维尔	34.3	-117.5		6.4	Ms	8										
1899	8	8				1				* * NOAA, Song	Chile:Iquique	智利:伊基克	-20.2	-70.1		7.7	Mk							3				
1899	9	4	0	22		4	3.1			* NOAA	Gulf of Alaska	阿拉斯加湾	60	-142	25	8.2	Ms	11						1				
1899	9	10	17	4						*	Gulf of Alaska	阿拉斯加湾	60	-140	25	7.8	Ms	7										
1899	9	10	21	41		4	61	5.9	2.5	* USGS,NOAA	Gulf of Alaska	阿拉斯加湾	60	-140	25	8.6	Ms	11						3				
1899	9	16	4	33						USGS,Song	Alaska:Lituya Bay	阿拉斯加:立图亚湾	59	-138		5.7	Mk	7										
1899	9	20	2	12						*	Turkey:Sultanhisar,Atca	土耳其:苏尔坦希萨,纳吉利	37.93	28.84		6.7	Ms	9	1117	4		4		3	7126	4		
1899	9	29	17	3		4	12	3.6	3	* NOAA	Indonesia:Maluku Islands	印度尼西亚:摩鹿加群岛	-3	128.5		7.8	Ms		2460	4	300	3		3				
1899	10	13	5							USGS,Song	US:California,Santa Rosa	美国:加利福尼亚州圣罗莎	38.4	-122.7		5.7	Mk	7										
1899	11	10	17	41						GSHAP,Japan	Japan:Akita	日本:秋田	40	140	33	7.2	Ms											1
1899	11	24	18	43		4	0.3	-17	-1	* NOAA	Japan:Miyazaki,Near Coast	日本:宫崎近海	31.9	132	60	7.2	Muk							1	2	1		
1899	11	25				4	0.2	-1	-2	* NOAA	Japan:Miyazaki,Near Coast	日本:宫崎近海	31.9	132		7.1	Ms											
1899	11	28								China	China:Guangxi,Wuxuan,S.	中国:广西武宣南	23.4	109.6		5	Ms	6										

年 Year	月 Mo	日 Dy	时 Hr	分 Mn	秒 Sec	海啸 Tsunami 源 Sr	浪高 Wh	级 I mI	级 S mS	资料来源 Information	震中 Earthquake Epicenter 地名(英文) Name(English)	地名(中文) Name(Chinese)	纬度(°) Latitude	经度(°) Longitude	深度 Depth	震级 Mag	标度 Scale	烈度 MMI	死亡人数 Deaths 数量/人 Num	级别 Dd	受伤人数 Injuries 数量/人 Num	级别 Dd	经济损失 Damage 数量/$ Mill $ Mill	级别 De	房屋毁坏 Houses Destroyed 数量/间 Num	级别 Dh	房屋受损 Houses Damaged 数量/间 Num	级别 Dh
1899	12	19	18	40						GSHAP	Russia:Dagestan, Makhachkala	俄罗斯:达吉斯坦共和国马哈奇卡拉	42.3	46.6	25	4.9	Ms	5.5										
1899	12	25	12	25		1			0.5	*CGS, USGS, NOAA	US:California,Temecula	美国:加利福尼亚州蒂梅丘拉	33.5	-117		6.7	Ms	9	6	1				2				
1899	12	25	20	20						Maso,Song	Philippines:Mindanao Island	菲律宾:棉兰老岛	8.2	126.11		5	Mk	6										
1899	12	31	7	50						*	Georgia:Borzhomi	格鲁吉亚:博尔若米	41.6	43.5		5.6	Muk		247	3				2				
1899	12									GSHAP	Brasil:Salvador	巴西:萨尔瓦多	-13.03	-39.6		4.3	Ms	5										
1899										China	China:Ningxia,Lingwu	中国:宁夏灵武	38.1	106.3		4.75	Ms	6										
1900	1	14								*Song	Indonesia:Java,Sukabumi	印度尼西亚:爪哇,苏卡布米	-6.9	106.8		6.2	Mk							3				
1900	1	20	6	33	30					*Engdahl	Mexico:Tomatlan	墨西哥:托马特兰	20	-105	10	7.3	Mw							1				
1900	3	21	15	55						Shi Z., Usami, Japan	Japan:Fukui	日本:福井	36	136.2		6.6	Ms				6	1			2	1	500	3
1900	4	17	2	25						GSHAP	Georgia:Gori,N.	格鲁吉亚:哥里北部	42.2	45.1	35	4.6	Ms	5										
1900	4	30	22	41	14					USGS	US:California,River Oaks	美国:加利福尼亚州里弗奥克斯	36.9	-121.6		4.5	Ms	5										
1900	5	6	1							GSHAP	Black Sea	黑海	45	35.4	22	4.5	Ms	5										
1900	5	11	17	23						Engdahl,GSHAP, Shi Z.,Usami	Japan:Oshu	日本:岩手奥州	39	141	33	7	Mj		4	1	17	1			44	1	1522	4
1900	5									China	China:Henan,Anyang,W.	中国:河南安阳西	36.1	114.2		5	Ms	6										
1900	6	7	22							*Song	Venezuela:Casanay (Casanai),Cariaco	委内瑞拉:卡萨奈,卡利亚科	10.3	-63.3		5.9	Mk							2				
1900	7	12	6	25						*	Turkey:Kars, Digor	土耳其:卡尔斯,季戈尔	40.3	43.1		5.9	Muk	8	140	3				3				
1900	8	1	7	45						USGS,Song	US:Utah,Eureka	美国:犹他州尤里卡	40	-112.1		5.6	Mk	7										
1900	8	11	4	40		4				*NOAA,Song	Canada:Southern Yukon Territory	加拿大:育空地区南部	62	-138		7	Mk		5	1				1				
1900	8	13	20	14						Maso,Song	Philippines:Masbate Island	菲律宾:马斯巴特岛	12	124		5	Mk	6										
1900	8									China	China:Sichuan,Qionglai	中国:四川邛崃	30.5	103.5		5	Ms	6										
1900	9	10	21	30		4				*NOAA	Bismarck Sea	俾斯麦海	-4	152		6.8	Ms											
1900	9	17	21	45		3	3			*Engdahl,NOAA	Bismarck Sea	俾斯麦海	-5	148		7.1	Mw											
1900	9	19								GSHAP	Colombia:Bogota	哥伦比亚:波哥达	4.6	-74		4	Ms	5										
1900	10	7	21	4		3		1	1.5	*Engdahl,NOAA	Indonesia:Papua	印度尼西亚:巴布亚	-4	140	33	6.9	Ms		5	1				1	1	1		
1900	10	9	12	28						*Engdahl,Shi Z	Alaska:Kodiak Island	阿拉斯加:科迪亚克岛	57.09	-153.48		7.7	Ms	8						1				
1900	10	29	8	11		3	10			*Engdahl,NOAA	Venezuela:Macuto	委内瑞拉:马库图	11.2	-66.5	60	7.7	Mw	10		3				3				
1900	11	5	7	42						Engdahl, Usami, Japan	Japan:Miyake Jima	日本:三宅岛	33.9	139.4	5	6.6	Mj				1	1			2	1	3	1
1900	12	25	5	9						*Engdahl	Kuril Islands,S.	千岛群岛南部	43	146	35	7.1	Mw	9										

时间						海啸				资料来源	震中				深度	震级	标度	烈度	死亡人数		受伤人数		经济损失		房屋毁坏		房屋受损	
年	月	日	时	分	秒	源	浪高	级 I	级 S		地名(英文)	地名(中文)	纬度(°)	经度(°)					数量/人	级别	数量/人	级别	数量/$ Mill	级别	数量/间	级别	数量/间	级别
Date						Tsunami				Information	Earthquake Epicenter				Depth	Mag	Scale	MMI	Deaths		Injuries		Damage		Houses Destroyed		Houses Damaged	
Year	Mo	Dy	Hr	Mn	Sec	Sr	Wh	mI	mS		Name(English)	Name(Chinese)	Latitude	Longitude					Num	Dd	Num	Dd	$ Mill	De	Num	Dh	Num	Dh
1900										China	China:Yunnan,Mile	中国:云南弥勒	24.4	103.4		5	Ms	6										
1901	2	6	15							GSHAP	Russia:Dagestan,Makhachkala	俄罗斯:达吉斯坦共和国马哈奇卡拉	42.8	46.7	22	4.8	Ms	5.5										
1901	2	14	16							*China,Engdahl	China:Yunnan,Dengchuan	中国:云南邓川	26	100.1		6.5	Ms	8		3				3		3		
1901	3	3	7	45		3				*NOAA	US:California,Bradley	美国:加利福尼亚州布拉德利	36	-120.5		6.7	Ms	8						1				
1901	3	31	7	11		1				*GSHAP,NOAA	Bulgaria:Balchik, Kavarna	保加利亚:巴尔奇克,卡瓦尔纳	43.4	28.7	14	7.2	Ms	8	4	1	50	1		3	1200	4		
1901	3	31	11	30						GSHAP	Bulgaria:Dobrich	保加利亚:多布里奇	43.6	27.8	30	5	Ms	5										
1901	4	25	16							China	China:Xizang (Tibet),Nyemo	中国:西藏尼木	29.5	90.1		6.75	Ms	9	18	1								
1901	4	25	22	25						GSHAP	Black Sea	黑海	43.3	28.5	10	5	Ms	6										
1901	4	26	1	10						GSHAP	Black Sea	黑海	43.3	28.5	10	4.5	Ms	6										
1901	5	12	12	32						GSHAP	Turkey:Eskisehir	土耳其:埃斯基城	39.8	30.5	15	5	Ms	6										
1901	5	17	6							USGS	US:Ohio,McDermott	美国:俄亥俄州麦克德莫特	38.75	-83		4.2	Ms	6										
1901	5	21	19							GSHAP	Kazakhstan:Zyryanovsk	哈萨克斯坦:济良诺夫斯克	50.3	83.5	17	5.6	Ms	7										
1901	6	7	0	5						China	China:Taiwan,Yilan	中国:台湾宜兰	24.7	121.8		6.4	Ms		1	1					1	1	57	2
1901	6	7	23	28						GSHAP	Black Sea	黑海	43.4	28.3	10	5.2	Ms	7										
1901	6	15	9	34		4				*Usami, Engdahl, NOAA	Japan:Iwate,Near Coast	日本:岩手近海	39	143	35	7	Ms											
1901	6	24	7	2		4	0.2	-2.3	-1.5	*Engdahl,NOAA	Ryukyu Islands	琉球群岛	27	130	35	7.2	Mw											
1901	7	26	22	20						USGS	US:Nevada,Elko	美国:内华达州埃尔科	40.8	-115.7		5	Ms	7										
1901	8	9	9	23	30	4	0.6	0	-0.5	*Usami, Japan, Engdahl,NOAA	Japan:Aomori, Near East Coast	日本:青森东部近海	40.5	142.5	35	7.2	Mw		18	1				2	10	1	31	1
1901	8	9	13	1		5	1.2	-0.7		*Engdahl,NOAA	New Caledonia:Loyalty Islands	新喀里多尼亚:罗亚尔特群岛	-22	170	60	7.9	Mw			1				2				
1901	8	9	18	33		4	0.3	-1	-1	*Engdahl, GSHAP,Japan,NOAA	Japan:Aomori, Near East Coast	日本:青森东部近海	40.6	142.3	35	7.5	Mw		18	1				2	8	1	615	3
1901	8	9	20			4	0	-1		*NOAA	Japan:Aomori,Near East Coast	日本:青森东部近海	40.5	142.5	33	6.3	Ms											
1901	8	18	7	44						GSHAP	Serbia:Cacak	塞尔维亚:查查克	44.2	20.7	4	4.6	Ms	7										
1901	9	10	0	30		1				*Nakamura,Maso,NOAA	Philippines:Tayabas	菲律宾:塔亚巴斯	14	121.6		7	Ms	7						2				
1901	10	8	2	14		3	1.5			*Engdahl,NOAA	Nicaragua:Chinandega	尼加拉瓜:奇南德加	13	-87		7.1	Mw							1				
1901	11	8	10	18						*	Turkey:Pasinler, Erzurum	土耳其:哈珊卡尔堡,埃尔佐鲁姆	40	41.5		6.1	Muk	8						3				
1901	11	14	4	32						USGS,Song	US:Utah,Richfield	美国:犹他州里奇菲尔德	38.7	-112.1		6.1	Mk	8										
1901	11	21	19	19						GSHAP,Song	Peru:Ica,Coast	秘鲁:伊卡近海	-14.177	-76.32	80	5	Mk	6										

年 Year	月 Mo	日 Dy	时 Hr	分 Mn	秒 Sec	海啸 Tsunami 源 Sr	浪高 Wh	级 I mI	级 S mS	资料来源 Information	震中 Earthquake Epicenter 地名(英文) Name(English)	地名(中文) Name(Chinese)	纬度(°) Latitude	经度(°) Longitude	深度 Depth	震级 Mag	标度 Scale	烈度 MMI	死亡人数 Deaths 数量/人 Num	级别 Dd	受伤人数 Injuries 数量/人 Num	级别 Dd	经济损失 Damage 数量/$ Mill $ Mill	级别 De	房屋毁坏 Houses Destroyed 数量/间 Num	级别 Dh	房屋受损 Houses Damaged 数量/间 Num	级别 Dh
1901	12	1								GSHAP	Turkmenistan:Lebap,E.	土库曼斯坦:列巴普东部	37.8	66.2	14	4.6	Ms	6										
1901	12	14	22	57						*Maso,Engdahl	Philippines:Lopez	菲律宾:洛佩斯	14	122	60	7	Ms	7										
1901	12	18	3	51						*	Turkey:Ayvalik	土耳其:艾伐利克	39.4	26.7		5.9	Ms	8						2				
1901	12	30	22	34						USGS	Aleutian Islands,S.	阿留申群岛南部	52	-160		7	Ms	6										
1901	12	31	9	2	30	1				*Engdahl, NOAA	Andreanof Islands, Aleutian Is.	阿留申群岛,安德烈亚诺夫群岛	52	-177		7.1	Mw											
1902	1	2	14	8						GSHAP,Song	Peru:Chimbote	秘鲁:钦博特	-9	-78.4	80	6.5	Mk	9										
1902	1	8	15	12						GSHAP	Black Sea	黑海	44.6	35.8	16	5.5	Ms	6.5										
1902	1	16								*Song	Mexico:Guerrero, Chilpancingo,W.	墨西哥:格雷罗州奇尔潘辛戈西部	17.7	-100		6.2	Mk		2	1				3				
1902	1	18	23	23		1				*NOAA	Guatemala:Quezaltenango	危地马拉:克萨尔特南戈	14.7	-91.6		6.3	Ms							1				
1902	1	21	21	40						GSHAP	Colombia:Vichada,S.	哥伦比亚:维查达南部	3	-71		4	Ms	5										
1902	1	24	10	48						USGS	US:Missouri,St Louis	美国:密苏里州圣路易斯	38.6	-90.3		4.5	Ms	6										
1902	1	30	14	1						Engdahl,Usami	Japan:Aomori,Hachinohe	日本:青森,八户	40.5	141.3	35	6.9	Ms		1	1					3	1		
1902	2	10	15	7						GSHAP	Russia:Kamchatka, Near East Coast	俄罗斯:堪察加东部近海	53	160	20	5.5	Ms	7.5										
1902	2	13	3	56						GSHAP	Kyrgyzstan:Kochkor	吉尔吉斯斯坦:科奇科尔	41.4	76	15	5.4	Ms	7										
1902	2	13	9	34	6					*	Azerbaijan:Samaxi	阿塞拜疆:沙马基区	40.7	48.6	15	6.9	Ms	9	86	2	60	2		4	3496	4		
1902	2	16	18	11						GSHAP	Azerbaijan:Agcabedi	阿塞拜疆:阿格贾贝迪区	40.2	47.4	32	5.2	Ms	5.5										
1902	2	26				1	5	2.3	2	*NOAA	El Salvador:La Libertad	萨尔瓦多:拉利伯塔德	13.5	-89.5		8.3	Ms		185	3				3				
1902	2	27	0	5						GSHAP	Azerbaijan:Samaxi	阿塞拜疆:沙马基区	40.5	48	18	4.6	Ms	5.5										
1902	3	9	7	46						*	Turkey:Cankiri	土耳其:钱克勒	40.7	33.6		5.5	Muk	9	4	1				3				
1902	3	11	20	14						GSHAP	Romania:Nereju	罗马尼亚:内雷茹	45.7	26.6	150	5.6	Ms	6										
1902	3	20	6	10	26					GSHAP	Georgia:Kutaisi	格鲁吉亚:库塔伊西	42.6	43.4	3	4.5	Ms	7										
1902	4	10	18	11						GSHAP	Finland:Kajaani	芬兰:卡亚尼	64.3	27.6	30	5.1	Ms	6										
1902	4	11	23	43						Engdahl,GSHAP	Russia:Lake Baykal	俄罗斯:贝加尔湖	51.6	104.5	16	6.6	Ms	8.5										
1902	4	17	21	10						GSHAP	Kyrgyzstan:Batken	吉尔吉斯斯坦:巴特肯	40	71	30	5.8	Ms	7										
1902	4	19	2	23	30	1				*Shi Z., Engdahl, NOAA	Guatemala:Quezaltenango, San Marcos	危地马拉:克萨尔特南戈,圣马科斯	14	-91	33	7.5	Mw		2000	4				3				
1902	4	27	16	2	21					GSHAP	Azerbaijan:Samaxi	阿塞拜疆:沙马基区	40.5	47.8	15	4.6	Ms	6										
1902	4	28	13	25						GSHAP	Russia:Khakassia,Sorsk	俄罗斯:哈卡斯州索尔斯克	53.8	90.5	15	6	Ms	7.5										
1902	4	29	6	57						*Song	US:California,Lompoc	美国:加利福尼亚州隆波克	34.5	-120.5		5.9	Mk	7						2				
1902	5	5				5	5		2	NOAA,Song	Martinique Island:Mount Pelee	马提尼克岛:培雷山	14.82	-61.17		7.7	Mk		23	1								

时间 Date						海啸 Tsunami				资料来源 Information	震中 Earthquake Epicenter				深度 Depth	震级 Mag	标度 Scale	烈度 MMI	死亡人数 Deaths		受伤人数 Injuries		经济损失 Damage		房屋毁坏 Houses Destroyed		房屋受损 Houses Damaged	
年 Year	月 Mo	日 Dy	时 Hr	分 Mn	秒 Sec	源 Sr	浪高 Wh	级I mI	级S mS		地名(英文) Name(English)	地名(中文) Name(Chinese)	纬度(°) Latitude	经度(°) Longitude					数量/人 Num	级别 Dd	数量/人 Num	级别 Dd	数量/$ Mill $ Mill	级别 De	数量/间 Num	级别 Dh	数量/间 Num	级别 Dh
1902	5	19	18	31						CGS, USGS	US: California, Napa	美国:加利福尼亚州那帕	38. 3	-122		5. 5	Ms	7										
1902	5	25	22	30						GSHAP	Black Sea	黑海	43. 5	28. 5	10	4. 5	Ms	6										
1902	5									China	China: Yunnan, Jianchuan	中国:云南剑川	26. 5	99. 9		5	Ms	6										
1902	6	9								* Song	Iran: Qeshm, Bandar Abbas	伊朗:格什姆,阿巴斯港	26. 6	56. 2		5. 9	Mk		10	1				2				
1902	6	11	2	45						USGS	US: California, Riverside	美国:加利福尼亚州里弗赛德	33. 7	-117. 1		4. 5	Ms	5										
1902	7	3								GSHAP	Russia: Vladikavkaz	俄罗斯:符拉迪克奥克兹	42. 8	44. 2	10	4. 7	Ms	7										
1902	7	5	14	56	30	3			2	* NOAA	Greece: Thessalonika	希腊:萨罗尼加	40. 8	23. 2	22	6. 6	Muk	10										
1902	7	9	3	38						* Iran	Iran: Bandar Abbas	伊朗:阿巴斯港	27. 1	56. 3		6. 4	Ms							2				
1902	7	12	13	47						Maso, Song	Philippines: Mindanao, Dapitan	菲律宾:棉兰老岛,达皮丹	8. 6	123. 4		5	Mk	6										
1902	7	28	6	57						USGS	US: California, Los Alamos	美国:加利福尼亚州洛斯阿拉莫斯	34. 8	-120. 4		5. 4	Ms	7										
1902	7	28	18							CGS, USGS	US: California, Los Alamos	美国:加利福尼亚州洛斯阿拉莫斯	34. 8	-120. 4		5. 8	Ms	6										
1902	7	31	9	20						CGS, USGS	US: California, Los Alamos	美国:加利福尼亚州洛斯阿拉莫斯	34. 7	-120. 3		5. 8	Ms	8										
1902	8	1	3	30						USGS, Song	US: California, Lompoc	美国:加利福尼亚州隆波克	34. 6	-120. 4		6. 1	Mk	8										
1902	8	12	17	16						GSHAP	Tadzhikistan: Sabah	塔吉克斯坦:萨巴赫	39. 5	68. 5	35	6	Ms	6. 5										
1902	8	16	8	11	36	1				NOAA, Song	Mexico: Culiacan, Off Coast of W.	墨西哥:库利亚坎西部沿海	24. 6	-107. 9		7	Mk											
1902	8	17	18	29						GSHAP	Russia: Buryatiya, Yanchukan	俄罗斯:布里亚特州扬丘坎镇	56. 7	112. 7	15	6. 5	Ms	9										
1902	8	21	11	17		1			2	* Nakamura, Maso, NOAA	Philippines: Mindanao, Lanao	菲律宾:棉兰老岛,拉瑙湖	7. 2	124. 2		7. 3	Ms	10		3				3		3		3
1902	8	22	3							* China, Engdahl	China: Xinjiang, Kashi, N.	中国:新疆喀什北部	39. 9	76. 2		8. 25	Mw	10	2500	4				4		4		
1902	8	25	17	9						* Maso, Song	Philippines: Iloilo, Panay	菲律宾:伊洛伊洛,班乃	10. 8	122. 6		6. 5	Mk	9						3				
1902	8	30	21	50						GSHAP	Afghan: Badakhshan	阿富汗:巴达赫尚	37	71	200	7. 7	Ms	7										
1902	8									* China	China: Yunnan, Jianchuan, S.	中国:云南剑川南	26. 3	99. 9		5. 5	Ms	7	6	1				2		3		
1902	9	5	4	33						GSHAP	Iran: Parsabad	伊朗:法尔萨巴德	39. 5	48	20	5	Ms	6										
1902	9	19								Australia	Australia: Yorke Peninsula	澳大利亚:约克半岛	-15	145		6	Ms		2	1								
1902	9	20	6	32						Afghan, GSHAP	Uzbekistan: Qashqadaryo	乌兹别克斯坦:卡什卡达里亚	38. 5	67		6. 2	Ms	7										
1902	9	22	1	46	30					* Maso, Engdahl	Mariana Ridge; Guam: Agana	马里亚纳海岭;关岛:阿加尼亚	18	146	60	7. 5	Mw	9				1		3				

年 Year	月 Mo	日 Dy	时 Hr	分 Mn	秒 Sec	海啸 源 Sr	海啸 浪高 Wh	海啸 级I mI	海啸 级S mS	资料来源 Information	震中 地名(英文) Name(English)	震中 地名(中文) Name(Chinese)	纬度(°) Latitude	经度(°) Longitude	深度 Depth	震级 Mag	标度 Scale	烈度 MMI	死亡人数 数量/人 Deaths Num	死亡人数 级别 Dd	受伤人数 数量/人 Injuries Num	受伤人数 级别 Dd	经济损失 数量/$ Mill Damage $ Mill	经济损失 级别 De	房屋毁坏 数量/间 Houses Destroyed Num	房屋毁坏 级别 Dh	房屋受损 数量/间 Houses Damaged Num	房屋受损 级别 Dh
1902	9	23	20	18	30					* Engdahl	Mexico: Venustiano Carranza, Chiapas	墨西哥:卡兰萨,恰帕斯	16.6	-92.6	100	7.8	Mw							3				
1902	9	27				1				NOAA, Song	Guatemala: Quezaltenango	危地马拉:克萨尔特南戈	14	-91		7	Mk							1				
1902	10	17	7	21						GSHAP	Georgia: Kakhetiya	格鲁吉亚:卡赫季州	42.1	45.8	7	4.5	Ms	7										
1902	10	26	11	37						GSHAP	Azerbaijan: Samaxi	阿塞拜疆:沙马基区	39.7	47.8	14	4.9	Ms	5.5										
1902	11	17	0	38						Maso, Song	Philippines: Luzon, Manila	菲律宾:吕宋岛马尼拉	14.3	120.05		5.5	Mk	7										
1902	11	17	19	50						USGS, Song	US: Utah, Pine Valley	美国:犹他州派恩瓦利	37.4	-113.5		6.1	Mk	8										
1902	12	4	22	18						GSHAP	Turkmenistan: Lebap, E.	土库曼斯坦:列巴普东部	37.8	65.5	20	4.9	Ms	6										
1902	12	5								USGS, Song	US: Utah, Pine Valley	美国:犹他州派恩瓦利	37.4	-113.5		5.1	Mk	6										
1902	12	12								USGS, Song	US: California, Los Alamos	美国:加利福尼亚州洛斯阿拉莫斯	34.8	-120.4		5.6	Mk	7										
1902	12	16	5	7						*	Uzbekistan: Andizhan	乌兹别克斯坦:安第札	40.8	72.3	9	6.4	Ms	9	4880	4				4	41704	5		
1902	12	23	23	15		4				Maso, Song	Guam	关岛(西太平洋)	14	143.3		7.2	Mk	6										
1902	12	28	1	43	19					GSHAP	Russia: Tuva, Khandagayty	俄罗斯:唐努图瓦州汉达盖特	50.7	91.3	30	6.6	Ms	7.5										
1903	1	2	0	7	15					GSHAP	Iran: Semnan, Dāmghān	伊朗:塞姆南,达姆甘	36.5	54.9	25	5.2	Ms	5										
1903	1	18	16	55						GSHAP	Azerbaijan: Gəncə	阿塞拜疆:占贾	40.7	46.4	12	4.6	Ms	5.5										
1903	1	20	8	24						GSHAP, Afghan	Afghan: Badakhshan	阿富汗:巴达赫尚	37	71	30	5.5	Ms	6										
1903	1	25	15	22						GSHAP	Ecuador: Quito	厄瓜多尔:基多	-0.2	-78.5		4.3	Ms	5										
1903	2	1	9	34						* GSHAP, Engdahl	Mongolia: North - East of Otgontenger	蒙古:恩赫泰万山东北	48	98	60	7.1	Mw	10										
1903	2	9	0	21						USGS	US: Illinois, Carbondale	美国:伊利诺斯州卡本代尔	37.8	-89.3		4.9	Ms	7										
1903	2	14								GSHAP	Brasil: Aracati	巴西:阿拉卡蒂	-4.38	-38.97		4.9	Ms	6										
1903	2	15								GSHAP	Brasil: Aracati	巴西:阿拉卡蒂	-4.38	-38.97		4.9	Ms	6										
1903	2	16	19	59	5					GSHAP, Italy	Slovenia: Idrija	斯洛文尼亚:伊德里亚	46	14.1	6	5.03	Ms	6										
1903	2	16								GSHAP	Brasil: Aracati	巴西:阿拉卡蒂	-4.38	-38.97		4.9	Ms	6										
1903	2	17	8	52						GSHAP	Russia: Kamchatka, Near East Coast	俄罗斯:堪察加东部近海	53	160	20	5.9	Ms	8										
1903	2	17	11	28						GSHAP	Caspian Sea	里海	40	53	20	5	Ms	6										
1903	2					1	0.2			* NOAA, Song	Mariana Islands	马里亚纳群岛	18	146		7	Mk											
1903	3	12	14	19						GSHAP	Russia: Kemerovo, Novokuzneck	俄罗斯:克麦罗沃州新库兹涅茨克	53.9	87	30	6.1	Ms	7										
1903	3	15	17	57						USGS, Song	US: Montana, Helena	美国:蒙大纳州海伦娜	46.6	-112		5.1	Mk	6										
1903	3	28	8	55	10					GSHAP	Uzbekistan: Andizhan	乌兹别克斯坦:安第札	40.8	72.7	14	6.1	Ms	8										
1903	3	29	22	30						*	Israel: Jerusalem	以色列:耶路撒冷	32.2	35.3		5.7	Muk		20	1								
1903	3	30				2	1	-0.5		* NOAA	Indonesia: Ceram Sea	印度尼西亚:塞兰海	-3	127.5	33	6.5	Ms											
1903	3									USGS, Song	Gulf of Alaska	阿拉斯加湾	61	-146		4.9	Mk	5										
1903	3									China	China: Xinjiang, Urumqi	中国:新疆乌鲁木齐	43.8	87.6		5	Ms	6										

年 Year	月 Mo	日 Dy	时 Hr	分 Mn	秒 Sec	源 Sr	浪高 Wh	级 I mI	级 S mS	资料来源 Information	地名(英文) Name(English)	地名(中文) Name(Chinese)	纬度(°) Latitude	经度(°) Longitude	深度 Depth	震级 Mag	标度 Scale	烈度 MMI	死亡人数 Deaths 数量/人 Num	死亡人数 Deaths 级别 Dd	受伤人数 Injuries 数量/人 Num	受伤人数 Injuries 级别 Dd	经济损失 Damage 数量/$ Mill	经济损失 Damage 级别 De	房屋毁坏 Houses Destroyed 数量/间 Num	房屋毁坏 Houses Destroyed 级别 Dh	房屋受损 Houses Damaged 数量/间 Num	房屋受损 Houses Damaged 级别 Dh
1903	4	19	13	25						Engdahl, GSHAP	Afghan:Badakhshan	阿富汗:巴达赫尚	37	71	160	6.9	Ms	6										
1903	4	19								* Turkey	Turkey:Mus	土耳其:穆什	39.1	42.4		7	Ms		1700	4				3				
1903	4	28	23	39						GSHAP	Turkey:Mus	土耳其:穆什	39.3	42.3	20	7	Ms	9										
1903	4	28	23	46						*	Turkey:Malazgirt	土耳其:马拉兹吉尔特	39.1	42.5		6.3	Ms	10	3560	4		4		4	12000	5		
1903	5	13				1			2	* NOAA	Italy:Sicily, Palermo	意大利:西西里岛,巴勒莫	38.1	13.4		5	Ms											
1903	5	16	5	20						GSHAP	Russia:Krasnoyarsk, S.	俄罗斯:克拉斯诺亚尔斯克南部	53.6	92.5	11	4.5	Ms	6										
1903	5	18	5	18						GSHAP	Russia:Krasnoyarsk, S.	俄罗斯:克拉斯诺亚尔斯克南部	53.6	92.5	11	4.5	Ms	6										
1903	5	23	22	11						Maso, Song	Philippines:Basud	菲律宾:巴苏德	14	123		5	Mk	6										
1903	5	26	20	30						GSHAP	Venezuela:Merida	委内瑞拉:梅里达	8.47	-71.43		4.9	Ms	6										
1903	5	28	3	58						*	Turkey:Ardahan	土耳其:阿尔达汉	40.9	42.7		5.8	Muk	8	1000	3				3				
1903	6	3	10							GSHAP	Ecuador:Tixan	厄瓜多尔:蒂克桑	-2.2	-78.83		4.3	Ms	5										
1903	6	3	11	29						GSHAP	Russia:Dagestan, Makhachkala	俄罗斯:达吉斯坦共和国马哈奇卡拉	42	46.4	10	4.5	Ms	6.5										
1903	6	8	15	8						GSHAP	Romania:Nereju	罗马尼亚:内雷茹	45.7	26.6	150	5.5	Ms	6										
1903	6	9	5	42						GSHAP	Ecuador:Quito	厄瓜多尔:基多	-0.22	-78.5		4.3	Ms	5										
1903	6	11	13	12						CGS, USGS	US:California, Morgan Hill	美国:加利福尼亚州摩根希尔	37.2	-121.8		6.1	Ms	7										
1903	6	18	16							China	China:Hebei, Shenxian	中国:河北深县	38	115.5		4.75	Ms	6										
1903	7	9	13	21	3					GSHAP	Armenia:Gyumri	亚美尼亚:久姆里	41.1	44.4	22	4.5	Ms	5.5										
1903	7	16				1				* NOAA, Song	Mexico:Cihuatlan, Off Coast of S.	墨西哥:锡瓦特兰南部海域	18.5	-107		7	Mk											
1903	7	24	20	26						USGS	US:California, Oroville Reservoir	美国:加利福尼亚州奥罗维尔水库	39.5	-122		4.5	Ms	7										
1903	7	28	4							* Song	Italy:Pontremoli	意大利:蓬特雷莫利	44.3	10		6.5	Mk	12										
1903	8	3	6	49						CGS, USGS	US:California, Morgan Hill	美国:加利福尼亚州莫干山	37.3	-121.8		6.2	Ms	7										
1903	8	8	1	10						GSHAP	Colombia:Bogota	哥伦比亚:波哥达	4.6	-74		4.5	Ms	5										
1903	8	11	4	32	54					* Engdahl	Greece:Mitata (Kythera)	希腊:歇拉岛	36.36	22.97	80	8.3	Muk	11	2	1				3				
1903	8	12	23							GSHAP	Argentina:San Juan	阿根廷:圣胡安	-32.1	-69.1	70	6	Ms	8										
1903	8	17	7	45	6					GSHAP	Croatia:Sisak	克罗地亚:西萨克	45.4	16.2	10	4.7	Ms	6										
1903	9	7				1				* NOAA, Song	Indonesia:Java Ridge	印度尼西亚:爪哇海岭	-9	111		7	Mk											
1903	9	13	8	2						GSHAP	Romania:Nereju	罗马尼亚:内雷茹	45.7	26.6	45	6.2	Ms	6										
1903	9	25	1	20						* Iran	Iran:Kashmar	伊朗:卡什马尔	35.2	58.2		6.5	Muk		350	3								
1903	9	26				2	0.7	-0.5		* NOAA, Song	Chile:Iquique	智利:伊基克	-20.2	-70.1	33	7	Mk											
1903	11	2	22	12						GSHAP	Azerbaijan:Gence, NE.	阿塞拜疆:占贾东北	41.1	47.1	36	5	Ms	6										
1903	11	4	18	18						USGS	US:Missouri, New Madrid	美国:密苏里州新马德里	36.5	-89.5		4.6	Ms	6										

时间						海啸				资料来源	震中				深度	震级	标度	烈度	死亡人数		受伤人数		经济损失		房屋毁坏		房屋受损	
年	月	日	时	分	秒	源	浪高	级 I	级 S		地名(英文)	地名(中文)	纬度(°)	经度(°)					数量/人	级别	数量/人	级别	数量/$ Mill	级别	数量/间	级别	数量/间	级别
Date						Tsunami				Information	Earthquake Epicenter				Depth	Mag	Scale	MMI	Deaths		Injuries		Damage		Houses Destroyed		Houses Damaged	
Year	Mo	Dy	Hr	Mn	Sec	Sr	Wh	mI	mS		Name(English)	Name(Chinese)	Latitude	Longitude					Num	Dd	Num	Dd	$ Mill	De	Num	Dh	Num	Dh
1903	11	4	19	14						USGS	US:Missouri, New Madrid	美国:密苏里州新马德里	36.5	-89.8		5.1	Ms	7										
1903	11	10	4	39		4				Maso, Song	Guam	关岛(西太平洋)	14	143.3		7.3	Mk	7										
1903	11	26	11	49						Engdahl, GSHAP	Russia:Lake Baykal	俄罗斯:贝加尔湖	52.7	107.6	30	6.7	Ms	8										
1903	11	30	2	34						GSHAP	Bulgaria:Blagoevgrad	保加利亚:布拉戈耶夫格勒	42.1	23.2	7	4.9	Ms	7										
1903	12	1	13	34						GSHAP	Bulgaria:Razlog Valley	保加利亚:拉兹洛格	42.1	23.4	10	4.6	Ms	6										
1903	12	1	13							GSHAP	Colombia:Urrao	哥伦比亚:乌劳	6.4	-76.4		5	Ms	7										
1903	12	7	14	44		3	0.7	-0.5		* NOAA, GSHAP, Engdahl	Chile:Vallenar	智利:巴耶纳尔	-28.5	-71	33	6.8	Ms	8		1				2		2		
1903	12	25	17	45						USGS, Song	US:California, Long Beach	美国:加利福尼亚州长滩	34	-118		5.1	Mk	6										
1903	12	28	2	56						* Engdahl	Philippines:Davao Gulf	菲律宾:达沃湾	7	126	60	7.1	Mw	8						2				3
1903										USGS, Song	US:Nevada, Fallon, NE.	美国:内华达州法伦东北	39.5	-118.1		5.1	Mk	6										
1904	1	1	1	48						GSHAP	Turkey:Denizli	土耳其:登尼资里	37.8	29.1	20	4.8	Ms	6										
1904	1	1	11	38						GSHAP	Turkey:Denizli	土耳其:登尼资里	37.8	29.1	20	4.8	Ms	6										
1904	1	20	14	52	6	1				* Engdahl, NOAA	Panama:Off Coast of S.	巴拿马:南部海域	7	-79	60	7.2	Mw											
1904	1	31	13	24						GSHAP, Song	Trinidad & Tobago:Port of Spain	特立尼达和多巴哥:西班牙港	10.68	-61.51		5	Mk	6										
1904	2	2				1			0.5	NOAA, Song	Celebes Sea	西里伯斯海	6.3	123.6		7	Mk											
1904	2	4	21							China	China:Xinjiang, Maralbishi, NW.	中国:新疆巴楚西北	40	78		6.1	Ms	7										
1904	2	6	2	49						GSHAP	Romania:Nereju	罗马尼亚:内雷茹	45.7	26.6	62	6.3	Ms	6										
1904	2	8	6	16						GSHAP	Black Sea	黑海	43.5	28.5	15	4.5	Ms	5										
1904	2	13	21	30						GSHAP	Russia:Omsk, Chugunly	俄罗斯:鄂木斯克州丘贡雷	56.4	73	30	5	Ms	6										
1904	3	4	4	45						GSHAP, Song	Peru:Lima	秘鲁:利马	-12.3	-76.2	90	6	Mk	7										
1904	3	4	10	17						GSHAP, Song	Peru:Lima	秘鲁:利马	-12.021	-76.951	60	6.5	Mk	9										
1904	3	17	4	20						USGS	US:Washington, Seattle	美国:华盛顿州西雅图	48.5	-122.8		5.3	Ms	5										
1904	3	18	13	42						* Engdahl	Japan:Hokkaido	日本:北海道	42.7	146.1	35	6.8	Mj	10						1				
1904	3	19	5	40						GSHAP, Song	Chile:Atacama	智利:阿塔卡马	-28.57	-70.78		6	Mk	8										
1904	3	20	9	59	50					GSHAP	Iran:Mashhad	伊朗:马什哈德	36.6	59.4	11	5.7	Ms	8										
1904	3	21	6	4						USGS	US:Maine, Alexander	美国:缅因州亚历山大	45	-67.2		5.1	Ms	7										
1904	3	28	10	17	10					GSHAP	Russia:Dagestan, Makhachkala	俄罗斯:达吉斯坦共和国马哈奇卡拉	42.8	46.9	12	4.5	Ms	6										
1904	4	4	10	3						*	Bulgaria:Struma	保加利亚:斯特鲁马河	41.8	23.2	15	7.5	Ms	10						3				
1904	4	4	10	26						* Turkey, Engdahl	Bulgaria:Struma	保加利亚:斯特鲁马河	41.8	23.2	15	7.1	Mw	11						3				
1904	4	4	18	9						USGS, Song	Hawaiian Islands	夏威夷群岛	19.25	-155		4.9	Mk	5										
1904	4	15	18							GSHAP	Kazakhstan:Zyryanovsk	哈萨克斯坦:济良诺夫斯克	50.5	84.8	15	5.4	Ms	6										

年 Year	月 Mo	日 Dy	时 Hr	分 Mn	秒 Sec	海啸 Tsunami 源 Sr	浪高 Wh	级 I mI	级 S mS	资料来源 Information	震中 Earthquake Epicenter 地名(英文) Name(English)	地名(中文) Name(Chinese)	纬度(°) Latitude	经度(°) Longitude	深度 Depth	震级 Mag	标度 Scale	烈度 MMI	死亡人数 Deaths 数量/人 Num	级别 Dd	受伤人数 Injuries 数量/人 Num	级别 Dd	经济损失 Damage 数量/$ Mill	级别 De	房屋毁坏 Houses Destroyed 数量/间 Num	级别 Dh	房屋受损 Houses Damaged 数量/间 Num	级别 Dh
1904	4	16	9	20						USGS	US:California,Redding	美国:加利福尼亚州雷丁	40.5	-122.4		4.5	Ms	5										
1904	4	17	13							GSHAP	Kazakhstan:Zyryanovsk	哈萨克斯坦:济良诺夫斯克	50.5	84.8	30	5.4	Ms	6										
1904	4	24	6	39						*China	China:Taiwan,Chiayi	中国:台湾嘉义	23.5	120.5		6.5	Ms	8	3	1	10	1		2	66	2	840	3
1904	4	28	15	25						GSHAP	Azerbaijan:Samaxi	阿塞拜疆:沙马基区	40.7	48.5	12	5.1	Ms	7										
1904	5	4	16							GSHAP	Ecuador:Loja	厄瓜多尔:洛哈	-4	-79.2		5.7	Ms	7										
1904	5	25	19	26						GSHAP	Russia:Khabarovsk,Amursk	俄罗斯:哈巴罗夫斯克区阿穆尔斯克	50.2	137	15	4.7	Ms	6										
1904	6	4	22	57						USGS,Song	Hawaiian Islands	夏威夷群岛	21	-156		4.9	Mk	5										
1904	6	6	14	25						GSHAP	Romania:Silistra	罗马尼亚:锡利斯特拉	44.1	27.3	30	4.7	Ms	5										
1904	6	25	14	45	36	4		1	2	*Engdahl,GSHAP,NOAA	Russia:Kamchatka,Near East Coast	俄罗斯:堪察加东部近海	52	159	30	7.5	Mw	10						1				
1904	6	25	21	0	30	3		1		*Engdahl,GSHAP,NOAA	Russia:Kamchatka,Near East Coast	俄罗斯:堪察加东部近海	52	159	30	7.6	Mw	10						1				
1904	6	27	0	9						*Engdahl	Russia:Kamchatka,Near East Coast	俄罗斯:堪察加东部近海	52	159	60	7.2	Mw	9										
1904	6	28	2	15						GSHAP	Bulgaria:Smolyan	保加利亚:斯莫梁	41.6	24.7	35	5	Ms	6										
1904	7	5				2			1	NOAA,Song	Indonesia:Maluku Islands	印度尼西亚:摩鹿加群岛	-3.6	128.7		7.3	Mk							1				
1904	7	24	10	44	36					Engdahl,GSHAP	Russia:Kamchatka,Near East Coast	俄罗斯:堪察加东部近海	52	159	30	6.7	Ms	8.5										
1904	7	30	10	26						USGS	US:California,Vacaville	美国:加利福尼亚州瓦卡维尔	38.5	-122		4.5	Ms	5										
1904	8	7	22	50		1				*Song	New Zealand:North Island,Near Coast of E.	新西兰:北岛东部近海	-40.5	177		7	Mk											
1904	8	8	22	49		1				*Engdahl	New Zealand:North Island,Near Coast of SE.	新西兰:北岛东南近海	-40.5	177	33	6.9	Ms											
1904	8	11	5	56						*	Greece:Samos Island	希腊:萨摩斯岛	37.75	27	10	6.2	Ms	10	4	1				3	540	3		
1904	8	27	21	56	6					*Engdahl	Alaska Peninsula,C.	阿拉斯加半岛中部	64.66	-148.08		7.3	Ms	6										
1904	8	30	11	42						*China,Engdahl	China:Sichuan,Dawu	中国:四川道孚	31	101.1		7	Ms	9	400	3				2		3		
1904	9	7				1				*NOAA,Song	Indonesia:Jawa Island,S.	印度尼西亚:爪哇岛南部	-7.7	109		7	Mk											
1904	9	8	16							China	China:Sichuan,Dawu	中国:四川道孚	31	101.1		5.5	Ms	7	19	1								
1904	9	10	16							China	China:Sichuan,Dawu	中国:四川道孚	31	101.1		5.5	Ms	7		1								
1904	9	13	5	36						GSHAP	Croatia:Rijeka	克罗地亚:里耶卡	45.3	14.5	5	4.6	Ms	7										
1904	10	1	10	16						Maso,Song	Philippines:Mindanao,Agusan River Valley	菲律宾:棉兰老岛,阿古桑河流域	8.2	126.1		5.5	Mk	7										
1904	10	1	13	40						GSHAP	Colombia:Supía	哥伦比亚:卡尔达斯的苏皮亚	5.7	-75.5		4	Ms	5										

时间 Date						海啸 Tsunami				资料来源 Information	震中 Earthquake Epicenter				深度 Depth	震级 Mag	标度 Scale	烈度 MMI	死亡人数 Deaths		受伤人数 Injuries		经济损失 Damage		房屋毁坏 Houses Destroyed		房屋受损 Houses Damaged	
年 Year	月 Mo	日 Dy	时 Hr	分 Mn	秒 Sec	源 Sr	浪高 Wh	级 I mI	级 S mS		地名(英文) Name(English)	地名(中文) Name(Chinese)	纬度(°) Latitude	经度(°) Longitude					数量/人 Num	级别 Dd	数量/人 Num	级别 Dd	数量/$ Mill $ Mill	级别 De	数量/间 Num	级别 Dh	数量/间 Num	级别 Dh
1904	10	8	18	39						Maso, Song	Philippines: Laoag, Near Coast	菲律宾:佬沃近海	18	120		5.5	Mk	7										
1904	10	23	10	26						GSHAP	Norway: Sandefjord	挪威:桑德尔福德	59.1	10.5	30	6	Ms	7.5										
1904	11	5	20	25						* China	China: Taiwan, Chiayi	中国:台湾嘉义	23.5	120.3		6.25	Ms	8	145	3	158	3		2	661	3	3179	4
1904	12	3	18	37						GSHAP, Song	Peru: Lima, Near Coast	秘鲁:利马近海	-12.362	-77.5	60	5	Mk	6										
1904	12	30				1				* Song	Cook Islands	库克群岛	-21	-160		7	Mk											
1905	1	6	14	30						USGS	US: California, Caliente	美国:加利福尼亚州卡连特	35.5	-118.7		5	Ms	5										
1905	1	9	6	17						GSHAP	Iran: Zanjān	伊朗:赞詹	37	48.7	19	6.2	Ms	8										
1905	1	20	2	32	30	2				NOAA	Aegean Sea	爱琴海	39.66	22.83		6.3	Ms											
1905	1	23	11	15						GSHAP, Song	Peru: Cusco	秘鲁:库斯科	-13.67	-71.87	7	5	Mk	6										
1905	2	25	10	35						GSHAP	Afghan: Fayzabad	阿富汗:法扎巴德	37	70.5	30	5.4	Ms	6										
1905	3	14	9	42						China, GSHAP	China: Xinjiang, Kashi, N.	中国:新疆喀什北部	40	76		6	Ms	7										
1905	3	15	17	55						GSHAP	Russia: Krasnoyarsk, S.	俄罗斯:克拉斯罗亚尔斯克南部	52.7	92.6	30	6.1	Ms	7.5										
1905	3	19				2	0.6		0.5	* NOAA, Song	Vanuatu Islands: Port Vila	瓦努阿图群岛:维拉港	-17.7	168.3		7	Mk											
1905	4	4	0	50						* Engdahl	India: Kangra	印度:坎格拉	33	76	60	7.8	Mw	10	20000	5				4				
1905	4	15								*	Turkey: Bursa	土耳其:布尔萨	40.2	29	33	6.5	Ms	10										
1905	4	25								* Iran	Iran: Hormozgan	伊朗:荷姆兹甘	27.67	56.03		5.8	Ms							2				
1905	4	30	16	13						GSHAP	Turkey: Eskisehir	土耳其:埃斯基城	39.8	30.5	22	5.4	Ms	6										
1905	5	4	2							USGS, Song	Hawaiian Islands	夏威夷群岛	19.25	-155		4.9	Mk	5										
1905	5	9								* Song	Mexico: Jalisco	墨西哥:哈利斯科	20.3	-103.4		6.2	Mk							3				
1905	5	26	23							GSHAP	Russia: Stavropol, Budyonnovsk	俄罗斯:斯塔夫罗波尔区布琼诺夫斯克	44.8	43.8	20	4.5	Ms	5.5										
1905	6	1	4	42						*	Albania: Shkoder	阿尔巴尼亚:斯库台	42.1	19.6	20	6.6	Muk	10	120	3			23.8	3				
1905	6	2	5	39	42					* Usami, Japan, Engdahl	Japan: Aki	日本:广岛安艺郡	34	132	100	7	mB		11	1	177	3		1	110	3	137	3
1905	7	6	16	21		3		-1		* Engdahl, NOAA	Japan: Fukushima, Off Coast	日本:福岛沿海	37.4	142.6	25	7.1	Mw		41	1								
1905	7	9	9	40	24					* GSHAP, Engdahl	Mongolia: South Hovsgol	蒙古:库苏古尔南部	49	99	33	8.4	M	10										
1905	7	9	10	57	24					GSHAP	Mongolia: Tselserleg	蒙古:车车尔格勒	49.5	97.3	20	6.7	Ms	8.5										
1905	7	9	11	21	21					GSHAP	Mongolia: Tselserleg	蒙古:车车尔格勒	49.5	97.3	20	6.8	Ms	8.5										
1905	7	15	10	10						USGS	US: Maine, Augusta	美国:缅因州奥古斯塔	44.3	-69.8		4.4	Ms	6										
1905	7	15	20	41						USGS, Song	US: California, San Bernardino	美国:加利福尼亚州圣贝纳迪诺	34.1	-117.3		5.1	Mk	6										
1905	7	16	18	52						GSHAP	Russia: Tuva, Kyzyl - Mazhalyk	俄罗斯:唐努图瓦州克孜勒马扎雷克	51.7	90.2	20	6	Ms	7										
1905	7	18	22	30						GSHAP	Brasil: Sr. Do Bonfim	巴西:塞纽尔杜邦芬	-10.2	-40.4	15	4.8	Ms	5										
1905	7	27	0	20						USGS	US: Michigan, Mohawk	美国:密歇根州莫霍克	47.24	-88.45		4.5	Ms	7										

年 Year	月 Mo	日 Dy	时 Hr	分 Mn	秒 Sec	源 Sr	浪高 Wh	级 I mI	级 S mS	资料来源 Information	地名(英文) Name(English)	地名(中文) Name(Chinese)	纬度(°) Latitude	经度(°) Longitude	深度 Depth	震级 Mag	标度 Scale	烈度 MMI	死亡人数 Deaths 数量/人 Num	死亡人数 Deaths 级别 Dd	受伤人数 Injuries 数量/人 Num	受伤人数 Injuries 级别 Dd	经济损失 Damage 数量/$ Mill $ Mill	经济损失 Damage 级别 De	房屋毁坏 Houses Destroyed 数量/间 Num	房屋毁坏 Houses Destroyed 级别 Dh	房屋受损 Houses Damaged 数量/间 Num	房屋受损 Houses Damaged 级别 Dh
1905	8	22	5	8						USGS	US:Missouri,Cape Girardeau	美国:密苏里州开普吉拉多	37.2	-89.3		4.8	Ms	6										
1905	8	26	14	45						* Song	Italy:Sulmona To Campobasso	意大利:阿布鲁佐	42.1	13.9		6.5	Mk	12										
1905	9	3	5	40						USGS,Song	US:California,Los Angeles	美国:加利福尼亚州洛杉矶	34	-118.3		5.1	Mk	6										
1905	9	8	1	43		4	1.3		4	* Italy, Engdahl, NOAA	Italy:Monteleone,Tropea	意大利:蒙特莱奥内,特罗佩阿	38.67	16.07		6.8	Ms	10	557	3				3				
1905	10	4	22	29		4	0.5	-1	2	* NOAA	Black Sea	黑海	44.7	37.4		5.1	Ms	7										
1905	10	8	7	27						*	Bulgaria:Blagoevgrad	保加利亚:布拉戈耶夫格勒	42	23	33	6.4	Muk	10										
1905	10	20	14	10						GSHAP	Turkey:Akcakoca	土耳其:阿克恰科贾	41	31	27	5.2	Ms	5										
1905	10	21	11	1	37					* GSHAP, Engdahl	Georgia:Poti	格鲁吉亚:波季	42	42	60	7.5	Muk	7										
1905	10	21	13	20	44					GSHAP	Russia:Karachaevo - Cherkess,Arkhyz	俄罗斯:卡拉恰伊 - 切尔克斯州阿尔赫兹	43.6	41.2	32	5.6	Ms	6										
1905	10	22	3	42						GSHAP	Turkey:Akcakoca	土耳其:阿克恰科贾	41	31	27	5.2	Ms	5										
1905	10	26								GSHAP,Song	Chile:Rancagua	智利:兰卡瓜	-34.17	-70.75		6	Mk	8										
1905	11	7	16							* China	China:Sichuan,Zigong	中国:四川自贡	29.4	104.7		5	Ms	6	13	1		1		1	3	1		
1905	11	8	21	41						* Turkey, GSHAP	Aegean Sea	爱琴海	40.25	24.2	30	7.8	Ms	10										
1905	11	11	21	29						USGS,Song	US:Idaho,Shoshone	美国:爱达荷州肖肖尼	42.9	-114.5		5.6	Mk	7										
1905	11	14	21	2						GSHAP	Venezuela:Lara	委内瑞拉:拉腊	10	-70.5		5.9	Ms	5										
1905	11	22				2				* NOAA,Song	Vanuatu Islands:Port Vila	瓦努阿图群岛:维拉港	-17.7	168.3		7	Mk											
1905	11	24				2				* NOAA,Song	Vanuatu Islands:Port Vila	瓦努阿图群岛:维拉港	-17.7	168.3		7	Mk											
1905	12	4	7	4						*	Turkey:Malatya	土耳其:马拉蒂亚	38.1	38.6		6.8	Muk	9		3				3				
1905	12	8	8	22		2		-0.5		* Maso,NOAA	Philippines:Tuburan	菲律宾:伯兰城	11	123.5		6.5	Ms	7						1				
1905	12	8								USGS,Song	South of Alaska	阿拉斯加南部	61	-160		4.9	Mk	5										
1905	12	10	18	12						Maso,Song	Philippines:Mindanao, Agusan River Valley	菲律宾:棉兰老岛,阿古桑河流域	8.2	126.1		6.1	Mk	8										
1905	12	17	22	16	18					GSHAP	Croatia:Bedekovcina	克罗地亚:贝代科夫契纳	45.9	16.1	7	5.6	Ms	7										
1905	12	23	22	23						CGS,USGS	US:California,Arvin	美国:加利福尼亚州阿尔文	35.3	-118.8		5.8	Ms	6										
1905										* Song	Syria:Halab (Aleppo)	叙利亚:阿勒颇	36.1	37.1		5.9	Mk	8						2		3		3
1905						2			3	NOAA,Song	Balearic Sea	巴利阿里海	38	8		6.7	Mk											
1905						1				NOAA,Song	Togo:Lome	多哥:洛美	6.1	1.2		7	Mk											
1906	1	2	4	26	30					GSHAP	Croatia:Bedekovcina	克罗地亚:贝代科夫契纳	45.9	16.1	14	6.1	Ms	8										
1906	1	3	13	42						USGS,Song	US:Nevada,Colville	美国:内华达州科尔维尔	48.5	-117.5		5.1	Mk	6										
1906	1	4	4	25						GSHAP	Croatia:Bedekovcina	克罗地亚:贝代科夫契纳	45.8	16	9	4.5	Ms	6										

年 Year	月 Mo	日 Dy	时 Hr	分 Mn	秒 Sec	海啸 Tsunami 源 Sr	浪高 Wh	级 I mI	级 S mS	资料来源 Information	震中 Earthquake Epicenter 地名(英文) Name(English)	地名(中文) Name(Chinese)	纬度(°) Latitude	经度(°) Longitude	深度 Depth	震级 Mag	标度 Scale	烈度 MMI	死亡人数 Deaths 数量/人 Num	级别 Dd	受伤人数 Injuries 数量/人 Num	级别 Dd	经济损失 Damage 数量/$ Mill	级别 De	房屋毁坏 Houses Destroyed 数量/间 Num	级别 Dh	房屋受损 Houses Damaged 数量/间 Num	级别 Dh
1906	1	6	16							* China	China: Yunnan, Xuanwei	中国:云南宣威	26.2	104.1		5.5	Ms	7	10	1				2		3		
1906	1	8	0	15						USGS	US: Kansas, Manhattan	美国:堪萨斯州曼哈顿	39.3	-96.6		4.9	Ms	7										
1906	1	9	10							GSHAP, Song	Peru: Sechura, Near Coast	秘鲁:塞丘拉近海	-5.6	-81.3	30	5	Mk	6										
1906	1	18	11							GSHAP, Song	Chile: Valparaiso	智利:瓦尔帕莱索	-33.05	-71.63		6	Mk	8										
1906	1	25	21	32	30					USGS, Song	US: Arizona, Flagstaff	美国:亚利桑那州弗拉格斯塔夫	35.2	-111.7		5.6	Mk	7										
1906	1	31	5	24		4				* NOAA, Song	Venezuela: Caracas	委内瑞拉:加拉加斯	10.5	-66.917		7	Mk											
1906	1	31	8							GSHAP	Ecuador: Near Coast of W.	厄瓜多尔:西部近海	1	-80.5		4.3	Ms	5										
1906	1	31	15	35	51	4	5	1	3	* Engdahl, NOAA	Ecuador: Off Coast of W.	厄瓜多尔:西部沿海	1	-81.5	25	8.8	M	9	1000	3				3		3		
1906	2	3								*	Colombia: Palmira	哥伦比亚:帕尔米拉	3.5	-76.2		7.7	Ms	10										
1906	2	5	3	44						GSHAP	Slovenia: Ljubljana	斯洛文尼亚:卢布尔雅那	46.1	14.5	8	4.6	Ms	5										
1906	2	7				2			0.5	* NOAA, Song	Ecuador: Near Coast of W.	厄瓜多尔:西部近海	1	-81		7	Mk											
1906	2	16				2				* NOAA, Song	Saint Lucia: Millet	圣卢西亚:米利特	13.88	-60.97		7.3	Mk	8						1				
1906	2	19	8							GSHAP	Ecuador: Ibarra	厄瓜多尔:伊瓦拉	0.3	-78.2		4.3	Ms	5										
1906	2	21				3				* NOAA, Song	Colombia: Buenaventura	哥伦比亚:布埃纳文图拉	3.9	-77.033		7	Mk											
1906	3	1	17	45						*	Albania: Elbasan	阿尔巴尼亚:爱尔巴桑	41.1	20	15	6.5	Muk	10						3				
1906	3	2	16							China	China: Xinjiang, Kuqa, SW.	中国:新疆库车西南	41.7	82.7		5	Ms	6										
1906	3	3	20	25						USGS	US: California, Poway	美国:加利福尼亚州波韦	33	-117		4.5	Ms	5										
1906	3	16	22	42	40					* China, Engdahl	China: Taiwan, Chiayi	中国:台湾嘉义	23.6	120.5	5	6.75	Ms	9	1258	4	745	3		3	6769	4	3633	4
1906	3	26	3	29						China	China: Taiwan, Yunlin	中国:台湾云林	23.7	120.5		5.5	Ms	7	1	1	5	1			29	1	529	3
1906	3	27	22	58	40					* China	China: Taiwan Strait	中国:台湾海峡	24.3	118.6		6.25	Ms	8		3		2		2		2		
1906	4	4	12	42						China	China: Taiwan, Chiayi	中国:台湾嘉义	23.6	120.5		4.75	Ms	6							5	1		
1906	4	5	18	59	19					China	China: Taiwan, Chiayi	中国:台湾嘉义	23.6	120.5		5	Ms	6							6	1		
1906	4	6	16	53						China	China: Taiwan, Chiayi	中国:台湾嘉义	23.4	120.4		5.5	Ms	7	12	1	6	1			63	2	283	3
1906	4	13	19	18						* China, Engdahl	China: Taiwan, Chiayi	中国:台湾嘉义	23.4	120.4	5	7.1	Ms	8	15	1	84	2		3	1794	4	10037	5
1906	4	16	9	48						GSHAP	Bulgarian: Kardzali	保加利亚:克尔贾利	41.7	25.3	20	4.7	Ms	5.5										
1906	4	18	13	12	21	4	0.1	-3.3	-2	* Engdahl, NOAA	US: California, San Francisco	美国:加利福尼亚州旧金山	37.67	-122.48	20	7.8	M	11	700	3			400	5				
1906	4	19	0	30						CGS, USGS	US: California, Brawley	美国:加利福尼亚州布劳利	32.9	-115.5		6.2	Ms	8										
1906	4	23	9	10						USGS	US: California, Eureka	美国:加利福尼亚州尤里卡	41	-124		6.4	Ms	7										
1906	4	28	18							GSHAP, Song	Peru: Máncora, Near Coast	秘鲁:曼科拉近海	-3.952	-81.356	30	5	Mk	6										
1906	5	2	5	30						USGS, Song	US: California, Cazadero	美国:加利福尼亚州卡扎德罗	38.5	-123		5.1	Mk	6										
1906	5	3	16							China	China: Taiwan, Chiayi	中国:台湾嘉义	23.4	120.4		5.25	Ms	6							3	1		
1906	5	5	0	36						GSHAP, Song	Peru: Tacna, Near Coast	秘鲁:塔克纳近海	-18.294	-71.021	30	6	Mk	7										

时间						海啸				资料来源	震中				深度	震级	标度	烈度	死亡人数		受伤人数		经济损失		房屋毁坏		房屋受损	
年	月	日	时	分	秒	源	浪高	级 I	级 S		地名(英文)	地名(中文)	纬度(°)	经度(°)					数量/人	级别	数量/人	级别	数量/$ Mill	级别	数量/间	级别	数量/间	级别
Date						Tsunami				Information	Earthquake Epicenter				Depth	Mag	Scale	MMI	Deaths		Injuries		Damage		Houses Destroyed		Houses Damaged	
Year	Mo	Dy	Hr	Mn	Sec	Sr	Wh	mI	mS		Name(English)	Name(Chinese)	Latitude	Longitude					Num	Dd	Num	Dd	$ Mill	De	Num	Dh	Num	Dh
1906	5	7	4	10						USGS, Song	US: California, Lucerne	美国:加利福尼亚州卢塞恩	39.2	-122.9		5.1	Mk	6										
1906	5	7	5							USGS, Song	US: California, Lucerne	美国:加利福尼亚州卢塞恩	39.2	-122.9		5.1	Mk	6										
1906	5	7				2				* NOAA, Song	Chile: Arica	智利:阿里卡	-18.5	-70.3	33	7	Mk											
1906	5	26	14	42						USGS	US: Michigan, Houghton	美国:密歇根州霍顿	47.1	-88.64		4.2	Ms	8										
1906	5									* China	China: Yunnan, Longling	中国:云南龙陵	24.6	98.7		5.5	Ms	7	1	1				2		3		
1906	6	1	4	30		1				Engdahl, NOAA	East Caroline Basin	东加罗林海盆	0	145	33	7.1	Mw											
1906	6	19	11	22	41					Engdahl, Maso	Philippines: Luzon, Coast N.	菲律宾:吕宋岛北部海域	20	122	60	7.1	Muk	6										
1906	7	1				1				NOAA, Song	Marshall Islands	马绍尔群岛	7.25	171.3		7	Mk											
1906	7	11								*	Colombia: Bogota	哥伦比亚:波哥达	4.6	-74		7.7	Ms	9										
1906	7	12	12	15						USGS, Song	US: New Mexico, Socorro	美国:新墨西哥州索科罗	34	-107		5.6	Mk	7										
1906	7	12	13	5						USGS, Song	US: New Mexico, Socorro	美国:新墨西哥州索科罗	34	-107		5.1	Mk	6										
1906	7	14	10	27						*	Colombia: Bogota	哥伦比亚:波哥达	4.6	-74		7.7	Ms	9										
1906	7	16	19							USGS, Song	US: New Mexico, Socorro	美国:新墨西哥州索科罗	34	-107		5.6	Mk	7										
1906	8	13	18	45						GSHAP	Kazakhstan: Almaty	哈萨克斯坦:阿拉木图	44.7	79.6	17	5.7	Ms	7										
1906	8	15	16							China	China: Hunan, Changde	中国:湖南常德	29.1	111.7		5	Ms	6										
1906	8	17	0	40		4	3.6	1.8	2	* Shi Z., Engdahl, NOAA	Chile: Valparaíso, Near Coast	智利:瓦尔帕莱索近海	-33	-72	25	8.2	M	11	1500	4			100	5				
1906	9	5	15	15						GSHAP, Song	Ecuador: Chimborazo, N.	厄瓜多尔:钦博腊索山北部	-1.6	-78.55		6	Mk	7										
1906	9	10	6	30						GSHAP	Ecuador: Cotopaxi	厄瓜多尔:科托帕希	-0.9	-78.6		5	Ms	6										
1906	9	14	16	4	18	4	1.5	0.6	1.5	* Engdahl, NOAA	New Britain Trench	新不列颠海沟[太平洋]	-7	149	33	8	Mw			3				3		3		
1906	9	17	10							* Song	Italy: Sicilia Island	意大利:西西里岛	38	13.7		6.5	Mk	12										
1906	9	25	0	48	36					GSHAP	Russia: Kabardino – Balkaria, Nalchik	俄罗斯:卡尔梅克州纳尔奇克	43.4	42.8	26	5	Ms	5.5										
1906	9	28	7	30	50					GSHAP	Turkey: Kars	土耳其:卡尔斯	40.6	43.1	9	4.8	Ms	7.5										
1906	9	28	15	24	54					* Engdahl	Ecuador: Chimborazo	厄瓜多尔:钦博腊索山	-2	-79	150	7.5	mB	7										
1906	10	2	1	50		3	1.2		1.5	* Engdahl, NOAA	Bismarck Sea	俾斯麦海	-4	149		7.2	Mw							1				
1906	10	4	6	52						GSHAP	Afghan: Balkh	阿富汗:巴尔赫	37.2	67.3	20	5.7	Ms	7										
1906	10	8	4	53	38					Engdahl, GSHAP	Sea of Okhotsk	鄂霍次克海	53.5	154.5	200	6.7	mB	5										
1906	10	16	22	15						GSHAP	Romania: Bacau	罗马尼亚:巴克乌	46.6	27.3	100	5.5	Ms	5.5										
1906	10	20	16	8	57					GSHAP	Armenia: Gyumri, N.	亚美尼亚:久姆里北部	41.2	44.3	26	5.2	Ms	6										
1906	10	24	15	39	30					Engdahl, Afghan, GSHAP	Afghan: Kholm	阿富汗:胡勒姆	36.5	68	32	6.8	Ms	8										
1906	10	25	2	52						GSHAP	Brasil: Corumbá	巴西:科伦巴	-19	-57.65		4.2	Ms	5										

时间 Date						海啸 Tsunami				资料来源 Information	震中 Earthquake Epicenter				深度 Depth	震级 Mag	标度 Scale	烈度 MMI	死亡人数 Deaths		受伤人数 Injuries		经济损失 Damage		房屋毁坏 Houses Destroyed		房屋受损 Houses Damaged	
年 Year	月 Mo	日 Dy	时 Hr	分 Mn	秒 Sec	源 Sr	浪高 Wh	级 I mI	级 S mS		地名(英文) Name(English)	地名(中文) Name(Chinese)	纬度(°) Latitude	经度(°) Longitude					数量/人 Num	级别 Dd	数量/人 Num	级别 Dd	数量/$ Mill	级别 De	数量/间 Num	级别 Dh	数量/间 Num	级别 Dh
1906	11	15	12	15						USGS, Song	US: New Mexico, Socorro	美国:新墨西哥州索科罗	34	-107		5.6	Mk	7										
1906	11	20	21			3				* NOAA	Ghana: Ho, Palime, Accra	加纳:霍城,帕利美,阿克拉	6.5	0.3		5	Mfa	8						2		3		
1906	12	4	11							GSHAP	Brasil: Campo Grande	巴西:大坎普	-20.95	-43.8		4	Ms	5										
1906	12	5	18	50	58					GSHAP	Russia: Dagestan, Mamedkala	俄罗斯:达吉斯坦共和国马梅德卡拉	42.2	47.9	22	4.7	Ms	5.5										
1906	12	7	6	40						CGS, USGS	US: California, San Simeon	美国:加利福尼亚州圣西米恩	35.5	-121.2		5.7	Ms	6										
1906	12	22	18	21						* China, Engdahl	China: Xinjiang, Shawan, SW.	中国:新疆沙湾西南	43.5	85		7.7	Mw	10	280	3				3	2000	4		
1906	12	26	5	54		2				* Engdahl, NOAA	Peru: Near Coast of S.	秘鲁:南部近海	-18	-71	60	7	Ms											
1906	12	26	18	12						GSHAP	Russia: Sakhalin Island	俄罗斯:库页岛(萨哈林岛)	50.9	142.1	25	6	Ms	7										
1907	1	4	5	19	12	4		1.5	2	* Engdahl, NOAA	Indonesia: Off West Coast of N. Sumatera	印度尼西亚:北苏门答腊西部海域	2	94.5	50	7.5	Mw		400	3				3		3		3
1907	1	10	0	32						GSHAP	Sweden: Karlstad	瑞典:卡尔斯塔德	59.6	12.3	24	4.5	Ms	5										
1907	1	14	13	3						GSHAP	Norway: West of Berg	挪威:贝格西部	65.5	11	42	4.9	Ms	5										
1907	1	14	21	36		4	2.5	1.3		* NOAA	Jamaica: Kingston	牙买加:金斯敦	18.2	-76.7		6.5	Muk		1000	3			30.0	4		3		
1907	1	22	2	41						GSHAP	Turkey: Istanbul	土耳其:伊斯坦布尔	41	29	12	4.5	Ms	5.5										
1907	1	27	4	58						GSHAP	Norway: West of Berg	挪威:贝格西部	65.5	11	41	5.2	Ms	6										
1907	2	11	13	22						USGS	US: Virginia, New Canton	美国:弗吉尼亚州新坎顿	37.7	-78.3		4	Ms	6										
1907	2	21	1							* Song	Italy: Sicilia Island	意大利:西西里岛	38	13.7		6.5	Mk	12										
1907	2	23	20	17						* GSHAP	Peru: Huancavelica	秘鲁:万卡韦利卡	-13.2	-75.4	90	7.6	Muk	6										
1907	3	29	20	46	30	3	4	2	1.5	* Engdahl, NOAA	Celebes Sea	西里伯斯海	3	122	500	7.2	mB											
1907	4	13	7	10						GSHAP	Afghan: Badakhshan	阿富汗:巴达赫尚	36.5	70.5	30	5.3	Ms	5.5										
1907	4	13	17	57	18					Engdahl, GSHAP	Afghan: Badakhshan	阿富汗:巴达赫尚	36.5	70.5	260	6.8	mB	6										
1907	4	15	6	8	6	4	2	1		* Engdahl, NOAA	Mexico: Guerrero, Acapulco, E.	墨西哥:格雷罗州阿卡普尔科东部	17	-100	60	7.9	Mw		8	1				3		3		
1907	4	18	20	59	48					* Engdahl	Philippines: Basud	菲律宾:巴苏德	14	123		7.1	Mw	9	2	1		1		3				
1907	4	18	23	52	24					Shi Z., Maso, Engdahl	Philippines: Libmanan	菲律宾:利马南	13.5	123		7	Ms	7						1				
1907	5	12	16							China	China: Xinjiang, Manas, S.	中国:新疆玛纳斯南	44.2	86.3		6	Ms	8	101	3						3		
1907	5	20	7	49						Maso, Song	Philippines: Leyte Island	菲律宾:莱特岛	11.2	124.3		6.1	Mk	8										
1907	5	25	15	32						* Maso, Song	Philippines: Laoag, Near Coast	菲律宾:佬沃近海	18	120		5.9	Mk	8						2				
1907	6	1	9	37	20					GSHAP	Ecuador: Quito	厄瓜多尔:基多	-0.2	-78.5		4.3	Ms	5										
1907	6	8				5				* * NOAA, Song	Samoa Islands	萨摩亚群岛	-13.612	-172.525		7	Mk											
1907	6	19				5				* * NOAA, Song	Samoa Islands	萨摩亚群岛	-13.612	-172.525		7	Mk											
1907	6	20	11	33						GSHAP, Song	Peru: Chiclayo, Near Coast	秘鲁:奇克拉约近海	-6.975	-80.493	58	5	Mk	6										

时间						海啸				资料来源	震中				深度	震级	标度	烈度	死亡人数		受伤人数		经济损失		房屋毁坏		房屋受损	
年	月	日	时	分	秒	源	浪高	级I	级S		地名(英文)	地名(中文)	纬度(°)	经度(°)					数量/人	级别	数量/人	级别	数量/$ Mill	级别	数量/间	级别	数量/间	级别
Date						Tsunami				Information	Earthquake Epicenter				Depth	Mag	Scale	MMI	Deaths		Injuries		Damage		Houses Destroyed		Houses Damaged	
Year	Mo	Dy	Hr	Mn	Sec	Sr	Wh	mI	mS		Name(English)	Name(Chinese)	Latitude	Longitude					Num	Dd	Num	Dd	$ Mill	De	Num	Dh	Num	Dh
1907	7	9				5				* * NOAA,Song	Samoa Islands	萨摩亚群岛	-13.612	-172.525		7	Mk											
1907	7	30								* Song	Indonesia:Sulawesi,Lemo	印度尼西亚:苏拉威西岛,勒莫	-2	121		5.9	Mk	8						2				
1907	8	13	2	18						GSHAP	Bulgaria:Tran	保加利亚:特伦	42.8	22.6	20	4.6	Ms	6										
1907	8	16	13							*	Albania:Elbasan	阿尔巴尼亚:爱尔巴桑	41.1	20.1	13	6.2	Muk	10										
1907	8	17	11	51						GSHAP	Greece:Kilkis	希腊:基尔基斯	41.3	22.5	6	4.9	Ms	7										
1907	8	17	17	27	54					Engdahl,GSHAP	Russia:Kamchatka Peninsula	俄罗斯:堪察加半岛	52	157	120	7.2	mB	7										
1907	8	21	5	11	24					GSHAP	Caspian Sea	里海	42.7	48.3	43	5.3	Ms	5.5										
1907	9	14	19	18						GSHAP	Turkmenistan:Mary	土库曼斯坦:马雷	37.6	61.9	10	4.6	Ms	6.5										
1907	9	15	17	46						GSHAP	Kyrgyzstan:Osh	吉尔吉斯斯坦:奥什	40.3	72.5	10	5.8	Ms	8										
1907	9	19	19	14						GSHAP	Kyrgyzstan:Osh	吉尔吉斯斯坦:奥什	40.3	72.5	14	5.5	Ms	7.5										
1907	9	20	1	54						CGS,USGS	US:California,Victorville	美国:加利福尼亚州维克托维尔	34.2	-117.1		5.8	Ms	7										
1907	9	24	12	59		3	0.7	-0.5		* NOAA	Canada:Yukon,Whitehorse	加拿大:育空地区白马市	59.5	-135.5		5.5	Ms	5						1				
1907	10	3	12	9						GSHAP	Russia:Jewish,Birobidzhan	俄罗斯:犹太州比罗比詹	48.7	132.2	22	5.2	Ms	6.5										
1907	10	11	15	47	18					GSHAP	Serbia:Novi Sad	塞尔维亚:诺威萨	45.2	19.9	30	4.8	Ms	5										
1907	10	14	16							China	China:Taiwan Strait	中国:台湾海峡	24.8	118.7		5	Ms	6										
1907	10	21	4	23	36					*GSHAP,Engdahl	Tadzhikistan:Khatlon	塔吉克斯坦:哈特隆州	38	69	33	7.2	Mw	9	12000	5				3		3		
1907	10	21	4	44						GSHAP	Tajikistan:Duachanbe	塔吉克斯坦:杜尚别	38.7	68.1	24	7.3	Ms	9										
1907	10	23	20	25						Afghan,GSHAP	Turkmenistan:Lebap,E.	土库曼斯坦:列巴普东部	37.7	65.4		6.1	Ms	7										
1907	10	23	20	28		3			3	* NOAA	Italy:Calabria	意大利:卡拉布里亚	38	16.1	33	5.9	Ms	10										
1907	10	24	5	10						GSHAP	Tadzhikistan:Khatlon	塔吉克斯坦:哈特隆州	38	68.8	18	5.2	Ms	6.5										
1907	10	27	5	17						GSHAP	Tajikistan:Duachanbe	塔吉克斯坦:杜尚别	38.8	68.4	24	6.5	Ms	8										
1907	11	2	22	15						GSHAP	Uzbekistan:Surxondaryo	乌兹别克斯坦:苏尔汉河	38.5	66.5	20	6.3	Ms	7										
1907	11	16	10	10						* GSHAP	Peru:Uchiza	秘鲁:乌奇萨	-8	-76.8	150	8.7	Ms	6										
1907	11	17	10	15						GSHAP	Ecuador:Loja	厄瓜多尔:洛哈	-4	-79.2		4.3	Ms	5										
1907	11	24	13	59						* Maso,Song	Philippines:Basud	菲律宾:巴苏德	14	123		6.5	Mk	9						2				
1907	12	15	17	35		2				* Engdahl,NOAA	Bismarck Sea	俾斯麦海	-3.1	142.5	33	6.9	Ms											
1907	12	25	22	36						Engdahl,GSHAP	Afghan:Badakhshan	阿富汗:巴达赫尚	36.5	70.5	240	6.8	Muk	6.5										
1908	1	5	14	40						GSHAP	Ukraine:Svalyava	乌克兰:斯瓦拉瓦	48.57	23.05	5	4.7	Ms	7										
1908	1	11	3	35						China,Engdahl	China:Taiwan,Hualien	中国:台湾花莲	23.7	121.4	5	6.8	Ms		2	1					3	1	5	1
1908	1	16	9	10						GSHAP	China:Xinjiang,Altay,N.	中国:新疆阿勒泰北部	49	87.2	15	5.3	Ms	6.5										
1908	1	20	20	5						Maso,Song	Philippines:Leyte Island	菲律宾:莱特岛	11.2	124.3		5	Mk	6										
1908	1	27	2							USGS,Song	US:California,Wendel	美国:加利福尼亚州文德尔	40.3	-120.3		5.6	Mk	7										
1908	1	31	4	50						GSHAP	Kazakhstan:Talas	哈萨克斯坦:塔拉兹	42.8	71.3	14	5.3	Ms	7										

时间 年 Date Year	月 Mo	日 Dy	时 Hr	分 Mn	秒 Sec	海啸 源 Tsunami Sr	浪高 Wh	级 I mI	级 S mS	资料来源 Information	震中 地名(英文) Earthquake Epicenter Name(English)	地名(中文) Name(Chinese)	纬度(°) Latitude	经度(°) Longitude	深度 Depth	震级 Mag	标度 Scale	烈度 MMI	死亡人数 数量/人 Deaths Num	级别 Dd	受伤人数 数量/人 Injuries Num	级别 Dd	经济损失 数量/$ Mill Damage $ Mill	级别 De	房屋毁坏 数量/间 Houses Destroyed Num	级别 Dh	房屋受损 数量/间 Houses Damaged Num	级别 Dh
1908	2	6				4	1.4	0.5	1	* NOAA	Indonesia: Southern Sumatra	印度尼西亚:苏门答腊南部	-2	100	130	7.5	Ms											
1908	2	14	11	25		2				* USGS, NOAA	Alaska Peninsula, S.	阿拉斯加半岛南部	61	-146.2		6	Ms	6						1				
1908	2	17	3							GSHAP	Turkey: Kozan	土耳其:科赞	37.4	35.8	33	6	Ms	8										
1908	3	5	2	16						* Maso, Engdahl	Philippines: Mindanao Island	菲律宾:棉兰老岛	9	126		6.9	Ms	6										
1908	3	13	0	40						GSHAP	Romania: Focsani	罗马尼亚:福克沙尼	45.5	27.9	25	4.5	Ms	5										
1908	3	23	12	20						*	Indonesia: Timor	印度尼西亚:帝汶	-10	129		6.6	Ms							1				
1908	3	24	22	7						GSHAP	Uzbekistan: Namangan	乌兹别克斯坦:纳曼干	40.9	71	26	5.4	Ms	6										
1908	3	26	23	3	30					* Engdahl	Mexico: Guerrero, NE.	墨西哥:格雷罗州东北	18	-99	80	7.7	mB							2				
1908	4	25	11	33						USGS	US: California, Seaside	美国:加利福尼亚州锡赛德	36.6	-121.8		4.5	Ms	5										
1908	4	29								GSHAP	Azerbaijan: Samaxi	阿塞拜疆:沙马基区	40.3	48.5	25	4.9	Ms	5.5										
1908	5	14	13	18						Maso, Song	Celebes Sea	西里伯斯海	7.3	123.75		5	Mk	6										
1908	5	15	8	31	36					Engdahl, USGS	Alaska: Lituya Bay	阿拉斯加:立图亚湾	59	-141		7	Ms	6										
1908	5	27	1	35	38					GSHAP	Russia: Dagestan, Derbent	俄罗斯:达吉斯坦共和国的杰尔宾特	42.2	48.1	19	4.9	Ms	6										
1908	5	30	22	15						GSHAP	Black Sea	黑海	44.4	34.3	14	4.7	Ms	5.5										
1908	5	31	17	42						USGS, Song	US: Pennsylvania, Allentown	美国:宾西法尼亚州阿伦敦	40.6	-75.5		5.1	Mk	6										
1908	6	16	17	50						GSHAP, Song	Peru: Near Coast of S.	秘鲁:南部近海	-18.158	-70.837	30	6	Mk	7										
1908	6	30	4	53						GSHAP	Norway: West of Bodo	挪威:博德西部	67.3	14.3	39	4.6	Ms	5										
1908	7	21	8	15						GSHAP	Ecuador: Guayaquil	厄瓜多尔:瓜亚基尔	-2.19	-79.89		4.3	Ms	5										
1908	8	18	10	59						CGS, USGS	US: California, Eureka	美国:加利福尼亚州尤里卡	40.8	-124		5.8	Ms	7										
1908	8	19	1	32						GSHAP	Russia: Adygeya, Maykop	俄罗斯:阿迪格州迈科普	44.6	40.2	18	4.6	Ms	5.5										
1908	9	11				2				NOAA, Song	Canada: Gulf of Saint Lawrence	加拿大:圣劳伦斯湾	48.958	-62.133		7	Mk											
1908	9	13	7	30						GSHAP	Tajikistan: Duachanbe	塔吉克斯坦:杜尚别	38.7	68.8	10	4.5	Ms	6										
1908	9	21	6	31		4	1.2	-0.5		* Engdahl, NOAA	Hawaiian Islands	夏威夷群岛	19.5	-155.4	33	6.8	Ms											
1908	9	22	17							GSHAP	Argentina: Cordoba	阿根廷:科尔多瓦	-30.5	-64.5	100	6.5	Ms	7										
1908	9	28	6	28						GSHAP, Iran	Turkey: Elazig	土耳其:埃拉泽	38.5	39.2	32	6.1	Ms	6										
1908	10	6	21	39	48					Engdahl, GSHAP	Romania: Vrancea	罗马尼亚:弗朗恰	45.8	26.5	150	6.8	Muk	8										
1908	10	11	23	30						GSHAP	Colombia: N Santander, Pamplona	哥伦比亚:北桑坦德,潘普洛纳	7.4	-72.7		4	Ms	5										
1908	11	4	8	37						USGS	US: California, Death Valley	美国:加利福尼亚州死谷	36	-117		6.5	Ms	6										
1908	11	6	19	40						GSHAP	Black Sea	黑海	44.6	33.4	7	4.5	Ms	6.5										
1908	12	10	4	39						GSHAP, Turkey	Georgia: Kutaisi	格鲁吉亚:库塔伊西	42.3	43	12	5.5	Ms	7										
1908	12	12	12	8		2				* Engdahl, NOAA	Peru: Lima, Near Coast	秘鲁:利马近海	-14	-78	60	8.2	Ms											

时间 年 Date Year	月 Mo	日 Dy	时 Hr	分 Mn	秒 Sec	海啸 源 Tsunami Sr	浪高 Wh	级I mI	级S mS	资料来源 Information	震中 地名(英文) Earthquake Epicenter Name(English)	地名(中文) Name(Chinese)	纬度(°) Latitude	经度(°) Longitude	深度 Depth	震级 Mag	标度 Scale	烈度 MMI	死亡人数 数量/人 Deaths Num	级别 Dd	受伤人数 数量/人 Injuries Num	级别 Dd	经济损失 数量/$ Mill Damage $ Mill	级别 De	房屋毁坏 数量/间 Houses Destroyed Num	级别 Dh	房屋受损 数量/间 Houses Damaged Num	级别 Dh
1908	12	27								USGS, Song	US: Montana, Helena	美国:蒙大纳州海伦娜	45.2	-111.9		5.1	Mk	6										
1908	12	28	4	20	24	4	13		5	* Italy, Engdahl, NOAA, GSHAP	Italy: Messina, Sicily	意大利:墨西拿,西西里岛	38.15	15.68	10	7.24	Ms	11	82220	5			116	5		4		
1908	12	28	22							GSHAP	Latvia: Madonas	拉脱维亚:马多纳	56.8	26.3	10	4.5	Ms	7										
1908	12	29	19							GSHAP	Latvia: Daugavpils	拉脱维亚:陶格夫匹尔斯	55.8	26.7	10	4.5	Ms	7										
1908	12	30	2							GSHAP	Belorussia: Minsk, NW.	白俄罗斯:明思克西北	54.5	25.8	10	4.5	Ms	7										
1908										China	China: Shaanxi, Lueyang, NW.	中国:陕西略阳西北	33.5	106		5.5	Ms	7										
1909	1	11	23	44						USGS	US: Washington, Seattle	美国:华盛顿州西雅图	49	-122.7		6	Ms	7										
1909	1	19	4	56						*	Turkey: Izmir	土耳其:伊兹密尔	38.6	26.9		5.8	Muk	9	8	1				3				
1909	1	22	10	10						GSHAP, Song	Russia: Sakhalin Island	俄罗斯:库页岛(萨哈林岛)	50.4	142.5	22	6.1	Mk	7										
1909	1	23	2	48	18					* Engdahl	Iran: Esfahan, W.	伊朗:伊斯法罕西部	33	50	33	7	Ms		5500	4				2				
1909	1	29								* Song	Morocco: Tetuan (Tetouan)	摩洛哥:特特万	35.6	-5.4		6.2	Mk		100	2				3				
1909	2	6	16	1						Maso, Song	Philippines: Mindanao, Agusan River Valley	菲律宾:棉兰老岛,阿古桑河流域	8.2	126.1		5	Mk	6										
1909	2	9	11	24	6					* Turkey, Engdahl	Turkey: Sivas	土耳其:锡瓦斯	40.2	37.8	60	6.8	Muk	9		3				3				
1909	2	14	15	55						USGS	US: California, Antioch	美国:加利福尼亚州安条克	38.1	-121.7		4.5	Ms	5										
1909	2	14	22	28	30					GSHAP	Bulgaria: Yambol	保加利亚:扬博尔	42.5	26.5	25	5.5	Ms	6										
1909	2	15	14	7	18					GSHAP	Bulgaria: Yambol	保加利亚:扬博尔	42.5	26.5	40	5.7	Ms	5										
1909	2	15	15	16						GSHAP	Bulgaria: Yambol	保加利亚:扬博尔	42.5	26.5	30	4.9	Ms	5										
1909	2	16	0	14						GSHAP	Bulgaria: Elhovo	保加利亚:埃尔霍沃	42.1	26.5	30	4.8	Ms	5										
1909	2	16	16	50						USGS, Song	Gulf of Alaska	阿拉斯加湾	60	-140		5.1	Mk	6										
1909	2	20	16							China	China: Shanxi, Heshun	中国:山西和顺	37.4	113.6		5	Ms	6										
1909	3	3	12							USGS	US: California, Omega	美国:加利福尼亚州欧米加	39.4	-120.9		5	Ms	5										
1909	3	7				2	3		2	NOAA, Song	Cook Islands	库克群岛	-21	-159		7.7	Mk							2				
1909	3	9								GSHAP	Sweden: Baltic Sea	瑞典:波的尼亚湾	64	22	19	4.6	Ms	6										
1909	3	10	22	36						GSHAP	Bulgarian: Pazardzhik	保加利亚:帕扎尔吉克	41.8	24.3	45	4.8	Ms	5										
1909	3	12	5	30						GSHAP	Russia: Dagestan, Kurakh	俄罗斯:达吉斯坦共和国库拉赫	41.6	48	7	4.6	Ms	7										
1909	3	12	23	19		4		-1		* Usami, Engdahl, NOAA	Japan Trench	日本海沟	34.5	141.5	35	7.1	Muk							1				
1909	3	13	14	29		4		-1		* Engdahl, NOAA	Japan Trench	日本海沟	34.5	141.5	35	7.6	mB							1				
1909	3	18	16	30						* Maso, Song	Philippine Trench	菲律宾海沟	8	127		5.9	Mk	8						2				
1909	3	23	3							* Song	Italy: Parma	意大利:帕尔马	44.5	10.5		6.5	Mk	12										
1909	4	12	8	5						GSHAP, Song	Peru: Vegueta	秘鲁:贝格塔	-11.57	-77.181	90	5	Mk	6										
1909	4	13	22	37						Maso, Song	Philippines: Basud	菲律宾:巴苏德	14	123		5	Mk	6										

时间						海啸				资料来源	震中				深度	震级	标度	烈度	死亡人数		受伤人数		经济损失		房屋毁坏		房屋受损	
年	月	日	时	分	秒	源	浪高	级 I	级 S		地名(英文)	地名(中文)	纬度(°)	经度(°)					数量/人	级别	数量/人	级别	数量/$ Mill	级别	数量/间	级别	数量/间	级别
Date						Tsunami				Information	Earthquake Epicenter				Depth	Mag	Scale	MMI	Deaths		Injuries		Damage		Houses Destroyed		Houses Damaged	
Year	Mo	Dy	Hr	Mn	Sec	Sr	Wh	mI	mS		Name(English)	Name(Chinese)	Latitude	Longitude					Num	Dd	Num	Dd	$ Mill	De	Num	Dh	Num	Dh
1909	4	14	19	53	42					* China, Engdahl	China: Taiwan, Taipei	中国:台湾台北	25	121.5	5	7.1	mB		9	1	51	2		1	122	3	1050	4
1909	4	18	10	45						GSHAP	Russia: Karachaevo – Cherkess, Ust – Dzheguta	俄罗斯:卡拉恰伊–切尔克斯州乌斯季杰古塔	44.1	42	9	4.6	Ms	6.5										
1909	4	23	17	39	36					*	Portugal: Ribatejo, Benavente	葡萄牙:里巴特茹,贝纳维特	38.9	−8.8		6.6	Ms	10	30	1				2		2		2
1909	4	26								* Song	Cameroon: Buea	喀麦隆:布埃亚	4.2	9.2		5.5	Mk							1				
1909	5	6								USGS, Song	Gulf of Alaska	阿拉斯加湾	59.5	−139.5		4.9	Mk	5										
1909	5	11	15	54	24					* China	China: Yunnan, Huaning, N.	中国:云南华宁北	24.4	103		6.5	Ms	8	21	1				2		3		
1909	5	14	11	17						* * Song	Indonesia: Makassar Strait	印度尼西亚:望加锡海峡	0.7	117.9		6.1	Mk	8						2				
1909	5	14	16							China	China: Yunnan, Ludian	中国:云南鲁甸	27.2	103.6		5.5	Ms	7										
1909	5	16	4	15						USGS	US: North Dakota, Fortuna	美国:北达科他州福图纳	49	−104		5.5	Ms	6										
1909	5	17	8	2	54					Engdahl, GSHAP	Bolivia: Chuquisaca	玻利维亚:丘基萨卡	−20	−64	250	7	mB	6										
1909	5	18	1	19						USGS, Song	US: California, Eureka	美国:加利福尼亚州尤里卡	41	−124		5.6	Mk	7										
1909	5	22	22	44						China	China: Taiwan, Nantou, N.	中国:台湾南投北	24	120.9		5.6	Ms	7			6	1			10	1	32	1
1909	5	26	14	42						USGS	US: Illinois, Joliet	美国:伊利诺斯州乔利埃特	41.6	−88.1		5.1	Ms	7										
1909	6	3	18	40	48	2		0.5	1	* Engdahl, NOAA	Indonesia: Southern Sumatra	印度尼西亚:苏门答腊南部	−2	101	40	7.2	Mw			3				3		3		3
1909	6	7	8	25						* Song	Italy: Toscana	意大利:托斯卡纳	43.2	11.5		6.5	Mk	12										
1909	6	8	5	46	30	2				* Engdahl, NOAA	Chile: Diego De Almagro	智利:迭戈德阿尔马格罗	−26.5	−70.5	60	7.2	Mw											
1909	6	9	1	32						GSHAP	Bulgaria: Yambol	保加利亚:扬博尔	42.6	26.3	30	4.7	Ms	5										
1909	6	11	21	6						*	France: Pertuis	法国:佩尔蒂	43.7	5.4		6.2	Ms	10	40	1				2				
1909	6	12	23							GSHAP	Ecuador: Near Coast of W.	厄瓜多尔:西部近海	−3.1	−80.5		4.3	Ms	5										
1909	6	23	7	24						CGS, USGS	US: California, Alleghany	美国:加利福尼亚州阿利甘尼	39.5	−121		5.9	Ms	7										
1909	7	2	16	37						GSHAP	Turkmenistan: Balkanabat	土库曼斯坦:巴尔坎纳巴德	39.7	54	14	4.6	Ms	6										
1909	7	6	5	48						GSHAP	Bulgaria: Asenovgrad	保加利亚:阿塞诺夫格勒	41.9	24.7	40	5.1	Ms	5										
1909	7	7	21	37	50					* Engdahl	Afghan: Badakhshan	阿富汗:巴达赫尚	36.5	70.5	230	7.6	mB	7										
1909	7	8	2	30						* Song	Pakistan: Mingora, N.	巴基斯坦:明戈拉北部	35.5	72.5		5.8	Mk		10	1				1				
1909	7	8				1				NOAA, Song	Vanuatu Islands	瓦努阿图群岛	−15.5	167.2		7.2	Mk							2		3		3
1909	7	15	0	28						*	Greece: Chavari (Elis)	希腊:伊利斯	37.9	21.5	4	5.7	Muk	10		1								
1909	7	19	4	34						USGS	US: Illinois, Havana	美国:伊利诺斯州哈瓦那	40.2	−90		4.8	Ms	7										
1909	7	23	17							GSHAP	Bolivia: Cochabamba	玻利维亚:科恰班巴	−17.43	−66.35		5.8	Ms	7										

时间						海啸				资料来源	震中				深度	震级	标度	烈度	死亡人数		受伤人数		经济损失		房屋毁坏		房屋受损	
年	月	日	时	分	秒	源	浪高	级 I	级 S		地名(英文)	地名(中文)	纬度(°)	经度(°)					数量/人	级别	数量/人	级别	数量/$ Mill	级别	数量/间	级别	数量/间	级别
Date						Tsunami				Information	Earthquake Epicenter				Depth	Mag	Scale	MMI	Deaths		Injuries		Damage		Houses Destroyed		Houses Damaged	
Year	Mo	Dy	Hr	Mn	Sec	Sr	Wh	mI	mS		Name(English)	Name(Chinese)	Latitude	Longitude					Num	Dd	Num	Dd	$ Mill	De	Num	Dh	Num	Dh
1909	7	30	10	51	54	3	9	3.2		* Shi Z., Engdahl, NOAA	Mexico:Acapulco	墨西哥:阿卡普尔科	16.8	-99.8		7.6	Mw							3		3		
1909	7									China	China:Yunnan,Jianchuan	中国:云南剑川	26.5	99.9		5.5	Ms	7	20	1								
1909	8	3	16							China,Engdahl	China:Xizang (Tibet),Nagarze	中国:西藏浪卡子	28.8	90.5		6.5	Ms	8								3		
1909	8	10	16							China	China:Guangdong,Zhaoqing	中国:广东肇庆	23.1	112.5		4.75	Ms	6										
1909	8	14	6	31		4	1.8	1		* Usami,Japan,Engdahl,NOAA	Japan:Nagahama	日本:滋贺长滨	35.4	136.3	5	6.7	Ms		41	1	784	3		3	2243	4	6124	4
1909	8	21	19	17		1			2	* NOAA	Celebes Sea	西里伯斯海	6.3	123.6		7.2	Ms											
1909	8	24	22	32						* Song	Italy:Toscana	意大利:托斯卡纳	43.2	11.5		6.5	Mk	12										
1909	8	29	10	27						Usami,Japan	Ryukyu Islands	琉球群岛	26	128		6	Ms		1	1	10	1					3	1
1909	9	8	16	49	48					USGS,Engdahl	Aleutian Islands	阿留申群岛	52.5	-169	90	7	mB	5										
1909	9	27	9	45						USGS	US:Indiana,Rockville	美国:印第安纳州罗克维尔	39.8	-87.2		5.1	Ms	7										
1909	10	6	2	41						USGS,Song	US:Utah,Tremonton	美国:犹他州特里蒙顿	41.8	-112.7		5.6	Mk	7										
1909	10	20	23	41	12					* Engdahl	Pakistan:Sibbi	巴基斯坦:锡比	30	68	60	7	Ms		231	3				2				
1909	10	21	16	27						* Song	Italy:Sicilia Island	意大利:西西里岛	37.7	15.2	5	6.5	Mk	12										
1909	10	23	7	10						USGS	US:Missouri,Sikeston	美国:密苏里州赛克斯顿	37	-89.5		4.5	Ms	5										
1909	10	29	6	45						USGS	US:California,Fortuna	美国:加利福尼亚州福图纳	40.5	-124.2		6.4	Ms	8										
1909	10	29	17	38						*	Turkey:Bursa	土耳其:布尔萨	40.3	29.6		5.8	Muk	8						3				
1909	10	31	10	23						*	Mexico:Guerrero,Michoacan	墨西哥:格雷罗,米却肯	17	-101.2		4.7	Muk							3				
1909	11	1	3	25						GSHAP	Tadzhikistan:Kuhistoni Badakhshon,E.	塔吉克斯坦:勾瑙-巴达科善东部	38.2	73.9	20	5.4	Ms	6.5										
1909	11	10	5	37	7					GSHAP	Croatia:Sisak	克罗地亚:西萨克	45.4	16.2	38	5.1	Ms	5										
1909	11	10	5	54	58					GSHAP	Croatia:Sisak	克罗地亚:西萨克	45.3	16.3	33	5.2	Ms	5.5										
1909	11	10	6	13	30					* Usami,Engdahl	Japan:Miyazzaki	日本:宫崎	32.3	131.1	150	7.5	mB				3	1			3	1		
1909	11	10	16							China	China:Hebei,Huolu	中国:河北获鹿	38.1	114.4		5.5	Ms	7								3		
1909	11	10	20	24						GSHAP	Black Sea	黑海	43.4	28.4	18	4.5	Ms	5										
1909	11	21	7	36						* China,Engdahl	China:Taiwan,Yilan	中国:台湾宜兰	24.4	121.8	5	7.3	Ms		4	1				1	14	1	39	1
1909	11	22	15	21						USGS	US:California,Paicines	美国:加利福尼亚州佩赛恩斯	36.7	-121.4		4.5	Ms	5										
1909	12	9	23	28	48	4				* Engdahl,NOAA	Mariana Islands,S.	马里亚纳群岛南部	12.5	145	50	6.8	Ms	8						2				
1909	12	9	23	28		4				* Maso	Guam	关岛(西太平洋)	14	143.3		8	Muk	8						2				
1909	12	13	0	21	39					GSHAP	Croatia:Sisak	克罗地亚:西萨克	45.4	15.9	38	4.9	Ms	5										
1910	1	8	14	49	30					* China,Engdahl	China:Yellow Sea	中国:黄海	35	122		6.75	Muk							2		3		
1910	1	10	13							USGS,Song	US:Utah,Richfield	美国:犹他州里奇菲尔德	38.7	-112.1		5.1	Mk	6										

时间 Date						海啸 Tsunami				资料来源 Information	震中 Earthquake Epicenter				深度 Depth	震级 Mag	标度 Scale	烈度 MMI	死亡人数 Deaths		受伤人数 Injuries		经济损失 Damage		房屋毁坏 Houses Destroyed		房屋受损 Houses Damaged	
年 Year	月 Mo	日 Dy	时 Hr	分 Mn	秒 Sec	源 Sr	浪高 Wh	级 I mI	级 S mS		地名(英文) Name(English)	地名(中文) Name(Chinese)	纬度(°) Latitude	经度(°) Longitude					数量/人 Num	级别 Dd	数量/人 Num	级别 Dd	数量/$ Mill $ Mill	级别 De	数量/间 Num	级别 Dh	数量/间 Num	级别 Dh
1910	1	12	3							USGS, Song	US: Utah, Richfield	美国:犹他州里奇菲尔德	38.7	-112.1		5.1	Mk	6										
1910	1	18	3	35						GSHAP	Azerbaijan: Gəncə	阿塞拜疆:占贾	40.7	46.3	18	4.5	Ms	5.5										
1910	1	23	18	49	42					GSHAP, Engdahl	Trinidad & Tobago: Northern Coast	特立尼达和多巴哥:北部近海	12	-60.5	100	6.9	mB	5										
1910	1	28	23	57	39					GSHAP	Croatia: Sisak	克罗地亚:西萨克	45.4	16.2	32	5.4	Ms	6.5										
1910	1	29	0	11	56					GSHAP	Croatia: Sisak	克罗地亚:西萨克	45.4	16.2	18	5.1	Ms	6										
1910	2	23	7	52						GSHAP	Bulgaria: Sandanski, N.	保加利亚:桑丹斯基北部	41.7	23.4	12	5.2	Ms	7.5										
1910	2	24				4				* NOAA, Song	Papua New Guinea: East New Britain	巴布亚新几内亚:东新不列颠	-4	152		7	Mk											
1910	3	8	2	25						GSHAP	Armenia: Kirovakan	亚美尼亚:瓦纳佐尔	40.8	44.6	10	4.5	Ms	6										
1910	3	11	6	52						USGS	US: California, Watsonville	美国:加利福尼亚州沃森维尔	36.9	-121.8		5.8	Ms	6										
1910	3	19	0	11						USGS	US: California, North Coast	美国:加利福尼亚州北部近海	40	-125		6	Ms	5										
1910	3	20	14	13						China	China: Taiwan, Taichung	中国:台湾台中	24	120.7		5.25	Ms	6										
1910	3	22	2	6	24					GSHAP	Macedonia: Prilep	马其顿:普里莱普	41.2	22	5	5	Ms	8										
1910	3	22								GSHAP, Song	Venezuela: Falcon	委内瑞拉:法尔孔	10.87	-69.45		5	Mk	6										
1910	3	25	18	38						China	China: Taiwan, Hualien	中国:台湾花莲	23.9	121.6		5.25	Ms	6										
1910	3									China	China: Yunnan, Longling	中国:云南龙陵	24.6	98.7		5.5	Ms	7										
1910	4	6	1	36						GSHAP	Bulgaria: Blagoevgrad	保加利亚:布拉戈耶夫格勒	42.1	23.2	8	4.5	Ms	6										
1910	4	11	7	57						CGS, USGS	US: California, Anza	美国:加利福尼亚州安萨	33.5	-116.5		5.8	Ms	5										
1910	4	12	0	22	13					* China, Engdahl	China: Taiwan, Keelung, Coast of NE.	中国:台湾基隆东北海域	25.5	122.5	200	7.75	mB		60	2				1	13	1	59	2
1910	4	13								* Song	Costa Rica: Cartago	哥斯达黎加:卡塔哥	9.8	-84		7	Mk		1750	4				2				
1910	4	19	8	30						USGS	US: Montana, Butte	美国:蒙大纳州比尤特	46	-112.5		5.4	Ms	5										
1910	5	4	23	50						* Song	Costa Rica: Cartago, San Jose	哥斯达黎加:卡塔哥,圣何塞	10	-84		6.4	Mk		700	3				3				
1910	5	6	16	40						CGS, USGS	US: California, Chalfant Valley	美国:加利福尼亚州夏芬谷	37.33	-118.42		6	Ms	6										
1910	5	13	6	20						USGS	US: California, Riverside	美国:加利福尼亚州里弗赛德	33.7	-117.4		5	Ms	5										
1910	5	15	15	47						USGS	US: California, Riverside	美国:加利福尼亚州里弗赛德	33.7	-117.4		6	Ms	7										
1910	5	18	19	30						GSHAP	Venezuela: San Timoteo	委内瑞拉:圣蒂莫特奥	9.84	-71.12		4.5	Ms	6										
1910	5	22	14	28						USGS, Song	US: Utah, Huntington	美国:犹他州亨廷顿	40.7	-111.8		5.6	Mk	7										
1910	6	7	2	5						*	Italy: Calitri	意大利:卡利特里	40.9	15.4	33	5.9	Muk	10										

时间						海啸				资料来源	震中				深度	震级	标度	烈度	死亡人数		受伤人数		经济损失		房屋毁坏		房屋受损	
年	月	日	时	分	秒	源	浪高	级 I	级 S		地名(英文)	地名(中文)	纬度(°)	经度(°)					数量/人	级别	数量/人	级别	数量/$ Mill	级别	数量/间	级别	数量/间	级别
Date						Tsunami				Information	Earthquake Epicenter				Depth	Mag	Scale	MMI	Deaths		Injuries		Damage		Houses Destroyed		Houses Damaged	
Year	Mo	Dy	Hr	Mn	Sec	Sr	Wh	mI	mS		Name(English)	Name(Chinese)	Latitude	Longitude					Num	Dd	Num	Dd	$ Mill	De	Num	Dh	Num	Dh
1910	6	24	13	27						*	Algeria:Masqueray, Kabylia	阿尔及利亚:卡比利亚	36	4	33	6.4	Ms	11	12	1				1				
1910	6	25	19	26						*	Turkey:Osmancik, Iskilip	土耳其:奥斯曼哲克,伊斯基利普	40.9	34.6		6.1	Muk	7						3				
1910	7	24	6	49		4				Shi Z., Usami	Japan:Hakodate, Date	日本:北海道伊达	42.5	140.8		6.5	Ms										15	1
1910	8	4	13							GSHAP	Venezuela:Merida	委内瑞拉:梅里达	8.7	-70.9		5.8	Ms	5										
1910	8	5								USGS, Song	South of Alaska	阿拉斯加南部	60	-160		4.9	Mk	5										
1910	9	24	3	32	42					* Engdahl	Mexico:Oaxaca	墨西哥:瓦哈卡	16.8	-95.9	80	6.9	Muk	9						2				
1910	9	24	4	5						USGS, Song	US:Arizona, Cameron	美国:亚利桑那州卡梅伦	35.8	-111.5		5.6	Mk	7										
1910	10	27								* Song	Morocco:Melilla	摩洛哥:梅利利亚	35.3	-2.97		5.9	Mk							2				
1910	11	5				1				NOAA, Song	Bering Strait	白令海峡	64	-165		7.1	Mk							2		2		
1910	11	7	17	20						USGS, Song	US:Nevada, Beatty	美国:内华达州比蒂	37.5	-117		5.1	Mk	6										
1910	11	10	12	19	54	3				* Engdahl, NOAA	Vanuatu Islands	瓦努阿图群岛	-14	166.5	90	7.1	mB							2				
1910	11	21	23	23						USGS, Song	US:Nevada, Coaldale	美国:内华达州科尔代尔	38	-118		5.6	Mk	7										
1910	12	3	8	15	54					GSHAP	Serbia:Jagodina	塞尔维亚:雅戈丁那	44	21.3	5	4.5	Ms	7										
1910	12	4	14	2						GSHAP	Iran:Parsabad	伊朗:法尔萨巴德	39.3	48	37	5.4	Ms	7										
1910	12	13	11	37	24					* Engdahl	Tanzania:Rukwa	坦桑尼亚:鲁夸	-8	31	0	7.6	Mw		2	1				2				
1910	12	16	14	45		2	0.4	-1.3	-1	* Engdahl, NOAA	Indonesia:Karakelong Island	印度尼西亚:卡拉克隆岛	4.5	126	0	7.6	Mw											
1910	12	18				2	0.4	-1.3	-1	* NOAA	Indonesia:Karakelong Island	印度尼西亚:卡拉克隆岛	4	127	33	6.7	Ms											
1910	12	23	1							GSHAP	Russia:Khabarovsk, Dva Stolba	俄罗斯:哈巴罗夫斯克区德瓦斯托尔巴村	59.5	144	15	5	Ms	6										
1910	12	25	19							GSHAP	Kyrgyzstan:Bishkek	吉尔吉斯斯坦:比什凯克	43	74.7	10	5.3	Ms	7.5										
1910	12	30				1			1	* Nakamura, NOAA	Philippines:Mindanao Island	菲律宾:棉兰老岛	9	125.5	60	6.3	Ms	7						1				
1910	12	31	12	11						CGS, USGS	US:California, Watsonville, Near Coast	美国:加利福尼亚州沃森维尔近海	36.8	-122.1		5.7	Ms	6										
1910										China	China:Guangxi, Xilin, SE.	中国:广西西林东南	24.5	105.2		4.75	Ms	6										
1911	1	3	23	25	45					* GSHAP, Engdahl	Kazakhstan:Almaty	哈萨克斯坦:阿拉木图	43.5	77.5	25	7.8	Mw	10.5	450	3				3				
1911	1	25	0	41	35					* China	China:Hebei, Yuxian	中国:河北蔚县	39.8	114.5		5.9	Ms	7		1		1		2		3		
1911	1	27	23	6	5	5	3			* Song	Philippines:Batangas	菲律宾:八打雁	14.002	120.993		7.8	Mk	9	1335	4	199	3		3	543	3		1
1911	2	5	16							China	China:Jiangxi, Jiujiang	中国:江西九江	29.7	116		5	Ms	6										
1911	2	18	18	41	3					* GSHAP, Afghan, Engdahl	Tajikistan:Pamir Mountains	塔吉克斯坦:帕米尔山脉	38.2	72.8	26	7.2	Mw	9	90	2				3		3		3
1911	2	18	21	36		3				* NOAA	Macedonia(Fyrom):Ohrid	马其顿:奥赫里德	41.1	20.7		6.7	Ms	10										
1911	2	21	18	55						GSHAP	Russia:Sakhalin Island	俄罗斯:库页岛(萨哈林岛)	46.4	142.3	20	4.7	Ms	5										

时间 Date						海啸 Tsunami				资料来源 Information	震中 Earthquake Epicenter				深度 Depth	震级 Mag	标度 Scale	烈度 MMI	死亡人数 Deaths		受伤人数 Injuries		经济损失 Damage		房屋毁坏 Houses Destroyed		房屋受损 Houses Damaged	
年 Year	月 Mo	日 Dy	时 Hr	分 Mn	秒 Sec	源 Sr	浪高 Wh	级 I mI	级 S mS		地名(英文) Name(English)	地名(中文) Name(Chinese)	纬度(°) Latitude	经度(°) Longitude					数量/人 Num	级别 Dd	数量/人 Num	级别 Dd	数量/$ Mill $ Mill	级别 De	数量/间 Num	级别 Dh	数量/间 Num	级别 Dh
1911	3	5	3	33						GSHAP	Serbia:Bosilegrad	塞尔维亚:博西莱格勒	42.5	22.5	30	5	Ms	5.5										
1911	3	11	19	15						GSHAP	Macedonia(Fyrom):Stip	马其顿:斯提普	41.6	22.4	30	5	Ms	5.5										
1911	3	11	20	40	18					GSHAP	Bulgaria:Blagoevgrad	保加利亚:布拉戈耶夫格勒	42	23	50	5.5	Ms	5.5										
1911	3	11	21	29						USGS	US:California,Hollister	美国:加利福尼亚州霍利斯特	36.83	-121.42		4.5	Ms	6										
1911	3	22	18							GSHAP	Brasil:Salvador	巴西:萨尔瓦多	-12.92	-38.67		4.7	Ms	7										
1911	3	31	16	57						USGS	US:Arkansas,Pine Bluff	美国:阿肯色州派恩布拉夫	34	-91.8		4.7	Ms	7										
1911	4	10	18	42	24					GSHAP,Engdahl	Colombia:Bolivar	哥伦比亚:波利瓦尔	9	-74	100	7	mB	9										
1911	4	18	18	14	36					* Engdahl	Oman:Ibri	阿曼:伊卜里	23	56	50	6.7	Muk		700	3				3		3		
1911	4	18	18	14						GSHAP,Iran	Iran:Kerman	伊朗:克尔曼	31.2	56.9	36	6.7	Ms	7										
1911	4	28	9	52	54					GSHAP,Engdahl	Colombia:Vaupes,S.	哥伦比亚:沃佩斯南部	0	-71	600	6.9	mB	8										
1911	5	4	23	36	54					* GSHAP,Engdahl	Russia:Kamchatka Peninsula	俄罗斯:堪察加半岛	51	157	240	7.4	mB	8										
1911	5	8				1				* NOAA,Song	Papua New Guinea:East New Britain	巴布亚新几内亚:东新不列颠	-6	151		7	Mk											
1911	5	11				2	5			NOAA	Togo:Lome	多哥:洛美	6.1	1.2		6.6	Ms							1				
1911	5	14	16	41						* China	China:Guangdong,Shanwei,Coast	中国:广东汕尾海域	22.5	115		6	Ms	7						2		3		
1911	6	2	22	34						USGS	US:South Dakota,Huron	美国:南达科他州休伦	44.2	-98.2		4.5	Ms	5										
1911	6	7	11	2	42					* Engdahl	Mexico:Near Coast of Michoacan	墨西哥:米却肯近海	17.5	-102.5	11	7.6	Mw		45	1	22	1						
1911	6	7	23	58	48					GSHAP	Caspian Sea	里海	41	50.5	52	6.4	Ms	6.5										
1911	6	15	14	26		4		1	1.5	* Usami,Japan,Engdahl,NOAA	Ryukyu Islands	琉球群岛	28	130	90	8.1	mB		12	1	26	1		3	428	3	565	3
1911	6	23	12	30	19					GSHAP	Azerbaijan:Samaxi	阿塞拜疆:沙马基区	40	48	18	5	Ms	6.5										
1911	6	30	7	10	20					GSHAP	Russia:Murmansk,Olenitsa	俄罗斯:摩尔曼斯克州奥列尼察	66.5	35.5	25	4.9	Ms	5.5										
1911	7	1	22	0	3					USGS,Engdahl	US:California,Morgan Hill	美国:加利福尼亚州莫干山	37.25	-121.75		6.5	Ms	8										
1911	7	4	13	33	26					* GSHAP,Engdahl	Afghan:Badakhshan	阿富汗:巴达赫尚	36	70.5	190	7.4	mB	8										
1911	7	12	4	7	36	1				* Bautista,Engdahl,NOAA	Philippines:Mindanao,Talacogon	菲律宾:棉兰老岛,塔拉科贡	9	126	50	7.5	Mw	10						3				3
1911	7	24								*	France:Aramits,Arros	法国:阿拉米,阿罗斯	43.2	0.2		5	Muk	7						2				
1911	7									China,Engdahl	China:Xizang (Tibet),Zayu	中国:西藏察隅	28.5	97.5		6.5	Ms	8										
1911	8	6								GSHAP	Russia:Amur,Berezovka	俄罗斯:阿穆尔州别列佐夫卡	53.5	127.1	10	5	Ms	7										
1911	8	11	23	40						USGS	US:California,Palm Springs	美国:加利福尼亚州棕泉	33.8	-116.7		4.5	Ms	6										

时间						海啸				资料来源	震中				深度	震级	标度	烈度	死亡人数		受伤人数		经济损失		房屋毁坏		房屋受损	
年	月	日	时	分	秒	源	浪高	级 I	级 S		地名(英文)	地名(中文)	纬度(°)	经度(°)					数量/人	级别	数量/人	级别	数量/$ Mill	级别	数量/间	级别	数量/间	级别
Date						Tsunami				Information	Earthquake Epicenter				Depth	Mag	Scale	MMI	Deaths		Injuries		Damage		Houses Destroyed		Houses Damaged	
Year	Mo	Dy	Hr	Mn	Sec	Sr	Wh	mI	mS		Name(English)	Name(Chinese)	Latitude	Longitude					Num	Dd	Num	Dd	$ Mill	De	Num	Dh	Num	Dh
1911	8	24	21	48						GSHAP	Norway:Bergen	挪威:卑尔根	60	5.2	45	4.7	Ms	5										
1911	9	8	22	43	59					GSHAP,Shi Z.	Russia:Kamchatka Peninsula	俄罗斯:堪察加半岛	52.5	158	80	6.5	Ms	7										
1911	9	15	13	10		2				*Chile,Shi Z.,Engdahl,NOAA	Chile:Iquique,Off Coast	智利:伊基克沿海	-20	-72	40	7.1	Mw											
1911	9	22	5	1	24	1			0.5	USGS, Engdahl, NOAA	Gulf of Alaska	阿拉斯加湾	60.5	-149	60	6.9	Muk	8						1				
1911	9	23	4	10						GSHAP,Song	Ecuador:Chimborazo,N.	厄瓜多尔:钦博腊索山北部	-1.7	-78.9		6	Mk	8										
1911	10	15	8	52						*Italy	Italy:Etna	意大利:埃特纳	37.7	15.15		5.28	Muk	10										
1911	10	16	16							China	China:Yunnan,Huize,N.	中国:云南会泽北	26.6	103.1		5.75	Ms	7										
1911	11	18	21	35						*Song	Albania:Korce, Pogradec	阿尔巴尼亚:科里察,波格拉德茨	40.4	20.5		6.2	Mk	10										
1912	1	2	16	21						USGS	US:Illinois,Aurora	美国:伊利诺斯州奥罗拉	41.5	-88.5		4.5	Ms	6										
1912	1	5	3	52						USGS	US:California,Chalfant Valley	美国:加利福尼亚州夏芬谷	37.33	-118.42		5.5	Ms	6										
1912	1	23								GSHAP	Uzbekistan:Namangan	乌兹别克斯坦:纳曼干	41	71.7	12	5.2	Ms	7										
1912	1	24	16	23	6	2				*Engdahl,NOAA	Greece:Kephallenia	希腊:坎发兰尼亚	38	20.5	60	6.8	Muk	10		2								
1912	2	17	13	38						GSHAP	Russia:Lake Baykal	俄罗斯:贝加尔湖	51.8	106	18	5.1	Ms	6										
1912	5	6	18	59						*Engdahl	Iceland:Hella	冰岛:海德拉	64	-20	60	7.5	Ms	11										
1912	5	6	19							GSHAP	Russia:Sakhalin Island	俄罗斯:库页岛(萨哈林岛)	46.7	142.3	15	5	Ms	5										
1912	5	8								*Song	Mexico:Jalisco,Guadalajara	墨西哥:哈利斯科,瓜达拉哈拉	20.4	-103.2		6.2	Mk							3				
1912	5	23	2	24	6					*Engdahl	Myanmar:Mandalay, Mogok	缅甸:曼德勒,抹谷	21	97	25	7	Ms	9		1				3				
1912	5	25	18	1	54					GSHAP	Romania:Nereju	罗马尼亚:内雷茹	45.7	27.2	90	6.4	Ms	8										
1912	5	25	20	15						GSHAP	Romania:Nereju	罗马尼亚:内雷茹	45.7	27.2	38	6.2	Ms	6.5										
1912	6	7	1	58						GSHAP	Romania:Nereju	罗马尼亚:内雷茹	45.7	26.6	100	5.5	Ms	6										
1912	6	7	13	17	5					GSHAP	Georgia:Akhalkalaki	格鲁吉亚:阿卡卡拉吉	41.4	44	19	4.8	Ms	6										
1912	6	8	4	41	30	3	0.5	-1		*GSHAP,Usami,Engdahl,NOAA	Japan:Aomori,Near Coast	日本:青森近海	40.5	142	35	6.8	Muk											
1912	6	12	10	30						USGS,Song	US:South Carolina,Charleston	美国:卡罗莱纳州查尔斯顿	32.9	-80		5.1	Mk	6										
1912	6	20								GSHAP	Kazakhstan:Almaty	哈萨克斯坦:阿拉木图	44.5	80	15	5.4	Ms	7										
1912	7	4	19	50						GSHAP	Russia:Stavropol,Mineralnye Vody	俄罗斯:斯塔夫罗波尔区矿水城	44.1	43.1	14	4.7	Ms	6										
1912	7	24	11	59						*Engdahl	Peru:Piura	秘鲁:皮乌拉	-5	-80	30	7	Ms	10		3		3		3		3		
1912	8	9	1	29		1				*Engdahl	Turkey:Marmara Sea	土耳其:马尔马拉海	40.5	27.2	60	7.6	Mw		3000	4	1575	4		4	5540	4		

年 Year	月 Mo	日 Dy	时 Hr	分 Mn	秒 Sec	源 Sr	浪高 Wh	级I mI	级S mS	资料来源 Information	地名(英文) Name(English)	地名(中文) Name(Chinese)	纬度(°) Latitude	经度(°) Longitude	深度 Depth	震级 Mag	标度 Scale	烈度 MMI	死亡人数 数量/人 Deaths Num	死亡人数 级别 Dd	受伤人数 数量/人 Injuries Num	受伤人数 级别 Dd	经济损失 数量/$ Mill Damage $ Mill	经济损失 级别 De	房屋毁坏 数量/间 Houses Destroyed Num	房屋毁坏 级别 Dh	房屋受损 数量/间 Houses Damaged Num	房屋受损 级别 Dh
1912	8	10	1	17	36					GSHAP	Russia: Chechnia, Grozny, NW.	俄罗斯:车臣共和国格罗兹尼北部	43.5	45.1	50	5.7	Ms	8										
1912	8	10	9	23						GSHAP	Turkey:Hellespont	土耳其:达达尼尔海峡	40.6	27.1	15	6.3	Ms	8										
1912	8	17								USGS,Song	Aleutian Islands	阿留申群岛	58.5	-157		4.9	Mk	5										
1912	8	18	21	12						USGS,Song	US:Arizona,Cameron	美国:亚利桑那州卡梅伦	36	-111.5		5.6	Mk	7										
1912	8	19	15	46	30					GSHAP	Azerbaijan:Sirvan,NW.	阿塞拜疆:希尔万西北	40	48.6	35	4.9	Ms	5										
1912	8	31	4	53						USGS	US:California,Jones Place	美国:加利福尼亚州琼斯普莱斯	38.92	-120.33		4.5	Ms	5										
1912	9	12	17	27						USGS	US:California,Cupertino	美国:加利福尼亚州库比蒂诺	37.33	-122.17		4.5	Ms	5										
1912	9	13	23	31						GSHAP	Turkey:Marmara Sea	土耳其:马尔马拉海	40.5	26.9	18	6.9	Ms	9										
1912	9	19								* Song	Mexico:Toluca de Lerdo	墨西哥:墨西哥州托卢卡	19.9	-99.9		6.2	Mk							3				
1912	9	30								GSHAP	Kazakhstan:Almaty	哈萨克斯坦:阿拉木图	44.5	80	15	5.4	Ms	7										
1912	10	12	19	48	41					GSHAP	Georgia:Akhalkalaki	格鲁吉亚:阿卡卡垃吉	41.4	43.8	14	6.3	Ms	6.5										
1912	10	13	2	22	56					GSHAP	Georgia:Bolnisi	格鲁吉亚:博尔尼西	41.5	44	30	5	Ms	6										
1912	10	13	16							USGS,Song	Hawaiian Islands	夏威夷群岛	20.5	-155.5		4.9	Mk	5										
1912	10	31	17	24	6	1				* Engdahl, NOAA	West Scotia Basin	西斯科舍海盆	7	138	33	6.9	Ms	3										
1912	11	7	7	40	24					* Engdahl	Aleutian Islands	阿留申群岛	57.5	-155	90	7.3	mB	5										
1912	11	8	7	54						* Song	Philippines:Sorsogon	菲律宾:索索贡	12.6	124		6.5	Mk	9						2				
1912	11	19	13	55						* Engdahl	Mexico:Toluca de Lerdo	墨西哥:墨西哥州托卢卡	19.9	-99.8	80	6.9	mB							3				
1912	11	30	23							GSHAP	Kazakhstan:Georgiyevka	哈萨克斯坦:格奥尔吉耶夫卡	43	75.2	15	4.7	Ms	6										
1912	12	2	1							GSHAP	Russia:Sakhalin Island	俄罗斯:库页岛(萨哈林岛)	50.5	142.5	15	5.5	Ms	7										
1912	12	6				1			0.5	* NOAA,Song	West Scotia Basin	西斯科舍海盆	7	138		7	Mk	3										
1912	12	14								USGS,Song	US:California,Oxnard	美国:加利福尼亚州奥克斯纳德	34	-119		5.1	Mk	6										
1912	12	24	15	2						GSHAP	Uzbekistan:Almalyk	乌兹别克斯坦:阿尔马雷克	40.8	70	25	5.2	Ms	6										
1913	1	1	18	28						USGS	US:South Carolina,Buffalo	美国:南卡罗来纳州布法罗	34.7	-81.7		4.8	Ms	7										
1913	1	7	22	50	43					China,Engdahl	China:Taiwan, Hualien,Coast of E.	中国:台湾花莲以东海域	23.8	121.7	0	6.7	Ms								2	1		
1913	1	19	23	47	55					* Shi Z., Engdahl	Kuril Islands	千岛群岛	46	152	150	6.9	mB							1				
1913	1	23	21	45						GSHAP	Croatia:Bedekovcina	克罗地亚:贝代科夫契纳	45.9	16	9	4.5	Ms	6										
1913	2	7								Wang S.	China:Henan,Xinyang	中国:河南信阳	32.2	114.1		5	Ms	6										
1913	2	7								Wang S.	China:Hubei,Macheng	中国:湖北麻城	31.2	115		5	Ms	6										

时间						海啸				资料来源	震中				深度	震级	标度	烈度	死亡人数		受伤人数		经济损失		房屋毁坏		房屋受损	
年	月	日	时	分	秒	源	浪高	级 I	级 S		地名(英文)	地名(中文)	纬度(°)	经度(°)					数量/人	级别	数量/人	级别	数量/$ Mill	级别	数量/间	级别	数量/间	级别
Date						Tsunami				Information	Earthquake Epicenter				Depth	Mag	Scale	MMI	Deaths		Injuries		Damage		Houses Destroyed		Houses Damaged	
Year	Mo	Dy	Hr	Mn	Sec	Sr	Wh	mI	mS		Name(English)	Name(Chinese)	Latitude	Longitude					Num	Dd	Num	Dd	$ Mill	De	Num	Dh	Num	Dh
1913	2	22	2	36		3	1.5	0.6	0.5	* NOAA	New Zealand: South Island, Westport	新西兰:南岛,韦斯特波特	-41.8	171.5	33	6.8	Ms	8						1		1		
1913	2	23	11							China	Kazakhstan: Koktal	哈萨克斯坦:科克塔尔	44	80	15	5.7	Ms	7.5										
1913	2	24	2	30						*	Ecuador: Gonzanama, San Pedro	厄瓜多尔:贡萨纳马,圣佩德罗	-3.4	-79.6	50	7.7	Muk	7		3				3		3		
1913	2	24	2	30						GSHAP	Ecuador: Loja	厄瓜多尔:洛哈	-4.2	-79.4		4.3	Ms	5										
1913	2	28	7							GSHAP	Ecuador: Azuay	厄瓜多尔:阿苏艾	-3.2	-79.2		5.7	Ms	7										
1913	3	11	3	42						GSHAP	Romania: Focsani	罗马尼亚:福克沙尼	45.6	27.8	15	4.5	Ms	5.5										
1913	3	14	3	40						GSHAP	Romania: Nereju	罗马尼亚:内雷茹	45.7	26.6	120	5.5	Ms	5.5										
1913	3	14	8	45		4				* Engdahl	Indonesia: Karakelong Island	印度尼西亚:卡拉克隆岛	4.5	126.5		7.9	Mw	9	138	3				2		2		
1913	3	24	10	34						*	Iran: Hormozgan	伊朗:荷姆兹甘	26.8	53.7		5.8	Ms		11	1								
1913	3	28	21	50						USGS	US: Tennessee, Washburn	美国:田纳西州沃什本	36.2	-83.7		4.1	Ms	7										
1913	4	3	10	39						China	China: Jiangsu, Zhenjiang	中国:江苏镇江	32.2	119.5		5.5	Ms	7										
1913	4	16	6							GSHAP	Azerbaijan: Lenkeran	阿塞拜疆:连科兰	39.1	48.6	12	5.1	Ms	7										
1913	6	14	9	33	12					* GSHAP, Turkey, Engdahl	Bulgaria: Tirnovo	保加利亚:特尔诺沃	43.5	25.5	30	6.8	Muk	11										
1913	6	28	8	53						* Italy	Italy: Cosenza, Rogliano, Bisigano	意大利:科森扎,罗利安诺	39.53	16.23		5.65	Ms	9						2				
1913	6	29	8	23						Usami, Japan	Japan: Kagoshima	日本:鹿岛	31.6	130.3		6	Ms				1	1			1	1		
1913	6	30	7	35						Japan	Japan: Kagoshima	日本:鹿岛	31.6	130.3		6.4	Ms				1	1			1	1		
1913	6	30	12							GSHAP	Uzbekistan: Fergana	乌兹别克斯坦:费尔干纳	40.4	71.8	10	4.8	Ms	6.5										
1913	7	15	16							China	China: Sichuan, Leshan	中国:四川乐山	29.6	103.7		5	Ms	6										
1913	7	19	15	50						GSHAP	Norwegian Sea	挪威海	64	8	44	4.6	Ms	5										
1913	7	23	22	3						GSHAP	Romania: Nereju	罗马尼亚:内雷茹	45.7	26.6	130	5.3	Ms	5.5										
1913	7	28	5	39	18	2	0.7	-0.5		* NOAA, Shi Z., Engdahl	Peru: Arequipa, Off Coast	秘鲁:阿雷基帕沿海	-17	-74		7	Ms	9						1				
1913	8	4	7	38						GSHAP	Norway: Sande	挪威:桑讷	61.4	5.8	45	5	Ms	5										
1913	8	6	22	14	24	2				* Shi Z., Engdahl, NOAA	Peru: Caraveli, Chuquibamba	秘鲁:卡拉威里,丘基班巴	-15.8	-73.5	40	7.8	Mw	10		2				3		3		3
1913	8	17	16							China	China: Sichuan, Beichuan	中国:四川北川	31.8	104.5		5	Ms	6										
1913	8									* China	China: Sichuan, Mianning	中国:四川冕宁	28.7	102.2		6	Ms	8	10	1				2		2		
1913	9	8	22	8						USGS, Song	Hawaiian Islands	夏威夷群岛	19	-155.5		4.9	Mk	5										
1913	9	9	18	43						GSHAP	Afghan: Qonduz	阿富汗:昆都士	37	69	18	5	Ms	7										
1913	9	11	2	34						GSHAP	Norway: West of Bodo	挪威:博德西部	67.5	13.5	20	4.7	Ms	6										
1913	9	25	16							China	China: Hainan, Haikou	中国:海南海口	20	110.3		5	Ms	6										
1913	9									China	China: Yunnan, Jinning	中国:云南晋宁	24.7	102.7		5	Ms	6										
1913	10	11	4	6	3	1	0.1	-3.3	1	* Engdahl, NOAA	Papua New Guinea: Huon Gulf	巴布亚新几内亚:休恩湾	-7	148	33	7	Ms											

年 Year	月 Mo	日 Dy	时 Hr	分 Mn	秒 Sec	源 Sr	浪高 Wh	级 I mI	级 S mS	资料来源 Information	地名(英文) Name(English)	地名(中文) Name(Chinese)	纬度(°) Latitude	经度(°) Longitude	深度 Depth	震级 Mag	标度 Scale	烈度 MMI	死亡人数 数量/人 Deaths Num	死亡人数 级别 Dd	受伤人数 数量/人 Injuries Num	受伤人数 级别 Dd	经济损失 数量/$ Mill Damage $ Mill	经济损失 级别 De	房屋毁坏 数量/间 Houses Destroyed Num	房屋毁坏 级别 Dh	房屋受损 数量/间 Houses Damaged Num	房屋受损 级别 Dh
1913	10	14	23							USGS, Song	US: Nevada, Helena	美国:内华达州海伦娜	45.2	-116.7		5.1	Mk	6										
1913	10	20								GSHAP	Kazakhstan: Almaty	哈萨克斯坦:阿拉木图	42.9	79.3	10	4.8	Ms	6										
1913	10	25	11	28						USGS, Song	Hawaiian Islands	夏威夷群岛	19	-155.5		4.9	Mk	5										
1913	11	4	21	33						*	Peru: Abancay, Soraya	秘鲁:阿班凯,索拉亚	-14.2	-72.9	10	6.3	Ms	10	150	3				3		3		
1913	11	11	21	55						USGS, Song	US: Colorado, Ouray	美国:科罗拉多州乌雷	38.1	-107.7		5.1	Mk	6										
1913	11	12	4	28	56					GSHAP	Iran: Tabriz, N.	伊朗:大不里士北部	38.8	45.8	25	4.7	Ms	5										
1913	11	17	20	30						GSHAP	Russia: Altai Krai, Onguday	俄罗斯:阿尔泰边疆区翁古达伊	50.5	85.5	24	5.4	Ms	5.5										
1913	12	12	5	35						GSHAP	Uzbekistan: Namangan	乌兹别克斯坦:纳曼干	41	71.5	10	4.8	Ms	6										
1913	12	14	2	45						GSHAP	Bolivia: Santa Cruz de la Sierra	玻利维亚:圣克鲁斯	-17.78	-63.17		5.4	Ms	5										
1913	12	21	15	37	38					* China, Engdahl	China: Yunnan, Eshan	中国:云南峨山	24.15	102.45		7.2	Mw	9	942	3	112	3		3		4		
1914	1	12	9	28	6	5	3	1.6	1.5	* Shi Z, Usami, Engdahl, NOAA	Japan: Shibushi	日本:鹿岛志布志	31.5	131	5	6.7	Ms		84	2	112	3		1	2268	4	1172	4
1914	1	12				4	1		1.5	* NOAA, Song	Peru: Lima	秘鲁:利马	-12	-76.6	33	7.3	Mk							1				
1914	1	13	21							GSHAP	Uzbekistan: Fergana	乌兹别克斯坦:费尔干纳	40.3	71.8	20	5.4	Ms	6.5										
1914	1	15	4	28		1			2	* Italy, NOAA	Italy: Livorno	意大利:里窝那	43.5	10.2		4.83	Ms	6										
1914	1	20	12	0	13					Engdahl, GSHAP	Russia: Kamchatka, Near East Coast	俄罗斯:堪察加东部近海	52	159.1	60	7.2	Muk	7										
1914	2	9	21	17	31					GSHAP	Russia: Dagestan, Chirkey	俄罗斯:达吉斯坦共和国奇尔克伊	42.9	46.9	14	4.9	Ms	6.5										
1914	2	10	18	31						USGS	Canada: Kingston	加拿大:金斯敦	44.98	-76.92		5.2	Ms	7										
1914	2	18	18	17						USGS	US: Nevada, Reno	美国:内华达州雷诺	39.5	-119.8		6	Ms	6										
1914	2	18	23	39						GSHAP	Bolivia: Santa Cruz de la Sierra	玻利维亚:圣克鲁斯	-17.78	-63.17		6	Ms	5										
1914	2	22	9	35						GSHAP	Bolivia: Santa Cruz de la Sierra	玻利维亚:圣克鲁斯	-17.78	-63.17		6	Ms	5										
1914	2	26	4	58	12	1				* Engdahl, NOAA	Peru: Arequipa	秘鲁:阿雷基帕	-17	-72	130	7.2	mB											
1914	2	27	8	10						GSHAP	Ecuador: Tungurahua	厄瓜多尔:东谷拉瓦	-1.4	-78.6		4.3	Ms	5										
1914	3	5	20	5						USGS	US: Georgia, Madison	美国:乔治亚州麦迪逊	33.5	-83.5		4.5	Ms	5										
1914	3	15	20	0	6					* GSHAP, Usami, Engdahl	Japan: Sakata	日本:山形酒田	39.2	139.8	5	7	Ms		94	2				3	931	3		
1914	3	27	17	50						Usami, Japan	Japan: Akita	日本:秋田	39.2	140.4		5.8	Ms								1	1		
1914	4	8	0	40	30					China	Tajikistan: Kuhistoni Badakhshon, NE.	塔吉克斯坦:勾瑙-巴达科善东北	38.5	73.6	16	5.4	Ms	7										
1914	4	11	17	38	10					GSHAP	Russia: Sakhalin Island	俄罗斯:库页岛(萨哈林岛)	47.1	141.8	15	4.5	Ms	5										
1914	4	20	13	19	50					GSHAP	Panama: Off Coast of S.	巴拿马:南部海域	7.6	-79.1		5.5	Ms	6										
1914	4	24	8	35						USGS	US: Nevada, Reno	美国:内华达州雷诺	39.5	-119.8		6.4	Ms	7										

时间 Date 年 Year	月 Mo	日 Dy	时 Hr	分 Mn	秒 Sec	海啸 Tsunami 源 Sr	浪高 Wh	级 I mI	级 S mS	资料来源 Information	震中 Earthquake Epicenter 地名(英文) Name(English)	地名(中文) Name(Chinese)	纬度(°) Latitude	经度(°) Longitude	深度 Depth	震级 Mag	标度 Scale	烈度 MMI	死亡人数 Deaths 数量/人 Num	级别 Dd	受伤人数 Injuries 数量/人 Num	级别 Dd	经济损失 Damage 数量/$ Mill $ Mill	级别 De	房屋毁坏 Houses Destroyed 数量/间 Num	级别 Dh	房屋受损 Houses Damaged 数量/间 Num	级别 Dh
1914	4	25	18	14	5					GSHAP	Russia:Altai Krai, Kamen – na – Obi	俄罗斯:阿尔泰边疆区鄂毕河畔卡缅	53.8	81.5	30	5.3	Ms	5.5										
1914	5	7	13	20	35					GSHAP	Turkmenistan:Balkanabat	土库曼斯坦:巴尔坎纳巴德	39.4	55.2	10	4.8	Ms	7										
1914	5	8	18	1						* Italy	Italy:Catania, Etna	意大利:卡塔尼亚,埃特纳	37.67	15.13		5.3	Ms	10	120	3				3	223	3		
1914	5	13	17	15						USGS, Song	US:Nevada, Wells	美国:内华达州韦尔斯	41.2	–112		5.6	Mk	7										
1914	5	26	14	22	42	4	0.1	1.5	2	* Engdahl, NOAA	Indonesia:Papua	印度尼西亚:巴布亚	–2	137	60	7.9	Mw	9	11	1				2		3		
1914	5	26	20	28	48					GSHAP	Poland:Presov	斯洛伐克:普雷绍夫	49.1	21.5	10	5.2	Ms	7										
1914	5	28	11	27						*	Turkey:Gemerek	土耳其:盖梅雷克	39.2	36		5.6	Muk	7						2				
1914	5	31								*	Ecuador:Monte Pullerina	厄瓜多尔:蒙特卡罗山	–0.2	–78.2	10	5.8	Muk	10										
1914	5					2				NOAA, Song	Canada:Gulf of Saint Lawrence	加拿大:圣劳伦斯湾	48.958	–62.133		7	Mk											
1914	6	1	9	21						GSHAP, Song	Ecuador:Quito	厄瓜多尔:基多	–0.5	–78.48		4.5	Mk	5										
1914	6	7	6	39	24					GSHAP, Song	Ecuador:Quito	厄瓜多尔:基多	–0.5	–78.48		5	Mk	6										
1914	6	25	19	7	18	1				* Engdahl, NOAA	Indonesia:Southern Sumatra	印度尼西亚:苏门答腊南部	–4.5	102.5		7.6	Mw		20	1	20	1		1		1		
1914	7	4	2	24	3					GSHAP	Azerbaijan:Gəncə	阿塞拜疆:占贾	40.8	46.8	30	4.6	Ms	5.5										
1914	7	26				1				* NOAA, Song	Indonesia:Sumatra, Lais	印度尼西亚:苏门答腊,莱斯	–3.5	102		7	Mk											
1914	7	31	18	23	12					GSHAP	Romania:Sfantu Gheorghe	罗马尼亚:圣格奥尔基	45.9	26.1	80	5.3	Ms	5.5										
1914	8	4	22	41	36					* China, Engdahl	China:Xinjiang, Barkol	中国:新疆巴里坤	43.5	91.5		7.2	Mw	8.5	1	1				1		2		
1914	8	16	18							GSHAP	Black Sea	黑海	44.8	37.6	30	4.7	Ms	5										
1914	8	17	4	57	1					GSHAP	Russia:Sverdlovsk, Bisert	俄罗斯:斯威尔德洛夫斯克州比谢尔季	56.8	59.4	25	5.5	Ms	7										
1914	9	11	11	48						* Song	Peru:Caraveli, Nazca, Ica	秘鲁:卡拉威里,纳斯卡	–15.5	–73.2		5.9	Mk			1				2				
1914	9	25	16							China	China:Yunnan, Huize	中国:云南会泽	26.4	103.3		5	Ms	6										
1914	10	3	22	6	34					* GSHAP, Engdahl	Turkey:Burdur, Kilinc	土耳其:布尔杜尔,克伦奇	37.82	30.27		7.1	Mw	9	4000	4	700	3		4	17000	5		
1914	10	17	6	22	30					*	Greece:Erythres	希腊:埃里斯雷	38.25	23.25		6	Ms	10										
1914	10	18	20	46						GSHAP	Kyrgyzstan:Osh, NE.	吉尔吉斯斯坦:奥什东北	40.7	73.1	16	5.1	Ms	6.5										
1914	10	26	2	52						GSHAP	Romania:Nereju	罗马尼亚:内雷茹	45.7	26.6	120	5	Ms	5										
1914	11	4	19	51						GSHAP, Afghan	Azerbaijan:Agcabədi	阿塞拜疆:阿格贾贝迪区	40.3	47.5	40	5.7	Ms	5										
1914	11	9	2	31						USGS	US: California, Lexington Hills	美国:加利福尼亚州列克星敦高地	37.17	–122		4.7	Ms	7										
1914	11	27	14	39	46	4	3	1.7	4	* NOAA	Greece:Leukas (Ionian Islands)	希腊:琉卡斯(伊奥尼亚群岛)	38.717	20.617	30	6.3	Ms	9	14	1				2		3		2

年 Year	月 Mo	日 Dy	时 Hr	分 Mn	秒 Sec	源 Sr	浪高 Wh	级 I mI	级 S mS	资料来源 Information	地名(英文) Name(English)	地名(中文) Name(Chinese)	纬度(°) Latitude	经度(°) Longitude	深度 Depth	震级 Mag	标度 Scale	烈度 MMI	死亡人数 Deaths 数量/人 Num	级别 Dd	受伤人数 Injuries 数量/人 Num	级别 Dd	经济损失 Damage 数量/$ Mill	级别 De	房屋毁坏 Houses Destroyed 数量/间 Num	级别 Dh	房屋受损 Houses Damaged 数量/间 Num	级别 Dh
1914	12	2	23	55						* Song	Peru: Pararca, Paysa, Colta	秘鲁:巴腊尔卡,巴伊萨,库尔塔	-15.2	-73.2		7	Mk	10	34	1				3				
1914	12	3				2				NOAA, Song	Indonesia: Ambon Island	印度尼西亚:安汶岛	-3.7	128.2		7	Mk											
1914	12	13	8	30						GSHAP	Ecuador: Cotopaxi	厄瓜多尔:科托帕希	-0.9	-78.7		5.7	Ms	7										
1914	12	28	10	42						USGS	US: California, Boulder Creek	美国:加利福尼亚州博尔德河	37.17	-122.17		4.5	Ms	5										
1915	1	12	4	31						CGS, USGS	US: California, Los Alamos	美国:加利福尼亚州洛斯阿拉莫斯	34.6	-120.2		5.7	Ms	8										
1915	1	13	6	52	42					* Italy, Engdahl	Italy: Marsica, Avezzano	意大利:马尔西卡山,阿韦扎偌	42.013	13.53	10	6.9	Ms	11	29978	5			60.0	4				
1915	1	14	5	9	43					GSHAP	Russia: Vladikavkaz, S.	俄罗斯:符拉迪克奥克兹南部	42.8	44.7	19	5.4	Ms	7										
1915	1	21	22	20						GSHAP, Iran	Russia: Vladikavkaz, S.	俄罗斯:符拉迪克奥克兹南部	42.8	44.7	30	5.2	Ms	6										
1915	1	25	7	55						GSHAP	Bulgaria: Razgrad	保加利亚:拉兹格勒	43.6	27.3	30	5	Ms	5.5										
1915	1	27	1	9	56	2				GSHAP, NOAA	Ionian Sea	爱奥尼亚海	38.36	20.6		6.6	Ms											
1915	2	22								USGS, Song	US: California, Redding	美国:加利福尼亚州雷丁	40.58	-121.83		5.6	Mk	7										
1915	2	24	15	41						GSHAP	Tajikistan: Panjakent	塔吉克斯坦:彭吉肯特	39.2	67.8	30	5.7	Ms	6.5										
1915	3	17	18	45						Shi Z., GSHAP, Usami, Engdahl	Japan: Off SE. Coast of Hokkaido	日本:北海道东南沿海	42.1	143.6	35	7.2	mB		2	1								
1915	3	26	16	2						GSHAP, Song	Trinidad & Tobago: Port of Spain	特立尼达和多巴哥:西班牙港	10.68	-61.51		5	Mk	6										
1915	4	1	5	41	50					GSHAP	Armenia: Razdan	亚美尼亚:赫拉兹丹	40.5	44.5	35	4.8	Ms	5.5										
1915	4	5	23	11						USGS	US: California, Coleville	美国:加利福尼亚州科尔维尔	38.58	-119.5		5	Ms	5										
1915	5	2	11	40						GSHAP	Kazakhstan: Gerasimovka	哈萨克斯坦:格拉西莫夫卡	45.6	80.6	15	4.8	Ms	6										
1915	5	6	12	9						USGS, Shi Z., Engdahl	US: California, Off Coast of N.	美国:加利福尼亚州北部沿海	39.5	-126.5		6.8	Muk	5										
1915	5	16	13	55						* Song	Philippines: Panay Island	菲律宾:班乃岛	11.3	122.3		5.9	Mk	8						2				
1915	5	23				1				* NOAA, Song	Molukka Sea	马鲁古海	-1.4	128.5		7	Mk											
1915	5	29	6	46						USGS	US: California, Springville	美国:加利福尼亚州斯普林维尔	36.08	-118.83		5	Ms	5										
1915	6	23	4	56						*	US: California, Imperial	美国:加利福尼亚州因皮里尔	32.8	-115.5		6.2	Muk	8	6	1			0.9	1				
1915	6	26	4	40	30					GSHAP	Turkmenistan: Turkmenbasy	土库曼斯坦:土库曼巴希	40.2	53.2	14	4.6	Ms	6										
1915	7	12	2	37	14					GSHAP	Caspian Sea	里海	40.2	52.9	15	5	Ms	6.5										
1915	7	15	22							USGS, Song	US: Utah, Huntington	美国:犹他州亨廷顿	40.4	-111.6		5.1	Mk	6										

时间 Date 年 Year	月 Mo	日 Dy	时 Hr	分 Mn	秒 Sec	海啸 Tsunami 源 Sr	浪高 Wh	级 I mI	级 S mS	资料来源 Information	震中 Earthquake Epicenter 地名(英文) Name(English)	地名(中文) Name(Chinese)	纬度(°) Latitude	经度(°) Longitude	深度 Depth	震级 Mag	标度 Scale	烈度 MMI	死亡人数 Deaths 数量/人 Num	级别 Dd	受伤人数 Injuries 数量/人 Num	级别 Dd	经济损失 Damage 数量/$ Mill $ Mill	级别 De	房屋毁坏 Houses Destroyed 数量/间 Num	级别 Dh	房屋受损 Houses Damaged 数量/间 Num	级别 Dh
1915	7	31	1	31	24					* Engdahl	Russia:Kamchatka, Near East Coast	俄罗斯:堪察加东部近海	54	162	0	7.5	Mw	10										
1915	8	7	15	4	3	3	1.5		3	* NOAA	Greece:Ionian Islands	希腊:伊奥尼亚群岛	38.5	20.617	14	6.7	Ms	9						3				
1915	8	11	9	10						*	Greece:Nisia Ionioy	希腊:伊奥尼亚群岛	38.5	20.5	10	5.9	Muk	10										
1915	8	18	14	4						USGS	US:Washington, Concrete	美国:华盛顿州康克里特	48.5	-121.4		5.6	Ms	5										
1915	8	21	19	23						GSHAP, Song	Peru:Lima, Near Coast	秘鲁:利马近海	-12.935	-76.815	40	5	Mk	6										
1915	8	22	9	18	16					GSHAP	Ecuador:Ibarra	厄瓜多尔:伊瓦拉	0.1	-78.7		5	Ms	6										
1915	8					1				NOAA, Song	Solomon Islands	所罗门群岛	-10.38	165.8		7	Mk											
1915	9	7	1	20	48	1			0.5	* Engdahl, NOAA	El Salvador:Chalatenango	萨尔瓦多:查拉特南戈	14	-89	80	7.4	mB											
1915	9	20	22	28						GSHAP, Song	Peru:Ica, Near Coast	秘鲁:伊卡近海	-14.412	-76.229	80	5	Mk	6										
1915	9	27								GSHAP	Rumania:Timisoara	罗马尼亚:蒂米什瓦拉	45.5	21.1	5	4.6	Ms	7										
1915	10	3	1	49						USGS, Song	US:Nevada, Imlay, SE.	美国:内华达州伊姆莱东南	40.5	-117.5		4.9	Mk	5										
1915	10	3	6	52	48					* Shi Z., Engdahl	US:Nevada, Imlay, SE.	美国:内华达州伊姆莱东南	40.5	-117.5		7.1	M	10						1				
1915	10	8	5	25	42					USGS	US:California, Montclair	美国:加利福尼亚州蒙特克莱尔	37.83	-122.25		4.5	Ms	6										
1915	10	19	8	43	54					GSHAP	Romania:Timisoara	罗马尼亚:蒂米什瓦拉	45.4	21.1	5	4.8	Ms	7.5										
1915	11	1	7	24		4	1			* Usami, Engdahl, NOAA	Japan:Oshu, Near Coast	日本:奥州近海	39	142.5	35	7.5	Mw											
1915	11	6	18	30						GSHAP	Brasil:Salvador	巴西:萨尔瓦多	-12.67	-38.63		4	Ms	6										
1915	11	6				2				* NOAA	Indonesia:Papua	印度尼西亚:巴布亚	-1	136		6	Ms											
1915	11	16	1	38						Usami, Japan	Japan:Chiba, Tokyo	日本:千叶县;东京	35.4	140.3		6.7	Ms				5	1						
1915	11	18	20	19	18	2			0.5	* China, NOAA	China:South China Sea	中国:南海	18	119.5		6.4	Ms	7						1				
1915	11	21	0	13	42					USGS, Engdahl	Mexico:Mexicali	墨西哥:墨西卡利	32	-115		7.1	Ms	9										
1915	12	3	2	39	19					* China, Engdahl	China:Xizang (Tibet), Sangri	中国:西藏桑日	29.5	91.5		7	Ms	9	170	3				2		3		
1915	12	7	18	40						USGS	US:Arkansas, Blytheville	美国:阿肯色州布莱斯维尔	36	-90		4.5	Ms	5										
1915	12	13	2	30						GSHAP	Venezuela:Caracas	委内瑞拉:加拉加斯	10.9	-66.8	25	5.6	Ms	6										
1915	12	28	23	40						GSHAP, Song	Peru:Nazca	秘鲁:纳斯卡	-15.155	-73.93	90	5	Mk	6										
1915	12	29								*	El Salvador:Ahuachapan, Ataco	萨尔瓦多:阿瓦查潘,亚他可	14.56	-88.76		6.6	Ms			1				2		3		
1915										China	China:Guangdong, Guangzhou	中国:广东广州	23.1	113.2		4.75	Ms	6										
1916	1	1	13	20	36	3	4.5	1.5	2	* Engdahl, NOAA	Papua New Guinea: New Ireland, E.	巴布亚新几内亚:新爱尔兰东部	-4	154	25	7.7	Mw							1		1		
1916	1	4	3	12						* Song	Philippines:Panay, Maasin	菲律宾:班乃,马阿辛	11.1	122.3		5.9	Mk	8						2				
1916	1	24	6	55	7					* GSHAP, Engdahl	Turkey:Ikizce	土耳其:伊基兹杰	41	37	33	7.2	Mw	8										

年 Year	月 Mo	日 Dy	时 Hr	分 Mn	秒 Sec	海啸 Tsunami 源 Sr	浪高 Wh	级 I mI	级 S mS	资料来源 Information	震中 Earthquake Epicenter 地名(英文) Name(English)	地名(中文) Name(Chinese)	纬度(°) Latitude	经度(°) Longitude	深度 Depth	震级 Mag	标度 Scale	烈度 MMI	死亡人数 Deaths 数量/人 Num	级别 Dd	受伤人数 Injuries 数量/人 Num	级别 Dd	经济损失 Damage 数量/$ Mill	级别 De	房屋毁坏 Houses Destroyed 数量/间 Num	级别 Dh	房屋受损 Houses Damaged 数量/间 Num	级别 Dh
1916	1	26	7	37	55					GSHAP	Romania:Câmpulung	罗马尼亚:肯普隆格	45.4	24.6	21	6.4	Ms	8										
1916	1	26	8	15						GSHAP	Romania:Râmnicu Vâlcea	罗马尼亚:勒姆尼库沃尔恰	45.4	24.2	10	5.2	Ms	8										
1916	1	26	8	30						GSHAP	Romania:Râmnicu Vâlcea	罗马尼亚:勒姆尼库沃尔恰	45.4	24.2	15	5	Ms	7										
1916	1	31				1		2.2	2.7	* NOAA,Song	Costa Rica:Pavones	哥斯达黎加:帕沃内斯	8.5	-83		7.7	Mk											
1916	2	3	4	24						USGS	US:New York,Galway	美国:纽约州戈尔韦	43	-74		4.1	Ms	6										
1916	2	3	5	3	4					USGS	US:Nevada,Dixie Valley	美国:内华达州迪克西瓦利	41	-117.8		5.9	Ms	5										
1916	2	8	15	35						GSHAP,Song	Peru: Ayacucho	秘鲁:阿亚库乔	-12.967	-74.064	120	5	Mk	6										
1916	2	11	20	53	20					GSHAP	Iran:Mashhad	伊朗:马什哈德	36	59.5	7	4.8	Ms	7.5										
1916	2	21	23	39						USGS	US:North Carolina,Asheville	美国:北卡罗来纳州阿什维尔	35.5	-82.5		5.2	Ms	7										
1916	2	22	9	12						Usami,Japan	Japan:Tsumagoi	日本:群马嬬恋村	36.5	138.5		6	Ms								7	1	3	1
1916	2	28	13	16						GSHAP	Kazakhstan:Almaty	哈萨克斯坦:阿拉木图	43	77.2	25	6	Ms	6.5										
1916	2	28	18	55						China	China:Xinjiang,Kalpin	中国:新疆柯坪	40.6	78.2	20	5.8	Ms	6.5										
1916	3	1	16							China	China:Yunnan,Huize,N.	中国:云南会泽北	26.7	103.3		5.25	Ms	6										
1916	3	30	5	47						USGS,Song	US:Arizona,Patagonia	美国:亚利桑那州巴塔哥尼亚	31.4	-110.9		5.1	Mk	6										
1916	4	10	22	30						GSHAP	Macedonia(Fyrom):Stip	马其顿:斯提普	41.7	22	35	4.8	Ms	6										
1916	4	24	4	26	42					* Engdahl	Dominica:Santo Domingo	多米尼加:圣多明哥	18.5	-68	80	7	mB	9						1				
1916	4	26	2	21	30	4	1.3			* Engdahl,NOAA	Panama:Bocas Del Toro	巴拿马:博卡斯德尔托罗	9.33	-82.55	33	7.1	Ms	9					0.025	1				
1916	5	13	2	26						USGS	US:Idaho,Weiser	美国:爱达荷州韦泽	44.2	-116.5		5.3	Ms	7										
1916	5	14	12	11						GSHAP	Azerbaijan:Sirvan	阿塞拜疆:希尔万	40	48.1	30	5	Ms	6										
1916	5	27	19	5						GSHAP	Netherlands Antilles:Willemstad	荷属安的列斯:威廉斯塔德	12.2	-68.94		4.9	Ms	5										
1916	6	2	3							GSHAP	Caspian Sea	里海	40.5	52.3	15	5.3	Ms	7										
1916	6	28	17	58	35					GSHAP	Azerbaijan:Quba,SW.	阿塞拜疆:库巴西南	41	48.5	25	4.9	Ms	5.5										
1916	7	3	23	21		5	10			Italy,NOAA	Tyrrhenian Sea	第勒尼安海(伊特鲁里亚海)	38.812	15.237		5.07	Ms											
1916	7	5	4	40						USGS,Song	US:California,North Coast	美国:加利福尼亚州北部近海	40.58	-124.25		5.1	Mk	6										
1916	7	14	20	27	1					GSHAP	Croatia:Senj	克罗地亚:塞尼	45.2	14.8	20	5.2	Ms	6.5										
1916	7	16	11	50						USGS	US:California,Newberry Springs	美国:加利福尼亚州纽贝里斯普林斯	34.7	-117		4.5	Ms	5										
1916	7	17	10	30						GSHAP	Colombia:Caqueta,E.	哥伦比亚:卡克塔东部	0	-72		4	Ms	5										
1916	8	5	22	52						Usami,Japan	Japan:Ehime	日本:爱媛	34	133.4		6.2	Ms				1	1						
1916	8	6	19	38						CGS,USGS	US:California,Tres Pinos,S.	美国:加利福尼亚州特雷斯皮诺斯南部	36.67	-121.25		5.8	Ms	7										

年 Year	月 Mo	日 Dy	时 Hr	分 Mn	秒 Sec	海啸 Tsunami 源 Sr	浪高 Wh	级 I mI	级 S mS	资料来源 Information	震中 Earthquake Epicenter 地名(英文) Name(English)	地名(中文) Name(Chinese)	纬度(°) Latitude	经度(°) Longitude	深度 Depth	震级 Mag	标度 Scale	烈度 MMI	死亡人数 Deaths 数量/人 Num	级别 Dd	受伤人数 Injuries 数量/人 Num	级别 Dd	经济损失 Damage 数量/$ Mill	级别 De	房屋毁坏 Houses Destroyed 数量/间 Num	级别 Dh	房屋受损 Houses Damaged 数量/间 Num	级别 Dh
1916	8	8	16	52	41					USGS	US:California,Davenport	美国:加利福尼亚州达文波特	37	-122		5	Ms	5										
1916	8	14	1	58	24					GSHAP	Russia:Sakhalin Island	俄罗斯:库页岛(萨哈林岛)	47	142	20	5	Ms	5										
1916	8	16	7	6	14	4			2	Italy, GSHAP, NOAA	Italy:Misano Adriatico	意大利:米萨诺阿德里亚蒂科	43.97	12.67		5.92	Ms											
1916	8	18	16	17	6					GSHAP	Russia:Sakhalin Island	俄罗斯:库页岛(萨哈林岛)	47	142	15	4.5	Ms	5										
1916	8	28	7	27	5					*China,Engdahl	China:Taiwan,Nantou	中国:台湾南投	23.7	120.9	5	7.2	Ms	8	180	3				2	614	3	4885	4
1916	8									China	China:Shanxi,Xinjiang	中国:山西新绛	35.7	111.3		5	Ms	6										
1916	9	11	6	36	30					*Engdahl	Indonesia:Java Ridge	印度尼西亚:爪哇海岭	-9	113	100	7.1	mB							3	340	3		
1916	9	30	2	11						CGS,USGS	US:California,Borrego Springs	美国:加利福尼亚州博雷戈斯普林斯	33.2	-116.1		5.7	Ms	5										
1916	10	18	22	4						USGS	US:Alabama,Sterrett	美国:阿拉巴马州斯特雷特	33.5	-86.5		5.1	Ms	7										
1916	10	23	2	44						USGS	US:California,Arvin	美国:加利福尼亚州阿尔文	34.9	-118.9		6	Ms	7										
1916	10	23	2	54						USGS	US:California,Ojai,N.	美国:加利福尼亚州奥海镇北部	34.7	-119		5.5	Ms	5										
1916	10	28	8	15	51					*Italy	Slovenia:Gornji Grad	斯洛文尼亚:格尔尼格勒	46.3	14.6	11	5.17	Muk	7						2				
1916	10	28	20	48						GSHAP	Armenia:Armavir	亚美尼亚:阿尔马维尔	40.1	44.1	20	4.9	Ms	6.5										
1916	11	10	5	57						GSHAP	Azerbaijan:Agdam	阿塞拜疆:阿格达姆区	40.1	46.4	19	4.7	Ms	5.5										
1916	11	10	9	11						USGS	US:California,Baker	美国:加利福尼亚州贝克	35.5	-116		6.1	Ms	5										
1916	11	12				2				*NOAA,Song	Venezuela:Independência	委内瑞拉:独立镇	10.1	-66.8		7	Mk											
1916	11	14	13	54	34					GSHAP	Armenia:Gyumri	亚美尼亚:久姆里	40.8	44.4	26	5.3	Ms	6.5										
1916	11	14	22	31	33					*China	China:Taiwan,Nantou,N.	中国:台湾南投北	24	121		6	Ms		1	1	20	1		1	97	2	972	3
1916	11	18	2	29						GSHAP	Greece:Kilkis	希腊:基尔基斯	41.3	22.5	15	4.5	Ms	6										
1916	11	26	5	8						Japan	Japan:Kobe	日本:神户	34.6	135		6.3	Ms		1	1	5	1			3	1	10	1
1916	11	26	6	8						Usami	Japan:Kobe	日本:神户	34.6	135		6.1	Ms		1	1					3	1		
1916	12	1	22	53						USGS,Song	US:California,San Luis Obispo	美国:加利福尼亚州圣路易斯－奥比斯保	35.17	-120.75		5.6	Mk	7										
1916										China	China:Xinjiang,Kuqa,W.	中国:新疆库车西	41.7	82.7		5.5	Ms	7										
1916										China	China:Xinjiang,Shanshan,NW.	中国:新疆鄯善西北	42.9	89.7		6	Ms	8										
1917	1	4	7	18	44					GSHAP	Georgia:Tbilisi	格鲁吉亚:第比利斯	41.3	44.5	25	4.6	Ms	5.5										
1917	1	4	16	55						*China,Engdahl	China:Taiwan,Nantou	中国:台湾南投	23.9	120.9	0	6.5	Ms		54	2	85	2		1	130	3	625	3
1917	1	21	23	11	34	3	2	1		*NOAA	Indonesia:Bali Island	印度尼西亚:巴厘岛	-7	116		6.6	Ms	9	1500	4				2		2		
1917	1	24	0	48	12					*China,Engdahl	China:Anhui,Heshan	中国:安徽霍山	31.3	116.2	0	6.5	Ms	8		3				3		3		
1917	1	24	16			4		1	1	*NOAA	China:Taiwan Strait	中国:台湾海峡	24.5	119.5		6.5	Ms							1				

时间 年 Date Year	月 Mo	日 Dy	时 Hr	分 Mn	秒 Sec	海啸 Tsunami 源 Sr	浪高 Wh	级 I mI	级 S mS	资料来源 Information	震中 Earthquake Epicenter 地名(英文) Name(English)	地名(中文) Name(Chinese)	纬度(°) Latitude	经度(°) Longitude	深度 Depth	震级 Mag	标度 Scale	烈度 MMI	死亡人数 Deaths 数量/人 Num	级别 Dd	受伤人数 Injuries 数量/人 Num	级别 Dd	经济损失 Damage 数量/$ Mill	级别 De	房屋毁坏 Houses Destroyed 数量/间 Num	级别 Dh	房屋受损 Houses Damaged 数量/间 Num	级别 Dh
1917	1	26	5	9	5					GSHAP	Russia: Kamchatka, Near East Coast	俄罗斯:堪察加东部近海	52	162	10	6.2	Ms	8.5										
1917	1	27	14	51	36					China	China: Fujian, Mingxi	中国:福建明溪	26.4	117.2		5	Ms	6										
1917	1	27	16							China	China: Sichuan, Ya – an	中国:四川雅安	30	103		4.75	Ms	6										
1917	1	29	8	22	55					* Italy	Slovenia: Brezice	斯洛文尼亚:布雷日采	45.9	15.6	13	5.75	Muk	8						3				
1917	1	29	10	29	15					GSHAP	Slovenia: Brezice	斯洛文尼亚:布雷日采	45.9	15.6	8	4.9	Ms	7										
1917	1	29	21	18	32					GSHAP	Slovenia: Brezice	斯洛文尼亚:布雷日采	45.9	15.6	16	4.6	Ms	6										
1917	1	30	2	45	36	2				* GSHAP, Engdahl, NOAA	Russia: Kamchatka Peninsula	俄罗斯:堪察加半岛	56.5	163	19	7.7	Mw	11										
1917	1	31	3	39	55	3	1.5	0.6		* NOAA	Philippines: Mindanao, Glan	菲律宾:棉兰老岛,格兰	6	125		6.4	Ms	9	7	1		1		2		2		
1917	2	6	21	50						GSHAP	Russia: Murmansk, Teriberka	俄罗斯:摩尔曼斯克州捷里别尔卡	69.1	35.3	20	4.5	Ms	5										
1917	2	20	21	28						GSHAP	Georgia: Tbilisi	格鲁吉亚:第比利斯	41.3	44.6	16	4.5	Ms	6										
1917	2	22	1	12						China	China: Anhui, Heshan	中国:安徽霍山	31.3	116.2		5.5	Ms	7										
1917	2	22	4	58	22					GSHAP	Georgia: Gori, N.	格鲁吉亚:哥里北部	42.7	44	9	4.5	Ms	6.5										
1917	3	3	16							USGS	US: California, North Coast	美国:加利福尼亚州北部近海	40.83	-124.17		4.6	Ms	5										
1917	3	16				2	1.5		1.5	NOAA, Song	Indonesia: Java Sea	印度尼西亚:爪哇海	-3.7	116.6		7.3	Mk							2				
1917	4	9	20	52						USGS	US: Missouri, Bloomsdale	美国:密苏里州布卢姆斯代尔	38.1	-90.2		5.1	Ms	7										
1917	4	10	2	14	8					GSHAP	Slovenia: Styria	斯洛文尼亚:斯特利亚	45.8	15.4	20	4.6	Ms	5.5										
1917	4	13	3	59						USGS	US: California, Santa Barbara	美国:加利福尼亚州圣巴巴拉	34.3	-119.5		4.5	Ms	5										
1917	4	26	9	36						* Italy	Italy: Sansepolcro	意大利:圣塞波尔克罗	43.5	12.1	33	5.8	Muk	10										
1917	4	29	11	55	33					GSHAP	Russia: Buryatiya, Severomuysk	俄罗斯:布里亚特州谢韦罗穆伊斯克城	56	113.8	20	6.6	Ms	9										
1917	5	1	18	26	30	4	0.3	3.6	3	* Shi Z., Engdahl, NOAA	Kermadec Ridge	克马德克海岭	-29.2	-177	50	8	Mw											
1917	5	5	7	50						GSHAP	Brasil: Campos	巴西:坎普斯	-21.6	-41.5	15	4.5	Ms	5										
1917	5	6	4	19		4	0.5	-1	-0.5	* NOAA	China: Taiwan, Taitung, Coast of E.	中国:台湾台东以东海域	23.2	121.6	33	5.8	Ms											
1917	5	17	19	7						Usami, Japan	Japan: Shimada	日本:静冈岛田	35	138.1		6.3	Ms		2	1	6	1						
1917	5	19	21							GSHAP	Romania: Nereju	罗马尼亚:内雷茹	45.7	26.6	150	5.5	Ms	6										
1917	5	21	4	45						GSHAP, Song	Peru: Trujillo, Near Coast	秘鲁:特鲁希略近海	-8.283	-79.502	40	5	Mk	6										
1917	5	21	8	56						GSHAP, Song	Peru: Chivay	秘鲁:奇瓦伊	-15.1	-71.5	20	6	Mk	7										
1917	5	28	6	6						USGS	US: California, Holtville	美国:加利福尼亚州霍尔特维尔	32.8	-115.3		5.5	Ms	6										
1917	5	31	8	47	20					* USGS, Engdahl	Aleutian Islands	阿留申群岛	54.5	-160		7.5	Mw	5										
1917	6	6	20	10						* Song	Italy: Terni	意大利:特尔尼	42.5	12.7		6.5	Mk	12										

时间 Date						海啸 Tsunami				资料来源	震中 Earthquake Epicenter				深度	震级	标度	烈度	死亡人数 Deaths		受伤人数 Injuries		经济损失 Damage		房屋毁坏 Houses Destroyed		房屋受损 Houses Damaged	
年	月	日	时	分	秒	源	浪高	级 I	级 S		地名(英文)	地名(中文)	纬度(°)	经度(°)					数量/人	级别	数量/人	级别	数量/$ Mill	级别	数量/间	级别	数量/间	级别
Year	Mo	Dy	Hr	Mn	Sec	Sr	Wh	mI	mS	Information	Name(English)	Name(Chinese)	Latitude	Longitude	Depth	Mag	Scale	MMI	Num	Dd	Num	Dd	$ Mill	De	Num	Dh	Num	Dh
1917	6	8	0	51	51	1				*	El Salvador:La Libertad	萨尔瓦多:拉利伯塔德	13.82	-89.31		6.7	Ms			3				4		3		
1917	6	18	9							GSHAP	Kazakhstan:Shymkent	哈萨克斯坦:奇姆肯特	42.5	68.8	10	5	Ms	7										
1917	6	26	5	49	42	4	12	3.6	3	*Engdahl,NOAA	Samoa Islands	萨摩亚群岛	-15.5	-173	25	8.5	Mw							2				
1917	7	6	11	1						USGS,Song	US:California,Owens Valley	美国:加利福尼亚州欧文斯谷	36.58	-118.08		5.1	Mk	6										
1917	7	9	22	22						USGS,Song	US:California, San Luis Obispo	美国:加利福尼亚州 圣路易斯-奥比斯保	35.25	-120.5		5.1	Mk	6										
1917	7	11	3	23	55					GSHAP	Romania:Nereju	罗马尼亚:内雷茹	45.7	26.6	100	5.5	Ms	6										
1917	7	26	8	33						USGS	US:California,Nipomo	美国:加利福尼亚州尼波莫	35	-120.5		4.8	Ms	5										
1917	7	27	2	51	48					GSHAP,Shi Z., Engdahl	Argentina:Mendoza	阿根廷:门多萨	-32.3	-68.9	60	6.9	Ms	7										
1917	7	29	21	52	24	2	0.9		1	*Engdahl,NOAA	Papua New Guinea:Dagua	巴布亚新几内亚:达呱区	-3	143.5		7.6	Mw											
1917	7	30	23	54	5					*China,Engdahl	China:Yunnan,Daguan,N.	中国:云南大关北	28	104		7.3	Mw	9	1800	4				4		4		
1917	8	23				1			0.5	NOAA,Song	Indonesia:Maluku Islands	印度尼西亚:摩鹿加群岛	-3.6	128.7		7	Mk											
1917	8	30	3	24	10					GSHAP	Colombia:Bogota	哥伦比亚:波哥达	4.6	-74		4	Ms	5										
1917	8	31	11	36	24					* Engdahl	Colombia:Bogota, Ubaque, Soacha, Caqueza	哥伦比亚:波哥达,乌巴克,索阿查	4	-74	40	7.1	Ms	8	6	1		2		1		1		
1917	9	3	21	30						USGS	US:Minnesota,Motley	美国:明尼苏达州莫特利	46.3	-94.5		4.3	Ms	6										
1917	9	17	1	20						* Song	Italy:Sora	意大利:索拉	41.7	13.6		6.5	Mk	12										
1917	9	30	18	30						GSHAP	Tajikistan: Khorog	塔吉克斯坦:霍罗格	37.3	71.5	15	5	Ms	6.5										
1917	10	5	23	33	40					GSHAP	Panama:Garachiné,S.	巴拿马:加拉奇内南部	7.5	-79		4.5	Ms	5										
1917	11	5	23	45						* Song	Italy:Ancona	意大利:安科纳	43.6	13.7		6.5	Mk	12										
1917	11	7	23	25						GSHAP	Brasil:Salvador	巴西:萨尔瓦多	-12.48	-38.66		4.3	Ms	7										
1917	11	16	3	19	30	3	2.5	1.3	1	*Engdahl,NOAA	Kermadec Ridge	克马德克海岭	-29	-177.5	60	7.3	Mw											
1917	12	12	10	50						USGS	US:Idaho,Wayan	美国:爱达荷州韦恩	43	-111.3		5.3	Ms	5										
1917	12	20	19	23	12					GSHAP	Bulgarian:Kardzali	保加利亚:克尔贾利	41.5	25.5	20	4.5	Ms	5.5										
1917	12	26	4	30						*	Guatemala:Guatemala City	危地马拉:危地马拉城	14	-90		6	Ms		2650	4				4				
1917										GSHAP	Brasil:Contagem	巴西:康塔根	-20.72	-46.61		4.3	Ms	5										
1917										China	China:Gansu,Gaotai	中国:甘肃高台	39.4	99.8		4.75	Ms	6										
1918	1	4	4	37						* Song	Guatemala:Guatemala City	危地马拉:危地马拉城	14	-90		6.2	Mk							3				
1918	1	26	20	44						GSHAP	Georgia:Gori,N.	格鲁吉亚:哥里北部	42.5	44.5	22	4.5	Ms	5.5										
1918	1									China	China:Yunnan,Xundian	中国:云南寻甸	25.6	103.3		5	Ms	6										
1918	2	13	6	7	14	4		1	-1	* China, Engdahl, NOAA	China:Guangdong, Nan-ao,Near Coast	中国:广东南澳近海	23.2	117.4	15	7.5	Ms	10	2000	4		4		4		4		
1918	2	24	23	0	20					GSHAP	Grenada:St Georges	格林纳达:圣乔治	12	-62		6.3	Ms	8										
1918	2	25	2	7						GSHAP	Romania:Nereju	罗马尼亚:内雷茹	45.7	26.6	120	5.6	Ms	6										

年 Year	月 Mo	日 Dy	时 Hr	分 Mn	秒 Sec	源 Sr	浪高 Wh	级I mI	级S mS	资料来源 Information	地名(英文) Name(English)	地名(中文) Name(Chinese)	纬度(°) Latitude	经度(°) Longitude	深度 Depth	震级 Mag	标度 Scale	烈度 MMI	死亡人数 Deaths 数量/人 Num	级别 Dd	受伤人数 Injuries 数量/人 Num	级别 Dd	经济损失 Damage 数量/$ Mill	级别 De	房屋毁坏 Houses Destroyed 数量/间 Num	级别 Dh	房屋受损 Houses Damaged 数量/间 Num	级别 Dh
1918	3	12	10	30						USGS, Song	US: California, Sierra City	美国:加利福尼亚州谢拉锡蒂	39.58	-120.83		5.6	Mk	7										
1918	3	21	16	58	22					GSHAP	Panama: Garachiné, S.	巴拿马:加拉奇内南部	7.5	-79		4.5	Ms	5										
1918	3	27	3	52	15					China	Ryukyu Islands	琉球群岛	25	123		6.25	Ms				3	1					6	1
1918	4	10	0	26						GSHAP	Norway: Vassenden	挪威:瓦森嫩	61.4	6.5	30	4.7	Ms	5										
1918	4	10	1	8	48					USGS	US: Virginia, Luray	美国:弗吉尼亚州卢雷	38.7	-78.4		4.6	Ms	6										
1918	4	21	22	32	30					* Engdahl	US: California, Riverside	美国:加利福尼亚州里弗赛德	33.7	-117	15	6.8	Muk						0.2	1				
1918	4	22	21	15						USGS, Song	US: California, Los Angeles	美国:加利福尼亚州洛杉矶	33.8	-117.6		5.1	Mk	6										
1918	5	1	4	32						CGS, USGS	US: California, Holtville	美国:加利福尼亚州霍尔特维尔	32.6	-115.4		5.6	Ms	6										
1918	5	20	17	55	11	2				* Chile, Shi Z, Engdahl, NOAA	Chile: Near Coast of Vallenar	智利:巴耶纳尔近海	-28.899	-71.893	35	7.6	mB											
1918	5	28	11	30						USGS, Song	US: New Mexico, Santa Fe	美国:新墨西哥州圣达菲	35.5	-106		5.6	Mk	7										
1918	6	6	22	32						CGS, USGS	US: California, Anza	美国:加利福尼亚州安萨	33.6	-116.7		5.5	Ms	6										
1918	6	7	16							China	China: Heilongjiang, Luobei, N.	中国:黑龙江萝北北	47.9	130.9		4.75	Ms	6										
1918	6	14	21	43						USGS, Song	Hawaiian Islands	夏威夷群岛	19	-155.5		4.9	Mk	5										
1918	6	21								GSHAP	Mongolia: Bayanbulag	蒙古:巴彦布拉格	47	98	20	5.4	Ms	6.5										
1918	7	8	10	22	8					* India, Engdahl	Bangladesh: Dhaka	孟加拉:达卡	24.809	90.725	15	7.5	Mw							2				
1918	7	15	0	23						USGS	US: California, North Coast	美国:加利福尼亚州北部近海	41	-125		6.5	Ms	6										
1918	7	18	2	30		5	0.1		0	* * NOAA, Song	Indonesia: Sangihe Islands	印度尼西亚:桑义赫群岛	3.138	125.491	33	7	Mk											
1918	8	9	0	31	44					China	China: Henan, Tongxu	中国:河南通许	34.5	114.5		5.25	Ms	6										
1918	8	13	16							* China	China: Yunnan, Qiaojia, S.	中国:云南巧家南	26.9	103		5.5	Ms	7						1				
1918	8	13	20	0	36					GSHAP, Italy	Slovenia: Idrija	斯洛文尼亚:伊德里亚	46	14	20	5.1	Ms	6										
1918	8	15	12	18	16	4	7.2	2.8	2.5	* Japan, Engdahl, NOAA	Philippines: Cotabato	菲律宾:哥打巴托	5.653	123.563	35	8.2	Mw	10	100	2				3				
1918	8	21	4	11	54					USGS	US: Maine, Paris	美国:缅因州帕里斯	44.2	-70.5		4.2	Ms	7										
1918	9	7	17	15	44	4	12	3.6	3	* Japan, Engdahl, Shi Z, Usami, NOAA	Kuril Islands	千岛群岛	46.812	150.253	242.4	7.6	mB		24	1	7	1		3				
1918	9	7	23	8	39					GSHAP	Ecuador: Tungurahua	厄瓜多尔:东谷拉瓦	-1.4	-78.4		5	Ms	6										
1918	9	13	6	55						* China	Philippines: Batanes, Ivana	菲律宾:巴坦群岛,伊瓦纳	20.3	121.5		5	Ms	8						2				
1918	10	11	14	14	41	4	6.1	2.6		* Shi Z, Engdahl, NOAA	Puerto Rico: Mona Passage	波多黎各:莫纳海峡	18.5	-67.5	60	7.3	Mw	9	142	3			29.0	4				

年 Year	月 Mo	日 Dy	时 Hr	分 Mn	秒 Sec	海啸 Tsunami 源 Sr	浪高 Wh	级 I mI	级 S mS	资料来源 Information	震中 Earthquake Epicenter 地名(英文) Name(English)	地名(中文) Name(Chinese)	纬度(°) Latitude	经度(°) Longitude	深度 Depth	震级 Mag	标度 Scale	烈度 MMI	死亡人数 Deaths 数量/人 Num	级别 Dd	受伤人数 Injuries 数量/人 Num	级别 Dd	经济损失 Damage 数量/$ Mill $ Mill	级别 De	房屋毁坏 Houses Destroyed 数量/间 Num	级别 Dh	房屋受损 Houses Damaged 数量/间 Num	级别 Dh
1918	10	16	2	15						USGS	US:Tennessee,Newbern	美国:田纳西州纽伯恩	36	-89.2		4.5	Ms	5										
1918	10	24	3	43		4				* NOAA,Song	Puerto Rico:Mona Passage	波多黎各:莫纳海峡	18.5	-67.5		7	Mk	7										
1918	11	2	10	1	10					USGS	Hawaiian Islands	夏威夷群岛	19.4	-155.3		6.2	Ms	7										
1918	11	6	19	26	8					GSHAP	Slovenia:Ljubljana	斯洛文尼亚:卢布尔雅那	46.2	14.4	35	5.4	Ms	5										
1918	11	8	4	38	11	4	0.5	1	2	* GSHAP,Engdahl,NOAA	Kuril Islands	千岛群岛	43.816	152.775	63.5	7.5	mB											
1918	11	11	7	4						Engdahl,Usami	Japan:Nagano	日本:长野	36.5	137.9	5	6.5	Mj								22	1		
1918	11	12	21	45						* Song	Puerto Rico:Mona Passage	波多黎各:莫纳海峡	18.2	-68.2		5.9	Mk	7						2				
1918	11	19	20	18						USGS,Song	US:California,Los Angeles	美国:加利福尼亚州洛杉矶	34	-118.5		5.1	Mk	6										
1918	12	4	11	47	39	4	5	2.3	2.5	* Chile,Engdahl,NOAA	Chile:Caldera,Off Coast	智利:卡尔德拉沿海	-27.275	-73.464	25	7.5	Mw			1				3		3		
1918	12	18	12	44						* *	Chile:Copiapo	智利:科皮亚波	-27.3	-70.5		8.2	Ms							3				
1918	12	21	9	24	40					GSHAP	Colombia:Vaupes,NE.	哥伦比亚:沃佩斯东北	1	-70	600	6.5	Ms	5										
1918										* Song	Iran:Razavi Khorasan	伊朗:呼罗珊	34.5	58.2		5.9	Mk	7						2				
1919	1	1	1	33	50	4	0.9	-0.1		* Japan,Engdahl	Philippine Trench	菲律宾海沟	7.184	126.937	35	7.1	Mw											
1919	1	1	3	0	4	1	0.4			* Engdahl,NOAA	Fiji Islands	斐济群岛	-19.971	-177.914	202.7	7.7	mB											
1919	1	2	1	33	42	4	0.9	-0.1		NOAA	Philippines:Mindanao Island	菲律宾:棉兰老岛	8	126	33	7.4	Ms											
1919	1	4	23							USGS,Song	US:California,Redding	美国:加利福尼亚州雷丁	40.58	-121.82		5.1	Mk	6										
1919	1	8	10	12	53					GSHAP,Iran	Turkey:Erzurum	土耳其:埃尔佐鲁姆	40.9	42.2	40	5.3	Ms	6										
1919	1	29	3	22						USGS,Song	Hawaiian Islands	夏威夷群岛	19	-155.5		4.9	Mk	5										
1919	2	13				2			1.5	NOAA,Song	Indonesia:Timor Sea	印度尼西亚:帝汶海	-9	124.85		7.3	Mk							1				
1919	2	16	15	57						CGS,USGS	US:California,Bakersfield	美国:加利福尼亚州贝克斯菲尔德	34.9	-119.2		5.7	Ms	7										
1919	2	25	22	38						USGS	US:California,Santa Rosa	美国:加利福尼亚州圣罗莎	38.33	-122.5		4.6	Ms	5										
1919	3									China	China:Yunnan,Luliang	中国:云南陆良	25	103.7		5	Ms	6										
1919	4	18	6	20	12					GSHAP	Romania:Nereju	罗马尼亚:内雷茹	45.7	26.8	100	5.7	Ms	6										
1919	4	27	0	22						* Shi Z.	Philippines:Burias Island	菲律宾:布里亚斯岛	13	123		6.4	Muk							2				
1919	4	28	6	45	45					*	El Salvador:San Salvador	萨尔瓦多:圣萨尔瓦多	13.69	-89.19		5.9	Ms			2				3				3
1919	4	30	7	17	13	4	2.5	1.3	1.5	* Engdahl,NOAA	Tonga Islands,E.	汤加群岛东部	-19.823	-172.215	35	8.2	Mw							1				
1919	5	6	19	40	38	3	2.5	2.6	1	* Engdahl,NOAA	Papua New Guinea:East New Britain,E.	巴布亚新几内亚:东新不列颠东部	-5.477	152.629	232.8	7.6	mB							1		1		
1919	6	1	21	30						GSHAP	Brasil:Coxim	巴西:科欣	-18	-56	15	4.9	Ms	5										
1919	6	5	4	20						GSHAP	Brasil:Campo Grande	巴西:大坎普	-21.03	-44.75		3.1	Ms	5										
1919	6	29	15	6	12					* Italy	Italy:Santa Sofia	意大利:圣索菲亚	44	11.5	33	6.2	Ms	10										
1919	7									China	China:Yunnan,Zhaotong	中国:云南昭通	27.3	103.7		5	Ms	6										
1919	8	5	9							GSHAP	Brasil:Sao Paulo	巴西:圣保罗	-25.01	-47.94		3.1	Ms	5										

年 Year	月 Mo	日 Dy	时 Hr	分 Mn	秒 Sec	海啸 源 Sr	浪高 Wh	级 I mI	级 S mS	资料来源 Information	地名(英文) Name(English)	地名(中文) Name(Chinese)	纬度(°) Latitude	经度(°) Longitude	深度 Depth	震级 Mag	标度 Scale	烈度 MMI	死亡人数 Deaths 数量/人 Num	级别 Dd	受伤人数 Injuries 数量/人 Num	级别 Dd	经济损失 Damage 数量/$ Mill	级别 De	房屋毁坏 Houses Destroyed 数量/间 Num	级别 Dh	房屋受损 Houses Damaged 数量/间 Num	级别 Dh
1919	8	9	14	38						GSHAP	Romania: Nereju	罗马尼亚:内雷茹	45.7	26.6	120	5.6	Ms	6										
1919	9	5	20	36	54					GSHAP, Italy	Croatia: Varazdin	克罗地亚:瓦拉日丁	46.5	16.5	16	5	Ms	6										
1919	9	6	1	45	45					USGS, Song	US: Virginia, Bentonville	美国:弗吉尼亚州本顿维尔	38.8	-78.2		5.1	Mk	6										
1919	9	15	3	50						USGS	Hawaiian Islands	夏威夷群岛	19	-155.5		6.1	Ms	7										
1919	9	15	14	7						USGS, Song	US: California, Eureka	美国:加利福尼亚州尤里卡	40.83	-124.17		5.6	Mk	7										
1919	10	3	9	37	20					*	Fiji Islands: Rabi	斐济群岛:拉比	-16.5	180		6.9	Ms	8						2				
1919	10	7	9	13						GSHAP	Serbia: Cacak	塞尔维亚:查查克	44	20	15	4.6	Ms	6										
1919	10	13	7	54	9					GSHAP	Turkey: Iznik, Izmit	土耳其:伊兹尼克,伊兹米特	40.08	28.86	10	4.5	Ms	5.5										
1919	10	22	6	6		4				* Italy	Italy: Aprilia	意大利:阿普里利亚	41.537	12.684	10	5.6	Ms	8										
1919	10	31	7	53						* Song	Italy: Sansepolcro	意大利:圣塞波尔克罗	43.5	12.1		6.5	Mk	12										
1919	11	13								GSHAP	Brasil: Salvador	巴西:萨尔瓦多	-12.55	-38.7		3.1	Ms	5										
1919	11	16	9	55						GSHAP	Brasil: Salvador	巴西:萨尔瓦多	-12.67	-38.68		3.5	Ms	5										
1919	11	20	14	11	34	1				Engdahl, NOAA	North Vanuatu Islands	瓦努阿图群岛北部	-12.675	166.434	113	6.8	mB											
1919	11	21				4				* Song	Indonesia: Papua	印度尼西亚:巴布亚	-4.13	138		7.3	Mk	8						1				
1919	11	23	4	20						GSHAP	Brasil: Salvador	巴西:萨尔瓦多	-12.65	-38.62		4.2	Ms	7										
1919	11	25	11	3						USGS	US: California, Aptos	美国:加利福尼亚州阿普托斯	37.08	-121.83		4.5	Ms	5										
1919	11	29	0	33						* Song	Italy: Isernia	意大利:伊塞尔尼亚	41.6	14.2		6.5	Mk	12										
1919	12	8	16							China	China: Yunnan, Mile	中国:云南弥勒	24.4	103.5		5.5	Ms	7										
1919	12	15	1	10						USGS, Song	Gulf of Alaska, SE.	阿拉斯加湾东南	57.5	-137		5.1	Mk	6										
1919	12	21	16							China	China: Yunnan, Kaiyuan	中国:云南开远	23.7	103.3		5.5	Ms	7										
1919	12	22	23	41	6					* Song, Turkey	Greece: Thesprotia	希腊:塞斯普罗蒂亚	39.4	20.5		6.3	Mk	9						3				
1919	12	25	21	42	20	1				GSHAP, NOAA	Black Sea	黑海	44.6	34.9	24	5.7	Ms	7										
1919	12	28	18	46	44					GSHAP	Bolivia: Tupiza	玻利维亚:图皮萨	-21.43	-65.72		5.3	Ms	5										
1920	1	1	2	35						USGS	US: California, Santa Ysabel	美国:加利福尼亚州圣伊莎贝尔	33.2	-116.7		5	Ms	6										
1920	1	3	21	48	3					*	Mexico: Veracruz; Puebla	墨西哥:韦拉克鲁斯;普埃布拉	19.26	-96.97		7.8	Ms	10	648	3	167	3		2				
1920	1	11	12	47						GSHAP, Song	Trinidad & Tobago: Port of Spain	特立尼达和多巴哥:西班牙港	10.68	-61.51		5	Mk	6										
1920	1	24	7	9	16					USGS	Canada: British Columbia, Vancouver	加拿大:英属哥伦比亚温哥华	48.8	-123		5.5	Ms	6										
1920	1	29				1	2	1	1	* NOAA, Song	Molukka Sea	马鲁古海	1	126		7.3	Mk											
1920	1	30	18	26	45					GSHAP	Colombia: Vichada, S.	哥伦比亚:维查达南部	3	-71.5		6	Ms	7										
1920	1	31	11	10						GSHAP	Brasil: Campo Grande	巴西:大坎普	-21.03	-44.75		4	Ms	6										
1920	2	2	11	22	14	1				* Engdahl, NOAA	New Britain Trench	新不列颠海沟[太平洋]	-6.474	151.685	35	7.6	Mw											
1920	2	20	0	1	30					GSHAP	Georgia: Gori	格鲁吉亚:哥里	42	44.1	22	4.8	Ms	6										

时间						海啸				资料来源	震中				深度	震级	标度	烈度	死亡人数		受伤人数		经济损失		房屋毁坏		房屋受损	
年	月	日	时	分	秒	源	浪高	级 I	级 S		地名(英文)	地名(中文)	纬度(°)	经度(°)					数量/人	级别	数量/人	级别	数量/$ Mill	级别	数量/间	级别	数量/间	级别
Date						Tsunami				Information	Earthquake Epicenter				Depth	Mag	Scale	MMI	Deaths		Injuries		Damage		Houses Destroyed		Houses Damaged	
Year	Mo	Dy	Hr	Mn	Sec	Sr	Wh	mI	mS		Name(English)	Name(Chinese)	Latitude	Longitude					Num	Dd	Num	Dd	$ Mill	De	Num	Dh	Num	Dh
1920	2	20	11	44	25					*	Georgia:Gori	格鲁吉亚:哥里	42	44.1	11	6.2	Ms		40	1				3				3
1920	6	5	4	21	35					* China, Engdahl	China:Taiwan, Hualien, Coast of E.	中国:台湾花莲以东海域	23.5	122.7	35	8	Mw		5	1	20	1		2	273	3	1257	4
1920	6	22	2	47						USGS	US:California, Los Angeles	美国:加利福尼亚州洛杉矶	34	-118.5		4.9	Ms	8										
1920	6									China	China:Yunnan, Pu-er	中国:云南普洱	22.8	101		4.75	Ms	6										
1920	7	16	18	8						USGS, Song	US:California, Los Angeles	美国:加利福尼亚州洛杉矶	34.1	-118.3		5.1	Mk	6										
1920	7	16	21	27						USGS, Song	US:California, Los Angeles	美国:加利福尼亚州洛杉矶	34.1	-118.3		5.1	Mk	6										
1920	7	16	21	30						USGS, Song	US:California, Los Angeles	美国:加利福尼亚州洛杉矶	34.1	-118.3		5.1	Mk	6										
1920	7	23	3	55						USGS, Song	US:California, Redding	美国:加利福尼亚州雷丁	40.5	-121.83		5.6	Mk	7										
1920	7	26	6	30						GSHAP	Ecuador:Guayaquil	厄瓜多尔:瓜亚基尔	-2.2	-79.9		5	Ms	6										
1920	8	20	16	15	38	3	1.4	0.5	1	* NOAA	Chile:Canete	智利:卡涅特	-38	-73.5	15	7	Ms							2		2		2
1920	9	7	5	55	40					* Italy	Italy:Carrara, Garfagnana	意大利:卡拉拉,弗加法格纳纳	44.18	10.28	10	6.48	Ms	10	1400	4								
1920	9	20	14	39	6	1		1	1.5	* Engdahl, NOAA	New Caledonia: Loyalty Islands	新喀里多尼亚:罗亚尔特群岛	-20.6	168.8	33	7.8	Mw											
1920	9	25								GSHAP	Kyrgyzstan: Jalal - Abad, NW.	吉尔吉斯斯坦:贾拉拉巴德西北	41.5	71	10	5.6	Ms	8										
1920	10	5	19	3	58					USGS	US:California, Salinas	美国:加利福尼亚州萨利纳斯	36.58	-121.67		5.2	Ms	5										
1920	10	7	20	54						GSHAP, Song	Peru:Puerto Maldonado	秘鲁:马尔多纳多港	-12	-69		6	Mk	7										
1920	10									China	China:Gansu, Gulang	中国:甘肃古浪	37.5	102.9		5	Ms	6										
1920	11	26	7	51						* Turkey	Albania:Tepelene, Dragoti	阿尔巴尼亚:台佩莱纳,丹瑞哥帝	40.2	20	25	6.3	Muk	11	600	3								
1920	12	5	11	58						USGS	US:California, Carpinteria	美国:加利福尼亚州卡平特里亚	34.5	-119.5		4.5	Ms	5										
1920	12	6	14	30						GSHAP	Macedonia(Fyrom):Stip	马其顿:斯提普	41.45	22.4	16	4.8	Ms	5.5										
1920	12	16	12	5	55					* China, Engdahl, Dis	China:Ningxia, Haiyuan	中国:宁夏海原	36.7	104.9	25	8.5	Ms	12	200000	5			25.0	4				
1920	12	17	18	59	49					*	Argentina:Mendoza	阿根廷:门多萨	-32.7	-68.4	10	6	Ms	8	400	3				3		3		
1920	12	18	2	1	4	1			5	* NOAA, GSHAP	Albania:Vlore	阿尔巴尼亚:发罗拉	40.5	19.5		6	Ms	10		3				3		3		
1920	12	21	21	33	42					China	China:Xizang (Tibet), Markam	中国:西藏芒康	29	98.5		6	Ms	8										
1920	12	22	5	53	45					GSHAP	Bolivia:Cochabamba	玻利维亚:科恰班巴	-16.97	-65.85		5.3	Ms	5										
1921	1	13	17	42						* Song	Italy:Faentino	意大利:法恩扎	44.3	11.9		6.5	Mk	12										
1921	1	30	16							China	China:Ningxia, Guyuan, W.	中国:宁夏固原西	36	106		5.5	Ms	7										
1921	2	14	16							China	China:Gansu, Wushan	中国:甘肃武山	34.7	104.8		5	Ms	6										

年 Year	月 Mo	日 Dy	时 Hr	分 Mn	秒 Sec	海啸 Tsunami 源 Sr	浪高 Wh	级 I mI	级 S mS	资料来源 Information	震中 Earthquake Epicenter 地名(英文) Name(English)	地名(中文) Name(Chinese)	纬度(°) Latitude	经度(°) Longitude	深度 Depth	震级 Mag	标度 Scale	烈度 MMI	死亡人数 Deaths 数量/人 Num	级别 Dd	受伤人数 Injuries 数量/人 Num	级别 Dd	经济损失 Damage 数量/$ Mill	级别 De	房屋毁坏 Houses Destroyed 数量/间 Num	级别 Dh	房屋受损 Houses Damaged 数量/间 Num	级别 Dh
1921	2	22	5	25						GSHAP	Venezuela:Caracas	委内瑞拉:加拉加斯	10.9	−66.8	15	4.8	Ms	5										
1921	2	22	16							China	China:Gansu,Tongwei	中国:甘肃通渭	35	105.2		5.5	Ms	7										
1921	3	14	12	15						USGS	US:Indiana,Terre Haute	美国:印第安纳州特雷霍特	39.5	−87.5		4.4	Ms	6										
1921	3	24	14	41	52					GSHAP	Russia:Kamchatka Peninsula	俄罗斯:堪察加半岛	51.5	158.2	50	6.7	Ms	7.5										
1921	3	26	16							China	China:Gansu,Jingtai	中国:甘肃景泰	37.1	104.1		5.5	Ms	7										
1921	4	12	9	36						China	China:Ningxia,Guyuan	中国:宁夏固原	35.8	106.2		6.5	Ms	8										
1921	5	3	16							China	China:Gansu,Jingtai	中国:甘肃景泰	37.2	104.2		5	Ms	6										
1921	5	14	11	17	45	2	1		0.5	* NOAA	Indonesia:Makassar Strait	印度尼西亚:望加锡海峡	0.7	117.9		6.2	Ms	8						2		1		1
1921	5	15	7	59						GSHAP	Serbia:Kraljevo	塞尔维亚:克拉列沃	43.4	20.1	22	4.6	Ms	5.5										
1921	7	1	11	48	17					GSHAP	Serbia:Jagodina	塞尔维亚:雅戈丁那	43.9	21.25	5	4.5	Ms	7										
1921	8	4				3				* NOAA,Song	China:Liaoning,Donggang	中国:辽宁东港	40.13	124.38		7.2	Mk							1		1		
1921	8	14	13	15	28					*	Eritrea:Zula	厄立特里亚:祖拉	15.6	39.6		5.9	Ms	8		2				3				
1921	9	11	4	1	26	4	0.1	−2.3	−2	* Engdahl,NOAA	Indonesia:Java Ridge	印度尼西亚:爪哇海岭	−11	111	25	7.3	Mw							1				
1921	9	16	0	51						*	Central African:Nola	中非:诺拉	3.8	16.3		4.8	Muk	8						1				
1921	9	24	1	15						* Song	Italy:Tolentino	意大利:托伦蒂诺	43.2	13.2		6.5	Mk	12										
1921	9	29	14	12						USGS	US:Utah,Richfield	美国:犹他州里奇菲尔德	38.7	−112.1		5.2	Ms	8										
1921	9	30	2	30						USGS,Song	US:Utah,Richfield	美国:犹他州里奇菲尔德	38.7	−112.1		5.6	Mk	7										
1921	10	1	15	32						USGS,Song	US:Utah,Richfield	美国:犹他州里奇菲尔德	38.7	−112.1		6.1	Mk	8										
1921	10	7	9	35	11					GSHAP	Russia:Sakhalin Island	俄罗斯:库页岛(萨哈林岛)	46.4	142.2	22	5.1	Ms	5.5										
1921	10	7								China	China:Shaanxi,Yichuan	中国:陕西宜川	36	110.1		5	Ms	6										
1921	10	10	2	6						* Song	Arafura Sea	亚拉科拉海	−5	135		5.9	Mk	7						2				
1921	11	7	16	2						* Song	Philippines:Mindanao Island	菲律宾:棉兰老岛	7.1	126.3		5.9	Mk	7						2				
1921	11	11	18	36	26	3		0.5	1	* Engdahl,NOAA	Philippine Trench	菲律宾海沟	8	127	35	7.3	Mw	7						1		1		
1921	11	22	16							China	China:Gansu,Huating,S.	中国:甘肃华亭南	35.1	106.7		4.75	Ms	6										
1921	11	28	14							China	China:Ningxia,Yinchuan	中国:宁夏银川	38.5	106.3		5.5	Ms	7										
1921	12	1	14	25						* Song	Italy:Castel Giorgio	意大利:乔治堡	42.7	12		6.5	Mk	12										
1921										GSHAP	China:Xinjiang,Ili	中国:新疆伊犁	43.9	81.4	15	6.5	Ms	8										
1922	1	2	14	50						USGS,Song	US:South Dakota,Chamberlain	美国:南达科他州张伯伦	43.8	−99.3		5.1	Mk	6										
1922	1	6	14	10	44	2				* Shi Z.,Engdahl,NOAA	Peru:Tarapaca,Off Coast of W.	秘鲁:塔拉帕卡西部沿海	−20.408	−76.389	25	7.1	Mw											
1922	1	19	21	58	50	3	1.8			* NOAA	Papua New Guinea:Honinabi,SW.	巴布亚新几内亚:霍尼纳比西南	−7	143		7.5	Ms							1		1		

时间						海啸				资料来源	震中				深度	震级	标度	烈度	死亡人数		受伤人数		经济损失		房屋毁坏		房屋受损	
年	月	日	时	分	秒	源	浪高	级 I	级 S		地名(英文)	地名(中文)	纬度(°)	经度(°)					数量/人	级别	数量/人	级别	数量/$ Mill	级别	数量/间	级别	数量/间	级别
Date						Tsunami				Information	Earthquake Epicenter				Depth	Mag	Scale	MMI	Deaths		Injuries		Damage		Houses Destroyed		Houses Damaged	
Year	Mo	Dy	Hr	Mn	Sec	Sr	Wh	mI	mS		Name(English)	Name(Chinese)	Latitude	Longitude					Num	Dd	Num	Dd	$ Mill	De	Num	Dh	Num	Dh
1922	1	27	6	50	40					GSHAP	Brasil:Sao Paulo	巴西:圣保罗	-22.17	-47.04	15	5.1	Ms	6										
1922	1	27	20	41						* Song	Philippines:Cebu Island	菲律宾:宿务岛	10.2	123.5		5.9	Mk	8						2				
1922	1	31	13	17	29					* Engdahl	US:California, Off Coast N.	美国:加利福尼亚州北部沿海	41	-125.5	15	7.3	M							1				
1922	2	16	3	14	48					*	Venezuela:Punto Fijo	委内瑞拉:蓬托菲霍	11.7	-70.85		6.4	Ms							3				
1922	2	22				1			0.5	* NOAA, Song	Indonesia:Maluku Islands	印度尼西亚:摩鹿加群岛	-3.3	128.9		7	Mk											
1922	2	28	1	14		4	0.7	-0.5		* Nakamura, NOAA	Philippines:Cebu Island	菲律宾:宿务岛	10.2	123.5		6.3	Ms		5	1				2				
1922	3	1	9	1		2			0.5	* Nakamura, NOAA	Philippines:Siaton	菲律宾:绍雷(绍拉)	9	123		6	Ms	8						2				
1922	3	4	13	7	45					GSHAP, Engdahl	Russia:Kamchatka Peninsula	俄罗斯:堪察加半岛	52.924	157.181	241.4	7.1	mB	5.5										
1922	3	10	11	21	20					USGS	US:California, Shandon	美国:加利福尼亚州尚登	35.75	-120.25		6.5	Ms	9										
1922	3	16	23	11						USGS	US:California, Parkfield	美国:加利福尼亚州帕克菲尔德	35.75	-120.33		5	Ms	5										
1922	3	22	22	29	10					USGS	US:Missouri, Cape Girardeau	美国:密苏里州开普吉拉多	37.4	-89.4		4.8	Ms	7										
1922	3	23	2	22						USGS	US:Missouri, Cape Girardeau	美国:密苏里州开普吉拉多	37.4	-89.4		4.6	Ms	6										
1922	3	24	12	22						*	Serbia:Cacak	塞尔维亚:查查克	44.4	20.4	12	6	Muk	10		3				3				
1922	4	6	2	36						GSHAP	Ecuador:Quito	厄瓜多尔:基多	-0.2	-78.6		5	Ms	6										
1922	4	10				1			0	* NOAA, Song	Indonesia:Southern Sumatra	印度尼西亚:苏门答腊南部	-3.5	102.5		7	Mk											
1922	4	26	1	11						Engdahl, Usami, Japan	Japan:Yokosuka	日本:神奈川横须贺	35.2	139.8	35	6.8	Mj		2	1	21	1			3	1	20	1
1922	5	2	20	24		2	0.6			* NOAA, Song	Puerto Rico:Vieques	波多黎各:别克斯岛	18.2	-65.5		7	Mk											
1922	5	11	6	45	35					GSHAP	Trinidad & Tobago: Northern Coast	特立尼达和多巴哥:北部近海	12	-59.5	33	6	Ms	5										
1922	5	22	17	33	18					GSHAP	Panama:Off Coast of S.	巴拿马:南部海域	7.5	-79		6	Ms	7										
1922	5	27	2	35						* Song	Italy:Venice	意大利:威尼斯	45.2	12.7		6.5	Mk	12										
1922	7	8				1			0	* NOAA, Song	Indonesia:Sumatera, Banda Aceh	印度尼西亚:苏门答腊,班达亚齐	5.467	95.233		7	Mk											
1922	8	8	3	49	6	2				Turkey, NOAA	Greece:Argolida	希腊:阿尔戈利斯	37.5	23.2		5.6	Ms											
1922	8	8								GSHAP, Song	Venezuela:Cariaco	委内瑞拉:卡利亚科	10.68	-63.14		5	Mk	6										
1922	8	16	15	56	33					GSHAP	Russia:Kamchatka Peninsula	俄罗斯:堪察加半岛	53.5	159	50	6.6	Ms	7.5										
1922	8	18	5	12						CGS, USGS	US:California, Shandon	美国:加利福尼亚州尚登	35.75	-120.25		5.5	Ms	5										

年 Year	月 Mo	日 Dy	时 Hr	分 Mn	秒 Sec	海啸 Tsunami 源 Sr	浪高 Wh	级 I mI	级 S mS	资料来源 Information	震中 Earthquake Epicenter 地名(英文) Name(English)	地名(中文) Name(Chinese)	纬度(°) Latitude	经度(°) Longitude	深度 Depth	震级 Mag	标度 Scale	烈度 MMI	死亡人数 Deaths 数量/人 Num	级别 Dd	受伤人数 Injuries 数量/人 Num	级别 Dd	经济损失 Damage 数量/$ Mill	级别 De	房屋毁坏 Houses Destroyed 数量/间 Num	级别 Dh	房屋受损 Houses Damaged 数量/间 Num	级别 Dh
1922	8	25	11	47	49					*	Algeria: Bordj Abou El Hasen, Dahra	阿尔及利亚:阿布哈桑堡,赫尔	36.3	1.3		5.1	Ms	10										
1922	8	25	19	29	40					GSHAP	Mongolia: Turgen	蒙古:图尔根	50	91	16	6.5	Ms	8.5										
1922	8	30	11	40						China	China: Ningxia, Guyuan	中国:宁夏固原	36	106.2		5.5	Ms	7										
1922	9	1	19	16	9	1				* China, Engdahl, NOAA	China: Taiwan, Yilan, Coast of E.	中国:台湾宜兰以东海域	24.5	122	35	7.6	Mw		5	1	7	1		2	139	3	161	3
1922	9	14	19	31	43					China, Engdahl	China: Taiwan, Yilan, Coast of E.	中国:台湾宜兰以东海域	24.6	122.3	35	7.1	Mw				5	1			24	1	389	3
1922	9	16	22	44	36					China	China: Taiwan, Hualien, Coast of E.	中国:台湾花莲以东海域	23.9	122.5		6.25	Ms				1	1			6	1	197	3
1922	10	11	14	50	6					* Shi Z., Engdahl	Peru: Arequipa	秘鲁:阿雷基帕	-16.125	-72.385	160	7.6	mB	7						2		3		2
1922	10	14	23	45						China, Engdahl	China: Taiwan, Yilan, Coast of E.	中国:台湾宜兰以东海域	24.5	122	35	6.9	Ms		6	1	2	1					14	1
1922	10	22				1				NOAA, Song	Australia: Tasman Sea	澳大利亚:塔斯曼海	-43.3	148.9		7	Mk											
1922	10	24	21	21	3					* Engdahl	Kuril Islands	千岛群岛	47	151.8	35	7.3	mB							1				
1922	11	7	23	0	15	2				* Engdahl, Shi Z., NOAA	Chile: Huasco, Near Coast	智利:瓦斯科近海	-28	-72	25	7.1	Ms											
1922	11	11	4	32	45	4	9	3.2	2.5	* Engdahl, NOAA	Chile: Atacama	智利:阿塔卡马	-28.553	-70.755	35	8.7	Mw		700	3				3				
1922	11	20	4	24	44					GSHAP	Turkey: Denizli	土耳其:登尼资里	37.5	29	28	4.9	Ms	5.5										
1922	11	24	2	15	40					GSHAP	Croatia: Osijek	克罗地亚:奥西耶克	45.6	18.7	18	5.3	Ms	7										
1922	11	24	2	28						GSHAP	Croatia: Osijek	克罗地亚:奥西耶克	45.7	18.8	26	4.8	Ms	5.5										
1922	11	27	3	31						USGS	US: Illinois, Eldorado	美国:伊利诺斯州埃尔多拉多	37.8	-88.5		4.8	Ms	7										
1922	12	2	3	46	36					China	China: Taiwan, Yilan, Coast of E.	中国:台湾宜兰以东海域	24.6	122		6.25	Ms		1	1	2	1			1	1	33	1
1922	12	7	16	50						* Engdahl, Usami, Japan	Japan: Nagasaki	日本:长崎	32.7	130.1	5	6.9	Mj		27	1	39	1		1	654	3	767	3
1922	12	8	2	2						Engdahl, Japan	Japan: Nagasaki	日本:长崎	32.7	130.1	5	6.5	Mj		3	1					70	2		
1922	12	25	3	33	10	3	0.4			* NOAA	New Zealand: South Island, Greta Valley	新西兰:南岛,格里塔瓦利	-43	173		6.3	Ms	7										
1923	1	1	17	55						GSHAP, Italy	Croatia: Rijeka	克罗地亚:里耶卡	45.9	14.4	7	5.03	Ms	6.5										
1923	1	11	4	29						USGS	US: Oregon, Lakeview	美国:俄勒冈州莱克维尤	42.2	-120.3		5	Ms	6										
1923	1	14	5	51						Usami, Japan	Japan: Ibaraki	日本:茨城	36.1	139.9		6.3	Ms				1	1						
1923	1	14	12	59	25					USGS, Song	Hawaiian Islands	夏威夷群岛	19	-155.5		5.1	Mk	6										
1923	1	22	9	4	20					* Engdahl	US: California, North Coast	美国:加利福尼亚州北部近海	40.8	-124.5	15	7.2	M	8						1				
1923	2	2	5	7	43					Shi Z., GSHAP, Engdahl	Russia: Kamchatka, Near East Coast	俄罗斯:堪察加东部近海	53.5	162	20	7.1	Mw	9.5										

时间 年 Year	月 Mo	日 Dy	时 Hr	分 Mn	秒 Sec	海啸 源 Sr	浪高 Wh	级I mI	级S mS	资料来源 Information	震中 地名(英文) Name(English)	地名(中文) Name(Chinese)	纬度(°) Latitude	经度(°) Longitude	深度 Depth	震级 Mag	标度 Scale	烈度 MMI	死亡人数 Deaths 数量/人 Num	级别 Dd	受伤人数 Injuries 数量/人 Num	级别 Dd	经济损失 Damage 数量/$ Mill	级别 De	房屋毁坏 Houses Destroyed 数量/间 Num	级别 Dh	房屋受损 Houses Damaged 数量/间 Num	级别 Dh
1923	2	3	16	1	49	4	8	3		* GSHAP, Engdahl, NOAA	Russia: Kamchatka Peninsula	俄罗斯:堪察加半岛	53.853	160.761	35	8.5	Mw	11	3	1			1.5	2				
1923	2	4								*	Iran: Bojnurd	伊朗:博季努尔德	37.6	57.3	10	5.5	Muk	8						2				
1923	2	5	12	22						GSHAP	Ecuador: Quito	厄瓜多尔:基多	-0.5	-78.6		6.3	Ms	8										
1923	2	12	18	19						USGS, Song	US: Washington, Seattle	美国:华盛顿州西雅图	48.8	-122.4		5.1	Mk	6										
1923	2	24	0	25						*	Ecuador: Quito	厄瓜多尔:基多	-0.4	-78.3		6.8	Ms	9		2								
1923	2	24	7	34	44					* GSHAP, Shi Z., Engdahl	Russia: Komandorsky Islands	俄罗斯:科曼多尔群岛	55	162.4	20	7.2	Mw							1				
1923	3	2	16	48	45	3			0.5	* Nakamura, Bautista, Engdahl, NOAA	Philippines: Mindanao Island	菲律宾:棉兰老岛	6.5	124	86.6	7.1	Mw	7										
1923	3	4				1	35		4	NOAA, Song	Chile: San Felix Island	智利:圣费利克斯岛	-26.3	-80.1		8.1	Mk											
1923	3	15	5	40						* GSHAP	Croatia: Split, SE.	克罗地亚:斯普利特东南	43.3	17.3	16	6.2	Mk	10						3				
1923	3	24	12	40	20					* China, Engdahl	China: Sichuan, Luhuo	中国:四川炉霍	31.5	101	25	7.2	Mw	10	4800	4				3		4		
1923	4	13	15	31	0	4	20	4.9	3.5	* GSHAP, Engdahl, NOAA	Russia: Kamchatka, Near East Coast	俄罗斯:堪察加东部近海	55.4	162.8	20	7.1	Mw	10	18	1	400	3		3		3		
1923	4	23	6	51	9					GSHAP	Russia: Vladikavkaz	俄罗斯:符拉迪克奥克兹	43	44.2	5	4.8	Ms	8										
1923	5	4	22	26	51	1				* Shi Z, Engdahl, NOAA, Chile	Chile: Near Coast of C.	智利:中部近海	-28.75	-71.75	105.8	6.7	mB							2		2		2
1923	5	9	9							* Song	Italy: Pieve Santo Stefano	意大利:皮耶韦-圣斯特凡诺	43.7	12		6.5	Mk	12										
1923	5	12	22	57	23					GSHAP	Georgia: Bolnisi	格鲁吉亚:博尔尼西	41.4	44.3	20	5.2	Ms	6										
1923	5	15								* Song	Indonesia: Java Island	印度尼西亚:爪哇岛	-7.7	109.2		6.5	Mk	9						2				
1923	5	16	15	46						GSHAP, Song	Ecuador: Quito	厄瓜多尔:基多	-0.22	-78.5		6	Mk	7										
1923	5	23	22	37						GSHAP	Russia: Kamchatka, Near East Coast	俄罗斯:堪察加东部近海	52.5	163.5	20	6.4	Ms	8.5										
1923	5	25	22	21						*	Iran: Torbat HEydarīyeh	伊朗:托尔巴特海达里耶	35.2	59.2		5.7	Ms	10	2200	4								
1923	6	1	17	24	47	4	0.4	-1.3		* Engdahl, NOAA	Japan Trench	日本海沟	35.674	141.767	35	7.1	Mw											
1923	6	13	16							China	China: Sichuan, Luhuo	中国:四川炉霍	31.3	100.8		5.75	Ms	7										
1923	7	1	7	54	55					China	China: Yunnan, Menghai	中国:云南勐海	22	100.5		6.5	Ms		1	1	10	1			420	3		
1923	7	13	11	13	41	4				Engdahl, Usami, Japan	Japan: Kagoshima, Near Coast	日本:鹿岛近海	31	130.9	35	7.1	Ms										20	1
1923	7	18				3		0.5	1	* NOAA	Philippines: Surigao	菲律宾:苏里高	9.5	125	33	5.5	Ms											
1923	7	23	7	30	26					USGS, Shi Z.	US: California, Riverside	美国:加利福尼亚州里弗赛德	34	-117.25		6.25	Ms	7										
1923	8	8	12	1	27					GSHAP	Venezuela: Cariaco	委内瑞拉:卡利亚科	10.5	-63.5	100	6.5	Ms	5										
1923	8	11	16							China	China: Gansu, Lanzhou	中国:甘肃兰州	36.2	103.7		5	Ms	6										
1923	8	12	12	11		2	0.7	-0.5		* NOAA, Song	Chile: Arica	智利:阿里卡	-18.5	-70.3	33	7	Mk											

年	月	日	时	分	秒	源	浪高	级 I	级 S	资料来源	地名(英文)	地名(中文)	纬度(°)	经度(°)	深度	震级	标度	烈度	死亡人数 数量/人	死亡人数 级别	受伤人数 数量/人	受伤人数 级别	经济损失 数量/$ Mill	经济损失 级别	房屋毁坏 数量/间	房屋毁坏 级别	房屋受损 数量/间	房屋受损 级别
Date						Tsunami				Information	Earthquake Epicenter				Depth	Mag	Scale	MMI	Deaths		Injuries		Damage		Houses Destroyed		Houses Damaged	
Year	Mo	Dy	Hr	Mn	Sec	Sr	Wh	mI	mS		Name(English)	Name(Chinese)	Latitude	Longitude					Num	Dd	Num	Dd	$ Mill	De	Num	Dh	Num	Dh
1923	8									China	China:Sichuan,Mianning	中国:四川冕宁	28.7	102.2		5.5	Ms	7										
1923	9	1	2	58	37	4	13	3.6	3	* Usami, Engdahl, NOAA	Japan:Tokyo, Yokohama	日本:东京,横滨	35.1	139.5	35	7.9	M		142807	5	103733	5	600	5	128266	5	574299	5
1923	9	1	16							China	China:Ningxia,Guyuan	中国:宁夏固原	36	106.2		5	Ms	6										
1923	9	2	2	46	46	4	0.3	-1.7		*Engdahl,NOAA	Japan:Miura	日本:神奈川三浦	35	139.5	35	7.6	Mw											
1923	9	2	22	38	8					GSHAP,Engdahl	Bolivia:El Alto	玻利维亚:埃尔阿尔托	-16	-68.5	35	6.8	mB	6										
1923	9	3	16							China	China:Ningxia,Haiyuan	中国:宁夏海原	36.6	105.6		5.5	Ms	7										
1923	9	4	1							GSHAP	Russia:Sakhalin Island	俄罗斯:库页岛(萨哈林岛)	47.7	142.3	14	5.2	Ms	6										
1923	9	9	4	16	25					GSHAP	Colombia:Puerto Leguizamo	哥伦比亚:莱吉萨莫港	0	-75		4.5	Ms	5										
1923	9	9	4	18	10					GSHAP	Panama:Garachiné,S.	巴拿马:加拉奇内南部	7.5	-79		4.5	Ms	5										
1923	9	11	10	14	48					GSHAP	Turkey:Denizli	土耳其:登尼资里	38	29.5	22	4.6	Ms	5.5										
1923	9	13	16							China	China:Hebei,Gaobeidian	中国:河北高碑店	39.4	115.8		5.5	Ms	7										
1923	9	14	12	57	31					GSHAP	Mongolia:North – West of Uliastay	蒙古:乌里雅苏台市西北	48	96	11	6	Ms	8.5										
1923	9	15	16							China	China:Henan,Fanxian	中国:河南范县	35.7	115.4		5	Ms	6										
1923	9	17	7	9	7					*	Iran:Bojnurd	伊朗:博季努尔德	37.2	57.7		6.4	Ms	9	157	3				3				
1923	9	22	20	47	45					* Engdahl	Iran:Kerman	伊朗:克尔曼	29.2	56.9	35	6.9	Muk		290	3								
1923	9	23								GSHAP	Mongolia:Bayan Ula	蒙古:巴彦乌拉	47	95	15	5.1	Ms	6.5										
1923	10	14	16							China	China:Inner Mongolia,Zalantun	中国:内蒙古扎兰屯	48.5	122.5		5	Ms	6										
1923	10	26	12	13	16					GSHAP	Turkey:Istanbul	土耳其:伊斯坦布尔	41.2	28.6	24	5	Ms	5.5										
1923	10	28	17	10						USGS	US:Arkansas,Marked Tree	美国:阿肯色州马克德特里	35.5	-90.4		4.8	Ms	7										
1923	10									China	China:Shaanxi,Ansai	中国:陕西安塞	37.1	109.2		5.5	Ms	7										
1923	11	2	21	8	11	3				* Engdahl, NOAA	Papua New Guinea: East New Britain	巴布亚新几内亚:东新不列颠	-4.5	151.5	50	7.2	mB											
1923	11	4	0	4	48	1				* Engdahl, NOAA	Papua New Guinea: East New Britain	巴布亚新几内亚:东新不列颠	-5	152	148.5	6.9	mB											
1923	11	5	22	7						USGS	Mexico:Mexicali	墨西哥:墨西卡利	32.5	-115.5		5	Ms	7										
1923	11	7	23	57						USGS	US:California,El Centro	美国:加利福尼亚州埃尔森特罗	32.5	-115.5		5.7	Ms	7										
1923	11	13	6	30						China	China:Shanxi,Kelan,W.	中国:山西岢岚西	38.7	111.1		5.5	Ms	7										
1923	12	14	10	31						* GSHAP	Colombia:Narino	哥伦比亚:纳里尼奥	1	-77.5		6.3	Muk	9	300	3				3				
1923	12	15	18	59						* Song	Italy:Alatri	意大利:阿特拉里	41.7	13.5		6.5	Mk	12										
1923	12	16	7	36	40					GSHAP	Colombia:Pasto	哥伦比亚:帕斯托	1	-77		4	Ms	5										
1923	12	22	9	55						* Song	Colombia:Gachala,Gacheta	哥伦比亚:嘎查拉,加奇塔	5.2	-73.2		7	Mk	10	7	1				3				
1923	12	23	17	4						GSHAP	Bulgaria:Asenovgrad	保加利亚:阿塞诺夫格勒	42.1	24.8	8	4.8	Ms	6.5										

时间 Date						海啸 Tsunami				资料来源 Information	震中 Earthquake Epicenter				深度 Depth	震级 Mag	标度 Scale	烈度 MMI	死亡人数 Deaths		受伤人数 Injuries		经济损失 Damage		房屋毁坏 Houses Destroyed		房屋受损 Houses Damaged	
年 Year	月 Mo	日 Dy	时 Hr	分 Mn	秒 Sec	源 Sr	浪高 Wh	级 I mI	级 S mS		地名(英文) Name(English)	地名(中文) Name(Chinese)	纬度(°) Latitude	经度(°) Longitude					数量/人 Num	级别 Dd	数量/人 Num	级别 Dd	数量/$ Mill $ Mill	级别 De	数量/间 Num	级别 Dh	数量/间 Num	级别 Dh
1923	12	28	22	24	48					GSHAP	Tajikistan:Leninobod	塔吉克斯坦:列宁纳巴德	39.6	69.2	18	6.4	Ms	8										
1924	1	1	3	5						USGS	US:Arkansas,Blytheville	美国:阿肯色州布莱斯维尔	36	-90		4.5	Ms	6										
1924	1	1	15	16	30					GSHAP	Tajikistan:Khodjend,N.	塔吉克斯坦:苦盏北部	41	70.5	20	5	Ms	6										
1924	1	7								GSHAP	Colombia:Medina	哥伦比亚:昆地那马加的梅迪纳	4.7	-73.5		6.3	Ms	8										
1924	1	13	3							GSHAP	Colombia:Narino	哥伦比亚:纳里尼奥	0.92	-77.78		7	Ms	9										
1924	1	15	20	50						*Engdahl,Usami	Japan:Kanagawa	日本:神奈川	35.5	139.5	5	7.3	Mj		19	1	638	3		3	1302	4	2439	4
1924	1	28	3	43	28					GSHAP	Colombia:Vaupes,NE.	哥伦比亚:沃佩斯东北	1	-70		5.5	Ms	5										
1924	3	3	8	1						*	Ecuador:Chimborazo,N.	厄瓜多尔:钦博腊索山北部	-1.6	-78.6		6.9	Muk		40	1				1				
1924	3	15	10	31	24	4				*GSHAP,Engdahl,Usami	Russia:Sakhalin Island	俄罗斯:库页岛(萨哈林岛)	49.126	143.142	35	6.9	Ms	8.5							4	1		
1924	3	15	12	46	44					GSHAP	Russia:Sakhalin Island	俄罗斯:库页岛(萨哈林岛)	49.2	141.9	13	5	Ms	6.5										
1924	3	16	1	22	36					GSHAP	Colombia:Amazonas,S.	哥伦比亚:亚马孙南部	-2	-72		5.5	Ms	6										
1924	3	16	20	51	3					GSHAP	Russia:Sakhalin Island	俄罗斯:库页岛(萨哈林岛)	49.3	141.9	13	5.5	Ms	7										
1924	3	16								*	Algeria:Batna	阿尔及利亚:巴特纳	35.1	5.2		5.6	Muk	9		3								
1924	3	17	14	4	9					GSHAP	Russia:Sakhalin Island	俄罗斯:库页岛(萨哈林岛)	49.3	141.9	18	5.2	Ms	5.5										
1924	4	3	23	54						USGS	US:California,Morgan Hill	美国:加利福尼亚州莫干山	37.33	-121.67		4.5	Ms	5										
1924	4	11	13	38	44					GSHAP	Russia:Sakhalin Island	俄罗斯:库页岛(萨哈林岛)	49.7	141.9	13	5.5	Ms	7										
1924	4	14	16	20	41	4			0.5	*Bautista,Engdahl,NOAA	Philippines:Mindanao,Mati	菲律宾:棉兰老岛,马蒂	6.5	126.5	35	8.2	Mw	9						3		3		
1924	4	16	4	21						GSHAP	Azerbaijan:Gence,N.	阿塞拜疆:占贾北部	41.7	46.5	10	4.6	Ms	6.5										
1924	5	6	16	9	31	2		1		*Bautista,Engdahl,Wang S.,NOAA	Philippines:Santa Cruz,Off Coast of W.	菲律宾:圣克鲁斯西部沿海	15.935	118.95	35	7	Ms							1				
1924	5	13	1	52	33					*GSHAP,Iran	Turkey:Erzurum	土耳其:埃尔佐鲁姆	40	42	30	5.3	Ms	9	50	1				2		3		
1924	5	31	11	38	1					GSHAP	Azerbaijan:Samaxi	阿塞拜疆:沙马基区	40.5	47.5	28	4.7	Ms	5.5										
1924	6	22	22	29	8					GSHAP	Colombia:Near Coast	哥伦比亚:近海	5.5	-78.5	60	6.5	Ms	7										
1924	6	26	1	37	33	3				*Engdahl,NOAA	Australia:Macquarie Island,S.	澳大利亚:麦加利岛南部	-56	157.5	25	8.3	Mw											
1924	6	30	15	44	26					*Engdahl	Kuril Islands	千岛群岛	45.1	147.4	120	7.2	mB							1				
1924	7	3	4	40	15					*China,Engdahl	China:Xinjiang,Niya,E.	中国:新疆民丰东	36.8	83.8	35	7.1	Mw	10	100	2				2		2		
1924	7	6	18	31	51					GSHAP	Kyrgyzstan:Osh,NE.	吉尔吉斯斯坦:奥什东北	40.5	73.1	22	6.4	Ms	7.5										

年 Year	月 Mo	日 Dy	时 Hr	分 Mn	秒 Sec	海啸 Tsunami 源 Sr	浪高 Wh	级 I mI	级 S mS	资料来源 Information	震中 Earthquake Epicenter 地名(英文) Name(English)	地名(中文) Name(Chinese)	纬度(°) Latitude	经度(°) Longitude	深度 Depth	震级 Mag	标度 Scale	烈度 MMI	死亡人数 Deaths 数量/人 Num	级别 Dd	受伤人数 Injuries 数量/人 Num	级别 Dd	经济损失 Damage 数量/$ Mill	级别 De	房屋毁坏 Houses Destroyed 数量/间 Num	级别 Dh	房屋受损 Houses Damaged 数量/间 Num	级别 Dh
1924	7	12	15	12	40					Engdahl,GSHAP	Kyrgyzstan:Osh,NE.	吉尔吉斯斯坦:奥什东北	40.565	73.397	25	6.8	Muk	8.5										
1924	7	20	0	21	40					GSHAP	Panama:Garachiné,S.	巴拿马:加拉奇内南部	7.5	-79		4.5	Ms	5										
1924	7	21				1			1	NOAA,Song	New Zealand:Chatham Islands	新西兰:查塔姆群岛	-43.95	-176.567		7.3	Mk							1				
1924	8	12	16	27	25					GSHAP	Croatia:Osijek	克罗地亚:奥西耶克	45.8	18.9	7	4.9	Ms	7										
1924	8	20	16	50						USGS	Hawaiian Islands	夏威夷群岛	19.25	-155.55		5	Ms	5										
1924	8	25	23	6	54					GSHAP	Russia:Komandorsky Islands	俄罗斯:科曼多尔群岛	55	162.5	20	6	Ms	8										
1924	8	28				1				* NOAA,Song	Iceland:Raudhamelur	冰岛:勒伊扎梅勒	64.15	-21.95		7	Mk											
1924	8	30	3	5	3	2			0.5	* Engdahl,NOAA	Philippines:Mindanao,Surigao	菲律宾:棉兰老岛,苏利高	8.5	126.5	35	7.2	Mw	9						2				
1924	9	11	3	33						USGS,Song	Hawaiian Islands	夏威夷群岛	19	-155.5		4.9	Mk	5										
1924	9	13	14	34	17					* Engdahl	Turkey:Erzurum	土耳其:埃尔佐鲁姆	39.864	41.876	35	6.8	Ms	10	60	2				2	380	3		
1924	9	23	2	22						GSHAP	Azerbaijan:Gəncə	阿塞拜疆:占贾	40.3	46.5	17	4.8	Ms	6										
1924	9	27	10	12						GSHAP	Caspian Sea	里海	37	53	16	5.1	Ms	6.5										
1924	10	9	5	41						GSHAP	Azerbaijan:Qebele,SE.	阿塞拜疆:盖贝莱区东南	40.9	48.6	18	5.2	Ms	6										
1924	10	20	19	52	44					GSHAP	Russia:Komandorsky Islands	俄罗斯:科曼多尔群岛	55	165.5	20	6.4	Ms	8.5										
1924	10	24	2							* Song	Italy:Ancona	意大利:安科纳	43.8	13.2		6.5	Mk	12										
1924	11	12								* Song	Indonesia:Java Island	印度尼西亚:爪哇岛	-7.2	109.5		6.1	Mk		60	2								
1924	11	25	7	10						USGS,Song	US:Idaho,Montpelier	美国:爱达荷州蒙特佩利尔	42.5	-111.5		5.1	Mk	6										
1924	11	28	8	45						* Song	Italy:Terni	意大利:特尔尼	42.5	12.7		6.5	Mk	12										
1924	12	2								* Song	Indonesia:Java Island	印度尼西亚:爪哇岛	-7.3	109.9		6.5	Mk	9	727	3				3				
1924	12	3	21	34	45					GSHAP,Italy	Slovenia:Brezice	斯洛文尼亚:布雷日采	45.9	15.6	7	5.3	Ms	7										
1924	12	23	17	4	50					GSHAP	Bulgaria:Asenovgrad	保加利亚:阿塞诺夫格勒	42.1	24.7	22	5.3	Ms	6										
1924	12	28	4	21						USGS	US:California,Salinas	美国:加利福尼亚州萨利纳斯	36.67	-121.67		4	Ms	6										
1924	12	28	22	55	5	1				* Shi Z,GSHAP,Engdahl	Kuril Islands	千岛群岛	43.397	146.579	35	7	Ms											
1925	1	7	11	6	42					GSHAP	Macedonia(Fyrom):Stip	马其顿:斯提普	42	22.4	30	4.7	Ms	5										
1925	1	8				2	0.7	-0.5		* NOAA,Song	Indonesia:Banda Sea	印度尼西亚:班达海	-5.25	130.5		7	Mk											
1925	1	9	17	38	24					* Turkey	Turkey:Ardahan	土耳其:阿尔达汉	41.1	42.4	60	6	Ms	8	200	3								
1925	1	11	16							China	China:Xizang(Tibet),Damxung	中国:西藏当雄	30.5	91.5		5.5	Ms	7										
1925	1	26	16							China	China:Guangdong,Heping	中国:广东和平	24.4	114.9		5	Ms	6										
1925	2	12	6	28	30					GSHAP	Georgia:Borzhomi	格鲁吉亚:博尔若米	41.5	43.5	23	4.8	Ms	6										
1925	2	23	23	53	36	3	1.4	0.5	1	* USGS,NOAA	Gulf of Alaska	阿拉斯加湾	60	-146		6	Ms	7						1				

时间 Date						海啸 Tsunami				资料来源 Information	震中 Earthquake Epicenter				深度 Depth	震级 Mag	标度 Scale	烈度 MMI	死亡人数 Deaths		受伤人数 Injuries		经济损失 Damage		房屋毁坏 Houses Destroyed		房屋受损 Houses Damaged	
年 Year	月 Mo	日 Dy	时 Hr	分 Mn	秒 Sec	源 Sr	浪高 Wh	级 I mI	级 S mS		地名(英文) Name(English)	地名(中文) Name(Chinese)	纬度(°) Latitude	经度(°) Longitude					数量/人 Num	级别 Dd	数量/人 Num	级别 Dd	数量/$ Mill $ Mill	级别 De	数量/间 Num	级别 Dh	数量/间 Num	级别 Dh
1925	3	1	23	42						* Song	Italy: Belluno	意大利:贝卢诺	46. 1	12. 2		6. 5	Mk	12										
1925	3	14	16							China	China: Yunnan, Dali	中国:云南大理	25. 7	100. 2		4. 75	Ms	6										
1925	3	16	14	42	19					* China, Engdahl	China: Yunnan, Dali	中国:云南大理	25. 7	100. 4	26	7	Ms	9	5000	4		4		4		4		
1925	3	20	2							* Song	Italy: Sinalunga	意大利:锡纳伦加	43. 2	10. 9		6. 5	Mk	12										
1925	4	2	16							China	China: Yunnan, Dali	中国:云南大理	25. 6	100. 2		5. 5	Ms	7										
1925	4	15	16							China	China: Yunnan, Midu	中国:云南弥渡	25. 3	100. 5		5	Ms	6										
1925	4	16	3	30						USGS, Song	Mexico: Mexicali	墨西哥:墨西卡利	32. 5	-115. 5		5. 1	Mk	6										
1925	4	27	4	5						USGS	US: Indiana, Evansville	美国:印第安纳州埃文斯维尔	38. 2	-87. 8		4. 8	Ms	6										
1925	5	5	10	6	6	2			0. 5	* NOAA	Philippines: Bayawan	菲律宾:巴亚万	9. 3	122. 7	35	6. 8	Ms		17	1				2		2		2
1925	5	7	4	30						* Song	Italy: Sinalunga	意大利:锡纳伦加	43. 2	10. 8		6. 5	Mk	12										
1925	5	13	22	51	17					GSHAP	Georgia: Akhalkalaki	格鲁吉亚:阿卡卡垃吉	41. 3	43. 6	18	5. 1	Ms	6. 5										
1925	5	15	11	57	5	2				* Engdahl, Chile, NOAA	Chile: Taltal	智利:塔尔塔尔	-25. 5	-70. 546	35	7. 1	Ms											
1925	5	23	2	9	50					* Usami, Japan, Engdahl	Japan: Toyooka	日本:兵库丰冈	35. 75	134. 75	5	6. 8	Ms		465	3	834	3		4	4061	4		
1925	5	25	3	43	6	3		-0. 5	0. 5	* NOAA	Philippines: Looc	菲律宾:洛克	12. 2	122. 1	10	6. 3	Ms	7										
1925	5									China	China: Guangxi, Pingguo	中国:广西平果	23. 4	107. 5		4. 75	Ms	6										
1925	6	7	23	41	39					Engdahl, GSHAP	Colombia: Tulua	哥伦比亚:图卢阿	4. 029	-76. 079	35	6. 8	Muk	7										
1925	6	28	1	21	11					* USGS, Engdahl	US: Montana, Townsend	美国:蒙大纳州汤森	46. 5	-111. 473	15	6. 6	M	8					0. 15	1				2
1925	6	28	2	5	27					USGS, Song	US: Montana, Townsend	美国:蒙大纳州汤森	46. 4	-111. 2		5. 6	Mk	7										
1925	6	28	4	20						USGS, Song	US: Montana, Townsend	美国:蒙大纳州汤森	46. 4	-111. 2		5. 1	Mk	6										
1925	6	29	14	42	16					*	US: California, Santa Barbara	美国:加利福尼亚州圣巴巴拉	34. 5	-119. 6		6. 2	Muk	9	13	1			8. 0	3				
1925	7	3	16	37						USGS, Song	US: California, Santa Barbara	美国:加利福尼亚州圣巴巴拉	34. 3	-119. 8		5. 1	Mk	6										
1925	7	3	18	19						USGS, Song	US: California, Santa Barbara	美国:加利福尼亚州圣巴巴拉	34. 3	-119. 8		5. 1	Mk	6										
1925	7	10	14	42						USGS, Song	US: Montana, Townsend	美国:蒙大纳州汤森	46. 4	-111. 2		4. 9	Mk	5										
1925	7	19	5							* Song	Italy: Pollino	意大利:波里诺	40. 2	16. 1		6. 5	Mk	12										
1925	7	26	16							China	China: Henan, Shangcheng	中国:河南商城	31. 7	115. 5		5	Ms	6										
1925	7	30	12	17						USGS	US: Texas, Panhandle	美国:德克萨斯州潘汉德尔	35. 4	-101. 3		4. 9	Ms	6										
1925	7	31	8	46	18					GSHAP	Colombia: Near Coast	哥伦比亚:近海	5. 5	-77. 5		5	Ms	7										
1925	8	5	20	11	33					China, GSHAP	China: Xinjiang, Maralbishi, NW.	中国:新疆巴楚西北	40	78		5. 25	Ms	6										
1925	8	7	6	46	37					*	Turkey: Dinar	土耳其:第纳尔	38	30. 5		5. 9	Ms	8	3	1				3	2043	4		
1925	8	8	10	13						USGS	US: California, Temecula	美国:加利福尼亚州蒂梅丘拉	33. 5	-117		4. 5	Ms	5										

时间						海啸				资料来源	震中				深度	震级	标度	烈度	死亡人数		受伤人数		经济损失		房屋毁坏		房屋受损	
年	月	日	时	分	秒	源	浪高	级 I	级 S		地名(英文)	地名(中文)	纬度(°)	经度(°)					数量/人	级别	数量/人	级别	数量/$ Mill	级别	数量/间	级别	数量/间	级别
Date						Tsunami				Information	Earthquake Epicenter				Depth	Mag	Scale	MMI	Deaths		Injuries		Damage		Houses Destroyed		Houses Damaged	
Year	Mo	Dy	Hr	Mn	Sec	Sr	Wh	mI	mS		Name(English)	Name(Chinese)	Latitude	Longitude					Num	Dd	Num	Dd	$ Mill	De	Num	Dh	Num	Dh
1925	8	19	12	7	34					GSHAP, Shi Z., Engdahl	Aleutian Islands	阿留申群岛	54.4	168.6	20	7	Ms	9										
1925	8	21	11	13	57					USGS	US: Nevada, Mina, SW.	美国:内华达州迈纳西南	38	-118.3		4.8	Ms	5										
1925	9	2	11	56						USGS	US: Kentucky, Henderson	美国:肯塔基州亨德森	37.8	-87.5		4.6	Ms	6										
1925	9	11	4	40	47					GSHAP	Croatia: Rijeka	克罗地亚:里耶卡	45.2	14.7	25	5.1	Ms	6										
1925	9	11	6	58	43					GSHAP	Croatia: Rijeka	克罗地亚:里耶卡	45	14.8	30	4.8	Ms	5										
1925	9	28	21	42	40					GSHAP	Kazakhstan: Karkaralinsk	哈萨克斯坦:卡尔卡拉林斯克	50	76	24	5.8	Ms	7										
1925	10	2	16							China	China: Yunnan, Dali	中国:云南大理	25.7	100.2		4.75	Ms	6										
1925	10	5	4	8	59					* Shi Z., Engdahl	Nicaragua: Managua	尼加拉瓜:马拉瓜	12.216	-85.871	35	6.8	Muk							3				
1925	10	9	13	55						USGS	US: New Hampshire, Center Ossipee	美国:新汉普郡州森特奥西皮	43.7	-71.1		4	Ms	6										
1925	10	14	17	5	8					* China	China: Yunnan, Lijiang	中国:云南丽江	27	100		5.75	Ms	7	12	1	10	1		2	500	3		
1925	10	25	4	31	9.3					GSHAP	Bolivia: Aiquile	玻利维亚:艾基莱	-18.2	-65.17		5.2	Ms	6										
1925	11	13	12	14	53	2			0.5	* Bautista, Engdahl, NOAA	Philippines: Samar, Laoang	菲律宾:萨马岛,拉旺	13	125	35	7.2	Mw	9		2		3		2		3		
1925	11	16	11	55	1	4	11	3.5	3	* Engdahl, NOAA	Mexico: Cihuatlan, Off Coast of S.	墨西哥:锡瓦特兰南部海域	18.375	-106.809	25	7	Ms							2				
1925	11	18	1	45						USGS, Song	US: Wyoming, Shell	美国:怀俄明州谢尔	44.4	-107.5		4.9	Mk	5										
1925	12	4								* Song	Italy: Forli´	意大利:弗利	44.2	12.2		6.5	Mk	12										
1925	12	10	4	59	32					GSHAP	Iran: Shirvan	伊朗:希尔凡	37.2	57.8	12	5.5	Ms	7.5										
1925	12	14								*	Iran: Razavi Khorasan	伊朗:呼罗珊	34.6	58.1		5.5	Muk		500	3								
1925	12	18	5	53						*	Iran: Bushehr	伊朗:布什尔	28.5	51.2		5.5	Muk		2	1				2				
1925	12	18	18	10	25					GSHAP	Afghan: Badakhshan	阿富汗:巴达赫尚	36.7	71	220	6.3	Ms	5										
1926	2	1	1	17	33					GSHAP	Venezuela: Cariaco	委内瑞拉:卡利亚科	10.5	-63.5	100	6.5	Ms	5										
1926	2	7	18	5	30					GSHAP	Uzbekistan: Samarqand	乌兹别克斯坦:撒马尔罕	39.4	67.2	10	4.5	Ms	6.5										
1926	2	7	21	59						USGS, Song	Hawaiian Islands	夏威夷群岛	21	-157		4.9	Mk	5										
1926	2	11	16							China	China: Jiangxi, Shicheng	中国:江西石城	26.4	116.3		4.75	Ms	6										
1926	2	18	18	20	45					USGS	US: California, Oxnard	美国:加利福尼亚州奥克斯纳德	34	-119.5		5.5	Ms	6										
1926	2	28	9	15						GSHAP	Russia: Khabarovsk, Ayan	俄罗斯:哈巴罗夫斯克区尼亚恰村	56.5	138	20	5	Ms	6										
1926	2	28	17	11						USGS, Song	Hawaiian Islands	夏威夷群岛	19	-155.5		4.9	Mk	5										
1926	3	8	18							GSHAP	Tajikistan: Khudzhand	塔吉克斯坦:苦盏	40.2	69.5	12	4.8	Ms	6.5										
1926	3	11	10	41	54					GSHAP, Song	Peru: Ucayali, SW.	秘鲁:乌卡亚利西南	-10	-74		5	Mk	6										
1926	3	20	9	3		1	1.5	0.6		* USGS, NOAA	Hawaiian Islands	夏威夷群岛	20.5	-155.5		6	Ms	5										
1926	4	3	20	9						USGS	US: California, Palm Springs	美国:加利福尼亚州棕泉	34	-116		5.5	Ms	5										
1926	4	11	6	26	24					GSHAP	Tajikistan: Thabo Shull	塔吉克斯坦:塔博沙尔	40.6	69.5	18	5.4	Ms	6.5										

时间						海啸				资料来源	震中				深度	震级	标度	烈度	死亡人数		受伤人数		经济损失		房屋毁坏		房屋受损	
年	月	日	时	分	秒	源	浪高	级 I	级 S		地名(英文)	地名(中文)	纬度(°)	经度(°)					数量/人	级别	数量/人	级别	数量/$ Mill	级别	数量/间	级别	数量/间	级别
Date						Tsunami				Information	Earthquake Epicenter				Depth	Mag	Scale	MMI	Deaths		Injuries		Damage		Houses Destroyed		Houses Damaged	
Year	Mo	Dy	Hr	Mn	Sec	Sr	Wh	mI	mS		Name(English)	Name(Chinese)	Latitude	Longitude					Num	Dd	Num	Dd	$ Mill	De	Num	Dh	Num	Dh
1926	4	18	18	18	30					GSHAP	Serbia:Cacak	塞尔维亚:查查克	43.9	20.4	24	4.7	Ms	5.5										
1926	4	19	7	49	58					GSHAP	Russia:Krasnodar,Krasnodar	俄罗斯:克拉斯诺达尔区克拉斯诺达尔	45.3	39.3	50	5.4	Ms	6.5										
1926	4	22	15	3						USGS,Song	Hawaiian Islands	夏威夷群岛	19.5	-155.5		5.1	Mk	6										
1926	5	19	10	11	6					GSHAP	Serbia:Cacak	塞尔维亚:查查克	44.5	20.6	10	4.6	Ms	6										
1926	5	28	22	31	33					GSHAP	Caspian Sea	里海	40.2	53.1	9	5	Ms	7.5										
1926	5	28	22	31	41					GSHAP	Kyrgyzstan:Jalal-Abad	吉尔吉斯斯坦:贾拉拉巴德	40.9	73.1	9	5.3	Ms	7.5										
1926	6	19	22							* Song	Italy:Montecassino	意大利:蒙特卡西诺	41.5	13.8		6.5	Mk	12										
1926	6	26	19	46	41					* Engdahl	Greece:Rhodes Island	希腊:罗德岛	36.5	27.5	101.8	7.7	mB	11		2				3				
1926	6	28	3	23	25	1				* Engdahl	Cocos Islands,SE.	科科斯群岛东南	-15	99.5		6.8	Ms	9	222	3								
1926	6	29	12	5						* Song	Italy:Reggiano	意大利:雷焦艾米利亚	44.6	10.7		6.5	Mk	12										
1926	6	29	23	21						USGS	US:California,Santa Barbara	美国:加利福尼亚州圣巴巴拉	34.5	-119.5		5.5	Ms	7										
1926	6	29	23	45						GSHAP	Bulgaria:Yambol	保加利亚:扬博尔	42.6	26.7	6	5	Ms	7										
1926	6	30	13	31						CGS,USGS	US:California,Caliente	美国:加利福尼亚州卡连特	35.8	-118.4		5.7	Ms	5										
1926	7	5								* Song	Indonesia:Southern Sumatra	印度尼西亚:苏门答腊南部	-2.9	104.7		6.4	Mk			3				2		3		3
1926	7	8	9	50						USGS,Song	US:North Carolina,Spruce Pine	美国:北卡罗来纳州斯普鲁斯派恩	35.9	-82.1		5.6	Mk	7										
1926	7	25	17	57	54					CGS,USGS	US:California,Three Rocks	美国:加利福尼亚州斯里罗克斯	36.5	-120.4	15	5.8	Ms	6										
1926	7	30				1				NOAA,Song	England:Jersey Island	英国:泽西岛	49.21	-2.131		7	Mk											
1926	8	17	1	43		3			3	* NOAA	Italy:Salina Island	意大利:萨利纳岛	39	14.8	100	6	Ms	7						3				
1926	8	18	13	57	36					GSHAP	Finland:Oulu	芬兰:奥卢	65.8	28.5	20	4.8	Ms	5.5										
1926	8	22				1				NOAA,Song	Portugal:Azores	葡萄牙:亚速尔群岛	38.3	-28.4		7	Mk											
1926	8	30	11	38	10	3				GSHAP, Engdahl,NOAA	Greece:Argolida	希腊:阿尔戈利斯	37.5	23	85.2	7.1	mB											
1926	8	31	10	40	8					* Song	Azores:Fayal Island	亚速尔群岛:法亚尔岛	38.5	-28		5.9	Mk		9	1	200	3		2				
1926	9	3	21	59	57					GSHAP	Bulgaria:Plovdiv	保加利亚:普罗夫迪夫	41.75	24.4	22	4.9	Ms	6										
1926	9	16	17	59	15	4	2	1		* Engdahl,NOAA	Solomon Islands	所罗门群岛	-9.674	159.519	35	6.9	Ms							1		1		
1926	9	27	6	43	9					GSHAP	Azerbaijan:Quba	阿塞拜疆:库巴	41.5	48.8	23	4.5	Ms	5										
1926	9	30	5	30						GSHAP	Venezuela:Merida	委内瑞拉:梅里达	8.6	-71.15		4.9	Ms	5										
1926	10	11	17	20						GSHAP	Venezuela:Merida	委内瑞拉:梅里达	8.55	-71.2		5.5	Ms	6										
1926	10	12	11	57	25					* GSHAP	Montenegro:Berane	门的内哥罗(黑山):贝拉内	42.8	19.9		5.2	Mk						1.1	2				
1926	10	21	9	29	45					GSHAP	Croatia:Rijeka	克罗地亚:里耶卡	45.1	14.9	26	4.7	Ms	5										
1926	10	22	12	35	11					USGS	US:California,Carmel,Near Coast	美国:加利福尼亚州卡梅尔近海	36.62	-122.35		6.1	Ms	7										

时间						海啸				资料来源	震中				深度	震级	标度	烈度	死亡人数		受伤人数		经济损失		房屋毁坏		房屋受损	
年	月	日	时	分	秒	源	浪高	级 I	级 S		地名(英文)	地名(中文)	纬度(°)	经度(°)					数量/人	级别	数量/人	级别	数量/$ Mill	级别	数量/间	级别	数量/间	级别
Date						Tsunami				Information	Earthquake Epicenter				Depth	Mag	Scale	MMI	Deaths		Injuries		Damage		Houses Destroyed		Houses Damaged	
Year	Mo	Dy	Hr	Mn	Sec	Sr	Wh	mI	mS		Name(English)	Name(Chinese)	Latitude	Longitude					Num	Dd	Num	Dd	$ Mill	De	Num	Dh	Num	Dh
1926	10	22	13	35	22					USGS	US:California,Carmel, Near Coast	美国:加利福尼亚州卡梅尔近海	36.55	-122.18		6.1	Ms	7										
1926	10	22	19	59						*	Turkey; Armenia	土耳其;亚美尼亚	40.7	43.7	7	5.7	Muk	9	360	3				4				
1926	10	25	14	2	9					GSHAP	Georgia:Akhalkalaki	格鲁吉亚:阿卡卡垃吉	41.3	44.3	18	4.6	Ms	5										
1926	10	27	16							China	China:Inner Mongolia,Zalantun	中国:内蒙古扎兰屯	48	122.7		5	Ms	6										
1926	10									China	China:Yunnan,Luxi	中国:云南泸西	24.5	103.8		5	Ms	6										
1926	11	3								GSHAP	Ecuador:Cotopaxi	厄瓜多尔:科托帕希	-0.8	-78.6		5	Ms	6										
1926	11	5	7	55	30					*Shi Z.,Engdahl	Nicaragua:Managua,Granada	尼加拉瓜:马拉瓜,格拉纳达	12.67	-86.736	35	7.1	mB							3				
1926	11	13	0	17	31					GSHAP	Bolivia:Cochabamba	玻利维亚:科恰班巴	-17.4	-66.12		5.4	Ms	6										
1926	11	13	16							China	China:Guangxi,Hechi	中国:广西河池	24.7	108.1		4.75	Ms	6										
1926	11	21	11	14	45					* China	China:Yunnan,Dali	中国:云南大理	25.6	100.3		5.5	Ms	7		3				1		2		
1926	12	9	22	38	48	2	1.5	0.6		* NOAA	Chile:Copiapo,Near Coast	智利:科皮亚波近海	-28	-71	33	6	Ms											
1926	12	13	0	44						USGS	US:Montana,Maudlow	美国:蒙大纳州莫德洛	46.1	-111.2		5.4	Ms	5										
1926	12	13								* Song	Indonesia:Java,Prupuk	印度尼西亚:爪哇,普鲁普克	-7	110		6.5	Mk	9						3				
1926	12	17	6	31	5					* Turkey	Albania:Durres	阿尔巴尼亚:都拉斯	41	19.5		6.1	Ms	10						3		3		
1926	12	18	5	30						GSHAP,Song	Ecuador:Concepcion	厄瓜多尔:康塞普西翁	0.8	-77.9		4.5	Mk	5										
1926	12	18	18	5						GSHAP	Ecuador:Concepcion	厄瓜多尔:康塞普西翁	0.8	-77.9		6.5	Ms	8										
1926	12	18				1				* NOAA,Song	Portugal:Coast SW.	葡萄牙:西南海域	36	-10		7	Mk							3				
1926	12	19	1	50						GSHAP	Colombia:Narino	哥伦比亚:纳里尼奥	1.1	-77.5		6.3	Ms	8										
1926	12	24	6	27	36					GSHAP	Armenia:Leninakan	亚美尼亚:列宁纳坎	41.5	44.1	18	4.5	Ms	6										
1926	12	27	18							GSHAP,Song	Ecuador:Carchi,E.	厄瓜多尔:卡尔奇东部	0.63	-77.8		6	Mk	7										
1927	1	1	8	16		1			1	* NOAA	US:California,El Centro	美国:加利福尼亚州埃尔森特罗	32.5	-115.5		5.8	Muk	8	1	1			3	2				
1927	1	24	5	18		2				GSHAP,NOAA	Norwegian Sea	挪威海	59	3	57	5.5	Ms	6										
1927	2	15	23	54	3.5					CGS,USGS	US:California,Davenport	美国:加利福尼亚州达文波特	36.95	-122.27		5.9	Ms	5										
1927	2	20	6	47	40					GSHAP	Croatia:Varazdin	克罗地亚:瓦拉日丁	46.3	16.9	5	4.5	Ms	7										
1927	3	7	9	27	42	4	11	0.4	3	* Engdahl,Usami,Japan,NOAA	Japan:Toyooka	日本:京都京丹后	35.802	134.924	9.6	7.6	Ms		2956	4	7806	4	40.0	4	21690	5	10841	5
1927	3	14	17	37	39					* China	China:Yunnan,Dongchuan	中国:云南东川	26	103		6	Ms	8		2				2		3		
1927	3	15	10	38	54					GSHAP	Panama:Garachiné,S.	巴拿马:加拉奇内南部	7.5	-79		4.5	Ms	5										
1927	3	19	16							* China	China:Yunnan,Xinping	中国:云南新平	24.1	102		5	Ms	6	7	1				1		1		
1927	3	20	15	21	42					USGS	Hawaiian Islands	夏威夷群岛	20.5	-155.25		6	Ms	5										
1927	3	25	18	14						GSHAP	Iran:Qūchān	伊朗:古昌	37.7	58.5	14	4.5	Ms	6										
1927	4	14	6	23	30					Engdahl,GSHAP	Argentina:Mendoza	阿根廷:门多萨	-32.477	-69.675	35	7.2	mB	8										
1927	4	17	19	7						* Song	Italy:Montecassino	意大利:蒙特卡西诺	41.5	13.8		6.5	Mk	12										
1927	4	18	15	2						GSHAP	Afghan:Badakhshan	阿富汗:巴达赫尚	37	71	200	6.8	Ms	6.5										

时间 Date 年 Year	月 Mo	日 Dy	时 Hr	分 Mn	秒 Sec	海啸 Tsunami 源 Sr	浪高 Wh	级 I mI	级 S mS	资料来源 Information	震中 Earthquake Epicenter 地名(英文) Name(English)	地名(中文) Name(Chinese)	纬度(°) Latitude	经度(°) Longitude	深度 Depth	震级 Mag	标度 Scale	烈度 MMI	死亡人数 Deaths 数量/人 Num	级别 Dd	受伤人数 Injuries 数量/人 Num	级别 Dd	经济损失 Damage 数量/$ Mill	级别 De	房屋毁坏 Houses Destroyed 数量/间 Num	级别 Dh	房屋受损 Houses Damaged 数量/间 Num	级别 Dh
1927	4	21	3	21	20					GSHAP	Russia: Altai Krai, Belyashi	俄罗斯:阿尔泰边疆区别利亚希镇	50.2	86.9	28	6	Ms	7										
1927	4									China	China: Qinghai, Ledu, E.	中国:青海乐都东	36.4	102.6		5.25	Ms	7										
1927	5	7	8	28						USGS	US: Arkansas, Jonesboro	美国:阿肯色州琼斯伯勒	35.8	-90.4		4.8	Ms	6										
1927	5	10	19	59	27					GSHAP	Russia: Khakassia, Bezymyanka, W.	俄罗斯:哈卡斯州别济米扬卡	52	88.5	22	5.3	Ms	7										
1927	5	14	20	29	21					GSHAP	Georgia: Gurdzhaani	格鲁吉亚:古祖尼	41.5	46	13	4.7	Ms	6.5										
1927	5	15	2	47						*	Serbia: Cacak	塞尔维亚:查查克	44.1	20.5	12	5.9	Muk	10										
1927	5	15	2	58	36					GSHAP	Serbia: Cacak	塞尔维亚:查查克	44.1	20.5	10	4.6	Ms	6										
1927	5	15	3	19	18					GSHAP	Serbia: Cacak	塞尔维亚:查查克	44.1	20.6	10	4.6	Ms	6										
1927	5	17	17	38	12					GSHAP	Serbia: Cacak	塞尔维亚:查查克	44.1	20.4	20	4.9	Ms	5.5										
1927	5	21	16							China	China: Sichuan, Zigong	中国:四川自贡	29.4	104.7		4.75	Ms	6										
1927	5	22	22	32	48					* China, Engdahl	China: Gansu, Gulang, W.	中国:甘肃古浪西	37.7	102.2	25	8	Ms	11	40912	5	524	3		4	26674	5		
1927	5	23	6	37	50					GSHAP	Mongolia: Southeast Uvs	蒙古:乌布苏东南部	49	94.6	24	5.6	Ms	6.5										
1927	5	28	17	36	17					USGS	US: California, North Coast	美国:加利福尼亚州北部近海	37.33	-122.92		4.9	Ms	5										
1927	6	1	12	20						USGS, Song	US: New Jersey, Long Branch	美国:新泽西州朗布兰奇	40.3	-74		5.6	Mk	7										
1927	6	18	6	26	48					GSHAP	Serbia: Cacak	塞尔维亚:查查克	43.9	20.6	18	4.9	Ms	6.5										
1927	6	20	17	24						* Song	Italy: Torino	意大利:托里诺(都灵)	45	7		6.5	Mk	12										
1927	6	26	11	20	50					* GSHAP, Song	Black Sea	黑海	44.5	34.3	35	5.5	Mk	7										
1927	7	1	8	18	59					* Engdahl	Greece: Oetylos (Laconia)	希腊:拉可尼亚	36.381	22.723	35	7	mB	10										
1927	7	11	13	4		2	1			* NOAA	Israel: Jerusalem	以色列:耶路撒冷	32	35.5	33	6.3	Ms		268	3				3				
1927	7	22	3	55	17					GSHAP, Iran	Iran: Semnan	伊朗:塞姆南	35	53.8	40	6.9	Ms	6.5										
1927	7	23	19	14	24					GSHAP	Macedonia(Fyrom): Bogdanci	马其顿:博丹奇区	41.7	22.7	21	4.9	Ms	6										
1927	7	23	22	40	34					GSHAP	Iran: Semnan	伊朗:塞姆南	34.5	53.9	13	6	Ms	8.5										
1927	8	3	20	12						USGS, Song	Hawaiian Islands	夏威夷群岛	19	-155.5		5.1	Mk	6										
1927	8	4	12	24						USGS	US: California, Los Angeles	美国:加利福尼亚州洛杉矶	34	-118.5		5.3	Ms	6										
1927	8	5	21	12	59	4	0.1	-3.3		* Engdahl, Usami, NOAA	Japan: Miyagi, Near Coast	日本:宫城近海	37.873	142.191	35	7.1	Ms											
1927	8	12	10	22	47					GSHAP	Uzbekistan: Namangan	乌兹别克斯坦:纳曼干	41	71.6	14	6	Ms	8										
1927	8	12	16	16	47					GSHAP	Uzbekistan: Namangan	乌兹别克斯坦:纳曼干	41	71.6	20	5.5	Ms	7										
1927	8	14	19	45						* Song	Slovenia: Ljubljana, S.	斯洛文尼亚:卢布尔雅那南部	45.8	14.2		6.3	Mk	12										
1927	8	16	1							* Song	Italy: Visso	意大利:维索	42.9	13.1		6.5	Mk	12										
1927	8	18	19	28	1	4	0.4	-1.3		* Engdahl, NOAA	Japan Trench	日本海沟	34.2	142	20	6.9	Ms											
1927	8	20	20	5	44					USGS	US: California, North Coast	美国:加利福尼亚州北部近海	41	-124.6		5.3	Ms	8										

时间						海啸				资料来源	震中				深度	震级	标度	烈度	死亡人数		受伤人数		经济损失		房屋毁坏		房屋受损	
年	月	日	时	分	秒	源	浪高	级 I	级 S		地名(英文)	地名(中文)	纬度(°)	经度(°)					数量/人	级别	数量/人	级别	数量/$ Mill	级别	数量/间	级别	数量/间	级别
Date						Tsunami				Information	Earthquake Epicenter				Depth	Mag	Scale	MMI	Deaths		Injuries		Damage		Houses Destroyed		Houses Damaged	
Year	Mo	Dy	Hr	Mn	Sec	Sr	Wh	mI	mS		Name(English)	Name(Chinese)	Latitude	Longitude					Num	Dd	Num	Dd	$ Mill	De	Num	Dh	Num	Dh
1927	8	24	18	9	3					* China, Engdahl	China:Taiwan,Tainan	中国:台湾台南	23	120.5	60	6.75	Muk		30	1	190	3		2	200	3	1209	4
1927	8	27	2	57	40					GSHAP	Uzbekistan:Namangan	乌兹别克斯坦:纳曼干	41	71.6	9	4.8	Ms	7										
1927	9	11	22	15						*	Ukraine:Crimea	乌克兰:克里米亚	44.3	34.3	17	6.8	Muk		10	1				4				
1927	9	18	2	7	7					USGS	US:California, Mammoth Lakes	美国:加利福尼亚州马姆莫斯湖	37.5	-118.75		6	Ms	6										
1927	9	23	13	54	23					China, Engdahl	China:Xinjiang,Hejing,W.	中国:新疆和静西	42.3	85.6		6.75	Muk	8										
1927	10	12	7	20	15					GSHAP	Serbia:Kragujevac	塞尔维亚:克拉古耶瓦茨	44	21	34	4.8	Ms	5										
1927	10	17	23	57						* Song	Italy:Avezzano	意大利:阿韦扎诺	41.9	13.5		6.5	Mk	12										
1927	10	24	15	59	56	3				* Engdahl, NOAA	Gulf of Alaska	阿拉斯加湾	57.44	-136.373	15	7.1	Ms	7						1				
1927	10	27	1	53						Usami, Japan	Japan:Niigata	日本:新潟	37.5	138.8		5.3	Ms				2	1					275	3
1927	10	30	23	49						* Song	Italy:Bedonia	意大利:贝多尼亚	44.5	9.6		6.5	Mk	12										
1927	10	31	23	30						China	China:Xinjiang,Artux,NE.	中国:新疆阿图什东北	40	76.6	20	5.4	Ms	7										
1927	11	4	13	51	5	4	1.8	1	1	* Engdahl, NOAA	US:California,Santa Maria,Near Coast	美国:加利福尼亚州圣玛丽亚近海	34.915	-121.031	15	7.1	M	8						2				
1927	11	14	0	12	6					GSHAP	Russia:Sakha,N.	俄罗斯:萨哈共和国北部	70.1	128.7	22	6.8	Ms	9										
1927	11	14	4	56	32					GSHAP, Engdahl	Russia:Sakha,N.	俄罗斯:萨哈共和国北部	70.033	128.69	15	6.8	Muk	9										
1927	11	15	17							* Song	Italy:Bedonia	意大利:贝多尼亚	44.5	9.6		6.5	Mk	12										
1927	11	18	20	2	50					GSHAP	Russia:Amur,Urusha	俄罗斯:阿穆尔州乌鲁沙	54.5	122.5	20	4.8	Ms	5.5										
1927	11	19	3	32	30					USGS	US:California,Nipomo	美国:加利福尼亚州尼波莫	35	-120.5		5	Ms	6										
1927	11	21	23	12	31	3	2.8	1.5	2	* Shi Z., Engdahl, NOAA	Chile:Aisen Region	智利:艾森区	-44.6	-73	33	7.1	Mw											
1927	11	23	3	15						* Song	Italy:Malcesine	意大利:马尔切西内	45.8	11.8		6.5	Mk	12										
1927	11	23	16							* China	China:Yunnan,Fumin	中国:云南富民	25.2	102.5		5.5	Ms	7		3				2		3		
1927	12	1	4	37	27	3	15	3.9	3	* NOAA	Indonesia:Sulawesi,Donggala	印度尼西亚:苏拉威西岛,栋加拉	-0.7	119.7		6.3	Ms	7	50	1	50	1		3		3		
1927	12	28	18	20	34	4	2	1		* Engdahl, NOAA	Russia:Kamchatka Peninsula	俄罗斯:堪察加半岛	55.663	160.039	35	7.5	Mw											
1927										China	China:Shaanxi,Lueyang	中国:陕西略阳	33.3	106.2		4.75	Ms	6										
1928	1	9	2	45						USGS	US:California,Gilroy	美国:加利福尼亚州吉尔罗伊	37	-121.58		4.6	Ms	5										
1928	1	25	20							* Song	Italy:Grosseto	意大利:格罗塞托	42.9	11.6		6.5	Mk	12										
1928	2	2	12	52						USGS, Song	US:Washington,Seattle	美国:华盛顿州西雅图	47.8	-121.7		5.1	Mk	6										
1928	2	3	13	47	38					GSHAP	Russia:Sakha,N.	俄罗斯:萨哈共和国北部	70.5	128.8	15	6.2	Ms	7.5										
1928	2	7								* Song	France:Cauro,Coti - Chiavari	法国:考罗,科蒂基亚瓦里	44.2	9.2		5.9	Mk	6						2				

时间						海啸				资料来源	震中				深度	震级	标度	烈度	死亡人数		受伤人数		经济损失		房屋毁坏		房屋受损	
年	月	日	时	分	秒	源	浪高	级 I	级 S		地名(英文)	地名(中文)	纬度(°)	经度(°)					数量/人	级别	数量/人	级别	数量/$ Mill	级别	数量/间	级别	数量/间	级别
Date						Tsunami				Information	Earthquake Epicenter				Depth	Mag	Scale	MMI	Deaths		Injuries		Damage		Houses Destroyed		Houses Damaged	
Year	Mo	Dy	Hr	Mn	Sec	Sr	Wh	mI	mS		Name(English)	Name(Chinese)	Latitude	Longitude					Num	Dd	Num	Dd	$ Mill	De	Num	Dh	Num	Dh
1928	2	9				2	0.7	-0.5		* NOAA	Canada:Vancouver Island	加拿大:温哥华岛	49	-125	33	5.8	Ms											
1928	2	10	4	39						*	Mexico:Oaxaca, Colima, Puebla	墨西哥:瓦哈卡,科利马,普埃布拉	17.8	-97.6	100	7.7	Muk							3				
1928	2	25	17	23	48					GSHAP	Afghan:Badakhshan	阿富汗:巴达赫尚	36.5	71	180	6.2	Ms	6										
1928	3	7	10	55						*	Italy:Sicily, Calabria	意大利:西西里岛,卡拉布里亚	38.8	16		6	Muk			2				2				
1928	3	8	18	13						* Iran	Iran:Nehbandan	伊朗:内赫班丹	31.6	60		5.5	Muk		4	1				2				
1928	3	18	15	20						USGS	US:New York, Lake Clear	美国:纽约州莱克克利尔	44.5	-74.3		4.1	Ms	6										
1928	3	18	23	49	35					GSHAP	Croatia:Pozega	克罗地亚:波热加	45.4	17.2	6	4.9	Ms	7										
1928	3	22	4	17	8	4				* Engdahl, NOAA	Mexico:Near Coast of Oaxaca	墨西哥:瓦哈卡近海	15.7	-96.1	35	7.5	Mw											
1928	3	27	8	32						*	Italy:Tolmezzo	意大利:托尔梅佐	46.4	13	33	5.8	Muk	10										
1928	3	28	11	57	55					GSHAP	Azerbaijan:Gəncə	阿塞拜疆:占贾	40.5	46.7	14	4.7	Ms	6.5										
1928	3	30	9	38	57					GSHAP	Romania:Tulnici	罗马尼亚:图尔尼奇	45.9	26.5	150	5.6	Ms	6										
1928	3	31	0	29	47	3	0.5		2	* NOAA	Turkey:Tepekoy, Torbali	土耳其:泰佩柯伊,托布雷	38.1	27.1		6.5	Ms	10	170	3	700	3		3	2600	4		
1928	4	9	17	34	18					* Engdahl	Peru:W. of Cuzco	秘鲁:库斯科西部	-13.731	-70.628	35	6.8	Ms	9	10	1				3		3		
1928	4	14	9	0	1					* Engdahl	Bulgaria:Chirpan	保加利亚:奇尔潘	42.2	25.3	15	6.8	Ms	10	105	3				4	74750	5		
1928	4	14	9	23	36					GSHAP	Bulgaria:Chirpan	保加利亚:奇尔潘	42.2	25.3	40	5.1	Ms	5										
1928	4	15	0	59						GSHAP	Brasil:Aracati	巴西:阿拉卡蒂	-4.56	-37.76		4	Ms	6										
1928	4	15	21	57	12					CGS, USGS	US:California, Elk Creek	美国:加利福尼亚州埃尔克里克	39.8	-122.65	15	5.5	Ms	6										
1928	4	16	21	26	15					*	Mexico:Oaxaca	墨西哥:瓦哈卡	17.75	-97.1		7.8	Ms							1				
1928	4	17	5	47	30					GSHAP	Bulgaria:Chirpan	保加利亚:奇尔潘	42.2	25.35	11	4.9	Ms	7										
1928	4	17	7	35						GSHAP	Bulgaria:Chirpan	保加利亚:奇尔潘	42.1	25.3	5	4.5	Ms	7										
1928	4	18	6	47	24					GSHAP	Bulgaria:Dimitrovgrad	保加利亚:季米特洛夫格勒	42.1	25.5	16	4.5	Ms	6										
1928	4	18	19	22	55					* Engdahl	Bulgaria:Popovitsa	保加利亚:普罗夫迪夫	42.386	25.087	15	6.8	Ms	11						4				
1928	4	20	8	16						GSHAP	Georgia:Kakhetiya	格鲁吉亚:卡赫季州	42.1	45.5	14	4.6	Ms	6										
1928	4	22	20	13	46	2	2.1	1.1	3	* Turkey, NOAA	Greece:Corinth (Corinthia)	希腊:科林斯(科林特)	38	23	14	6.3	Ms	11	20	1				4	3000	4		
1928	4	24	11	14	48	2			3	* NOAA	Aegean Sea	爱琴海	38	23.5		5	Ms											
1928	4	25	0	31	18	1				* NOAA	Greece:Megara	希腊:墨伽拉	38	23		5.2	Ms	6										
1928	4	27	20	35	1	4				* Engdahl	Peru:W. of Cuzco	秘鲁:库斯科西部	-13	-69.5	35	6.8	Muk	5										
1928	4	27				2	0.6			NOAA, Song	Turkey:Izmir	土耳其:伊兹密尔	38.5	27		6.6	Mk											
1928	4									China	China:Sichuan, Luxian	中国:四川泸县	28.5	105.5		4.75	Ms	6										
1928	5	1	15	58	25					GSHAP	Turkmenistan:Asgabat	土库曼斯坦:阿什哈巴德	38.2	58.4	20	4.6	Ms	5.5										
1928	5	2	21	54	32	1				* * GSHAP, NOAA	Turkey:Demirci	土耳其:代米尔吉	39.6	29.1	20	6.3	Ms	8										
1928	5	3	1	25	13	2			2	* NOAA	Turkey:Malkara	土耳其:马尔卡拉	40.8	26.8		4.3	Ms	7										

时间						海啸				资料来源	震中				深度	震级	标度	烈度	死亡人数		受伤人数		经济损失		房屋毁坏		房屋受损	
年	月	日	时	分	秒	源	浪高	级I	级S		地名(英文)	地名(中文)	纬度(°)	经度(°)					数量/人	级别	数量/人	级别	数量/$ Mill	级别	数量/间	级别	数量/间	级别
Date						Tsunami				Information	Earthquake Epicenter				Depth	Mag	Scale	MMI	Deaths		Injuries		Damage		Houses Destroyed		Houses Damaged	
Year	Mo	Dy	Hr	Mn	Sec	Sr	Wh	mI	mS		Name(English)	Name(Chinese)	Latitude	Longitude					Num	Dd	Num	Dd	$ Mill	De	Num	Dh	Num	Dh
1928	5	6	18							GSHAP	Turkey:Eskisehir	土耳其:埃斯基城	39.8	30.5	12	5	Ms	6.5										
1928	5	9	20	1	30					GSHAP	Georgia:Borzhomi	格鲁吉亚:博尔若米	41.9	43.1	28	4.6	Ms	5.5										
1928	5	14	22	14	51					* Engdahl	Peru:Huancabamba,Cajamarca	秘鲁:宛卡班巴,卡哈马尔卡	-5	-78	35	7.2	Mw	10	29	1			8.0	3				
1928	5	17	10	55						GSHAP,Song	Peru:Cuzco	秘鲁:库斯科	-13	-72		5	Mk	6										
1928	5	18				2			0.5	* NOAA,Song	Tonga Islands,E.	汤加群岛东部	-19	-172.5		7	Mk											
1928	5	25	16							China	China:Yunnan,Huize,NE.	中国:云南会泽东北	26.6	103.7		4.75	Ms	6										
1928	5	27	9	50	28	4	0.2	-2.3	-2	* GSHAP,Engdahl,NOAA	Japan:Iwate,Near Coast	日本:岩手近海	40	143.2	35	7.1	Ms											
1928	6	4	5	30						USGS	US:California,Weaverville	美国:加利福尼亚州威弗维尔	40.75	-122.92		4.5	Ms	6										
1928	6	15	6	12	42	3				* Bautista,Engdahl,NOAA	Philippines:Mindoro,SW.	菲律宾:民都洛岛西南	12.732	120.819	35	7	Ms	8						2				
1928	6	17	3	19	33	4	0.2	3	1	* Engdahl,NOAA	Mexico:Oaxaca	墨西哥:瓦哈卡	16.25	-98	35	7.7	Mw		4	1				2				
1928	6	21	16	27	19					USGS,Shi Z.,Engdahl	Gulf of Alaska	阿拉斯加湾	60	-146.5	35	6.8	Ms	6										
1928	7	6	4	24	4					GSHAP	Bolivia:Cochabamba	玻利维亚:科恰班巴	-17.24	-66.29		5.3	Ms	5										
1928	7	11	23	46	55					GSHAP	Uzbekistan:Uzgut	乌兹别克斯坦:乌尔古特	39.4	67.2	20	5.4	Ms	6.5										
1928	7	18	18	45						GSHAP	Ecuador:Napo	厄瓜多尔:纳波	-1	-78		5.7	Ms	7										
1928	7	18	19	5	9	2				* GSHAP,Engdahl,NOAA	Peru:Jaén	秘鲁:哈恩	-5.359	-78.738	35	6.9	Ms	6										
1928	7	19	20	13	50					* China	China:Sichuan,Xiaojin,N.	中国:四川小金北	31.5	102.5		5.75	Ms	7	6	1	10	1		2		2		
1928	8	4				5	10	3.3	3	NOAA,Song	Indonesia:Flores Islands	印度尼西亚:弗洛勒斯群岛	-8.32	121.708	1	7.8	Mk		226	3								
1928	8	21	19	1						*	Iran:Shirvan	伊朗:希尔凡	37.3	57.9	9	5.4	Muk	8	10	1				2				
1928	8	23	3	53	38					GSHAP	Kyrgyzstan:Talas,SE.	吉尔吉斯斯坦:塔拉斯东南	41.8	72.9	21	5.5	Ms	7										
1928	8	24	11	50	30					GSHAP	Russia:Dagestan,Tpig	俄罗斯:达吉斯坦共和国特皮格	41.7	47.5	22	4.5	Ms	5.5										
1928	8	25	1	48	12					GSHAP	Russia:Sakhalin Island	俄罗斯:库页岛(萨哈林岛)	49.6	141.9	12	5.5	Ms	7.5										
1928	8	26	5	15	3					GSHAP	Uzbekistan:Samarkand	乌兹别克斯坦:撒马尔罕	39.6	67.1	10	4.6	Ms	6.5										
1928	9	5	14	42						CGS,USGS	US:California,Fort Irwin	美国:加利福尼亚州欧文堡	35	-117		5.5	Ms	5										
1928	9	22	16							China	China:Yunnan,Lufeng,NW.	中国:云南禄丰西北	25.4	101.8		5.5	Ms	7										
1928	9	27	0	44	5					GSHAP	Trinidad & Tobago:Northern Coast	特立尼达和多巴哥:北部近海	12	-60	33	6.5	Ms	7										
1928	10	5	19	47	21					GSHAP	Russia:Chechnia,Grozny,S.	俄罗斯:车臣共和国格罗兹尼北部	42.8	45.6	8	4.7	Ms	7										

时间 Date 年 Year	月 Mo	日 Dy	时 Hr	分 Mn	秒 Sec	海啸 Tsunami 源 Sr	浪高 Wh	级 I mI	级 S mS	资料来源 Information	震中 Earthquake Epicenter 地名(英文) Name(English)	地名(中文) Name(Chinese)	纬度(°) Latitude	经度(°) Longitude	深度 Depth	震级 Mag	标度 Scale	烈度 MMI	死亡人数 Deaths 数量/人 Num	级别 Dd	受伤人数 Injuries 数量/人 Num	级别 Dd	经济损失 Damage 数量/$ Mill $ Mill	级别 De	房屋毁坏 Houses Destroyed 数量/间 Num	级别 Dh	房屋受损 Houses Damaged 数量/间 Num	级别 Dh
1928	10	23	17	52	6					GSHAP	Russia:Kamchatka, Near East Coast	俄罗斯:堪察加东部近海	51.1	157.3	50	6.1	Ms	7										
1928	11	1	16	8	18					GSHAP	Colombia:Trinidad	哥伦比亚:特立尼达	5.5	-71.5		5.7	Ms	7										
1928	11	3	4	2	50					USGS	US:Tennessee, Greeneville	美国:田纳西州格林维尔	36.11	-82.83	5	4.5	Ms	6										
1928	11	6	13	42	36					GSHAP	Caspian Sea	里海	40	52.8	40	5.4	Ms	5.5										
1928	11	7	13	44	36					GSHAP	Russia:Sakhalin Island	俄罗斯:库页岛(萨哈林岛)	47.3	142.5	20	4.9	Ms	5.5										
1928	11	7	18	37	20					GSHAP	Russia:Tuva, Kyzyl - Mazhalyk	俄罗斯:唐努图瓦州克孜勒马扎雷克	51.9	90.6	20	5.3	Ms	6.5										
1928	11	20	16	35	10	2				* Chile, Engdahl, NOAA	Chile:Tocopilla, Near Coast	智利:托科皮亚近海	-23.111	-69.931	35	6.9	Ms											
1928	11	23	4	23	12					GSHAP	Romania:Nereju	罗马尼亚:内雷茹	45.7	26.6	150	5.7	Ms	5.5										
1928	12	1	4	6	15	3	1.5	0.6	0.5	* Chile, Engdahl, NOAA	Chile:Talca, Chillan, Santiago	智利:塔尔卡,奇廉,圣地亚哥	-35.086	-71.683	35	7.7	Mw	9	279	3				3		3		
1928	12	2	23	41	35					GSHAP	Kyrgyzstan:Issyk - Kul, N.	吉尔吉斯斯坦:伊塞克湖州北部	42.8	77.3	15	4.6	Ms	6										
1928	12	15	14	54	18					GSHAP	Kyrgyzstan:Naryn, N.	吉尔吉斯斯坦:纳伦北部	42.1	74.9	15	4.7	Ms	6										
1928	12	18	3	44	26					GSHAP	Mongolia:South - West of Uliastay	蒙古:乌里雅苏台市西南	47.5	96	30	5.5	Ms	6										
1928	12	19	11	39	17	4				* Shi Z, Engdahl, NOAA	Philippines:Cotabato	菲律宾:哥打巴托	7.1	124.1	35	7.3	Mw	7	97	2	102	3		2		2		2
1928	12	20	7	27	8					GSHAP	Croatia:Zagreb	克罗地亚:萨格勒布	45.7	15.5	26	4.5	Ms	5										
1928						1				NOAA, Song	Canada:Newfoundland	加拿大:纽芬兰(岛)	48.967	-58		7	Mk											
1929	1	13	0	3	3					* Engdahl	Kuril Islands	千岛群岛	49.8	154.8	35	7.4	mB	7										
1929	1	13	18	44	39					* China	China:Inner Mongolia, Tumed Zuoqi	中国:内蒙古土默特左旗	40.7	111.3		6	Ms	8	2	1	10	1		2	100	2		
1929	1	17	11	45	42	4				* Engdahl, NOAA	Venezuela:Anaco	委内瑞拉:阿纳科	9.499	-64.381	35	6.9	Muk	9	50	1	800	3		3				
1929	1	19	11	19	33					* China	Myanmar:Myitkyina	缅甸:密支那	25.5	98		5.5	Ms	9						2				
1929	1	19	16							China	China:Inner Mongolia, Tumed Zuoqi	中国:内蒙古土默特左旗	40.7	111.3		5.5	Ms	7										
1929	1	21	10	30	53					USGS	Alaska Peninsula, C.	阿拉斯加半岛中部	64	-148		6.25	Ms	6										
1929	1	30	1	55						GSHAP	Venezuela:Trujillo	委内瑞拉:特鲁希略	9.33	-70.64		4.9	Ms	6										
1929	2	1	17	14	26					* Engdahl	Afghan:Badakhshan	阿富汗:巴达赫尚	36.459	70.931	207.9	7	mB							3				
1929	2	16	3							USGS	US:Montana, Maudlow	美国:蒙大纳州莫德洛	46.1	-111.3		5.6	Ms	5										
1929	2	20	7	59	53					GSHAP	Georgia:Gori, N.	格鲁吉亚:哥里北部	42.3	44.3	22	4.5	Ms	5.5										
1929	2	22	19	38	22					GSHAP	Azerbaijan:Gəncə	阿塞拜疆:占贾	40.4	45.9	16	4.7	Ms	6										
1929	3	7	1	34	43	4	1			* Engdahl, NOAA	Aleutian Islands	阿留申群岛	50.786	-169.524	25	7.8	Mw	5						1				
1929	3	11	13	25	32					GSHAP	Colombia:Cartagena	哥伦比亚:卡塔赫纳	10.5	-75.5		5	Ms	6										

时间 Date						海啸 Tsunami				资料来源	震中 Earthquake Epicenter				深度	震级	标度	烈度	死亡人数 Deaths		受伤人数 Injuries		经济损失 Damage		房屋毁坏 Houses Destroyed		房屋受损 Houses Damaged	
年	月	日	时	分	秒	源	浪高	级 I	级 S		地名(英文)	地名(中文)	纬度(°)	经度(°)					数量/人	级别	数量/人	级别	数量/$ Mill	级别	数量/间	级别	数量/间	级别
Year	Mo	Dy	Hr	Mn	Sec	Sr	Wh	mI	mS	Information	Name(English)	Name(Chinese)	Latitude	Longitude	Depth	Mag	Scale	MMI	Num	Dd	Num	Dd	$ Mill	De	Num	Dh	Num	Dh
1929	3	16	8							GSHAP	Venezuela:Lara	委内瑞拉:拉腊	9.9	-69.39		5.5	Ms	6										
1929	3	17	2							GSHAP	Venezuela:Lara	委内瑞拉:拉腊	9.9	-69.39		5.5	Ms	6										
1929	4	5	17	46	34					GSHAP	Turkey:Damal	土耳其:达马尔	41.3	43.1	31	4.6	Ms	5.5										
1929	5	1	15	37	37					* Engdahl	Iran:Bojnurd	伊朗:博季努尔德	37.957	57.693	25	7.1	Mw		3800	4				4				
1929	5	1	22	42	44					GSHAP	Iran:Qūchān	伊朗:古昌	37.3	58.2	15	4.8	Ms	6.5										
1929	5	3	16	20	1					GSHAP	Iran:Qūchān	伊朗:古昌	37.7	58.2	13	5.1	Ms	7										
1929	5	4	6	31	19					Iran,GSHAP	Turkmenistan:Asgabat	土库曼斯坦:阿什哈巴德	38.64	58.02	33	5.2	Ms	6										
1929	5	13	13	27	9					GSHAP	Iran:Bojnurd	伊朗:博季努尔德	37.8	57.4	13	5.7	Ms	8										
1929	5	18	6	37						*	Turkey:Susehri	土耳其:苏谢赫里	40.2	37.9	10	6.5	Muk	8	64	2								
1929	5	20	12	17	56					GSHAP	Romania:Vrancea	罗马尼亚:弗朗恰	45.8	26.5	100	5.6	Ms	6										
1929	5	21	16	35		4	0.7	-0.5		* Usami,NOAA	Japan:Miyazaki,Near Coast	日本:宫崎近海	31.7	132.2	30	7.1	Ms											
1929	5	23	18	36	24					GSHAP	Norwegian Sea	挪威海	57.2	6.6	33	4.6	Ms	6										
1929	5	26	22	40	3	4	1.5	0.6		* Engdahl,Shi Z., NOAA	Canada:British Columbia, Kunghit Island	加拿大:英属哥伦比亚康吉特岛	51.235	-130.556	15	7	Ms							1				
1929	5	29	23	31	11					GSHAP	Norwegian Sea	挪威海	57.3	6.4	11	4.5	Ms	5										
1929	5	30	9	43	31					Engdahl,GSHAP	Argentina:San Rafael	阿根廷:圣拉斐尔	-34.768	-67.598	35	6.8	Muk	9										
1929	6	3	8	25	45					GSHAP	Macedonia:Prilep	马其顿:普里莱普	41.5	22	22	4.5	Ms	5.5										
1929	6	3	20	29	54					GSHAP	Kazakhstan:Qyzylorda	哈萨克斯坦:克孜勒奥尔达	43.2	67.1	51	6.4	Ms	7										
1929	6	4	7	4	45					GSHAP	Afghan:Jowzjan,N.	阿富汗:朱兹詹北部	37.3	66.5	14	5.7	Ms	8										
1929	6	4								* Song	Myanmar:Myitkyina	缅甸:密支那	25.2	97.2		5.9	Mk							2				
1929	6	13	9	24	39	4				* Shi Z, Bautista,Engdahl,NOAA	Philippines:Mindanao, Hinatuan	菲律宾:棉兰老岛,海纳特	8.5	127	35	7.2	Mw	10						2				
1929	6	16	22	47	32	4	2.5	1.3	1.5	* Engdahl, NOAA	New Zealand:South Island, Murchison	新西兰:南岛,默奇森	-41.75	172.25	35	7.5	Mw		17	1				3		3		
1929	6	19	8	30	35					GSHAP	Serbia:Cacak	塞尔维亚:查查克	44.3	20.6	8	4.5	Ms	6										
1929	7	8	16	46	7					USGS	US:California,Long Beach	美国:加利福尼亚州长滩	33.91	-118.04	13	4.7	Ms	7										
1929	7	10	9	40						GSHAP	Macedonia(Fyrom):Stip	马其顿:斯提普	41.45	22.3	18	4.5	Ms	5.5										
1929	7	13	7	36						*	Iran:Shirvan	伊朗:希尔凡	37.5	58	57	5.8	Muk		5	1				2				
1929	7	15	7	44	14					*	Iran:Khuzestan	伊朗:胡齐斯坦	32.2	49.7	65	6.2	Muk		6	1				2				
1929	7	20	8							GSHAP	Russia:Altai Krai,Belyashi	俄罗斯:阿尔泰边疆区别利亚希镇	49.9	87	10	4.7	Ms	6.5										
1929	7	23	18	42						*	Iceland:Reykjavik	冰岛:雷克雅末克	63.9	-21.7	33	6.3	Muk	10										
1929	7	25	0	17	21					GSHAP	Iran:Shirvan	伊朗:希尔凡	37.6	57.9	13	5.7	Ms	8										
1929	7	25	8	39	12					GSHAP	Ecuador:Quito	厄瓜多尔:基多	-0.4	-78.55		6.3	Ms	8										
1929	8	4	14	45						GSHAP	Ecuador:Quito	厄瓜多尔:基多	-0.4	-78.55		5	Ms	6										
1929	8	12	11	24		1				* Song	US:New York,Darien	美国:纽约州达里恩	42.9	-78.3		7	Mk											

时间						海啸				资料来源	震中				深度	震级	标度	烈度	死亡人数		受伤人数		经济损失		房屋毁坏		房屋受损	
年	月	日	时	分	秒	源	浪高	级 I	级 S		地名(英文)	地名(中文)	纬度(°)	经度(°)					数量/人	级别	数量/人	级别	数量/$ Mill	级别	数量/间	级别	数量/间	级别
Date						Tsunami				Information	Earthquake Epicenter				Depth	Mag	Scale	MMI	Deaths		Injuries		Damage		Houses Destroyed		Houses Damaged	
Year	Mo	Dy	Hr	Mn	Sec	Sr	Wh	mI	mS		Name(English)	Name(Chinese)	Latitude	Longitude					Num	Dd	Num	Dd	$ Mill	De	Num	Dh	Num	Dh
1929	9	4	22	24	58					GSHAP	Kazakhstan:Qyzylorda	哈萨克斯坦:克孜勒奥尔达	43.2	66.8	30	5.3	Ms	5.5										
1929	9	16	2	49						GSHAP	Iran:Shirvan	伊朗:希尔凡	37.6	57.9	10	4.8	Ms	7										
1929	9	24	13	52	17					GSHAP	Afghan:Badakhshan	阿富汗:巴达赫尚	36.7	70.7	200	6.4	Ms	6.5										
1929	9	26	4	50	56					USGS	Hawaiian Islands	夏威夷群岛	19.75	-156		5.6	Ms	7										
1929	9	27	21	20						USGS, Song	Hawaiian Islands	夏威夷群岛	19.75	-156		5.1	Mk	6										
1929	9	28	17	38						USGS, Song	Hawaiian Islands	夏威夷群岛	19.75	-156		5.6	Mk	7										
1929	9	29	1	48						USGS, Song	Hawaiian Islands	夏威夷群岛	19.75	-156		5.1	Mk	6										
1929	9	30	22	25						USGS, Song	Hawaiian Islands	夏威夷群岛	19.75	-156		5.1	Mk	6										
1929	10	5	16	59	56					GSHAP	Russia:Kamchatka, Near East Coast	俄罗斯:堪察加东部近海	53.4	160	20	6.1	Ms	8										
1929	10	6	7	51	31					USGS	Hawaiian Islands	夏威夷群岛	19.75	-156		6.5	Ms	7										
1929	10	16	16	28	8					GSHAP	Uzbekistan:Tashkent	乌兹别克斯坦:塔什干	41.2	69	14	4.6	Ms	6										
1929	10	20	3	50						GSHAP, Song	Trinidad & Tobago: Port of Spain	特立尼达和多巴哥:西班牙港	10.68	-61.51		5	Mk	6										
1929	11	1	6	57	21					GSHAP	Romania:Tulnici	罗马尼亚:图尔尼奇	45.9	26.5	150	6.7	Ms	6.5										
1929	11	9				2				NOAA, Song	Indonesia:Off West Coast of N. Sumatera	印度尼西亚:北苏门答腊西部海域	4.633	95.567		7	Mk		6	1								
1929	11	11	21	41	31					GSHAP	Kyrgyzstan:Batken, W.	吉尔吉斯斯坦:巴特肯西部	39.9	70.4	12	4.8	Ms	6.5										
1929	11	18	20	32	1	4	7	2.2		* Engdahl, NOAA	Canada:Grand Banks of Newfoundland	加拿大:纽芬兰大浅滩	44.539	-56.008	15	7.3	M	6	52	2				3				
1929	11	19								GSHAP	Iran:Shirvan	伊朗:希尔凡	37.5	57.9	12	5	Ms	7										
1929	11	28	19	49						USGS	US:California, Blackrock	美国:加利福尼亚州布莱克罗克	36.9	-118.2		5.5	Ms	7										
1929	12	4	12	29						USGS	US:California, Bridgeville	美国:加利福尼亚州布里奇维尔	40.5	-124		4.5	Ms	5										
1929	12	20	20	19	34					GSHAP	Aegean Sea	爱琴海	40.2	23.8	6	5	Ms	7										
1929	12	24	22	12	14					GSHAP	Caspian Sea	里海	41	49.5	15	4.7	Ms	6										
1930	1	2	16							* China	China:Jiangsu, Zhenjiang	中国:江苏镇江	32.2	119.4		5.5	Ms	7				2		1				
1930	1	9	8	6	13					USGS	US:California, San Juan Bautista	美国:加利福尼亚州圣胡安包蒂斯塔	36.8	-121.5		4.5	Ms	5										
1930	1	9	8	16						USGS	US:California, San Juan Bautista	美国:加利福尼亚州圣胡安包蒂斯塔	36.8	-121.5		4.5	Ms	5										
1930	1	16	0	34						CGS, USGS	US:California, Landers	美国:加利福尼亚州兰德斯	34.2	-116.9		5.5	Ms	7										
1930	1	28	6	25						*	Albania:Korce, Lavdar	阿尔巴尼亚:科里察,拉夫达里	40.4	20.5	33	5.6	Muk	10										
1930	2	4	17							GSHAP	Venezuela:Maracaibo	委内瑞拉:马拉开波湾	10.64	-71.62		4.9	Ms	5										
1930	2	11	0	11						Usami, Japan	Japan:Wakayama	日本:和歌山附近	34.2	135.1	10	5.2	Ms				1	1					5	1
1930	2	14	18	38	12					* Engdahl	Aegean Sea	爱琴海	36.067	24.789	35	6.8	Muk	11		2								

时间						海啸				资料来源	震中				深度	震级	标度	烈度	死亡人数		受伤人数		经济损失		房屋毁坏		房屋受损	
年	月	日	时	分	秒	源	浪高	级 I	级 S		地名(英文)	地名(中文)	纬度(°)	经度(°)					数量/人	级别	数量/人	级别	数量/$ Mill	级别	数量/间	级别	数量/间	级别
Date						Tsunami				Information	Earthquake Epicenter				Depth	Mag	Scale	MMI	Deaths		Injuries		Damage		Houses Destroyed		Houses Damaged	
Year	Mo	Dy	Hr	Mn	Sec	Sr	Wh	mI	mS		Name(English)	Name(Chinese)	Latitude	Longitude					Num	Dd	Num	Dd	$ Mill	De	Num	Dh	Num	Dh
1930	2	16				2				*NOAA, Song	Spain:El Ejido, Off Coast of S.	西班牙:埃尔埃希多南部近海	36	-3		7	Mk											
1930	2	26	2	30						USGS	US:California,Brawley	美国:加利福尼亚州布劳利	33	-115.5		5	Ms	7										
1930	3	1	23	44						USGS	US:California,Brawley	美国:加利福尼亚州布劳利	33	-115.5		4.5	Ms	7										
1930	3	8	3	45	30					GSHAP	Panama:Off Coast of N.	巴拿马:北部沿海	9.7	-78.7		6.3	Ms	8										
1930	3	26								*Italy	Italy:Filicudi Island	意大利:非里库地岛	38.6	14.6		5	Ms	9						2				
1930	3	31								*Song	Nicaragua:Managua	尼加拉瓜:马拉瓜	12.1	-86.2		6.4	Mk		1000	3			15.0	3				
1930	4	9	21	56	47					USGS	US:California,Truckee	美国:加利福尼亚州特拉基	39.25	-120		4.3	Ms	6										
1930	4	12	12	56	40					USGS	US:Nevada,Wabuska	美国:内华达州沃布斯卡	39.25	-119.17		4.5	Ms	6										
1930	5	5	13	45	58	4				*Engdahl, NOAA	Myanmar:Pegu, Rangoon	缅甸:勃固,仰光	17.3	96.5	35	7.2	Mw	9	550	3				3		3		3
1930	5	6	22	34	28					*Engdahl	Iran:Orumiyeh	伊朗:乌尔米耶	38.152	44.685	25	7.1	Mw		1360	4								
1930	5	14	19	48	22					*China	China:Yunnan,Qiaojia,S.	中国:云南巧家南	26.8	103		6	Ms	8	42	1	10	1		2		3		
1930	5	26	6	47						USGS	Hawaiian Islands	夏威夷群岛	19.4	-155.4		4.7	Ms	5										
1930	6	12	9	15						USGS,Song	US:Wyoming,Afton	美国:怀俄明州阿夫顿	42.6	-111		5.1	Mk	6										
1930	6	15	16							China	China:Guangxi,Pingguo	中国:广西平果	23.5	107.5		4.75	Ms	6										
1930	6	17	20	7	22					GSHAP	Russia:Altayskiy Kray, Bulatovo	俄罗斯:阿尔泰边疆区布拉托沃	51.8	84.8	15	5.3	Ms	6										
1930	6	19	13	7	27	3	1.5	-0.5		*NOAA	Indonesia:Bandar Lampung	印度尼西亚:班达楠榜	-5.6	105.3	33	6	Ms											
1930	6									China	China:Yunnan,Gejiu	中国:云南个旧	23.4	103.2		5.25	Ms	6										
1930	7	2	21	3	45					*Engdahl, GSHAP,India	India:Meghalaya	印度:梅加拉亚邦	25.641	90.245	35	7.1	Ms	9						3				
1930	7	5	23	12						*	Spain:Montilla	西班牙:梦提拉	37.8	-4.5		5.6	Muk							2				
1930	7	18	9	42						Japan,Song	Japan:Aso Mountain	日本:阿苏山	32.9	131.1		6.1	Mk											1
1930	7	18								*Song	Myanmar:Tharrawaddy	缅甸:沙耶瓦岛	17.4	95.5		5.9	Mk		50	1				2				
1930	7	19	2	38						USGS,Song	US:Oregon,Dallas	美国:俄勒冈州达拉斯	45	-123.2		5.1	Mk	6										
1930	7	19	15	20	12	2	0.1	-3.3		*NOAA	Indonesia:Java Ridge	印度尼西亚:爪哇海岭	-9.3	114.3	100	6.5	Ms											
1930	7	23	0	9						*Italy	Italy:Irpinia	意大利:伊尔皮尼亚	41.05	15.37	7	6.72	Ms	10	1430	4				3	3188	4		
1930	8	5	11	25						USGS	US:California,Santa Barbara	美国:加利福尼亚州圣巴巴拉	34.5	-119.5		5	Ms	6										
1930	8	24	10	51	16					*China	China:Sichuan,Litang,NW.	中国:四川理塘西北	30	100		5.5	Ms		200	3				1				
1930	8	31	0	40	38	3	3.1	-1	-0.5	*NOAA	US:California,Topanga	美国:加利福尼亚州托潘加	34.03	-118.643	15	5.2	Ms	7	1	1				1				
1930	9	11	17	20	12					GSHAP	Afghan:Taloqan	阿富汗:塔卢坎	36.7	70.1	220	6.2	Ms	6										
1930	9	11				2	0.7	-0.5		*NOAA,Song	Indonesia:North West of Sumatera	印度尼西亚:苏门答腊西北沿海	5.5	94		7	Mk											
1930	9	13	3	57	48					GSHAP,Song	Tajikistan:Roghun	塔吉克斯坦:罗格汉	38.56	69.41	1	5.5	Mk	7										

时间						海啸				资料来源	震中				深度	震级	标度	烈度	死亡人数		受伤人数		经济损失		房屋毁坏		房屋受损	
年	月	日	时	分	秒	源	浪高	级I	级S		地名(英文)	地名(中文)	纬度(°)	经度(°)					数量/人	级别	数量/人	级别	数量/$ Mill	级别	数量/间	级别	数量/间	级别
Date						Tsunami				Information	Earthquake Epicenter				Depth	Mag	Scale	MMI	Deaths		Injuries		Damage		Houses Destroyed		Houses Damaged	
Year	Mo	Dy	Hr	Mn	Sec	Sr	Wh	mI	mS		Name(English)	Name(Chinese)	Latitude	Longitude					Num	Dd	Num	Dd	$ Mill	De	Num	Dh	Num	Dh
1930	9	21	23	4	14					* China	Myanmar:Myitkyina	缅甸:密支那	25.8	98.4		6.5	Ms	8						2		2		
1930	9	22	16	26	40					* GSHAP	Tajikistan:Dushanbe	塔吉克斯坦:杜桑贝	38.4	68.5	5	6.3	Muk	8	175	3								
1930	9	23	2	56	55					CGS,USGS	US:California,Eureka	美国:加利福尼亚州尤里卡	40.95	-124.2		5.5	Ms	7										
1930	9	30	20	40						USGS	US:Ohio,Sidney	美国:俄亥俄州悉尼	40.3	-84.3		4.2	Ms	7										
1930	9	30	21	20	54	3				* Engdahl,NOAA	Bismarck Sea	俾斯麦海	-4.423	145.46	35	6.8	Muk											
1930	10	2								* Iran	Iran:Tehran,Damāvand	伊朗:德黑兰,达马万德	35.8	52.1		5.5	Muk		1	1				2				
1930	10	12	15	6	41					GSHAP	Tajikistan:Khudzhand	塔吉克斯坦:苦盏	40.2	69.7	12	5.1	Ms	6.5										
1930	10	16	21	36						Usami,Japan	Japan:Kaga	日本:石川加贺	36.33	136.33	20	6.4	Ms		1	1								
1930	10	19	12	17						USGS	US:Louisiana,Napoleonville	美国:路易斯安那州拿破仑维尔	30	-91		4.2	Ms	6										
1930	10	29	12	37						USGS	US:California,Whitmore	美国:加利福尼亚州惠特莫尔	40.67	-121.92		4.5	Ms	6										
1930	10	30	7	13	10	4			4	* NOAA	Italy:Senigallia	意大利:塞尼加利亚	43.75	13.5		6	Ms	9	18	1				3				
1930	11	5				3	6			* NOAA	Kenya:Mombasa	肯尼亚:蒙巴萨	-4.05	39.667		7	Ms											
1930	11	7	5	56	52					GSHAP	Georgia:Zugdidi	格鲁吉亚:祖格迪迪	42.7	42	25	4.8	Ms	6										
1930	11	21	2	0	25					* Turkey	Albania:Vlore	阿尔巴尼亚:发罗拉	40.5	19.5	12	6.3	Ms	11	35	1	108	3		3	980	3		
1930	11	25	19	2	52					* Engdahl	Japan:Izu	日本:静冈伊豆	34.977	139.103	35	6.9	Mw		259	3	1285	4		4	8099	4		
1930	11	27	18	47						GSHAP	Turkmenistan:Balkanabat	土库曼斯坦:巴尔坎纳巴德	39.7	54.5	15	4.7	Ms	6.5										
1930	12	2	13	29						*	Albania:Vlore, Tepelene	阿尔巴尼亚:发罗拉,德培雷恩	40.3	19.6	4	5	Muk	9	25	1				2				
1930	12	3	18	51	50					* Engdahl	Myanmar:Pyu	缅甸:彪关	17.972	96.422	35	7.3	Mw		36	1		3		2		2		2
1930	12	5	5	57	54					GSHAP	Azerbaijan:Quba	阿塞拜疆:库巴	41.4	48.7	24	5.2	Ms	6										
1930	12	7	12							* Song	Italy:Senigallia	意大利:塞尼加利亚	43.7	13.3		6.5	Mk	12										
1930	12	8	8	1	5					* China	China:Taiwan,Tainan	中国:台湾台南	23.2	120.6		6.25	Ms		5	1	10	1		2	297	3	165	3
1930	12	11	8	58	55					USGS	US:California,North Coast	美国:加利福尼亚州北部近海	40.08	-124.5		5	Ms	5										
1930	12	12	9	32						USGS	US:California,Leggett	美国:加利福尼亚州莱格特	39.83	-123.58		4.5	Ms	5										
1930	12	12	20	16						USGS	US:California,North Coast	美国:加利福尼亚州北部近海	40.67	-124.32		4.5	Ms	5										
1930	12	18	9	27	30					GSHAP	Kazakhstan:Almaty	哈萨克斯坦:阿拉木图	43	78.7	15	4.6	Ms	6										
1930	12	20	14	2						Usami,Japan	Japan:Miyoshi	日本:广岛三次	34.9	132.8	20	6	Ms										1	1
1930	12	21	23	51	53					* China	China:Taiwan,Nantou	中国:台湾南投	23.5	120.9		5.5	Ms							2	121	3		
1930	12	23	21	35	36	4	12	3.4	1.5	* NOAA	Bismarck Sea	俾斯麦海	-1.3	144.3	33	6.5	Ms		23	1				1	56	2		
1930	12	24	6	2	50					*	Argentina:Salta	阿根廷:萨尔塔	-24.7	-66.3	30	6	Ms	8	39	1		3		3		3		3
1930	12	25	19	3						*	Japan:Okuizumo	日本:岛根奥出云町	35.1	133	5	7	Muk		272	3				3				
1930	12	29	8	26	24	3	1		0.5	* NOAA	Chile:Vallenar	智利:巴耶纳尔	-28.5	-71		6	Ms											

年 Year	月 Mo	日 Dy	时 Hr	分 Mn	秒 Sec	海啸 源 Sr	浪高 Wh	级 I mI	级 S mS	资料来源 Information	地名(英文) Name(English)	地名(中文) Name(Chinese)	纬度(°) Latitude	经度(°) Longitude	深度 Depth	震级 Mag	标度 Scale	烈度 MMI	死亡人数 数量/人 Deaths Num	级别 Dd	受伤人数 数量/人 Injuries Num	级别 Dd	经济损失 数量/$ Mill Damage $ Mill	级别 De	房屋毁坏 数量/间 Houses Destroyed Num	级别 Dh	房屋受损 数量/间 Houses Damaged Num	级别 Dh
1931	1	4	0	0	43					* Turkey	Greece:Corinth – Isthmia (Corinthia)	希腊:科林斯 – 伊斯米亚(科林特)	38	23		5.6	Muk	8		2								
1931	1	6	16							China	China:Yunnan,Tengchong	中国:云南腾冲	25	98.5		5	Ms	6										
1931	1	6	23	28	40					USGS	US:California,Off Coast of C.	美国:加利福尼亚州中部沿海	36.5	–124.4		5	Ms	5										
1931	1	14								* * Song	Indonesia:Java,Sukabumi	印度尼西亚:爪哇,苏卡布米	–6.9	106.8		6.2	Mk							3				
1931	1	15	1	50	47					* Engdahl	Mexico:Oaxaca	墨西哥:瓦哈卡	16.1	–96.8	35	7.8	Mw	10										
1931	1	20	9	27	25					GSHAP	Afghan:Badakhshan	阿富汗:巴达赫尚	36.5	70.6	300	6.3	Ms	6										
1931	1	26	7	50						* Song	Italy:Carrara	意大利:卡拉拉	44.3	10.1		6.5	Mk	12										
1931	1	28	5	55						*	Albania:Korce	阿尔巴尼亚:科里察	40.6	20.8	33	5.8	Muk	9	90	2				3				
1931	1	28	20	9						* Song	Myanmar:Myitkyina	缅甸:密支那	25.4	96.8		6.5	Mk	9						2				
1931	2	1	6	30						* Song	Italy:Carrara	意大利:卡拉拉	44.3	10.1		6.5	Mk	12										
1931	2	2	22	46	51	4		3.9		* Engdahl, NOAA	New Zealand:North Island, Maraekakaho	新西兰:北岛,马拉卡卡霍	–39.772	176.025	35	7.7	Mw	9	256	3			25.0	4				
1931	2	5	4	48						USGS,Song	US: New Mexico, Albuquerque	美国:新墨西哥州阿尔伯克基	35.1	–106.6		5.1	Mk	6										
1931	2	6	5	20	12					GSHAP	Armenia:Kapan	亚美尼亚:卡潘	39.5	46.3	27	4.5	Ms	5.5										
1931	2	13	1	27	23	1	0.1			* Engdahl, NOAA	New Zealand:North Island, Hastings	新西兰:北岛,黑斯廷斯	–39.479	176.813	35	7.1	Ms											
1931	2	19				1				* NOAA,Song	New Zealand:North Island, Hastings	新西兰:北岛,黑斯廷斯	–39.5	177		7	Mk											
1931	2	23	10	1						USGS	US:California,Bradley	美国:加利福尼亚州布拉德利	35.83	–120.5		4.7	Ms	5										
1931	3	7	0	16	47					GSHAP	Greece:Kilkis	希腊:基尔基斯	41.2	22.5	18	6	Ms	8										
1931	3	7	1	50						GSHAP	Greece:Kilkis	希腊:基尔基斯	41.3	22.5	22	4.9	Ms	6										
1931	3	8	1	50	24					* Engdahl	Greece:Kilkis	希腊:基尔基斯	41	22.5	120	6.9	Muk	10										
1931	3	8	5	3	9					GSHAP	Greece:Kilkis	希腊:基尔基斯	41.3	22.5	6	4.6	Ms	7										
1931	3	9	3	48	57	4	0.4	–1.3	–1	* Engdahl, NOAA	Japan:Aomori, Near East Coast	日本:青森东部近海	40.484	142.664	35	7.7	Mw											
1931	3	10	3	28	53					USGS	US:California,North Coast	美国:加利福尼亚州北部近海	40	–125		5.6	Ms	5										
1931	3	18	8	2	23	3				* Chile, Engdahl, NOAA	Chile:Near Coast of C.	智利:中部近海	–33.825	–71.546	35	7.1	Ms											
1931	3	19	6	25	7					* Engdahl	Philippines:Laoag,Batac	菲律宾:拉瓦格,巴塔克	18.11	120.354	35	6.9	Muk	9						2				
1931	3	26	23							* Song	Italy:Verona	意大利:维罗那	44.9	11.4		6.5	Mk	12										
1931	3	31	16	2						*	Nicaragua:Matagalpa	尼加拉瓜:马塔加尔帕	13.2	–85.7		5.6	Muk		2450	4			15.0	3				
1931	4	4	18	40						GSHAP	Russia:Sakhalin Island	俄罗斯:库页岛(萨哈林岛)	49.5	142	10	4.5	Ms	6										
1931	4	18	4							USGS,Song	US:Washington,Seattle	美国:华盛顿州西雅图	48.75	–122.25		5.1	Mk	6										

时间 Date						海啸 Tsunami				资料来源 Information	震中 Earthquake Epicenter				深度 Depth	震级 Mag	标度 Scale	烈度 MMI	死亡人数 Deaths		受伤人数 Injuries		经济损失 Damage		房屋毁坏 Houses Destroyed		房屋受损 Houses Damaged	
年 Year	月 Mo	日 Dy	时 Hr	分 Mn	秒 Sec	源 Sr	浪高 Wh	级 I mI	级 S mS		地名(英文) Name(English)	地名(中文) Name(Chinese)	纬度(°) Latitude	经度(°) Longitude					数量/人 Num	级别 Dd	数量/人 Num	级别 Dd	数量/$ Mill $ Mill	级别 De	数量/间 Num	级别 Dh	数量/间 Num	级别 Dh
1931	4	20	19	54	31					USGS	US: New York, Chestertown	美国:纽约州切斯特敦	43.47	-73.79	5	4.7	Ms	7										
1931	4	21	15	17						* Song	Italy: Bologna	意大利:博洛尼亚	44.4	11.6		6.5	Mk	12										
1931	4	24	22	27						* Song	Italy: Claut	意大利:克劳特	46.3	12.5		6.5	Mk	12										
1931	4	27	16	50						* Iran	Armenia: Kapan	亚美尼亚:卡潘	39.48	46.09	15	6.4	Ms	8	2890	4				4				
1931	5	1	22	36	58					GSHAP	Venezuela: Barinas	委内瑞拉:巴里纳斯	8.1	-69.64	25	6.3	Ms	5										
1931	5	5	12	18						USGS	US: Alabama, Birmingham	美国:阿拉巴马州伯明翰	33.7	-86.6		4	Ms	6										
1931	5	12	1	37	3					Shi Z., GSHAP	Russia: Kamchatka Peninsula	俄罗斯:堪察加半岛	52	158	50	6.5	Ms	8										
1931	5	12	10	25	13					GSHAP	Iran: Tabriz, N.	伊朗:大不里士北部	38.8	46.3	21	5.3	Ms	6.5										
1931	5	17	15	23	19					GSHAP	Azerbaijan: Samaxi	阿塞拜疆:沙马基区	40.5	48.5	26	5	Ms	5.5										
1931	5	30	11	34	16					USGS	Aleutian Islands	阿留申群岛	52.2	173.3		6	Ms	6										
1931	6	18	14	35						GSHAP, Song	Peru: Espinar	秘鲁:埃斯皮纳尔	-14.139	-71.36	15	6	Mk	7										
1931	7	1	7	48	39					China	China: Hubei, Lichuan, S.	中国:湖北利川南	30	109		5	Ms	6										
1931	7	5	17	57	9					GSHAP	Iran: Parsabad	伊朗:法尔萨巴德	39.3	47.8	60	5.3	Ms	6										
1931	7	6	0	30						* Song	Italy: Sicilia Island	意大利:西西里岛	37.7	15.1		6.5	Mk	12										
1931	7	16	20	26	12					GSHAP	Ecuador: Cotopaxi	厄瓜多尔:科托帕希	-0.9	-78.7		5.7	Ms	7										
1931	7	24	16							China	China: Shandong, Boshan, E.	中国:山东博山东部	36.5	118.1		4.75	Ms	6										
1931	7	25	7	39	10					GSHAP	Caspian Sea	里海	41.4	49.5	16	4.8	Ms	6										
1931	8	4	15	18	26					GSHAP	Russia: Sakhalin Island	俄罗斯:库页岛(萨哈林岛)	49.5	142	9	4.5	Ms	6.5										
1931	8	7	2	11	43	1				* Engdahl, NOAA	Bismarck Sea	俾斯麦海	-2.859	142.079	35	7.1	Mw											
1931	8	10	21	18	48					* China, Engdahl	China: Xinjiang, Fuyun	中国:新疆富蕴	47.1	89.8	35	8	Mw	11	10000	5				4		4		
1931	8	11	16							China	China: Hunan, Xiangxiang, S.	中国:湖南湘乡南	27.5	112.4		4.75	Ms	6										
1931	8	15	4	1	5					GSHAP	Afghan: Fayzabad	阿富汗:法扎巴德	36.5	70.8	200	5.9	Ms	6										
1931	8	16	11	40	22					USGS	US: Texas, Marfa	美国:德克萨斯州马尔法	30.5	-104.57	1	5.8	Ms	8										
1931	8	21	12	35						GSHAP	Ecuador: Ambato	厄瓜多尔:安巴托	-0.9	-77.8		5	Ms	6										
1931	8	23	18	1	46					USGS	US: California, North Coast	美国:加利福尼亚州北部近海	40	-125		5.3	Ms	6										
1931	8	27	15	27	25					* GSHAP, Engdahl	Pakistan: Mach, Baluchistan	巴基斯坦:默杰,俾路支	29.473	67.172	35	7.1	Mw							3				
1931	9	9	13	40	30					USGS	US: California, North Coast	美国:加利福尼亚州北部近海	40.8	-125		5.8	Ms	6										
1931	9	12	15	41	32					GSHAP	Colombia: Near Coast	哥伦比亚:近海	5	-77.5		6.2	Ms	7										
1931	9	12	16							China	China: Xizang (Tibet), Lhozhag	中国:西藏洛扎	28.3	90.8		6.5	Ms	8										
1931	9	14	0	10						* Song	Italy: Cascia	意大利:卡夏	42.7	13		6.5	Mk	12										
1931	9	17	19	30						GSHAP	China: Heilongjiang, Heihe	中国:黑龙江黑河	50.1	127	80	5.5	Ms	6										

年 Year	月 Mo	日 Dy	时 Hr	分 Mn	秒 Sec	海啸 Tsunami 源 Sr	浪高 Wh	级 I mI	级 S mS	资料来源 Information	地名(英文) Name(English)	地名(中文) Name(Chinese)	纬度(°) Latitude	经度(°) Longitude	深度 Depth	震级 Mag	标度 Scale	烈度 MMI	死亡人数 Deaths 数量/人 Num	级别 Dd	受伤人数 Injuries 数量/人 Num	级别 Dd	经济损失 Damage 数量/$ Mill	级别 De	房屋毁坏 Houses Destroyed 数量/间 Num	级别 Dh	房屋受损 Houses Damaged 数量/间 Num	级别 Dh
1931	9	20	23	5	3					USGS	US:Ohio,New Bremen	美国:俄亥俄州新不来梅	40.43	-84.27	5	4.7	Ms	7										
1931	9	21	2	20	4					* Usami, Japan, Engdahl	Japan:Yorii	日本:埼玉寄居	36.021	139.381	35	6.8	Muk		16	1	146	3		2	207	3	285	3
1931	9	25	5	59	52	3	1	4.9		* Engdahl, NOAA	Indonesia:Sumatra, Coast of SW.	印度尼西亚:苏门答腊西南海域	-5.178	102.511	35	7.3	Mw	8						1				
1931	10	3	19	13	21	4	9	3.3	2.5	* Engdahl, NOAA	Solomon Islands:San Cristobal Island	所罗门群岛:圣克里斯托瓦尔岛	-10.5	161.75	35	7.8	Mw		50	1				3		3		
1931	10	5	22	31	29					Engdahl,GSHAP	Afghan:Badakhshan	阿富汗:巴达赫尚	36.535	70.854	206.4	6.8	Muk	7										
1931	10	17	12	34	50					USGS	Alaska Peninsula,S.	阿拉斯加半岛南部	63	-147		5.6	Ms	5										
1931	10	20	15	58	32					GSHAP	Caspian Sea	里海	41.7	51.1	110	6.2	Ms	7										
1931	11	2	10	3	3	4	0.8	-0.3		* Usami,Japan, Engdahl,NOAA	Japan:Miyazzaki	日本:宫崎	32	131.5	60	7.5	Mw		5		29	1			5	1	21	1
1931	11	4	15	21	30					GSHAP	Tadzhikistan:Khatlon	塔吉克斯坦:哈特隆州	38.1	69	30	5.5	Ms	6										
1931	11	16	3	20	49					GSHAP	Finland:Laukaa	芬兰:劳卡	62.5	25.8	15	4.6	Ms	6										
1931	11	22								GSHAP	Iran:Bojnurd	伊朗:博季努尔德	37.8	57.5	11	5	Ms	7										
1931	12	1				1				NOAA,Song	Cuba:Rodrigo	古巴:罗德里戈	22.8	-80.4		7	Mk											
1931	12	17	3	36						USGS	US:Mississippi,Philipp	美国:密西西比州菲利普	33.8	-90.1		4.6	Ms	6										
1931	12	31	15	25						USGS	US:Washington,Belfair	美国:华盛顿州贝尔费尔	47.5	-123		4.8	Ms	6										
1932	1	20	2	30	46					* Engdahl	Peru:Lima,Near Coast	秘鲁:利马近海	-11.866	-77.386	35	6.8	Muk	9										
1932	1	26	10	13						USGS,Song	US:Wyoming,Jackson	美国:怀俄明州杰克逊	43.5	-110.7		5.1	Mk	6										
1932	2	3	6	16	3	2				* Engdahl, NOAA	Cuba:Santiago De Cuba	古巴:圣地亚哥	19.77	-75.85	25	6.8	Muk		8	1				3				
1932	2	5	6	40	52					GSHAP	Uzbekistan:Andijan	乌兹别克斯坦:安集延	40.9	72.2	17	4.7	Ms	6										
1932	2	17	16	6	57					GSHAP	Colombia:La Guajira, Near Coast	哥伦比亚:瓜希拉省近海	12	-73.5		5.6	Ms	7										
1932	3	5	16							* China	China:Sichuan,Garze,SW.	中国:四川甘孜西南	30.1	101.8		6	Ms	8	200	3				1		2		
1932	3	8	18	1	4					*	Fiji Islands:Koro,Mudu	斐济群岛:科罗海,穆杜	-17.5	179.6		6.2	Muk	7						2				
1932	3	13	2	53						GSHAP	Romania:Nereju	罗马尼亚:内雷茹	45.7	26.6	120	5	Ms	5.5										
1932	3	14	22	42	57					Engdahl,GSHAP	Venezuela:El Palmar	委内瑞拉:埃尔帕尔马	8.149	-71.974	35	6.8	Muk	9										
1932	3	15	7	44	34					Turkey,GSHAP	Armenia:Idzhevan	亚美尼亚:伊杰万	41	45	15	5.6	Ms	7										
1932	3	25	23	58	39					Engdahl,USGS	Alaska Peninsula,S.	阿拉斯加半岛南部	62.355	-153.451	35	6.9	Muk	7										
1932	4	6	0	14	7					GSHAP	Russia:Vladikavkaz	俄罗斯:符拉迪克奥克兹	42.8	44.6	20	4.7	Ms	6										
1932	4	6	9	11	18					* China	China:Hubei,Macheng,N.	中国:湖北麻城北	31.4	115		6	Ms	8	6	1	27	1		2		3		
1932	4	12	7	0	40					GSHAP	Georgia:Akhalkalaki	格鲁吉亚:阿卡卡垃吉	41	43.7	32	4.7	Ms	5.5										
1932	4	18	21	2	50					GSHAP	Kyrgyzstan:Bishkek	吉尔吉斯斯坦:比什凯克	42.8	74.6	15	4.5	Ms	6										

年 Year	月 Mo	日 Dy	时 Hr	分 Mn	秒 Sec	源 Sr	浪高 Wh	级 I mI	级 S mS	资料来源 Information	地名(英文) Name(English)	地名(中文) Name(Chinese)	纬度(°) Latitude	经度(°) Longitude	深度 Depth	震级 Mag	标度 Scale	烈度 MMI	死亡人数 Deaths 数量/人 Num	死亡人数 级别 Dd	受伤人数 Injuries 数量/人 Num	受伤人数 级别 Dd	经济损失 Damage 数量/$ Mill	经济损失 级别 De	房屋毁坏 Houses Destroyed 数量/间 Num	房屋毁坏 级别 Dh	房屋受损 Houses Damaged 数量/间 Num	房屋受损 级别 Dh
1932	4	23	9	58						GSHAP	Macedonia(Fyrom):Berovo	马其顿:贝罗沃区	41.3	22.7	24	5	Ms	6										
1932	5	14	13	11	6					* Engdahl	Molukka Sea	马鲁古海	0.258	126.169	35	8.1	Mw	7	6	1				3				
1932	5	20	19	16						*	Iran:Mazanderan	伊朗:马赞德兰	36.6	53.4	12	5.4	Muk	8	1070	4				3				
1932	5	27	10	42	15					GSHAP	Romania:Nereju	罗马尼亚:内雷茹	45.7	26.6	120	5.6	Ms	6										
1932	6	3	10	36	54	4	3	1.5	2	*Engdahl,NOAA	Mexico:Cihuatlán	墨西哥:锡瓦特兰	19.457	-104.146	25	7.9	Mw	10	400	3				3		3		
1932	6	6	8	44	22					USGS	US:California, North Coast	美国:加利福尼亚州北部近海	40.75	-124.5		6.4	Ms	8										
1932	6	6	16							China	China:Yunnan, Gejiu	中国:云南个旧	23.4	103.2		5	Ms	6										
1932	6	14	9	44	17					USGS	US:California, Los Gatos	美国:加利福尼亚州洛斯加托斯	37.25	-122.08		4.5	Ms	5										
1932	6	16	12	9	25					GSHAP	Armenia:Zangezur	亚美尼亚:休尼克	39.3	46	26	4.8	Ms	6										
1932	6	18	10	12	16	4	1	1	0.5	* Engdahl, NOAA	Mexico:Colima	墨西哥:科利马	19.452	-103.632	54.3	7.9	Mw	10						2				
1932	6	20	9	1	47					* * Shi Z.	El Salvador:Off Coast of W.	萨尔瓦多:西部海域	12.5	-89	80	6	Ms							3				
1932	6	22	12	59	31	4	10	3.3	1.5	* Engdahl, NOAA	Mexico:Manzanillo	墨西哥:曼萨尼约	19.028	-104.379	25	6.9	Muk		75	2	100	2		3	400	3		
1932	6	29	22	20	12					GSHAP	Colombia:Bahia Solano	哥伦比亚:巴伊阿索拉诺	7	-77.5		5.6	Ms	7										
1932	7	3	3	7						GSHAP	Russia:Sakhalin Island	俄罗斯:库页岛(萨哈林岛)	49.5	142	17	4.5	Ms	6										
1932	7	8	8	30	49					USGS, Song	Hawaiian Islands	夏威夷群岛	19.4	-155.3	10	4.9	Mk	5										
1932	7	8	11	17	7					GSHAP	Turkey:Hacibektas	土耳其:哈吉贝克塔什	38.9	34.5	12	4.8	Ms	6										
1932	7	10	0	43	25					GSHAP, Song	Russia:Sakhalin Island	俄罗斯:库页岛(萨哈林岛)	53.1	143.3	15	5.5	Mk	7										
1932	7	18	6	1	55					USGS	US:Washington, Seattle	美国:华盛顿州西雅图	47.75	-121.83		5.2	Ms	6										
1932	7	26	6	51	58					USGS	US:California, Posey, E.	美国:加利福尼亚州波西东部	35.8	-118.53	16	4.5	Ms	6										
1932	8	6	3	57						GSHAP, Song	Peru:Arequipa	秘鲁:阿雷基帕	-16.7	-71.7	90	5	Mk	6										
1932	8	6	22	16						USGS, Song	US:Washington, Seattle	美国:华盛顿州西雅图	47.7	-122.3		5.1	Mk	6										
1932	8	14	4	39	39					* Engdahl. GSHAP	India:Assam	印度:阿萨姆邦	25.765	95.655	143.9	7	mB							2				
1932	8	24	12	10	32					* Song, Shi Z.	Philippines:Baguio	菲律宾:碧瑶	16.5	120.5		6.25	Mk	7						2				
1932	9	9	13	39	4	2	0.7	-0.5		*Shi Z. ,NOAA	Indonesia:Banda Sea	印度尼西亚:班达海	-3.6	128.3	17	6.25	Ms	7						3	73	2		3
1932	9	14	8	43	23					USGS	Gulf of Alaska	阿拉斯加湾	61	-148	50	6.25	Ms	5										
1932	9	15	13	54	58	1		-0.5		* Engdahl, NOAA	New Zealand:Gisborne, Wairoa	新西兰:吉斯伯恩,威洛亚	-38.956	177.455	35	6.8	Ms				5	1		2		2		
1932	9	26	19	20	49	4	1		3	*Engdahl,NOAA	Greece:Chalkidiki	希腊:哈尔基迪基	40.333	23.732	35	6.9	Muk	10	491	3								
1932	9	29	3	57						*	Greece:Chalkidiki	希腊:哈尔基迪基	40.5	23.8		6.2	Muk	11										
1932	10	2	3	22	5					GSHAP	Uzbekistan:Navoiy	乌兹别克斯坦:纳沃伊州	41.4	65.6	30	6.2	Ms	7										
1932	10	29	11	8	50					GSHAP	Tadzhikistan:Dzhirgatal	塔吉克斯坦:吉尔加塔尔	39.2	72.2	20	5.9	Ms	6.5										

时间 Date						海啸 Tsunami				资料来源 Information	震中 Earthquake Epicenter				深度 Depth	震级 Mag	标度 Scale	烈度 MMI	死亡人数 Deaths		受伤人数 Injuries		经济损失 Damage		房屋毁坏 Houses Destroyed		房屋受损 Houses Damaged	
年 Year	月 Mo	日 Dy	时 Hr	分 Mn	秒 Sec	源 Sr	浪高 Wh	级 I mI	级 S mS		地名(英文) Name(English)	地名(中文) Name(Chinese)	纬度(°) Latitude	经度(°) Longitude					数量/人 Num	级别 Dd	数量/人 Num	级别 Dd	数量/$ Mill $ Mill	级别 De	数量/间 Num	级别 Dh	数量/间 Num	级别 Dh
1932	11	2	16							China	China:Yunnan,Chengjiang,SE.	中国:云南澄江东南	24.5	103.1		5	Ms	6										
1932	11	3	18	54	40					USGS	US:California,Boulder Creek	美国:加利福尼亚州博尔德河	37.16	-122.16		4.9	Ms	5										
1932	11	4				1				* NOAA,Song	Venezuela:Cumana	委内瑞拉:库马纳	10.5	-64.2		7	Mk											
1932	11	10				4	5.4			* Song	US:New York,Breezy Point	美国:纽约州布里齐波恩特	40.5	-74		7	Mk											
1932	12	9	8	34	55					GSHAP	Peru:Nazca	秘鲁:纳斯卡	-15	-75	75	6.5	Ms	6										
1932	12	20								*	US:Nevada,Cedar Mountain	美国:内华达州雪松山	38.7	-117.8		7.2	Muk	12										
1932	12	24	4	17	20					GSHAP	Kyrgyzstan:Issyk-Kul,N.	吉尔吉斯斯坦:伊塞克湖州北部	42.8	78.2	23	5.6	Ms	6.5										
1932	12	25	1	4	32					*China,Engdahl	China:Gansu,Yumen	中国:甘肃玉门	39.771	96.69	25	7.6	Mw	10	275	3	320	3		3	1167	4		
1932	12	25	12	32	3					GSHAP	Bolivia:Potosi	玻利维亚:波托西	-18.69	-66.01		5.4	Ms	6										
1932	12	30	21	20						GSHAP	Kyrgyzstan:Issyk-Kul,N.	吉尔吉斯斯坦:伊塞克湖州北部	42.8	78.2	20	5.1	Ms	6										
1932										* China	China:Sichuan,Barkam,S.	中国:四川马尔康南	31.8	102.2		5	Ms	7		1				1		1		
1933	1	2	7	56	52					GSHAP	Bulgaria:Dospat	保加利亚:多斯帕特	41.7	24.2	50	4.6	Ms	5.5										
1933	1	4	3	59	28					USGS,Shi Z.	Gulf of Alaska	阿拉斯加湾	61	-148		6.25	Ms	6										
1933	1	8	16			5	9	3.2	2	NOAA	Kuril Islands	千岛群岛	49.12	154.508	33	6	Ms		2	1								
1933	1	9	2	1	46					GSHAP	Afghan:Taloqan	阿富汗:塔卢坎	36.4	69.6	180	7.1	Ms	6.5										
1933	1	18	2	35	21					GSHAP	Serbia:Cacak	塞尔维亚:查查克	44	20.2	7	4.5	Ms	6.5										
1933	1	20	13	5						USGS,Song	US:Utah,Parowan	美国:犹他州帕罗万	37.8	-112.8		5.1	Mk	6										
1933	2	10	22	0	50					GSHAP	Colombia:Narino	哥伦比亚:纳里尼奥	1.2	-77.5		5.7	Ms	7										
1933	2	22	17	57	4					GSHAP	China:Xinjiang,Ili	中国:新疆伊犁	43	81.5	30	5.5	Ms	6.5										
1933	2	23	8	9	21	2				* Engdahl,NOAA	Chile:Iquique,Near Coast	智利:伊基克近海	-20	-71	40	7.2	Mw											
1933	2	26	21	25						* Song	Italy:Sicilia Island	意大利:西西里岛	37.4	13		6.5	Mk	12										
1933	3	1								China	China:Yunnan,Lijiang	中国:云南丽江	26.9	100.2		5	Ms	6										
1933	3	2	17	31	1	4	29	4.9	3.5	* GSHAP, Shi Z, Usami,Japan, Engdahl,NOAA	Japan Trench	日本海沟	39.1	144.7	10	8.4	M		3064	4	1092	4		4	6067	4	4329	4
1933	3	11	1	54	8	4	0.1	-3.3		*	US:California,Huntington Beach	美国:加利福尼亚州亨廷顿海滩	33.62	-117.97	16	6.3	ML	9	120	3			40.0	4				
1933	3	17	15	55	30					Engdahl,GSHAP	Russia:Kamchatka Peninsula	俄罗斯:堪察加半岛	54.857	161.601	35	7	Ms	9										
1933	3	22	2	22	50					GSHAP	Kyrgyzstan:Chui,C.	吉尔吉斯斯坦:楚河州中部	42.6	74.5	20	5.2	Ms	6.5										
1933	3	23	17	38	16					GSHAP	Mongolia:West Dundgovi	蒙古:中戈壁西部	45.7	104.2	30	6.2	Ms	8										
1933	4	23	5	57	37	1				* Turkey,Engdahl,NOAA	Greece:Dodecanese Islands	希腊:多德卡尼斯群岛	36.516	27.15	35	6.8	Muk	10										

年 Year	月 Mo	日 Dy	时 Hr	分 Mn	秒 Sec	海啸 Tsunami 源 Sr	浪高 Wh	级 I mI	级 S mS	资料来源 Information	震中 Earthquake Epicenter 地名(英文) Name(English)	地名(中文) Name(Chinese)	纬度(°) Latitude	经度(°) Longitude	深度 Depth	震级 Mag	标度 Scale	烈度 MMI	死亡人数 Deaths 数量/人 Num	级别 Dd	受伤人数 Injuries 数量/人 Num	级别 Dd	经济损失 Damage 数量/$ Mill $ Mill	级别 De	房屋毁坏 Houses Destroyed 数量/间 Num	级别 Dh	房屋受损 Houses Damaged 数量/间 Num	级别 Dh
1933	4	27	2	36	12					USGS, Shi Z., Engdahl	Alaska Peninsula, S.	阿拉斯加半岛南部	61.25	-150.75	35	6.9	Ms	7										
1933	5	16	11	45	26					USGS	US: California, Fremont	美国:加利福尼亚州弗里蒙特	37.6	-122		4.5	Ms	7										
1933	5	18	4	28	35					GSHAP	Ecuador: Ibarra	厄瓜多尔:伊瓦拉	0.5	-78.5	60	5.6	Ms	6										
1933	5	19				3				* NOAA, Song	Togo: Kpalime	多哥:帕利梅	6.9	0.6		7	Mk											
1933	5	21	10	10						*	El Salvador: Near Coast	萨尔瓦多:近海	12	-87.5	90	6.9	Muk							2				
1933	6	4	14	8	22					USGS	US: Nevada, Luning	美国:内华达州卢宁	38.5	-118.16	16	5.2	Ms	5										
1933	6	18	21	37	38	4	0.2	-2.3		* Japan, Engdahl, NOAA	Japan: Miyagi, Near Coast	日本:宫城近海	38.28	142.51	35	7.2	Mw											
1933	6	25	20	45	27					USGS	US: Nevada, Yerington	美国:内华达州耶灵顿	39.08	-119.33		6.1	Ms	7										
1933	7	2	19	59	13					GSHAP	Romania: Nehoiu	罗马尼亚:内霍尤	45.2	26.2	140	5.6	Ms	6										
1933	7	19	18	43	15					GSHAP	Turkey: Denizli	土耳其:登尼资里	38.7	29.9	18	5.3	Ms	7										
1933	7	28	11	48	8					USGS, Song	Andreanof Islands, Aleutian Is.	阿留申群岛,安德烈亚诺夫群岛	52.6	-168.7		4.9	Mk	5										
1933	8	6	2	54	52					GSHAP	Peru: Perene	秘鲁:佩雷内	-11	-75.5	100	6.5	Ms	6										
1933	8	25	7	50	33					* China, Engdahl	China: Sichuan, Maoxian, W.	中国:四川茂县西	31.9	103.4	25	7.3	Mw	10	9300	4				4		4		
1933	9	9	19	34	21					GSHAP	Tajikistan: Isfala	塔吉克斯坦:伊斯法拉	40.1	70.7	26	5.5	Ms	6										
1933	9	19	4	46	30					GSHAP	Russia: Maritime Kray, Nakhodka	俄罗斯:滨海边疆区纳霍德卡	43.2	133	4	4.5	Ms	7										
1933	9	19	16							* *	China: Sichuan, Hanyuan, N.	中国:四川汉源北	29.5	102.5		5	Ms	6	200	3				1	30	1		
1933	9	21	3	14	26					Shi Z., Usami, Japan	Japan: Nanao	日本:石川七尾	37.2	137.2		6	Ms		3	1	55	2			2	1	143	3
1933	9	26	3	33						* Italy	Italy: Sulmona	意大利:苏尔莫纳	42.05	14.18	33	5.68	Ms	9	10	1				2				
1933	10	2	9	10	18					USGS	US: California, Long Beach	美国:加利福尼亚州长滩	33.78	-118.13	16	5.4	Ms	6										
1933	10	2	15	29	30	3		0.6	1.5	* Engdahl, NOAA	Ecuador: Near Coast of W.	厄瓜多尔:西部近海	-2.044	-81.099	35	6.9	Ms											
1933	10	5	13	29	46					GSHAP	Iran: Razavi Khorasan	伊朗:呼罗珊	34.6	57.3	10	6	Ms	8.5										
1933	10	14	16							China	China: Sichuan, Maoxian	中国:四川茂县	31.8	104		5.75	Ms	7										
1933	10	24	16	24	59					GSHAP	Russia: Chechnia, Grozny, S.	俄罗斯:车臣共和国格罗兹尼北部	42.9	45.9	10	5.2	Ms	7.5										
1933	10	25	7	0	46					USGS	US: California, Long Beach	美国:加利福尼亚州长滩	33.95	-118.13	16	4.3	Ms	6										
1933	10	27	10	58	54					USGS	US: Nevada, Round Mountain	美国:内华达州朗德芒廷	38.9	-117.6		5.5	Ms	5										
1933	11	3	4	14						*	Chile: Antofagasta, Coast	智利:安托法加斯塔近海	-22	-70.5	70	5.5	Muk	10										
1933	11	4	8	41	18					GSHAP	Venezuela: Merida	委内瑞拉:梅里达	8.36	-71.81	25	6	Ms	6										
1933	11	23	16							China	China: Sichuan, Maoxian, Diexi	中国:四川茂县叠溪	32	103.7		4.75	Ms	6										
1933	11	23	16							China	China: Yunnan, Pu-er	中国:云南普洱	23	101.1		4.75	Ms	6										

年 Year	月 Mo	日 Dy	时 Hr	分 Mn	秒 Sec	源 Sr	浪高 Wh	级 I mI	级 S mS	资料来源 Information	地名(英文) Name(English)	地名(中文) Name(Chinese)	纬度(°) Latitude	经度(°) Longitude	深度 Depth	震级 Mag	标度 Scale	烈度 MMI	死亡人数 Deaths 数量/人 Num	死亡人数 Deaths 级别 Dd	受伤人数 Injuries 数量/人 Num	受伤人数 Injuries 级别 Dd	经济损失 Damage 数量/$ Mill	经济损失 Damage 级别 De	房屋毁坏 Houses Destroyed 数量/间 Num	房屋毁坏 Houses Destroyed 级别 Dh	房屋受损 Houses Damaged 数量/间 Num	房屋受损 Houses Damaged 级别 Dh
1933	11	28	11	9						* GSHAP	Iran: Yazd	伊朗:亚兹德	32.1	56	27	6.3	Muk	9	4	1				3				
1933	12	8								GSHAP, Song	Trinidad & Tobago: Port of Spain	特立尼达和多巴哥:西班牙港	10.68	-61.51		5	Mk	6										
1933	12	12	14	11	17	3				* Engdahl, NOAA	Papua New Guinea: New Ireland	巴布亚新几内亚:新爱尔兰	-4.294	153.154	35	6.8	Muk							1				
1934	1	9	14	10						USGS	US: California, Glendora	美国:加利福尼亚州格伦多拉	34.1	-117.68	16	4.5	Ms	5										
1934	1	12	13	31	52					* China	China: Yunnan, Jianshui, NW.	中国:云南建水西北	23.7	102.7		6	Ms	8	1	1	14	1		2		3		
1934	1	15	8	43	25					* India, Engdahl	India: Bihar; Nepal: Kathmandu	印度:比哈尔;尼泊尔:加德满都	26.5	86.5	35	8.1	M	11	10600	5				4		4		4
1934	1	17	8	22	30					GSHAP	Caspian Sea	里海	42.3	51	60	5.2	Ms	5.5										
1934	1	20	17	56	16					* China	China: Inner Mongolia, Wuyuan	中国:内蒙古五原	41	108.8		6.25	Ms	8		1				2		3		
1934	1	30	19	23	29					USGS	US: Nevada, Mina	美国:内华达州迈纳	38.3	-118.4		5.5	Ms	7										
1934	1	30	20	16	31					USGS	US: Nevada, Mina, SW.	美国:内华达州迈纳西南	38.28	-118.36		6.5	Ms	8										
1934	2	1	11	18	51					USGS	US: Nevada, Luning	美国:内华达州卢宁	38.5	-118.25		5.2	Ms	5										
1934	2	1	11	45	54					USGS	US: Nevada, Mina	美国:内华达州迈纳	38.3	-118.4		5.4	Ms	5										
1934	2	2	19	59	13					GSHAP	Romania: Nehoiu	罗马尼亚:内霍尤	45.5	26.2	140	5.6	Ms	6										
1934	2	14	3	59	42	4				* Shi Z., Bautista, Engdahl, NOAA	China: South China Sea, Zhongsha Islands, E.	中国:南海中沙群岛东	17.5	119	35	7.5	Mw							1				
1934	2	18	1	17						China	China: Liaoning, Jinzhou	中国:辽宁金州	39.1	121.7		4.75	Ms	6										
1934	3	4	11	17	30					GSHAP	Russia: Kamchatka, Near East Coast	俄罗斯:堪察加东部近海	56	164	20	6.3	Ms	8.5										
1934	3	12	15	5	40					USGS	US: Utah, Tremonton	美国:犹他州特里蒙顿	41.7	-112.8		6.6	Ms	8										
1934	3	12	18	20	13					USGS	US: Utah, Brigham City	美国:犹他州布里格姆城	41.5	-112.5		6	Ms	7										
1934	3	13	16	20	19					USGS	US: Nevada, Coaldale	美国:内华达州科尔代尔	38	-118		4.7	Ms	5										
1934	3	15	12	1						USGS	US: Utah, Brigham City	美国:犹他州布里格姆城	41.5	-112.5		5.1	Ms	6										
1934	3	29	20	6	48					GSHAP	Romania: Nereju	罗马尼亚:内雷茹	45.7	26.5	150	6.8	Ms	8										
1934	4	3	7	36	27					GSHAP	Colombia: Near Coast	哥伦比亚:近海	4	-78		6	Ms	7										
1934	4	6	12	7	9					GSHAP	Colombia: Near Coast	哥伦比亚:近海	3.4	-77.8		5	Ms	6										
1934	4	15	2	58	13					USGS	US: New York, West Chazy	美国:纽约州西谢齐	44.7	-73.8		4.5	Ms	6										
1934	5	2	16							China	China: Yunnan, Huize	中国:云南会泽	26.6	103.1		5.25	Ms	6										
1934	5	4	4	36	11					USGS, Shi Z., Engdahl	Alaska Peninsula, S.	阿拉斯加半岛南部	61.25	-147.5	35	7.1	mB	6										
1934	5	6	8	9	49					USGS	US: Utah, Park Valley	美国:犹他州帕克瓦利	41.5	-113		5.5	Ms	6										

时间 Date						海啸 Tsunami				资料来源 Information	震中 Earthquake Epicenter				深度 Depth	震级 Mag	标度 Scale	烈度 MMI	死亡人数 Deaths		受伤人数 Injuries		经济损失 Damage		房屋毁坏 Houses Destroyed		房屋受损 Houses Damaged	
年 Year	月 Mo	日 Dy	时 Hr	分 Mn	秒 Sec	源 Sr	浪高 Wh	级 I mI	级 S mS		地名(英文) Name(English)	地名(中文) Name(Chinese)	纬度(°) Latitude	经度(°) Longitude					数量/人 Num	级别 Dd	数量/人 Num	级别 Dd	数量/$ Mill $ Mill	级别 De	数量/间 Num	级别 Dh	数量/间 Num	级别 Dh
1934	5	14	22	12	46					USGS	Alaska: Kodiak Island	阿拉斯加:科迪亚克岛	57.75	−152.25	60	6.5	Ms	6										
1934	5	21	4	36	48					China	China: Fujian, Quanzhou	中国:福建泉州	25	118.2		5.75	Ms	7										
1934	5									China	China: Sichuan, Maoxian, Diexi	中国:四川茂县叠溪	32	103.7		4.75	Ms	6										
1934	6	2	13	43		2				* Iceland, NOAA	Iceland: Grenivik	冰岛:格雷尼维克	66	−18.25	3	6.2	Ms	8										
1934	6	5	21	48						USGS	US: California, Parkfield	美国:加利福尼亚州帕克菲尔德	35.8	−120.33	16	5	Ms	5										
1934	6	5	22	52						USGS	US: California, Parkfield	美国:加利福尼亚州帕克菲尔德	35.8	−120.33	16	4	Ms	6										
1934	6	8	4	30						USGS	US: California, Parkfield	美国:加利福尼亚州帕克菲尔德	35.8	−120.33	16	5	Ms	7										
1934	6	8	4	47	47					USGS	US: California, Parkfield	美国:加利福尼亚州帕克菲尔德	35.8	−120.33	16	6	Ms	8										
1934	6	8	16							China	China: Sichuan, Maoxian, Diexi	中国:四川茂县叠溪	32	103.7		5.5	Ms	7										
1934	6	11	3	7	9					GSHAP	Argentina: Río Cuarto	阿根廷:里奥夸尔托	−33.5	−64.5	30	6	Ms	9										
1934	6	18	9	13	51					Engdahl, USGS, Shi Z.	Alaska Peninsula, S.	阿拉斯加半岛南部	60.785	−151.244	50.2	6.8	Muk	5										
1934	7	6	22	48	55					USGS	US: California, North Coast	美国:加利福尼亚州北部近海	41.22	−125.27	5	6.5	Ms	5										
1934	7	18	1	36	28	4		1	1.5	* Engdahl, NOAA	Panama: Off Coast of S.	巴拿马:南部海域	8	−82.5	25	7.6	Mw				4	1	0.75	1		2		
1934	7	18	19	40	24	3	0.7	−0.7		* Engdahl, NOAA	Solomon Islands: Santa Cruz Islands	所罗门群岛:圣克鲁斯岛	−11.907	166.731	35	7.8	Mw											
1934	7	19	1	27	33	4				* * NOAA, Engdahl	Indonesia: Irian Jaya Barat	印度尼西亚:西巴布亚	−0.5	133.3	35	7	Ms											
1934	7	21	6	18	23	1				* Engdahl	North Vanuatu Islands	瓦努阿图群岛北部	−11.139	165.503	35	7.1	Mw											
1934	7	22	19	56	36					Engdahl, GSHAP	Afghan: Badakhshan	阿富汗:巴达赫尚	35.712	70.683	35	6.8	Muk	7										
1934	7	30	7	20						USGS	US: Nebraska, Chadron	美国:奈伯拉斯卡州沙德伦	42.7	−103		4.3	Ms	6										
1934	7	30								* * Song	Indonesia: Sulawesi, Lemo	印度尼西亚:苏拉威西岛,勒莫	−2	121		5.9	Mk	8						2				
1934	8	2	7	13	8					USGS	Alaska Peninsula, S.	阿拉斯加半岛南部	61.5	−147.5		6	Ms	5										
1934	8	6	12	7	8					GSHAP	Colombia: Near Coast	哥伦比亚:近海	3.2	−77.7		6	Ms	7										
1934	8	11	8	18	21					* China	China: Taiwan, Wulai	中国:台湾新北乌来	24.8	121.5		6.5	Ms		3	1				1	6	1	11	1
1934	8	15	19	10						GSHAP	Ecuador: Chimborazo	厄瓜多尔:钦博腊索山	−2.3	−79		5	Ms	6										
1934	8	20	0	47	27					USGS	US: Missouri, Wyatt	美国:密苏里州怀厄特	36.95	−89.2		4.7	Ms	7										
1934	8	31	14	57	47					GSHAP	Tadzhikistan: Tajikabad	塔吉克斯坦:塔吉卡巴德	38.9	70.9	7	6.5	Ms	9										
1934	9	8	6	44	55					GSHAP	Tajikistan: Kalaihongbu	塔吉克斯坦:卡莱洪布	38.4	71.2	11	5.4	Ms	6										
1934	9	11	14	7	5					GSHAP	Tadzhikistan: Tajikabad	塔吉克斯坦:塔吉卡巴德	38.8	70.9	7	5	Ms	7										

时间						海啸				资料来源	震中				深度	震级	标度	烈度	死亡人数		受伤人数		经济损失		房屋毁坏		房屋受损	
年	月	日	时	分	秒	源	浪高	级 I	级 S		地名(英文)	地名(中文)	纬度(°)	经度(°)					数量/人	级别	数量/人	级别	数量/$ Mill	级别	数量/间	级别	数量/间	级别
Date						Tsunami				Information	Earthquake Epicenter				Depth	Mag	Scale	MMI	Deaths		Injuries		Damage		Houses Destroyed		Houses Damaged	
Year	Mo	Dy	Hr	Mn	Sec	Sr	Wh	mI	mS		Name(English)	Name(Chinese)	Latitude	Longitude					Num	Dd	Num	Dd	$ Mill	De	Num	Dh	Num	Dh
1934	9	22	16							China	China:Ningxia,Haiyuan	中国:宁夏海原	36.6	105.7		5	Ms	6										
1934	9	27	22	51	20					GSHAP	Kyrgyzstan:Issyk – Kul,W.	吉尔吉斯斯坦:伊塞克湖州西部	42.4	75.8	18	4.9	Ms	6										
1934	10	26	16							China	China:Hebei,Funing	中国:河北抚宁	39.9	119.2		5	Ms	6										
1934	11	2	16	41	50					GSHAP	Turkey:Yusufeli	土耳其:优素费利	41	41.6	22	4.7	Ms	5										
1934	11	2	22	6	16					GSHAP	Azerbaijan:Lenkeran	阿塞拜疆:连科兰	39.9	48.7	22	4.5	Ms	5										
1934	11	12	14	45						USGS	US:Iowa,Davenport	美国:爱荷华州达文波特	41.5	-90.5		4	Ms	6										
1934	11	17	17	42						USGS	US:California,Fortuna	美国:加利福尼亚州福图纳	40.5	-124.08		5	Ms	5										
1934	11	18	3	21	20					GSHAP	Afghan:Badakhshan	阿富汗:巴达赫尚	36.4	70.6	200	6.7	Ms	6										
1934	11	18	9	18	31					Shi Z., GSHAP	Russia:Kamchatka Peninsula	俄罗斯:堪察加半岛	54	160.5	20	6	Ms	8										
1934	11	27								* Song	Turkey:Diyarbakir	土耳其:迪亚巴克尔	37.919	40.211		6.2	Mk		100	2				3				
1934	11	30	2	5	19	4	0.1			* Engdahl, NOAA	Mexico:Off Coast of Jalisco	墨西哥:哈利斯科沿海	18.679	-105.319	25	7	Ms							3				
1934	12	3	2	38	30					* Shi Z.	Honduras:San Jorge, La Encarnacion	洪都拉斯:圣乔治湾,恩卡纳西翁	15	-89		6.25	Ms							2				
1934	12	4	17	24	35	2				* Engdahl, shi Z., NOAA	Chile:Iquique, Pisagua	智利:伊基克,皮萨瓜	-19.298	-69.752	35	6.9	Muk					2		2		3		
1934	12	13	10	12						GSHAP	Ecuador:Quito	厄瓜多尔:基多	0.1	-78.4		5	Ms	6										
1934	12	13				1				NOAA,Song	East Caroline Basin	东加罗林海盆	0	150		7	Mk											
1934	12	15	17	0	10					USGS	US:California,North Coast	美国:加利福尼亚州北部近海	40.6	-124.2		4.8	Ms	5										
1934	12	15								* Song	Turkey:Diyarbakir	土耳其:迪亚巴克尔	37.919	40.211		5.9	Mk		20	1				2				
1934	12	17	11	10						USGS	US:California,Lompoc	美国:加利福尼亚州隆波克	34.58	-120.33	16	4.5	Ms	6										
1934	12	24	15	23						* Song	North Atlantic Ocean,E.	北大西洋东部	38.2	-20.6		7	Mk	10										
1934	12	26	0	25	26					GSHAP	Black Sea	黑海	44.4	34.3	18	4.6	Ms	5.5										
1934	12	30	13	52	14					USGS	Mexico:Mexicali	墨西哥:墨西卡利	32.25	-115.5		6.5	Ms	9										
1934	12	31	18	45	57					* Engdahl	US:California,Baja, Imperial Valley	美国:加利福尼亚州巴哈,帝王谷	32.685	-115.761	15	7.1	Ms	10										
1935	1	2	7	30						USGS,Song	US:Arizona,Roll	美国:亚利桑那州罗尔	32.8	-114.2		5.1	Mk	6										
1935	1	2	17	17						USGS	Hawaiian Islands	夏威夷群岛	19.42	-155.28	4	5.9	Ms	5										
1935	1	2	22	40	58					CGS,USGS	US:California,North Coast	美国:加利福尼亚州北部近海	40.25	-125.25		5.8	Ms	5										
1935	1	4	14	41						*	Turkey:Marmara Sea	土耳其:马尔马拉海	40.5	27.5	7	6.2	Muk	10	5	1				2				
1935	1	10	8	10						USGS,Song	US:Arizona,Tusayan	美国:亚利桑那州图萨扬	36	-112.1		5.1	Mk	6										
1935	1	18	16							China	China:Hebei,Tangshan	中国:河北唐山	39.6	118.3		4.75	Ms	6										
1935	1	19	0	49	14					GSHAP	Black Sea	黑海	42.4	40	22	4.7	Ms	6										

年 Year	月 Mo	日 Dy	时 Hr	分 Mn	秒 Sec	海啸 Tsunami 源 Sr	浪高 Wh	级 I mI	级 S mS	资料来源 Information	震中 Earthquake Epicenter 地名(英文) Name(English)	地名(中文) Name(Chinese)	纬度(°) Latitude	经度(°) Longitude	深度 Depth	震级 Mag	标度 Scale	烈度 MMI	死亡人数 Deaths 数量/人 Num	级别 Dd	受伤人数 Injuries 数量/人 Num	级别 Dd	经济损失 Damage 数量/$ Mill $ Mill	级别 De	房屋毁坏 Houses Destroyed 数量/间 Num	级别 Dh	房屋受损 Houses Damaged 数量/间 Num	级别 Dh
1935	1	25	14	38						GSHAP	Armenia:Gyumri	亚美尼亚:久姆里	41.1	43.9	30	5	Ms	5.5										
1935	2	3	2	10	40					GSHAP	Afghan:Badakhshan	阿富汗:巴达赫尚	36.5	70.5	220	6.1	Ms	5.5										
1935	2	21	1	25						USGS,Song	US:New Mexico,La Joya	美国:新墨西哥州拉霍亚	34.5	-106.8		5.1	Mk	6										
1935	2	25	2	51	27					* GSHAP,Engdahl	Aegean Sea	爱琴海	35.8	25	35	6.8	Muk	8		2								
1935	2									China	China:Yunnan,Zhaotong,SE.	中国:云南昭通东南	27	104		5.5	Ms	7										
1935	3	1	11							USGS	US:Nebraska,Nebraska	美国:内布拉斯加州林肯市	40.3	-96.2		4.6	Ms	6										
1935	3	5	10	26	35					* Shi Z.	Iran:Mazandaran	伊朗:马赞德兰	36.3	53.3		6	Muk		60	2								
1935	3	5	22	35						GSHAP,Song	Peru:Huari	秘鲁:瓦里	-9.82	-77.43	25	5	Mk	6										
1935	4	3	11	11	57					GSHAP	Afghan:Badakhshan	阿富汗:巴达赫尚	36.7	70.9	160	6.3	Ms	6										
1935	4	10	22	32	31					GSHAP	Venezuela:Macuro	委内瑞拉:马库罗	10.5	-62	100	6.5	Ms	6										
1935	4	11	23	14	50					* Iran,Engdahl	Iran:Mazanderan	伊朗:马赞德兰	36.432	53.621	35	6.8	Muk	9	690	3				3				
1935	4	15	23	4	35					GSHAP	Iran:Semnan,Dāmghān	伊朗:塞姆南,达姆甘	35.9	54	17	4.6	Ms	6										
1935	4	20	22	2	3					* China,Engdahl	China:Taiwan,Taichung	中国:台湾台中	24.364	120.613	35	7.1	Ms	9	3276	4	12053	5		4	17907	5	21211	5
1935	4	20	22	26	26					China	China:Taiwan,Miaoli	中国:台湾苗栗	24.7	120.9		6	Ms	8										
1935	4	22	13	15	27					GSHAP	Uzbekistan:Samarqand	乌兹别克斯坦:撒马尔罕	39.8	67.5	25	5.3	Ms	6										
1935	4	27	16							* * China	China:Sichuan,Luding,S.	中国:四川泸定南	29.4	102.3		6	Ms	8	2	1				1		1		
1935	4									China	China:Yunnan,Jianshui,E.	中国:云南建水东	23.5	103		5.5	Ms	7										
1935	5	1	10	24						*	Turkey:Bingol	土耳其:宾格尔	39.3	40.6		6.1	Muk		540	3								
1935	5	4	23	2	24					* China	China:Taiwan,Miaoli,Coast of W.	中国:台湾苗栗西部海域	24.8	120.8		6	Ms				37	1		1	28	1	571	3
1935	5	16	17	24	16					GSHAP	Tadzhikistan:Khatlon,S.	塔吉克斯坦:哈特隆州南部	37.5	69.2	52	5.5	Ms	5										
1935	5	30	21	32	57	1				* Engdahl	Pakistan:Quetta	巴基斯坦:奎达	28.894	66.176	35	8.1	Mw	10	60000	5			25.0	4		4		4
1935	6	7	1	50	58					* China	China:Taiwan,Taichung	中国:台湾台中	24.2	120.5		5.75	Ms				5	1		1	15	1	415	3
1935	6	19	9	55						USGS	US:California,Bishop,W.	美国:加利福尼亚州毕晓普西部	37.25	-118.5	16	4.5	Ms	5										
1935	6	28	19	30	5					USGS	Hawaiian Islands	夏威夷群岛	19.5	-155.25		5.6	Ms	6										
1935	7	5	17	53						GSHAP	Tajikistan:Dushanbe (Stalinabad)	塔吉克斯坦:杜桑贝	38.3	67.4	18	6.2	Ms	8										
1935	7	6	5	20	23					GSHAP	Kazakhstan:Almaty	哈萨克斯坦:阿拉木图	43.1	77.1	14	4.7	Ms	6										
1935	7	11	18	35						* Usami	Japan:Tenryu	日本:静冈滨松天龙区	35	138	10	6.3	Muk		9	1				1	814	3		
1935	7	13	0	3	46					GSHAP	Romania:Nehoiu	罗马尼亚:内霍尤	45.3	26.6	140	5.6	Ms	6										
1935	7	13	10	54	17					USGS	US:California,Glendora	美国:加利福尼亚州格伦多拉	34.2	-117.9	16	4.7	Ms	5										
1935	7	13	22	40	50					GSHAP	Russia:Sakhalin Island	俄罗斯:库页岛(萨哈林岛)	51	142	17	5.5	Ms	6.5										
1935	7	16	16	18	58					* China	China:Taiwan,Miaoli	中国:台湾苗栗	24.6	120.8	30	6.5	Ms	8	2746	4	6004	4		4	30000	5		

年 Year	月 Mo	日 Dy	时 Hr	分 Mn	秒 Sec	海啸 源 Sr	海啸 浪高 Wh	海啸 级 I mI	海啸 级 S mS	资料来源 Information	震中 地名(英文) Name(English)	震中 地名(中文) Name(Chinese)	纬度(°) Latitude	经度(°) Longitude	深度 Depth	震级 Mag	标度 Scale	烈度 MMI	死亡人数 Deaths 数量/人 Num	死亡人数 级别 Dd	受伤人数 Injuries 数量/人 Num	受伤人数 级别 Dd	经济损失 Damage 数量/$ Mill	经济损失 级别 De	房屋毁坏 Houses Destroyed 数量/间 Num	房屋毁坏 级别 Dh	房屋受损 Houses Damaged 数量/间 Num	房屋受损 级别 Dh
1935	7	19	0	50		4	0.2	-2.3		* Japan, NOAA	Japan: Ibaraki, Near Coast	日本:茨城近海	36.6	141.4		6.9	Ms											
1935	8	7	4	15						GSHAP	Colombia: Narino	哥伦比亚:纳里尼奥	1	-77.5		4	Ms	5										
1935	8	7	9	2						* Song	Colombia: Narino	哥伦比亚:纳里尼奥	1	-77.5	95	6	Mk	7	8	1				3				
1935	8	10	5	10						* Song	Italy: Foligno	意大利:福利尼奥	42.9	12.7		6.5	Mk	12										
1935	8	10	18							GSHAP	Colombia: Narino	哥伦比亚:纳里尼奥	1	-77.5		4	Ms	5										
1935	8	24	19	49	2					GSHAP	Russia: Chechnia, Grozny	俄罗斯:车臣共和国格罗兹尼	42.9	45.8	30	4.5	Ms	5										
1935	9	3	6	47						USGS	US: California, San Bernardino	美国:加利福尼亚州圣贝纳迪诺	34.03	-117.32	16	4.5	Ms	5										
1935	9	5	6							GSHAP	Romania: Vrancea	罗马尼亚:弗朗恰	45.8	26.7	130	5.6	Ms	6										
1935	9	18	4	58						GSHAP	Colombia: Bagado	哥伦比亚:乔科的巴加多	5.5	-76	80	6.3	Ms	8										
1935	9	20	1	46	43	3				* Engdahl, NOAA	Papua New Guinea: Green River	巴布亚新几内亚:格林河	-3.92	141.33	35	8.1	Mw											
1935	10	7	19	30						USGS, Song	US: Montana, Helena	美国:蒙大纳州海伦娜	47	-111.9		5.1	Mk	6										
1935	10	8	9	19	6					GSHAP	Tadzhikistan: Tajikabad	塔吉克斯坦:塔吉卡巴德	38.8	70.8	15	6.1	Ms	9										
1935	10	11	4	20	15					GSHAP	Afghan: Taloqan, S.	阿富汗:塔卢坎南部	36.3	70.4	200	5.8	Ms	6										
1935	10	12	7	50	39					USGS	US: Montana, Helena	美国:蒙大纳州海伦娜	46.6	-112	5	5.9	Ms	7										
1935	10	12	16	45	25	4	0.3	-1.7	-1	* Japan, GSHAP, Engdahl, NOAA	Japan Trench	日本海沟	39.9	143.7	10	7.1	Mw											
1935	10	14	20	20	12					GSHAP	Tadzhikistan: Kalaihongbu	塔吉克斯坦:卡莱洪布	38.8	70.5	8	5	Ms	8										
1935	10	15	20	30						USGS, Song	US: Montana, Helena	美国:蒙大纳州海伦娜	46.6	-112		5.1	Mk	6										
1935	10	18	0	11	60	4	0.2	-2.3	-2	* Japan, GSHAP, Engdahl, NOAA	Japan Trench	日本海沟	40.7	144.3	10	7.1	Mw											
1935	10	19	4	48	2					*	US: Montana, Helena	美国:蒙大纳州海伦娜	46.6	-112		6.2	Ms	8	2	1		3	19.0	3	300	3		
1935	10	24	14	48	8					USGS	US: California, Landers	美国:加利福尼亚州兰德斯	34.1	-116.8	16	5.1	Ms	5										
1935	10	27	1	45						GSHAP	Colombia: Narino	哥伦比亚:纳里尼奥	1	-77.5		4	Ms	5										
1935	10	27	19	21						USGS, Song	US: Montana, Helena	美国:蒙大纳州海伦娜	46.6	-112		5.1	Mk	6										
1935	10	27	22	5	5					GSHAP	Colombia: Tulua	哥伦比亚:图卢阿	4	-76	150	5.5	Ms	7										
1935	10	31	18	37	47					*	US: Montana, Helena	美国:蒙大纳州海伦娜	46.6	-112		6	Ms	8	2	1			6.0	3				
1935	11	1	6	3	34					USGS	Canada: Ontario, North Bay	加拿大:安大略,诺斯贝	46.87	-79.05	1	6.2	Ms	7										
1935	11	4	11	23						USGS, Song	US: Montana, Helena	美国:蒙大纳州海伦娜	46.6	-112		5.1	Mk	6										
1935	11	21	11	41		1			2	USGS, NOAA	Hawaiian Islands	夏威夷群岛	19.52	-155.52	8	5.6	Ms	5						1				
1935	11	25	10	3	3	2				* NOAA	Indonesia: North West of Sumatera	印度尼西亚:苏门答腊西北沿海	5.5	94		6.5	Ms											
1935	11	28	14	41	48					USGS	US: Montana, Helena	美国:蒙大纳州海伦娜	46.6	-112		5	Ms	6										

时间 Date 年 Year	月 Mo	日 Dy	时 Hr	分 Mn	秒 Sec	海啸 Tsunami 源 Sr	浪高 Wh	级 I mI	级 S mS	资料来源 Information	震中 Earthquake Epicenter 地名(英文) Name(English)	地名(中文) Name(Chinese)	纬度(°) Latitude	经度(°) Longitude	深度 Depth	震级 Mag	标度 Scale	烈度 MMI	死亡人数 Deaths 数量/人 Num	级别 Dd	受伤人数 Injuries 数量/人 Num	级别 Dd	经济损失 Damage 数量/$ Mill	级别 De	房屋毁坏 Houses Destroyed 数量/间 Num	级别 Dh	房屋受损 Houses Damaged 数量/间 Num	级别 Dh
1935	12	14	22	5	25					* Shi Z. , Engdahl	Mexico:Tapachula	墨西哥:恰帕斯的塔帕丘拉	14. 75	-92. 5	35	7. 2	Mw							3				
1935	12	16	18							USGS,Song	US:New Mexico,Albuquerque	美国:新墨西哥州阿尔伯克基	34. 7	-106. 8		5. 1	Mk	6										
1935	12	18	5	33	18					USGS,Song	US:New Mexico,Albuquerque	美国:新墨西哥州阿尔伯克基	34. 7	-106. 8		5. 1	Mk	6										
1935	12	18	7	10	36					* China	China:Sichuan,Mabian	中国:四川马边	28. 7	103. 6		6	Ms	8	100	2				2		3		
1935	12	20	10	30						USGS,Song	US:New Mexico,Albuquerque	美国:新墨西哥州阿尔伯克基	34. 7	-106. 8		5. 1	Mk	6										
1935	12	24	12	24	11					Engdahl,GSHAP	Colombia:Near Coast	哥伦比亚:近海	2. 753	-79. 293	15	6. 8	Muk	8										
1935	12	25	17	15						USGS	US:California,Huntington Beach	美国:加利福尼亚州亨廷顿海滩	33. 6	-118. 02	16	4. 5	Ms	5										
1935	12	28	2	35	30	1				* Engdahl, NOAA	Indonesia:Northern Sumatra	印度尼西亚:苏门答腊北部	-0. 345	98. 147	35	7. 8	Mw	8				1		2		2		
1935										China	China:Yunnan,Lancang	中国:云南澜沧	22. 6	99. 9		4. 75	Ms	6										
1936	1	5								GSHAP	Colombia:Narino	哥伦比亚:纳里尼奥	1. 1	-77. 6		4	Ms	5										
1936	1	9	9	23						*	Colombia:Narino	哥伦比亚:纳里尼奥	1. 1	-77. 6		7	Muk		250	3				2				
1936	1	10	4	30						GSHAP	Colombia:Narino	哥伦比亚:纳里尼奥	1. 1	-77. 6		5. 7	Ms	7										
1936	1	15	4	40						USGS,Song	US:Wyoming,Moran	美国:怀俄明州莫兰	44	-111		5. 1	Mk	6										
1936	1	23	5							GSHAP	Russia:Maritime Kray,Kamenka	俄罗斯:滨海边疆区卡缅卡	66	44	10	4. 5	Ms	6										
1936	2	7	7	56	30					* China,Engdahl	China:Gansu,Linxia	中国:甘肃临夏	35. 633	103. 265	25	6. 8	Muk	9		3		3		3	9650	4		
1936	2	12	16							China	China:Hebei,Chengde,S.	中国:河北承德南	40. 4	118. 3		4. 75	Ms	6										
1936	2	14	0	30						USGS,Song	US:Montana,Helena	美国:蒙大纳州海伦娜	46. 6	-112		5. 1	Mk	6										
1936	2	21	1	7	58					Shi Z. ,Usami	Japan:Kashihara	日本:奈良橿原	34. 5	135. 8	20	6. 4	Ms		9	1					18	1		
1936	2	23	22	20	43					USGS	US:California,San Bernardino	美国:加利福尼亚州圣贝纳迪诺	34. 13	-117. 34	10	4. 5	Ms	5										
1936	3	5	16							China	China:Ningxia,Haiyuan	中国:宁夏海原	36. 6	105. 6		4. 75	Ms	6										
1936	3	24	16	36	3					GSHAP	Azerbaijan:Shemakha (Semacha)	阿塞拜疆:舍马罕	40. 8	48. 9	32	4. 8	Ms	5										
1936	4	1	2	9	28	4	3	1. 5	1. 5	* Engdahl, NOAA	Indonesia:Karakelong Island	印度尼西亚:卡拉克隆岛	4. 165	126. 521	35	7. 7	Mw	9			3	1		2	169	3		
1936	4	1								* China	China:Guangxi,Lingshan,NE.	中国:广西灵山东北	22. 5	109. 4	7	6. 75	Ms	9		4				4		4		
1936	4	7	22	53						USGS	US:California,Holtville	美国:加利福尼亚州霍尔特维尔	32. 9	-115. 22	16	4. 5	Ms	5										
1936	4	17	22	15	8					GSHAP	Iran:Shirvan	伊朗:希尔凡	37. 5	57. 7	12	5	Ms	7										
1936	4	22	16							China	China:Guangdong,Shunde	中国:广东顺德	22. 7	113. 2		5	Ms	6										
1936	4	26	23	59	12					* China, Engdahl	China:Sichuan,Mabian	中国:四川马边	28. 733	103. 497	25	6. 8	Muk	9		3				2		3		

时间 年 Year	月 Mo	日 Dy	时 Hr	分 Mn	秒 Sec	海啸 Tsunami 源 Sr	浪高 Wh	级 I mI	级 S mS	资料来源 Information	震中 Earthquake Epicenter 地名(英文) Name(English)	地名(中文) Name(Chinese)	纬度(°) Latitude	经度(°) Longitude	深度 Depth	震级 Mag	标度 Scale	烈度 MMI	死亡人数 Deaths 数量/人 Num	级别 Dd	受伤人数 Injuries 数量/人 Num	级别 Dd	经济损失 Damage 数量/$ Mill $ Mill	级别 De	房屋毁坏 Houses Destroyed 数量/间 Num	级别 Dh	房屋受损 Houses Damaged 数量/间 Num	级别 Dh
1936	5	7	11	47						USGS	US:California,Borrego Springs	美国:加利福尼亚州博雷戈斯普林斯	33.13	-116.08	16	4.5	Ms	5										
1936	5	7	21	31	15					GSHAP	Russia:Vladikavkaz	俄罗斯:符拉迪克奥克兹	43.1	44.3	12	4.5	Ms	6										
1936	5	9	20	20	40					USGS	US:California,Shingletown	美国:加利福尼亚州欣格尔敦	40.5	-121.65		4.5	Ms	5										
1936	5	10	17	40	13					USGS	US:California,Chalfant Valley	美国:加利福尼亚州夏芬谷	37.61	-118.37	10	5	Ms	5										
1936	5	17	17	38	2					GSHAP	Romania:Nehoiu	罗马尼亚:内霍尤	45.3	26.3	140	5.6	Ms	5.5										
1936	5	22	0	15	58					GSHAP	Argentina:San Luis	阿根廷:圣路易斯	-32	-66	40	6	Ms	8										
1936	6	3	9	15						USGS	US:California,Off Coast N.	美国:加利福尼亚州北部沿海	40.16	-126.45		5.8	Ms	5										
1936	6	20	3	24	4					USGS	US:Texas,Lefors	美国:德克萨斯州利弗斯	35.31	-100.77	5	4.4	Ms	6										
1936	6	29	14	30	12					Engdahl,GSHAP	Afghan:Badakhshan	阿富汗:巴达赫尚	36.502	70.836	222.2	6.8	Muk	7.5										
1936	6	30	15	6	45					* Engdahl	Russia:Komandorsky Islands	俄罗斯:科曼多尔群岛	55	165	20	7.2	Mw	10										
1936	6	30	19	26						*	Iran:Birjand	伊朗:比尔詹德	33	60		6.2	Muk		12	1				2				
1936	7	3	21	2						* GSHAP	South Korea:Gurye	韩国:求礼郡	35.2	127.6		5.8	Muk		9	1				3				
1936	7	4								Korea	South Korea:Gurye	韩国:求礼郡	35.2	127.6		6	Ms	8										
1936	7	13	11	12	17	4	1		0.5	* Chile, Engdahl, NOAA	Chile:Antofagasta,S.	智利:安托法加斯塔南部	-24.5	-70	60	7.1	Mw		1	1	40	1		2		3		
1936	7	15	23							GSHAP	Colombia:Narino	哥伦比亚:纳里尼奥	1.1	-77.6		6.3	Ms	8										
1936	7	16	7	7	48					USGS	US:Washington,Walla Walla	美国:华盛顿州沃拉沃拉	45.97	-118.21	5	5.7	Ms	7										
1936	7	17	17	29	11					GSHAP	Colombia:Narino	哥伦比亚:纳里尼奥	1.5	-77		4	Ms	7										
1936	7	19	2	36	54					GSHAP	Colombia:Narino	哥伦比亚:纳里尼奥	1	-77.3		5	Ms	6										
1936	8	1	6	24	30					* China	China:Gansu,Tianshui,S.	中国:甘肃天水南	34.2	105.7		6	Ms	8	115	3	31	1		3	4459	4		
1936	8	4	14	9	47					Wang S.	China:Taiwan,Coast of S.	中国:台湾南部海域	20	121		5.5	Ms	9										
1936	8	14								* Song	Colombia:Narino	哥伦比亚:纳里尼奥	1.2	-77.3		5.8	Mk		18	1								
1936	8	16	16							* China	China:Yunnan,Huize,W.	中国:云南会泽西	26.6	103		5.5	Ms	7	30	1				2	30	1		
1936	8	20	23	32	42					GSHAP	Afghan:Badakhshan	阿富汗:巴达赫尚	36.7	71.2	100	6.1	Ms	6										
1936	8	22	6	51	35					* China	China:Taiwan,Taitung	中国:台湾台东	22.3	120.8		7.2	Ms		10	1	10	1		1	15	1	200	3
1936	8	23	21	12	14	2				* Engdahl, NOAA	Indonesia:North West of Sumatera	印度尼西亚:苏门答腊西北沿海	5.296	94.759	35	7.1	Ms	8	9	1	20	1		2				
1936	8	26	7	22						GSHAP	Ecuador:Quito	厄瓜多尔:基多	-0.05	-78.45		4.3	Ms	5										
1936	8	29	12	41	50					GSHAP	Tajikistan:Pamir Mountains	塔吉克斯坦:帕米尔山脉	38.2	72	30	5.5	Ms	6										
1936	9	2	10	1	3					GSHAP	Azerbaijan:Gence,N.	阿塞拜疆:占贾北部	41.7	46.5	17	4.7	Ms	6.5										
1936	9	2	11	57	19					GSHAP	Azerbaijan:Gence,N.	阿塞拜疆:占贾北部	41.5	46.6	21	4.8	Ms	6										

时间 年 Year	月 Mo	日 Dy	时 Hr	分 Mn	秒 Sec	海啸 Tsunami 源 Sr	浪高 Wh	级I mI	级S mS	资料来源 Information	震中 Earthquake Epicenter 地名(英文) Name(English)	地名(中文) Name(Chinese)	纬度(°) Latitude	经度(°) Longitude	深度 Depth	震级 Mag	标度 Scale	烈度 MMI	死亡人数 Deaths 数量/人 Num	级别 Dd	受伤人数 Injuries 数量/人 Num	级别 Dd	经济损失 Damage 数量/$ Mill	级别 De	房屋毁坏 Houses Destroyed 数量/间 Num	级别 Dh	房屋受损 Houses Damaged 数量/间 Num	级别 Dh
1936	9	2	13	12	25					GSHAP	Azerbaijan:Gence,N.	阿塞拜疆:占贾北部	41.5	46.6	22	5.3	Ms	6										
1936	9	6	4	49	2					GSHAP	Romania:Timisoara	罗马尼亚:蒂米什瓦拉	45.7	21.1	5	4.8	Ms	7										
1936	9	9								*	Indonesia:Sumatera,Aceh	印度尼西亚:苏门答腊亚齐	3.8	97.5		7.2	Muk	8	17	1				2				
1936	10	23	6	24	25					USGS,Song	Alaska Peninsula,S.	阿拉斯加半岛南部	61.3	-150.7		5.1	Mk	6										
1936	10	27	1	45						GSHAP	Colombia:Narino	哥伦比亚:纳里尼奥	1	-77.8		4	Ms	5										
1936	11	2	20	45	59	4	0.7	-0.5		* Engdahl,Usami, Japan, NOAA, GSHAP	Japan:Miyagi,Near Coast	日本:宫城近海	38.2	142.2	40	7.1	Mw		4						3	1		
1936	11	3	4	43	33					GSHAP	Sea of Okhotsk	鄂霍次克海	59	151.2	16	5.7	Ms	7.5										
1936	11	11	17	11	24					* China	China:Xinjiang,Ulugqat,W.	中国:新疆乌恰西	39.5	74.2		5.5	Ms			2				1				
1936	11	13	12	31	34	2	13	3.7	2	* Engdahl, NOAA	Russia:Kamchatka, Near East Coast	俄罗斯:堪察加东部近海	55.2	164	35	7.1	Ms	10						1				
1936	11	18	1	48	27					GSHAP	Kyrgyzstan:Issyk-Kul,N.	吉尔吉斯斯坦:伊塞克湖州北部	42.8	77.2	19	4.8	Ms	6										
1936	11	23	20	6	22					GSHAP,Song	Venezuela:Coro	委内瑞拉:科罗	11.49	-69.55		4.5	Mk	5										
1936	12	16	16	15						GSHAP	Colombia:Narino	哥伦比亚:纳里尼奥	1.1	-77.6		5.7	Ms	7										
1936	12	19	2	57	37					* Song	El Salvador:Usulutan	萨尔瓦多:乌苏卢坦	13.2	-88.7		6.4	Mk		400	3								
1936	12	27	0	14						* Shi Z., Usami	Japan:Shizuoka,Near Coast	日本:静冈近海	34.4	139.2		6.3	Ms		3	1				1	39	1		
1937	1	7	13	20	41					* China, Engdahl	China:Qinghai,Maduo,NW.	中国:青海玛多西北	35.404	97.667	15	7.6	Mw	10						1				
1937	1	7	20	47	42					GSHAP	Armenia:Echmiadzin	亚美尼亚:埃奇米阿津	40.13	44.43	10	4.6	Ms	7										
1937	1	12	18	32	58					* Song	Nicaragua:Chinandega, Port Corinto	尼加拉瓜:奇南德加,科林多港	12.6	-87.2		5.9	Mk							2				
1937	1	24	16	12	44					GSHAP	Russia:Amur,Gornyy,N.	俄罗斯:阿穆尔州戈尔内北部	56	130	15	5.5	Ms	7										
1937	2	7	4	41	34					CGS,USGS	US:California,North Coast	美国:加利福尼亚州北部近海	40.5	-125.25		5.8	Ms	5										
1937	2	10								*	Algeria:Guelma, Lapaine	阿尔及利亚:盖勒马	36.1	7.1		5.4	Muk	8		1								
1937	2	19	9	9	10					USGS	US:Nevada,Mina,SW.	美国:内华达州迈纳西南	38.3	-118.3		5	Ms	5										
1937	2	21	7	2	44					* Engdahl	Kuril Islands	千岛群岛	44.5	149.4	45	7.3	Mw							1				
1937	3	2	14	47	33					USGS	US:Ohio,St Marys	美国:俄亥俄州圣玛丽斯	40.49	-84.27	2	5	Ms	7										
1937	3	5	12	47						USGS	US:California,Salinas	美国:加利福尼亚州萨利纳斯	36.7	-121.7		4.5	Ms	5										
1937	3	8	10	31	12					USGS	US:California,Montclair	美国:加利福尼亚州蒙特克莱尔	37.8	-122.2		4.5	Ms	7										
1937	3	9	5	44	36					USGS	US:Ohio,New Bremen	美国:俄亥俄州新不来梅	40.47	-84.28	3	5.4	Ms	8										

时间						海啸				资料来源	震中				深度	震级	标度	烈度	死亡人数		受伤人数		经济损失		房屋毁坏		房屋受损	
年	月	日	时	分	秒	源	浪高	级 I	级 S		地名(英文)	地名(中文)	纬度(°)	经度(°)					数量/人	级别	数量/人	级别	数量/$ Mill	级别	数量/间	级别	数量/间	级别
Date						Tsunami				Information	Earthquake Epicenter				Depth	Mag	Scale	MMI	Deaths		Injuries		Damage		Houses Destroyed		Houses Damaged	
Year	Mo	Dy	Hr	Mn	Sec	Sr	Wh	mI	mS		Name(English)	Name(Chinese)	Latitude	Longitude					Num	Dd	Num	Dd	$ Mill	De	Num	Dh	Num	Dh
1937	3	25	16	49	2					USGS	US:California,Borrego Springs	美国:加利福尼亚州博雷戈斯普林斯	33.41	-116.26	10	6	Ms	6										
1937	4	4	15	40	13					GSHAP	Bosnia:Banja Luka	波斯尼亚:巴尼亚卢卡	45.3	17.9	6	4.7	Ms	7										
1937	4	8								GSHAP,Song	Peru:Huamachuco	秘鲁:瓦马丘科	-7.729	-77.981	20	5	Mk	6										
1937	4	17								GSHAP,Song	Peru:Huamachuco	秘鲁:瓦马丘科	-7.73	-77.98	10	5	Mk	6										
1937	4	25	4	27	48					USGS	US:Nevada,Round Mountain	美国:内华达州朗德芒廷	39	-117		4.5	Ms	5										
1937	5	21	13	12	25					GSHAP	Colombia:Cauca	哥伦比亚:考卡	2.5	-77.5	90	6.5	Ms	8										
1937	6	10	17							China	China:Jilin,Jilin,N.	中国:吉林吉林市北	44.2	126.6		5	Ms	6										
1937	6	18	9	7	26					USGS	US:California,Cedarville	美国:加利福尼亚州锡达维尔	41.25	-120		5.2	Ms	5										
1937	6	21	15	13	5.9					Engdahl,GSHAP	Peru:Trujillo,Near Coast	秘鲁:特鲁希略近海	-8.443	-79.853	42	7.1	Ms	7										
1937	6	27	16							China	China:Fujian,Putian	中国:福建莆田	25.4	119.1		4.75	Ms	6										
1937	7	22	17	9	35					Engdahl,USGS	Alaska Peninsula,C.	阿拉斯加半岛中部	64.494	-146.854	35	7.3	Ms	8										
1937	7	23	20	44	17					GSHAP	Tadzhikistan:Kuhistoni Badakhshon,E.	塔吉克斯坦:勾瑙-巴达科善东部	38.5	73.8	100	5.8	Ms	6										
1937	7	26	3	47	9					*Shi Z.,Engdahl	Mexico:Puebla,Esperanza	墨西哥:普埃布拉,埃斯佩兰萨	18.523	-95.878	35	7.2	mB		34	1				2				
1937	7	31	20	35	51					*China,Engdahl	China:Shandong,Heze	中国:山东菏泽	35.4	115.1	25	7	Muk	9	390	3		3		4		4		
1937	8	1	10	41	8					Wang S.,Engdahl	China:Shandong,Heze	中国:山东菏泽	35.3	115.2	25	6.8	Muk	8										
1937	8	6	3	24						USGS	US:California,Meyers	美国:加利福尼亚州迈尔斯	38.8	-120.1		4.5	Ms	5										
1937	8	19	7	5	15					USGS	US:Nevada,Mina,SW.	美国:内华达州迈纳西南	38.1	-118.2		4.6	Ms	5										
1937	8	20	11	59	22	3		0.5		*Engdahl,NOAA	Philippines:Tanay	菲律宾:塔奈	14.5	121.5	60	7.3	Mw	8	1	1		3		3		3		3
1937	9	1	13	48	8					USGS	US:California,Victorville	美国:加利福尼亚州维克托维尔	34.21	-117.53	10	4.5	Ms	5										
1937	9	1	16	35	34					USGS	US:California,Ontario	美国:加利福尼亚州安大略	34.18	-117.55	10	4.5	Ms	5										
1937	9	8	2	51	11					GSHAP	Bulgaria:Dospat	保加利亚:多斯帕特	41.6	24.1	70	4.8	Ms	5.5										
1937	9	14	2	16	54					GSHAP	Armenia:Gyumri	亚美尼亚:久姆里	41	44.4	28	4.5	Ms	5.5										
1937	9	14	16							* *China	China:Shanxi,Taiyuan	中国:山西太原	37.8	112.5		5	Ms	7		2				2		3		
1937	9	21	21	2		3			1	*NOAA	Russia:Kamchatka Peninsula	俄罗斯:堪察加半岛	56	162.5	33	5.7	Ms											
1937	9	22				1				NOAA	Russia:Kamchatka,Near East Coast	俄罗斯:堪察加东部近海	58	165		5.8	Ms											
1937	9	24	2	40	7					GSHAP	Colombia:Montería	哥伦比亚:蒙特里亚	9	-76	100	5.5	Ms	7										
1937	9	27	8	55	17					*Engdahl	Indonesia:Java,Jogyakarta	印度尼西亚:爪哇,日惹	-8.7	110.8	35	7	Ms	9	1	1				3	326	3	2200	4
1937	9	29	3	30						GSHAP	Bulgaria:Radnevo	保加利亚:拉德内沃	42.2	25.8	24	4.8	Ms	5.5										
1937	10	2	14	15	46					GSHAP	Azerbaijan:Quba,SW.	阿塞拜疆:库巴西南	41.1	48.3	10	4.5	Ms	6.5										

年 Year	月 Mo	日 Dy	时 Hr	分 Mn	秒 Sec	海啸 Tsunami 源 Sr	浪高 Wh	级 I mI	级 S mS	资料来源 Information	震中 Earthquake Epicenter 地名(英文) Name(English)	地名(中文) Name(Chinese)	纬度(°) Latitude	经度(°) Longitude	深度 Depth	震级 Mag	标度 Scale	烈度 MMI	死亡人数 Deaths 数量/人 Num	级别 Dd	受伤人数 Injuries 数量/人 Num	级别 Dd	经济损失 Damage 数量/$ Mill	级别 De	房屋毁坏 Houses Destroyed 数量/间 Num	级别 Dh	房屋受损 Houses Damaged 数量/间 Num	级别 Dh
1937	10	6	9	47	18					* Engdahl	Mexico:Chilpancingo,Tixtla	墨西哥:奇尔潘辛戈,蒂科斯特拉	18.43	-98.921	35	6.9	Muk							3				
1937	10	24	11	35	57					USGS,Song	Gulf of Alaska	阿拉斯加湾	60	-150.5		4.9	Mk	5										
1937	10	29	7	26	37					GSHAP	Afghan:Taloqan	阿富汗:塔卢坎	36.6	70.1	200	6.5	Ms	7										
1937	11	3	6	6						GSHAP	Bolivia:La Paz	玻利维亚:拉巴斯	-15.5	-68.5	33	5.4	Ms	6										
1937	11	6				2	0.5	-1		* NOAA	Indonesia:Yogyakarta	印度尼西亚:雍亚卡他	-8.7	110.8	33	6	Ms											
1937	11	9	16							China	China:Yunnan,Chenggong	中国:云南呈贡	24.9	102.8		5	Ms	6										
1937	11	13	11	50	37					Afghan,GSHAP	Tadzhikistan:Khatlon	塔吉克斯坦:哈特隆州	38	69.5	10	5.7	Ms	6										
1937	11	14	10	58	13					* GSHAP,Engdahl	Afghan:Fayzabad	阿富汗:法扎巴德	36.5	70.5	240	7.1	mB	9						3				
1937	11	18	4	39	56					China,GSHAP	Kazakhstan:Narynkol	哈萨克斯坦:纳伦郭勒	42.6	80.1	20	5.1	Ms	6.5										
1937	11	22	4	12	54					USGS	US:California,Lompoc,Near Coast	美国:加利福尼亚州隆波克近海	34.37	-120.62	10	4.5	Ms	5										
1937	12	8	8	32	15					* China,Engdahl	China:Taiwan,Taitung	中国:台湾台东	22.9	121.2	38.8	7	Ms				1	1		1	5	1	37	1
1937	12	18	13	18						GSHAP	Uzbekistan:Tashkent,NE.	乌兹别克斯坦:塔什干东北	42.1	70.9	25	6.5	Ms	7.5										
1937	12	18	20	22	41					GSHAP	Azerbaijan:Quba,SW.	阿塞拜疆:库巴西南	41	48.5	18	4.6	Ms	5.5										
1937	12	23	13	18	6					* Engdahl	Mexico:Guerrero,Ometepec	墨西哥:格雷罗,奥美特佩克	16.7	-98.5	60	7.4	Mw		4	1								
1937	12	24	6	20	40					* Shi Z.	Peru:Huancabamba,Oxapampa	秘鲁:宛卡班巴,奥克萨潘帕	-10.5	-76.5	10	6.25	Muk	10	15	1				2				
1937	12	25	9	55	50					GSHAP	Russia:Buryatiya,Krasnyy	俄罗斯:布里亚特州克拉斯内	55.6	111.7	15	6.5	Ms	8										
1937	12	26								* Song	El Salvador:Ahuachapan,Atiquizaya	萨尔瓦多:阿华查邦,阿替基寨雅	13.5	-89.5		6.2	Mk							3				
1938	1	2								* Song	Mexico:Ometepec	墨西哥:奥美特佩克	16.1	-98.3		6.2	Mk	7						3				
1938	1	7	18	27	21					GSHAP	Mongolia:Altay	蒙古:阿尔泰	46	96	15	5.1	Ms	6.5										
1938	1	12	1	8	21					GSHAP	Tadzhikistan:Tajikabad	塔吉克斯坦:塔吉卡巴德	38.8	71	10	5.4	Ms	6.5										
1938	1	18	9	28	57					GSHAP	Afghan:Badakhshan	阿富汗:巴达赫尚	36.7	70.8	200	6.1	Ms	6										
1938	1	23	8	32	51					Engdahl,USGS	Hawaiian Islands	夏威夷群岛	20.96	-156.18	25	6.8	Ms	7										
1938	2	1	19	4	22	4	1	1	1.5	* Engdahl,NOAA	Indonesia:Banda Sea	印度尼西亚:班达海	-5.05	131.62	35	8.4	Mw							2	24	1	8	1
1938	2	4	14	23						* Song	Colombia:Manizales	哥伦比亚:卡尔达斯的马尼萨莱斯	5.1	-75.5	130	6.2	Mk	8	2	1				3				
1938	2	5	2	23	41					GSHAP,Engdahl	Colombia:Sipi	哥伦比亚:乔科的锡皮	4.555	-75.919	155.7	6.9	mB	8										
1938	2	8	6							GSHAP	Ecuador:Chimborazo,Bolivar	厄瓜多尔:钦博拉索山,玻利瓦	-1.7	-79.03		4.3	Ms	5										
1938	2	12	20	0	14					USGS	US:California,Live Oak	美国:加利福尼亚州莱夫奥克	37	-122		4.5	Ms	6										
1938	2	13				2	0.5	-1		* NOAA,Song	Indonesia:Banda Sea	印度尼西亚:班达海	-5.25	130.5		7	Mk							1				

年 Year	月 Mo	日 Dy	时 Hr	分 Mn	秒 Sec	海啸 Tsunami 源 Sr	浪高 Wh	级 I mI	级 S mS	资料来源 Information	震中 Earthquake Epicenter 地名(英文) Name(English)	地名(中文) Name(Chinese)	纬度(°) Latitude	经度(°) Longitude	深度 Depth	震级 Mag	标度 Scale	烈度 MMI	死亡人数 Deaths 数量/人 Num	级别 Dd	受伤人数 Injuries 数量/人 Num	级别 Dd	经济损失 Damage 数量/$ Mill	级别 De	房屋毁坏 Houses Destroyed 数量/间 Num	级别 Dh	房屋受损 Houses Damaged 数量/间 Num	级别 Dh
1938	2	14	2	54	15					GSHAP	Turkmenistan:Balkanabat	土库曼斯坦:巴尔坎纳巴德	40.4	53.7	30	6.2	Ms	7.5										
1938	2	15	7	45	40					USGS	US:California,Landers	美国:加利福尼亚州兰德斯	34.17	-116.26	10	4.5	Ms	5										
1938	2	21	13	49	37					GSHAP	Russia:Tuva,Turan	俄罗斯:唐努图瓦州图兰	52	93.5	28	5.4	Ms	6										
1938	2	27								GSHAP	Turkmenistan:Turkmenbasy	土库曼斯坦:土库曼巴希	40.5	53.5	30	5.1	Ms	5.5										
1938	3	5	12							GSHAP,Song	Peru:Cuzco	秘鲁:库斯科	-14	-72	20	5	Mk	6										
1938	3	6	1	56		1	0.1	-3.3		* NOAA,Song	New Britain Trench	新不列颠海沟[太平洋]	-5.1	153.1		7	Mk											
1938	3	6	18	30						GSHAP,Song	Peru:Espinar	秘鲁:埃斯皮纳尔	-14.2	-71.3	30	5	Mk	6										
1938	3	27	11	16	27					GSHAP	Croatia:Varazdin	克罗地亚:瓦拉日丁	46.05	16.9	7	5.6	Ms	8										
1938	4	13	19	29						USGS	US:California,Brawley	美国:加利福尼亚州布劳利	32.88	-115.58	16	4.5	Ms	5										
1938	4	19	10	59	23					* Engdahl	Turkey:Kirsehir	土耳其:克尔谢希尔	39.439	34.015	35	6.8	Muk	10	224	3				3				
1938	4	24	20	21	6					GSHAP	Colombia:Guainia	哥伦比亚:瓜伊尼亚	2	-69		5	Ms	6										
1938	4	25	10	13	39					GSHAP	Russia:Krasnoyarsk,SE.	俄罗斯:克拉斯诺亚尔斯克东南	55.2	94.6	15	4.9	Ms	6.5										
1938	4	25	17	7						* Song	Nicaragua:Leon,Chinandega	尼加拉瓜:里昂,奇南德加	12.2	-86.9		5.9	Mk							2				
1938	5	2	23	40	30					GSHAP	Colombia:Antioquia	哥伦比亚:安提奥基亚	7.5	-75	100	5.8	Ms	7										
1938	5	6	18	17						* Song	Nicaragua:Leon (Telica Volcano)	尼加拉瓜:里昂(特利卡火山)	12.3	-86.9		6.2	Mk							3				
1938	5	12	15	39	6	3		1		* Engdahl, NOAA	Papua New Guinea: West New Britain	巴布亚新几内亚:西新不列颠	-6	147.8	60	7.3	Mw							1		1		1
1938	5	14	12	3	9					* China	Myanmar:Keng Tung	缅甸:肯格塔恩	21.7	99.5		6	Ms	8		2				1		1		
1938	5	19	17	8	36	4	3	1.6		* Engdahl, NOAA	Indonesia:Tinombo	印度尼西亚:蒂农博	-0.366	119.525	49.4	7.5	Mw	9	17	1				3	942	3		
1938	5	23	7	18	33	4	0.8	-0.3		* Engdahl, Usami, NOAA	Japan Trench	日本海沟	36.458	141.755	35	7.7	Mw								1	1	250	3
1938	5	28	10	14	1					USGS	US:Off Coast of W. Oregon	美国:俄勒冈州西部沿海	42.75	-126.1		6	Ms	5										
1938	5	28	16	42	3	4	0.9	-0.1		* GSHAP, Usami, NOAA	Japan:Hokkaido	日本:北海道	43.6	144.3	20	6.7	Ms		1	1				1	7	1		
1938	5	31	8	34	55					USGS	US:California,Los Angeles	美国:加利福尼亚州洛杉矶	33.7	-117.51	10	5.5	Ms	5										
1938	6	10	9	53	45	4	1.5	0.6		* Usami, China, NOAA	Ryukyu Islands,SW.	琉球群岛西南	25.208	125.115	35	7.6	Mw											
1938	6	13	11	30						USGS,Song	US:Montana,Manhattan	美国:蒙大纳州曼哈顿	45.9	-111.3		5.1	Mk	6										
1938	6	14	5	32						USGS,Song	US:Montana,Manhattan	美国:蒙大纳州曼哈顿	45.9	-111.3		5.1	Mk	6										
1938	6	20	23	50	36					GSHAP,China	Kazakhstan:Almaty	哈萨克斯坦:阿拉木图	42.72	76.12	10	6.9	Muk	8.5										

年 Year	月 Mo	日 Dy	时 Hr	分 Mn	秒 Sec	海啸 Tsunami 源 Sr	浪高 Wh	级 I mI	级 S mS	资料来源 Information	震中 Earthquake Epicenter 地名(英文) Name(English)	地名(中文) Name(Chinese)	纬度(°) Latitude	经度(°) Longitude	深度 Depth	震级 Mag	标度 Scale	烈度 MMI	死亡人数 Deaths 数量/人 Num	级别 Dd	受伤人数 Injuries 数量/人 Num	级别 Dd	经济损失 Damage 数量/$ Mill	级别 De	房屋毁坏 Houses Destroyed 数量/间 Num	级别 Dh	房屋受损 Houses Damaged 数量/间 Num	级别 Dh
1938	6	28	19	17	43					* Shi Z.	Mexico:Teloloapan	墨西哥:特洛瓦潘	18.2	-99.5	110	6.5	Ms							2				
1938	7	2	11	50						GSHAP, Song	Peru:Perene	秘鲁:佩雷内	-11.272	-75.951	15	6	Mk	7										
1938	7	5	18	6	56					USGS	US:California, Los Angeles	美国:加利福尼亚州洛杉矶	33.68	-117.55	10	4.5	Ms	5										
1938	7	7	4	50						GSHAP, Song	Peru:Piura	秘鲁:皮乌拉	-5.692	-80.042	80	5	Mk	6										
1938	7	7	12	50	9					GSHAP	Caspian Sea	里海	40.3	53.2	26	4.9	Ms	6										
1938	7	13	20	15	17					GSHAP	Romania:Tulnici	罗马尼亚:图尔尼奇	45.9	26.7	120	5.6	Ms	6										
1938	8	10	2	2						* GSHAP	Ecuador:Sangolqui, Tingo - Pichincha	厄瓜多尔:桑戈尔基,廷戈-皮钦查	-0.3	-78.4	10	7.2	Muk	10										
1938	8	11	9	50	36					GSHAP	Georgia:Kakhetiya	格鲁吉亚:卡赫季州	42.3	45.6	20	4.7	Ms	5.5										
1938	8	13	18	30						GSHAP, Song	Ecuador:Quito	厄瓜多尔:基多	-0.31	-78.42		4.5	Mk	5										
1938	8	25	0	4	54					GSHAP	Colombia:Near Coast	哥伦比亚:近海	4	-78		5	Ms	6										
1938	8	31	3	18	14					USGS	US:California, Long Beach	美国:加利福尼亚州长滩	33.76	-118.25	10	4.5	Ms	6										
1938	9	6	13	28	20					GSHAP	Caspian Sea	里海	41	50	22	5	Ms	6										
1938	9	11	8	21	36					GSHAP	Russia:Kabardino - Balkaria, Nalchik	俄罗斯:卡尔梅克州纳尔奇克	43.4	43.2	30	4.6	Ms	5.5										
1938	9	12	6	10						USGS	US:California, Whitethorn	美国:加利福尼亚州怀特索恩	40	-124		5.5	Ms	6										
1938	9	17	3	34	28					USGS	US:Arkansas, Gilmore	美国:阿肯色州吉尔摩	35.41	-90.25	1	4.8	Ms	5										
1938	9	17	17	20	17					USGS	US:New Mexico, Glenwood	美国:新墨西哥州格伦伍德	33.3	-108.5		4.9	Ms	6										
1938	9	20	5	39						USGS	US:New Mexico, Glenwood	美国:新墨西哥州格伦伍德	33.3	-108.5		4.3	Ms	6										
1938	9	20	22	4	30					China, GSHAP	Mongolia:Hongo, W.	蒙古:洪戈西部	48.2	90.5		5.25	Ms	6.5										
1938	9	27	12	23	48					USGS	US:California, Soledad	美国:加利福尼亚州索莱达	36.45	-121.25		5	Ms	5										
1938	9	29	23	34	57					USGS	US:New Mexico, Glenwood	美国:新墨西哥州格伦伍德	33.3	-108.5		4.8	Ms	6										
1938	10	19	4	13	26					Engdahl, GSHAP	Mongolia:Nogoonnuur	蒙古:瑙贡努尔	49.5	90.3	36	6.8	Muk	8										
1938	11	2	8	59	58					USGS	US:New Mexico, Glenwood	美国:新墨西哥州格伦伍德	33.3	-108.5		4.3	Ms	6										
1938	11	5	8	43	23	4	1.1	0.1		* Shi Z., Usami, Engdahl, NOAA	Japan Trench	日本海沟	37.009	142.045	35	7.9	Mw		1	1				1	20	1		
1938	11	5	10	50	17	4	1.1	0.1		* Engdahl, NOAA	Japan Trench	日本海沟	37.108	142.081	35	7.8	Mw											
1938	11	6	8	53	55	4	1.3	0.4		* Engdahl, NOAA	Japan Trench	日本海沟	37.287	142.283	35	7.7	Mw											
1938	11	6	21	38	46	4	1.3	0.3		Shi Z., Engdahl, NOAA	Japan Trench	日本海沟	36.867	142.625	60	7	Ms											
1938	11	9	2	22		4				* NOAA	Japan:Fukushima, Near Coast	日本:福岛近海	37.5	141.2	20	6.5	Ms											

时间 年 Year	月 Mo	日 Dy	时 Hr	分 Mn	秒 Sec	海啸 源 Sr	浪高 Wh	级 I mI	级 S mS	资料来源 Information	震中 地名(英文) Name(English)	地名(中文) Name(Chinese)	纬度(°) Latitude	经度(°) Longitude	深度 Depth	震级 Mag	标度 Scale	烈度 MMI	死亡人数 数量/人 Num	级别 Dd	受伤人数 数量/人 Num	级别 Dd	经济损失 数量/$ Mill	级别 De	房屋毁坏 数量/间 Num	级别 Dh	房屋受损 数量/间 Num	级别 Dh
1938	11	10	20	18	47	4	0.3	-1.7		* USGS, Engdahl, NOAA	Aleutian Islands	阿留申群岛	55.328	-158.37	35	8.2	M	6										
1938	11	13	22	31	33	4	0.8	-0.5		* Shi Z., Engdahl, NOAA	Japan: Fukushima, Near Coast	日本:福岛近海	37	141.5	60	7	Ms											
1938	11	14	12	6	39					GSHAP	Turkey: Kars	土耳其:卡尔斯	40.4	43.5	20	4.5	Ms	6										
1938	11	15	13	48						USGS, Song	US: California, Potter Valley	美国:加利福尼亚州波特瓦利	39.25	-123		5.1	Mk	6										
1938	11	22	1	14		4	0.3	-1.7		* NOAA	Japan Trench	日本海沟	36.7	142.1	10	6.9	Ms											
1938	11	27	0	12	39					USGS	US: New Mexico, Glenwood	美国:新墨西哥州格伦伍德	33.3	-108.5		4.6	Ms	5										
1938	11	30	2	29	52	4	0.2	-2.3		* Engdahl, NOAA	Japan Trench	日本海沟	37.026	142.133	35	6.9	Ms											
1938	12	1	16	17						USGS	US: California, Fremont	美国:加利福尼亚州弗里蒙特	37.5	-121.8		4.5	Ms	6										
1938	12	3	17	42	53					USGS	US: California, Huntington Lake, NE.	美国:加利福尼亚州亨廷顿莱克东北	37.45	-118.6	10	5.7	Ms	6										
1938	12	6	23	0	56					* China, Engdahl	China: Taiwan, Taitung, Coast of E.	中国:台湾台东以东海域	22.9	121.5	39	7	Ms				1	1		1	13	1	180	3
1938	12	12	22	2	46					GSHAP	Colombia: Near Coast	哥伦比亚:近海	6.5	-78		5	Ms	6										
1938	12	17	16	35	25					GSHAP	Mongolia: North Hovo	蒙古:科布多北部	47.5	92.8	18	6.5	Ms	8.5										
1938										* * Song	Iran: Razavi Khorasan	伊朗:呼罗珊	34.5	58.2		5.9	Mk	7						2				
1939	1	2	4	35						*	Mediterranean Sea	地中海	36.3	30.7		5.3	Muk							3				
1939	1	7	16							China	China: Shandong, Rushan, N.	中国:山东乳山北	37.1	121.6		5.5	Ms	8										
1939	1	11	22							USGS	US: Nevada, Yerington	美国:内华达州耶灵顿	39	-119.2		5.5	Ms	6										
1939	1	13	16	47	14					GSHAP	Russia: Komi, Sholomka	俄罗斯:科米州绍洛姆卡村	60.6	51.2	10	4.7	Ms	7										
1939	1	22	4	41	4					GSHAP	Russia: Sakhalin Island	俄罗斯:库页岛(萨哈林岛)	53.6	143	13	5.5	Ms	7										
1939	1	23	2	34	23					GSHAP	Armenia: Gyumri	亚美尼亚:久姆里	40.6	43.9	25	4.5	Ms	5										
1939	1	25	3	32	14	2				* Engdahl, NOAA	Chile: Chillan	智利:奇廉	-36.2	-72.2	60	7.7	Mw	10	30000	5			920	5		4		
1939	1	27	20	10	15	1			2	* Italy, NOAA	Italy: Calabria	意大利:卡拉布里亚	38.467	14.883	15	5.15	Ms											
1939	1	30	2	18	30	3		0.9	1	* Engdahl, NOAA	Papua New Guinea: Bougainville Island	巴布亚新几内亚:布干维尔岛	-7.08	155.386	35	7.7	Mw		5	1		3		2		3		
1939	2	6	7	23	17					Italy, GSHAP	Croatia: Rijeka	克罗地亚:里耶卡	45.2	14.6		5.03	Ms	6										
1939	2	17	3	24	24					GSHAP	Bulgaria: Razlog Valley	保加利亚:拉兹洛格	42.1	23.4	40	5.1	Ms	5										
1939	2	24	14	15	56					USGS	Aleutian Islands	阿留申群岛	54.05	-162.01	79	6.25	Ms	5										
1939	3	12	16							China	China: Gansu, Jingyuan	中国:甘肃靖远	36.6	104.7		5	Ms	6										
1939	3	20	3	22		4	0.8	-0.3		* NOAA	Japan: Miyazaki, Near Coast	日本:宫崎近海	32.3	132	20	6.6	Ms		1	1					1	1		
1939	3	23	5	44						GSHAP	Hungary: Debrecen	匈牙利:德布勒森	47.43	21.97	23	5.1	Ms	6										

时间						海啸				资料来源	震中				深度	震级	标度	烈度	死亡人数		受伤人数		经济损失		房屋毁坏		房屋受损	
年	月	日	时	分	秒	源	浪高	级 I	级 S		地名(英文)	地名(中文)	纬度(°)	经度(°)					数量/人	级别	数量/人	级别	数量/$ Mill	级别	数量/间	级别	数量/间	级别
Date						Tsunami				Information	Earthquake Epicenter				Depth	Mag	Scale	MMI	Deaths		Injuries		Damage		Houses Destroyed		Houses Damaged	
Year	Mo	Dy	Hr	Mn	Sec	Sr	Wh	mI	mS		Name(English)	Name(Chinese)	Latitude	Longitude					Num	Dd	Num	Dd	$ Mill	De	Num	Dh	Num	Dh
1939	4	18	6	22	44	2				* Chile, Engdahl, NOAA	Chile: Copiapo	智利:科皮亚波	-27	-70.5	35	7.3	mB											
1939	4	20	17	46	14					GSHAP	St Vincent & Grenadines: Port Elizabeth, E.	圣文森特和格林纳丁斯:伊丽莎白港东部	13	-60.5	130	5.3	Ms	7										
1939	4	25	12	53	37					GSHAP	Peru: Huancayo	秘鲁:万卡约	-12.5	-75.5	150	6.3	Ms	6										
1939	4	30	2	55	29	3	11	3.4	1.5	* Engdahl, NOAA	Solomon Islands	所罗门群岛	-9.295	159.234	35	7.9	Mw		12	1				2		2		
1939	5	1	5	58	33	4	0.3	-1.7	-1	* Usami, Engdahl, NOAA	Japan: Akita, Near West Coast	日本:秋田西部近海	40.1	139.5	35	7	Ms		27	1	52	2		2	585	3		
1939	5	1	21	53	18					USGS	US: California, North Coast	美国:加利福尼亚州北部近海	40.2	-124.7		4.5	Ms	5										
1939	5	4	20	44	47					USGS	US: Nevada, Las Vegas	美国:内华达州拉斯维加斯	35.97	-114.82		5	Ms	6										
1939	5	7	17	0	7	1			0.5	* Shi Z., NOAA	Philippines: Calapan	菲律宾:卡拉潘	13.5	121.2	110	6.5	Ms		27	1					585	3		
1939	5	8	1	46	53	4			1	* Engdahl, NOAA	North Atlantic Ocean, Azores Islands	北大西洋:亚速尔群岛	37.053	-24.427	15.7	6.5	Ms	10										
1939	5	11	18	4						USGS	US: Nevada, Mina	美国:内华达州迈纳	38.58	-117.83		5.5	Ms	6										
1939	5	12								USGS, Song	US: Montana, Manhattan	美国:蒙大纳州曼哈顿	45.9	-111.3		5.1	Mk	6										
1939	5	15	20	57	31					USGS, Song	Hawaiian Islands	夏威夷群岛	19.37	-155.13	16	5.1	Mk	6										
1939	5	19	18	51	34					GSHAP	Russia: Tuva, NE.	俄罗斯:唐努图瓦州东北	52.3	98.6	30	6	Ms	7.5										
1939	5	26	9	40	37					GSHAP	Russia: Lake Baykal	俄罗斯:贝加尔湖	53.9	108.8	23	6	Ms	8										
1939	5	29	5	47						GSHAP	Russia: Sakhalin Island	俄罗斯:库页岛(萨哈林岛)	46.5	141.5	12	4.5	Ms	5.5										
1939	5	30	0	4						GSHAP	Japan Sea, N.	日本海北部	46.4	141.6	14	4.8	Ms	6										
1939	5	30	10	7	6					GSHAP	Tadzhikistan: Garm	塔吉克斯坦:加尔姆	38.98	70.45	6	5.8	Ms	8.5										
1939	5	31								GSHAP, Song	Venezuela: Barcelona	委内瑞拉:巴塞罗纳	10.18	-64.61		5	Mk	6										
1939	6	3	9	30						GSHAP, Song	Venezuela: Barcelona	委内瑞拉:巴塞罗纳	10.13	-64.7		5	Mk	6										
1939	6	4	1	19	10					USGS	US: New Mexico, Glenwood	美国:新墨西哥州格伦伍德	33.3	-108.5		4.6	Ms	6										
1939	6	22	19	19	26	2				* NOAA	Ghana: Accra	加纳:阿克拉	5.18	-0.13	13	6.8	mB	9	22	1	130	3		3	1500	4		
1939	6	24	4	22	24					* GSHAP, Song	Peru: Pomacanchi	秘鲁:波马奇	-12.5	-72		5.8	Mk	6	37	1				1				
1939	6	24	13	2	6					USGS	US: California, Tres Pinos	美国:加利福尼亚州特雷斯皮诺斯	36.8	-121.45		5.5	Ms	7										
1939	6	28	11	32	22					GSHAP	Brasil: Criciuma	巴西:克里西乌马	-29	-49	15	5.5	Ms	7										
1939	7	14	14	21						USGS	Hawaiian Islands	夏威夷群岛	19.32	-155.12		5.5	Ms	5										
1939	7	17	9	24	54					USGS	US: California, Las Lomas	美国:加利福尼亚州拉斯洛马斯	36.85	-121.68		4.5	Ms	5										
1939	8	2	9	25	17					GSHAP	Greece: Drama, NE.	希腊:兹拉马东北	41.5	24.5	24	4.9	Ms	5										
1939	8	9	12	29	41					GSHAP	Bulgaria: Chirpan	保加利亚:奇尔潘	42.2	25.2	6	4.8	Ms	7										
1939	8	11	6	2	4					GSHAP, Song	Venezuela: Carabobo	委内瑞拉:卡拉沃沃	11.61	-67.59	25	4.5	Mk	5										

时间 Date						海啸 Tsunami				资料来源 Information	震中 Earthquake Epicenter				深度 Depth	震级 Mag	标度 Scale	烈度 MMI	死亡人数 Deaths		受伤人数 Injuries		经济损失 Damage		房屋毁坏 Houses Destroyed		房屋受损 Houses Damaged	
年 Year	月 Mo	日 Dy	时 Hr	分 Mn	秒 Sec	源 Sr	浪高 Wh	级 I mI	级 S mS		地名(英文) Name(English)	地名(中文) Name(Chinese)	纬度(°) Latitude	经度(°) Longitude					数量/人 Num	级别 Dd	数量/人 Num	级别 Dd	数量/$ Mill $ Mill	级别 De	数量/间 Num	级别 Dh	数量/间 Num	级别 Dh
1939	8	15	3	52		2				* NOAA	Cuba:Santa Clara	古巴:圣塔克莱拉	22.4	-80		8.1	Ms											
1939	8	20	7	17	26					USGS	Aleutian Islands	阿留申群岛	54	-164	75	6.25	Ms	5										
1939	9	5	6	2						GSHAP	Romania:Tulnici	罗马尼亚:图尔尼奇	45.9	26.6	150	5.1	Ms	6										
1939	9	6	11	27	32					GSHAP	Afghan:Sheberghan	阿富汗:希比尔甘	36.6	66.5	30	5.2	Ms	5										
1939	9	18	16							* China	China:Yunnan,Yuxi	中国:云南玉溪	24.4	102.6		5.5	Ms	7	2	1				1		1		
1939	9	19	3	24						GSHAP	Iran:Shirvan	伊朗:希尔凡	37.8	57.7	17	5.5	Ms	7										
1939	9	21	0	37						*	Turkey:Izmir	土耳其:伊兹密尔	39.1	26.8		6.5	Muk	9	41	1				2				
1939	10	11	14	51						* GSHAP	Peru:Orcopampa	秘鲁:奥尔科潘帕	-15.3	-72.2	120	8.6	Ms	7						2		3		
1939	10	14	6	2	24					GSHAP	Venezuela:Cariaco	委内瑞拉:卡利亚科	10.7	-63.8		5.6	Ms	7										
1939	10	19	21	32	44					GSHAP	Turkey:Kütahya	土耳其:屈塔希亚	39.8	29.6	8	5.3	Ms	7.5										
1939	11	13	7	45	54					USGS	US:Washington,Seattle	美国:华盛顿州西雅图	47.5	-122.5		5.7	Ms	7										
1939	11	21	8	43						*	Turkey:Erzincan	土耳其:埃尔津占	39.7	40.4	80	5.9	Muk	7	13	1				2				
1939	11	21	11	1	48					* GSHAP, Engdahl	Afghan:Badakhshan	阿富汗:巴达赫尚	36.42	71.134	216	6.9	Muk							2				
1939	11	23	15	14	52					USGS	US:Missouri,House Springs	美国:密苏里州豪斯斯普林斯	38.18	-90.14		4.6	Ms	5										
1939	12	21	21	0	33	3				* Engdahl, NOAA	Indonesia:Kalo,Luwuk, Sula Island	印度尼西亚:卡洛,卢武克,苏拉岛	-0.208	122.565	35	7.8	mB							2		3		
1939	12	26	23	57	23	4	0.5		4	* Engdahl, NOAA	Turkey:Erzincan	土耳其:埃尔津占	39.77	39.533	35	7.8	Ms	12	32700	5			20.0	3		4		
1939	12	27	19	28	49					USGS	US:California,Long Beach	美国:加利福尼亚州长滩	33.78	-118.2	16	4.7	Ms	6										
1939	12	28	12	15	38					USGS	US:California,Parkfield	美国:加利福尼亚州帕克菲尔德	35.8	-120.33		5	Ms	6										
1940	1	15	13	19	24	2			3	* Italy,NOAA	Italy:Sicily,Palermo	意大利:西西里岛,巴勒莫	38.08	13.43	15	5.34	Ms	8										
1940	1	15								* Song	Argentina:San Juan	阿根廷:圣胡安	-31	-69		7	Mk		10000	5								
1940	1	19	4	23	48					* China	China:Inner Mongolia, Hure Qi,W.	中国:内蒙古库伦旗西	42.7	121.3		6	Ms	7		2				2		3		
1940	1	26	23	11	41					GSHAP	Kazakhstan:Almaty	哈萨克斯坦:阿拉木图	44.4	79.3	30	5.5	Ms	6										
1940	2	1	6	20						GSHAP	Greece:Thessalonika	希腊:萨罗尼加	40.5	22.8	12	5.4	Ms	7										
1940	2	8	8	5	59					USGS,Shi Z.	US:California,Chico	美国:加利福尼亚州奇科	40	-121.6	35	6	Ms	7										
1940	2	12	9	17	49					Engdahl,USGS	Aleutian Islands	阿留申群岛	54.958	-161.182	35	6.8	Muk	5										
1940	2	13	23	53						USGS,Song	US:California,Whitethorn	美国:加利福尼亚州怀特索恩	40	-124		5.1	Mk	6										
1940	2	19	12	6	56					USGS	US: California, San Bernardino	美国:加利福尼亚州圣贝纳迪诺	34.02	-117.05	16	4.6	Ms	5										
1940	2	20								* Turkey	Turkey:Kayseri,Develi	土耳其:开塞利,德韦利	38.4	35.5		5.3	Ms	9	37	1				2				
1940	2	20								* Song	Nicaragua:Corinto,Chinandega	尼加拉瓜:科林托,奇南德加	12.5	-87.5		5.9	Mk							2				
1940	2	23	9	27	46					GSHAP	Bulgaria:Popovitsa	保加利亚:普罗夫迪夫	42.2	25	30	5	Ms	5.5										

时间						海啸				资料来源	震中				深度	震级	标度	烈度	死亡人数		受伤人数		经济损失		房屋毁坏		房屋受损	
年	月	日	时	分	秒	源	浪高	级I	级S		地名(英文)	地名(中文)	纬度(°)	经度(°)					数量/人	级别	数量/人	级别	数量/$ Mill	级别	数量/间	级别	数量/间	级别
Date						Tsunami				Information	Earthquake Epicenter				Depth	Mag	Scale	MMI	Deaths		Injuries		Damage		Houses Destroyed		Houses Damaged	
Year	Mo	Dy	Hr	Mn	Sec	Sr	Wh	mI	mS		Name(English)	Name(Chinese)	Latitude	Longitude					Num	Dd	Num	Dd	$ Mill	De	Num	Dh	Num	Dh
1940	3	9	20	8	43					GSHAP	Georgia:Akhalkalaki	格鲁吉亚:阿卡卡拉吉	41.4	43.6	22	4.9	Ms	6										
1940	4	2	16							China	China:Yunnan,Yuxi	中国:云南玉溪	24.4	102.4		5	Ms	7										
1940	4	6	13	43	2					* China	China:Yunnan,Shiping,NW.	中国:云南石屏西北	23.9	102.3		6	Ms	8	181	3	475	3		3	11556	5	4153	4
1940	5	6	12	54	6					GSHAP	Kyrgyzstan:Suluktu	吉尔吉斯斯坦:苏柳克塔	39.6	69.5	12	4.9	Ms	6.5										
1940	5	7	22	23						*	Georgia:Gori,S.	格鲁吉亚:哥里南部	41.7	43.8	19	6	Muk		16	1				2				
1940	5	14	0	45						GSHAP	Bulgaria:Plovdiv	保加利亚:普罗夫迪夫	41.8	24.5	9	4.7	Ms	6.5										
1940	5	18	5	3	59					USGS	US:California,Landers	美国:加利福尼亚州兰德斯	34.08	-116.3	16	5.4	Ms	5										
1940	5	19	4	36	49					* Engdahl	US:California,Imperial	美国:加利福尼亚州因皮里尔	33.222	-115.697	15	6.9	M	10	9	1			33.0	4				
1940	5	19	5	51	34					USGS	US:California,Holtville	美国:加利福尼亚州霍尔特维尔	32.76	-115.48	16	5.5	Ms	9										
1940	5	23	11							USGS,Song	US:California,Holtville	美国:加利福尼亚州霍尔特维尔	32.76	-115.48		5.1	Mk	6										
1940	5	23	17	30						USGS,Song	US:California,Holtville	美国:加利福尼亚州霍尔特维尔	32.77	-115.48		5.1	Mk	6										
1940	5	23	18	45						USGS,Song	US:California,Holtville	美国:加利福尼亚州霍尔特维尔	32.76	-115.48		5.1	Mk	6										
1940	5	24	16	33	58	3	2	1	1.5	* Engdahl, NOAA	Peru:Sayán	秘鲁:萨扬	-11.119	-77.629	50.1	7.5	Mw	10	179	3	3500	4		3		3		
1940	6	4	10	35	8					USGS	US:California,Descanso	美国:加利福尼亚州德斯坎索	33	-116.43	16	5.1	Ms	5										
1940	6	17	10	26	47					USGS	Hawaiian Islands	夏威夷群岛	20.4	-154.7		6	Ms	5										
1940	6	17	18	17						USGS,Song	Hawaiian Islands	夏威夷群岛	20.5	-155.25		4.9	Mk	5										
1940	6	17	23	9						USGS,Song	Hawaiian Islands	夏威夷群岛	20.5	-155.25		4.9	Mk	5										
1940	6	18	16							* China	China:Yunnan,Yuxi,N.	中国:云南玉溪北	24.5	102.6		5.75	Ms	7	2	1	20	1		2		3		
1940	6	23	18	59	36					GSHAP,Song	Venezuela:Valencia	委内瑞拉:巴伦西亚	10.05	-68.05	25	5	Mk	6										
1940	6	24	9	57	23					GSHAP	Romania:Vrancea	罗马尼亚:弗朗恰	45.8	26.5	120	5	Ms	5.5										
1940	7	6	3	40	18					GSHAP	St Vincent & Grenadines:Port Elizabeth	圣文森特和格林纳丁斯:伊丽莎白港	13	-61.25	160	6.5	Ms	6										
1940	7	10	13	10	48					GSHAP	Georgia:Bolnisi	格鲁吉亚:博尔尼西	41.5	44	18	5.1	Ms	6.5										
1940	7	11	1	23	33					GSHAP	Iran:Parsabad	伊朗:法尔萨巴德	39.5	47.6	18	4.9	Ms	6.5										
1940	7	16	3	17	33					USGS	Hawaiian Islands	夏威夷群岛	20.5	-155		5.6	Ms	5										
1940	7	19	16	27						USGS,Song	Alaska Peninsula,S.	阿拉斯加半岛南部	61	-150		5.1	Mk	6										
1940	8	1	15	8	26	4	3.5	1.8		* GSHAP,Usami,Engdahl,NOAA	Japan:W. Hokkaido Island	日本:北海道岛西部海域	44.508	139.829	35	7.5	Mw	9	10	1				2	20	1	612	3
1940	8	5	9	55	15					* China	China:Liaoning,Gaozhou	中国:辽宁盖州	40.2	122		5.75	Ms	8						3	1190	4	9376	4
1940	8	19	20	43	36					GSHAP	Turkey:Eskisehir	土耳其:埃斯基城	40	30	14	4.5	Ms	5.5										
1940	8	22	3	27	18					USGS,Shi Z.,Engdahl	Aleutian Islands	阿留申群岛	53	-165.5	60	7	Ms	5										

时间						海啸				资料来源	震中				深度	震级	标度	烈度	死亡人数		受伤人数		经济损失		房屋毁坏		房屋受损	
年	月	日	时	分	秒	源	浪高	级I	级S		地名(英文)	地名(中文)	纬度(°)	经度(°)					数量/人	级别	数量/人	级别	数量/$ Mill	级别	数量/间	级别	数量/间	级别
Date						Tsunami				Information	Earthquake Epicenter				Depth	Mag	Scale	MMI	Deaths		Injuries		Damage		Houses Destroyed		Houses Damaged	
Year	Mo	Dy	Hr	Mn	Sec	Sr	Wh	mI	mS		Name(English)	Name(Chinese)	Latitude	Longitude					Num	Dd	Num	Dd	$ Mill	De	Num	Dh	Num	Dh
1940	8	30	15	2	1					China, GSHAP	Kazakhstan: Taldy Kurgan, SE.	哈萨克斯坦:塔尔迪库尔干东南	44.6	79.6	20	5.5	Ms	7										
1940	10	4	7	54	50	2				* GSHAP, Engdahl, NOAA	Chile: Tocopilla, Near Coast	智利:托科皮亚近海	-20.592	-70.718	23.5	7.1	mB											
1940	10	10	2	6						* * Song	Arafura Sea	亚拉科拉海	-5	135		5.9	Mk	7						2				
1940	10	11	5	57	12					USGS	US: California, Torrance	美国:加利福尼亚州托伦斯	33.77	-118.45	16	4.7	Ms	6										
1940	10	11	14	41	14	2				* Chile, Shi Z, Engdahl, NOAA	Chile: Ancud	智利:安库德	-42.042	-73.933	15	7	Ms											
1940	10	22	6	37						GSHAP	Romania: Tulnici	罗马尼亚:图尔尼奇	45.9	26.5	150	6.8	Ms	7										
1940	10	22	11	1						USGS	US: California, North Coast	美国:加利福尼亚州北部近海	40.5	-124.1		4.5	Ms	6										
1940	10	27	22	29	18					USGS	US: Washington, Seattle	美国:华盛顿州西雅图	47.2	-123.4		5.1	Ms	5										
1940	11	8	12	0	42					GSHAP	Romania: Nehoiu	罗马尼亚:内霍尤	45.4	26.2	100	5.3	Ms	6										
1940	11	10	1	39	8					* GSHAP, Engdahl	Romania: Vrancea	罗马尼亚:弗朗恰	45.773	26.655	122	7.3	mB	10	1000	3			10.0	3				
1940	11	11	6	34	12					GSHAP	Romania: Tulnici	罗马尼亚:图尔尼奇	46	26.8	130	5	Ms	6										
1940	11	19	18	35						USGS	US: California, North Coast	美国:加利福尼亚州北部近海	40.75	-124.9		4.7	Ms	6										
1940	11	19	20	27	13					GSHAP	Romania: Panciu	罗马尼亚:潘丘	45.9	27.1	100	5.3	Ms	6										
1940	11	20	17	59	57					GSHAP	Afghan: Badakhshan	阿富汗:巴达赫尚	36.6	70.8	200	5.8	Ms	7										
1940	12	20	7	27	26					USGS	US: New Hampshire, Glen	美国:新汉普郡州格伦	43.87	-71.37	10	5.5	Ms	7										
1940	12	20	23	40	42					USGS	US: California, Whitethorn	美国:加利福尼亚州怀特索恩	40	-124		5.5	Ms	6										
1940	12	23	21	50	29					USGS, Song	US: Montana, Sheridan	美国:蒙大纳州谢立丹	46.5	-112.5		5.1	Mk	6										
1940	12	24	13	43	45					USGS	US: New Hampshire, Glen	美国:新汉普郡州格伦	43.91	-71.28	8	5.5	Ms	7										
1940										China	China: Sichuan, Maoxian	中国:四川茂县	31.6	103.9		5.5	Ms	7										
1941	1	11	8	32	59					*	Yemen: Sanaa	也门:萨纳	16.4	43.5		6.5	mB	8	1200	4	200	3			700	3	1000	3
1941	1	13	16	27	40	3	0.2	-3.3		* Engdahl, NOAA	Papua New Guinea: East New Britain	巴布亚新几内亚:东新不列颠	-4.72	152.316	35	7	Ms		4	1				1	1	1		1
1941	1	23	12	3						USGS	US: California, Off Coast N.	美国:加利福尼亚州北部沿海	40.5	-125		4.7	Ms	5										
1941	2	2	23	38	32					GSHAP	Colombia: Bahia Solano	哥伦比亚:巴伊阿索拉诺	6	-77.5		5.6	Ms	6										
1941	2	9	9	44	4	1				*	US: California, North Coast	美国:加利福尼亚州北部近海	40.5	-125.25		6.6	Ms	6						1				
1941	2	16	16	38						*	Iran: Razavi Khorasan	伊朗:呼罗珊	33.5	58.6		6.3	Muk		730	3				3				
1941	3	16	18	48		2			2	* NOAA	Italy: Marsala, Near Coast of N.	意大利:马尔萨拉北部近海	38.3	12.2		5	Ms											
1941	4	7	9	25						USGS	US: Washington, Omak	美国:华盛顿州奥马克	48.3	-119.6		4.5	Ms	6										
1941	4	11	12	5						GSHAP	Brasil: Cuiabá	巴西:库亚巴	-16.45	-54.64		4.3	Ms	5										

时间						海啸				资料来源	震中				深度	震级	标度	烈度	死亡人数		受伤人数		经济损失		房屋毁坏		房屋受损	
年	月	日	时	分	秒	源	浪高	级I	级S		地名(英文)	地名(中文)	纬度(°)	经度(°)					数量/人	级别	数量/人	级别	数量/$ Mill	级别	数量/间	级别	数量/间	级别
Date						Tsunami				Information	Earthquake Epicenter				Depth	Mag	Scale	MMI	Deaths		Injuries		Damage		Houses Destroyed		Houses Damaged	
Year	Mo	Dy	Hr	Mn	Sec	Sr	Wh	mI	mS		Name(English)	Name(Chinese)	Latitude	Longitude					Num	Dd	Num	Dd	$ Mill	De	Num	Dh	Num	Dh
1941	4	15	19	9	57					* Engdahl	Mexico: Michoacan, Colima, Jalisco	墨西哥:米却肯,科利马,哈利斯科	18.677	-102.957	35	7.6	Mw	7										
1941	4	20	17	38	27					GSHAP	Tadzhikistan: Tajikabad	塔吉克斯坦:塔吉卡巴德	39.2	70.5	20	6.4	Ms	9										
1941	4	26	23	10	58					GSHAP	Tadzhikistan: Garm	塔吉克斯坦:加尔姆	39.3	70.6	10	5.5	Ms	7.5										
1941	5	5	15	18	27					* China	China: Heilongjiang, Suihua	中国:黑龙江绥化	47	127.2		6	Ms	8	132	3	203	3		3	6321	4	4134	4
1941	5	6	16	55	29					GSHAP	Tadzhikistan: Garm	塔吉克斯坦:加尔姆	39.3	70.6	10	5.6	Ms	7.5										
1941	5	11	5	8						GSHAP, Song	Peru: Sayán	秘鲁:萨扬	-11.5	-76.9		5	Mk	6										
1941	5	13	16	1	54					USGS	US: California, Off Coast N.	美国:加利福尼亚州北部沿海	40.3	-126.4		6	Ms	5										
1941	5	16	7	14	34					* China, Engdahl	China: Yunnan, Gengma	中国:云南耿马	23.6	99.4	25	7	Muk	9		1				2		3		
1941	5	28	6	23	18					USGS	US: California, Morgan Hill	美国:加利福尼亚州摩根希尔	37.08	-121.75		4.5	Ms	5										
1941	6	15	1	28	24					GSHAP	Georgia: Zugdidi	格鲁吉亚:祖格迪迪	42.3	42.1	13	4.7	Ms	6.5										
1941	6	26	11	52	7	4	1.5			* Engdahl, India, GSHAP, NOAA	India: Andaman Islands, Madras	印度:安达曼群岛,马德拉斯	12.149	92.478	49.1	7.7	Mw		5000	4		1		4		4		4
1941	7	1	7	50	55					USGS	US: California, Santa Barbara	美国:加利福尼亚州圣巴巴拉	34.37	-119.58	16	5.9	Ms	8										
1941	7	3	7	11	43					GSHAP	Argentina: San Juan	阿根廷:圣胡安	-31.8	-67.8	20	6.25	Ms	7										
1941	7	15	14	45	26					Shi Z., Usami	Japan: Shinano	日本:长野信浓町	36.8	138.2		6.2	Ms		5	1					77	2		
1941	7	20	1	10						GSHAP	Colombia: Bucaramanga	哥伦比亚:布卡拉曼加	7.1	-73.2		4.5	Ms	5										
1941	7	22	18	52	5					USGS	US: California, Holtville	美国:加利福尼亚州霍尔特维尔	32.73	-115.45	16	4.5	Ms	5										
1941	7	30	1	51	21					USGS, Shi Z.	Alaska Peninsula, S.	阿拉斯加半岛南部	61	-151		6.25	Ms	6										
1941	8	7								* Song	Tunisia: Al – Qayrawan	突尼斯:凯鲁万	36	10		5.5	Mk							1				
1941	8	13	0	55	53					GSHAP	Uzbekistan: Fergana	乌兹别克斯坦:费尔干纳	40.8	71.3	20	5.1	Ms	6										
1941	8	30	4	41	44					GSHAP	Rumania: Timisoara	罗马尼亚:蒂米什瓦拉	45.8	20.8	7	4.8	Ms	7										
1941	9	1	14	18	40					GSHAP	Bulgaria: Chepelare	保加利亚:切佩拉雷	41.7	24.7	6	5.1	Ms	7.5										
1941	9	8	3	12	45					USGS	US: California, Santa Barbara	美国:加利福尼亚州圣巴巴拉	34.33	-119.58	16	4.5	Ms	5										
1941	9	10	21	53						* Iran	Turkey: Agri	土耳其:阿勒	39.5	43.3	28	6	Muk	8	430	3								
1941	9	14	16	43	32					USGS	US: California, Mammoth Lakes	美国:加利福尼亚州马姆莫斯湖	37.57	-118.73	16	5.8	Ms	6										
1941	9	14	18	21	19					USGS	US: California, Mammoth Lakes	美国:加利福尼亚州马姆莫斯湖	37.57	-118.73	16	5.5	Ms	6										
1941	9	14	18	39	12					USGS	US: California, Mammoth Lakes	美国:加利福尼亚州马姆莫斯湖	37.57	-118.73	16	6	Ms	6										
1941	9	18	13	14	10					Engdahl, GSHAP	Peru: Apurimac	秘鲁:阿普里马克	-13.928	-72.294	61	7	mB	6										
1941	9	21	6	19	45					China	China: Jiangxi, Xunwu, N.	中国:江西寻邬北	25.15	115.6		5.75	Ms	7										

时间 年 Year	月 Mo	日 Dy	时 Hr	分 Mn	秒 Sec	海啸 源 Sr	浪高 Wh	级 I mI	级 S mS	资料来源 Information	地名(英文) Name(English)	地名(中文) Name(Chinese)	纬度(°) Latitude	经度(°) Longitude	深度 Depth	震级 Mag	标度 Scale	烈度 MMI	死亡人数 数量/人 Num	死亡人数 级别 Dd	受伤人数 数量/人 Num	受伤人数 级别 Dd	经济损失 数量/$ Mill	经济损失 级别 De	房屋毁坏 数量/间 Num	房屋毁坏 级别 Dh	房屋受损 数量/间 Num	房屋受损 级别 Dh
1941	9	21	19	53	7.2					USGS	US:California,Arvin	美国:加利福尼亚州阿尔文	34.87	-118.93	16	5.2	Ms	5										
1941	9	25	17	48	38					USGS	Hawaiian Islands	夏威夷群岛	19.5	-155.5		6	Ms	7										
1941	10	3	16	13	8					USGS	US:California,North Coast	美国:加利福尼亚州北部近海	40.4	-124.8		6.4	Ms	6										
1941	10	8	15	24	20					* China	China:Sichuan,Barkam,S.	中国:四川马尔康南	31.7	102.3		6	Ms	8	15	1	10	1		1	70	2		
1941	10	22	6	57	19					USGS	US:California,Long Beach	美国:加利福尼亚州长滩	33.82	-118.22	16	4.9	Ms	7										
1941	10	25	7	9						USGS	US:California,Oroville Reservoir	美国:加利福尼亚州奥罗维尔水库	39.5	-122.17		4.6	Ms	5										
1941	11	12	10	4						*	Turkey:Erzincan	土耳其:埃尔津占	39.7	39.4	70	5.9	Muk	8	15	1								
1941	11	14	8	41	36					USGS	US:California,Long Beach	美国:加利福尼亚州长滩	33.78	-118.25	16	5.4	Ms	8										
1941	11	16	20	11						USGS,Song	Hawaiian Islands	夏威夷群岛	20	-155.8		4.9	Mk	5										
1941	11	18	13	26						USGS,Song	Hawaiian Islands	夏威夷群岛	20	-155.8		4.9	Mk	5										
1941	11	18	16	46		4	1.2	0.3		* Usami, Engdahl, NOAA	Japan:Miyazaki,Near Coast	日本:宫崎近海	32	132.1	10	7.7	Mw		2	1				1	27	1		
1941	11	25	18	3	59	4			2	* Engdahl,NOAA	North Atlantic Ocean,E.	北大西洋东部	37.171	-18.96	25	8.1	Mw	9										
1941	11	28	12	23	25					GSHAP	Afghan:Fayzabad	阿富汗:法扎巴德	36.6	70.6	200	6.3	Ms	8										
1941	12	2	23	38	32					GSHAP	Colombia:Bahia Solano	哥伦比亚:巴伊阿索拉诺	6	-77.5		5.6	Ms	7										
1941	12	5	20	47	4	4	0.2	-3.3	-3	* Engdahl, NOAA	Costa Rica:Piedras Blancas	哥斯达黎加:彼德拉斯布兰卡斯	8.752	-83.158	35	7.3	Mw	4	6	1		3		2		3		
1941	12	6	16							China	China:Yunnan,Mojiang	中国:云南墨江	23.4	101.7		5	Ms	6										
1941	12	6	21	24	45	4	0.1	-3.3	-4	* Shi Z., Engdahl, NOAA	Costa Rica:Off Coast	哥斯达黎加:沿海	8.143	-84.401	35	7	Ms											
1941	12	14	16							China	China:Yunnan,Shiping	中国:云南石屏	23.7	102.5		5	Ms	6										
1941	12	16	19	19	46					* China,Engdahl	China:Taiwan,Tainan	中国:台湾台南	23.251	120.391	35	7.1	Mw	9	319	3				2	1768	4		
1941	12	26	14	48	3					* China,Engdahl	Myanmar:Keng Tung	缅甸:肯格塔恩	21.076	99.145	25	7	Ms	8		2				1		2		
1941	12	29	18	37						USGS,Song	US:Oregon,Portland	美国:俄勒冈州波特兰	45.5	-122.7		5.1	Mk	6										
1941	12	31	6	48	44					USGS	US:California,Mammoth Lakes	美国:加利福尼亚州马姆莫斯湖	37.57	-118.73	16	5.4	Ms	6										
1942	1	18	16	36	31					GSHAP	Uzbekistan:Namangan	乌兹别克斯坦:纳曼干	41.1	71.6	21	5.9	Ms	7										
1942	1	18	16							China	China:Yunnan,Pu-er	中国:云南普洱	22.8	101		5	Ms	6										
1942	1	31	17	30	47					* China	China:Yunnan,Pu-er,NW.	中国:云南普洱西北	23.1	100.3		6.75	Ms	8	90	2		4		4		4		
1942	2	14	10	44	59					GSHAP	Uzbekistan:Namangan	乌兹别克斯坦:纳曼干	40.9	72.1	15	5.5	Ms	7										
1942	3	22	2	8	27					GSHAP	Afghan:Fayzabad	阿富汗:法扎巴德	36.6	70.7	200	6.3	Ms	5.5										
1942	3	27	18	38	3					GSHAP	Turkmenistan:Balkanabat	土库曼斯坦:巴尔坎纳巴德	39.5	55.3	24	5.2	Ms	6										
1942	4	3	17	45						GSHAP	Caspian Sea	里海	39.8	53.4	18	5.3	Ms	6.5										
1942	4	4								GSHAP	Caspian Sea	里海	39.8	53.4	20	5	Ms	6										

年 Year	月 Mo	日 Dy	时 Hr	分 Mn	秒 Sec	海啸 Tsunami 源 Sr	浪高 Wh	级 I mI	级 S mS	资料来源 Information	震中 Earthquake Epicenter 地名(英文) Name(English)	地名(中文) Name(Chinese)	纬度(°) Latitude	经度(°) Longitude	深度 Depth	震级 Mag	标度 Scale	烈度 MMI	死亡人数 Deaths 数量/人 Num	级别 Dd	受伤人数 Injuries 数量/人 Num	级别 Dd	经济损失 Damage 数量/$ Mill	级别 De	房屋毁坏 Houses Destroyed 数量/间 Num	级别 Dh	房屋受损 Houses Damaged 数量/间 Num	级别 Dh
1942	4	15	19							GSHAP	Caspian Sea	里海	39. 8	53. 4	20	5	Ms	6										
1942	5	2								GSHAP, Song	Venezuela: La Guaira (La Guaayra)	委内瑞拉:拉瓜伊拉	11	-66		6	Mk	7										
1942	5	11								GSHAP	Turkmenistan: Turkmenbasy	土库曼斯坦:土库曼巴希	40. 5	53. 5	20	5. 3	Ms	6. 5										
1942	5	14	2	13	28					* Shi Z., Engdahl	Ecuador: Bahía de Caráquez	厄瓜多尔:卡拉克斯港	0. 012	-79. 902	35	7. 8	Mw	9	200	3			2. 5	2		3		
1942	5	15								* * Song	Indonesia: Java Island	印度尼西亚:爪哇岛	-7. 7	109. 2		6. 5	Mk	9						2				
1942	5	22	10	30	36	1	1		1	* NOAA	Colombia: Santa Fe	哥伦比亚:圣达菲	4. 6	-74. 5	130	5. 8	Ms							2				
1942	5	23	15	47	29					USGS	US: California, Brawley	美国:加利福尼亚州布劳利	32. 98	-115. 98	16	5	Ms	5										
1942	6	5								* Song	Argentina: San Rafael	阿根廷:圣拉斐尔	-34. 6	-67. 9		6. 2	Mk							3				
1942	7	8	21	22	27					* China	China: Inner Mongolia, Horqin Zuoyi Houqi	中国:内蒙古科尔沁左翼后旗	43	122		6	Ms	8		2		2		2		2		
1942	7	27	11	5	29					GSHAP	Kuril Islands	千岛群岛	44	146. 5	80	6	Ms	6										
1942	7									GSHAP	Russia: Amur, SW.	俄罗斯:阿穆尔州西南	51. 9	132. 1	15	4. 5	Ms	7										
1942	8	18	21	55	24					USGS	US: Nevada, Hawthorne, N.	美国:内华达州霍索恩北部	38. 6	-118. 5		5	Ms	6										
1942	8	23	6	35	18					GSHAP	Russia: Kamchatka, Near East Coast	俄罗斯:堪察加东部近海	53	163. 8	20	6. 7	Ms	9										
1942	8	24	22	50	32	3	2	1	1	* Engdahl, NOAA	Peru: Ica, Near Coast	秘鲁:伊卡近海	-14. 975	-74. 92	35	8. 2	Ms	9	30	1	25	1		3		3		
1942	8	27	6	14						*	Albania: Peshkopia	阿尔巴尼亚:佩什科比	41. 7	20. 4	33	6	Ms	10	43	1	110	3		3		3		
1942	8	30	23	8						USGS, Song	US: Utah, Cedar City	美国:犹他州锡达城	37. 7	-113. 1		5. 1	Mk	6										
1942	9	3	14	6	1					USGS	US: California, Fillmore	美国:加利福尼亚州菲尔莫尔	34. 48	-118. 98	16	4. 5	Ms	5										
1942	9	4	6	34	33					USGS	US: California, Fillmore	美国:加利福尼亚州菲尔莫尔	34. 48	-118. 98	16	4. 5	Ms	5										
1942	9	13	8	21						GSHAP	Turkmenistan: Balkanabat	土库曼斯坦:巴尔坎纳巴德	39. 7	54. 5	15	4. 7	Ms	6										
1942	9	19	7	26	34					GSHAP	Azerbaijan: Gәncә	阿塞拜疆:占贾	40. 5	46. 4	12	4. 6	Ms	6. 5										
1942	9	26	15	50						USGS, Song	US: Utah, Cedar City	美国:犹他州锡达城	37. 7	-113. 1		5. 1	Mk	6										
1942	10	21	16	22	13					USGS	US: California, Seeley, NW.	美国:加利福尼亚州西利西北	32. 97	-116	16	6. 5	Ms	6										
1942	10	22	1	50	38					CGS, USGS	US: California, Salton City	美国:加利福尼亚州索尔顿城	33. 233	-115. 717	16	6	Ms	5										
1942	11	1	18	50	6					USGS, Song	US: Idaho, Cocolalla	美国:爱达荷州科科拉拉	48. 1	-116. 6		4. 9	Mk	5										
1942	11	12	4	55	32					* Shi Z., Engdahl	Mexico: Juchitan	墨西哥:胡齐坦	16. 592	-94. 296	69. 5	6. 8	Muk							3				
1942	11	15	17	1						*	Turkey: Balikesir, Bigadic	土耳其:巴里开赛,比加迪克	39. 2	28. 2		6. 1	Muk	8	16	1				2				

时间						海啸				资料来源	震中				深度	震级	标度	烈度	死亡人数		受伤人数		经济损失		房屋毁坏		房屋受损	
年	月	日	时	分	秒	源	浪高	级 I	级 S		地名(英文)	地名(中文)	纬度(°)	经度(°)					数量/人	级别	数量/人	级别	数量/$ Mill	级别	数量/间	级别	数量/间	级别
Date						Tsunami				Information	Earthquake Epicenter				Depth	Mag	Scale	MMI	Deaths		Injuries		Damage		Houses Destroyed		Houses Damaged	
Year	Mo	Dy	Hr	Mn	Sec	Sr	Wh	mI	mS		Name(English)	Name(Chinese)	Latitude	Longitude					Num	Dd	Num	Dd	$ Mill	De	Num	Dh	Num	Dh
1942	11	21	14	1						* Song	Turkey:Kastamonu, Kargi	土耳其:卡斯塔木努,卡尔古	40.3	34.6		5.9	Mk	8	17	1				2				
1942	11	26	14	27	32					Engdahl,GSHAP	Kuril Islands	千岛群岛	45.405	150.175	76	7.4	mB	6.5										
1942	11	26	22	20						*	Turkey:Havza, Ladik	土耳其:哈佛扎,拉迪克	40.5	34		7.6	Muk		4000	4				4				
1942	12	2	19	4						* Song	Turkey:Corum	土耳其:乔鲁姆	40.6	35		6.2	Mk	8	4	1				3				
1942	12	3	9	44	42					CGS, USGS	US:Nevada, Nixon	美国:内华达州尼克松	39.7	-119.3		5.9	Ms	6										
1942	12	11	2	39						* Song	Turkey:Merzifon	土耳其:梅尔济丰	40.8	35.1		6.2	Mk	8						3				
1942	12	17	15	7	43					USGS	US:Nevada, Johnson Lane, S.	美国:内华达州约翰逊巷南部	38.87	-119.9		5.1	Ms	5										
1942	12	20	14	3	11					* Engdahl	Turkey:Niksar, Erbaa	土耳其:尼克萨尔,埃尔巴	40.9	36.5	35	7.2	Mw	10	1000	3				4				
1942	12	25	8	0	28					GSHAP	Bolivia:Cochabamba	玻利维亚:科恰班巴	-17.28	-65.81		5.7	Ms	6										
1942	12	26	12	31	40					GSHAP	Colombia:Cordoba	哥伦比亚:科尔多巴	8.5	-75.5		6.5	Ms	8										
1942	12	29	3	42						*	Croatia:Split, SE.	克罗地亚:斯普利特东南	43.4	17.2	15	6	Muk	10										
1943	1	11	19	50	18					GSHAP	Tajikistan:Roghun	塔吉克斯坦:罗格汉	38.62	69.3	18	6	Ms	9										
1943	1	12	9	5	9					GSHAP	Tajikistan:Duachanbe	塔吉克斯坦:杜尚别	38.47	69.26	5	5.6	Ms	9										
1943	1	12	10	41	42					GSHAP	Tajikistan:Roghun	塔吉克斯坦:罗格汉	38.53	69.51	3	4.7	Ms	8.5										
1943	1	20	15	32						*	Turkey:Hendek	土耳其:亨达克	40.8	30.5		6.6	Muk		285	3								
1943	1	22	12							GSHAP	Sea of Okhotsk	鄂霍次克海	59	151	20	5	Ms	6										
1943	1	29								* Song	Bosnia:Zenica	波斯尼亚:泽尼察	44.3	17		5.8	Mk		19	1				1				
1943	1	30	5	33	3					* Engdahl	Ecuador:Guayaquil	厄瓜多尔:瓜亚基尔	-2	-80.5	100	6.9	Muk	6						2				3
1943	1	31	5	1						* GSHAP	Peru:Espinar	秘鲁:埃斯皮纳尔	-14.2	-71.5	25	5	Ms	7	75	2	200	3		1				
1943	2	18	15	38	46					GSHAP	Bolivia:Cochabamba	玻利维亚:科恰班巴	-17.38	-66.19	33	5.2	Ms	6										
1943	2	22	9	20	45					* Engdahl	Mexico:Guerrero, Paricutin Volcano Forms	墨西哥:格雷罗,帕里库廷火山	16.7	-101.5	60	7.4	Mw	7	11	1				3				
1943	2	22	14	20						USGS, Song	US:Utah, Salt Lake City	美国:犹他州盐湖城	40.7	-112		5.1	Mk	6										
1943	3	4	10	13						Shi Z., Usami	Japan:Tottori	日本:鸟取	35.6	134.2	20	6.1	Ms				11	1			68	2		
1943	3	7	3	1	36					GSHAP	Bering Sea, W.	白令海西部	58.5	166	20	6.7	Ms	9										
1943	3	9	3	25	25					USGS	US:Ohio, Mentor	美国:俄亥俄州门托	41.63	-81.31	7	4.5	Ms	6										
1943	3	17	0	40	44					USGS	US:California, Holtville	美国:加利福尼亚州霍尔特维尔	32.73	-115.43	16	4.5	Ms	5										
1943	3	30	16							China	China:Yunnan, Dali	中国:云南大理	25.7	100.1		5.5	Ms	7										
1943	3	30	21	7	28					USGS	US:California, Sierraville	美国:加利福尼亚州谢拉维尔	39.43	-120.4		5.3	Ms	5										
1943	4	5	1	56	1					* China	Tajikistan:Kuhistoni Badakhshon, N.	塔吉克斯坦:勾瑙－巴达科善北部	39.3	73.3		6.5	Ms			3				2		3		
1943	4	6	16	7	15	4	1			* Engdahl, NOAA	Chile:Illapel	智利:伊拉帕尔	-30.75	-72	60	8.2	Mw		11	1				1		1		
1943	4	16								*	Algeria:Mansourah	阿尔及利亚:曼苏拉	36.1	4.5		5	Muk			2								
1943	4	28	19	46	50					GSHAP	Romania:Vrancea	罗马尼亚:弗朗恰	45.8	27.1	100	5.5	Ms	5.5										

年 Year	月 Mo	日 Dy	时 Hr	分 Mn	秒 Sec	海啸 Tsunami 源 Sr	浪高 Wh	级 I mI	级 S mS	资料来源 Information	震中 Earthquake Epicenter 地名(英文) Name(English)	地名(中文) Name(Chinese)	纬度(°) Latitude	经度(°) Longitude	深度 Depth	震级 Mag	标度 Scale	烈度 MMI	死亡人数 Deaths 数量/人 Num	级别 Dd	受伤人数 Injuries 数量/人 Num	级别 Dd	经济损失 Damage 数量/$ Mill	级别 De	房屋毁坏 Houses Destroyed 数量/间 Num	级别 Dh	房屋受损 Houses Damaged 数量/间 Num	级别 Dh
1943	4	29	15	24	56					GSHAP	Kuril Islands	千岛群岛	44.5	147.2	120	6.2	Ms	6										
1943	5	12	12	25						* Song	Italy: Sarnano	意大利:萨尔纳诺	43.1	13.3		6.5	Mk	12										
1943	5	31	20	16	53					USGS	US: California, Bishop, W.	美国:加利福尼亚州毕晓普西部	37.38	-118.6	16	4.5	Ms	5										
1943	6	13	5	11	49	4	0.6	-07		* GSHAP, Engdahl, NOAA	Japan: SE. Hokkaido Island	日本:北海道东南	42.75	143.25	60	7.1	Mw											
1943	6	15	11	10						GSHAP	Japan: Hokkaido	日本:北海道	41.33	142.45	20	6.9	Ms	8										
1943	6	20	15	33						*	Turkey: Hendek, Adapazari	土耳其:亨达克,阿达帕札勒	40.6	30.5	15	6.2	Muk	10	285	3				3				
1943	6	20	16	47	55					GSHAP	Turkey: Sakarya	土耳其:萨卡里亚	40.8	30.4	32	5.5	Ms	6										
1943	6	20	16							*	China: Sichuan, Chengdu	中国:四川成都	30.6	104.1		5	Ms	6		1				1		1		
1943	6	25	4	25						USGS	US: Montana, Homestead, NW.	美国:蒙大纳州霍姆斯特德西北	48.5	-105		4	Ms	6										
1943	7	23	14	53	9					* Engdahl	Indonesia: Java Ridge	印度尼西亚:爪哇海岭	-9.5	110	90	7.6	mB	8	213	3	2096	4		3			2800	4
1943	8	9	5	30	4					USGS	US: Nevada, Mina, SW.	美国:内华达州迈纳西南	38.2	-118.2		5.5	Ms	6										
1943	8	12	4	50						Usami, Japan	Japan: Fukushima	日本:福岛	37.3	139.8	15	6.1	Ms				3	1						1
1943	8	29	3	45	13					USGS	US: California, Landers	美国:加利福尼亚州兰德斯	34.27	-116.97	16	5.5	Ms	6										
1943	8									China	China: Guangxi, Hechi	中国:广西河池	24.5	108.1		4.75	Ms	6										
1943	9	9	4	6	13					GSHAP	Afghan: Badakhshan	阿富汗:巴达赫尚	36.3	70.8	160	6.3	Ms	6.5										
1943	9	10	8	36	53					* Usami, Engdahl	Japan: Misasa	日本:鸟取三朝	35.3	133.9	10	7	Mw		1400	4				4	7736	4		
1943	10	13	5	43	3					Shi Z., Usami	Japan: Shinano	日本:长野信浓町	36.8	138.2		6.1	Ms		1	1					34	1		
1943	10	13								GSHAP, Song	Venezuela: Lara	委内瑞拉:拉腊	9.92	-69.59		5	Mk	6										
1943	10	23	17	23	16					* GSHAP, Engdahl	India: Mariani	印度:阿萨姆的默里亚尼	26.8	94		7.1	Mw							2				
1943	10	26	4	50	33					USGS	US: California, San Jose	美国:加利福尼亚州圣何塞	37.43	-121.68		4.9	Ms	6										
1943	10									GSHAP, Song	Venezuela: Yaracuy	委内瑞拉:亚拉奎	10.46	-68.58		5	Mk	6										
1943	11	2	3	39	17					GSHAP	Tajikistan: Garm	塔吉克斯坦:加尔姆	38.7	70.65	5	5.2	Ms	7										
1943	11	3	14	32	17					USGS, Engdahl	Alaska Peninsula, S.	阿拉斯加半岛南部	61.9	-150.84		7.2	Mw	5										
1943	11	11	2	52						USGS, Song	Hawaiian Islands	夏威夷群岛	19	-155.5		4.9	Mk	5										
1943	11	12								* * Song	Indonesia: Java, Wonosobo	印度尼西亚:爪哇,索博	-7.2	109.5		6.1	Mk		60	2								
1943	11	26	22	20	36					* Engdahl	Turkey: Ladik	土耳其:拉迪克	41	33.7	33	7.5	Mw	11	4020	4				3				
1943	11	28	17	11						*	Russia: Kamchatka Peninsula	俄罗斯:堪察加半岛	54.9	156.8	350	7.6	Muk							1				
1943	11	29	0	43						USGS	US: Washington, Lopez	美国:华盛顿州洛佩斯	48.4	-122.9		4.8	Ms	6										
1943	12	2								* * Song	Indonesia: Java, Wonosobo	印度尼西亚:爪哇,索博	-7.3	109.9		6.5	Mk	9	727	3				3				
1943	12	5								* Song	Turkey: Erzincan	土耳其:埃尔津詹	40	40		6.4	Mk		550	3				3				

年 Year	月 Mo	日 Dy	时 Hr	分 Mn	秒 Sec	源 Sr	浪高 Wh	级I mI	级S mS	资料来源 Information	地名(英文) Name(English)	地名(中文) Name(Chinese)	纬度(°) Latitude	经度(°) Longitude	深度 Depth	震级 Mag	标度 Scale	烈度 MMI	死亡人数 Deaths 数量/人 Num	死亡人数 Deaths 级别 Dd	受伤人数 Injuries 数量/人 Num	受伤人数 Injuries 级别 Dd	经济损失 Damage 数量/$ Mill	经济损失 Damage 级别 De	房屋毁坏 Houses Destroyed 数量/间 Num	房屋毁坏 Houses Destroyed 级别 Dh	房屋受损 Houses Damaged 数量/间 Num	房屋受损 Houses Damaged 级别 Dh
1943	12	14	16							China	China:Yunnan,Kunming	中国:云南昆明	25.1	102.7		4.75	Ms	6										
1944	1	3	10	19	13					GSHAP	Columbia:Uribia	哥伦比亚:乌里维亚北部海域	13	-71		5	Ms	6										
1944	1	4	0	57	54					GSHAP	Columbia:Uribia	哥伦比亚:乌里维亚北部海域	13	-71		5.5	Ms	6										
1944	1	12	15	2	40					USGS	US:California,North Coast	美国:加利福尼亚州北部近海	40.3	-124.9		5.1	Ms	5										
1944	1	15	23	49	30					* Engdahl	Argentina:San Juan	阿根廷:圣胡安	-31.5	-68.5	50	7.1	Mw		8000	4			100	5				
1944	1	20	1							GSHAP	Russia:Magadan,Ola	俄罗斯:马加丹州奥拉	60	152	20	5	Ms	6										
1944	2	1	3	22	36					* Engdahl	Turkey:Karabük	土耳其:卡拉比克	41.4	32.7	33	7.2	Mw	10	2381	4				3				
1944	2	3	11	25	24					GSHAP	Colombia:Trinidad	哥伦比亚:特立尼达	5.6	-71.6		5	Ms	6										
1944	2	3	14	10	12					GSHAP	Colombia:Tame	哥伦比亚:塔梅	6.5	-72		5	Ms	6										
1944	2	6	3	50	30					GSHAP,Song	Venezuela:Maturín	委内瑞拉:马图林	10	-62		6	Mk	7										
1944	3	9	22	12	58					* China, Engdahl	China: Xinjiang, Xinyuan, NE.	中国:新疆新源东北	44	84		7.1	Ms	8	3	1				1		2		
1944	3	14	23	59	26					GSHAP	Bulgaria:Satovcha	保加利亚:萨托夫恰	41.7	23.9	22	5.1	Ms	6.5										
1944	4	5	18	5	53					* GSHAP,Iran	Iran:Gorgan	伊朗:戈尔甘	36.8	54.5	7	5.4	Muk	8	20	1				2				
1944	4	12	10	15	32					GSHAP	Colombia:El Carmen	哥伦比亚:埃尔卡门	6.2	-76.4		4.5	Ms	5										
1944	5	9	14	29	57					GSHAP	Colombia:Huila	哥伦比亚:乌伊拉	2.5	-75.5	100	6	Ms	7										
1944	6	10	11	11	51					USGS	US:California,Palm Springs	美国:加利福尼亚州棕泉	34.01	-116.77	10	4.5	Ms	5										
1944	6	12	10	45	35					USGS	US:California,Palm Springs	美国:加利福尼亚州棕泉	33.98	-116.72	10	5.1	Ms	6										
1944	6	12	11	16	36					USGS	US:California,Palm Springs	美国:加利福尼亚州棕泉	33.99	-116.71	10	5.3	Ms	6										
1944	6	13	8	27	32					USGS	US:California,Lompoc	美国:加利福尼亚州隆波克	34.67	-120.5	16	4.6	Ms	5										
1944	6	19	0	3	33					USGS	US:California,Long Beach	美国:加利福尼亚州长滩	33.87	-118.22	16	4.5	Ms	6										
1944	6	19	3	6	7					USGS	US:California,Long Beach	美国:加利福尼亚州长滩	33.87	-118.22	16	4.4	Ms	6										
1944	6	25	4	16	25					* GSHAP	Turkey:Usak	土耳其:乌沙克	38.9	29.3	40	6.2	Muk	8	21	1								
1944	6	25	6	57	44					GSHAP	Turkey:Gediz	土耳其:盖迪兹	39	29.5	12	5.4	Ms	7										
1944	7	3	5	38	24					USGS	US:California,Ridgecrest	美国:加利福尼亚州里奇克雷斯特	35.35	-117.83		4.7	Ms	5										
1944	7	12	19	30	21					USGS	US:Idaho,Custer,NW.	美国:爱达荷州卡斯特西北	44.41	-115.06	10	6.1	Ms	7										
1944	7	30	4	0	35					* Turkey	Greece:Gytheio	希腊:吉雄	36.7	22.5	8	6	Muk	10										
1944	8	29	7	28	15					GSHAP	Colombia:Apartado	哥伦比亚:阿帕尔塔多	7.6	-76.7		4	Ms	5										
1944	9	3	21	29	52					GSHAP	Colombia:Antioquia	哥伦比亚:安提奥基亚	7	-75		4	Ms	5										
1944	9	5	4	38	46					*	US:New York,Massena	美国:纽约州马塞纳	44.957	-74.723	12	5.6	Ms	8					2	2				

年 Year	月 Mo	日 Dy	时 Hr	分 Mn	秒 Sec	源 Sr	浪高 Wh	级 I mI	级 S mS	资料来源 Information	地名(英文) Name(English)	地名(中文) Name(Chinese)	纬度(°) Latitude	经度(°) Longitude	深度 Depth	震级 Mag	标度 Scale	烈度 MMI	死亡人数 Deaths 数量/人 Num	死亡人数 Deaths 级别 Dd	受伤人数 Injuries 数量/人 Num	受伤人数 Injuries 级别 Dd	经济损失 Damage 数量/$ Mill	经济损失 Damage 级别 De	房屋毁坏 Houses Destroyed 数量/间 Num	房屋毁坏 Houses Destroyed 级别 Dh	房屋受损 Houses Damaged 数量/间 Num	房屋受损 Houses Damaged 级别 Dh
1944	9	9	4	12	20					USGS, Song	US: Colorado, Somerset	美国:科罗拉多州萨默塞特	39	-107.5		5.1	Mk	6										
1944	9	15	14	20						* * GSHAP	Ecuador: Puerto Limón	厄瓜多尔:利蒙港	-0.5	-79		5.7	Ms	7						3				
1944	9	23	12	13	20					GSHAP, Shi Z., Engdahl	Russia: Kamchatka, Near East Coast	俄罗斯:堪察加东部近海	53	162.5	20	7.1	Mw	9										
1944	9	27	16	25	2					* China, Engdahl	China: Xinjiang, Ulugqat	中国:新疆乌恰	39.1	75	40	7	Ms	8						1		2		
1944	10	5	15	21	24					GSHAP	Colombia: Choco, Near Coast	哥伦比亚:乔科近海	4.5	-78		4.5	Ms	5										
1944	10	6	2	34	36					*	Turkey: Izmir	土耳其:伊兹密尔	39.4	26.7		6.8	Ms	9	30	1				4	5500	4		
1944	12	6	16	27						Usami	Japan: Yamagata	日本:山形	38.3	140.2		5.8	Ms								1	1		
1944	12	7	4	35	42	4	10	2.9	2.5	* Shi Z., Engdahl, NOAA	Japan: Mie, Near Coast	日本:三重近海	34	137.1	30	8.1	M		1223	4	2135	4		3	29205	5	46950	5
1944	12	7	4	48						USGS, Song	US: Washington, Aberdeen	美国:华盛顿州阿伯丁	46.9	-123.8		5.1	Mk	6										
1944	12	27	14	11	40					USGS	Hawaiian Islands	夏威夷群岛	19.5	-155.5		5.6	Ms	6										
1945	1	7	22	25	33					USGS	US: California, Paicines	美国:加利福尼亚州佩赛恩斯	36.73	-121.2		4.7	Ms	6										
1945	1	12	18	38	26	4	1	-0.7		* Usami, Engdahl, NOAA	Japan: Tahara	日本:爱知田原市	34.7	137.2		6.8	Ms		2306	4	896	3		4	7221	4		
1945	1	15	5	30						GSHAP	Turkey: Saray	土耳其:萨拉伊	38.4	44.2	32	5.1	Ms	6										
1945	2	8	9	40						GSHAP, Song	Peru: Arequipa	秘鲁:阿雷基帕	-16.5	-71.7	15	4.5	Mk	5										
1945	2	10	4	57	56	4	0.4	-1.3	-1	* GSHAP, Engdahl, Usami, NOAA	Japan: Aomori, Near Coast	日本:青森近海	41.25	142.5	50	7.1	Ms		2	1					2	1		
1945	2	11	1	20	50					GSHAP	Russia: Sakhalin Island	俄罗斯:库页岛(萨哈林岛)	52.7	141.9	10	5	Ms	7										
1945	2	14	3	1	11					USGS	US: Idaho, Custer, NW.	美国:爱达荷州卡斯特西北	44.61	-115.09	10	6	Ms	6										
1945	3	6	21	5						GSHAP, Song	Peru: Trujillo	秘鲁:特鲁希略	-7.738	-79.003	70	4.5	Mk	5										
1945	3	12	20	51	47					GSHAP	Romania: Nehoiu	罗马尼亚:内霍尤	45.6	26.4	150	5.8	Ms	6										
1945	3	15	21	20						GSHAP, Song	Peru: Talara, Near Coast	秘鲁:塔拉拉近海	-4.4	-81.6	30	4.5	Mk	5										
1945	3	17	23	57	54					Engdahl, GSHAP	Colombia: Near Coast	哥伦比亚:近海	6.6	-78.5	0	6.8	Muk	8										
1945	3	18	8	1	26					*	Uganda: Mpigi	乌干达:姆皮吉	0	32		6	Ms	9	5	1				2				
1945	3	18	8	10	14					GSHAP	Colombia: Bahía Solano, Near Coast	哥伦比亚:巴伊阿索拉诺近海	6.6	-78.5		4.5	Ms	5										
1945	3	20	7	59						*	Turkey: Aelana, Ceyhan	土耳其:伊利安那港,杰伊汉	37.4	35.8	60	6	Muk	7	300	3								
1945	3	27	1	45						GSHAP, Song	Peru: Pararca	秘鲁:巴腊尔卡	-15.2	-73.1	25	4.5	Mk	5										
1945	3	29	15	30						GSHAP, Song	Peru: Arequipa. NW.	秘鲁:阿雷基帕西北	-15.9	-73.2	20	4.5	Mk	5										
1945	4	7	9	32						GSHAP, Song	Peru: Máncora, Near Coast	秘鲁:曼科拉近海	-4.161	-82.098	30	4.5	Mk	5										
1945	4	12	0	21	7					GSHAP	Colombia: Off Coast of W.	哥伦比亚:西部沿海	2.5	-80		5	Ms	6										
1945	4	14	6	47						GSHAP, Song	Peru: Arequipa	秘鲁:阿雷基帕	-17	-71.6	25	4.5	Mk	5										
1945	4	14	7							GSHAP, Song	Peru: Ilo, Near Coast	秘鲁:伊洛近海	-17.746	-71.72	30	5	Mk	6										

时间 Date 年 Year	月 Mo	日 Dy	时 Hr	分 Mn	秒 Sec	海啸 Tsunami 源 Sr	浪高 Wh	级 I mI	级 S mS	资料来源 Information	震中 Earthquake Epicenter 地名(英文) Name(English)	地名(中文) Name(Chinese)	纬度(°) Latitude	经度(°) Longitude	深度 Depth	震级 Mag	标度 Scale	烈度 MMI	死亡人数 Deaths 数量/人 Num	级别 Dd	受伤人数 Injuries 数量/人 Num	级别 Dd	经济损失 Damage 数量/$ Mill $ Mill	级别 De	房屋毁坏 Houses Destroyed 数量/间 Num	级别 Dh	房屋受损 Houses Damaged 数量/间 Num	级别 Dh
1945	4	15	2	35	22					Engdahl,GSHAP	Bering Sea,W.	白令海西部	57	164	0	7.1	Mw	9										
1945	4	19	17	46	51					GSHAP	Kyrgyzstan:Issyk－Kul,N.	吉尔吉斯斯坦:伊塞克湖州北部	42.9	77.5	20	5.7	Ms	7										
1945	4	29	13	45						GSHAP,Song	Peru:Moquegua	秘鲁:莫克瓜	－17	－70.6	100	4.5	Mk	5										
1945	4	29	20	16	17					USGS	US:Washington,Seattle	美国:华盛顿州西雅图	47.4	－121.7		5.5	Ms	7										
1945	5	2	5	58						GSHAP,Song	Peru:Talara,Near Coast	秘鲁:塔拉拉近海	－4.6	－81.6	30	5	Mk	6										
1945	5	2	19	47	54					USGS	US:California,Hoopa	美国:加利福尼亚州胡帕	41.2	－123.5		5	Ms	5										
1945	5	10	17	53	15					GSHAP,Song	Peru:Ica,Near Coast	秘鲁:伊卡近海	－15	－77		4.5	Mk	5										
1945	5	11	20	17						* Iran	Iran:Garmsar	伊朗:伽姆萨尔	35.18	52.4	33	4.7	Ms		20	1				3				
1945	5	17	15	6	47					USGS	US:California,Hollister	美国:加利福尼亚州霍利斯特	36.82	－121.37		4.6	Ms	6										
1945	5	19	12	18						USGS,Song	Hawaiian Islands	夏威夷群岛	19.5	－155.5		4.9	Mk	5										
1945	5	19	15	7	4					USGS,Shi Z.	US:California,Off Coast of N.	美国:加利福尼亚州北部沿海	40.25	－126.5		6.2	Ms	5										
1945	6	15	9	8						GSHAP,Song	Peru:Lima,Near Coast	秘鲁:利马近海	－12.345	－77.699	40	5	Mk	6										
1945	6	21	1	33						* Song	Turkey:Van,Nemrut	土耳其:凡城,尼姆鲁特	38.5	43.3		5.9	Mk	7						2				
1945	6	21	11	55						GSHAP,Song	Peru:Arequipa	秘鲁:阿雷基帕	－16.138	－72.415	30	5	Mk	6										
1945	6	22	9	18	40					GSHAP,Engdahl	Kuril Islands	千岛群岛	43.9	146.5	120	6.9	mB	6.5										
1945	6	30	18	18	28					GSHAP	Colombia:Sincelejo	哥伦比亚:苏克雷的辛塞莱霍	9.5	－75.3		5	Ms	6										
1945	7	9	11	56	44					GSHAP	Colombia:Near Coast	哥伦比亚:近海	6.7	－78.9		5	Ms	6										
1945	7	9	16	42	8					GSHAP	Colombia:Cauca	哥伦比亚:考卡	2.5	－76.5	100	6.5	Ms	7										
1945	7	26	10	32	16					USGS	US:South Carolina,Swansea	美国:南卡罗来纳州斯旺西	33.75	－81.38	5	4.3	Ms	6										
1945	7	29	8	56						* Iran	Turkey:Van,Bolgesi	土耳其:凡城,沃尔季什	38.5	43.3	33	6.4	Ms	7	300	3				3				
1945	8	6	23	2	10					GSHAP,Song	Peru:Tarapoto	秘鲁:塔拉波托	－6	－76.5	100	6	Mk	7										
1945	8	8	19	50						GSHAP,Song	Peru:Pucallpa,SW.	秘鲁:普卡尔帕西南	－8.9	－75.7	30	5	Mk	6										
1945	8	9	3	13	32					GSHAP,Song	Peru:Tarapoto	秘鲁:塔拉波托	－6	－76.5		5	Mk	6										
1945	8	15	17	56	24					USGS	US:California,Borrego Springs	美国:加利福尼亚州博雷戈斯普林斯	33.22	－116.13	16	5.7	Ms	6										
1945	8	21	16	29	37					GSHAP,Engdahl	Peru:Pasco,W.	秘鲁:帕斯科东部	－10.5	－75	120	6.8	Muk	6										
1945	8	21	16							China	China:Yunnan,Gejiu	中国:云南个旧	23.4	103.2		5	Ms	6										
1945	8	27	9	13	4					USGS	US:California,San Jose	美国:加利福尼亚州圣何塞	37.27	－121.8		4.5	Ms	6										
1945	9	9	12	56	20					GSHAP,Song	Peru:Ica	秘鲁:伊卡	－14.5	－76		4.5	Mk	5										
1945	9	12	0	51						*	Cameroon:Moloundou;Congo:Babali	喀麦隆:莫隆杜;刚果:巴巴利	2.5	15.6		6.2	Muk	8						1				

时间						海啸				资料来源	震中				深度	震级	标度	烈度	死亡人数		受伤人数		经济损失		房屋毁坏		房屋受损	
年	月	日	时	分	秒	源	浪高	级 I	级 S		地名(英文)	地名(中文)	纬度(°)	经度(°)					数量/人	级别	数量/人	级别	数量/$ Mill	级别	数量/间	级别	数量/间	级别
Date						Tsunami				Information	Earthquake Epicenter				Depth	Mag	Scale	MMI	Deaths		Injuries		Damage		Houses Destroyed		Houses Damaged	
Year	Mo	Dy	Hr	Mn	Sec	Sr	Wh	mI	mS		Name(English)	Name(Chinese)	Latitude	Longitude					Num	Dd	Num	Dd	$ Mill	De	Num	Dh	Num	Dh
1945	9	23	9	57	48					USGS	US:Idaho,Lakeside	美国:爱达荷州莱克赛德	48	-114.3		5.5	Ms	6										
1945	9	23	15	34	21					* China	China:Hebei,Luanxian	中国:河北滦县	39.5	119		6.25	Ms	8	17	1	30	1		1	600	3		
1945	9	29	4	27	46					GSHAP	Peru:Tarapoto	秘鲁:塔拉波托	-6	-77		5.6	Ms	6										
1945	10	5	4	15						GSHAP,Song	Peru:Tarapoto	秘鲁:塔拉波托	-6.47	-77.17	40	4.5	Mk	5										
1945	10	9	14	36	33					Engdahl,GSHAP	Kuril Islands	千岛群岛	43.5	147.5	80	7	mB	7										
1945	11	13	2	46	38					GSHAP,Song	Peru:Trujillo,Near Coast	秘鲁:特鲁希略近海	-8.5	-79.5		4.5	Mk	5										
1945	11	18	1	7	41					USGS,Song	US:Utah,Richfield	美国:犹他州里奇菲尔德	38.8	-112		5.1	Mk	6										
1945	11	23	8	10	1					GSHAP	Venezuela:Maturín	委内瑞拉:马图林	10	-62	100	6.5	Ms	6										
1945	11	27	21	56	50	4	15	3.9		* Engdahl, NOAA	Gulf of Oman,E.	阿曼湾东部	24.2	62.6	25	8	Mw	10	4000	4			25.0	4				
1945	12	9	6	8	46					GSHAP	Romania:Focsani	罗马尼亚:福克沙尼	45.6	26.8	90	6.2	Ms	7										
1945	12	21	18	35						GSHAP	Turkey:Denizli	土耳其:登尼资里	37.9	29	4	4.7	Ms	8										
1945	12	21								* Turkey	Turkey:Denizli, Burdur	土耳其:丹兹利,布尔杜尔	38	28.9		5.3	Ms	8	7	1				2				
1945	12	23	8	10	1					GSHAP	Venezuela:Maturín	委内瑞拉:马图林	10	-62	100	6.5	Ms	6										
1946	1	8	18	54	18					USGS	US:California,Westmorland	美国:加利福尼亚州威斯特莫兰	33	-115.83	16	5.4	Ms	5										
1946	1	13	16	31	15					USGS	US:California,Bishop,W.	美国:加利福尼亚州毕晓普西部	37.32	-118.65	16	4.7	Ms	6										
1946	1	23	6	22						GSHAP,Song	Peru:La Unión	秘鲁:拉乌尼翁	-9.483	-76.77	100	4.5	Mk	5										
1946	1	25	4	28	27					GSHAP,Song	Venezuela:Cariaco	委内瑞拉:卡利亚科	10.7	-63.8		5	Mk	6										
1946	1	28	8	9						GSHAP,Song	Peru:Lima,Near Coast	秘鲁:利马近海	-12.389	-77.632	60	4.5	Mk	5										
1946	2	3	7	22						GSHAP,Song	Peru:Ilo,Near Coast	秘鲁:伊洛近海	-17.634	-72.463	70	5	Mk	6										
1946	2	10								* Iran	Iran:Birjand	伊朗:比尔詹德	32.55	59.26	33	5.5	Ms	8	3	1				3				
1946	2	12	2	43	24					*	Algeria:Hodna Mountains	阿尔及利亚:荷德纳山脉	35.75	5		5.6	Ms	9	264	3				3				
1946	2	15	3	17	48					USGS	US:Washington,Olympia	美国:华盛顿州奥林匹亚	47.4	-122.67	18	5.7	Ms	7										
1946	2	17	8	40						GSHAP,Song	Peru:Bagua Grande	秘鲁:大巴瓜	-5.65	-78	40	4.5	Mk	5										
1946	2	21	15	43						*	Turkey: Konya	土耳其:科尼亚	38.2	31.8	60	5.6	Muk	8	12	1								
1946	3	5	4	45	7					GSHAP	Azerbaijan:Lenkeran	阿塞拜疆:连科兰	39.6	49.3	11	4.8	Ms	7										
1946	3	12	2	21						* Iran	Iran:Bushehr	伊朗:布什尔	29.4	51.4	33	6	Ms							3				
1946	3	15	13	21	1					USGS	US:California,Brown	美国:加利福尼亚州布朗	35.75	-117.99	16	5.2	Ms	6										
1946	3	15	13	49	36					USGS	US:California,Inyo,W.	美国:加利福尼亚州因约县西部	35.72	-118.06	22	6.3	Ms	7										
1946	3	15	14	0	35					USGS	US:California,Inyo,W.	美国:加利福尼亚州因约县西部	35.72	-118.07	16	5.3	Ms	6										
1946	3	17	14	45	53					USGS	US:Nevada,Mina	美国:内华达州迈纳	38.3	-117.9		5	Ms	5										

时间 Date						海啸 Tsunami				资料来源 Information	震中 Earthquake Epicenter				深度 Depth	震级 Mag	标度 Scale	烈度 MMI	死亡人数 Deaths		受伤人数 Injuries		经济损失 Damage		房屋毁坏 Houses Destroyed		房屋受损 Houses Damaged	
年 Year	月 Mo	日 Dy	时 Hr	分 Mn	秒 Sec	源 Sr	浪高 Wh	级I mI	级S mS		地名(英文) Name(English)	地名(中文) Name(Chinese)	纬度(°) Latitude	经度(°) Longitude					数量/人 Num	级别 Dd	数量/人 Num	级别 Dd	数量/$ Mill $ Mill	级别 De	数量/间 Num	级别 Dh	数量/间 Num	级别 Dh
1946	3	18	15	49	26					USGS	US:California,Brown	美国:加利福尼亚州布朗	35.78	-117.92	16	4.8	Ms	5										
1946	3	18	15	50	43					USGS	US:California,Brown	美国:加利福尼亚州布朗	35.75	-117.91	4	5.3	Ms	5										
1946	3	29	7	17	28					GSHAP	Colombia:Huila	哥伦比亚:乌伊拉	2.3	-76.3		5.7	Ms	7										
1946	3	29	7	26	4					GSHAP,Song	Ecuador:Near Coast of W.	厄瓜多尔:西部近海	-1.7	-80.9		6	Mk	7										
1946	3	29	19	55	11					GSHAP	Colombia:Huila	哥伦比亚:乌伊拉	2.3	-76.3		4	Ms	5										
1946	3	29	20	7	1					GSHAP	Colombia:Huila	哥伦比亚:乌伊拉	2.3	-76.3		4.5	Ms	5										
1946	3	30	0	2	18					GSHAP	Colombia:Huila	哥伦比亚:乌伊拉	2.3	-76.3		4.5	Ms	5										
1946	3	30	17	22	31					GSHAP	Colombia:Huila	哥伦比亚:乌伊拉	2.3	-76.3		4.5	Ms	5										
1946	4	1	12	28	54	4	35	5.1	4	* USGS, Engdahl, NOAA	Alaska:Unimak Island	阿拉斯加:乌尼马克岛	53.32	-163.19	50	7.3	Ms	6	164	3			26.3	4		3		
1946	4	17	17	30						GSHAP,Song	Peru:Cuzco	秘鲁:库斯科	-13.44	-72.51	25	4.5	Mk	5										
1946	5	2	1	26	12					USGS	US:California,Livermore	美国:加利福尼亚州利弗莫尔	37.68	-121.6		4.6	Ms	5										
1946	5	9	19	49	8					GSHAP	Georgia:Gori,N.	格鲁吉亚:哥里北部	42.7	44.4	20	4.8	Ms	6										
1946	5	19	0	31	16					GSHAP	Russia:Komandorsky Islands	俄罗斯:科曼多尔群岛	55	165.2	20	6	Ms	8										
1946	5	29	17	51	3					USGS	US:California,Tres Pinos	美国:加利福尼亚州特雷斯皮诺斯	36.77	-121.42		4.5	Ms	5										
1946	5	31	3	12						* Iran	Turkey:Ustukran	土耳其:埃尔祖鲁姆	40	41.5		6	Muk	8	840	3								
1946	6	6	2							GSHAP,Song	Peru:North Ica	秘鲁:伊卡北部	-13.5	-76	90	4.5	Mk	5										
1946	6	8	21	15						GSHAP,Song	Peru:Torata	秘鲁:塔克纳	-17.4	-70.2	110	4.5	Mk	5										
1946	6	11	6	8	6					GSHAP	Colombia:Magdalena,Near Coast	哥伦比亚:马格达莱纳近海	11.6	-74.2		4.5	Ms	5										
1946	6	15	19	46	53					USGS	US:California,Jacumba	美国:加利福尼亚州哈昆巴	32.6	-116.32	16	4.8	Ms	5										
1946	6	23	17	13	22	4	9	4.9	2	* Engdahl,NOAA	Canada:British Columbia,Powell River	加拿大:英属哥伦比亚鲍威尔里弗	49.75	-124.5	0	7.6	Mw							1				
1946	7	5								* * Song	Indonesia:Southern Sumatra	印度尼西亚:苏门答腊南部	-2.9	104.7		6.4	Mk			3				2		3		
1946	7	7	6	55	15					USGS	US:California,Redding	美国:加利福尼亚州雷丁	40.5	-121.5		5	Ms	5										
1946	7	16	19	45	23					GSHAP	Turkey:Cay	土耳其:恰伊	38.5	31	30	5.2	Ms	5										
1946	7	18	7	15						GSHAP	Brasil:Sao Paulo	巴西:圣保罗	-25.1	-47	15	4.6	Ms	5										
1946	7	18	11	51						GSHAP,Song	Peru:Tacna	秘鲁:塔克纳	-18.1	-70	30	4.5	Mk	5										
1946	7	18	14	27	58					USGS	US:California,Landers,NE.	美国:加利福尼亚州兰德斯东北	34.53	-115.98	16	5.6	Ms	5										
1946	7	23	6	45						USGS	US:South Dakota,Wessington Springs	美国:南达科他州韦辛顿斯普林斯	44.1	-98.6		4.1	Ms	6										

年 Year	月 Mo	日 Dy	时 Hr	分 Mn	秒 Sec	海啸 Tsunami 源 Sr	浪高 Wh	级 I mI	级 S mS	资料来源 Information	震中 Earthquake Epicenter 地名(英文) Name(English)	地名(中文) Name(Chinese)	纬度(°) Latitude	经度(°) Longitude	深度 Depth	震级 Mag	标度 Scale	烈度 MMI	死亡人数 Deaths 数量/人 Num	级别 Dd	受伤人数 Injuries 数量/人 Num	级别 Dd	经济损失 Damage 数量/$ Mill	级别 De	房屋毁坏 Houses Destroyed 数量/间 Num	级别 Dh	房屋受损 Houses Damaged 数量/间 Num	级别 Dh
1946	8	1	21	21						GSHAP, Song	Peru: Huánuco, E.	秘鲁:瓦努科东部	-9	-75.2	30	4.5	Mk	5										
1946	8	2	5	15	36					GSHAP	Colombia: Bucaramanga	哥伦比亚:布卡拉曼加	7	-72.7		4.5	Ms	5										
1946	8	2	19	18	48	2			9	* NOAA, Engdahl	Chile: Diego De Almagro	智利:迭戈德阿尔马格罗	-26.5	-70.5	50	7.1	Ms		2	1				3				
1946	8	4	17	51	5	4	5	2.2		* Engdahl, NOAA	Dominica: Samana	多米尼加:萨马纳	19.3	-68.9	60	7.9	Mw		1790	4				3		3		
1946	8	8	13	28	28	4	0.6			* Engdahl, NOAA	Dominica: Northeastern Coast	多米尼加:东北海域	19.71	-69.51	50	7.5	Mw		75	2								
1946	8	24	14	30						GSHAP, Song	Peru: Ica, Near Coast	秘鲁:伊卡近海	-14.4	-76.3	40	4.5	Mk	5										
1946	9	2	10	10						GSHAP, Song	Peru: Jaén	秘鲁:哈恩	-5	-78.9	30	4.5	Mk	5										
1946	9	8	8	22						GSHAP, Song	Peru: Lima, Near Coast	秘鲁:利马近海	-12.4	-77.8	30	4.5	Mk	5										
1946	9	13	18	59	9					GSHAP	Russia: Kamchatka Peninsula	俄罗斯:堪察加半岛	52.4	158.2	80	7	Ms	7.5										
1946	9	15	5	21	22					GSHAP	Colombia: Near Coast	哥伦比亚:近海	5	-78		5	Ms	6										
1946	9	22	14	21	35					GSHAP	Russia: Chechnia, Grozny, S.	俄罗斯:车臣共和国格罗兹尼北部	42.6	45.9	14	4.5	Ms	5.5										
1946	9	24	21	22						GSHAP, Song	Peru: Nazca	秘鲁:纳斯卡	-14.9	-75.1	90	4.5	Mk	5										
1946	9	24	22	2	56					GSHAP	Russia: Chechnia, Grozny, S.	俄罗斯:车臣共和国格罗兹尼北部	42.6	45.6	19	4.7	Ms	6										
1946	9	28	7	19	9					USGS	US: California, Palm Springs	美国:加利福尼亚州棕泉	33.95	-116.85	16	5	Ms	6										
1946	9	30	0	59	40	2				* Engdahl, Shi Z., NOAA	Peru: Canete	秘鲁:卡涅特	-13	-76	70	6.9	Ms	7						2				3
1946	10	2	4	46	5					GSHAP, Engdahl	Russia: Kamchatka, Near East Coast	俄罗斯:堪察加东部近海	51	159	60	6.8	Muk	8										
1946	10	3	7	17	9					GSHAP	Romania: Nereju	罗马尼亚:内雷茹	45.7	26.6	100	5.5	Ms	6										
1946	10	3	15	37	38					GSHAP	Turkey: Dogubeyazit	土耳其:多乌巴亚泽特	39.5	44	25	4.7	Ms	5										
1946	10	9	8	30						GSHAP, Song	Peru: North Ica	秘鲁:伊卡北部	-13.5	-76	90	4.5	Mk	5										
1946	10	30	13							GSHAP, Song	Peru: Arequipa, Near Coast	秘鲁:阿雷基帕近海	-15.8	-75.5	30	4.5	Mk	5										
1946	11	1	11	14	24	1				* Engdahl, NOAA	Andreanof Islands, Aleutian Is.	阿留申群岛,安德烈亚诺夫群岛	51.5	-174.5	40	7	Ms											
1946	11	2	18	28	25					* Engdahl	Kyrgyzstan: Jalal - Abad	吉尔吉斯斯坦:贾拉拉巴德	41.5	72.5	35	7.3	Mw	10						2				
1946	11	3	18	47						GSHAP	Romania: Vrancea	罗马尼亚:弗朗恰	45.8	26.6	150	5.6	Ms	6										
1946	11	4	21	47	47					* Engdahl	Turkmenistan: Balkanabat	土库曼斯坦:巴尔坎纳巴德	39.3	55.4	26	7.1	Mw		400	3				3				
1946	11	10	17	42	53					* Engdahl	Peru: Caraz	秘鲁:卡拉斯	-8.5	-77.5	12	6.8	Mw	11	800	3				3				
1946	11	10	22	2	31					GSHAP, Song	Peru: Caraz, N.	秘鲁:卡拉斯北部	-8.3	-77.8		4.5	Mk	5										
1946	11	11	9							GSHAP, Song	Peru: Caraz	秘鲁:卡拉斯	-9.15	-77.73		4.5	Mk	5										
1946	11	12	5							GSHAP, Song	Peru: Caraz	秘鲁:卡拉斯	-9.15	-77.73		4.5	Mk	5										
1946	11	12								GSHAP, Song	Peru: Caraz	秘鲁:卡拉斯	-8.57	-77.62		4.5	Mk	5										

年 Year	月 Mo	日 Dy	时 Hr	分 Mn	秒 Sec	海啸 Tsunami 源 Sr	浪高 Wh	级I mI	级S mS	资料来源 Information	震中 Earthquake Epicenter 地名(英文) Name(English)	地名(中文) Name(Chinese)	纬度(°) Latitude	经度(°) Longitude	深度 Depth	震级 Mag	标度 Scale	烈度 MMI	死亡人数 Deaths 数量/人 Num	级别 Dd	受伤人数 Injuries 数量/人 Num	级别 Dd	经济损失 Damage 数量/$ Mill	级别 De	房屋毁坏 Houses Destroyed 数量/间 Num	级别 Dh	房屋受损 Houses Damaged 数量/间 Num	级别 Dh
1946	11	16	9	59						GSHAP, Song	Peru: Tacna	秘鲁:塔克纳	-18.1	-70	30	4.5	Mk	5										
1946	11	18								GSHAP, Song	Peru: Caraz	秘鲁:卡拉斯	-8.57	-77.62		4.5	Mk	5										
1946	11	19	8	48						GSHAP, Song	Peru: Lima	秘鲁:利马	-12.87	-76.406	90	4.5	Mk	5										
1946	11	20	5	30						GSHAP, Song	Peru: Chimbote	秘鲁:钦博特	-9.07	-78.59		4.5	Mk	5										
1946	11	21								GSHAP, Song	Peru: Santa Clara	秘鲁:圣克拉拉	-8.42	-77.45		4.5	Mk	5										
1946	11	22	11	50						GSHAP, Song	Peru: Santa Clara	秘鲁:圣克拉拉	-8.42	-77.45		4.5	Mk	5										
1946	11	24								GSHAP, Song	Peru: Santa Clara	秘鲁:圣克拉拉	-8.42	-77.45		4.5	Mk	5										
1946	11	26								GSHAP, Song	Peru: Santa Clara	秘鲁:圣克拉拉	-8.42	-77.45		4.5	Mk	5										
1946	11	28	18							GSHAP, Song	Peru: Santa Clara	秘鲁:圣克拉拉	-8.42	-77.45		4.5	Mk	5										
1946	11	30	10							GSHAP, Song	Peru: Santa Clara	秘鲁:圣克拉拉	-8.82	-77.46		4.5	Mk	5										
1946	12	1	17	30						GSHAP, Song	Peru: Caraz, N.	秘鲁:卡拉斯北部	-8.26	-77.66		4.5	Mk	5										
1946	12	2	16	30						GSHAP, Song	Peru: Caraz, N.	秘鲁:卡拉斯北部	-8.26	-77.66		4.5	Mk	5										
1946	12	3	11							GSHAP, Song	Peru: Caraz, N.	秘鲁:卡拉斯北部	-8.26	-77.66		4.5	Mk	5										
1946	12	4	22	46	39					* China, Engdahl	China: Taiwan, Tainan	中国:台湾台南	23.1	120.3		6.75	Ms	9	58	2	384	3		2	700	3	10700	5
1946	12	10	2	35						GSHAP, Song	Peru: Lima	秘鲁:利马	-12.05	-77.05		4.5	Mk	5										
1946	12	10	18	45						GSHAP, Song	Peru: Caraz	秘鲁:卡拉斯	-8.47	-77.72	25	4.5	Mk	5										
1946	12	11	13	9						USGS, Song	US: Idaho, Whitefish	美国:爱达荷州怀特菲什	48.4	-114.4		5.1	Mk	6										
1946	12	13								* * Song	Indonesia: Java, Prupuk	印度尼西亚:爪哇,普鲁普克	-7	110		6.5	Mk	9						3				
1946	12	18	14	20	28					USGS	US: California, North Coast	美国:加利福尼亚州北部近海	40.3	-124.6		4.7	Ms	5										
1946	12	20	19	19	5	4	6.6	2.7	2	* Engdahl, NOAA, Japan	Ryukyu Trench	琉球海沟	33	135.6	20	8.1	M		1432	4				4	14259	5		
1946										GSHAP	Brasil: Contagem	巴西:康塔根	-20.72	-46.61		4.3	Ms	5										
1947	1	16	2	37	40					GSHAP	Argentina: Cordoba	阿根廷:科尔多瓦	-31.1	-64.5	50	5.5	Ms	7										
1947	1	21								GSHAP, Song	Peru: Caraz, N.	秘鲁:卡拉斯北部	-8.3	-77.6	30	4.5	Mk	5										
1947	1	26	10	6	46					* Engdahl	Nicaragua: Managua	尼加拉瓜:马拉瓜	12.5	-86.25	170	7	mB							2				
1947	2	5	6	14	23					USGS	US: California, Tres Pinos, S.	美国:加利福尼亚州特雷斯皮诺斯南部	36.23	-120.65		5	Ms	6										
1947	2	6	17	20	40					USGS	US: California, Ridgecrest	美国:加利福尼亚州里奇克雷斯特	35.68	-118.07	16	4.6	Ms	5										
1947	2	9	15	18						GSHAP, Song	Peru: Perene	秘鲁:佩雷内	-11.2	-75.4	15	5	Mk	6										
1947	2	18	11							GSHAP, Song	Venezuela: Maracaibo	委内瑞拉:马拉开波湾	10.74	-71.62		5	Mk	6										
1947	2	24	17	31	36					GSHAP	Bolivia: La Paz	玻利维亚:拉巴斯	-15.5	-68.8	32	6.8	Ms	8										
1947	2	25	8	55						GSHAP, Song	Peru: Vinas	秘鲁:比尼亚斯	-7.95	-77.7	25	5	Mk	6										
1947	3	14	18							USGS, Song	US: Montana, Seeley Lake	美国:蒙大纳州锡利莱克	47.2	-113.5		5.1	Mk	6										
1947	3	25	20	32	14	4	10	3.3	1.5	* Engdahl, NOAA	New Zealand: North Island, Off Coast of E.	新西兰:北岛东部沿海	-38.85	178.87	12	7	Ms	4						1		1		
1947	3	26	20	48	32					* China	China: Yunnan, Dayao	中国:云南大姚	25	102		5.5	Ms	7	1	1		1		2		3		

时间 年 Year	月 Mo	日 Dy	时 Hr	分 Mn	秒 Sec	海啸 Tsunami 源 Sr	浪高 Wh	级 I mI	级 S mS	资料来源 Information	震中 Earthquake Epicenter 地名(英文) Name(English)	地名(中文) Name(Chinese)	纬度(°) Latitude	经度(°) Longitude	深度 Depth	震级 Mag	标度 Scale	烈度 MMI	死亡人数 Deaths 数量/人 Num	级别 Dd	受伤人数 Injuries 数量/人 Num	级别 Dd	经济损失 Damage 数量/$ Mill $ Mill	级别 De	房屋毁坏 Houses Destroyed 数量/间 Num	级别 Dh	房屋受损 Houses Damaged 数量/间 Num	级别 Dh
1947	3	30	7	44						USGS	US:California,North Coast	美国:加利福尼亚州北部近海	40.38	-124.68		4.6	Ms	5										
1947	4	10	15	58	6					*	US:California,Victorville	美国:加利福尼亚州维克托维尔	35	-116.6		6.4	Muk	7						2				
1947	4	19	8	6						GSHAP,Song	Peru:Satipo	秘鲁:萨蒂波	-11.1	-74.8	30	4.5	Mk	5										
1947	5	1								China	China:Taiwan,Nantou,N.	中国:台湾南投北	24.2	121.2		5.25	Ms	7										
1947	5	6	20	30	32	4				* Engdahl,NOAA	New Britain Trench	新不列颠海沟[太平洋]	-6.5	148.5	60	7.3	Mw											
1947	5	17	7	6		4	6	2.6		* NOAA	New Zealand:North Island,Near Coast of NE.	新西兰:北岛东北近海	-38.42	178.88	12	7.2	Ms											
1947	5	27	20	59	42					USGS	US:California,North Coast	美国:加利福尼亚州北部近海	40.4	-124.7		5.2	Ms	6										
1947	6	7	4	5						* China	China:Sichuan,Huidong,SE.	中国:四川会东东南	26.7	102.9		5.5	Ms	7	3	1				1		2		
1947	6	20	22	8	18					GSHAP	Bulgaria:Chirpan	保加利亚:奇尔潘	42.2	25.3	6	4.6	Ms	7										
1947	6	22	23	29	33					USGS	US:California,Aptos	美国:加利福尼亚州阿普托斯	37	-121.77		4.7	Ms	6										
1947	6	30	4	23	53					USGS	US:Missouri,St Louis	美国:密苏里州圣路易斯	38.4	-90.2		4.2	Ms	6										
1947	7	10	8	30						GSHAP,Song	Peru:Caraz	秘鲁:卡拉斯	-8.57	-77.62		5	Mk	6										
1947	7	10	15							*	Iran:Shirvan	伊朗:希尔凡	37.5	57.8	9	4.1	Muk	7						2				
1947	7	12	4	27						GSHAP	Peru:Chimbote,Near Coast	秘鲁:钦博特近海	-9.392	-79.122	40	6.1	Ms	6										
1947	7	14	7	1						* GSHAP	Colombia:Narino	哥伦比亚:纳里尼奥	1.2	-77.2	10	7	Ms	9	2	1				2				
1947	7	14	12	45						GSHAP	Colombia:Narino	哥伦比亚:纳里尼奥	1.4	-77		4.5	Ms	6										
1947	7	14	15							GSHAP	Colombia:Narino	哥伦比亚:纳里尼奥	1.4	-77		4.5	Ms	6										
1947	7	15	14	30						GSHAP	Bulgaria:Dimitrovgrad	保加利亚:季米特洛夫格勒	42	25.5	5	4.6	Ms	7										
1947	7	17								GSHAP	Colombia:Narino	哥伦比亚:纳里尼奥	1.4	-77		4	Ms	5										
1947	7	24	22	10	46					USGS	US:California,Palm Springs	美国:加利福尼亚州棕泉	34.02	-116.5	16	5.5	Ms	5										
1947	7	25	9	55						GSHAP,Song	Peru:Trujillo,Near Coast	秘鲁:特鲁希略近海	-8.2	-79.3	40	4.5	Mk	5										
1947	7	29	12	45						GSHAP,Song	Peru:Caraz,N.	秘鲁:卡拉斯北部	-8.33	-77.5	20	5	Mk	6										
1947	7	30	4							GSHAP,Song	Peru:Arequipa	秘鲁:阿雷基帕	-16.2	-71.8	120	5	Mk	6										
1947	8	2	23	45						GSHAP,Song	Peru:Caraz,N.	秘鲁:卡拉斯北部	-8.33	-77.5	20	4.5	Mk	5										
1947	8	6	9	36	40					*	Algeria:Aae	阿尔及利亚:安纳巴	37	8		5.3	Ms	9	3	1		3		2				
1947	8	10	2	46	41					USGS	US:Michigan,Coldwater	美国:密歇根州科尔德沃特	41.93	-85	2	4.6	Ms	6										
1947	8	10	21	58	24					USGS	US:California,Hollister	美国:加利福尼亚州霍利斯特	36.88	-121.42		4.4	Ms	6										
1947	8	15	4	58	42					GSHAP	Georgia:Gori,N.	格鲁吉亚:哥里北部	42.5	45	15	4.5	Ms	6										
1947	8	25	8	50						GSHAP,Song	Peru:Moquegua	秘鲁:莫克瓜	-16.9	-70.8	120	4.5	Mk	5										

时间 Date						海啸 Tsunami				资料来源 Information	震中 Earthquake Epicenter				深度 Depth	震级 Mag	标度 Scale	烈度 MMI	死亡人数 Deaths		受伤人数 Injuries		经济损失 Damage		房屋毁坏 Houses Destroyed		房屋受损 Houses Damaged	
年 Year	月 Mo	日 Dy	时 Hr	分 Mn	秒 Sec	源 Sr	浪高 Wh	级 I mI	级 S mS		地名(英文) Name(English)	地名(中文) Name(Chinese)	纬度(°) Latitude	经度(°) Longitude					数量/人 Num	级别 Dd	数量/人 Num	级别 Dd	数量/$ Mill $ Mill	级别 De	数量/间 Num	级别 Dh	数量/间 Num	级别 Dh
1947	8	28	14	29	30					GSHAP	Russia:Kamchatka Peninsula	俄罗斯:堪察加半岛	52.5	160	10	6.2	Ms	9										
1947	9	5	1	41						GSHAP,Song	Peru:Pucallpa,SW.	秘鲁:普卡尔帕西南	-8.6	-75.8	30	4.5	Mk	5										
1947	9	8	5	52						USGS	US:California,Truckee	美国:加利福尼亚州特拉基	39.3	-120.2		4.5	Ms	5										
1947	9	8	7	13						USGS	US:California,Truckee	美国:加利福尼亚州特拉基	39.3	-120.2		4.7	Ms	6										
1947	9	15	4							GSHAP,Song	Peru:Perene	秘鲁:佩雷内	-10.2	-75.8	40	4.5	Mk	5										
1947	9	23	12	28	9					* Engdahl	Iran:Razavi Khorasan	伊朗:呼罗珊	33.4	58.7		6.8	Muk		500	3				3				
1947	9	23	13	52	55					USGS	US:California,North Coast	美国:加利福尼亚州北部近海	40.4	-125.2		5.3	Ms	5										
1947	9	25	1	34	30					USGS	US:Idaho,Lowman	美国:爱达荷州洛曼	44.3	-115.4		4.7	Ms	6										
1947	9	29	5	45						GSHAP,Song	Peru:Piura	秘鲁:皮乌拉	-4.526	-80.364	80	4.5	Mk	5										
1947	10	1	12	30						GSHAP,Song	Peru:Caraz,N.	秘鲁:卡拉斯北部	-8.264	-77.588	20	5	Mk	6										
1947	10	6	19	55	37	1	1		2	* Engdahl, NOAA	Greece:Kyparissia (Messinia)	希腊:麦锡尼	36.967	21.683	28	6.9	Ms	9	3	1	20	1		4	7000	4		
1947	10	13	8	45						GSHAP,Song	Peru:Arequipa	秘鲁:阿雷基帕	-16.5	-71.7	30	4.5	Mk	5										
1947	10	15	8							GSHAP,Song	Peru:North Ica	秘鲁:伊卡北部	-13.6	-76	90	4.5	Mk	5										
1947	10	16	2	9	47					USGS,Engdahl	Alaska Peninsula,C.	阿拉斯加半岛中部	64.28	-148.23	66	7.2	M	8										
1947	10	17	16							China	China:Sichuan,Zigong	中国:四川自贡	29.4	104.8		4.75	Ms	6										
1947	10	19	21	12						GSHAP,Song	Peru:Perene	秘鲁:佩雷内	-11.15	-75.9	40	4.5	Mk	5										
1947	10	31	15							GSHAP	Peru:Cuzco	秘鲁:库斯科	-13	-72.5	20	4	Ms	5										
1947	11	1	14	58	53					* Engdahl	Peru:Satipo,Acobamba	秘鲁:萨蒂波,阿科班巴	-10.5	-75	0	7.7	Mw	10	233	3				3				
1947	11	1	16	2						GSHAP,Song	Peru:Ucayali,SW.	秘鲁:乌卡亚利西南	-10.74	-74.25		4.5	Mk	5										
1947	11	1	17	12						GSHAP,Song	Peru:Ucayali,SW.	秘鲁:乌卡亚利西南	-10.74	-74.25		4.5	Mk	5										
1947	11	1	18	55						GSHAP,Song	Peru:Ucayali,SW.	秘鲁:乌卡亚利西南	-10.74	-74.25		4.5	Mk	5										
1947	11	2	1	32						GSHAP,Song	Peru:Ucayali,SW.	秘鲁:乌卡亚利西南	-10.74	-74.25		4.5	Mk	5										
1947	11	2	6	55						GSHAP,Song	Peru:Ucayali,SW.	秘鲁:乌卡亚利西南	-10.74	-74.25		4.5	Mk	5										
1947	11	2	9	3						GSHAP,Song	Peru:Ucayali,SW.	秘鲁:乌卡亚利西南	-10.74	-74.25		4.5	Mk	5										
1947	11	2	17	23						GSHAP,Song	Peru:Ucayali,SW.	秘鲁:乌卡亚利西南	-10.74	-74.25		4.5	Mk	5										
1947	11	2	21							GSHAP,Song	Peru:Huánuco	秘鲁:瓦努科	-9.92	-76.23		4.5	Mk	5										
1947	11	2	22	3						GSHAP,Song	Peru:Ucayali,SW.	秘鲁:乌卡亚利西南	-10.74	-74.25		4.5	Mk	5										
1947	11	4	0	9	10	4	2	1	1	* GSHAP, Engdahl, Usami,NOAA	Japan:W. Hokkaido Island	日本:北海道西部	43.8	141.5	33	7.1	Ms							1				
1947	11	6	9	42						GSHAP,Song	Peru:Ucayali,SW.	秘鲁:乌卡亚利西南	-10.74	-74.25		4.5	Mk	5										
1947	11	6	16	50						USGS,Song	US:New Mexico,Sandia Park	美国:新墨西哥州桑迪亚公园	35.2	-106.3		5.1	Mk	6										
1947	11	7	23							GSHAP,Song	Peru:Perene	秘鲁:佩雷内	-10.565	-75.101	200	5	Mk	6										
1947	11	18	17	32						GSHAP,Song	Peru:Huánuco	秘鲁:瓦努科	-9.92	-76.23		4.5	Mk	5										

时间						海啸				资料来源	震中				深度	震级	标度	烈度	死亡人数		受伤人数		经济损失		房屋毁坏		房屋受损	
年	月	日	时	分	秒	源	浪高	级 I	级 S		地名(英文)	地名(中文)	纬度(°)	经度(°)					数量/人	级别	数量/人	级别	数量/$ Mill	级别	数量/间	级别	数量/间	级别
Date						Tsunami				Information	Earthquake Epicenter				Depth	Mag	Scale	MMI	Deaths		Injuries		Damage		Houses Destroyed		Houses Damaged	
Year	Mo	Dy	Hr	Mn	Sec	Sr	Wh	mI	mS		Name(English)	Name(Chinese)	Latitude	Longitude					Num	Dd	Num	Dd	$ Mill	De	Num	Dh	Num	Dh
1947	11	18	21	59	3					USGS	US:California, San Nicolas Island	美国:加利福尼亚州圣尼古拉斯岛	33.27	-119.45	16	5	Ms	5										
1947	11	23	9	46	3					USGS	US:Montana, Hebgen Lake	美国:蒙大纳州赫伯根湖	44.82	-111.71	5	6.2	Ms	8										
1947	12	7	1	44	18					GSHAP	Afghan:Badakhshan	阿富汗:巴达赫尚	36.7	70.5	200	5.7	Ms	5										
1947	12	7	19	22	55					GSHAP	Turkey:Horasan	土耳其:霍拉桑	40	42.2	8	4.5	Ms	7										
1947	12	15	19	5						GSHAP	Brasil:Porto Murtinho	巴西:穆尔蒂纽港	-21.7	-57.9		4.3	Ms	5										
1947	12	25	21	22	7					GSHAP	Georgia:Gori, N.	格鲁吉亚:哥里北部	42.5	45	30	4.7	Ms	5.5										
1947	12	28	19	58	18					USGS	US:Maine, Dover – Foxcroft	美国:缅因州多佛 – 福克斯克罗夫特	45.2	-69.3		4.5	Ms	5										
1948	1	18	1	17						GSHAP, Song	Peru:Satipo	秘鲁:萨蒂波	-11.1	-74.8	40	4.5	Mk	5										
1948	1	21	16	47	40					GSHAP	Argentina:Cordoba	阿根廷:科尔多瓦	-30.5	-58	30	5.5	Ms	6										
1948	1	21	18	19	19					GSHAP, Song	Venezuela:Lara	委内瑞拉:拉腊	10.24	-69.85	25	5	Mk	6										
1948	1	24	17	46	40	4		1	1.5	*Engdahl, NOAA	Philippines:Panay, Iloilo City	菲律宾:班乃,伊洛伊洛城	10.5	122	33	8.1	Mw	9	72	2			3.5	2		3		
1948	1	28	14	26						GSHAP, Song	Peru:Santa Clara	秘鲁:圣克拉拉	-8.6	-77.42	25	4.5	Mk	5										
1948	2	9	12	58	15	4	2.5		4	*Turkey, Engdahl, NOAA	Greece:Karpathos Island	希腊:皮加贾岛	35.5	27.1	40	6.9	Ms	10						1				
1948	2	11	3	29	28					USGS	US:California, Springville	美国:加利福尼亚州斯普林维尔	36.1	-118.8		4.9	Ms	6										
1948	2	14	22							GSHAP, Song	Peru:Tayabamba	秘鲁:塔亚班巴	-8.3	-77.2	20	6	Mk	7										
1948	2	18	16							China	China:Hubei, Baokang	中国:湖北保康	31.9	111.4		4.75	Ms	6										
1948	2	27	3	4						GSHAP, Song	Peru:Lima, Near Coast	秘鲁:利马近海	-12	-77.8	40	4.5	Mk	5										
1948	3	1	8	12	13					USGS	US:California, Ontario	美国:加利福尼亚州安大略	34.17	-117.53	16	4.7	Ms	6										
1948	3	4	1	53						GSHAP, Song	Peru:Perene	秘鲁:佩雷内	-10.2	-75.2	80	5	Mk	6										
1948	3	6	5	17						GSHAP, Song	Peru:Satipo	秘鲁:萨蒂波	-11.1	-74.8	40	4.5	Mk	5										
1948	3	12	4	29	6					USGS	US:Texas, Dalhart	美国:德克萨斯州达尔哈特	36.22	-102.48	5	4.5	Ms	6										
1948	3	22	0	7						GSHAP, Song	Peru:Arequipa. NW.	秘鲁:阿雷基帕西北	-15.638	-74.858	30	4.5	Mk	5										
1948	3	28	1	30	7					GSHAP	Bolivia:Sucre	玻利维亚:苏克雷	-18.96	-65.17	33	6.1	Ms	7										
1948	3	28	22	38	3					USGS	US:California, San Juan Bautista	美国:加利福尼亚州圣胡安包蒂斯塔	36.85	-121.57		4.6	Ms	5										
1948	3	28	22	45						USGS	US:California, San Juan Bautista	美国:加利福尼亚州圣胡安包蒂斯塔	36.85	-121.57		4.5	Ms	5										
1948	4	14	4	38						GSHAP, Song	Peru:Paccha	秘鲁:帕克查	-11.8	-75.1	30	5	Mk	6										
1948	4	16	22	26	24					USGS	US: California, Thousand Oaks	美国:加利福尼亚州绍曾德奥克斯	34.02	-118.97	16	4.7	Ms	6										
1948	4	17	16	11	28	4	0.6	-0.7		*Engdahl, NOAA	Ryukyu Trench	琉球海沟	33	135.75	40	7.2	Mw											
1948	4	18	0	5						GSHAP, Song	Peru:Chiclayo, Near Coast	秘鲁:奇克拉约近海	-7	-80.3	40	4.5	Mk	5										
1948	4	22	10	42	45	3	1		4	*Turkey, NOAA	Greece:Nisia Ionioy	希腊:伊奥尼亚群岛	38.5	20.3	33	6.7	Ms	10		2								

时间						海啸				资料来源	震中				深度	震级	标度	烈度	死亡人数		受伤人数		经济损失		房屋毁坏		房屋受损	
年	月	日	时	分	秒	源	浪高	级 I	级 S		地名(英文)	地名(中文)	纬度(°)	经度(°)					数量/人	级别	数量/人	级别	数量/$ Mill	级别	数量/间	级别	数量/间	级别
Date						Tsunami				Information	Earthquake Epicenter				Depth	Mag	Scale	MMI	Deaths		Injuries		Damage		Houses Destroyed		Houses Damaged	
Year	Mo	Dy	Hr	Mn	Sec	Sr	Wh	mI	mS		Name(English)	Name(Chinese)	Latitude	Longitude					Num	Dd	Num	Dd	$ Mill	De	Num	Dh	Num	Dh
1948	4	24	1	15						GSHAP,Song	Peru:Arequipa	秘鲁:阿雷基帕	-16.5	-71.7	30	4.5	Mk	5										
1948	4	24	8	45						GSHAP,Song	Peru:Arequipa	秘鲁:阿雷基帕	-16.5	-71.7	30	4.5	Mk	5										
1948	5	7	7	15						* Song	Italy:Modena	意大利:摩德纳	44.6	10.9		6.5	Mk	12										
1948	5	11	8	55	41					* Engdahl	Peru:Arequipa, Moquegua	秘鲁:阿雷基帕,莫克瓜	-17.5	-70.25	70	7.4	mB	10	1	1				2				
1948	5	12	1	44						GSHAP,Song	Peru:Arequipa	秘鲁:阿雷基帕	-16.5	-71.7	30	4.5	Mk	5										
1948	5	23	9	13	18	4				China,NOAA	China:Shandong,Wendeng,W.	中国:山东文登西部	37.2	121.8		6	Ms											
1948	5	23	15	28	54					GSHAP	Armenia:Gyumri	亚美尼亚:久姆里	41.1	44	20	4.5	Ms	6										
1948	5	25	7	11	21					* China,Engdahl	China:Sichuan,Litang	中国:四川理塘	29.5	100.5		7.2	Mw	10	800	3	200	3		3	600	3	1000	3
1948	5	28	5	36	16					* Engdahl	Peru:Canete	秘鲁:卡涅特	-13	-76.5	60	7	Muk	7	4	1				2				
1948	5	29	4	48	58					GSHAP	Romania:Tulnici	罗马尼亚:图尔尼奇	45.9	26.7	150	6	Ms	6.5										
1948	6	2	18	58	18	2		-0.5		* NOAA	India:Nicobar Islands	印度:尼科巴群岛	6	95		6.3	Ms											
1948	6	10	20	45						GSHAP,Song	Peru:Torata	秘鲁:塔克纳	-17.1	-71.1	30	4.5	Mk	5										
1948	6	14	9	20						GSHAP	Peru:Pucallpa	秘鲁:普卡尔帕	-7.7	-74.3	200	6.1	Ms	6										
1948	6	15	11	44	43					Engdahl,Usami	Japan:Tanabe	日本:和歌山田边	33.75	135.25		6.9	Muk		2	1					60	2		
1948	6	18	7	27	15					China	China:Sichuan,Muli,N.	中国:四川木里北	28.7	101.4		5.75	Ms	7										
1948	6	23	0	39						GSHAP,Song	Peru:Piura	秘鲁:皮乌拉	-4.682	-80.39	90	4.5	Mk	5										
1948	6	23	7	25						GSHAP,Song	Peru:Torata	秘鲁:塔克纳	-17.3	-70.8	30	6	Mk	7										
1948	6	27	0	8	23					* China	China:Yunnan,Jianchuan	中国:云南剑川	26.4	99.7		6.25	Ms	8	110	3	100	2		2	600	3		
1948	6	28	7	13	30					* Usami,Engdahl	Japan:Fukui,Near Coast	日本:福井近海	36.5	136	20	7	Mw		5131	4	11000	5		4	63000	5		
1948	6	28	11	41						USGS	Hawaiian Islands	夏威夷群岛	21.2	-157.9	5	4.8	Ms	6										
1948	6	30	12	21						*	Greece: Ionian Islands, Levkas	希腊:伊奥尼亚群岛,莱夫卡斯	38.5	20.5	33	6.4	Muk	11	6	1				2				
1948	7	3	4	18						GSHAP,Song	Peru:Pucallpa	秘鲁:普卡尔帕	-8.3	-74.7	95	5	Mk	6										
1948	7	10	16							China	China:Yunnan,Lanping	中国:云南兰坪	26.4	99.4		5.25	Ms	6										
1948	7	20	11	2	17					GSHAP,Engdahl	Peru:Arequipa,Off Coast	秘鲁:阿雷基帕沿海	-17	-75	70	7.1	mB	6										
1948	7	26	3	33	35					GSHAP	Colombia:Riosucio	哥伦比亚:里奥苏西奥	7.5	-77.4		5	Ms	6										
1948	7	26	17	50	1					USGS	US:California,Ridgecrest	美国:加利福尼亚州里奇克雷斯特	35.58	-118.16	5	4.5	Ms	5										
1948	7	28	8	0	56					GSHAP	Kyrgyzstan:Naryn,C.	吉尔吉斯斯坦:纳伦中部	41.4	75.3	6	4.9	Ms	7.5										
1948	8	6	9	56	2					GSHAP	Colombia:Yacopi	哥伦比亚:昆地那马加的亚科皮	5.2	-74.5	130	5	Ms	6										
1948	8	10	13	26	49					Turkey,GSHAP	Mediterranean Sea	地中海	36.9	28.8	33	5.6	Ms	5.5										
1948	8	16	11	15						GSHAP,Song	Peru:Cuzco	秘鲁:库斯科	-13.42	-72.8	25	4.5	Mk	5										
1948	8	18	19	11	57					USGS	US:California,North Coast	美国:加利福尼亚州北部近海	40.5	-124.7		5	Ms	5										
1948	8	19	2	18						GSHAP,Song	Peru:Near Coast of S.	秘鲁:南部近海	-17.9	-71.8	30	4.5	Mk	5										
1948	8	19	13	50	46					USGS,Shi Z.	Alaska Peninsula,S.	阿拉斯加半岛南部	63	-150.5	100	6.25	Ms	5										
1948	8	25	6	9	24					GSHAP,Engdahl	Argentina:Salta	阿根廷:萨尔塔	-24.4	-64.6	50	6.9	Ms	9										

年 Year	月 Mo	日 Dy	时 Hr	分 Mn	秒 Sec	海啸 Tsunami 源 Sr	浪高 Wh	级 I mI	级 S mS	资料来源 Information	震中 Earthquake Epicenter 地名(英文) Name(English)	地名(中文) Name(Chinese)	纬度(°) Latitude	经度(°) Longitude	深度 Depth	震级 Mag	标度 Scale	烈度 MMI	死亡人数 Deaths 数量/人 Num	级别 Dd	受伤人数 Injuries 数量/人 Num	级别 Dd	经济损失 Damage 数量/$ Mill $ Mill	级别 De	房屋毁坏 Houses Destroyed 数量/间 Num	级别 Dh	房屋受损 Houses Damaged 数量/间 Num	级别 Dh
1948	8	30	21	42	1					GSHAP	Russia: Dagestan, Derbent, SW.	俄罗斯:达吉斯坦共和国杰尔宾特西南	41.9	48	31	5.4	Ms	6										
1948	9	8	15	9	11	4	2	1	1.5	* Engdahl, NOAA	Tonga Islands	汤加群岛	-21	-174	0	8	Mw											
1948	10	2	18	10						GSHAP, Song	Peru: Apurimac	秘鲁:阿普里马克	-14	-72.8	30	5	Mk	6										
1948	10	5	20	12	5					* Engdahl	Turkmenistan: Asgabat	土库曼斯坦:阿什哈巴德	37.9	58.6	18	7.2	Mw	10	19800	5		4	25.0	4		4		
1948	10	8	19	1	7					* China	China: Guizhou, Weining, N.	中国:贵州威宁北	27.4	104		5.75	Ms	8	3	1	75	2		2		3		
1948	10	9	16							China	China: Sichuan, Maoxian, Diexi	中国:四川茂县叠溪	32	103.7		5	Ms	6										
1948	10	13	4	44	50					GSHAP	Turkey: Istanbul	土耳其:伊斯坦布尔	40.8	29.2	20	5.6	Ms	6.5										
1948	10	22	16							China	China: Sichuan, Mabian	中国:四川马边	28	103.6		5.5	Ms	7										
1948	11	2	16	48	8					USGS, Song	US: Nevada, Las Vegas	美国:内华达州拉斯维加斯	35.98	-114.78		5.1	Mk	6										
1948	11	18	8	18						GSHAP, Song	Peru: Lima, Near Coast	秘鲁:利马近海	-12.345	-77.293	70	4.5	Mk	5										
1948	11	22	16	6	4					GSHAP	Tajikistan: Chimtarga	塔吉克斯坦:奇姆塔尔加山	39.2	68.1	30	5.4	Ms	5.5										
1948	11	24	18	45						GSHAP, Song	Peru: Arequipa	秘鲁:阿雷基帕	-16.5	-71.7	25	4.5	Mk	5										
1948	12	4	0	22	48	2	5	1	1.5	* Engdahl, NOAA	Mexico: Maria Madre Island	墨西哥:玛丽亚马德雷岛	22	-106		6.9	Ms		4	1	21	1		3				
1948	12	4	16							China	China: Yunnan, Qiaojia, S.	中国:云南巧家南	26.4	103.1		5	Ms	6										
1948	12	4	23	43	17					USGS	US: California, Palm Springs	美国:加利福尼亚州棕泉	33.93	-116.38	16	6.5	Ms	7										
1948	12	22	0	35						GSHAP, Song	Peru: Casma, Near Coast	秘鲁:卡斯马近海	-9.5	-78.6	40	4.5	Mk	5										
1948	12	26	7	12	21	3	0.7	-0.5		* NOAA	Chile: Calama	智利:卡拉马	-22.5	-69	100	7	Ms	7										
1948	12	29	12	53	28					USGS	US: California, Sierraville, W.	美国:加利福尼亚州谢拉维尔西部	39.55	-120.08		6	Ms	7										
1948	12	31	14	35	46					USGS	US: California, San Simeon	美国:加利福尼亚州圣西米恩	35.67	-121.4		4.6	Ms	5										
1949	1	1	1	17	54					USGS	US: California, River Oaks	美国:加利福尼亚州里弗奥克斯	36.9	-121.62		4.5	Ms	7										
1949	1	7	7							GSHAP	Peru: Perene	秘鲁:佩雷内	-11.5	-75	30	4.7	Ms	5										
1949	1	8	12	20						GSHAP, Song	Peru: Chincha Alta, Near Coast	秘鲁:上钦查近海	-13.852	-76.545	60	5	Mk	6										
1949	1	9	8	30						GSHAP, Song	Venezuela: Barinas	委内瑞拉:巴里纳斯	8.49	-70.53		5	Mk	6										
1949	1	11	10	20						GSHAP, Song	Peru: Arequipa	秘鲁:阿雷基帕	-16.442	-71.223	100	5	Mk	6										
1949	1	12	21	22						GSHAP, Song	Peru: Arequipa	秘鲁:阿雷基帕	-16.5	-71.7	25	4.5	Mk	5										
1949	1	25	23	49						GSHAP, Song	Peru: Caraz	秘鲁:卡拉斯	-8.51	-77.68	20	4.5	Mk	5										
1949	1	26	12	45						GSHAP, Song	Peru: Arequipa	秘鲁:阿雷基帕	-16.5	-71.7	25	4.5	Mk	5										
1949	1	27	11			4				* NOAA	Russia: Kamchatka, Near East Coast	俄罗斯:堪察加东部近海	54.6	163.5	150	5.9	Ms											
1949	2	5	0	28	15					GSHAP	Turkey: Bursa	土耳其:布尔萨	39.9	29.2	9	5.1	Ms	7										

年 Year	月 Mo	日 Dy	时 Hr	分 Mn	秒 Sec	源 Sr	浪高 Wh	级 I mI	级 S mS	资料来源 Information	地名(英文) Name(English)	地名(中文) Name(Chinese)	纬度(°) Latitude	经度(°) Longitude	深度 Depth	震级 Mag	标度 Scale	烈度 MMI	死亡人数 Deaths 数量/人 Num	死亡人数 Deaths 级别 Dd	受伤人数 Injuries 数量/人 Num	受伤人数 Injuries 级别 Dd	经济损失 Damage 数量/$ Mill	经济损失 Damage 级别 De	房屋毁坏 Houses Destroyed 数量/间 Num	房屋毁坏 Houses Destroyed 级别 Dh	房屋受损 Houses Damaged 数量/间 Num	房屋受损 Houses Damaged 级别 Dh
1949	2	9	13	28	30	1				* NOAA, Song	Greece: Nisia Ionioy	希腊:伊奥尼亚群岛	38.2	20	15	6.6	Mk											
1949	2	11	21	5	24					USGS	US: California, Bishop	美国:加利福尼亚州毕晓普	37.08	-117.75	16	5.6	Ms	6										
1949	2	16	22	29	32					GSHAP	Colombia: Narino	哥伦比亚:纳里尼奥	1.6	-77		4	Ms	5										
1949	2	23	16	8	8					* China, Engdahl	China: Xinjiang, Kuqa, NE.	中国:新疆库车东北	42	84		7.3	Mw	9	21	1	17	1		3	1010	4		
1949	2	24	5	28	12					China, GSHAP, Dis	China: Xinjiang, Kuqa	中国:新疆库车	41.9	82.9		5.5	Ms		23	1	21	1						
1949	3	3	6	35						GSHAP, Song	Peru: Caraz	秘鲁:卡拉斯	-9.36	-77.95	90	4.5	Mk	5										
1949	3	4	10	19	25					* Engdahl	Afghan: Fayzabad	阿富汗:法扎巴德	36	70.5	230	7.4	mB	8						2				
1949	3	5	2	56						GSHAP, Song	Peru: Lima	秘鲁:利马	-11.771	-77.25	50	5	Mk	6										
1949	3	6	4	1	4					GSHAP	Georgia: Zugdidi	格鲁吉亚:祖格迪迪	42.3	41.4	13	4.6	Ms	6.5										
1949	3	6	8	45						GSHAP, Song	Peru: Vegueta	秘鲁:贝格塔	-11.365	-77.177	50	4.5	Mk	5										
1949	3	7	6	25						GSHAP, Song	Peru: Tacna	秘鲁:塔克纳	-18.1	-70	30	4.5	Mk	5										
1949	3	7	6	50						USGS, Song	US: Utah, Huntington	美国:犹他州亨廷顿	40.7	-111.8		5.1	Mk	6										
1949	3	9	12	28	39					USGS	US: California, Gilroy	美国:加利福尼亚州吉尔罗伊	37.02	-121.48		5.2	Ms	7										
1949	3	16								GSHAP, Song	Venezuela: Merida	委内瑞拉:梅里达	8.49	-71.53		5	Mk	6										
1949	4	2	9							GSHAP, Song	Peru: Nazca	秘鲁:纳斯卡	-14.9	-75.1	90	4.5	Mk	5										
1949	4	13	19	55	43	3				* Shi Z., Engdahl, NOAA	US: Washington: Olympia	美国:华盛顿州奥林匹亚	47.167	-122.617	60	6.5	Ms	8	8	1			25.0	4				
1949	4	20	3	29	7	2				* Engdahl, NOAA	Chile: Canete	智利:卡涅特	-38	-73.5	70	7.1	mB		57	2				2				
1949	4	23	0	30	14					GSHAP, Song	Peru: Perene	秘鲁:佩雷内	-11.26	-75	90	4.5	Mk	5										
1949	4	24	4	22						*	Iran: Bandar Abbas	伊朗:阿巴斯港	27.28	56.46	100	6.3	Ms							3				
1949	5	2	11	25	47					USGS	US: California, Landers, E.	美国:加利福尼亚州兰德斯东部	34.02	-115.68	16	5.9	Ms	5										
1949	5	2	15	2						USGS, Song	Hawaiian Islands	夏威夷群岛	19.5	-155.7		4.9	Mk	5										
1949	5	6	8	51						GSHAP, Song	Peru: Lima	秘鲁:利马	-12.5	-76.5	100	4.5	Mk	5										
1949	5	9	13	36	15	2				* Engdahl, NOAA	Indonesia: Off West Coast of N. Sumatera	印度尼西亚:北苏门答腊西部海域	4.5	95.5	0	6.8	Muk											
1949	5	17	6	22						GSHAP, Song	Peru: Lima	秘鲁:利马	-12.833	-76.522	60	4.5	Mk	5										
1949	5	30	8	36						GSHAP, Song	Peru: Mácora, Near Coast	秘鲁:曼科拉近海	-4	-81.5	30	4.5	Mk	5										
1949	6	10	3	6	40					USGS	US: California, Morgan Hill	美国:加利福尼亚州莫干山	37.3	-121.67		4.6	Ms	6										
1949	6	20	21							GSHAP, Song	Peru: Ica	秘鲁:伊卡	-13.549	-75.306	90	5	Mk	6										
1949	7	8	7	50	40					GSHAP	Tadzhikistan: Tajikabad	塔吉克斯坦:塔吉卡巴德	39.2	70.8	28	5.1	Ms	6										
1949	7	8	8	2	16					GSHAP	Tadzhikistan: Tajikabad	塔吉克斯坦:塔吉卡巴德	39.2	70.8	12	5.7	Ms	7										
1949	7	10	3	53	36					* Engdahl	Tadzhikistan: Tajikabad	塔吉克斯坦:塔吉卡巴德	39	70.5	16	7.6	Mw	10	3500	4				4		4		

时间 年 Date Year	月 Mo	日 Dy	时 Hr	分 Mn	秒 Sec	海啸 Tsunami 源 Sr	浪高 Wh	级 I mI	级 S mS	资料来源 Information	震中 Earthquake Epicenter 地名(英文) Name(English)	地名(中文) Name(Chinese)	纬度(°) Latitude	经度(°) Longitude	深度 Depth	震级 Mag	标度 Scale	烈度 MMI	死亡人数 Deaths 数量/人 Num	级别 Dd	受伤人数 Injuries 数量/人 Num	级别 Dd	经济损失 Damage 数量/$ Mill $ Mill	级别 De	房屋毁坏 Houses Destroyed 数量/间 Num	级别 Dh	房屋受损 Houses Damaged 数量/间 Num	级别 Dh
1949	7	10	15	19						GSHAP	Tadzhikistan:Dzhirgatal	塔吉克斯坦:吉尔加塔尔	39. 1	71	10	5. 8	Ms	8										
1949	7	10	15	49	17					GSHAP	Tadzhikistan:Dzhirgatal	塔吉克斯坦:吉尔加塔尔	39. 2	71. 1	19	6. 2	Ms	8										
1949	7	10	16	24						Engdahl,GSHAP	Tadzhikistan:Dzhirgatal	塔吉克斯坦:吉尔加塔尔	39. 2	70. 7	0	6. 5	Ms	8										
1949	7	11	16	10						Usami,Japan	Japan:Yamaguchi	日本:山口	34	132. 5	40	6. 2	Ms		2	1								
1949	7	14	10	9	55					GSHAP	Serbia:Kragujevac	塞尔维亚:克拉古耶瓦茨	44. 1	21	7	4. 9	Ms	7										
1949	7	15	5	30						GSHAP,Song	Peru:Caraz,N.	秘鲁:卡拉斯北部	-8. 32	-77. 51	20	5	Mk	6										
1949	7	21	8	1	39					GSHAP	Peru:Pampacolca	秘鲁:潘帕科尔卡	-15. 5	-73	150	6. 5	Ms	6										
1949	7	23	15	3	30	3	2		2	*Turkey, Engdahl,NOAA	Greece:Chios	希腊:希俄斯岛	38. 6	26. 3	10	6. 8	Muk	9	3	1	50	1		3				
1949	7	25	5	45						GSHAP	Peru:Perene	秘鲁:佩雷内	-11. 15	-75. 9	20	4. 3	Ms	5										
1949	8	5	7	49	29					GSHAP,Song	Peru:Tarapoto	秘鲁:塔拉波托	-6. 5	-77	100	4. 5	Mk	5										
1949	8	5	19	8	47					*Engdahl, Shi Z.	Ecuador:Tungurahua	厄瓜多尔:东谷拉瓦	-1. 5	-78. 2	60	6. 8	Muk	10	6000	4			7. 5	3				
1949	8	7	23	53	52					GSHAP,Song	Peru:Espinar	秘鲁:埃斯皮纳尔	-15	-71. 5		4. 5	Mk	5										
1949	8	10	1	30						GSHAP,Song	Peru:Caraz,N.	秘鲁:卡拉斯北部	-8. 33	-77. 53	25	4. 5	Mk	5										
1949	8	11	3	13	10					GSHAP	Ecuador:Ambato	厄瓜多尔:安巴托	-1. 2	-78. 5		5	Ms	6										
1949	8	17	18	34	13					GSHAP	Kuril Islands	千岛群岛	43. 5	146. 2	75	7. 3	Ms	7										
1949	8	17	18	44	13					*Engdahl	Turkey:Bingol,N.	土耳其:宾格尔北部	39. 5	40. 6	0	6. 8	Muk	10	320	3				3				
1949	8	22	4	1	11	4	0. 6	-1		*Engdahl, NOAA	Canada:Queen Charlotte Islands	加拿大:夏洛特皇后群岛	53. 62	-133. 27	25	8. 1	Ms											
1949	8	23	15	13	44					GSHAP,Song	Peru:Arequipa	秘鲁:阿雷基帕	-16	-73	150	4. 5	Mk	5										
1949	8	23	22	3	54					GSHAP	Tadzhikistan:Dzhirgatal	塔吉克斯坦:吉尔加塔尔	39. 2	71. 1	25	5. 5	Ms	6										
1949	8	25	18	45						GSHAP,Song	Peru:Moquegua	秘鲁:莫克瓜	-17	-71	30	4. 5	Mk	5										
1949	8	27	14	51	46					USGS	US:California,Lompoc	美国:加利福尼亚州隆波克	34. 5	-120. 5	16	4. 9	Ms	6										
1949	9	5				4				Nakamura	Philippines:Santiago	菲律宾:圣地亚哥	17	121	80	6	Ms											
1949	9	12	13							GSHAP	Ecuador:Quito	厄瓜多尔:基多	-0. 05	-78. 45		4. 3	Ms	6										
1949	9	15	3	45						*Song	Italy:Terni	意大利:特尔尼	42. 5	12. 7		6. 5	Mk	12										
1949	9	15	15	56						GSHAP	Russia:Sakhalin Island	俄罗斯:库页岛(萨哈林岛)	51	142. 5	10	5. 2	Ms	7										
1949	9	15	16							China	China:Yunnan,Huaning	中国:云南华宁	24. 2	103		5. 25	Ms	7										
1949	9	17	4	10						GSHAP,Song	Peru:Ica	秘鲁:伊卡	-14. 3	-75. 8	90	4. 5	Mk	5										
1949	9	27	15	30	45					USGS,Shi Z., Engdahl	Gulf of Alaska	阿拉斯加湾	59. 75	-149	50	6. 7	Ms	5										
1949	10	8	20	34	18					Wang S.	China:Taiwan,Coast of S.	中国:台湾南部海域	21. 5	122		5. 5	Ms	9										
1949	10	11	9	5	27					GSHAP	Japan:Hokkaido	日本:北海道	42. 8	144	105	5. 9	Ms	5										
1949	10	18	5	28						GSHAP,Song	Peru:Arequipa	秘鲁:阿雷基帕	-16. 365	-73. 164	60	4. 5	Mk	5										

年 Year	月 Mo	日 Dy	时 Hr	分 Mn	秒 Sec	海啸 Tsunami 源 Sr	浪高 Wh	级 I mI	级 S mS	资料来源 Information	震中 Earthquake Epicenter 地名(英文) Name(English)	地名(中文) Name(Chinese)	纬度(°) Latitude	经度(°) Longitude	深度 Depth	震级 Mag	标度 Scale	烈度 MMI	死亡人数 Deaths 数量/人 Num	级别 Dd	受伤人数 Injuries 数量/人 Num	级别 Dd	经济损失 Damage 数量/$ Mill	级别 De	房屋毁坏 Houses Destroyed 数量/间 Num	级别 Dh	房屋受损 Houses Damaged 数量/间 Num	级别 Dh
1949	10	19	21	0	19	4	0.3	-1.7	-1	* Engdahl, NOAA	New Britain Trench	新不列颠海沟[太平洋]	-5.5	154	60	7.5	Mw											
1949	10	21	6	9						Wang S.	China:Taiwan,Coast of S.	中国:台湾南部海域	21.5	122		5.2	Ms	9										
1949	10	22	21	45	20					USGS	US:California,San Benito	美国:加利福尼亚州圣贝尼托	36.58	-121.17		4.7	Ms	5										
1949	10	28	2	29	16					USGS	US:California,North Coast	美国:加利福尼亚州北部近海	40.9	-124.2		4.5	Ms	5										
1949	10	30	6							GSHAP	Russia:Sakhalin Island	俄罗斯:库页岛(萨哈林岛)	47	142.6	10	5.2	Ms	7										
1949	11	2	2	29	38					USGS	US:Utah,St George	美国:犹他州圣乔治	37	-113.5		4.7	Ms	5										
1949	11	4	20	42	38					USGS	Mexico:Tijuana	墨西哥:提华纳	32.2	-116.55	16	5.7	Ms	6										
1949	11	5	4	35	24					USGS	Mexico:Tijuana	墨西哥:提华纳	32.2	-116.55	16	5.1	Ms	6										
1949	11	5	15	5	45					GSHAP	Iran:Gorgan	伊朗:戈尔甘	36.7	54.7	24	5.5	Ms	6.5										
1949	11	7	20	59	52					GSHAP	Bolivia:Santa Cruz de la Sierra,S.	玻利维亚:圣克鲁斯南部	-18.5	-63.5		5	Ms	5										
1949	11	13	5	27	11					* China	China:Sichuan,Luding,NW.	中国:四川泸定西北	30	102.5		5.5	Ms	7		2				1	4	1		
1949	11	15	16	30						GSHAP,Song	Peru:Caraz,N.	秘鲁:卡拉斯北部	-8.32	-77.57	20	4.5	Mk	5										
1949	11	17	1	19	52					* Song	US:California,Long Beach	美国:加利福尼亚州长滩	33.75	-118.25		6.2	Mk	5					9.0	3				
1949	11	20	4	43	56					GSHAP,Song	Peru:Perene	秘鲁:佩雷内	-11	-75		4.5	Mk	5										
1949	12	14	15	55						GSHAP,Song	Peru:North Ica	秘鲁:伊卡北部	-13.5	-76	90	4.5	Mk	5										
1949	12	17	6	53	30	2	0.7			* Engdahl, NOAA	Chile:Punta Arenas	智利:蓬塔阿雷纳斯	-54	-71	33	7.8	Mw		1	1				1				
1949	12	17	15	7	55	2	0.7	-0.5		* Shi Z., Engdahl, NOAA	Chile:Punta Arenas	智利:蓬塔阿雷纳斯	-54	-71	0	7.8	Mw		3	1				1				
1949	12	22	7	58						GSHAP,Song	Peru:Satipo	秘鲁:萨蒂波	-11.25	-74.9	100	4.5	Mk	5										
1949	12	25	23	24	54					Shi Z.,Usami	Japan:Utsunomiya	日本:宇都宫市	36.5	140		6.25	Ms		10	1					908	3		
1949	12	26	3	36	10					GSHAP	Romania:Nereju	罗马尼亚:内雷茹	45.7	26.7	135	5.3	Ms	5.5										
1949	12	29	3	3	54	3		1	1.5	* Engdahl, NOAA	Philippines:Laoag	菲律宾:拉瓦格	18	121		7.2	Mw	6	16	1				2		2		2
1949	12	31								GSHAP	Brasil:Lajes	巴西:拉日斯	-5.69	-36.24		4.9	Ms	6										
1950	1	12	17	10						GSHAP	Japan:Hokkaido	日本:北海道	42.3	142.4	120	6.2	Ms	5										
1950	1	13	3							GSHAP,Song	Peru:Caraz	秘鲁:卡拉斯	-8.43	-77.55	20	4.5	Mk	5										
1950	1	14	19	52	30					USGS	US:California,North Coast	美国:加利福尼亚州北部近海	40.22	-124.42		4.6	Ms	6										
1950	1	17	0	51						USGS,Song	US:Arizona,Ganado	美国:亚利桑那州加纳多	35.7	-109.5		5.1	Mk	6										
1950	1	17	5							GSHAP,Song	Peru:Yanaoca	秘鲁:亚纳奥卡	-13.5	-71.2	15	4.5	Mk	5										
1950	1	18	1	55	51					USGS	US:Utah,Talmage	美国:犹他州塔尔米奇	40.5	-110.5		5.3	Ms	5										
1950	1	19	17	27						* Iran	Iran:Hormozgan	伊朗:荷姆兹甘	27.3	53.2		5.8	Ms		20	1				3				

时间						海啸				资料来源	震中				深度	震级	标度	烈度	死亡人数		受伤人数		经济损失		房屋毁坏		房屋受损	
年	月	日	时	分	秒	源	浪高	级I	级S		地名(英文)	地名(中文)	纬度(°)	经度(°)					数量/人	级别	数量/人	级别	数量/$ Mill	级别	数量/间	级别	数量/间	级别
Date						Tsunami				Information	Earthquake Epicenter				Depth	Mag	Scale	MMI	Deaths		Injuries		Damage		Houses Destroyed		Houses Damaged	
Year	Mo	Dy	Hr	Mn	Sec	Sr	Wh	mI	mS		Name(English)	Name(Chinese)	Latitude	Longitude					Num	Dd	Num	Dd	$ Mill	De	Num	Dh	Num	Dh
1950	1	21	14	9	49					GSHAP, Song	Chile: Chillan	智利:奇廉	-36	-71.5	64	5	Mk	6										
1950	1	22	3	18	18					GSHAP	Colombia: Near Coast	哥伦比亚:近海	4.2	-78.6		5	Ms	6										
1950	1	22	4	7						* * Iran	Iran: Hormozgan	伊朗:荷姆兹甘	27.3	53.2		5.8	Ms		30	1								
1950	1	30	0	56	32	2				* Engdahl, NOAA	Chile: Punta Arenas	智利:蓬塔阿雷纳斯	-53.5	-71.5	0	6.9	Ms	6		1								
1950	2	2	23	33	39					* China, Engdahl	China: Yunnan, Menghai, SW.	中国:云南勐海西南	21.7	100.1		7.1	Mw							1	1	1		
1950	2	4	9	30	52					* GSHAP	Turkey: Sason	土耳其:萨松	38.34	41.47	40	4.6	Ms		20	1				1				
1950	2	24	6	1	42					GSHAP	Colombia: Bahia Solano	哥伦比亚:巴伊阿索拉诺	6	-77.5		6	Ms	7										
1950	2	25	5	47	11					GSHAP	Mongolia: West Bayanhongor	蒙古:巴彦洪戈尔西部	45.8	98.5	15	6.1	Ms	9										
1950	2	26	0	6	22					USGS	US: California, Ventura, N.	美国:加利福尼亚州文图拉北部	34.62	-119.08	16	4.7	Ms	6										
1950	2	27	11	58						GSHAP	Brasil: Sao Paulo	巴西:圣保罗	-21.82	-46.71		3.9	Ms	5										
1950	2	28	10	20	57					* Engdahl	Sea of Okhotsk	鄂霍次克海	46	144	340	7.5	mB	6										
1950	3	5	2	17	18					GSHAP, Song	Peru: Lima, Near Coast	秘鲁:利马近海	-12.2	-77.5	40	4.5	Mk	5										
1950	3	5	18	1	23					GSHAP, Song	Chile: Antofagasta, N.	智利:安托法加斯塔北部	-22.1	-68.7	160	5	Mk	6										
1950	3	7	8	3						*	Brazil: Amazonas	巴西:亚马孙州	-8	-71	550	8.6	Ms	5										
1950	3	14	3	10	4					GSHAP, Engdahl	Peru: Pucallpa	秘鲁:普卡尔帕	-8	-74	150	6.8	Muk	6										
1950	3	14	18	10	41	3		-0.5		* NOAA	New Zealand: North Island, Near Coast of NE.	新西兰:北岛东北近海	-37.8	177.2		5.8	Ms											
1950	3	20	15	22	17					USGS	US: California, Mill Creek	美国:加利福尼亚州米尔克里克	40.45	-121.47		5.5	Ms	5										
1950	3	22	23	43						GSHAP, Song	Peru: Satipo	秘鲁:萨蒂波	-11.1	-74.8	30	4.5	Mk	5										
1950	3	31	12	47	42					GSHAP, Song	Peru: Lima, Near Coast	秘鲁:利马近海	-10.958	-78.194	50	5	Mk	6										
1950	4	3	19	3	13					GSHAP	Colombia: Cauca	哥伦比亚:考卡	2	-77		4	Ms	5										
1950	4	4	18	44	10					GSHAP, Engdahl	Russia: Buryatiya, Khokhorzon	俄罗斯:布里亚特州霍霍尔宗村	51.77	101	24	6.8	Muk	9										
1950	4	6	2	43	28					GSHAP	Turkmenistan: Asgabat	土库曼斯坦:阿什哈巴德	37.9	58.6	17	5.4	Ms	7										
1950	4	10	16	48	48					GSHAP	Colombia: Ibagué	哥伦比亚:托利马的伊瓦格	4.6	-75.4	128	6	Ms	7										
1950	4	14	11	3	48					USGS, Song	US: Washington, Seattle	美国:华盛顿州西雅图	48	-122.5		5.1	Mk	6										
1950	4	26	6	11	48					GSHAP, Song	Peru: Satipo	秘鲁:萨蒂波	-11.1	-74.8	30	4.5	Mk	5										
1950	4	30	18	21	37					GSHAP, Song	Peru: Perene	秘鲁:佩雷内	-10.3	-75.4		5	Mk	6										
1950	5	9	11	16	57					GSHAP, Afghan	Turkmenistan: Asgabat	土库曼斯坦:阿什哈巴德	38.4	58.6	25	6.4	Ms	7.5										
1950	5	10	2	8	50					GSHAP	Ukraine: Chernivtsi	乌克兰:切尔诺夫策	48.1	25.6	8	4.5	Ms	6										
1950	5	19	14	40						GSHAP, Song	Peru: Moquegua	秘鲁:莫克瓜	-16.8	-71.3	110	4.5	Mk	5										
1950	5	20	18	53	50					GSHAP	Afghan: Badakhshan	阿富汗:巴达赫尚	37.1	70.9	80	5.7	Ms	5										
1950	5	21	18	37						*	Peru: Cusco	秘鲁:库斯科	-13.5	-72		6	Muk		83	2				3				
1950	5	25	18	3						GSHAP, Song	Peru: Cusco	秘鲁:库斯科	-13.544	-71.964	25	4.5	Mk	5										
1950	5	30	1	16	15					USGS	Hawaiian Islands	夏威夷群岛	19.5	-156		6.2	Ms	7										

年 Year	月 Mo	日 Dy	时 Hr	分 Mn	秒 Sec	源 Sr	浪高 Wh	级 I mI	级 S mS	资料来源 Information	地名(英文) Name(English)	地名(中文) Name(Chinese)	纬度(°) Latitude	经度(°) Longitude	深度 Depth	震级 Mag	标度 Scale	烈度 MMI	死亡人数 Deaths 数量/人 Num	级别 Dd	受伤人数 Injuries 数量/人 Num	级别 Dd	经济损失 Damage 数量/$ Mill	级别 De	房屋毁坏 Houses Destroyed 数量/间 Num	级别 Dh	房屋受损 Houses Damaged 数量/间 Num	级别 Dh
1950	5	31	0	45						GSHAP, Song	Peru: Lima, Near Coast	秘鲁:利马近海	-12.4	-77.5	40	4.5	Mk	5										
1950	5	31	9	21	45					GSHAP, Song	Peru: Pucallpa	秘鲁:普卡尔帕	-8	-74	150	4.5	Mk	5										
1950	6	7	16	52	34					GSHAP, Engdahl	Peru: Loreto, NW.	秘鲁:洛雷托西北	-4	-76.5	110	6.8	Muk	6										
1950	6	9	18	40						GSHAP, Song	Peru: Cuzco	秘鲁:库斯科	-13.4	-73.2	30	4.5	Mk	5										
1950	6	19	12	36	58					* Engdahl	Indonesia: Java Island	印度尼西亚:爪哇岛	-6.2	112		6.8	Muk		16	1				1				
1950	6	20	1	18	53					GSHAP	Romania: Tulnici	罗马尼亚:图尔尼奇	45.9	26.6	150	5.5	Ms	6										
1950	6	22	22	53	37					GSHAP	Peru: Azangaro	秘鲁:阿桑加罗	-15	-70		4.9	Ms	5										
1950	6	26	1	57						GSHAP, Song	Peru: Sayán	秘鲁:萨扬	-10.54	-76.6	100	5	Mk	6										
1950	7	2	22	49	25					GSHAP	Colombia: Villavicencio	哥伦比亚:比亚维森西奥	4.2	-73.7		6	Ms	7										
1950	7	6	8	30						GSHAP, Song	Peru: Puerto Maldonado	秘鲁:马尔多纳多港	-12.61	-69.18		4.5	Mk	5										
1950	7	9	2	35						* GSHAP	Colombia: Anboledas	哥伦比亚:阿沃莱达斯	7.8	-72.5	41	7	Ms	9	211	3			5.0	3				
1950	7	9	3	28	59					GSHAP	Colombia: Abrego	哥伦比亚:北桑坦德的阿夫雷戈	7.8	-73.1		5	Ms	6										
1950	7	9	5	20						GSHAP, Song	Peru: Pucallpa	秘鲁:普卡尔帕	-8.9	-74.3	40	4.5	Mk	5										
1950	7	9	16	10	24					Engdahl, GSHAP	Afghan: Fayzabad	阿富汗:法扎巴德	36.7	70.5	223	7.5	Ms	6										
1950	7	17	12	25						GSHAP, Song	Peru: Cusco	秘鲁:库斯科	-14.1	-71.5	20	5	Mk	6										
1950	7	27	11	29	26					USGS	US: California, Calipatria	美国:加利福尼亚州卡利帕特里亚	33.12	-115.57	16	4.8	Ms	6										
1950	7	28	3	25						USGS	US: California, Calipatria	美国:加利福尼亚州卡利帕特里亚	33.12	-115.57	16	4.7	Ms	5										
1950	7	28	17	50	48					USGS	US: California, Calipatria	美国:加利福尼亚州卡利帕特里亚	33.12	-115.57	16	5.4	Ms	6										
1950	7	29	14	36	32					USGS	US: California, Calipatria	美国:加利福尼亚州卡利帕特里亚	33.12	-115.57	16	5.5	Ms	8										
1950	8	1	8	37	20					USGS	US: California, Calipatria	美国:加利福尼亚州卡利帕特里亚	33.12	-115.57	16	4.7	Ms	6										
1950	8	3	22	18	19	2				* NOAA	Venezuela: El Tocuyo	委内瑞拉:托丘约	10.5	-68	8	6.8	Ms		100	2								
1950	8	5	3	54						GSHAP, Song	Venezuela: Lara	委内瑞拉:拉腊	9.8	-69.85		5	Mk	6										
1950	8	5	10	45	14					GSHAP, Song	Venezuela: Lara	委内瑞拉:拉腊	9.66	-69.74	25	5	Mk	6										
1950	8	5	19	8						*	Ecuador: Tungurahua	厄瓜多尔:东谷拉瓦	-1.5	-78.2	60	6.8	Muk	11										
1950	8	6	10	30						GSHAP, Song	Venezuela: Guanare	委内瑞拉:瓜纳里	9.29	-70.67		6	Mk	7										
1950	8	6	14	30						GSHAP, Song	Venezuela: Lara	委内瑞拉:拉腊	9.98	-69.93		5	Mk	6										
1950	8	6	20	35						GSHAP, Song	Peru: Caraz	秘鲁:卡拉斯	-8.4	-77.58	20	5	Mk	6										
1950	8	7	10	56	30					GSHAP	Georgia: Gurdzhaani	格鲁吉亚:古祖尼	41.2	45.3	18	4.5	Ms	6										
1950	8	7	22	30						GSHAP, Song	Venezuela: Cojedes	委内瑞拉:科赫德斯	8.99	-68.29		5	Mk	6										
1950	8	8	3	35						GSHAP, Song	Peru: Chiclayo, Near Coast	秘鲁:奇克拉约近海	-7	-80.3	40	4.5	Mk	5										
1950	8	8	5	29	16					GSHAP	Turkmenistan: Asgabat	土库曼斯坦:阿什哈巴德	38.2	58.5	17	4.9	Ms	6										
1950	8	9	0	45						GSHAP, Song	Venezuela: Lara	委内瑞拉:拉腊	9.58	-69.89		5	Mk	6										
1950	8	12	11							GSHAP, Song	Venezuela: Trujillo	委内瑞拉:特鲁希略	9.67	-70.25		5	Mk	6										

时间						海啸				资料来源	震中				深度	震级	标度	烈度	死亡人数		受伤人数		经济损失		房屋毁坏		房屋受损	
年	月	日	时	分	秒	源	浪高	级 I	级 S		地名(英文)	地名(中文)	纬度(°)	经度(°)					数量/人	级别	数量/人	级别	数量/$ Mill	级别	数量/间	级别	数量/间	级别
Date						Tsunami				Information	Earthquake Epicenter				Depth	Mag	Scale	MMI	Deaths		Injuries		Damage		Houses Destroyed		Houses Damaged	
Year	Mo	Dy	Hr	Mn	Sec	Sr	Wh	mI	mS		Name(English)	Name(Chinese)	Latitude	Longitude					Num	Dd	Num	Dd	$ Mill	De	Num	Dh	Num	Dh
1950	8	14	6	31	35					GSHAP, Song	Peru: Torata	秘鲁:塔克纳	-17.4	-71		4.5	Mk	5										
1950	8	15	14	9	30					* China, Engdahl, Dis	China: Xizang (Tibet), Zayu	中国:西藏察隅	28.5	96.5		8.6	M	11	3986	4			20.0	3				
1950	8	20	1	44	55					USGS, Song	US: Montana, Seeley Lake, NE.	美国:蒙大纳州锡利莱克东北	47.25	-113.25		5.1	Mk	6										
1950	8	25	3	35						GSHAP, Song	Peru: Cusco	秘鲁:库斯科	-13.7	-71.85	25	4.5	Mk	5										
1950	9	2	4	19	32					GSHAP	Azerbaijan: Gence, N.	阿塞拜疆:占贾北部	41.7	46.2	16	4.6	Ms	6										
1950	9	4	17	45						GSHAP, Song	Peru: Yanaoca	秘鲁:亚纳奥卡	-13.5	-71.2	15	4.5	Mk	5										
1950	9	5	19	19	56					USGS	US: California, Palm Springs	美国:加利福尼亚州棕泉	33.65	-116.75	16	4.8	Ms	6										
1950	9	9	5	37	38					GSHAP, Song	Chile: Copiapo	智利:科皮亚波	-27	-70.6		5	Mk	6										
1950	9	11								GSHAP, Song	Venezuela: Lara	委内瑞拉:拉腊	9.8	-69.85		5	Mk	6										
1950	9	13	0	3	7					* China	China: Yunnan, Gejiu, N.	中国:云南个旧北	23.5	103.1		5.75	Ms	8						2	320	3	200	3
1950	9	19	5	45						GSHAP, Song	Venezuela: Lara	委内瑞拉:拉腊	9.92	-69.59		5	Mk	6										
1950	9	23	10	20						GSHAP, Song	Peru: Máncora, Near Coast	秘鲁:曼科拉近海	-3.6	-81.6	30	4.5	Mk	5										
1950	9	25	18	9	27					GSHAP, Song	Chile: Valparaiso	智利:瓦尔帕莱索	-32.5	-71.3		5	Mk	6										
1950	10	5	16	9	31	4	0.1	-3.3	-2	* Engdahl, NOAA	Costa Rica: Upala	哥斯达黎加:乌帕拉	11	-85	60	7.8	Mw											
1950	10	8	3	23	9	3		1.5	2	* Engdahl, NOAA	Indonesia: Ceram Sea	印度尼西亚:塞兰海	-3.8	128.3	60	7.5	Mw			2				3				
1950	10	16	5	25	22					GSHAP, Song	Peru: Piura	秘鲁:皮乌拉	-5	-80	60	5	Mk	6										
1950	10	23	16	13	20	4	0.2	-1.3	-1	* Shi Z., Engdahl, NOAA	Mexico: Mazatenango	危地马拉:马萨特南戈	14.5	-91.5	0	7.5	Mw							3		3		3
1950	10	26	8	45						GSHAP, Song	Peru: Satipo	秘鲁:萨蒂波	-11.1	-74.8	30	4.5	Mk	5										
1950	10	26	9	30						GSHAP, Song	Venezuela: Coro	委内瑞拉:科罗	11.42	-69.68		5	Mk	6										
1950	10	28	16	47	18					GSHAP	Russia: Altai Krai, Rubtsovsk, Nw.	俄罗斯:阿尔泰边疆区鲁布佐夫斯克西北	52.3	79.3	25	5	Ms	5.5										
1950	11	4	1	30						GSHAP	Peru: North Ica	秘鲁:伊卡北部	-13.6	-76	90	4.8	Ms	5										
1950	11	6	7							GSHAP	Peru: Caraz	秘鲁:卡拉斯	-8.44	-77.57	20	3.5	Ms	5										
1950	11	8	2	18	12	3				* Engdahl, NOAA	Solomon Islands	所罗门群岛	-10	159.5	0	7.1	Mw											
1950	11	9	7	32	36					GSHAP	Russia: Chechnia, Grozny, E.	俄罗斯:车臣共和国格罗兹尼北部	43.3	46.1	19	5	Ms	6										
1950	11	14	2	35	50					USGS	US: California, Shingletown	美国:加利福尼亚州欣格尔敦	40.48	-121.5		4.6	Ms	5										
1950	11	15	17	45						GSHAP	Peru: Torata	秘鲁:塔克纳	-17.3	-70.6	30	4.1	Ms	5										
1950	11	16	16	48						GSHAP	Peru: Ica, Coast	秘鲁:伊卡近海	-14.3	-76.5	50	4.6	Ms	5										
1950	11	17	19	28	16					* Engdahl	Mexico: Near Coast of Guerrero	墨西哥:格雷罗近海	16.5	-100.4		6.8	Muk	11						2				
1950	11	17	22	1	4					GSHAP	Tadzhikistan: Kalaihongbu	塔吉克斯坦:卡莱洪布	38.75	70.5	5	5.3	Ms	7										
1950	11	20	13	15						GSHAP, Song	Venezuela: Lara	委内瑞拉:拉腊	9.61	-69.8		5	Mk	6										
1950	11	20	21	48						GSHAP	Peru: Torata	秘鲁:塔克纳	-17.3	-70.6	30	4.3	Ms	5										
1950	11	21	20	53	57					GSHAP	Tajikistan: Garm	塔吉克斯坦:加尔姆	38.6	70.5	5	5.2	Ms	7										

年 Year	月 Mo	日 Dy	时 Hr	分 Mn	秒 Sec	海啸 Tsunami 源 Sr	浪高 Wh	级 I mI	级 S mS	资料来源 Information	震中 Earthquake Epicenter 地名(英文) Name(English)	地名(中文) Name(Chinese)	纬度(°) Latitude	经度(°) Longitude	深度 Depth	震级 Mag	标度 Scale	烈度 MMI	死亡人数 Deaths 数量/人 Num	级别 Dd	受伤人数 Injuries 数量/人 Num	级别 Dd	经济损失 Damage 数量/$ Mill	级别 De	房屋毁坏 Houses Destroyed 数量/间 Num	级别 Dh	房屋受损 Houses Damaged 数量/间 Num	级别 Dh
1950	11	27	14	13						GSHAP	Peru:Tacna	秘鲁:塔克纳	-18	-69.9	30	4.1	Ms	5										
1950	12	9	21	38	48					* Engdahl	Chile:Antofagasta, C.	智利:安托法加斯塔中部	-23.5	-67.5	100	7.7	mB	7	1	1		2		1				
1950	12	10	2	50	42	2	0.7	-0.5	0	* Engdahl, NOAA	Peru:Ica, Chimbote, Huaraz	秘鲁:伊卡,钦博塔,安卡什	-14.25	-75.75	80	7.1	mB	7	4	1	12	1		2		2		
1950	12	10	9	8	45					GSHAP, Song	Peru:Ica, Near Coast	秘鲁:伊卡近海	-15	-77		4.5	Mk	5										
1950	12	14	1	52	49					* Engdahl	Tonga Islands	汤加群岛	-19.5	-176	200	7.5	mB	6										
1950	12	14	13	24	19					USGS	US:California, Doyle	美国:加利福尼亚州多伊尔	40.08	-120.07		5.6	Ms	7										
1950	12	14	14	15	51	4	0.3	-1.5		* Engdahl, NOAA	Mexico:Oaxaca	墨西哥:瓦哈卡	16.48	-98.22	50	7.3	Mw	5						3				
1950	12	15	23	37	51					GSHAP	Kazakhstan:Almaty	哈萨克斯坦:阿拉木图	45	78	23	5	Ms	6										
1950	12	21	11	36	48					GSHAP, Song	Chile:La Higuera	智利:拉伊格拉	-29.5	-71	100	5	Mk	6										
1950	12	27	4	30						GSHAP, Song	Peru:Moquegua	秘鲁:莫克瓜	-17	-71.2	30	4.5	Mk	5										
1950	12	28	21	6	16					GSHAP, Song	Peru:Ica, Near Coast	秘鲁:伊卡近海	-14.6	-76.3	33	4.5	Mk	5										
1950										GSHAP	Russia:Sakha, Artyk	俄罗斯:萨哈共和国阿尔特克	65	145.5	20	5	Ms	6										
1951	1	1	17	53	30					GSHAP, Song	Peru:Ica	秘鲁:伊卡	-14.3	-75.8	80	4.5	Mk	5										
1951	1	2	23	12	4					GSHAP, Song	Peru:Chimbote, Near Coast	秘鲁:钦博特近海	-9.5	-79.5	200	4.5	Mk	5										
1951	1	6	5	17	20					GSHAP, Engdahl	Afghan:Badakhshan	阿富汗:巴达赫尚	36.5	71	223	6.8	Muk	6										
1951	1	10	2	52						GSHAP, Song	Peru:Lima, Near Coast	秘鲁:利马近海	-11.8	-77.5	40	4.5	Mk	5										
1951	1	16	17	53	53					GSHAP	Azerbaijan:Lenkeran, N.	阿塞拜疆:连科兰北部	39.1	49.6	25	4.9	Ms	6										
1951	1	17	17							GSHAP, Song	Peru:Ica	秘鲁:伊卡	-14.3	-75.8	80	4.5	Mk	5										
1951	1	22	15	14	53					USGS	US:Nevada, Johnson Lane	美国:内华达州约翰逊巷	39.08	-119.95		4.8	Ms	5										
1951	1	22	23	20						GSHAP, Song	Venezuela:Isla Cubagua	委内瑞拉:库巴瓜岛	10.43	-63.8		5	Mk	6										
1951	1	24	7	17	2.6					CGS, USGS	US:California, Brawley	美国:加利福尼亚州布劳利	32.983	-115.733	16	5.8	Ms	7										
1951	1	26	2	51						GSHAP, Song	Peru:Piura	秘鲁:皮乌拉	-5.794	-79.751	30	5	Mk	6										
1951	1	31	16	39						GSHAP, Song	Peru:Lima	秘鲁:利马	-12.209	-76.935	50	5	Mk	6										
1951	2	2	16	44	36					GSHAP	Russia:Sakhalin Island	俄罗斯:库页岛(萨哈林岛)	46.7	142.5	10	5.5	Ms	7.5										
1951	2	2	18	25	53					GSHAP	Russia:Sakhalin Island	俄罗斯:库页岛(萨哈林岛)	46.8	142.4	11	4.9	Ms	7										
1951	2	3	16	30						GSHAP, Song	Peru:Huari	秘鲁:瓦里	-9.561	-77.363	80	4.5	Mk	5										
1951	2	4	11	6						GSHAP, Song	Peru:Lima	秘鲁:利马	-11.9	-77.1	30	4.5	Mk	5										
1951	2	9	4	34	43					GSHAP, Song	Chile:Illapel	智利:伊亚佩尔	-31.5	-71	96	4.5	Mk	5										
1951	2	10	1	56						GSHAP, Song	Peru:Lima	秘鲁:利马	-11.9	-77.1	30	4.5	Mk	5										
1951	2	10	8	38	14					GSHAP	Kuril Islands	千岛群岛	43.5	146.2	70	6	Ms	6										
1951	2	12	17	22	6					GSHAP	Russia:Sakha, Artyk, NW.	俄罗斯:萨哈共和国阿尔特克西北	65.8	137	18	6.4	Ms	8										

时间						海啸				资料来源	震中				深度	震级	标度	烈度	死亡人数		受伤人数		经济损失		房屋毁坏		房屋受损	
年	月	日	时	分	秒	源	浪高	级 I	级 S		地名(英文)	地名(中文)	纬度(°)	经度(°)					数量/人	级别	数量/人	级别	数量/$ Mill	级别	数量/间	级别	数量/间	级别
Date						Tsunami				Information	Earthquake Epicenter				Depth	Mag	Scale	MMI	Deaths		Injuries		Damage		Houses Destroyed		Houses Damaged	
Year	Mo	Dy	Hr	Mn	Sec	Sr	Wh	mI	mS		Name(English)	Name(Chinese)	Latitude	Longitude					Num	Dd	Num	Dd	$ Mill	De	Num	Dh	Num	Dh
1951	2	15	10	47	59					USGS	US:California,Anza	美国:加利福尼亚州安萨	33.48	-116.5	16	4.8	Ms	5										
1951	2	15	10	49	57					USGS	US:California,Anza	美国:加利福尼亚州安萨	33.48	-116.5	16	4.8	Ms	5										
1951	2	17	21	7	7					* Engdahl	Papua New Guinea:Lea Lea	巴布亚新几内亚:莱阿莱阿	-9.3	147.1	180	7.2	mB		3000	4								
1951	2	22	1	45	42	2	6		3	* NOAA,Song	Papua New Guinea:Nuku	巴布亚新几内亚:努库	-3.7	142.2		7.8	Mk											
1951	3	3	21	41	23					GSHAP	Georgia:Tbilisi	格鲁吉亚:第比利斯	41.8	44.5	14	4.6	Ms	6										
1951	3	4	11	17	24					GSHAP, Engdahl	Peru:Nazca	秘鲁:纳斯卡	-16	-74.5	64	6.9	Muk	6										
1951	3	6	10	45						GSHAP,Song	Peru:Jaén	秘鲁:哈恩	-5.52	-79	20	4.5	Mk	5										
1951	3	13	0	21	9					GSHAP,Song	Peru:Pucallpa	秘鲁:普卡尔帕	-9	-74.1	96	4.5	Mk	5										
1951	3	15	16							China	China:Sichuan,Hanyuan	中国:四川汉源	29.3	102.6		5	Ms	6										
1951	3	29	9	48						GSHAP,Song	Peru:Ica	秘鲁:伊卡	-14	-76	80	4.5	Mk	5										
1951	4	8	19	31						GSHAP,Song	Peru:Torata	秘鲁:塔克纳	-17.2	-71.2	30	4.5	Mk	5										
1951	4	14	4	10	6					GSHAP	Tadzhikistan:Dzhirgatal	塔吉克斯坦:吉尔加塔尔	39.1	71.6	25	5.9	Ms	6.5										
1951	4	14	13	32	59					GSHAP	Russia:Sakha,Allakh - Yun	俄罗斯:萨哈共和国阿拉赫云	61.3	137.4	30	6.5	Ms	7.5										
1951	4	22	3	40						GSHAP,Song	Peru:Ica	秘鲁:伊卡	-14.3	-75.8	80	4.5	Mk	5										
1951	4	23	0	52	23					USGS	Hawaiian Islands	夏威夷群岛	19.2	-155.5		6.5	Ms	7										
1951	4	30	12	11						GSHAP,Song	Peru:Arequipa	秘鲁:阿雷基帕	-16.5	-71.7	25	4.5	Mk	5										
1951	5	3	19	54						GSHAP,Song	Peru:Satipo	秘鲁:萨蒂波	-11.25	-74.9	100	4.5	Mk	5										
1951	5	4	11	53	14					GSHAP	Japan:Hokkaido	日本:北海道	44.4	142.2	240	6.5	Ms	5										
1951	5	6	23	8						*	El Salvador:La Unión	萨尔瓦多:拉乌尼翁	13	-87.8	100	6.5	Muk		1100	4			23.0	3				
1951	5	8	20	0	51					GSHAP,Song	Peru:Trujillo,Near Coast	秘鲁:特鲁希略近海	-8.3	-79.8	64	5	Mk	6										
1951	5	10	9	50						GSHAP,Song	Peru:Satipo	秘鲁:萨蒂波	-11	-74	83	4.5	Mk	5										
1951	5	12	22	7	52					GSHAP	Kyrgyzstan:Bazar Dare	吉尔吉斯斯坦:扎尔达雷	39.62	71.2	25	5.6	Ms	6										
1951	5	13								GSHAP	Turkmenistan:Balkanabat	土库曼斯坦:巴尔坎纳巴德	39.3	55	13	4.8	Ms	6.5										
1951	5	16	13	23						* GSHAP	Peru:Azangaro	秘鲁:阿桑加罗	-15	-69.5	250	7.9	Muk	5										
1951	5	18	11	38						GSHAP,Song	Peru:Cusco	秘鲁:库斯科	-13.55	-71.97	30	4.5	Mk	5										
1951	5	18	17	20						GSHAP,Song	Peru:Santa Clara	秘鲁:圣克拉拉	-8.5	-77.37	20	4.5	Mk	5										
1951	5	24	18	25						GSHAP,Song	Peru:Arequipa	秘鲁:阿雷基帕	-16	-72.8	20	4.5	Mk	5										
1951	5	25	0	2	52					GSHAP,Song	Venezuela:Lara	委内瑞拉:拉腊	9.71	-69.76	25	4.5	Mk	5										
1951	5	28	20	5						GSHAP,Song	Peru:Arequipa	秘鲁:阿雷基帕	-16.17	-71.8	30	4.5	Mk	5										
1951	6	12	5	42	35					GSHAP,Song	Peru:Canete	秘鲁:卡涅特	-13.1	-76.2		5	Mk	6										
1951	6	24	1	44	26					GSHAP	Peru:Trujillo,Near Coast	秘鲁:特鲁希略近海	-8.3	-79.8		5.5	Ms	6										
1951	6	24	2	26	34					GSHAP,Song	Peru:Ica,Near Coast	秘鲁:伊卡近海	-14.6	-76.3		4.5	Mk	5										
1951	6	25	16	12	37					USGS	Alaska Peninsula,S.	阿拉斯加半岛南部	61.1	-150.1	128	6.2	Ms	5										

年 Year	月 Mo	日 Dy	时 Hr	分 Mn	秒 Sec	海啸 源 Sr	海啸 浪高 Wh	海啸 级 I mI	海啸 级 S mS	资料来源 Information	地名(英文) Name(English)	地名(中文) Name(Chinese)	纬度(°) Latitude	经度(°) Longitude	深度 Depth	震级 Mag	标度 Scale	烈度 MMI	死亡人数 数量/人 Deaths Num	死亡人数 级别 Dd	受伤人数 数量/人 Injuries Num	受伤人数 级别 Dd	经济损失 数量/$ Mill Damage $ Mill	经济损失 级别 De	房屋毁坏 数量/间 Houses Destroyed Num	房屋毁坏 级别 Dh	房屋受损 数量/间 Houses Damaged Num	房屋受损 级别 Dh
1951	6	25	19	45	42					USGS	US:California,Brown	美国:加利福尼亚州布朗	35.77	-117.95	12	4.6	Ms	5										
1951	6	27	17	40						GSHAP,Song	Peru:Chimbote,Near Coast	秘鲁:钦博特近海	-9.293	-79.752	60	4.5	Mk	5										
1951	6	28	3	7	46					GSHAP	Bolivia:Chuquisaca	玻利维亚:丘基萨卡	-19.3	-63.8		6.2	Ms	5										
1951	6	28	3	36	52					GSHAP,Song	Peru:Arequipa	秘鲁:阿雷基帕	-17	-71.5		5	Mk	6										
1951	7	2	18	13	19					GSHAP,Song	Peru:Ancash,Near Coast	秘鲁:安卡什省近海	-10.3	-79.5	150	4.5	Mk	5										
1951	7	9	0	4						*	Mexico:Oaxaca	墨西哥:瓦哈卡	16.1	-96.8	50	6.2	Muk		1	1				2				
1951	7	12	14	41						GSHAP,Song	Peru:Moquegua	秘鲁:莫克瓜	-16.7	-71	120	4.5	Mk	5										
1951	7	14	4	59						GSHAP,Song	Peru:Máncora,Near Coast	秘鲁:曼科拉近海	-4	-81.3	30	5	Mk	6										
1951	7	17	7	34	17					GSHAP	Colombia:Narino	哥伦比亚:纳里尼奥	1	-78	200	4	Ms	5										
1951	7	17	9	19	17					GSHAP	Colombia:Narino	哥伦比亚:纳里尼奥	1	-78	200	4	Ms	5										
1951	7	29	10	53	45					USGS	US:California,Tres Pinos,S.	美国:加利福尼亚州特雷斯皮诺斯南部	36.58	-121.18		5	Ms	6										
1951	7	30	5	16	10					GSHAP,Song	Peru:Torata	秘鲁:塔克纳	-17.3	-71.3	70	4.5	Mk	5										
1951	8	1	3	18						GSHAP,Song	Venezuela:Lara	委内瑞拉:拉腊	10.05	-69.3		5	Mk	6										
1951	8	3	0	23	58	5				* NOAA	Nicaragua:Gulf of Fonseca,Potosi	尼加拉瓜:丰塞卡湾,波多西	13	-87.5	100	6	Ms		1000	3				3				
1951	8	4	11	20	42					Wang S.	Luzon Ridge,W.	吕宋海岭西部	19.6	120.6		5.1	Ms	9										
1951	8	6	8	8	56					*	Nicaragua:Gulf of Fonseca,Jinotega	尼加拉瓜:丰塞卡湾,希诺特加	13	-87.5	100	5.5	Ms							3		2		
1951	8	6	9	5	2					USGS	US:California,Paicines	美国:加利福尼亚州佩赛恩斯	36.62	-121.22		4.9	Ms	6										
1951	8	7	5	37	30					GSHAP,Song	Peru:Santa Clara	秘鲁:圣克拉拉	-8.443	-77.256	100	5	Mk	6										
1951	8	8	9							GSHAP,Song	Peru:Satipo	秘鲁:萨蒂波	-11.25	-74.85	100	4.5	Mk	5										
1951	8	8	22	9						* Song	Italy:Montecassino	意大利:蒙特卡西诺	41.6	13.8		6.5	Mk	12										
1951	8	10	0	5	24					GSHAP,Song	Peru:Pisco,Near Coast	秘鲁:皮斯科近海	-14	-77		5	Mk	6										
1951	8	12	23	26	24					GSHAP,Song	Peru:Chincha Alta,Near Coast	秘鲁:上钦查近海	-13.8	-77	50	4.5	Mk	5										
1951	8	13	18	33	30					* Engdahl	Turkey:Kursunlu	土耳其:库鲁修鲁	40.8	33.4		6.7	Muk	9	50	1				3				
1951	8	14	8	15						GSHAP,Song	Peru:Torata	秘鲁:塔克纳	-17.4	-70.4	30	4.5	Mk	5										
1951	8	14	20	1	28					GSHAP	Colombia:Yacopi	哥伦比亚:昆地那马加的亚科皮	5.2	-74.5	223	5	Ms	6										
1951	8	15	7	23						* Song	US:California,Huntington Beach	美国:加利福尼亚州亨廷顿比奇	33.5	-118.2		5.9	Mk	5					3	2				
1951	8	21	10	57		4	3.6	1.8		*Engdahl,NOAA	Hawaiian Islands	夏威夷群岛	19.7	-156	60	6.9	Ms							2				
1951	8	27	5							GSHAP,Song	Peru:Arequipa	秘鲁:阿雷基帕	-16.2	-72.4	30	4.5	Mk	5										
1951	8	30	14	30						GSHAP,Song	Peru:Santa Clara	秘鲁:圣克拉拉	-8.55	-77.34	20	4.5	Mk	5										
1951	9	4	23	45						GSHAP,Song	Peru:Talara,Near Coast	秘鲁:塔拉拉近海	-4.4	-81.6	30	4.5	Mk	5										
1951	9	8	9	53						GSHAP,Song	Peru:Chiclayo,Near Coast	秘鲁:奇克拉约近海	-6.9	-80.2	40	5	Mk	6										
1951	9	10	12	15						GSHAP,Song	Peru:Pucallpa,SW.	秘鲁:普卡尔帕西南	-8.9	-75.7	40	4.5	Mk	5										

年 Year	月 Mo	日 Dy	时 Hr	分 Mn	秒 Sec	海啸 Tsunami 源 Sr	浪高 Wh	级 I mI	级 S mS	资料来源 Information	震中 Earthquake Epicenter 地名(英文) Name(English)	地名(中文) Name(Chinese)	纬度(°) Latitude	经度(°) Longitude	深度 Depth	震级 Mag	标度 Scale	烈度 MMI	死亡人数 Deaths 数量/人 Num	级别 Dd	受伤人数 Injuries 数量/人 Num	级别 Dd	经济损失 Damage 数量/$ Mill $ Mill	级别 De	房屋毁坏 Houses Destroyed 数量/间 Num	级别 Dh	房屋受损 Houses Damaged 数量/间 Num	级别 Dh
1951	9	14	7	45						GSHAP, Song	Peru: Zana	秘鲁:萨尼亚	-7.75	-79.18		4.5	Mk	5										
1951	9	16	11	42	51					USGS, Song	Hawaiian Islands	夏威夷群岛	19.32	-155.42		4.9	Mk	5										
1951	9	20	1							GSHAP, Song	Peru: Mάncora, Near Coast	秘鲁:曼科拉近海	-4	-81.4	30	4.5	Mk	5										
1951	9	20	5	48	13					GSHAP, Song	Peru: Mάncora	秘鲁:曼科拉	-4.2	-81.2		5	Mk	6										
1951	9	29	22	44						GSHAP, Song	Peru: Torata	秘鲁:塔克纳	-17.4	-70.2	100	4.5	Mk	5										
1951	10	3	11	7	9					GSHAP, Song	Chile: Arica, Near Coast	智利:阿里卡近海	-18.8	-70.5	64	4.5	Mk	5										
1951	10	7	6	0	19					GSHAP	Colombia: Antioquia	哥伦比亚:安提奥基亚	7.2	-75	96	5	Ms	6										
1951	10	8	4	10	35					CGS, USGS	US: California, North Coast	美国:加利福尼亚州北部近海	40.25	-124.5		6	Ms	7										
1951	10	9	10	13	11					GSHAP, Song	Venezuela: Lara	委内瑞拉:拉腊	10	-69.77	25	4.5	Mk	5										
1951	10	17	2	33	21					GSHAP	Venezuela: Zulia	委内瑞拉:苏利亚	9.5	-73		5	Ms	6										
1951	10	21	21	34	14	4	0.3			* China, Engdahl, Dis	China: Taiwan, Hualien	中国:台湾花莲	23.75	121.5	0	7.5	Mw	9	113	2	856	3		3	2382	4		
1951	10	22	3	29	27					China, Engdahl	China: Taiwan, Hualien	中国:台湾花莲	23.75	121.25	0	7.2	Mw	9										
1951	10	22	5	43	1	4	0.3			Engdahl, China, NOAA	China: Taiwan, Nantou, N.	中国:台湾南投北	24	121.25	0	7.1	Mw		68	2	586	3		3	2382	4		
1951	10	31	20	58	19					USGS	US: California, Hollister	美国:加利福尼亚州霍利斯特	36.9	-121.42		4.8	Ms	5										
1951	11	2	21	55	42					GSHAP	Georgia: Kakhetiya	格鲁吉亚:卡赫季州	42.3	45.3	20	5.3	Ms	7										
1951	11	3	8	51	15					GSHAP	Colombia: Buenaventura	哥伦比亚:布埃纳文图拉	4	-77	100	4	Ms	5										
1951	11	8	19	34	12					USGS, Song	Hawaiian Islands	夏威夷群岛	19.19	-155.72		5.1	Mk	6										
1951	11	9	22	7	55					GSHAP, Engdahl	Bolivia: Tupiza	玻利维亚:图皮萨	-21.75	-68	120	6.8	Muk	5										
1951	11	9	22	10						GSHAP, Song	Peru: Arequipa	秘鲁:阿雷基帕	-16.596	-71.796	30	4.5	Mk	5										
1951	11	13	11	24	42					USGS	US: California, Off Coast N.	美国:加利福尼亚州北部沿海	40.4	-125.3		4.8	Ms	5										
1951	11	14	8	39	53					USGS	US: California, Petrolia	美国:加利福尼亚州彼得罗利亚	40.43	-124.05		4.7	Ms	6										
1951	11	18	9	35	47					* China, Engdahl, Dis	China: Xizang (Tibet), Damxung	中国:西藏当雄	31.1	91.4		8	Ms	10						1		1		
1951	11	24	18	50	18					* China, Engdahl, Dis	China: Taiwan, Taitung, Coast of E.	中国:台湾台东以东海域	22.9	121.5		7.3	Mw	9	17	1	326	3		2	1016	4	582	3
1951	12	5	5	55						GSHAP, Song	Peru: Arequipa	秘鲁:阿雷基帕	-16.55	-71.6	30	4.5	Mk	5										
1951	12	5	15	53	14					USGS	US: California, Calipatria	美国:加利福尼亚州卡利帕特里亚	33.1	-115.4	16	4.5	Ms	7										
1951	12	6	14	29	19					GSHAP	Colombia: Nuquí, Near Coast	哥伦比亚:努基近海	5.7	-77.4		5	Ms	6										
1951	12	21	7	37	29					* China, Dis	China: Yunnan, Jianchuan	中国:云南剑川	26.7	100		6.25	Ms	9	423		2395	4	39.0	4	29890	5		
1951	12	26	0	46	54					USGS	US: California, Near Coast of San Diego	美国:加利福尼亚州圣地牙哥近海	32.82	-118.35	16	5.9	Ms	6										

时间 Date 年 Year	月 Mo	日 Dy	时 Hr	分 Mn	秒 Sec	海啸 Tsunami 源 Sr	浪高 Wh	级 I mI	级 S mS	资料来源 Information	震中 Earthquake Epicenter 地名(英文) Name(English)	地名(中文) Name(Chinese)	纬度(°) Latitude	经度(°) Longitude	深度 Depth	震级 Mag	标度 Scale	烈度 MMI	死亡人数 Deaths 数量/人 Num	级别 Dd	受伤人数 Injuries 数量/人 Num	级别 Dd	经济损失 Damage 数量/$ Mill $ Mill	级别 De	房屋毁坏 Houses Destroyed 数量/间 Num	级别 Dh	房屋受损 Houses Damaged 数量/间 Num	级别 Dh
1951	12	28	2	49	27					USGS	US:California, Mammoth Lakes	美国:加利福尼亚州马姆莫斯湖	37.57	-118.58	16	5.2	Ms	5										
1952	1	3	6	3						*	Turkey:Pasinler, Erzurum	土耳其:哈珊卡尔堡,埃尔佐鲁姆	39.9	41.7		6	Muk	8	103	3				2				
1952	1	11	7	3	7					GSHAP	Kuril Islands	千岛群岛	44.6	148.9	80	5.9	Ms	5										
1952	1	15	7	0	51					GSHAP	Ecuador:Loja	厄瓜多尔:洛哈	-4.26	-80.06	100	6.5	Ms	5										
1952	1	18	22	53	15					GSHAP	Colombia:Near Coast	哥伦比亚:近海	3.5	-78		4	Ms	5										
1952	1	28	15	23						GSHAP,Song	Peru:Ica	秘鲁:伊卡	-14.3	-75.8	80	4.5	Mk	5										
1952	1	30	4							USGS,Song	US:Vermont,Burlington	美国:维莫特州伯灵顿	44.5	-73.2		5.1	Mk	6										
1952	2	5	16							China	China:Sichuan,Xichang	中国:四川西昌	27.9	102.3		5	Ms	6										
1952	2	9	8	43	31					USGS	US:California,Lone Pine	美国:加利福尼亚州隆派恩	36.61	-117.9	8	4.1	Ms	6										
1952	2	12	1	58	29					GSHAP,Song	Peru:Pucallpa	秘鲁:普卡尔帕	-8.5	-74	223	5	Mk	6										
1952	2	14	21	2	37					Engdahl, GSHAP	Colombia:Mutata	哥伦比亚:安提奥基亚的穆塔塔	7.3	-76.5	0	6.8	Muk	8										
1952	2	20	9	10	3					GSHAP,Song	Peru:Arequipa,Near Coast	秘鲁:阿雷基帕近海	-16	-74.5	96	5	Mk	6										
1952	2	26	11	31	10					*Shi Z., Engdahl	Peru:Puno,N.	秘鲁:普诺北部	-14.1	-69.9	260	6.9	mB	6										
1952	2	27	4	5	47					GSHAP	Tajikistan:Duachanbe	塔吉克斯坦:杜尚别	38.6	68.9	8	4.7	Ms	6.5										
1952	3	4	1	22	43	4	6.5	2.7	2	*GSHAP,Usami, Engdahl,NOAA	Japan:Hokkaido	日本:北海道	42.15	143.85	45	8.1	Mw	9	33	1	572	3		3	2422	4		
1952	3	7	7	32						Shi Z.,Usami	Japan:Fukui,Near Coast	日本:福井近海	36.5	136.2		6.8	Ms		7	1					10	1		
1952	3	9	17	3	47	4	0.3	-1.7	-1	*Engdahl,NOAA	Japan:Hokkaido	日本:北海道	42.5	143	20	7.2	Mw							2				
1952	3	15	8	49						GSHAP,Song	Peru:Arequipa	秘鲁:阿雷基帕	-16.2	-72.4	30	4.5	Mk	5										
1952	3	17	3	58		4	1			*NOAA	Hawaiian Islands	夏威夷群岛	19.11	-155.033	33	4.5	Ms											
1952	3	19	10	57	12	4	0.3			*Engdahl,NOAA	Philippines:Mindanao Island	菲律宾:棉兰老岛	9.5	126	25	7.7	Mw											
1952	3	31	0	50	40					GSHAP,Song	Peru:Piura	秘鲁:皮乌拉	-6	-79.5		5	Mk	6										
1952	4	1	0	37	41					USGS	US:Montana,Bigfork	美国:蒙大纳州比格福克	48	-113.8		5.5	Ms	7										
1952	4	6	18	12	55					GSHAP,Song	Peru:Lima,Near Coast	秘鲁:利马近海	-11	-78.2		5	Mk	6										
1952	4	7	10	23	13					GSHAP	Colombia:Narino	哥伦比亚:纳里尼奥	1.5	-77.75		4	Ms	5										
1952	4	9	16	29	28					USGS	US:Oklahoma,Oklahoma City	美国:奥克拉荷马州奥克拉荷马城	35.53	-97.85	10	5.5	Ms	7										
1952	4	13	12	50						GSHAP,Song	Peru:Torata	秘鲁:塔克纳	-17.2	-70.7	30	4.5	Mk	5										
1952	4	17	11	43	23					GSHAP,Song	Chile:Illapel	智利:伊拉帕尔	-30.8	-71.5	33	4.5	Mk	5										
1952	4	19	9	58	59					Engdahl,GSHAP	Colombia:Norte de Santander	哥伦比亚:北桑坦德	7.2	-72.1	64	6.9	Muk	7										
1952	4	21	9	11						GSHAP,Song	Peru:Lima	秘鲁:利马	-12	-76.7	90	4.5	Mk	5										
1952	4	22	16	54	43					USGS,Song	US:Montana,Toston	美国:蒙大纳州托斯顿	46.2	-111.4		5.1	Mk	6										
1952	4	29	19	42	30					GSHAP,Song	Chile:Pichilemu	智利:披市勒亩	-34.6	-71.9		4.5	Mk	5										
1952	5	3	12	14	11					GSHAP,Song	Peru:Ica,Near Coast	秘鲁:伊卡近海	-14.6	-76.3		5	Mk	6										

年 Year	月 Mo	日 Dy	时 Hr	分 Mn	秒 Sec	海啸 Tsunami 源 Sr	浪高 Wh	级 I mI	级 S mS	资料来源 Information	震中 Earthquake Epicenter 地名(英文) Name(English)	地名(中文) Name(Chinese)	纬度(°) Latitude	经度(°) Longitude	深度 Depth	震级 Mag	标度 Scale	烈度 MMI	死亡人数 Deaths 数量/人 Num	级别 Dd	受伤人数 Injuries 数量/人 Num	级别 Dd	经济损失 Damage 数量/$ Mill	级别 De	房屋毁坏 Houses Destroyed 数量/间 Num	级别 Dh	房屋受损 Houses Damaged 数量/间 Num	级别 Dh
1952	5	3	20	41						GSHAP, Song	Peru: Ica	秘鲁:伊卡	-14.3	-75.8	80	4.5	Mk	5										
1952	5	4	0	14						GSHAP, Song	Peru: Ica	秘鲁:伊卡	-14.4	-76.1		5	Mk	6										
1952	5	8	8	11	3					GSHAP	Colombia: Santander	哥伦比亚:桑坦德	7.5	-73		4.5	Ms	5										
1952	5	9	15	31	32					USGS	US: Nevada, Reno	美国:内华达州雷诺	39.42	-119.78		5.1	Ms	6										
1952	5	13	19	31	45	2	0.1	-3.3		* Engdahl, NOAA	Costa Rica: Santa Cruz	哥斯达黎加:圣克鲁斯	10.3	-85.3	64	6.9	Muk											
1952	5	16	20	45	41					GSHAP, Engdahl	Colombia: Near Coast	哥伦比亚:近海	6.7	-78.9		6.9	Muk	8										
1952	5	17	15	47	27					GSHAP	Colombia: Near Coast	哥伦比亚:近海	6.7	-78.9		5	Ms	6										
1952	5	23	10	3						GSHAP, Song	Peru: Tacna	秘鲁:塔克纳	-18.1	-70	30	4.5	Mk	5										
1952	5	23	22	12	26					USGS	Hawaiian Islands	夏威夷群岛	19.48	-155.98	10	6	Ms	6										
1952	5	24	4	15	15					USGS	US: Nevada, Boulder City	美国:内华达州博尔德城	36.1	-114.7	16	4.9	Ms	6										
1952	6	3	5	53	27					GSHAP	Romania: Focsani	罗马尼亚:福克沙尼	45.5	27.1	21	4.5	Ms	5										
1952	6	3	12	24	12					GSHAP	Colombia: Acandí	哥伦比亚:阿坎迪	8.5	-77	96	5	Ms	6										
1952	6	3								* Song	Turkey: Pasinler, Erzincan	土耳其:哈珊卡尔堡,埃尔津占	39.8	39.5		6.2	Mk	7	94	2				3				
1952	6	4	21	30	47					GSHAP	Colombia: Bahia Solano	哥伦比亚:巴伊阿索拉诺	6	-77.5		6.1	Ms	8										
1952	6	5	5	56	33					GSHAP	Colombia: Bahia Solano	哥伦比亚:巴伊阿索拉诺	6	-77.5		6.2	Ms	8										
1952	6	11	0	31	42					GSHAP, Engdahl	Argentina: San Juan	阿根廷:圣胡安	-31.581	-68.467	25	6.5	Ms	8										
1952	6	19	12	12	59					* China	China: Yunnan, Lancang, NW.	中国:云南澜沧西北	22.7	99.8		6.5	Ms	8						1	10	1		
1952	6	20	9	38	9					USGS	US: Ohio, San Toy	美国:俄亥俄州圣托伊	39.64	-82.02	9	4	Ms	6										
1952	6	20	16	33						GSHAP, Song	Peru: Santa Clara	秘鲁:圣克拉拉	-8.8	-77.4	25	4.5	Mk	5										
1952	6	22	4	7	56					GSHAP, Song	Ecuador: Portoviejo	厄瓜多尔:波托维耶霍	-1.5	-80.5		4.5	Mk	5										
1952	6	23	8	44						GSHAP, Song	Peru: Lima, Near Coast	秘鲁:利马近海	-12.4	-77.4	40	4.5	Mk	5										
1952	6	27	13	9	14					GSHAP	Greece: Chalkidiki	希腊:哈尔基迪基	40.8	23.5	14	4.7	Ms	6										
1952	6	29	9	56	38					GSHAP	Colombia: Bucarasica	哥伦比亚:北桑坦德的布卡拉西卡	8.15	-72.92	157	5.5	Ms	6										
1952	7	3	0	52	24					GSHAP	Colombia: Nuquí, Near Coast	哥伦比亚:努基近海	5.7	-77.4		6	Ms	7										
1952	7	6	7							GSHAP, Song	Peru: Cusco	秘鲁:库斯科	-13.55	-71.97	25	4.5	Mk	5										
1952	7	16	23	48	10					USGS, Song	US: Missouri, New Madrid	美国:密苏里州新马德里	36.2	-89.6		5.1	Mk	6										
1952	7	17	16	9	50					Engdahl, Usami, Shi Z.	Japan: Oyodo	日本:奈良大淀	34.4	135.8	64	6.8	Muk		9	1					20	1		
1952	7	19	8	2						GSHAP, Song	Peru: Lima, Near Coast	秘鲁:利马近海	-12.572	-76.873	70	5	Mk	6										
1952	7	21	11	52	16					* Engdahl	US: California, Bakersfield	美国:加利福尼亚州贝克斯菲尔德	34.949	-119.046	10	7.3	M	11	12	1			60.0	4				
1952	7	21	12	5	31					USGS	US: California, Bakersfield	美国:加利福尼亚州贝克斯菲尔德	35	-119	16	6.4	Ms	5										

时间 年 Year	月 Mo	日 Dy	时 Hr	分 Mn	秒 Sec	海啸 源 Sr	浪高 Wh	级 I mI	级 S mS	资料来源 Information	震中 地名(英文) Name(English)	地名(中文) Name(Chinese)	纬度(°) Latitude	经度(°) Longitude	深度 Depth	震级 Mag	标度 Scale	烈度 MMI	死亡人数 数量/人 Num	级别 Dd	受伤人数 数量/人 Num	级别 Dd	经济损失 数量/$ Mill	级别 De	房屋毁坏 数量/间 Num	级别 Dh	房屋受损 数量/间 Num	级别 Dh
1952	7	21	15	13	58					USGS	US: California, Caliente	美国:加利福尼亚州卡连特	35.18	-118.65	16	5.1	Ms	6										
1952	7	21	15	53						USGS	US: California, Bakersfield	美国:加利福尼亚州贝克斯菲尔德	35	-119	16	4.5	Ms	5										
1952	7	21	19	41	22					USGS	US: California, Arvin	美国:加利福尼亚州阿尔文	35.13	-118.77	16	5.5	Ms	5										
1952	7	22	13	31	43					USGS	US: California, Bakersfield	美国:加利福尼亚州贝克斯菲尔德	35	-119	16	4.8	Ms	5										
1952	7	22	18	5						GSHAP, Song	Peru: Lima, Near Coast	秘鲁:利马近海	-11.6	-77.8	40	4.5	Mk	5										
1952	7	23	0	38	32					USGS	US: California, Caliente	美国:加利福尼亚州卡连特	35.37	-118.58	16	6.1	Ms	6										
1952	7	23	3	19	23					USGS	US: California, Caliente	美国:加利福尼亚州卡连特	35.37	-118.58	16	5	Ms	5										
1952	7	23	7	53	19					USGS	US: California, Arvin	美国:加利福尼亚州阿尔文	35	-118.83	16	5.4	Ms	7										
1952	7	23	13	17	5					USGS	US: California, Arvin	美国:加利福尼亚州阿尔文	35.22	-118.82	16	5.7	Ms	7										
1952	7	23	18	13	51					USGS	US: California, Arvin	美国:加利福尼亚州阿尔文	35	-118.83	16	5.2	Ms	6										
1952	7	25	19	9	45					CGS, USGS	US: California, Caliente	美国:加利福尼亚州卡连特	35.315	-118.516	6	6	Ms	6										
1952	7	25	19	43	24					CGS, USGS	US: California, Caliente	美国:加利福尼亚州卡连特	35.317	-118.494	11	5.8	Ms	6										
1952	7	29	7	3	47					USGS	US: California, Bakersfield	美国:加利福尼亚州贝克斯菲尔德	35.38	-118.85	16	6.1	Ms	7										
1952	7	29	8	1	46					USGS	US: California, Arvin	美国:加利福尼亚州阿尔文	35.4	-118.82	16	5.1	Ms	5										
1952	7	31	12	9	9					USGS	US: California, Caliente	美国:加利福尼亚州卡连特	35.33	-118.6	16	5.8	Ms	6										
1952	8	1	13	4	30					USGS	US: California, Arvin	美国:加利福尼亚州阿尔文	34.9	-118.95	16	5.1	Ms	5										
1952	8	3	4	22						GSHAP, Song	Peru: Lima, Near Coast	秘鲁:利马近海	-12.3	-77.4	40	4.5	Mk	5										
1952	8	3	13	13	44					GSHAP, Song	Peru: Lima, Near Coast	秘鲁:利马近海	-12.8	-78.5		5	Mk	6										
1952	8	3	16	36	14					GSHAP	Romania: Nehoiu	罗马尼亚:内霍尤	45.6	26.5	150	5.1	Ms	5										
1952	8	6	13	36						GSHAP, Song	Peru: Lima, Near Coast	秘鲁:利马近海	-12.05	-77.5	30	4.5	Mk	5										
1952	8	7	16	31	51					USGS	US: California, Bakersfield	美国:加利福尼亚州贝克斯菲尔德	35.03	-119.05	16	4.9	Ms	5										
1952	8	11	21	44						GSHAP, Song	Peru: Tumbes, Near Coast	秘鲁:通贝斯近海	-3.6	-80.9	30	4.5	Mk	5										
1952	8	13	17	39	25					USGS	US: California, Caliente	美国:加利福尼亚州卡连特	35.15	-118.68	16	4.7	Ms	6										

年 Year	月 Mo	日 Dy	时 Hr	分 Mn	秒 Sec	海啸 Tsunami 源 Sr	浪高 Wh	级 I mI	级 S mS	资料来源 Information	震中 Earthquake Epicenter 地名(英文) Name(English)	地名(中文) Name(Chinese)	纬度(°) Latitude	经度(°) Longitude	深度 Depth	震级 Mag	标度 Scale	烈度 MMI	死亡人数 Deaths 数量/人 Num	级别 Dd	受伤人数 Injuries 数量/人 Num	级别 Dd	经济损失 Damage 数量/$ Mill $ Mill	级别 De	房屋毁坏 Houses Destroyed 数量/间 Num	级别 Dh	房屋受损 Houses Damaged 数量/间 Num	级别 Dh
1952	8	17	16	2	11					China, Engdahl	China: Xizang (Tibet), Damxung, NE.	中国:西藏当雄东北	30.797	91.648	10	7.7	Mw	10	54	2				2	774	3		
1952	8	19	19	12	26					USGS	US: California, Bakersfield	美国:加利福尼亚州贝克斯菲尔德	35.05	-119.23	16	4.5	Ms	5										
1952	8	22	22	41	24					*	US: California, Bakersfield	美国:加利福尼亚州贝克斯菲尔德	35.333	-118.917	16	5.8	ML	8	2	1		2	10.0	3	90	2		
1952	8	23	10	9	7					USGS	US: California, Lancaster	美国:加利福尼亚州兰开斯特	34.52	-118.2	13	5	Ms	6										
1952	8	24								GSHAP, Song	Venezuela: Villa De Rosario	委内瑞拉:维拉代罗萨里奥	10.53	-72.47		5	Mk	6										
1952	8	25	6	20	26					USGS	US: California, Arvin	美国:加利福尼亚州阿尔文	35.1	-118.97	16	4.7	Ms	5										
1952	8	26	10	45						GSHAP, Song	Peru: Cusco	秘鲁:库斯科	-13.55	-71.97	20	4.5	Mk	5										
1952	8	30	4	55	60					USGS	US: California, Caliente	美国:加利福尼亚州卡连特	35.31	-118.48	5	4.7	Ms	5										
1952	8									China	China: Yunnan, Kaiyuan, S.	中国:云南开远南	23.6	103.2		5	Ms	6										
1952	9	2	12	41	32					USGS	US: California, Caliente	美国:加利福尼亚州卡连特	35.13	-118.7	16	4.6	Ms	5										
1952	9	2	20	45	56					USGS	US: California, Bakersfield	美国:加利福尼亚州贝克斯菲尔德	34.97	-119	16	4.7	Ms	5										
1952	9	3	13	47	42					GSHAP	Turkey: Adilcevaz	土耳其:阿迪尔杰瓦兹	39	43	12	4.7	Ms	7										
1952	9	11	2	1						GSHAP, Song	Peru: Pucallpa, SW.	秘鲁:普卡尔帕西南	-8.9	-75.7	30	5	Mk	6										
1952	9	12	10	35	25					USGS	US: California, Bakersfield	美国:加利福尼亚州贝克斯菲尔德	35	-119.05	16	4.5	Ms	5										
1952	9	14	15	55						GSHAP, Song	Peru: Pucallpa, SW.	秘鲁:普卡尔帕西南	-8.9	-75.7	30	5	Mk	6										
1952	9	15	4	31	22					GSHAP	Iran: Qūchān	伊朗:古昌	37.9	58	18	5.1	Ms	6.5										
1952	9	16	2	50		5	0.3	-1.7	-1	Usami, Japan, NOAA, Song	Japan Trench	日本海沟	31.9	140		7	Mk											
1952	9	20	21	10	24					GSHAP, Song	Peru: Ica, Near Coast	秘鲁:伊卡近海	-15.5	-76.4	33	4.5	Mk	5										
1952	9	21	2	33						GSHAP, Song	Peru: Moquegua	秘鲁:莫克瓜	-16.8	-71.3	30	4.5	Mk	5										
1952	9	22	11	41	25					USGS	US: California, North Coast	美国:加利福尼亚州北部近海	40.2	-124.42		5.2	Ms	7										
1952	9	24	3	23		5	0.3	-1.7		Usami, Japan, NOAA, Song	Japan Trench	日本海沟	31.9	140		7	Mk		31	1				1				
1952	9	25	3	33		5	0.1	-3.3	-1	Usami, Japan, NOAA, Song	Japan Trench	日本海沟	31.9	140		7	Mk											
1952	9	30	12	52	2					* China, Dis	China: Sichuan, Mianning, S.	中国:四川冕宁南	28.3	102.2		6.75	Ms	9	271				5.1	3	4196	4		
1952	10	2	7	39						GSHAP, Song	Peru: Pucallpa, SW.	秘鲁:普卡尔帕西南	-8.9	-75.7	30	4.5	Mk	5										
1952	10	2	11	4						GSHAP, Song	Peru: Torata	秘鲁:塔克纳	-17.4	-70.5	30	4.5	Mk	5										
1952	10	6	14	7	12					GSHAP, Song	Peru: Perene	秘鲁:佩雷内	-10.3	-75.4	33	4.5	Mk	5										
1952	10	8	14	24	1					* China	China: Shanxi, Daixian, SW.	中国:山西代县西南	39	112.7		5.5	Ms	8						3	5043	4		

年 Year	月 Mo	日 Dy	时 Hr	分 Mn	秒 Sec	源 Sr	浪高 Wh	级I mI	级S mS	资料来源 Information	地名(英文) Name(English)	地名(中文) Name(Chinese)	纬度(°) Latitude	经度(°) Longitude	深度 Depth	震级 Mag	标度 Scale	烈度 MMI	死亡人数 Deaths 数量/人 Num	级别 Dd	受伤人数 Injuries 数量/人 Num	级别 Dd	经济损失 Damage 数量/$ Mill	级别 De	房屋毁坏 Houses Destroyed 数量/间 Num	级别 Dh	房屋受损 Houses Damaged 数量/间 Num	级别 Dh
1952	10	17	12	42						GSHAP, Song	Peru: Trujillo, Near Coast	秘鲁:特鲁希略近海	-8.302	-79.941	30	4.5	Mk	5										
1952	10	22	17							*	Turkey: Ceyhan, Misis	土耳其:杰伊汗,米西斯	36.5	35.5		5	Muk	7	20	1				3				
1952	10	27	6	31						GSHAP, Song	Peru: Lima, Near Coast	秘鲁:利马近海	-11.639	-78.132	40	4.5	Mk	5										
1952	10	30	13	13	7					GSHAP	Colombia: Montería	哥伦比亚:蒙特里亚	8.7	-76.3		5.7	Ms	7										
1952	11	4	16	58	28	4	18	4.2	4	* Engdahl, NOAA	Russia: Kamchatka, Near East Coast	俄罗斯:堪察加东部近海	52.755	160.057	22.2	9	M	11	4000	4				3				
1952	11	7	8	55	35					USGS	US: California, Bakersfield	美国:加利福尼亚州贝克斯菲尔德	35	-119.08	16	4.6	Ms	5										
1952	11	14	11	40	44					GSHAP, Song	Peru: Juanjui	秘鲁:胡安惠	-6.6	-76.9		5	Mk	6										
1952	11	22	7	46	36					USGS	US: California, San Simeon	美国:加利福尼亚州圣西米恩	35.77	-121.14	10	6	Ms	7										
1952	11	27	7	20	32					GSHAP	Afghan: Taloqan	阿富汗:塔卢坎	36.6	70	150	6.2	Ms	6										
1952	11	28	1	12	55					GSHAP	Colombia: Near Coast	哥伦比亚:近海	6.7	-78.9		5	Ms	6										
1952	12	3	2	5						GSHAP, Song	Peru: Ilo, Near Coast	秘鲁:伊洛近海	-17.547	-71.767	30	4.5	Mk	5										
1952	12	7	0	50	17					USGS	Aleutian Islands	阿留申群岛	52.5	174.2		6.2	Ms	6										
1952	12	8	15	9	32					* China	China: Yunnan, Lancang, NW.	中国:云南澜沧西北	22.9	99.7		5.75	Ms	7						1	60	2		
1952	12	13	18	35						GSHAP, Song	Peru: Lima, Near Coast	秘鲁:利马近海	-11.7	-78	40	4.5	Mk	5										
1952	12	17	4	40						GSHAP, Song	Peru: Satipo	秘鲁:萨蒂波	-11.25	-74.9	100	4.5	Mk	5										
1952	12	29	17	36	50					GSHAP	Turkmenistan: Asgabat	土库曼斯坦:阿什哈巴德	38.1	58	6	5	Ms	8.5										
1952	12	30	12	7						* Song	Costa Rica: La Paz	哥斯达黎加:拉巴斯	10.3	-83.5		5.8	Mk		29	1								
1953	1	1								China	China: Guangdong, Heyuan	中国:广东河源	23.8	114.7		4.75	Ms	6										
1953	1	2	11	23						GSHAP, Song	Peru: Bayóvar, Near Coast	秘鲁:巴约瓦尔近海	-6	-81.3		4.5	Mk	5										
1953	1	9	16	14						GSHAP, Song	Peru: Talara, Near Coast	秘鲁:塔拉拉近海	-4.4	-81.6	30	4.5	Mk	5										
1953	1	15	12	5						USGS	Hawaiian Islands	夏威夷群岛	19.32	-155.43	24	5.2	Ms	5										
1953	1	15	21	56						* Song	Iran: Bushehr	伊朗:布什尔	28.5	52.3		5.5	Mk		11	1								
1953	1	25	19	47						*	Haiti: Port - Au - Prince	海地:太子港	18.4	-73.4		5.7	Muk		2	1				2				
1953	2	12	0	16						GSHAP, Song	Peru: Ilo, Near Coast	秘鲁:伊洛近海	-17.5	-71.7	40	5	Mk	6										
1953	2	12	8	15	32					* Iran, GSHAP	Iran: Semnan	伊朗:塞姆南	35.39	54.88	13	6.9	Muk	8.5	970	3								
1953	2	15	8	8	24					GSHAP	Kyrgyzstan: Talas, SW.	吉尔吉斯斯坦:塔拉斯西南	42.2	71.8	16	4.8	Ms	6										
1953	2	15	9	32	25					GSHAP, Song	Peru: Lima, Near Coast	秘鲁:利马近海	-12	-77.5		5	Mk	6										
1953	2	15				2	0.7	-0.5		* NOAA	Peru: Lima, Near Coast	秘鲁:利马近海	-12	-77.5		5.5	Ms											
1953	3	7	5	25						GSHAP, Song	Peru: Lima	秘鲁:利马	-12.13	-76.87	20	4.5	Mk	5										
1953	3	8	3	5						GSHAP, Song	Peru: Zana	秘鲁:萨尼亚	-7.7	-79.6	30	4.5	Mk	5										
1953	3	11				5	0.1	-3.3	-1.8	Usami, Japan, NOAA, Song	Japan Trench	日本海沟	31.9	140		7	Mk											
1953	3	17	13	4		3	3	0.6		* NOAA	Kuril Islands	千岛群岛	50	156.5		5.8	Ms											

时间						海啸				资料来源	震中				深度	震级	标度	烈度	死亡人数		受伤人数		经济损失		房屋毁坏		房屋受损	
年	月	日	时	分	秒	源	浪高	级 I	级 S		地名(英文)	地名(中文)	纬度(°)	经度(°)					数量/人	级别	数量/人	级别	数量/$ Mill	级别	数量/间	级别	数量/间	级别
Date						Tsunami				Information	Earthquake Epicenter				Depth	Mag	Scale	MMI	Deaths		Injuries		Damage		Houses Destroyed		Houses Damaged	
Year	Mo	Dy	Hr	Mn	Sec	Sr	Wh	mI	mS		Name(English)	Name(Chinese)	Latitude	Longitude					Num	Dd	Num	Dd	$ Mill	De	Num	Dh	Num	Dh
1953	3	18	19	6	17					* Engdahl	Turkey: Yenice, Onon	土耳其:图穆鲁斯,森扁	40.12	27.621	15	7.2	Mw		1070	4			3.57	2				
1953	3	21	19	35	17					GSHAP	Bosnia: Banja Luka	波斯尼亚:巴尼亚卢卡	45.2	18.1	8	4.5	Ms	7										
1953	3	22	5	19						USGS	US: California, Woodfords	美国:加利福尼亚州伍德福兹	38.82	-119.98		5	Ms	5										
1953	3	30	22	16						GSHAP, Song	Peru: Apurimac	秘鲁:阿普里马克	-13.6	-72.6	20	5	Mk	6										
1953	4	5	14	29	48					GSHAP, Song	Peru: Chimbote, Near Coast	秘鲁:钦博特近海	-9	-79		4.5	Mk	5										
1953	4	14	23	45						GSHAP, Song	Peru: Pucallpa	秘鲁:普卡尔帕	-8.5	-74.4	200	4.5	Mk	5										
1953	4	15	7	46						GSHAP, Song	Peru: Moquegua	秘鲁:莫克瓜	-16.7	-71	120	4.5	Mk	5										
1953	4	17	0	2	50					GSHAP, Shi Z.	Peru: Loreto, SW.	秘鲁:洛雷托西南	-5.2	-77.2		6.1	Ms	6										
1953	4	23	14	18						GSHAP, Song	Peru: Satipo	秘鲁:萨蒂波	-11.25	-74.9	100	4.5	Mk	5										
1953	4	23	16	24	32	1				* Engdahl	Papua New Guinea: New Ireland	巴布亚新几内亚:新爱尔兰	-4.402	152.708	35	7.6	Mw											
1953	4	24	7	55						GSHAP, Song	Chile: Arica	智利:阿里卡	-18.2	-69.95	30	4.5	Mk	5										
1953	4	26	0	28						GSHAP, Song	Peru: Trujillo	秘鲁:特鲁希略	-7.3	-78.46	20	5	Mk	6										
1953	4	30	15	45	24					GSHAP	Azerbaijan: Qebele	阿塞拜疆:盖贝莱区	41	48.1	20	5	Ms	6										
1953	4									* Song	Iran: Fars	伊朗:法尔斯	29	52		5.8	Mk		1	1								
1953	5	2	23	50						GSHAP, Song	Peru: Torata	秘鲁:塔克纳	-17.2	-71.1	20	5	Mk	6										
1953	5	3	23	57	6					* China	China: Yunnan, Mile, SW.	中国:云南弥勒西南	24.2	103.2		5	Ms	7						1		2		
1953	5	6	17	16	48	2				* Engdahl, NOAA	Chile: Coelemu	智利:科埃莱穆	-37.254	-72.92	68.4	7.5	mB	10	9	1	26	1	500	5				
1953	5	12	12	39	6					USGS, Song	Andreanof Islands, Aleutian Is.	阿留申群岛,安德烈亚诺夫群岛	52.3	-177.3	96	6	Mk	5										
1953	5	17	2	33	54					GSHAP	Romania: Focsani	罗马尼亚:福克沙尼	45.3	27.3	140	5	Ms	5										
1953	5	20	16							China	China: Yunnan, Jianchuan	中国:云南剑川	26.5	99.9		5	Ms	6										
1953	5	25	3	24	1					USGS	US: California, Bakersfield	美国:加利福尼亚州贝克斯菲尔德	35	-119.02	16	4.8	Ms	5										
1953	5	26	1	43	12					GSHAP	Japan: SE. Hokkaido Island	日本:北海道东南	41.8	143	50	6.2	Ms	6.5										
1953	5	27	7	45						GSHAP	Peru: Mollendo, Near Coast	秘鲁:莫延多近海	-17.2	-72.3	30	4.5	Ms	5										
1953	5	28	20	49						GSHAP	Peru: Chimbote	秘鲁:钦博特	-9.3	-78.2	90	5	Ms	5										
1953	5	31	19	58	39	2	0.1	-3.3		* Engdahl, NOAA	Dominica: Puerto Plata	多米尼加:普拉塔港	19.8	-70.7	33	6.9	Ms											
1953	6	6	0	2	24					GSHAP	Iran: Kashmar	伊朗:卡什马尔	35.3	58.6	13	4.6	Ms	6.5										
1953	6	7	1	58	6					GSHAP	Russia: Sakhalin Island	俄罗斯:库页岛(萨哈林岛)	53.6	143	13	5.2	Ms	7										
1953	6	11	14	35	57					GSHAP	Colombia: Near Coast	哥伦比亚:近海	3	-79.5		4	Ms	5										
1953	6	14	4	17	30					USGS	US: California, Brawley	美国:加利福尼亚州布劳利	32.95	-115.72	16	5.5	Ms	7										
1953	6	14	4	29	58					USGS	US: California, Brawley	美国:加利福尼亚州布劳利	32.95	-115.72	16	4.8	Ms	5										
1953	6	17	14	8	36					GSHAP, Song	Peru: Nazca	秘鲁:纳斯卡	-15.6	-74.6	64	5	Mk	6										
1953	6	18	5	44						* Song	Greece: Didymoteicho	希腊:季季莫蒂霍	41.4	26.3		5.9	Mk		37	1				2				
1953	6	18	13	30						GSHAP, Song	Peru: Ica	秘鲁:伊卡	-14.3	-75.8	80	4.5	Mk	5										

年 Year	月 Mo	日 Dy	时 Hr	分 Mn	秒 Sec	海啸 Tsunami 源 Sr	浪高 Wh	级 I mI	级 S mS	资料来源 Information	震中 Earthquake Epicenter 地名(英文) Name(English)	地名(中文) Name(Chinese)	纬度(°) Latitude	经度(°) Longitude	深度 Depth	震级 Mag	标度 Scale	烈度 MMI	死亡人数 Deaths 数量/人 Num	级别 Dd	受伤人数 Injuries 数量/人 Num	级别 Dd	经济损失 Damage 数量/$ Mill	级别 De	房屋毁坏 Houses Destroyed 数量/间 Num	级别 Dh	房屋受损 Houses Damaged 数量/间 Num	级别 Dh
1953	6	30	1	15	10					GSHAP, Song	Peru: Perene	秘鲁:佩雷内	-11.5	-75.5		4.5	Mk	5										
1953	7	4	1	41						GSHAP, Song	Peru: Espinar	秘鲁:埃斯皮纳尔	-14.811	-71.251	130	4.5	Mk	5										
1953	7	18	4	25						GSHAP, Song	Peru: Arequipa	秘鲁:阿雷基帕	-16.63	-71.5	35	4.5	Mk	5										
1953	7	26	13	5	22					GSHAP, Song	Peru: Nazca	秘鲁:纳斯卡	-15	-75	60	5	Mk	6										
1953	7	28	1	30						GSHAP, Song	Peru: Piura	秘鲁:皮乌拉	-4.6	-80.6	80	4.5	Mk	5										
1953	7	28	9	38						GSHAP, Song	Peru: Sayán	秘鲁:萨扬	-10.547	-76.777	100	4.5	Mk	5										
1953	8	4	3	55						GSHAP, Song	Peru: Torata	秘鲁:塔克纳	-17.2	-71.4	70	4.5	Mk	5										
1953	8	8	16	50						USGS, Song	US: Idaho, Proctor	美国:爱达荷州普罗克托	47.9	-114		5.1	Mk	6										
1953	8	11	3	32	22					* Engdahl	Greece: Asprogerakas (Kephallenia)	希腊:坎发兰尼亚	38.1	20.6	33	6.8	Ms	9										
1953	8	12	9	23	55	2				* Engdahl, NOAA	Greece: Lixouri - Argostoli	希腊:利克苏里 - 阿尔戈斯托利	38.046	20.766	15	7.2	Mw	10	476	3	2412	4	100	5	27773	5		
1953	8	14	17	15						GSHAP, Song	Peru: Lima	秘鲁:利马	-11.9	-76.54	30	4.5	Mk	5										
1953	8	16	3	9	55					GSHAP, Song	Peru: Contamana	秘鲁:孔塔马纳	-7.1	-74.7	160	5	Mk	6										
1953	8	21	16	45	58					GSHAP	Colombia: Tulua	哥伦比亚:图卢阿	4.1	-76.7	96	4	Ms	5										
1953	8	22	5	47						USGS, Song	Hawaiian Islands	夏威夷群岛	19.75	-155.8		4.9	Mk	5										
1953	8	22	17	48						GSHAP, Song	Peru: Nazca	秘鲁:纳斯卡	-14.9	-75.1	80	4.5	Mk	5										
1953	8	29	6	30						GSHAP, Song	Venezuela: Trujillo	委内瑞拉:特鲁希略	9.35	-70.63		5	Mk	6										
1953	9	2	0	36	1					GSHAP	Azerbaijan: Gence, NE.	阿塞拜疆:占贾东北	41.1	47.4	5	4.9	Ms	7										
1953	9	9	15	51	14					GSHAP, Song	Indonesia: Northern Sumatera	印度尼西亚:苏门答腊北部	2	99		5	Mk	5										
1953	9	10	4	6		3				* NOAA	Cyprus: Nea Pafos (Paphos)	塞浦路斯:帕福斯	35	32.5		6.5	Ms	10	40	1				2				
1953	9	11	18	26	28					USGS	US: Missouri, St Louis	美国:密苏里州圣路易斯	38.8	-90.1		4	Ms	6										
1953	9	11	19	32						GSHAP, Song	Peru: Chincha Alta, Near Coast	秘鲁:上钦查近海	-13.6	-76.6	80	4.5	Mk	5										
1953	9	14	0	26	36	4	15	1	1	* Engdahl, NOAA	Fiji Islands	斐济群岛	-18.2	178.3	60	6.8	Muk		7	1	12	1		2		2		
1953	9	16	11	15	29					GSHAP	Azerbaijan: Gence, NE.	阿塞拜疆:占贾东北	41.2	47.4	28	4.8	Ms	5										
1953	9	26	3	34	29					USGS	US: Nevada, Reno	美国:内华达州雷诺	39.53	-119.98		5.3	Ms	6										
1953	9	29	4	39	43					GSHAP	Colombia: Uribia, Near Coast	哥伦比亚:乌里维亚近海	12.04	-72.66		4	Ms	5										
1953	10	7	14	59	21					USGS	US: California, Arvin	美国:加利福尼亚州阿尔文	35.03	-118.85	16	4.9	Ms	5										
1953	10	14	14	47	23					Engdahl, GSHAP	Japan: Hokkaido	日本:北海道	42.8	144.6	128	6.9	Ms	5										
1953	10	27	3	40	52					GSHAP, Shi Z.	Japan: Hokkaido	日本:北海道	42.7	145.5	45	6.2	Ms	6.5										
1953	11	2	7							GSHAP, Song	Peru: Apurimac	秘鲁:阿普里马克	-13.9	-72.3	20	4.5	Mk	5										
1953	11	5	8	21	38					GSHAP	Afghan: Badakhshan	阿富汗:巴达赫尚	36.5	70.6	200	5.8	Ms	5										

时间						海啸				资料来源	震中				深度	震级	标度	烈度	死亡人数		受伤人数		经济损失		房屋毁坏		房屋受损	
年	月	日	时	分	秒	源	浪高	级 I	级 S		地名(英文)	地名(中文)	纬度(°)	经度(°)					数量/人	级别	数量/人	级别	数量/$ Mill	级别	数量/间	级别	数量/间	级别
Date						Tsunami				Information	Earthquake Epicenter				Depth	Mag	Scale	MMI	Deaths		Injuries		Damage		Houses Destroyed		Houses Damaged	
Year	Mo	Dy	Hr	Mn	Sec	Sr	Wh	mI	mS		Name(English)	Name(Chinese)	Latitude	Longitude					Num	Dd	Num	Dd	$ Mill	De	Num	Dh	Num	Dh
1953	11	17	11	43	50					GSHAP	Russia:Chechnia,Grozny,S.	俄罗斯:车臣共和国格罗兹尼北部	43.1	45.9	16	4.5	Ms	5.5										
1953	11	18	5	50						GSHAP,Song	Peru:Chimbote,Near Coast	秘鲁:钦博特近海	-9.2	-78.9	40	5	Mk	6										
1953	11	24	3	48	50					GSHAP	Georgia:Kutaisi	格鲁吉亚:库塔伊西	42.7	43.3	32	4.7	Ms	5.5										
1953	11	25	17	48	56	4	3	1.5	1.5	* Usami, Engdahl, NOAA	Japan Trench	日本海沟	34.034	141.786	35	7.9	Mw		1	1				1				
1953	12	7	2	5	40					* Engdahl	Chile:Antofagasta,C.	智利:安托法加斯塔中部	-22.538	-68.845	107.9	7.2	mB		3	1			7.3	3				
1953	12	12	16	35	10					GSHAP,Song	Ecuador:Near Coast of W.	厄瓜多尔:西部近海	-3.5	-81		4.5	Mk	5										
1953	12	12	17	31	28	4	1	-1	0.5	*Engdahl,NOAA	Peru:Tumbes,Near Coast	秘鲁:通贝斯近海	-3.597	-80.847	19	7.5	Mw	9	6	1	20	1		2	200	3		
1953	12	15	12	44	36					USGS	US:California,Arvin	美国:加利福尼亚州阿尔文	35.22	-118.82	16	4.6	Ms	5										
1953	12	16	4	32	12					USGS	US:Oregon,Portland	美国:俄勒冈州波特兰	45.5	-122.7		5	Ms	6										
1953	12	16	21	52						GSHAP,Song	Peru:Arequipa	秘鲁:阿雷基帕	-16.66	-71.5	25	4.5	Mk	5										
1953	12	18	2	15						GSHAP,Song	Peru:Zana	秘鲁:萨尼亚	-6.5	-79.25	25	4.5	Mk	5										
1953	12	22	11	50						GSHAP,Song	Peru:Chimbote,Near Coast	秘鲁:钦博特近海	-8.9	-79	40	4.5	Mk	5										
1953	12	23	4	45	23					GSHAP	Colombia:Pasto	哥伦比亚:帕斯托	1	-77		6	Ms	8										
1953	12	28	8	39	40					GSHAP,Song	Ecuador:Near Coast of W.	厄瓜多尔:西部近海	-3	-81		4.5	Mk	5										
1954	1	2	3	25						USGS	US:Kentucky,Middlesboro	美国:肯塔基州米德尔斯伯勒	36.6	-83.7		4.3	Ms	6										
1954	1	7	7	25						USGS,Song	US:Pennsylvania,Reading	美国:宾西法尼亚州里丁	40.3	-76		5.1	Mk	6										
1954	1	8	18	50						GSHAP,Song	Peru:Chimbote,Near Coast	秘鲁:钦博特近海	-9.2	-78.9	40	4.5	Mk	5										
1954	1	9	2	8						GSHAP,Song	Peru:Lima	秘鲁:利马	-12	-76.5	90	4.5	Mk	5										
1954	1	12	23	33	49					USGS,Shi Z.	US:California,Bakersfield	美国:加利福尼亚州贝克斯菲尔德	35	-119.02	16	6	Ms	7										
1954	1	23	4	30						GSHAP,Song	Peru:Chimbote,Near Coast	秘鲁:钦博特近海	-9.2	-78.9	40	4.5	Mk	5										
1954	1	23	16	6	31					GSHAP	Tajikistan:Pamir Mountains	塔吉克斯坦:帕米尔山脉	37.4	72.5	8	5.8	Ms	8										
1954	1	27	14	19	48					USGS	US:California,Caliente	美国:加利福尼亚州卡连特	35.15	-118.63	16	5	Ms	5										
1954	1	29	4	40						GSHAP,Song	Ecuador:Near Coast of W.	厄瓜多尔:西部近海	-3.4	-80.6	30	4.5	Mk	5										
1954	2	5	15	17						*	Mexico:Chiapas	墨西哥:恰帕斯州	17.3	-92.6	100	6.2	Muk		6	1			17.0	3				
1954	2	5	18	40						GSHAP,Song	Peru:Pucallpa,SW.	秘鲁:普卡尔帕西南	-8.9	-75.7	30	4.5	Mk	5										
1954	2	7	20	57	56					China	China:Hubei,Chibi	中国:湖北赤壁	29.7	113.9		4.75	Ms	6										
1954	2	8	14	19	9					* GSHAP	Chile:La Higuera,E.	智利:拉伊格拉东部	-29	-70.5	150	7.7	Muk	6										
1954	2	10	23	58	38					USGS	US:California,Bakersfield	美国:加利福尼亚州贝克斯菲尔德	34.93	-119.07	16	4.5	Ms	5										
1954	2	11	0	30	21					* China, Engdahl, Dis	China:Gansu,Shandan,NE.	中国:甘肃山丹东北	39	101.3	35	7.1	Mw	10	47		332	3		3		3		
1954	2	12	10	8	46					GSHAP,Song	Peru:Torata	秘鲁:塔克纳	-17.5	-70	150	4.5	Mk	5										

年 Year	月 Mo	日 Dy	时 Hr	分 Mn	秒 Sec	源 Sr	浪高 Wh	级 I mI	级 S mS	资料来源 Information	地名(英文) Name(English)	地名(中文) Name(Chinese)	纬度(°) Latitude	经度(°) Longitude	深度 Depth	震级 Mag	标度 Scale	烈度 MMI	死亡人数 数量/人 Num	死亡人数 级别 Dd	受伤人数 数量/人 Num	受伤人数 级别 Dd	经济损失 数量/$ Mill	经济损失 级别 De	房屋毁坏 数量/间 Num	房屋毁坏 级别 Dh	房屋受损 数量/间 Num	房屋受损 级别 Dh
1954	2	16	1	18						GSHAP, Song	Peru: Lima, Near Coast	秘鲁:利马近海	-12.272	-77.913	40	4.5	Mk	5										
1954	2	21	20							USGS, Song	US: Pennsylvania, Wilkes - Barre	美国:宾西法尼亚州威尔克斯 - 巴里	41.2	-75.9		5.6	Mk	7										
1954	2	24	3	55						USGS, Song	US: Pennsylvania, Wilkes - Barre	美国:宾西法尼亚州威尔克斯 - 巴里	41.2	-75.9		5.1	Mk	6										
1954	2	26	18	46	17					GSHAP	Afghan: Badakhshan	阿富汗:巴达赫尚	36.8	71.3	120	6	Ms	6										
1954	2	28	18	9						*	Australia: Adelaide, S.	澳大利亚:阿得雷德南部	-34.9	138.7	4	5.4	Muk	8						2				
1954	3	3	20	46	8					USGS	Alaska Peninsula, S.	阿拉斯加半岛南部	61.54	-146.78	56	6.2	Ms	5										
1954	3	9	19	38	54					GSHAP	Colombia: Santander	哥伦比亚:桑坦德	7.5	-73.5	183	4.5	Ms	5										
1954	3	16	15	19	1					GSHAP, Song	Peru: Yanaoca	秘鲁:亚纳奥卡	-13.5	-71.25		4.5	Mk	5										
1954	3	18	7	17	14					GSHAP	Turkmenistan: Balkanabat	土库曼斯坦:巴尔坎纳巴德	39.9	54	18	4.5	Ms	5.5										
1954	3	19	9	54	29					USGS	US: California, Borrego Springs	美国:加利福尼亚州博雷戈斯普林斯	33.28	-116.18	16	6.2	Ms	6										
1954	3	21	23	42	16					* Engdahl	Myanmar: Sagaing	缅甸:实皆	24.42	95.104	186.1	7.4	mB							2				
1954	3	22	22	50						GSHAP, Song	Peru: Torata	秘鲁:塔克纳	-17.4	-70.5	30	4.5	Mk	5										
1954	3	23	4	14	50					USGS	US: California, Borrego Springs	美国:加利福尼亚州博雷戈斯普林斯	33.28	-116.18	16	5.1	Ms	5										
1954	3	27				4				NOAA, Song	Marshall Islands	马绍尔群岛	7.25	171.3		7	Mk											
1954	3	29	6	17	8					* Engdahl	Spain: Granada	西班牙:格拉纳达	37.032	-3.513	627.3	7.9	M							3				
1954	3	30	16	40	2					USGS	Hawaiian Islands	夏威夷群岛	19.38	-155.02	9	6	Ms	6										
1954	3	30	18	41	56					USGS	Hawaiian Islands	夏威夷群岛	19.35	-155.02	9	6.5	Ms	7										
1954	4	5	17	52	22					GSHAP, Song	Chile: Antofagasta, C.	智利:安托法加斯塔中部	-23	-67.5	150	5	Mk	6										
1954	4	8	4	18	4					GSHAP	Turkey: Tavas	土耳其:塔瓦斯	37.2	29.2	25	4.8	Ms	5										
1954	4	10	10	15	46					GSHAP	Panama: Off Coast of N.	巴拿马:北部沿海	10.5	-78		4.5	Ms	5										
1954	4	11	10	53	32					GSHAP	Afghan: Fayzabad	阿富汗:法扎巴德	36.6	70.6	200	6.4	Ms	5.5										
1954	4	20								*	Greece: Larissa	希腊:拉里萨	39.8	22.1		7	Muk		25	1								
1954	4	21	9	57	37					GSHAP	Russia: Chechnia, Grozny, S.	俄罗斯:车臣共和国格罗兹尼北部	42.8	45.8	18	4.9	Ms	6										
1954	4	21	20	23	5					GSHAP, Song	Peru: Mala, Near Coast	秘鲁:马拉近海	-13	-77	100	5	Mk	6										
1954	4	22	18	50	13					USGS	US: California, Watsonville	美国:加利福尼亚州沃森维尔	36.9	-121.68		4.3	Ms	6										
1954	4	25	3	57	6					GSHAP	Colombia: Bucarasica	哥伦比亚:北桑坦德的布卡拉西卡	8	-72.9		5	Ms	6										
1954	4	25	20	33	28					CGS, USGS	US: California, San Juan Bautista	美国:加利福尼亚州圣胡安包蒂斯塔	36.903	-121.61		5.6	Ms	8										
1954	4	26				4				* NOAA, Song	Marshall Islands	马绍尔群岛	7.25	171.3		7	Mk											
1954	4	30	13	2	40					* Engdahl	Greece: Sophades (Karditsa)	希腊:卡尔季察	39.187	22.239	25	6.8	Ms	10	31	1			3.15	2				

时间						海啸				资料来源	震中				深度	震级	标度	烈度	死亡人数		受伤人数		经济损失		房屋毁坏		房屋受损	
年	月	日	时	分	秒	源	浪高	级 I	级 S		地名(英文)	地名(中文)	纬度(°)	经度(°)					数量/人	级别	数量/人	级别	数量/$ Mill	级别	数量/间	级别	数量/间	级别
Date						Tsunami				Information	Earthquake Epicenter				Depth	Mag	Scale	MMI	Deaths		Injuries		Damage		Houses Destroyed		Houses Damaged	
Year	Mo	Dy	Hr	Mn	Sec	Sr	Wh	mI	mS		Name(English)	Name(Chinese)	Latitude	Longitude					Num	Dd	Num	Dd	$ Mill	De	Num	Dh	Num	Dh
1954	5	12	2	50						GSHAP, Song	Peru: Lima	秘鲁:利马	-12	-76.8	90	4.5	Mk	5										
1954	5	14	0	54	58					GSHAP	Colombia: Near Coast	哥伦比亚:近海	6.6	-78.9	40	4	Ms	5										
1954	5	15	13	2	14					USGS	US: Washington, Seattle	美国:华盛顿州西雅图	48	-122		5	Ms	6										
1954	5	18	5	11	5					GSHAP, Song	Peru: Perene	秘鲁:佩雷内	-10.5	-75.5		4.5	Mk	5										
1954	5	18	15	45						GSHAP, Song	Peru: Chimbote, Near Coast	秘鲁:钦博特近海	-9.2	-78.9	40	4.5	Mk	5										
1954	5	21	0	59						GSHAP, Song	Peru: Arequipa	秘鲁:阿雷基帕	-16.45	-71.75	25	5	Mk	6										
1954	5	25	0	20						GSHAP, Song	Peru: Arequipa	秘鲁:阿雷基帕	-16.25	-71.8	15	5	Mk	6										
1954	5	27	9	36						GSHAP, Song	Peru: Vegueta	秘鲁:贝格塔	-11.168	-77.251	50	4.5	Mk	5										
1954	5	29	18	30						GSHAP, Song	Peru: Arequipa	秘鲁:阿雷基帕	-16.25	-71.9	15	4.5	Mk	5										
1954	6	1	20	32	36					GSHAP, Song	Peru: Huancayo, E.	秘鲁:万卡约东部	-12	-74		5	Mk	6										
1954	6	2	2	15						GSHAP, Song	Peru: Apurimac	秘鲁:阿普里马克	-13.5	-72.7	25	4.5	Mk	5										
1954	6	10								* Song	Afghan: Sar - E Pol	阿富汗:萨尔普勒	36	66		7	Mk		2000	4								
1954	6	11	11	25	36					Turkey, GSHAP	Georgia: Akhalkalaki	格鲁吉亚:阿卡卡拉吉	41.4	44.1	33	5.5	Ms	7										
1954	6	12	7	54						GSHAP, Song	Peru: Arequipa	秘鲁:阿雷基帕	-16.65	-71.5	25	4.5	Mk	5										
1954	6	15	13	30	3					Engdahl, GSHAP	Peru: Loreto, SW.	秘鲁:洛雷托西南	-5.4	-76.7	128	6.7	Ms	6										
1954	6	17	1	8	39					* China	China: Anhui, Liuan	中国:安徽六安	31.6	116.6		5.25	Ms	6						1		1		
1954	6	23	8	30						GSHAP, Song	Ecuador: Morona Santiago, C.	厄瓜多尔:莫罗纳-圣地亚哥中部	-2.27	-78.11		4.5	Mk	5										
1954	6	24	15	25						GSHAP, Song	Peru: Tacna	秘鲁:塔克纳	-18	-69.8	120	4.5	Mk	5										
1954	7	2	2	45	9					* Engdahl	Philippines: Sorsogon	菲律宾:索索贡	13	123.9		6.8	Ms	9	22	1	101	3		2				
1954	7	3	21	52	35					USGS	Hawaiian Islands	夏威夷群岛	19.4	-155.2	12	5.4	Ms	6										
1954	7	6	11	13	20					*	US: Nevada, Fallon	美国:内华达州法伦	39.4	-118.5		6.8	Muk	9						2				
1954	7	6	22	7	41					USGS, Shi Z.	US: Nevada, Fallon	美国:内华达州法伦	39.3	-118.5		6.5	Ms	7										
1954	7	7	0	25	16					GSHAP	Norway: West of Lykling	挪威:吕克灵西部	59.7	4.9	54	5.1	Ms	5										
1954	7	8	9							GSHAP, Song	Peru: Caraz	秘鲁:卡拉斯	-8.44	-77.52	25	4.5	Mk	5										
1954	7	8	12	55	10					USGS	US: Nevada, Fallon	美国:内华达州法伦	39.42	-118.53		4.7	Ms	5										
1954	7	8	19	31	57					USGS	US: Nevada, Fallon	美国:内华达州法伦	39.42	-118.53		5.3	Ms	5										
1954	7	10	5	20						GSHAP, Song	Peru: Arequipa	秘鲁:阿雷基帕	-16.6	-71.6	15	5	Mk	6										
1954	7	10	22	56	55					GSHAP	Afghan: Badakhshan	阿富汗:巴达赫尚	36.8	71.2	200	6.1	Ms	5										
1954	7	13	21	54						GSHAP, Song	Peru: Arequipa. NW.	秘鲁:阿雷基帕西北	-15.9	-73.2	20	5	Mk	6										
1954	7	25	11	0	20					GSHAP	Venezuela: Machiques	委内瑞拉:马奇克斯	9.87	-72.71	25	4.3	Ms	5										
1954	7	31	0	59	57					* China, Engdahl	China: Inner Mongolia, Alxa Zuoqi, W.	中国:内蒙古阿拉善左旗西	38.8	104.2		7	Ms	9						2	542	3		
1954	7									GSHAP	Russia: Sakha, Artyk	俄罗斯:萨哈共和国阿尔特克	66	141	16	5	Ms	7										
1954	8	2	10	18	53					USGS	US: Nevada, Fallon	美国:内华达州法伦	39.42	-118.53		5.4	Ms	5										
1954	8	7	20	10						GSHAP, Song	Peru: Yanaoca	秘鲁:亚纳奥卡	-13.5	-71.2	15	4.5	Mk	5										
1954	8	12	11	36						GSHAP, Song	Peru: Perene	秘鲁:佩雷内	-10.3	-75.7	150	4.5	Mk	5										
1954	8	15	17	18	27					GSHAP	Colombia: Villavicencio	哥伦比亚:梅塔的比亚维森西奥	3.8	-74.1	40	4.5	Ms	5										

年 Year	月 Mo	日 Dy	时 Hr	分 Mn	秒 Sec	海啸 Tsunami 源 Sr	浪高 Wh	级 I mI	级 S mS	资料来源 Information	震中 Earthquake Epicenter 地名(英文) Name(English)	地名(中文) Name(Chinese)	纬度(°) Latitude	经度(°) Longitude	深度 Depth	震级 Mag	标度 Scale	烈度 MMI	死亡人数 Deaths 数量/人 Num	级别 Dd	受伤人数 Injuries 数量/人 Num	级别 Dd	经济损失 Damage 数量/$ Mill	级别 De	房屋毁坏 Houses Destroyed 数量/间 Num	级别 Dh	房屋受损 Houses Damaged 数量/间 Num	级别 Dh
1954	8	19	15	6	30					GSHAP,Song	Peru:Jaén	秘鲁:哈恩	-5	-79		4.5	Mk	5										
1954	8	20	15	30						*	Iran:Kangan,Akhtar	伊朗:坎根,阿赫塔尔	27.5	52		5	Muk		1	1				3				
1954	8	22	21	40						GSHAP,Song	Peru:Moquegua	秘鲁:莫克瓜	-16.7	-70.9	120	4.5	Mk	5										
1954	8	24	5	51	30					* Engdahl	US:Nevada,Stillwater	美国:内华达州斯蒂尔沃特	39.5	-118.3	0	6.6	M	12										
1954	8	26	13	48	3					USGS	US:California,Oxnard	美国:加利福尼亚州奥克斯纳德	33.92	-119.5	16	4.8	Ms	6										
1954	8	29	22	55						GSHAP,Song	Peru:Lima	秘鲁:利马	-12.1	-76.8	90	4.5	Mk	5										
1954	8	30	7	57	24					GSHAP	Kuril Islands	千岛群岛	43.9	147.7	60	6.3	Ms	6										
1954	8	31	22	20	32					USGS,Shi Z.	US:Nevada,Fallon,NE.	美国:内华达州法伦东北	39.58	-118.45		6.2	Ms	7										
1954	9	8	21	40	24					GSHAP	Colombia:Neiva	哥伦比亚:内瓦	3.2	-74.5		4	Ms	5										
1954	9	9	1	4	37	4	0.3			* Engdahl,NOAA	Algeria:El Asnam	阿尔及利亚:亚斯南	36.2	1.6	5	6.7	Ms	11	1243	4	5000	4	6.0	3	20000	5		
1954	9	9	2	52						*	Algeria:El Asnam	阿尔及利亚:亚斯南	36	1.5		6.7	Muk	11										
1954	9	9	4	50	13					GSHAP	Colombia:Bahia Solano	哥伦比亚:巴伊阿索拉诺	6	-77.6		4	Ms	5										
1954	9	9	9	28						* Song	Algeria:El Asnam	阿尔及利亚:亚斯南	36	1.5		6.2	Mk	10										
1954	9	15	6	38	4					GSHAP,Song	Peru:Talara,Near Coast	秘鲁:塔拉拉近海	-4.5	-82	60	4.5	Mk	5										
1954	9	16	5	55	25					GSHAP	Colombia:Aguachica	哥伦比亚:阿瓜奇卡	8.2	-73.5		4.5	Ms	5										
1954	9	17	4	28						GSHAP,Song	Peru:Arequipa	秘鲁:阿雷基帕	-16.5	-71.9	100	4.5	Mk	5										
1954	9	17	19	1	48					GSHAP	Colombia:Tame	哥伦比亚:塔梅	6.4	-71.59	2	5	Ms	6										
1954	9	20	14	34						GSHAP,Song	Peru:Lima	秘鲁:利马	-11.803	-77.362	40	4.5	Mk	5										
1954	10	3	11	18	47					USGS,Shi Z., Engdahl	Alaska Peninsula,S.	阿拉斯加半岛南部	60.7	-150.3	64	6.8	Ms	8										
1954	10	8	7	41						GSHAP,Song	Peru:Loreto,SW.	秘鲁:洛雷托西南	-5.95	-77	100	4.5	Mk	5										
1954	10	10	23	21	40					GSHAP	Colombia:Jurado,Near Coast	哥伦比亚:胡拉多近海	7	-78		4.5	Ms	5										
1954	10	13	22	11	43					GSHAP	Tadzhikistan:Khatlon	塔吉克斯坦:哈特隆州	37.4	69.3	11	5.1	Ms	7										
1954	10	16	19	48	48					GSHAP	Colombia:Bagado	哥伦比亚:乔科的巴加多	5.6	-76		4.5	Ms	5										
1954	10	22	22	47	29					GSHAP	Iran:Tabriz,N.	伊朗:大不里士北部	38.7	45.8	26	4.8	Ms	5										
1954	10	24	11	41	6					* China	China:Sichuan,Zigong	中国:四川自贡	29.4	104.8		5	Ms	7						1	67	2	538	3
1954	10	25	13	19	27					GSHAP	Iran:Qūchān	伊朗:古昌	37.6	58.2	19	4.9	Ms	6										
1954	10	30	23	43	29					Iran, GSHAP	Armenia:Idzhevan	亚美尼亚:伊杰万	40.5	45.25	6	6	Ms	7.5										
1954	10					2	18	4.2	4	NOAA,Song	Greenland Sea	格陵兰海	67.47	-32.283		8.1	Mk											
1954	11	1	21	9	58					GSHAP	Iran:Bojnurd	伊朗:博季努尔德	37.1	57.3	22	5.1	Ms	6										
1954	11	2	8	24	12					*	Indonesia:Sumba	印度尼西亚:萨姆巴	-8	119		6.8	Muk	8						1				
1954	11	10	18	7	21					USGS	US:California,Hopland	美国:加利福尼亚州霍普兰	39.07	-123.03		4.4	Ms	6										
1954	11	12	6	30						GSHAP,Song	Peru:Arequipa	秘鲁:阿雷基帕	-16.4	-71.8	30	4.5	Mk	5										

时间 Date						海啸 Tsunami				资料来源 Information	震中 Earthquake Epicenter				深度 Depth	震级 Mag	标度 Scale	烈度 MMI	死亡人数 Deaths		受伤人数 Injuries		经济损失 Damage		房屋毁坏 Houses Destroyed		房屋受损 Houses Damaged	
年 Year	月 Mo	日 Dy	时 Hr	分 Mn	秒 Sec	源 Sr	浪高 Wh	级 I mI	级 S mS		地名(英文) Name(English)	地名(中文) Name(Chinese)	纬度(°) Latitude	经度(°) Longitude					数量/人 Num	级别 Dd	数量/人 Num	级别 Dd	数量/$ Mill $ Mill	级别 De	数量/间 Num	级别 Dh	数量/间 Num	级别 Dh
1954	11	12	11	27	40					GSHAP	Russia:Karachaevo - Cherkess,Kurdzhinovo	俄罗斯:卡拉恰伊－切尔克斯州库尔吉诺沃	43.9	40.9	17	4.6	Ms	6										
1954	11	25	11	16	36					CGS,USGS,Shi Z.,Engdahl	US:California,Off Coast N.	美国:加利福尼亚州北部沿海	40.27	-125.63		6.7	Ms	5										
1954	12	3	21	38	16					GSHAP	Kyrgyzstan:Naryn,C.	吉尔吉斯斯坦:纳伦中部	41.4	74.8	15	5.4	Ms	7										
1954	12	4	18	31	12					GSHAP	Trinidad & Tobago:Northern Coast	特立尼达和多巴哥:北部近海	10.93	-61.43	53	6.5	Ms	8										
1954	12	4	22	5	18					GSHAP,Song	Trinidad & Tobago:Northern Coast	特立尼达和多巴哥:北部近海	10.9	-61.3		4.5	Mk	5										
1954	12	5	7	28						GSHAP,Song	Peru:Arequipa	秘鲁:阿雷基帕	-16.28	-71.7	30	4.5	Mk	5										
1954	12	6	4	45	10					GSHAP,Song	Trinidad & Tobago:Northern Coast	特立尼达和多巴哥:北部近海	10.9	-61.5		4.5	Mk	5										
1954	12	8	7	47						GSHAP,Song	Peru:Paramonga	秘鲁:帕拉蒙加	-10.762	-77.48	40	4.5	Mk	5										
1954	12	16	11	7	15					*USGS,Engdahl	US:Nevada,Fallon,E.	美国:内华达州法伦东部	39.3	-118.2	10	7.2	M	10										
1954	12	17	7	8	58					USGS	US:California,San Leandro	美国:加利福尼亚州圣莱安德罗	37.72	-122.13		4.5	Ms	6										
1954	12	17	11	24	26					GSHAP	Azerbaijan:Gence,NE.	阿塞拜疆:占贾东北	41.1	46.9	25	4.6	Ms	5										
1954	12	19	10	25						GSHAP,Song	Peru:Torata	秘鲁:塔克纳	-17.1	-71.15	30	4.5	Mk	5										
1954	12	21	19	56	24					USGS,Shi Z.	US:California,Eureka	美国:加利福尼亚州尤里卡	40.78	-124.17		6.6	Ms	7										
1954	12	26	8	15						GSHAP,Song	Peru:Santa Clara	秘鲁:圣克拉拉	-8.69	-77.25	20	4.5	Mk	5										
1954	12	28	17							GSHAP,Song	Peru:Arequipa	秘鲁:阿雷基帕	-16.5	-71.66	20	5	Mk	6										
1954	12	30	2	7	22					GSHAP	Greece:Thessalonika	希腊:萨罗尼加	40.6	22.7	9	4.6	Ms	6										
1954	12	30	9	16	13					USGS	US:California,Eureka	美国:加利福尼亚州尤里卡	40.78	-123.87		4.7	Ms	6										
1954	12	30	9	18	36					GSHAP	Russia:Lipeck,Ratchino	俄罗斯:利佩茨克州拉奇诺	53	40	15	4.8	Ms	6										
1955	1	3	18	41	57					GSHAP	Peru:Nazca	秘鲁:纳斯卡	-15	-75.4	64	5.9	Ms	5										
1955	1	5	8	20	40					USGS,Song	US:Nevada,Fallon,E.	美国:内华达州法伦东部	39	-118		4.9	Mk	5										
1955	1	8	3							GSHAP,Song	Peru:Espinar	秘鲁:埃斯皮纳尔	-14.4	-71.49	25	4.5	Mk	5										
1955	1	8	20	19						GSHAP,Song	Peru:Lima,Near Coast	秘鲁:利马近海	-12.586	-76.9	90	4.5	Mk	5										
1955	1	10	4	25	50					GSHAP	Afghan:Badakhshan	阿富汗:巴达赫尚	37.2	70.8	100	5.8	Ms	5.5										
1955	1	18				2				*NOAA	Panama:Off Coast of N.	巴拿马:北部沿海	9.7	-79.6		5.5	mb							1				
1955	1	22	16	19	1					GSHAP	Colombia:Riosucio	哥伦比亚:里奥苏西奥	7.6	-77.5	40	4	Ms	5										
1955	1	25	7	24	39					USGS	US:Missouri,New Madrid	美国:密苏里州新马德里	36.07	-89.83	8	4.4	Ms	6										
1955	1	25	12	23						*Song	US:California,Long Beach	美国:加利福尼亚州长滩	33.8	-118.2		5.9	Mk	4					3	2				

年 Year	月 Mo	日 Dy	时 Hr	分 Mn	秒 Sec	海啸 Tsunami 源 Sr	浪高 Wh	级 I mI	级 S mS	资料来源 Information	地名(英文) Name(English)	地名(中文) Name(Chinese)	纬度(°) Latitude	经度(°) Longitude	深度 Depth	震级 Mag	标度 Scale	烈度 MMI	死亡人数 Deaths 数量/人 Num	级别 Dd	受伤人数 Injuries 数量/人 Num	级别 Dd	经济损失 Damage 数量/$ Mill	级别 De	房屋毁坏 Houses Destroyed 数量/间 Num	级别 Dh	房屋受损 Houses Damaged 数量/间 Num	级别 Dh
1955	1	31	5	3	7					GSHAP	Brasil:Mato Grosso	巴西:马托格罗索	-12.42	-57.3		6.8	Ms	9										
1955	2	9	16	6						GSHAP,Song	Peru:Lima	秘鲁:利马	-12	-77		5	Mk	6										
1955	2	10	4	6	12					GSHAP,Song	Peru:Vegueta	秘鲁:贝格塔	-11.5	-77.5		5	Mk	6										
1955	2	18	22	48	33					*GSHAP,Song	Pakistan:Quetta	巴基斯坦:奎达	30.5	67		6.3	Mk	7	12	1		3		2				
1955	2	20	12	20						GSHAP,Song	Peru:Yanaoca	秘鲁:亚纳奥卡	-13.5	-71.2	15	4.5	Mk	5										
1955	2	26	18	19						GSHAP,Song	Peru:Chiclayo,Near Coast	秘鲁:奇克拉约近海	-7.194	-80.259	30	5	Mk	6										
1955	3	1	1	46	13					GSHAP	Brasil:Serra,Off Coast of E.	巴西:塞拉东部沿海	-19.84	-36.75	15	6.3	Ms	9										
1955	3	2	15	59	1					USGS	US:California,San Ardo	美国:加利福尼亚州圣阿多	36	-120.93		4.8	Ms	6										
1955	3	5	10	23	2					GSHAP	Afghan:Badakhshan	阿富汗:巴达赫尚	36.8	71.3	100	5.2	Ms	5										
1955	3	6	20	55	27					GSHAP	Tadzhikistan:Kuda La	塔吉克斯坦:库达拉	38.3	72.7	100	5.5	Ms	5										
1955	3	9	17	11	23					GSHAP,Song	Peru:Jaén	秘鲁:哈恩	-5	-79		5	Mk	6										
1955	3	15	6	25						GSHAP,Song	Peru:Chimbote,Near Coast	秘鲁:钦博特近海	-9.2	-78.9	40	4.5	Mk	5										
1955	3	28	2	2	20					USGS,Song	Hawaiian Islands	夏威夷群岛	19.4	-155.3		5.1	Mk	6										
1955	3	28	19	42	9					GSHAP	Georgia:Gori,N.	格鲁吉亚:哥里北部	42.4	44.9	9	4.5	Ms	6.5										
1955	3	31	18	17	12					*Shi Z.,Engdahl	Philippines:Mindanao,Lanao	菲律宾:棉兰老岛,拉瑙湖	7.386	122.878	54.2	7.7	Mw	8	400	3			5.0	3				
1955	4	1	14	24	26					USGS	Hawaiian Islands	夏威夷群岛	19.41	-155.3	10	5.2	Ms	5										
1955	4	4	19	24	5					*	Nicaragua:Chinandega	尼加拉瓜:奇南德加	13	-87		6.2	Muk							2				
1955	4	9	13	1	23					USGS	US:Illinois,Marissa	美国:伊利诺斯州马里萨	38.23	-89.79	11	4.3	Ms	6										
1955	4	9	15	21	41					GSHAP,Song	Peru:Pasco,W.	秘鲁:帕斯科东部	-10	-75	100	4.5	Mk	5										
1955	4	13	20	45						*Turkey	Greece:Kyparissia (Messinia)	希腊:麦锡尼	37.5	22		5.9	Ms							2				
1955	4	14	1	29	3					*China,Engdahl, Dis	China:Sichuan,Garze,SW.	中国:四川甘孜西南	30	101.8	10	7.5	Mw	10	84	1	224	3		2	600	3	500	3
1955	4	15	3	40	59					*China,Engdahl	China:Xinjiang,Ulugqat,W.	中国:新疆乌恰西	39.816	74.64	35	7.1	Mw	9						2		2		
1955	4	19	16	47	19	3				*Turkey,NOAA	Greece:Magnesia	希腊:马格尼西亚	39.3	23.1	33	6.3	Ms	10	8	1				3				
1955	4	19	20	24	6	4	1		1	*Engdahl,NOAA	Chile:Near Coast of C.	智利:中部近海	-30	-72	30	6.9	Ms	6	1	1				1		1		
1955	4	21	7	18						*	Aegean Sea	爱琴海	39.5	23		6	Muk	10	7	1				3				
1955	4	22	16	27	38					Engdahl,GSHAP	Kuril Islands	千岛群岛	46	150.5	128	6.7	Ms	5										
1955	4	24	12	59	12					*China	China:Xinjiang,Usu,SW.	中国:新疆乌苏西南	44.2	83.6		6.5	Ms							1		1		
1955	4	24	21	7	52					GSHAP	Colombia:Saravena	哥伦比亚:萨拉韦纳	6.86	-71.76		4	Ms	5										
1955	4	25	8	25	21					GSHAP	Colombia:Huila	哥伦比亚:乌伊拉	2	-75.5		4.5	Ms	6										
1955	5	1	21	22	52					GSHAP	Romania:Nehoiu	罗马尼亚:内霍尤	45.5	26.3	135	5.4	Ms	5										
1955	5	3	12	50	5					GSHAP,Song	Peru:Trujillo,Near Coast	秘鲁:特鲁希略近海	-8.5	-79.5		5	Mk	6										
1955	5	7	11	50	39					USGS	US:California,Kelseyville	美国:加利福尼亚州凯尔西维尔	38.93	-122.87		4.6	Ms	6										
1955	5	11	11	4	1					GSHAP,Engdahl	Ecuador:Napo,N.	厄瓜多尔:纳波北部	-0.2	-77.8		6.8	Muk	8										

时间						海啸				资料来源	震中				深度	震级	标度	烈度	死亡人数		受伤人数		经济损失		房屋毁坏		房屋受损	
年	月	日	时	分	秒	源	浪高	级 I	级 S		地名(英文)	地名(中文)	纬度(°)	经度(°)					数量/人	级别	数量/人	级别	数量/$ Mill	级别	数量/间	级别	数量/间	级别
Date						Tsunami				Information	Earthquake Epicenter				Depth	Mag	Scale	MMI	Deaths		Injuries		Damage		Houses Destroyed		Houses Damaged	
Year	Mo	Dy	Hr	Mn	Sec	Sr	Wh	mI	mS		Name(English)	Name(Chinese)	Latitude	Longitude					Num	Dd	Num	Dd	$ Mill	De	Num	Dh	Num	Dh
1955	5	14	13	35	43					GSHAP	Afghan:Badakhshan	阿富汗:巴达赫尚	36.7	70.9	200	5.7	Ms	5										
1955	5	17	14	49	55	2				*Engdahl,NOAA	India:Nicobar Islands	印度:尼科巴群岛	6.738	93.754	29.1	7.2	Mw											
1955	5	19	7	9						GSHAP,Song	Peru:Moquegua	秘鲁:莫克瓜	-16.8	-70.2	150	4.5	Mk	5										
1955	5	21	15	17	6					GSHAP,Song	Ecuador:Near Coast of W.	厄瓜多尔:西部近海	-3.5	-81.5		4.5	Mk	5										
1955	5	22	23	45	17					GSHAP,Song	Peru:Satipo	秘鲁:萨蒂波	-11	-74	100	6	Mk	7										
1955	5	26	21	18						China	China:Guizhou,Xingren,NW.	中国:贵州兴仁西北	25.5	105		5	Ms	6										
1955	5	28	6	20	41					GSHAP,Engdahl	Argentina:Cordoba	阿根廷:科尔多瓦	-30.8	-65.198	192	6.7	Ms	6										
1955	5	28	19	44	20					USGS	US:California,Ridgecrest	美国:加利福尼亚州里奇克雷斯特	35.53	-118.26	12	4.5	Ms	5										
1955	6	2	1	20						GSHAP,Song	Peru:Lima	秘鲁:利马	-12.8	-76.4	90	4.5	Mk	5										
1955	6	3	11	39	41					GSHAP	Norway:West of Kalvag	挪威:卡尔沃格西部	61.7	4.4	64	5.2	Ms	5										
1955	6	7	0	48	54					*China	China:Yunnan,Huaping,SW.	中国:云南华坪西南	26.5	101.1		6	Ms	8						3	4524	4		
1955	6	12	14	51						GSHAP,Song	Peru:Lima	秘鲁:利马	-11.73	-76.66	30	4.5	Mk	5										
1955	6	14	3	42	50					GSHAP	Colombia:Near Coast	哥伦比亚:近海	6	-78.5		4	Ms	5										
1955	6	20	2							GSHAP,Song	Peru:Cuzco	秘鲁:库斯科	-13.5	-72	20	5	Mk	6										
1955	6	21	21	35	7					GSHAP,Song	Peru:Chiclayo,Near Coast	秘鲁:奇克拉约近海	-7	-80.5		4.5	Mk	5										
1955	7	3	14	1	53					GSHAP	Afghan:Badakhshan	阿富汗:巴达赫尚	36.9	70.8	80	6.3	Ms	5.5										
1955	7	10	4	17	50					GSHAP	Greece:Edhessa, Kilkis	希腊:埃泽萨,基尔基斯	40.9	22.1	8	4.5	Ms	6										
1955	7	16	7	7	10					*Engdahl	Turkey:Soke, Aydin	土耳其:瑟凯,艾登	37.6	27.2		6.8	Ms	9	4	1				3				
1955	7	16	13	31	43					GSHAP	Peru:Lima,Near Coast	秘鲁:利马近海	-14	-78.5	50	5	Ms	6										
1955	7	19	8	47	38					GSHAP	Uzbekistan:Jazzakh	乌兹别克斯坦:吉扎克	39.7	68	14	5.2	Ms	7										
1955	7	20	21	1	43					*	Ecuador:Ibarra	厄瓜多尔:伊瓦拉	0.2	-78.4		6	Muk							3				
1955	7	21	11	45	40					GSHAP	Peru:Nazca	秘鲁:纳斯卡	-15.4	-74	60	6.8	Ms	6										
1955	7	27	1	20	51					Shi Z. ,Usami	Japan:Tokushima	日本:德岛	33.8	134.3	10	6	Ms		1	1								
1955	7	27	12	30						GSHAP,Song	Ecuador:Ibarra	厄瓜多尔:伊瓦拉	0.35	-78.35		4.5	Mk	5										
1955	7	31	6	45						GSHAP,Song	Ecuador:Ibarra	厄瓜多尔:伊瓦拉	0.2	-78.4		4.5	Mk	5										
1955	8	3	6	39	42					USGS,Song	US:Colorado,Lake City	美国:科罗拉多州莱克城	38	-107.3		5.1	Mk	6										
1955	8	5	10	20	50					GSHAP	Russia:Dagestan,Chirkey,E.	俄罗斯:达吉斯坦共和国奇尔克伊东部	43	47.2	9	4.8	Ms	6.5										
1955	8	7	17	17	44					USGS,Song	Hawaiian Islands	夏威夷群岛	20	-155.8	40	4.9	Mk	5										
1955	8	8	3	21	51					USGS	US:California,Caliente	美国:加利福尼亚州卡连特	35.4	-118.62	4	4.7	Ms	5										
1955	8	8	10	35	35					USGS	US:California,Benton	美国:加利福尼亚州本顿	38.33	-118.67		5.2	Ms	5										
1955	8	14	12	28						USGS	Hawaiian Islands	夏威夷群岛	19.31	-155.29	29	5.7	Ms	6										
1955	8	17	10	42	37					GSHAP,Song	Peru:Uchiza	秘鲁:乌奇萨	-8.5	-76	150	5	Mk	6										
1955	8	19	7	44	44					GSHAP,Song	Peru:Trujillo,Near Coast	秘鲁:特鲁希略近海	-8	-79.5	60	5	Mk	6										

时间 Date 年 Year	月 Mo	日 Dy	时 Hr	分 Mn	秒 Sec	海啸 Tsunami 源 Sr	浪高 Wh	级 I mI	级 S mS	资料来源 Information	震中 Earthquake Epicenter 地名(英文) Name(English)	地名(中文) Name(Chinese)	纬度(°) Latitude	经度(°) Longitude	深度 Depth	震级 Mag	标度 Scale	烈度 MMI	死亡人数 Deaths 数量/人 Num	级别 Dd	受伤人数 Injuries 数量/人 Num	级别 Dd	经济损失 Damage 数量/$ Mill $ Mill	级别 De	房屋毁坏 Houses Destroyed 数量/间 Num	级别 Dh	房屋受损 Houses Damaged 数量/间 Num	级别 Dh
1955	8	21	0	42	52					GSHAP	Tajikistan:Roghun	塔吉克斯坦:罗格汉	38.58	69.65	10	4.9	Ms	6.5										
1955	8	23	20	56	53					GSHAP	Russia:Chechnia,Grozny	俄罗斯:车臣共和国格罗兹尼	43.2	46.1	40	4.6	Ms	5										
1955	8	27	2	49						GSHAP,Song	Peru:Torata	秘鲁:塔克纳	-17.2	-70.9	25	5	Mk	6										
1955	8	29	8	6						GSHAP,Song	Peru:Lima	秘鲁:利马	-11.902	-75.862	120	4.5	Mk	5										
1955	9	1	17	33						*	Costa Rica:Cartago	哥斯达黎加:卡塔哥	10	-84.5		5.8	Muk		10	1				2				
1955	9	5	2	1	18					USGS	US:California,Morgan Hill	美国:加利福尼亚州莫干山	37.37	-121.78		5.5	Ms	7										
1955	9	5	11	46						GSHAP,Song	Peru:Lima,Near Coast	秘鲁:利马近海	-12.064	-77.525	40	4.5	Mk	5										
1955	9	8	3	27	16	3				*NOAA	Solomon Islands	所罗门群岛	-6.9	155.7	33	6.5	Ms											
1955	9	8	3	31	25					GSHAP	Colombia:Apartado	哥伦比亚:阿帕尔塔多	8	-77		5	Ms	6										
1955	9	12	2	52						GSHAP,Song	Peru:Pucallpa,SW.	秘鲁:普卡尔帕西南	-8.9	-75.7	30	4.5	Mk	5										
1955	9	12	6	9	24					*Turkey, Engdahl	Mediterranean Sea	地中海	32.2	29.6	33	6.7	Ms		22	1	12	1		3				
1955	9	13	22	15						GSHAP,Song	Peru:Lima	秘鲁:利马	-12	-76.5	30	4.5	Mk	5										
1955	9	19	23	58	51					GSHAP	Azerbaijan:Gence,NE.	阿塞拜疆:占贾东北	41.3	47.6	25	4.6	Ms	5										
1955	9	23	15	6	18					*China, Engdahl, Dis	China:Sichuan,Panzhihua	中国:四川攀枝花	26.6	101.8		6.9	Ms	9	602	1	1153	4	16.7	3	15000	5		
1955	9	28	1	46	40					China	China:Sichuan,Panzhihua	中国:四川攀枝花	26.5	101.8		5.5	Ms	7										
1955	10	1	6	29	55					*China	China:Sichuan,Garze,SW.	中国:四川甘孜西南	29.9	101.4		5.75	Ms	7						1		1		
1955	10	9	21	3						*GSHAP,Song	Peru:La Union Prov,Arequipa	秘鲁:拉乌尼翁,阿雷基帕	-16.2	-71.3	25	5.9	Mk	6	1	1				2				
1955	10	10	8	57	53	1				*Engdahl	New Britain Trench	新不列颠海沟[太平洋]	-5.1	152.924	35	7.3	Mw											
1955	10	15	4	31	15					GSHAP	Colombia:Bahia Solano	哥伦比亚:巴伊阿索拉诺	6	-77.5		5	Ms	6										
1955	10	17	3	52						GSHAP,Song	Peru:North Ica	秘鲁:伊卡北部	-13.5	-76.1	90	4.5	Mk	5										
1955	10	19	1	45						Usami,Japan	Japan:Akita	日本:秋田	40.3	140.2		5.7	Ms								1	1		1
1955	10	24	4	10	44					USGS	US:California,Concord	美国:加利福尼亚州康科德市	37.97	-122.05		5.4	Ms	7										
1955	10	24	15	6	51					GSHAP	Colombia:Tamara	哥伦比亚:塔马拉	5.8	-72.2		4	Ms	5										
1955	11	2	19	40	6					USGS	US:California,San Ardo	美国:加利福尼亚州圣阿多	36	-120.92		5.2	Ms	6										
1955	11	6	6	5						GSHAP,Song	Peru:Moquegua	秘鲁:莫克瓜	-16.7	-70.8	130	4.5	Mk	5										
1955	11	7	19	57						GSHAP,Song	Peru:Lima	秘鲁:利马	-12.1	-76.7	90	4.5	Mk	5										
1955	11	13	10	10						GSHAP,Song	Venezuela:Merida	委内瑞拉:梅里达	8.6	-71.69		5	Mk	6										
1955	11	18	3	57						GSHAP,Song	Peru:Lima,Near Coast	秘鲁:利马近海	-11.611	-78.088	40	4.5	Mk	5										
1955	12	6	0	53	59					GSHAP	Colombia:Hacari	哥伦比亚:北桑坦德的阿卡里	8.4	-73		4	Ms	5										
1955	12	10	20	24	16					GSHAP	Russia:Magadan,Poselok	俄罗斯:马加丹州波谢洛克村	64	152	12	5.2	Ms	7										
1955	12	14	12	52	12					GSHAP	Colombia:Near Coast	哥伦比亚:近海	6.3	-78.8		4	Ms	5										

时间						海啸				资料来源	震中				深度	震级	标度	烈度	死亡人数		受伤人数		经济损失		房屋毁坏		房屋受损	
年	月	日	时	分	秒	源	浪高	级 I	级 S		地名(英文)	地名(中文)	纬度(°)	经度(°)					数量/人	级别	数量/人	级别	数量/$ Mill	级别	数量/间	级别	数量/间	级别
Date						Tsunami				Information	Earthquake Epicenter				Depth	Mag	Scale	MMI	Deaths		Injuries		Damage		Houses Destroyed		Houses Damaged	
Year	Mo	Dy	Hr	Mn	Sec	Sr	Wh	mI	mS		Name(English)	Name(Chinese)	Latitude	Longitude					Num	Dd	Num	Dd	$ Mill	De	Num	Dh	Num	Dh
1955	12	14	20	50						GSHAP, Song	Peru: Talara, Near Coast	秘鲁:塔拉拉近海	-4.4	-81.6	30	4.5	Mk	5										
1955	12	14	20	52						GSHAP, Song	Peru: Talara, Near Coast	秘鲁:塔拉拉近海	-4.4	-84.6	30	4.5	Mk	5										
1955	12	17	6	7	29					USGS	US: California, Brawley	美国:加利福尼亚州布劳利	33	-115.5	16	5.4	Ms	7										
1955	12	20	13	42	10					GSHAP	Colombia: Narino	哥伦比亚:纳里尼奥	0.8	-77.7		4.5	Ms	5										
1955	12	25	18	43	29					GSHAP	Georgia: Zugdidi	格鲁吉亚:祖格迪迪	42.7	42.3	10	4.8	Ms	6.5										
1956	1	3	0	25	49					USGS	US: California, Los Angeles	美国:加利福尼亚州洛杉矶	33.72	-117.5	14	4.7	Ms	6										
1956	1	6	11	58	7					USGS	UA: Kansas, Wichita	美国:堪萨斯州威奇托	37.58	-98.35	29	4.4	Ms	6										
1956	1	8	7	11	26					*	Mexico: Guerrero, Acapulco, E.	墨西哥:格雷罗州阿卡普尔科东部	17	-99.5		6.5	Ms					3		3				
1956	1	8	20	54	22	2				Shi Z., Engdahl, NOAA	Chile: Arica, Near Coast	智利:阿里卡近海	-19.029	-70.671	51.9	6.7	Ms	5		1				1				
1956	1	12	5	46						*	Hungary: Budapest	匈牙利:布达佩斯	47.5	19.3		5.8	Muk		2	1				3				
1956	1	12	7	45	27					GSHAP	Colombia: Manizales	哥伦比亚:卡尔达斯的马尼萨莱斯	5	-75.5	200	4	Ms	5										
1956	1	16	23	37	46					* Engdahl	Ecuador: Portoviejo	厄瓜多尔:波托维耶霍	-0.825	-80.283	35	6.9	Ms	9						2				
1956	1	19	3	52	3					GSHAP	Colombia: Near Coast	哥伦比亚:近海	4.25	-78		4	Ms	5										
1956	1	22	22	32	22					GSHAP	Georgia: Gurdzhaani	格鲁吉亚:古祖尼	41.3	45.5	33	4.5	Ms	5										
1956	1	24								*	Nicaragua: Puerto Samoza	尼加拉瓜:波多黎各	12.2	-86.7		7.3	Muk							2				
1956	1	29	4	44	16					USGS	US: Missouri, New Madrid	美国:密苏里州新马德里	35.76	-89.8	16	4	Ms	6										
1956	1	29	9	45						GSHAP	Russia: Sakha, Altantsy	俄罗斯:萨哈共和国阿尔坦齐镇	61.5	131.5	12	4.8	Ms	6										
1956	1	31	2	25						* Italy	Slovenia: Ilirska Bistrica	斯洛文尼亚:伊利尔斯卡比斯特里察	45.5	14.3	7	5.1	Muk	7						2				
1956	2	7	3	16	39					USGS	US: California, Santa Clarita	美国:加利福尼亚州圣塔克拉利塔	34.59	-118.61	3	4.6	Ms	5										
1956	2	7	7	3	29					GSHAP	Colombia: Murindo	哥伦比亚:穆林多	6.68	-76.63	24	4	Ms	5										
1956	2	9	14	32	41					USGS, Engdahl	Mexico: Baja California	墨西哥:下加利福尼亚	31.75	-115.92	16	6.8	Ms	6										
1956	2	18	1	37	16					GSHAP, Song	Peru: Casma, Huaraz	秘鲁:卡斯马,安卡什(瓦拉斯)	-10	-79		4.5	Mk	5										
1956	2	18	17	48	40					GSHAP, Song	Peru: Trujillo, Near Coast	秘鲁:特鲁希略近海	-8.5	-79.5		5	Mk	6										
1956	2	20	20	31						*	Turkey: Eskisehir	土耳其:埃斯基城	40	30.5		5.8	Muk	8	4	1				2				
1956	2	23	6	4	42					GSHAP	Turkey: Eskisehir	土耳其:埃斯基城	39.9	30.5	14	4.5	Ms	6										
1956	3	5	23	29	46	4	0.4	-1.3	-1	* Shi Z., NOAA	Japan: Hokkaido	日本:北海道	44.3	144.1	20	6.4	Ms	7.5										
1956	3	8	7	26	20					USGS	US: Nevada, Fallon, E.	美国:内华达州法伦东部	39.03	-118.07		4.6	Ms	5										
1956	3	10	5	56	14					USGS	US: California, North Coast	美国:加利福尼亚州北部近海	40.3	-124.23		4.5	Ms	5										
1956	3	16	19	32	40					* Shi Z.	Lebanon: Litani	黎巴嫩:利塔尼河	35.5	35.5	6	6	Muk		148	3				3				

时间 年 Year	月 Mo	日 Dy	时 Hr	分 Mn	秒 Sec	海啸 源 Sr	浪高 Wh	级 I mI	级 S mS	资料来源 Information	地名(英文) Name(English)	地名(中文) Name(Chinese)	纬度(°) Latitude	经度(°) Longitude	深度 Depth	震级 Mag	标度 Scale	烈度 MMI	死亡人数 数量/人 Num	级别 Dd	受伤人数 数量/人 Num	级别 Dd	经济损失 数量/$ Mill	级别 De	房屋毁坏 数量/间 Num	级别 Dh	房屋受损 数量/间 Num	级别 Dh
1956	3	16	20	29	34					USGS	US:California,Landers	美国:加利福尼亚州兰德斯	34.31	-116.76	1	4.8	Ms	5										
1956	3	18	3	55	39					GSHAP	Azerbaijan:Qebele,SE.	阿塞拜疆:盖贝莱区东南	40.8	48.1	11	4.5	Ms	5.5										
1956	3	20	16	19	20					GSHAP	Azerbaijan:Quba,SW.	阿塞拜疆:库巴西南	41	48.3	11	4.5	Ms	5.5										
1956	3	21	4	54	48					GSHAP	Azerbaijan:Qebele,SE.	阿塞拜疆:盖贝莱区东南	40.92	48.39	8	5.3	Ms	7.5										
1956	3	22	6	34						GSHAP	Ecuador:Azuay	厄瓜多尔:阿苏艾	-3.3	-79	96	6.5	Ms	7										
1956	3	31	8	19	30					GSHAP	Colombia:Near Coast of W.	哥伦比亚:西部近海	3.5	-78.5	100	5	Ms	6										
1956	4	5	4	29	13					USGS	US:California,Pope Valley	美国:加利福尼亚州波普瓦利	38.53	-122.52		4.4	Ms	6										
1956	4	6	7	11	39					Engdahl,GSHAP	Afghan:Fayzabad	阿富汗:法扎巴德	36.392	70.781	212.3	6.8	Ms	7.5										
1956	4	9	2	15	40					GSHAP	Russia:Amur,Novopokrovka	俄罗斯:阿穆尔州新波克罗夫卡	49	130.5	20	5	Ms	6										
1956	4	11	1	45	10					GSHAP	Tadzhikistan:Garm	塔吉克斯坦:加尔姆	38.85	70.42	5	5	Ms	7										
1956	4	18	12	52	30					GSHAP	Romania:Feldioara	罗马尼亚:费尔迪瓦拉	46.1	27.4	22	4.9	Ms	5										
1956	4	19	18	38						* Song	Spain:Alhama,Malaga	西班牙:阿哈马,马拉加	37	-4		6.2	Mk		7	1				3				
1956	4	24	0	22	30					GSHAP	Colombia:Near Coast	哥伦比亚:近海	3.5	-79		4	Ms	5										
1956	4	30	12	14	21					GSHAP	Georgia:Gori,N.	格鲁吉亚:哥里北部	42.5	44.9	8	4.6	Ms	7										
1956	5	3	17	25	48					GSHAP	Kazakhstan:Almaty	哈萨克斯坦:阿拉木图	42.6	78.7	16	4.8	Ms	6										
1956	5	11	16	30	51					USGS	US:California,Landers	美国:加利福尼亚州兰德斯	34.23	-116.79	13	4.7	Ms	5										
1956	5	13	7	50	33					GSHAP	Pakistan:Multan	巴基斯坦:木尔坦	29.9	70		6.1	Ms	8										
1956	5	14	7	53	36					USGS	Hawaiian Islands	夏威夷群岛	20.28	-155.28	20	4.5	Ms	5										
1956	5	20				4				NOAA,Song	Marshall Islands	马绍尔群岛	7.25	171.3		7	Mk											
1956	5	27				4				NOAA,Song	Marshall Islands	马绍尔群岛	7.25	171.3		7	Mk											
1956	6	9	23	13	56					* GSHAP,Engdahl	Afghan:Bamyan	阿富汗:巴米扬	35.042	67.479	35	7.6	Mw		100	2								
1956	7	3	0	31	31					GSHAP	Colombia:Santander	哥伦比亚:桑坦德	7.41	-72.8	72	4.5	Ms	5										
1956	7	3	23	26	18					GSHAP	Afghan:Badakhshan	阿富汗:巴达赫尚	37	70.9	230	5.8	Ms	6										
1956	7	9	3	11	45	4	30	5	6	* Engdahl,NOAA	Greece:Amorgos	希腊:阿莫尔戈斯	36.617	26.026	35	7.8	Mw	9	56	2				3				
1956	7	9	3	24	8	3	10			* Engdahl,NOAA	Aegean Sea	爱琴海	36.508	25.956	35	6.9	Ms											
1956	7	10				4				NOAA,Song	Marshall Islands	马绍尔群岛	7.25	171.3		7	Mk											
1956	7	16	15	7	9					* Engdahl	Myanmar:Sagaing,S.	缅甸:实皆南部	21.969	95.802	32.1	7.1	Mw		38	1				2				
1956	7	20				4				NOAA,Song	Marshall Islands	马绍尔群岛	7.25	171.3		7	Mk											
1956	7	21	15	32						*	India:Anjar, Bhuj,Gandhidham	印度:安杰尔,普杰,甘地达姆	23	70		6.1	Muk	9	156	3				3				
1956	7	23	8	3	48					USGS	US:California,Greenfield	美国:加利福尼亚州格林菲尔德	36.3	-121.3		4.7	Ms	5										

年 Year	月 Mo	日 Dy	时 Hr	分 Mn	秒 Sec	源 Sr	浪高 Wh	级 I mI	级 S mS	资料来源 Information	地名(英文) Name(English)	地名(中文) Name(Chinese)	纬度(°) Latitude	经度(°) Longitude	深度 Depth	震级 Mag	标度 Scale	烈度 MMI	死亡人数 Deaths 数量/人 Num	死亡人数 Deaths 级别 Dd	受伤人数 Injuries 数量/人 Num	受伤人数 Injuries 级别 Dd	经济损失 Damage 数量/$ Mill	经济损失 Damage 级别 De	房屋毁坏 Houses Destroyed 数量/间 Num	房屋毁坏 Houses Destroyed 级别 Dh	房屋受损 Houses Damaged 数量/间 Num	房屋受损 Houses Damaged 级别 Dh
1956	7	26	9	53	17					USGS	US:Nevada,Fallon,NE.	美国:内华达州法伦东北	39. 55	-118. 45		5. 1	Ms	5										
1956	7	28	21	2	42					GSHAP	Russia:Perm,Berezovka	俄罗斯:彼尔姆州别列佐夫卡	57. 7	57. 6	15	4. 8	Ms	6										
1956	8	2	7	11	18					GSHAP	Colombia:Valle Del Cauca	哥伦比亚:考卡山谷	5. 13	-76. 22	103	4. 5	Ms	5										
1956	8	12	16	59	38	4		-1	-1	* NOAA	Japan:Mie,Near Coast	日本:三重近海	33. 8	138. 8	50	6. 5	Ms											
1956	8	19	0	44	33					* China	China:Shanxi,Pingding,E.	中国:山西平定东	37. 8	114		5	Ms	7						1	76	2	360	3
1956	8	23	13	48	26					GSHAP,Shi Z.	Bolivia:La Paz	玻利维亚:拉巴斯	-15. 27	-68. 67	33	6. 4	Ms	6										
1956	8	27	15	37	24					GSHAP	Russia:Dagestan,Buynaksk	俄罗斯:达吉斯坦共和国布伊纳克斯克	42. 9	47. 1	14	4. 6	Ms	5. 5										
1956	9	6	1	30	43					GSHAP	Colombia:Riosucio	哥伦比亚:乔科的里奥苏西奥	7. 5	-77		4. 5	Ms	5										
1956	9	7	13	35	51					USGS	US:Tennessee,Tazewell	美国:田纳西州塔兹韦尔	36. 44	-83. 79	5	4. 1	Ms	6										
1956	9	22	14	2	24					GSHAP	Tajikistan:Garm	塔吉克斯坦:加尔姆	38. 95	70. 51	4	4. 5	Ms	7. 5										
1956	9	22	15	54	21					GSHAP	Tadzhikistan:Khatlon,C.	塔吉克斯坦:哈特隆州中部	38	69	7	5. 8	Ms	7										
1956	9	29	21	20	55					Shi Z. ,Usami	Japan:Miyagi	日本:宫城	38	140. 5	20	6. 1	Ms		1	1								
1956	10	11	2	24	38					* Engdahl	Kuril Islands	千岛群岛	45. 967	150. 548	104. 8	7. 3	mB	7										
1956	10	11	16	48	50					USGS	US:California,Off Coast N.	美国:加利福尼亚州北部沿海	40. 67	-125. 77		6	Ms	5										
1956	10	13	5	4	43					GSHAP	Venezuela:Guanare	委内瑞拉:瓜纳里	9. 25	-69. 85		4. 4	Ms	6										
1956	10	16	10	44	55					USGS	Hawaiian Islands	夏威夷群岛	19. 67	-156. 47	25	5. 5	Ms	5										
1956	10	29	15	42	8					GSHAP	Peru:Pueblo Libre	秘鲁:普韦布洛利布雷	-8. 5	-77	60	6. 4	Ms	6										
1956	10	30	10	36	21					USGS	US:Oklahoma,Owasso	美国:奥克拉荷马州奥瓦索	36. 2	-95. 8		4	Ms	7										
1956	10	30	22	52	27					GSHAP	Colombia:Near Coast	哥伦比亚:近海	5	-79		4. 5	Ms	5										
1956	10	31	0	3	4					GSHAP	Colombia:Near Coast	哥伦比亚:近海	5	-79		4	Ms	5										
1956	10	31	14	3	50					* Engdahl	Iran:Hormozgan	伊朗:荷姆兹甘	27. 283	54. 405	35	6. 8	Ms		347	3				4				
1956	11	1	3	5						GSHAP,Song	Venezuela:Coro	委内瑞拉:科罗	11. 42	-69. 68		5	Mk	6										
1956	11	2	16	4	30	3	1. 2	0. 3	3	* Turkey,NOAA	Greece:Volos - Agria (Magnesia)	希腊:伏洛斯 - 阿格里	39. 5	23		5. 75	Ms	8		2								
1956	11	14	0	51	30					GSHAP	Afghan:Badakhshan	阿富汗:巴达赫尚	36. 7	70. 8	190	7	Ms	6										
1956	11	16	3	23	9					USGS	US:California,Parkfield	美国:加利福尼亚州帕克菲尔德	35. 95	-120. 47		5	Ms	6										
1956	11	16	11	54						GSHAP	Venezuela:El Palmar	委内瑞拉:埃尔帕尔马	8. 2	-71. 23	25	5	Ms	8										
1956	11	21	6	22	10					GSHAP	Russia:Sakhalin Island	俄罗斯:库页岛(萨哈林岛)	49. 1	141. 9	14	5	Ms	6. 5										
1956	11	23	4	46						GSHAP	Venezuela:Merida	委内瑞拉:梅里达	8. 3	-71. 2	12	5. 7	Ms	6										
1956	11	24								GSHAP,Song	Venezuela:El Palmar	委内瑞拉:埃尔帕尔马	8. 13	-71. 47		5	Mk	6										

时间						海啸				资料来源	震中				深度	震级	标度	烈度	死亡人数		受伤人数		经济损失		房屋毁坏		房屋受损	
年	月	日	时	分	秒	源	浪高	级 I	级 S		地名(英文)	地名(中文)	纬度(°)	经度(°)					数量/人	级别	数量/人	级别	数量/$ Mill	级别	数量/间	级别	数量/间	级别
Date						Tsunami				Information	Earthquake Epicenter				Depth	Mag	Scale	MMI	Deaths		Injuries		Damage		Houses Destroyed		Houses Damaged	
Year	Mo	Dy	Hr	Mn	Sec	Sr	Wh	mI	mS		Name(English)	Name(Chinese)	Latitude	Longitude					Num	Dd	Num	Dd	$ Mill	De	Num	Dh	Num	Dh
1956	11	26	4	12	43					USGS	US:Missouri,Poplar Bluff	美国:密苏里州波普勒布拉夫	36.91	-90.39	1	4.3	Ms	6										
1956	12	16	1	41	58					GSHAP	Colombia:Bahia Solano	哥伦比亚:巴伊阿索拉诺	6.33	-77.63	39	6.5	Ms	7										
1956	12	18	2	31	11	2				*NOAA,GSHAP,Shi Z.,Engdahl	Chile:Antofagasta,S.	智利:安托法加斯塔南部	-25.492	-70.182	43.7	6.9	Ms											
1956	12	31	17	37	45					USGS	US:California,Mammoth Lakes	美国:加利福尼亚州马姆莫斯湖	38.25	-118.93		5	Ms	6										
1956	12	31	17	39	24					USGS	US:California,Mammoth Lakes	美国:加利福尼亚州马姆莫斯湖	38.28	-118.97		5.1	Ms	6										
1956	12	31	21	33	22					*China	China:Hebei,Zhuolu	中国:河北涿鹿	40.5	115.5		5	Ms	6						1	3	1		
1957	1	4	12	36	10					GSHAP	Colombia:Near Coast	哥伦比亚:近海	7	-78		5	Ms	6										
1957	1	13	11	38	16					GSHAP	Tajikistan:Garm	塔吉克斯坦:加尔姆	38.77	70.55	15	5.2	Ms	7										
1957	1	24	20	54	50					USGS	US:California,Descanso	美国:加利福尼亚州德斯坎索	33.11	-116.52	4	4.6	Ms	5										
1957	1	26	1	16	6					USGS	US:Washington,Seattle	美国:华盛顿州西雅图	48.33	-122.43		5	Ms	6										
1957	1	26	16	30	48					GSHAP	Georgia:Zugdidi	格鲁吉亚:祖格迪迪	42.58	42.3	19	5.3	Ms	7										
1957	1	26	20	26	48					GSHAP	Georgia:Zugdidi	格鲁吉亚:祖格迪迪	42.6	42.3	12	4.5	Ms	6.5										
1957	1	28	21	1	40					GSHAP	Tajikistan:Roghun	塔吉克斯坦:罗格汉	38.45	69.3	6	4.5	Ms	6.5										
1957	1	29	15	17	28					GSHAP	Georgia:Zugdidi	格鲁吉亚:祖格迪迪	42.47	42.45	16	5.1	Ms	7										
1957	1	29	15	21	24					GSHAP	Georgia:Zugdidi	格鲁吉亚:祖格迪迪	42.5	42.4	9	5.3	Ms	8										
1957	1	29	21	19	53					USGS	US:California,Big Sur,Coast of W.	美国:加利福尼亚州大瑟尔西部近海	35.87	-122.12		4.9	Ms	5										
1957	2	1	7	52	15					USGS	US:California,Palm Springs	美国:加利福尼亚州棕泉	33.99	-116.34	11	4.6	Ms	5										
1957	2	6	20	34	58					GSHAP	Mongolia:Suhbaatar	蒙古:苏赫巴托尔	50	105.5	20	6.5	Ms	8										
1957	2	11	17	4	57					USGS,Song	US:Washington,Easton	美国:华盛顿州伊斯顿	47.53	-121.07		5.1	Mk	6										
1957	2	17	7	23						GSHAP	Turkmenistan:Lebap,E.	土库曼斯坦:列巴普东部	37.6	65.3	17	4.7	Ms	5.5										
1957	2	18	23	49	52					GSHAP	Peru:Lima,Near Coast	秘鲁:利马近海	-11.5	-78	100	6.6	Ms	6										
1957	2	20	4	41	1					*	Tunisia:Sidi Touil	突尼斯:西迪泰维	36.2	8.9		5.6	Ms		13	1	96	2		2				
1957	2	23	20	26	18					*China,Engdahl	China:Taiwan,Hualien	中国:台湾花莲	23.917	121.517	56.8	7.2	Mw		11	1		3		2				
1957	3	4	3	28	58					GSHAP	Kyrgyzstan:Osh	吉尔吉斯斯坦:奥什	40.5	72.3	16	4.7	Ms	6										
1957	3	8	12	21	16					*Engdahl	Greece:Magnesia	希腊:马格尼西亚	39.4	22.8	10	6.9	Ms	10	2	1		3		2				
1957	3	9	14	22	33	5	23	3.9	3.5	*Engdahl,USGS, NOAA	Andreanof Islands,Aleutian Is.	阿留申群岛,安德烈亚诺夫群岛	51.556	-175.392	30	9.1	M	8					5.0	3		1		
1957	3	18	18	56	28					USGS	US:California,Oxnard	美国:加利福尼亚州奥克斯纳德	34.12	-119.22	14	4.7	Ms	6										
1957	3	18	23	17	28					GSHAP	Black Sea	黑海	44.5	33	15	5.5	Ms	6.5										
1957	3	22	14	21	14					*Engdahl,USGS	Alaska:Unimak Island	阿拉斯加:乌尼马克岛	53.678	-165.681	45.2	7.1	Mw	5										

时间 年 Year	月 Mo	日 Dy	时 Hr	分 Mn	秒 Sec	海啸 Tsunami 源 Sr	浪高 Wh	级I mI	级S mS	资料来源 Information	震中 Earthquake Epicenter 地名(英文) Name(English)	地名(中文) Name(Chinese)	纬度(°) Latitude	经度(°) Longitude	深度 Depth	震级 Mag	标度 Scale	烈度 MMI	死亡人数 Deaths 数量/人 Num	级别 Dd	受伤人数 Injuries 数量/人 Num	级别 Dd	经济损失 Damage 数量/$ Mill $ Mill	级别 De	房屋毁坏 Houses Destroyed 数量/间 Num	级别 Dh	房屋受损 Houses Damaged 数量/间 Num	级别 Dh
1957	3	22	19	44	21					USGS	US: California, San Francisco	美国:加利福尼亚州旧金山	37.67	-122.48		5.3	Ms	7										
1957	3	23	8	13	48					USGS	US: California, San Francisco	美国:加利福尼亚州旧金山	37.7	-122.52		4.2	Ms	6										
1957	4	21	21	12	29					GSHAP, Shi Z., Engdahl	Colombia: Cubara	哥伦比亚:北桑坦德的库瓦拉	6.933	-72.066	16.3	7.1	Ms	8										
1957	4	22	13	43	20					GSHAP	Colombia: Cubara	哥伦比亚:北桑坦德的库瓦拉	6.99	-71.97	66	5	Ms	7										
1957	4	23	9	23	39					USGS	US: Alabama, Birmingham	美国:阿拉巴马州伯明翰	33.77	-86.72	5	4.1	Ms	6										
1957	4	23	17	57	17					GSHAP	Colombia: Saravena	哥伦比亚:阿劳卡的萨拉韦纳	6.97	-71.82		5	Ms	7										
1957	4	23								* Song	Iran: Esfahan	伊朗:伊斯法罕	33.4	52.5		5.8	Mk		16	1								
1957	4	24	19	10	15					* Engdahl	Greece: Dodecanese Islands	希腊:多德卡尼斯群岛	36.356	28.649	58.7	6.9	Ms							2				
1957	4	25	0	45	23					GSHAP	Iran: Qūchān	伊朗:古昌	37.3	58.4	15	4.5	Ms	6										
1957	4	25	2	25	44					* Engdahl	Turkey: Fethiye	土耳其:费特希耶	36.387	28.609	63.4	7	mB	10	18	1								
1957	4	25	21	57	39					USGS	US: California, Salton City	美国:加利福尼亚州索尔顿城	33.22	-115.81		5.2	Ms	7										
1957	4	26	11	40	9					USGS	US: Maine, Portland	美国:缅因州波特兰	43.53	-70.25	5	4.7	Ms	6										
1957	5	8	14	24	34					GSHAP	Kyrgyzstan: Naryn, C.	吉尔吉斯斯坦:纳伦中部	41.5	74.7	7	4.8	Ms	7										
1957	5	12	6	48	30					GSHAP	Russia: Sakhalin Island	俄罗斯:库页岛(萨哈林岛)	53.1	142.7	20	5.5	Ms	6.5										
1957	5	13	14	24	51					USGS	US: North Carolina, Marion	美国:北卡罗来纳州马里恩	35.8	-82.14	5	4	Ms	6										
1957	5	24	2	37	50					GSHAP	Colombia: Buenaventura	哥伦比亚:布埃纳文图拉	3.74	-76.77	60	6.7	Ms	8										
1957	5	26	6	33	35					* Shi Z., Engdahl	Turkey: Abant	土耳其:阿邦特	40.7	30.9	15	7.2	Mw	9	500	3				3				
1957	5	29	10	2	55					GSHAP	Iran: Orumiyeh	伊朗:乌尔米耶	38.3	45.1	21	4.6	Ms	5.5										
1957	5	31	21	57	48					GSHAP	Colombia: Buenaventura	哥伦比亚:布埃纳文图拉	3.66	-76.82	62	4	Ms	5										
1957	6	5	16	27	18					China	China: Shanxi, Yuci	中国:山西榆次	37.6	112.8		5	Ms	6										
1957	6	10	20	2	2					* China	China: Shanxi, Taiyuan	中国:山西太原	38	112.5		5	Ms	6						1	3	1	221	3
1957	6	21	0	41	25					USGS	US: California, June Lake	美国:加利福尼亚州琼莱克	37.7	-119.28		4.6	Ms	5										
1957	6	22	23	50	30	3	1.8	0.8		* Engdahl, NOAA	Indonesia: Papua	印度尼西亚:巴布亚	-1.5	137	35	7.3	Mw							3				
1957	6	26	19	5						GSHAP, Song	Venezuela: Lara	委内瑞拉:拉腊	10.3	-70.14		6	Mk	7										
1957	6	27	0	9	35					* Engdahl	Russia: Chita, Kuanda	俄罗斯:赤塔州库安达村镇	56.3	116.5	16	7.4	Mw	10	1200	4				2				
1957	7	2	0	42	29					* Engdahl, Iran	Iran: Mazanderan	伊朗:马赞德兰	36.09	52.701	35	7.1	Mw	9	1100	4				3				

年 Year	月 Mo	日 Dy	时 Hr	分 Mn	秒 Sec	源 Sr	浪高 Wh	级 I mI	级 S mS	资料来源 Information	地名(英文) Name(English)	地名(中文) Name(Chinese)	纬度(°) Latitude	经度(°) Longitude	深度 Depth	震级 Mag	标度 Scale	烈度 MMI	死亡人数 Deaths 数量/人 Num	死亡人数 Deaths 级别 Dd	受伤人数 Injuries 数量/人 Num	受伤人数 Injuries 级别 Dd	经济损失 Damage 数量/$ Mill	经济损失 Damage 级别 De	房屋毁坏 Houses Destroyed 数量/间 Num	房屋毁坏 Houses Destroyed 级别 Dh	房屋受损 Houses Damaged 数量/间 Num	房屋受损 Houses Damaged 级别 Dh
1957	7	28	8	40	10	4	1.3	1.3	0.5	* Engdahl, NOAA	Mexico: Acapulco, Mexico City	墨西哥:阿卡普尔科,墨西哥城	16.881	-99.297	37.2	7.8	Mw	7	65	2		3	25.0	4		3		
1957	7	29	13	15	19	2				* NOAA, Shi Z.	Chile: Mejillones, Near Coast	智利:梅希约内斯近海	-23.5	-71.5	33	7	Ms											
1957	8	8	13	50						GSHAP, Song	Peru: Mɑ́ncora, Near Coast	秘鲁:曼科拉近海	-4.279	-81.921	40	5	Mk	6										
1957	8	18	10	41	56					USGS	Hawaiian Islands	夏威夷群岛	21.8	-155.47	10	5.6	Ms	5										
1957	8	20	15	21	11					GSHAP	Afghan: Badakhshan	阿富汗:巴达赫尚	36.9	71	210	6	Ms	5										
1957	8	26	11	28	52					GSHAP, Shi Z.	Bolivia: Chuquisaca	玻利维亚:丘基萨卡	-18.74	-63.73	33	6.4	Ms	7										
1957	8	26	15	24	19					GSHAP	Colombia: Santander	哥伦比亚:桑坦德	6.97	-73.14	140	4.5	Ms	5										
1957	8	26	18	22	18					GSHAP	Bolivia: Santa Cruz de la Sierra, S.	玻利维亚:圣克鲁斯南部	-19	-63	33	6.2	Ms	5										
1957	8	30	16	18	1					GSHAP	Uzbekistan: Andizhan	乌兹别克斯坦:安第札	39.37	72.93	46	5.5	Ms	5.5										
1957	9	2	21	27	38					GSHAP	Afghan: Badakhshan, NE.	阿富汗:巴达赫尚东北	36.6	72	200	6.2	Ms	6										
1957	9	5								* Iran	Iran: Jahrom	伊朗:贾赫罗姆	28.2	53.7		5	Ms			3				3				
1957	9	7	1	10	36					GSHAP	Venezuela: El Palmar	委内瑞拉:埃尔帕尔马	8.24	-72.12	25	4.1	Ms	5										
1957	9	26				3	0.7	-0.5		* NOAA	Indonesia: Java Ridge	印度尼西亚:爪哇海岭	-8.2	107.3		5.5	Ms											
1957	10	3	6	39	9					GSHAP	Venezuela: Pilar	委内瑞拉:比拉尔	10.65	-62.82		4.6	Ms	5										
1957	10	4	5	26	7					GSHAP	Venezuela: Pilar	委内瑞拉:比拉尔	10.92	-62.81	32	6.8	Ms	9										
1957	10	5	22	40	46					GSHAP	Tadzhikistan: Khatlon	塔吉克斯坦:哈特隆州	37.6	69.4	50	5.2	Ms	5										
1957	10	6	0	54	9					GSHAP	Venezuela: Pilar	委内瑞拉:比拉尔	10.82	-62.79	35	5.1	Ms	7										
1957	10	10	1	30						GSHAP, Song	Venezuela: El Palmar	委内瑞拉:埃尔帕尔马	8.19	-72.23		5	Mk	6										
1957	10	14	8	17	34					GSHAP	Venezuela: Pilar	委内瑞拉:比拉尔	11.02	-62.97		4	Ms	5										
1957	10	24	20	7	21					GSHAP	Argentina: La Rioja	阿根廷:拉里奥哈	-28.9	-68	37	6	Ms	7										
1957	10	26	14	17	9	2	0.7	-0.5		* Shi Z., NOAA	Indonesia: Makassar Strait	印度尼西亚:望加锡海峡	-2	116	87	6.4	Ms											
1957	10	31	2	47	46					USGS	US: California, Cape Horn	美国:加利福尼亚州凯普霍恩	39.18	-123.68		4.7	Ms	5										
1957	11	10	2	36	25	2	2.7	1.4	2	* NOAA, Shi Z.	Solomon Islands	所罗门群岛	-7.2	155.6		6.5	Ms											
1957	11	10	10	21	20					GSHAP	Colombia: Antioquia	哥伦比亚:安提奥基亚	7.88	-74.48	52	5	Ms	7										
1957	11	10	19	20	6					Shi Z., Usami	Japan: Miyake Jima	日本:三宅岛	34.2	139.4		6.3	Ms								2	1		
1957	11	17	6	0	29					USGS	US: Oregon, Tillamook	美国:俄勒冈州蒂拉穆克	45.3	-123.8		4	Ms	6										
1957	11	27	3	22	17					GSHAP	Colombia: Bucaramanga	哥伦比亚:布卡拉曼加	7.03	-73.21	129	4.5	Ms	5										
1957	11	29	22	19	43					* Engdahl	Bolivia: Tupiza	玻利维亚:图皮萨	-20.402	-67.307	156.9	7.4	mB							1				
1957	12	4	3	37	52					* Engdahl	Mongolia: Boon Tsagaan Nuur, S.	蒙古:本查干湖南部	45.153	99.206	35	8.1	M	11	30	1				2				
1957	12	13	1	31	58					Engdahl, GSHAP	Colombia: Murindo	哥伦比亚:穆林多	6.72	-76.82	51.1	6.7	Ms	8										
1957	12	13	1	45	6					* Engdahl, Iran	Iran: Kermanshah	伊朗:克尔曼沙赫	34.278	47.712	35	6.8	Ms		1200	4				3				
1957	12	18	2	11	40					GSHAP	Venezuela: Pilar	委内瑞拉:比拉尔	11.068	-62.848	10	4.5	Ms	5										
1957	12	19	6	25						USGS, Song	US: Idaho, Murray	美国:爱达荷州默里	47.5	-116		5.1	Mk	6										

时间 年 Date Year	月 Mo	日 Dy	时 Hr	分 Mn	秒 Sec	海啸 Tsunami 源 Sr	浪高 Wh	级 I mI	级 S mS	资料来源 Information	震中 Earthquake Epicenter 地名(英文) Name(English)	地名(中文) Name(Chinese)	纬度(°) Latitude	经度(°) Longitude	深度 Depth	震级 Mag	标度 Scale	烈度 MMI	死亡人数 Deaths 数量/人 Num	级别 Dd	受伤人数 Injuries 数量/人 Num	级别 Dd	经济损失 Damage 数量/$ Mill	级别 De	房屋毁坏 Houses Destroyed 数量/间 Num	级别 Dh	房屋受损 Houses Damaged 数量/间 Num	级别 Dh
1958	1	2	22	35	35					GSHAP	Trinidad & Tobago: Northern Coast	特立尼达和多巴哥:北部近海	11.299	-60.743	35	4.5	Ms	6										
1958	1	5	11	30	48					GSHAP	Russia: Sakha, SW.	俄罗斯:萨哈共和国西南	56.7	121.2	14	6.5	Ms	9										
1958	1	6	1	54	37					GSHAP	Afghan: Badakhshan	阿富汗:巴达赫尚	37	71	70	5.8	Ms	5.5										
1958	1	6	16	53						GSHAP	Bolivia: Sucre	玻利维亚:苏克雷	-18.31	-64.67		5.2	Ms	6										
1958	1	13	20	28	43					GSHAP	Kyrgyzstan: Kara Mack	吉尔吉斯斯坦:卡拉梅克	39.5	71.8	20	5.4	Ms	6										
1958	1	15	19	14	31					* Engdahl	Peru: Arequipa	秘鲁:阿雷基帕	-16.779	-72.503	68.6	7	mB	9	28	1				2				
1958	1	16	2	4						* Song	Iran: Mazanderan	伊朗:马赞德兰	36.5	53		6.4	Mk			3				2				
1958	1	19	14	7	27	4			2	* Shi Z., Engdahl, NOAA	Colombia: Near Coast	哥伦比亚:近海	1.5	-79.5	60	7.8	Mw	9	115	3	46	1		2		2		
1958	1	23	13	35	4					GSHAP	Norwegian Sea	挪威海	65	6.5	48	5.3	Ms	6										
1958	1	24	5	54	1					GSHAP	Russia: Kamchatka, Near East Coast	俄罗斯:堪察加东部近海	56	164	60	6.6	Ms	7										
1958	1	24	13	50						GSHAP	Ecuador: Cotopaxi	厄瓜多尔:科托帕希	-0.93	-78.61		5	Ms	6										
1958	2	1	14	9						* Song	Colombia: Near Coast	哥伦比亚:近海	2	-79		7	Mk	10	22	1				3				
1958	2	1	18	2	39					GSHAP	Colombia: Near Coast	哥伦比亚:近海	1.76	-79.16		6.5	Ms	8										
1958	2	1	20	45	52					GSHAP	Colombia: Near Coast	哥伦比亚:近海	1.66	-79.19	46	6.7	Ms	8										
1958	2	2	2	34	59					GSHAP	Ecuador: Near Coast of W.	厄瓜多尔:西部近海	1.57	-79.28		5	Ms	6										
1958	2	2	8	16	20					GSHAP	Colombia: Off Coast of W.	哥伦比亚:西部沿海	2	-80		5	Ms	6										
1958	2	2	8	49	15					GSHAP	Colombia: Near Coast	哥伦比亚:近海	1.62	-79.26		5.5	Ms	7										
1958	2	3	14	2	16					GSHAP	Colombia: Bahia Solano	哥伦比亚:巴伊阿索拉诺	7	-77.5		4.5	Ms	5										
1958	2	7	23	23	37					* Engdahl, China	China: Sichuan, Maoxian	中国:四川茂县	31.577	103.912	14.2	6.8	Ms	7						1		1		
1958	2	9	2	30	58					GSHAP	Colombia: Ibagué	哥伦比亚:托利马的伊瓦格	4.8	-75.3	32	4.5	Ms	5										
1958	2	13	22	52						USGS, Song	US: Utah, Huntington	美国:犹他州亨廷顿	40.5	-111.5		5.1	Mk	6										
1958	2	17	5	18	42					GSHAP	Afghan: Badakhshan	阿富汗:巴达赫尚	36.5	70.6	180	6.6	Ms	6										
1958	2	21	13	47	10					GSHAP	Ecuador: Near Coast of W.	厄瓜多尔:西部近海	1.5	-80		4	Ms	5										
1958	2	21	19	30						GSHAP, Song	Venezuela: Anaco	委内瑞拉:阿纳科	9.45	-64.84		5	Mk	6										
1958	3	1	9	5	40					GSHAP	Peru: Chincha Alta, Near Coast	秘鲁:上钦查近海	-13.5	-76.5		7	Ms	6										
1958	3	3	16	18	23					GSHAP, Shi Z.	Russia: Komandorsky Islands	俄罗斯:科曼多尔群岛	55.5	166	40	6.4	Ms	6.5										
1958	3	3	17	13	14					GSHAP	Colombia: Suaita	哥伦比亚:苏艾塔	6	-73.5	150	5	Ms	6										
1958	3	6	5	47	21					GSHAP	Colombia: Bucaramanga	哥伦比亚:布卡拉曼加	7.01	-73.11	149	4.5	Ms	6										
1958	3	11	0	22	56					*	Ryukyu Islands	琉球群岛	25	125	70	7.5	Ms			2		3						
1958	3	17	4	10	12					GSHAP	Colombia: Guican	哥伦比亚:圭坎	6.5	-72.5		4	Ms	5										
1958	3	28	4	9	37					GSHAP	Afghan: Badakhshan	阿富汗:巴达赫尚	36.6	70.9	210	5.8	Ms	5										
1958	3	28	12	6	26					Engdahl, GSHAP	Afghan: Badakhshan	阿富汗:巴达赫尚	36.543	70.996	183.6	6.8	Ms	6										

时间 Date						海啸 Tsunami				资料来源	震中 Earthquake Epicenter				深度	震级	标度	烈度	死亡人数 Deaths		受伤人数 Injuries		经济损失 Damage		房屋毁坏 Houses Destroyed		房屋受损 Houses Damaged	
年	月	日	时	分	秒	源	浪高	级 I	级 S		地名(英文)	地名(中文)	纬度(°)	经度(°)					数量/人	级别	数量/人	级别	数量/$ Mill	级别	数量/间	级别	数量/间	级别
Year	Mo	Dy	Hr	Mn	Sec	Sr	Wh	mI	mS	Information	Name(English)	Name(Chinese)	Latitude	Longitude	Depth	Mag	Scale	MMI	Num	Dd	Num	Dd	$ Mill	De	Num	Dh	Num	Dh
1958	3	30	14	23	20					GSHAP	Colombia:Buenaventura	哥伦比亚:布埃纳文图拉	4	-77	60	4.5	Ms	5										
1958	4	3	8	25	44					GSHAP	Ecuador:Esmeraldas	厄瓜多尔:埃斯梅拉达斯	1.38	-79.5		4.5	Ms	5										
1958	4	4	9	18	50					GSHAP	Hungary:Kiskunhalas	匈牙利:基斯孔哈拉斯	46.3	19.5	15	4.7	Ms	6										
1958	4	7	15	30	47					Engdahl, USGS	Alaska Peninsula, C.	阿拉斯加半岛中部	65.823	-156.243	35	7.3	M	8										
1958	4	8	4	35	21					GSHAP	Colombia:Bucaramanga	哥伦比亚:布卡拉曼加	7	-73	54	5	Ms	6										
1958	4	9	6	15	12					USGS	Gulf of Alaska, SE.	阿拉斯加湾东南	56.14	-139.23		5.5	Ms	5										
1958	4	12	22	37	11					USGS	US:Washington, Methow	美国:华盛顿州梅特豪	48	-120		4.1	Ms	6										
1958	4	13	9	7	25					USGS	Alaska Peninsula, C.	阿拉斯加半岛中部	65.83	-155.55		6.7	Ms	5										
1958	4	13	12	29	14					GSHAP, Shi Z., Engdahl	Russia:Kamchatka Peninsula	俄罗斯:堪察加半岛	52.918	160.801	35	6.7	Ms	8.5										
1958	4	16	8	17	18					GSHAP	Colombia:Valle Del Cauca	哥伦比亚:考卡山谷	5	-77		4	Ms	5										
1958	4	19	9	1	2					USGS, Song	US:Nevada, Las Vegas	美国:内华达州拉斯维加斯	36	-114.8		5.1	Mk	6										
1958	4	21	22	37	38	2			0.5	* Shi Z., NOAA	Indonesia:Southern Sumatra	印度尼西亚:苏门答腊南部	-4.4	104.2	161	6.7	Ms											
1958	4	22	10	2	43					GSHAP	Mediterranean Sea	地中海	36.5	30.4	80	5.3	Ms	5.5										
1958	5	4	1	36	22					GSHAP	Colombia:Gacheta	哥伦比亚:昆地那马加的加切塔	4.7	-73.7	40	4	Ms	5										
1958	5	10	22	54	40					USGS	Alaska Peninsula, C.	阿拉斯加半岛中部	65.12	-152.09		6.3	Ms	5										
1958	5	11	5	23	56					USGS	Alaska Peninsula, C.	阿拉斯加半岛中部	65.01	-151.97		6.3	Ms	5										
1958	5	14	2	34						* Song	Azores Islands	亚速尔群岛	38.5	-28.8		5.9	Mk							2				
1958	5	22	1	28	36					GSHAP	Colombia:Chocontá	哥伦比亚:昆地那马加的乔孔塔	5.2	-73.7	9	4	Ms	5										
1958	5	24	23	4	47					USGS	US:California, Humboldt	美国:加利福尼亚州洪堡	40.3	-124.05		4.9	Ms	5										
1958	5	25	21	11	42					GSHAP	Ecuador:Morona Santiago	厄瓜多尔:莫罗纳－圣地亚哥	-3.12	-78.09	100	6.5	Ms	7										
1958	5	28	16	45	54					USGS	US:Montana, Sheridan	美国:蒙大纳州谢立丹	46.5	-113		4.4	Ms	6										
1958	5	31	3	50	7					GSHAP	Georgia:Akhalkalaki	格鲁吉亚:阿卡卡垃吉	41.4	43.9	17	4.7	Ms	6.5										
1958	5	31	9	31	15					GSHAP	Georgia:Akhalkalaki	格鲁吉亚:阿卡卡垃吉	41.3	44	15	4.5	Ms	6.5										
1958	6	10	20	21	16					GSHAP	Colombia:Near Coast	哥伦比亚:近海	5.6	-79.5	87	4.5	Ms	6										
1958	6	23	5	10	4					GSHAP	Mongolia:West Bulgan	蒙古:布尔干西部	48.7	102.9	15	6.2	Ms	8										
1958	7	5	2	5	57					GSHAP	Georgia:Zugdidi	格鲁吉亚:祖格迪迪	42.7	41.65	6	4.6	Ms	7										
1958	7	10	6	15	60	4	53	4.6	5	* Engdahl, NOAA	Alaska:Lituya Bay	阿拉斯加:立图亚湾	58.37	-136.665	35	7.3	M	11	5	1			0.1	1		1		
1958	7	14	5	25	55					USGS	US:California, Santa Barbara	美国:加利福尼亚州圣巴巴拉	34.35	-119.49	16	4.7	Ms	5										
1958	7	26	17	37	14					* Engdahl	Peru:Puno, N.	秘鲁:普诺北部	-13.238	-69.389	611.7	7.2	mB							1				
1958	8	6	17	16	10					GSHAP	Norway:Etne	挪威:埃特讷	59.6	6.1	43	5	Ms	5										
1958	8	15	6	20	52					GSHAP	Colombia:Bucaramanga	哥伦比亚:布卡拉曼加	6.81	-72.98	159	5	Ms	6										

时间						海啸				资料来源	震中				深度	震级	标度	烈度	死亡人数		受伤人数		经济损失		房屋毁坏		房屋受损	
年	月	日	时	分	秒	源	浪高	级 I	级 S		地名(英文)	地名(中文)	纬度(°)	经度(°)					数量/人	级别	数量/人	级别	数量/$ Mill	级别	数量/间	级别	数量/间	级别
Date						Tsunami				Information	Earthquake Epicenter				Depth	Mag	Scale	MMI	Deaths		Injuries		Damage		Houses Destroyed		Houses Damaged	
Year	Mo	Dy	Hr	Mn	Sec	Sr	Wh	mI	mS		Name(English)	Name(Chinese)	Latitude	Longitude					Num	Dd	Num	Dd	$ Mill	De	Num	Dh	Num	Dh
1958	8	15	19	55	44					GSHAP, Shi Z., Engdahl	Russia: Kamchatka, Near East Coast	俄罗斯:堪察加东部近海	53.51	160.253	46.1	6.8	Ms	9										
1958	8	16	19	13	51					* Engdahl	Iran: Hamadan	伊朗:哈马丹	34.259	47.869	35	6.7	Ms		132	3				3				
1958	8	18	10	16	39					GSHAP	Colombia: Jurado	哥伦比亚:胡拉多	7.36	-77.66		4	Ms	5										
1958	8	30	17	56	9					GSHAP	Colombia: Bolivar	哥伦比亚:波利瓦尔	7.3	-74.3	40	4	Ms	5										
1958	9	1	14	40	55					* GSHAP	Bolivia: Cochabamba	玻利维亚:科恰班巴	-18	-65		5.2	Ms	7	4	1				4				
1958	9	2	12	44	47					GSHAP	Georgia: Akhalkalaki	格鲁吉亚:阿卡卡垃吉	41.2	44	5	4.5	Ms	5.5										
1958	9	4	21	51	17					* Engdahl	Argentina: Tunuyán	阿根廷:图努扬	-33.785	-70.112	35	6.8	Ms		7	1				3				
1958	9	6	7	32	39					GSHAP	Colombia: Casanare	哥伦比亚:卡萨纳雷	5.9	-70.8	40	4	Ms	5										
1958	9	7	2	48	14					GSHAP	Colombia: Bucaramanga	哥伦比亚:布卡拉曼加	7	-73	150	4	Ms	5										
1958	9	14	14	21	44					GSHAP	Russia: Sakha, SW.	俄罗斯:萨哈共和国西南	56.73	121.08	10	6.4	Ms	9										
1958	9	17	12	24		2	0.2	-2.3	-1	* NOAA, Song	Kuril Islands	千岛群岛	49.3	156.4		7	Mk											
1958	9	18	20	53	2					GSHAP	Afghan: Taloqan	阿富汗:塔卢坎	36.8	70.4	200	5.8	Ms	5										
1958	9	21	7	24	55					USGS	US: California, Greenfield	美国:加利福尼亚州格林菲尔德	36.35	-121.12		4.6	Ms	6										
1958	9	21	16	18						* Iran	Iran: Kermanshah	伊朗:克尔曼沙赫	34.52	47.42	71	5.5	Ms		20	1				3				
1958	9	22	6	58	10					GSHAP	Colombia: Barrancabermeja	哥伦比亚:巴兰卡韦梅哈	6.7	-73.7	74	4	Ms	5										
1958	9	25	1	5	36					* China	China: Guangxi, Lingshan, NE.	中国:广西灵山东北	22.5	109.5	5	5.75	Ms	7						1		1		
1958	10	1	21	42	11					USGS	US: California, Sierra City	美国:加利福尼亚州谢拉锡蒂	39.57	-120.3		4.6	Ms	6										
1958	10	10	13	5	16					USGS	US: California, Bradley	美国:加利福尼亚州布拉德利	35.93	-120.5		4.5	Ms	5										
1958	10	13	8	58	13					GSHAP	Kyrgyzstan: Naryn, C.	吉尔吉斯斯坦:纳伦中部	41.6	75.01	12	5.2	Ms	6.5										
1958	10	13	10	11	55					GSHAP	Tajikistan: Dushanbe (Stalinabad)	塔吉克斯坦:杜桑贝	38.27	68.67	22	5	Ms	6										
1958	10	18	6	34	13					GSHAP	Colombia: Guican	哥伦比亚:圭坎	6.71	-72.18	100	5.5	Ms	6										
1958	10	20	1	12						*	Indonesia: Java Ridge	印度尼西亚:爪哇海岭	-9.5	112.5	100	6.7	Muk	8	8	1				3				
1958	11	2	0	6	3					GSHAP	Russia: Sakha, SW.	俄罗斯:萨哈共和国西南	57	121	15	4.8	Ms	5.5										
1958	11	4	9	16	44					GSHAP	Colombia: Bucaramanga	哥伦比亚:布卡拉曼加	7	-73	150	5.5	Ms	6										
1958	11	4	22	55	16	1	0.1			* Shi Z.	Southern Pacific Ridge	南太平洋海岭	-50	-115	266	6.1	Ms											
1958	11	6	22	58	10	4	5	2	2.5	* Engdahl, GSHAP, NOAA	Kuril Islands	千岛群岛	44.329	148.623	35	8.4	Mw	10						2				
1958	11	8	2	41	13					USGS	US: Illinois, Bone Gap	美国:伊利诺斯州布尼加普	38.44	-88.01	5	4.4	Ms	6										
1958	11	12	6	9	13					GSHAP	Venezuela: Guanare	委内瑞拉:瓜纳里	9.26	-69.75	25	4.4	Ms	5										
1958	11	12	20	23	33	2	1		-1	* Engdahl, NOAA	Kuril Islands	千岛群岛	44.052	148.837	35	7	Mw											

时间 Date						海啸 Tsunami				资料来源 Information	震中 Earthquake Epicenter				深度 Depth	震级 Mag	标度 Scale	烈度 MMI	死亡人数 Deaths		受伤人数 Injuries		经济损失 Damage		房屋毁坏 Houses Destroyed		房屋受损 Houses Damaged	
年 Year	月 Mo	日 Dy	时 Hr	分 Mn	秒 Sec	源 Sr	浪高 Wh	级 I mI	级 S mS		地名(英文) Name(English)	地名(中文) Name(Chinese)	纬度(°) Latitude	经度(°) Longitude					数量/人 Num	级别 Dd	数量/人 Num	级别 Dd	数量/$ Mill $ Mill	级别 De	数量/间 Num	级别 Dh	数量/间 Num	级别 Dh
1958	11	13	9	6	22					GSHAP	Venezuela:Barinas	委内瑞拉:巴里纳斯	8.93	-69.67	25	4.5	Ms	5										
1958	11	18	10	45						* Song	Italy:Pontremoli	意大利:蓬特雷莫利	44.3	9.9		6.5	Mk	12										
1958	11	23	19	26	54					GSHAP	Colombia:Salgar	哥伦比亚:萨尔加	6	-76		4	Ms	5										
1958	11	26	0	12	7					GSHAP	Georgia:Gurdzhaani	格鲁吉亚:古祖尼	41.6	45.9	19	4.6	Ms	6										
1958	11	26	14	11	2					GSHAP	Colombia:Santander	哥伦比亚:桑坦德	7.2	-73.5	218	4.5	Ms	5										
1958	11	29	9	30						* Song	Italy:Genova	意大利:热那亚	44.4	8.8		6.5	Mk	12										
1958	12	1	3	21	18					USGS,CGS	Mexico:Mexicali	墨西哥:墨西卡利	32.25	-115.75	16	5.8	Ms	6										
1958	12	5	14	19	54					GSHAP	Colombia:Bahia Solano	哥伦比亚:巴伊阿索拉诺	7	-77		4.5	Ms	5										
1958	12	9	15	13	16					GSHAP	Colombia:Antioquia	哥伦比亚:安提奥基亚	7	-74	209	4.5	Ms	5										
1958	12	11	9	52	27					USGS	US:California,San Francisco	美国:加利福尼亚州旧金山	37.7	-122.57		4.7	Ms	6										
1958	12	19	0	50	29					GSHAP	Norway:Mo I Rana	挪威:摩城	66.2	13.7	25	4.7	Ms	5										
1958	12	19	3	27	24					GSHAP	Turkey:Tavas	土耳其:塔瓦斯	37.4	29.1	16	5	Ms	6.5										
1958	12	20	2	12	22					GSHAP	Colombia:Cesar	哥伦比亚:恺撒	9.84	-73.49	90	4.5	Ms	5										
1958	12	21	4	46	29					China,GSHAP	China:Xinjiang,Ili	中国:新疆伊犁	44.55	80.87		6.5	Ms	8										
1958	12	23	6	27	14					GSHAP	Colombia:Narino,Near Coast	哥伦比亚:纳里尼奥近海	2.15	-78.98		5	Ms	6										
1959	1	5	12	36	3.3					USGS	US:California,Inyo,W.	美国:加利福尼亚州因约县西部	36.15	-118.03	3	4.7	Ms	5										
1959	1	11	4	27	25					GSHAP	Turkey:Fethiye	土耳其:费特希耶	36.6	29.1	14	4.5	Ms	6										
1959	1	13	16	32	37					GSHAP	Colombia:Antioquia	哥伦比亚:安提奥基亚	7.5	-74.5	134	4	Ms	5										
1959	1	22	5	10	31	4	0.8	-0.3	-2	* Engdahl,NOAA	Japan Trench	日本海沟	37.56	142.483	35	7.2	Mw											
1959	1	26	6	46						* Song	Italy:Bedonia	意大利:贝多尼亚	44.5	9.6		6.5	Mk	12										
1959	1	30	15	7	45					GSHAP	Colombia:Narino	哥伦比亚:纳里尼奥	1	-77.5		4.5	Ms	5										
1959	1	30	20	38	58					Shi Z.,Usami	Japan:Hokkaido	日本:北海道	43.5	144.2		6.4	Ms								1	1		
1959	1	30	22	52	54					China	China:Ningxia,Xiji,N.	中国:宁夏西吉北	36.3	105.8		5	Ms	6										
1959	2	7	9	36	55	1			-2	* GSHAP,Shi Z,Engdahl,NOAA	Peru:Máncora,Near Coast	秘鲁:曼科拉近海	-3.786	-81.685	35	6.9	Ms							1				1
1959	2	16	12	16	27					GSHAP	Colombia:Off Coast of W.	哥伦比亚:西部沿海	2	-80		4	Ms	5										
1959	2	23				2	1		3	NOAA,Song	Greece:Thessalonika	希腊:萨罗尼加	40.63	22.97		6.7	Mk											
1959	2	26	12	54	34					GSHAP	Colombia:Murindo	哥伦比亚:穆林多	6.75	-76.5	36	4	Ms	5										
1959	2	27	22	19	52					USGS,Song	US:Utah,Parowan	美国:犹他州帕罗万	38	-112.5		5.1	Mk	6										
1959	3	1	1	39	48					GSHAP	Colombia:Riosucio	哥伦比亚:乔科的里奥苏西奥	7.5	-77		4	Ms	5										
1959	3	2	15	51	43					GSHAP	Afghan:Fayzabad	阿富汗:法扎巴德	37	70.5	220	6	Ms	5										
1959	3	2	23	27	17					USGS	US:California,Gilroy	美国:加利福尼亚州吉尔罗伊	36.98	-121.6		5.3	Ms	6										
1959	3	3	21	31	21					GSHAP	Azerbaijan:Sirvan,NW.	阿塞拜疆:希尔万西北	40	48.7	25	4.5	Ms	5										
1959	3	23	7	10	20					USGS	US:Nevada,Fallon,NE.	美国:内华达州法伦东北	39.6	-118.02		6.3	Ms	6										

年 Year	月 Mo	日 Dy	时 Hr	分 Mn	秒 Sec	海啸 Tsunami 源 Sr	浪高 Wh	级 I mI	级 S mS	资料来源 Information	震中 Earthquake Epicenter 地名(英文) Name(English)	地名(中文) Name(Chinese)	纬度(°) Latitude	经度(°) Longitude	深度 Depth	震级 Mag	标度 Scale	烈度 MMI	死亡人数 Deaths 数量/人 Num	级别 Dd	受伤人数 Injuries 数量/人 Num	级别 Dd	经济损失 Damage 数量/$ Mill $ Mill	级别 De	房屋毁坏 Houses Destroyed 数量/间 Num	级别 Dh	房屋受损 Houses Damaged 数量/间 Num	级别 Dh
1959	3	26	11	4	38					GSHAP	Tajikistan:Sughd	塔吉克斯坦:索格特州	39. 26	70. 93	10	4. 8	Ms	6. 5										
1959	4	1	18	18	30					USGS	US:California,Chilcoot	美国:加利福尼亚州奇尔库特	39. 72	-120. 2		5. 6	Ms	7										
1959	4	2	4	34	19					GSHAP	Turkey:Bursa	土耳其:布尔萨	40. 1	29. 5	10	4. 6	Ms	7										
1959	4	4	19	28	11					GSHAP	Colombia:Los Santos	哥伦比亚:洛斯桑托斯	6. 6	-73		4	Ms	5										
1959	4	5	10	48						* Italy	France:St Paul D'Ubaye, Jausiers	法国:圣保罗,若西耶	44	6. 8		5. 5	Muk	8						2				
1959	4	5	20	32	48					GSHAP	Colombia:Bahia Solano	哥伦比亚:巴伊阿索拉诺	6	-77. 5		4	Ms	5										
1959	4	6	1	59	24					GSHAP	Colombia:Bucaramanga	哥伦比亚:布卡拉曼加	7	-73. 3		4. 5	Ms	5										
1959	4	6	13	52	4					GSHAP	Colombia:Guaviare	哥伦比亚:瓜维亚雷	2. 5	-72		4. 5	Ms	6										
1959	4	7	10	29	42					GSHAP	Colombia:Bolivar	哥伦比亚:波利瓦尔	7. 5	-74		4	Ms	5										
1959	4	9	12	24		2	0. 1	-3. 3	-2	* NOAA	Kuril Islands	千岛群岛	44. 5	149	60	6	Ms											
1959	4	11	22							* Song	Italy:Montefalco	意大利:蒙特法尔科	42. 9	12. 6		6. 5	Mk	12										
1959	4	13	14	25	46					GSHAP	Colombia:Santander	哥伦比亚:桑坦德	7	-73. 75		4	Ms	5										
1959	4	15	21	35	18					GSHAP	Colombia:Barrancabermeja	哥伦比亚:巴兰卡韦梅哈	6. 9	-73. 7	175	4	Ms	5										
1959	4	17								* Song	Italy:Formigine	意大利:福尔米吉内	44. 5	10. 8		6. 5	Mk	12										
1959	4	25	0	26						*	Turkey:Koycegiz, Mugla	土耳其:克伊杰伊兹,穆拉	37	28. 7		6. 3	Muk	8						2				
1959	4	26	20	40	39					* China, Engdahl	China:Taiwan,Yilan, Coast of E.	中国:台湾宜兰以东海域	24. 687	122. 792	126. 3	7. 5	Ms		2	1				1				
1959	5	4	7	15	46	4	0. 2	1	1	* Engdahl, NOAA	Russia:Kamchatka Peninsula	俄罗斯:堪察加半岛	53. 351	159. 645	35	8	Mw	10	1	1	13	1		2		2		
1959	5	12	3	42	47					GSHAP	Colombia:Riosucio	哥伦比亚:乔科的里奥苏西奥	7. 5	-77	6	4	Ms	5										
1959	5	12	9	46	59					Engdahl, GSHAP	Argentina:Jujuy	阿根廷:胡胡伊	-23. 149	-64. 944	35	6. 8	Ms	8										
1959	5	20	19	49	13					GSHAP	Georgia:Poti	格鲁吉亚:波季	41. 87	41. 86	13	5. 1	Ms	7. 5										
1959	5	24	19	17	42					* Shi Z. , Engdahl	Mexico:Oaxaca	墨西哥:瓦哈卡	17. 45	-97. 145	69. 6	7	mB							3				
1959	5	26	13	44	40					GSHAP	Romania:Vrancea	罗马尼亚:弗朗恰	45. 8	26. 5	135	4. 9	Ms	5										
1959	5	26	15	58	1					USGS	US:California,Natividad	美国:加利福尼亚州纳蒂维达	36. 72	-121. 62		4. 6	Ms	6										
1959	5	27	20	38	26					GSHAP	Romania:Timisoara	罗马尼亚:蒂米什瓦拉	45. 7	21. 1	5	5	Ms	7. 5										
1959	5	28	4	6	57					GSHAP	Colombia:Santander	哥伦比亚:桑坦德	7. 1	-73. 6	168	5	Ms	6										
1959	5	30	7	26	34					GSHAP	Romania:Nehoiu	罗马尼亚:内霍尤	45. 5	26. 3	150	4. 8	Ms	5										
1959	5	31	12	15	48					GSHAP	Romania:Nereju	罗马尼亚:内雷茹	45. 7	27. 4	20	4. 7	Ms	6										
1959	6	3	3	43	42					GSHAP	Colombia:Buenaventura	哥伦比亚:布埃纳文图拉	3. 69	-77. 11	60	4. 5	Ms	6										
1959	6	3	22	18	36					GSHAP	Colombia:Ibagué	哥伦比亚:伊瓦格	4. 2	-75. 5	40	4. 5	Ms	5										
1959	6	14	1	26	32					USGS	US:California,Calpine	美国:加利福尼亚州卡尔派恩	39. 67	-120. 55		4. 5	Ms	5										

时间 Date						海啸 Tsunami				资料来源 Information	震中 Earthquake Epicenter				深度 Depth	震级 Mag	标度 Scale	烈度 MMI	死亡人数 Deaths		受伤人数 Injuries		经济损失 Damage		房屋毁坏 Houses Destroyed		房屋受损 Houses Damaged	
年 Year	月 Mo	日 Dy	时 Hr	分 Mn	秒 Sec	源 Sr	浪高 Wh	级 I mI	级 S mS		地名(英文) Name(English)	地名(中文) Name(Chinese)	纬度(°) Latitude	经度(°) Longitude					数量/人 Num	级别 Dd	数量/人 Num	级别 Dd	数量/$ Mill $ Mill	级别 De	数量/间 Num	级别 Dh	数量/间 Num	级别 Dh
1959	6	17	10	27	11					USGS	US:Oklahoma,Marlow	美国:奥克拉荷马州马洛	34.64	-98.06	5	4.2	Ms	6										
1959	6	18	0	29	40					USGS	US:California,Mammoth Lakes	美国:加利福尼亚州马姆莫斯湖	37.55	-118.57		4.7	Ms	5										
1959	6	18	15	31	32					* Engdahl	Russia:Kamchatka Peninsula	俄罗斯:堪察加半岛	54.129	160.265	35	6.8	Ms	10										
1959	6	23	14	35						USGS	US:Nevada,Yerington	美国:内华达州耶灵顿	39.08	-118.82		6.2	Ms	6										
1959	6	23	15	4	34					USGS	US:Nevada,Yerington	美国:内华达州耶灵顿	39.1	-118.8		5.5	Ms	5										
1959	6	30	22	42	30					GSHAP,Song	Venezuela:Merida	委内瑞拉:梅里达	8.3	-71.23	25	6	Mk	8										
1959	7	1	23	49	23					USGS	US:California,Bakersfield	美国:加利福尼亚州贝克斯菲尔德	35.19	-119.1	9	4.7	Ms	5										
1959	7	2	18	33	54					* China	China:Henan,Huangchuan	中国:河南潢川	31.8	115.3		5	Ms	6				1		1		1		
1959	7	3	23	20	49					GSHAP	Colombia:Charalá	哥伦比亚:查腊拉	6.2	-72.8	40	4.5	Ms	5										
1959	7	6	18	3	33					GSHAP	Colombia:Bucaramanga	哥伦比亚:布卡拉曼加	7	-73	200	4	Ms	5										
1959	7	10	17	40	50					GSHAP	Kyrgyzstan:Jalal - Abad	吉尔吉斯斯坦:贾拉拉巴德	41.05	73.5	15	4.8	Ms	6										
1959	7	12	19	21	58					GSHAP	Kyrgyzstan:Talas,SE.	吉尔吉斯斯坦:塔拉斯东南	41.72	72.8	14	5	Ms	6										
1959	7	19	15	6	16					Engdahl,GSHAP	Peru:Ayaviri	秘鲁:阿亚维里	-15.092	-70.391	208	7.1	mB	7										
1959	7	21	17	39	29					USGS	US:Arizona,Fredonia	美国:亚利桑那州弗里多尼亚	36.8	-112.37		5.6	Ms	6										
1959	7	22	19	32	31					GSHAP	Russia:Sakhalin Island	俄罗斯:库页岛(萨哈林岛)	50.2	142.5	13	5.5	Ms	7										
1959	7	23	3	48	12					GSHAP	Colombia:Cauca, Huila	哥伦比亚:考卡,乌伊拉	2.7	-76.2	60	4.5	Ms	6										
1959	7	23	4	24	35					GSHAP	Colombia:Cauca	哥伦比亚:考卡	2.5	-76.5		4	Ms	5										
1959	7	25	15	58	54					GSHAP	Russia:Sakhalin Island	俄罗斯:库页岛(萨哈林岛)	50.2	142.5	15	4.7	Ms	5.5										
1959	7	26	9	36	31					GSHAP,Song	Venezuela:Soro,Coast	委内瑞拉:索罗近海	11.24	-62.27	144	4.5	Mk	5										
1959	7	26	17	7	3					GSHAP	Turkey:Marmara Sea	土耳其:马尔马拉海	40.9	27.5	30	5	Ms	5										
1959	7	28	3	33	44					GSHAP	Colombia:Galan	哥伦比亚:加兰	6.5	-73.4	31	4	Ms	5										
1959	7	31	19	53	2					GSHAP	Tadzhikistan:Khatlon	塔吉克斯坦:哈特隆州	38.5	70	6	5.9	Ms	7										
1959	8	3	6	8	37					USGS	US:South Carolina,Summerville	美国:南卡罗来纳州萨默维尔	33.05	-80.13	1	4.4	Ms	6										
1959	8	4	7	36	59					USGS	US: California, Chalfant Valley	美国:加利福尼亚州夏芬谷	37.35	-118.55	16	5.2	Ms	5										
1959	8	4	23	53	30					USGS	US:Oregon,Portland	美国:俄勒冈州波特兰	45.68	-122.27		4.7	Ms	5										
1959	8	6	3	44	35					USGS	US:Washington,Manson	美国:华盛顿州曼森	47.82	-120		4.4	Ms	6										
1959	8	10	23	7	29					* China	China:Shanxi,Jishan	中国:山西稷山	35.6	110.9		5.4	Ms	7						1	43	1		
1959	8	13	0	33	13					Iran,GSHAP	Azerbaijan:Lenkeran	阿塞拜疆:连科兰	39.85	48.51	48	5.3	Ms	6.5										

时间 Date 年 Year	月 Mo	日 Dy	时 Hr	分 Mn	秒 Sec	海啸 Tsunami 源 Sr	浪高 Wh	级 I mI	级 S mS	资料来源 Information	震中 Earthquake Epicenter 地名(英文) Name(English)	地名(中文) Name(Chinese)	纬度(°) Latitude	经度(°) Longitude	深度 Depth	震级 Mag	标度 Scale	烈度 MMI	死亡人数 Deaths 数量/人 Num	级别 Dd	受伤人数 Injuries 数量/人 Num	级别 Dd	经济损失 Damage 数量/$ Mill $ Mill	级别 De	房屋毁坏 Houses Destroyed 数量/间 Num	级别 Dh	房屋受损 Houses Damaged 数量/间 Num	级别 Dh
1959	8	15	8	57	5					* China, Engdahl, Dis	China: Taiwan, Pingtung, Coast of E.	中国:台湾屏东以东海域	21.952	120.97	25	7.2	Mw		17	1	63	2		3	1541	4	1126	4
1959	8	17	21	4	50	4	1	1.3		* Engdahl, NOAA	Solomon Islands	所罗门群岛	-7.895	156.338	35	7.1	Mw							3				
1959	8	18	6	37	20					* Engdahl	US: Wyoming, Shell	美国:怀俄明州谢尔	44.548	-110.636	15	7.3	M	10	28	1			11.0	3				
1959	8	18	8	41	48					USGS	US: Montana, West Yellowstone	美国:蒙大纳州西黄石	44.85	-111.05	5	6	Ms	6										
1959	8	19	4	4	2					USGS	US: Wyoming, Mammoth	美国:怀俄明州马默斯	44.65	-110.84	5	6	Ms	5										
1959	8	19	15	32	3					GSHAP	Romania: Tulnici	罗马尼亚:图尔尼奇	45.9	26.8	150	5.1	Ms	5										
1959	8	19	19	6	27					USGS	US: Montana, Cameron	美国:蒙大纳州卡梅伦	44.82	-111.59	5	5	Ms	5										
1959	8	20	19	11	27					USGS	US: Montana, Dillon, SE.	美国:蒙大纳州狄龙东南	44.7	-111.68	5	5	Ms	5										
1959	8	23	8	40						USGS, Song	US: Montana, West Yellowstone	美国:蒙大纳州西黄石	44.7	-111.2		5.1	Mk	6										
1959	8	26	8	25	37					* Shi Z., Engdahl	Mexico: Gulf of Campeche	墨西哥:坎佩切海湾	18.2	-94.4	32.4	6.9	Ms		25	1				3				
1959	8	29	17	3	14					GSHAP, Shi Z.	Russia: Lake Baykal	俄罗斯:贝加尔湖	52.68	106.98	20	6.8	Ms	9										
1959	9	1	11	37						*	Albania: Kucove	阿尔巴尼亚:库乔亚区	40.9	19.8	11	6.1	Muk	10	2	1				3				
1959	9	5	12	4						USGS, Song	US: Montana, West Yellowstone	美国:蒙大纳州西黄石	44.7	-111.2		5.1	Mk	6										
1959	9	13	19	49	35					USGS	US: Montana, West Yellowstone	美国:蒙大纳州西黄石	44.72	-111.13	5	4.4	Ms	6										
1959	9	16	18	18	57					GSHAP	Colombia: Bolivar	哥伦比亚:波利瓦尔	7.5	-74		4	Ms	5										
1959	9	16	19	14	53					GSHAP	Colombia: Bahia Solano	哥伦比亚:巴伊阿索拉诺	7	-77.5		4	Ms	5										
1959	9	16	20	53	54					GSHAP	Colombia: Riosucio	哥伦比亚:里奥苏西奥	7.5	-77.5		4	Ms	5										
1959	9	19	3	50	50					GSHAP	Bolivia: Cochabamba	玻利维亚:科恰班巴	-17.73	-65.19		4.6	Ms	5										
1959	9	23	9	38	27					GSHAP	Colombia: Bahia Solano	哥伦比亚:巴伊阿索拉诺	7	-77.5		4	Ms	5										
1959	9	25	7	18	37					GSHAP	Black Sea	黑海	43.8	39.4	5	4.5	Ms	7										
1959	10	1	4	35	35					USGS	US: California, Lompoc	美国:加利福尼亚州隆波克	34.46	-120.52	14	4.5	Ms	5										
1959	10	2	2	16	42					GSHAP	Colombia: Saravena	哥伦比亚:萨拉韦纳	7	-72		4	Ms	5										
1959	10	5	13	51	32					GSHAP	Colombia: Chipata	哥伦比亚:奇帕塔	6.1	-73.7	40	4	Ms	5										
1959	10	13	8	15						USGS	US: Arizona, Flagstaff	美国:亚利桑那州弗拉格斯塔夫	35.5	-111.5		5	Ms	5										
1959	10	16	8	53	24					GSHAP	Colombia: Antioquia	哥伦比亚:安提奥基亚	7	-74	178	4	Ms	5										
1959	10	19	14	29	45					GSHAP	Bolivia: Cochabamba	玻利维亚:科恰班巴	-17.38	-66.19		5.4	Ms	5										
1959	10	24	15	35	15					USGS	US: California, Inyo, W.	美国:加利福尼亚州因约县西部	35.74	-118.02	7	4.2	Ms	6										
1959	10	24	23	40	38					GSHAP	Uzbekistan: Tashkent	乌兹别克斯坦:塔什干	41.67	70	13	5.7	Ms	7.5										
1959	10	25	15	57						* GSHAP	Turkey: Varto, Mus	土耳其:瓦尔托,穆什	39.1	41.6	50	6.2	Muk		18	1				2				

年 Year	月 Mo	日 Dy	时 Hr	分 Mn	秒 Sec	海啸 Tsunami 源 Sr	浪高 Wh	级 I mI	级 S mS	资料来源 Information	震中 Earthquake Epicenter 地名(英文) Name(English)	地名(中文) Name(Chinese)	纬度(°) Latitude	经度(°) Longitude	深度 Depth	震级 Mag	标度 Scale	烈度 MMI	死亡人数 Deaths 数量/人 Num	级别 Dd	受伤人数 Injuries 数量/人 Num	级别 Dd	经济损失 Damage 数量/$ Mill $ Mill	级别 De	房屋毁坏 Houses Destroyed 数量/间 Num	级别 Dh	房屋受损 Houses Damaged 数量/间 Num	级别 Dh
1959	10	26	7	35	10	4	0.1	-3.3	-1	* Shi Z., Engdahl, NOAA	Japan Trench	日本海沟	37.531	143.051	13	6.7	Ms											
1959	10	27	6	52	49	4				* GSHAP, Shi Z.	Kuril Islands	千岛群岛	44.9	151.6	70	7.2	Ms											
1959	10	31	5	1	31					GSHAP	Colombia: Neiva	哥伦比亚:内瓦	3	-76		4	Ms	5										
1959	10	31	18	31	18					GSHAP	Colombia: Narino	哥伦比亚:纳里尼奥	2	-77.5	100	4.5	Ms	5										
1959	11	3	17	3	8					USGS, Song	US: Montana, West Yellowstone	美国:蒙大纳州西黄石	44.7	-111.2		5.1	Mk	6										
1959	11	7								*	Algeria: Bou - Medfa	阿尔及利亚:布迈德法	36.4	2.6		5.5	Muk	8						2				
1959	11	15	10	25	16					* China, GSHAP	China: Xinjiang, Ulugqat, SW.	中国:新疆乌恰西南	38.75	75.32	40	6.4	Ms	7		1				1				
1959	11	23	18	15	25					USGS	US: Washington, Packwood	美国:华盛顿州帕克伍德	46.67	-121.75		4.8	Ms	5										
1959	11	30	11	13						China, GSHAP	China: Xinjiang, Ili	中国:新疆伊犁	44.4	80.6	20	5.8	Ms	7										
1959	12	5	7	53	36					GSHAP	Colombia: Santander	哥伦比亚:桑坦德	7.3	-73.3	40	4	Ms	5										
1959	12	5	8	13	42					USGS	US: California, Off Coast N.	美国:加利福尼亚州北部沿海	40.3	-125.42		5.1	Ms	5										
1959	12	21	14	58	5					GSHAP	Colombia: Santander	哥伦比亚:桑坦德	7.5	-72.9	80	4	Ms	5										
1959	12	22	2	38	57					USGS	US: California, North Coast	美国:加利福尼亚州北部近海	40.27	-124.52		4.7	Ms	5										
1959	12	22	3	4						GSHAP	Bolivia: Tupiza	玻利维亚:图皮萨	-21.43	-65.72		5.4	Ms	6										
1959	12	24	12	50						* Song	Peru: Ayacucho, Pomabamba	秘鲁:阿亚库乔,波马班巴	-13.5	-74		5.9	Mk	7	7	1				2				
1959	12	29	2	32	53					USGS	US: California, Hollister	美国:加利福尼亚州霍利斯特	36.9	-121.48		4.7	Ms	6										
1960	1	1	10	58	5					GSHAP	Colombia: Murindo	哥伦比亚:穆林多	7	-76.5		4	Ms	5										
1960	1	13	15	40	30	4	5.7	2.6	3	* Shi Z., Engdahl, NOAA	Peru: Arequipa, Chuquibamba	秘鲁:阿雷基帕,丘基班巴	-15.814	-72.788	95.4	7.5	mB	10	63	2	200	3		3		3		
1960	1	15	9	30	24					* Shi Z., Engdahl	Peru: Lima, Nazca, Ica	秘鲁:利马,纳斯卡,伊卡	-14.961	-75.162	97.2	6.9	mB		63	2				1				
1960	1	17	2	57	58					GSHAP, Shi Z.	Peru: Ayacucho	秘鲁:阿亚库乔	-14.5	-74.5	150	6.4	Ms	6										
1960	1	18	19	30	18					GSHAP	Colombia: Acandí, Near Coast	哥伦比亚:阿坎迪近海	9	-77	100	5	Ms	6										
1960	1	20	3	25	53					USGS	US: California, Tres Pinos	美国:加利福尼亚州特雷斯皮诺斯	36.78	-121.43		5	Ms	6										
1960	1	30	1	42	42					GSHAP	Colombia: Bucaramanga	哥伦比亚:布卡拉曼加	6.77	-73.14	168	4	Ms	5										
1960	2	2	12	32	30					GSHAP	Russia: Murmansk, Alakurtti, E.	俄罗斯:摩尔曼斯克州阿拉库尔季东部	67	30.9	18	4.8	Ms	5.5										
1960	2	2	23	51	59					* China	China: Gansu, Zhouqu	中国:甘肃舟曲	33.8	104.5		5.25	Ms	6						1		1		
1960	2	7	4	24	53					GSHAP	Colombia: Norte de Santander	哥伦比亚:北桑坦德	7.19	-72.23	36	5	Ms	6										
1960	2	10	22	52	53					GSHAP	Colombia: Bucaramanga	哥伦比亚:布卡拉曼加	6.85	-72.72	152	4	Ms	5										

时间 年 Year	月 Mo	日 Dy	时 Hr	分 Mn	秒 Sec	海啸 Tsunami 源 Sr	浪高 Wh	级 I mI	级 S mS	资料来源 Information	震中 Earthquake Epicenter 地名(英文) Name(English)	地名(中文) Name(Chinese)	纬度(°) Latitude	经度(°) Longitude	深度 Depth	震级 Mag	标度 Scale	烈度 MMI	死亡人数 Deaths 数量/人 Num	级别 Dd	受伤人数 Injuries 数量/人 Num	级别 Dd	经济损失 Damage 数量/$ Mill $ Mill	级别 De	房屋毁坏 Houses Destroyed 数量/间 Num	级别 Dh	房屋受损 Houses Damaged 数量/间 Num	级别 Dh
1960	2	19	3	38	12					GSHAP	Colombia:Santander	哥伦比亚:桑坦德	7.6	-73.6	245	4.5	Ms	5										
1960	2	19	5	9	28					USGS,Song	Gulf of Alaska	阿拉斯加湾	60.87	-150.36	44	4.9	Mk	5										
1960	2	19	10	36	54					GSHAP	Afghan:Badakhshan	阿富汗:巴达赫尚	36.8	71	190	7.1	Ms	7										
1960	2	21	8	13	31					*	Algeria:Melouza	阿尔及利亚:迈卢扎	36	4.1	33	5.6	Ms		47	1	88	2		2				
1960	2	21	23	25	48					GSHAP	Uzbekistan:Fergana	乌兹别克斯坦:费尔干纳	40.2	71.68	19	4.6	Ms	6										
1960	2	23	2	9	5					GSHAP	Afghan:Badakhshan	阿富汗:巴达赫尚	36.7	71.1	160	5.9	Ms	5										
1960	2	25	15	15	20					GSHAP	Colombia:Bucaramanga	哥伦比亚:布卡拉曼加	7	-72.4	40	4	Ms	5										
1960	2	26	6	3						Korea	North Korea:Pyongyang	朝鲜:平壤	38.87	125.8		5.1	Ms	6										
1960	2	29	23	40	12	1				* NOAA	Morocco:Agadir	摩洛哥:阿加迪尔	30.5	-9.5		6.8	Ms	10	13100	5	25000	5	120	5		3		
1960	3	5	7	55	6					GSHAP	Colombia:Bucaramanga	哥伦比亚:布卡拉曼加	7	-73		4	Ms	5										
1960	3	6	22	26	49					GSHAP	Colombia:Los Santos	哥伦比亚:洛斯桑托斯	6.5	-73	200	4.5	Ms	5										
1960	3	9	23	54	25					GSHAP,Shi Z.	Peru:Arequipa	秘鲁:阿雷基帕	-16.5	-72.5	150	6.2	Ms	6										
1960	3	13	23	53	32					GSHAP	Colombia:Riosucio	哥伦比亚:乔科的里奥苏西奥	7.5	-77	60	6.1	Ms	8										
1960	3	14	0	40	43					GSHAP	Colombia:Riosucio	哥伦比亚:乔科的里奥苏西奥	7.5	-77	60	4.5	Ms	6										
1960	3	20	17	7	29	4	1		-2	* Engdahl, GSHAP, Shi Z., Usami, NOAA	Japan Trench	日本海沟	39.871	143.435	20	7.8	Mw							1				
1960	3	21	0	2	44					GSHAP	Caspian Sea	里海	42.9	47.8	8	4.6	Ms	7										
1960	3	23	0	23		4	0.8	0.6	-2.5	* NOAA	Japan Trench	日本海沟	39.4	143.7		6.7	Ms											
1960	3	26	8	44	33					GSHAP	Colombia:Bucaramanga	哥伦比亚:布卡拉曼加	7	-73		4	Ms	5										
1960	4	2	15	0	36					GSHAP	Colombia:Jambalo	哥伦比亚:考卡的汉巴洛	3	-76.5		4	Ms	5										
1960	4	13	6	57	49					* China	China:Jilin,Yushu	中国:吉林榆树	44.7	127		5.8	Ms	8						1	29	1		
1960	4	15	10	52						GSHAP,Song	Venezuela:Caracas	委内瑞拉:加拉加斯	10.5	-66.92		5	Mk	6										
1960	4	24	12	14						*	Iran:Lar	伊朗:拉尔	28	54.5		6	Muk		420	3			20.0	3				
1960	4	29	9	16	12					* Shi Z.	Indonesia:Sulawesi	印度尼西亚:苏拉威西岛	-0.5	121.5		6.4	Ms	8						3				
1960	4	29	12	47	16					GSHAP	Ecuador:Cotopaxi	厄瓜多尔:科托帕希	-1	-78.5	100	5.9	Ms	5										
1960	5	6	4	55						GSHAP	Colombia:Cauca	哥伦比亚:考卡	2.5	-77		4	Ms	5										
1960	5	19	2	6	55					GSHAP	Afghan:Badakhshan	阿富汗:巴达赫尚	36.5	71	100	6.2	Ms	6										
1960	5	21	10	2	58	4	0.3		-1	* Engdahl,NOAA	Chile:Curanilahue	智利:库拉尼拉韦	-37.872	-73.243	35	8.2	Mw			3		3		1				
1960	5	22	19	11	18	4	25	4.6	4	* Engdahl, NOAA	Chile:Puerto Montt, Valdivia	智利:蒙特港,巴尔迪维亚	-38.235	-73.047	35	9.5	M	12	2223	4	3000	4	1000	5	58622	5		
1960	5	26	5	10						*	Albania:Delvine	阿尔巴尼亚:德维纳区	40	20		6.5	Muk		8	1				2				
1960	6	5	7	47	7					USGS	US:California,Mammoth Lakes,S.	美国:加利福尼亚州马姆莫斯湖南部	37.52	-118.73	16	5.2	Ms	5										
1960	6	6	1	17	46					USGS	US:California,North Coast	美国:加利福尼亚州北部近海	40.84	-124.91		5.7	Ms	6										

时间 Date						海啸 Tsunami				资料来源 Information	震中 Earthquake Epicenter				深度 Depth	震级 Mag	标度 Scale	烈度 MMI	死亡人数 Deaths		受伤人数 Injuries		经济损失 Damage		房屋毁坏 Houses Destroyed		房屋受损 Houses Damaged	
年 Year	月 Mo	日 Dy	时 Hr	分 Mn	秒 Sec	源 Sr	浪高 Wh	级 I mI	级 S mS		地名(英文) Name(English)	地名(中文) Name(Chinese)	纬度(°) Latitude	经度(°) Longitude					数量/人 Num	级别 Dd	数量/人 Num	级别 Dd	数量/$ Mill $ Mill	级别 De	数量/间 Num	级别 Dh	数量/间 Num	级别 Dh
1960	6	7	18	9	48					GSHAP	Colombia: Antioquia	哥伦比亚:安提奥基亚	7	-74		4	Ms	5										
1960	6	8	21	47	48					GSHAP	Colombia: Valle Del Cauca	哥伦比亚:考卡山谷	5	-77	100	4	Ms	5										
1960	6	11	15	14	9	3	0.7	-0.5		* NOAA	Solomon Sea, W.	所罗门海西部	-9.4	152.3	33	6.6	Ms											
1960	6	18	21	18	39					GSHAP	Venezuela: El Tocuyo	委内瑞拉:托丘约	10.75	-67.17		4.9	Ms	6										
1960	6	25	13	53	37					GSHAP	Colombia: Guican	哥伦比亚:圭坎	6.5	-72.5	150	5	Ms	7										
1960	7	6	5	16	48					GSHAP	Afghan: Fayzabad	阿富汗:法扎巴德	36.8	70.5	210	6	Ms	5										
1960	7	19	2	42	30					GSHAP	Carnegie Ridge	卡内基海岭	1	-87.5		6	Ms	5										
1960	7	23	14	15						USGS, Song	US: New Mexico, La Joya	美国:新墨西哥州拉霍亚	34.35	-106.85		5.1	Mk	6										
1960	7	29	17	31	43	4	0.1	-3.3	-3	* Shi Z., Engdahl, NOAA	Japan: Iwate, Near Coast	日本:岩手近海	40.365	142.454	50.5	6.8	Ms											
1960	7	30	2	4						* Song	Ecuador: Chimborazo, Bolivar	厄瓜多尔:钦博拉索山,玻利瓦	-1.5	-79	21	5.8	Mk	7	11	1				1				
1960	8	7	16	27	16					USGS, Song	US: Idaho, Montpelier	美国:爱达荷州蒙特佩利尔	42.4	-111.5	49	5.1	Mk	6										
1960	8	9	7	39	18					USGS, Shi Z.	US: California, Off Coast N.	美国:加利福尼亚州北部沿海	40.32	-127.07	17	6.3	Ms	5										
1960	8	9	14	2	34					GSHAP	Russia: Sakhalin Island	俄罗斯:库页岛(萨哈林岛)	46.9	142.7	9	4.7	Ms	6.5										
1960	8	15	23	17	14					GSHAP	Colombia: Santander	哥伦比亚:桑坦德	6.9	-73.1	157	4	Ms	5										
1960	8	21	21	43	45					GSHAP	Colombia: Near Coast	哥伦比亚:近海	5.4	-78.5	29	4	Ms	5										
1960	8	27	15	58						* GSHAP, Song	India: New Delhi	印度:新德里	28.6	76.7	58	6	Mk							2				
1960	8	29	4	53	23					GSHAP, Song	Carnegie Ridge	卡内基海岭	1	-85.2	48	4.5	Mk	5										
1960	9	1	5	59	55					GSHAP	Colombia: Bahia Solano	哥伦比亚:巴伊阿索拉诺	7	-77.3	56	4	Ms	5										
1960	9	10	5	17	24					GSHAP, Song	Ecuador: La Libertad	厄瓜多尔:拉利伯塔德	-2.5	-82		4.5	Mk	5										
1960	9	10	15	6	33					USGS	US: Washington, Bremerton	美国:华盛顿州布雷默顿	47.7	-122.7	25	4.6	Ms	6										
1960	9	16	1	38	59					GSHAP	Tadzhikistan: Duachanbe	塔吉克斯坦:杜尚别	38.6	68.6	45	5.5	Ms	6										
1960	9	18	14	3	56					GSHAP	Colombia: Santander	哥伦比亚:桑坦德	6.9	-73.1	177	4	Ms	5										
1960	9	19	18	51	53					GSHAP	Colombia: Near Coast	哥伦比亚:近海	6.5	-78		4	Ms	5										
1960	9	19	18	58	27					GSHAP	Colombia: Bahia Solano	哥伦比亚:巴伊阿索拉诺	7	-77.2	60	4	Ms	5										
1960	9	19	19	1	21					GSHAP, Shi Z.	Colombia: Bahia Solano	哥伦比亚:巴伊阿索拉诺	6.97	-77.44	66	6.2	Ms	7										
1960	9	19	21	18	15					GSHAP	Colombia: Near Coast	哥伦比亚:近海	7	-78		4	Ms	5										
1960	9	22	9	5	33					*	Congo: Lake Tanganyika	刚果:坦噶尼喀湖	-3.6	29	28	6.6	Ms		24	1				2				3
1960	9	22	15	11	46					GSHAP	Colombia: Murindo	哥伦比亚:穆林多	7.2	-77.2	56	4.5	Ms	6										
1960	9	23	2	27	1					GSHAP	Colombia: Riosucio	哥伦比亚:里奥苏西奥	7.6	-77.4	63	4	Ms	5										
1960	9	28	1	27	57					GSHAP	Colombia: Santander	哥伦比亚:桑坦德	7.3	-73	40	4	Ms	5										

时间 Date						海啸 Tsunami				资料来源 Information	震中 Earthquake Epicenter				深度 Depth	震级 Mag	标度 Scale	烈度 MMI	死亡人数 Deaths		受伤人数 Injuries		经济损失 Damage		房屋毁坏 Houses Destroyed		房屋受损 Houses Damaged	
年 Year	月 Mo	日 Dy	时 Hr	分 Mn	秒 Sec	源 Sr	浪高 Wh	级 I mI	级 S mS		地名(英文) Name(English)	地名(中文) Name(Chinese)	纬度(°) Latitude	经度(°) Longitude					数量/人 Num	级别 Dd	数量/人 Num	级别 Dd	数量/$ Mill $ Mill	级别 De	数量/间 Num	级别 Dh	数量/间 Num	级别 Dh
1960	10	7	19	7	31					GSHAP	Colombia: Santa Marta, Cartagena	哥伦比亚:圣玛尔塔,卡塔赫纳	10.8	-74.3	131	4	Ms	5										
1960	10	7								* Song	Philippines: Panay Island	菲律宾:班乃岛	11.1	122.3		5.9	Mk		3	1				2				
1960	10	11	8	5	31					USGS	US: Colorado, Cimarron	美国:科罗拉多州锡马龙	38.3	-107.6	49	5.5	Ms	6										
1960	10	13	2	21	26					GSHAP	Romania: Nereju	罗马尼亚:内雷茹	45.7	26.5	150	5.5	Ms	6										
1960	10	17	15	45	37					GSHAP	Colombia: Near Coast	哥伦比亚:近海	4.8	-78.4	83	4.7	Ms	6										
1960	10	17	15	56	14					GSHAP	Colombia: Off Coast of W.	哥伦比亚:西部沿海	5	-78.2	79	5	Ms	6										
1960	10	18	10	26	47					GSHAP	Kyrgyzstan: Karakol	吉尔吉斯斯坦:普热瓦利斯克	42.3	78.4	17	4.9	Ms	6										
1960	11	1	8	46	1	2				* Shi Z., Engdahl, NOAA	Chile: Near Coast of C.	智利:中部近海	-38.379	-74.848	35	6.8	Ms			1				1				
1960	11	5	4	43	49					China	China: Guangxi, Du-an	中国:广西都安	24	108.5		5	Ms	6										
1960	11	9	9	43	42					* China, Dis	China: Sichuan, Songpan	中国:四川松潘	32.7	103.7	20	6.75	Ms	9						3	733	3		
1960	11	14	23	2	26					GSHAP	Colombia: Santander	哥伦比亚:桑坦德	6.9	-73.2	190	4	Ms	5										
1960	11	16	15	38	22					GSHAP	Colombia: Fundación	哥伦比亚:马格达雷那的丰达西翁	10.3	-74.07	47	4.4	Ms	5										
1960	11	20	22	2	2	4	9	3.2	2.5	* Engdahl, NOAA	Peru: Chiclayo, Near Coast	秘鲁:奇克拉约近海	-6.727	-80.606	52	7.8	Mw		66	2	2	1	0.55	1				
1960	11	22	2	32	21					GSHAP, Song	Peru: Chiclayo, Near Coast	秘鲁:奇克拉约近海	-7.1	-80.8	51	5	Mk	6										
1960	12	3	4	24	18					Engdahl, GSHAP	Mongolia: Namgon	蒙古:瑙木贡	43.122	104.411	12.4	6.9	Ms	9										
1960	12	10	6	5	36					GSHAP	Ecuador: Off Coast of W.	厄瓜多尔:西部沿海	0	-82		4.3	Ms	6										
1960	12	25	11	24	43					GSHAP, Iran	Azerbaijan: Sirvan, NW.	阿塞拜疆:希尔万西北	40.1	48.6	23	5	Ms	5										
1960	12	27	10	35	26					USGS	US: California, North Coast	美国:加利福尼亚州北部近海	41.52	-125.05		5.4	Ms	5										
1960	12	29	10	10	4					GSHAP, Song	Venezuela: Lara	委内瑞拉:拉腊	9.7	-69.4		4.5	Mk	5										
1961	1	10	14	22		1				* Song	Kuril Islands	千岛群岛	50	156.1	70	7	Mk											
1961	1	14	16	17	26					GSHAP	Colombia: Bucaramanga	哥伦比亚:布卡拉曼加	6.8	-73	159	5.2	Ms	7										
1961	1	16	7	20	13	4	0.4	-1.3	-2	* Engdahl, NOAA	Japan Trench	日本海沟	36.136	141.912	35	6.9	Ms											
1961	1	16	11	19	47	4	0.4	-1.3	-1	Shi Z., NOAA	Japan: Sosa	日本:千叶匝瑳	35.7	140.6	157	6.4	Ms											
1961	1	16	12	12	35	4	0.4	-1.3	-2	Shi Z., NOAA	Japan Trench	日本海沟	36.2	141.7	105	6.9	Ms											
1961	1	28	3	24	46					GSHAP	Peru: Chincha Alta, Near Coast	秘鲁:上钦查近海	-13.6	-76.3	86	5.8	Ms	6										
1961	1	28	8	12	46					USGS	US: California, Inyo, W.	美国:加利福尼亚州因约县西部	35.78	-118.05	6	5.3	Ms	6										
1961	1	30	12	12	36					USGS	Alaska Peninsula, C.	阿拉斯加半岛中部	65.23	-150.25		5.5	Ms	5										
1961	2	1	18	39						Usami	Japan: Niigata	日本:新潟	37.45	138.83	20	5.2	Ms		5	1					259	3		
1961	2	2	0	4	16					USGS	US: California, Huntington Lake, NE.	美国:加利福尼亚州亨廷顿莱克东北	37.45	-118.63	16	5.3	Ms	5										
1961	2	2	0	7	42					USGS	US: California, Huntington Lake, NE.	美国:加利福尼亚州亨廷顿莱克东北	37.42	-118.67	16	5.1	Ms	5										
1961	2	11	9	0	20					GSHAP	Colombia: Santander	哥伦比亚:桑坦德	6.9	-73.1	182	4	Ms	5										

时间 年 Year	月 Mo	日 Dy	时 Hr	分 Mn	秒 Sec	海啸 Tsunami 源 Sr	浪高 Wh	级I mI	级S mS	资料来源 Information	震中 Earthquake Epicenter 地名(英文) Name(English)	地名(中文) Name(Chinese)	纬度(°) Latitude	经度(°) Longitude	深度 Depth	震级 Mag	标度 Scale	烈度 MMI	死亡人数 Deaths 数量/人 Num	级别 Dd	受伤人数 Injuries 数量/人 Num	级别 Dd	经济损失 Damage 数量/$ Mill	级别 De	房屋毁坏 Houses Destroyed 数量/间 Num	级别 Dh	房屋受损 Houses Damaged 数量/间 Num	级别 Dh
1961	2	12	21	53	46	4	1		−0.5	* Shi Z., Engdahl, NOAA	Kuril Islands	千岛群岛	43.744	147.729	35	6.9	Ms											
1961	2	17	6	11	53					GSHAP	Colombia: Santander	哥伦比亚:桑坦德	6.9	−73.1	159	4	Ms	5										
1961	2	26	18	10	52	4	0.7		−1	* Usami, Engdahl, NOAA	Japan: Miyazaki, Near Coast	日本:宫崎近海	31.632	131.548	49.9	7.7	Mw		2	1	7	1		2	170	3		
1961	2	27	1	7	51					GSHAP	Colombia: Bucaramanga	哥伦比亚:布卡拉曼加	6.7	−73	200	5.1	Ms	6										
1961	3	7	19	0	48					* China	China: Hubei, Changyang	中国:湖北长阳	30.5	111		4.9	Ms	7						2	25	1	800	3
1961	3	11	22	7	2					GSHAP	Colombia: Cordoba	哥伦比亚:科尔多巴	8.2	−75.6	40	4.2	Ms	5										
1961	3	16	13	45	36					*	Indonesia: Flores Islands	印度尼西亚:弗洛勒斯群岛	−8.2	122	74	6.3	Muk		2	1				3				
1961	3	17	12	14						Japan	Japan: Hyogo	日本:兵库	35.1	134.3	40	5.9	Ms											1
1961	3	18				2	3.6		2	NOAA, Song	Solomon Islands	所罗门群岛	−10.38	165.8		7.7	Mk							1				1
1961	3	20	3	30	27					GSHAP	Afghan: Badakhshan	阿富汗:巴达赫尚	36.6	71.1	80	5.8	Ms	6										
1961	3	24	10	36						* Italy	Italy: Scilla	意大利:希拉	38.175	15.654		4.63	Ms		15	1				2				
1961	4	3	1	10	32					GSHAP	Colombia: Bucaramanga	哥伦比亚:布卡拉曼加	6.8	−72.9	221	5.1	Ms	6										
1961	4	3	1	22	40					GSHAP	Colombia: Abrego	哥伦比亚:北桑坦德的阿夫雷戈	7.8	−73.2	84	4	Ms	5										
1961	4	4	21	32						* Song	US: California, Long Beach	美国:加利福尼亚州长滩	34	−118	16	5.9	Mk						4.5	2				
1961	4	4	22	42	35					GSHAP	Norwegian Sea	挪威海	61.8	1.5	41	4.9	Ms	5										
1961	4	6	4	4	45					USGS	US: California, North Coast	美国:加利福尼亚州北部近海	40.18	−124.75		5.1	Ms	5										
1961	4	7	21	17	48					GSHAP	Uzbekistan: Andizhan	乌兹别克斯坦:安第札	39.64	72.89	26	5.5	Ms	6										
1961	4	8	9	3	48					GSHAP	Ecuador: Tixan	厄瓜多尔:蒂克桑	−2.2	−78.9		6.1	Ms	8										
1961	4	9	7	23	16					USGS	US: California, Tres Pinos, S.	美国:加利福尼亚州特雷斯皮诺斯南部	36.68	−121.3		5.6	Ms	7										
1961	4	9	7	25	41					USGS	US: California, Tres Pinos, S.	美国:加利福尼亚州特雷斯皮诺斯南部	36.68	−121.3		5.5	Ms	7										
1961	4	12	11	36	44					GSHAP	Colombia: Barrancabermeja	哥伦比亚:巴兰卡韦梅哈	6.9	−73.5	35	4	Ms	5										
1961	4	13	16	34	41					* China, Engdahl	China: Xinjiang, Maralbishi, W.	中国:新疆巴楚西	39.8	77.7	10.7	6.8	Ms	9						2	53	2		
1961	4	16	5	2	39					USGS, Song	US: Utah, Ephraim	美国:犹他州伊弗雷姆	39.33	−111.65		5.1	Mk	6										
1961	4	24	13	55	17					GSHAP, Song	Venezuela: Merida	委内瑞拉:梅里达	8.3	−71.1		4.5	Mk	5										
1961	4	25	9	42	9					GSHAP, Song	Venezuela: Merida	委内瑞拉:梅里达	8.75	−70.85	25	4.5	Mk	5										
1961	4	30	20	1	16					GSHAP	Colombia: Bucaramanga	哥伦比亚:布卡拉曼加	7	−73.3	182	4	Ms	5										
1961	5	10	8	55	59					GSHAP, Song	Venezuela: San Carlos Del Zulia	委内瑞拉:圣卡洛斯－德尔苏利亚	9.22	−71.17	25	4.5	Mk	5										
1961	5	15	21	6	26					GSHAP	Colombia: Bucaramanga	哥伦比亚:布卡拉曼加	6.8	−73.1	169	4	Ms	5										
1961	5	23	2	45		3				* NOAA	Greece: Rhodes Island	希腊:罗德岛	36.7	28.5		6.5	Ms											
1961	6	1	23	29	22					* Engdahl	Ethiopia: Karakore	埃塞俄比亚:卡拉科雷	10.44	39.858	23.9	6.6	Muk	9	30	1		3		2				

时间 Date						海啸 Tsunami				资料来源	震中 Earthquake Epicenter				深度	震级	标度	烈度	死亡人数 Deaths		受伤人数 Injuries		经济损失 Damage		房屋毁坏 Houses Destroyed		房屋受损 Houses Damaged	
年	月	日	时	分	秒	源	浪高	级 I	级 S	资料来源	地名(英文)	地名(中文)	纬度(°)	经度(°)	深度	震级	标度	烈度	数量/人	级别	数量/人	级别	数量/$ Mill	级别	数量/间	级别	数量/间	级别
Year	Mo	Dy	Hr	Mn	Sec	Sr	Wh	mI	mS	Information	Name(English)	Name(Chinese)	Latitude	Longitude	Depth	Mag	Scale	MMI	Num	Dd	Num	Dd	$ Mill	De	Num	Dh	Num	Dh
1961	6	6				2	0.9	-0.1	2	NOAA, Song	Greece: Thessalonika	希腊:萨罗尼加	40.63	22.97		6.7	Mk											
1961	6	9	5	53	55					GSHAP	Colombia: Narino	哥伦比亚:纳里尼奥	1.5	-76.7	33	4	Ms	5										
1961	6	9	9	36	50					Iran	Caspian Sea	里海	41	50.75	50	6	Ms	6										
1961	6	11	5	10	29					* Engdahl	Iran: Lar	伊朗:拉尔	27.865	54.558	35	6.8	Ms		60	2				3				
1961	6	11	17	15	33					* China	China: Yunnan, Tengchong	中国:云南腾冲	24.97	98.63	27	5.8	Ms	8						3	5740	4		
1961	6	15	0	51	31					GSHAP	Colombia: Santander	哥伦比亚:桑坦德	6.9	-73.1	146	4	Ms	5										
1961	6	16	10	31	56	1				*	Colombia: Convención	哥伦比亚:北桑坦德的孔本西翁	8.9	-73.4	120	6.5	Ms	8										
1961	6	19	17	4	37					GSHAP	Afghan: Badakhshan	阿富汗:巴达赫尚	36.7	70.7	180	6.2	Ms	6										
1961	6	23	4	18	49					GSHAP, Song	Venezuela: Cariaco	委内瑞拉:卡利亚科	10.5	-63.6		4.5	Mk	5										
1961	6	25	10	58	19					GSHAP	Colombia: Magdalena, Near Coast	哥伦比亚:马格达莱纳近海	11.3	-74.7	33	4.5	Ms	5										
1961	6	26	16	43	39					GSHAP	Colombia: Magdalena, Near Coast	哥伦比亚:马格达莱纳近海	11.3	-74.2	59	4	Ms	6										
1961	6	27	0	49						* Song	Iran: Lorestan	伊朗:洛雷斯坦	33.5	49.4		5.9	Mk		5	1				2				
1961	6	27	7	3	41					* China	China: Yunnan, Deqen	中国:云南迪庆	27.73	99.75	10	6	Ms	8						3	11400	5		
1961	7	3	7	6						USGS, Song	US: New Mexico, Socorro	美国:新墨西哥州索科罗	34.1	-106.95		5.1	Mk	6										
1961	7	3	14	49	30					GSHAP	Peru: Chimbote, Near Coast	秘鲁:钦博特近海	-8.7	-79.1	57	5.5	Ms	6										
1961	7	4	4	56						USGS	US: Nevada, Winnemucca	美国:内华达州温尼马卡	40.9	-118.4		5.4	Ms	5										
1961	7	8	11	20	56					GSHAP	Azerbaijan: Gence, NE.	阿塞拜疆:占贾东北	41.1	46.7	10	4.5	Ms	5.5										
1961	7	9	9							GSHAP, Song	Venezuela: Coro	委内瑞拉:科罗	11.42	-69.68		5	Mk	6										
1961	7	18	14	3	42	4	0.2	-2.3		* Japan, Engdahl, NOAA	Ryukyu Islands	琉球群岛	29.655	131.743	36.2	6.9	Ms											
1961	7	23	15	24	16					USGS	Hawaiian Islands	夏威夷群岛	19.38	-155.28	26	4.6	Ms	5										
1961	7	23	21	51	10	4	1.5		-0.5	* Engdahl, NOAA	Vanuatu Islands	瓦努阿图群岛	-18.421	168.411	35	7.3	Mw							1				
1961	7	31	0	7	8					USGS	US: California, Parkfield	美国:加利福尼亚州帕克菲尔德	35.82	-120.37		4.7	Ms	5										
1961	8	1	5	39	53	2	0.9			* NOAA	Solomon Islands	所罗门群岛	-9.3	160.5	50	6.6	Ms											
1961	8	11	15	51	35	4	0.1	-3.3	-4	* Usami, Engdahl, NOAA	Japan: SE. Hokkaido Island	日本:北海道东南	42.913	145.304	35	7.2	Mw											
1961	8	17	8	2	11					Wang S.	China: Xizang (Tibet), Damxung	中国:西藏当雄	30.5	91.5	60	7	Ms	10	54	2				2	774	3		
1961	8	19	4	56	24					USGS	US: Oregon, Klamath Falls	美国:俄勒冈州克拉马斯福尔斯	44.7	-122.5	33	4.5	Ms	6										
1961	8	19	5	33	38					* Usami, Engdahl	Japan: Fukui	日本:福井	36.07	136.7	35	6.9	Ms		10	1				2	12	1		
1961	8	23	1	0	48					USGS	US: California, Descanso	美国:加利福尼亚州德斯坎索	33.05	-116.24	12	4.7	Ms	5										
1961	8	23	4	12	36					GSHAP	Tajikistan: Gissar	塔吉克斯坦:吉萨尔	38.55	68.5	19	5.4	Ms	6										
1961	8	26	1	19	39					GSHAP	Colombia: Bucaramanga	哥伦比亚:布卡拉曼加	7.1	-73.2	183	4	Ms	5										

时间 Date						海啸 Tsunami				资料来源 Information	震中 Earthquake Epicenter				深度 Depth	震级 Mag	标度 Scale	烈度 MMI	死亡人数 Deaths		受伤人数 Injuries		经济损失 Damage		房屋毁坏 Houses Destroyed		房屋受损 Houses Damaged	
年 Year	月 Mo	日 Dy	时 Hr	分 Mn	秒 Sec	源 Sr	浪高 Wh	级 I mI	级 S mS		地名(英文) Name(English)	地名(中文) Name(Chinese)	纬度(°) Latitude	经度(°) Longitude					数量/人 Num	级别 Dd	数量/人 Num	级别 Dd	数量/$ Mill $ Mill	级别 De	数量/间 Num	级别 Dh	数量/间 Num	级别 Dh
1961	9	5	6	13						China, GSHAP	Tajikistan: Kuhistoni Badakhshon, N.	塔吉克斯坦:勾瑙-巴达科善北部	38.5	73.2	100	6.4	Ms	6										
1961	9	5	11	34	31					USGS, Shi Z.	Alaska Peninsula, S.	阿拉斯加半岛南部	59.77	-150.8		6.2	Ms	6										
1961	9	5	14	9	52					GSHAP	Iran: Gorgan	伊朗:戈尔甘	36.8	54.5	19	5.6	Ms	7										
1961	9	16	3	24	56					USGS	US: Washington, Carson	美国:华盛顿州卡森	46.01	-122.13	7	4.8	Ms	5										
1961	9	17	5	30	10					GSHAP	Iran: Bojnurd	伊朗:博季努尔德	37.51	57.3	25	4.5	Ms	5.5										
1961	9	17	15	55	56					USGS	US: Washington, Cougar	美国:华盛顿州库格	46.02	-122.12	7	5.1	Ms	6										
1961	9	18	11	1	4					GSHAP	Caspian Sea	里海	41.1	50.2	64	6	Ms	7										
1961	9	23	3	1	33					USGS	Hawaiian Islands	夏威夷群岛	19.32	-155.11	4	4.5	Ms	5										
1961	9	25	5	28	54					USGS	Hawaiian Islands	夏威夷群岛	19.3	-155	9	4.5	Ms	5										
1961	9	29	22	38	4					GSHAP	Colombia: Near Coast	哥伦比亚:近海	1.7	-79.3	33	4	Ms	5										
1961	10	1	0	16	1					* China	China: Gansu, Minxian, E.	中国:甘肃岷县东	34.33	104.78		5.7	Ms	7						1	10	1	36	1
1961	10	7	9	55	55					GSHAP	Ecuador: Portoviejo	厄瓜多尔:波托维耶霍	-0.4	-80.4	56	6.2	Ms	6										
1961	10	14	7	1						* Iran	Iran: Hamadan	伊朗:哈马丹	34.11	48.46	84	5.3	Ms		2	1				2				
1961	10	18	16	51	58	2				* Shi Z., Engdahl, NOAA	Chile: Concepcion, Near Coast	智利:康塞普西翁近海	-36.803	-73.433	25	6.8	Ms			1				1				
1961	10	19	5	9	44					USGS	US: California, Brown	美国:加利福尼亚州布朗	35.83	-117.76		5.2	Ms	6										
1961	10	20	19	49	51					USGS	US: California, Huntington Beach	美国:加利福尼亚州亨廷顿海滩	33.65	-117.99	5	4.3	Ms	6										
1961	10	26	21	56	17					GSHAP	Colombia: Santander	哥伦比亚:桑坦德	6.9	-73.1	154	5	Ms	6										
1961	11	7	1	29	8					USGS	US: Oregon, Gresham	美国:俄勒冈州格雷舍姆	45.7	-122.4	33	4.5	Ms	6										
1961	11	8	19	30						GSHAP, Song	Peru: Cusco	秘鲁:库斯科	-13.98	-71.9	20	5	Mk	6										
1961	11	15	5	38	56					USGS	US: California, Arvin	美国:加利福尼亚州阿尔文	34.94	-118.99	11	5	Ms	6										
1961	11	15	7	17	14	4	0.1	-3.3	-3.5	* Japan, Engdahl, NOAA	Japan: SE. Hokkaido Island	日本:北海道东南	42.723	145.315	52.3	6.8	Ms		2									1
1961	12	3	18	31	52					GSHAP	Armenia: Leninakan	亚美尼亚:列宁纳坎	41.04	44.08	10	4.9	Ms	6.5										
1961	12	4	12	38	3					China	China: Qinghai, Zaduo	中国:青海杂多	33	95		5.9	Ms	8										
1961	12	6	16	39	38					GSHAP	Kuril Islands	千岛群岛	49.28	155.44	55	6.5	Ms	6										
1961	12	20	13	25	35					* Engdahl	Colombia: Pereira	哥伦比亚:利萨拉尔达的佩雷拉	4.587	-75.542	162.9	6.9	Ms		23	1				3				
1961	12	23	14	36	27					GSHAP	Colombia: Contratación	哥伦比亚:孔特拉塔西翁	6.4	-73.4	197	4.7	Ms	5										
1961	12	31	16	36	6					USGS	US: South dakota, Hayes	美国:南达科他州海斯	44.25	-100.72	23	4.2	Ms	6										
1962	1	1	13	24	42					GSHAP	Colombia: Santander	哥伦比亚:桑坦德	6.9	-73	176	5	Ms	6										
1962	1	7	10	3						*	Croatia: Split, SE.	克罗地亚:斯普利特东南	43.3	17.1	33	6	Muk		4	1				2				
1962	1	9	12	40	48					GSHAP	Japan: Hokkaido	日本:北海道	43.09	144.89	40	6	Ms	6										

时间 Date 年 Year	月 Mo	日 Dy	时 Hr	分 Mn	秒 Sec	海啸 Tsunami 源 Sr	浪高 Wh	级I mI	级S mS	资料来源 Information	震中 Earthquake Epicenter 地名(英文) Name(English)	地名(中文) Name(Chinese)	纬度(°) Latitude	经度(°) Longitude	深度 Depth	震级 Mag	标度 Scale	烈度 MMI	死亡人数 Deaths 数量/人 Num	级别 Dd	受伤人数 Injuries 数量/人 Num	级别 Dd	经济损失 Damage 数量/$ Mill	级别 De	房屋毁坏 Houses Destroyed 数量/间 Num	级别 Dh	房屋受损 Houses Damaged 数量/间 Num	级别 Dh
1962	1	11	5	5						*	Croatia:Split,SE.	克罗地亚:斯普利特东南	43. 3	17. 1	33	5. 8	Muk		1	1				2				
1962	1	16	2	4						* * Song	Iran:Mazanderan	伊朗:马赞德兰	36. 5	53		6. 4	Mk			3				2				
1962	1	17	2	27	44					GSHAP	Brasil:Rio De Janeiro	巴西:里约热内卢	-22. 93	-43. 23		3. 2	Ms	5										
1962	1	31	0	5	52					GSHAP	Tadzhikistan:Khatlon	塔吉克斯坦:哈特隆州	38. 67	70. 13	5	5	Ms	7										
1962	2	1	6	37	57					USGS	US:California,Guadalupe	美国:加利福尼亚州瓜达卢普	34. 88	-120. 68	16	4. 5	Ms	5										
1962	2	2	6	43	30					USGS	US:Missouri,New Madrid	美国:密苏里州新马德里	36. 37	-89. 51	4	4. 3	Ms	6										
1962	2	3	21	38	18					GSHAP	Colombia:Bucaramanga	哥伦比亚:布卡拉曼加	6. 8	-73	160	4	Ms	5										
1962	2	5	14	45	51					USGS	US:Colorado,Ridgway	美国:科罗拉多州里奇韦	38. 2	-107. 6	25	4. 7	Ms	5										
1962	2	14	6	36	3					* Engdahl	Chile:Angol	智利:安戈尔	-38. 091	-73. 05	32. 9	7. 5	mB							2				
1962	2	15	7	12	43					USGS	US:Arizona,Fredonia	美国:亚利桑那州弗里多尼亚	36. 9	-112. 4	26	4. 5	Ms	5										
1962	2	18	17	25	13					GSHAP	Colombia:Antioquia	哥伦比亚:安提奥基亚	8. 08	-74. 87	24	5. 6	Ms	8										
1962	2	18	23	25	20					GSHAP,Song	Carnegie Ridge	卡内基海岭	-0. 6	-91. 7	33	5	Mk	6										
1962	2	18								*	Tunisia:Gafour	突尼斯:加弗尔	36	9		5. 3	Muk	8						2				
1962	2	20	16	2	14					GSHAP	Colombia:Bucaramanga	哥伦比亚:布卡拉曼加	6. 8	-73. 1	150	4	Ms	5										
1962	2	20	16	5	45					GSHAP	Japan:Hokkaido	日本:北海道	43	144. 76	45	6. 3	Ms	6										
1962	2	27	6	34	53					China	China:Sichuan,Dechang,NW.	中国:四川德昌西北	27. 6	101. 9		5. 5	Ms	6										
1962	3	4	0	41	42					GSHAP,Song	Peru:Perene	秘鲁:佩雷内	-10. 6	-75. 2	33	5	Mk	7										
1962	3	12	11	40	17	3	0. 1	-3. 3		* GSHAP, Shi Z. , Engdahl,NOAA	Panama:Puerto Armuelles, Near Coast of S.	巴拿马:阿穆埃耶斯港南部近海	8. 008	-82. 757	35	6. 8	Ms							1				
1962	3	12	15	2	41					GSHAP	Russia:Sakhalin Island	俄罗斯:库页岛(萨哈林岛)	47. 1	143. 2	30	4. 8	Ms	5										
1962	3	18	15	30						* Turkey	Albania:Elbasan	阿尔巴尼亚:爱尔巴桑	40. 9	19. 5	33	6. 1	Muk		15	1				2				
1962	3	18	20	18	53					* China,Dis	China:Guangdong,Heyuan	中国:广东河源	23. 72	114. 67	5	6. 1	Ms	8	6	1	63	2		3	1200	4	9400	4
1962	3	19	23	5	8					GSHAP	Caspian Sea	里海	37. 46	54. 28	10	4. 5	Ms	6. 5										
1962	3	25	15	28	54					GSHAP	Colombia:El Carmen	哥伦比亚:北桑坦德的埃尔卡门	8. 5	-73. 3	92	4	Ms	5										
1962	3	28	0	51	55					GSHAP	Afghan:Badakhshan	阿富汗:巴达赫尚	36. 9	71. 4	110	6	Ms	5										
1962	4	1	0	45						* GSHAP	Iran:Razavi Khorasan	伊朗:呼罗珊	33. 6	59	33	5. 5	Ms	7	5	1				2				
1962	4	11	23	21	26					GSHAP	Carnegie Ridge	卡内基海岭	-0. 2	-91. 5	25	6. 4	Ms	5										
1962	4	12	0	52	43	4	1		-2	* Japan, GSHAP, Engdahl,NOAA	Japan Trench	日本海沟	38. 073	142. 741	24. 5	7. 2	Mw											
1962	4	13	15	38	52					USGS	US:California,Coleville	美国:加利福尼亚州科尔维尔	38. 22	-119. 46	6	5. 1	Ms	5										

年 Year	月 Mo	日 Dy	时 Hr	分 Mn	秒 Sec	海啸 Tsunami 源 Sr	浪高 Wh	级 I mI	级 S mS	资料来源 Information	震中 Earthquake Epicenter 地名(英文) Name(English)	地名(中文) Name(Chinese)	纬度(°) Latitude	经度(°) Longitude	深度 Depth	震级 Mag	标度 Scale	烈度 MMI	死亡人数 Deaths 数量/人 Num	级别 Dd	受伤人数 Injuries 数量/人 Num	级别 Dd	经济损失 Damage 数量/$ Mill	级别 De	房屋毁坏 Houses Destroyed 数量/间 Num	级别 Dh	房屋受损 Houses Damaged 数量/间 Num	级别 Dh
1962	4	18	19	14	37					* Shi Z.	Peru: Casma, Huaraz	秘鲁:卡斯马,安卡什(瓦拉斯)	-10	-79	39	6.3	Muk		9	1				2				
1962	4	19	23	16	5					GSHAP	Russia: Sakha, N.	俄罗斯:萨哈共和国北部	69.5	138.5	24	6.2	Ms	7.5										
1962	4	23	4	18	1					* China	China: Yunnan, Funing, E.	中国:云南富宁东	23.6	106.1		5.5	Ms	7						1				
1962	4	23	5	58	10	4	0.1	-3.3	-3.5	* GSHAP, Engdahl, Usami, Japan, NOAA	Japan: Hokkaido	日本:北海道	42.529	144.069	35	6.9	Ms	7	3									
1962	4	25	8	48	58					USGS	US: Nevada, Luning	美国:内华达州卢宁	38.5	-118.1	25	4.6	Ms	5										
1962	4	25								*	France: Le Gua	法国:勒瓜	45	5.6		5.3	Muk	8						2				
1962	4	27	9	12	32					USGS	US: California, Riverside	美国:加利福尼亚州里弗赛德	33.74	-117.19	6	4.1	Ms	6										
1962	4	30	2	26						* Usami	Japan: Kurihara	日本:宫城栗原	38.7	141.1	100	6.5	Muk		3	1				3	340	3		
1962	4	30	7	48	46					GSHAP	Colombia: Santander	哥伦比亚:桑坦德	6.9	-73	130	4	Ms	5										
1962	5	7	17	39	52					Engdahl, GSHAP	Kuril Islands	千岛群岛	45.166	147.025	19.8	6.7	Ms	8.5										
1962	5	10	0	3	40					USGS	Alaska Peninsula, S.	阿拉斯加半岛南部	61.96	-150.11	82	6	Ms	5										
1962	5	11	14	11	56	4	0.8	-0.3	0	* Engdahl, NOAA	Mexico: Acapulco	墨西哥:阿卡普尔科	17.171	-99.651	35	7.3	Mw	8	4	1		3		2		2		
1962	5	13	9	12	34					GSHAP	Colombia: Santander	哥伦比亚:桑坦德	6.9	-73	183	4	Ms	5										
1962	5	19	14	58	16	3	0.3			* Engdahl, NOAA	Mexico: Guerrero, Acapulco, E.	墨西哥:格雷罗州阿卡普尔科东部	17.008	-99.764	35	6.7	Ms		3	1	16	1		2		2		
1962	5	21	12	2	53					* China, Engdahl	China: Qinghai, Golmud, NE.	中国:青海格尔木东北	36.991	95.896	15.7	6.9	Ms							1		1		1
1962	5	21	12	21		2	0.1		-2	* NOAA	Japan: Hokkaido	日本:北海道	41.8	142.7	60	5.7	Ms											
1962	5	28	22	57	47	3				* NOAA	Aegean Sea	爱琴海	39.8	25		4.5	Ms											
1962	6	6	17	50	7					USGS	US: California, Ukiah	美国:加利福尼亚州尤凯亚	39.12	-123.1	10	5.2	Ms	7										
1962	6	11	7	15						*	Bosnia: Gorazde	波斯尼亚:戈拉日代	43.6	18.3		6.3	Muk						40.0	4				
1962	6	11	15	41	44					GSHAP	Colombia: Bucaramanga	哥伦比亚:布卡拉曼加	6.8	-73.1	40	4	Ms	5										
1962	6	24	1	21	18					* China, Dis	China: Yunnan, Nanhua	中国:云南南华	25.2	101.2		6.2	Ms	7	7		77	2		3	2550	4	1960	4
1962	6	27				4				NOAA, Song	Kiribati: Line Islands	基里巴斯:莱恩群岛	1.5	-157.2		7	Mk											
1962	6	28	4	27	14					USGS	Hawaiian Islands	夏威夷群岛	19.4	-155.45	10	6.1	Ms	6										
1962	7	1	11	46	30					GSHAP	Azerbaijan: Baki	阿塞拜疆:巴库	40.7	49.6	13	4.5	Ms	6										
1962	7	6	23	5	35					GSHAP, Engdahl	Afghan: Taloqan	阿富汗:塔卢坎	36.547	70.375	211.8	6.9	Ms	7										
1962	7	11	13	58	29					GSHAP	Colombia: Bucaramanga	哥伦比亚:布卡拉曼加	7	-73.1	182	4	Ms	5										
1962	7	14	19	43	46					USGS	US: California, Off Coast N.	美国:加利福尼亚州北部沿海	40.43	-125.51	30	5.1	Ms	5										
1962	7	16	12	54	43					USGS	Alaska Peninsula, S.	阿拉斯加半岛南部	62.27	-152.58	50	6	Ms	5										
1962	7	20	9	2	10					USGS	US: Nevada, Fallon, E.	美国:内华达州法伦东部	39.5	-118.2	33	4.7	Ms	5										
1962	7	25	3	48	16					USGS	Hawaiian Islands	夏威夷群岛	19.54	-155.96	2	4.7	Ms	5										

时间 Date						海啸 Tsunami				资料来源 Information	震中 Earthquake Epicenter				深度 Depth	震级 Mag	标度 Scale	烈度 MMI	死亡人数 Deaths		受伤人数 Injuries		经济损失 Damage		房屋毁坏 Houses Destroyed		房屋受损 Houses Damaged	
年 Year	月 Mo	日 Dy	时 Hr	分 Mn	秒 Sec	源 Sr	浪高 Wh	级I mI	级S mS		地名(英文) Name(English)	地名(中文) Name(Chinese)	纬度(°) Latitude	经度(°) Longitude					数量/人 Num	级别 Dd	数量/人 Num	级别 Dd	数量/$ Mill	级别 De	数量/间 Num	级别 Dh	数量/间 Num	级别 Dh
1962	7	26	8	14	46					* Engdahl	Panama:Off Coast of S.	巴拿马:南部海域	7.499	-82.781	23	7.2	Mw							2				
1962	7	30	20	19	3					*Shi Z ,Engdahl	Colombia:Mistrato	哥伦比亚:米斯特拉托	5.096	-76.626	150	6.9	Ms		47	1	300	3		3				3
1962	8	3	4	6	8					GSHAP	Colombia:Mistrato	哥伦比亚:米斯特拉托	5.2	-76.4	79	4	Ms	5										
1962	8	9	4	21	55					GSHAP	Colombia:Bucaramanga	哥伦比亚:布卡拉曼加	6.7	-73.1	180	4.5	Ms	6										
1962	8	15	10	6	55					GSHAP	Russia:Maritime Kray, Kirovsky	俄罗斯:滨海边疆区基洛夫斯基	45.1	133.1	30	5	Ms	5.5										
1962	8	18	6	59	33					GSHAP, Song	Ecuador:Off Coast of W.	厄瓜多尔:西部沿海	0.8	-82.3	33	4.5	Mk	5										
1962	8	18	16	43	56					USGS	Alaska Peninsula, S.	阿拉斯加半岛南部	62.26	-152.54	46	6.1	Ms	5										
1962	8	18	17	46	16					USGS	Alaska Peninsula, S.	阿拉斯加半岛南部	62.21	-152.5	40	6.3	Ms	5										
1962	8	19	18	26	38					* China	China:Xinjiang, Wenquan, SE.	中国:新疆温泉东南	44.68	81.58		6.4	Ms	8						1		1		
1962	8	21	18	19						* Italy	Italy:Benevento	意大利:贝内文托	41.13	14.97	34	6.19	Muk		16	1				2				
1962	8	23	19	29	15					USGS	US:California, North Coast	美国:加利福尼亚州北部近海	41.84	-124.39	59	5.6	Ms	6										
1962	8	26	6	49						Usami, Japan	Japan:Miyake Jima	日本:三宅岛	34.11	139.45	40	5.9	Ms								5	1		
1962	8	28	10	59	58					* Engdahl	Greece:Argolida	希腊:阿尔戈利斯	37.874	22.737	107.7	6.8	Ms		1	1				2				
1962	8	30	13	35						*	US:Utah, Logan	美国:犹他州洛根	41.8	-111.8	37	5.8	Muk	7					2	2				
1962	9	1	19	20	41					* Engdahl	Iran:Qazvin	伊朗:加兹温	35.556	49.81	17.6	6.9	Ms	9	12225	5	2776	4	30.0	4	21310	5		
1962	9	4	17	17	26					USGS	US:California, North Coast	美国:加利福尼亚州北部近海	41.01	-124.21	45	4.9	Ms	6										
1962	9	4	22	59	16					* Iran, GSHAP	Turkey:Igdir	土耳其:伊迪尔	39.9	43.9	10	5.8	Muk	7.5	1	1				2				
1962	9	5	6	39	17					GSHAP	Colombia:Galan	哥伦比亚:加兰	6.6	-73.4	200	4	Ms	5										
1962	9	5	16	4	28					USGS	US:Utah, Salt Lake City	美国:犹他州盐湖城	40.72	-112.09	7	5.2	Ms	6										
1962	9	12	20	10						GSHAP	Ecuador:Ambato	厄瓜多尔:安巴托	-1.04	-78.59		5.6	Ms	7										
1962	9	12	20	57	0					GSHAP, Afghan	Afghan:Qonduz	阿富汗:昆都士	36.5	69.2	50	6.63	Ms	7										
1962	9	14	0	33						*	Aegean Sea	爱琴海	39.6	23.3		5.5	Muk							2				
1962	9	15	22	50	49					GSHAP	Kuril Islands	千岛群岛	48.56	156.86	50	6.4	Ms	6.5										
1962	9	16	5	36	16					USGS	US:California, Inyo, W.	美国:加利福尼亚州因约县西部	35.76	-118.04	4	4.9	Ms	5										
1962	9	28	18	56	9					GSHAP	Colombia:Mistrato	哥伦比亚:米斯特拉托	5.2	-76.2	127	4	Ms	5										
1962	10	4	22	47	46					GSHAP	Colombia:S. of Armenia	哥伦比亚:亚美尼亚南部	4.2	-75.8	166	4.5	Ms	5										
1962	10	5	20	2						* Iran	Iran:Kashmar	伊朗:卡什马尔	35.1	58.7	8	5.3	Muk	8	6	1				2				
1962	10	6	13	33	37					GSHAP, Song	Venezuela:Carache	委内瑞拉:卡拉切	9.5	-70		4.5	Mk	5										
1962	10	9	13	22	25					China	China:Ningxia, Xiji, N.	中国:宁夏西吉北	36.1	105.7		4.7	Ms	6										
1962	10	21	2	5	24					USGS	Gulf of Alaska	阿拉斯加湾	61.39	-149.21	71	6	Ms	6										
1962	10	23	9	2	3					GSHAP	Venezuela:Carache	委内瑞拉:卡拉切	9.5	-70.21	25	4	Ms	5										
1962	10	29	2	42	54					USGS	US:California, Big Bear Lake	美国:加利福尼亚州大熊湖	34.33	-116.86	9	4.8	Ms	6										
1962	10	30				4				NOAA, Song	Kiribati:Line Islands	基里巴斯:莱恩群岛	1.5	-157.2		7	Mk											
1962	11	1	13	46	32					GSHAP	Tadzhikistan:Khatlon	塔吉克斯坦:哈特隆州	37.66	70.2	5	5	Ms	7										

年 Year	月 Mo	日 Dy	时 Hr	分 Mn	秒 Sec	源 Sr	浪高 Wh	级 I mI	级 S mS	资料来源 Information	地名(英文) Name(English)	地名(中文) Name(Chinese)	纬度(°) Latitude	经度(°) Longitude	深度 Depth	震级 Mag	标度 Scale	烈度 MMI	死亡人数 Deaths 数量/人 Num	死亡人数 Deaths 级别 Dd	受伤人数 Injuries 数量/人 Num	受伤人数 Injuries 级别 Dd	经济损失 Damage 数量/$ Mill	经济损失 Damage 级别 De	房屋毁坏 Houses Destroyed 数量/间 Num	房屋毁坏 Houses Destroyed 级别 Dh	房屋受损 Houses Damaged 数量/间 Num	房屋受损 Houses Damaged 级别 Dh
1962	11	6	0	9						*	Iran:Hormozgan	伊朗:荷姆兹甘	28.1	55.6	40	5.5	Muk							2				
1962	11	6	3	36	44					USGS	US:Oregon, Portland	美国:俄勒冈州波特兰	45.64	-122.59	16	5.2	Ms	7										
1962	11	11	3	52	19					GSHAP	Ecuador:Ambato	厄瓜多尔:安巴托	-1.2	-78.8	59	6.3	Ms	6										
1962	11	15	4	7	30					GSHAP	Colombia:Bucaramanga	哥伦比亚:布卡拉曼加	7.1	-73.2	40	4	Ms	5										
1962	11	15	23	25	15					GSHAP, Shi Z.	Peru:Chimbote, Near Coast	秘鲁:钦博特近海	-8.7	-79.8	45	6.1	Ms	6										
1962	11	16	6	39	8					GSHAP	Ecuador:Cotopaxi	厄瓜多尔:科托帕希	-1	-78.6	33	6.3	Ms	8										
1962	11	19	14	30	32					GSHAP	Colombia:Bucaramanga	哥伦比亚:布卡拉曼加	6.8	-73	135	4	Ms	5										
1962	12	7	9	36	1					China	China:Ningxia, Lingwu	中国:宁夏灵武	38.12	106.27		5.5	Ms	7										
1962	12	8	9	2	54					GSHAP	Iran:Gorgan	伊朗:戈尔甘	36.63	54.85	40	5	Ms	5.5										
1962	12	11	3	12	50					China	China:Gansu, Gangu, N.	中国:甘肃甘谷西北	34.75	105.05		5	Ms	6										
1962	12	15	3	48	35					GSHAP	Norway:West of Bodo	挪威:博德西部	67.5	14.2	30	4.5	Ms	6										
1962	12	17	17	25	39					* China	China:Ningxia, Wuzhong	中国:宁夏吴忠	38.03	106.18		5.5	Ms	7						1		1		
1962	12	21	8	42	43	1				* USGS, NOAA	Aleutian Islands	阿留申群岛	52.47	-168.54	33	6.5	Ms											
1962	12	31	20	49	35					USGS	US:Washington, Mt St Helens	美国:华盛顿州圣海伦山	47.1	-122	33	4.7	Ms	6										
1963	1	1	4	5	28					GSHAP	Colombia:Santander	哥伦比亚:桑坦德	6.9	-73.1	150	4.9	Ms	5										
1963	1	1	12	50	26					GSHAP	Colombia:Santander	哥伦比亚:桑坦德	6.9	-73	33	4.2	Ms	5										
1963	1	1	19	27	33					GSHAP	Iran:Mashhad	伊朗:马什哈德	35.4	58.9	11	4.6	Ms	6.5										
1963	1	4	21	17	10					GSHAP	Colombia:Santander	哥伦比亚:桑坦德	6.9	-73.1	160	4.4	Ms	5										
1963	1	8	19	39	45					USGS	Hawaiian Islands	夏威夷群岛	19.39	-155.22	31	4.6	Ms	5										
1963	1	11	0	7	25					China	China:Qinghai, Menyaun	中国:青海门源	37.4	101.6		4.75	Ms	7										
1963	1	12	3	40	33					GSHAP	Colombia:Sipi	哥伦比亚:乔科的锡皮	4.7	-76.7	84	5.8	Ms	6										
1963	1	12	6	20	18					GSHAP	Afghan:Kalafgan	阿富汗:卡拉夫甘	36.6	70	48	5.1	Ms	5										
1963	1	12	10	43	44					GSHAP	Colombia:Bucaramanga	哥伦比亚:布卡拉曼加	7.1	-73.5		3.5	Ms	5										
1963	1	14	18	33	24					GSHAP	Romania:Nereju	罗马尼亚:内雷茹	45.7	26.6	118	5.9	Ms	6										
1963	1	16	3	52	56					GSHAP	Colombia:Antioquia	哥伦比亚:安提奥基亚	7.5	-74.5	33	4.4	Ms	5										
1963	1	24	21	43	12					USGS	US:Washington, Seattle	美国:华盛顿州西雅图	47.6	-122.1	17	4.5	Ms	6										
1963	1	26	21	20	43					GSHAP	Colombia:Sipi	哥伦比亚:乔科的锡皮	4.5	-76.4	127	4	Ms	5										
1963	1	27	15	24	44					USGS	US:Idaho, Clayton	美国:爱达荷州克莱顿	44.19	-114.53	11	4.8	Ms	6										
1963	1	27	19	35	15					GSHAP	Caspian Sea	里海	41.08	49.84	55	6.2	Ms	7.5										
1963	1	31	2	27						*	Iran:Qūchān	伊朗:古昌	36.9	57.8	3	4.5	Muk	9	4	1				2				
1963	1	31	17	6	2					GSHAP	Azerbaijan:Baki	阿塞拜疆:巴库	40.8	49.8	5	4.5	Ms	5.5										
1963	2	13	8	50	5	4	0.2	-2.3	-2	* China, Engdahl, NOAA	China:Taiwan, Hualien, Coast of E.	中国:台湾花莲以东海域	24.356	122.06	35	7.3	Mw		15	1	18	1		2		2		
1963	2	16	3	1	41					USGS	US:Montana, Maudlow	美国:蒙大纳州莫德洛	46.1	-111	33	4.5	Ms	5										
1963	2	21	17	14	31					*	Libya:Barce (Al Marj)	利比亚:迈尔季	32.6	21	5	5.4	Ms		300	3	375	3	5.0	3		3		3
1963	2	27	0	10	1					GSHAP	Ecuador:Bolivar, N.	厄瓜多尔:波利瓦尔北部	-1.2	-79	33	4.3	Ms	6										
1963	2	28	16	5	46					GSHAP	Colombia:Santander	哥伦比亚:桑坦德	6.9	-73	40	4.2	Ms	5										

时间 年 Year	月 Mo	日 Dy	时 Hr	分 Mn	秒 Sec	海啸 源 Sr	浪高 Wh	级 I mI	级 S mS	资料来源 Information	震中 地名(英文) Name(English)	地名(中文) Name(Chinese)	纬度(°) Latitude	经度(°) Longitude	深度 Depth	震级 Mag	标度 Scale	烈度 MMI	死亡人数 数量/人 Deaths Num	级别 Dd	受伤人数 数量/人 Injuries Num	级别 Dd	经济损失 数量/$ Mill Damage $ Mill	级别 De	房屋毁坏 数量/间 Houses Destroyed Num	级别 Dh	房屋受损 数量/间 Houses Damaged Num	级别 Dh
1963	3	1	0	25	58					USGS	US:California,Arvin	美国:加利福尼亚州阿尔文	34.93	−118.97	14	5	Ms	5										
1963	3	1	3	20	2					GSHAP	Iran:Mashhad	伊朗:马什哈德	35.97	60.03	16	4.5	Ms	6										
1963	3	2	19	41	55					GSHAP	Colombia:Bucaramanga	哥伦比亚:布卡拉曼加	6.8	−73	165	4.2	Ms	5										
1963	3	3	17	30	11					USGS	US:Missouri,Bernie	美国:密苏里州伯尼	36.64	−90.05	9	4.8	Ms	6										
1963	3	7	23	53	27					USGS	US:Oregon,Salem	美国:俄勒冈州塞勒姆	44.88	−122.74		4.4	Ms	5										
1963	3	11	11	30	16					GSHAP	Colombia:Valle Del Cauca	哥伦比亚:考卡山谷	5.1	−76.4	95	4.3	Ms	5										
1963	3	16	8	44	49	1				* GSHAP, Engdahl	Kuril Islands	千岛群岛	46.641	154.951	13.7	7.2	Mw	8										
1963	3	24	12	44						*	Iran:Hamadan	伊朗:哈马丹	34.4	47.9	40	7.2	Muk		100	2				3				
1963	3	25	9	28	43					USGS	US:Nevada,Boulder City	美国:内华达州博尔德城	36	−114.8	19	4.9	Ms	6										
1963	3	26	21	34	41					Shi Z., Usami, Japan	Japan Sea	日本海	36	135.7		6.9	Ms				1	1			5	1		
1963	3	27	2	31	52					GSHAP	Colombia:Barrancabermeja	哥伦比亚:巴兰卡韦梅哈	6.8	−73.8	33	4.1	Ms	5										
1963	3	27	12	31	52					GSHAP	Colombia:Bucaramanga	哥伦比亚:布卡拉曼加	6.8	−73	176	4.6	Ms	5										
1963	3	27	13	15	30					GSHAP	Colombia:Charalá	哥伦比亚:查腊拉	6.3	−73.1	147	5	Ms	6										
1963	3	28	12	45						* Song	Italy:Calitri	意大利:卡利特里	40.8	15.6		6.5	Mk	12										
1963	3	31	2	27	7					* GSHAP	Iran:Qūchān	伊朗:古昌	37	57.9	33	7	Muk	8.5	4	1		3		2	100	2		
1963	4	1	6	42	46					GSHAP,Song	Venezuela:Coro	委内瑞拉:科罗	11.3	−69.9		4.5	Mk	5										
1963	4	2	0	57	45					GSHAP	Colombia:Santander	哥伦比亚:桑坦德	6.9	−73.1	159	5.2	Ms	6										
1963	4	4	6	7	21					GSHAP	Colombia:Tolima	哥伦比亚:托利马	3.9	−75	33	4	Ms	5										
1963	4	10	6	56	33					GSHAP	Colombia:Santander	哥伦比亚:桑坦德	6.9	−73.1	152	5.3	Ms	6										
1963	4	19	7	35	25					* China,Engdahl,	China:Qinghai,Maduo,NW.	中国:青海玛多西北	35.631	96.979	35	6.9	Ms	8						1		1		1
1963	4	23	9	55	7					* China	China:Yunnan,Yunlong,SE.	中国:云南云龙东南	25.8	99.5	20	6	Ms	7						2	5	1		
1963	5	4	4	41	16					GSHAP	Colombia:Guayabetal	哥伦比亚:瓜亚韦塔尔	4.2	−74.1	43	4	Ms	5										
1963	5	7	18	0	23					GSHAP	Colombia:Uribia,Near Coast	哥伦比亚:乌里维亚近海	12.1	−72.2	58	4.5	Ms	5										
1963	5	9	15	3	44					*	Nicaragua:Leon	尼加拉瓜:里昂	12.4	−87	50	5.5	Ms							1				
1963	5	10	22	22	44					GSHAP	Ecuador:Morona Santiago,N.	厄瓜多尔:莫罗纳－圣地亚哥北部	−2.12	−77.51	25	6.8	Ms	7										
1963	5	13	1	32	37					GSHAP	Colombia:Santander	哥伦比亚:桑坦德	6.9	−73.3	145	4.8	Ms	5										
1963	5	14	11	23	2					GSHAP	Ecuador:Near Coast of W.	厄瓜多尔:西部近海	0.7	−80.2	25	4.4	Ms	8										
1963	5	18	12	20	34					*	Indonesia:Bali Island	印度尼西亚:巴厘岛	−8.2	115.6	65	6	Muk							3				
1963	5	19	10	0	5					* Italy	Slovenia:Ljubljana	斯洛文尼亚:卢布尔雅那	46.1	14.8	13	5.17	Muk	7						2				
1963	5	20	13	22	9					GSHAP	Colombia:Narino	哥伦比亚:纳里尼奥	1.1	−77.6	148	4.2	Ms	5										
1963	5	22	13	56	49					Engdahl,GSHAP	Kuril Islands	千岛群岛	48.626	154.815	50.6	6.5	Muk	6										
1963	5	22	22	41	5					USGS	US:California,Pescadero	美国:加利福尼亚州佩斯卡德罗	37.27	−122.32		4.6	Ms	6										

年 Year	月 Mo	日 Dy	时 Hr	分 Mn	秒 Sec	海啸 Tsunami 源 Sr	浪高 Wh	级 I mI	级 S mS	资料来源 Information	震中 Earthquake Epicenter 地名(英文) Name(English)	地名(中文) Name(Chinese)	纬度(°) Latitude	经度(°) Longitude	深度 Depth	震级 Mag	标度 Scale	烈度 MMI	死亡人数 Deaths 数量/人 Num	级别 Dd	受伤人数 Injuries 数量/人 Num	级别 Dd	经济损失 Damage 数量/$ Mill	级别 De	房屋毁坏 Houses Destroyed 数量/间 Num	级别 Dh	房屋受损 Houses Damaged 数量/间 Num	级别 Dh
1963	5	23	15	53	2					USGS	US:California,Calipatria	美国:加利福尼亚州卡利帕特里亚	33.03	-115.68		4.8	Ms	6										
1963	5	26	23	6	54					GSHAP	Russia:Kamchatka Peninsula	俄罗斯:堪察加半岛	55.3	160.1	10	6	Ms	8										
1963	5	28	8	22	45					GSHAP	Colombia:Santander	哥伦比亚:桑坦德	6.9	-73	149	4.5	Ms	5										
1963	6	2	22	26	20					GSHAP	Colombia:Sucre	哥伦比亚:苏克雷	8.4	-74.8	34	4.8	Ms	5										
1963	6	3	11	31	51					GSHAP	Colombia:Sogamoso	哥伦比亚:索加莫索	5.4	-73	32	5	Ms	7										
1963	6	7	5	7	48					GSHAP,Song	Venezuela:Isla Cubagua	委内瑞拉:库巴瓜岛	10.6	-64.1		4.5	Mk	5										
1963	6	8	12	46	4					GSHAP	Colombia:Santander	哥伦比亚:桑坦德	6.9	-73.2	140	4.7	Ms	5										
1963	6	8	20	18	48					GSHAP	Colombia:Bahia Solano	哥伦比亚:巴伊阿索拉诺	6	-77		4	Ms	5										
1963	6	11	18	34	7					GSHAP	Tajikistan:Roghun	塔吉克斯坦:罗格汉	38.42	69.62	7	4.5	Ms	6.5										
1963	6	11	18	34	31					GSHAP	Colombia:Near Coast	哥伦比亚:近海	4.9	-77.5	33	4.4	Ms	5										
1963	6	21	13	44	24					* China	China:Heilongjiang,Luobei,N.	中国:黑龙江萝北北	47.9	130.6		5.8	Ms	7						1				
1963	6	24	4	26	37					Engdahl,USGS	Gulf of Alaska	阿拉斯加湾	59.273	-152.184	33	6.7	Ms	7										
1963	6	26	14	23	8					GSHAP	Colombia:Bucaramanga	哥伦比亚:布卡拉曼加	6.8	-73.1	142	4.5	Ms	5										
1963	6	30	7	41						*	Iran:Lorestan	伊朗:洛雷斯坦	33.2	49.2	38	5.1	Muk							2				
1963	7	4	8	3	48					GSHAP	Colombia:Riosucio	哥伦比亚:乔科的里奥苏西奥	7.5	-76.9	41	4.4	Ms	5										
1963	7	7	19	20	40					USGS	US:Utah, Levan	美国:犹他州勒万	39.53	-111.91	7	4.4	Ms	6										
1963	7	8	21	2	57					GSHAP	Colombia:Bucaramanga	哥伦比亚:布卡拉曼加	6.8	-73	166	4	Ms	5										
1963	7	11	14	18	30					GSHAP	Colombia:Bucaramanga	哥伦比亚:布卡拉曼加	6.8	-72.9	164	4	Ms	5										
1963	7	12	6	43	52					GSHAP	Colombia:Bucaramanga	哥伦比亚:布卡拉曼加	7	-73.2	127	4.5	Ms	5										
1963	7	14	5	41	45					GSHAP,Shi Z.	Venezuela:Yaguaraparo	委内瑞拉:亚瓜拉帕罗	10.45	-62.73	34	6.3	Ms	6										
1963	7	16	18	27	20					Engdahl,GSHAP	Russia:Karachaevo - Cherkess,Dombay	俄罗斯:卡拉恰伊-切尔克斯州栋巴伊	43.163	41.527	35	6.7	Ms	9										
1963	7	17	11	57	2					GSHAP	Georgia:Tkvarcheli	格鲁吉亚:特克瓦谢利	43.2	41.7	14	4.7	Ms	6.5										
1963	7	24	12	45	4					GSHAP	Venezuela:Aragua	委内瑞拉:阿拉瓜	10.2	-67.1		4	Ms	5										
1963	7	25	7	4	22					GSHAP	Colombia:Bucaramanga	哥伦比亚:布卡拉曼加	6.8	-73	152	5.2	Ms	6										
1963	7	26	4	17	13					* Turkey	Macedonia:Skopje	马其顿:斯科普里	42.1	21.5	5	6	Ms	10	1070	4	3300	4	1000	5		4		
1963	7	29	6	10						*	Iran:Hormozgan	伊朗:荷姆兹甘	28.2	55.7	46	5.2	Muk		5	1				2				
1963	7	30	6	34	57					USGS	US:California,Landers	美国:加利福尼亚州兰德斯	34.15	-116.21	13	4.7	Ms	5										
1963	8	7	4	33	43					GSHAP	Russia:Sakhalin Island	俄罗斯:库页岛(萨哈林岛)	53.8	142.7	17	5	Ms	5.5										
1963	8	14	14	32	37					GSHAP	Chile:Antofagasta,N.	智利:安托法加斯塔北部	-22.3	-68.7	120	5.1	Ms	5										
1963	8	15	0	47	5					GSHAP	Colombia:Cauca, Huila	哥伦比亚:考卡,乌伊拉	2.8	-76.1	33	4.3	Ms	5										
1963	8	15	17	25	8					* Engdahl	Peru:Puno,N.	秘鲁:普诺北部	-13.742	-69.332	552.1	7.7	Mw							1				

年 Year	月 Mo	日 Dy	时 Hr	分 Mn	秒 Sec	海啸 Tsunami 源 Sr	浪高 Wh	级 I mI	级 S mS	资料来源 Information	震中 Earthquake Epicenter 地名(英文) Name(English)	地名(中文) Name(Chinese)	纬度(°) Latitude	经度(°) Longitude	深度 Depth	震级 Mag	标度 Scale	烈度 MMI	死亡人数 Deaths 数量/人 Num	级别 Dd	受伤人数 Injuries 数量/人 Num	级别 Dd	经济损失 Damage 数量/$ Mill	级别 De	房屋毁坏 Houses Destroyed 数量/间 Num	级别 Dh	房屋受损 Houses Damaged 数量/间 Num	级别 Dh
1963	8	20	13	19	50					GSHAP	Colombia:Tulua	哥伦比亚:图卢阿	4.1	-76.5	50	4.5	Ms	5										
1963	8	22	23	20	21					GSHAP	Colombia:Tulua	哥伦比亚:图卢阿	4.3	-76.4	100	4.9	Ms	6										
1963	8	27								GSHAP	Brasil:Lajes	巴西:拉日斯	-5.69	-36.24		4.6	Ms	6										
1963	8	29	7	53	50					* China	China:Xinjiang,Ulugqat,W.	中国:新疆乌恰西	39.8	74.2		6.5	Ms	8	1	1				1	40	1		
1963	8	29	15	30	31					GSHAP,Shi Z.	Peru:Chiclayo,Near Coast	秘鲁:奇克拉约近海	-7.1	-81.6	23	6.5	Ms	6										
1963	9	2	1	34						*	India:Kashmir,SW.	印度:克什米尔西南	33.9	74.8	25	5.3	Muk		80	2				2				
1963	9	3	18	37	43					GSHAP	Colombia:Santander	哥伦比亚:桑坦德	6.9	-73.1	143	4.4	Ms	5										
1963	9	11	2	8	44					USGS	US:Idaho,Clayton	美国:爱达荷州克莱顿	44.18	-114.61	8	4.8	Ms	6										
1963	9	14	19	46	17					USGS	US:California,San Juan Bautista	美国:加利福尼亚州圣胡安包蒂斯塔	36.89	-121.6	3	5.4	Ms	7										
1963	9	17	5	54	36					Engdahl,GSHAP	Peru:Lima,Near Coast	秘鲁:利马近海	-10.69	-78.146	65.4	6.8	Muk	6										
1963	9	18	15	41	58					Iran,GSHAP	Turkmenistan:Asgabat	土库曼斯坦:阿什哈巴德	38.67	57.22	12	5.2	Ms	6.5										
1963	9	18	16	58	13	4			3	GSHAP,NOAA	Turkey:Istanbul	土耳其:伊斯坦布尔	40.9	29.2	33	6.38	Ms											
1963	9	23	14	41	53					USGS	US:California,Palm Springs	美国:加利福尼亚州棕泉	33.71	-116.93	17	5	Ms	6										
1963	9	24	6	35	52					USGS	US:Wyoming,Mammoth	美国:怀俄明州马默斯	44.9	-111	33	4.7	Ms	5										
1963	9	24	16	30	17	2				* Shi Z.,Engdahl,NOAA	Peru:Cajacay	秘鲁:卡哈凯	-10.694	-78.212	65.3	6.9	mB		1	1				2				
1963	9	29	21	58	23					GSHAP	Colombia:Santander	哥伦比亚:桑坦德	6.9	-73	157	4	Ms	5										
1963	9	30	3	46	51					GSHAP	Colombia:Riosucio	哥伦比亚:乔科的里奥苏西奥	7.3	-76.9	33	4.4	Ms	5										
1963	10	1	2	43	27					GSHAP	Colombia:Bucaramanga	哥伦比亚:布卡拉曼加	6.8	-73.1	132	4.6	Ms	5										
1963	10	2								GSHAP	Brasil:Lajes	巴西:拉日斯	-5.69	-36.24		4.9	Ms	6										
1963	10	12	11	27		4	0.1	-3.3	-2	* GSHAP,Engdahl,NOAA	Kuril Islands	千岛群岛	44.426	149.272	48.3	7.1	Mw											
1963	10	13	5	17	53	4	4.5	2.3	2.5	* Engdahl,NOAA	Kuril Islands	千岛群岛	44.77	149.798	13.4	8.6	Mw	9						1				
1963	10	16	15	42	59					China,GSHAP	Tajikistan:Kuhistoni Badakhshon,N.	塔吉克斯坦:勾瑙-巴达科善北部	38.8	73.3		6.6	Ms	8										
1963	10	19	6	46	4					GSHAP	Uzbekistan:Namangan	乌兹别克斯坦:纳曼干	41.17	71.63	8	4.7	Ms	6.5										
1963	10	20	0	53	11	4	15	3.9	3	* Japan,Engdahl,NOAA	Kuril Islands	千岛群岛	44.772	150.563	27.9	7.9	Mw											
1963	10	23	20	24	7					USGS	Hawaiian Islands	夏威夷群岛	19.38	-155.42	9	4.6	Ms	5										
1963	10	24	6	44	19					GSHAP	Colombia:Near Coast	哥伦比亚:近海	4.3	-78.4	38	5	Ms	6										
1963	10	24	7	24	3					GSHAP	Colombia:Near Coast	哥伦比亚:近海	4.4	-78.5	33	4.4	Ms	5										
1963	10	27	12	2	58					GSHAP	Colombia:Near Coast	哥伦比亚:近海	5.6	-79.4	32	4	Ms	5										
1963	11	4	1	3	13					GSHAP	Colombia:Off Coast of W.	哥伦比亚:西部沿海	2.3	-79.7	62	4.1	Ms	5										
1963	11	4	1	17	6					* Engdahl	Indonesia:Banda Sea	印度尼西亚:班达海	-6.733	129.684	35	7.8	mB							1				

年 Year	月 Mo	日 Dy	时 Hr	分 Mn	秒 Sec	源 Sr	浪高 Wh	级 I mI	级 S mS	资料来源 Information	地名(英文) Name(English)	地名(中文) Name(Chinese)	纬度(°) Latitude	经度(°) Longitude	深度 Depth	震级 Mag	标度 Scale	烈度 MMI	死亡人数 Deaths 数量/人 Num	死亡人数 级别 Dd	受伤人数 Injuries 数量/人 Num	受伤人数 级别 Dd	经济损失 Damage 数量/$ Mill $ Mill	经济损失 级别 De	房屋毁坏 Houses Destroyed 数量/间 Num	房屋毁坏 级别 Dh	房屋受损 Houses Damaged 数量/间 Num	房屋受损 级别 Dh
1963	11	13	9	1	13					GSHAP	Colombia:Santander	哥伦比亚:桑坦德	7	-73.5	149	4	Ms	5										
1963	11	24	16	49	31					GSHAP	Colombia:La Guajira, Near Coast	哥伦比亚:瓜希拉省近海	11.4	-73.8	111	4.1	Ms	5										
1963	11	25	6	50	9					GSHAP	Colombia:Santander	哥伦比亚:桑坦德	6.9	-73.3	167	4.2	Ms	5										
1963	11	25	17	53	37					GSHAP	Colombia:Bucaramanga	哥伦比亚:布卡拉曼加	6.8	-73	160	4	Ms	5										
1963	11	27	9	40	41					GSHAP	Colombia:Santander	哥伦比亚:桑坦德	7.2	-73.3	114	4	Ms	5										
1963	12	3	23	3	42					GSHAP,Shi Z.	Chile:Calama	智利:卡拉马	-22.4	-69.3	16	6.3	Ms	6										
1963	12	5	11	29	49					GSHAP	Colombia:Riosucio	哥伦比亚:里奥苏西奥	7.4	-77.3	33	4.7	Ms	5										
1963	12	6	8	34	22					USGS	US:California,Chalfant Valley	美国:加利福尼亚州夏芬谷	37.65	-118.4	2	4.7	Ms	6										
1963	12	8	11	8	5					GSHAP	Azerbaijan:Sirvan,NW.	阿塞拜疆:希尔万西北	40.1	48.7	19	4.5	Ms	5										
1963	12	10	3	31	21					Shi Z.	Indonesia:Banda Sea	印度尼西亚:班达海	-6.2	128.1	366	6	Ms							1				
1963	12	12	20	54	35					GSHAP	Colombia:Sogamoso	哥伦比亚:索加莫索	5.7	-73.1	140	4.9	Ms	6										
1963	12	13	5	28	7					GSHAP	Colombia:Bahia Solano	哥伦比亚:巴伊阿索拉诺	6.9	-77.1	33	4	Ms	5										
1963	12	16	1	51	31	2		-0.5	0	* Shi Z.,NOAA	Indonesia:Java Island	印度尼西亚:爪哇岛	-6.2	105.4	64	6.6	Ms							1				1
1963	12	18	0	30	3	2			0.5	* Shi Z., Engdahl, NOAA	Tonga Islands,SW.	汤加群岛西南	-24.776	-176.52	35	7.7	Mw											
1963	12	22	23	13	55					GSHAP	Colombia:Santander	哥伦比亚:桑坦德	6.9	-73	153	5.2	Ms	6										
1963	12	23	22	34	22					GSHAP	Colombia:Uribia,Near Coast	哥伦比亚:乌里维亚近海	12.3	-72.8	33	4.5	Ms	5										
1963	12	27	2	36	22					USGS	US:Oregon,Hillsboro	美国:俄勒冈州希尔斯伯勒	45.7	-123.4	33	4.1	Ms	6										
1963	12	31	15	18	7					GSHAP	Iran:Tabriz,N.	伊朗:大不里士北部	38.7	45.4	18	4.8	Ms	5.5										
1964	1	8	22	30	48					* ISC,Engdahl	Indonesia:Sulawesi	印度尼西亚:苏拉威西岛	-3.737	119.419	60	5.5	mb		8	1				3				
1964	1	18	12	4	40					* China, Engdahl, Dis	China:Taiwan,Kaohsiung	中国:台湾高雄	23.15	120.656	21	7	Ms	9	106	3	650	3		3	10502	5	25818	5
1964	2	13	9	3	53					* China	China:Yunnan,Binchuan,NE.	中国:云南宾川东北	26.1	101		5.4	Ms	7						1				
1964	2	18	12	19						*	Azores Islands	亚速尔群岛	38.8	-28.4	33	4.6	Muk							3				
1964	3	28	3	36	13	4	67	6.1	5	* Engdahl, NOAA	Gulf of Alaska	阿拉斯加湾	61.017	-147.648	6.6	9.2	M	10	139	3			430	5		3		
1964	4	2	1	11	58	3		-0.5	0	* Engdahl, NOAA	Indonesia:North of Banda Aceh	印度尼西亚:班达亚齐北部	5.987	95.404	129.2	5.6	mb	7						3		3		
1964	4	13	8	30						*	Croatia:Pozega	克罗地亚:波热加	45.3	18.1	32	6	Muk	8	3	1				3				
1964	4	29	9	16						* * Song	Indonesia:Sulawesi	印度尼西亚:苏拉威西岛	-0.5	121.5		6.2	Mk	8						3				
1964	5	5	2	53	11					GSHAP	Colombia:Santander	哥伦比亚:桑坦德	7.2	-73.4	122	4.8	Ms	5										
1964	5	7	5	45	32					* ISC,Engdahl	Tanzania:Singida	坦桑尼亚:辛吉达	-3.93	35.112	31.6	6.3	mb		1	1	19	1		3				
1964	5	7	7	58	14	4	0.9	-0.1	-3	* Usami, Engdahl, NOAA	Japan:Akita,Near West Coast	日本:秋田西部近海	40.407	139.024	21.1	6.6	Ms								3	1		

年	月	日	时	分	秒	源	浪高	级 I	级 S	资料来源	地名(英文)	地名(中文)	纬度(°)	经度(°)	深度	震级	标度	烈度	死亡人数 数量/人	死亡人数 级别	受伤人数 数量/人	受伤人数 级别	经济损失 数量/$ Mill	经济损失 级别	房屋毁坏 数量/间	房屋毁坏 级别	房屋受损 数量/间	房屋受损 级别
Date						Tsunami				Information	Earthquake Epicenter				Depth	Mag	Scale	MMI	Deaths		Injuries		Damage		Houses Destroyed		Houses Damaged	
Year	Mo	Dy	Hr	Mn	Sec	Sr	Wh	mI	mS		Name(English)	Name(Chinese)	Latitude	Longitude					Num	Dd	Num	Dd	$ Mill	De	Num	Dh	Num	Dh
1964	5	31	13	19	46					China	China:Gansu,Lintao	中国:甘肃临洮	35.3	103.3		5	Ms	6										
1964	6	14	12	15	34					* Engdahl	Turkey:Malatya,Adiyaman	土耳其:马拉蒂亚,阿德亚曼	38.08	38.475	10.4	6.1	Muk	8	8	1				2				
1964	6	16	4	1	41	4	5.8	2.7	2	* ISC,Usami,Engdahl,NOAA	Japan Sea	日本海	38.434	139.226	13.1	7.5	M	5	26	1	450	3	800	5	2250	4		
1964	6	23	1	26	38					* Japan,Engdahl	Kuril Islands	千岛群岛	43.27	146.151	75.3	7.2	mb				1	1						
1964	7	6	7	22	13					* Engdahl	Mexico:Guerrero,N.	墨西哥:格雷罗州北部	18.194	-100.51	92.7	7.2	mb		78	2				3				
1964	7	24	8	12	39	4	0.1	-3.3	-2	* ISC, Engdahl, NOAA	Kuril Islands	千岛群岛	47.159	153.876	14.9	6.8	Ms											
1964	8	27	12	25	22					GSHAP	Colombia:Cartago	哥伦比亚:卡塔戈	4.89	-76.19	109	4.8	Ms	5										
1964	9	1	22	20	30					* China	China:Shanxi,Yuanqu,SW.	中国:山西垣曲西南	35.1	111.6		4.7	Ms	7						1	23	1		
1964	9	5	7	49	3					Wang S.	China:Shaanxi,Shangnan,S.	中国:陕西商南南部	33.2	110.7	9	4.9	Ms	7										
1964	9	23	0	4	39					China	China:Guangdong,Heyuan	中国:广东河源	23.73	114.68	4	5.1	Ms	6										
1964	10	6	14	31	24					* Engdahl	Turkey:Manyas, Bursa	土耳其:马尼亚斯,布尔萨	40.25	28.208	31	7	Muk	10	19	1			5.0	3				
1964	10	18	2	49	18					GSHAP	Colombia:Narino	哥伦比亚:纳里尼奥	2.79	-78.03	76	4.8	Ms	5										
1964	10	30	16	47	54					GSHAP	Colombia:Bucaramanga	哥伦比亚:布卡拉曼加	6.84	-73.06	157	4.7	Ms	5										
1964	11	17	8	15	41	3	0.5	-1	-4	* Engdahl,NOAA	Papua New Guinea:East New Britain	巴布亚新几内亚:东新不列颠	-5.753	150.732	50.1	7.1	Mw							1				
1964	11	29	9	11	4					GSHAP	Colombia:Bucaramanga	哥伦比亚:布卡拉曼加	6.83	-73.14	154	4.9	Ms	5										
1964	12	7	21	3	48					GSHAP	Colombia:Off Coast of W.	哥伦比亚:西部沿海	2.7	-79.83	38	4.7	Ms	5										
1964	12	11	15	11	8	4	0.1	-3.3		* ISC,Usami,Engdahl,NOAA	Japan:Akita,Near West Coast	日本:秋田西部近海	40.474	139.056	34.3	5.8	mb											
1964	12	27								* Song	Iran:Hormozgan	伊朗:荷姆兹甘	27	54		5.9	Mk							2				
1965	1	1	21	38	29					*	Algeria:M'Sila	阿尔及利亚:姆西拉	35.7	4.4	10	5.5	Ms		4	1	350	3	2	2	25000	5		
1965	1	10	14	53	59					* China	China:Shanxi,Yuanqu,SW.	中国:山西垣曲西南	35	111.5	10	5.2	Ms	7						2		3		
1965	1	12	16	18	9					China	China:Shanxi,Yuanqu,S.	中国:山西垣曲南	35	111.63		5.5	Ms	7										
1965	1	24	0	11	17	4		2	1.5	* Engdahl,NOAA	Indonesia:Sanana Island	印度尼西亚:萨纳纳岛	-2.455	125.965	28.4	8.2	Mw		71	2				2	3000	4		
1965	2	4	5	1	22	4	11	3.3	2.5	* Engdahl,NOAA	Aleutian Islands	阿留申群岛	51.209	178.499	30.1	7.5	M	6					0.01	1				
1965	2	10	16	9						*	Iran:Tabriz	伊朗:大不里士	37.6	47.1	52	5.1	Muk		20	1				3				
1965	2	23	18	11	48	2				* Shi Z, Engdahl, NOAA	Chile:Taltal,Near Coast	智利:塔尔塔尔近海	-25.667	-70.71	38.5	7	Ms											
1965	3	9	17	57	54	3				* Engdahl,NOAA	Greece:Alonisos, Skopelos	希腊:爱琴海,斯科派洛斯岛	39.229	23.825	18	6.3	Mw		38	1	253	3	8.0	3		3		
1965	3	14	15	53	8					* Engdahl	Afghan:Badakhshan	阿富汗:巴达赫尚	36.4	70.716	209.7	7.5	mb	7						1				
1965	3	22	22	56	28	2				* ISC, Engdahl, NOAA	Chile:Los Vilos	智利:洛斯比洛斯	-31.99	-71.523	46.3	6	Muk	6										
1965	3	28	16	33	17					* Shi Z,Engdahl	Chile:Valparaiso	智利:瓦尔帕莱索	-32.492	-71.212	69.9	7.4	mb		400	3			125	5				
1965	3	30	2	27	5	4	0.1	-2.3	-1	* Engdahl,NOAA	Aleutian Islands,Rat Island	阿留申群岛,拉特岛	50.314	177.935	20	7.7	Mw											
1965	3	31	9	47	28					* Engdahl	Greece:Kato - Makrinou	希腊:下马克里努	38.339	22.299	50.3	6.3	mb	10	6	1				2				

年 Year	月 Mo	日 Dy	时 Hr	分 Mn	秒 Sec	源 Sr	浪高 Wh	级I mI	级S mS	资料来源 Information	地名(英文) Name(English)	地名(中文) Name(Chinese)	纬度(°) Latitude	经度(°) Longitude	深度 Depth	震级 Mag	标度 Scale	烈度 MMI	死亡人数 Deaths 数量/人 Num	级别 Dd	受伤人数 Injuries 数量/人 Num	级别 Dd	经济损失 Damage 数量/$ Mill	级别 De	房屋毁坏 Houses Destroyed 数量/间 Num	级别 Dh	房屋受损 Houses Damaged 数量/间 Num	级别 Dh
1965	4	4	20	31	35					GSHAP	Colombia:Cartago	哥伦比亚:卡塔戈	4.87	-76.09	104	4.9	Ms	5										
1965	4	5	3	12	54					*	Greece:Dukat	希腊:杜卡特	37.7	21.8	34	6.2	Ms	10	32	1	200	3		3		3		
1965	4	19	23	42	1					* ISC, Usami, Engdahl	Japan:Makinohara	日本:静冈牧之原	34.842	138.278	38.7	6	Ms		2	1	4	1		1				
1965	4	29	15	28	46					*Shi Z, Engdahl	US:Washington, Seattle	美国:华盛顿州西雅图	47.317	-122.335	65.4	6.8	Ms	8	7	1			28.0	4				
1965	5	1	16	35	40					GSHAP	Colombia:Bucaramanga	哥伦比亚:布卡拉曼加	6.83	-72.99	162	4.7	Ms	5										
1965	5	3	10	1	35					*	El Salvador:San Marcos	萨尔瓦多:圣马科斯	13.5	-89.3	23	6.3	Ms	6	125	3	1138	4	35.0	4				
1965	5	19	10	58	27					GSHAP	Colombia:Cartago	哥伦比亚:卡塔戈	4.9	-76.06	107	4.8	Ms	5										
1965	5	23	16	5	27					China	China:Yunnan, Eshan, SE.	中国:云南峨山东南	24	102.5		5.2	Ms	6										
1965	6	11	3	33	47	4	0.1	-3.3	-3	* ISC, Engdahl, NOAA	Kuril Islands	千岛群岛	44.614	148.941	44.3	7.1	Mw											
1965	6	21	0	21	14					* Engdahl	Iran:Hormozgan	伊朗:荷姆兹甘	28.098	55.841	14.3	5.6	Muk							3				
1965	6	29	20	0	14					GSHAP	Colombia:Bucaramanga	哥伦比亚:布卡拉曼加	7.17	-73.3	109	4.8	Ms	5										
1965	7	2	20	58	41	4	0.1	-3.3		* ISC, Shi Z., Engdahl, NOAA	Aleutian Islands	阿留申群岛	52.976	-167.569	57.7	6.5	Ms							1				
1965	7	3	11	26	13					*China, Engdahl	China:Yunnan, Sipsongpanna, NE.	中国:云南西双版纳东北	22.468	101.425	29	5.9	Muk	7						1				
1965	7	6	3	18	45	1	3	4.3	2	*Engdahl, NOAA	Greece:Gulf of Corinth	希腊:科林斯海湾	38.391	22.426	23.3	5.8	mb		1	1	6	1		2				
1965	7	26	11	1	22					GSHAP	Colombia:Santander	哥伦比亚:桑坦德	7.43	-72.94	159	4.8	Ms	5										
1965	8	2	18	4	58					GSHAP	Panama:Off Coast of S.	巴拿马:南部海域	7.63	-78.56	33	4.8	Ms	5										
1965	8	2	20	43	30					GSHAP	Panama:Off Coast of S.	巴拿马:南部海域	7.44	-78.53	24	4.8	Ms	5										
1965	8	11	20	4	15					GSHAP	Colombia:Bucaramanga	哥伦比亚:布卡拉曼加	6.87	-73.11	154	4.9	Ms	5										
1965	8	11	22	31	52	4	7	2.8	2.5	* ISC, Engdahl, NOAA	Vanuatu Islands	瓦努阿图群岛	-15.797	167.268	45.8	7.6	Mw							2				
1965	8	13	12	40	8	3	2	1	1.5	*Engdahl, NOAA	Vanuatu Islands	瓦努阿图群岛	-15.9	167.6	21.5	7.3	Mw											
1965	8	23	19	46	2	4	0.4	-1.3		*Engdahl, NOAA	Mexico:Oaxaca	墨西哥:瓦哈卡	16.178	-95.846	10.5	7.4	Mw		5	1				1				1
1965	8	27	15	58						* * Song	India:New Delhi	印度:新德里	28.6	76.7	58	5.9	Mk							2				
1965	9	7	4	37	54					China	China:Yunnan, Jianshui	中国:云南建水	23.7	102.7		4.7	Ms	6										
1965	10	3	16	14	56	2				* ISC, Shi Z., Engdahl, NOAA	Chile:Off Coast of S.	智利:南部沿海	-42.962	-75.381	20.2	6.5	Muk	3										
1965	11	13	4	33	55					* China, Engdahl, ISC, Dis	China:Xinjiang, Urumqi, E.	中国:新疆乌鲁木齐东	43.9	87.8	60	7	Ms	8	7		40	1			2000	4		
1965	11	25	23	29	48					GSHAP	Colombia:Bucaramanga	哥伦比亚:布卡拉曼加	6.67	-73.05	167	4.8	Ms	5										
1965	11	30	9	16	14					GSHAP	Colombia:Bucaramanga	哥伦比亚:布卡拉曼加	6.85	-73.15	173	4.7	Ms	5										
1965	12	3	18	48	26					GSHAP	Colombia:Bucaramanga	哥伦比亚:布卡拉曼加	6.83	-72.97	164	4.7	Ms	5										
1965	12	21	12	25	47					GSHAP	Colombia:Santander	哥伦比亚:桑坦德	6.93	-72.76	209	4.7	Ms	5										
1965	12	23	1	57	51					GSHAP	Colombia:Yacopi	哥伦比亚:亚科皮	5.29	-74.3	57	4.9	Ms	5										
1966	1	31	1	35	3					* China	China:Yunnan, Deqen, NW.	中国:云南迪庆西北	27.9	99.7		5.1	Ms	7						1		1		
1966	2	5	2	1	47					* Engdahl	Greece:Sophades (Karditsa)	希腊:卡尔季察	39.044	21.757	21.4	6.2	Muk		1	1	60	2	4	2	450	3		

年 Year	月 Mo	日 Dy	时 Hr	分 Mn	秒 Sec	海啸 Tsunami 源 Sr	浪高 Wh	级 I mI	级 S mS	资料来源 Information	震中 Earthquake Epicenter 地名(英文) Name(English)	地名(中文) Name(Chinese)	纬度(°) Latitude	经度(°) Longitude	深度 Depth	震级 Mag	标度 Scale	烈度 MMI	死亡人数 Deaths 数量/人 Num	级别 Dd	受伤人数 Injuries 数量/人 Num	级别 Dd	经济损失 Damage 数量/$ Mill	级别 De	房屋毁坏 Houses Destroyed 数量/间 Num	级别 Dh	房屋受损 Houses Damaged 数量/间 Num	级别 Dh
1966	2	5	15	12	31					* China, Engdahl, Dis	China: Yunnan, Dongchuan	中国:云南东川	26.16	103.171	9.2	6.5	Ms	9	305					2		3		
1966	2	13	10	44	39					* China, Engdahl	China: Yunnan, Dongchuan	中国:云南东川	26.174	103.252	2.2	6.2	Ms	8						1		1		
1966	2	18	3	45	12					China	China: Yunnan, Dongchuan	中国:云南东川	26.1	103.2		5.2	Ms	6										
1966	2	20	4	10	28					GSHAP	Colombia: Santander	哥伦比亚:桑坦德	6.94	-73.09	151	4.7	Ms	5										
1966	3	5	2	29	20					GSHAP	Venezuela: Lara	委内瑞拉:拉腊	9.93	-69.32	25	4.8	Ms	5										
1966	3	6	0	12	19					* China	China: Hebei, Ningjin, S.	中国:河北宁晋南	37.47	115.03		5.2	Ms	7						1	11	1		
1966	3	7	1	16	9					*	Turkey: Varto, Mus	土耳其:瓦尔托,穆什	39.1	41.6	38	6	Muk	8	10	1				3				
1966	3	7	21	29	16					* China, Engdahl, Dis	China: Hebei, Longyao, E.	中国:河北隆尧东	37.388	114.963	7.7	6.8	Ms	9		3				4		4		
1966	3	12	16	31	20	3	0.1	-3.3	0	* China, Engdahl, NOAA	China: Taiwan, Hualien, Coast of E.	中国:台湾花莲以东海域	24.307	122.695	28.9	7.4	Mw		7	1	11	1		2		2		
1966	3	18	4	59	28					GSHAP	Colombia: Bucaramanga	哥伦比亚:布卡拉曼加	6.73	-73.09	168	4.7	Ms	5										
1966	3	19	16	59	31					* China	China: Hebei, Julu, NW.	中国:河北巨鹿西北	37.27	114.97	20	5.6	Ms	6						1		2		
1966	3	20	1	42	51					* Engdahl	Uganda: Kichwamba	乌干达:基丘万巴	0.842	29.873	15	7.2	Muk		140	3		3	1.5	2				
1966	3	22	7	19	27					* China, Dis	China: Hebei, Ningjin, SE.	中国:河北宁晋东南	37.5	115.1	9	7.2	Ms	10	8064	3	38451	5	1637	5	5000000	5		
1966	3	26	2	14	10					GSHAP	Colombia: Santander	哥伦比亚:桑坦德	6.91	-73.09	159	4.7	Ms	5										
1966	3	26	15	19	1					* China, Engdahl, Dis	China: Hebei, Xinji, S.	中国:河北辛集南	37.74	115.172	5.7	6.2	Ms	7						2	8458	4	74415	5
1966	4	20	14	31	15					* China	China: Hebei, Longyao, S.	中国:河北隆尧南	37.25	114.78	14	5.3	Ms							1	22	1		
1966	4	21	8	18	25					GSHAP	Colombia: Bucaramanga	哥伦比亚:布卡拉曼加	6.87	-73.08	162	4.7	Ms	5										
1966	4	26								* Song	Uzbekistan: Tashkent	乌兹别克斯坦:塔什干	41.2	69.1		7.7	Mk		10	1			300	5				
1966	4	29	6	45	22					GSHAP	Colombia: Bucaramanga	哥伦比亚:布卡拉曼加	6.77	-73.18	169	4.7	Ms	5										
1966	5	2	23	13						*	Turkey: Siirt	土耳其:锡尔特	38	42.6	41	4.8	Muk							2				
1966	6	15	0	59	43	3	0.2	0.5	1	* Engdahl, NOAA	Solomon Islands	所罗门群岛	-10.4	160.8	31	7.1	Mw											
1966	6	26	23	30	55					China	China: Sichuan, Anxian	中国:四川安县	31.6	104.2	46	4.8	Ms	6										
1966	6	27	10	41	8					* ISC, Wang S., Engdahl	Nepal: Athpali	尼泊尔:阿特巴利	29.554	80.854	22.7	6.3	Muk		80	2			1	2				
1966	7	3								*	Turkey: Mus	土耳其:穆什	38.5	41.3		5.8	Ms		14	1								
1966	7	12	0	4	12					*	Turkey: Varto	土耳其:瓦尔托	38.9	41.3	64	4.6	Ms		12	1	20	1		3				
1966	7	12	18	53		4	0.2		1	* NOAA	Black Sea	黑海	44.75	37		5.5	Ms	6										
1966	8	15	2	15	33					* Engdahl	India: Delhi	印度:德里	28.616	78.892	25	5.6	mb		15	1				1				
1966	8	19	12	22	10					* Engdahl	Turkey: Varto	土耳其:瓦尔托	39.161	41.58	17.5	6.8	Muk	9	2394	4			20.0	3				
1966	9	1	14	13	48					*	Greece: Kyparissia (Messinia)	希腊:麦锡尼	37.5	22.1	17	5.9	Ms	8	1	1	25	1	14.0	3	180	3		
1966	9	4	22	14						*	Colombia: Bogota	哥伦比亚:波哥达	4.6	-73.9	8	5.2	Muk		6	1				3				
1966	9	19	4	3	53					* China	China: Yunnan, Ruili	中国:云南瑞丽	24	97.7		5.4	Ms	7						1				
1966	9	19	18	40						*	Venezuela: Falcon	委内瑞拉:法尔孔	10.8	-69.5	12	5	Muk							3				
1966	9	22	21	54	13					China	China: Yunnan, Xuanwei, E.	中国:云南宣威东	26.2	104.5		5	Ms	6										

时间						海啸				资料来源	震中				深度	震级	标度	烈度	死亡人数		受伤人数		经济损失		房屋毁坏		房屋受损	
年	月	日	时	分	秒	源	浪高	级 I	级 S		地名(英文)	地名(中文)	纬度(°)	经度(°)					数量/人	级别	数量/人	级别	数量/$ Mill	级别	数量/间	级别	数量/间	级别
Date						Tsunami				Information	Earthquake Epicenter				Depth	Mag	Scale	MMI	Deaths		Injuries		Damage		Houses Destroyed		Houses Damaged	
Year	Mo	Dy	Hr	Mn	Sec	Sr	Wh	mI	mS		Name(English)	Name(Chinese)	Latitude	Longitude					Num	Dd	Num	Dd	$ Mill	De	Num	Dh	Num	Dh
1966	9	28	14	0	21					* China, ISC, Engdahl	China: Yunnan, Deqen, SE.	中国:云南迪庆东南	27.457	100.089	5.5	6.4	Ms	9						3		3		
1966	10	2	2	24	57					* China	China: Jilin, Changchun	中国:吉林长春	43.83	125.12	10	5.2	Ms	7						3				
1966	10	11	9	6	20					China	China: Yunnan, Yongshan, S.	中国:云南永善南	27.9	103.81		5.2	Ms	6										
1966	10	17	21	41	55	4	3	-1	1.5	* Engdahl, NOAA	Peru: Lima, Huacho, Huaura	秘鲁:利马,瓦乔,窝拉河	-10.807	-78.684	20.7	8.2	Mw	9	110	3	3000	4	35.0	4				
1966	10	19	14	28	28					GSHAP	Colombia: Narino	哥伦比亚:纳里尼奥	2.84	-78.73	32	4.8	Ms	5										
1966	10	29	2	39	28					* Engdahl	Greece: Janina	希腊:伊欧亚里纳	38.874	21.176	11.3	5.7	mb		1	1	23	1		3		3		
1966	11	28				1			-0.5	NOAA, Song	Solomon Islands	所罗门群岛	-10	168		7	Mk											
1966	11	29	19	25	37					GSHAP	Colombia: Acandí, Near Coast	哥伦比亚:阿坎迪近海	9.11	-77.4	36	4.7	Ms	5										
1966	12	3	11	19	24					GSHAP	Colombia: Sogamoso	哥伦比亚:索加莫索	5.76	-72.53	25	4.7	Ms	5										
1966	12	28	8	18	7	4	0.4		0.5	* Engdahl, NOAA	Chile: Taltal, Catalina	智利:塔尔塔尔,卡特琳娜	-25.502	-70.655	30	7.7	Mw	8	3	1	6	1	0.4	1		3		
1966	12	31	18	23	11	4	2			* Engdahl, NOAA	Solomon Islands: Santa Cruz Islands	所罗门群岛:圣克鲁斯群岛	-11.893	166.445	82.8	7.3	mb							1				
1966	12	31	22	15	17	4	1.5			* Engdahl, NOAA	Solomon Islands: Santa Cruz Islands	所罗门群岛:圣克鲁斯群岛	-12.334	166.684	22.6	7.2	Mw											
1967	1	1	18	23	4	4	2	1		* NOAA	North Vanuatu Islands	瓦努阿图群岛北部	-11.8	166.5	33	8.1	Ms											
1967	1	3	17	21	42					GSHAP	Colombia: Bucaramanga	哥伦比亚:布卡拉曼加	6.79	-73.02	163	4.7	Ms	5										
1967	1	4	5	58						*	Greece: Patrai	希腊:帕特雷	38.4	22	10	6	Muk							2				
1967	1	5	0	14	40					* ISC, Engdahl	Mongolia: Southwest Bulgan	蒙古:布尔干西南	48.202	102.925	14.7	7	Mw	10						1				
1967	1	16	7	22	12					GSHAP	Colombia: Near Coast	哥伦比亚:近海	5.17	-77.61	43	4.7	Ms	5										
1967	1	22	8	18	15					GSHAP	Colombia: Bucaramanga	哥伦比亚:布卡拉曼加	6.8	-72.98	168	4.7	Ms	5										
1967	1	24	14	45	12					* China	China: Sichuan, Renshou, N.	中国:四川仁寿北	30.2	104.1		5.5	Ms	7						2	417	3		
1967	2	9	14	4	48					*	Albania: Gjirokastev	阿尔巴尼亚:吉诺卡斯特	40	20.2	33	5.6	Ms							2	77	2		
1967	2	9	15	24	47					* ISC, Shi Z., Engdahl	Colombia: Huila, Neiva, Rivera	哥伦比亚:乌伊拉,内瓦,里维埃拉	2.889	-74.799	40.4	7.2	Mw	9	98	2			20.0	3				
1967	2	19	22	14	39					* Engdahl	Indonesia: Java Ridge	印度尼西亚:爪哇海岭	-9.168	112.946	97.9	6.8	Muk	9	54	2				3				
1967	3	19	4	1	36	1				* NOAA, ISC, Engdahl	Kuril Islands	千岛群岛	45.626	151.197	8.7	7	Ms	8										
1967	3	25	14	29	12					GSHAP	Panama: Off Coast of S.	巴拿马:南部海域	7.35	-79.85	20	4.7	Ms	5										
1967	3	27	8	58	24					* China, Engdahl, Dis	China: Hebei, Hejian	中国:河北河间	38.516	116.601	26.8	6.3	Ms	7	19		916	3		3	15700	5		
1967	4	6	6	17						Usami	Japan: Shizuoka, Near Coast	日本:静冈近海	34.11	139.15	10	5.3	Ms								7	1		
1967	4	11	5	9	12	3		1.6	1.5	* NOAA	Indonesia: Makassar Strait	印度尼西亚:望加锡海峡	-3.7	119.3	33	5.5	Ms		71	2	100	2		2		2		

时间 年 Date Year	月 Mo	日 Dy	时 Hr	分 Mn	秒 Sec	海啸 Tsunami 源 Sr	浪高 Wh	级 I mI	级 S mS	资料来源 Information	震中 Earthquake Epicenter 地名(英文) Name(English)	地名(中文) Name(Chinese)	纬度(°) Latitude	经度(°) Longitude	深度 Depth	震级 Mag	标度 Scale	烈度 MMI	死亡人数 Deaths 数量/人 Num	级别 Dd	受伤人数 Injuries 数量/人 Num	级别 Dd	经济损失 Damage 数量/$ Mill $ Mill	级别 De	房屋毁坏 Houses Destroyed 数量/间 Num	级别 Dh	房屋受损 Houses Damaged 数量/间 Num	级别 Dh
1967	4	12	4	51	37	3		1	1.5	* Engdahl, NOAA	Indonesia: Sumatera, Aceh	印度尼西亚:苏门答腊亚齐	5.084	96.232	18.6	6.1	mb		14	1				3	2000	4		
1967	4	20	2	24	45					GSHAP	Colombia: Bucaramanga	哥伦比亚:布卡拉曼加	6.71	-73.2	156	4.8	Ms	5										
1967	5	1	7	9	2					* Engdahl	Greece: Janina	希腊:伊欧亚尼纳	39.552	21.291	13	5.9	Muk		9	1			5.0	3				
1967	5	6	19	39	21					GSHAP	Colombia: Bahia Solano	哥伦比亚:巴伊阿索拉诺	6.7	-77.3	33	4.8	Ms	5										
1967	5	12	9	28	47					GSHAP	Colombia: Bucaramanga	哥伦比亚:布卡拉曼加	6.87	-73	155	4.8	Ms	5										
1967	7	13	2	10	20					*	Algeria: Mascara	阿尔及利亚:马斯卡拉	35.5	-0.1	13	5	Ms		10	1	15	1		1	40	1		
1967	7	22	16	56	55					* Engdahl	Turkey: Mudurnu, Adapazari	土耳其:穆杜尔努,阿达帕札勒	40.632	30.74	4.2	7.4	Mw	10	86	2			3	2				
1967	7	26	18	52	60					* Engdahl	Turkey: Tunceli	土耳其:通杰利	39.502	40.408	8.7	6.2	Muk		97	2				3				
1967	7	28	4	55	58					China	China: Hebei, Huailai, NE.	中国:河北怀来东北	40.55	115.55	10	5.4	Ms	6										
1967	7	29	0	0	3	4	0.1			* Engdahl, NOAA	Venezuela: El Tocuyo	委内瑞拉:托丘约	10.555	-67.31	23.7	6.5	Mw	8	300	3	1536	4	140	5				
1967	7	29	10	24	26					* Engdahl	Colombia: Bucaramanga	哥伦比亚:布卡拉曼加	6.788	-73.073	160.9	6.8	Ms		20	1				3				
1967	8	13	22	7	48					* ISC	France: Arette, Aramits	法国:阿雷特,阿拉米	43.2	-0.5	15	5.9	Muk	8	1	1	80	2		2		3		
1967	8	13	22	15	10	4	0.1	-3.3	3	* NOAA	Papua New Guinea: East New Britain	巴布亚新几内亚:东新不列颠	-4.4	152.5	30	6.4	Ms							3				
1967	8	15	4	6	57					GSHAP	Colombia: Bucaramanga	哥伦比亚:布卡拉曼加	6.87	-73.02	168	4.7	Ms	5										
1967	8	19	7	3	9					GSHAP	Colombia: Bucaramanga	哥伦比亚:布卡拉曼加	6.86	-73.07	159	4.9	Ms	5										
1967	8	19	23	31	41					China	China: Sichuan, Nanjiang, N.	中国:四川南江北部	32.7	106.8		4.8	Ms	6										
1967	8	30	4	22	4					* China, Engdahl	China: Sichuan, Luhuo, NW.	中国:四川炉霍西北	31.631	100.232	8.1	7	Muk	9						4		4		
1967	9	1	2	49	19					GSHAP	Colombia: Bucaramanga	哥伦比亚:布卡拉曼加	6.83	-73.15	155	4.9	Ms	5										
1967	9	3	21	7	32	4	2	1	1.5	* Shi Z, Engdahl, NOAA	Peru: Chimbote, Off Coast	秘鲁:钦博特沿海	-10.601	-79.689	36.5	6.8	Ms											
1967	10	15	21	43	59					China	China: Gansu, Jingyuan, NE.	中国:甘肃靖远东北	36.8	105		4.8	Ms	6										
1967	10	25	0	59	24					* China, Engdahl	China: Taiwan, Hualien, Coast of E.	中国:台湾花莲以东海域	24.464	122.221	67.1	7	mb		2	1				2	23	1		
1967	10	25	4	49	38					GSHAP	Colombia: Bucaramanga	哥伦比亚:布卡拉曼加	6.89	-73.02	159	4.8	Ms	5										
1967	11	5	14	23	54					GSHAP	Colombia: Neiva	哥伦比亚:内瓦	3.13	-74.81	36	4.9	Ms	5										
1967	11	15	21	31	56	2				* ISC, Shi Z, Engdahl, NOAA	Chile: Vallenar	智利:巴耶纳尔	-28.792	-71.165	35.9	6	mb											
1967	11	30	7	23	54					* ISC, Engdahl	Albania: Durres, NE.	阿尔巴尼亚:都拉斯东北	41.379	20.456	36.5	6.7	Muk	10	18	1			20.0	3				
1967	12	2	20	5	48					* China	China: Hebei, Xinji, S.	中国:河北辛集南	37.72	115.22	25	5.7	Ms	7						2		1		
1967	12	10	22	51	22					* India, ISC, Engdahl	India: Satara	印度:萨达拉	17.394	73.774	10.7	6.3	M	8	180	3			0.4	1				
1967	12	18	14	7	45					* China	China: Shanxi, Puxian	中国:山西蒲县	36.47	111.22	30	5.4	Ms	6						1		1		
1967	12	21	2	25	24	4	0.7	-0.5	0	* Shi Z, Engdahl, NOAA	Chile: Antofagasta, N.	智利:安托法加斯塔北部	-21.864	-69.948	42.5	7.4	Mw		1	1		3		2		2		
1968	1	4	10	3						*	Nicaragua: Managua	尼加拉瓜:马拉瓜	12.1	-86.2	5	4.6	Ms						2	2				

年 Year	月 Mo	日 Dy	时 Hr	分 Mn	秒 Sec	海啸 Tsunami 源 Sr	浪高 Wh	级 I mI	级 S mS	资料来源 Information	震中 Earthquake Epicenter 地名(英文) Name(English)	地名(中文) Name(Chinese)	纬度(°) Latitude	经度(°) Longitude	深度 Depth	震级 Mag	标度 Scale	烈度 MMI	死亡人数 Deaths 数量/人 Num	级别 Dd	受伤人数 Injuries 数量/人 Num	级别 Dd	经济损失 Damage 数量/$ Mill	级别 De	房屋毁坏 Houses Destroyed 数量/间 Num	级别 Dh	房屋受损 Houses Damaged 数量/间 Num	级别 Dh
1968	1	15	2	1	9					* Italy	Italy:Sicily,Belice Valley	意大利:西西里岛,贝利切谷	37.77	12.98	33	6.12	Ms		216	3	563	3	320	5				
1968	1	25	9	56	49					*	Italy:Sicily,Belice Valley	意大利:西西里岛,贝利切谷	37.8	13.2	33	5.1	Ms		8	1	55	2		1				
1968	1	28	1	50	48					GSHAP	Colombia:Neiva	哥伦比亚:内瓦	3.08	-75.02	66	4.7	Ms	5										
1968	1	29	10	19	7	4	0.3	-1.7	-1	* ISC,Engdahl,NOAA	Kuril Islands	千岛群岛	43.586	146.701	39.7	7.3	Mw											
1968	2	12	5	44	44					* ISC,Engdahl	New Britain Trench	新不列颠海沟[太平洋]	-5.502	153.404	23.2	7.4	Mw	8						1				
1968	2	19	22	45	44	3	1.2	0.3	3	* ISC,Engdahl,NOAA	Aegean Sea	爱琴海	39.372	24.946	8.1	7.2	Mw	10	20	1			0.6	1				
1968	2	21	1	45						* Usami	Japan:Kagoshima	日本:鹿岛	32	130.6	3	6.3	Muk		3	1				2	368	3		
1968	2	25								*	Algeria:Setif	阿尔及利亚:塞提夫	36.08	5.07		4.9	Ms	8	1	1	4	1		2	100	2		
1968	3	20	19	2	50					*	Kenya:Homa Bay	肯尼亚:霍马湾	-0.6	34.4	33	4.6	Ms		1	1	1	1		1				
1968	4	1	0	42	5	4	3.1	1.3	1.5	* Usami, Engdahl, NOAA	Japan:Miyazzaki,Near Coast	日本:宫崎近海	32.482	132.192	30.2	7.5	Mw	7	1	1	22	1		2		2		
1968	4	1	9	5	5					China	China:Fujian,Hua - an	中国:福建华安	25.1	117.6		5.2	Ms	6										
1968	4	29	17	1	58					*	Iran:Maku	伊朗:马库	39.2	44.3	34	5.3	Ms	7	38	1	100	2	1	2	1000	3		
1968	5	2	10	2						*	Iran:Maku	伊朗:马库	39.3	44.4		6.2	Ms	6						3				
1968	5	4				3				NOAA,Song	Easter Island	复活节岛	-27.15	-109.45		7	Mk											
1968	5	16	0	49	0	4	6	2.3	-0.5	* ISC,Engdahl,NOAA	Japan Trench	日本海沟	40.903	143.346	25.8	8.3	Mw	6	52	2	329	3	131	5	1218	4		
1968	5	16	10	39	1	4	0.6			* ISC,Engdahl,NOAA	Japan:Aomori,Near Coast of E.	日本:青森东部近海	41.593	142.786	11.8	7.8	Mw											
1968	5	23	17	24	20					* ISC, Shi Z., Engdahl	New Zealand:South Island,Murchison	新西兰:南岛,默奇森	-41.743	172.123	46.7	7.2	Mw		3	1			3	2				
1968	5	28	13	27	20					* ISC,Engdahl	Indonesia:Papua,N.	印度尼西亚:巴布亚北部	-2.919	139.411	63.7	7.2	mb							1				
1968	6	9								*	Armenia:Zangezur	亚美尼亚:休尼克	39.1	46.1	31	5	Muk	7						2				
1968	6	12	13	41	51	4	0.1	1.6		* Engdahl,NOAA	Japan:Miyako,Near Coast	日本:宫古近海	39.501	142.893	31.2	7.1	Mw							1				
1968	6	19	8	13	35					* Shi Z., Engdahl	Peru:San Martin,Moyobamba	秘鲁:圣马丁,莫约班巴	-5.558	-77.151	15.6	6.9	Ms		15	1			0.1	1				
1968	6	23	9	16	18					*	Iran:Bushehr	伊朗:布什尔	29.8	51.2	32	5.3	Muk							3				
1968	7	25	7	23	9	3	0.1			* ISC,Engdahl,NOAA	Kermadec Ridge	克马德克海岭	-30.811	-178.148	65.1	7.1	mb							1				
1968	8	1	20	19	25	4	0.2	-1.7		* Bautista,Engdahl,NOAA	Philippines:Santiago,SE.	菲律宾:圣地亚哥东南	16.384	122.078	52.2	7.7	Mw		270	3	261	3	8.0	3		3		
1968	8	2	14	6	46					* ISC,Shi Z., Engdahl	Mexico:Oaxaca,Guerrero	墨西哥:瓦哈卡,格雷罗	16.494	-97.771	49.8	7.3	Mw	7	18	1			2.4	2				
1968	8	5	7	17	5	1				* NOAA,ISC	Japan:Osaka	日本:大阪	33.3	132.2	10	6.5	Ms											

时间 Date						海啸 Tsunami				资料来源	震中 Earthquake Epicenter				深度	震级	标度	烈度	死亡人数 Deaths		受伤人数 Injuries		经济损失 Damage		房屋毁坏 Houses Destroyed		房屋受损 Houses Damaged	
年	月	日	时	分	秒	源	浪高	级 I	级 S		地名(英文)	地名(中文)	纬度(°)	经度(°)					数量/人	级别	数量/人	级别	数量/$ Mill	级别	数量/间	级别	数量/间	级别
Year	Mo	Dy	Hr	Mn	Sec	Sr	Wh	mI	mS	Information	Name(English)	Name(Chinese)	Latitude	Longitude	Depth	Mag	Scale	MMI	Num	Dd	Num	Dd	$ Mill	De	Num	Dh	Num	Dh
1968	8	5	16	17	7					ISC, Usami, Engdahl	Japan: Ehime	日本:爱媛	33.327	132.225	45.1	6.2	mb								1	1		
1968	8	10	2	7	4	4	0.4	-1.3		* ISC, Engdahl, NOAA	Molukka Sea	马鲁古海	1.422	126.26	19.6	7.6	Mw							1				
1968	8	14	22	14	20	4	10	3.3	3	* ISC, Engdahl, NOAA	Indonesia: Sulawesi, Tambu	印度尼西亚:苏拉威西岛,坦布	0.058	119.69	18.8	7.3	Mw	8	200	3	58	2		3	800	3		
1968	8	31	10	47	40					* ISC, Engdahl	Iran: Razavi Khorasan	伊朗:呼罗珊	34.045	58.96	12.3	7.2	Mw	10	12100	5	17000	5	35.0	4	12000	5		
1968	9	1	5	39						*	Armenia: Zangezur	亚美尼亚:休尼克	39.1	46.2	24	5	Muk	8						3				
1968	9	1	7	27	31					* ISC, Engdahl	Iran: Razavi Khorasan	伊朗:呼罗珊	34.072	58.212	15	6.3	Ms		700	3				3	1500	4		
1968	9	3	8	19	54	3	3			* Engdahl, NOAA	Turkey: Bartin, Amasra	土耳其:巴尔腾,阿马斯腊	41.771	32.452	4.9	6.6	Mw	8	24	1	200	3		3	2000	4		
1968	9	4	23	24						*	Iran: Razavi Khorasan	伊朗:呼罗珊	33.9	58.2	15	5.4	Muk							3				
1968	9	20	6	0	5	2				* Shi Z, Engdahl, NOAA	Venezuela: Carupano	委内瑞拉:卡鲁帕诺	10.731	-62.719	102.6	6.2	mb	9	3	1				2				
1968	9	24	4	19						*	Turkey: Bingol	土耳其:宾格尔	39.2	40.1	14	5.1	Muk		2	1				3				
1968	9	25	10	38	38	1	2		1	* ISC, Engdahl, NOAA	Mexico: Chiapas	墨西哥:恰帕斯州	15.551	-92.66	122.4	5.8	mb		20	1	500	3		2				
1968	10	7	19	20	22					* Engdahl	Japan: South Honshu Ridge	日本:本州南部海岭	26.291	140.682	519.8	7.3	Mw	5										
1968	10	14	2	58	51					* ISC, Engdahl	Australia: Meckering, Northam	澳大利亚:梅克林,诺瑟姆	-31.523	116.978	5	6.8	Ms	9					2.2	2				
1968	10	21	14	3	38					GSHAP	Colombia: Urrao	哥伦比亚:乌劳	6.54	-76.54	25	4.7	Ms	5										
1968	10	23	21	4	43					* Engdahl	Papua New Guinea: Wewak, Dagua	巴布亚新几内亚:威瓦克,达呱区	-3.375	143.322	9.4	7.1	Mw							2				
1968	11	3	4	49						*	Montenegro: Bar	蒙特尼哥罗(黑山):巴尔	42.1	19.3	17	5.3	Muk		1	1			38.6	4				
1969	1	2	0	45	1					China	China: Hubei, Baokang	中国:湖北保康	31.5	111.2		4.8	Ms	6										
1969	1	3	3	16						*	Iran: Shirvan	伊朗:希尔凡	37.1	57.9	11	5.6	Muk	8	50	1				2				
1969	1	5	13	26	43					* Engdahl	Solomon Islands: Santa Isabel Island	所罗门群岛:圣伊萨贝尔岛	-7.991	158.968	62.8	7.3	mb							1				
1969	1	19	7	2	9					* ISC, Engdahl	Japan: Hokkaido, Coast N.	日本:北海道北部海域	44.891	143.207	237.1	7.3	mb							1				
1969	2	11	22	8	54					* China, ISC, Engdahl	China: Xinjiang, Uqturpan	中国:新疆乌什	41.426	79.239	13.1	7.1	Muk	8	4	1		1		3		3		
1969	2	23	0	37	5	4	4	2	2	* Shi Z, Engdahl, NOAA	Indonesia: Sulawesi	印度尼西亚:苏拉威西岛	-3.179	118.799	60.6	5.9	mb		664	3				3	1287	4		
1969	2	28	2	40	35	4	1.1			* Engdahl, NOAA	Portugal: Lisboa; Morocco: Raba	葡萄牙:里斯本;摩洛哥:拉巴特	35.923	-10.568	32.5	7.8	Mw	7	13	1	80	2		2				
1969	3	23	21	8	45					* ISC, Engdahl	Turkey: Demirci, Gordes	土耳其:代米尔吉,戈尔德	39.127	28.492	16.3	5.6	mb	8						3				
1969	3	28	1	48	32					* ISC, Engdahl	Turkey: Alasehir, Sarigol	土耳其:阿拉谢希尔,萨里格尔	38.535	28.467	9.3	6.4	Ms		53	2				3				
1969	3	29	9	15	53					* ISC, Engdahl	Ethiopia: Afar	埃塞俄比亚:阿法尔区	11.939	41.219	12	6.3	Ms	9	40	1	160	3	0.32	1		3		

年 Year	月 Mo	日 Dy	时 Hr	分 Mn	秒 Sec	海啸 Tsunami 源 Sr	浪高 Wh	级 I mI	级 S mS	资料来源 Information	震中 Earthquake Epicenter 地名(英文) Name(English)	地名(中文) Name(Chinese)	纬度(°) Latitude	经度(°) Longitude	深度 Depth	震级 Mag	标度 Scale	烈度 MMI	死亡人数 Deaths 数量/人 Num	级别 Dd	受伤人数 Injuries 数量/人 Num	级别 Dd	经济损失 Damage 数量/$ Mill	级别 De	房屋毁坏 Houses Destroyed 数量/间 Num	级别 Dh	房屋受损 Houses Damaged 数量/间 Num	级别 Dh
1969	3	31	7	15	51	3				* ISC, Engdahl, NOAA	Egypt: South of Gulf of Suez	埃及:苏伊士湾南端	27.511	33.936	3.5	6.8	Ms		2	1	16	1		3	107	3		
1969	4	3	22	12						*	Albania: Kuçovë	阿尔巴尼亚:库乔亚区	40.7	19.8	33	5.5	Muk		1	1				2				
1969	4	21	7	19	28	4	0.2	-2.3	-3	* Usami, Engdahl, NOAA	Japan: Miyazzaki, Near Coast	日本:宫崎近海	32.149	131.868	37.1	7	Muk											
1969	4	30	20	20						*	Turkey: Demirci	土耳其:代米尔吉	39.2	28.6	9	5.1	Muk							2				
1969	7	18	4	24	47					* China, Engdahl, ISC, Dis	China: Bohai Sea	中国:渤海	38.421	119.453	12	7.4	Ms	7	10		353	3	72.3	4	15290	5		
1969	7	24	2	59	23					* Engdahl	Peru: Lampa – Junin	秘鲁:兰姆帕–胡宁	-11.863	-75.083	2.1	5.7	Ms	11						3				
1969	7	25	14	49	38					* China, Engdahl, Dis	China: Guangdong, Yangjiang	中国:广东阳江	21.612	111.809	3.4	6.4	Ms	8	33	1	998	3	35.5	4	10762	5	35965	5
1969	8	2	4	30	29	4			-1	* NOAA	Papua New Guinea: Lae	巴布亚新几内亚:莱城	-6.6	146.9	17	5.4	Ms											
1969	8	11	13	55						* Italy	Italy: Perugia	意大利:佩鲁贾	43.036	12.226	33	5.09	Muk	7						2				
1969	8	11	21	27	38	4	5	1.4	2	* ISC, Engdahl, NOAA	Kuril Islands	千岛群岛	43.478	147.815	45.6	8.2	Mw	9						2				
1969	9	9	5	15	38					ISC, Usami, Engdahl	Japan: Gujo	日本:岐阜郡上	35.786	137.093	7.5	6	Ms		1	1								
1969	9	14	16	15	27					* China, Engdahl	China: Xinjiang, Ulugqat, W.	中国:新疆乌恰西	39.739	74.807	31.2	5.6	Ms	7						1	10	1		
1969	9	29	20	3	30					* Engdahl	South Africa: Ceres	南非:锡里斯	-33.19	19.336	15	6.3	Ms		12	1			24.0	3				
1969	10	1	5	5	46					* ISC, Shi Z., Engdahl	Peru: Huancayo	秘鲁:万卡约	-11.835	-75.195	6.5	6.2	Ms	11	150	3			5.0	3				
1969	10	2	4	56	47					* USGS	US: California, Santa Rosa	美国:加利福尼亚州圣罗莎	38.467	-122.692	10	5.6	ML	8	1	1			8.4	3				
1969	10	5	1	22						*	South Africa: Tulbagh	南非:图尔巴	-33.1	19.6	33	5.8	Muk							2				
1969	10	26	15	36	52					* Engdahl	Bosnia: Banja Luka	波斯尼亚:巴尼亚卢卡	44.807	17.353	15	5.6	Ms	8	14	1			50.0	4				
1969	10	27	8	10	58					* ISC, Engdahl	Bosnia: Kakasi	波斯尼亚:卡卡西	44.837	17.234	15	6.1	Ms	9	9	1				3				
1969	11	6	11	33	16					GSHAP	Colombia: Valle Del Cauca	哥伦比亚:考卡山谷	5.18	-76.29	108	4.9	Ms	5										
1969	11	22	23	9	35	4	15	3.9	3	* Engdahl, NOAA	Russia: Kamchatka, Near East Coast	俄罗斯:堪察加东部近海	57.729	163.595	9.1	7.8	Mw	10						1				
1969	12	6	9	39	44					GSHAP	Colombia: Near Coast	哥伦比亚:近海	2.99	-79.02	38	4.7	Ms	5										
1969	12	17	7	13						*	Ecuador: Pujili, Latacunga	厄瓜多尔:普希利,拉塔昆加	-0.8	-78.3	27	4.2	Muk							3				
1969	12	25	21	32	29	4	0.5	-3.3		* ISC, Shi Z., Engdahl, NOAA	Guadeloupe: Grand Bourg	瓜德罗普岛:格兰堡	15.727	-59.648	9.7	7.2	Mw	6						1				
1970	1	4	17	0	40					* China, Engdahl, Dis	China: Yunnan, Tonghai	中国:云南通海	24.147	102.462	14	7.8	Ms	10	15621	4	26783	5	411	5	166117	5	172339	5
1970	1	10	12	7	9	4	0.1			* ISC, Engdahl, NOAA	Philippines: Mindanao Island	菲律宾:棉兰老岛	6.788	126.687	61.4	7.6	Mw	6										
1970	1	20	17	33	6					ISC, Usami, Engdahl	Japan: Hokkaido	日本:北海道	42.523	143.024	34.9	6.4	Ms								2	1		

年 Year	月 Mo	日 Dy	时 Hr	分 Mn	秒 Sec	源 Sr	浪高 Wh	级 I mI	级 S mS	资料来源 Information	地名(英文) Name(English)	地名(中文) Name(Chinese)	纬度(°) Latitude	经度(°) Longitude	深度 Depth	震级 Mag	标度 Scale	烈度 MMI	死亡人数 数量/人 Num	死亡人数 级别 Dd	受伤人数 数量/人 Num	受伤人数 级别 Dd	经济损失 数量/$ Mill	经济损失 级别 De	房屋毁坏 数量/间 Num	房屋毁坏 级别 Dh	房屋受损 数量/间 Num	房屋受损 级别 Dh
											Earthquake Epicenter								Deaths		Injuries		Damage		Houses Destroyed		Houses Damaged	
1970	2	5	22	5	60					* Bautista, Engdahl	Philippines: Romblon Island	菲律宾:朗布隆岛	12.6	122.058	7.7	6.6	Ms		3	1		2		2				
1970	2	6	22	10	41					China, Engdahl	China: Yunnan, Ninger, W.	中国:云南宁洱西	23.051	100.753	6	6.1	Ms	7										
1970	2	14	11	18	16					* Shi Z.	Peru: Panao, Chaclla	秘鲁:帕瑙,奎罗	−9.9	−75.6	35	6	mb	9	12	1				3		3		
1970	2	24	2	7	34					China, Engdahl	China: Sichuan, Dayi, W.	中国:四川大邑西	30.604	103.054	3	6.2	Ms	7										
1970	3	11	22	38	37	4	0			* ISC, Shi Z., Engdahl, NOAA	Alaska: Kodiak Island	阿拉斯加:科迪亚克岛	57.328	−153.94	38.7	6	Ms	5						1				
1970	3	14	1	51	44					*	Iran: Orumiyeh	伊朗:乌尔米耶	38.5	44.7	23	5.3	Ms		5	1				2		3		
1970	3	22	10	42	6					China	China: Sichuan, Maoxian	中国:四川茂县	31.63	104.03	16	4.8	Ms	6										
1970	3	23	1	52	59					* India	India: Broach	印度:古杰拉特的布罗奇	21.7	73	3	5.4	mb		26	1	200	3		2				
1970	3	28	21	2	26					* Shi Z, Engdahl	Turkey: Gediz	土耳其:盖迪兹	39.172	29.55	24.2	7.4	Ms	10	1086	4	1174	4	55.6	4	8229	4	5586	4
1970	4	7	5	34	6	3		1	1	* Bautista, Engdahl, NOAA	Philippines: San Jose, Coast E.	菲律宾:圣琼斯东部海域	15.772	121.659	28.3	7.2	Mw	6	15	1	200	3		2				
1970	4	23	9	1						*	Turkey: Demirci, Manisa	土耳其:代米尔吉,马尼萨	39.1	28.7	18	5.7	Ms	8	411	3	43	1			150	3		
1970	5	14	9	20	23					* Engdahl	Russia: Dagestan, Chirkey, NE.	俄罗斯:达吉斯坦共和国奇尔克伊东北	43.079	47.08	13.2	5.5	mb							1		1		
1970	5	14	18	12	26	3				* ISC, Engdahl, NOAA	Russia: Dagestan, Chirkey, NE.	俄罗斯:达吉斯坦共和国奇尔克伊东北	43.102	47.071	12.7	6.5	Ms	8		3				3		2		
1970	5	31	20	23	32	4	0.4	0.8		* Engdahl, Shi Z., NOAA	Peru: Casma, Near Coast	秘鲁:卡斯马近海	−9.248	−78.84	73	7.9	M	10	66794	5	50000	5	530	5		3		
1970	6	5	4	53	6					* ISC, Engdahl	Kazakhstan: Almaty	哈萨克斯坦:阿拉木图	42.492	78.719	4	6.6	Ms							3	5000	4		
1970	6	14	0	0	9	2				* ISC, Shi Z., Engdahl, NOAA	Chile: Punta Arenas, NW.	智利:蓬塔阿雷纳斯西北	−51.988	−74.328	0.6	6.5	Ms											
1970	6	19	10	56	16	2				* ISC, Shi Z., Engdahl, NOAA	Chile: Tocopilla, Near Coast	智利:托科皮亚近海	−22.265	−70.502	49	6.4	Ms											
1970	7	2	2	24	36					*	Turkey: Kangal	土耳其:坎加尔	38.8	36.7	27	4.9	Ms		1	1				2	150	3		
1970	7	25	22	41	14	4	0.3	−0.7		* Engdahl, NOAA	Japan: Miyazaki, Near Coast	日本:宫崎近海	32.246	131.68	45.6	7	Mw				13	1		1				
1970	7	29	4	50	59					China, Engdahl	China: Xinjiang, Maralbishi, W.	中国:新疆巴楚西	39.899	77.773	16.5	5.9	Ms	7										
1970	7	30	0	52	20					* ISC, Engdahl	Iran: Gorgan, NE.	伊朗:戈尔甘东北	37.836	55.887	10.9	6.6	Ms	8	176	3	483	3	8.0	3	2000	4		
1970	7	31	13	10	49					China	China: Sichuan, Leibo, NE.	中国:四川雷波东北	28.63	103.73	44	5.4	Ms	7										
1970	7	31	17	8	6					* Shi Z, Engdahl	Colombia: Amazonas	哥伦比亚:亚马孙	−1.486	−72.563	644.6	8	M		1	1		2		2				
1970	9	7	20	58	49					* ISC	Croatia: Knin	克罗地亚:克宁	44	16	5	5.5	Ms	7			8	1		2				
1970	9	26	12	2	32					* Engdahl	Colombia: Bahia Solano	哥伦比亚:巴伊阿索拉诺	6.237	−77.527	12.6	6.6	Ms				2	1	0.4	1	104	3		
1970	9	28	19	1		4				* NOAA	New Zealand: South Island, Christchurch	新西兰:南岛,基督城	−44.6	173.6		5.1	Ms											

时间						海啸				资料来源	震中				深度	震级	标度	烈度	死亡人数		受伤人数		经济损失		房屋毁坏		房屋受损	
年	月	日	时	分	秒	源	浪高	级 I	级 S		地名(英文)	地名(中文)	纬度(°)	经度(°)					数量/人	级别	数量/人	级别	数量/$ Mill	级别	数量/间	级别	数量/间	级别
Date						Tsunami				Information	Earthquake Epicenter				Depth	Mag	Scale	MMI	Deaths		Injuries		Damage		Houses Destroyed		Houses Damaged	
Year	Mo	Dy	Hr	Mn	Sec	Sr	Wh	mI	mS		Name(English)	Name(Chinese)	Latitude	Longitude					Num	Dd	Num	Dd	$ Mill	De	Num	Dh	Num	Dh
1970	9	30	9	52	23	3			0.5	* Wang S., NOAA	Luzon Ridge	吕宋海岭	20.6	122	33	5.3	Ms	7						2		3		
1970	10	5	23	24						* *	Croatia: Knin	克罗地亚:克宁	44	15.8	49	5	Ms							2				
1970	10	16	5	26	15					ISC, Usami, Engdahl	Japan: Yokote	日本:横手	39.279	140.738	23.7	5.8	Ms								1	1		
1970	10	25	11	22						* *	Iran: Piranshahr	伊朗:皮兰沙赫尔	36.8	45.1	19	5.5	Ms							2				
1970	10	31	17	53	7	4	3	0.3	0.5	* Engdahl, NOAA	Papua New Guinea: Madang	巴布亚新几内亚:马当	-4.907	145.471	8.1	7.3	Ms	8	18	1	20	1	1.75	2	800	3		
1970	11	8	9	15	55					China	China: Sichuan, Zamtang, SE.	中国:四川壤塘东南	32.15	101.4		5.5	Ms	7										
1970	11	28	14	45	34	2				* Shi Z., Engdahl, NOAA	Chile: Tarapaca, S.	智利:塔拉帕卡南部	-20.971	-69.899	43.9	5.7	mb											
1970	12	2	19	12	50					China, Dis	China: Ningxia, Xiji, W.	中国:宁夏西吉西	35.93	105.58	15	5.5	Ms	7	117		408	3			1540	4		
1970	12	4	1	59	25	4	0.8		2	* NOAA	Russia: Krasnodar, Sochi	俄罗斯:克拉斯诺达尔区索契	43.7	39.5	7	5.1	Ms											
1970	12	10	4	34	39					* Shi Z., ISC, Engdahl	Peru: Tumbes	秘鲁:通贝斯	-4.079	-80.662	20.1	7.8	Ms	10	82	2	350	3	6.0	3				
1971	1	10	7	17	8					* Engdahl	Indonesia: Papua	印度尼西亚:巴布亚	-3.232	139.744	54.9	7.7	Mw	9						2				
1971	2	4	15	33	33					* Engdahl	Indonesia: Natal, Sibolga	印度尼西亚:纳塔尔,实武牙	0.552	98.665	60	7.1	Ms	9						2				
1971	2	5	9	10	36					China, Engdahl	China: Yunnan, Baoshan	中国:云南保山东	25.247	99.352	16.2	5.8	Ms	7										
1971	2	6	18	9	9					* Italy	Italy: Tuscania	意大利:图斯卡尼亚	42.442	11.846	33	4.9	mb	8	24	1	100	2	41.0	4				
1971	2	9	14	0	42					* Shi Z., Engdahl	US: California, San Fernando	美国:加利福尼亚州圣费尔南多	34.401	-118.392	6.4	6.7	M	11	65	2	2000	4	505	5				
1971	2	14	16	27	36					* ISC	Iran: Shāhrūd	伊朗:沙赫鲁德	36.62	55.73	25	5.5	Muk		1	1				2				
1971	4	3	12	50	43					China	China: Qinghai, Zaduo, S.	中国:青海杂多南部	32.2	95.4	20	6.5	Ms	9										
1971	4	6	6	49	53					*	Iran: Fars	伊朗:法尔斯	29.8	51.9	10	5.2	MS							3				
1971	4	12	19	3	22					* Iran, ISC, Engdahl	Iran: Hormozgan	伊朗:荷姆兹甘	28.264	55.608	5.6	6	Ms		1	1				3				
1971	4	28	15	32	2					China, Engdahl	China: Yunnan, Pu-er	中国:云南普洱	22.953	100.993	8	6.7	Ms	8										
1971	5	2	6	8	26	4	0		-3	* Shi Z., ISC, Engdahl, NOAA	Aleutian Islands	阿留申群岛	51.433	-177.248	21	7.1	Ms	6										
1971	5	12	6	25	16					* Engdahl	Turkey: Burdur	土耳其:布尔杜尔	37.555	29.746	28.8	5.9	Ms	6	100	2		3		3				
1971	5	22	16	44	1					* Engdahl	Turkey: Bingol	土耳其:宾格尔	38.868	40.542	3.6	6.7	Ms	8	1000	3		2	5.0	3				
1971	6	5	10	21	22					China	China: Shanxi, Heshun, NW.	中国:山西和顺西北	37.5	113.4	10	4.7	Ms	6										
1971	6	11	12	56	7					* Shi Z, Engdahl	Dominica: Santo Domingo	多米尼加:多米尼加	17.984	-69.808	59	6.5	Muk					2		2				
1971	6	15	22	4	10					China	China: Xinjiang, Uqturpan	中国:新疆乌什	41.52	79.28	12	5.8	Ms	7										
1971	6	16	14	44	23					*	Indonesia: Java Island	印度尼西亚:爪哇岛	-7.2	109.1	35	5.2	mb		1	1	6	1		3				
1971	6	17	21	0	42					* Chile, Shi Z., Engdahl	Chile: Catalina, Antofagasta	智利:卡特琳娜,安托法加斯塔	-25.423	-69.052	90.1	7.2	mb	5	1	1				2				
1971	6	26	19	0	37					China	China: Guizhou, Wangmo	中国:贵州望谟	25.22	106.13	33	4.9	Ms	6										
1971	6	28	4	1	46					China, Dis	China: Ningxia, Wuzhong	中国:宁夏吴忠	37.9	106.32	23	5.1	Ms	6										

时间 年 Date Year	月 Mo	日 Dy	时 Hr	分 Mn	秒 Sec	海啸 Tsunami 源 Sr	浪高 Wh	级 I mI	级 S mS	资料来源 Information	震中 Earthquake Epicenter 地名(英文) Name(English)	地名(中文) Name(Chinese)	纬度(°) Latitude	经度(°) Longitude	深度 Depth	震级 Mag	标度 Scale	烈度 MMI	死亡人数 Deaths 数量/人 Num	级别 Dd	受伤人数 Injuries 数量/人 Num	级别 Dd	经济损失 Damage 数量/$ Mill	级别 De	房屋毁坏 Houses Destroyed 数量/间 Num	级别 Dh	房屋受损 Houses Damaged 数量/间 Num	级别 Dh
1971	7	9	3	3	20	4	1.2	0.3	0	* Shi Z., Engdahl, NOAA	Chile: Valparaiso	智利:瓦尔帕莱索	-32.558	-71.085	59	7.8	Mw	9	83	2	447	3	236	5		3		
1971	7	14	6	11	31	4	6	1.6	1	* Engdahl, NOAA	New Britain Trench	新不列颠海沟[太平洋]	-5.519	153.906	44.5	8	Mw	9	4	1	5	1		1				
1971	7	15	1	33	22					* Italy	Italy: Parma	意大利:帕尔马	44.8	10.3	7	5.61	Ms		2	1				2				
1971	7	26	1	23	22	4	10	3.3	1.5	* Engdahl, NOAA	Papua New Guinea: New Ireland	巴布亚新几内亚:新爱尔兰	-4.889	153.183	37.1	8.1	Mw	6						2				
1971	7	26	1	48	36					China, ISC, Engdahl, Dis	China: Xinjiang, Payzawat, NE.	中国:新疆伽师东北	39.848	77.246	41.1	5.8	mb	8	5		50	1			1000	3		
1971	7	27	2	2	46					* GSHAP, Engdahl, CSN	Ecuador: Morona Santiago	厄瓜多尔:莫罗纳-圣地亚哥	-2.825	-77.362	94.5	7.3	mb	7	1	1		2		2				
1971	7	31	19	1	50					China	China: Xinjiang, Usu, SW.	中国:新疆乌苏西南	44.2	84.4	22	4.8	Ms	6										
1971	8	2	7	24	59	4	0.2	-2.3	-0.5	* Engdahl, NOAA	Japan: SE. Hokkaido Island	日本:北海道东南	41.378	143.459	53.8	7.2	Mw							1				
1971	8	9	2	54	37					* CSN	Iran: Mazanderan	伊朗:马赞德兰	36.3	52.7	27	5.8	Mw		1	1				2				
1971	8	16	4	58	1					* China, Engdahl	China: Sichuan, Mabian	中国:四川马边	28.879	103.672	22.7	5.5	mb	7		1				1		1		
1971	8	26	6	55	9					*	Iran: Bushehr	伊朗:布什尔	30	50.7	45	4.8	mb							3				
1971	9	5	18	35	29	4	2			* Engdahl, NOAA	Russia: Sakhalin Island	俄罗斯:库页岛(萨哈林岛)	46.555	141.187	18.3	7.3	Mw	9						1				
1971	9	6	13	37	12	4	0.3			* ISC, Engdahl, NOAA	Russia: Sakhalin Island	俄罗斯:库页岛(萨哈林岛)	46.755	141.382	20.8	6.2	Mw											
1971	9	8	11	48	28	4	0.1		-3	* ISC, Engdahl, NOAA	Russia: Sakhalin Island	俄罗斯:库页岛(萨哈林岛)	46.445	141.122	24.1	6.6	Ms											
1971	9	8	16	59	56	4	0.1	-0.7	-3	* ISC, Engdahl, NOAA	Russia: Sakhalin Island	俄罗斯:库页岛(萨哈林岛)	46.302	141.055	20.6	6.2	Ms											
1971	9	25	4	36	15	2	1.8	0.8	0.5	* Engdahl, NOAA	Papua New Guinea: Lae	巴布亚新几内亚:莱城	-6.558	146.673	111.6	6.3	mb	7						1				
1971	9	27	19	1	47	4	0		-4	* ISC, Engdahl, NOAA	Russia: Sakhalin Island	俄罗斯:库页岛(萨哈林岛)	46.419	141.159	19.6	6.1	Ms											
1971	10	15	10	33	51					* Engdahl	Peru: Apurimac	秘鲁:阿普里马克	-14.183	-73.399	80	5.7	mb	9	5	1				3				
1971	10	27	17	58	40					* Engdahl	Vanuatu Islands: Espiritu Santo Islands	瓦努阿图群岛:圣埃斯皮里图岛	-15.578	167.32	60.9	6.3	mb	7	1	1		2		3				
1971	11	6	22	0	0	2	0.1			* ISC, NOAA	Aleutian Islands, Rat Island	阿留申群岛,拉特岛	51.5	179.1	21	6.8	Mw											
1971	12	15	8	29	54	4	0.5			* Engdahl, NOAA	Russia: Kamchatka, Near East Coast	俄罗斯:堪察加东部近海	56.023	163.17	9	7.8	Mw	10										
1972	1	4	3	16	56					* China, Engdahl	China: Taiwan, Taitung, Coast of E.	中国:台湾台东以东海域	22.536	122.017	28.9	7.2	Ms	5										
1972	1	15	20	21	49					Wang S., Engdahl	China: Xinjiang, Kalpin	中国:新疆柯坪	40.225	78.969	11.1	5.9	Ms	7										
1972	1	23	1	5	56					Wang S.	China: Yunnan, Shiping, SE.	中国:云南石屏东南	23.5	102.6	6	5.6	Ms	7										
1972	1	25	1	6	21	4	0.1	-3.3	-2	* China, Engdahl, NOAA	China: Taiwan, Taitung, Coast of E.	中国:台湾台东以东海域	22.549	122.325	10.1	8	Ms	6	1	1				1	5	1		

年 Year	月 Mo	日 Dy	时 Hr	分 Mn	秒 Sec	海啸 Tsunami 源 Sr	浪高 Wh	级 I mI	级 S mS	资料来源 Information	震中 Earthquake Epicenter 地名(英文) Name(English)	地名(中文) Name(Chinese)	纬度(°) Latitude	经度(°) Longitude	深度 Depth	震级 Mag	标度 Scale	烈度 MMI	死亡人数 Deaths 数量/人 Num	级别 Dd	受伤人数 Injuries 数量/人 Num	级别 Dd	经济损失 Damage 数量/$ Mill $ Mill	级别 De	房屋毁坏 Houses Destroyed 数量/间 Num	级别 Dh	房屋受损 Houses Damaged 数量/间 Num	级别 Dh
1972	1	25	3	41	22					* China, Engdahl	China: Taiwan, Taitung, Coast of E.	中国:台湾台东以东海域	23.037	122.118	11.9	7.6	Ms							1				
1972	2	4	2	42	19					* Italy	Italy: Ancona	意大利:安科纳	43.633	13.55	25	5.18	Ms		1	1	2	1		2				
1972	2	10	6	49	16					*	Iran: Bushehr	伊朗:布什尔	29.7	50.9	21	4.5	mb							3				
1972	2	29	9	23	2	4	0.4	-1.3	0.5	* Engdahl, NOAA	Japan Trench	日本海沟	33.377	140.881	58.8	7.5	Mw	10						2				
1972	3	20	7	33	50					* GSHAP, Shi Z., Engdahl	Peru: Juanjui	秘鲁:胡安惠	-6.81	-76.78	49.8	6.9	Muk	9	7	1	50	1	20.0	3				
1972	4	8	9	33	39					China	China: Sichuan, Garze, SW.	中国:四川甘孜西南	29.6	101.8	28	5.2	Ms	6										
1972	4	9	3	10	50					China	China: Xinjiang, Luntai, NE.	中国:新疆轮台东北	42.3	84.8	30	5.6	Ms	7										
1972	4	10	2	6	51					* Engdahl	Iran: Fars, Qir, Karzin	伊朗:法尔斯,吉尔,卡尔津	28.408	52.789	11	6.9	Ms	9	30000	5	1700	4		4		4		
1972	4	24	9	57	21					* China, Engdahl, CSN	China: Taiwan, Hualien	中国:台湾花莲	23.604	121.534	21	7.3	Ms	5	4	1	11	1		2				
1972	4	25	19	30	9					* Bautista, Engdahl, CSN	Philippines: Mindoro Island	菲律宾:民都洛岛	13.388	120.312	33.9	7.2	Mw	7						2				
1972	5	6	22	5	22					China	China: Sichuan, Xichang, E.	中国:四川西昌东	27.9	102.4		4.8	Ms	6										
1972	6	8	18	53	46	2				* Shi Z., Engdahl, NOAA	Chile: Andacollo	智利:安达科约	-30.375	-71.528	58.9	6.6	Ms	7										
1972	6	21	15	6	53					*	Italy: Ancona	意大利:安科纳	43.8	13.3	4	4.4	mb		2	1			300	5				
1972	6	24	15	29	22					* ISC, Engdahl	Afghan: Taloqan	阿富汗:塔卢坎	36.255	69.684	31.1	6.1	Ms	6	11	1	15	1		2		3		
1972	7	2	12	56	7					* CSN	Iran: Fars	伊朗:法尔斯	30.1	50.8	31	5.8	MS							2				
1972	7	22	16	41	1					Wang S.	China: Xizang (Tibet), Nagqu, W.	中国:西藏那曲西	31.5	91.7	15	6	Ms	7										
1972	7	30	21	45	14	4	0.1	-2.3	-2	* Shi Z., Engdahl, NOAA	Alaska: Sitka, Juneau	阿拉斯加:锡特卡,朱诺	56.696	-136.098	6.8	7.6	Ms	7						1				
1972	8	17	23	44	8	4	0.6	-1		* Engdahl, NOAA	New Britain Trench	新不列颠海沟[太平洋]	-6.002	152.928	12.9	7.1	Ms	5										
1972	8	27	14	49	31					China	China: Yunnan, Pu-er, W.	中国:云南普洱西	22.8	100.5	25	5.4	Ms	6										
1972	9	3	16	48	30					* Engdahl	Pakistan: Gupis, Rawalpindi	巴基斯坦:古比斯,拉瓦尔品第	35.949	73.321	32.9	6.2	Ms		100	2				3	1000	3	1000	3
1972	9	7	22	26	58					* ISC	France: Rochefort	法国:罗什福尔	46	-1.1	60	5.6	Muk	8						2				
1972	9	13	4	13	22					* Engdahl	Greece: Corinthia, Arcadia	希腊:科林特,阿卡迪亚	37.953	22.444	81.3	5.8	mb	8						2				
1972	9	17	14	7	12					* Engdahl	Greece: Lixouri	希腊:利克苏里	38.239	20.269	0.7	6.3	Ms	7						2	40	1		
1972	9	27	0	8	33					China, Engdahl	China: Sichuan, Garze, NW.	中国:四川甘孜西北	30.274	101.567	43.2	5.6	Ms	7										
1972	11	2	19	55	25					* Engdahl	Vanuatu Islands	瓦努阿图群岛	-20.034	169.007	38.4	7	Ms	5										
1972	12	2	0	19	54	2	0.5	-2.3		* Engdahl, Bautista, Engdahl, NOAA	Philippines: Mindanao, Davao	菲律宾:棉兰老岛,达沃	6.466	126.657	82.1	7.4	mb	6						1				
1972	12	4	10	16	14	4	0.5	-1	-1	* ISC, Engdahl, NOAA	Japan Trench	日本海沟	33.331	140.713	70.6	7.4	Mw	10						2				

时间						海啸				资料来源	震中				深度	震级	标度	烈度	死亡人数		受伤人数		经济损失		房屋毁坏		房屋受损	
年	月	日	时	分	秒	源	浪高	级 I	级 S		地名(英文)	地名(中文)	纬度(°)	经度(°)					数量/人	级别	数量/人	级别	数量/$ Mill	级别	数量/间	级别	数量/间	级别
Date						Tsunami				Information	Earthquake Epicenter				Depth	Mag	Scale	MMI	Deaths		Injuries		Damage		Houses Destroyed		Houses Damaged	
Year	Mo	Dy	Hr	Mn	Sec	Sr	Wh	mI	mS		Name(English)	Name(Chinese)	Latitude	Longitude					Num	Dd	Num	Dd	$ Mill	De	Num	Dh	Num	Dh
1972	12	23	6	29	45					* Engdahl	Nicaragua:Managua	尼加拉瓜:马拉瓜	12.347	-86.128	7.3	6.2	Ms		10000	5	20000	5	800	5				
1972	12	29	4	51	2	2				* Shi Z., Engdahl, NOAA	Chile:Ovalle	智利:奥瓦耶	-30.61	-71.189	54.4	6	Ms											
1973	1	30	21	1	13	4	1.1	0.1		* Shi Z., Engdahl, NOAA	Mexico:Farias, Tecoman	墨西哥:法里亚斯,特科曼	18.455	-102.96	37.2	7.6	Mw		56	2	390	3		2		2		
1973	2	6	10	37	9					* China, Engdahl, Dis	China:Sichuan, Luhuo, NW.	中国:四川炉霍附近	31.361	100.504	6.6	7.6	Ms	10	2175		2756	4		2	15700	5	2867	4
1973	2	21	14	42	23					* ISC	New Zealand:North Island, Maraekakaho	新西兰:北岛,马拉卡卡霍	-39.58	176.57	38	5.7	mb	6						2				
1973	2	21	14	45	57					* USGS, ISC	US:California, Oxnard	美国:加利福尼亚州奥克斯纳德	34.1	-119	8	5.9	ML	7					1	2				
1973	2	24	0	2	41					*	Iran:Fars	伊朗:法尔斯	28.58	52.62	27	5.2	Mw							3				
1973	2	28	6	37	55	4	1.5	0.6	0.5	* Engdahl, ISC, NOAA	Kuril Islands, S.	千岛群岛南部	50.484	156.624	60.6	7.2	Mw	8						2				
1973	3	9	19	9	13					* USGS	Australia:Wollongong, Sydney	澳大利亚:卧龙岗,悉尼	-34.13	150.27	13	5.5	mb	6					0.5	1				
1973	3	11	13	37	47					USGS, ISC	Japan:Hokkaido	日本:北海道	41.59	142.01	73	5.5	mb	5										
1973	3	17	8	30	55	4	1.3			* Bautista, Engdahl, NOAA	Philippines:San Andres	菲律宾:圣安德烈斯	13.399	122.795	42.3	7.5	Mw	9	15	1	64	2	0.45	1				
1973	3	22	1	6	57					China	China:Xizang (Tibet), Tingri, S.	中国:西藏日喀则定日南部	28.1	87.2	33	5.3	Ms	6										
1973	3	22	6	10	24					China	China:Yunnan, Sipsongpanna	中国:云南西双版纳	22	100.9	10	5.5	Ms	7										
1973	3	27	2	8	31					USGS	Japan:Ichihara	日本:千叶市原	35.48	139.92	64	5	mb	6										
1973	3	27	12	32	5					USGS, ISC	Aleutian Islands	阿留申群岛	52.58	172.87	43	5.6	mb	5										
1973	4	1	7	12	38					* Engdahl	Djibouti:Djibouti	吉布提:吉布提	11.631	43.019	18.8	5.9	Ms							2				
1973	4	7	19	30	7					USGS	Adriatic Sea	亚得里亚海	41.49	19.98	16	4.7	mb	6										
1973	4	8	22	51	56					USGS	Bismarck Sea	俾斯麦海	-5.54	146.48	66	4.9	mb	6										
1973	4	13	8	12	15					USGS	Italy:Crotone	意大利:克罗托内	39.09	16.96	45	4.7	mb	6										
1973	4	14	8	34	2					* Shi Z., Engdahl	Costa Rica:Arenal	哥斯达黎加:阿雷纳	10.673	-84.858	31.5	6.5	Ms		26	1	100	2	0.2	1				
1973	4	22	4	46	21					China	China:Yunnan, Yiliang	中国:云南彝良	27.7	104.2		5.1	Ms	6										
1973	4	24	21	30	7					* ISC, Shi Z., Engdahl	Colombia:Off Coast of W.	哥伦比亚:西部沿海	4.911	-78.114	20.2	6.5	Ms		1	1				2				
1973	4	26	20	26	33					* Engdahl	Hawaiian Islands, Hilo	夏威夷群岛,希洛市	19.936	-155.098	48	6.3	Muk	8					5.6	3				
1973	4	29	14	37	54					USGS	Morocco:Tangiers	摩洛哥:丹吉尔	34.64	-4.07	19	4.6	mb	6										
1973	5	1	10	40	45					ISC, USGS	Papua New Guinea:Milne Bay	巴布亚新几内亚:米尔恩湾区	-10	150.2	15	6	Mw	6										
1973	5	5	7	40	58					USGS	Japan:Aomori	日本:青森	40.89	140.31	17	5.1	mb	6										
1973	5	17	15	44	20					USGS, ISC	Japan Trench	日本海沟	33.14	140.67	62	5.5	mb	5										

时间 Date						海啸 Tsunami				资料来源 Information	震中 Earthquake Epicenter				深度 Depth	震级 Mag	标度 Scale	烈度 MMI	死亡人数 Deaths		受伤人数 Injuries		经济损失 Damage		房屋毁坏 Houses Destroyed		房屋受损 Houses Damaged	
年 Year	月 Mo	日 Dy	时 Hr	分 Mn	秒 Sec	源 Sr	浪高 Wh	级 I mI	级 S mS		地名(英文) Name(English)	地名(中文) Name(Chinese)	纬度(°) Latitude	经度(°) Longitude					数量/人 Num	级别 Dd	数量/人 Num	级别 Dd	数量/$ Mill $ Mill	级别 De	数量/间 Num	级别 Dh	数量/间 Num	级别 Dh
1973	5	22	22	4	58					USGS, ISC	Papua New Guinea: Milne Bay	巴布亚新几内亚:米尔恩湾区	-10.01	150.32	13	5.5	mb	5										
1973	6	1	16	39	48					China	China: Yunnan, Tengchong	中国:云南腾冲	24.9	98.5		5	Ms	6										
1973	6	2	23	57	6					Wang S., Engdahl	China: Xinjiang, Jinghe, SE.	中国:新疆精河东南	44.142	83.592	22.3	5.6	Ms	7										
1973	6	6	21	11	21					USGS	Macedonia: Budva	蒙特尼哥罗(黑山):布德瓦	42.38	18.65	16	4.6	mb	7										
1973	6	11	3	15	39					USGS	Croatia: Varazdin	克罗地亚:瓦拉日丁	46.19	16.09	11	4.5	mb	7										
1973	6	17	3	55	4	4	6	2.2	1	* ISC, Engdahl, NOAA	Japan: Hokkaido	日本:北海道	43.223	145.743	43.3	7.8	Mw	8	27	1			5.0	3	2	1		
1973	6	17	12	14	26					USGS	Japan: Hokkaido	日本:北海道	42.92	145.57	41	5.5	mb	6										
1973	6	17	13	33	28					USGS	Japan: Hokkaido	日本:北海道	43.07	145.38	46	5.6	mb	8										
1973	6	17	20	37	58					ISC, Engdahl	Japan: Off SE. Coast of Hokkaido	日本:北海道东南沿海	42.717	145.983	37.1	6	Ms	6										
1973	6	23	5	26	49					USGS, ISC	Andreanof Islands, Aleutian Is.	阿留申群岛,安德烈亚诺夫群岛	51.88	-176.9	62	5.5	mb	5										
1973	6	24	2	43	25	4	0.6	2.2		* ISC, Engdahl, NOAA	Kuril Islands	千岛群岛	43.356	146.422	33.1	7.3	Mw	8			1	1		1				
1973	6	26	22	31	59	4	0.2			* ISC, Engdahl, NOAA, CSN	Japan: Off SE. Coast of Hokkaido	日本:北海道东南沿海	43.112	146.601	28.6	7	Ms											
1973	6	28	21	59	27					China	China: Sichuan, Mabian, E.	中国:四川马边东	28.9	103.7	10	5.4	Ms	6										
1973	6	29	3	26	53					USGS	Japan: Hokkaido	日本:北海道	43.4	145.8	50	5.9	mb	6										
1973	7	3	16	10	12					USGS	Adriatic Sea	亚得里亚海	44.08	13.27	47	5.3	mb	6										
1973	8	2	8	58	15					China	China: Yunnan, Yiliang, NE.	中国:云南彝良东北	27.9	104.6		5.4	Ms	7										
1973	8	8	14	36	11					USGS	Italy: Avellino, Potenza, Caserta	意大利:艾维连奴,波坦察,卡塞塔	40.82	15.39	33	4.6	ML	7										
1973	8	11	7	15	38					China, Engdahl, Dis	China: Sichuan, Songpan, NE.	中国:四川松潘东北	32.916	104.019	7.2	6.5	Ms	7										
1973	8	13	8	28	21					ISC, Engdahl, USGS	Papua New Guinea: East Sepik	巴布亚新几内亚:东塞皮克	-4.489	144.124	112.8	5.9	mb	7										
1973	8	16	3	58	10					China	China: Yunnan, Pu-er	中国:云南普洱	23.05	101.11	33	6.4	Ms	8										
1973	8	18	22	38	29					*	Italy: Sicilia Island	意大利:西西里岛	37.7	15		3.5	Mw	6					0.5	1				
1973	8	23	23	50	32					USGS, ISC	Japan Trench	日本海沟	37.21	142.13	34	5.7	mb	5										
1973	8	28	9	50	41					* Engdahl	Mexico: Veracruz, Mexico City	墨西哥:韦拉克鲁斯,墨西哥城	18.233	-96.608	80.7	7.3	mb	7	600	3				3				
1973	9	7	9	31	15					USGS	Papua New Guinea: East New Britain	巴布亚新几内亚:东新不列颠	-5.62	151.5	61	5.5	mb	6										
1973	9	9	2	13	37					China, Engdahl	China: Sichuan, Garze, N.	中国:四川甘孜北	31.564	99.986	5.8	5.8	Ms	6										
1973	9	30	6	17	53					USGS	Japan: Sanmu	日本:千叶山武	35.61	140.45	62	5.9	mb	6										
1973	10	1	14	16	23					USGS	Japan: Sosa	日本:千叶匝瑳	35.72	140.56	56	5.6	mb	6										

年 Year	月 Mo	日 Dy	时 Hr	分 Mn	秒 Sec	海啸 Tsunami 源 Sr	浪高 Wh	级 I mI	级 S mS	资料来源 Information	震中 Earthquake Epicenter 地名(英文) Name(English)	地名(中文) Name(Chinese)	纬度(°) Latitude	经度(°) Longitude	深度 Depth	震级 Mag	标度 Scale	烈度 MMI	死亡人数 Deaths 数量/人 Num	级别 Dd	受伤人数 Injuries 数量/人 Num	级别 Dd	经济损失 Damage 数量/$ Mill $ Mill	级别 De	房屋毁坏 Houses Destroyed 数量/间 Num	级别 Dh	房屋受损 Houses Damaged 数量/间 Num	级别 Dh
1973	10	5	5	47	51	4	0. 4	-1. 3	-1	* Shi Z., Engdahl, NOAA	Chile: Valparaiso, La Ligua	智利:瓦尔帕莱索,拉里瓜	-33. 068	-71. 942	34	6. 3	Muk	7						2				
1973	11	4	15	52	16					* ISC, Engdahl	Greece: Ionian Sea	希腊:爱奥尼亚海	38. 846	20. 615	22. 9	5. 5	Ms	8						2				
1973	11	11	7	14	52					*	Iran: Fars, N.	伊朗:法尔斯北部	30. 57	52. 89	11	5. 5	Mw		1	1				3				
1973	11	12	3	53	44					USGS	New Britain Trench	新不列颠海沟[太平洋]	-6. 15	154. 46	50	5. 9	Ms	6										
1973	11	13	1	12	12					USGS	Japan: Miyagi, Near Coast	日本:宫城近海	38. 62	142. 15	78	5. 5	mb	6										
1973	11	19	13	1	58					ISC, Engdahl, USGS	Japan: Miyagi, Near Coast	日本:宫城近海	38. 955	141. 94	55. 4	6. 5	Muk	6										
1973	11	19	18	40	5					USGS	Chile: Coquimbo	智利:科金博	-28. 46	-70. 85	58	5. 7	mb	7										
1973	11	19	21	11	17					USGS, ISC	Japan: Miyagi, Near Coast	日本:宫城近海	38. 89	141. 92	60	5. 5	mb	6										
1973	11	23	13	36	19					* USGS	Azores: Pico, Fayal	亚速尔群岛:皮可,法亚尔岛	38. 46	-28. 31	5	5. 2	Mw	8	1	1				2				
1973	11	25	9	19	15					USGS, Engdahl	Japan: Tanabe	日本:和歌山田边	33. 82	135. 38	56	5. 6	mb	6										
1973	11	29	10	57	45					* ISC, Engdahl, USGS	Greece: Crete Island	希腊:克里特岛	35. 173	23. 846	30. 3	5. 6	Ms	8						2				
1973	11	30	7	48	41					USGS, ISC	US: Tennessee, Maryville	美国:田纳西州玛丽维尔	35. 8	-83. 96	3	5. 6	mb	6										
1973	11	30	8	9	57					ISC, Engdahl, USGS	Vanuatu Islands	瓦努阿图群岛	-15. 223	167. 5	130. 6	6. 2	mb	6										
1973	12	28	13	41	47					* Engdahl, USGS	Vanuatu Islands: Espiritu Santo Islands	瓦努阿图群岛:圣埃斯皮里图岛	-14. 5	166. 784	23. 6	7. 3	Mw	7						2				
1973	12	29	0	19	33					* Engdahl	Vanuatu Islands	瓦努阿图群岛	-15. 155	167. 002	51	6. 9	Mw	8						2				
1973	12	31	11	0	54					China, Dis	China: Hebei, Hejian, E.	中国:河北河间东	38. 4	116. 8	19	5. 3	Ms	6										
1974	1	2	10	42	33					ISC, Shi Z., Engdahl, USGS	Chile: Calama	智利:卡拉马	-22. 45	-68. 326	119. 8	7. 5	Mw	8										
1974	1	5	8	33	51					* Engdahl	Peru: Lima, Yauyos	秘鲁:利马,尧约斯	-12. 351	-76. 307	92. 2	6. 1	mb		10	1		3		3				
1974	1	10	8	51	17					ISC, Engdahl	Vanuatu Islands	瓦努阿图群岛	-14. 525	166. 959	53. 8	7. 1	Mw	6										
1974	1	24	19	12	53					ISC, Engdahl, USGS	Japan: Hokkaido	日本:北海道	42. 072	143. 866	38. 2	5. 7	Muk	6										
1974	1	31	7	3	58					USGS, ISC	Japan: Miyazzaki, Near Coast	日本:宫崎近海	31. 84	131. 64	37	5. 6	mb	5										
1974	1	31	23	30	7	4	1. 5	2. 2	1	* Engdahl, NOAA, USGS	Solomon Islands	所罗门群岛	-7. 405	155. 946	37. 7	7. 3	Mw	6										
1974	2	1	0	1	2					*	Turkey: Izmir	土耳其:伊兹密尔	38. 6	27	29	5. 2	mb		2	1	20	1						
1974	2	1	3	12	36	4	4. 5	2. 2	2	* Engdahl, NOAA	Solomon Islands	所罗门群岛	-7. 213	155. 737	35. 1	7. 4	Mw	6						2				
1974	3	3	4	50	51					ISC, Engdahl, USGS	Japan: Asahi	日本:千叶旭市	35. 591	140. 625	52	6	Muk	6										
1974	3	12	15	11	6					USGS, ISC	East Scotia Basin	东斯科舍海盆	8. 76	150. 95	33	5. 5	mb	5										

年 Year	月 Mo	日 Dy	时 Hr	分 Mn	秒 Sec	海啸 Tsunami 源 Sr	浪高 Wh	级 I mI	级 S mS	资料来源 Information	震中 Earthquake Epicenter 地名(英文) Name(English)	地名(中文) Name(Chinese)	纬度(°) Latitude	经度(°) Longitude	深度 Depth	震级 Mag	标度 Scale	烈度 MMI	死亡人数 Deaths 数量/人 Num	级别 Dd	受伤人数 Injuries 数量/人 Num	级别 Dd	经济损失 Damage 数量/$ Mill	级别 De	房屋毁坏 Houses Destroyed 数量/间 Num	级别 Dh	房屋受损 Houses Damaged 数量/间 Num	级别 Dh
1974	4	3	23	5	3					USGS	US:Illinois, Olney	美国:伊利诺斯州奥尔尼	38.59	-88.09	11	4.7	MLg	6										
1974	4	13	8	59	15					USGS	Kazakhstan:Shymkent, W.	哈萨克斯坦:奇姆肯特西部	41.95	68.92	36	4.6	mb	6										
1974	4	18	1	19	23					*	Colombia:Cepita, San Andreas	哥伦比亚:塞皮塔,圣安德里亚	6.89	-72.93	24	5	mb		3	1				2				
1974	4	22	0	29	17					* China, Dis	China:Jiangsu, Liyang	中国:江苏溧阳	31.6	119.1	16	5.5	Ms	7	8		214	3	144	5	11081	5	77700	5
1974	5	8	23	33	29	4	0.2	-2.3	-2.5	* ISC, Usami, Engdahl, NOAA	Japan:Minamiizu	日本:静冈南伊豆	34.569	138.773	10.7	7.2	Mw	9	38	1	102	3		2	134	3		
1974	5	10	19	25	17					* China, Engdahl, Dis	China:Yunnan, Daguan, N.	中国:云南大关北	28.184	103.995	9	7.1	Ms	9	1423	5	1600	4		3	28000	5	66000	5
1974	5	13	17	40	28					USGS	Afghan:Badakhshan	阿富汗:巴达赫尚	36.47	70.91	208	5.5	mb	6										
1974	5	23	19	51	30					USGS	Croatia:Split	克罗地亚:斯普利特	43.38	17.07	33	4.7	mb	6										
1974	6	6	12	30	55					China	China:Hebei, Ningjin, SE.	中国:河北宁晋东南	37.5	115	24	4.7	Ms	6										
1974	6	12	16	25	46					* Engdahl	Venezuela:Cariaco	委内瑞拉:卡利亚科	10.511	-63.431	8.3	6.1	Ms	8	5	1			2.5	2				
1974	6	19	3	9	38					USGS	Russia:Magadan, Poselok	俄罗斯:马加丹州波谢洛克村	63.16	150.85	33	5	mb	7										
1974	6	20	9	28	33					USGS	Bosnia:Banja Luka	波斯尼亚:巴尼亚卢卡	44.35	17.71	33	5.1	mb	7										
1974	6	20	17	8	27					* USGS	Croatia:Karlovac	克罗地亚:卡尔洛维克	44.97	15.53	7	5.1	Muk	7						2				
1974	6	30	8	33	47					USGS	Vanuatu Islands	瓦努阿图群岛	-17.99	168.29	61	5.7	mb	6										
1974	7	1	16	51	54					* GSHAP, Engdahl	Bolivia:Tarija	玻利维亚:塔里哈	-22.124	-64.638	18	6.5	Mw							2				
1974	7	8	5	45	40					ISC, Engdahl, USGS	Japan:Ibaraki, Near Coast	日本:茨城近海	36.426	141.139	44.5	6	Ms	6										
1974	7	13	1	18	23					* Shi Z., Engdahl	Colombia:Bogota, Cali, Pereira	哥伦比亚:波哥达,卡利,佩雷拉	7.737	-77.631	5.5	7.7	Ms		11	1				1				
1974	8	3	18	16	36					* Engdahl	Japan:Bando	日本:茨城坂东	36.015	139.901	51.9	5.5	Muk	6	2	1	17	1		2				
1974	8	18	10	44	10	1				* CSN, Shi Z., Engdahl, NOAA	Chile:La Union, Valdivia	智利:拉乌尼翁,巴尔迪维亚	-38.433	-73.462	8.4	7.1	Ms	6						1				
1974	9	4	9	20	3					USGS, ISC	Japan:Morioka	日本:岩手盛冈	40.2	141.74	55	5.6	mb	6										
1974	9	17	5	10	32					USGS	Albania:Erseke	阿尔巴尼亚:爱尔塞克	40.29	20.64	17	4.9	ML	7										
1974	9	20	21	20	12					USGS	Papua New Guinea:Eastern Highlands	巴布亚新几内亚:东高地区	-6.24	146.06	111	5.8	mb	6										
1974	9	23	14	51	5					China	China:Sichuan, Zoige, NW.	中国:四川若尔盖西北	33.8	102.6	12	5.6	Ms	7										
1974	9	23	19	28	14					* Engdahl	Gabon:Ogooue - Lolo	加蓬:奥果韦-洛洛	-0.297	12.759	2.4	6.2	Ms							2				
1974	9	27	5	47	30	4	0.4	0.6	-1	* Engdahl, NOAA, USGS	Japan:Hokkaido, Near Coast of E.	日本:北海道东部海域	43.18	146.537	30	6.9	Mw	6										
1974	10	3	14	21	34	4	0.9	0.8	1	* Engdahl, NOAA	Peru:Lima, Callao	秘鲁:利马,卡亚俄	-12.254	-77.524	33.9	8.1	Mw	9	78	2	2414	4	10.0	3		3		
1974	10	8	9	50	57					* CSN, Shi Z., ISC, Engdahl	Antigua And Barbuda:St Kitts	安提瓜和巴布达:圣基茨	17.347	-61.977	23.3	6.9	Mw	8			4	1		2				

时间 Date 年 Year	月 Mo	日 Dy	时 Hr	分 Mn	秒 Sec	海啸 Tsunami 源 Sr	浪高 Wh	级 I mI	级 S mS	资料来源 Information	震中 Earthquake Epicenter 地名(英文) Name(English)	地名(中文) Name(Chinese)	纬度(°) Latitude	经度(°) Longitude	深度 Depth	震级 Mag	标度 Scale	烈度 MMI	死亡人数 Deaths 数量/人 Num	级别 Dd	受伤人数 Injuries 数量/人 Num	级别 Dd	经济损失 Damage 数量/$ Mill $ Mill	级别 De	房屋毁坏 Houses Destroyed 数量/间 Num	级别 Dh	房屋受损 Houses Damaged 数量/间 Num	级别 Dh
1974	10	29	1	5	16					USGS	Bosnia and Herzegovina: Tuzla	波斯尼亚和黑塞哥维那:图兹拉	44. 62	18. 41	33	5. 1	mb	7										
1974	11	8	21	23	24					ISC, Usami, Engdahl, USGS	Japan: Hokkaido	日本:北海道	42. 543	141. 788	128. 2	6. 5	Mw	8										
1974	11	11	5	17	51					USGS	Andreanof Islands, Aleutian Is.	阿留申群岛,安德烈亚诺夫群岛	51. 63	-178. 11	68	5. 8	mb	6										
1974	11	12	5	59	51					USGS	Chile: Colina	智利:科利纳	-33. 15	-70. 62	90	5. 5	mb	7										
1974	11	13	2	36	26					USGS	Russia: Dagestan, Igali	俄罗斯:达吉斯坦共和国伊加利	42. 72	46. 56	42	5. 1	mb	6										
1974	11	15	23	32	45					ISC, Engdahl, USGS	Japan: Chiba, Near Coast	日本:千叶近海	35. 821	141. 06	43. 9	5. 6	Ms	6										
1974	11	20	4	14	52					ISC, Engdahl, USGS	Vanuatu Islands	瓦努阿图群岛	-15. 153	167. 226	68. 3	6. 2	mb	7										
1974	11	22	5	25	56					USGS	US: South Carolina, Summerville	美国:南卡罗来纳州萨默维尔	32. 9	-80. 14	18	4. 7	mb	6										
1974	11	28	23	1	25					USGS	US: California, San Juan Bautista	美国:加利福尼亚州圣胡安包蒂斯塔	36. 91	-121. 5	9	5. 2	ML	6										
1974	11	29	22	5	24					ISC, Engdahl, USGS	Japan: South Honshu Ridge	日本:南本州海岭	30. 682	138. 354	424. 7	7. 1	Mw	6										
1974	12	2	1	55	16					USGS	Italy: Romagna	意大利:弗里	42. 99	12. 97	7	4. 9	mb	6										
1974	12	2	9	5	44					*	Iran: Hormozgan	伊朗:荷姆兹甘	28	55. 8	36	5. 4	mb							2				
1974	12	10	1	41	6					USGS, ISC	Afghan: Kabul	阿富汗:喀布尔	36. 46	70. 48	204	5. 5	mb	5										
1974	12	28	12	11	44					* Engdahl	Pakistan: Balakot, Patan	巴基斯坦:巴拉考特,巴丹	35. 023	72. 9	14. 5	6. 2	Ms	7	5300	4	17000	5	3. 255	2		3		3
1975	1	2	19	31	44					USGS, ISC	Aleutian Islands	阿留申群岛	53. 01	159. 45	47	5. 5	mb	5										
1975	1	9	23	9	47					* USGS	Russia: Dagestan, Chirkey	俄罗斯:达吉斯坦共和国奇尔克伊	42. 89	46. 99	31	5. 2	mb	8						2				
1975	1	11	21	22	28					China	China: Yunnan, Chuxiong	中国:云南楚雄	24. 9	101. 61		5. 4	Ms	6										
1975	1	15	9	42	24	1				* NOAA	Indonesia: Banda Sea	印度尼西亚:班达海	-5	130		5. 9	Ms	7						1	81	2		
1975	1	15	11	34	44					China, Engdahl, Dis	China: Sichuan, Garze, SW.	中国:四川甘孜西南	29. 41	101. 745	32. 9	6. 2	Ms				1	1			61	2		
1975	1	16	0	9	47					USGS	Italy: Villa San Giovanni	意大利:圣乔瓦尼镇	38. 17	15. 63	21	4. 9	ML	7										
1975	1	19	8	1	60					* India, Wang S., Engdahl	India: Kashmir	印度:克什米尔	32. 375	78. 489	2. 7	6. 8	Ms		47	1				2				
1975	1	22	4	40	51					USGS	Japan: Kumamoto	日本:熊本	33. 06	131. 08	9	5	Ms	6										
1975	1	22	12	59	38					China	China: Yunnan, Qiaojia, S.	中国:云南巧家南	26. 5	103		4. 7	Ms	6										
1975	1	23	14	19	17					* Usami, Engdahl, USGS	Japan: Kumamoto	日本:熊本	32. 991	131. 053	9. 5	5. 8	Ms	8						2	16	1		
1975	1	23	17	57	3					USGS	Japan: Kumamoto	日本:熊本	32. 92	131. 16	17	4. 8	mb	6										
1975	2	2	8	43	42					* Engdahl, USGS	Aleutian Islands	阿留申群岛	53. 036	173. 595	13. 1	7. 6	Ms	9						2				

年 Year	月 Mo	日 Dy	时 Hr	分 Mn	秒 Sec	海啸 Tsunami 源 Sr	浪高 Wh	级 I mI	级 S mS	资料来源 Information	震中 Earthquake Epicenter 地名(英文) Name(English)	地名(中文) Name(Chinese)	纬度(°) Latitude	经度(°) Longitude	深度 Depth	震级 Mag	标度 Scale	烈度 MMI	死亡人数 Deaths 数量/人 Num	级别 Dd	受伤人数 Injuries 数量/人 Num	级别 Dd	经济损失 Damage 数量/$ Mill	级别 De	房屋毁坏 Houses Destroyed 数量/间 Num	级别 Dh	房屋受损 Houses Damaged 数量/间 Num	级别 Dh
1975	2	4	1	32	52					USGS	US:Montana,Kalispell	美国:蒙大纳州卡利斯佩尔	48.21	-114.11	8	5	ML	6										
1975	2	4	11	36	5					* China, Engdahl, Dis	China:Liaoning,Haicheng	中国:辽宁海城	40.717	122.734	8	7.3	Ms	10	1328	3	16980	5	1001	5		4		
1975	2	7	16	41	16					USGS,ISC	Japan:Tokyo	日本:东京	35.74	139.97	56	5.5	mb	6										
1975	2	9	4	45	24					* CSN,Engdahl	Indonesia:Java Island	印度尼西亚:爪哇岛	-6.777	106.63	11.3	5.6	Ms		1	1				2				
1975	2	22	8	36	9					Shi Z., Engdahl, USGS	Aleutian Islands	阿留申群岛	51.324	-179.404	48.8	6.5	Ms	6										
1975	3	7	7	4	44					* Engdahl	Iran:Hormozgan	伊朗:荷姆兹甘	27.484	56.225	22.4	6.1	Ms		7	1				2				
1975	3	7	17	36	8					China	China:Yunnan,Yanjin,N.	中国:云南盐津北	28.4	104.2	30	5.3	Ms	6										
1975	3	13	15	26	48	2				* Shi Z., Engdahl, NOAA	Chile:Coquimbo	智利:科金博	-29.912	-71.396	31.4	6.9	Ms	8	2	1	25	1		1				
1975	3	27	5	15	8					* Engdahl,USGS	Turkey:Canakkale, Eceabat	土耳其:肯纳卡莱,伊赛巴特	40.42	26.147	3.4	6.7	Ms	6						2				
1975	3	28	2	31	8					* Engdahl	US:Idaho,Pocatello Valley	美国:爱达荷州波卡提洛峡谷	42.012	-112.476	5.3	6	Ms	8					1	2				
1975	4	2	8	44	0					USGS	Japan:Miyake Jima	日本:三宅岛	33.6	140.37	71	5.6	mb	6										
1975	4	5	9	34	37					* Shi Z., Engdahl	Venezuela:Lara	委内瑞拉:拉腊	10.067	-69.663	21.6	6.1	Ms	8	3	1			1.2	2				
1975	4	8	6	27	13					USGS	Japan:Fukushima,Near Coast	日本:福岛近海	37.72	141.65	46	5.8	mb	6										
1975	4	17	18	41	8					USGS	Japan:Satte	日本:埼玉幸手	36.15	139.75	65	5.1	mb	6										
1975	4	20	17	35	52					* Usami, Engdahl	Japan:Oita	日本:大分	33.143	131.26	6.7	6.1	Ms	6			8	1		3	95	2		
1975	5	10	14	27	43					* Engdahl	Chile:Canete	智利:卡涅特	-38.215	-72.999	28	7.7	Mw							2				
1975	5	26	9	11	49	4	0.8			* Engdahl,NOAA	North Atlantic Ocean,E.	北大西洋东部	35.97	-17.645	4.9	7.9	Mw	6						1				
1975	6	4	2	24	31					Wang S., Engdahl	China:Xinjiang,Hotan,S.	中国:新疆和田南	35.872	79.925	8	5.8	Ms	7										
1975	6	7	8	46	22					USGS, Engdahl, ISC	US:California,Fortuna	美国:加利福尼亚州福图纳	40.57	-124.14	21	5.7	Ms	8										
1975	6	10	13	47	19	4	5.5	2.3	2	* Engdahl, NOAA	Japan:Hokkaido, Near Coast of E.	日本:北海道东部海域	43.129	147.655	28.2	7	Ms							2				
1975	6	14	10	40	21					USGS	Chile:San Felipe	智利:圣费利佩	-32.49	-70.68	94	5.6	mb	7										
1975	6	18	2	35	60					USGS	Venezuela:Pilar	委内瑞拉:比拉尔	10.61	-63.28	16	4.6	mb	6										
1975	6	19	10	11	14					USGS	Italy:Foggia	意大利:福查	41.7	15.77	16	5.2	ML	6										
1975	6	23	13	17	38					USGS	Germany:Fulda	德国:富尔达	50.59	9.86	33	5.2	ML	7										
1975	6	30	18	54	13					USGS	US:Wyoming,Mammoth	美国:怀俄明州马默斯	44.673	-110.736	15	5.9	Ms	7										
1975	7	8	12	4	41					* Engdahl	Myanmar:Pagan	缅甸:蒲甘	21.449	94.597	119.7	6.8	Muk		1	1			1	2				
1975	7	9	13	55	41					China	China:Yunnan,Kaiyuan,NE.	中国:云南开远东北	23.9	103.3	18	5.3	Ms	6										
1975	7	9	14	54	15					USGS	US:Minnesota,Morris	美国:明尼苏达州莫里斯	45.67	-96.04	10	4.6	mb	7										
1975	7	11	7	18	47					*	Algeria:Setif	阿尔及利亚:塞提夫	36.32	5.241	30	4.3	mb		1	1	18	1		2				

时间 Date						海啸 Tsunami				资料来源 Information	震中 Earthquake Epicenter				深度 Depth	震级 Mag	标度 Scale	烈度 MMI	死亡人数 Deaths		受伤人数 Injuries		经济损失 Damage		房屋毁坏 Houses Destroyed		房屋受损 Houses Damaged	
年 Year	月 Mo	日 Dy	时 Hr	分 Mn	秒 Sec	源 Sr	浪高 Wh	级 I mI	级 S mS		地名(英文) Name(English)	地名(中文) Name(Chinese)	纬度(°) Latitude	经度(°) Longitude					数量/人 Num	级别 Dd	数量/人 Num	级别 Dd	数量/$ Mill $ Mill	级别 De	数量/间 Num	级别 Dh	数量/间 Num	级别 Dh
1975	7	20	14	37	42	4	2	1	1	* Engdahl, NOAA, CSN	Solomon Sea, N.	所罗门海北部	-6.612	155.097	59.7	7.7	Mw	8						3		2		
1975	7	20	19	54	30					* Engdahl, USGS, CSN	Solomon Islands	所罗门群岛	-7.081	155.214	44.2	7.3	Mw	7										
1975	7	24	6	42	35					USGS	Chile:Los Andes, SE.	智利:洛斯安第斯东南	-33	-70.28	112	4.7	mb	6										
1975	7	30	16	25	20					USGS	Turkey:Afyon	土耳其:阿菲永	39.47	32.1	20	4.6	mb	6										
1975	8	1	20	20	14					* CGS, USGS, Engdahl	US: California, Oroville Reservoir	美国:加利福尼亚州奥罗维尔水库	39.503	-121.39	9.4	5.8	M	8			10	1	6.0	3				
1975	8	3	6	35	17					USGS	US:California, Three Rocks	美国:加利福尼亚州斯里罗克斯	36.46	-120.35	5	4.9	ML	6										
1975	8	12	14	21	7					ISC, Engdahl, USGS	Ryukyu Trench	琉球海沟	32.064	137.783	399.3	6.9	Mw	5										
1975	8	18	12	49	33					USGS	Papua New Guinea:East New Britain	巴布亚新几内亚:东新不列颠	-4.75	152.39	55	5.2	mb	6										
1975	9	2	12	10	6					China, Dis	China:South Yellow Sea	中国:南黄海	32.9	121.71	16	5.3	Ms	5										
1975	9	3	21	50	29					China	China:Yunnan, Yangbi, N.	中国:云南漾濞北	25.9	99.9	5	5	Ms	6										
1975	9	6	9	20	14					* Engdahl	Turkey:Lice	土耳其:利杰	38.516	40.768	39.7	6.7	Ms	9	2311	4	3372	4	17.0	3				
1975	9	13	21	20	60					USGS	US:California, Bradley	美国:加利福尼亚州布拉德利	36	-120.56	13	4.8	ML	6										
1975	9	21	14	16	38					* Iran	Iran: Aharmahal And Bakhtiari	伊朗:恰哈马哈勒－巴赫蒂亚里	31.599	51.037	33	5.2	Ms	7	2	1				3				
1975	10	20	3	20	0					USGS	Russia:Dagestan, Belidzhi	俄罗斯:达吉斯坦共和国别利吉	41.66	48.25	33	4.7	mb	6										
1975	10	27	23	18	53					Wang S.	Laos:Boun Neua	老挝:奔讷	21.5	101.8	39	5.7	Ms	7										
1975	10	30	1	41	34					ISC, Engdahl, USGS	Japan:Hokkaido	日本:北海道	42.115	142.622	60.3	6	Mw	6										
1975	10	31	8	28	4	4	4	-0.7	-1.5	* Bautista, Engdahl, NOAA	Philippines:Samar Island	菲律宾:萨马岛	12.536	125.999	51.1	7.5	Mw	6	1	1				1	30	1		
1975	11	1	1	17	35					* Engdahl	Guam	关岛(西太平洋)	13.851	144.813	107.8	7.1	mb	7						1				
1975	11	16	17	29	32					USGS	US:California, Off Coast N.	美国:加利福尼亚州北部沿海	40.43	-126.11	33	4.9	ML	6										
1975	11	29	14	47	41	4	14	3	3	* Engdahl, NOAA	Hawaiian Islands	夏威夷群岛	19.451	-155.033	2.1	7.2	Ms	9	2	1	19	1	4	2		3		
1975	11	30	18	22	22					China	China:Yunnan, Lijiang, N.	中国:云南丽江北	27.2	100.3	18	4.9	Ms	6										
1975	12	3	7	14	32					USGS	Japan:Hokkaido	日本:北海道	43.22	145.65	76	5.3	mb	6										
1975	12	5	20	14	18					USGS	Japan:Hokkaido	日本:北海道	43.6	146.39	68	5.8	mb	6										
1975	12	9	9	14	44					ISC, Engdahl, USGS	Samoa Islands, S.	萨摩亚群岛南部	-14.923	-172.776	48.5	6.2	Ms	6										
1975	12	14	18	16	20					USGS	US:California, Landers	美国:加利福尼亚州兰德斯	34.27	-116.33	8	4.7	ML	6										
1975	12	25	23	22	23					ISC, Engdahl, USGS	Papua New Guinea: East Sepik	巴布亚新几内亚:东塞皮克	-4.083	142.148	113	6.4	mb	6										

年 Year	月 Mo	日 Dy	时 Hr	分 Mn	秒 Sec	海啸 Tsunami 源 Sr	浪高 Wh	级 I mI	级 S mS	资料来源 Information	震中 Earthquake Epicenter 地名(英文) Name(English)	地名(中文) Name(Chinese)	纬度(°) Latitude	经度(°) Longitude	深度 Depth	震级 Mag	标度 Scale	烈度 MMI	死亡人数 Deaths 数量/人 Num	级别 Dd	受伤人数 Injuries 数量/人 Num	级别 Dd	经济损失 Damage 数量/$ Mill $ Mill	级别 De	房屋毁坏 Houses Destroyed 数量/间 Num	级别 Dh	房屋受损 Houses Damaged 数量/间 Num	级别 Dh
1975	12	26	15	56	38	4	0.8	-0.3		*Engdahl,NOAA	Samoa Islands	萨摩亚群岛	-16.241	-172.364	15	7.7	Mw	5										
1975	12	27	4	31	51					USGS	Italy:Loiano	意大利:洛亚诺	44.53	11.86	34	4.9	mb	6										
1975	12	31	9	45	48					*Engdahl	Greece:Kato - Makrinou	希腊:下马克里努	38.527	21.714	15	5.5	Ms	9	1	1	10	1		3				
1976	1	5	6	23	33					USGS	US:New Mexico,Crownpoint	美国:新墨西哥州克朗波因特	35.84	-108.34	25	4.6	ML	6										
1976	1	10	12	51	28					China	China:Xinjiang,Kuqa,NE.	中国:新疆库车东北	42.2	83.3		5.8	Ms	7										
1976	1	13	13	29	19					*Engdahl	Iceland:Thvera	冰岛:斯韦尔	66.226	-16.576	15	6.3	Mw							2				
1976	1	14	15	56	34					*Engdahl	Kermadec Ridge	克马德克海岭	-29.213	-177.638	43.7	7.8	Mw	8										
1976	1	14	16	47	38	4	0.9	-0.1		*Engdahl,NOAA	Kermadec Ridge	克马德克海岭	-29.172	-177.316	31.7	7.9	Mw							1				
1976	1	14	21	43	59					USGS	US:California,Coalinga	美国:加利福尼亚州科灵加	36.01	-120.27	11	4.8	ML	6										
1976	1	21	10	5	25	4	0.4	-1.3	-2.5	*Engdahl,NOAA	Kuril Islands	千岛群岛	44.777	149.141	38.9	7.2	Mw											
1976	2	4	0	4	58					USGS	US:Arizona,Prescott	美国:亚利桑那州普雷斯科特	34.65	-112.5	12	5.2	ML	6										
1976	2	4	9	1	46	4	0.1			* Shi Z.,CSN,ISC,Engdahl,NOAA	Guatemala: Chimaltenango,Guatemala City	危地马拉:奇马尔特南戈,危地马拉城	15.297	-89.145	12.1	7.5	M	9	23000	5	76000	5	2147	5				
1976	2	16	14	45	38					China	China:Yunnan,Pu - er	中国:云南普洱	22.8	100.7	10	5.8	Ms	6										
1976	2	22	16	15	17					USGS	Croatia:Knin	克罗地亚:克宁	44.15	15.72	33	5.2	mb	6										
1976	3	4	2	50	3					ISC, Engdahl, USGS	Vanuatu Islands	瓦努阿图群岛	-14.785	167.217	101.4	6.9	Mw	6										
1976	3	13	16	30	42					*ISC	Guatemala:Panajachel	危地马拉:帕纳哈切尔	14.77	-91.06	5	5.4	mb		4	1	50	1		2				
1976	3	19	13	3	38					* ISC, Engdahl, USGS	Afghan:Termez, Narin	阿富汗:铁尔梅兹,纳林	36.589	67.76	18.7	5.6	mb	8	50	1				3				
1976	3	24	4	46	5					ISC, Engdahl, USGS	Kermadec Ridge	克马德克海岭	-29.875	-177.697	28.9	7.1	Mw	7										
1976	3	25	0	41	21					USGS	US:Arkansas,Marked Tree	美国:阿肯色州马克德特里	35.59	-90.48	15	5	MLg	6										
1976	3	25	11	55	39					*	Turkey:Cildir	土耳其:彻尔德尔	41.13	43.01	18	4.8	mb		1	1				2				
1976	4	5	16	54	39					Wang S.,Dis,Engdahl,USGS	China: Inner Mongolia, Horinger,SE.	中国:内蒙古和林格尔东南	40.231	112.222	7.7	6.2	Ms	7	28		865	3			30542	5	114204	5
1976	4	8	2	40	25					*Engdahl	Uzbekistan:Gazli	乌兹别克斯坦:加兹利	40.352	63.738	7.7	6.7	Mw	7						3				
1976	4	8	15	21	38					USGS	US:California,Simi Valley	美国:加利福尼亚州西米谷	34.35	-118.67	16	4.8	ML	6										
1976	4	9	7	8	51					*Shi Z.,Engdahl	Ecuador:Esmeraldos	厄瓜多尔:埃斯梅拉达斯	0.849	-79.577	17.9	6.7	Mw		10	1			4	2				
1976	4	13	0	47	17					USGS	US:Oregon,Wasco	美国:俄勒冈州沃斯科	45.22	-120.77	15	4.8	ML	6										
1976	4	21	20	0	19					USGS	Bosnia and Herzegovina:Mostar	波斯尼亚和黑塞哥维那:莫斯塔尔	43.4	17.49	32	5.5	mb	6										
1976	4	29	22	18	6					*Engdahl	Turkey:Ardahan	土耳其:阿尔达汉	40.939	42.872	7.6	5.5	Ms		4	1				2				
1976	5	5	4	52	55					ISC, Engdahl, USGS	Kermadec Ridge	克马德克海岭	-29.845	-177.641	59.8	7.1	Mw	6										

年 Year	月 Mo	日 Dy	时 Hr	分 Mn	秒 Sec	海啸 Tsunami 源 Sr	浪高 Wh	级 I mI	级 S mS	资料来源 Information	震中 Earthquake Epicenter 地名(英文) Name(English)	地名(中文) Name(Chinese)	纬度(°) Latitude	经度(°) Longitude	深度 Depth	震级 Mag	标度 Scale	烈度 MMI	死亡人数 Deaths 数量/人 Num	级别 Dd	受伤人数 Injuries 数量/人 Num	级别 Dd	经济损失 Damage 数量/$ Mill	级别 De	房屋毁坏 Houses Destroyed 数量/间 Num	级别 Dh	房屋受损 Houses Damaged 数量/间 Num	级别 Dh
1976	5	6	19	59	7					USGS	Italy: Udine	意大利:乌迪内	46.2	13.26	33	4.5	mb	7										
1976	5	6	20	0	15					* Italy, Engdahl	Italy: Udine	意大利:乌迪内	46.385	13.266	20.9	6.5	Mw	10	978	3	1700	4	3600	5				
1976	5	7	0	23	50					USGS	Italy: Udine	意大利:乌迪内	46.17	13.31	33	4.7	mb	6										
1976	5	7	9	41	19					USGS	Italy: Udine	意大利:乌迪内	46.35	12.94	33	5.9	mb	6										
1976	5	9	0	53	44					USGS, ISC	Italy: Udine	意大利:乌迪内	46.24	13.31	14	5.5	mb	9										
1976	5	11	22	44	0					USGS	Italy: Udine	意大利:乌迪内	46.27	12.99	11	5.2	mb	8										
1976	5	11	23	36	47					USGS	Italy: Udine	意大利:乌迪内	46.36	12.84	33	5	mb	6										
1976	5	15	8	9	57					USGS, ISC	Congo: Bosobolo	刚果:博索博洛	4.46	19.35	23	5.6	mb	5										
1976	5	16	8	35	15					USGS	Canada: British Columbia, Vancouver	加拿大:英属哥伦比亚温哥华	48.8	-123.36	62	5.1	mb	6										
1976	5	17	2	58	43					* Engdahl	Uzbekistan: Gazli, Bukhara	乌兹别克斯坦:加兹利,布哈拉	40.377	63.437	16.6	6.7	Mw	10					85.0	4				
1976	5	19	4	7	16					USGS, Engdahl, ISC	Colombia: Armenia	哥伦比亚:金迪奥的亚美尼亚	4.46	-75.78	157	6.4	Muk	6										
1976	5	29	11	58	15					Wang S.	China: Yunnan, Longling, E.	中国:云南龙陵东	24.5	98.9	20	5.2	Ms	6										
1976	5	29	12	23	21					* China, Engdahl, Dis	China: Yunnan, Longling, E.	中国:云南龙陵东	24.514	98.915	6	7.3	Ms	9	98	2	2442	4	171	5	420000	5		
1976	5	29	14	0	19					* China, Engdahl, USGS	China: Yunnan, Longling, E.	中国:云南龙陵东	24.531	98.71	10	7.4	Ms	9										
1976	5	31	5	8	30					Wang S., Engdahl	China: Yunnan, Dehong, SE.	中国:云南德宏东南	24.349	98.624	10.5	6.5	Ms	8										
1976	6	3	16	44	40					ISC, Engdahl, USGS	Papua New Guinea: East New Britain, E.	巴布亚新几内亚:东新不列颠东部	-5.099	153.591	80.2	7.2	Mw	6										
1976	6	4	23	39	36					USGS	Chile: Antofagasta, C.	智利:安托法加斯塔中部	-23.1	-68.54	101	5.4	mb	6										
1976	6	7	14	26	42					* CSN, Shi Z., Engdahl	Mexico: Guerrero, Zihuatanejo	墨西哥:格雷罗州锡瓦塔塔内霍	17.38	-100.692	56.3	6.5	Mw							2				
1976	6	9	0	20	38					Wang S., Engdahl	China: Yunnan, Tengchong	中国:云南腾冲	24.942	98.749	5.3	6.2	Ms	7										
1976	6	20	4	38	11					ISC, Engdahl, USGS	Ryukyu Islands, SW.	琉球群岛西南	24.822	125.956	50.5	5.8	Ms	6										
1976	6	25	7	47	46					USGS, ISC	Japan: South Honshu Ridge	日本:本州南部海岭	29.91	138.58	433	5.5	mb	5										
1976	6	25	19	18	55					* Engdahl	Indonesia: Papua, E.	印度尼西亚:巴布亚东部	-4.523	140.105	3.2	7.2	Mw		5150	4				3				
1976	7	10	4	11	25					USGS	Italy: Udine	意大利:乌迪内	46.23	13.16	33	4.9	mb	6										
1976	7	14	7	13	24					* Engdahl	Indonesia: Bali Island	印度尼西亚:巴厘岛	-8.227	114.775	25.4	6.5	Mw		563	3			195	5				
1976	7	17	21	6	35					ISC, Engdahl, USGS	Papua New Guinea: New Ireland	巴布亚新几内亚:新爱尔兰	-4.182	152.8	62.6	6.6	Mw	6										
1976	7	26	2	56	38					* Engdahl	Malaysia: Sabah	马来西亚:沙巴	4.935	118.255	10.4	6.3	Mw	7						2				
1976	7	27	19	42	56					* China, Engdahl, Dis	China: Hebei, Tangshan	中国:河北唐山	39.606	117.888	16.6	7.8	Ms	11	242000	5	164000	5	12232	5				
1976	7	28	10	45	36					* China, Engdahl	China: Hebei, Luanxian	中国:河北滦县	39.723	118.36	18.4	7.1	Ms	9		2				1				

时间 Date						海啸 Tsunami				资料来源 Information	震中 Earthquake Epicenter				深度 Depth	震级 Mag	标度 Scale	烈度 MMI	死亡人数 Deaths		受伤人数 Injuries		经济损失 Damage		房屋毁坏 Houses Destroyed		房屋受损 Houses Damaged	
年 Year	月 Mo	日 Dy	时 Hr	分 Mn	秒 Sec	源 Sr	浪高 Wh	级I mI	级S mS		地名(英文) Name(English)	地名(中文) Name(Chinese)	纬度(°) Latitude	经度(°) Longitude					数量/人 Num	级别 Dd	数量/人 Num	级别 Dd	数量/$ Mill $ Mill	级别 De	数量/间 Num	级别 Dh	数量/间 Num	级别 Dh
1976	7	28	20	17	44					ISC, Engdahl, USGS	Russia:Chechnia,Grozny,N.	俄罗斯:车臣共和国格罗兹尼北部	43.264	45.654	15.2	6.2	Mw	6										
1976	8	16	14	6	47					Wang S., Engdahl, Dis	China:Sichuan,Songpan	中国:四川松潘	32.753	104.095	12.1	7.2	Ms	9	38						5000	4		
1976	8	16	16	11	12	4	8.5	2.3	2.5	* Bautista, Engdahl, NOAA	Philippines:Mindanao,Lebak	菲律宾:棉兰老岛,莱巴克	6.292	124.09	57.7	8	Mw	6	5066	4	10000	5	130	5				
1976	8	17	4	19	29					* Engdahl	Philippines:Mindanao Island	菲律宾:棉兰老岛	7.261	122.961	21.2	7.1	Mw			1				1				
1976	8	19	1	12	37					* ISC	Turkey:Denizli	土耳其:登尼资里	37.7	28.89	3	5.6	Muk		4	1	50	1		2	1800	4		
1976	8	23	3	30	5					Wang S., Engdahl	China:Sichuan,Songpan,E.	中国:四川松潘东	32.485	104.184	7	7.2	Ms	8.5										
1976	8	24	21	26	12					USGS,ISC	Chile:Taltal,Near Coast	智利:塔尔塔尔近海	-25.33	-70.69	8	5.6	mb	5										
1976	9	8	8	21	2					USGS	US:Washington,Seattle	美国:华盛顿州西雅图	47.38	-123.08	48	4.5	Md	6										
1976	9	11	16	31	12					* Engdahl, USGS, ISC	Italy:Udine	意大利:乌迪内	46.337	13.181	4.2	5.5	Ms	7	5	1				2				
1976	9	12	19	53	28					USGS	Italy:Udine	意大利:乌迪内	46.22	13.15	3	4.6	Muk	7										
1976	9	15	3	15	20					* Italy, ISC, Engdahl	Italy:Udine	意大利:乌迪内	46.314	13.206	0.9	6	Mw	9	11	1				2				
1976	9	17	1	23	56					USGS	Italy:Sicilia Island	意大利:西西里岛	37.99	14.66	45	4.9	mb	6										
1976	9	19	13	56	11					China	China: Yunnan, Sipsongpanna, N.	中国:云南西双版纳北	22.48	101.07		5.2	Ms	6										
1976	9	22	20	7	5					Wang S., Engdahl, Dis	China:Inner Mongolia,Wuhai	中国:内蒙古乌海	40.061	106.3	28.1	6.2	Ms	7										
1976	10	6	13	38	42					USGS	Japan:Fukushima,Near Coast	日本:福岛近海	37.09	141.27	81	5.6	mb	6										
1976	10	9	6	11	35					China	China:Yunnan,Eshan	中国:云南峨山	24.1	102.3		5.3	Ms	6										
1976	10	29	2	51	8					* Engdahl	Indonesia:Papua	印度尼西亚:巴布亚	-4.475	139.991	15	6.8	Mw	8	133	3								
1976	11	4	10	41	38					USGS	US:California,Salton City	美国:加利福尼亚州索尔顿城	33.08	-115.6	6	4.9	ML	6										
1976	11	6	18	4	7					Wang S., Engdahl, Dis	China:Sichuan,Muli,SW.	中国:四川木里西南	27.63	101.003	7.9	6.7	Ms	9	33		462	3			413	3		
1976	11	7	4	0	52					* Engdahl	Iran:Razavi Khorasan	伊朗:呼罗珊	33.821	59.184	7	6	Mw	8	17	1				3				
1976	11	15	13	53	3					Wang S., Engdahl, Dis	China:Tianjin,Ninghe,N.	中国:天津宁河北	39.475	117.743	22.9	6.9	Ms	8	12		7	1			1000	3		
1976	11	24	12	22	17					* Engdahl	Turkey:Muradiye	土耳其:姆拉迪艾	39.083	44.03	9.7	7.3	Mw	10	5000	4			60.0	4				
1976	11	27	21	42	13					* ISC,Engdahl	Afghan:Badakhshan	阿富汗:巴达赫尚	36.49	71.061	188.2	5.9	Mw	5						2				
1976	11	30	0	41	5					* CSN,Shi Z., Engdahl	Chile:Pozo Almonte,E.	智利:波索阿尔蒙特东部	-20.472	-68.893	133.7	7.6	Mw	8	1	1	13	1		2				
1976	12	7	12	59	56					USGS	Mexico:Mexicali	墨西哥:墨西卡利	31.98	-114.78	8	5.2	ML	6										
1976	12	8	8	38	26					*	South Africa:Welkom	南非:威尔康姆	-27.953	26.653	33	5.2	mb		4	1	36	1		2				

时间						海啸				资料来源	震中				深度	震级	标度	烈度	死亡人数		受伤人数		经济损失		房屋毁坏		房屋受损	
年	月	日	时	分	秒	源	浪高	级I	级S		地名(英文)	地名(中文)	纬度(°)	经度(°)					数量/人	级别	数量/人	级别	数量/$ Mill	级别	数量/间	级别	数量/间	级别
Date						Tsunami				Information	Earthquake Epicenter				Depth	Mag	Scale	MMI	Deaths		Injuries		Damage		Houses Destroyed		Houses Damaged	
Year	Mo	Dy	Hr	Mn	Sec	Sr	Wh	mI	mS		Name(English)	Name(Chinese)	Latitude	Longitude					Num	Dd	Num	Dd	$ Mill	De	Num	Dh	Num	Dh
1976	12	13	6	36	59					Wang S., Engdahl	China: Sichuan, Yanyuan, SW.	中国:四川盐源西南	27.358	100.997	8.7	6.4	Ms	8										
1976	12	15	13	15	17					USGS,ISC	Mariana Islands,S.	马里亚纳群岛南部	13.1	145.06	77	5.5	mb	5										
1976	12	27								* Song	Turkey:Caldiran	土耳其:恰尔德兰	39	44		5.7	Mk		1	1				2				
1977	1	1	21	39	41					Wang S., Engdahl	China: Qinghai, Haixi Mang-ai,NW.	中国:青海海西茫崖西北	38.189	91.017	5	6.4	Ms	8										
1977	1	8	9	38	7					USGS	US:California,Richmond	美国:加利福尼亚州里奇蒙	37.91	-122.2	10	4.6	ML	6										
1977	1	13	9	19	6					USGS	Bosnia and Herzegovina:Livno	波斯尼亚和黑塞哥维那:利夫诺	43.55	17.1	20	5.3	mb	7										
1977	1	17	21	27	21					Shi Z., Engdahl, USGS	Chile:Antofagasta,SE.	智利:安托法加斯塔东南	-24.911	-68.652	100	6.9	Mw	7										
1977	1	26	13	11	30					*	Indonesia:Bali Island	印度尼西亚:巴厘岛	-8.22	115.19	33	5.2	mb	6						1				
1977	1	31	14	26	19					* ISC, Engdahl, USGS	Kyrgyzstan:Khaydarken	吉尔吉斯斯坦:海达尔肯	40.08	70.858	39.2	6	Mw	8						2				
1977	2	18	20	51	33					ISC, Engdahl, USGS	Japan Trench	日本海沟	33.131	140.927	58.1	6.2	Mw	6										
1977	2	22	6	24	7					USGS	US:Nevada,Wellington,	美国:内华达州惠灵顿	38.48	-119.29	5	4.8	ML	6										
1977	2	24	11	39	58					ISC,USGS	Japan:Hokkaido	日本:北海道	42.5	142.6	65	6.6	Mw	6										
1977	3	4	19	21	56					*Engdahl,USGS	Romania:Paltin	罗马尼亚:帕尔廷	45.777	26.703	88.9	7.5	Mw	9	1581	4	10500	5	800	5				
1977	3	7	9	12	28					USGS	Japan:Hokkaido	日本:北海道	43.1	145.77	24	5.4	mb	6										
1977	3	8	23	17	29					* Shi Z., Engdahl	Indonesia:Northern Sumatra	印度尼西亚:苏门答腊北部	0.502	99.772	14.5	6.1	Mw	8						1				
1977	3	11	5	9	37					USGS	US:Montana,Toston	美国:蒙大纳州托斯顿	46.13	-111.48	5	4.8	ML	6										
1977	3	16	23	54	53					China	China:Yunnan,Yangbi,NW.	中国:云南漾濞西北	25.85	99.68		5.4	Ms	6										
1977	3	18	21	43	54					* Bautista, Engdahl	Philippines:Santiago,E.	菲律宾:圣地亚哥东部	16.753	122.283	34	7.3	Mw	8	1	1			0.1	1				
1977	3	21	21	18	57					* Engdahl	Iran:Hormozgan	伊朗:荷姆兹甘	27.608	56.358	35.6	6.7	Mw		167	3	556	3		3				
1977	3	23	2	11	15					USGS,ISC	Colombia:Los Santos	哥伦比亚:洛斯桑托斯	6.79	-73.04	164	5.5	mb	5										
1977	3	25	2	39	58					*	Turkey:Elazig	土耳其:埃拉泽	38.56	40.02	21	5.2	mb		30	1				3				
1977	4	2	7	15	26	4	0.1	-3.3	-2	*Engdahl,NOAA	Samoa Islands	萨摩亚群岛	-16.795	-171.947	50.3	7.3	Mw	6						1				
1977	4	6	13	36	36					* Engdahl	Iran: Aharmahal And Bakhtiari	伊朗:恰哈马哈勒-巴赫蒂亚里	31.961	50.649	16.3	6	Mw		366	3	200	3		2				
1977	4	17	2	41	18					USGS	Argentina:Mendoza	阿根廷:门多萨	-33.26	-68.88	47	5.1	mb	6										
1977	4	19	6	14	60					USGS	Japan:Naka	日本:茨城那珂	36.46	140.56	65	5.3	mb	6										
1977	4	20	0	31	54					USGS	Bosnia:Banja Luka	波斯尼亚:巴尼亚卢卡	44.92	17.39	33	4.6	mb	6										
1977	4	20	23	13	8	4	0.2	-3.3	-1	*Engdahl,NOAA	Solomon Islands	所罗门群岛	-9.813	160.471	11	6.8	Mw	6										
1977	4	20	23	42	55	4				*Engdahl,NOAA	Solomon Islands	所罗门群岛	-9.903	160.456	39.4	7.3	Mw	7						1				
1977	4	20	23	49	12					* ISC,Engdahl	Solomon Islands	所罗门群岛	-9.571	160.652	16.4	7.1	Mw					1		1				
1977	4	21	1	20	33					USGS,ISC	Solomon Islands	所罗门群岛	-9.89	159.95	32	5.5	mb	5										
1977	4	21	4	24	12	4	0	-3.3	-1.5	*Engdahl,NOAA	Solomon Islands	所罗门群岛	-10.01	160.817	44.9	7.4	Mw	7	18	1	1	1		3				

年 Year	月 Mo	日 Dy	时 Hr	分 Mn	秒 Sec	源 Sr	浪高 Wh	级 I mI	级 S mS	资料来源 Information	地名(英文) Name(English)	地名(中文) Name(Chinese)	纬度(°) Latitude	经度(°) Longitude	深度 Depth	震级 Mag	标度 Scale	烈度 MMI	死亡人数 Deaths 数量/人 Num	级别 Dd	受伤人数 Injuries 数量/人 Num	级别 Dd	经济损失 Damage 数量/$ Mill $ Mill	级别 De	房屋毁坏 Houses Destroyed 数量/间 Num	级别 Dh	房屋受损 Houses Damaged 数量/间 Num	级别 Dh
1977	4	21	13	38	49					USGS	Uzbekistan:Gazli	乌兹别克斯坦:加兹利	40.49	63.78	33	4.9	mb	6										
1977	5	12	11	17	54					Wang S., Engdahl, Dis	China:Tianjin,Ninghe	中国:天津宁河	39.277	117.734	20.1	6.2	Ms	7			30	1						
1977	5	26	1	35	14					*	Iran:Maku	伊朗:马库	38.93	44.38	37	5.4	Ms		3	1	9	1		3				
1977	5	28								* Song	Turkey:Caldiran	土耳其:恰尔德兰	39	44		5.8	Mk		6	1				3				
1977	6	3	1	5	24					USGS	Kyrgyzstan:Batken	吉尔吉斯斯坦:巴特肯	39.87	71.79	24	5.1	mb	7										
1977	6	3	2	31	6					Engdahl, USGS	Afghan:Badakhshan	阿富汗:巴达赫尚	36.373	70.761	208	6.1	Mw	5										
1977	6	5	13	59	22					USGS	Italy:Sicilia Island	意大利:西西里岛	37.88	14.46	8	4.9	mb	7										
1977	6	8	14	25	47					USGS, Engdahl	Japan:Miyagi	日本:宫城	38.54	141.49	78	5.8	Mw	6										
1977	6	21	2	43	7					USGS	US:California, Livermore	美国:加利福尼亚州利弗莫尔	37.65	-121.64	10	4.7	ML	6										
1977	6	22	7	11	28					USGS	Japan:Oamishirasato	日本:千叶大网白里	35.48	140.43	35	5.1	mb	6										
1977	6	22	12	8	34	4	0.4			* CSN, Engdahl, NOAA, USGS	Tonga Islands	汤加群岛	-22.912	-175.744	65.5	8.1	Ms	7	1	1	5	1	1.2	2				
1977	6	28	2	46	42					USGS	Japan:Kumamoto	日本:熊本	32.8	130.75	18	4.7	mb	6										
1977	7	14	5	49	9					USGS	Uzbekistan:Gazli	乌兹别克斯坦:加兹利	40.32	63.68	33	5.5	mb	7										
1977	7	16	13	13	30					* USGS	Slovenia:Trstenik, Bela	斯洛文尼亚:克拉尼	46.29	14.29	6	4.6	mb	6						2				
1977	7	21	13	45	56					ISC, Bautista, Engdahl, USGS	Philippines:Santiago, E.	菲律宾:圣地亚哥东部	16.888	122.377	34.5	6.9	Ms	7										
1977	7	23	6	57	2					China, Dis	China:Xinjiang, Kuqa, NE.	中国:新疆库车东北	42.3	83.5	30	5.4	Ms	6										
1977	8	6	19	27	16					USGS	Japan:Arida	日本:和歌山有田	34.07	135.18	6	4.7	mb	6										
1977	8	16	15	32	42					USGS	Japan:Kainan	日本:和歌山海南	34.15	135.16	9	4.5	mb	6										
1977	8	19	6	8	55	4	15	3.9	3	* Engdahl, NOAA	Indonesia:Sumba Islands, S.	印度尼西亚:松巴岛南部	-11.126	118.38	21.3	8.3	Mw		189	3	75	2	1.2	2				
1977	8	21	5	19	34					USGS, ISC	Japan:Chiba, Near Coast	日本:千叶近海	35.24	141.12	42	5.5	mb	5										
1977	8	28	9	45	15					USGS	Tyrrhenian Sea	第勒尼安海(伊特鲁里亚海)	38.21	8.21	10	5.2	ML	8										
1977	8	28	20	10	3	2	0.6	-0.7	-0.5	* Engdahl, NOAA	East Caroline Basin, S.	东加罗林海盆南部	-1.072	146.278	7.1	5.9	Mw											
1977	8	31	0	42	6					* Shi Z., Engdahl	Colombia: Apartado, Medellin	哥伦比亚:阿帕尔坦多,麦德林	7.352	-76.159	22	6.6	Mw	6	3	1				2				
1977	9	12	22	20	29					USGS	France:Pau	法国:波城	43.09	-1	33	4.5	ML	6										
1977	9	16	23	48	8					USGS	Italy:Udine	意大利:乌迪内	46.27	12.97	25	5.1	mb	7										
1977	9	20	20	28	19					USGS	Bosnia and Herzegovina:Gacko	波斯尼亚和黑塞哥维那:加茨科	43.21	18.59	33	4.6	mb	6										
1977	9	23	2	58	1					USGS	Adriatic Sea	亚得里亚海	41.5	20.07	23	5.1	ML	7										
1977	9	30	10	19	21					USGS	US:Utah, Talmage	美国:犹他州塔尔米奇	40.52	-110.44	5	5.1	ML	6										
1977	10	4	15	38	57					USGS	Japan:Satte	日本:埼玉幸手	36.09	139.74	66	5.4	mb	6										
1977	10	10	11	53	51	2	0		-3	* Engdahl, NOAA	Tonga Islands, S.	汤加群岛南部	-25.846	-175.283	6.9	7.3	Mw											
1977	10	19	1	44	47					China, Dis	China:Guangxi, Pingguo	中国:广西平果	23.4	107.6	16	5	Ms	6			37	1			35	1	2097	4

时间 年 Year	月 Mo	日 Dy	时 Hr	分 Mn	秒 Sec	海啸 Tsunami 源 Sr	浪高 Wh	级 I mI	级 S mS	资料来源 Information	震中 Earthquake Epicenter 地名(英文) Name(English)	地名(中文) Name(Chinese)	纬度(°) Latitude	经度(°) Longitude	深度 Depth	震级 Mag	标度 Scale	烈度 MMI	死亡人数 Deaths 数量/人 Num	级别 Dd	受伤人数 Injuries 数量/人 Num	级别 Dd	经济损失 Damage 数量/$ Mill $ Mill	级别 De	房屋毁坏 Houses Destroyed 数量/间 Num	级别 Dh	房屋受损 Houses Damaged 数量/间 Num	级别 Dh
1977	10	19	16	50	51					USGS	US:Montana, Dillon, SE.	美国:蒙大纳州狄龙东南	44.77	-111.81	10	4.7	ML	6										
1977	10	30	12	53	25					Engdahl, USGS	Vanuatu Islands	瓦努阿图群岛	-14.863	167.019	107.9	6.2	Mw	5										
1977	11	3	2	22	55					* ISC, USGS	Bulgaria:Velingrad	保加利亚:韦林格勒	42.11	23.97	6	5.5	ML	7						2				
1977	11	4	9	52	59					ISC, Shi Z., Engdahl, USGS	Andreanof Islands, Aleutian Is.	阿留申群岛,安德烈亚诺夫群岛	51.646	-175.991	46.1	6.8	Mw	7										
1977	11	9	11	20	33					*	Iran:Gorgan	伊朗:戈尔甘	36.73	55.04	33	5	Muk							2				
1977	11	17	17	20	33					USGS, ISC	Japan:Miyake Jima	日本:三宅岛	33.64	139.87	112	5.5	mb	5										
1977	11	22	21	15	53					USGS	US:California, Willits	美国:加利福尼亚州威利茨	39.45	-123.26	5	4.8	ML	8										
1977	11	23	9	26	27					* Engdahl	Argentina:San Juan, Mendoza	阿根廷:圣胡安,门多萨	-31.083	-67.778	18.3	7.5	Mw	9	70	2	300	3	80.0	4				
1977	11	26	22	46	51					China, Dis	China:Tianjin, Ninghe	中国:天津宁河	39.35	117.83	20.1	5.5	Ms	5										
1977	11	27	9	25	55					USGS	US:Idaho, Indian Valley	美国:爱达荷州印第安瓦利	44.58	-116.27	5	4.5	ML	6										
1977	11	28	4	19	36					USGS, ISC	Argentina:San Juan	阿根廷:圣胡安	-31.68	-67.75	36	5.5	mb	5										
1977	12	2	4	13	54					Engdahl, USGS	Papua New Guinea:Madang	巴布亚新几内亚:马当	-5	145.083	56.1	6.1	Mw	6										
1977	12	2	12	57	11					USGS, ISC	Russia:Kamchatka Peninsula	俄罗斯:堪察加半岛	52.93	159.71	15	5.8	mb	5										
1977	12	6	10	52	54					USGS	Tajikistan:Khudzhand	塔吉克斯坦:苦盏	41.42	69.73	33	5.2	mb	7										
1977	12	16	15	10	28					USGS	Japan:Ibaraki, Near Coast	日本:茨城近海	36.62	140.99	46	5.6	mb	6										
1977	12	18	16	47	18					Wang S., Engdahl, Dis	China: Xinjiang, Payzawat, NE.	中国:新疆伽师东北	39.857	77.285	23.4	6.2	Ms	7			8	1			314	3		
1977	12	19	23	34	33					* Engdahl	Iran:Kerman, N.	伊朗:克尔曼北部	30.915	56.414	14.2	5.9	Mw		584	3	1000	3		3				
1978	1	2	6	31	28					USGS	Georgia:Bolnisi	格鲁吉亚:博尔尼西	41.54	44.24	10	5.3	mb	7										
1978	1	14	0	36	15					USGS	Japan:Oshima	日本:东京大岛	34.73	139.24	18	4.9	mb	6										
1978	1	14	0	45	34					USGS	Japan:Oshima	日本:东京大岛	34.7	139.27	18	5.2	mb	6										
1978	1	14	0	47	38					USGS	Japan:Oshima	日本:东京大岛	34.81	139.23	7	5.2	mb	6										
1978	1	14	3	24	40	4	0.6	-0.7		* Engdahl, NOAA, USGS	Japan:Oshima	日本:东京大岛	34.802	139.294	9.2	6.7	Mw	8	25	1	129	3		3	94	2		
1978	1	14	22	31	46					USGS, Engdahl	Japan:Nishiizu	日本:静冈西伊豆	34.8	138.8	10	5.9	Mw	6										
1978	1	17	11	33	15					Engdahl, USGS	Argentina:San Juan	阿根廷:圣胡安	-31.333	-67.913	21.4	6	Mw	6										
1978	1	20	0	24	26					USGS, ISC	Solomon Islands	所罗门群岛	-9.79	159.48	73	5.5	mb	5										
1978	1	25	23	18	54					ISC, Engdahl, USGS	Papua New Guinea:Kalip	巴布亚新几内亚:卡利普	-5.294	151.75	12.6	6.6	Mw	7										
1978	1	27	7	22	8					USGS	Mariana Islands	马里亚纳群岛	13.45	144.82	41	5.2	mb	7										
1978	2	8	4	10	32					USGS	Italy:San Guiliano Di Puglia, Campobasso	意大利:圣安诺迪普利亚,坎布巴索	41.11	14.89	95	5	mb	6										
1978	2	8	16	14	39					USGS	Tunisia:Al - Hammah	突尼斯:哈迈	34.29	9.11	23	4.9	mb	6										

年 Year	月 Mo	日 Dy	时 Hr	分 Mn	秒 Sec	海啸 Tsunami 源 Sr	浪高 Wh	级 I mI	级 S mS	资料来源 Information	震中 Earthquake Epicenter 地名(英文) Name(English)	地名(中文) Name(Chinese)	纬度(°) Latitude	经度(°) Longitude	深度 Depth	震级 Mag	标度 Scale	烈度 MMI	死亡人数 Deaths 数量/人 Num	级别 Dd	受伤人数 Injuries 数量/人 Num	级别 Dd	经济损失 Damage 数量/$ Mill	级别 De	房屋毁坏 Houses Destroyed 数量/间 Num	级别 Dh	房屋受损 Houses Damaged 数量/间 Num	级别 Dh
1978	2	9	16	30	38					USGS	Bosnia and Herzegovina: Livno	波斯尼亚和黑塞哥维那:利夫诺	44.13	16.92	20	4.5	ML	6										
1978	2	15	3	17	37					*	Turkey: Erzincan	土耳其:埃尔津占	39.69	39.79	33	4.8	mb				20	1		2	525	3		
1978	2	16	0	26	34					USGS	Bosnia and Herzegovina: Livno	波斯尼亚和黑塞哥维那:利夫诺	43.93	16.92	33	5.1	mb	6										
1978	2	20	4	37	1					* ISC, Engdahl	Japan: Miyagi, Near Coast	日本:宫城近海	38.832	141.969	67.2	6.5	Mw	8			30	1		2				
1978	2	23	9	49	23					USGS	Switzerland: Maloja	瑞士:马洛亚	46.53	9.77	10	4.5	ML	6										
1978	3	7	2	48	40					ISC, Engdahl, USGS	Ryukyu Trench	琉球海沟	31.945	137.467	442.5	5.9	mb	6										
1978	3	11	15	52	11					USGS	US: Washington, Seattle	美国:华盛顿州西雅图	47.42	-122.71	25	4.8	ML	6										
1978	3	11	19	20	49					* Italy	Italy: Brancaleone	意大利:布兰卡莱奥内	37.967	16.183	33	5.6	mb		2	1		2		2				
1978	3	11	23	57	46					USGS	Mexico: Mexicali	墨西哥:墨西卡利	32.29	-115.08	5	5	ML	6										
1978	3	12	17	59	49					USGS	Japan: Miyagi, Near Coast	日本:宫城近海	38.81	141.93	64	5.1	mb	6										
1978	3	12	18	42	23					USGS	Mexico: Mexicali	墨西哥:墨西卡利	32.23	-115.08	5	4.9	ML	6										
1978	3	15	22	4	43					ISC, Engdahl, USGS	Japan: South Honshu Ridge	日本:本州南部海岭	26.433	140.734	274.2	6.5	Mw	6										
1978	3	16	1	59	60					* Engdahl	Pakistan: Quetta, Nushki	巴基斯坦:奎塔,努士启	29.93	66.236	10.6	6.1	Mw		1	1				2				
1978	3	16	6	8	41					USGS	Bosnia and Herzegovina: Mostar	波斯尼亚和黑塞哥维那:莫斯塔尔	43.13	17.82	33	4.6	ML	6										
1978	3	19	1	39	11					* Shi Z., Engdahl	Mexico: Acapulco	墨西哥:阿卡普尔科	16.932	-99.782	11	6.6	Mw		1	1	25	1		2				
1978	3	20	10	24	14					USGS	Japan: Kuki	日本:埼玉久喜	36.05	139.68	66	5.7	mb	6										
1978	3	22	0	50	34	4	0.1	0.1	-2.5	* ISC, Engdahl, NOAA	Kuril Islands	千岛群岛	44.015	148.988	35.6	6.7	Mw											
1978	3	22	21	34	35	4	0.1		-3	* ISC, Engdahl, NOAA	Kuril Islands	千岛群岛	44.125	149.018	32.5	6.4	Mw	5										
1978	3	23	0	31	2	4	0.2	-2.3	-1.5	* ISC, Engdahl, NOAA	Kuril Islands	千岛群岛	44.293	148.947	26.1	7.1	Mw	5										
1978	3	23	3	14	21	4	0.3	-2.3	0	CSN, Engdahl, NOAA, USGS	Kuril Islands	千岛群岛	44.359	149.113	8.2	7.5	Ms	6										
1978	3	23	3	15	20					* ISC, CSN, Engdahl	Kuril Islands	千岛群岛	44.982	148.523	21	7.6	Mw	6										
1978	3	23	18	45	39					USGS	Croatia: Split	克罗地亚:斯普利特	43.64	16.69	33	4.9	ML	6										
1978	3	24	19	47	49	4	0.7	-1.7	0	* Engdahl, NOAA	Kuril Islands	千岛群岛	44.233	148.923	12.2	7.5	Mw	6										
1978	3	24	21	5	49					* ISC, Engdahl	Kazakhstan: Almaty	哈萨克斯坦:阿拉木图	42.835	78.574	23.8	6.9	Mw	8						3				
1978	3	26	0	27	4					USGS	US: California, Ukiah	美国:加利福尼亚州尤凯亚	39.19	-123.2	10	4.6	ML	6										
1978	3	29	17	51	19					USGS, ISC	Japan: South Honshu Ridge	日本:本州南部海岭	27.92	141.78	22	5.5	mb	5										
1978	4	6	23	29	55					ISC, Engdahl, USGS	Japan: Chiba, Near Coast	日本:千叶近海	35.254	141.107	31	6	Mw	6										

年 Year	月 Mo	日 Dy	时 Hr	分 Mn	秒 Sec	海啸 Tsunami 源 Sr	浪高 Wh	级 I mI	级 S mS	资料来源 Information	震中 Earthquake Epicenter 地名(英文) Name(English)	地名(中文) Name(Chinese)	纬度(°) Latitude	经度(°) Longitude	深度 Depth	震级 Mag	标度 Scale	烈度 MMI	死亡人数 Deaths 数量/人 Num	级别 Dd	受伤人数 Injuries 数量/人 Num	级别 Dd	经济损失 Damage 数量/$ Mill $ Mill	级别 De	房屋毁坏 Houses Destroyed 数量/间 Num	级别 Dh	房屋受损 Houses Damaged 数量/间 Num	级别 Dh
1978	4	7	16	21	21					USGS	Japan:Asahi	日本:千叶旭市	35. 72	140. 62	57	5	mb	6										
1978	4	11	2	41	45					Engdahl, USGS	Papua New Guinea:Northern	巴布亚新几内亚:北部区	-9. 431	148. 961	28. 7	6	Mw	6										
1978	4	13	18	5	26					*	Serbia:Kraljevo	塞尔维亚:克拉列沃	43. 269	20. 919	33	5. 7	Ms							2				
1978	4	15	23	33	50					* Italy, Engdahl	Italy:Sicilia Island	意大利:西西里岛	38. 383	15. 072	16. 8	6. 1	Mw		5	1				2	400	3		
1978	4	22	15	4	16					China, Dis	China:Xinjiang, Korla	中国:新疆库尔勒	41. 9	85. 9	24	5. 4	Ms	6										
1978	5	5	21	3	16					USGS	Mexico:Mexicali	墨西哥:墨西卡利	32. 22	-115. 32	5	5. 5	ML	6										
1978	5	10	15	36	26					USGS, ISC	Japan:Fukushima, Near Coast	日本:福岛近海	37. 32	141. 78	40	5. 5	mb	5										
1978	5	16	3	40	46					USGS	Afghan:Taloqan	阿富汗:塔卢坎	37. 71	69. 87	12	4. 7	mb	6										
1978	5	16	5	32	10					USGS	Macedonia:Pluzine	蒙特尼哥罗(黑山):普卢日内	43. 17	18. 68	33	4. 9	ML	6										
1978	5	16	7	35	47					USGS	Japan:Aomori	日本:青森	40. 99	141. 26	32	5. 7	mb	6										
1978	5	16	8	23	58					USGS	Japan:Aomori	日本:青森	41	141. 26	23	5. 8	mb	6										
1978	5	18	2	37	6					USGS	Serbia:Krusevac	塞尔维亚:克鲁舍瓦茨	43. 29	20. 98	10	5	mb	7										
1978	5	18	12	33	31					China, Dis	China:Liaoning, Haicheng	中国:辽宁海城	40. 72	122. 62	13	5. 9	Ms	7			11	1	15. 3	3			2419	4
1978	5	18	17	14	30					USGS	Turkmenistan:Balkanabat	土库曼斯坦:巴尔坎纳巴德	39. 73	54. 76	33	5	mb	6										
1978	5	19	12	58	56					China, Dis	China:Yunnan, Xiaguan	中国:云南下关	25. 53	100. 3		5. 1	Ms	6										
1978	5	21	12	8	46					USGS	Japan: Aomori, Near East Coast	日本:青森东部近海	40. 8	142. 44	55	5. 2	mb	6										
1978	5	23	7	50	30					ISC, Engdahl, USGS	Japan:Kagoshima	日本:鹿岛	31. 083	130. 148	163. 7	6. 7	Mw	6										
1978	5	23	23	34	13					* ISC, Engdahl	Greece:Thessaloniki, Volvi	希腊:塞萨洛尼基,沃尔维	40. 733	23. 314	9. 2	5. 8	Mw	7			2	1		2				
1978	5	26	13	21	2					USGS	Uzbekistan:Gazli	乌兹别克斯坦:加兹利	40. 17	63. 56	33	4. 5	mb	6										
1978	5	26	13	43	38					USGS	Russia:Dagestan, Gerel′	俄罗斯:达吉斯坦共和国格列利镇	41. 96	46. 55	38	5. 6	mb	6										
1978	6	3	20	3	53					* ISC, Japan, USGS	Japan:Misato	日本:岛根美乡町	35. 1	132. 6	4	6. 1	Mw	6			1	1		2				
1978	6	4	19	30	23					ISC, USGS	Uzbekistan:Gazli	乌兹别克斯坦:加兹利	40. 38	63. 62	33	6	mb	7										
1978	6	12	8	14	29	4	0. 6		0. 5	* Engdahl, NOAA	Japan:Miyagi, Near Coast	日本:宫城近海	38. 224	142. 009	53. 3	7. 7	Mw	8	28	1	10000	5	800	5		3		
1978	6	14	11	34	22					ISC, Engdahl, USGS	Japan:Miyagi, Off Coast	日本:宫城沿海	38. 416	142. 392	41. 2	6. 4	Mw	6										
1978	6	14	12	32	36	2	0	-3. 3		* Engdahl, NOAA	Philippines:Mindanao Island	菲律宾:棉兰老岛	8. 285	122. 395	30. 1	7	Mw											
1978	6	20	20	3	24	4	0. 5			* Engdahl, NOAA	Greece:Thessaloniki	希腊:塞萨洛尼基	40. 765	23. 304	7. 7	6. 3	Mw		50	1		3	1000	5				
1978	6	21	10	54	23					USGS	Japan:Miyagi, Near Coast	日本:宫城近海	38. 33	141. 76	52	5. 9	Mw	6										
1978	6	21	11	10	38					USGS, ISC, Engdahl	Sea of Okhotsk	鄂霍次克海	48. 266	148. 641	401. 2	6. 5	Mw	5										
1978	6	22	2	33	24					USGS	Romania:Timisoara	罗马尼亚:蒂米什瓦拉	46. 72	21. 06	10	4. 8	ML	7										

年 Year	月 Mo	日 Dy	时 Hr	分 Mn	秒 Sec	海啸 Tsunami 源 Sr	浪高 Wh	级 I mI	级 S mS	资料来源 Information	震中 Earthquake Epicenter 地名(英文) Name(English)	地名(中文) Name(Chinese)	纬度(°) Latitude	经度(°) Longitude	深度 Depth	震级 Mag	标度 Scale	烈度 MMI	死亡人数 Deaths 数量/人 Num	级别 Dd	受伤人数 Injuries 数量/人 Num	级别 Dd	经济损失 Damage 数量/$ Mill	级别 De	房屋毁坏 Houses Destroyed 数量/间 Num	级别 Dh	房屋受损 Houses Damaged 数量/间 Num	级别 Dh
1978	6	22	6	20		2	0.6		5	* NOAA, Song	Adriatic Sea	亚得里亚海	44	14		6.7	Mk							1				
1978	6	24	0	14	28					USGS	Adriatic Sea	亚得里亚海	41.71	20.29	10	5.5	ML	6										
1978	7	4	2	40	56					ISC, Engdahl, USGS	Japan: Kumamoto	日本:熊本	32.691	131.169	120.3	5.8	Mw	6										
1978	7	12	21	49	55					China, Dis	China: Sichuan, Heishui	中国:四川黑水	31.93	102.95	23	5.4	Ms	6										
1978	7	15	17	44	55					USGS, ISC	Japan: Hokkaido	日本:北海道	41.87	142.52	62	5.6	mb	6										
1978	7	23	14	42	41	2	0.1	-3.3	-1	* Wang S., Engdahl, NOAA	China: Taiwan, Taitung, Coast of E.	中国:台湾台东以东海域	22.243	121.419	39.2	7.3	Mw											
1978	7	25	23	30	51					USGS	Canada: Vancouver Island	加拿大:温哥华岛	50.3	-127.58	11	5.6	ML	5										
1978	7	29	14	37	33					*	Guatemala: Panajachel	危地马拉:帕纳哈切尔	14.84	-91.02	10	4.9	mb		17	1		3		2				
1978	8	3	18	11	21					* Engdahl	Chile: Copiapo – Taltai	智利:科皮亚波–塔尔塔尔	-26.541	-70.542	76.4	6.9	Mw	9			13	1		3				
1978	8	4	16	16	16					USGS	Peru: Moquegua	秘鲁:莫克瓜	-16.95	-71.33	30	5.1	mb	6										
1978	8	13	22	54	53					* CGS, USGS, Engdahl	US: California, Santa Barbara	美国:加利福尼亚州圣巴巴拉	34.385	-119.638	7.7	5.8	Mw	7			65	2	15.0	3				
1978	8	14	14	17	50	4	0.1		1	* NOAA	Spain: Cadiz	西班牙:加的斯	36.63	-6.871	30	5	mb											
1978	8	15	9	4	24					USGS	Georgia: Akhalkalaki	格鲁吉亚:阿卡卡垃吉	41.29	44.02	15	4.8	mb	6										
1978	8	16	14	56	45					China	China: Gansu, Minle	中国:甘肃民乐	38.6	101.3	33	4.8	Ms	6										
1978	8	18	20	53	20					USGS	Adriatic Sea	亚得里亚海	41.86	20.3	5	5	ML	7										
1978	8	21	0	28	23					USGS	Argentina: San Juan	阿根廷:圣胡安	-31.27	-67.77	10	5.6	mb	6										
1978	8	22	22	48	11					USGS	Georgia: Gori	格鲁吉亚:哥里	41.95	43.92	10	4.8	mb	6										
1978	9	3	0	21	16					USGS	Black Sea	黑海	44.4	38.05	33	5.7	mb	6										
1978	9	3	5	8	30					* ISC, USGS	Germany: Bisingen	德国:毕森根市	48.29	9.01	8	5.9	ML	8				3	150	5				
1978	9	4	21	54	53					USGS	US: California, Woodfords	美国:加利福尼亚州伍德福兹	38.81	-119.81	14	5.2	ML	6										
1978	9	9	23	11	7					China	China: Yunnan, Pu – er	中国:云南普洱	22.95	101.17		5.8	Ms	7										
1978	9	11	7	40	53					ISC, Engdahl, USGS	Ryukyu Islands, SW.	琉球群岛西南	24.984	124.865	15	6	Mw	6										
1978	9	16	15	35	55					* Engdahl	Iran: Razavi Khorasan	伊朗:呼罗珊	33.268	57.387	15	7.4	Mw		20000	5			50.0	4		4		
1978	9	25	21	23	52					USGS	Uzbekistan: Gazli	乌兹别克斯坦:加兹利	40.38	63.7	33	4.5	mb	6										
1978	10	2	20	28	53					USGS	Romania: Vrancea	罗马尼亚:弗朗恰	45.72	26.48	164	5	mb	6										
1978	10	4	16	42	49					USGS	US: California, Chalfant Valley	美国:加利福尼亚州夏芬谷	37.53	-118.63	9	5.8	ML	6										
1978	10	6	21	26	32					USGS	US: California, North Coast	美国:加利福尼亚州北部近海	40.45	-124.59	32	4.7	ML	6										
1978	10	11	1	49	1					USGS	Japan Trench	日本海沟	33.42	140.79	57	5.9	mb	6										
1978	10	28	22	46	35					USGS	Japan: Hokkaido	日本:北海道	42.68	144.21	82	5.1	mb	6										
1978	11	1	19	48	28					* Engdahl, USGS	Tajikistan: Kuhistoni Badakhshon	塔吉克斯坦:勾瑙–巴达科善	39.363	72.59	24.2	6.6	Mw	9						3				
1978	11	6	15	8	57					USGS, ISC	Japan: Hokkaido	日本:北海道	42.23	142.98	63	5.5	mb	6										

年 Year	月 Mo	日 Dy	时 Hr	分 Mn	秒 Sec	海啸 Tsunami 源 Sr	浪高 Wh	级 I mI	级 S mS	资料来源 Information	震中 Earthquake Epicenter 地名(英文) Name(English)	地名(中文) Name(Chinese)	纬度(°) Latitude	经度(°) Longitude	深度 Depth	震级 Mag	标度 Scale	烈度 MMI	死亡人数 Deaths 数量/人 Num	级别 Dd	受伤人数 Injuries 数量/人 Num	级别 Dd	经济损失 Damage 数量/$ Mill	级别 De	房屋毁坏 Houses Destroyed 数量/间 Num	级别 Dh	房屋受损 Houses Damaged 数量/间 Num	级别 Dh
1978	11	17	21	44	30					China	China:Qinghai,Haixi,S.	中国:青海海西南	37	97.2		4.8	Ms	6										
1978	11	23	1	43	50					USGS	Japan:Higashiizu	日本:静冈东伊豆	34.72	139.05	7	5	mb	8										
1978	11	29	19	52	50	2	1.5	0.6		* Shi Z., Engdahl, NOAA	Mexico:Oaxaca	墨西哥:瓦哈卡	16.012	-96.602	24.5	7.8	Mw		9	1		3		2				
1978	11	30	3	26	25					USGS	China:Xinjiang,Ulugqat,W.	中国:新疆乌恰西	39.59	74.04	62	4.5	mb	7										
1978	12	3	13	15	55					USGS	Japan:Higashiizu	日本:静冈东伊豆	34.81	139.15	17	5.3	mb	6										
1978	12	5	15	39	4					USGS	Italy:Loiano	意大利:洛亚诺	44.46	11.99	35	4.6	ML	7										
1978	12	6	14	2	12					* ISC,Engdahl	Kuril Islands	千岛群岛	44.455	146.475	181	7.8	Mw	8						2				
1978	12	14	7	5	21					* Engdahl	Iran:Khuzestan	伊朗:胡齐斯坦	32.132	49.639	19	6.2	Mw		76	2		2		2				
1978	12	21	1	13	55					USGS,Engdahl	Chile:Concepcion	智利:康塞普西翁	-36.29	-72.46	47	5.9	Mw	6										
1978	12	23	11	23	15					* China, Engdahl	China:Taiwan,Taitung,Coast of E.	中国:台湾台东以东海域	23.224	122.015	48	7	Mw		2	1	3	1						
1979	1	1	23	14	39					USGS	US:California,Topanga	美国:加利福尼亚州托潘加	33.95	-118.68	11	5	ML	6										
1979	1	16	9	50	8					* ISC,Engdahl	Iran:Razavi Khorasan	伊朗:呼罗珊	33.901	59.471	8.6	6.5	Mw		200	3		3		2				
1979	1	19	11	56	15					USGS,ISC	Japan:Hokkaido	日本:北海道	41.53	143.92	17	5.5	mb	5										
1979	2	3	9	58	16					USGS	US:California,North Coast	美国:加利福尼亚州北部近海	40.89	-124.41	28	5.2	ML	7										
1979	2	6	14	45	12					China	China:Inner Mongolia, New Barag Youqi	中国:内蒙古新巴尔虎右旗	48.9	116.8	20	4.9	Ms	6										
1979	2	9	14	44	17					USGS	Italy:Milano	意大利:米兰	45.65	9.45	33	4.5	mb	6										
1979	2	14	3	41	2					USGS	Tajikistan:Khudzhand	塔吉克斯坦:苦盏	40.24	69.94	48	4.8	mb	6										
1979	2	16	10	8	55					* Shi Z., Engdahl	Peru:Arequipa	秘鲁:阿雷基帕	-16.535	-72.551	55.2	7.2	Mw		18	1		2		2				
1979	2	20	6	32	36	4	0.2	-1.7		* Engdahl, NOAA	Japan Trench	日本海沟	40.298	143.717	19.9	6.3	Mw											
1979	2	22	15	57	28					USGS	US:California,Doyle	美国:加利福尼亚州多伊尔	40.01	-120.07	17	5.2	ML	6										
1979	2	26	22	9	45					USGS	Adriatic Sea	亚得里亚海	41.54	20.15	28	4.5	ML	6										
1979	2	28	21	27	8	4	0.1	-1.7		* Shi Z., Engdahl, NOAA	Gulf of Alaska	阿拉斯加湾	60.691	-141.671	18	7.5	Mw	7						1				
1979	3	2	7	20	13					China,Dis	China:Anhui,Guzhen	中国:安徽固镇	33.18	117.42	11	4.9	Ms	6										
1979	3	7	12	54	50					China	China:Sichuan,Yanyuan,NW.	中国:四川盐源西北	27.5	101.1		4.9	Ms	6										
1979	3	14	11	7	15	4	1.3	-3.3		* Shi Z., Engdahl, NOAA	Mexico:Guerrero,Zihuatanejo	墨西哥:格雷罗州锡瓦塔塔内霍	17.759	-101.222	24.6	7.5	Mw		5	1	35	1	30.0	4	200	3		
1979	3	15	12	52	27					Wang S., Engdahl, Dis	China:Yunnan,Pu-er	中国:云南普洱	23.175	101.055	2.5	6.8	Ms	9	12		563	3	19.6	3	31746	5		
1979	3	15	21	7	17					USGS	US:California,Landers	美国:加利福尼亚州兰德斯	34.32	-116.45	1	5.7	ML	8										
1979	3	20	21	41	21					USGS	Chile:Talca	智利:塔尔卡	-35.68	-71.15	91	5.5	mb	6										

时间						海啸				资料来源	震中				深度	震级	标度	烈度	死亡人数		受伤人数		经济损失		房屋毁坏		房屋受损	
年	月	日	时	分	秒	源	浪高	级 I	级 S		地名(英文)	地名(中文)	纬度(°)	经度(°)					数量/人	级别	数量/人	级别	数量/$ Mill	级别	数量/间	级别	数量/间	级别
Date						Tsunami				Information	Earthquake Epicenter				Depth	Mag	Scale	MMI	Deaths		Injuries		Damage		Houses Destroyed		Houses Damaged	
Year	Mo	Dy	Hr	Mn	Sec	Sr	Wh	mI	mS		Name(English)	Name(Chinese)	Latitude	Longitude					Num	Dd	Num	Dd	$ Mill	De	Num	Dh	Num	Dh
1979	3	29	2	1	31					Wang S. ,Dis	China:Xinjiang,Kuqa,NE.	中国:新疆库车东北	42	83.4	20	6	Ms	6			1	1						
1979	3	29	7	7	18					Wang S. , Engdahl, Dis	China:Qinghai,Yushu,SE.	中国:青海玉树东南	32.478	97.184	7.7	6.2	Ms	6							36	1		
1979	4	9	2	10	20	1				* ISC,NOAA, USGS	Montenegro:Ulcinj	门的内哥罗(黑山):乌尔齐尼	41.956	19.023	10	5.5	Mw	6										
1979	4	12	4	58	57					USGS	Japan:Minamiyamashiro	日本:京都南山城村	34.78	135.99	26	4.6	mb	6										
1979	4	15	6	19	45	4	0.6		1	* Engdahl, NOAA	Adriatic Sea	亚得里亚海	42.001	19.154	15	7	Mw	9	131	3	1001	4	2700	5		4		
1979	4	18	19	51	13					USGS	Montenegro:Ulcinj	门的内哥罗(黑山):乌尔齐尼	42.13	19.01	10	4.8	ML	6										
1979	4	19	0	17	35					USGS	Adriatic Sea	亚得里亚海	41.98	19.1	10	4.6	ML	6										
1979	4	19	5	42	50					USGS	Montenegro:Ulcinj	门的内哥罗(黑山):乌尔齐尼	42.04	18.97	9	4.6	ML	6										
1979	4	28	3	38	3					USGS	Macedonia:Budva	蒙特尼哥罗(黑山):布德瓦	42.25	18.76	10	4.8	ML	7										
1979	5	5	20	4	55					ISC,USGS	Venezuela:Pedraza La Vieja	委内瑞拉:旧佩德拉萨	8.07	-71	13	6	Mw	6										
1979	5	8	5	11	8					USGS	US:California,Morgan Hill	美国:加利福尼亚州莫干山	37.31	-121.67	9	4.9	ML	6										
1979	5	14	23	4	3					Engdahl,USGS	Chile:Antofagasta,C.	智利:安托法加斯塔中部	-22.919	-69.087	82.7	6.3	Mw	6										
1979	5	17	9	56	22					USGS	Japan:Hokkaido	日本:北海道	42.9	144.63	57	5	mb	6										
1979	5	21	16	31	5					* ISC	Indonesia:Bali Island	印度尼西亚:巴厘岛	-8.299	115.934	76	5.7	Mw							3				
1979	5	21	22	46	58					China	China:Hubei,Badong	中国:湖北巴东	31.08	110.5	16	5.1	Ms	7										
1979	5	24	17	23	20					* Engdahl	Adriatic Sea	亚得里亚海	42.241	18.826	9.6	6.2	Mw	8			65	2		2				
1979	5	30	9	38	54					* ISC,Engdahl	Indonesia:Sumbawa	印度尼西亚:松巴哇	-8.342	115.863	20	6.2	Mw		22	1			4.15	2				
1979	5	30	23	47	16					USGS	Macedonia:Budva	蒙特尼哥罗(黑山):布德瓦	42.32	18.8	10	4.6	ML	6										
1979	5	31	7	20	6					USGS	Romania: Bucharest, Kishinev	罗马尼亚:布加勒斯特,基希讷乌	45.55	26.33	120	5.1	mb	6										
1979	6	2	9	47	60					* Engdahl	Australia:Perth	澳大利亚:珀斯	-30.784	117.132	3	6.1	Mw						1.5	2				
1979	6	14	7	39	28					USGS	US:California,Ridgecrest	美国:加利福尼亚州里奇克雷斯特	35.72	-118.02	5	4.6	ML	6										
1979	6	19	4	15	14					Wang S. ,Dis	China:Shanxi,Jiexiu	中国:山西介休	37.1	111.87		5.2	Ms	7	3		178	3	24.1	3	809	3	17376	5
1979	6	25	5	29	7					* Engdahl	Papua New Guinea:Madang	巴布亚新几内亚:马当	-5	145.65	187.8	6.6	Mw							2				
1979	6	29	5	53	21					USGS	US:California,Landers	美国:加利福尼亚州兰德斯	34.25	-116.9	6	4.5	ML	6										
1979	6	30	0	34	12					USGS	US:California,Landers	美国:加利福尼亚州兰德斯	34.25	-116.9	10	4.9	ML	6										
1979	7	1	20	38	6					* Shi Z. , Engdahl	Costa Rica:Puerto Armuelles	哥斯达黎加:阿摩叶斯港	8.375	-82.845	28	6.2	Mw						2	2				

时间						海啸				资料来源	震中				深度	震级	标度	烈度	死亡人数		受伤人数		经济损失		房屋毁坏		房屋受损	
年	月	日	时	分	秒	源	浪高	级I	级S		地名(英文)	地名(中文)	纬度(°)	经度(°)					数量/人	级别	数量/人	级别	数量/$ Mill	级别	数量/间	级别	数量/间	级别
Date						Tsunami				Information	Earthquake Epicenter				Depth	Mag	Scale	MMI	Deaths		Injuries		Damage		Houses Destroyed		Houses Damaged	
Year	Mo	Dy	Hr	Mn	Sec	Sr	Wh	mI	mS		Name(English)	Name(Chinese)	Latitude	Longitude					Num	Dd	Num	Dd	$ Mill	De	Num	Dh	Num	Dh
1979	7	4	6	7	45					ISC, Engdahl, USGS	Kuril Islands	千岛群岛	43.965	146.701	63.6	6	mb	6										
1979	7	6	2	1	17					ISC, Engdahl, USGS	Chile:La Ligua	智利:拉利瓜	-32.196	-71.382	46.5	5.8	Mw	6										
1979	7	9	10	57	23					* China, Dis, USGS,ISC	China:Jiangsu,Liyang,SW.	中国:江苏溧阳西南	31.45	119.25	12	6	Ms	8	41	1	2954	4	164	5	113909	5	229750	5
1979	7	13	8	10	13					ISC, Engdahl, USGS	Japan:Yamaguchi	日本:山口	33.887	131.848	69.1	6.1	Mw	6										
1979	7	18	13	12	3					* ISC	Turkey:Dursunbey, Anatolia	土耳其:杜尔孙贝伊,安纳托利亚	39.672	28.66	3	5.5	Mw							2	200	3		
1979	8	6	17	5	23					USGS	US:California,Morgan Hill	美国:加利福尼亚州摩根希尔	37.1	-121.5	6	5.7	Mw	7										
1979	8	8	17	0	48					Wang S.	China: Yunnan, Baoshan, SW.	中国:云南保山西南	25	98.8	10	5	Ms	7										
1979	8	24	16	59	28					* China,Dis	China: Inner Mongolia, Wuyuan	中国:内蒙古五原	41.2	108.1	18	6	Ms	7			124	3	15.6	3	400	3		
1979	9	3	2	12		2				NOAA	Venezuela:Puerto Cumarebo	委内瑞拉:库马雷沃港	11.517	-69.5	0	5	Ms											
1979	9	11	11	52	47					USGS,ISC	Philippines:Mindanao Island	菲律宾:棉兰老岛	8.12	125	13	5.5	mb	5										
1979	9	12	5	17	56	4	2	1		* Engdahl, NOAA	Indonesia:Papua	印度尼西亚:巴布亚	-1.688	135.966	18.9	7.5	Mw		115	3		3		3	1000	3		
1979	9	19	21	35	40					* Italy, Engdahl, USGS	Italy:Cascia	意大利:卡夏	42.773	13.01	15	5.9	mb	8	5	1	5000	4		3				
1979	9	22	7	59	38					USGS,ISC	Hawaiian Islands	夏威夷群岛	19.35	-155.07	9	5.5	ML	5										
1979	9	25	13	5	54					USGS	Kazakhstan:Taldy - Kurgan	哈萨克斯坦:塔尔迪库尔干	45.08	77.01	40	5.9	mb	6										
1979	10	9	7	49	29					* ISC,USGS	Guatemala:Antigua	危地马拉:安地瓜	14.321	-90.082	33	5.1	Mw	7			40	1		2				
1979	10	9	22	23	54					USGS,ISC	Antigua and Barbuda:St John$s,E.	安提瓜和巴布达:圣约翰斯东部	16.64	-61.24	62	5.6	mb	6										
1979	10	12	10	25	19					* Engdahl	New Zealand: South Island, SW.	新西兰:南岛西南近海	-46.695	165.826	5.9	7.3	Mw	5										
1979	10	15	23	17	0					* Engdahl, USGS	US:California,Imperial	美国:加利福尼亚州因皮里尔	32.815	-115.646	12	6.4	M	9			91	2	30.0	4				
1979	10	20	1	41	13					* Engdahl	Indonesia:Sumbawa	印度尼西亚:松巴哇	-8.365	115.782	51.8	6.4	Mw		2	1	40	1		2				
1979	10	23	9	51	8					ISC, Engdahl, USGS	Solomon Islands	所罗门群岛	-10.628	161.352	17.2	7	Mw	6										
1979	10	27	14	35	59					* Shi Z., Engdahl	Guatemala:Near Coast	危地马拉:近海	13.829	-90.841	57.7	6.9	Mw		4	1	23	1		2				
1979	10	28	5	39	36					USGS	Japan:Chiba,Near Coast	日本:千叶近海	35.02	140.6	88	5.5	mb	6										
1979	11	2	15	53	6					* Engdahl	Indonesia:Java Island	印度尼西亚:爪哇岛	-7.745	108.164	72.3	6.5	Mw		30	1	200	3	16.0	3				
1979	11	6	5	26	18					* ISC	Greece:Thesprotia	希腊:塞斯普罗蒂亚	39.536	20.398	40	5.9	Mw	8	1	1	3	1		3				

年 Year	月 Mo	日 Dy	时 Hr	分 Mn	秒 Sec	源 Sr	浪高 Wh	级 I mI	级 S mS	资料来源 Information	地名(英文) Name(English)	地名(中文) Name(Chinese)	纬度(°) Latitude	经度(°) Longitude	深度 Depth	震级 Mag	标度 Scale	烈度 MMI	死亡人数 Deaths 数量/人 Num	级别 Dd	受伤人数 Injuries 数量/人 Num	级别 Dd	经济损失 Damage 数量/$ Mill	级别 De	房屋毁坏 Houses Destroyed 数量/间 Num	级别 Dh	房屋受损 Houses Damaged 数量/间 Num	级别 Dh
1979	11	8	2	3	53					USGS	Albania:Kavaje	阿尔巴尼亚:卡瓦亚	41.07	19.6	10	4.7	mb	6										
1979	11	10	4	19	34					USGS	Adriatic Sea	亚得里亚海	41.81	19.07	10	4.5	mb	6										
1979	11	14	2	21	21					* Engdahl	Iran:Razavi Khorasan	伊朗:呼罗珊	33.959	59.723	8.9	6.6	Mw		350	3				3				
1979	11	16	15	21	25	2				* Engdahl, NOAA	Fiji Islands	斐济群岛	-16.686	-179.913	11	6.8	Mw							2				
1979	11	23	23	40	31					* ISC, Shi Z., Engdahl	Colombia: Manizales - Armenia	哥伦比亚:马尼萨莱斯 - 亚美尼亚	4.793	-76.19	108.5	7.2	Mw		72	2	600	3	20.0	3				
1979	11	27	17	10	35					* Engdahl	Iran:Razavi Khorasan	伊朗:呼罗珊	34.059	59.757	8	7.1	Mw	5	17	1	24	1		3				
1979	12	6	9	48	55					China	China: Xizang (Tibet), Bowo, NW.	中国:西藏波密西北	30.1	95.6	10	5.1	Ms	6										
1979	12	7	9	24	0					* Engdahl	Iran:Razavi Khorasan	伊朗:呼罗珊	34.083	59.851	16.5	6.1	Mw							3				
1979	12	12	7	59	5	4	6	2.3	2.5	* Shi Z., Engdahl, NOAA	Colombia:Near Coast	哥伦比亚:近海	1.603	-79.362	24.4	8.1	Mw	9	600	3	20000	5	8.0	3	10000	5		
1979	12	14	7	19	14					USGS	Japan:Hokkaido	日本:北海道	42.82	144.3	67	5.5	mb	6										
1979	12	15	0	2	40					* Engdahl	Indonesia:Southern Sumatra	印度尼西亚:苏门答腊南部	-3.333	102.576	13.5	6.6	Mw		8	1	162	3		2	2500	4		
1979	12	17	19	58	23					* ISC, Engdahl	Indonesia:Sumbawa; Bali	印度尼西亚:松巴哇;巴厘岛	-8.487	115.754	15	6.5	Mw		27	1	200	3		2				
1979	12	21	20	40	25					USGS	US:California, Holtville	美国:加利福尼亚州霍尔特维尔	32.78	-115.38	5	4.6	ML	6										
1979	12	26	3	57	4					USGS	England:Carlisle	英国:卡莱尔	54.9	-2.68	10	4.5	mb	6										
1979	12	26	19	43	38					USGS, ISC	Chile:Talca	智利:塔尔卡	-36	-71.34	92	5.6	mb	5										
1979	12	29	15	6	7					USGS, ISC	Japan:Hokkaido	日本:北海道	42.39	142.96	66	5.7	mb	6										
1979	12	30	6	25	49					USGS	Chile:Putaendo	智利:普塔恩多	-32.6	-70.53	78	5.2	mb	6										
1980	1	1	16	42	42	4			1	* Engdahl, NOAA	Azores: Terceira, Angra Do Heroismo	亚速尔群岛:特塞拉岛,英雄港	38.727	-27.75	12.9	6.9	Mw	8	56	2	400	3	5.0	3				
1980	1	12	15	57	3					ISC, Engdahl, USGS	Japan:Hokkaido	日本:北海道	41.742	143.662	32.2	6.1	Mw	6										
1980	1	13	5	54	38					USGS	Uzbekistan:Andizhan	乌兹别克斯坦:安第札	39.33	72.71	44	5.1	mb	6										
1980	1	14	21	51	2					USGS, ISC	Argentina:Mendoza	阿根廷:门多萨	-33.19	-69.46	14	5.6	mb	5										
1980	1	23	3	48	5					USGS	Macedonia:Budva	蒙特尼哥罗(黑山):布德瓦	42.35	18.89	10	4.6	ML	6										
1980	1	24	19	0	13					* Engdahl	US:California, Livermore	美国:加利福尼亚州利弗莫尔	37.713	-121.727	15	5.8	M	7			50	1	11.5	3				
1980	1	27	2	33	36					USGS	US:California, Livermore	美国:加利福尼亚州利弗莫尔	37.74	-121.74	15	5.8	ML	6										
1980	2	2	12	29	14					China	China:Sichuan, Muli	中国:四川木里	27.85	101.29	16	5.8	Ms	6										
1980	2	10	3	46						China	China:Inner Mongolia, Yakeshi, E.	中国:内蒙古牙克石东部	48.88	122.22	5	5.6	Ms	6										
1980	2	10	11	54	33					USGS, ISC	Kuril Islands	千岛群岛	43.99	147.23	73	5.5	mb	5										
1980	2	13	22	9	35					China, ISC, Engdahl	China:Xinjiang, Mazar, W.	中国:新疆麻扎西	36.472	76.858	94.3	6.1	Ms	7										

年 Year	月 Mo	日 Dy	时 Hr	分 Mn	秒 Sec	源 Sr	浪高 Wh	级 I mI	级 S mS	资料来源 Information	地名(英文) Name(English)	地名(中文) Name(Chinese)	纬度(°) Latitude	经度(°) Longitude	深度 Depth	震级 Mag	标度 Scale	烈度 MMI	死亡人数 Deaths 数量/人 Num	级别 Dd	受伤人数 Injuries 数量/人 Num	级别 Dd	经济损失 Damage 数量/$ Mill	级别 De	房屋毁坏 Houses Destroyed 数量/间 Num	级别 Dh	房屋受损 Houses Damaged 数量/间 Num	级别 Dh
1980	2	17	19	2	32					USGS, ISC	Russia: Kamchatka Peninsula	俄罗斯:堪察加半岛	52.66	158.9	33	5.5	mb	5										
1980	2	18	13	3	25					Engdahl, USGS	Ecuador: Guayaquil	厄瓜多尔:瓜亚基尔	-2.25	-79.73	90	5.7	Mw	6										
1980	2	22	3	2	45					Wang S., Engdahl	China: Xizang (Tibet), Xainza, W.	中国:西藏申扎南	30.548	88.617	7.3	6.6	Ms	8										
1980	2	23	5	51	4	4	0.6	-0.7	-2	* Engdahl, NOAA	Kuril Islands	千岛群岛	43.591	146.678	37.6	7.1	Mw	7										
1980	2	23	22	38	53					ISC, Engdahl, CSN, USGS	Japan: Off SE. Coast of Hokkaido	日本:北海道东南沿海	43.281	146.883	29.1	6.1	Mw	6										
1980	2	25	10	47	39					USGS	US: California, Anza	美国:加利福尼亚州安萨	33.52	-116.55	6	5.6	ML	6										
1980	3	12	3	21	53					USGS, ISC	Japan: Chiba, Near Coast	日本:千叶近海	34.87	140.42	85	5.5	mb	5										
1980	4	16	12	18	20					* Engdahl	Indonesia: Java Island	印度尼西亚:爪哇岛	-8.045	108.741	64.3	6.2	Mw							3				
1980	4	17	19	25	32					China, Dis	China: Qinghai, Tianjun, N.	中国:青海天峻北	37.86	99.13	15	5.2	Ms	6										
1980	5	14	1	41	4					*	Italy: Potenza	意大利:波坦察	40.459	15.855	24	4.5	Mw	8						2				
1980	5	18	7	9	39					* Engdahl	Guatemala: San Lucas Tolimán	危地马拉:圣卢卡斯-托利曼	14.727	-91.272	103.3	5.9	Mw							2				
1980	5	18	15	32	18					* Engdahl	US: Washington, Mt St Helens	美国:华盛顿州圣海伦山	46.36	-121.993	15	5.7	Mw	5	57	2			2000	5				
1980	5	18	20	2	60					* ISC, Engdahl	Serbia: Kraljevo	塞尔维亚:克拉列沃	43.26	20.908	10	5.9	Mw	8			30	1	5.0	3				
1980	5	24	20	16	6					USGS	Italy: Cascia	意大利:卡夏	42.85	13.16	10	4.5	ML	6										
1980	5	25	16	33	47					* Shi Z., Engdahl	US: California, Mammoth Lakes	美国:加利福尼亚州马姆莫斯湖	37.526	-118.835	12.3	6.2	M	7			7	1	2	2				
1980	5	25	19	44	53					ISC, Shi Z., Engdahl, USGS	US: California, Huntington Lake, NE.	美国:加利福尼亚州亨廷顿莱克东北	37.376	-118.836	5.5	5.9	M	7										
1980	5	27	14	50	58					ISC, Engdahl, USGS	US: California, Huntington Lake, NE.	美国:加利福尼亚州亨廷顿莱克东北	37.418	-118.798	0.4	5.9	M	6										
1980	5	28	19	51	19					USGS, ISC	Italy: Sicily, Palermo	意大利:西西里岛,巴勒莫	38.48	14.25	14	5.7	mb	6										
1980	6	9	3	28	22					* Shi Z., Engdahl	Mexico: Mexicali	墨西哥:墨西卡利	32.269	-114.906	2.2	6.4	Mw	5	1	1	100	2		2				
1980	6	17	21	45	53					China	China: Yunnan, Wenshan, NW.	中国:云南文山西北	23.53	103.87	20	5.8	Ms	6										
1980	6	22	19	14	34					USGS	Croatia: Split, SE.	克罗地亚:斯普利特东南	43.1	17.42	10	5.1	ML	7										
1980	6	25	12	4	59					Engdahl, USGS	Colombia: S. of Armenia	哥伦比亚:亚美尼亚南部	4.471	-75.756	165.3	6.4	Mw	6										
1980	6	25	18	48	11					USGS	Papua New Guinea: Morobe	巴布亚新几内亚:莫罗贝	-6.59	146.84	21	5.7	mb	6										
1980	6	26	21	6	24					USGS	Japan: Atami	日本:静冈热海	35	139.19	17	4.9	mb	6										
1980	6	28	3	4	60					USGS	Japan: Higashiizu	日本:静冈东伊豆	34.82	139.17	12	4.5	mb	6										
1980	6	29	7	20	8	4	0.6	-0.7		* ISC, Engdahl, NOAA	Japan: Oshima	日本:东京大岛	34.854	139.273	17	6.4	Mw	8			7	1		2				

年	月	日	时	分	秒	源	浪高	级 I	级 S	资料来源	地名(英文)	地名(中文)	纬度(°)	经度(°)	深度	震级	标度	烈度	死亡人数 数量/人	死亡人数 级别	受伤人数 数量/人	受伤人数 级别	经济损失 数量/$ Mill	经济损失 级别	房屋毁坏 数量/间	房屋毁坏 级别	房屋受损 数量/间	房屋受损 级别
Date						Tsunami				Information	Earthquake Epicenter				Depth	Mag	Scale	MMI	Deaths		Injuries		Damage		Houses Destroyed		Houses Damaged	
Year	Mo	Dy	Hr	Mn	Sec	Sr	Wh	mI	mS		Name(English)	Name(Chinese)	Latitude	Longitude					Num	Dd	Num	Dd	$ Mill	De	Num	Dh	Num	Dh
1980	6	29	7	46	14					USGS	US:California,Benton	美国:加利福尼亚州本顿	37.97	-118.67	15	5	ML	6										
1980	7	5	20	25	26					USGS,ISC	Kyrgyzstan:Issyk Kul	吉尔吉斯斯坦:伊塞克湖州	41.85	77.46	28	5.6	mb	6										
1980	7	8	23	19	24					* Engdahl	Solomon Islands: Santa Cruz Islands	所罗门群岛:圣克鲁斯群岛	-12.487	166.482	56	7.5	Mw							1				
1980	7	9	2	11	55					* Engdahl	Greece:Magnisia	希腊:马格尼西亚	39.257	23.009	17.2	6.6	Mw	9	1	1		3	5.0	3				
1980	7	11	11	47	27					* USGS	Tajikistan:Isfala	塔吉克斯坦:伊斯法拉	40.113	70.596	33	5.2	mb	6						1				
1980	7	12	5	32	9					*	Greece:Volos	希腊:伏洛斯	39.203	22.729	10	4	mb		1	1			5.0	3				
1980	7	17	19	42	24	4	0.1	-1.7		* Engdahl, NOAA	Solomon Islands: Santa Cruz Islands	所罗门群岛:圣克鲁斯群岛	-12.504	166.011	31.6	7.8	Mw											
1980	7	19	0	37	57					USGS	Adriatic Sea	亚得里亚海	41.46	20.28	19	4.9	mb	6										
1980	7	22	5	17	10					* ISC	Iran:Rudbar, Rasht	伊朗:鲁德巴,拉什特	37.19	50.201	47	5.9	Mw		1	1		3		2				
1980	7	27	18	52	22					*	US:Kentucky,Olympia	美国:肯塔基州奥林匹亚	38.174	-83.907	8	5.1	Ms	7			2	1	1	2				
1980	7	29	14	58	42					* ISC,Engdahl	Nepal:Seti	尼泊尔:塞蒂	29.616	81.1	13.8	6.6	Mw		200	3		3	245	5				
1980	8	9	5	45	10					* ISC,Shi Z., Engdahl	Honduras; Guatemala:Izabel Province	洪都拉斯;危地马拉:古拉特	15.915	-88.488	15.4	6.5	Mw		2	1		3		2				
1980	8	18	15	7	54					* GSHAP, Engdahl	Ecuador:Guayaquil	厄瓜多尔:瓜亚基尔	-1.986	-80.002	55.9	6	Mw	8	8	1	100	2	5.0	3				
1980	8	23	21	36	51					* ISC	India:Kashmir	印度:克什米尔	32.913	75.633	25	5.7	Mw		15	1	40	1		2		3		
1980	8	23	21	50	3					* ISC	India:Kashmir	印度:克什米尔	32.834	75.629	33	5.5	mb			1				1				
1980	8	29	10	38	14					USGS	Chile:Mafil	智利:马菲尔	-39.66	-73.1	34	5.4	mb	6										
1980	9	7	4	36	38					USGS,ISC	US:California,Benton	美国:加利福尼亚州本顿	38.03	-118.58	15	5.6	ML	5										
1980	9	23	19	10	23					USGS,ISC	Japan:Saitama	日本:埼玉	35.95	139.63	89	5.6	mb	6										
1980	9	24	17	54	25					* Engdahl	Japan:Tokyo, Yokohama	日本:东京,横滨	35.525	140.062	71.5	6	Mw	6	2	1	73	2	1	2				
1980	10	5	15	32	50					* USGS	New Zealand:Gisborne, Hawera	新西兰:吉斯伯恩,哈维拉	-39.542	176.478	32	5.6	Mw	6						2				
1980	10	9	2	7	34					USGS	Japan:Ibaraki,Near Coast	日本:茨城近海	36.3	140.87	52	5.2	mb	6										
1980	10	10	12	25	26	4	0.7		2	* Engdahl, NOAA	Algeria:Bordj Abou El Hasen, Dahra	阿尔及利亚:阿布哈桑堡,赫尔	36.154	1.417	15	7.7	Mw	10	5000	4	9000	4	5200	5	25000	5		
1980	10	20	3	29	21					USGS	Japan Trench	日本海沟	33.08	140.38	81	5.6	mb	6										
1980	10	24	14	53	36					* Shi Z., Engdahl	Mexico: Huajapan De Leon, Oaxaca	墨西哥:瓦华潘 - 德莱昂,瓦哈卡	18.176	-98.236	64.9	7.4	Ms	9	300	3		3	5.0	3		3		
1980	10	31	12	55	37					USGS	US:California,El Centro	美国:加利福尼亚州埃尔森特罗	32.67	-115.58	4	4.5	ML	6										
1980	11	6	1	34	25					China,Dis	China:Xinjiang,Manas,S.	中国:新疆玛纳斯南	43.81	86.14	15	5.7	Ms	7										
1980	11	8	10	27	35					* CGS,USGS, Shi Z., Engdahl	US:California,North Coast	美国:加利福尼亚州北部近海	41.112	-124.299	16.4	7.6	Mw	7	5	1			2.75	2				
1980	11	12	6	58	12					*	Peru:Huancavelica	秘鲁:万卡韦利卡	-13.347	-74.545	71	4.9	mb		7	1			1	2				
1980	11	12	21	23	4					USGS	Brazil:Para,SE.	巴西:帕拉东南	-8.06	-50.19	33	4.9	mb	7										

年 Year	月 Mo	日 Dy	时 Hr	分 Mn	秒 Sec	源 Sr	浪高 Wh	级 I mI	级 S mS	资料来源 Information	地名(英文) Name(English)	地名(中文) Name(Chinese)	纬度(°) Latitude	经度(°) Longitude	深度 Depth	震级 Mag	标度 Scale	烈度 MMI	死亡人数 Deaths 数量/人 Num	级别 Dd	受伤人数 Injuries 数量/人 Num	级别 Dd	经济损失 Damage 数量/$ Mill	级别 De	房屋毁坏 Houses Destroyed 数量/间 Num	级别 Dh	房屋受损 Houses Damaged 数量/间 Num	级别 Dh
1980	11	20	3	29	43					USGS	Brazil: Sobral	巴西:索布腊儿尔	-4.49	-38.27	10	5.1	mb	6										
1980	11	23	18	34	55					* Engdahl	Italy: Avellino, Potenza, Caserta	意大利:艾维连奴,波坦察,卡塞塔	40.794	15.312	6.8	6.9	Mw	10	4689	4	7700	4	20000	5				
1980	11	26	17	35	39					*	Venezuela: San Cristobal	委内瑞拉:圣克里斯托瓦尔	8.045	-72.441	40	5	Ms				36	1		2	30	1		
1980	11	26	23	49	2					USGS	Japan: Morioka	日本:岩手盛冈	40.38	141.31	95	5.8	mb	6										
1980	12	11	14	35	30					USGS	Kazakhstan: Shymkent, W.	哈萨克斯坦:奇姆肯特西部	41.27	69.17	33	5.1	mb	7										
1980	12	11	23	10	3					ISC, Engdahl, USGS	Japan: Miyazzaki	日本:宫崎	32.472	131.695	49.4	5.8	Mw	6										
1980	12	19	1	16	55					* ISC, Engdahl	Iran: Qom	伊朗:库姆	34.476	50.646	12.9	6.2	Mw		26	1			5.0	3				
1980	12	22	12	51	20					* Engdahl	Iran: Qom	伊朗:库姆	34.425	50.634	18.4	5.8	Mw		3	1	139	3	1	2				
1981	1	2	15	39	48					ISC, Engdahl, USGS	Ryukyu Islands	琉球群岛	29.318	128.1	225	6.9	Mw	6										
1981	1	14	6	1	14					USGS, ISC	Japan: Kagoshima, Near Coast of S.	日本:鹿岛南部近海	30.68	130.97	33	5.6	mb	6										
1981	1	18	18	17	28	4	0.4	-1.3		* Engdahl, NOAA, USGS	Japan: Miyagi, Near Coast	日本:宫城近海	38.708	142.788	47.3	7	Mw	6										
1981	1	19	15	11	2					* Engdahl	Indonesia: Papua	印度尼西亚:巴布亚	-4.514	139.284	20	6.7	Mw		305	3		2		3				
1981	1	23	21	13	49					* China, Engdahl, Dis	China: Sichuan, Dawu	中国:四川道孚	30.936	101.101	5.5	6.9	Ms	8	123	3	489	3	27.7	4	2992	4		
1981	1	28	3	47	44					USGS	Japan: Kazo	日本:埼玉加须	36.17	139.66	69	5.2	mb	6										
1981	1	29	21	19	36					USGS	Japan: Nagasaki	日本:长崎	32.44	129.79	33	5	mb	6										
1981	2	12	1	50	7					USGS, ISC	Azores: Sao Miguel (San Miguel)	亚速尔群岛:圣米格尔	38.46	-26.75	10	5.7	mb	6										
1981	2	14	6	9	27					USGS	US: Washington, Mt St Helens	美国:华盛顿州圣海伦山	46.35	-122.24	7	5.5	ML	6										
1981	2	14	17	27	44					* Italy	Italy: Salerno	意大利:萨勒诺	40.985	14.613	10	4.91	Ms	7	12	1			0.5	1				
1981	2	23	4	6	40					USGS	Georgia: Gurdzhaani	格鲁吉亚:古祖尼	41.79	45.97	33	5.1	mb	6										
1981	2	24	6	45	10					USGS	Ryukyu Islands	琉球群岛	28.31	129.41	43	5.9	Ms	6										
1981	2	24	20	53	38	4			3	* ISC, Engdahl, NOAA	Greece: Gulf of Corinth	希腊:科林斯海湾	38.16	22.974	16.9	6.6	Mw	8	22	1	400	3	900	5				
1981	3	4	21	58	6					* ISC, Engdahl	Greece: Athens, Corinth	希腊:雅典,科林斯	38.196	23.301	15	6.3	Mw	9	1	1	9	1		2				
1981	3	5	14	9	40					USGS	Hawaiian Islands	夏威夷群岛	21.02	-156.99	10	5.5	ML	6										
1981	3	10	15	16	20					*	Greece: Preveza	希腊:普雷韦扎	39.481	20.699	31	5.6	mb	8	2	1				2	150	3		
1981	3	15	21	33	10					USGS, Engdahl, ISC	Ryukyu Islands	琉球群岛	29.313	129.406	15.4	5.5	Ms	6										
1981	3	23	19	28	9					ISC, Engdahl, USGS	Chile: Near Coast of C.	智利:中部近海	-33.664	-71.962	22.7	6.4	Mw	6										
1981	3	26	18	4	45					Engdahl, USGS	Chile: Tarapaca	智利:塔拉帕卡	-19.492	-69	131	6.5	Mw	5										

时间 Date						海啸 Tsunami				资料来源 Information	震中 Earthquake Epicenter				深度 Depth	震级 Mag	标度 Scale	烈度 MMI	死亡人数 Deaths		受伤人数 Injuries		经济损失 Damage		房屋毁坏 Houses Destroyed		房屋受损 Houses Damaged	
年 Year	月 Mo	日 Dy	时 Hr	分 Mn	秒 Sec	源 Sr	浪高 Wh	级 I mI	级 S mS		地名(英文) Name(English)	地名(中文) Name(Chinese)	纬度(°) Latitude	经度(°) Longitude					数量/人 Num	级别 Dd	数量/人 Num	级别 Dd	数量/$ Mill $ Mill	级别 De	数量/间 Num	级别 Dh	数量/间 Num	级别 Dh
1981	4	13	3	4	8					USGS,ISC	Japan Trench	日本海沟	37.23	142.18	28	5.7	mb	5										
1981	4	18	0	32	40					* GSHAP	Peru:Ayacucho	秘鲁:阿亚库乔	-13.144	-74.376	38	5.5	Mw	7	8	1	15	1		2				
1981	4	25	23	6	9					China	China: Inner Mongolia, Yakeshi,E.	中国:内蒙古牙克石东部	48.89	122.02	20	5.1	Ms	6										
1981	4	26	12	9	31					* ISC,Engdahl	US:California,Westmorland	美国:加利福尼亚州威斯特莫兰	33.126	-115.643	10.1	6.0	Mw	7					1.5	2				
1981	5	22	11	36	20					China	China:Sichuan,Yanyuan,W.	中国:四川盐源西	27.33	101.18	10	5	Ms	5										
1981	5	25	5	25	12	4	0.3	-1.7		* Engdahl, NOAA	New Zealand:Auckland Islands,N.	新西兰:奥克兰群岛以北	-48.721	164.658	8.6	7.6	Mw											
1981	6	7	13	0	57					USGS	Italy:Marsala	意大利:马尔萨拉	37.67	12.47	18	4.9	mb	6										
1981	6	11	7	24	24					* Engdahl	Iran:Kerman	伊朗:克尔曼	29.858	57.686	14.3	6.6	Mw		3000	4		3	5.0	3				
1981	6	22	17	53	22					* Engdahl	Peru:Huancavelica	秘鲁:万卡韦利卡	-13.186	-74.464	16.7	5.8	Mw		10	1		2	5.0	3				
1981	7	7	1	29	8					China	Myanmar:Myitkyina	缅甸:密支那	25.42	97.67	25	5.1	Ms	6										
1981	7	28	3	3	22					USGS,ISC	Chile:Puerto Montt	智利:蒙特港	-41.57	-73.2	43	5.5	mb	5										
1981	7	28	17	22	24					* Engdahl	Iran:Kerman	伊朗:克尔曼	29.964	57.766	13.8	7.3	Mw		3000	4	1000	3	1000	5				
1981	8	4	18	35	41					USGS,ISC	Caspian Sea	里海	38.07	49.34	27	5.6	Ms	5										
1981	8	13	2	58	12					* USGS	Bosnia:Banja Luka	波斯尼亚:巴尼亚卢卡	44.849	17.312	16	5.8	ML	8			44	1	5.0	3				
1981	8	13	3	1	34					China,Dis	China:Inner Mongolia,Fengzhen,E.	中国:内蒙古丰镇东	40.58	113.41	18	5.8	Ms	7	1		11	1			616	3	21854	5
1981	9	1	9	29	31	4	1	-3.3	-2	* Engdahl, NOAA	Samoa Islands:Apia	萨摩亚群岛:阿皮亚	-15.112	-173.019	14.2	7.7	Mw	6		1				1		1		
1981	9	2	9	24	46					USGS	Japan:Chiba,Near Coast	日本:千叶近海	35.71	140.9	57	5.5	mb	6										
1981	9	3	5	35	46					ISC, Engdahl, USGS	Kuril Islands	千岛群岛	43.622	146.978	45.3	6.6	Mw	8										
1981	9	4	15	50	55					ISC, Engdahl, USGS	US:California,Oxnard,S.	美国:加利福尼亚州奥克斯纳德南部	33.895	-119.028	15	6.0	Mw	6										
1981	9	12	7	15	54					* ISC,Engdahl	India:Kashmir,Gilgit	印度:克什米尔,吉尔吉特	35.68	73.593	17	6.2	Mw		220	3	2500	4	5.0	3				
1981	9	19	6	50	59					China	China:Yunnan,Pu-er	中国:云南普洱	23.02	101.46	33	6	Ms	7										
1981	9	30	11	53	27					USGS	US: California, Mammoth Lakes	美国:加利福尼亚州马姆莫斯湖	37.59	-118.89	5	5.9	ML	6										
1981	10	16	3	25	42					* Chile, ISC, Engdahl	Chile:Off Coast of C.	智利:中部沿海	-33.2	-73.072	25	7.1	Mw	6	1	1								
1981	10	18	4	31	3					* ISC,Engdahl	Colombia:Cúcuta	哥伦比亚:北桑坦德的库库塔	8.111	-72.5	39.2	5.9	Mw	7	15	1		3	5.0	3				
1981	10	25	3	22	16	4	0.1			* ISC, Engdahl, NOAA	Mexico: Michoacan, Lazaro Cardenas	墨西哥:米却肯,拉萨罗卡德纳斯	18.161	-101.99	19	7.2	Mw		9	1				3				
1981	11	6	16	47	48					ISC, Engdahl, USGS	Papua New Guinea: East Sepik,Near Coast of N.	巴布亚新几内亚:东塞皮克北部近海	-3.492	143.844	15	6.6	Mw	6										

时间 Date						海啸 Tsunami				资料来源 Information	震中 Earthquake Epicenter				深度 Depth	震级 Mag	标度 Scale	烈度 MMI	死亡人数 Deaths		受伤人数 Injuries		经济损失 Damage		房屋毁坏 Houses Destroyed		房屋受损 Houses Damaged	
年 Year	月 Mo	日 Dy	时 Hr	分 Mn	秒 Sec	源 Sr	浪高 Wh	级 I mI	级 S mS		地名(英文) Name(English)	地名(中文) Name(Chinese)	纬度(°) Latitude	经度(°) Longitude					数量/人 Num	级别 Dd	数量/人 Num	级别 Dd	数量/$ Mill	级别 De	数量/间 Num	级别 Dh	数量/间 Num	级别 Dh
1981	11	7	3	29	52					ISC, Engdahl, USGS	Chile:La Ligua	智利:拉利瓜	-32.232	-71.379	63.9	7	Mw	7										
1981	11	8	18	1	2					China,Dis	China:Hebei,Longyao,E.	中国:河北隆尧东	37.4	114.99	20	5.8	Ms	6										
1981	11	13	9	7	8					USGS	Romania:Galati	罗马尼亚:加拉茨	45.21	28.95	7	4.9	mb	8										
1981	11	14	9	5	32					* ISC,Engdahl	Egypt:Aswan	埃及:阿斯旺	23.688	32.657	18.4	5.8	Mw	8						1	11	1		
1981	11	17	7	11	23					USGS,ISC	Chile:Chanaral,NE.	智利:查尼亚拉尔东北	-25.95	-70.08	70	5.5	mb	6										
1981	11	23	10	17	25					ISC, Engdahl, USGS	Kuril Islands,S.	千岛群岛南部	43.051	146.172	40.1	6	Mw	6										
1981	11	29	5	6	47					USGS	Italy:Potenza	意大利:波坦察	40.74	15.64	33	4.9	ML	6										
1981	12	2	6	24	46					ISC, Engdahl, USGS	Japan: Aomori, Near East Coast	日本:青森东部近海	40.943	142.512	77.7	6.3	Mw	6										
1981	12	12	20	26	47					* CSN	Pakistan:Quetta	巴基斯坦:奎达	29.856	66.962	33	4.7	Ms		6	1	12	1		2	45	1	45	1
1981	12	19	14	10	52					* ISC,Engdahl	Greece:Aegean Sea,Lesbos	希腊:爱琴海,莱斯沃斯	39.184	25.313	10	6.9	Mw							1				
1982	1	7	20	37	58					USGS	Japan:Akita	日本:秋田	40.12	140.32	46	5.1	mb	6										
1982	1	9	12	53	52					USGS	Canada:Gaspe Peninsula	加拿大:加斯佩半岛	46.98	-66.66	10	5.8	MLg	6										
1982	1	11	6	10	7	2	0.1			* ISC,Bautista, NOAA,USGS	Philippines: Virac, Catanduanes	菲律宾:比拉克,卡坦端内斯	13.835	124.336	32.6	7.4	Ms	7						1				
1982	1	11	21	41	8					* USGS	Canada:Gaspe Peninsula	加拿大:加斯佩半岛	46.97	-66.66	7	5.5	MLg	6						1				
1982	1	12	5	48	20					* Engdahl	Honduras:Masaya	洪都拉斯:马萨亚	13.172	-87.54	7.9	6.1	Mw				2	1		2				
1982	1	19	0	14	42					USGS	US:New Hampshire,Laconia	美国:新汉普郡州拉科尼亚	43.5	-71.6	8	4.7	Md	6										
1982	1	20	4	25	15					* ISC,Engdahl	India:Nicobar Islands	印度:尼科巴群岛	7.061	93.953	26.2	6.3	Mw					2		2				
1982	1	21	21	52	41					USGS,ISC	Hawaiian Islands	夏威夷群岛	19.23	-155.59	10	5.7	mb	6										
1982	1	21	22	29	14					USGS	Hawaiian Islands	夏威夷群岛	19.22	-155.55	13	5.6	mb	6										
1982	2	10	16	17	52					*	Indonesia:Java, Sukabumi	印度尼西亚:爪哇,苏卡布米	-6.863	106.936	40	5.5	mb				17	1	3.5	2				
1982	2	10	20	38	5					Engdahl,USGS	Argentina:Jujuy,N.	阿根廷:胡胡伊北部	-22.682	-66.603	220	6.8	Mw	5										
1982	2	20	9	17	4					USGS,ISC	Fiji Islands	斐济群岛	-16.71	177.23	14	5.5	mb	5										
1982	2	24	4	22	36	4	0.1			* Engdahl, NOAA	Indonesia:Sumatera,Aceh	印度尼西亚:苏门答腊亚齐	4.398	97.578	11.3	5.9	Mw											
1982	2	25	0	39	11					China,Dis	China:Jiangxi,Longnan	中国:江西龙南	24.78	114.74	23	5	Ms	6									1917	4
1982	3	6	23	14	36					USGS	Japan:Mito	日本:茨城美图	36.44	140.45	67	5.6	mb	6										
1982	3	11	10	32	28	1	0.1			* Engdahl, NOAA	Indonesia:Sumbawa Island	印度尼西亚:松巴哇岛	-9.429	118.356	31.4	6.5	Mw											
1982	3	16	13	52	24					USGS	Croatia:Varazdin	克罗地亚:瓦拉日丁	46.17	16.26	14	5	ML	7										
1982	3	20	11	17	33					China	China:Xinjiang,Burqin,SW.	中国:新疆布尔津西南	47.62	86.38	28	4.9	Ms	6										
1982	3	21	2	32	7	4	1.3	0.4		* Engdahl, NOAA	Japan: Hokkaido, Urakawa, Hiroo	日本:北海道,浦河,広尾	42.262	142.423	27.4	6.9	Mw	10	110	3			1	2				
1982	3	21	9	44	3					USGS	Italy:Potenza	意大利:波坦察	39.92	15.77	28	5.2	ML	6										
1982	3	28	4	16	53					*	Mexico:Chiapas	墨西哥:恰帕斯州	17.36	-93.228	9	3.5	MS		10	1	200	3	3.3	2				

年	月	日	时	分	秒	源	浪高	级I	级S	资料来源	地名(英文)	地名(中文)	纬度(°)	经度(°)	深度	震级	标度	烈度	死亡人数 数量/人	死亡人数 级别	受伤人数 数量/人	受伤人数 级别	经济损失 数量/$ Mill	经济损失 级别	房屋毁坏 数量/间	房屋毁坏 级别	房屋受损 数量/间	房屋受损 级别
Date						Tsunami				Information	Earthquake Epicenter				Depth	Mag	Scale	MMI	Deaths		Injuries		Damage		Houses Destroyed		Houses Damaged	
Year	Mo	Dy	Hr	Mn	Sec	Sr	Wh	mI	mS		Name(English)	Name(Chinese)	Latitude	Longitude					Num	Dd	Num	Dd	$ Mill	De	Num	Dh	Num	Dh
1982	3	28	23	24	52					* Engdahl	Peru: Lima, Coast	秘鲁:利马近海	-12.743	-76.01	91.4	6.3	Mw	6	3	1			5.0	3				
1982	4	14	6	36	55					* China, Dis	China: Ningxia, Haiyuan	中国:宁夏海原	36.71	105.63	20	5.5	Ms	7			18	1		1	2226	4	7940	4
1982	5	6	15	42	21					USGS, Engdahl	Uzbekistan: Batken	乌兹别克斯坦:巴特肯	40.146	71.533	30.8	5.8	Mw	7										
1982	5	15	22	2	20					USGS	Bosnia and Herzegovina: Mostar	波斯尼亚和黑塞哥维那:莫斯塔尔	43.44	17.36	10	4.5	ML	6										
1982	5	22	1	35	37					USGS, ISC	Japan: Hokkaido	日本:北海道	42.08	142.62	50	5.5	mb	6										
1982	5	29	12	21	8					USGS, ISC	Japan: Hokkaido	日本:北海道	42.81	143.16	75	5.8	mb	5										
1982	5	31	20	13	10					ISC, Engdahl, USGS	Japan: Miyagi, Near Coast	日本:宫城近海	38.773	142.153	50	6.1	Mw	6										
1982	6	7	10	59	39					* Engdahl	Mexico: Guerrero, Orziba, Oaxaca, Guadalupe	墨西哥:格雷罗,瓦哈卡,瓜达卢佩	16.517	-98.344	18.4	6.9	Mw	6	9	1		3		2				
1982	6	15	23	24	32					* China, Dis	China: Sichuan, Garze, NW.	中国:四川甘孜西北	31.96	100.03	15	6.0	Ms	7	11	1	13	1	2.08	2				
1982	6	19	6	21	58					* CSN, ISC, Engdahl	El Salvador: La Libertad, Coast	萨尔瓦多:拉利伯塔德近海	13.337	-89.312	73.1	7.3	Mw	7	43	1		3	5.0	3				
1982	6	28	9	57	30					USGS	Germany: Siegen	德国:锡根	50.73	7.8	10	4.8	ML	6										
1982	7	3	8	13	33					China, Dis	China: Yunnan, Jianchuan	中国:云南剑川	26.65	100.14	15	5.4	Ms	7	2		10	1	0.71	1	3749	4	3352	4
1982	7	5	8	56	56					USGS, ISC	Japan: Kagoshima	日本:鹿岛	31	130.45	116	5.7	mb	5										
1982	7	23	14	23	54	4	0.4	-1.3	-1	* ISC, Engdahl, NOAA, USGS	Japan Trench	日本海沟	36.307	141.763	27.4	7	Mw	6										
1982	8	5	9	16	41					USGS, ISC	Chile: Copiapo	智利:科皮亚波	-26.68	-70.66	39	5.5	mb	7										
1982	8	6	20	40	52					* ISC, Engdahl	Indonesia: Flores Islands, Ruteng	印度尼西亚:弗洛勒斯群岛,鲁滕	-8.332	120.357	31.3	5.8	Mw							2				
1982	8	12	4	33	0					USGS	Japan: Oshima	日本:东京大岛	34.9	139.48	34	5.4	Ms	6										
1982	8	26	5	23	1					Engdahl, USGS	Ecuador: Guayaquil	厄瓜多尔:瓜亚基尔	-2.702	-79.875	66.5	6.0	Mw	6										
1982	9	20	16	26	44					USGS	Trinidad & Tobago: Northern Coast	特立尼达和多巴哥:北部近海	11.22	-60.85	6	5.2	mb	6										
1982	9	22	10	39	9					USGS	Japan: Hokkaido	日本:北海道	41.98	143.11	10	4.8	mb	6										
1982	9	29	5	50	32					* ISC	Honduras: Ocotepeque	洪都拉斯:奥科特佩克	14.487	-89.121	12	5.5	Mw		3	1	2	1		2		3	554	3
1982	10	1	14	29	5					USGS	US: California, Ridgecrest	美国:加利福尼亚州里奇克雷斯特	35.73	-117.75	8	5.4	ML	6										
1982	10	8	13	34	57					China	China: Yunnan, Jianchuan	中国:云南剑川	26.45	100.02	25	5.1	Ms	6										
1982	10	17	10	56	48					* Italy, USGS	Italy: Perugia	意大利:佩鲁贾	43.3355	13.0152	16	4.75	Mw	7					35.0	4				
1982	10	18	15	29	24					USGS	Italy: Perugia	意大利:佩鲁贾	43.13	12.63	19	4.6	ML	8										
1982	10	19	12	45	58					China	China: Hebei, Lulong	中国:河北卢龙	39.96	118.98	10	4.9	Ms	6										
1982	10	25	22	26	4					USGS, ISC	US: California, Coalinga	美国:加利福尼亚州科灵加	36.32	-120.51	11	5.5	mb	6										
1982	10	26	3	24	31					USGS, Engdahl	Chile: Coquimbo	智利:科金博	-29.68	-71.37	71	5.8	Mw	7										
1982	10	27	15	36	31					China	China: Yunnan, Funing, E.	中国:云南富宁东	23.8	105.96	15	5.8	Ms	7										
1982	10	31	6	3	6					Engdahl, USGS	Guatemala: Antigua	危地马拉:安地瓜	14.069	-90.288	96.9	6.2	Mw	6										

年 Year	月 Mo	日 Dy	时 Hr	分 Mn	秒 Sec	海啸 源 Sr	海啸 浪高 Wh	海啸 级 I mI	海啸 级 S mS	资料来源 Information	地名(英文) Name(English)	地名(中文) Name(Chinese)	纬度(°) Latitude	经度(°) Longitude	深度 Depth	震级 Mag	标度 Scale	烈度 MMI	死亡人数 数量/人 Num	死亡人数 级别 Dd	受伤人数 数量/人 Num	受伤人数 级别 Dd	经济损失 数量/$ Mill	经济损失 级别 De	房屋毁坏 数量/间 Num	房屋毁坏 级别 Dh	房屋受损 数量/间 Num	房屋受损 级别 Dh
1982	11	14	8	29	20					USGS, ISC	Russia: Kamchatka Peninsula	俄罗斯:堪察加半岛	52.99	158.67	92	5.7	mb	5										
1982	11	16	23	41	21					* USGS	Albania: Elbasan	阿尔巴尼亚:爱尔巴桑	40.883	19.59	21	5.6	mb	8	1	1	12	1	5.0	3				
1982	11	17	0	37	52					USGS	Albania: Elbasan	阿尔巴尼亚:爱尔巴桑	40.86	19.52	10	4.9	mb	6										
1982	12	13	9	12	51					* ISC, Engdahl	Yemen: Dhamar	也门:扎马尔	14.669	44.246	7	6.2	Mw	8	2800	4	1500	4	2000	5		4		
1982	12	16	0	40	50					* ISC, Engdahl	Afghan: Puli Khumri	阿富汗:普勒胡姆里	36.115	68.981	35.9	6.4	Mw		500	3	3000	4	1	2				
1982	12	16	6	53	1					USGS	US: California, Bull Creek	美国:加利福尼亚州比尔河	40.37	-124.06	5	4.6	ML	6										
1982	12	19	17	43	57	4	0.2	-2.3		* ISC, Engdahl, NOAA	Tonga Islands, S.	汤加群岛南部	-24.193	-175.575	31.6	7.7	Mw											
1982	12	25	12	28	0	1				* Engdahl, NOAA	Indonesia: Flores Island, E.	印度尼西亚:弗洛勒斯岛东部	-8.428	122.971	6.3	6	Mw		13	1	390	3	1.45	2	1875	4		
1982	12	28	6	37	44	4	0.4	-1.3	-1	* ISC, Engdahl, NOAA, USGS	Japan: Miyake Jima	日本:三宅岛	33.881	139.446	20.3	6.2	Mw	6										
1982	12	28	7	30	4					China	China: Yunnan, Sipsongpanna, NE.	中国:云南西双版纳东北	22.34	101.14	12	5.3	Ms	7										
1982	12	28	7							China	China: Yunnan, Yongping	中国:云南永平	25.56	99.42	15	5.4	Ms	6										
1982	12	29	7	2	33					USGS, ISC, Engdahl	Japan: Miyake Jima	日本:三宅岛	33.76	139.34	19	5.8	Mw	5										
1983	1	4	7	3	13					USGS	Japan: Hokkaido	日本:北海道	42.23	142.74	59	5.2	mb	6										
1983	1	7	1	38	11					USGS	US: California, Mammoth Lakes	美国:加利福尼亚州马姆莫斯湖	37.63	-118.92	14	5.4	ML	6										
1983	1	7	3	24	19					USGS	US: California, Mammoth Lakes	美国:加利福尼亚州马姆莫斯湖	37.62	-118.98	12	5.4	ML	6										
1983	1	17	12	41	30	3				* Engdahl, NOAA	Ionian Sea	爱奥尼亚海	38.015	20.324	6	6.9	Mw											
1983	1	24	8	17	40					* ISC, Engdahl	Mexico: Oaxaca, Salina Cruz	墨西哥:瓦哈卡,萨利纳克鲁斯	16.132	-95.238	49.3	6.8	Mw	7						2				
1983	1	30	22	45	42					USGS	Japan Trench	日本海沟	33.41	140.81	63	5.7	mb	6										
1983	2	13	1	40	12					* China, Engdahl, ISC, Dis	China: Xinjiang, Ulugqat, N.	中国:新疆乌恰北	40.015	75.235	7.5	6.7	Ms	8			2	1			3000	4		
1983	2	13	6	35	32					Engdahl, USGS	Guam	关岛(西太平洋)	13.867	144.974	108.8	6.1	Mw	6										
1983	2	25	18	22	13					* USGS	Macedonia: Skopje	马其顿:斯科普里	41.959	21.54	24	4.7	mb	7	12	1			0.5	1				
1983	2	25	22	49	54					ISC, Engdahl, USGS	Chile: Arica, SE.	智利:阿里卡东南	-18.612	-69.356	138.8	6.7	Mw	6										
1983	2	26	20	7	50					* USGS	Tadzhikistan: Garm	塔吉克斯坦:加尔姆	38.841	70.727	49	5.3	mb	7						3				
1983	2	27	12	14	21					ISC, Engdahl, USGS	Japan: Tsukubamirai	日本:茨城筑波未来	35.949	140.037	67	6.0	Mw	6										
1983	3	3	3	32	16					China, Dis	China: Xinjiang, Hutubi, S.	中国:新疆呼图壁南	43.99	86.66	68	5.4	Ms	5										
1983	3	4	6	32	19					USGS	US: South Dakota, Stephan	美国:南达科他州斯蒂芬	44.21	-99.41	5	4.6	MLg	6										

时间 Date						海啸 Tsunami				资料来源 Information	震中 Earthquake Epicenter				深度	震级	标度	烈度	死亡人数 Deaths		受伤人数 Injuries		经济损失 Damage		房屋毁坏 Houses Destroyed		房屋受损 Houses Damaged	
年	月	日	时	分	秒	源	浪高	级 I	级 S		地名(英文)	地名(中文)	纬度(°)	经度(°)					数量/人	级别	数量/人	级别	数量/$ Mill	级别	数量/间	级别	数量/间	级别
Year	Mo	Dy	Hr	Mn	Sec	Sr	Wh	mI	mS		Name(English)	Name(Chinese)	Latitude	Longitude	Depth	Mag	Scale	MMI	Num	Dd	Num	Dd	$ Mill	De	Num	Dh	Num	Dh
1983	3	4	14	11	36					USGS,ISC	Japan:Miyako,Off Coast	日本:宫古沿海	39.5	143.23	33	5.7	Ms	5										
1983	3	8	17	6	38					ISC, Engdahl, USGS	Grenada:St Georges,S.	格林纳达:圣乔治南部	10.997	-62.386	85.3	5.9	Mw	6										
1983	3	12	0	53	42					ISC, Engdahl, USGS	Indonesia:Banda Sea	印度尼西亚:班达海	-4.052	127.896	35.4	6.1	Mw	6										
1983	3	12	1	36	39	4	3	1.6	1.5	* Engdahl, NOAA	Indonesia:Banda Sea	印度尼西亚:班达海	-4.084	127.854	30.4	6.6	Mw							1				
1983	3	14	12	12	48					USGS, Engdahl, ISC	Turkmenistan:Balkanabat	土库曼斯坦:巴尔坎纳巴德	39.17	54.47	33	5.6	Ms	7										
1983	3	15	17	27	26					USGS,ISC	Japan:Hamamatsu	日本:静冈滨松	34.78	137.57	43	5.7	mb	6										
1983	3	18	9	5	51	4	0.3	-1.7		* Engdahl, NOAA, USGS	Papua New Guinea:New Ireland,E.	巴布亚新几内亚:新爱尔兰东部	-4.887	153.589	88.7	7.7	Mw	7						2				
1983	3	23	23	51	9					* Engdahl	Greece:Nisia Ionioy	希腊:伊奥尼亚群岛	38.221	20.362	25.1	6.2	Mw	7			7	1		2	160	3		
1983	3	25	11	57	49					* Iran	Iran:Tehran,Damāvand	伊朗:德黑兰,达马万德	35.953	52.264	33	5.2	Ms		30	1	61	2	5.0	3				
1983	3	31	13	12	53					* GSHAP	Colombia:Popayan	哥伦比亚:波帕扬	2.461	-76.686	22	7.0	Mw	9	350	3	1200	4	411	5				
1983	4	2	0	32	28					*	Azerbaijan:Lenkeran	阿塞拜疆:连科兰	39.042	48.714	33	4.6	mb	5					5.0	3				
1983	4	3	2	50	2					* Engdahl	Costa Rica:Puntarenas	哥斯达黎加:蓬塔雷纳斯	8.777	-83.032	25	7.5	Mw		6	1		2	1	2				
1983	4	4	2	51	37					* Engdahl	Indonesia: North West of Sumatera	印度尼西亚:苏门答腊西北沿海	5.724	94.694	94.5	7	Mw	7		2	100	2	1	2				
1983	4	5	6	50	32					* China, Engdahl	China:Xinjiang,Ulugqat,N.	中国:新疆乌恰北	39.963	75.262	10.7	6.1	Ms			1				1				
1983	4	12	12	7	58					* Engdahl	Peru:Chimbote	秘鲁:钦博特	-4.845	-78.091	125.7	7	Mw		10	1			0.5	1				
1983	4	15	18	30	43					USGS	Alaska Peninsula,C.	阿拉斯加半岛中部	64.85	-147.53	10	4.8	ML	6										
1983	4	22	0	37	41					* Engdahl	Thailand:Ban Rai	泰国:班赖	14.91	99.026	27.9	5.8	Mw							2				
1983	4	24	11	21	55					USGS	Japan:Bando	日本:茨城坂东	36.04	139.89	63	4.7	mb	6										
1983	4	26	15	26	42					ISC, Engdahl, USGS	China:Taiwan,Yilan,Coast of E.	中国:台湾宜兰以东海域	24.694	122.607	119.7	6.5	Mw	5										
1983	5	2	23	42	39					* ISC,Engdahl	US:California,Coalinga	美国:加利福尼亚州科灵加	36.234	-120.304	10	6.5	M	8			45	1	31.0	4	500	3		
1983	5	26	3	0	1	4	15	3.9	2	* ISC, Engdahl, NOAA	Japan:Akita,Near West Coast	日本:秋田西部近海	40.468	139.08	20	7.7	Mw	8	104	3	324	3	800	5	3513	4		
1983	5	28	3	28	6					China	China: Yunnan, Sipsongpanna,NE.	中国:云南西双版纳东北	22.41	101.4	5	5.2	Ms	6										
1983	5	29	20	53	58					USGS,ISC	Japan:Hokkaido	日本:北海道	42.64	143.46	80	5.7	mb	6										
1983	5	29	22	1	50					USGS,ISC	Japan: Near West Coast of Honshu	日本:本州西部近海	40.7	139.37	36	5.6	mb	5										
1983	6	1	11	17	38					China,Dis	China:Xinjiang,Fukang,SE.	中国:新疆阜康东南	44.03	88.61	21	5.3	Ms	6										
1983	6	9	12	49	5	4	0.6			* Engdahl, NOAA, USGS	Japan:Noshiro	日本:能代	40.242	139.004	27.3	6	Mw	6										

年 Year	月 Mo	日 Dy	时 Hr	分 Mn	秒 Sec	海啸 Tsunami 源 Sr	浪高 Wh	级 I mI	级 S mS	资料来源 Information	震中 Earthquake Epicenter 地名(英文) Name(English)	地名(中文) Name(Chinese)	纬度(°) Latitude	经度(°) Longitude	深度 Depth	震级 Mag	标度 Scale	烈度 MMI	死亡人数 Deaths 数量/人 Num	级别 Dd	受伤人数 Injuries 数量/人 Num	级别 Dd	经济损失 Damage 数量/$ Mill	级别 De	房屋毁坏 Houses Destroyed 数量/间 Num	级别 Dh	房屋受损 Houses Damaged 数量/间 Num	级别 Dh
1983	6	9	13	4	2					ISC, Engdahl, USGS	Japan: Akita, Near West Coast	日本:秋田西部近海	40.24	139.012	28.7	5.9	Mw	6										
1983	6	11	3	9	52					USGS, ISC	US: California, Coalinga	美国:加利福尼亚州科灵加	36.24	-120.46	4	5.5	mb	6										
1983	6	18	22	13	32					USGS, ISC	Japan Sea, E.	日本海东部	40.18	138.94	21	5.5	mb	5										
1983	6	21	6	25	30	4	1			* ISC, Engdahl, NOAA, USGS	Japan: Off SW. Coast of Hokkaido	日本:北海道西南沿海	41.358	139.124	17.1	6.8	Mw	6						1				
1983	6	24	7	18	23					ISC, Engdahl, USGS	Vietnam: Muong Lay	越南:孟来	21.738	103.259	15.3	6.3	Mw	6										
1983	6	29	8	8	36					USGS	US: California, San Diego	美国:加利福尼亚州圣地亚哥	32.63	-117.38	5	4.6	ML	6										
1983	7	1	22	3	42					USGS	Japan: Ibaraki, Near Coast	日本:茨城近海	36.94	141.12	51	5.5	mb	6										
1983	7	3	17	14	22					* Engdahl	Costa Rica: Cartago	哥斯达黎加:卡塔戈	9.629	-83.69	14.2	6.5	Mw	9	2	1	60	2	5.0	3				
1983	7	5	12	1	28					* Engdahl	Turkey: Biga, Erdek	土耳其:比噶,埃尔德克	40.312	27.255	4.5	6.1	Mw	8	5	1	26	1		2				
1983	7	9	7	40	51					USGS	US: California, Coalinga	美国:加利福尼亚州科灵加	36.24	-120.41	9	5.5	ML	6										
1983	7	12	15	10	5					* ISC, Engdahl	Alaska: Prince William Sound	阿拉斯加:威廉王子湾	61.024	-147.434	32.6	6.5	Mw	6					1	2				
1983	7	15	9	38	29					USGS	Costa Rica: San Jose, SE.	哥斯达黎加:圣何塞东南	9.66	-83.93	33	4.7	mb	6										
1983	7	19	6	9	28					USGS	Fiji Islands	斐济群岛	-19.19	177.65	33	5.1	mb	6										
1983	7	22	2	39	53					ISC, USGS	US: California, Coalinga	美国:加利福尼亚州科灵加	36.23	-120.42	9	6.0	Mw	6										
1983	7	22	2	41	1					* Iran	Iran: Zanjān	伊朗:赞詹	36.948	49.18	41	5.6	Ms	6	3	1	41	1	5.0	3	75	2		
1983	7	25	22	31	39					USGS, ISC	US: California, Coalinga	美国:加利福尼亚州科灵加	36.22	-120.41	9	5.6	mb	6										
1983	7	27	0	31	28					China	China: Qinghai, Qilian, NW.	中国:青海祁连西北	38.71	99.05	25	4.9	Ms	5										
1983	7	28	15	6	45					USGS, ISC	Japan: Hokkaido	日本:北海道	41.97	142.65	62	5.5	mb	5										
1983	8	6	4	52	54					*	Pakistan: Ziarat	巴基斯坦:加拉特	30.349	67.84	10	4.7	mb							2	25	1	25	1
1983	8	6	15	43	55	2	0.1		2	* Engdahl, NOAA	Aegean Sea	爱琴海	40.107	24.763	10	6.7	Mw	6						2				
1983	8	8	3	47	57					* ISC, USGS	Japan: Fujiyoshida	日本:山梨富士吉田	35.5	139.07	25	6.0	Mw	6	1	1	28	1		1		2		
1983	8	12	19	36	31					USGS	Italy: Abruzzo	意大利:阿布鲁佐	41.75	13.85	10	4.8	ML	6										
1983	8	17	10	55	59	4	0.1	-3.3		* ISC, Engdahl, NOAA	Russia: Kamchatka Peninsula	俄罗斯:堪察加半岛	55.788	161.321	92.8	7	Mw											
1983	8	17	12	17	58	4	0.1			* Bautista, Engdahl, NOAA	Philippines: Laoag	菲律宾:佬沃	18.219	120.803	29	6.6	Mw	8	16	1	471	3	2.227	2		3		
1983	8	24	13	36	32					Engdahl, USGS	US: California, North Coast	美国:加利福尼亚州北部近海	40.29	-124.63	20.8	6.2	Mw	5										
1983	8	25	20	23	34					ISC, Engdahl, USGS	Japan: Oita	日本:大分	33.55	131.471	123.4	6.5	Mw	6										

时间 年 Year	月 Mo	日 Dy	时 Hr	分 Mn	秒 Sec	海啸 Tsunami 源 Sr	浪高 Wh	级 I mI	级 S mS	资料来源 Information	震中 Earthquake Epicenter 地名(英文) Name(English)	地名(中文) Name(Chinese)	纬度(°) Latitude	经度(°) Longitude	深度 Depth	震级 Mag	标度 Scale	烈度 MMI	死亡人数 Deaths 数量/人 Num	级别 Dd	受伤人数 Injuries 数量/人 Num	级别 Dd	经济损失 Damage 数量/$ Mill	级别 De	房屋毁坏 Houses Destroyed 数量/间 Num	级别 Dh	房屋受损 Houses Damaged 数量/间 Num	级别 Dh
1983	9	7	19	22	5					ISC, Engdahl, USGS	Gulf of Alaska	阿拉斯加湾	60.934	-147.535	30	6.4	Mw	6										
1983	9	10	6	14	22					* USGS	Serbia:Kraljevo	塞尔维亚:克拉列沃	43.246	20.859	10	5.1	mb	8						2				
1983	9	16	23	10	48					USGS, ISC	Philippines:Bucay	菲律宾:布凯	17.97	120.77	33	5.6	mb	5										
1983	10	3	13	33	37					* ISC, Engdahl	Japan:Miyakejima, Oshima	日本:三宅岛,大岛	33.986	139.48	10.8	6	Mw	8						2				
1983	10	4	18	52	16	4	0.2	-2.3	0.2	* Engdahl, NOAA	Chile:Copoapo - Chanaral	智利:科皮亚波 - 查尼亚拉尔	-26.539	-70.503	24.6	7.7	Mw	7	5	1	12	1	1	2	40	1		
1983	10	7	10	18	46					USGS	US:New York, Newcomb	美国:纽约州纽科姆	43.94	-74.26	12	5.3	MLg	6										
1983	10	8	11	57	54					USGS	US:Utah, Salt Lake City	美国:犹他州盐湖城	40.75	-111.99	4	4.5	ML	6										
1983	10	15	2	58	8					USGS	Japan:Sakai	日本:茨城境町	36.12	139.81	63	5.1	mb	6										
1983	10	16	5	32	28					* Engdahl	Indonesia:Biau	印度尼西亚:比奥	1.08	120.963	18.5	6.4	Mw							2	20	1	15	1
1983	10	23	4	44	44					USGS	Japan:Hokkaido	日本:北海道	41.83	142.51	67	5.5	mb	6										
1983	10	25	0	36	24					* Engdahl	Indonesia:Sulawesi Utara	印度尼西亚:北苏拉威西	1.151	120.842	26.6	6.5	Mw	7	2	1	4	1		2	20	1	4	1
1983	10	28	1	50	32					USGS	Japan:Chikusei	日本:茨城筑西	36.18	139.9	70	5.2	mb	6										
1983	10	28	14	6	10					* Engdahl	US:Idaho, Borah Peak, Challis	美国:爱达荷州博拉峰,查利斯	44.086	-113.805	16	7.3	Ms	9	2	1	2	1	12.5	3				
1983	10	30	4	12	30					* Engdahl	Turkey:Erzurum, Kars	土耳其:埃尔佐鲁姆,卡尔斯	40.328	42.177	15	6.6	Mw		1342	4	1142	4	25.0	4		4		
1983	10	30	16	51	57					* Japan	Japan:Tottori	日本:鸟取	35.464	133.899	27	6.2	Mw	6			11	1		2				
1983	11	6	21	9	43					* China, Dis	China:Shandong, Heze	中国:山东菏泽	35.17	115.25	15	6.0	Ms	7	46	1	5138	4	162	5	61208	5	280171	5
1983	11	8	0	49	32					*	Belgium:Liege	比利时:列日	50.696	5.346	10	5	mb	7	2	1	30	1	50.0	4		3		
1983	11	9	16	29	52					* Italy, USGS	Italy: Parma	意大利:帕尔马	44.765	10.27	37	5.2	ML	8			100	2		2				
1983	11	16	16	13	3					* Engdahl	Hawaiian Islands	夏威夷群岛	19.438	-155.376	12.5	6.7	M	8			6	1	6.5	3				
1983	11	22	14	21	4					ISC, Engdahl, USGS	Ecuador:Muisne	厄瓜多尔:穆伊斯内	0.518	-79.767	49.8	6.8	Mw	6										
1983	11	30	2	56	48					ISC, Engdahl, USGS	Japan:Hokkaido	日本:北海道	41.868	142.752	50.5	6	Mw	6										
1983	11	30	17	46	3	4	1.5	-1.3		* Engdahl, NOAA, USGS	Chagos Archipelago Region	查戈斯群岛地区[印度洋]	-6.835	72.065	11	7.7	Mw	6						1				
1983	12	2	3	9	3					CSN, Engdahl, USGS	Guatemala:Near Coast	危地马拉:近海	14.055	-91.914	31	7	Mw	6										
1983	12	5	1	53	39					USGS	Japan:Miyazzaki, Near Coast	日本:宫崎近海	32.47	131.85	56	5	mb	6										
1983	12	15	4	22	35					Engdahl, USGS	Chile:Los Andes, W.	智利:洛斯安第斯西部	-33.111	-70.195	99.5	6.0	Mw	6										
1983	12	15	10	52	54					China, ISC, Dis	China:Xinjiang, Urumqi	中国:新疆乌鲁木齐	42.99	87.28	30	5.2	Ms	6										
1983	12	22	1	2	7					* Engdahl	Papua New Guinea:East New Britain	巴布亚新几内亚:东新不列颠	-5.4	151.916	54.3	6.5	Mw	5	10	1			25.0	4				
1983	12	22	4	11	30					* Engdahl	Guinea:Gaoual - Koumbia	几内亚:高瓦尔 - 昆比亚	11.862	-13.511	8.2	6.3	Mw	9	443	3	1436	4	8.0	3	4000	4		

年 Year	月 Mo	日 Dy	时 Hr	分 Mn	秒 Sec	海啸 Tsunami 源 Sr	浪高 Wh	级 I mI	级 S mS	资料来源 Information	地名(英文) Name(English)	地名(中文) Name(Chinese)	纬度(°) Latitude	经度(°) Longitude	深度 Depth	震级 Mag	标度 Scale	烈度 MMI	死亡人数 Deaths 数量/人 Num	级别 Dd	受伤人数 Injuries 数量/人 Num	级别 Dd	经济损失 Damage 数量/$ Mill	级别 De	房屋毁坏 Houses Destroyed 数量/间 Num	级别 Dh	房屋受损 Houses Damaged 数量/间 Num	级别 Dh
1983	12	23	22	56	7					USGS	Chile:Copiapo,Near Coast	智利:科皮亚波近海	-27.54	-71.46	33	5.3	mb	6										
1983	12	25	2	56	12					USGS	Adriatic Sea	亚得里亚海	41.96	19.07	11	4.5	ML	6										
1983	12	30	23	52	41					* Engdahl	Afghan:Badakhshan	阿富汗:巴达赫尚	36.401	70.713	213.6	7.4	Mw	7	26	1	483	3	3	2				
1983	12	31	0	44	43					USGS,ISC	Chile:Antofagasta,S.	智利:安托法加斯塔南部	-26.05	-70.08	55	5.5	mb	5										
1984	1	5	23	33	59					China, USGS, Dis	China:Gansu,Wuwei,NW.	中国:甘肃武威西北	37.96	102.17	17	5.3	Ms	6			4	1						
1984	1	8	15	24	16	1	0.1			* Engdahl, NOAA	Indonesia:Sulawesi,W	印度尼西亚:苏拉威西岛西部	-2.866	118.725	42.5	6.7	Mw		2	1	89	2	0.5	1				2
1984	1	10	12	12	60					USGS	Bosnia and Herzegovina:Trebinje	波斯尼亚和黑塞哥维那:特雷比涅	42.78	18.13	10	4.7	ML	6										
1984	1	13	19	41	40					USGS	Adriatic Sea	亚得里亚海	42.03	19.05	10	4.9	ML	6										
1984	1	17	11	13	40					USGS,ISC	Japan:Ibaraki,Near Coast	日本:茨城近海	36.44	141.23	39	5.6	mb	5										
1984	2	1	14	22	7					* ISC,Engdahl	Afghan:Khorog, Jalalabad	阿富汗:霍罗格,贾拉拉巴德	34.577	70.475	17	6.1	Mw		1	1	35	1	5.0	3				
1984	2	3	8	29	49					USGS,ISC	Chile:La Serena	智利:塞雷那	-29.5	-71.26	46	5.6	mb	5										
1984	2	7	21	33	23					* Engdahl, USGS	Solomon Islands:Guadalcanal	所罗门群岛:瓜达康纳尔岛	-9.957	160.522	17	7.6	Mw	6						2				
1984	2	11	8	2	52	4			3	* NOAA	Greece:Amfissa	希腊:阿姆菲萨	38.396	22.094	29	5.4	Ms							1				
1984	2	15	10	49	48					USGS	Uzbekistan:Samarqand	乌兹别克斯坦:撒马尔罕	39.93	67.63	22	5.2	mb	6										
1984	2	16	17	18	43					* Engdahl	Afghan:Fayzabad	阿富汗:法扎巴德	36.448	70.849	208.5	6.4	Mw	6	4	1	13	1	5.0	3				
1984	2	17	1	37	26					China,Dis	China:Qinghai,Qilian,SE.	中国:青海祁连东南	37.74	100.74	28	5.3	Ms	6			1	1	0.03	1				
1984	2	17	23	26	52					USGS	Uzbekistan:Namangan	乌兹别克斯坦:纳曼干	40.81	71.05	18	5.4	mb	6										
1984	2	23	15	22	49					USGS	Uzbekistan:Samarqand	乌兹别克斯坦:撒马尔罕	39.97	67.68	33	5.2	mb	6										
1984	3	6	2	17	22					ISC, Engdahl, USGS	Japan:South Honshu Ridge	日本:本州南部海岭	29.374	138.872	459.8	7.4	Mw	6										
1984	3	11	11	55	32					USGS	Slovenia:Novo Mesto	斯洛文尼亚:新梅斯托	45.87	15.48	10	4.6	ML	6										
1984	3	16	17	10	47					USGS,ISC	Japan:Hokkaido	日本:北海道	42.93	145.48	49	5.5	mb	5										
1984	3	19	20	28	39					* Engdahl, USGS	Uzbekistan:Gazli	乌兹别克斯坦:加兹利	40.356	63.344	9	7	Mw	9			100	2	5.0	3				
1984	3	20	6	28	40					USGS,ISC	Uzbekistan:Gazli	乌兹别克斯坦:加兹利	40.25	63.23	12	5.5	mb	6										
1984	3	24	9	44	4	4	0.2	-2.3	-2	* Engdahl, NOAA	Kuril Islands	千岛群岛	44.171	148.164	37.4	7.2	Mw											
1984	3	27	20	6	34					* Engdahl, USGS	Papua New Guinea:Madang	巴布亚新几内亚:马当	-4.593	145.85	20.6	6.5	Mw	8			11	1		2		3		
1984	4	15	10	56	53					USGS	Austria:Ternitz	奥地利:泰尔尼茨	47.67	15.85	25	4.5	ML	7										
1984	4	22	17	39	23					USGS	Italy:Livorno	意大利:来航	43.62	10.19	15	4.7	ML	6										
1984	4	24	21	15	21					* ISC,Engdahl	US:California,Morgan Hill	美国:加利福尼亚州莫干山	37.304	-121.708	8.8	6.2	M	8			27	1	8.0	3				
1984	4	29	5	3	0					* Italy,USGS	Italy:Perugia - Assissi - Gubbio	意大利:佩鲁贾 - 阿西西 - 古比欧	43.256	12.53	12	6.1	ML	8	3	1	200	3	25.0	4				

时间						海啸				资料来源	震中				深度	震级	标度	烈度	死亡人数		受伤人数		经济损失		房屋毁坏		房屋受损	
年	月	日	时	分	秒	源	浪高	级 I	级 S		地名(英文)	地名(中文)	纬度(°)	经度(°)					数量/人	级别	数量/人	级别	数量/$ Mill	级别	数量/间	级别	数量/间	级别
Date						Tsunami				Information	Earthquake Epicenter				Depth	Mag	Scale	MMI	Deaths		Injuries		Damage		Houses Destroyed		Houses Damaged	
Year	Mo	Dy	Hr	Mn	Sec	Sr	Wh	mI	mS		Name(English)	Name(Chinese)	Latitude	Longitude					Num	Dd	Num	Dd	$ Mill	De	Num	Dh	Num	Dh
1984	5	6	19	54	49					USGS,ISC	Andreanof Islands, Aleutian Is.	阿留申群岛,安德烈亚诺夫群岛	51.69	-176.77	58	5.6	mb	5										
1984	5	7	17	49	45					* Italy, Engdahl, USGS	Italy:Abruzzo	意大利:阿布鲁佐	41.737	13.891	21.5	6	ML	8	3	1	100	2	5.0	3				
1984	5	11	10	41	50					* USGS	Italy:Abruzzo	意大利:阿布鲁佐	41.831	13.961	14	5.4	ML	8	3	1	63	2		2				
1984	5	13	12	45	56					* USGS	Bosnia and Herzegovina:Mostar	波斯尼亚和黑塞哥维那:莫斯塔尔	42.967	17.734	30	5.1	mb	7	1	1				2				
1984	5	21	15	37	55					China, Engdahl, Dis	China:South Yellow Sea	中国:南黄海	32.604	121.603	44	6.4	Ms	6									900	3
1984	5	21	15	39	4					China, Engdahl, Dis	China:South Yellow Sea	中国:南黄海	32.697	121.517	45.1	6.2	Ms	6										
1984	5	23	7	50	17					China	China:Inner Mongolia, Alxa Youqi	中国:内蒙古阿拉善右旗	39.86	102.71	15	4.9	Ms	6										
1984	5	30	0	39	45					USGS,ISC	Japan:Himeji	日本:兵库姬路	34.89	134.6	26	5.6	mb	6										
1984	5	30	1	2	55					USGS	Japan:Himeji	日本:兵库姬路	34.93	134.63	10	4.7	mb	6										
1984	5	30	7	49	45					ISC, Engdahl, USGS	Papua New Guinea:East New Britain	巴布亚新几内亚:东新不列颠	-4.838	151.596	171.7	7.1	Mw	6										
1984	6	13	2	29	25	4	0.5	0.6		* NOAA	Japan:South Honshu Ridge	日本:本州南部海岭	31.448	140.036	41	5.5	Ms											
1984	6	24	11	17	16					* Engdahl	Dominica:Santo Domingo	多米尼加:多米尼加	17.982	-69.369	44.1	6.7	Mw	5	5	1				1				
1984	6	24	14	30	53					USGS	Spain:Mdlaga	西班牙:马拉加	37.12	-3.7	16	4.8	mb	6										
1984	6	29	17	45	26					USGS	Japan:Sakai	日本:茨城境町	36.12	139.84	73	5.1	mb	6										
1984	7	1	7	47	13					USGS	Italy:Abruzzo	意大利:阿布鲁佐	41.83	13.94	10	4.5	ML	6										
1984	7	9	18	57	10					USGS	Greece:Edhessa	希腊:埃泽萨	40.68	21.83	10	5.2	ML	7										
1984	7	19	6	56	10					USGS	England:Gwynedd	英国:圭内斯	52.88	-4.2	12	5.4	ML	6										
1984	7	19	23	25	15					ISC, Engdahl, USGS	Ryukyu Islands	琉球群岛	28.16	129.46	49.7	5.9	Mw	8										
1984	8	6	19	6	40	4	0.2	-2.3		* ISC, Engdahl, NOAA	Japan:Miyazzaki,Near Coast	日本:宫崎近海	32.447	131.865	45.5	6.9	Mw	6	20	1	9	1		2				
1984	8	12	16	51	20					USGS,ISC	Philippines:Laoag	菲律宾:佬沃	18.39	120.81	13	5.5	mb	5										
1984	8	14	1	2	8					USGS	Gulf of Alaska	阿拉斯加湾	61.86	-149.1	19	5.7	ML	6										
1984	8	14	11	45	48					USGS	Uzbekistan:Gazli	乌兹别克斯坦:加兹利	40.28	63.22	11	5.3	mb	7										
1984	8	14	18	30	13					USGS,ISC	Japan:Kagoshima	日本:鹿岛	31.58	130.07	19	5.6	mb	6										
1984	8	22	9	46	30					USGS	US:Idaho,Challis	美国:爱达荷州查利斯	44.47	-114.01	10	5.8	ML	5										
1984	8	27	6	41	26					*	Indonesia:Northern Sumatra	印度尼西亚:苏门答腊北部	1.761	99.075	33	5.2	Ms				123	3	1	2	415	3		
1984	8	28	19	4	31					USGS,Engdahl	Ryukyu Islands	琉球群岛	27.507	128.547	47.6	5.8	Mw	6										
1984	9	2	15	14	2					USGS	Bosnia:Banja Luka	波斯尼亚:巴尼亚卢卡	44.9	17.34	10	4.5	ML	6										
1984	9	7	0	44	42					* ISC,USGS	Serbia:Krusevac	塞尔维亚:克鲁舍瓦茨	43.314	20.957	13	5.3	ML	8			2	1		2				
1984	9	13	10	9	1					USGS	Philippines:Mindoro Island	菲律宾:民都洛岛	13.35	121.26	13	4.9	mb	6										

时间						海啸				资料来源	震中				深度	震级	标度	烈度	死亡人数		受伤人数		经济损失		房屋毁坏		房屋受损	
年	月	日	时	分	秒	源	浪高	级 I	级 S		地名(英文)	地名(中文)	纬度(°)	经度(°)					数量/人	级别	数量/人	级别	数量/ $ Mill	级别	数量/间	级别	数量/间	级别
Date						Tsunami				Information	Earthquake Epicenter				Depth	Mag	Scale	MMI	Deaths		Injuries		Damage		Houses Destroyed		Houses Damaged	
Year	Mo	Dy	Hr	Mn	Sec	Sr	Wh	mI	mS		Name(English)	Name(Chinese)	Latitude	Longitude					Num	Dd	Num	Dd	$ Mill	De	Num	Dh	Num	Dh
1984	9	13	23	48	50					* ISC, Engdahl	Japan: Mt Ontake	日本:御岳山	35.801	137.466	1.1	6.2	Mw	6	29	1			43.0	4				
1984	9	14	22	14	32					USGS, ISC	Japan: Gero	日本:岐阜下吕	35.77	137.42	10	5.6	mb	5										
1984	9	18	13	26	2					*	Turkey: Erzurum, Olur	土耳其:埃尔佐鲁姆,奥卢尔	40.885	42.219	10	6.4	Ms	8	3	1	38	1		2	75000	5		
1984	9	18	17	2	45	4	0.1	-3.3		* ISC, Engdahl, NOAA, USGS	Japan Trench	日本海沟	34.016	141.521	43.3	6.8	Mw	6										
1984	9	20	16	56	24					USGS, ISC	Japan Trench	日本海沟	34.01	141.59	29	5.8	Ms	5										
1984	9	20	21	53	55					USGS, ISC	Japan Trench	日本海沟	33.97	141.55	32	5.8	Ms	5										
1984	9	27	11	33	53					USGS	Uzbekistan: Gazli	乌兹别克斯坦:加兹利	40.29	63.27	33	5	mb	6										
1984	10	9	4	30	42					* ISC	Greece: Messina	希腊:墨西拿	37.013	21.757	27	5.5	Mw	7			1	1		2		3		
1984	10	18	9	46	25					*	Turkey: Senkaya	土耳其:申卡亚	40.545	42.403	60	5.3	mb		3	1	35	1		3	75000	5		
1984	10	18	15	30	23					* USGS	US: Wyoming, Douglas	美国:怀俄明州道格拉斯	42.375	-105.72	33	5.5	ML	6						1				
1984	10	19	12	58	3					USGS	Japan: Nagasaki	日本:长崎	32.72	130.13	25	5.1	mb	6										
1984	10	23	22	28	60					USGS, ISC	Guam	关岛(西太平洋)	13.71	144.92	122	5.8	mb	6										
1984	10	25	10	36	2					USGS	US: California, Los Alamos	美国:加利福尼亚州洛斯阿拉莫斯	34.75	-120.15	6	4.6	ML	6										
1984	10	26	20	22	20					* Engdahl, USGS	Tajikistan: Dzhirgatal, Garm	塔吉克斯坦:吉尔加塔尔,加尔姆	39.176	71.358	9	6.1	Mw	7						2		2		
1984	11	3	9	30	9					USGS	US: Wyoming, Lander	美国:怀俄明州兰德	42.49	-108.85	5	4.9	ML	6										
1984	11	5	6	6	18					USGS	Afghan: Badakhshan, Takhar	阿富汗:巴达赫尚,塔哈尔	37.4	70.22	33	5.2	mb	6										
1984	11	23	9	45	23					China, Dis	China: Ningxia, Lingwu	中国:宁夏灵武	38.05	106.3	14	5.3	Ms	7										
1984	11	26	7	25	43					USGS, ISC	Papua New Guinea: Bougainville Island	巴布亚新几内亚:布干维尔岛	-6.28	154.78	67	5.6	mb	5										
1984	11	26	16	21	47					USGS, ISC	US: California, Mammoth Lakes, S.	美国:加利福尼亚州马姆莫斯湖南部	37.47	-118.7	10	5.6	ML	5										
1984	12	11	3	56	43					USGS	Japan: Utsunomiya	日本:宇都宫市	36.58	139.47	34	4.7	mb	6										
1984	12	11	23	22	23					Engdahl, USGS	Chile: Calama	智利:卡拉马	-22.589	-68.671	115.4	6.5	Mw	5										
1984	12	18	19	35	27					USGS, ISC	Japan: Fukushima, Near Coast	日本:福岛近海	37.16	141.48	43	5.5	mb	5										
1984	12	28	10	37	53	4	0.2	-2.3		* Engdahl, NOAA	Russia: Kamchatka, Near East Coast	俄罗斯:堪察加东部近海	56.21	163.391	16.7	6.7	Mw											
1984	12	30	23	33	39					* Engdahl	India: Assam, Cachar District	印度:阿萨姆邦,察查地区	24.678	92.866	15	6	Mw		20	1	100	2		3				
1985	1	5	13	6	33					USGS	Serbia: Vranje	塞尔维亚:弗拉涅	42.56	22.12	27	4.5	ML	7										
1985	1	5	15	45	38					USGS, Engdahl	Japan: Koya	日本:和歌山高野	34.198	135.544	69.5	5.7	Mw	6										
1985	1	16	7	45	35					China	China: Qinghai, Zaduo	中国:青海杂多	32.94	95.26	15	5.2	Ms	7										
1985	1	26	3	7	1					* Engdahl	Argentina: Mendoza, La Ligua	阿根廷:门多萨,拉里瓜	-33.11	-68.592	18.6	6	Mw	7	6	1	238	3	5.0	3	12000	5		

时间 年 Date Year	月 Mo	日 Dy	时 Hr	分 Mn	秒 Sec	海啸 Tsunami 源 Sr	浪高 Wh	级I mI	级S mS	资料来源 Information	震中 Earthquake Epicenter 地名(英文) Name(English)	地名(中文) Name(Chinese)	纬度(°) Latitude	经度(°) Longitude	深度 Depth	震级 Mag	标度 Scale	烈度 MMI	死亡人数 Deaths 数量/人 Num	级别 Dd	受伤人数 Injuries 数量/人 Num	级别 Dd	经济损失 Damage 数量/$ Mill $ Mill	级别 De	房屋毁坏 Houses Destroyed 数量/间 Num	级别 Dh	房屋受损 Houses Damaged 数量/间 Num	级别 Dh
1985	2	2	20	52	34					*	Iran:Fars,Firuzabad	伊朗:法尔斯,菲鲁扎巴德	28.399	52.997	37	5.3	Ms		1	1	80	2		2	1500	4		
1985	2	8	6	58	17					USGS	US:California,Bakersfield	美国:加利福尼亚州贝克斯菲尔德	35.45	-118.9	11	4.7	ML	6										
1985	2	11	0	13	54					USGS	Mexico:Oaxaca	墨西哥:瓦哈卡	16.64	-94.97	90	5.2	mb	6										
1985	2	21	18	53	11					USGS	Chile:Near Coast of C.	智利:中部近海	-33.21	-71.77	55	5.2	Ms	6										
1985	2	23	4	35	52					USGS	Chile:San Antonio, Valparaiso	智利:圣安东尼奥,瓦尔帕莱索	-33.15	-71.88	64	5	mb	6										
1985	2	28	20	53	49					ISC, Engdahl, USGS	Ryukyu Islands	琉球群岛	27.52	128.467	55.4	6	Mw	6										
1985	3	3	22	47	10	4	3.5	1.6		* Chile, Engdahl, NOAA	Chile:San Antonio, Valparaiso	智利:圣安东尼奥,瓦尔帕莱索	-33.132	-71.708	40	8	Mw	8	200	3	2575	4	1500	5		3		
1985	3	16	14	54	3	4	0.1	-3.3		* Engdahl, NOAA, USGS	Saint Kitts and Nevis: Charlestown	圣基茨和尼维斯:查尔斯敦	16.982	-62.446	15.8	6.4	Mw	6			6	1		2				
1985	3	17	10	41	38					* ISC,Engdahl	Chile: Valparaiso, Vina Del Mar	智利:瓦尔帕莱索,维尼亚德尔马	-32.708	-71.61	22	6.6	Mw	7	1	1				2				
1985	3	18	19	49	46					* Engdahl	Philippines: Pagadian, Zamboanga	菲律宾:帕加迪安,三宝颜	7.775	123.512	27.1	6.5	Mw	5	2	1	25	1		2	30	1		
1985	3	19	4	1	6					ISC, Engdahl, USGS	Chile:Valparaiso	智利:瓦尔帕莱索	-33.272	-71.703	20	6.7	Mw	6										
1985	3	20	5	53	50					USGS	Japan:Satte	日本:埼玉幸手	36.07	139.79	65	4.9	mb	6										
1985	3	27	12	48	13					ISC, Engdahl, USGS	Kuril Islands	千岛群岛	44.402	146.649	147	6.1	Mw	6										
1985	3	28	16	7	8					ISC, Engdahl, USGS	Japan:Akita	日本:秋田	40.327	140.335	164.6	6.3	Mw	6										
1985	3	29	11	15	6					China,Dis	China:Sichuan,Zigong	中国:四川自贡	29.41	105	7	4.8	Ms	7			4	1	41.2	4				
1985	4	1	9	13	14					USGS	US: Montana, Seeley Lake, NE.	美国:蒙大纳州锡利莱克东北	47.28	-113.23	10	4.8	mb	6										
1985	4	9	1	57	1					* Chile, Engdahl, USGS	Chile:Santiago - Valparaiso	智利:圣地亚哥 - 瓦尔帕莱索	-34.143	-71.463	38	7.1	Mw	6	2	1		2		2				
1985	4	10	16	26	21					ISC, Engdahl, USGS	Japan:South Honshu Ridge	日本:本州南部海岭	29.978	138.88	414.7	6.3	Mw	6										
1985	4	13	1	5	60	2	2			* Engdahl, NOAA	Indonesia:Denpasar, Bali	印度尼西亚:登巴萨,巴厘岛	-9.205	114.195	82.4	5.9	Mw							2		2		
1985	4	18	5	52	55					* China, Engdahl, Dis	China:Yunnan,Luquan,NE.	中国:云南禄劝东北	25.914	102.863	3.9	6.2	Ms	8	22	1	300	3	8.2	3	20000	5		
1985	4	23	15	16	22					USGS	El Salvador:Usulutan	萨尔瓦多:乌苏卢坦	13.47	-88.61	37	4.8	mb	6										
1985	4	24	1	7	13					* ISC, Bautista, Engdahl	Philippines:Baguio	菲律宾:碧瑶	16.542	120.813	6	6.1	Mw	7	6	1	11	1		2				
1985	4	27	4	14	27					USGS	Uzbekistan:Namangan	乌兹别克斯坦:纳曼干	40.72	71.18	33	5	mb	6										

时间 年 Date Year	月 Mo	日 Dy	时 Hr	分 Mn	秒 Sec	海啸 Tsunami 源 Sr	浪高 Wh	级 I mI	级 S mS	资料来源 Information	震中 Earthquake Epicenter 地名(英文) Name(English)	地名(中文) Name(Chinese)	纬度(°) Latitude	经度(°) Longitude	深度 Depth	震级 Mag	标度 Scale	烈度 MMI	死亡人数 Deaths 数量/人 Num	级别 Dd	受伤人数 Injuries 数量/人 Num	级别 Dd	经济损失 Damage 数量/$ Mill $ Mill	级别 De	房屋毁坏 Houses Destroyed 数量/间 Num	级别 Dh	房屋受损 Houses Damaged 数量/间 Num	级别 Dh
1985	4	27	4	49	51					USGS	Uzbekistan:Namangan	乌兹别克斯坦:纳曼干	40. 72	71. 15	33	5. 1	mb	6										
1985	4	29	2	19	60					USGS,Engdahl	Japan:Hokkaido	日本:北海道	41. 513	142. 008	68. 2	5. 8	Mw	6										
1985	4	30	18	14	13					*	Greece:Magnisia	希腊:马格尼西亚	39. 266	22. 81	27	5. 5	Ms	6						1	7	1		
1985	5	10	15	35	54					* Engdahl, USGS	Papua New Guinea:West New Britain	巴布亚新几内亚:西新不列颠	-5. 601	151. 056	47. 4	7. 2	Mw	8	1	1			1	2				
1985	5	10	23	45	30					USGS	Serbia:Kraljevo	塞尔维亚:克拉列沃	43. 31	20. 93	18	5	ML	8										
1985	5	11	10	40	40					USGS,ISC	Japan:Fukushima,Near Coast	日本:福岛近海	37. 09	141. 43	55	5. 5	mb	5										
1985	5	13	10	41	0					ISC,USGS	Japan:Ehime	日本:爱媛	32. 99	132. 59	39	6. 0	Mw	6										
1985	5	19	18	9	17					ISC, Engdahl, USGS	Chile:Coquimbo	智利:科金博	-30. 257	-71. 339	40. 5	6. 2	Mw	6										
1985	5	26	18	5	9					USGS	Spain:Cordoba	西班牙:科尔多瓦	37. 85	-4. 59	13	4. 5	Ms	6										
1985	6	2	16	26	55					ISC, Engdahl, USGS	Chile:Curanilahue	智利:库拉尼拉韦	-37. 873	-73. 912	1. 8	5. 9	Mw	5										
1985	6	5	23	4	58					ISC, Engdahl, USGS	Papua New Guinea:New Ireland	巴布亚新几内亚:新爱尔兰	-4. 66	153. 231	72. 8	6. 3	Mw	6										
1985	6	10	15	37	4					ISC, Engdahl, USGS	Argentina:Catamarca	阿根廷:卡塔马卡	-27. 964	-66. 869	169. 2	6. 4	Mw	5										
1985	6	21	2	33	0					China,Dis	China:Inner Mongolia,Sonid Youqi	中国:内蒙古苏尼特右旗	42. 57	112. 51		5. 3	Ms	6										
1985	6	24	0	42	29					China	China:Gansu,Tanchang	中国:甘肃宕昌	34. 02	104. 29	14	4. 9	Ms	5										
1985	7	1	7	49	29					USGS,ISC	Philippines:Mindanao Island	菲律宾:棉兰老岛	8. 27	126. 52	77	5. 5	mb	5										
1985	7	3	4	36	55	2	1. 3	0. 4		* Engdahl, NOAA	Papua New Guinea:New Ireland	巴布亚新几内亚:新爱尔兰	-4. 452	152. 879	46. 7	7. 2	Mw	7					1	2				
1985	7	17	8	9	31					Engdahl,USGS	Papua New Guinea:New Ireland	巴布亚新几内亚:新爱尔兰	-4. 238	152. 932	31. 3	6. 0	Mw	6										
1985	7	29	7	54	46					* ISC,Engdahl	Afghan:Badakhshan	阿富汗:巴达赫尚	36. 164	70. 864	99. 8	7. 4	Mw	8	5	1	38	1	2	2				
1985	8	1	12	13	43					China	China:Xizang (Tibet), Miling,E.	中国:西藏米林东	29. 17	95. 16	25	5. 7	Ms	6										
1985	8	1	14	35	3					USGS	Romania:Vrancea	罗马尼亚:弗朗恰	45. 71	26. 51	107	5. 3	mb	6										
1985	8	4	12	1	58					Engdahl,USGS	US:California,Huron	美国:加利福尼亚州休伦	36. 137	-120. 104	10	6. 1	Mw	6										
1985	8	10	16	36	8					USGS,ISC	Papua New Guinea:New Ireland	巴布亚新几内亚:新爱尔兰	-4. 25	152. 88	32	5. 7	mb	5										
1985	8	12	3	49	20					ISC, Engdahl, USGS	Japan:Fukushima,Near Coast	日本:福岛近海	37. 796	141. 726	51. 4	6. 5	Mw	6										
1985	8	15	4	28	47					USGS	Hungary:Budapest	匈牙利:布达佩斯	47. 04	18. 05	10	4. 9	ML	7										
1985	8	15	18	58	3					USGS	Italy:Genova	意大利:热那亚	44. 58	9. 74	10	4. 7	ML	7										
1985	8	21	11	26	30					* ISC,Engdahl	Peru:Chimbote,Near Coast	秘鲁:钦博特近海	-9. 18	-78. 853	55. 6	6. 4	Mw	6			100	2		2	60	2		

年 Year	月 Mo	日 Dy	时 Hr	分 Mn	秒 Sec	源 Sr	浪高 Wh	级 I mI	级 S mS	资料来源 Information	地名(英文) Name(English)	地名(中文) Name(Chinese)	纬度(°) Latitude	经度(°) Longitude	深度 Depth	震级 Mag	标度 Scale	烈度 MMI	死亡人数 Deaths 数量/人 Num	级别 Dd	受伤人数 Injuries 数量/人 Num	级别 Dd	经济损失 Damage 数量/$ Mill	级别 De	房屋毁坏 Houses Destroyed 数量/间 Num	级别 Dh	房屋受损 Houses Damaged 数量/间 Num	级别 Dh
1985	8	23	12	41	60					* China, Engdahl, Dis	China: Xinjiang, Ulugqat	中国:新疆乌恰	39.445	75.248	20	7.1	Ms	9	64	2	200	3	41.2	4	10000	5		
1985	9	1	19	7	41					China, Dis	China: Yunnan, Jianshui	中国:云南建水	23.72	102.75	6	5.4	Ms	7			3	1					1015	4
1985	9	15	2	42	55					* Engdahl	Indonesia: Papua	印度尼西亚:巴布亚	-4.065	136.094	4.5	6.3	Mw		10	1	7	1		2				
1985	9	15	7	57	55					ISC, Engdahl, USGS	Mexico: Oaxaca	墨西哥:瓦哈卡	17.94	-97.185	68.1	6	Mw	6										
1985	9	19	13	17	49	4	3	1.6		* Engdahl, NOAA	Mexico: Michoacan, Mexico City	墨西哥:米却肯,墨西哥城	18.437	-102.358	15	8	M	9	9500	4	30000	5	4000	5		4		
1985	9	21	1	37	14	4	1.2	0.3		* Engdahl, NOAA	Mexico: Guerrero, Zihuatanejo	墨西哥:格雷罗州锡瓦塔塔内霍	17.827	-101.622	18.4	7.6	Mw	6		2				2				
1985	9	26	8	33	27					USGS	Chile: San Antonio	智利:圣安东尼奥	-33.62	-71.6	47	5.7	Ms	6										
1985	9	27	3	39	10					* Engdahl, USGS	Solomon Islands: Honiara	所罗门群岛:霍尼亚拉	-9.794	159.914	33.3	6.6	Mw	7						1		3		
1985	9	28	14	50	15					* USGS	Macedonia(Fyrom): Stip	马其顿:斯提普	41.581	22.254	7	5.3	ML	7			16	1		2	500	3		
1985	10	4	8	41	38					USGS, ISC, Engdahl	Japan: South Honshu Ridge	日本:本州南部海岭	27.56	139.96	478	6.1	Mw	5										
1985	10	4	12	25	52					ISC, Engdahl, USGS	Japan: Abiko	日本:千叶我孙子	35.862	140.085	71.6	5.9	mb	8										
1985	10	5	15	24	3					ISC, Engdahl, USGS	Canada: NW. Territories	加拿大:西北地区	62.171	-124.279	7	6.6	Mw	6										
1985	10	9	9	33	34					ISC, Engdahl, USGS	Aleutian Islands	阿留申群岛	54.731	-159.638	32.2	6.6	Mw	6										
1985	10	11	3	39	11					*	Guatemala: San Miguel	危地马拉:圣米格尔	15.299	-90.863	5	4.5	mb	7				3		2	500	3		3
1985	10	13	15	59	53					* Engdahl, USGS	Tajikistan: Khudzhand	塔吉克斯坦:苦盏	40.338	69.814	16.2	5.8	Mw	9	29	1	80	2	200	5		3		
1985	10	18	3	22	24					USGS	Japan: Wajima	日本:石川轮岛	37.62	136.9	35	5.9	mb	6										
1985	10	27	19	35	2					* ISC, Engdahl	Algeria: Annaba - Setif	阿尔及利亚:安纳巴-塞提夫	36.386	6.847	30.6	5.8	Mw		6	1				1				
1985	11	7	8	26	21					* Iran	Turkey: Erzurum, Kars	土耳其:埃尔佐鲁姆,卡尔斯	40.36	42.29	31	5.3	Ms				14	1		2	113	3		
1985	11	17	9	40	23					* Engdahl	Indonesia: Irian Jaya Barat	印度尼西亚:西巴布亚	-1.67	134.937	11.4	7.1	Mw	8						1				
1985	11	19	14	3	35					USGS, ISC	Ryukyu Islands	琉球群岛	28.67	128.88	134	5.5	mb	5										
1985	11	21	21	57	15					USGS, ISC	Adriatic Sea	亚得里亚海	41.7	19.39	24	5.7	mb	6										
1985	11	24	12	53	46					USGS	Macedonia: Budva	蒙特尼哥罗(黑山):布德瓦	42.3	18.75	6	4.5	Md	6										
1985	11	25	16	43	56					USGS	Macedonia: Budva	蒙特尼哥罗(黑山):布德瓦	42.3	18.75	17	4.9	Md	6										
1985	11	30	14	38	26					China, Dis	China: Hebei, Qiuxian	中国:河北任县	37.2	114.8	15	5.3	Ms	5										
1985	12	2	7	14	37					USGS	Japan: Off SW. Coast of Hokkaido	日本:北海道西南沿海	41.16	139.81	21	5.6	Ms	6										
1985	12	11	15	28	48					USGS	Chile: Near Coast of C.	智利:中部近海	-32.92	-71.73	81	4.8	mb	6										
1985	12	16	2	44	39					* Engdahl	Nicaragua: Rivas, Masaya	尼加拉瓜:里瓦斯,马萨亚	11.716	-85.88	35.9	6.1	Mw	6			6	1		1				

年 Year	月 Mo	日 Dy	时 Hr	分 Mn	秒 Sec	源 Sr	浪高 Wh	级 I mI	级 S mS	资料来源 Information	地名(英文) Name(English)	地名(中文) Name(Chinese)	纬度(°) Latitude	经度(°) Longitude	深度 Depth	震级 Mag	标度 Scale	烈度 MMI	死亡人数 Deaths 数量/人 Num	死亡人数 Deaths 级别 Dd	受伤人数 Injuries 数量/人 Num	受伤人数 Injuries 级别 Dd	经济损失 Damage 数量/$ Mill	经济损失 Damage 级别 De	房屋毁坏 Houses Destroyed 数量/间 Num	房屋毁坏 Houses Destroyed 级别 Dh	房屋受损 Houses Damaged 数量/间 Num	房屋受损 Houses Damaged 级别 Dh
1985	12	18	22	36	26					USGS	Colombia:Falan	哥伦比亚:托利马的法兰	5. 16	-74. 85	11	5	mb	6										
1985	12	21	10	4	11					USGS	Czech:Praha	捷克:布拉格	50. 18	12. 44	24	4. 6	ML	6										
1985	12	21	10	16	17					USGS	Czech:Praha	捷克:布拉格	50. 33	12. 32	10	5. 1	ML	7										
1985	12	23	5	16	5					ISC, Engdahl, USGS	Canada:NW. Territories	加拿大:西北地区	62. 164	-124. 311	6	6. 8	M	6										
1986	1	6	0	9	11					USGS	Azerbaijan:Baki	阿塞拜疆:巴库	40. 54	49. 3	33	4. 9	mb	6										
1986	1	11	19	42	22					*	Peru:Huarmey, Casma	秘鲁:瓦尔梅,卡斯马	-9. 505	-77. 512	39	5. 3	mb	5	1	1				2	80	2		
1986	1	20	23	38	28					USGS	Czech:Praha	捷克:布拉格	50. 18	12. 31	10	5	ML	6										
1986	1	26	7	48	24					USGS, ISC	Chile:Caldera, Near Coast	智利:卡尔德拉近海	-27. 07	-70. 91	31	5. 7	mb	5										
1986	1	26	19	20	51					USGS	US:California, Tres Pinos	美国:加利福尼亚州特雷斯皮诺斯	36. 81	-121. 28	7	5. 5	ML	6										
1986	1	27	16	35	53					USGS, ISC	Azerbaijan:Lenkeran	阿塞拜疆:连科兰	38. 88	48. 62	71	5. 5	mb	7										
1986	1	27	23	13	52					China	China:Guangdong, Yangjiang	中国:广东阳江	21. 9	111. 75	7	4. 8	Ms	6										
1986	1	29	11	56	35					*	Indonesia:Southern Sumatra	印度尼西亚:苏门答腊南部	-3. 904	103. 461	33	5	mb				2	1		3				
1986	1	31	16	46	43					USGS	US:Ohio, Painesville	美国:俄亥俄州佩恩斯维尔	41. 65	-81. 16	10	5	mb	6										
1986	2	3	15	12	47					*	Guatemala: Ixchiguan, San Marcos Province	危地马拉:伊思奇古安,圣马科斯	15. 075	-92. 072	16	4. 7	mb							2	500	3		
1986	2	5	17	53	33					USGS	Norway:Gurskoya	挪威:居什克岛	62. 78	4. 81	29	4. 7	ML	6										
1986	2	5	21	59	32					China	China: Xizang (Tibet), Markam	中国:西藏芒康附近	29. 82	98. 37	9	5	Ms	6										
1986	2	9	12	42	52					China, Dis	China:Inner Mongolia, Dedu, NE.	中国:内蒙古德都东北	48. 67	126. 61	12	5	Ms	7										
1986	2	12	2	59	34					ISC, Engdahl, USGS	Japan:Ibaraki, Near Coast	日本:茨城近海	36. 429	140. 975	45. 4	6. 2	Mw	6										
1986	2	18	14	34	3					USGS	Greece:Edhessa	希腊:埃泽萨	40. 75	22. 04	21	4. 5	ML	6										
1986	2	28	17	7	25					China, Dis	China:Inner Mongolia, Dedu, NE.	中国:内蒙古德都东北	48. 64	126. 68	10	5. 3	Ms	7										
1986	3	2	7	9	29					ISC, Engdahl, USGS	Japan:Miyagi, Near Coast	日本:宫城近海	38. 506	142. 209	40. 5	5. 8	Mw	6										
1986	3	3	1	24	5					USGS	Adriatic Sea	亚得里亚海	41. 97	20. 29	18	5	ML	6										
1986	3	3	4	25	53					USGS	Adriatic Sea	亚得里亚海	41. 95	20. 29	16	4. 7	ML	6										
1986	3	6	0	5	38					ISC, Engdahl, USGS	Caspian Sea	里海	40. 342	51. 6	22. 4	6. 5	Mw	6										
1986	3	13	8	41	17					China, Dis	China:Yunnan, Heqing, S.	中国:云南鹤庆南	26. 19	100. 19	10	5. 4	Ms	6			7	1					3310	4
1986	3	24	2	1	33					ISC, Engdahl, USGS	Ryukyu Islands	琉球群岛	28. 592	129. 987	44. 9	6. 3	Mw	6										

年 Year	月 Mo	日 Dy	时 Hr	分 Mn	秒 Sec	源 Sr	浪高 Wh	级 I mI	级 S mS	资料来源 Information	地名(英文) Name(English)	地名(中文) Name(Chinese)	纬度(°) Latitude	经度(°) Longitude	深度 Depth	震级 Mag	标度 Scale	烈度 MMI	死亡人数 Deaths 数量/人 Num	死亡人数 Deaths 级别 Dd	受伤人数 Injuries 数量/人 Num	受伤人数 Injuries 级别 Dd	经济损失 Damage 数量/$ Mill $ Mill	经济损失 Damage 级别 De	房屋毁坏 Houses Destroyed 数量/间 Num	房屋毁坏 Houses Destroyed 级别 Dh	房屋受损 Houses Damaged 数量/间 Num	房屋受损 Houses Damaged 级别 Dh
1986	3	25	23	49	34					USGS	Uzbekistan:Gazli	乌兹别克斯坦:加兹利	40.34	63.66	33	5.2	mb	6										
1986	3	30	8	53	54					ISC, Engdahl, USGS	Australia:S. Australia,N.	澳大利亚:南澳北部	-26.288	132.701	5	5.7	Mw	6										
1986	3	31	11	55	40					USGS	US:California,San Jose	美国:加利福尼亚州圣何塞	37.48	-121.69	8	5.7	ML	6										
1986	4	4	11	23	22					China	China:Qinghai,Yushu,NW.	中国:青海玉树西北	33.11	95.99	10	5.1	Ms	5										
1986	4	5	20	14	29					* GSHAP	Peru:Cuzco	秘鲁:库斯科	-13.41	-71.785	51	6.1	Mw	6	16	1	170	3	22.0	3	2000	4		
1986	4	23	15	17	6					China,Dis	China:Xinjiang,Fuyun,N.	中国:新疆富蕴北	47.51	89.6	17	5.4	Ms	6										
1986	4	24	0	22	15					China,Dis	China:Xinjiang,Fuyun,N.	中国:新疆富蕴北	47.51	89.7	17	5.4	Ms	6										
1986	4	26	7	35	16					*	India: Kashmir, Dharmsala, Lahore	印度:克什米尔,达兰萨拉	32.128	76.374	33	5.5	mb		6	1	30	1		3				3
1986	4	30	14	9	40					USGS,ISC	Chile:Putre	智利:普特雷	-18.04	-69.45	105	5.5	mb	5										
1986	4	30	23	14	44					USGS,ISC	Ryukyu Islands	琉球群岛	28.7	130.05	43	5.5	mb	5										
1986	5	5	3	35	40					* ISC,Engdahl	Turkey:Dogansehir	土耳其:多安谢希尔	37.998	37.785	4.5	6.1	Mw		15	1	100	2	5.0	3	4000	4		
1986	5	7	22	47	12	4	0.9	-0.1		* Engdahl, NOAA	Andreanof Islands, Aleutian Is.	阿留申群岛,安德烈亚诺夫群岛	51.557	-174.813	28.2	8	M	6						1				
1986	5	13	8	44	3					* Engdahl	Georgia:Akhalkalaki,Susuz	格鲁吉亚:阿卡卡拉吉,苏苏兹	41.408	43.714	3.7	5.8	Mw	7	2	1				3	1500	4		
1986	5	15	6	38	36					ISC, Engdahl, USGS	Andreanof Islands, Aleutian Is.	阿留申群岛,安德烈亚诺夫群岛	52.314	-174.676	9.9	6.4	Mw	6										
1986	5	15	14	38	9					*	Pakistan:Barkham	巴基斯坦:巴克姆	29.627	69.363	18	5.2	mb							3				
1986	5	17	16	20	23	1				* Engdahl, NOAA, USGS	Andreanof Islands, Aleutian Is.	阿留申群岛,安德烈亚诺夫群岛	52.255	-174.324	12.8	6.5	Mw	6										
1986	5	20	4	25	48					* China, Engdahl	China:Taiwan,Hualien	中国:台湾花莲	24.146	121.644	15.8	6.8	Ms		1	1	5	1		1				
1986	6	4	15	48	21					USGS	Alaska Peninsula,C.	阿拉斯加半岛中部	65.64	-152.6	10	5.7	ML	5										
1986	6	11	13	48	2					* Engdahl	Venezuela:Pilar	委内瑞拉:比拉尔	10.578	-62.909	14.1	6.3	Mw	7	2	1	45	1	1	2				
1986	6	12	22	19	50					China,Dis	China:Xinjiang,Urumqi	中国:新疆乌鲁木齐	43.78	87.4	21	5	Ms	6										
1986	6	20	17	12	45					China,Engdahl	China: Xizang (Tibet), Coqen,SE.	中国:西藏措勤东南	31.179	86.759	7.5	6.4	Ms	8										
1986	6	24	2	53	13					ISC, Engdahl, USGS	Japan:South Honshu Ridge	日本:本州南部海岭	34.832	140.545	62.5	6.6	Mw	6										
1986	6	24	3	11	35					* Engdahl	Papua New Guinea: East Sepik	巴布亚新几内亚:东塞皮克	-4.443	144.003	123.3	7.2	Mw	7					0.5	1				
1986	7	8	9	20	45					* USGS, Engdahl	US:California,Palm Springs	美国:加利福尼亚州棕泉	33.97	-116.779	11.7	6.1	M	7			29	1	4.5	2				
1986	7	10	0	15	30					China	China:Sichuan,Yanyuan	中国:四川盐源	27.45	101.48	31	4.9	Ms	6										
1986	7	12	7	54	27					*	Iran:Fars	伊朗:法尔斯	29.962	51.582	10	5.7	mb		1	1	4	1		2	300	3		
1986	7	12	8	19	38					USGS	US:Ohio,St Marys	美国:俄亥俄州圣玛丽斯	40.54	-84.37	10	4.5	mb	6										

时间						海啸				资料来源	震中				深度	震级	标度	烈度	死亡人数		受伤人数		经济损失		房屋毁坏		房屋受损	
年	月	日	时	分	秒	源	浪高	级 I	级 S		地名(英文)	地名(中文)	纬度(°)	经度(°)					数量/人	级别	数量/人	级别	数量/$ Mill	级别	数量/间	级别	数量/间	级别
Date						Tsunami				Information	Earthquake Epicenter				Depth	Mag	Scale	MMI	Deaths		Injuries		Damage		Houses Destroyed		Houses Damaged	
Year	Mo	Dy	Hr	Mn	Sec	Sr	Wh	mI	mS		Name(English)	Name(Chinese)	Latitude	Longitude					Num	Dd	Num	Dd	$ Mill	De	Num	Dh	Num	Dh
1986	7	13	13	47	11					* Engdahl	US：California, San Diego, Newport Beach	美国：加利福尼亚州圣地亚哥，新港海滩	33.066	-117.84	15	5.8	Mw	6					0.7	1				
1986	7	18	17	22	38					* GSHAP	Venezuela：Churuguara, Falcon, Lara	委内瑞拉：丘鲁瓜拉，法拉孔，拉腊	10.77	-69.428	7	5.9	mb		1	1				1	30	1		
1986	7	21	14	42	28					* ISC, Engdahl	US：California, Chalfant Valley	美国：加利福尼亚州夏芬谷	37.495	-118.436	9.7	6.4	M	6					1	2				
1986	7	21	14	51	11					USGS, ISC	US：California, Chalfant Valley	美国：加利福尼亚州夏芬谷	37.52	-118.41	10	5.7	ML	5										
1986	7	31	7	22	40					USGS, ISC	US：California, Chalfant Valley	美国：加利福尼亚州夏芬谷	37.46	-118.37	5	5.9	ML	5										
1986	8	3	1	33	20					*	Turkey：Gaziantep	土耳其：加济安泰普	37.2	37.3	12	5	mb							1	73	2		
1986	8	6	19	55	12					China, Dis	China：Sichuan, Litang, SE.	中国：四川理塘东南	29.3	100.85	11	5.5	Ms	7	1		2	1			14	1	47	1
1986	8	12	9	45	50					China, Dis	China：Sichuan, Yanyuan	中国：四川盐源	27.48	101.47	6	5.4	Ms	7	1		43	1	4.14	2	175	3	10000	5
1986	8	15	20	20	36					China, Dis	China：Inner Mongolia, Dedu, NE.	中国：内蒙古德都东北	48.59	126.53	28	5.5	Ms	7										
1986	8	26	9	43	1					China, Engdahl	China：Gansu, Yongchang, SW.	中国：甘肃永昌西南	37.77	101.568	2.4	6.5	Ms	8										
1986	8	29	14	57	3					USGS	Italy：Udine	意大利：乌迪内	46.34	12.47	10	4.8	ML	6										
1986	8	30	21	28	37					* Engdahl	Romania：Bucharest, Kishinev	罗马尼亚：布加勒斯特，基希讷乌	45.525	26.272	135.9	7.2	Mw	8	2	1	558	3	730	5	55000	5		
1986	9	9	0	30	47					China	Mongolia：Ovoot	蒙古：敖包特	45.45	114.73	15	4.9	Ms	6										
1986	9	9	1	30	42					China, Dis	China：Inner Mongolia, Abag	中国：内蒙古阿巴嘎旗	45.2	114.95	22	5.6	Ms	6										
1986	9	13	17	24	35					* Engdahl	Greece：Kalami, Lakonia, Zakinthos	希腊：卡拉米，拉科尼亚，扎金索斯	37.077	22.176	23.3	6	Mw	10	20	1	300	3	5.0	3	1500	4		
1986	9	15	11	41	28					*	Greece：Messinia, Berga	希腊：麦锡尼，贝尔加	36.93	22.175	10	4.9	mb	7			37	1		1				
1986	9	17	12	8	9					USGS, ISC	Tajikistan：Kuhistoni Badakhshon, S.	塔吉克斯坦：勾瑙－巴达科善南部	37.29	71.73	119	5.5	mb	5										
1986	10	1	19	53	41					USGS	Italy：Reggio nell'Emilia	意大利：雷焦艾米利亚	44.34	10.19	28	4.7	ML	6										
1986	10	5	18	53	21					* GSHAP	South Africa：Mount Frere, Durban	南非：弗里尔山，德班	-30.546	28.737	5	5.1	Mw							1				
1986	10	6	23	28	7					China, Dis	China：Yunnan, Luquan	中国：云南禄劝	25.43	102.49	9	5.2	Ms	6			30	1			280	3		
1986	10	10	17	49	26					* Engdahl	El Salvador：San Salvador	萨尔瓦多：圣萨尔瓦多	13.796	-89.155	10.9	5.7	Mw		1100	4	10000	5	1030	5				
1986	10	11	9	0	11					*	Turkey：Aydin, Denizli－Izmir	土耳其：艾登，丹兹利－伊兹密尔	37.931	28.574	5	5.5	Ms				3	1		1	50	1		
1986	10	13	21	17	51					USGS	Japan：Fukushima	日本：福岛	37.1	141.01	65	5.7	mb	6										
1986	10	16	19	54	10					*	Pakistan：Khuzdar	巴基斯坦：胡兹达尔	27.727	66.65	43	5.2	mb							1	150	3	150	3
1986	10	20	6	46	11	4	0.2	-2.2		* Engdahl, NOAA	Kermadec Ridge	克马德克海岭	-28.15	-176.291	26.7	7.7	Mw							1				
1986	10	20	12	15	32					USGS	Italy：Porto San Giorgio, Permo	意大利：圣佐治港，巴马	43.17	13.85	10	4.5	ML	6										

时间 年 Year	月 Mo	日 Dy	时 Hr	分 Mn	秒 Sec	海啸 Tsunami 源 Sr	浪高 Wh	级 I mI	级 S mS	资料来源 Information	震中 Earthquake Epicenter 地名(英文) Name(English)	地名(中文) Name(Chinese)	纬度(°) Latitude	经度(°) Longitude	深度 Depth	震级 Mag	标度 Scale	烈度 MMI	死亡人数 Deaths 数量/人 Num	级别 Dd	受伤人数 Injuries 数量/人 Num	级别 Dd	经济损失 Damage 数量/$ Mill	级别 De	房屋毁坏 Houses Destroyed 数量/间 Num	级别 Dh	房屋受损 Houses Damaged 数量/间 Num	级别 Dh
1986	10	20	14	48	19					USGS	Portugal:Faro	葡萄牙:法鲁	36. 78	-8. 76	32	4. 8	mb	6										
1986	10	27	22	32	21					USGS	Adriatic Sea	亚得里亚海	41. 93	19. 46	19	4. 9	ML	6										
1986	11	9	14	10	45					China	China:Qinghai,Qumalai,SE.	中国:青海曲麻莱东南	34. 04	96. 2	10	4. 7	Ms	6										
1986	11	14	21	20	7	4	0. 3			* China, Engdahl, NOAA	China:Taiwan,Hualien,Coast of E.	中国:台湾花莲以东海域	23. 989	121. 731	34	7. 4	Mw	8	15	1	44	1		1				
1986	11	21	23	33	2					USGS	US:California,North Coast	美国:加利福尼亚州北部近海	40. 37	-124. 44	15	5. 1	ML	6										
1986	11	22	0	41	44					ISC, Engdahl, USGS	Japan:South Honshu Ridge	日本:本州南部海岭	34. 517	139. 564	2. 1	6	Mw	6										
1986	11	25	13	59	42					* ISC	Bosnia:Strmica, Knin	波斯尼亚:斯特尔米察,克宁	44. 12	16. 339	30	6. 0	Mw	8			12	1		2				
1986	11	27	12	10	31					USGS	Bosnia:Strmica, Knin	波斯尼亚:斯特尔米察,克宁	44. 06	16. 22	10	4. 5	Md	6										
1986	11	28	22	29	35					USGS	Japan:Ibaraki,Near Coast	日本:茨城近海	36. 35	141. 17	41	5. 7	mb	6										
1986	11	30	5	19	48					* GSHAP	Brazil:Natal	巴西:纳塔尔	-5. 494	-35. 769	5	5. 1	Mw		1	1			5. 0	3	1500	4		
1986	11	30	20	15	32					ISC, Engdahl, USGS	Japan:Oshu,Near Coast	日本:奥州近海	39. 003	142. 032	37	6	Mw	6										
1986	12	7	14	17	10					* ISC	Bulgaria:Veliko Turnovo	保加利亚:大特尔偌沃	43. 274	25. 912	21	6. 1	Mw	7	3	1	60	2	5. 0	3				
1986	12	16	6	22	51					USGS	Croatia:Rijeka	克罗地亚:里耶卡	45. 06	14. 8	10	5	ML	8										
1986	12	18	17	16	15					USGS	Bulgaria:Veliko Turnovo	保加利亚:大特尔偌沃	43. 31	26. 07	6	4. 5	mb	6										
1986	12	19	5	47	29					*	Chile:Valparaiso	智利:瓦尔帕莱索	-33. 071	-72. 084	33	5	mb					2		1	16	1		
1986	12	20	23	8	13					China,Dis	China:Qinghai,Golmud,NW.	中国:青海格尔木西北	36. 72	93. 7	20	5. 3	Ms	6										
1986	12	20	23	47	9					* Iran	Iran:Fars	伊朗:法尔斯	29. 99	51. 62	25	5. 5	Ms							2	80	2		
1986	12	24	16	48	6					USGS	Bosnia:Strmica, Knin	波斯尼亚:斯特尔米察,克宁	44. 09	16. 35	31	4. 9	Md	7										
1986	12	30	0	38	30					USGS	Japan:Hakuba	日本:长野白马村	36. 67	137. 9	10	5. 5	mb	6										
1987	1	5	22	52	46					* China,Dis	China: Xinjiang, Baicheng, NW.	中国:新疆拜城西北	41. 95	81. 31	16	5. 9	Ms	6										
1987	1	6	5	7	48					USGS	China:Taiwan,Hualien,Coast of E.	中国:台湾花莲以东海域	23. 98	121. 73	38	5. 8	mb	6										
1987	1	7	0	39	28					USGS	Albania:Korce	阿尔巴尼亚:科里察	40. 44	20. 58	13	4. 9	ML	6										
1987	1	7	18	19	6					China,Dis	China:Gansu,Tewo,N.	中国:甘肃迭部北	34. 26	103. 36	20	5. 8	Ms	7										
1987	1	9	6	14	46					ISC, Japan, Engdahl,USGS	Japan:Miyako	日本:岩手宫古	39. 889	141. 616	68	6. 6	Mw	8			1	1						1
1987	1	9	17	40	35					USGS	Japan:Iwate	日本:岩手	39. 82	141. 64	84	5	mb	6										
1987	1	14	11	3	50					ISC, Engdahl, USGS	Japan:Hokkaido	日本:北海道	42. 597	142. 793	102	6. 8	Mw	8										
1987	1	15	19	41	42					USGS	China:Taiwan,Kaohsiung	中国:台湾高雄	22. 91	120. 2	17	4. 9	mb	6										
1987	1	17	10	4	8					USGS,ISC	Japan:Iwate	日本:岩手	39. 82	141. 67	83	5. 6	mb	6										

时间 年 Year	月 Mo	日 Dy	时 Hr	分 Mn	秒 Sec	海啸 Tsunami 源 Sr	浪高 Wh	级 I mI	级 S mS	资料来源 Information	震中 Earthquake Epicenter 地名(英文) Name(English)	地名(中文) Name(Chinese)	纬度(°) Latitude	经度(°) Longitude	深度 Depth	震级 Mag	标度 Scale	烈度 MMI	死亡人数 Deaths 数量/人 Num	级别 Dd	受伤人数 Injuries 数量/人 Num	级别 Dd	经济损失 Damage 数量/$ Mill $ Mill	级别 De	房屋毁坏 Houses Destroyed 数量/间 Num	级别 Dh	房屋受损 Houses Damaged 数量/间 Num	级别 Dh
1987	1	24	8	9	20					* China, Engdahl, Dis	China: Xinjiang, Uqturpan	中国：新疆乌什	41.488	79.343	8.2	6.4	Ms	8					4.63	2	800	3	4100	4
1987	1	26	11	11	42					*	Algeria: Mohammadia	阿尔及利亚：穆罕默迪耶	35.964	1.374	10	4.9	mb		1	1	7	1	1	2	629	3		
1987	2	6	12	23	50					ISC, Engdahl, USGS	Japan: Fukushima, Near Coast	日本：福岛近海	37.025	141.705	36	6.4	Mw	6										
1987	2	6	13	16	19	4	0.1	-3.3		* ISC, Engdahl, NOAA, USGS	Japan: Fukushima, Near Coast	日本：福岛近海	37.023	141.723	41.5	6.7	Mw	8										
1987	2	8	18	33	59	4	1.5	1		* Engdahl, NOAA, USGS	Papua New Guinea: Huon Peninsula	巴布亚新几内亚：休昂港半岛	-6.024	147.668	42.5	7.3	Mw	7	3	1			2.625	2		3		
1987	2	13	10	1	39					USGS, ISC	Japan: Hitachi	日本：茨城日立	36.63	140.88	63	5.5	mb	6										
1987	2	13	13	58	8					USGS	Albania: Tepelene	阿尔巴尼亚：德培雷恩	40.2	19.82	14	5	ML	6										
1987	2	17	3	3	22					China, Dis	China: Jiangsu, Seyang, SE.	中国：江苏射阳东南	33.57	120.76	11	5	Ms	6					0.93	1				
1987	2	18	0	0	55					ISC, Engdahl, USGS	Aleutian Islands	阿留申群岛	51.279	-179.259	41.3	6.2	Mw	5										
1987	2	23	0	21	21					USGS	Tadzhikistan: Garm	塔吉克斯坦：加尔姆	38.98	70.71	33	5	mb	6										
1987	2	25	19	56	34					China, Engdahl, Dis	China: Qinghai, Haixi Mang-ai, NW.	中国：青海海西茫崖西北	38.081	91.162	24	6.1	Ms	6										
1987	3	2	1	42	34					* Engdahl, USGS	New Zealand: North Island, Whakatane	新西兰：北岛，瓦卡塔尼	-38.015	176.921	15	6.5	Mw	10	1	1	25	1	210	5				
1987	3	5	9	17	5	4	0.2	-2.3		* ISC, Engdahl, NOAA	Chile: Antofagasta, C.	智利：安托法加斯塔中部	-24.395	-70.102	45.3	7.6	Mw	6	1	1				2				
1987	3	6	4	10	44					* GSHAP, Engdahl	Ecuador: Napo, Quito	厄瓜多尔：纳波，基多	0.083	-77.785	16.4	7.2	Mw	9	1000	3			700	5				
1987	3	10	3	24	13					USGS, ISC	Japan: Ibaraki, Near Coast	日本：茨城近海	36.92	141.66	47	5.5	Ms	5										
1987	3	18	3	36	32	4	0	-3.3		* Engdahl, NOAA, USGS	Japan: Miyazaki, Naze	日本：宫崎山甲	32.057	131.773	54	6.7	Mw	7	2	1	5	1		2				
1987	3	21	12	8	59					USGS, Engdahl	Costa Rica: Puerto Cortes	哥斯达黎加：科尔特斯港	8.878	-83.381	35.1	5.8	Mw	6										
1987	3	24	12	49	47	4	0.2			* NOAA, USGS	Japan: Joetsu	日本：新泻上越	37.447	137.865	23	5.7	mb	6										
1987	3	26	11	56	54					USGS	Tajikistan: Khudzhand	塔吉克斯坦：苦盏	41.69	69.84	20	5.1	mb	6										
1987	4	7	0	40	45					ISC, Engdahl, USGS	Japan: Fukushima, Near Coast	日本：福岛近海	37.392	141.722	29	6.7	Mw	7										
1987	4	10	10	59	41					USGS	Japan: Satte	日本：埼玉幸手	36.06	139.72	69	5.1	mb	6										
1987	4	18	2	1	39					USGS, ISC	Gulf of Alaska	阿拉斯加湾	61.37	-150.66	68	5.7	mb	5										
1987	4	22	20	13	25					ISC, Engdahl, USGS	Japan: Fukushima, Near Coast	日本：福岛近海	37.187	141.484	30	6.7	Mw	7										
1987	4	24	2	30	30					USGS	Italy: Novellara	意大利：诺菲拉腊	44.83	10.67	32	4.8	Md	7										
1987	4	25	12	16	50					* ISC, Engdahl, USGS	Philippines: Manila, Cubi Point	菲律宾：马尼拉，骄碧角	15.92	120.268	107	6.9	Mw	5						1				

时间 Date						海啸 Tsunami				资料来源 Information	震中 Earthquake Epicenter				深度 Depth	震级 Mag	标度 Scale	烈度 MMI	死亡人数 Deaths		受伤人数 Injuries		经济损失 Damage		房屋毁坏 Houses Destroyed		房屋受损 Houses Damaged	
年 Year	月 Mo	日 Dy	时 Hr	分 Mn	秒 Sec	源 Sr	浪高 Wh	级 I mI	级 S mS		地名(英文) Name(English)	地名(中文) Name(Chinese)	纬度(°) Latitude	经度(°) Longitude					数量/人 Num	级别 Dd	数量/人 Num	级别 Dd	数量/$ Mill $ Mill	级别 De	数量/间 Num	级别 Dh	数量/间 Num	级别 Dh
1987	4	25	19	22	9					* ISC, Engdahl	Indonesia: Northern Sumatera	印度尼西亚:苏门答腊北部	2.404	98.902	7.8	6.4	Mw		2	1	22	1	1	2	300	3		
1987	4	30	1	10	34					USGS	Ryukyu Islands	琉球群岛	28.58	129.34	34	5	mb	7										
1987	4	30	4	17	38					China	China: Xinjiang, Ulugqat, W.	中国:新疆乌恰西	39.78	74.53	26	5.8	Ms	8										
1987	5	2	19	21	30					USGS, ISC	Aleutian Islands	阿留申群岛	54.8	-160.1	33	5.8	ML	5										
1987	5	2	20	43	53					USGS	Italy: Novellara	意大利:诺菲拉腊	44.82	10.72	10	5.2	ML	7										
1987	5	5	15	40	48					USGS, ISC, Engdahl	Afghan: Badakhshan	阿富汗:巴达赫尚	36.48	70.67	202	6.2	Mw	5										
1987	5	11	20	51	44					USGS, Engdahl	Japan: Miyagi, Near Coast	日本:宫城近海	38.953	141.96	55.2	5.8	Mw	6										
1987	5	18	1	3	9					China	China: Yunnan, Heqing, S.	中国:云南鹤庆南	26.22	100.26	4	5	Ms	6										
1987	5	23	17	9	4					* Bautista	Philippines: Mindanao, Talakag	菲律宾:棉兰老岛,塔拉卡格	8.047	125.41	32	5.2	Mw		1	1	2	1		1				
1987	5	29	6	27	51					* Iran	Iran: Hamadan	伊朗:哈马丹	34.08	48.27	40	4.9	mb		2	1	50	1		1				
1987	6	10	23	48	55					USGS	US: Indiana, Olney	美国:印第安纳州奥尔尼	38.71	-87.95	9	5.1	MLg	6										
1987	6	18	14	3	17	1	0.1			* Engdahl, NOAA	Solomon Islands	所罗门群岛	-10.724	162.318	73	6.3	Mw											
1987	6	30	9	17	8					USGS	Japan: Chikusei	日本:茨城筑西	36.17	139.99	69	5	mb	6										
1987	7	3	10	21	58					USGS	Italy: Porto San Giorgio, Permo	意大利:圣佐治港,巴马	43.25	13.94	12	5.3	Md	7										
1987	7	6	2	49	43	3	0.1			* Engdahl, NOAA	Vanuatu Islands	瓦努阿图群岛	-14.039	167.925	36.4	6.6	Mw											
1987	7	11	23	9	20					USGS	Serbia: Kraljevo	塞尔维亚:克拉列沃	43.71	20.45	17	4.6	Md	7										
1987	7	20	21	54	38					USGS, ISC	Solomon Sea, N.	所罗门海北部	-6.41	154.86	54	5.6	mb	5										
1987	7	31	23	56	59					ISC, Engdahl, USGS	US: California, North Coast	美国:加利福尼亚州北部近海	40.389	-124.196	17.7	6	Mw	6										
1987	8	2	9	7	32					* China, Dis	China: Jiangxi, Xunwu, W.	中国:江西寻乌西	24.96	115.56	12	5.4	Ms	7			84	2	5.7	3	484	3	37000	5
1987	8	4	15	4	40					USGS, ISC	Chile: Osorno	智利:奥索尔诺	-40.47	-73.19	38	5.9	mb	5										
1987	8	8	15	48	58					* Chile, Engdahl	Chile: Tarapaca	智利:塔拉帕卡	-19.092	-70.006	71.2	7.2	Mw	7	5	1	112	3	1	2	1000	3		
1987	8	10	12	12	13					China, Dis	China: Ningxia, Lingwu	中国:宁夏灵武	38.11	106.42	9	5.2	Ms	7			1	1	2.56	2	18	1		
1987	8	13	15	23	9					* Engdahl	Peru: Tacna	秘鲁:塔克纳	-17.9	-70.908	37.9	6.5	Mw	5	1	1	1	1		1				
1987	8	14	6	24	5					USGS	Serbia: Kraljevo	塞尔维亚:克拉列沃	43.73	20.41	13	4.7	ML	7										
1987	8	15	18	4	25					ISC, Engdahl, USGS	Chile: Copiapo	智利:科皮亚波	-28.097	-70.774	37	6.4	Mw	6										
1987	9	4	16	42	49					* USGS	Italy: Porto San Giorgio, Permo	意大利:圣佐治港,巴马	43.242	13.874	19	5.1	mb	8			2	1	1	2				
1987	9	15	2	4	31					China	China: Guangdong, Heyuan	中国:广东河源	23.83	114.44	13	4.7	Ms	6										
1987	9	18	8	43	29					USGS, ISC	Chile: Antofagasta, C.	智利:安托法加斯塔中部	-24.27	-69.15	96	5.5	mb	5										
1987	9	18	21	58	37					China, Dis	China: Xinjiang, Fuyun	中国:新疆富蕴	47.31	89.64	16	5.8	Ms	7									1000	3
1987	9	22	13	43	38					* Engdahl	Ecuador: Ambato, Latacunga	厄瓜多尔:安巴托,拉塔昆加	-1.008	-78.032	5.2	6.4	Mw		2	1	12	1		2		3		

时间 年 Year	月 Mo	日 Dy	时 Hr	分 Mn	秒 Sec	海啸 源 Sr	浪高 Wh	级 I mI	级 S mS	资料来源 Information	震中 地名(英文) Name(English)	地名(中文) Name(Chinese)	纬度(°) Latitude	经度(°) Longitude	深度 Depth	震级 Mag	标度 Scale	烈度 MMI	死亡人数 Deaths 数量/人 Num	级别 Dd	受伤人数 Injuries 数量/人 Num	级别 Dd	经济损失 Damage 数量/$ Mill	级别 De	房屋毁坏 Houses Destroyed 数量/间 Num	级别 Dh	房屋受损 Houses Damaged 数量/间 Num	级别 Dh
1987	10	1	14	42	20					* USGS, ISC, Engdahl	US: California, Whittier	美国:加利福尼亚州惠提尔	34.061	-118.134	14.4	6.0	Mw	8	8	1	200	3	358	5				
1987	10	2	22	27	56					* GSHAP	Peru: Trujillo, Chimbote	秘鲁:特鲁希略,钦博塔	-8.143	-77.954	20	5.8	Mw		3	1				2		3		
1987	10	4	10	27	20					USGS	Japan: Fukushima, Near Coast	日本:福岛近海	37.31	141.62	43	5.8	mb	6										
1987	10	4	10	59	38					* USGS	US: California, Whittier	美国:加利福尼亚州惠提尔	34.07	-118.1	8	5.2	mb	7	1	1		2		2				
1987	10	6	4	19	8	4	0.3	-3.3		* Engdahl, NOAA	Tonga Islands, N.	汤加群岛北部	-17.963	-172.212	22.3	7.3	Mw											
1987	10	12	13	57	6	4	0.1	-0.5		* Engdahl, NOAA	Solomon Sea	所罗门海	-7.269	154.425	25	7	Mw											
1987	10	16	20	48	3	4	0.1	-3.3		* Engdahl, NOAA, USGS	Papua New Guinea: West New Britain	巴布亚新几内亚:西新不列颠	-6.215	149.036	48	7.4	Mw	8						2				
1987	10	24	19	12	33					China	China: Gansu, Lixian, S.	中国:甘肃礼县南	34.07	105.22	33	4.8	Ms	6										
1987	11	6	22	27	13					USGS	Japan: Hokkaido	日本:北海道	43.42	146.26	61	5.2	mb	6										
1987	11	9	17	46	19					USGS, ISC	Chile: Calama	智利:卡拉马	-22.12	-69.57	43	5.5	mb	6										
1987	11	11	15	4	52					USGS	Colombia: Dabeiba	哥伦比亚:达韦瓦	6.8	-76.34	30	5.4	mb	6										
1987	11	17	8	46	53	4	0.1	-3.3		* Engdahl, NOAA	Gulf of Alaska	阿拉斯加湾	58.79	-143.193	15	7.2	Mw											
1987	11	24	1	54	20					* Engdahl, USGS	US: California, Imperial	美国:加利福尼亚州因皮里尔	33.264	-115.759	15	6.5	ML	6	2	1			3	2				
1987	11	24	13	15	58					ISC, Engdahl, USGS	US: California, Salton City	美国:加利福尼亚州索尔顿城	33.07	-115.952	1.9	6.5	Mw	7										
1987	11	26	1	43	15					* Engdahl	Indonesia: Timor; Pantar	印度尼西亚:帝汶;班达岛	-8.259	124.15	27.5	6.6	Mw		125	3	108	3	5.0	3	237	3		
1987	11	30	19	23	17	4	0.4	-1		* Engdahl, NOAA	Gulf of Alaska	阿拉斯加湾	58.836	-142.601	8.7	7.9	M	6						1				
1987	12	17	2	8	20					* ISC, Engdahl	Japan: Chiba, Tokyo	日本:千叶县;东京	35.421	140.322	47.3	6.5	Mw	8	2	1			5.0	3				
1987	12	21	4	28	24					USGS	Tadzhikistan: Garm	塔吉克斯坦:加尔姆	38.7	70.67	14	4.8	mb	6										
1988	1	3	21	32	24					* China, USGS, Dis	China: Ningxia, Lingwu	中国:宁夏灵武	38.07	106.34	14	5.4	Ms	7							688	3		
1988	1	9	1	2	49					* Engdahl, USGS	Albania: Tirana	阿尔巴尼亚:地拉那	41.209	19.758	23.4	5.9	Mw	7						2				
1988	1	10	7	43	13					China, ISC, Dis	China: Yunnan, Ninglang, SE.	中国:云南宁蒗东南	27.23	100.96	9	5.5	Ms	7			12	1	10.3	3	180	3	4796	4
1988	1	19	23	14	55					USGS	Bosnia: Banja Luka	波斯尼亚:巴尼亚卢卡	44.58	17.67	10	4.5	ML	7										
1988	1	22	0	35	60					* Engdahl	Australia: Tennant Creek	澳大利亚:滕南特克里克	-19.874	133.778	5	6.3	M							2				
1988	1	22	12	4	59					* ISC, Engdahl	Australia: Northern Territory, C.	澳大利亚:北领地中部	-19.897	133.828	5	6.6	M	9										
1988	2	1	14	21	38					USGS	Italy: Udine	意大利:乌迪内	46.31	13.12	8	5.4	ML	6										
1988	2	5	14	1	4					ISC, Engdahl, USGS	Chile: Antofagasta, S.	智利:安托法加斯塔南部	-24.743	-70.423	37	7.2	Mw	6										
1988	2	5	18	1	3	4	0.1			* NOAA	Chile: Antofagasta, S.	智利:安托法加斯塔南部	-24.753	-70.433	37	7.2	Ms											

时间 年 Year	月 Mo	日 Dy	时 Hr	分 Mn	秒 Sec	海啸 Tsunami 源 Sr	浪高 Wh	级I mI	级S mS	资料来源 Information	震中 Earthquake Epicenter 地名(英文) Name(English)	地名(中文) Name(Chinese)	纬度(°) Latitude	经度(°) Longitude	深度 Depth	震级 Mag	标度 Scale	烈度 MMI	死亡人数 Deaths 数量/人 Num	级别 Dd	受伤人数 Injuries 数量/人 Num	级别 Dd	经济损失 Damage 数量/$ Mill	级别 De	房屋毁坏 Houses Destroyed 数量/间 Num	级别 Dh	房屋受损 Houses Damaged 数量/间 Num	级别 Dh
1988	2	6	14	50	47					* Engdahl	Bangladesh:Sylhet	孟加拉:锡尔赫特(锡莱特)	24.68	91.52	30.2	5.9	Mw		2	1	100	2		2				
1988	2	6	18	42	17					USGS	Montenegro:Ulcinj	门的内哥罗(黑山):乌尔齐尼	42.14	19.11	15	4.6	Md	6										
1988	2	7	8	46	59					Engdahl, USGS,ISC	Alaska Peninsula,S.	阿拉斯加半岛南部	60.304	-153.279	137.7	6.5	Mw	5										
1988	2	11	15	25	56					USGS	US:California,Whittier	美国:加利福尼亚州惠提尔	34.08	-118.05	12	4.8	ML	6										
1988	2	22	19	13	19					ISC, Engdahl, USGS	Chile:Pica	智利:皮卡	-20.919	-69.728	70	6.6	Mw	5										
1988	2	25	4	59	27					China	China:Liaoning,Zhangwu,S.	中国:辽宁彰武南	42.25	122.52	17	4.8	Ms	6										
1988	3	6	22	35	37	4	0.2	-2.3		* Engdahl, NOAA	Alaska:Anchorage	阿拉斯加:安克雷奇	57.262	-142.747	6.1	7.8	M	5					0.005	1				
1988	3	10	6	17	25					ISC, Engdahl, USGS	Trinidad & Tobago: Near Coast of S.	特立尼达和多巴哥:南部近海	10.27	-60.586	56	6.7	Mw	6										
1988	3	11	3	44	58					ISC, Engdahl, USGS	Panama:Bocas Del Toro	巴拿马:博卡斯德尔托罗	9.106	-82.945	17.3	6	Mw	7										
1988	3	17	20	34	29					ISC,USGS	Japan:Tokyo	日本:东京	35.66	139.65	96	6.0	Mw	6										
1988	3	26	20	35	13					USGS,ISC	Albania:Tepelene	阿尔巴尼亚:德培雷恩	40.18	19.89	39	5.5	mb	6										
1988	3	28	3	33	41					USGS,ISC	Hawaiian Islands	夏威夷群岛	19.94	-156.45	1	5.6	mb	5										
1988	3	30	2	12	44					* Iran, Engdahl, USGS	Iran:Deh Dasht,Bahbahan	伊朗:代赫达什特,贝赫贝汉	30.846	50.177	28.6	5.9	Mw							2				
1988	4	15	10	58	14					China,ISC,Dis	China:Sichuan,Huidong,SE.	中国:四川会东东南	26.36	102.76	9	5.4	Ms	7			20	1	0.59	1	100	2	1500	4
1988	5	6	14	46	18					ISC, Engdahl, USGS	Nicaragua:Rivas	尼加拉瓜:里瓦斯	11.505	-85.872	87	6.6	Mw	6										
1988	5	7	1	59	28					ISC, Engdahl, USGS	Japan:Hokkaido	日本:北海道	42.662	143.68	72	5.9	Mw	6										
1988	5	9	16	23	60					USGS	Jamaica:St Andrew	牙买加:圣安德鲁	18.09	-76.5	10	4.5	mb	6										
1988	5	20	3	19	54					USGS	Peru:Torata	秘鲁:塔克纳	-17.47	-69.47	124	5.5	mb	6										
1988	5	25	18	21	57					China,Dis	China:Xinjiang,Korla,NW.	中国:新疆库尔勒西北	41.97	85.64	21	5.2	Ms	6										
1988	6	2	6	11	42					China,Dis	China:Sichuan,Dawu,SE.	中国:四川道孚东南	30.61	101.49	9	5	Ms	6	1						4	1		
1988	6	13	1	45	37					USGS	US:California,Morgan Hill	美国:加利福尼亚州莫干山	37.38	-121.77	7	5.4	ML	6										
1988	6	19	19	52	7					* Bautista	Philippines:Mindoro,San Jose	菲律宾:民都洛岛,圣何塞	12.376	121.067	17	6.4	Mw	7	2	1				2				
1988	6	19	20	19	53					* USGS	Philippines:Panay Island	菲律宾:班乃岛	12.356	121.086	12.5	6.2	Mw	7										
1988	6	24	2	6	26	4	1			* NOAA	Philippines:Claveria	菲律宾:克拉韦里亚	18.606	121.013	53	5.4	mb							1				
1988	6	27	18	43	22					USGS	US:California,Los Gatos	美国:加利福尼亚州洛斯加托斯	37.13	-121.88	13	5.7	ML	6										

年 Year	月 Mo	日 Dy	时 Hr	分 Mn	秒 Sec	海啸 Tsunami 源 Sr	浪高 Wh	级 I mI	级 S mS	资料来源 Information	震中 Earthquake Epicenter 地名(英文) Name(English)	地名(中文) Name(Chinese)	纬度(°) Latitude	经度(°) Longitude	深度 Depth	震级 Mag	标度 Scale	烈度 MMI	死亡人数 Deaths 数量/人 Num	级别 Dd	受伤人数 Injuries 数量/人 Num	级别 Dd	经济损失 Damage 数量/$ Mill	级别 De	房屋毁坏 Houses Destroyed 数量/间 Num	级别 Dh	房屋受损 Houses Damaged 数量/间 Num	级别 Dh
1988	7	5	20	32	8	4	0.1			* Engdahl, NOAA	Papua New Guinea: West New Britain	巴布亚新几内亚:西新不列颠	-6.125	148.793	58.5	6.7	Mw	5						2				
1988	7	8	16	35	36					USGS, ISC	Papua New Guinea: Bougainville Island	巴布亚新几内亚:布干维尔岛	-6.29	154.68	74	5.8	mb	5										
1988	7	20	23	15	38					* China, Engdahl	China: Taiwan, Hualien	中国:台湾花莲	23.977	121.685	51	6.0	Ms		1	1	1	1		1				
1988	7	30	23	40	41					USGS, ISC	Japan: Oshima	日本:东京大岛	34.81	139.33	10	5.5	mb	6										
1988	8	1	1	39	22					USGS	Japan: Oshima	日本:东京大岛	34.85	139.28	10	4.9	mb	6										
1988	8	3	5	43	15					USGS, ISC	Afghan: Badakhshan	阿富汗:巴达赫尚	36.48	70.95	201	5.5	mb	5										
1988	8	6	0	36	26					* Engdahl, China	Myanmar: Sagaing, N.	缅甸:实皆北部	25.09	95.108	90.5	7.3	Mw	6	38	1			1	2				
1988	8	10	4	38	29	4	0.1	-3.3		* Engdahl, NOAA	Solomon Islands: San Cristobal	所罗门群岛:圣克里斯托瓦尔	-10.258	160.896	36.1	7.6	Mw		1	1				1	100	2		
1988	8	11	16	4	45					* Engdahl	Iran: Fars	伊朗:法尔斯	29.9	51.657	15	6.1	Mw		1	1				2				
1988	8	12	5	14	54					USGS, ISC	Japan: Tateyama	日本:千叶馆山	35.02	139.8	70	5.5	mb	6										
1988	8	14	17	50	49					China	China: Yunnan, Lancang, N.	中国:云南澜沧北	22.83	99.86	15	5	Ms	6										
1988	8	14	17	53	11					ISC, Engdahl, USGS	Chile: Copiapo, Near Coast	智利:科皮亚波近海	-27.345	-71.09	34.9	6.7	Mw	6										
1988	8	14	20	3	4					USGS, Engdahl, ISC	US: Utah, Castle Dale	美国:犹他州代尔堡	39.13	-110.87	17.3	5.5	Ms	6										
1988	8	15	9	59	25					ISC, Engdahl, USGS	Philippines: Mindanao Island	菲律宾:棉兰老岛	8.729	126.291	51.3	6.1	Mw	6										
1988	8	20	23	9	11					* Engdahl	Nepal: Sagarmatha	尼泊尔:萨加玛塔	26.758	86.624	57	6.9	Mw	8	1091	4			132	5				
1988	9	4	15	49	22					USGS, ISC	Japan: Yamakita	日本:神奈川山北	35.42	138.96	51	5.6	mb	6										
1988	9	5	6	13	17					USGS	Dominica: Santo Domingo	多米尼加:多米尼加	18.42	-70.38	27	5.5	mb	6										
1988	9	6	0	42	34					*	Papua New Guinea: Kaiapit	巴布亚新几内亚:卡亚皮特	-6.06	146.23		4.3	ML		74	2				2				
1988	9	6	19	16	37					USGS, ISC	Georgia: Poti	格鲁吉亚:波季	42.01	41.72	10	5.5	mb	6										
1988	9	7	2	28	10					USGS	US: Kentucky, Owingsville	美国:肯塔基州奥因斯维尔	38.14	-83.88	10	4.6	MLg	6										
1988	9	20	17	56	20					USGS, Engdahl	Colombia: Bajo Baudo, Buenaventura	哥伦比亚:巴霍包,布埃纳文图拉	4.671	-77.386	39.8	5.8	Mw	6										
1988	9	25	20	52	15					* USGS	Tajikistan: Kuhistoni Badakhshon, S.	塔吉克斯坦:勾瑙-巴达科善南部	37.18	71.811	11	5.5	mb	6						2				
1988	9	26	7	17	0					USGS, ISC	Afghan: Badakhshan	阿富汗:巴达赫尚	36.29	71.37	106	5.6	mb	5										
1988	9	26	8	23	20					USGS, Engdahl	Japan: Chiba, Near Coast	日本:千叶近海	35.53	141.07	29	5.7	Mw	6										
1988	10	10	5	52	13					ISC, Engdahl, USGS	Japan: Hokkaido	日本:北海道	42.698	144.385	64.1	5.8	Mw	6										
1988	10	14	16	12	23					USGS	Albania: Tepelene	阿尔巴尼亚:德培雷恩	40.15	19.74	50	4.5	Md	6										
1988	10	16	6	15	29					USGS, ISC	Azores: Sao Miguel Island	亚速尔群岛:圣米格尔岛	37.53	-25.36	10	5.6	mb	6										

时间						海啸				资料来源	震中				深度	震级	标度	烈度	死亡人数		受伤人数		经济损失		房屋毁坏		房屋受损	
年	月	日	时	分	秒	源	浪高	级 I	级 S		地名(英文)	地名(中文)	纬度(°)	经度(°)					数量/人	级别	数量/人	级别	数量/$ Mill	级别	数量/间	级别	数量/间	级别
Date						Tsunami				Information	Earthquake Epicenter				Depth	Mag	Scale	MMI	Deaths		Injuries		Damage		Houses Destroyed		Houses Damaged	
Year	Mo	Dy	Hr	Mn	Sec	Sr	Wh	mI	mS		Name(English)	Name(Chinese)	Latitude	Longitude					Num	Dd	Num	Dd	$ Mill	De	Num	Dh	Num	Dh
1988	10	16	12	34	6					* Engdahl	Greece:Ionian Sea, Vartholomion	希腊:爱奥尼亚海,瓦尔索洛米翁	37.874	20.986	15.8	5.9	Mw	8						2				
1988	10	31	10	12	58					*	Algeria:Blida	阿尔及利亚:布利达	36.443	2.759	12	5.6	Ms							2				
1988	11	3	14	47	13					* Engdahl	Guatemala:San Vicente Pacaya	危地马拉:圣维森特省帕卡亚	13.908	-90.502	75.4	6.6	Mw	6	5	1		2		2			100	2
1988	11	3	19	42	21					* ISC, Engdahl	Puerto Rico: Mona Passage, Catano	波多黎各:莫纳海峡,坦诺	19.002	-67.328	40.3	6	Mw	5						2				
1988	11	5	2	14	29					China, Engdahl, USGS, Dis	China:Qinghai, Golmud, SW.	中国:青海格尔木西南	34.27	91.87	7	6.8	Ms	9										
1988	11	6	13	3	21					* China, Engdahl, Dis	China:Yunnan, Ximeng, N.	中国:云南临沧东北	22.814	99.605	18	7.4	Ms	10	748	3	7700	4	606	5	412000	5		
1988	11	6	13	15	45					* China, Engdahl	China: Yunnan, Cangyuan, NE.	中国:云南临沧东北	23.228	99.436	9.5	6.9	Ms	10										
1988	11	10	0	17	49					* China	China:Guangxi, Qinzhou	中国:广西钦州	21.28	108.55	9	4.8	Ms	6			71	2		1				
1988	11	12	3	34	49					* USGS	Jamaica: St Andrew, Jacks Hill	牙买加:圣安德鲁,杰克斯山	18.068	-76.597	16	5.4	mb	6						2				
1988	11	17	6	55	48					* Bautista, Engdahl	Philippines:Samar;Catarman	菲律宾:萨马岛;卡塔曼	12.327	124.576	19	6.6	Mw	6						2				
1988	11	21	16	55	55					* Engdahl, USGS	Azores:Sao Miguel Island	亚速尔群岛:圣米格尔岛	37.912	-26.121	16.1	5.9	Mw	7						2				
1988	11	21	17	46	2					China, Dis	China:Gansu, Sunan, S.	中国:甘肃肃南南	38.57	99.6	24	5.7	Ms	6										
1988	11	25	23	46	5					* ISC, Engdahl	Canada:Quebec, Saguenay	加拿大:魁北克,萨奎尼	48.065	-71.269	24	5.9	M	7						2				
1988	11	27	4	17	55					China	China:Yunnan, Lancang	中国:云南澜沧	22.74	99.94	14	5.8	Ms	6										
1988	11	29	11	23	39					USGS	Colombia:Manizales - Armenia	哥伦比亚:马尼萨莱斯 - 亚美尼亚	5.1	-76.57	85	5.8	mb	6										
1988	12	3	3	13	46					USGS, ISC	Japan:South Honshu Ridge	日本:本州南部海岭	27.8	141.06	106	5.5	mb	5										
1988	12	3	11	38	26					USGS	US:California, Whittier	美国:加利福尼亚州惠提尔	34.15	-118.13	13	5	ML	6										
1988	12	7	7	41	26					* Engdahl	Armenia:Leninakan, Spitak	亚美尼亚:列宁纳坎,斯皮塔克	40.928	44.114	5	6.8	M	10	25000	5			16200	5		4		
1988	12	16	11	35	51					USGS	Adriatic Sea	亚得里亚海	44.74	14.97	10	4.5	ML	6										
1988	12	21	8	21	4					USGS, ISC	Kyrgyzstan:Jalal - Abad	吉尔吉斯斯坦:贾拉拉巴德	41.22	72.3	33	5.9	mb	6										
1989	1	6	19	8	27					USGS, ISC	Japan Trench	日本海沟	36.4	141.75	43	5.8	Ms	5										
1989	1	19	6	53	29					USGS, ISC	US:California, Topanga	美国:加利福尼亚州托潘加	33.92	-118.63	12	5.6	mb	6										
1989	1	22	23	2	4					* Engdahl	Tajikistan:Dushanbe (Stalinabad)	塔吉克斯坦:杜桑贝	38.478	68.697	1.6	5.5	Ms	7	274	3			24.8	3				
1989	1	24	20	3	39					USGS	Japan:Hokkaido	日本:北海道	42.23	142.69	50	5.6	mb	6										
1989	1	30	4	6	23					USGS	US:Utah, Salina	美国:犹他州萨利纳	38.82	-111.61	24	5.4	ML	6										

年 Year	月 Mo	日 Dy	时 Hr	分 Mn	秒 Sec	海啸 Tsunami 源 Sr	浪高 Wh	级 I mI	级 S mS	资料来源 Information	震中 Earthquake Epicenter 地名(英文) Name(English)	地名(中文) Name(Chinese)	纬度(°) Latitude	经度(°) Longitude	深度 Depth	震级 Mag	标度 Scale	烈度 MMI	死亡人数 Deaths 数量/人 Num	级别 Dd	受伤人数 Injuries 数量/人 Num	级别 Dd	经济损失 Damage 数量/$ Mill	级别 De	房屋毁坏 Houses Destroyed 数量/间 Num	级别 Dh	房屋受损 Houses Damaged 数量/间 Num	级别 Dh
1989	2	3	17	49	58					China	China: Xizang (Tibet), Nyemo, N.	中国:西藏尼木北	30. 11	90	8	5. 6	Ms	6										
1989	2	5	1	59	49					USGS, ISC	Japan Trench	日本海沟	33. 38	140. 81	59	5. 6	mb	5										
1989	2	19	12	27	10					USGS	Japan: Kasukabe	日本:埼玉春日部	35. 96	139. 79	60	5. 5	mb	6										
1989	2	26	12	21	11					USGS	Costa Rica: San Jose, S.	哥斯达黎加:圣何塞东南	9. 67	−84. 18	22	4. 7	Md	7										
1989	3	1	13	0	33					China	China: Sichuan, Xiaojin, N.	中国:四川小金北	31. 5	102. 49	13	5	Ms	6										
1989	3	2	7	13	46					USGS, ISC	Dominica: La Altagracia	多米尼加:阿尔塔格拉西亚	18. 38	−68. 66	134	5. 6	mb	5										
1989	3	5	13	48	42					USGS	Kyrgyzstan: Chui	吉尔吉斯斯坦:楚河州	42. 51	74. 63	33	4. 8	mb	6										
1989	3	6	14	39	44					ISC, Engdahl, USGS	Japan: Sosa	日本:千叶匝瑳	35. 665	140. 584	42	6. 1	Mw	7										
1989	3	8	11	44	34					* Engdahl	Indonesia: Molucca Sea	印度尼西亚:马鲁古海	1. 023	126. 205	33. 6	6. 1	Mw							3				
1989	3	10	8	0	49					*	Turkey: Erzurum, Kars	土耳其:埃尔佐鲁姆,卡尔斯	40. 027	41. 816	10	4. 4	mb							2				
1989	3	10	14	14	11					* Engdahl	Papua New Guinea: New Ireland	巴布亚新几内亚:新爱尔兰	−4. 333	152. 842	49. 6	5. 8	Mw	5	1	1				2				
1989	3	10	21	49	48					* ISC, Engdahl	Malawi: Salima, Dedza	马拉维:萨利马,代扎	−13. 74	34. 48	30	6. 3	Mw		9	1	100	2	28. 0	4				
1989	4	1	21	58	14					USGS, ISC	Argentina: Mendoza	阿根廷:门多萨	−32. 8	−69. 95	109	5. 5	mb	5										
1989	4	3	17	46	34					USGS	US: California, San Jose	美国:加利福尼亚州圣何塞	37. 42	−121. 79	9	4. 7	ML	6										
1989	4	7	20	7	30					USGS	US: California, Huntington Beach	美国:加利福尼亚州亨廷顿海滩	33. 62	−117. 9	13	4. 6	ML	6										
1989	4	8	4	25	5					USGS	Montenegro: Niksic	蒙特内哥罗(黑山):尼克希奇	42. 83	18. 73	39	4. 5	ML	6										
1989	4	9	2	31	35					China	China: Xizang (Tibet), Rinbung, SE.	中国:西藏仁布东南	29. 1	90. 08	10	4. 9	Ms	7										
1989	4	15	20	34	11					* China, Engdahl, Dis	China: Sichuan, Batang, SE.	中国:四川巴塘东南	30. 007	99. 237	13	6. 6	Ms	8	9	1	121	3	112	5	75604	5	267594	5
1989	4	20	22	59	56					ISC, Engdahl, USGS	Russia: Sakha, SW.	俄罗斯:萨哈共和国西南	57. 166	122. 074	26	6. 3	Mw	6										
1989	4	25	1	13	23					China, Engdahl	China: Sichuan, Batang, E.	中国:四川巴塘东	30. 004	99. 414	8	6. 6	Ms	8										
1989	4	25	14	29	2					* ISC, Engdahl	Mexico: Mexico City, Acapulco	墨西哥:墨西哥城,阿卡普尔科	16. 794	−99. 251	19	6. 9	Mw	6	3	1				2				
1989	4	25	17	18	38					USGS, ISC	Japan: Narita	日本:千叶成田	35. 84	140. 36	71	5. 5	mb	5										
1989	4	27	16	47	50					USGS	US: Missouri, New Madrid	美国:密苏里州新马德里	36. 01	−89. 77	10	4. 7	MLg	6										
1989	5	3	5	53	3					China, Engdahl, Dis	China: Sichuan, Batang, E.	中国:四川巴塘东	30. 091	99. 471	14	6. 3	Ms				24	1	7. 1	3	7968	4		
1989	5	3	9	13	24					*	Iran: Fars	伊朗:法尔斯	29. 964	51. 655	33	5. 1	mb							3				

年 Year	月 Mo	日 Dy	时 Hr	分 Mn	秒 Sec	源 Sr	浪高 Wh	级 I mI	级 S mS	资料来源 Information	地名(英文) Name(English)	地名(中文) Name(Chinese)	纬度(°) Latitude	经度(°) Longitude	深度 Depth	震级 Mag	标度 Scale	烈度 MMI	死亡人数 Deaths 数量/人 Num	级别 Dd	受伤人数 Injuries 数量/人 Num	级别 Dd	经济损失 Damage 数量/$ Mill $ Mill	级别 De	房屋毁坏 Houses Destroyed 数量/间 Num	级别 Dh	房屋受损 Houses Damaged 数量/间 Num	级别 Dh
1989	5	4	0	22	7					* GSHAP	Venezuela: Falcon, Carabobo	委内瑞拉:法拉孔,卡拉沃沃	11.038	-68.27	16	5.7	Mw							2				
1989	5	6	1	40	56					China	China: Yunnan, Menglian, NE.	中国:云南孟连东北	22.33	99.9	12	5.1	Ms	6										
1989	5	7	0	38	17					* China, USGS, Dis	China: Yunnan, Gengma	中国:云南耿马	23.52	99.62	34	6.2	Ms	7	1	1	91	2	54.0	4	5300	4		
1989	5	23	10	54	47	4	0.1	-1.7		* Engdahl, NOAA	Macquarie Ridge	麦夸里海岭	-52.507	160.602	4.3	8.1	Mw	7						1				
1989	5	27	20	8	39					* ISC, Engdahl	Iran: Fars	伊朗:法尔斯	30.146	50.886	29	6	Mw		114	3			5.0	3				
1989	5	29	22	22	31					USGS, ISC	Chile: Antofagasta, C.	智利:安托法加斯塔中部	-23.9	-70.34	32	5.5	mb	5										
1989	6	9	14	46	4					China, Dis	China: Sichuan, Shimian, N.	中国:四川石棉北	29.34	102.38	9	5	Ms	7	1		7	1	1.12	2	79	2	1660	4
1989	6	12	0	4	12					* ISC, Engdahl	Bangladesh: Khulna, S.	孟加拉:库尔纳南部	21.831	89.788	6	5.8	Mw		1	1				2				
1989	6	12	16	57	18					USGS	US: California, Los Angeles	美国:加利福尼亚州洛杉矶	34.03	-118.18	16	4.5	ML	6										
1989	6	25	20	37	34					* Engdahl	Ecuador: Esmeraldas, Guayaquil	厄瓜多尔:埃斯梅拉尔达斯,瓜亚基尔	1.137	-79.568	15	6.3	Mw	7						2				
1989	6	26	3	27	7	4	0.3	-1.7		* Engdahl, NOAA	Hawaiian Islands	夏威夷群岛	19.464	-155.174	9	6.4	Mw	6			5	1		2	105	3		
1989	6	26	10	38	41					* Engdahl	Azores: Graciosa, Terceira	亚速尔群岛:格拉秀沙,特塞拉岛	39.109	-28.234	11	5.7	Mw	6						2				
1989	7	4	17	28	23					USGS	Japan: Atami	日本:静冈热海	35.04	139.18	32	4.6	mb	6										
1989	7	6	15	1	41					USGS	Japan: Ito	日本:静冈伊东	34.93	139.2	5	4.9	mb	6										
1989	7	9	2	9	9					* ISC, USGS	Japan: Ito	日本:静冈伊东	34.942	139.193	5	5.5	Mw	6						2				
1989	7	14	20	42	42					* ISC, Engdahl	Indonesia: Timor, Alor	印度尼西亚:帝汶,阿勒群岛	-8.089	125.114	12.4	6.7	Mw							2				
1989	8	1	0	18	7					* ISC, Engdahl	Indonesia: Papua	印度尼西亚:巴布亚	-4.482	138.974	14	6.1	Mw		120	3			1	2				
1989	8	3	7	42	41					* USGS	Russia: Chechnia, Grozny, NW.	俄罗斯:车臣共和国格罗兹尼北部	43.522	45.362	18	5	mb	6	1	1				2				
1989	8	6	22	53	57					USGS, ISC	Japan: Hokkaido	日本:北海道	42.8	145.12	44	5.7	mb	5										
1989	8	8	8	13	28					USGS	US: California, Loma Prieta	美国:加利福尼亚州洛马普里埃塔	37.13	-121.95	15	5.4	ML	6										
1989	8	8	23	44	4					USGS	Chile: Calama	智利:卡拉马	-22.72	-68.48	102	5.3	mb	6										
1989	8	20	11	16	58					* Engdahl, USGS	Djibouti: Yoboki	吉布提:约博基	11.743	41.963	12	6.5	Mw	9	2	1	2	1		1				
1989	9	4	5	20	57					* Engdahl	Indonesia: Tembagapura	印度尼西亚:特巴加普拉	-4.248	136.704	9	6.4	Mw							2				
1989	9	4	13	15	0	4	0.1	-3.3		* Engdahl, NOAA	Aleutian Islands	阿留申群岛	55.629	-156.912	11	7.1	Mw											
1989	9	13	21	53	60					USGS	Italy: Brescia	意大利:布雷西亚	45.8	11.21	10	5.1	ML	7										
1989	9	16	2	5	10					ISC, Engdahl, USGS	Caspian Sea	里海	40.337	51.551	47	6.4	Mw	6										
1989	9	20	0	26	13					China, Dis	China: Yunnan, Songming	中国:云南嵩明	25.47	103.21	15	5	Ms	6			73	2	8.9	3	842	3		
1989	9	20	16	21	57					China	China: Gansu, Subei, E.	中国:甘肃肃北东	39.16	97.18	13	4.9	Ms	5										
1989	9	22	1	25	53					* China, Engdahl, Dis	China: Sichuan, Xiaojin, N.	中国:四川小金北	31.541	102.451	15	6.5	Ms	8	1	1	151	3	55.8	4	1381	4	2888	4

年 Year	月 Mo	日 Dy	时 Hr	分 Mn	秒 Sec	源 Sr	浪高 Wh	级 I mI	级 S mS	资料来源 Information	地名(英文) Name(English)	地名(中文) Name(Chinese)	纬度(°) Latitude	经度(°) Longitude	深度 Depth	震级 Mag	标度 Scale	烈度 MMI	死亡人数 Deaths 数量/人 Num	级别 Dd	受伤人数 Injuries 数量/人 Num	级别 Dd	经济损失 Damage 数量/$ Mill	级别 De	房屋毁坏 Houses Destroyed 数量/间 Num	级别 Dh	房屋受损 Houses Damaged 数量/间 Num	级别 Dh
1989	10	1	2	59	6					* Iran	Iran: Iluyeh & Boyer Ahmad	伊朗:科吉卢耶-博韦艾哈迈德	30.96	51.421	42	5.2	mb							2				
1989	10	13	21	19	58					USGS, ISC	Japan: Oshima	日本:东京大岛	34.73	139.53	25	5.7	mb	6										
1989	10	18	0	4	18	4	1	-3.3		* Engdahl, NOAA	US: California, Loma Prieta	美国:加利福尼亚州洛马普里埃塔	37.144	-121.756	16	6.9	M	9	62	2	3757	4	5.6	3		3		
1989	10	18	14	57	22					* China, Dis	China: Shanxi, Datong, E.	中国:山西大同东	39.92	113.91	13	6.0	Ms	8	15	1	145	3	102	5	39000	5	76000	5
1989	10	29	5	25	41	4	0.1			* Engdahl, NOAA	Japan: Miyako, Off Coast	日本:宫古沿海	39.676	143.298	12.1	6.5	Mw											
1989	10	29	19	9	15	2				* Engdahl, NOAA	Algeria: Algiers, Cherchell	阿尔及利亚:阿尔及尔,舍尔沙勒	36.729	2.433	6	6	Mw	8	30	1	245	3	5.0	3				
1989	11	1	10	25	52	3	0.1			* NOAA	Dominica: Miches	多米尼加:米切斯	18.986	-68.833	26	5.2	mb											
1989	11	1	18	25	37	3	0.9	-0.7		* Engdahl, NOAA	Japan: Aomori, Misawa	日本:青森,三泽	39.923	142.757	29	7.4	Mw	6						1				
1989	11	20	3	21	6					* China, Dis	China: Chongqing, Changshou	中国:重庆长寿	29.91	106.85	23	5.3	Ms	7	3	1	146	3	41.8	4	305	3	17853	5
1989	11	20	4	19	7					* Engdahl	Iran: Kerman	伊朗:克尔曼	29.9	57.716	19.9	5.9	Mw		3	1				2				
1989	11	25	16	13	48					China	China: Guangdong, Heyuan, S.	中国:广东河源南	23.71	114.56	33	4.7	Ms	6										
1989	12	6	5	33	12					USGS	Croatia: Split	克罗地亚:斯普利特	43.65	16.87	10	4.9	ML	7										
1989	12	8	17	23	30					USGS, ISC	Japan: Ibaraki, Near Coast	日本:茨城近海	36.55	140.92	46	5.6	mb	6										
1989	12	15	18	43	48					* Bautista, Engdahl	Philippines: Mindanao, Cotabato	菲律宾:棉兰老岛,哥打巴托	8.377	126.642	26.2	7.5	Mw	6	1	1			1	2				
1989	12	27	23	26	57					* USGS	Australia: Newcastle	澳大利亚:纽卡斯尔	-32.967	151.619	10	5.5	mb	8	12	1			1.1	2				
1990	1	7	11	2	6					USGS	Central Alaska	阿拉斯加中部	64.78	-148.87	20	5.5	ML	5										
1990	1	11	11	10	51					USGS	Japan: Kusatsu	日本:滋贺草津	35.07	135.95	25	4.8	mb	6										
1990	1	14	3	3	21					China, Engdahl, Dis	China: Qinghai, Haixi, Shatu Liang	中国:青海海西沙土梁	37.805	92.005	12	6.5	Ms	8					2.09	2	1333	4		
1990	1	15	3	19	44					China	China: Sichuan, Dayi, W.	中国:四川大邑西	30.63	103.31	21	4.7	Ms	6										
1990	1	16	20	8	22					USGS, ISC	US: California, Petrolia	美国:加利福尼亚州佩脱里亚	40.23	-124.14	2	5.6	mb	7										
1990	1	17	6	38	6					USGS	Australia: Perth	澳大利亚:珀斯	-31.67	117	6	5.5	ML	6										
1990	1	23	7	47	10					USGS, ISC	Peru: Lima, Callao	秘鲁:利马,卡亚俄	-12.45	-75.07	104	5.5	mb	5										
1990	1	29	13	16	11					USGS	US: New Mexico, La Joya	美国:新墨西哥州拉霍亚	34.46	-106.88	12	4.8	MLg	6										
1990	1	31	10	16	15					USGS	Macedonia: Bogdanci	马其顿:博丹奇区	41.42	22.66	15	4.5	ML	6										
1990	2	5	5	16	48					ISC, Engdahl, USGS	Afghan: Badakhshan	阿富汗:巴达赫尚	37.066	71.288	110	6.3	Mw	6										
1990	2	8	7	15	34					* Bautista, Engdahl	Philippines: Bohol, Cebu	菲律宾:保和岛	9.773	124.64	26	6.8	Mw	7	1	1			1	2				
1990	2	9	17	57	25					China, Dis	China: Jiangsu, Taicang, NW.	中国:江苏太仓西北	31.63	121.02	9	4.9	Ms	6	2		24	1	33.4	4			100000	5
1990	2	11	17	46	6					USGS, ISC	Japan: Ibaraki, Near Coast	日本:茨城近海	36.33	140.92	46	5.7	mb	6										
1990	2	13	21	13	8					China	China: Yunnan, Nujiang, N.	中国:云南怒江北	26.11	98.98	32	4.8	Ms	6										

年 Year	月 Mo	日 Dy	时 Hr	分 Mn	秒 Sec	海啸 Tsunami 源 Sr	浪高 Wh	级 I mI	级 S mS	资料来源 Information	震中 Earthquake Epicenter 地名(英文) Name(English)	地名(中文) Name(Chinese)	纬度(°) Latitude	经度(°) Longitude	深度 Depth	震级 Mag	标度 Scale	烈度 MMI	死亡人数 Deaths 数量/人 Num	级别 Dd	受伤人数 Injuries 数量/人 Num	级别 Dd	经济损失 Damage 数量/$ Mill	级别 De	房屋毁坏 Houses Destroyed 数量/间 Num	级别 Dh	房屋受损 Houses Damaged 数量/间 Num	级别 Dh
1990	2	19	5	34	38					ISC, Engdahl, USGS	New Zealand: North Island, Waitahora	新西兰:北岛,怀霍拉	-40.368	176.2	25.4	6.2	Mw	7										
1990	2	20	6	53	42	4	0.2	-1.7		* ISC, Engdahl, NOAA, USGS	Japan: Oshima	日本:东京大岛	34.747	139.257	14	6.4	Mw	6										
1990	2	28	23	43	37					* USGS	US: California, Claremont, Covina	美国:加利福尼亚州克莱蒙特,科维那	34.14	-117.7	5	5.5	Mw	7					12.7	3				
1990	3	4	19	46	20					* Engdahl	Pakistan: Kalat, Quetta	巴基斯坦:卡拉特,奎塔	28.908	66.36	3.9	6.1	Mw		11	1			1	2				
1990	3	25	13	22	57	4	1			* ISC, Engdahl, NOAA	Costa Rica: Puntarenas, San Jose	哥斯达黎加:彭塔雷纳斯,圣何塞	9.948	-84.757	22	7.3	Mw	8			10	1		2	60	2		
1990	3	25	14	17	22					* Engdahl	Afghan: Langar, NW.	阿富汗:兰加尔西北	37.002	72.925	49.3	6.4	Ms	6						1				
1990	3	26	22	47	20					* Bautista, Engdahl	Philippines: Mindanao Island	菲律宾:棉兰老岛	9.282	125.56	52.7	5.9	Mw		1	1				2				
1990	4	2	13	46	32					* USGS	England: Manchester, Liverpool	英国:曼彻斯特,利物浦	52.314	-2.985	18	5.2	ML	6						2				
1990	4	3	22	2	37					USGS	Bosnia and Herzegovina: Mostar	波斯尼亚和黑塞哥维那:莫斯塔尔	43.42	17.39	10	5.6	ML	7										
1990	4	5	21	12	38	4	1.8	-1		* Engdahl, NOAA	Northern Mariana Islands	北马利亚纳群岛	15.15	147.596	18	7.4	Mw							1				
1990	4	11	7	53	38					USGS	Japan: Hokkaido	日本:北海道	42.54	144.05	71	5.5	mb	6										
1990	4	14	5	33	27					USGS	US: Washington, Bellingham	美国:华盛顿州贝灵厄姆	48.85	-122.16	12	5.2	ML	6										
1990	4	17	1	59	32					* China, Engdahl, Dis	China: Xinjiang, Ulugqat	中国:新疆乌恰	39.394	74.958	15	6.3	Ms	8			2	1	0.73	1		3		
1990	4	17	22	32	27					USGS	US: California, Claremont, Covina	美国:加利福尼亚州克莱蒙特,科维那	34.11	-117.72	4	4.7	ML	6										
1990	4	18	13	39	21					* Engdahl	Indonesia: South Sulawesi sea	印度尼西亚:苏拉威西海南部	1.186	122.799	26	7.6	Mw		3	1				3				
1990	4	18	13	53	51					USGS	US: California, Watsonville	美国:加利福尼亚州沃森维尔	36.92	-121.68	5	5.4	ML	6										
1990	4	18	19	38	9					*	Iran: Hanna	伊朗:哈纳	31.107	51.678	47	4.7	mb							2				
1990	4	24	19	30	40					USGS	Montenegro: Ulcinj	门的内哥罗(黑山):乌尔齐尼	42.13	19.13	21	4.9	Md	6										
1990	4	26	9	37	13					* China, Engdahl, USGS, Dis	China: Qinghai, Gonghe, SW.	中国:青海共和西南	36.04	100.279	8	7.0	Ms	9	119	3	2149	4	564	5	6000	4		
1990	4	26	11	27	43					USGS	Albania: Peqin	阿尔巴尼亚:佩令区	41.01	19.78	39	4.9	Md	6										
1990	4	28	4	41	48					USGS	US: California, Concord	美国:加利福尼亚州康科德市	37.88	-121.98	6	4.6	ML	6										
1990	5	3	7	45	41					ISC, USGS	Japan: Hitachi	日本:茨城日立	36.65	140.66	49	6.0	Mw	6										
1990	5	5	7	21	19					* Italy, Engdahl	Italy: Potenza	意大利:波坦察	40.716	15.812	7.8	5.84	Mw	7	2	1				2				
1990	5	13	4	23	11					* Engdahl	New Zealand: North Island, Dannevirke	新西兰:北岛,丹尼弗克	-40.282	176.116	21	6.4	Mw	8						2				

年	月	日	时	分	秒	源	浪高	级 I	级 S	资料来源	地名(英文)	地名(中文)	纬度(°)	经度(°)	深度	震级	标度	烈度	死亡人数 数量/人	死亡人数 级别	受伤人数 数量/人	受伤人数 级别	经济损失 数量/$ Mill	经济损失 级别	房屋毁坏 数量/间	房屋毁坏 级别	房屋受损 数量/间	房屋受损 级别
Date						Tsunami				Information	Earthquake Epicenter				Depth	Mag	Scale	MMI	Deaths		Injuries		Damage		Houses Destroyed		Houses Damaged	
Year	Mo	Dy	Hr	Mn	Sec	Sr	Wh	mI	mS		Name(English)	Name(Chinese)	Latitude	Longitude					Num	Dd	Num	Dd	$ Mill	De	Num	Dh	Num	Dh
1990	5	14	21	34	6					Engdahl, USGS	Chile: Talca	智利:塔尔卡	-35.853	-71.403	83.4	6.1	Mw	6										
1990	5	20	2	22	3					* ISC, Engdahl	Sudan: Juba	苏丹:朱巴	5.126	32.197	15	7.1	Mw		31	1				1				
1990	5	22	20	35	39					USGS	Cuba: Santiago, Near Coast	古巴:圣地亚哥近海	19.74	-76.02	13	5.1	Md	6										
1990	5	24	20	0	10					* Engdahl	Sudan: Juba	苏丹:朱巴	5.355	31.868	16	7.1	Mw							1				
1990	5	27	18	27	57					USGS	Armenia: Gyumri, Spitak	亚美尼亚:久姆里,斯皮塔克	40.87	44.24	10	4.9	mb	6										
1990	5	29	12	34	42	1	5			ISC, NOAA	Philippines: Mindanao Island	菲律宾:棉兰老岛	7.7	125.6	33	6.1	Mw											
1990	5	30	2	34	8					* Engdahl	Peru: Rioja, Neuva Cajamarca	秘鲁:利奥哈,卡哈马尔卡	-6.015	-77.148	24	6.6	Mw	7	135	3			1	2				
1990	5	30	10	40	8					* ISC, Engdahl	Romania: Vrancea	罗马尼亚:弗朗恰	45.861	26.64	89	7	Mw	6	14	1			23.7	3				
1990	5	31	0	17	50					* Engdahl	Romania: Vrancea	罗马尼亚:弗朗恰	45.825	26.732	91	6.3	Mw	5						2				
1990	6	1	1	22	12					ISC, Engdahl, USGS	Japan: Yokoshibahikari	日本:千叶横芝光	35.639	140.518	58.7	6.3	Mw	6										
1990	6	3	11	39	12					USGS	Bosnia: Banja Luka	波斯尼亚:巴尼亚卢卡	44.64	17.58	10	4.7	ML	7										
1990	6	5	13	42	51					USGS, ISC	Japan: Yamakita	日本:神奈川山北	35.41	139.04	121	5.6	mb	6										
1990	6	8	0	31	50					*	Costa Rica: Santiago De Puriscal	哥斯达黎加:圣地亚哥	9.855	-84.327	10	4.7	mb							2			14	1
1990	6	9	1	14	35					* GSHAP, USGS	Peru: Rioja, Moyobamba	秘鲁:利奥哈,莫约班巴	-6.062	-77.136	26	5.5	mb	6	1	1				2				
1990	6	13	2	44	8					USGS	Western Caroline Islands	卡罗琳群岛西部	9.46	138.2	20	5.6	mb	6										
1990	6	14	3	47	29					* China	Kazakhstan: Zaysan	哈萨克斯坦:蒂桑	47.869	85.076	58	7.2	Ms	5	1	1				3				
1990	6	14	7	40	56					* Bautista, Engdahl	Philippines: Culasi, Panay	菲律宾:库拉西,班乃	11.39	122.046	18.1	7.1	Mw	6	4	1				2				
1990	6	17	4	51	47					* Engdahl	Pakistan: Baluchistan	巴基斯坦:俾路支	27.425	65.739	15	6.1	Mw							2				
1990	6	20	21	0	14					* Iran, Engdahl	Iran: Rasht, Qazvin, Zanjan	伊朗:拉什特,加兹温,赞詹	37.001	49.186	19	7.9	Ms	7	40000	5	105000	5	8000	5		4		
1990	6	21	9	2	16					* Iran, Engdahl	Iran: Rudbar, Rasht	伊朗:鲁德巴,拉什特	36.631	49.786	14.7	5.8	Mw		20	1				2				
1990	7	5	1	9	27					USGS	Afghan: Taloqan	阿富汗:塔卢坎	37.59	69.24	31	4.8	mb	6										
1990	7	6	0	16	20					*	Indonesia: Java, Kuningan	印度尼西亚:爪哇,库宁	-6.904	108.12	14	5.8	mb							3				
1990	7	11	15	14	5					USGS, ISC	Gulf of Alaska	阿拉斯加湾	59.33	-136.47	10	5.7	ML	5										
1990	7	12	23	8	23					ISC, Engdahl, USGS	Martinique Island	马提尼克岛(拉丁美洲)	14.63	-60.469	20.9	5.8	Mw	6										
1990	7	13	14	20	45					* Engdahl	Afghan: Badakhshan	阿富汗:巴达赫尚	36.438	70.78	211.6	6.4	Mw		43	1				1				
1990	7	16	7	26	36					* Bautista, Engdahl	Philippines: Baguio, Cabanatuan, Dagupan	菲律宾:碧瑶,卡巴纳端,达古潘	15.721	121.181	24.9	7.7	Mw	9	2412	4			370	5				
1990	7	16	14	51	36					USGS	Argentina: Uspallata	阿根廷:乌斯帕亚塔	-32.46	-69.96	102	5.7	mb	6										
1990	7	18	11	29	25					* ISC	Turkey: Cameli, Denizli	土耳其:恰梅利,丹兹利	36.99	29.595	17	5.6	Mw							2				
1990	7	27	12	38	1					* Engdahl	Vanuatu Islands	瓦努阿图群岛	-15.341	167.492	127.8	7.2	Mw	5						2				

年 Year	月 Mo	日 Dy	时 Hr	分 Mn	秒 Sec	海啸 源 Sr	浪高 Wh	级 I mI	级 S mS	资料来源 Information	地名(英文) Name(English)	地名(中文) Name(Chinese)	纬度(°) Latitude	经度(°) Longitude	深度 Depth	震级 Mag	标度 Scale	烈度 MMI	死亡人数 Deaths 数量/人 Num	级别 Dd	受伤人数 Injuries 数量/人 Num	级别 Dd	经济损失 Damage 数量/$ Mill	级别 De	房屋毁坏 Houses Destroyed 数量/间 Num	级别 Dh	房屋受损 Houses Damaged 数量/间 Num	级别 Dh
1990	7	31	15	50	53					USGS	Bosnia and Herzegovina: Mostar	波斯尼亚和黑塞哥维那:莫斯塔尔	43.02	17.81	10	4.9	ML	7										
1990	8	3	9	15	8					* China, Engdahl	Kazakhstan: Rechnoy	哈萨克斯坦:列奇诺伊	47.971	85.008	33	6.6	Ms	7						2				
1990	8	4	12	52	27					China, Dis	China: Sichuan, Emeishan, SW.	中国:四川峨眉山西南	29.54	103.29	14	4.7	Ms	6					3.87	2				
1990	8	5	3	36	24					ISC, Engdahl, USGS	Japan: Ibaraki, Near Coast	日本:茨城近海	36.413	141.182	27	6.1	Mw	6										
1990	8	11	2	59	55					*	Ecuador: Quito	厄瓜多尔:基多	-0.059	-78.449	5	5	mb	7	4	1				2				
1990	8	18	13	38	17					China, USGS	China: Sichuan, Yanyuan, SW.	中国:四川盐源西南	27.03	101.23	17	5.7	Ms	6										
1990	8	22	23	47	6					USGS, ISC	Japan: Isumi	日本:千叶夷隅	35.22	140.42	26	5.5	mb	6										
1990	8	23	2	44	57					USGS	Japan: Mobara	日本:千叶茂原	35.3	140.36	44	4.9	mb	6										
1990	9	2	4	26	50					ISC, Engdahl, USGS	Ecuador: Bahia De Caraquez, Canoa	厄瓜多尔:加拉加斯湾,卡诺亚	-0.142	-80.215	14	6.2	Mw	6										
1990	9	3	10	48	33					USGS	Slovenia: Novo Mesto	斯洛文尼亚:新梅斯托	45.92	15.87	20	5.1	ML	7										
1990	9	4	2	56	58					USGS	Russia: Sakhalin Island	俄罗斯:库页岛(萨哈林岛)	49.79	142.39	15	4.9	mb	6										
1990	9	23	21	13	8	4	0.2			* Engdahl, NOAA	Japan: South Honshu Ridge	日本:本州南部海岭	33.27	138.616	10	6.5	Mw											
1990	9	26	13	18	51					USGS	US: Missouri, Sikeston	美国:密苏里州赛克斯顿	37.17	-89.58	12	5	MLg	6										
1990	9	26	23	8	24					*	South Africa: Welkom	南非:威尔康姆	-28.014	26.727	5	5.4	mb		2	1	5	1		1				
1990	9	27	21	12	33					* USGS	Kazakhstan: Zaysan	哈萨克斯坦:蒂桑	47.903	84.961	33	5	mb	6						2				
1990	10	18	9	30	44					*	South Africa: Charletonville	南非:卡尔顿维尔	-26.39	27.349	5	4	mb		10	1	6	1						
1990	10	20	8	7	28					* China, Engdahl, Dis	China: Gansu, Jingtai, W.	中国:甘肃景泰西	37.097	103.728	4.2	6.1	Ms	8	2	1	27	1	31.4	4	15431	5		
1990	10	24	6	15	21					USGS, ISC	US: California, Mono City	美国:加利福尼亚州莫诺锡蒂	38.05	-119.16	12	5.7	ML	5										
1990	10	24	23	38	14					ISC, Dis	China: Xinjiang, Jinghe, SE.	中国:新疆精河东南	44.22	83.95	21	5.6	mb	6										
1990	10	25	4	54	1					* Engdahl	Afghan: Chitral, Mardan	阿富汗:吉德拉尔,马尔丹	35.091	70.475	112.2	5.8	Mw		11	1				2				
1990	10	31	14	39	27					USGS	Chile: Copiapo	智利:科皮亚波	-26.63	-70.48	59	5.5	mb	6										
1990	11	3	16	39	58					USGS	Tajikistan: Dzhirgatal, Garm	塔吉克斯坦:吉尔加塔尔,加尔姆	39.03	71.43	51	5.6	mb	6										
1990	11	6	18	45	54					* Engdahl	Iran: Darab	伊朗:达拉卜	28.266	55.484	11	6.6	Mw		22	1			232	5				
1990	11	11	22	16	25					USGS	Slovenia: Kranj	斯洛文尼亚:克拉尼	46.14	14.05	22	4.7	ML	6										
1990	11	12	12	28	53					ISC, Engdahl, USGS	Kazakhstan: Almaty	哈萨克斯坦:阿拉木图	42.962	78.082	19	6.3	Mw	7										
1990	11	15	2	34	29					* Engdahl	Indonesia: Sumatera, Aceh	印度尼西亚:苏门答腊亚齐	3.932	97.393	13.3	6.7	Mw		1	1			2.1	2				
1990	11	23	10	33	31					USGS	Japan: Hino	日本:鸟取日野	35.19	133.4	10	4.6	mb	6										

年 Year	月 Mo	日 Dy	时 Hr	分 Mn	秒 Sec	海啸 源 Sr	浪高 Wh	级 I mI	级 S mS	资料来源 Information	地名(英文) Name(English)	地名(中文) Name(Chinese)	纬度(°) Latitude	经度(°) Longitude	深度 Depth	震级 Mag	标度 Scale	烈度 MMI	死亡人数 数量/人 Num	死亡人数 级别 Dd	受伤人数 数量/人 Num	受伤人数 级别 Dd	经济损失 数量/$ Mill	经济损失 级别 De	房屋毁坏 数量/间 Num	房屋毁坏 级别 Dh	房屋受损 数量/间 Num	房屋受损 级别 Dh
1990	11	25	12	32	45					USGS,ISC	Ecuador:Morona Santiago	厄瓜多尔:莫罗纳-圣地亚哥	-2.69	-77.77	25	5.6	mb	5										
1990	11	27	4	37	59					* USGS	Croatia:Split	克罗地亚:斯普利特	43.853	16.633	24	5.6	Ms	8						2				
1990	12	1	18	9	29					*	Kyrgyzstan:Jalal-Abad	吉尔吉斯斯坦:贾拉拉巴德	40.854	73.553	29	5	mb	6						3				
1990	12	3	5	48	18					USGS,ISC	New Caledonia:Noumea	新喀里多尼亚:努美阿	-22.73	166.7	11	5.7	mb	5										
1990	12	7	9	38	16					USGS	Japan:Joetsu	日本:新潟上越	37.22	138.49	10	5.4	mb	6										
1990	12	7	9	40	44					USGS	Japan:Joetsu	日本:新潟上越	37.31	138.47	14	5.1	mb	6										
1990	12	13	0	24	26	4	0.1			* Italy,NOAA	Italy:Sicily,Carlentini	意大利:西西里岛,卡抡蒂尼	37.266	15.121	11	5.68	Ms	7	19	1	200	3	500	5				
1990	12	13	3	1	49					* China, Engdahl, USGS	China:Taiwan,Hualien	中国:台湾花莲	23.884	121.646	9.5	6.3	Mw	6	2	1	3	1		1				
1990	12	13	19	50	21	4	0			* China,Engdahl, NOAA,USGS	China:Taiwan,Hualien,Coast of E.	中国:台湾花莲以东海域	23.749	121.598	14.5	7.0	Ms	7						1				
1990	12	13	23	28	6					China, Engdahl, USGS	China:Taiwan,Hualien,Coast of E.	中国:台湾花莲以东海域	23.856	121.71	6	6.3	Ms	7										
1990	12	14	11	22	39					USGS,ISC	Peru:Chimbote,Near Coast	秘鲁:钦博特近海	-9.69	-78.98	38	5.8	mb	6										
1990	12	14	17	23	31					USGS	China:Taiwan,Hualien,Coast of E.	中国:台湾花莲以东海域	23.96	121.7	10	4.6	mb	6										
1990	12	16	15	45	41					USGS,ISC	Georgia:Akhalkalaki	格鲁吉亚:阿卡卡垃吉	41.36	43.72	33	5.7	mb	7										
1990	12	20	7	2	59					USGS,ISC	Afghan:Fayzabad,N.	阿富汗:法扎巴德北部	37.61	70.34	8	5.5	mb	5										
1990	12	21	6	57	45					* ISC,Engdahl	Greece:Edhessa, Kilkis	希腊:埃泽萨,基尔基斯	40.98	22.347	13	6.1	Mw	7	1	1				2				
1990	12	22	17	27	56					* ISC,Engdahl	Costa Rica:Alajuela, Santiago De Puriscal	哥斯达黎加:阿拉辉拉,圣地亚哥	9.979	-84.23	12.9	6	Mw	8	2	1	350	3	19.5	3				
1990	12	30	19	14	21					* ISC,Engdahl	Bismarck Sea	俾斯麦海	-5.118	150.962	177	7.5	Mw							1				
1991	1	5	14	57	13					* Engdahl	Myanmar:Thabeikkyin, Mandalay	缅甸:德贝金,曼德勒	23.582	95.878	17.7	7	Mw							2				
1991	1	13	11	53	38					Engdahl, ISC, Dis	China:Inner Mongolia,Bayan Nur,W.	中国:内蒙巴彦淖尔西	40.622	105.799	12.2	5.6	Ms	5					0.04	1			25	1
1991	1	28	12	58	50					ISC, Engdahl, USGS	New Zealand: South Island, Lower Buller	新西兰:南岛,下布勒	-41.968	171.774	28	5.7	Mw	6										
1991	1	28	18	0	55					ISC, Engdahl, USGS	New Zealand: South Island, Lower Buller	新西兰:南岛,下布勒	-41.968	171.769	18.9	5.9	Mw	6										
1991	1	28	22	28	4					ISC,Dis	China:Shanxi,Xinzhou	中国:山西忻州	38.46	112.71	32	5.6	mb	6										
1991	1	31	23	3	35					* Engdahl	Afghan:Badakhstan, Baghlan	阿富汗:库纳尔,巴格兰	35.979	70.471	142	6.9	Mw	7	845	3			36.0	4				
1991	2	9	16	19	2	4	0.1	-3.3		* Engdahl, NOAA	Solomon Islands	所罗门群岛	-9.892	159.217	24.3	6.9	Mw							1				
1991	2	13	15	49	39					*	France:Le Bourget	法国:布尔歇	44.885	6.76	5	3.8	ML		9	1				1				
1991	2	16	1	23	40	4	0.1	-3.3		* NOAA	Kuril Islands	千岛群岛	48.268	154.328	39	6.1	Mw											
1991	2	18	9	6	18					China,Dis	China:Sichuan,Xiaojin	中国:四川小金	31.6	102.4		5	Ms	7					7.1	3				

时间 Date						海啸 Tsunami				资料来源	震中 Earthquake Epicenter				深度	震级	标度	烈度	死亡人数 Deaths		受伤人数 Injuries		经济损失 Damage		房屋毁坏 Houses Destroyed		房屋受损 Houses Damaged	
年	月	日	时	分	秒	源	浪高	级 I	级 S		地名(英文)	地名(中文)	纬度(°)	经度(°)					数量/人	级别	数量/人	级别	数量/$ Mill	级别	数量/间	级别	数量/间	级别
Year	Mo	Dy	Hr	Mn	Sec	Sr	Wh	mI	mS	Information	Name(English)	Name(Chinese)	Latitude	Longitude	Depth	Mag	Scale	MMI	Num	Dd	Num	Dd	$ Mill	De	Num	Dh	Num	Dh
1991	2	21	2	35	36	4	0.2	-1.7		* Engdahl, NOAA	Bering Sea	白令海	58.438	-175.476	20	6.7	Mw											
1991	2	23	6	25	8					USGS	Canada: Vancouver Island	加拿大:温哥华岛	49.49	-126.8	34	4.9	ML	6										
1991	2	24	6	8	9					USGS	El Salvador: Near Coast	萨尔瓦多:近海	13	-88.08	39	4.5	mb	6										
1991	2	25	14	30	30					* China, Engdahl, Dis	China: Xinjiang, Kalpin	中国:新疆柯坪	40.33	78.97	24.7	6.5	Ms	8	1		9	1	2.44	2	1155	4		
1991	3	11	4	47	11					China, Dis	China: Qinghai, Gade	中国:青海甘德	33.8	99.6		4.4	Ms	6					1.92	2				
1991	3	12	6	3	56					China, USGS	China: Taiwan, Tainan	中国:台湾台南	23	120.3	17	6	Ms	7										
1991	3	24	6	39	22					USGS, ISC	Fiji Islands	斐济群岛	-16.83	177.3	11	5.5	Mw	5										
1991	3	25	18	2	41					* China, Dis	China: Shanxi, Datong	中国:山西大同	40	113.8	10	5.8	Ms	7	1		131	3	18.7	3	314	3	235	3
1991	3	26	3	58	25					China, Engdahl, USGS	China: Taiwan, Coast of S.	中国:台湾南部海域	21.708	121.728	18.8	6.7	Ms	7										
1991	4	4	15	23	23					* Engdahl	Peru: Rioja, Neuva Cajamarca	秘鲁:利奥哈,卡哈马尔卡	-6.045	-77.096	21	6.4	Mw	5	10	1				2				
1991	4	5	4	19	51					* ISC, Engdahl	Peru: Rioja, Moyobamba	秘鲁:利奥哈,莫约班巴	-5.976	-77.05	20	6.9	Mw	7	53	2				3				
1991	4	5	15	50	49					ISC, Engdahl	Peru: Ica	秘鲁:伊卡	-14.193	-75.465	50	6.3	Mw	6										
1991	4	18	9	18	30					* USGS	Tadzhikistan: Khatlon	塔吉克斯坦:哈特隆州	37.457	68.273	33	5.5	Mw	7	3	1				3				
1991	4	19	10	12	47					USGS	Brazil: Sobral	巴西:索布腊儿尔	-3.89	-39.74	10	4.8	mb	6										
1991	4	20	17	8	20					*	Afghan: Badakhshan	阿富汗:巴达赫尚	36.416	70.912	33	4.1	mb							2				
1991	4	22	21	56	54	4	3	1		* ISC, Engdahl, NOAA	Costa Rica: Limon, Pandora	哥斯达黎加:利蒙,潘多拉	9.675	-83.072	12.3	7.6	Mw	10	87	2			510	5				
1991	4	24	10	54	36					*	Turkey: Erzurum Province	土耳其:埃尔佐鲁姆	39.597	41.118	33	4.5	mb		1	1				2				
1991	4	24	22	12	3					USGS	Japan: Shimada	日本:静冈岛田	34.88	138.14	41	4.7	mb	6										
1991	4	29	9	12	50					* Engdahl	Georgia: Kutaisi	格鲁吉亚:库塔伊西	42.448	43.669	17	7.3	Mw	9	270	3			1700	5		4		
1991	4	29	18	12	23					USGS, ISC, Engdahl	Peru: Vegueta	秘鲁:贝格塔	-11.26	-77.67	58	6.7	Mw	5										
1991	5	4	1	18	55					USGS	US: Missouri, New Madrid	美国:密苏里州新马德里	36.56	-89.82	5	5	MLg	6										
1991	5	4	3	42	56					* ISC, Engdahl	Panama: Changuinola	巴拿马:昌金努拉	9.549	-82.439	6.3	6.2	Mw				36	1		2				
1991	5	15	14	28	50					*	Georgia: Kutaisi	格鲁吉亚:库塔伊西	42.565	43.349	14	4.9	mb	5						2				
1991	5	24	20	50	57					ISC, Engdahl, USGS	Peru: Moquegua	秘鲁:莫克瓜	-16.553	-70.657	128	6.9	Mw	6										
1991	5	26	10	59	49					*	Malaysia: Kalimantan, Ranau	马来西亚:加里曼丹,兰瑙	5.865	116.746	33	5.1	mb		1	1				2				
1991	5	29	11	2	11					China	China: Hebei, Tangshan	中国:河北唐山	39.72	118.3		4.8	Ms	7										
1991	5	29	23	6	55					China, Dis	China: Hebei, Tangshan	中国:河北唐山	39.68	118.27		5.1	Ms	7			6	1	15.6	3				
1991	6	6	8	2	6					China	China: Xinjiang, Hejing	中国:新疆和静	42.68	87.25	22	5.1	Ms	5										
1991	6	15	0	59	22					* Engdahl	Georgia: Gori, N.	格鲁吉亚:哥里北部	42.415	44.025	9	6.3	Mw	8	8	1				3				
1991	6	15	1	21	42					USGS, ISC	Japan: Miyako	日本:岩手宫古	39.49	141.75	71	5.5	mb	6										

时间 年 Year	月 Mo	日 Dy	时 Hr	分 Mn	秒 Sec	海啸 Tsunami 源 Sr	浪高 Wh	级I mI	级S mS	资料来源 Information	震中 Earthquake Epicenter 地名(英文) Name(English)	地名(中文) Name(Chinese)	纬度(°) Latitude	经度(°) Longitude	深度 Depth	震级 Mag	标度 Scale	烈度 MMI	死亡人数 Deaths 数量/人 Num	级别 Dd	受伤人数 Injuries 数量/人 Num	级别 Dd	经济损失 Damage 数量/$ Mill	级别 De	房屋毁坏 Houses Destroyed 数量/间 Num	级别 Dh	房屋受损 Houses Damaged 数量/间 Num	级别 Dh
1991	6	15	11	15	28					*	Philippines: Pinatubo Eruption	菲律宾:皮纳图博火山	15.119	120.355	10	5.7	mb		137	3				3				
1991	6	16	11	7	11					*	Turkey:Kagizman	土耳其:卡厄兹曼	39.984	42.875	26	4.6	mb							2				
1991	6	20	5	18	54					* Engdahl	Indonesia:South Sulawesi sea	印度尼西亚:苏拉威西海南部	1.226	122.789	32.5	7.5	Mw	6						3				
1991	6	24	4	59	4					USGS,ISC	Gulf of Alaska	阿拉斯加湾	58.32	-137.01	10	5.7	MS	5										
1991	6	25	3	49	18					USGS,ISC	Japan:Hitachi	日本:茨城日立	36.6	140.88	61	5.5	mb	6										
1991	6	27	0	11	4					USGS	Japan:Kumamoto	日本:熊本	32.47	130.34	33	4.5	mb	6										
1991	6	28	14	43	55					* CGS	US:California,Arcadia	美国:加利福尼亚州阿卡迪亚	34.262	-118.002	11	5.8	mb	7	2	1	104	3	33.5	4				
1991	7	1	6	18	4					China,Dis	China:Yunnan,Shidian	中国:云南施甸	24.9	99		5.0	Ms	7			22	1	9.6	3				
1991	7	4	6	26	32					USGS,ISC	Georgia:Gori,N.	格鲁吉亚:哥里北部	42.39	44.12	20	5.5	mb	7										
1991	7	4	11	43	12					* Engdahl	Indonesia:Timor,Kalabahi	印度尼西亚:帝汶,卡拉巴希	-8.13	124.558	29	6.7	Mw		23	1			7.7	3				
1991	7	6	12	19	50					ISC, Engdahl, USGS	Peru:Cuzco	秘鲁:库斯科	-13.245	-72.153	105	6.8	Mw	6										
1991	7	12	10	42	21					* USGS	Romania:Timisoara	罗马尼亚:蒂米什瓦拉	45.364	21.057	11	5.7	Mw	8	2	1	30	1		1				2
1991	7	18	11	56	31					* USGS	Romania:Caras - Severin	罗马尼亚:卡拉什 - 塞维林	44.888	22.407	12	5.7	mb	8						2			615	3
1991	7	22	11	58	52					China	China:Yunnan,Shidian	中国:云南施甸	24.8	99		5.2	Ms	7										
1991	7	23	19	44	50					*	Peru:Maca, Chivay	秘鲁:玛卡,奇瓦伊	-15.679	-71.574	5	5	mb	5	92	2				2				
1991	7	24	9	45	42					* USGS	Iraq:Arbil	伊拉克:阿尔贝拉	36.52	44.066	26	5.5	Mw	8	20	1		3		2	100	2		
1991	8	9	9	33	50					*	Costa Rica:Cartago	哥斯达黎加:卡塔哥	9.737	-84.054	5	4.7	Ms							1			30	1
1991	8	15	1	34	34					USGS	Romania:Voiteg, Deta	罗马尼亚:沃伊泰格,代塔	45.49	21.29	10	4.5	Md	6										
1991	8	17	6	18	34					*	Venezuela:Lara	委内瑞拉:拉腊	10.045	-69.948	10	5.5	mb	5						2			100	2
1991	8	17	19	29	41					* CGS, Engdahl	US:California,Petrolia	美国:加利福尼亚州佩脱里亚	40.281	-124.151	12	5.6	M	7						2				
1991	8	28	1	29	2					USGS,ISC	Japan:Yasugi	日本:岛根安来	35.34	133.21	12	5.9	mb	6										
1991	9	2	11	5	50					USGS,ISC,Dis	China:Qinghai,Haixi,NW.	中国:青海海西西北	37.44	95.4	10	5.5	mb	6					0.51	1				
1991	9	3	8	44	50					ISC, Engdahl, USGS	Japan:South Honshu Ridge	日本:本州南部海岭	33.688	138.793	27.2	6.3	Mw	6										
1991	9	8	13	50	31					*	New Zealand: Wellington, Wanganui	新西兰:惠灵顿,旺加努伊	-40.25	175.053	88	5.6	mb							2				
1991	9	8	19	45	22					USGS	Macedonia:Budva	蒙特尼哥罗(黑山):布德瓦	42.16	18.75	10	4.9	Md	6										
1991	9	17	21	10	29					USGS,ISC	US:California,San Simeon	美国:加利福尼亚州圣西米恩	35.83	-121.32	8	5.5	mb	6										
1991	9	18	9	48	15					* Engdahl	Guatemala: Guatemala City, Solola	危地马拉:危地马拉城,索洛拉	14.603	-90.931	11	6.2	Mw	6	25	1	200	3		3				
1991	9	20	11	16	11					China,ISC,Dis	China:Qinghai,Gonghe	中国:青海共和	36.19	100.06	13	5.3	Ms	6					1.90	2				

年 Year	月 Mo	日 Dy	时 Hr	分 Mn	秒 Sec	海啸 Tsunami 源 Sr	浪高 Wh	级 I mI	级 S mS	资料来源 Information	震中 Earthquake Epicenter 地名(英文) Name(English)	地名(中文) Name(Chinese)	纬度(°) Latitude	经度(°) Longitude	深度 Depth	震级 Mag	标度 Scale	烈度 MMI	死亡人数 Deaths 数量/人 Num	级别 Dd	受伤人数 Injuries 数量/人 Num	级别 Dd	经济损失 Damage 数量/$ Mill	级别 De	房屋毁坏 Houses Destroyed 数量/间 Num	级别 Dh	房屋受损 Houses Damaged 数量/间 Num	级别 Dh
1991	10	6	1	46	48					USGS	Turkey: Cildir	土耳其:彻尔德尔	41.1	43.41	18	5	mb	6										
1991	10	14	15	58	15	4	0.2	-3.3	-2.5	* Engdahl, NOAA	Solomon Islands	所罗门群岛	-9.048	158.549	24.8	7.2	Mw											
1991	10	19	21	23	16					* India, Engdahl	India: Chamoli, Uttarkashi, New Delhi	印度:查莫利,乌塔卡西,新德里	30.736	78.808	10	6.8	Mw	8	1500	4	1800	4	60.0	4	7500	4		
1991	10	28	1	9	12					ISC, USGS	Japan: Oita	日本:大分	33.92	131.17	19	6.0	Mw	6										
1991	11	4	1	50	32					*	Iran: Behbahan	伊朗:贝赫贝汉	30.666	50.218	39	5.4	Ms							2				
1991	11	8	15	13	44					*	India: Jodhpur, Jaisalmer	印度:焦特布尔,杰伊瑟尔梅尔	26.323	70.607	22	5.6	mb							1				
1991	11	10	8	20	21					USGS, ISC	Costa Rica: Turrialba, Cartago	哥斯达黎加:杜黎阿勒巴,卡塔哥	10	-83.26	37	5.6	mb	6										
1991	11	19	8	24	3					USGS	Japan: Tokyo	日本:东京	35.57	139.97	78	4.9	mb	6										
1991	11	19	22	28	53					* GSHAP, Engdahl	Colombia: Chaco, Buenaventura	哥伦比亚:查科省,布埃纳文图拉	4.585	-77.295	21	7.2	Mw	6	2	1				2				
1991	11	22	0	40	24					*	Yemen: Adan	也门:艾顿	13.887	44.068	10	4.7	mb		10	1				2				
1991	11	26	19	40	50					ISC, Engdahl, USGS	Japan: Hokkaido	日本:北海道	42.074	142.541	56	6.4	Mw	6										
1991	11	28	17	19	56					* Iran	Iran: Rudbar, Rasht	伊朗:鲁德巴,拉什特	36.924	49.603	16	5.6	mb		1	1				2				
1991	12	2	8	49	40					*	Romania: Voiteg, Deta	罗马尼亚:沃伊泰格,代塔	45.498	21.115	10	5.6	Ms	8				2		2			5000	4
1991	12	19	3	12	22					USGS	Romania: Voiteg, Deta	罗马尼亚:沃伊泰格,代塔	45.91	21.57	10	4.5	ML	6										
1991	12	22	8	43	15	1	0.5		0.5	* Engdahl, NOAA	Kuril Islands	千岛群岛	45.615	151.01	25	7.6	Mw											
1992	1	2	19	41	46					ISC, Engdahl, USGS	Colombia: Chiquinquira	哥伦比亚:奇金基拉	5.609	-73.794	134	5.8	Mw	6										
1992	1	5	6	30	17	4	0.8	-0.3		* NOAA, CSN	China: Hainan, Dongfang, Coast	中国:海南东方海岸	18.85	108.67	8	3.7	Ms							1				
1992	1	12	0	12	31					ISC, Dis	China: Gansu, Jiayuguan, N.	中国:甘肃嘉峪关北部	40.05	98.14	33	5.7	mb	6										
1992	1	22	21	41	26					USGS, ISC, Dis	China: Yellow Sea	中国:黄海	35.35	121.11	33	5.5	ML	6										
1992	2	1	19	4	5					* USGS	Japan: Miura	日本:神奈川三浦	35.11	139.64	100	5.8	Mw	8			37	1		1				
1992	2	4	1	58	40					* ISC	Indonesia: Jawa, Brebes	印度尼西亚:爪哇,伯利伯斯	-7.138	109.067	58	5.2	Mw							2				
1992	2	18	11	16	14					China	China: Fujian, Putian, Nanri Dao	中国:福建福建莆田南日岛	25.02	119.67	13	5.2	Ms	5										
1992	3	4	11	57	53					* Iran	Iran: Aharmahal And Bakhtiari	伊朗:恰哈马哈勒-巴赫蒂亚里	31.726	50.778	18	4.9	mb		6	1				2				
1992	3	8	3	43	4					USGS	US: California, North Coast	美国:加利福尼亚州北部近海	40.23	-124.29	13	5.5	Mw	6										
1992	3	12	13	5	55					USGS, ISC	Algeria: Ain Temouchent	阿尔及利亚:艾因蒂姆尚特	35.31	-2.53	21	5.8	mb	6										
1992	3	13	17	18	39					* Engdahl	Turkey: Erzincan	土耳其:埃尔津占	39.728	39.654	27	6.7	Mw	8	498	3			13.5	3				

时间 年 Year	月 Mo	日 Dy	时 Hr	分 Mn	秒 Sec	海啸 Tsunami 源 Sr	浪高 Wh	级I mI	级S mS	资料来源 Information	震中 Earthquake Epicenter 地名(英文) Name(English)	地名(中文) Name(Chinese)	纬度(°) Latitude	经度(°) Longitude	深度 Depth	震级 Mag	标度 Scale	烈度 MMI	死亡人数 Deaths 数量/人 Num	级别 Dd	受伤人数 Injuries 数量/人 Num	级别 Dd	经济损失 Damage 数量/$ Mill $ Mill	级别 De	房屋毁坏 Houses Destroyed 数量/间 Num	级别 Dh	房屋受损 Houses Damaged 数量/间 Num	级别 Dh
1992	3	21	3	11	58					USGS	China:Taiwan,Hualien	中国:台湾花莲	23.95	121.68	24	4.5	ML	7										
1992	3	30	19	32	2					USGS	Macedonia:Ohrid	马其顿:奥赫里德	41.13	20.99	10	4.9	ML	7										
1992	4	5	7	47	48					China, USGS, ISC, Dis	China:Xinjiang,Hotan,S.	中国:新疆和田南	35.7	80.66	17	5.9	Ms	7					1.82	2				
1992	4	13	1	20	1					* USGS	Netherlands:Roermond	荷兰:鲁尔蒙德	51.153	5.798	21	5.9	ML	8	1	1			100	5				
1992	4	13	5	58	46					USGS	Japan:Oshu,Near Coast	日本:奥州近海	39.12	142.27	58	5.2	Mw	6										
1992	4	19	18	32	21					China,Eng-dahl, USGS	China:Taiwan,Hualien	中国:台湾花莲	23.885	121.567	16	6.8	Ms	7										
1992	4	23	4	50	25					* Engdahl	US:California,Palm Springs	美国:加利福尼亚州棕泉	33.868	-116.546	12	6.1	M	7						2				
1992	4	23	12	18	34					China,Dis	China:Yunnan,Menglian	中国:云南孟连	22.3	99.1		6.7	Ms	7	4		44	1	10.9	3				
1992	4	25	18	6	6	4	1.8	0.8	0.5	* CGS, Engdahl, NOAA	US:California,Humboldt	美国:加利福尼亚州洪堡	40.381	-124.048	15	7.2	M	8			98	2	66.0	4				
1992	5	1	8	55	60					USGS	Tajikistan:Roghun	塔吉克斯坦:罗格汉	38.47	70.08	33	4.5	mb	6										
1992	5	3	3	40	41					USGS,ISC	Chile:Near Coast of C.	智利:中部近海	-32.37	-71.59	68	5.5	Mw	5										
1992	5	8	5	15	50					USGS	Albania:Tepelene	阿尔巴尼亚:德培雷恩	40.11	19.75	17	4.7	ML	6										
1992	5	8	6	44	39					USGS	Switzerland:St. Gallen	瑞士:圣加伦	47.27	9.5	5	5	ML	6										
1992	5	11	10	7	51					USGS,ISC	Japan:Naka	日本:茨城那珂	36.47	140.52	59	5.6	mb	6										
1992	5	12	15	46	56					USGS,ISC	Peru:Casma,Near Coast	秘鲁:卡斯马近海	-9.52	-78.75	62	5.7	Mw	5										
1992	5	15	8	8	2					* Engdahl	Kyrgyzstan:Jalal-Abad	吉尔吉斯斯坦:贾拉拉巴德	40.997	72.467	32.1	6.2	Ms	7	3	1			31.0	4				
1992	5	17	10	15	32	4	0.1			* Engdahl, NOAA	Philippines:Mindanao, Tandag	菲律宾:棉兰老岛,坦达	7.245	126.759	28.7	7.5	Mw							1				
1992	5	20	12	20	34					* Engdahl	Pakistan:Peshawar, Kohat	巴基斯坦:白沙瓦,戈哈特	33.323	71.35	16	6.1	Mw		50	1				2				
1992	5	25	16	55	6					* ISC,Engdahl	Cuba:Pilon, Manzanillo	古巴:皮隆,曼萨尼约	19.618	-77.883	23.1	6.8	Mw				40	1		2			820	3
1992	5	27	5	13	41	1	0.1			* Engdahl, NOAA	Solomon Islands	所罗门群岛	-11.085	165.252	23.4	7	Mw											
1992	5	27	22	30	36					ISC, Engdahl, USGS	New Zealand:Wairau Valley	新西兰:怀劳瓦利	-41.589	173.635	71.2	5.9	Mw	6										
1992	6	7	11	45	60					USGS	Bosnia and Herzegovina: Sokolac	波斯尼亚和黑塞哥维那:索科拉茨	43.84	18.81	11	4.8	ML	6										
1992	6	15	1	46	35					USGS	Japan:Shizuoka,Near Coast	日本:静冈近海	34.15	139.07	27	5.3	Mw	7										
1992	6	28	11	57	39					* Engdahl	US:California,Landers	美国:加利福尼亚州兰德斯	34.198	-116.515	15	7.6	Mw	9	3	1	400	3	92.0	4				
1992	6	28	15	5	33					* Engdahl	US:California,Big Bear Lake	美国:加利福尼亚州大熊湖	34.289	-116.817	12.4	6.5	Mw	8				2		2				
1992	6	29	10	14	24					* ISC,Engdahl	US:Nevada,Amargosa Valley	美国:内华达州阿马戈萨瓦利	36.77	-116.315	9.8	5.7	M							2				

时间 Date						海啸 Tsunami				资料来源 Information	震中 Earthquake Epicenter				深度 Depth	震级 Mag	标度 Scale	烈度 MMI	死亡人数 Deaths		受伤人数 Injuries		经济损失 Damage		房屋毁坏 Houses Destroyed		房屋受损 Houses Damaged	
年 Year	月 Mo	日 Dy	时 Hr	分 Mn	秒 Sec	源 Sr	浪高 Wh	级 I mI	级 S mS		地名(英文) Name(English)	地名(中文) Name(Chinese)	纬度(°) Latitude	经度(°) Longitude					数量/人 Num	级别 Dd	数量/人 Num	级别 Dd	数量/$ Mill $ Mill	级别 De	数量/间 Num	级别 Dh	数量/间 Num	级别 Dh
1992	7	5	21	18	27					USGS, ISC	US: California, Newberry Springs	美国:加利福尼亚州纽贝里斯普林斯	34.58	-116.32	10	5.7	mb	6										
1992	7	9	1	43	58					USGS, ISC	US: California, Landers	美国:加利福尼亚州兰德斯	34.24	-116.84	8	5.5	mb	6										
1992	7	11	18	14	16					USGS, ISC	US: California, Caliente, W.	美国:加利福尼亚州卡连特西部	35.21	-118.07	10	5.7	ML	5										
1992	7	13	15	34	6					Engdahl, USGS	Russia: Kamchatka Peninsula	俄罗斯:堪察加半岛	51.189	157.606	45	6.2	Mw	6										
1992	7	18	8	37	1	4	0.3	-2.3	-0.5	* Engdahl, NOAA	Japan: Oshu, Off Coast	日本:奥州沿海	39.453	143.298	31.3	6.9	Mw											
1992	7	30	8	24	49					China, Eng-dahl, Dis	China: Xizang (Tibet), Lhasa, NW.	中国:西藏拉萨西北	29.576	90.241	14	6.5	Ms	7			3	1	6.6	3				
1992	8	9	12	1	30					USGS	Tajikistan: Khudzhand	塔吉克斯坦:苦盏	39.83	69.9	33	4.6	mb	6										
1992	8	13	4	52	30					USGS	Macedonia: Ohrid	马其顿:奥赫里德	40.98	20.93	10	4.6	ML	6										
1992	8	19	2	4	39					* Engdahl	Kyrgyzstan: Chui, SW.	吉尔吉斯斯坦:楚河州西南	42.122	73.621	27	7.5	Mw	9	54	2			130	5				
1992	8	24	6	59	41					ISC, Engdahl, USGS	Japan: Nanae	日本:北海道七饭町	41.982	140.682	121	6.1	Mw	6										
1992	8	26	18	42	2					USGS	Macedonia: Podgorica	蒙特尼哥罗(黑山):波德戈里察	42.38	19.34	36	5.1	Md	7										
1992	8	28	0	50	50					*	Pakistan: Kalat	巴基斯坦:卡拉特	29.087	66.74	9	5.5	Ms		4	1				2				
1992	9	2	0	16	4	4	9.9	3.3	2.8	* Engdahl, NOAA	Nicaragua: Masachapa	尼加拉瓜:马萨查帕	11.766	-87.352	45	7.7	M		170	3	489	3	30.0	4	1500	4		
1992	9	2	10	26	21					USGS	US: Utah, St George	美国:犹他州圣乔治	37.09	-113.47	15	5.6	Mw	6										
1992	9	8	0	38	15					* Iran	Iran: Firuzabad	伊朗:菲鲁扎巴德	29.134	52.187	17	5.2	mb		1	1				2				
1992	9	11	3	57	28					* Engdahl	Congo: Kabalo	刚果:卡巴洛	-6.165	26.656	11	6.3	Mw		8	1	37	1		2		3		
1992	10	11	19	24	28					ISC, Engdahl, USGS	Vanuatu Islands	瓦努阿图群岛	-19.265	168.997	129	7.4	Mw	8										
1992	10	12	13	9	57					* Engdahl	Egypt: Cairo	埃及:开罗	29.729	31.158	22	5.8	Mw		545	3	6512	4	1200	5	9350	4		
1992	10	17	8	32	42					* Engdahl	Colombia: Murindo, Cali	哥伦比亚:穆林多,卡利	6.852	-76.71	14	6.7	Mw							2				
1992	10	18	15	11	60					* Engdahl	Colombia: Murindo, Apartado	哥伦比亚:穆林多,阿帕尔坦多	7.094	-76.763	2.9	7.4	Mw		11	1				2				
1992	10	20	7	18	50					USGS	Ryukyu Islands	琉球群岛	24.5	123.66	21	5.3	Mw	7										
1992	10	23	9	11	9					USGS	Morocco: Errachidia	摩洛哥:拉希迪耶	31.35	-4.32	28	5.6	Mw	6										
1992	10	23	23	19	47					ISC, Engdahl, USGS	Georgia: Gori, N.	格鲁吉亚:哥里北部	42.572	45.086	16	6.4	Mw	8										
1992	10	30	5	38	28					USGS	Montenegro: Ulcinj	门的内哥罗(黑山):乌尔齐尼	42.42	19.02	26	4.6	ML	7										
1992	10	30	10	43	58					USGS	Morocco: Errachidia	摩洛哥:拉希迪耶	31.28	-4.37	25	5.6	Mw	6										
1992	11	8	10	22	53					USGS	Chile: Antofagasta, C.	智利:安托法加斯塔中部	-23.63	-70.38	33	5.6	Mw	5										
1992	11	26	10	47	56					China, Dis	China: Fujian, Longyan	中国:福建龙岩	25.5	117		5	Ms	6			292	3	18.5	3				

时间 Date						海啸 Tsunami				资料来源 Information	震中 Earthquake Epicenter				深度 Depth	震级 Mag	标度 Scale	烈度 MMI	死亡人数 Deaths		受伤人数 Injuries		经济损失 Damage		房屋毁坏 Houses Destroyed		房屋受损 Houses Damaged	
年 Year	月 Mo	日 Dy	时 Hr	分 Mn	秒 Sec	源 Sr	浪高 Wh	级 I mI	级 S mS		地名(英文) Name(English)	地名(中文) Name(Chinese)	纬度(°) Latitude	经度(°) Longitude					数量/人 Num	级别 Dd	数量/人 Num	级别 Dd	数量/$ Mill $ Mill	级别 De	数量/间 Num	级别 Dh	数量/间 Num	级别 Dh
1992	11	27	16	0	57					USGS	US:California,Victorville	美国:加利福尼亚州维克托维尔	34.34	-116.9	1	5.6	ML	6										
1992	11	27	21	9	17					USGS,ISC	Turkmenistan:Asgabat	土库曼斯坦:阿什哈巴德	37.47	59.86	24	5.5	mb	6										
1992	11	29	17	39	42					China,CSN,Dis	China:Sichuan,Shiqu,N.	中国:四川石渠北	33.16	98.04	24	5.1	Ms	7			1	1	7.9	3				
1992	12	2	18	3	44					USGS,ISC	South of Alaska	阿拉斯加南部	61.81	-151.19	74	5.5	Mw	5										
1992	12	7	2	11	44					ISC, Engdahl, USGS	Kuril Islands	千岛群岛	43.983	147.148	45	6	Mw	7										
1992	12	9	20	29	47					USGS	Armenia:Gavar	亚美尼亚:卡莫	40.06	45.31	15	4.8	mb	7										
1992	12	12	5	29	28	4	26	4.7	2.7	* Engdahl, NOAA	Indonesia:Flores Islands	印度尼西亚:弗洛勒斯群岛	-8.482	121.844	28	7.8	Mw		2500	4	500	3	100	5	31785	5		
1992	12	18	3	14	6					ISC, Engdahl, USGS	Papua New Guinea:Lae	巴布亚新几内亚:莱城	-6.478	147.217	27.9	6.1	Mw	6										
1992	12	18	11	21	41					China,Dis	China:Yunnan,Yongsheng	中国:云南永胜	26.37	100.58	15	5.4	Ms	6	1		142	3	1.99	2	255	3	17578	5
1992	12	19	9	34	6					USGS	Romania:Timisoara	罗马尼亚:蒂米什瓦拉	45.56	20.95	22	4.8	ML	6										
1992	12	21	6	13	38					USGS,ISC	Aleutian Islands,Rat Island	阿留申群岛,拉特岛	52.01	179.07	99	5.5	mb	5										
1992	12	23	2	20	6					USGS,ISC	Chile:Iquique	智利:伊基克	-19.77	-68.81	105	5.7	Mw	5										
1992	12	28	5	23	26					USGS	China:Taiwan,Hualien,Coast of E.	中国:台湾花莲以东海域	23.92	121.74	34	5	mb	6										
1992	12	31	7	26	6					USGS	Japan:Miyagi,Near Coast	日本:宫城近海	38.9	142.42	39	5.8	Mw	6										
1993	1	13	17	11	8					USGS	Jamaica:St Andrew	牙买加:圣安德鲁	17.95	-76.58	16	5.5	Mw	7										
1993	1	15	11	6	8					* Engdahl, USGS	Japan: Hokkadio, Kushiro, Hachinohe	日本:北海道,钏路,八户	43.022	144.124	102	6.1	mb	9	2	1			358	5				
1993	1	20	14	49	12					USGS	Azores:Fayal Island	亚速尔群岛:法亚尔岛	38.54	-29.28	10	5.4	Mw	6										
1993	1	26	20	32	3					* China, USGS,Dis	China:Yunnan,Pu-er	中国:云南普洱	23.1	101.1	14	6.3	Ms	8			154	3	12.7	3	28417	5		
1993	1	27	10	27	6					*	Iran:Nehbandan	伊朗:内赫班丹	32.104	60.088	33	5.1	mb							1				
1993	1	31	19	33	29					China,Dis	China:Yunnan,Dayao	中国:云南大姚	25.85	101.35	10	5.3	Ms	6			4	1	2.00	2	1202	4	3227	4
1993	2	2	16	5	14					USGS,ISC,Dis	China:Xinjiang,Bayingol	中国:新疆巴音郭楞	42.22	86.13	33	5.7	mb	6	4		5	1	0.13	1	11	1	147	3
1993	2	7	13	27	44	4	0.5	-1	-0.5	* ISC,Engdahl, NOAA,USGS	Japan:Ishikawa, Toyama	日本:石川富山	37.691	137.271	11	6.3	Mw	8						1				
1993	3	6	11	30	33					ISC,USGS	Nicaragua:Chinandega	尼加拉瓜:奇南德加	12.74	-87.4	54	6.3	Mw	6										
1993	3	12	14	1	37					* Engdahl	North of Fiji Islands	斐济群岛北部	-14.393	-178.213	11.8	6.4	Mw		5	1				2				
1993	3	15	16	8	59					ISC, Engdahl, USGS	Chile:Copiapo	智利:科皮亚波	-26.718	-70.896	29	6.5	Mw	6										
1993	3	17	10	15	4					USGS	Uzbekistan:Namangan	乌兹别克斯坦:纳曼干	41.06	72.05	20	4.8	mb	6										
1993	3	20	14	52	1					* China, Engdahl, Dis	China:Xizang (Tibet),Lhatse,SW.	中国:西藏拉孜西南	29	87.345	12	6.6	Ms	8	2		3	1	12.0	3				
1993	3	25	13	34	35					* USGS	US:Oregon,Salem	美国:俄勒冈州塞勒姆	45.035	-122.607	21	5.6	Mw	7					28.4	4				
1993	3	26	22	52	47					*	Iran:Iluyeh & Boyer Ahmad	伊朗:科吉卢耶-博韦艾哈迈德	30.692	50.886	30	5.1	mb							2				

年 Year	月 Mo	日 Dy	时 Hr	分 Mn	秒 Sec	海啸 Tsunami 源 Sr	浪高 Wh	级 I mI	级 S mS	资料来源 Information	震中 Earthquake Epicenter 地名(英文) Name(English)	地名(中文) Name(Chinese)	纬度(°) Latitude	经度(°) Longitude	深度 Depth	震级 Mag	标度 Scale	烈度 MMI	死亡人数 Deaths 数量/人 Num	级别 Dd	受伤人数 Injuries 数量/人 Num	级别 Dd	经济损失 Damage 数量/$ Mill	级别 De	房屋毁坏 Houses Destroyed 数量/间 Num	级别 Dh	房屋受损 Houses Damaged 数量/间 Num	级别 Dh
1993	4	18	9	16	25					* Engdahl	Peru: Lima	秘鲁:利马	-11.701	-76.469	106	6.3	Mw		6	1				1				
1993	5	5	18	21	32					USGS, ISC	Japan: Oshu	日本:岩手奥州	39.1	141.68	99	5.6	mb	6										
1993	5	13	11	59	48					ISC, Engdahl, USGS	Aleutian Islands	阿留申群岛	54.964	-160.502	32	6.9	Mw	6										
1993	5	23	23	57	44					China, Dis	China: Sichuan, Dege	中国:四川德格	31.78	98.8		5.0	Ms	6					1.50	2				
1993	5	25	23	16	45					ISC, Engdahl, USGS	Aleutian Islands	阿留申群岛	55.021	-160.581	37	6.1	Mw	6										
1993	5	28	4	47	41					USGS	US: California, Bakersfield	美国:加利福尼亚州贝克斯菲尔德	35.15	-119.1	21	5.2	ML	6										
1993	5	31	6	12	59					USGS	Japan: Ito	日本:静冈伊东	34.91	139.25	33	4.5	mb	6										
1993	6	1	19	51	11					USGS	Croatia: Varazdin	克罗地亚:瓦拉日丁	46.17	16.47	30	5	ML	7										
1993	6	8	12	57	49					USGS, ISC	Hawaiian Islands	夏威夷群岛	19.33	-155.22	6	5.5	mb	6										
1993	6	8	13	3	38	4	0.1	-1	-0.5	* Engdahl, NOAA, USGS	Russia: Kamchatka Peninsula	俄罗斯:堪察加半岛	51.203	157.736	71	7.5	Mw	7						1				
1993	6	8	23	17	43					ISC, Engdahl, USGS	Argentina: San Juan	阿根廷:圣胡安	-31.59	-69.202	113	6.3	Mw	6										
1993	6	22	16	32	44					* ISC	Iran: Fars	伊朗:法尔斯	30.149	50.814	39	5.7	Mw		24	1								
1993	7	10	20	40	60					* ISC, Engdahl	Costa Rica: Turrialba, Cartago	哥斯达黎加:杜黎阿勒巴,卡塔哥	9.821	-83.609	15.6	5.8	Mw		2	1	9	1		1				
1993	7	11	13	36	23					ISC, Engdahl, USGS	Chile: Antofagasta, S.	智利:安托法加斯塔南部	-25.258	-70.049	48	6.6	Mw	6										
1993	7	12	13	17	14	4	54	5	3.1	* ISC, Engdahl, NOAA	Japan Sea, N.	日本海北部	42.883	139.225	20.4	7.7	Mw	8	230	3	233	3	1207	5	2374	4		
1993	7	14	12	31	49					*	Greece: Patras	希腊:佩特雷	38.224	21.756	23	5.6	Mw							1				
1993	7	17	9	46	33					China, ISC, Dis	China: Yunnan, Deqen	中国:云南迪庆	27.98	99.67	16	5.8	Ms	6	1		15	1	3.61	2				
1993	8	1	0	20	41					*	Sudan: Khartoum	苏丹:喀土穆	15.385	31.69	13	5.5	Mw		2	1	9	1		1				
1993	8	7	8	36	6					China, Dis	China: Sichuan, Muchuan	中国:四川沐川	29.02	103.6	5	5	Ms	7			3	1	1.88	2	389	3	3221	4
1993	8	7	19	42	44	4	0.2			* Engdahl, NOAA, USGS	Japan: Yakumo	日本:北海道八云町	42.081	139.854	14	6.3	Mw	8										
1993	8	8	8	34	27	4	2.1	-1		* Engdahl, NOAA	Guam: Tuman Bay, Apra Harbor	关岛(西太平洋):图曼湾,阿普拉港	12.983	144.838	62.1	7.8	Mw	9			48	1	250	5				
1993	8	10	0	51	55					ISC, Engdahl, USGS	New Zealand: South Island, Secretary Island	新西兰:南岛,塞克勒特里岛	-45.207	166.958	28	7	Mw	6										
1993	8	10	9	46	36					ISC, Engdahl, USGS	New Zealand: North Island, Te Karaka	新西兰:北岛,蒂卡拉卡	-38.495	177.795	14.4	6.4	Mw	7										
1993	8	13	5	3	50					USGS	Montenegro: Niksic	蒙特内哥罗(黑山):尼克希奇	42.82	18.65	10	4.5	Md	6										
1993	8	14	14	30	0					China, Dis	China: Yunnan, Yaoan	中国:云南姚安	25.45	101.25	8	5.6	Ms	7			152	3	5.3	3				
1993	9	4	20	22	33					China, Dis	China: Qinghai, Golmud, E.	中国:青海格尔木	37.1	94.7		5.1	Ms	6					0.28	1				

时间 Date						海啸 Tsunami				资料来源 Information	震中 Earthquake Epicenter				深度 Depth	震级 Mag	标度 Scale	烈度 MMI	死亡人数 Deaths		受伤人数 Injuries		经济损失 Damage		房屋毁坏 Houses Destroyed		房屋受损 Houses Damaged	
年 Year	月 Mo	日 Dy	时 Hr	分 Mn	秒 Sec	源 Sr	浪高 Wh	级 I mI	级 S mS		地名(英文) Name(English)	地名(中文) Name(Chinese)	纬度(°) Latitude	经度(°) Longitude					数量/人 Num	级别 Dd	数量/人 Num	级别 Dd	数量/$ Mill $ Mill	级别 De	数量/间 Num	级别 Dh	数量/间 Num	级别 Dh
1993	9	10	19	12	56					* Engdahl	Guatemala:Southwest;Mexico:Chiapas	危地马拉:西南;墨西哥:恰帕斯	14.702	−92.656	34	7.3	Ms		1	1	3	1		2				
1993	9	11	4	55	33					ISC,USGS	Japan:Hokkaido	日本:北海道	41.99	142.45	53	6.0	Mw	6										
1993	9	21	3	28	57					* Engdahl	US:Oregon,Klamath Falls	美国:俄勒冈州克拉马斯福尔斯	42.316	−122.021	11	6	Mw	7	2	1			7.5	3				
1993	9	29	22	25	50					* India, ISC, Engdahl	India:Latur − Osmanabad	印度:拉土尔 − 奥斯马纳巴德	18.079	76.516	7	6.2	M	8	9748	4	30000	5	1300	5		4		
1993	10	2	8	42	34					China, Engdahl, Dis	China:Xinjiang,Ruoqiang	中国:新疆若羌	38.185	88.711	14	6.6	Ms	8			1	1	0.83	1				
1993	10	11	15	54	23					ISC, Engdahl, USGS	Ryukyu Trench	琉球海沟	32.043	137.905	354.9	6.9	Mw	6										
1993	10	13	2	6	2					* Engdahl	Papua New Guinea:Madang,S.	巴布亚新几内亚:马当南部	−5.852	146.084	25	6.9	Mw		60	2	200	3	5.0	3				
1993	10	20	16	15	60					*	Nepal:Dali	尼泊尔:达利	28.723	82.28	37	5.1	mb							1				
1993	10	24	7	52	17					ISC, Engdahl, USGS	Mexico:Acapulco	墨西哥:阿卡普尔科	16.761	−98.756	21	6.6	Mw	7										
1993	10	26	11	38	21					China,Dis	China:Qinghai,Qilian	中国:青海祁连	38.6	98.7		6	Ms	5										
1993	10	30	17	59	3					USGS	Argentina:San Juan	阿根廷:圣胡安	−31.7	−68.23	107	5.8	Mw	6										
1993	11	11	0	6	7					USGS,ISC	Japan:Oshu,Near Coast	日本:奥州近海	39.03	142.27	29	5.5	mb	6										
1993	11	12	13	27	28					*	India:Latur	印度:拉土尔	18.12	76.533	10	4.6	mb				25	1		1			100	2
1993	11	13	1	18	6	4	0.1	−3.3	−3	* Engdahl. NOAA, USGS	Russia:Kamchatka Peninsula	俄罗斯:堪察加半岛	51.942	158.591	34	7	Mw	6						1				
1993	11	19	1	43	23					ISC, Engdahl, USGS	Aleutian Islands	阿留申群岛	54.19	−164.278	16.7	6.5	Mw	6										
1993	11	19	3	58	53					USGS	Alaska:Unimak Island	阿拉斯加:乌尼马克岛	54.28	−164.15	33	5.8	ML	5										
1993	11	27	6	11	23					USGS	Japan:Miyagi	日本:宫城	38.62	141.16	104	5.8	Mw	6										
1993	11	30	20	37	9					* China,Dis	China:Xinjiang,Ulugqat	中国:新疆乌恰	39.4	75.4	18	6.0	Ms	8	2		37	1	10.3	3	842	3	4862	4
1993	12	4	9	30	14					USGS,ISC	Japan:Hokkaido	日本:北海道	41.76	141.94	84	5.5	mb	6										
1993	12	4	22	15	20					USGS,ISC	US:Oregon,Klamath Falls	美国:俄勒冈州克拉马斯福尔斯	42.3	−122.01	8	5.6	mb	7										
1993	12	15	21	49	42					USGS,ISC	China:Taiwan,Tainan	中国:台湾台南	23.18	120.57	17	5.9	mb	8										
1993	12	17	3	19	4					USGS,ISC	Japan:Oshu,Near Coast	日本:奥州近海	39.19	142.18	54	5.7	mb	6										
1993	12	23	14	22	35					USGS,ISC	Spain:Málaga	西班牙:马拉加	36.76	−2.94	27	5.5	mb	7										
1993	12	29	9	34	38					USGS	Alaska Peninsula,C.	阿拉斯加半岛中部	64.42	−146.9	9	4.8	ML	6										
1994	1	3	5	52	26					* China,Dis	China:Qinghai,Gonghe	中国:青海共和	36.1	100.1	8	6.0	Ms	8			9	1	6.7	3	1130	4		
1994	1	4	8	3	16					USGS	Spain:Málaga	西班牙:马拉加	36.65	−2.82	22	5	MLg	7										
1994	1	5	13	24	11					ISC, Engdahl, USGS	Tyrrhenian Sea	第勒尼安海(伊特鲁里亚海)	39.173	15.189	275.2	5.8	Mw	7										
1994	1	16	1	49	16					*	US:Pennsylvania,Reading	美国:宾西法尼亚州里丁	40.33	−76.037	5	4.6	mb	5						1				

时间						海啸				资料来源	震中				深度	震级	标度	烈度	死亡人数		受伤人数		经济损失		房屋毁坏		房屋受损	
年	月	日	时	分	秒	源	浪高	级 I	级 S		地名(英文)	地名(中文)	纬度(°)	经度(°)					数量/人	级别	数量/人	级别	数量/$ Mill	级别	数量/间	级别	数量/间	级别
Date						Tsunami				Information	Earthquake Epicenter				Depth	Mag	Scale	MMI	Deaths		Injuries		Damage		Houses Destroyed		Houses Damaged	
Year	Mo	Dy	Hr	Mn	Sec	Sr	Wh	mI	mS		Name(English)	Name(Chinese)	Latitude	Longitude					Num	Dd	Num	Dd	$ Mill	De	Num	Dh	Num	Dh
1994	1	17	12	30	57	3	0.1	-3.3	-3	* ISC, Engdahl, NOAA	US:California,Northridge	美国:加利福尼亚州北岭	34.185	-118.563	19	6.7	M	9	60	2	7000	4	40000	5	40000	5		
1994	1	20	5	50	11					USGS	China:Taiwan,Hualien,Coast of E.	中国:台湾花莲以东海域	23.98	121.81	36	5.5	Mw	6										
1994	1	21	2	24	32	4	2	1	1.5	* Engdahl, NOAA	Indonesia:Maluku Utara	印度尼西亚:北马鲁古	1.05	127.759	20	7.2	Ms		9	1	300	3		2	550	3		
1994	2	1	10	1	55					USGS	Hawaiian Islands	夏威夷群岛	19.24	-155.29	32	5.6	Mw	5										
1994	2	3	9	5	6					* ISC,Engdahl	US:Wyoming,Afton	美国:怀俄明州阿夫顿	42.781	-110.969	5.8	5.8	Mw	7						1				
1994	2	5	23	34	11					* Engdahl	Uganda:Fort Portal	乌干达:弗持波德尔	0.547	30.08	14	6.2	Mw		7	1		2	70.0	4				
1994	2	11	14	59	51					USGS	US:Wyoming,Afton	美国:怀俄明州阿夫顿	42.76	-111	5	5.3	ML	6										
1994	2	12	17	6	58					USGS,ISC	Japan:Kagoshima	日本:鹿岛	32.06	130.58	31	5.7	mb	6										
1994	2	15	17	7	46					* ISC,Engdahl	Indonesia:Southern Sumatra	印度尼西亚:苏门答腊南部	-4.976	104.286	23	6.9	Mw		207	3	2000	4	169	5	6000	4		
1994	2	15	21	9	41					China, Engdahl, ISC,Dis	China:Qinghai,Gonghe	中国:青海共和	36.143	100.152	14	5.8	Ms	7			30	1	2.19	2				
1994	2	23	8	2	6					* ISC,Engdahl	Iran:Zahedan	伊朗:扎黑丹	30.814	60.565	6	6.1	Mw		6	1		3	1.4	2				
1994	2	25	7	42	14					China,Dis	China:Sichuan,Jiangyou	中国:四川江油	31.63	104.75	10	4.7	Ms	6			3	1	0.41	1				
1994	2	25	16	3	7					USGS	Croatia:Split	克罗地亚:斯普利特	43.57	16.51	35	4.5	Md	6										
1994	3	1	3	49	3					* ISC,Engdahl	Iran:Firuzabad	伊朗:菲鲁扎巴德	29.149	52.662	13	6.1	Mw		2	1	50	1		2				1
1994	3	2	3	38	4					*	Haiti:Saint - Louis Du Nord	海地:圣路易北	19.803	-72.799	59	5.4	Mw		4	1				2				1
1994	3	11	3	12	11					USGS	Japan:Shizuoka,Near Coast	日本:静冈近海	34.22	139.17	10	5.5	Mw	6										
1994	3	16	12	9	26					USGS	Japan:Shizuoka,Near Coast	日本:静冈近海	34.04	139.08	10	4.5	mb	6										
1994	3	20	21	20	12					USGS,ISC	US:California,Burbank	美国:加利福尼亚州伯班克	34.23	-118.47	13	5.6	mb	6										
1994	3	31	9	41	42					USGS	Austria:Vorarlberg	奥地利:福拉尔贝格	47.25	10.15	13	4.7	ML	6										
1994	4	8	1	10	43	4	0.1	-2.3	-1.5	* ISC, Engdahl, NOAA	Japan Trench	日本海沟	40.653	143.695	16.4	6.4	Mw											
1994	4	15	19	41	8					USGS	Mariana Islands,S.	马里亚纳群岛南部	12.99	144.56	33	5.5	Mw	5										
1994	4	21	3	51	47					ISC, Engdahl, USGS	Papua New Guinea:Bougainville Island	巴布亚新几内亚:布干维尔岛	-5.713	154.15	29.6	6.7	Mw	6										
1994	4	30	3	28	43					ISC, Engdahl, USGS	Japan:Miyazzaki	日本:宫崎	31.427	131.329	50.5	5.9	Mw	6										
1994	5	1	12	0	38					* ISC,Engdahl	Afghan:Balkh	阿富汗:巴尔赫	36.948	67.158	19	6.1	Mw	6	160	3								
1994	5	3	16	36	46					ISC, Engdahl, USGS	Trinidad & Tobago: Near Coast of S.	特立尼达和多巴哥:南部近海	10.275	-60.729	36	6	Mw	6										
1994	5	24	4	0	44					* China, Engdahl, USGS	China:Taiwan,Hualien,Coast of E.	中国:台湾花莲以东海域	23.938	122.433	18.9	7	Ms	6										
1994	5	28	8	4	32					USGS,ISC	Japan:Nagahama	日本:滋贺长滨	35.41	136.13	48	5.5	mb	6										
1994	6	2	18	17	39	4	14	3.7	2.5	* Engdahl, NOAA	Indonesia:Java Ridge	印度尼西亚:爪哇海岭	-10.411	112.935	34.5	7.1	Ms		250	3	423	3	2.2	2	1500	4		

时间 Date						海啸 Tsunami				资料来源 Information	震中 Earthquake Epicenter				深度 Depth	震级 Mag	标度 Scale	烈度 MMI	死亡人数 Deaths		受伤人数 Injuries		经济损失 Damage		房屋毁坏 Houses Destroyed		房屋受损 Houses Damaged	
年 Year	月 Mo	日 Dy	时 Hr	分 Mn	秒 Sec	源 Sr	浪高 Wh	级 I mI	级 S mS		地名(英文) Name(English)	地名(中文) Name(Chinese)	纬度(°) Latitude	经度(°) Longitude					数量/人 Num	级别 Dd	数量/人 Num	级别 Dd	数量/$ Mill $ Mill	级别 De	数量/间 Num	级别 Dh	数量/间 Num	级别 Dh
1994	6	3	21	7	2	4	3.7			* Engdahl, NOAA	Indonesia: Java Ridge	印度尼西亚：爪哇海岭	-10.383	112.962	29.1	6.6	Mw											
1994	6	4	0	57	53	4	3			* Engdahl, NOAA	Indonesia: Java Ridge	印度尼西亚：爪哇海岭	-10.728	113.411	15.7	6.5	Mw											
1994	6	5	1	9	32					* China, Engdahl, USGS	China: Taiwan, Hualien, Coast of E.	中国：台湾花莲以东海域	24.442	121.873	11	7.0	Ms	7	1	1	2	1		2		2		
1994	6	6	9	3	1					ISC, USGS	Ryukyu Islands	琉球群岛	28.66	129.1	61	6.0	Mw	6										
1994	6	6	20	47	42					* ISC, Engdahl	Colombia: Cauca, Huila	哥伦比亚：考卡，乌伊拉	2.904	-75.963	12	6.8	Mw		295	3			2.4	2	200	3		
1994	6	9	0	33	18					* Engdahl	Brazil: Rio Branco	巴西：里奥布朗库	-13.856	-67.489	631	8.2	M		5	1		3		2				
1994	6	18	3	25	17					* Engdahl, USGS	New Zealand: South Island, Christchurch	新西兰：南岛，基督城	-43.081	171.61	14	6.7	Mw	6						1				
1994	6	19	13	43	51					USGS	New Zealand: South Island, Christchurch	新西兰：南岛，基督城	-43.27	171.61	10	6	Mw	6										
1994	6	20	9	9	5					* Engdahl	Iran: Firuzabad, Shiraz	伊朗：菲鲁扎巴德，设拉子	29.066	52.693	9	5.9	Mw		3	1	100	2		3		3		3
1994	6	29	2	1	58					USGS	Japan: Tateyama	日本：千叶馆山	34.91	139.96	48	4.5	mb	6										
1994	6	29	18	22	36					China, Engdahl, Dis	China: Qinghai, Zhiduo, W.	中国：青海治多西部	32.546	93.68	10	6.3	Ms	8					0.18	1				
1994	6	30	9	55	10					USGS, ISC	Caspian Sea	里海	40.94	50.61	33	5.5	mb	7										
1994	7	1	5	14	49					USGS	Japan: Hokkaido	日本：北海道	42.29	143.01	63	5	mb	6										
1994	7	1	10	12	41					USGS, ISC	Turkmenistan: Turkmenbasy	土库曼斯坦：土库曼巴希	40.23	53.38	40	6.4	Mw	5										
1994	7	1	22	43	18					USGS	Japan: Hokkaido	日本：北海道	42.13	142.92	64	5.5	mb	6										
1994	7	2	12	8	47					USGS	Ryukyu Islands	琉球群岛	28.37	129.55	46	5.3	Mw	6										
1994	7	12	13	47	35					USGS	Dominica: Puerto Plata, Santiago	多米尼加：普拉塔港，圣地亚哥	19.76	-70.92	33	5.6	Mw	6										
1994	7	13	2	35	58					ISC, Engdahl, USGS	Vanuatu Islands	瓦努阿图群岛	-16.6	167.537	32.8	7.2	Mw	6										
1994	8	14	9	6	55					ISC, Engdahl, USGS	Japan: Miyagi, Near Coast	日本：宫城近海	38.798	142.084	49.6	6.0	Mw	6										
1994	8	14	10	58	20					USGS, ISC	Chile: Near Coast of C.	智利：中部近海	-29.81	-71.59	42	5.5	Mw	5										
1994	8	18	1	13	8					* ISC, Engdahl	Algeria: Mascara	阿尔及利亚：马斯卡拉	35.48	-0.092	9	6.0	Mw		171	3				4		4		
1994	8	25	1	24	47					USGS, ISC	Japan: Off SE. Coast of Hokkaido	日本：北海道东南沿海	42.77	145.05	72	5.9	mb	6										
1994	8	31	9	7	27					ISC, Engdahl, USGS	Japan: Hokkaido	日本：北海道	43.709	145.991	76	6.2	Mw	7										
1994	9	1	15	15	55	4	0.1	-3.3	-3	* Engdahl, NOAA	US: California, Off Coast N.	美国：加利福尼亚州北部沿海	40.382	-125.777	10.3	7.1	M	6						1				
1994	9	1	16	12	43					ISC, Engdahl, USGS	Macedonia: Bitola Municipality	马其顿：比托拉市	41.167	21.241	20.4	6.3	Mw	7										
1994	9	4	14	50	37					China, ISC, Dis	China: Qinghai, Gonghe	中国：青海共和	36.01	100.31	33	5.3	Ms	6					0.24	1				

年 Year	月 Mo	日 Dy	时 Hr	分 Mn	秒 Sec	海啸 Tsunami 源 Sr	浪高 Wh	级 I mI	级 S mS	资料来源 Information	震中 Earthquake Epicenter 地名(英文) Name(English)	地名(中文) Name(Chinese)	纬度(°) Latitude	经度(°) Longitude	深度 Depth	震级 Mag	标度 Scale	烈度 MMI	死亡人数 Deaths 数量/人 Num	级别 Dd	受伤人数 Injuries 数量/人 Num	级别 Dd	经济损失 Damage 数量/$ Mill $ Mill	级别 De	房屋毁坏 Houses Destroyed 数量/间 Num	级别 Dh	房屋受损 Houses Damaged 数量/间 Num	级别 Dh
1994	9	12	12	23	43					ISC, Engdahl, USGS	US: Nevada, Johnson Lane, S.	美国:内华达州约翰逊巷南部	38.859	-119.711	4.5	6.0	Mw	6										
1994	9	13	6	1	23					USGS	US: Colorado, Ridgway	美国:科罗拉多州里奇韦	38.15	-107.98	10	4.6	ML	6										
1994	9	16	6	20	22					China, Engdahl, Dis	China: Taiwan Strait	中国:台湾海峡	22.566	118.711	13	7.3	Ms	6	4		799	3	23.2	3				
1994	9	19	15	28	36					China, Dis	China: Yunnan, Jinggu	中国:云南景谷	23.6	100.35		5.2	Ms	6			11	1	1.76	2				
1994	9	23	19	15	41					China, Dis	China: Qinghai, Gonghe	中国:青海共和	36.33	100.5		5.5	Ms	7			1	1	1.23	2				
1994	10	4	13	22	58	4	10	2.3	2.6	* Engdahl, NOAA, USGS	Japan: Hokkaido, Near Coast of E.	日本:北海道东部海域	43.945	147.224	14	8.3	Mw	9	11	1	242	3	11700	5				
1994	10	7	2	36	9					USGS, ISC	Kuril Islands	千岛群岛	43.61	147.29	52	6.6	Mw	5										
1994	10	8	21	44	10	4	3	1.6	1.5	* Engdahl, NOAA	Indonesia: Halmahera	印度尼西亚:哈马黑拉	-1.25	127.916	17	6.8	Mw		1	1	52	2		2			500	3
1994	10	9	7	55	42	4	0.2	-3.3	-3	* ISC, Engdahl, NOAA, USGS	Kuril Islands	千岛群岛	43.999	147.813	38	7.6	Mw	6										
1994	10	10	14	7	0					China, Dis	China: Qinghai, Gonghe	中国:青海共和	36.17	100.33		5.3	Ms	5					0.61	1				
1994	10	11	1	37	22					ISC, Engdahl, USGS	Chile: Los Vilos	智利:洛斯比洛斯	-32.164	-71.501	47	5.7	Mw	6										
1994	10	15	23	21	6					USGS	Japan: Kainan	日本:和歌山海南	34.16	135.24	10	4.5	mb	6										
1994	10	16	10	9	53					USGS	Iran: Bojnurd	伊朗:博季努尔德	38.09	56.7	33	4.9	ML	6										
1994	10	19	12	54	8					USGS	Solomon Islands	所罗门群岛	-9.52	159.45	5	5.5	Mw	5										
1994	11	14	19	15	32	4	7.3	2.9	2.1	* Bautista, Engdahl, NOAA	Philippines: Mindoro Island	菲律宾:民都洛岛	13.537	121.075	32	7.1	Mw		81	2	225	3	3.7	2	797	3	3288	4
1994	11	20	2	57	16					USGS, ISC	Solomon Islands	所罗门群岛	-9.79	159.71	23	5.6	Mw	5										
1994	12	3	12	28	49					USGS	Austria: Ternitz	奥地利:泰尔尼茨	47.72	16.17	12	4.6	ML	6										
1994	12	18	11	7	34					USGS, ISC	Japan: Aizumisato	日本:福岛会津美里	37.37	139.8	14	5.5	Mw	6										
1994	12	19	14	59	59					USGS	Azerbaijan: Qebele	阿塞拜疆:盖贝莱区	40.93	47.82	33	4.6	mb	6										
1994	12	26	14	10	29					* USGS	US: California, Eureka	美国:加利福尼亚州尤里卡	40.741	-124.31	23	5.5	Mw	7					2.1	2				
1994	12	28	12	19	26	4	0.5			* Engdahl, NOAA, USGS	Japan Trench	日本海沟	40.53	143.403	29.2	7.8	Mw	10	3	1	200	3	170	5				
1994	12	29	18	58	27					China, ISC, Dis	China: Sichuan, Muchuan	中国:四川沐川	29.05	103.85	16	5.7	Ms	7			133	3	3.69	2	1175	4	2965	4
1994	12	31	2	57	21					China, Dis	China: Beibu Bay	中国:北部湾	20.43	109.47		5.1	Ms	5										
1994	12	31	2	57	57					* China, Dis	China: Beibu Bay	中国:北部湾	21	109.4		6.1	Ms	6			327	3	0.19	1				
1995	1	4	23	14	42					USGS, ISC	Kuril Islands	千岛群岛	43.25	147.45	49	5.9	mb	6										
1995	1	6	9	40	29					USGS	Japan: Shizuoka, Near Coast	日本:静冈近海	34.02	139.14	18	4.8	mb	6										
1995	1	6	22	37	36					ISC, Engdahl, USGS	Japan: Morioka, Near East Coast	日本:盛冈东部近海	40.343	142.208	27	7	Mw	7										
1995	1	7	12	34	39					USGS	Japan: Oyama	日本:栃木小山	36.35	139.89	69	4.9	mb	6										

年 Year	月 Mo	日 Dy	时 Hr	分 Mn	秒 Sec	海啸 Tsunami 源 Sr	浪高 Wh	级 I mI	级 S mS	资料来源 Information	震中 Earthquake Epicenter 地名(英文) Name(English)	地名(中文) Name(Chinese)	纬度(°) Latitude	经度(°) Longitude	深度 Depth	震级 Mag	标度 Scale	烈度 MMI	死亡人数 Deaths 数量/人 Num	级别 Dd	受伤人数 Injuries 数量/人 Num	级别 Dd	经济损失 Damage 数量/$ Mill	级别 De	房屋毁坏 Houses Destroyed 数量/间 Num	级别 Dh	房屋受损 Houses Damaged 数量/间 Num	级别 Dh
1995	1	10	10	9	45					China, USGS, ISC, Dis	China: Beibu Bay	中国:北部湾	20.5	109.4		6.2	Ms	6	1		8	1	0.38	1				
1995	1	11	7	48	23					USGS, ISC	Japan: Hokkaido	日本:北海道	41.93	142.48	57	5.6	Mw	5										
1995	1	12	10	26	49					ISC, Engdahl, USGS	Kuril Islands	千岛群岛	44.104	147.124	35	6	Mw	7										
1995	1	12	23	29	40					USGS	Japan: Shizuoka, Near Coast	日本:静冈近海	34.28	139.1	25	5.1	mb	6										
1995	1	15	2	40	18					ISC, USGS	Ryukyu Islands	琉球群岛	27.74	128.4	33	6.1	Mw	6										
1995	1	16	20	46	54	4	0.2	-2.3	-2	* ISC, Engdahl, NOAA	Japan: Kobe	日本:神户	34.572	135.03	22	7.3	Mw	11	5502	4	36896	5	131500	5	200000	5		
1995	1	19	15	5	5					* Engdahl	Colombia: Bogota, Manizales	哥伦比亚:波哥达,马尼萨莱斯	5.045	-72.929	17	6.5	Mw		7	1		2		2	512	3	20	1
1995	1	20	3	35	46					USGS, ISC	Japan: Off SE. Coast of Hokkaido	日本:北海道东南沿海	43.33	146.8	57	6.2	Mw	5										
1995	1	21	8	47	31					ISC, Engdahl, USGS	Japan: Off SE. Coast of Hokkaido	日本:北海道东南沿海	43.382	146.72	59	6.3	Mw	6										
1995	2	8	18	40	27					* Engdahl	Colombia: Cali, Pereira	哥伦比亚:卡利,佩雷拉	4.053	-76.574	74	6.4	Mw		42	1	400	3	50.0	4	2000	4		
1995	2	14	23	55	31					USGS	Japan: Hokkaido	日本:北海道	42.51	144.69	33	5	mb	6										
1995	2	15	0	56	41					USGS	Japan: Hokkaido	日本:北海道	42.5	144.74	33	4.8	mb	6										
1995	2	18	0	14	41					China, Dis	China: Yunnan, Lancang	中国:云南澜沧	22.98	99.68		5.2	Ms	6					0.87	1	9	1	316	3
1995	2	18	12	37	32					USGS	Japan: Sumoto	日本:兵库洲本	34.44	134.76	10	4.7	mb	6										
1995	2	23	5	19	2					USGS	China: Taiwan, Hualien	中国:台湾花莲	24.14	121.61	40	6.2	Mw	6										
1995	2	23	21	3	4					* ISC, Engdahl	Cyprus: Paphos, Nicosia	塞浦路斯:帕菲斯,尼科西亚	35.078	32.273	18	5.9	Mw	7	2	1	5	1	4.34	2	70	2	570	3
1995	2	23	21	40	31					USGS, ISC	Cyprus: Paphos, Nicosia	塞浦路斯:帕菲斯,尼科西亚	35.04	32.31	10	5.5	mb	6										
1995	2	25	3	15	6					ISC, Dis	China: Taiwan Strait	中国:台湾海峡	24.36	118.56	36	5.6	mb	5										
1995	3	18	18	2	36					China, Dis	China: Xinjiang, Hoxud	中国:新疆和硕	42.57	87.2	24	5.1	Ms	6					0.05	1				
1995	3	19	23	53	15					* Engdahl	Indonesia: Papua	印度尼西亚:巴布亚	-4.143	135.118	26.8	6.9	Mw							1				1
1995	3	22	20	5	55					USGS, ISC	Chile: Concepcion	智利:康塞普西翁	-36.27	-72.96	39	5.5	Ms	5										
1995	3	22	22	24	32					USGS, ISC	Japan: Bando	日本:茨城坂东	36	139.89	62	5.5	mb	6										
1995	3	23	9	18	21					USGS, ISC	Chile: Concepcion	智利:康塞普西翁	-36.27	-72.96	41	5.5	Mw	5										
1995	3	26	5	21	20					USGS, ISC	Aleutian Islands	阿留申群岛	54.82	-161.39	42	6.2	Mw	5										
1995	4	1	3	49	34					* USGS	Japan: Niigata, Sado	日本:新潟,佐渡	37.925	139.186	11	5.8	mb	6						2				
1995	4	2	1	29	5					USGS	Japan: Niigata	日本:新潟	37.97	139.18	10	4.7	mb	6										
1995	4	5	4	25	8					USGS	Japan: Niigata	日本:新潟	37.92	139.29	10	4.6	mb	6										
1995	4	7	22	6	58	4	0.1	-1.7	-1.5	* ISC, Engdahl, NOAA	Samoa Islands: Apia	萨摩亚群岛:阿皮亚	-15.308	-173.492	21	7.4	Mw											
1995	4	14	0	32	55					ISC, USGS	US: Texas, Alpine	美国:德克萨斯州阿尔派恩	30.27	-103.31	10	6.1	Mw	6										

时间 Date						海啸 Tsunami				资料来源 Information	震中 Earthquake Epicenter				深度 Depth	震级 Mag	标度 Scale	烈度 MMI	死亡人数 Deaths		受伤人数 Injuries		经济损失 Damage		房屋毁坏 Houses Destroyed		房屋受损 Houses Damaged	
年 Year	月 Mo	日 Dy	时 Hr	分 Mn	秒 Sec	源 Sr	浪高 Wh	级I mI	级S mS		地名(英文) Name(English)	地名(中文) Name(Chinese)	纬度(°) Latitude	经度(°) Longitude					数量/人 Num	级别 Dd	数量/人 Num	级别 Dd	数量/$ Mill $ Mill	级别 De	数量/间 Num	级别 Dh	数量/间 Num	级别 Dh
1995	4	17	17	56	27					USGS	Russia:Sakhalin Island,N.	俄罗斯:库页岛(萨哈林岛)北部	54.32	142.93	33	4.6	mb	6										
1995	4	17	23	28	9					ISC, Engdahl, USGS	Kuril Islands	千岛群岛	45.952	151.251	23	6.8	Mw	6										
1995	4	18	11	26	24					USGS	Japan:Shizuoka	日本:静冈静冈	34.95	138.56	26	4.8	mb	6										
1995	4	21	0	34	49	4	0.2	-3.3	-2	* ISC, Engdahl, NOAA	Philippines:Samar Island	菲律宾:萨马岛	12.086	125.587	22.7	7.6	Mw											
1995	4	21	5	17	4	4	0.2	-2.3	-2	* ISC, Engdahl, NOAA	Philippines:Samar Island,E.	菲律宾:萨马岛东部	12.048	125.858	31.6	6.8	Mw											
1995	4	24	16	13	8					China,Dis	China:Yunnan,Jianping	中国:云南金平	22.77	102.73		5.5	Ms	7			20	1	1.32	2				
1995	4	25	8	29	3					USGS,ISC	China:Taiwan,Pingtung	中国:台湾屏东	22.67	120.69	41	5.5	mb	6										
1995	4	26	3	46	29					China,Dis	China:Sichuan,Muchuan	中国:四川沐川	28.98	103.65	10	5.1	Ms	6			7	1	2.15	2	290	3	3645	4
1995	4	28	16	30	3					ISC, Engdahl, USGS	Kuril Islands	千岛群岛	44.112	147.95	33.5	6.9	Mw	7										
1995	5	2	11	48	12					China,USGS,Dis	China:Xinjiang,Manas,S.	中国:新疆玛纳斯南	43.78	84.66	29	5.8	Ms	6	2		3	1	0.12	1				
1995	5	11	13	49	20					USGS	Hawaiian Islands	夏威夷群岛	20.07	-155.33	23	4.5	Md	6										
1995	5	13	8	47	14					* ISC,Engdahl	Greece:Grevena - Kozani	希腊:格莱维纳 - 科札尼	40.151	21.713	14	6.6	Mw	8			25	1	450	5	12000	5		
1995	5	14	11	33	21	4	4	2	1.5	* Engdahl, NOAA	Indonesia:Timor, Dili	印度尼西亚:帝汶,帝利	-8.452	125.049	12.7	6.9	Mw		11	1	19	1		1		2		
1995	5	16	20	12	46	4	0.5	-1.3	-2	* Engdahl, NOAA	Vanuatu Islands,SE.	瓦努阿图群岛东南	-22.968	169.945	23.6	7.7	Mw											
1995	5	22	12	50	32					USGS	Slovenia:Ljubljana	斯洛文尼亚:卢布尔雅那	45.62	14.23	27	4.9	ML	6										
1995	5	23	10	1	30					ISC,USGS	Japan:W. Hokkaido Island	日本:北海道西部	43.71	141.76	33	6.2	Mw	6										
1995	5	24	11	2	13					USGS,ISC	Gulf of Alaska	阿拉斯加湾	61.01	-150.12	41	5.6	Mw	5										
1995	5	27	13	3	54	4	0.1	-2.3	-2	* ISC, Engdahl, NOAA	Russia:Sakhalin Island	俄罗斯:库页岛(萨哈林岛)	52.597	142.827	11	7.5	Mw	9	1989	4	750	3	300	5				
1995	5	28	19	59	13					USGS,ISC	Chile:Vallenar	智利:巴耶纳尔	-28.98	-71.22	42	5.7	Mw	5										
1995	5	28	21	46	54					China,Dis	China:Xinjiang,Jeminay	中国:新疆吉木乃	47.67	85.6	25	5	Ms	6					0.46	1				
1995	6	2	19	7	22					USGS,ISC	Chile:Illapel	智利:伊亚佩尔	-31.77	-71.3	69	5.6	Mw	5										
1995	6	13	10	42	40					USGS	Russia:Sakhalin Island	俄罗斯:库页岛(萨哈林岛)	53.1	142.91	12	5.2	Mw	6										
1995	6	13	21	35	0					USGS,ISC	Russia:Sakhalin Island	俄罗斯:库页岛(萨哈林岛)	53	142.75	10	5.6	mb	6										
1995	6	15	0	15	51	4	1	-1		* Engdahl, NOAA	Greece:Patrai	希腊:帕特雷	38.448	22.31	14	6.5	Mw	7	26	1	60	2	660	5				
1995	6	29	23	2	28					USGS	Russia:Irkutsk,Slyudyanka	俄罗斯:伊尔库茨克州斯柳江卡	51.96	103.1	11	5.8	Mw	7										
1995	7	2	23	53	22					USGS,ISC	Japan:Miura	日本:神奈川三浦	35.04	139.39	119	5.9	mb	6										
1995	7	3	19	50	52					ISC, Engdahl, USGS	Kermadec Ridge	克马德克海岭	-29.411	-177.502	38	7.2	Mw	6										
1995	7	9	15	56	28					China,Dis	China:Qinghai,Gonghe	中国:青海共和	36.03	100.17	14	5.3	Ms	6					0.20	1				

年 Year	月 Mo	日 Dy	时 Hr	分 Mn	秒 Sec	海啸 Tsunami 源 Sr	浪高 Wh	级 I mI	级 S mS	资料来源 Information	震中 Earthquake Epicenter 地名(英文) Name(English)	地名(中文) Name(Chinese)	纬度(°) Latitude	经度(°) Longitude	深度 Depth	震级 Mag	标度 Scale	烈度 MMI	死亡人数 Deaths 数量/人 Num	级别 Dd	受伤人数 Injuries 数量/人 Num	级别 Dd	经济损失 Damage 数量/$ Mill $ Mill	级别 De	房屋毁坏 Houses Destroyed 数量/间 Num	级别 Dh	房屋受损 Houses Damaged 数量/间 Num	级别 Dh
1995	7	11	21	46	41					* China, Engdahl, Dis	China: Yunnan, Menglian, W.	中国:云南孟连西	21.965	99.122	9.4	7.3	Ms		11	1	136	3	24.6	3	100000	5		
1995	7	14	16	52	47					USGS, ISC	China: Taiwan, Hualien, Coast of E.	中国:台湾花莲以东海域	24.32	121.87	10	5.8	mb	9										
1995	7	21	22	44	1					* China, Dis	China: Gansu, Yongdeng	中国:甘肃永登	36.5	103	13	5.8	Ms	8	12	1	592	3	8.5	3	10000	5		
1995	7	25	7	49	21					USGS	Mariana Islands	马里亚纳群岛	13.44	145.18	57	4.7	mb	6										
1995	7	30	5	11	25	4	3	1.6	1.5	* Engdahl, NOAA	Chile: Antofagasta, C.	智利:安托法加斯塔中部	-23.285	-70.103	46	8	Mw	7	3	1	58	2	1.791	2	115	3		
1995	7	30	5	26	9					ISC, Engdahl, USGS	Chile: Antofagasta, C.	智利:安托法加斯塔中部	-23.23	-70.48	33	6.7	Mw	6										
1995	7	30	6	39	29					USGS, ISC	Chile: Antofagasta	智利:安托法加斯塔	-24.27	-70.57	33	5.8	mb	6										
1995	7	30	7	34	18					USGS	Chile: Mejillones	智利:梅希约内斯	-23.45	-70.36	33	5	mb	6										
1995	7	30	11	51	17					USGS	Ryukyu Islands	琉球群岛	28.66	129.38	48	5.5	mb	6										
1995	8	9	8	23	1					USGS, ISC	Chile: Antofagasta, C.	智利:安托法加斯塔中部	-23.1	-70.15	35	5.5	Mw	5										
1995	8	16	10	27	31	4	0.6	-1	-1.5	* ISC, Engdahl, NOAA	Papua New Guinea: Rabaul, Kokopo	巴布亚新几内亚:拉布尔,科可波	-5.788	154.213	30	7.7	Mw							1				
1995	8	22	22	11	57					USGS, ISC	Kermadec Ridge	克马德克海岭	-29.16	-177.37	23	5.5	Mw	5										
1995	8	25	9	27	21					USGS	Bosnia: Banja Luka	波斯尼亚:巴尼亚卢卡	45.37	17.64	23	4.8	ML	7										
1995	9	14	14	4	33	3	0.4	-1.3	-1	* Engdahl, NOAA	Mexico: Guerrero, Oaxaca, Puebla	墨西哥:格雷罗,瓦哈卡,普埃布拉	16.852	-98.588	23	7.4	Mw		3	1				2				
1995	9	20	3	14	31					China, Dis	China: Shandong, Cangshan	中国:山东苍山	34.95	118.1	12	5.2	Ms	6			320	3	2.38	2	500	3		
1995	9	20	23	27	36					USGS, ISC	US: California, Ridgecrest	美国:加利福尼亚州里奇克雷斯特	35.76	-117.64	5	5.6	Mw	5										
1995	9	26	4	39	5					ISC, Dis	China: Xinjiang, Baicheng, NW.	中国:新疆拜城西北	41.85	81.64	33	5.8	mb	6					0.42	1				
1995	9	28	23	44	42					USGS, ISC	Croatia: Dubrovnik	克罗地亚:杜布罗夫尼克	42.62	18.16	10	5.5	mb	6										
1995	9	30	13	56	36					USGS	Russia: Sakhalin Island	俄罗斯:库页岛(萨哈林岛)	51.89	142.98	33	5.5	Mw	5										
1995	10	1	2	42	48					USGS	Japan: Ito	日本:静冈伊东	34.94	139.17	26	4.6	mb	6										
1995	10	1	15	57	18					* Engdahl	Turkey: Evciler, Dinar	土耳其:艾布西雷尔,第纳尔	38.077	30.143	31.2	6.4	Mw	8	101	3	348	3	206	5	5100	4		
1995	10	3	1	51	26					* ISC, Engdahl	Ecuador: Morona Santiago	厄瓜多尔:莫罗纳-圣地亚哥	-2.75	-77.801	24	7.5	Mw		10	1				3				
1995	10	5	22	26	54					China, Dis	China: Hebei, Tangshan	中国:河北唐山	39.67	118.33	5	5	Ms	6			3	1	0.23	1				
1995	10	6	5	23	20					* ISC, Engdahl, USGS	Alaska: Fairbanks	阿拉斯加:费尔班克斯	65.128	-148.528	9	6	Mw	6						1				
1995	10	6	12	43	43					USGS	Japan: Shizuoka, Near Coast	日本:静冈近海	34.07	139.08	33	5.9	Mw	7										

年 Year	月 Mo	日 Dy	时 Hr	分 Mn	秒 Sec	海啸 Tsunami 源 Sr	浪高 Wh	级 I mI	级 S mS	资料来源 Information	震中 Earthquake Epicenter 地名(英文) Name(English)	地名(中文) Name(Chinese)	纬度(°) Latitude	经度(°) Longitude	深度 Depth	震级 Mag	标度 Scale	烈度 MMI	死亡人数 Deaths 数量/人 Num	级别 Dd	受伤人数 Injuries 数量/人 Num	级别 Dd	经济损失 Damage 数量/$ Mill $ Mill	级别 De	房屋毁坏 Houses Destroyed 数量/间 Num	级别 Dh	房屋受损 Houses Damaged 数量/间 Num	级别 Dh
1995	10	6	18	9	48					* Engdahl	Indonesia: Sumatera, Jambi	印度尼西亚:苏门答腊占碑	-2.006	101.45	35.7	6.7	Mw		84	2	1868	4		4	17600	5		
1995	10	8	8	55	48					ISC, USGS	Uzbekistan: Namangan	乌兹别克斯坦:纳曼干	41	72	34	6.2	Mw	6										
1995	10	9	15	35	54	4	11	2.3	2.5	* Engdahl, NOAA	Mexico: Jalisco, Manzanillo	墨西哥:哈利斯科,曼萨尼约	19.052	-104.208	26.2	8	Mw		50	1	200	3		2		2		
1995	10	13	17	4	5					USGS	Japan: Kobe	日本:神户	34.61	135.11	17	4.9	mb	6										
1995	10	18	10	37	29	4	2.6	0.8	1.5	* ISC, Engdahl, NOAA, USGS	Ryukyu Islands	琉球群岛	28.065	130.28	30.3	7.1	Mw	7			1	1		1				
1995	10	18	23	26	1					ISC, Engdahl, USGS	Ryukyu Islands	琉球群岛	28.243	130.257	29.7	6.1	Mw	6										
1995	10	19	2	41	39	4	1.5	0.6	0.5	* Engdahl, NOAA, USGS	Ryukyu Islands	琉球群岛	28.173	130.154	20	6.8	Mw	7										
1995	10	23	22	46	53					* China, Engdahl, Dis	China: Yunnan, Wuding	中国:云南武定	25.99	102.228	10	6.5	Ms	9	53	2	13903	5	93.4	4				
1995	10	31	22	27	4					USGS	China: Taiwan, Tainan	中国:台湾台南	23.2	120.5	16	4.9	mb	6										
1995	11	1	0	35	34	4	0.1	-3.3	-3	* ISC, Engdahl, NOAA, USGS	Chile: Vallenar	智利:巴耶纳尔	-28.88	-71.365	20	6.7	Mw	6										
1995	11	13	8	43	16					ISC, Engdahl, USGS	Russia: Buryatiya, Taksimo	俄罗斯:布里亚特州塔克西莫村镇	56.078	114.572	22	5.8	Mw	6										
1995	11	22	4	15	14	2	0.1			* Engdahl, NOAA	Egypt: Gulf of Aqaba	埃及:亚喀巴湾	28.763	34.807	14	7.2	Mw	8	12	1		2		2				
1995	11	23	4	41	47					USGS, ISC	Japan: Hokkaido	日本:北海道	41.34	142.49	63	5.5	mb	6										
1995	11	29	23	56	28					USGS	Spain: Galicia	西班牙:加利西亚	42.93	-7.2	17	4.6	MLg	6										
1995	12	3	18	1	9	4	1.1	0.1	0.5	* Engdahl, NOAA	Kuril Islands, Iturup, Matua	千岛群岛,择捉岛,马图亚	44.708	149.262	24.4	7.9	Mw	5										
1995	12	18	4	56	59					China, Dis	China: Qinghai, Maduo	中国:青海玛多	34.6	97.3		6.2	Ms	7					0.26	1				
1995	12	20	11	39	18					USGS, ISC	Ryukyu Islands	琉球群岛	27.37	128.38	33	5.5	mb	6										
1995	12	24	14	29	19					USGS	Spain: Galicia	西班牙:加利西亚	42.94	-7.21	10	4.6	MLg	6										
1995	12	25	4	43	26					ISC, Engdahl, USGS	Indonesia: Banda Sea	印度尼西亚:班达海	-6.915	129.187	144.6	7.1	Mw	6										
1995	12	26	3	31	10					China, Dis	China: Chongqing, Rongchang	中国:重庆荣昌	29.4	105.5	5	4.5	Ms	6			2	1	0.58	1				
1995	12	28	18	27	60					USGS	US: Nevada, Johnson Lane, S.	美国:内华达州约翰逊巷南部	38.78	-119.55	5	5.5	ML	5										
1996	1	1	8	5	13	4	3.4	2.3	1.8	* Engdahl, NOAA	Indonesia: Sulawesi	印度尼西亚:苏拉威西岛	0.725	119.932	24	7.9	Mw	6	9	1	63	2	1.2	2	400	3		
1996	1	1	9	38	25					USGS, ISC	Trinidad & Tobago: Northern Coast	特立尼达和多巴哥:北部近海	11.23	-61.72	70	5.7	mb	6										
1996	1	1	9	57	55	5	30			ISC, Engdahl, NOAA	Russia: Kamchatka Peninsula	俄罗斯:堪察加半岛	53.914	159.445	31.5	6.7	Ms											

年 Year	月 Mo	日 Dy	时 Hr	分 Mn	秒 Sec	海啸 Tsunami 源 Sr	浪高 Wh	级 I mI	级 S mS	资料来源 Information	震中 Earthquake Epicenter 地名(英文) Name(English)	地名(中文) Name(Chinese)	纬度(°) Latitude	经度(°) Longitude	深度 Depth	震级 Mag	标度 Scale	烈度 MMI	死亡人数 Deaths 数量/人 Num	级别 Dd	受伤人数 Injuries 数量/人 Num	级别 Dd	经济损失 Damage 数量/$ Mill $ Mill	级别 De	房屋毁坏 Houses Destroyed 数量/间 Num	级别 Dh	房屋受损 Houses Damaged 数量/间 Num	级别 Dh
1996	1	8	10	4	48					ISC, USGS	Russia: Sakhalin Island	俄罗斯:库页岛(萨哈林岛)	53.21	143.04	20	6.2	Mw	7										
1996	1	9	1	7	22					USGS	Austria: Bad Voslau	奥地利:巴特弗斯劳	47.96	16.38	10	4.5	ML	6										
1996	1	9	6	27	52					China, Dis	China: Xinjiang, Shawan	中国:新疆沙湾	43.8	85.58	24	5.2	Ms	6					0.38	1				
1996	1	16	0	8	34					China, Dis	China: Chongqing, Rongchang	中国:重庆荣昌	29.31	105.5		4.3	Ms	6					0.32	1				
1996	1	17	10	6	47					Engdahl, USGS	Indonesia: Papua	印度尼西亚:巴布亚	-4.399	140.12	98.1	6.1	Mw	6										
1996	1	19	19	2	0					ISC, USGS	Peru: Casma, Huaraz	秘鲁:卡斯马,安卡什(瓦拉斯)	-10.42	-78.66	39	6.4	Mw	5										
1996	2	3	11	14	22					* China, Engdahl, Dis	China: Yunnan, Lijiang	中国:云南丽江	27.317	100.333	11	7.0	Ms	9	309	3	17057	5	367	5	959000	5		
1996	2	7	1	33	19					USGS, ISC	Japan: Ono	日本:福井大野	35.92	136.57	41	5.6	mb	6										
1996	2	16	15	23	0					ISC, Engdahl, USGS	Japan Trench	日本海沟	37.344	142.433	41	6.7	Mw	6										
1996	2	17	5	59	32	4	7.7	2.9	1.8	* Engdahl, NOAA	Indonesia: Papua	印度尼西亚:巴布亚	-0.919	136.973	36.5	8.2	Mw		166	3	423	3	4.2	2	5043	4		
1996	2	20	14	12	12					USGS	Bosnia: Banja Luka	波斯尼亚:巴尼亚卢卡	44.51	17.24	10	5	Md	6										
1996	2	21	12	51	4	4	5.1	2.3	1.9	* Engdahl, NOAA	Peru: Chimbote, Near Coast	秘鲁:钦博特近海	-9.708	-79.845	15	7.5	Mw		12	1	57	2			15	1	22	1
1996	2	22	13	40	55					ISC, Engdahl, USGS	Chile: San Antonio	智利:圣安东尼奥	-33.595	-71.528	43	5.9	Mw	7										
1996	2	25	3	8	18	4	0.1	-3.3	-3	* Engdahl, NOAA	Mexico: Near Coast of Guerrero	墨西哥:格雷罗近海	15.949	-98.104	22.6	7.1	Mw											
1996	2	28	11	22	1					China, ISC, Dis	China: Sichuan, Nanxi	中国:四川南溪	28.92	104.86	15	5.4	Ms	7	1		50	1	6.3	3				
1996	3	6	14	35	28					USGS	Japan: Yamakita	日本:神奈川山北	35.43	138.99	33	5.6	Mw	7										
1996	3	9	22	35	38					USGS, ISC	Azores Islands	亚速尔群岛	37.03	-24.37	10	5.7	Mw	5										
1996	3	12	18	43	43					China, USGS, Dis	China: Xinjiang, Altay	中国:新疆阿勒泰	48.8	88	16	6.1	Ms	7					3.56	2				
1996	3	19	15	0	26					* China, Engdahl, Dis	China: Xinjiang, Artux, N.	中国:新疆阿图什以北	40.055	76.659	12	6.9	Ms	9	24	1	128	3	46.5	4	22833	5		
1996	3	26	22	58	31					USGS	Adriatic Sea	亚得里亚海	44.33	15.38	33	4.7	ML	6										
1996	3	28	23	3	48					* ISC, Engdahl	Ecuador: Cotopaxi, Pastaza	厄瓜多尔:科托帕希,帕斯塔萨	-1.023	-78.647	9	5.9	Mw	6	27	1			7.0	3				
1996	4	19	0	19	33					ISC, Engdahl, USGS	Chile: Antofagasta, C.	智利:安托法加斯塔中部	-23.866	-69.947	46	6.6	Mw	6										
1996	4	29	14	40	42					* Engdahl	Solomon Sea, N.	所罗门海北部	-6.521	155.087	38	7.5	Ms		1	1				1				
1996	5	2	6	30	25					USGS, ISC	Philippines: Baguio	菲律宾:碧瑶市	16.13	120.6	33	5.5	Mw	5										
1996	5	3	3	32	49					* China, Engdahl, Dis	China: Inner Mongolia, Baotou	中国:内蒙包头	40.778	109.714	24.5	6.4	Ms	8	26	1	453	3	323	5				
1996	5	10	10	19	38					USGS, ISC	Peru: Ayacucho	秘鲁:阿亚库乔	-14.01	-74.47	101	5.5	Mw	5										
1996	6	1	12	49	13					China, ISC, Dis	China: Gansu, Menyuan, E.	中国:甘肃门源东部	37.33	102.91	16	5.4	Ms	6			20	1	3.61	2	3263	4		
1996	6	10	4	3	36	4	0.5		0.5	* Engdahl, NOAA	Andreanof Islands, Aleutian Is.	阿留申群岛,安德烈亚诺夫群岛	51.613	-177.615	28	7.9	Mw	6										

年 Year	月 Mo	日 Dy	时 Hr	分 Mn	秒 Sec	海啸 Tsunami 源 Sr	浪高 Wh	级I mI	级S mS	资料来源 Information	震中 Earthquake Epicenter 地名(英文) Name(English)	地名(中文) Name(Chinese)	纬度(°) Latitude	经度(°) Longitude	深度 Depth	震级 Mag	标度 Scale	烈度 MMI	死亡人数 Deaths 数量/人 Num	级别 Dd	受伤人数 Injuries 数量/人 Num	级别 Dd	经济损失 Damage 数量/$ Mill	级别 De	房屋毁坏 Houses Destroyed 数量/间 Num	级别 Dh	房屋受损 Houses Damaged 数量/间 Num	级别 Dh
1996	6	10	15	24	59	4	0.1	-3.3	-1.5	* ISC, Engdahl, NOAA	Aleutian Islands	阿留申群岛	51.415	-176.887	27.5	7.3	Mw											
1996	6	18	8	11	6					USGS	Azerbaijan: Naxcivan	阿塞拜疆:纳希切万	39.16	45.8	51	4.7	mb	6										
1996	7	2	7	5	2					China, Dis	China: Yunnan, Lijiang	中国:云南丽江	26.93	100.1	10	5.2	Ms	6	2		57	2	2.62	2				
1996	7	3	6	44	46					China, USGS, Dis	China: Xizang (Tibet), Xaitongmoin, N.	中国:西藏谢通门北	29.7	87.8	26	6	Ms	6					0.15	1				
1996	7	9	10	23	8					USGS	Adriatic Sea	亚得里亚海	42.96	14	33	4.5	ML	6										
1996	7	22	14	19	36					ISC, Engdahl, USGS	Indonesia: Dondo	印度尼西亚:东都	1.016	120.405	27.1	7	Mw	8										
1996	8	10	18	12	19					ISC, Engdahl, USGS	Japan: Miyagi	日本:宫城	38.987	140.541	9	6	Mw	7										
1996	8	10	18	54	12					ISC, USGS	Japan: Yuzawa	日本:秋田汤泽	39.11	140.52	10	6.1	Mw	7										
1996	9	4	18	16	4	4	0.3	-2.3	-2	* ISC, Engdahl, NOAA	Japan Trench	日本海沟	31.642	140.16	24.4	5.7	Mw											
1996	9	5	8	14	16	4	0.1	-3.3	-2.5	* ISC, Engdahl, NOAA	Easter Island, W.	复活节岛西部	-22.182	-113.458	9.1	6.9	Mw											
1996	9	5	20	44	11					* Engdahl	Croatia: Dubrovnik	克罗地亚:杜布罗夫尼克	42.77	17.985	12	6	Mw	8				2		3				
1996	9	11	2	37	17					ISC, Engdahl, USGS	Japan: Chiba, Near Coast	日本:千叶近海	35.596	140.962	56.9	6.2	Mw	8										
1996	9	17	23	47	7					USGS, ISC	Kuril Islands	千岛群岛	43.65	147.21	33	5.5	mb	5										
1996	9	24	19	24	50					China, USGS, Dis	China: Yunnan, Lijiang	中国:云南丽江	27.22	100.37	15	5.7	Ms	7	1		141	3	3.70	2				
1996	10	1	23	4	13					USGS, ISC	Peru: Mala, Near Coast	秘鲁:马拉近海	-12.68	-76.81	61	5.6	Mw	5										
1996	10	15	0	22	39					USGS, ISC	Kuril Islands	千岛群岛	43.71	147.11	33	5.5	mb	5										
1996	10	15	9	55	59					ISC, USGS	Italy: Novellara	意大利:诺菲拉腊	44.7	10.7	10	6.2	Mw	7										
1996	10	15	12	18	24					USGS	Italy: Novellara	意大利:诺菲拉腊	44.78	10.73	10	4.7	ML	6										
1996	10	18	10	50	25	4	0.2	-2.3	-2.5	* Engdahl, NOAA, USGS	Japan: Kagoshima, Near Coast of S.	日本:鹿岛南部近海	30.592	131.089	25	6.6	Mw	6										
1996	10	19	14	44	42	4	0.6	0.1	0.5	* ISC, Engdahl, NOAA, USGS	Japan: Miyazzaki, Near Coast	日本:宫崎近海	31.921	131.567	18	6.7	Mw	7						1				
1996	10	25	19	59	41					USGS, ISC	Peru: Torata	秘鲁:塔克纳	-17.38	-69.99	116	5.7	Mw	5										
1996	11	9	13	56	6					China, Dis	China: Yangtze Delta, E.	中国:长江口以东	31.7	123.1		6.1	Ms	5										
1996	11	12	16	59	44	4	0.4	-1.7	-1	* ISC, Engdahl, NOAA	Peru: Chincha Alta, Acari	秘鲁:钦查阿尔塔,阿卡里	-14.95	-75.532	21	7.7	Mw	8	14	1				4				
1996	11	19	10	44	45					China, Engdahl, Dis	China: Xinjiang, Karakorum Mountains	中国:新疆喀喇昆仑山	35.387	78.209	12	7.1	Ms	8										
1996	11	28	7	40	43					USGS	Japan: South Honshu Ridge	日本:本州南部海岭	34.56	140.12	66	5.6	Mw	6										
1996	12	2	22	17	58	4	0.2	-2.3	-2	* ISC, Engdahl, NOAA, USGS	Japan: Miyazzaki	日本:宫崎	31.835	131.323	29	6.7	Mw	7										
1996	12	15	21	36	33					China, Dis	China: Beijing, Shunyi	中国:北京顺义	40.17	116.48	10	4	Ms	5			6	1	0.17	1				

时间						海啸				资料来源	震中				深度	震级	标度	烈度	死亡人数		受伤人数		经济损失		房屋毁坏		房屋受损	
年	月	日	时	分	秒	源	浪高	级I	级S		地名(英文)	地名(中文)	纬度(°)	经度(°)					数量/人	级别	数量/人	级别	数量/$ Mill	级别	数量/间	级别	数量/间	级别
Date						Tsunami				Information	Earthquake Epicenter				Depth	Mag	Scale	MMI	Deaths		Injuries		Damage		Houses Destroyed		Houses Damaged	
Year	Mo	Dy	Hr	Mn	Sec	Sr	Wh	mI	mS		Name(English)	Name(Chinese)	Latitude	Longitude					Num	Dd	Num	Dd	$ Mill	De	Num	Dh	Num	Dh
1996	12	16	6	59	51					USGS	Kyrgyzstan:Issyk Kul	吉尔吉斯斯坦:伊塞克湖州	42.74	78.15	23	4.5	mb	6										
1996	12	16	7	0	13					USGS	Kyrgyzstan:Issyk Kul	吉尔吉斯斯坦:伊塞克湖州	42.75	78.23	22	4.9	mb	6										
1996	12	18	10	12	27					USGS,ISC	Chile:Taltal,Near Coast	智利:塔尔塔尔近海	-25.12	-70.68	32	6.1	Mw	5										
1996	12	21	1	28	46					ISC,USGS	Japan:Tochigi	日本:栃木	36.38	139.72	43	6.3	Mw	7										
1996	12	21	8	39	39					China,ISC,Dis	China:Sichuan,Batang,E.	中国:四川巴塘东	30.56	99.51	10	5.5	Ms	7	2		60	2	5.0	3				
1997	1	9	13	43	32					* ISC,Engdahl	Kyrgyzstan:Naryn,SW.	吉尔吉斯斯坦:纳伦西南	41.05	74.319	15	5.8	Mw	7						1				
1997	1	11	20	28	28					* ISC,Engdahl	Mexico:Michoacan, Arteaga	墨西哥:米却肯,阿特亚加	18.211	-102.791	35	7.2	Mw		1	1				2				
1997	1	12	12	10	51					*	Albania:Berat, Gramsh	阿尔巴尼亚:培拉特,格拉姆什	40.956	19.672	10	4.8	mb	6						1				
1997	1	21	1	47	15					* China, Engdahl, Dis	China:Xinjiang,Payzawat	中国:新疆伽师	39.432	76.935	17	6.4	Ms	8	12	1	44	1	4.61	2	743	3		
1997	1	25	2	38	53					China,Dis	China:Yunnan,Mengna	中国:云南勐腊	21.87	101.08		5.1	Ms	6					1.88	2			17960	5
1997	1	30	9	59	2					China,Dis	China:Yunnan,Jinghong	中国:云南景洪	22.4	101.4	5	5.6	Ms	7			2	1	6.4	3	1412	4	55427	5
1997	2	4	10	37	49					* ISC,Engdahl	Iran:Bojnurd	伊朗:博季努尔德	37.712	57.333	8	6.5	Mw	8	88	2	1948	4	30.0	4	5500	4	11000	5
1997	2	19	20	21	48					USGS	Japan:Fukushima	日本:福岛	37.4	141.07	84	5.5	Mw	6										
1997	2	20	7	55	2					Engdahl,USGS	Japan:Hokkaido	日本:北海道	41.85	142.686	53.9	6.0	Mw	7										
1997	2	27	21	8	3					* ISC,Engdahl	Pakistan:Harnai - Sibi, Quetta	巴基斯坦:哈奈-锡比,奎塔	29.97	68.22	22	7.1	Mw		60	2		3		2	500	3		
1997	2	28	12	57	25					* Engdahl	Iran:Ardabil	伊朗:阿尔达比勒	38.096	48.035	44.2	6.1	Mw	7	1100	4	2600	4		4	12000	5		
1997	3	1	6	4	12					* China,Dis	China:Xinjiang,Payzawat	中国:新疆伽师	39.5	76.9		6.0	Ms	7	1	1	6	1	10.9	3	190	3		
1997	3	3	11	10	57					USGS	Japan:Oshima	日本:东京大岛	34.85	139.27	10	4.8	mb	6										
1997	3	3	14	9	43					USGS	Japan:Ito	日本:静冈伊东	34.96	139.15	10	4.7	mb	7										
1997	3	4	3	51	26					USGS	Japan:Izu	日本:静冈伊豆	34.89	139.04	10	5.6	Mw	6										
1997	3	16	5	51	37					ISC,USGS	Japan:Shinshiro	日本:爱知新城市	34.95	137.51	33	6.0	Mw	7										
1997	3	18	15	24	48					USGS	US:California,Victorville	美国:加利福尼亚州维克托维尔	34.97	-116.82	1	5.1	Md	6										
1997	3	19	19	57	12					* ISC	Pakistan:Chitral	巴基斯坦:吉德拉尔	34.872	71.62	50	5.1	Mw		15	1				1				
1997	3	25	0	14	45					USGS	Chile:Santiago	智利:圣地亚哥	-33.48	-70.55	84	5.5	Mw	6										
1997	3	26	8	31	52					* ISC, Engdahl, USGS	Japan:Kagoshima	日本:鹿岛	31.973	130.395	29.8	6.1	Mw	6						2				
1997	4	2	6	14	33					ISC, Engdahl, USGS	Trinidad & Tobago: Scarborough	特立尼达和多巴哥:斯卡伯勒	11.398	-61.17	50.4	6.1	Mw	6										
1997	4	2	19	33	22					USGS	Japan:Kagoshima	日本:鹿岛	31.82	130.09	10	5.5	Mw	8										
1997	4	2	21	47	31					USGS	Japan:Ehime	日本:爱媛	33.36	132.22	45	5.1	Mw	6										
1997	4	5	4	24	51					USGS	Japan:Kagoshima	日本:鹿岛	31.95	130.43	33	5.1	Mw	7										
1997	4	5	23	46	21					* China, Engdahl	China:Xinjiang,Payzawat	中国:新疆伽师	39.514	76.869	29	6.3	Ms	8										
1997	4	6	4	36	34					* China, Engdahl	China:Xinjiang,Payzawat	中国:新疆伽师	39.513	77.022	11	6.4	Ms	8						3				

年 Year	月 Mo	日 Dy	时 Hr	分 Mn	秒 Sec	源 Sr	浪高 Wh	级 I mI	级 S mS	资料来源 Information	地名(英文) Name(English)	地名(中文) Name(Chinese)	纬度(°) Latitude	经度(°) Longitude	深度 Depth	震级 Mag	标度 Scale	烈度 MMI	死亡人数 Deaths 数量/人 Num	死亡人数 级别 Dd	受伤人数 Injuries 数量/人 Num	受伤人数 级别 Dd	经济损失 Damage 数量/$ Mill	经济损失 级别 De	房屋毁坏 Houses Destroyed 数量/间 Num	房屋毁坏 级别 Dh	房屋受损 Houses Damaged 数量/间 Num	房屋受损 级别 Dh
1997	4	11	5	34	45					* China, Engdahl, Dis	China:Xinjiang,Payzawat	中国:新疆伽师	39.552	76.976	15	6.6	Ms	8	8	1	62	2	56.5	4	5834	4		
1997	4	15	18	19	11					China,Engdahl	China:Xinjiang,Payzawat	中国:新疆伽师	39.592	77.007	16	6.3	Ms	8										
1997	4	18				1				NOAA,Song	Australia:Norfolk Island	澳大利亚:诺福克岛	-29	168		7	Mk											
1997	4	21	12	2	28	4	3	-2.3	-2	* ISC, Engdahl, NOAA	Solomon Islands:Santa Cruz Islands	所罗门群岛:圣克鲁斯群岛	-12.56	166.738	29.8	7.7	Mw							1	7	1		
1997	4	22	9	31	27					* Engdahl	Trinidad & Tobago:Scarborough	特立尼达和多巴哥:斯卡伯勒	11.122	-61.058	18	6.7	Mw				2	1	25.0	4	3	1		
1997	4	23	19	44	30					* Engdahl	Guam	关岛(西太平洋)	13.991	144.992	101	6.5	Mw	7			4	1		1				
1997	5	9	9	6	39					Engdahl,USGS	Mariana Islands,S.	马里亚纳群岛南部	13.208	144.798	29	6.0	Mw	7										
1997	5	10	7	57	32					* ISC,Engdahl	Iran:Birjand	伊朗:比尔詹德	33.833	59.796	12.8	7.5	Mw	10	1728	4	2300	4	100	5	10533	5		
1997	5	11	22	59	41					ISC, Engdahl, USGS	Japan:Fukushima	日本:福岛	37.119	140.979	63	5.9	Mw	6										
1997	5	13	5	38	29					ISC, Engdahl, USGS	Japan:Kagoshima	日本:鹿岛	31.945	130.282	14.2	6.1	Mw	9										
1997	5	13	14	13	47					* Engdahl	Afghan:Badakhshan	阿富汗:巴达赫尚	36.471	71.044	196	6.4	Mw		1	1				2				
1997	5	13	23	32	8					USGS	Japan:Kagoshima	日本:鹿岛	31.87	130.38	33	4.6	Ms	6										
1997	5	17	2	10	19					USGS,ISC	Chile:Copiapo	智利:科皮亚波	-27.16	-69.5	106	5.5	Mw	5										
1997	5	21	22	51	31					* India, Engdahl	India:Jabalpur	印度:贾巴尔普尔	23.066	80.121	36	5.8	M	8	56	2	1000	3	143	5	8546	4	52690	5
1997	5	31	6	51	1					China,Dis	China:Fujian,Yongan	中国:福建永安	25.58	117.18	6	5.2	Ms	6					8.9	3				
1997	6	23	19	13	27					USGS	US:Washington,Seattle	美国:华盛顿州西雅图	47.6	-122.57	7	4.9	Md	6										
1997	6	25	9	50	16					ISC, Engdahl, USGS	Japan:Hiroshima, Okayama	日本:广岛冈山	34.433	131.58	19.7	5.9	Mw	7										
1997	6	25	19	38	43					* ISC,Engdahl	Iran:Razavi Khorasan	伊朗:呼罗珊	33.894	59.433	12	5.9	Mw							3	100	2	5000	4
1997	7	9	19	24	13	3				* ISC, Engdahl, NOAA	Venezuela:Cariaco - Cumana	委内瑞拉:卡利亚科 - 库马纳	10.448	-63.533	10	7.4	Mw	5	81	2	522	3	81.0	4				
1997	7	15	11	5	31					USGS,ISC	China:Taiwan,Yilan,Coast of E.	中国:台湾宜兰东南海域	24.71	122.45	102	5.6	Mw	5										
1997	7	21	8	45	49					* ISC	South Africa:Klerksdorp	南非:克拉克斯多普	-26.857	26.619	5	5.1	Mw		15	1	46	1						
1997	8	13	4	45	6					ISC, Engdahl, USGS	Ryukyu Islands	琉球群岛	25.158	125.852	55	6.1	Mw	6										
1997	8	13	8	13	33					China,Dis	China:Chongqing,Rongchang	中国:重庆荣昌	29.45	105.55	13	5.2	Ms	7			33	1	7.7	3	1125	4	1084	4
1997	8	20	7	15	14					* Engdahl	Indonesia:Sumatera,Aceh	印度尼西亚:苏门答腊亚齐	4.342	96.478	12	6	Mw							2				
1997	9	26	0	33	12					* Italy,USGS	Italy:Marche,Umbria	意大利:马尔凯,翁布里亚	43.019	12.879	10	6.1	Mw	8						1				
1997	9	26	5	26	50					China,Dis	China:Guangdong,Fushan	中国:广东佛山	23.27	112.91	4.8	4.2	ML	5					8.6	3				
1997	9	26	9	40	28					* ISC, Engdahl, USGS	Italy:Romagna	意大利:弗里	43.078	12.79	10	6	Mw	10	14	1	100	2	4525	5	80000	5		

时间 Date						海啸 Tsunami				资料来源 Information	震中 Earthquake Epicenter				深度 Depth	震级 Mag	标度 Scale	烈度 MMI	死亡人数 Deaths		受伤人数 Injuries		经济损失 Damage		房屋毁坏 Houses Destroyed		房屋受损 Houses Damaged	
年 Year	月 Mo	日 Dy	时 Hr	分 Mn	秒 Sec	源 Sr	浪高 Wh	级 I mI	级 S mS		地名(英文) Name(English)	地名(中文) Name(Chinese)	纬度(°) Latitude	经度(°) Longitude					数量/人 Num	级别 Dd	数量/人 Num	级别 Dd	数量/$ Mill $ Mill	级别 De	数量/间 Num	级别 Dh	数量/间 Num	级别 Dh
1997	9	26	9	47	39					USGS,ISC	Italy:Romagna	意大利:弗里	43.16	12.75	10	5.6	mb	7										
1997	9	28	1	38	27					*Engdahl	Indonesia:Sulawesi,Parepare	印度尼西亚:苏拉威西岛,巴里巴里	-3.754	119.674	13	5.9	Mw		17	1			1.1	2				
1997	9	28	23	13	14					USGS,ISC	Chile:Calama	智利:卡拉马	-22.41	-68.45	106	5.6	Mw	5										
1997	9	30	6	27	30	4	0			* ISC, Engdahl, NOAA	Japan Trench	日本海沟	31.986	141.945	31.9	6.2	Mw											
1997	10	3	8	55	22					USGS,ISC	Italy:Romagna	意大利:弗里	43.08	12.79	10	5.7	mb	7										
1997	10	6	23	24	53					USGS	Italy:Romagna	意大利:弗里	43.04	12.84	10	5.5	Mw	8										
1997	10	7	5	9	57					USGS	Italy:Romagna	意大利:弗里	43.01	12.85	10	4.8	ML	6										
1997	10	9	20	42	2					USGS,ISC	Japan Sea,N.	日本海北部	41.98	138.86	33	5.5	Mw	5										
1997	10	10	18	45	53					Engdahl,USGS	Solomon Islands	所罗门群岛	-9.306	158.81	25	6.0	Mw	6										
1997	10	11	18	24	24					USGS,ISC	China:Taiwan,Gongliao,Coast of E.	中国:台湾新北贡寮以东海域	25.03	122.45	143	5.5	Mw	5										
1997	10	12	11	8	36					USGS,ISC	Italy:Romagna	意大利:弗里	42.9	12.9	10	5.7	mb	7										
1997	10	14	9	53	19	4	0.1			*Engdahl, NOAA	Tonga Islands,W.	汤加群岛西部	-22.271	-176.672	169.2	7.7	Mw											
1997	10	14	15	23	13					ISC, Engdahl, USGS	Italy:Gualdo	意大利:瓜尔多	42.931	12.876	13.8	5.6	Ms	8										
1997	10	15	1	3	35	3				*ISC,Engdahl, NOAA,USGS	Chile: Pueblo Nuevo, Coquimbo	智利:新普韦布洛,科金博	-30.906	-71.17	58	7.4	Mw	7	8	1	300	3	48.0	4	5000	4	15700	5
1997	10	15	4	28	47					USGS,ISC	Chile:Ovalle	智利:奥瓦耶	-30.81	-71.25	47	5.5	mb	5										
1997	10	16	12	0	31					USGS	Italy:Romagna	意大利:弗里	43.02	12.85	10	4.8	ML	6										
1997	10	21	6	32	33					China,Dis	China:Inner Mongolia,Hangjin Houqi	中国:内蒙古航锦后旗	41.15	107.37	18	5	Ms	7			18	1	6.1	3	145	3		
1997	10	23	12	28	33					China,ISC,Dis	China:Yunnan,Lijiang	中国:云南丽江	26.98	100.49	10	5.3	Ms	6					3.23	2				
1997	10	24	8	35	18					USGS	US:Alabama,Brewton	美国:阿拉巴马州布鲁顿	31.12	-87.34	10	4.9	MLg	6										
1997	10	26	1	35	38					USGS	Chile:Chanaral,E.	智利:查尼亚拉尔东部	-26.33	-70.15	57	5.3	Mw	6										
1997	11	3	2	29	52					China, USGS, ISC,Dis	China:Xizang (Tibet), Gyirong,E.	中国:西藏吉隆东	29.08	85.38	5	5.6	Ms	7					0.96	1				
1997	11	3	19	17	35					ISC, Engdahl, USGS	Chile:Ovalle	智利:奥瓦耶	-30.774	-71.255	45	6.2	Mw	7										
1997	11	9	19	7	33					USGS	Italy:Romagna	意大利:弗里	42.9	12.95	10	5	ML	7										
1997	11	14	4	29	53					USGS	China:Taiwan,Hualien,Coast of E.	中国:台湾花莲以东海域	24.16	121.86	33	5.2	mb	8										
1997	11	15	7	5	17					ISC, Engdahl, USGS	Japan:Hokkaido	日本:北海道	43.875	144.973	150	6.1	Mw	6										
1997	11	18	13	7	42					*Engdahl	Greece:Ionian Sea, Amalias	希腊:爱奥尼亚海,亚美雅斯	37.481	20.777	22.9	6.6	Mw							1				
1997	11	21	11	23	8					*Engdahl	India:Mizoram	印度:米佐拉姆	22.25	92.721	54	6.1	Mw		23	1	200	3		1	1	1		2
1997	11	23	3	51	2					ISC,USGS	Japan Sea	日本海	39.96	138.84	33	6.2	Mw	6										

年	月	日	时	分	秒	海啸 源	浪高	级 I	级 S	资料来源	震中 地名(英文)	地名(中文)	纬度(°)	经度(°)	深度	震级	标度	烈度	死亡人数 数量/人	级别	受伤人数 数量/人	级别	经济损失 数量/$ Mill	级别	房屋毁坏 数量/间	级别	房屋受损 数量/间	级别
Date						Tsunami				Information	Earthquake Epicenter				Depth	Mag	Scale	MMI	Deaths		Injuries		Damage		Houses Destroyed		Houses Damaged	
Year	Mo	Dy	Hr	Mn	Sec	Sr	Wh	mI	mS		Name(English)	Name(Chinese)	Latitude	Longitude					Num	Dd	Num	Dd	$ Mill	De	Num	Dh	Num	Dh
1997	11	25	12	14	35					* Engdahl, USGS	Indonesia:South Sulawesi sea	印度尼西亚:苏拉威西海南部	1. 219	122. 516	24	7	Mw	6						1				
1997	11	27	17	34	30					USGS,ISC	Georgia:Gurdzhaani	格鲁吉亚:古祖尼	41. 85	45. 33	37	5. 7	mb	6										
1997	12	5	11	26	57	4	8	0. 6	0. 5	* Engdahl, NOAA	Russia:Kamchatka,Near East Coast	俄罗斯:堪察加东部近海	54. 799	162. 003	36. 1	7. 8	Mw	7										
1997	12	7	3	50	40					USGS,ISC	Japan:Fukushima,Near Coast	日本:福岛近海	37. 7	141. 59	87	5. 8	mb	6										
1997	12	9	14	23	45					USGS,ISC	Bolivia:Potosi,W.	玻利维亚:波托西西部	-20. 24	-68. 36	132	5. 7	Mw	5										
1997	12	19	13	7	53					USGS	Japan:Komatsu	日本:石川小松	36. 24	136. 11	15	4. 6	mb	6										
1997	12	26	8			5	3		2	NOAA,Song	Montserrat:Plymouth	蒙特塞拉特:普利茅斯	16. 72	-62. 18		7. 6	Mk											
1998	1	2	18	19	54					USGS	Japan:Hokkaido	日本:北海道	42. 96	145. 4	33	5. 1	Mw	6										
1998	1	10	3	50	40					* China, Engdahl, Dis	China:Hebei,Shangyi,E.	中国:河北尚义东	41. 133	114. 532	5	6. 2	Ms	8	49	2	656	3	101	5	169150	5		
1998	1	10	8	20	12					* Engdahl	Guatemala: Quezaltenango, San Marcos	危地马拉:克萨尔特南戈,圣马科斯	14. 449	-91. 52	74. 1	6. 6	Mw				27	1		1		2		1
1998	1	12	4	12	6					USGS	Chile:Antofagasta,S.	智利:安托法加斯塔南部	-24. 95	-70. 01	53	5. 6	Mw	5										
1998	1	12	10	14	9					NEIC,Engdahl, USGS	Chile:Ovalle	智利:奥瓦耶	-31. 046	-71. 466	35	6. 6	Mw	6										
1998	1	28	19	19	48					USGS	Chile:Maule,SE.	智利:马乌莱东南	-35. 75	-70. 86	33	4. 7	Md	6										
1998	1	30	12	16	10					NEIC,Engdahl, USGS	Chile:Antofagasta,C.	智利:安托法加斯塔中部	-23. 841	-70. 13	42	7. 1	Mw	7										
1998	2	3	3	2	1					* Engdahl	Mexico:Near Coast of Oaxaca	墨西哥:瓦哈卡近海	15. 906	-96. 253	24	6. 3	Mw							1				
1998	2	4	14	33	23					* Engdahl	Afghan:Rostaq	阿富汗:罗斯塔奇	37. 071	70. 042	31. 8	5. 9	Mw		2323	4				3				
1998	2	6	6	37	14					USGS	Chile:Antofagasta,C.	智利:安托法加斯塔中部	-22. 67	-70. 13	57	5. 5	Mw	5										
1998	2	20	12	18	8					* Engdahl	Afghan:Astor	阿富汗:阿斯托尔	36. 475	71. 104	236	6. 4	Mw		1	1				2				
1998	2	21	0	55	42					USGS	Japan:Niigata	日本:新潟	37. 22	138. 68	33	5. 1	Mw	6										
1998	3	8	4	46	49					USGS	Japan:Kazo	日本:埼玉加须	36. 09	139. 6	69	4. 6	mb	6										
1998	3	10	23	32	44					USGS	Brazil:Mato Grosso	巴西:马托格罗索	-11. 67	-57	10	5. 2	mb	6										
1998	3	11	13	18	1					China,Dis	China:Hebei,Zhangbei	中国:河北张北	41. 15	114. 38		5. 5	Ms	7			3	1	1. 33	2	364	3		
1998	3	14	19	40	29					* Engdahl	Iran:Kerman	伊朗:克尔曼	30. 167	57. 606	9	6. 6	Mw		5	1	50	1		3	2000	4		
1998	3	19	13	51	31					* China,Dis	China:Xinjiang,Artux,NE.	中国:新疆阿图什东北	40. 2	76. 8	33	6. 0	Ms	7					2. 67	2	400	3		
1998	3	23	9	37	9					USGS	Japan:Ibaraki,Near Coast	日本:茨城近海	36. 32	141. 07	41	5. 5	Mw	5										
1998	3	25	3	12	29	3	0. 1			* Engdahl, NOAA	Balleny Islands	巴雷尼群岛	-62. 857	149. 569	21. 8	8. 1	Mw											
1998	3	26	16	26	12					USGS	Italy:Porto San Giorgio, Permo	意大利:圣佐治港,巴马	43. 26	12. 97	10	5. 4	Mw	7										
1998	4	3	7	26	37					*	Italy:Gualdo	意大利:瓜尔多	43. 164	12. 701	10	5. 2	Mw							1				
1998	4	9	8	45	41					USGS	Japan:Hitachi	日本:茨城日立	36. 92	140. 82	110	5. 5	Mw	6										

年 Year	月 Mo	日 Dy	时 Hr	分 Mn	秒 Sec	海啸 Tsunami 源 Sr	浪高 Wh	级 I mI	级 S mS	资料来源 Information	震中 Earthquake Epicenter 地名(英文) Name(English)	地名(中文) Name(Chinese)	纬度(°) Latitude	经度(°) Longitude	深度 Depth	震级 Mag	标度 Scale	烈度 MMI	死亡人数 Deaths 数量/人 Num	级别 Dd	受伤人数 Injuries 数量/人 Num	级别 Dd	经济损失 Damage 数量/$ Mill	级别 De	房屋毁坏 Houses Destroyed 数量/间 Num	级别 Dh	房屋受损 Houses Damaged 数量/间 Num	级别 Dh
1998	4	10	15	0	55					* Engdahl	Iran: Birjand, Gonabad	伊朗:比尔詹德,戈纳巴德	32.432	60.056	35	5.8	Mw		12	1	10	1		2			600	3
1998	4	12	10	55	33					* USGS	Slovenia: Bovec	斯洛文尼亚:波维克	46.245	13.652	10	5.7	Mw	8	1	1				2				
1998	4	14	2	47	49					China, Dis	China: Hebei, Tangshan	中国:河北唐山	39.67	118.48	10	4.7	Ms	6			7	1						
1998	4	16	3	13	27					China, Dis	China: Guangxi, Huanjiang	中国:广西环江	25.12	107.98	11	4.9	Ms	6			2	1	3.11	2	35	1	4575	4
1998	4	22	11	32	50					USGS	Japan: Higashiomi	日本:滋贺东近江市	35.15	136.42	33	5.2	Mw	6										
1998	4	25	22	37	38					USGS	Japan: Ito	日本:静冈伊东	34.92	139.08	33	4.8	mb	6										
1998	5	3	2	9	8					USGS	Japan: Izu	日本:静冈伊豆	34.87	138.98	34	5.6	Mw	6										
1998	5	3	15	30	22	4	0.1			* Engdahl, NOAA	Ryukyu Islands	琉球群岛	22.43	125.375	25.4	7.5	Mw											
1998	5	22	4	48	52					* Engdahl	Bolivia: Aiquile, Totora	玻利维亚:艾基莱,托托拉	-17.777	-65.439	24	6.6	Mw		105	3				3				
1998	5	22	19	49	34					USGS	Japan: Oita	日本:大分	33.62	131.51	81	5.5	Mw	6										
1998	5	28	21	11	44					* China, USGS, Dis	China: Xinjiang, Hotan	中国:新疆和田	37.8	79.2		6.2	Ms	7			28	1	6.6	3	2000	4		
1998	5	29	22	49	34					USGS, NEIC	Kyrgyzstan: Naryn	吉尔吉斯斯坦:纳伦州	41.17	75.65	19	5.6	Mw	6										
1998	5	30	6	22	31					* Engdahl	Afghan: Badakhshan, Takhar	阿富汗:巴达赫尚,塔哈尔	37.137	70.094	35	6.6	Mw		4000	4		4		4				
1998	5	30	6	22	38					USGS	China: Taiwan, Hualien, Coast of E.	中国:台湾花莲以东海域	24.3	122.19	54	4.9	mb	6										
1998	6	22	7	7	8					USGS	Ryukyu Islands	琉球群岛	28.04	129.39	63	5.5	Mw	6										
1998	6	25	6	39	18					China, Dis	China: Xinjiang, Wensu	中国:新疆温宿	41.55	80.68	25	5.2	Ms	6	1				0.57	1				
1998	6	27	13	55	52					* Engdahl	Turkey: Adana, Ceyhan	土耳其:阿达纳,杰伊汗	36.923	35.329	16	6.3	Mw	8	145	3				3				
1998	6	30	17	22	50					USGS	Japan: Omachi	日本:长野大町	36.43	137.72	33	4.7	mb	6										
1998	7	9	5	19	9					* Engdahl	Azores: Fayal Island	亚速尔群岛:法亚尔岛	38.67	-28.566	9	6.2	Mw		10	1			72.0	4				
1998	7	9	14	19	20					* Engdahl	Azerbaijan: Lenkeran	阿塞拜疆:连科兰	38.715	48.542	26	6	Mw							2				
1998	7	11	11	4	40					China, Dis	China: Shanxi, Linyi	中国:山西临猗	35.03	110.7	15	5	Ms	6			1	1	2.11	2				
1998	7	17	4	51	16					* China, USGS	China: Taiwan, Yunlin	中国:台湾云林	23.7	120.4		6.3	Ms	8	5	1	27	1		1				
1998	7	17	8	49	16	4	15			* Engdahl, NOAA	Bismarck Sea	俾斯麦海	-2.943	142.582	25	7.1	Ms		2205	4	1000	3		3				
1998	7	18	9	57	14					USGS	Chile: Copiapo	智利:科皮亚波	-28.31	-70.84	46	5.5	Mw	5										
1998	7	20	1	5	57					China, Engdahl, Dis	China: Xizang (Tibet), Xaitongmoin	中国:西藏谢通门	30.21	88.282	11	6.1	Ms	7										
1998	7	28	4	51	42					China, Dis	China: Xinjiang, Baicheng	中国:新疆拜城	41.73	81.53	15	5.4	Ms	6			15	1	1.12	2				
1998	7	29	1	15	22					China, Dis	China: Ningxia, Haiyuan	中国:宁夏海原	36.8	105.45	25	4.9	Ms	6			2	1	0.14	1				
1998	8	2	4	40	42					China, Dis	China: Xinjiang, Payzawat	中国:新疆伽师	39.6	77.5	11	6	Ms	7			3	1	6.3	3	809	3		
1998	8	4	18	59	21					* Engdahl	Ecuador: Bahia De Caraquez, Canoa	厄瓜多尔:加拉加斯湾,卡诺亚	-0.56	-80.23	20	7.2	Mw		3	1				3				
1998	8	15	5	18	9					USGS	Italy: Cascia	意大利:卡夏	42.41	12.98	10	4.8	ML	7										
1998	8	15	18	31	9					USGS	Japan: Matsumoto	日本:长野松本	36.27	137.64	10	5.5	Mw	6										
1998	8	27	9	3	36					* China, Engdahl, Dis	China: Xinjiang, Payzawat	中国:新疆伽师	39.558	77.33	17	6.6	Ms	8	3	1	18	1	15.6	3	3600	4		

年 Year	月 Mo	日 Dy	时 Hr	分 Mn	秒 Sec	源 Sr	浪高 Wh	级I mI	级S mS	资料来源 Information	地名(英文) Name(English)	地名(中文) Name(Chinese)	纬度(°) Latitude	经度(°) Longitude	深度 Depth	震级 Mag	标度 Scale	烈度 MMI	死亡人数 Deaths 数量/人 Num	死亡人数 Deaths 级别 Dd	受伤人数 Injuries 数量/人 Num	受伤人数 Injuries 级别 Dd	经济损失 Damage 数量/$ Mill	经济损失 Damage 级别 De	房屋毁坏 Houses Destroyed 数量/间 Num	房屋毁坏 Houses Destroyed 级别 Dh	房屋受损 Houses Damaged 数量/间 Num	房屋受损 Houses Damaged 级别 Dh
1998	8	31	2	32	4					USGS	Slovenia:Ljubljana	斯洛文尼亚:卢布尔雅那	45.95	14.78	10	4.9	ML	6										
1998	9	3	7	58	21					USGS, Engdahl	Japan:Senboku	日本:秋田仙北	39.793	140.742	6.2	5.8	Mw	9										
1998	9	3	17	37	60					NEIC, Engdahl, USGS	Chile:Near Coast of C.	智利:中部近海	-29.437	-71.652	27	6.6	Mw	6										
1998	9	4	10	40	53					USGS	China:Taiwan, Hualien	中国:台湾花莲	23.77	121.45	33	4.7	mb	6										
1998	9	15	7	24	7					USGS	Japan:Miyagi	日本:宫城	38.35	140.51	50	5.1	mb	6										
1998	9	18	3	53	12					China, Dis	China:Xinjiang, Akqi	中国:新疆阿合奇	40.97	78.5	15	4.8	Ms	6			35	1	0.89	1				
1998	9	25	19	52	52					USGS	US:Pennsylvania, Adamsville	美国:宾西法尼亚州亚当斯维尔	41.49	-80.39	5	4.5	Mw	6										
1998	9	28	13	34	31					* Engdahl	Indonesia: Jawa, Malang, Blitar	印度尼西亚:爪哇,玛琅,布里达	-8.183	112.337	146.4	6.6	Mw		1	1				1				
1998	9	29	6	39	13					USGS	Hawaiian Islands	夏威夷群岛	19.35	-155.13	9	4.8	Md	6										
1998	9	29	22	14	50					* USGS	Serbia:Belgrade, Ljig	塞尔维亚:贝尔格来德,利格	44.209	20.08	10	5.5	Mw	8	1	1				1				
1998	9	30	23	42	54					*	Albania:Kukes, Peshkopi	阿尔巴尼亚:库奇斯,佩什科比	41.925	20.39	10	5.3	Mw							1				
1998	10	2	12	49	30					China, Dis	China:Yunnan, Ninglang	中国:云南宁蒗	27.2	100.9	13	5.3	Ms	6										
1998	10	5	2	20	34					*	Iran:Lorestan	伊朗:洛雷斯坦	33.199	47.225	39	5.4	Mw							1			100	2
1998	10	10	4	12	9					USGS	Chile:Near Coast of C.	智利:中部近海	-33.52	-72.08	33	5.7	Mw	5										
1998	10	10	16	32	19					Engdahl, USGS	Indonesia:Tinombo	印度尼西亚:蒂农博	-0.421	119.727	18	6.0	Mw	6										
1998	10	26	20	1	3					China, Dis	China:Yunnan, Ninglang	中国:云南宁蒗	27.23	101	10	5.2	Ms	6			32	1	11.0	3				
1998	11	8	12	40	46					USGS	Japan:Kawasaki	日本:神奈川川崎	35.51	139.9	92	4.9	mb	6										
1998	11	13	13	1	11					*	Iran:Jahrom, S.	伊朗:贾赫罗姆南部	27.791	53.608	33	5.4	Mw		5	1	105	3				2	850	3
1998	11	19	11	38	11					* China, USGS, NEIC, Dis	China:Yunnan, Ninglang	中国:云南宁蒗	27.3	100.9		6.2	Ms	8	5	1	1600	4	60.8	4	5172	4		
1998	11	23	9	30	19					USGS, NEIC	Chile:Antofagasta, C.	智利:安托法加斯塔中部	-23.72	-70.51	33	5.6	Mw	5										
1998	11	23	19	48	10					USGS	Japan:Fukushima, Near Coast	日本:福岛近海	37.98	141.48	78	5.2	Mw	6										
1998	11	24	1	6	12					USGS	Chile:Calama	智利:卡拉马	-22.62	-69.24	79	5.2	Mw	6										
1998	11	27	10	27	3					USGS	Argentina:Mendoza	阿根廷:门多萨	-32.14	-69.33	126	5.5	Mw	5										
1998	11	29	14	10	31	2	2.8			* Engdahl, NOAA	Indonesia:Mangole, Manado	印度尼西亚:芒俄勒,马纳都	-1.916	124.823	16	7.7	Mw	7	41	1	107	3		3	1000	3		
1998	12	1	7	37	56					* China, Dis	China:Yunnan, Xuanwei	中国:云南宣威	26.4	104.1		5.1	Ms	7			84	2	13.3	3	21872	5		
1998	12	14	0	59	3					USGS	China:Taiwan, Hualien, Coast of E.	中国:台湾花莲以东海域	24.42	122.2	62	4.7	mb	6										
1998	12	16	0	18	45					Engdahl, USGS	Japan:Miyazzaki, Near Coast	日本:宫崎近海	31.344	131.345	30	6.0	Mw	6										
1999	1	14	22	45	19					USGS	Georgia:Akhalkalaki	格鲁吉亚:阿卡卡垃吉	41.27	43.98	33	4.8	mb	6										

时间 Date						海啸 Tsunami				资料来源 Information	震中 Earthquake Epicenter				深度 Depth	震级 Mag	标度 Scale	烈度 MMI	死亡人数 Deaths		受伤人数 Injuries		经济损失 Damage		房屋毁坏 Houses Destroyed		房屋受损 Houses Damaged	
年 Year	月 Mo	日 Dy	时 Hr	分 Mn	秒 Sec	源 Sr	浪高 Wh	级 I mI	级 S mS		地名(英文) Name(English)	地名(中文) Name(Chinese)	纬度(°) Latitude	经度(°) Longitude					数量/人 Num	级别 Dd	数量/人 Num	级别 Dd	数量/$ Mill $ Mill	级别 De	数量/间 Num	级别 Dh	数量/间 Num	级别 Dh
1999	1	18	19	41	30					USGS	Puerto Rico:Vega Baja	波多黎各:下维加	18. 86	-67. 22	33	5	Mw	6										
1999	1	24	0	37	6					NEIC, Eng - dahl, USGS	Japan:Kagoshima, Near Coast of S.	日本:鹿岛南部近海	30. 656	131. 125	34	6. 4	Mw	6										
1999	1	25	18	19	18					* Engdahl	Colombia:Armenia, Calarca	哥伦比亚:亚美尼亚,卡拉卡	4. 449	-75. 652	17	6. 2	Mw		1185	4	4750	4	2900	5		4		
1999	1	28	1	25	43					USGS	Japan:Matsumoto	日本:长野松本	36. 24	137. 92	10	4. 9	mb	6										
1999	1	29	5	44	22					China, Dis	China: Inner Mongolia, Xilin Gol	中国:内蒙古锡林郭勒盟	44. 55	115. 75	18	5. 2	Ms	6					2. 69	2				
1999	1	31	5	7	14					USGS	Russia: Dagestan, Makhachkala	俄罗斯:达吉斯坦共和国马哈奇卡拉	43. 16	46. 84	33	5. 8	Mw	6										
1999	2	1	23	57	53					*	Russia: Dagestan, Makhachkala	俄罗斯:达吉斯坦共和国马哈奇卡拉	42. 962	46. 954	33	3. 2	mb						0. 9	1				
1999	2	2	13	45	17					* USGS	Spain:Mula, Puebla De Mula	西班牙:穆拉,普埃布拉	38. 193	-1. 566	10	5. 2	MLg	7			20	1	44. 0	4				3
1999	2	11	14	8	53					* Engdahl	Afghan:Lowgar, Vardak	阿富汗:洛加尔,瓦尔达克	34. 319	69. 188	15. 7	6	Mw		70	2	500	3		3	7000	4		
1999	2	17	21	58	55					USGS, NEIC	Chile:Iquique	智利:伊基克	-21. 14	-70. 04	33	5. 6	Mw	5										
1999	2	21	18	14	38					USGS	Russia: Dagestan, Makhachkala	俄罗斯:达吉斯坦共和国马哈奇卡拉	43. 21	46. 83	65	5. 3	Mw	6										
1999	2	25	3	6	17					USGS	Russia:Chita, Syulban	俄罗斯:赤塔州休利班	56. 53	116. 11	10	4. 8	mb	6										
1999	2	25	18	58	29					USGS	Russia:Lake Baykal	俄罗斯:贝加尔湖	51. 6	104. 86	10	5. 9	mb	6										
1999	2	26	5	18	18					USGS	Japan:Sakata	日本:山形酒田	39. 15	139. 87	33	5. 3	Mw	7										
1999	3	1	21	51	22					USGS	El Salvador:San Vicente	萨尔瓦多:圣维森特	13. 64	-88. 73	33	4. 7	Md	6										
1999	3	4	5	38	27					* Engdahl	Iran:Kerman	伊朗:克尔曼	28. 306	57. 232	23	6. 6	Mw		1	1				1			517	3
1999	3	11	13	18	2					* China, Dis	China:Hebei, Zhangbei	中国:河北张北	41. 2	114. 6		5. 6	Ms	6			3	1	1. 33	2	200	3		
1999	3	14	0	4	45					USGS	Japan:Shizuoka, Near Coast	日本:静冈近海	34. 13	139. 09	33	5. 1	mb	6										
1999	3	15	10	42	55					China, USGS, Dis	China:Xinjiang, Kuqa	中国:新疆库车	41. 89	82. 69	10	5. 6	Ms	6			3	1	1. 98	2			2400	4
1999	3	16	7	43	37					USGS	Japan:Kyoto	日本:京都	35. 21	135. 82	33	5. 1	mb	6										
1999	3	21	16	16	2					USGS	Russia:Buryatiya, Kichera	俄罗斯:布里亚特州基切拉镇	55. 9	110. 21	10	5. 9	Mw	6										
1999	3	25	23	31	11					USGS	Japan:Mito	日本:茨城美图	36. 4	140. 47	82	5. 2	Mw	6										
1999	3	27	16	37	6					USGS	Japan:Shizuoka, Near Coast	日本:静冈近海	34. 06	138. 9	39	4. 8	mb	6										
1999	3	28	19	5	13					* India, Engdahl	India:Chamoli, Rudraprayag	印度:查莫利,鲁德拉普拉亚格	30. 476	79. 425	15	6. 6	Mw	8	100	2	394	3	70. 0	4	21100	5		
1999	4	1	21	36	23					NEIC, Eng - dahl, USGS	Papua New Guinea:New Ireland	巴布亚新几内亚:新爱尔兰	-4. 365	152. 772	36. 6	6. 2	Mw	6										
1999	4	3	6	17	20					* Engdahl, USGS	Peru:Camana, Arequipa	秘鲁:卡马那,阿雷基帕	-16. 599	-72. 482	85	6. 8	Mw	6	1	1	50	1		2			300	3

年 Year	月 Mo	日 Dy	时 Hr	分 Mn	秒 Sec	源 Sr	浪高 Wh	级I mI	级S mS	资料来源 Information	地名(英文) Name(English)	地名(中文) Name(Chinese)	纬度(°) Latitude	经度(°) Longitude	深度 Depth	震级 Mag	标度 Scale	烈度 MMI	死亡人数 Deaths 数量/人 Num	死亡人数 级别 Dd	受伤人数 Injuries 数量/人 Num	受伤人数 级别 Dd	经济损失 Damage 数量/$ Mill	经济损失 级别 De	房屋毁坏 Houses Destroyed 数量/间 Num	房屋毁坏 级别 Dh	房屋受损 Houses Damaged 数量/间 Num	房屋受损 级别 Dh
1999	4	4	4	59	0					USGS	China: Taiwan, Yilan, Coast of E.	中国:台湾宜兰东南海域	24.81	121.99	93	4.8	mb	6										
1999	4	10	7	52	22					USGS	China: Taiwan, Hualien, Coast of E.	中国:台湾花莲以东海域	24.04	121.83	10	4.8	mb	6										
1999	4	15	6	29	6					China, Dis	China: Gansu, Wenxian	中国:甘肃文县	32.9	104.95	8	4.7	Ms	6	1		30	1	0.76	1				
1999	4	25	12	27	5					USGS	Japan: Mito	日本:茨城美图	36.44	140.47	81	5.3	Mw	6										
1999	4	30	19	28	49					USGS	Chile: Near Coast of C.	智利:中部近海	-31.65	-71.68	52	5.6	Mw	5										
1999	5	6	23	0	53					* Engdahl	Iran: Fars	伊朗:法尔斯	29.52	51.903	19.5	6.2	Mw		26	1	100	2		2	800	3		
1999	5	7	1	3	23					USGS	China: Taiwan, Yilan, Coast of E.	中国:台湾宜兰东南海域	24.71	121.89	10	5	mb	6										
1999	5	12	17	59	24					Engdahl, USGS	Japan: Hokkaido	日本:北海道	43.13	143.789	97	6.2	Mw	6										
1999	5	17	3	29	26					China, Dis	China: Hainan, Wanning	中国:海南万宁	18.62	110.5	20	5.2	Ms	6										
1999	5	27	16	1	23					USGS	Russia: Buryatiya, Kichera	俄罗斯:布里亚特州基切拉镇	55.81	110.04	10	5.1	Mw	6										
1999	5	30	15	56	45					USGS	Russia: Buryatiya, Kichera	俄罗斯:布里亚特州基切拉镇	55.8	110.03	10	5.2	Mw	6										
1999	6	3	16	11	43					USGS	China: Taiwan, Hualien, Coast of E.	中国:台湾花莲以东海域	24.45	122.36	75	5.4	Mw	6										
1999	6	4	9	12	50					*	Azerbaijan: Agali	阿塞拜疆:阿加利	40.802	47.448	33	5.4	Mw	5	1	1	18	1	5.0	3			50	1
1999	6	13	11	51	13					USGS	Russia: Buryatiya, Kichera	俄罗斯:布里亚特州基切拉镇	55.81	110.04	10	4.7	mb	6										
1999	6	15	20	42	7					* Engdahl, USGS	Mexico: Puebla, Veracruz	墨西哥:普埃布拉,韦拉克鲁斯	18.374	-97.457	63	7	Mw	8	20	1	200	3	227	5			2000	4
1999	6	17	15	2	16					China	China: Xinjiang, Baicheng	中国:新疆拜城	41.87	81.8	22	5	Ms	5										
1999	6	21	17	43	4					* Engdahl	Mexico: Guerrero, Michoacan, Cuitzeo	墨西哥:格雷罗,米却肯,奎特绍	18.284	-101.64	47	6.3	Mw							3			1300	4
1999	6	29	23	18	6					USGS, NEIC	Afghan: Badakhshan	阿富汗:巴达赫尚	36.62	71.35	189	5.7	Mw	5										
1999	7	1	7	40	56					USGS	Serbia: Kraljevo	塞尔维亚:克拉列沃	43.69	20.99	10	5.2	Mw	7										
1999	7	3	1	43	54					USGS	US: Washington, W.	美国:华盛顿州西部沿海	47.08	-123.46	40	5.8	Mw	7										
1999	7	7	13	53	14					USGS	China: Taiwan, Kaohsiung	中国:台湾高雄	23.37	120.85	33	4.9	mb	6										
1999	7	11	14	14	19					* Engdahl	Guatemala: Livingston	危地马拉:利文斯顿	15.789	-88.278	15	6.7	Mw		1	1	40	1		2	7	1	4	1
1999	7	22	10	42	12					* NEIC	Bangladesh: Chittagong, S.	孟加拉:吉大港南部	21.544	91.895	10	5.2	mb		6	1	200	3		3	700	3		
1999	7	26	2	45	47					USGS	Japan: Aomori, Near East Coast	日本:青森东部近海	40.78	141.68	104	5.7	Mw	5										
1999	8	2	1	6	38					USGS	Argentina: Mendoza	阿根廷:门多萨	-33.02	-70.15	95	5.5	Mw	5										
1999	8	11	4	27	55					USGS	Cyprus: Paphos, Nicosia	塞浦路斯:帕菲斯,尼科西亚	34.79	32.94	33	5.6	Mw	7										
1999	8	12	5	45	1					Engdahl, USGS	Indonesia: Sulawesi, Tojo	印度尼西亚:苏拉威西岛,台基	-1.757	122.473	29.9	6.2	Mw	6										

年 Year	月 Mo	日 Dy	时 Hr	分 Mn	秒 Sec	海啸 Tsunami 源 Sr	浪高 Wh	级 I mI	级 S mS	资料来源 Information	震中 Earthquake Epicenter 地名(英文) Name(English)	地名(中文) Name(Chinese)	纬度(°) Latitude	经度(°) Longitude	深度 Depth	震级 Mag	标度 Scale	烈度 MMI	死亡人数 Deaths 数量/人 Num	级别 Dd	受伤人数 Injuries 数量/人 Num	级别 Dd	经济损失 Damage 数量/$ Mill $ Mill	级别 De	房屋毁坏 Houses Destroyed 数量/间 Num	级别 Dh	房屋受损 Houses Damaged 数量/间 Num	级别 Dh
1999	8	17	0	1	40	4	2.5			* Engdahl, NOAA	Turkey: Istanbul, Kocaeli	土耳其:伊斯坦布尔,科贾埃利	40.773	30.002	13.3	7.6	M	10	17118	5	50000	5	20000	5			73342	5
1999	8	20	20	33	11					USGS	Japan: Aridagawa	日本:和歌山有田川	34.02	135.4	65	5.7	Mw	8										
1999	8	31	8	10	50					*	Turkey: Izmit	土耳其:伊兹米特	40.711	29.949	10	5.2	Mw		1	1	166	3		1				
1999	9	7	11	56	51					* Engdahl	Greece: Athens	希腊:雅典	38.13	23.613	10	6	Mw	9	143	3	1600		655	5	53000	5		
1999	9	10	14	18	19					USGS	China: Taiwan, Taitung, Coast of E.	中国:台湾台东以东海域	22.25	121.8	10	5.4	Mw	6										
1999	9	13	11	55	30					* Engdahl	Turkey: Izmit	土耳其:伊兹米特	40.745	30.094	13	5.8	mb		7	1	422	3		1				
1999	9	14	12	54	31					China, Dis	China: Sichuan, Mianzhu	中国:四川绵竹	31.6	104.08		5	Ms	6			4	1	0.55	1				
1999	9	18	21	28	35					Engdahl, USGS	Russia: Kamchatka Peninsula	俄罗斯:堪察加半岛	51.233	157.446	60	6.0	Mw	6										
1999	9	20	17	47	19					* China, Engdahl, Dis	China: Taiwan, Nantou	中国:台湾南投	23.819	120.863	21	7.7	M	10	2297	4	8700	4	14000	5	82000	5		
1999	9	25	8	43						* China, USGS	China: Taiwan, Nantou	中国:台湾南投	23.9	121.1	17	6.5	Mw	8		1				1				
1999	9	27	11	49	13					China	China: Qinghai, Henan	中国:青海河南县	34.75	101.3	15	5.1	Ms	6										
1999	9	30	16	31	15					* Engdahl, USGS	Mexico: Oaxaca	墨西哥:瓦哈卡	16.046	-96.912	40	7.5	Mw	8	33	1	215	3	165	5			2000	4
1999	10	16	9	46	49					* Engdahl	US: California, Ludlow, Landers	美国:加利福尼亚州勒德罗,兰德斯	34.555	-116.436	15	7.4	Ms	7			4	1		1				
1999	10	22	2	18	58					* China, Engdahl, USGS, Dis	China: Taiwan, Chiayi	中国:台湾嘉义	23.538	120.456	14	6.4	Ms	9	1	1	254	3	0.79	1	15	1		
1999	10	29	21	25	53					USGS	Japan: Shikokuchuo	日本:爱媛县四国中央	34.03	133.42	37	4.5	mb	6										
1999	10	31	13	27	42					* USGS	Peru: Chuschi, Cangallo	秘鲁:丘斯奇,坎加约	-13.64	-74.43	62	4.4	mb	6			30	1		3	210	3	1100	4
1999	11	1	13	25	17					* China, Dis	China: Shanxi, Datong, E.	中国:山西大同东	39.8	113.9	10	5.6	Ms	7			70	2	16.9	3	13235	5		
1999	11	6	18	34	1					USGS	Japan: Tsuruga	日本:福井敦贺	35.64	135.74	10	4.7	mb	6										
1999	11	11	14	41	26					*	Turkey: Adapazari, Golcuk	土耳其:阿达帕札勒,格尔居克	40.744	30.266	22	5.7	Mw		2	1	171	3		1				
1999	11	12	16	57	21					* Engdahl	Turkey: Adapazari, Zonguldak	土耳其:阿达帕札勒,松古达克	40.821	31.227	11	7.5	Ms	9	834	3	4948	4	10000	5				
1999	11	15	1	34	36					USGS, NEIC	Japan: Miyagi, Off Coast	日本:宫城沿海	38.3	142.31	50	5.7	Mw	5										
1999	11	24	16	40	21					* China, Dis	China: Yunnan, Chengjiang	中国:云南澄江	24.5	102.8		5.2	Ms	6	1	1	12	1	9.2	3	90	2		
1999	11	25	20	51	16					China, Dis	China: Qinghai, Golog	中国:青海果洛	34.52	99.87		5.1	Ms	6					1.49	2				
1999	11	26	4	27	25					*	Iran: Gorgan	伊朗:戈尔甘	36.92	54.9	33	5.3	Mw							1			50	1
1999	11	26	13	21	17	4	6.6			* Engdahl, NOAA	Vanuatu Islands	瓦努阿图群岛	-16.322	168.19	33	7.4	Mw		10	1	100	2		3		3		
1999	11	29	4	10	41					* China, Dis	China: Liaoning, Xiuyan	中国:辽宁岫岩	40.4	123.2	10	5.4	Ms	7					10.3	3	160	3		
1999	11	29	12	34	3					USGS	Japan: Higashiura	日本:爱知东浦町	34.99	136.97	45	4.6	mb	6										
1999	11	30	8	24	52					China, Dis	China: Sichuan, Mianzhu	中国:四川绵竹	31.43	104.33	26	5	Ms	6	1		3	1	0.43	1				
1999	12	3	17	6	55					*	Turkey: Erzurum	土耳其:埃尔佐鲁姆	40.358	42.346	19	5.7	Mw		1	1	6	1		2			340	3
1999	12	4	17	6	51					USGS, NEIC	Chile: Vallenar	智利:巴耶纳尔	-28.5	-71.22	34	5.7	Mw	5										
1999	12	6	23	12	34					NEIC, Engdahl, USGS	Alaska: Kodiak Island	阿拉斯加:科迪亚克岛	57.366	-154.532	52	7	Mw	6										

时间						海啸				资料来源	震中				深度	震级	标度	烈度	死亡人数		受伤人数		经济损失		房屋毁坏		房屋受损	
年	月	日	时	分	秒	源	浪高	级 I	级 S		地名(英文)	地名(中文)	纬度(°)	经度(°)					数量/人	级别	数量/人	级别	数量/$ Mill	级别	数量/间	级别	数量/间	级别
Date						Tsunami				Information	Earthquake Epicenter				Depth	Mag	Scale	MMI	Deaths		Injuries		Damage		Houses Destroyed		Houses Damaged	
Year	Mo	Dy	Hr	Mn	Sec	Sr	Wh	mI	mS		Name(English)	Name(Chinese)	Latitude	Longitude					Num	Dd	Num	Dd	$ Mill	De	Num	Dh	Num	Dh
1999	12	11	18	3	39					* Engdahl, USGS	Philippines: Hermana Mayor Island	菲律宾:大埃尔马纳岛	15.78	119.789	40	7.3	Mw	6	5	1	40	1	1.794	2				
1999	12	21	11	0	49					USGS	Russia: Buryatiya, Kichera	俄罗斯:布里亚特州基切拉镇	55.83	110.03	10	5.5	Mw	6										
1999	12	21	14	14	58					* Engdahl	Indonesia: Java Island	印度尼西亚:爪哇岛	-6.8	105.527	42	6.5	Mw		5	1	220	3	3.9	2			2800	4
1999	12	22	17	36	56					* USGS	Algeria: Ain Temouchent	阿尔及利亚:艾因蒂姆尚特	35.321	-1.281	10	5.6	Mw	7	24	1	175	3	60.9	4	3000	4		
2000	1	3	22	34	13					*	India: Mizoram, S.	印度:米佐拉姆南部	22.132	92.771	33	4.6	mb							1			100	2
2000	1	8	1	19	46					NEIC, Engdahl, USGS	Solomon Islands	所罗门群岛	-9.872	159.902	11	6.4	Mw	6										
2000	1	11	23	43	56					* China, Dis	China: Liaoning, Xiuyan	中国:辽宁岫岩	40.5	123.1	10	5.1	Ms	7			14	1	3.20	2	3600	4		
2000	1	14	23	37	8					* China, Dis	China: Yunnan, Yaoan	中国:云南姚安	25.624	101.051	17.4	6.5	Ms	8	7	1	2591	4	129	5	41000	5		
2000	1	26	20	55	16					China, Dis	China: Yunnan, Mile	中国:云南弥勒	24.2	103.63	10	5.5	Ms	7			69	2	12.1	3				
2000	1	28	14	21	7					NEIC, Engdahl	Japan: Off SE. Coast of Hokkaido	日本:北海道东南沿海	43.072	146.773	42.6	6.8	Mw	6										
2000	1	31	7	25	60					China, NEIC, Dis	China: Xinjiang, Ruoqiang	中国:新疆若羌	38.114	88.604	33	5.6	Ms	6					0.56	1				
2000	2	2	22	58	2					*	Iran: Kashmar	伊朗:卡什马尔	35.288	58.218	33	5.3	Mw		1	1	15	1		2	100	2	300	3
2000	2	7	19	34	57					*	Swaziland: Manzini	斯威士兰:曼齐尼	-26.288	30.888	5	4.5	mb				1	1		1				
2000	2	15	21	33	19					USGS	China: Taiwan, Kaohsiung	中国:台湾高雄	23.35	120.93	33	5.3	Mw	6										
2000	4	2	6	18	20					USGS	Hawaiian Islands	夏威夷群岛	19.34	-155.21	4	5	Md	6										
2000	4	5	4	36	59	2	0.1			* NOAA	Mediterranean Sea	地中海	34.22	25.69	38	5.5	Mw											
2000	4	15	8	32	38					China, Dis	China: Qinghai, Zaduo	中国:青海杂多	33.22	95.47	33	5.3	Ms	7					0.39	1				
2000	4	20	8	41	30					USGS, NEIC	Uzbekistan: Qashqadaryo	乌兹别克斯坦:卡什卡达里亚	38.62	66.44	10	5.5	Mw	6										
2000	5	2	23	59	18					USGS	Gulf of Alaska	阿拉斯加湾	59.74	-139.4	10	5.4	Mw	6										
2000	5	4	4	21	18	4	6			* Engdahl, NOAA, USGS	Molukka Sea	马鲁古海	-1.153	123.478	26	7.6	Mw	7	46	1	264	3	30.0	4	10000	5		
2000	5	6	13	41	53					USGS	China: Taiwan, Hualien	中国:台湾花莲	24.09	121.67	33	4.8	mb	6										
2000	5	7	23	10	54					*	Turkey: Puturge	土耳其:皮蒂尔盖	38.164	38.777	5	4.5	mb				1	1		2			200	3
2000	5	12	18	43	20					NEIC, Engdahl	Argentina: Jujuy	阿根廷:胡胡伊	-23.757	-66.766	225	7.2	Mw	6										
2000	5	17	3	25	49					* China	China: Taiwan, Nantou, N.	中国:台湾南投北	24	121.1		6.1	Ms		3	1	13	1		1				
2000	6	3	8	54	49					Engdahl, USGS	Japan: Sanmu	日本:千叶山武	35.568	140.464	47.5	6.1	Mw	6										
2000	6	4	16	28	28					* Engdahl	Indonesia: Southern Sumatera, Lahat	印度尼西亚:苏门答腊南部,拉哈特	-4.762	102.007	34.6	7.9	Ms	6	103	3	2174	4	6.0	3				
2000	6	6	2	41	51					* Engdahl	Turkey: Cerkes, Cubuk	土耳其:切鲁开斯,查布克	40.716	32.998	7	6	Mw	7	2	1	80	2		3			4600	4
2000	6	6	10	59	13					China, Engdahl, NEIC, Dis	China: Gansu, Jingtai, W.	中国:甘肃景泰西	37.035	103.821	15	5.9	Ms	8			24	1	8.7	3				
2000	6	6	21	16	42					USGS	Japan Sea	日本海	36.83	135.46	10	5.9	Mw	6										
2000	6	7	13	46	56					*	Myanmar: Kachin	缅甸:克钦	26.856	97.238	33	6.5	Ms							1		2		

年 Year	月 Mo	日 Dy	时 Hr	分 Mn	秒 Sec	海啸 源 Sr	海啸 浪高 Wh	海啸 级 I mI	海啸 级 S mS	资料来源 Information	地名(英文) Name(English)	地名(中文) Name(Chinese)	纬度(°) Latitude	经度(°) Longitude	深度 Depth	震级 Mag	标度 Scale	烈度 MMI	死亡人数 数量/人 Num	死亡人数 级别 Dd	受伤人数 数量/人 Num	受伤人数 级别 Dd	经济损失 数量/$ Mill	经济损失 级别 De	房屋毁坏 数量/间 Num	房屋毁坏 级别 Dh	房屋受损 数量/间 Num	房屋受损 级别 Dh
2000	6	7	23	45	28					* Engdahl	Indonesia:Southern Sumatera, Lahat	印度尼西亚:苏门答腊南部,拉哈特	-4.622	101.852	32	6.7	Mw		1	1				2			600	3
2000	6	8	0	32	47					USGS	Japan:Kumamoto	日本:熊本	32.68	130.68	21	5	mb	6										
2000	6	10	18	23	29					* China, Engdahl, USGS	China:Taiwan, Nantou	中国:台湾南投	23.877	121.237	19	6.8	Ms	8	2	1	36	1		1				
2000	6	14	21	49	19					USGS	US:California, Brawley	美国:加利福尼亚州布劳利	32.88	-115.5	4	4.5	ML	6										
2000	6	16	7	55	36					NEIC, Engdahl, USGS	Chile:Santiago	智利:圣地亚哥	-33.893	-70.095	114	6.4	Mw	6										
2000	6	17	15	40	43					* Engdahl	Iceland: Vestmannaeyjar, Hella	冰岛:韦斯特曼纳埃亚尔,赫拉	63.924	-20.478	8	6.5	Mw				1	1	20.0	3	11	1	19	1
2000	6	18	14	44	14	4	0.3			* Engdahl, NOAA	Australia:Cocos Islands	澳大利亚:科科斯群岛	-13.896	97.328	7.1	7.9	Mw											
2000	6	19	21	56	25					USGS	China:Taiwan, Hualien	中国:台湾花莲	23.87	121.29	50	5.3	Mw	6										
2000	6	21	0	51	49					* Engdahl	Iceland:Grimsnes, Selfoss	冰岛:格里姆斯内斯,塞尔福斯	63.929	-20.712	8	6.5	Mw						12.0	3	12	1		
2000	6	22	12	16	32					USGS, CSN	Italy:Perugia	意大利:佩鲁贾	43.3	12.48	10	5.5	mB	6										
2000	6	29	3	11	51					USGS	Japan:Shizuoka, Near Coast	日本:静冈近海	34.15	139.18	10	5.3	mb	6										
2000	7	1	7	1	58	4	0.1			* Engdahl, NOAA, USGS	Japan:Shizuoka, Near Coast	日本:静冈近海	34.232	139.127	14.1	6.1	Mw	8	1	1		3		1				
2000	7	6	19	30	20					*	Nicaragua:Granada	尼加拉瓜:格拉纳达	11.884	-85.988	33	5.4	Mw		7	1	42	1		3	357	3	1130	4
2000	7	8	18	57	44					USGS	Japan:Shizuoka, Near Coast	日本:静冈近海	34.05	139.13	10	5.9	Mw	6										
2000	7	11	2	49	48					USGS	Austria:Schwechat	奥地利:施韦夏特	48.01	16.42	10	5.3	ML	6										
2000	7	12	1	10	43					*	Indonesia:Bogor	印度尼西亚:茂物	-6.675	106.845	33	5.4	Mw				6	1		2			225	3
2000	7	15	1	30	33	4	0.1			* Engdahl, NOAA, USGS	Japan:Shizuoka, Near Coast	日本:静冈近海	34.37	139.274	16.6	6.1	Mw	8			10	1		1				
2000	7	16	3	21	46					* Engdahl	Philippines:Luzon, Coast N.	菲律宾:吕宋岛北部海域	20.258	122.069	27.9	6.4	Mw				6	1		2				3
2000	7	20	18	39	19					NEIC, Engdahl, USGS	Japan:Ibaraki, Near Coast	日本:茨城近海	36.55	140.918	31	6	Mw	6										
2000	7	23	21	52	44					USGS	Japan:Shizuoka, Near Coast	日本:静冈近海	34.13	139.12	10	5.6	Mw	7										
2000	7	27	1	49	53					USGS	Japan:Shizuoka, Near Coast	日本:静冈近海	34.21	139.37	10	5.6	Mw	6										
2000	7	30	0	18	0					USGS	Japan:Miyake Jima	日本:三宅岛	33.93	139.35	10	5.7	Mw	7										
2000	7	30	12	25	48	4	0.1			* Engdahl, NOAA, USGS	Japan:Miyake Jima	日本:三宅岛	33.923	139.366	15	6.5	Mw	8			1	1		1				
2000	8	3	1	9	41					NEIC, Engdahl, USGS	Solomon Islands: Santa Cruz Islands	所罗门群岛:圣克鲁斯群岛	-12.043	166.501	36.8	6.6	Mw	6										

时间						海啸				资料来源	震中				深度	震级	标度	烈度	死亡人数		受伤人数		经济损失		房屋毁坏		房屋受损	
年	月	日	时	分	秒	源	浪高	级 I	级 S		地名(英文)	地名(中文)	纬度(°)	经度(°)					数量/人	级别	数量/人	级别	数量/$ Mill	级别	数量/间	级别	数量/间	级别
Date						Tsunami				Information	Earthquake Epicenter				Depth	Mag	Scale	MMI	Deaths		Injuries		Damage		Houses Destroyed		Houses Damaged	
Year	Mo	Dy	Hr	Mn	Sec	Sr	Wh	mI	mS		Name(English)	Name(Chinese)	Latitude	Longitude					Num	Dd	Num	Dd	$ Mill	De	Num	Dh	Num	Dh
2000	8	4	21	13	5					* NEIC, Engdahl	Russia:Sakhalin Island	俄罗斯:库页岛(萨哈林岛)	48.776	142.182	16	6.8	Mw	6			8	1	0.92	1			1390	4
2000	8	18	1	52	21					USGS	Japan:Shizuoka, Near Coast	日本:静冈近海	34.13	139.18	10	5.7	Mw	8										
2000	8	20	10	48	14					USGS	China:Taiwan, Kaohsiung	中国:台湾高雄	23.07	120.76	10	4.8	ML	6										
2000	8	20	19	2	22					USGS	China:Taiwan, Kaohsiung	中国:台湾高雄	23.02	120.68	10	4.5	ML	6										
2000	8	20	19	4	35					USGS	China:Taiwan, Kaohsiung	中国:台湾高雄	22.99	120.65	10	4.6	ML	6										
2000	8	21	13	25						* China, Dis	China:Yunnan, Wuding	中国:云南武定	25.8	102.2		5.1	Ms		1	1	406	3	43.0	4				
2000	9	3	8	36	30					* USGS	US:California, Napa	美国:加利福尼亚州那帕	38.379	-122.413	10	5	Mw	7			41	1	50.0	4				
2000	9	10	8	54	46					China, USGS, Engdahl	China:Taiwan, Hualien	中国:台湾花莲	24.039	121.579	55.1	6.3	Ms	6										
2000	9	11	10	49	34					USGS	China:Taiwan, Hualien, Coast of E.	中国:台湾花莲以东海域	24.37	121.83	33	4.7	mb	6										
2000	9	12	0	28	0					China, Engdahl, Dis	China:Qinghai, Wenquan, N.	中国:青海温泉北	35.426	99.443	10	6.6	Ms	8			5	1	0.65	1	20	1		
2000	10	2	2	25	33					* Engdahl	Tanzania:Lake Tanganyika	坦桑尼亚:坦噶尼喀湖	-8.002	30.769	34	6.5	Mw				6	1		1	7	1	150	3
2000	10	4	14	37	46					Engdahl, USGS	Grenada:St Georges, S.	格林纳达:圣乔治南部	11.114	-62.541	110	6.2	Mw	6										
2000	10	6	4	30	21					* Engdahl	Japan:Okayama, Tottori	日本:冈山,鸟取	35.454	133.107	9	6.7	Mw	9			130	3	150	5	104	3	2230	4
2000	10	6	12	5	36					China, Dis	China: Yunnan, Longchuan, W.	中国:云南陇川西	24.3	97.6	18	5.8	Ms	6			17	1	6.1	3				
2000	10	30	12	1	33					Engdahl, USGS	Indonesia:Sumba Island	印度尼西亚:松巴岛	-9.762	119.014	39.5	6.0	Mw	6										
2000	10	30	22	39	7					* NEIC	Afghan:Taloqan	阿富汗:塔卢坎	37.542	69.582	33	5.2	mb							2			800	3
2000	11	8	7	0	0					* Engdahl	Colombia:Off Coast of W.	哥伦比亚:西部沿海	7.048	-77.802	17	6.5	Mw				2	1		2			86	2
2000	11	16	4	54	56	4	3			* Engdahl, NOAA	Papua New Guinea:East New Britain	巴布亚新几内亚:东新不列颠	-4.001	152.327	16.8	8	Mw		2	1				2				
2000	11	16	7	42	19					* Engdahl	Papua New Guinea:East New Britain, E.	巴布亚新几内亚:东新不列颠东部	-5.243	153.127	32.6	7.8	Mw							1				
2000	11	25	18	9	13					* Engdahl	Azerbaijan:Baki	阿塞拜疆:巴库	40.226	49.974	50	6.8	Mw		28	1	430	3		1				
2000	12	2	15	35	23					USGS	Russia:Dagestan, Derbent	俄罗斯:达吉斯坦共和国杰尔宾特	42.43	47.35	33	4.6	mb	6										
2000	12	6	17	11	8					* Engdahl, USGS	Turkmenistan:Balkanabat	土库曼斯坦:巴尔坎纳巴德	39.552	54.831	30	7.5	Ms	7	11	1		2		1				
2000	12	10	19	30	44					USGS	China:Taiwan, Tainan	中国:台湾台南	23.03	120.3	17	5.3	ML	6										
2000	12	15	16	44	54					* Engdahl	Turkey:Afyon - Bolvadin	土耳其:阿夫永 - 博尔瓦丁	38.456	31.281	41.4	5.8	Ms	7	6	1	41	1		1				2
2000	12	29	18	3	31					USGS	China:Taiwan, Hualien, Coast of E.	中国:台湾花莲以东海域	24.39	121.86	33	4.9	mb	6										
2001	1	7	6	26	58					USGS	Russia:Magadan, Sheltinga	俄罗斯:马加丹州舍利京加村	59.43	147.23	14	5.4	Mw	6										

年 Year	月 Mo	日 Dy	时 Hr	分 Mn	秒 Sec	海啸 源 Sr	海啸 浪高 Wh	海啸 级 I mI	海啸 级 S mS	资料来源 Information	地名(英文) Name(English)	地名(中文) Name(Chinese)	纬度(°) Latitude	经度(°) Longitude	深度 Depth	震级 Mag	标度 Scale	烈度 MMI	死亡人数 数量/人 Deaths Num	死亡人数 级别 Dd	受伤人数 数量/人 Injuries Num	受伤人数 级别 Dd	经济损失 数量/$ Mill Damage $ Mill	经济损失 级别 De	房屋毁坏 数量/间 Houses Destroyed Num	房屋毁坏 级别 Dh	房屋受损 数量/间 Houses Damaged Num	房屋受损 级别 Dh
2001	1	10	16	2	44					NEIC, Engdahl, USGS	Alaska: Kodiak Island	阿拉斯加:科迪亚克岛	56.97	-153.491	25	7	Mw	6										
2001	1	13	17	33	32					* Engdahl	El Salvador: Near Coast	萨尔瓦多:近海	13.038	-88.661	38	7.7	M	8	844	3	4723	4	753	5	108226	5	169632	5
2001	1	26	3	16	42					* India, Engdahl	India: Gujarat, Bhuj	印度:古吉拉特,普杰	23.394	70.234	16	7.7	M	10	20005	5	166836	5	2623	5	339000	5		
2001	2	13	14	22	8					* Engdahl	El Salvador: La Paz	萨尔瓦多:拉巴斯	13.627	-89.021	11	6.6	Mw	6	315	3	3399	4	349	5	41302	5	15706	5
2001	2	14	7	27	28					China, Dis	China: Sichuan, Yajiang	中国:四川雅江	29.4	101.19	8	5.0	Ms	6										
2001	2	23	0	9	0					* China, Dis	China: Sichuan, Yajiang	中国:四川雅江	29.4	101.19	15	6.0	Ms	8	10	1	156	3	22.7	3	60000	5		
2001	2	25	8	28	15					USGS	Honduras: San Andres	洪都拉斯:圣安德烈斯	14.06	-88.62	10	4.6	Md	6										
2001	2	28	18	54	33					* Engdahl	US: Washington, Olympia, Seattle	美国:华盛顿州奥林匹亚,西雅图	47.112	-122.603	54	6.8	M	8	1	1	400	3	2000	5				
2001	3	12	8	57	50					China, Dis	China: Yunnan, Lancang	中国:云南澜沧	22.5	99.8	28	5	Ms	6			6	1	6.7	3				
2001	3	19	5	52	16					NEIC, Engdahl, USGS	Indonesia: Banda Sea	印度尼西亚:班达海	-4.025	128.005	20.9	6.5	Mw	6										
2001	3	24	6	27	54					* Engdahl	Japan: Hiroshima, Okayama	日本:广岛冈山	34.074	132.496	42	6.8	Mw	9	2	1			500	5			3700	4
2001	4	3	14	57	11					USGS	Japan: Kakegawa	日本:静冈挂川	34.9	138.02	33	5.4	Mw	7										
2001	4	10	3	13	7					China, Dis	China: Yunnan, Shidian	中国:云南施甸	24.807	99.009	10	5.2	Ms	6										
2001	4	12	10	47	1					China, Engdahl, USGS, Dis	China: Yunnan, Shidian	中国:云南施甸	24.807	99.009	5	5.9	Ms	8	4		250	3	65.2	4				
2001	4	26	17	48	58					Engdahl, USGS	Japan: Hokkaido	日本:北海道	43.167	145.862	72	6.0	Mw	6										
2001	5	4	6	42	13					USGS	US: Arkansas, Greenbrier	美国:阿肯色州格林布赖尔	35.21	-92.19	10	4.7	MLg	6										
2001	5	8	18	2	17					*	El Salvador: Conchagua	萨尔瓦多:孔查瓜火山附近	13.605	-88.795	10	5.7	Mw		1	1				2	84	2	70	2
2001	5	23	21	10	44					* China, Engdahl, Dis	China: Sichuan, Muli, SW.	中国:四川木里西南	27.6	100.9	5	5.8	Ms	7	1	1	71	2	16.8	3				
2001	6	1	14	0	44					*	Afghan: Parvan	阿富汗:帕尔旺	35.169	69.389	62	5	Mw		4	1	20	1		1		2		
2001	6	7	18	3	28					China, Engdahl, USGS, Dis	China: Yunnan, Shidian	中国:云南施甸	24.807	99.009	12	5.3	Ms	6										
2001	6	14	2	35	26					China, USGS, Engdahl	China: Taiwan, Yilan, Coast of E.	中国:台湾宜兰以东海域	24.557	122.048	42.6	6.4	Ms	7										
2001	6	19	5	43	41					USGS	China: Taiwan, Taitung	中国:台湾台东	23.09	121.22	33	5.1	Mw	6										
2001	6	23	20	33	15	4	7			* Engdahl, NOAA	Peru: Arequipa, Moquegua, Tacna	秘鲁:阿雷基帕,莫克瓜,塔克纳	-16.305	-73.55	29.8	8.4	M	8	103	3	2713	4	200	5	22399	5		
2001	6	25	13	28	47					*	Turkey: Osmaniye	土耳其:奥斯曼尼耶	37.238	36.206	5	5.5	Mw				130	3		1			66	2
2001	6	30	4	7	37					USGS	China: Taiwan, Hualien	中国:台湾花莲	23.99	121.64	33	4.8	mb	6										
2001	7	5	13	53	50					* Engdahl	Peru: Caraveli, Chala	秘鲁:卡拉威里,查拉	-16.051	-73.71	62	6.6	Mw							2	300	3		
2001	7	7	9	38	43					* Engdahl, USGS	Peru: Arequipa, Arica	秘鲁:阿雷基帕,阿里卡	-17.522	-71.938	17.4	7.6	Mw	6	1	1	30	1		2	200	3		
2001	7	9	23	51	32					China, Dis	China: Yunnan, Chuxiong	中国:云南楚雄	24.93	101.4	13	5.3	Ms	6			1	1	2.33	2				

时间 Date						海啸 Tsunami				资料来源 Information	震中 Earthquake Epicenter				深度 Depth	震级 Mag	标度 Scale	烈度 MMI	死亡人数 Deaths		受伤人数 Injuries		经济损失 Damage		房屋毁坏 Houses Destroyed		房屋受损 Houses Damaged	
年 Year	月 Mo	日 Dy	时 Hr	分 Mn	秒 Sec	源 Sr	浪高 Wh	级I mI	级S mS		地名(英文) Name(English)	地名(中文) Name(Chinese)	纬度(°) Latitude	经度(°) Longitude					数量/人 Num	级别 Dd	数量/人 Num	级别 Dd	数量/$ Mill $ Mill	级别 De	数量/间 Num	级别 Dh	数量/间 Num	级别 Dh
2001	7	10	21	41	4					China, Dis	China: Gansu, Sunan	中国:甘肃肃南	39.03	97.9	4	5.3	Ms	6										
2001	7	14	18	36	8					* China, Dis	China: Yunnan, Jiangchuan	中国:云南江川	24.3	102.6	8	5.1	Ms	6			4	1	4.55	2	150	3		
2001	7	24	5	0	8					NEIC, Engdahl, USGS	Chile: Tarapaca	智利:塔拉帕卡	-19.55	-69.232	17.1	6.3	Mw	7										
2001	7	26	0	21	38					* Engdahl	Greece: Skyros	希腊:斯基罗斯	39.064	24.291	6.1	6.5	Mw							1			100	2
2001	8	6	4	53	13					USGS	Russia: Sakhalin Island	俄罗斯:库页岛(萨哈林岛)	47.25	142.74	10	4.9	mb	6										
2001	8	8	3	15	25					USGS	Russia: Sakhalin Island	俄罗斯:库页岛(萨哈林岛)	47.24	142.59	10	4.9	mb	6										
2001	8	9	2	6	60					* Engdahl	Peru: Abancay	秘鲁:阿班凯	-14.351	-72.663	41.4	5.8	Mw		4	1	15	1		2		3		
2001	8	10	20	19	27					USGS	US: California, Portola	美国:加利福尼亚州波托拉	39.82	-120.65	17	5.2	Mw	6										
2001	9	1	13	8	12					USGS, NEIC	Russia: Sakhalin Island	俄罗斯:库页岛(萨哈林岛)	47.33	142.55	10	5.5	Mw	7										
2001	9	4	4	5	56					China, Dis	China: Yunnan, Jinggu	中国:云南景谷	23.63	100.55	8	5	Ms	6			9	1	4.54	2				
2001	9	9	23	59	18					* USGS	US: California, Los Angeles	美国:加利福尼亚州洛杉矶	34.059	-118.387	5	4.2	mb	6						1				
2001	9	17	22	44	42					USGS	China: Taiwan, Kaohsiung	中国:台湾高雄	23.2	120.76	5	5	mb	6										
2001	10	10	1	49	57					USGS	Russia: Lake Baykal	俄罗斯:贝加尔湖	52.49	106.72	10	5.2	Ms	6										
2001	10	12	15	2	19					* Engdahl	Mariana Islands, S.	马里亚纳群岛南部	12.724	145.051	42.8	7.3	Ms	8			1	1		2		3		
2001	10	27	5	35	44					* China, Engdahl, Dis	China: Yunnan, Yongsheng	中国:云南永胜	26.2	100.6	10	6.0	Ms	7	1	1	220	3	49.5	4	3400	4		
2001	11	14	9	26	12					* China, Engdahl, Dis	China: Qinghai, Kunlun Mountain Pass	中国:青海昆仑山口	35.918	90.543	10.8	8.1	Ms	10					5.3	3		2		2
2001	12	2	13	1	55					NEIC, Engdahl, USGS	Japan: Oshu	日本:岩手奥州	39.424	141.047	125	6.5	Mw	6										
2001	12	8	20	29	36					Engdahl, USGS	Ryukyu Islands	琉球群岛	28.284	129.552	36.6	6.2	Mw	6										
2001	12	18	4	3	0	4	0.1			* NEIC, Engdahl, NOAA	China: Taiwan, Hualien, Coast of E.	中国:台湾花莲以东海域	23.984	122.736	16.3	7.3	Ms											
2001	12	19	7	54	8					* USGS	Bangladesh: Dhaka	孟加拉:达卡	23.632	90.376	10	4.5	mb	6			100	2		1				2
2002	1	2	17	22	50	4	0.4	-4.6	-4.1	* Engdahl, NOAA	Vanuatu Islands: Efate	瓦努阿图群岛:埃法特岛	-17.609	167.917	23.2	7.5	Ms					2		1				
2002	1	9	6	45	58					*	Tajikistan: Roghun	塔吉克斯坦:罗格汉	38.673	69.902	33	5.3	Mw		3	1	50	1		2			209	3
2002	1	10	11	14	59					* Engdahl	Papua New Guinea: Aitape	巴布亚新几内亚:爱塔佩	-3.21	142.405	11	6.7	Mw		1	1				2	200	3		
2002	1	14	15	36	26					*	Chile: Tarapaca	智利:塔拉帕卡	-19.384	-69.231	33	5.6	Mw							1				1
2002	1	15	7	13	2					NEIC, Engdahl, USGS	Indonesia: Sumatra, Coast of SW.	印度尼西亚:苏门答腊西南海域	-6.324	105.19	25.2	6.1	Mw	6										
2002	1	17	20	1	29					*	Congo: Goma	刚果:戈马	-1.684	29.077	15	4.7	mb		1001	4	400	3		3	307	3		
2002	1	30	8	42	3					*	Mexico: Veracruz	墨西哥:韦拉克鲁斯	18.194	-95.908	109	5.9	Mw							1				2
2002	2	3	7	11	35					* Engdahl	Turkey: Afyon	土耳其:阿菲永	38.452	31.206	40.1	6.5	Mw		44	1	318	3		2			622	3

时间						海啸				资料来源	震中				深度	震级	标度	烈度	死亡人数		受伤人数		经济损失		房屋毁坏		房屋受损	
年	月	日	时	分	秒	源	浪高	级 I	级 S		地名(英文)	地名(中文)	纬度(°)	经度(°)					数量/人	级别	数量/人	级别	数量/$ Mill	级别	数量/间	级别	数量/间	级别
Date						Tsunami				Information	Earthquake Epicenter				Depth	Mag	Scale	MMI	Deaths		Injuries		Damage		Houses Destroyed		Houses Damaged	
Year	Mo	Dy	Hr	Mn	Sec	Sr	Wh	mI	mS		Name(English)	Name(Chinese)	Latitude	Longitude					Num	Dd	Num	Dd	$ Mill	De	Num	Dh	Num	Dh
2002	2	3	20	59	28					*	Tajikistan: Duachanbe	塔吉克斯坦:杜尚别	38.773	69.924	44	4.9	mb					2		1				2
2002	2	4	20	9	31					USGS	Spain: Málaga	西班牙:马拉加	37.1	-2.61	20	5	Mw	6										
2002	2	12	3	27	26					USGS	China: Taiwan, Hualien	中国:台湾花莲	23.72	121.56	54	5.7	Mw	6										
2002	2	12	13	44	37					USGS	Japan: Ibaraki, Near Coast	日本:茨城近海	36.59	140.95	45	5.6	Mw	6										
2002	2	17	13	3	53					* NEIC	Iran: Bushehr	伊朗:布什尔	28.093	51.755	33	5.6	mb		1	1	30	1		2				3
2002	2	22	19	32	42					*	Mexico: Mexicali	墨西哥:墨西卡利	32.319	-115.322	7	5.5	Ms							1				
2002	2	26	8	32	49					USGS, NEIC	Chile: Putre	智利:普特雷	-18.3	-69.71	91	5.6	Mw	5										
2002	3	3	12	8	22					* Engdahl, USGS	Afghan: Kabul	阿富汗:喀布尔	36.465	70.458	230	7.4	Mw		166	3		2		3	300	3	400	3
2002	3	5	21	16	11	4	3			* Engdahl, NOAA, USGS	Philippines: Mindanao Island	菲律宾:棉兰老岛	6.073	124.226	32.7	7.5	Mw	10	15	1	100	2	1.714	2			800	3
2002	3	11	20	6	37					USGS	United Arab Emirates: Dubai	阿拉伯联合酋长国:迪拜	25.24	56.15	10	5	Mw	7										
2002	3	25	14	56	36					* Engdahl	Afghan: Puli Khumri	阿富汗:普勒胡姆里	36.044	69.32	8	6.2	Ms		1000	3	200	3		4	1500	4		
2002	3	26	3	45	49	3	0.1			* Engdahl, NOAA	Ryukyu Islands, SW.	琉球群岛西南	23.355	124.085	26.3	6.6	Ms											
2002	3	31	6	52	53	4	0.2			* China, Engdahl, NOAA, USGS	China: Taiwan, Hualien, Coast of E.	中国:台湾花莲以东海域	24.315	122.179	41.1	7.5	Ms	9	5	1	200	3		2	100	2		
2002	3	31	17	9	37					USGS	China: Taiwan, Hualien, Coast of E.	中国:台湾花莲以东海域	24.42	122.08	33	4.8	ML	6										
2002	4	1	19	59	34					* Engdahl	Chile: Coquimbo, La Serena	智利:科金博,拉塞雷纳	-29.654	-71.264	71	6.4	Mw							1				
2002	4	3	18	6	11					USGS	China: Taiwan, Hualien, Coast of E.	中国:台湾花莲以东海域	24.29	121.84	33	5.3	Mw	6										
2002	4	4	13	4	49					USGS	China: Taiwan, Yilan	中国:台湾宜兰	24.31	121.77	33	4.9	ML	6										
2002	4	12	4	0	24					*	Kyrgyzstan: Suluktu	吉尔吉斯斯坦:苏柳克塔	39.959	69.417	10	5.9	Ms		50	1	150	3		2	160	3	250	3
2002	4	18	16	8	37					* USGS	Chile: Copiapo, Taltal	智利:科皮亚波,塔尔塔尔	-27.535	-70.586	62	6.6	Mw	7			19	1		2	34	1	575	3
2002	4	20	10	50	48					* USGS	US: New York, Saranac	美国:纽约州萨拉纳克	44.513	-73.699	11	5.2	Mw	7						1				
2002	4	22	15	14	29					USGS	China: Taiwan, Hualien, Coast of E.	中国:台湾花莲以东海域	24.32	122.14	33	4.6	mb	6										
2002	4	24	10	51	51					* USGS	Kosovo: Prishtine, SE.	科索沃:普里什蒂纳东南	42.436	21.466	10	5.7	Mw	7	1	1	60	2		1				
2002	4	24	19	48	7					*	Iran: Kermanshah	伊朗:克尔曼沙赫	34.642	47.4	33	5.4	Mw		2	1	56	2		2		4		
2002	4	25	17	41	22					* CSN, USGS	Georgia: Tbilisi	格鲁吉亚:第比利斯	41.765	44.96	10	4.8	mb	7	5	1	52	2		3			2400	4
2002	4	26	16	6	7					* USGS	Mariana Islands, S.	马里亚纳群岛南部	13.088	144.619	86	7.1	Mw	7			5	1		1				
2002	5	14	5	0	30					USGS	US: California, Gilroy	美国:加利福尼亚州吉尔罗伊	36.97	-121.6	7	4.9	Mw	6										
2002	5	15	3	46	1					China, USGS	China: Taiwan, Yilan, Coast of E.	中国:台湾宜兰以东海域	24.5	122.1		6.5	Ms	6										
2002	5	18	15	15	9					*	Tanzania: Bariadi	坦桑尼亚:巴里亚迪河	-2.907	33.733	10	5.5	Ms		2	1				2	690	3	700	3
2002	5	23	15	52	15					USGS	Chile: Ovalle	智利:奥瓦耶	-30.75	-71.2	52	6	Mw	6										

年 Year	月 Mo	日 Dy	时 Hr	分 Mn	秒 Sec	源 Sr	浪高 Wh	级 I mI	级 S mS	资料来源 Information	地名(英文) Name(English)	地名(中文) Name(Chinese)	纬度(°) Latitude	经度(°) Longitude	深度 Depth	震级 Mag	标度 Scale	烈度 MMI	死亡人数 Deaths 数量/人 Num	死亡人数 级别 Dd	受伤人数 Injuries 数量/人 Num	受伤人数 级别 Dd	经济损失 Damage 数量/$ Mill	经济损失 级别 De	房屋毁坏 Houses Destroyed 数量/间 Num	房屋毁坏 级别 Dh	房屋受损 Houses Damaged 数量/间 Num	房屋受损 级别 Dh
2002	5	24	0	23	16					USGS	Chile:Illapel	智利:伊亚佩尔	-31.97	-70.95	60	5.7	Mw	6										
2002	5	28	4	4	23					*	Argentina:Aminga, Anillaco	阿根廷:阿明加,阿尼亚科	-28.937	-66.797	22	6.0	Mw				27	1		2	40	1		3
2002	6	18	13	56	23					NEIC,USGS	Chile:Ovalle	智利:奥瓦耶	-30.805	-71.124	54	6.6	Mw	7										
2002	6	18	17	37	15					USGS	US:Indiana,Mt Vernon	美国:印第安纳州芒特弗农	37.99	-87.78	5	4.6	Mw	6										
2002	6	20	5	40	43					*	Bangladesh:Syedpur	孟加拉:赛伊德布尔	25.842	88.932	40	4.5	mb				55	2		1				2
2002	6	22	2	58	21					* USGS	Iran:Qazvin,W.	伊朗:加兹温西部	35.626	49.047	10	6.5	Mw	8	261	3	1300	4	300	5		4		
2002	6	23	11	10	42					USGS,NEIC	Chile:Monte Patria	智利:蒙特帕特里亚	-30.84	-71.17	67	5.6	Mw	6										
2002	6	24	1	12	20					USGS	China:Taiwan,Hualien,Coast of E.	中国:台湾花莲以东海域	23.96	121.75	33	4.5	mb	6										
2002	7	22	5	45	3					*	Germany:Wurselen	德国:维尔瑟伦	50.889	6.103	17	4.8	mb							1				
2002	7	28	20	28	31					USGS	Russia:Lake Baykal	俄罗斯:贝加尔湖	52.98	107.77	10	4.7	mb	6										
2002	7	31	0	16	45					* USGS	Panama:Baru,Near Coast	巴拿马:巴鲁近海	7.929	-82.793	10	6.5	Mw	7			11	1		2		2		3
2002	8	8	11	42	1					* China	China:Sichuan,Xinlong	中国:四川新龙	30.9	100		5.3	Ms							1	8	1		
2002	8	10	9	3	18					USGS	China:Taiwan,Hualien	中国:台湾花莲	24.17	121.67	33	5.2	Mw	6										
2002	8	14	13	57	52					*	Mariana Islands	马里亚纳群岛	14.101	146.199	30	6.5	Mw							1				1
2002	8	15	5	30	26					*	Indonesia:Sulawesi	印度尼西亚:苏拉威西岛	-1.196	121.333	10	6.2	Mw		48	1				2			200	3
2002	8	24	20	1	18					*	Egypt:Cairo	埃及:开罗	30.2	31.41	10	4.4	mb							1			44	1
2002	8	26	14	55	14					USGS,NEIC	Indonesia:Sunda Strait	印度尼西亚:巽他海峡	-6.75	105.71	62	5.8	Mw	5										
2002	8	28	17	5	34					USGS	China: Taiwan, Pingtung, Coast of E.	中国:台湾屏东以东海域	22.11	121.58	33	5.6	Mw	6										
2002	9	2	1	0	3					*	Iran:Qazvin,SW.	伊朗:加兹温西南	35.701	48.838	10	5.2	Mw							1				1
2002	9	3	14	23	45					USGS,NEIC	Philippines:Mindoro Island	菲律宾:民都洛岛	13.54	120.75	10	5.8	Mw	5										
2002	9	5	11	3	6					*	Kyrgyzstan:Osh,SW.	吉尔吉斯斯坦:奥什西南	39.77	72.007	32	5.5	Mw							1				
2002	9	6	1	21	29					*	Italy:Sicily,Palermo	意大利:西西里岛,巴勒莫	38.381	13.701	5	6.0	Mw		2	1	20	1	500	5				2
2002	9	6	11	2	1					USGS	China:Taiwan,Nantou	中国:台湾南投	23.72	120.79	33	4.8	mb	6										
2002	9	8	18	44	24	4	5.5	0.58	1.08	* NOAA	Papua New Guinea:Wewak	巴布亚新几内亚:威瓦克	-3.302	142.945	13	7.8	Ms		4	1	70	2		3				
2002	9	13	22	28	29	4				* NOAA	India:Andaman Islands	印度:安达曼群岛	13.036	93.068	21	6.7	Ms		2	1				1	40	1		
2002	9	20	15	43	35					*	Indonesia:Irian Jaya Barat	印度尼西亚:西巴布亚	-1.68	134.234	10	6.4	Mw							1			31	1
2002	9	22	23	53	15					* USGS	England:Birmingham	英国:伯明翰	52.52	-2.15	9	5	ML	6			1	1		1				
2002	9	25	18	14	49					*	Mexico:Acapulco	墨西哥:阿卡普尔科	16.87	-100.113	6	5.3	Mw				2	1		1				2
2002	9	25	22	28	12					*	Iran:Ahwaz	伊朗:阿瓦士	31.995	49.329	10	5.6	Mw				5	1		2				3
2002	9	30	6	44	48					*	France:Talhouet	法国:塔卢埃	47.832	-3.207	10	4.5	ML							1				1
2002	10	10	10	50	21	2	5	2.32	2.82	* NOAA	Indonesia:Irian Jaya Barat	印度尼西亚:西巴布亚	-1.757	134.297	10	7.7	Ms		8	1	632	3		3	1000	3		

时间 Date						海啸 Tsunami				资料来源 Information	震中 Earthquake Epicenter				深度 Depth	震级 Mag	标度 Scale	烈度 MMI	死亡人数 Deaths		受伤人数 Injuries		经济损失 Damage		房屋毁坏 Houses Destroyed		房屋受损 Houses Damaged	
年 Year	月 Mo	日 Dy	时 Hr	分 Mn	秒 Sec	源 Sr	浪高 Wh	级 I mI	级 S mS		地名(英文) Name(English)	地名(中文) Name(Chinese)	纬度(°) Latitude	经度(°) Longitude					数量/人 Num	级别 Dd	数量/人 Num	级别 Dd	数量/$ Mill $ Mill	级别 De	数量/间 Num	级别 Dh	数量/间 Num	级别 Dh
2002	10	16	10	12	21					NEIC,USGS	Russia:Kamchatka Peninsula	俄罗斯:堪察加半岛	51.952	157.323	102.4	6.2	Mw	6										
2002	10	18	6	43	21					USGS	China:Taiwan,Hualien,Coast of E.	中国:台湾花莲以东海域	24.24	122.01	33	4.9	ML	6										
2002	10	23	11	27	19					* USGS	Alaska:Cantwell	阿拉斯加:坎特威尔	63.514	-147.912	4	6.7	Ms	8						2				
2002	10	24	6	8	38					*	Congo:Goma,Bukavu	刚果:哥马,布卡武	-1.884	29.004	11	6.3	Ms		2	1				1		2		
2002	10	29	10	2	22					* USGS	Italy:Sicilia Island	意大利:西西里岛	37.67	15.27	10	4.5	ML	8			9	1		1				2
2002	10	31	10	32	59					* Italy,USGS	Italy:San Guiliano Di Puglia,Campobasso	意大利:圣安诺迪普利亚,坎布巴索	41.694	14.925	10	5.9	Mw	8	29	1	135	3	796	5				4
2002	11	1	22	9	29					*	India:Kashmir,Gilgit	印度:克什米尔,吉尔吉特	35.517	74.654	33	5.4	Mw		11	1	40	1		3			1000	3
2002	11	2	1	26	11					* USGS	Indonesia:Simeulue Island	印度尼西亚:锡默卢岛	2.824	96.085	30	7.6	Ms	6	3	1	65	2		3			994	3
2002	11	3	22	12	41					* USGS,CSN	Alaska:Slana, Mentasta Lake	阿拉斯加:斯拉纳,门湖	63.517	-147.444	5	8.1	Mw	9			1	1	56.0	4				
2002	11	3	22	50	45					USGS	Central Alaska	阿拉斯加中部	63.41	-145.07	5	5.5	ML	5										
2002	11	4	4	35	58					USGS	Japan:Miyazzaki	日本:宫崎	32.39	131.55	33	5.4	mb	6										
2002	11	9	2	18	12					USGS	Sea of Azov	亚速海	45	37.77	10	5.5	Mw	6										
2002	11	20	21	32	31					*	India:Kashmir,Gilgit	印度:克什米尔,吉尔吉特	35.414	74.515	33	6.5	Ms		19	1	40	1		3	100	2	1256	4
2002	11	27	16	43	18					*	Vanuatu Islands: Mere Lava Island	瓦努阿图群岛:火山岛附近	-14.49	167.827	33	5.9	Mw				3	1		2			100	2
2002	12	2	4	58	55					*	Greece:Amalias	希腊:阿马利阿斯	37.747	21.087	10	5.7	Mw				17	1		2	8	1	100	2
2002	12	14	13	27	27					* China,Dis	China:Gansu,Yumen	中国:甘肃玉门	39.8	97.3	22	5.9	Ms	7	2	1	350	3	8.5	3	13380	5		
2002	12	24	17	3	3					*	Iran:Kermanshah	伊朗:克尔曼沙赫	34.594	47.454	33	5.2	Mw				15	1		3	3000	4		
2002	12	25	12	57	10					* China,Dis	China:Xinjiang,Ulugqat	中国:新疆乌恰	39.6	75.4	10	5.7	Ms	6					3.68	2		2		
2002	12	25	19	13	43					*	Afghan:Baghlan,W.	阿富汗:巴格兰西部	35.704	69.868	91	5.5	Mw							1				1
2002	12	30				5	11		3	NOAA,Song	Italy:Stromboli	意大利:斯特龙博利岛	38.789	15.213		6.7	Mk					2		2				2
2003	1	4	11	7						China,Dis	China:Xinjiang,Payzawat	中国:新疆伽师	39.6	77.9	17	5.4	Ms	6					3.77	2	190	3		
2003	1	11	17	45	31					*	Iran:Fars	伊朗:法尔斯	29.59	51.474	33	5.2	Mw					2		3	650	3	1350	4
2003	1	20	8	43	6	4	2			* NOAA	Solomon Islands:Honiara	所罗门群岛:霍尼亚拉	-10.491	160.77	33	7.8	Ms											
2003	1	22	2	6	35	4	0.6		0.5	* NOAA	Mexico:Near Coast of Jalisco	墨西哥:哈利斯科近海	18.77	-104.104	24	7.6	Ms	8	29	1	300	3		3	2005	4	6615	4
2003	1	23	0	8	23					* USGS	Indonesia: Sumbawa Island,Dompu	印度尼西亚:松巴哇岛,栋普	-8.807	118.524	33	5.5	Mw	6			2	1		2			500	3
2003	1	26	19	57	3					*	Italy:Spinello, Santa Sofia	意大利:斯皮纳罗,圣安娜索非亚	43.883	11.96	7	4.7	mb	7						1				1
2003	1	27	5	26	23					*	Turkey:Tunceli	土耳其:通杰利	39.5	39.878	10	6.1	Mw		1	1		2		1				2
2003	2	13	17	34	21					* China,Dis	China:Xinjiang,Shihezi	中国:新疆石河子	43.897	85.923	24	5.4	Ms	6					0.06	1				
2003	2	15	5	47	59					* USGS	Philippines:Cawayan	菲律宾:卡瓦延	12.171	123.921	10	5.8	Mw	6						1				
2003	2	15	11	1	58					* CSN,USGS	Philippines:Samar Island	菲律宾:萨马岛	12.13	124.21	17	6.5	Ms	7						1				2

年 Year	月 Mo	日 Dy	时 Hr	分 Mn	秒 Sec	海啸 Tsunami 源 Sr	浪高 Wh	级 I mI	级 S mS	资料来源 Information	地名(英文) Name(English)	地名(中文) Name(Chinese)	纬度(°) Latitude	经度(°) Longitude	深度 Depth	震级 Mag	标度 Scale	烈度 MMI	死亡人数 Deaths 数量/人 Num	级别 Dd	受伤人数 Injuries 数量/人 Num	级别 Dd	经济损失 Damage 数量/$ Mill	级别 De	房屋毁坏 Houses Destroyed 数量/间 Num	级别 Dh	房屋受损 Houses Damaged 数量/间 Num	级别 Dh
2003	2	22	12	19	11					* USGS	US: California, Landers	美国:加利福尼亚州兰德斯	34. 31	-116. 848	1	5. 2	Mw	6						1				
2003	2	22	20	41	3					*	France: Lorraine	法国:洛林	48. 342	6. 57	10	5. 7	ML							1				
2003	2	24	1	3	41					* China, Dis	China: Xinjiang, Maralbishi, W.	中国:新疆巴楚西	39. 5	77. 2	11	6. 8	Ms	9	268	3	4853	4	169	5	71000	5		
2003	2	25	3	52	41					* China	China: Xinjiang, Maralbishi, W.	中国:新疆巴楚西	39. 483	77. 393	10	5. 5	Ms		5	1				1				
2003	3	2	22	46	47					USGS, NEIC	Japan: Fukushima, Near Coast	日本:福岛近海	37. 68	141. 72	42	5. 8	Mw	5										
2003	3	11	7	27	33					NEIC, USGS	Papua New Guinea: New Ireland	巴布亚新几内亚:新爱尔兰	-4. 694	153. 238	40. 2	6. 8	Mw	7										
2003	3	12	4	47	51					* China, USGS, NEIC	China: Xinjiang, Maralbishi, W.	中国:新疆巴楚西	39. 5	77. 4	10	5. 9	Ms		5	1				1				
2003	3	21	11	38	20					* CSN, USGS	Indonesia: Java, Caracas	印度尼西亚:爪哇,加拉加斯	-6. 983	108. 468	33	4. 8	mb	6						2			800	3
2003	3	22	13	36	16					*	Germany: Albstadt	德国:阿尔布施塔特	48. 21	9	6	4. 7	ML							1				
2003	3	25	2	53	25					*	Indonesia: Flores Islands	印度尼西亚:弗洛勒斯群岛	-8. 294	120. 743	33	6. 5	Mw		4	1	20	1		1				2
2003	3	25	18	51	26					*	Bhutan: Haa	不丹:哈阿宗	27. 264	89. 331	47	5. 5	Mw							1				1
2003	4	3	6	59	33					USGS	China: Taiwan, Kaohsiung	中国:台湾高雄	23	120. 61	28	4. 5	mb	6										
2003	4	10	0	40	15					*	Turkey: Izmir, Seferihisar	土耳其:伊兹密尔,塞费里希萨尔	38. 221	26. 958	10	5. 7	Mw				90	2		2		2		2
2003	4	17	0	48	39					* China, Dis	China: Qinghai, Haixi, NW.	中国:青海海西西北	37. 5	96. 8	14	6. 6	Ms	8					8. 8	3	490	3		1
2003	4	23	22	37						China, Dis	China: Shaanxi, Shiquan	中国:陕西石泉	33. 2	108. 3	12	4. 5	Ms	6			1	1	1. 57	2			152	3
2003	4	29	8	59	39					* CSN, USGS	US: Alabama, Fort Payne	美国:阿拉巴马州佩恩堡	34. 494	-85. 629	20	5	Ms	6						1				
2003	5	1	0	27	5					*	Turkey: Bingol	土耳其:宾格尔	39. 007	40. 464	10	6. 4	Ms		177	3	521	3		3	718	3	2593	4
2003	5	4	15	44	36					* China, Dis	China: Xinjiang, Maralbishi, W.	中国:新疆巴楚西	39. 4	77. 3	10	5. 8	Ms	7	1	1	3	1	9. 3	3	1600	4		
2003	5	21	18	44	20	4	3	1	1. 5	* NOAA	Algeria: Algiers, Cherchell	阿尔及利亚:阿尔及尔,舍尔沙勒	36. 964	3. 634	12	6. 9	Ms	10	2266	4	10261	5	5000	5	43000	5	43000	5
2003	5	26	9	24	33					* USGS	Japan: Iwate, Miyagi	日本:岩手,宫城	38. 849	141. 568	68	7. 0	Mw	8			143	3	233	5			720	3
2003	5	26	19	23	28					*	Indonesia: Maluku Utara, Coast of E.	印度尼西亚:北马鲁古东部海域	2. 354	128. 855	31	7. 1	Ms		1	1	7	1		1	28	1	20	1
2003	5	27	17	11	29	4	0. 1			* NOAA	Algeria: Algiers, Cherchell	阿尔及利亚:阿尔及尔,舍尔沙勒	36. 939	3. 578	8	5. 7	Mw		9	1				1				
2003	6	6	12	29	34					* USGS	US: Kentucky, Bardwell	美国:肯塔基州巴德韦尔	36. 87	-88. 98	3	4	Mw	6						1				
2003	6	9	1	52	51					USGS, NEIC	China: Taiwan, Hualien, Coast of E.	中国:台湾花莲以东海域	24. 41	122. 02	48	5. 8	Mw	5										
2003	6	9	7	6	39					*	Greece: Gonnoi, Larisa	希腊:贡尼,拉里萨	39. 893	22. 309	18	5. 2	Mw							2			50	1

时间						海啸				资料来源	震中				深度	震级	标度	烈度	死亡人数		受伤人数		经济损失		房屋毁坏		房屋受损	
年	月	日	时	分	秒	源	浪高	级 I	级 S		地名(英文)	地名(中文)	纬度(°)	经度(°)					数量/人	级别	数量/人	级别	数量/$ Mill	级别	数量/间	级别	数量/间	级别
Date						Tsunami				Information	Earthquake Epicenter				Depth	Mag	Scale	MMI	Deaths		Injuries		Damage		Houses Destroyed		Houses Damaged	
Year	Mo	Dy	Hr	Mn	Sec	Sr	Wh	mI	mS		Name(English)	Name(Chinese)	Latitude	Longitude					Num	Dd	Num	Dd	$ Mill	De	Num	Dh	Num	Dh
2003	6	10	8	40	31					China, USGS	China: Taiwan, Hualien, Coast of E.	中国:台湾花莲以东海域	23.6	121.6		6	Mw	6										
2003	6	16	18	33	40					USGS	China: Taiwan, Hualien, Coast of E.	中国:台湾花莲以东海域	23.53	121.61	57	5.5	Mw	6										
2003	6	17	14	46						China, Dis	China: Sichuan, Xichang	中国:四川西昌	27.87	102.3		4.8	Ms						0.22	1			34	1
2003	6	19	23	4	60					USGS	Chile: Ovalle	智利:奥瓦耶	−30.69	−71.54	51	5.6	Mw	5										
2003	6	20	13	30	42					* USGS	Chile: Ovalle, Coquimbo	智利:奥瓦耶,科金博	−30.608	−71.637	33	6.8	Ms	6			1	1		1				2
2003	6	26	14	11	45					USGS	Philippines: Aroroy	菲律宾:阿罗罗伊	12.25	123.85	10	6	Mw	6										
2003	7	3	14	59	32					*	Iran: Mashhad	伊朗:马什哈德	35.476	60.784	41	5.2	Mw							1			90	2
2003	7	7	19	55	0					USGS	Philippines: Luzon, Coast N.	菲律宾:吕宋岛北部海域	20.37	122	10	5.6	Mw	5										
2003	7	10	1	54						China, Dis	China: Sichuan, Xichang	中国:四川西昌	27.78	102.46		4.8	Ms				1	1	0.68	1			1100	4
2003	7	10	17	6	38					* NEIC	Iran: Jahrom	伊朗:贾赫罗姆	28.355	54.169	10	5.9	mb		1	1	25	1		3	3500	4		
2003	7	21	13	15	58					USGS	Austria: Murau	奥地利:穆劳	47.16	14.33	10	4.7	ML	6										
2003	7	21	15	16	32					* China, Dis	China: Yunnan, Dayao	中国:云南大姚	26	101.2	10	6.2	Ms	8	16	1	793	3	71.5	4	650	3	6828	4
2003	7	25	15	13	8					* NEIC, USGS	Japan: Miyagi, Iwate	日本:宫城,岩手	38.432	141.003	10	5.6	Mw	8			569	3	411	5			1025	4
2003	7	26	1	0	58					*	Turkey: Denizli	土耳其:登尼资里	38.111	28.887	10	5	ML					2		1			48	1
2003	7	26	1	22	23					USGS	Japan: Miyagi	日本:宫城	38.51	141.05	10	5.1	mb	6										
2003	7	26	7	56	43					USGS	Japan: Miyagi	日本:宫城	38.48	141	10	5.3	Mw	8										
2003	7	26	8	36	49					*	Turkey: Denizli	土耳其:登尼资里	38.019	28.927	10	5.4	Mw				10	1		1	1	1		1
2003	7	26	14	10	16					USGS	Chile: Copiapo	智利:科皮亚波	−28.2	−70.94	36	5.5	Mw	5										
2003	7	26	23	18	18					*	Bangladesh: Rangamati	孟加拉:兰加马蒂	22.854	92.306	10	5.7	Mw		2	1	25	1		2	500	3		
2003	7	27	19	8	4					USGS	Japan: Miyagi	日本:宫城	38.54	141.02	10	5.1	Mw	6										
2003	8	4	4	37	20					*	East Scotia Basin	东斯科舍海盆	−60.532	−43.411	10	7.6	Mw							1				
2003	8	11	0	19	9					*	Indonesia: Maluku Utara	印度尼西亚:北马鲁古	1.142	128.152	10	6.0	Mw							2			200	3
2003	8	11	16	30	12					USGS	China: Taiwan, Yilan	中国:台湾宜兰	24.58	121.6	60	4.8	mb	6										
2003	8	13	8	29	27					*	Panama: Colon	巴拿马:科隆	9.355	−79.941	54	5.4	Mw							1				
2003	8	14	5	14	55					*	Ionian Sea	爱奥尼亚海	39.16	20.605	10	6.3	Mw				50	1		2				2
2003	8	16	10	58	43					* China, Dis	China: Inner Mongolia, Bairin Zuoqi	中国:内蒙巴林左旗	43.9	119.7	24	5.9	Ms	8	4	1	1064	4	97.4	4	7900	4		
2003	8	18	9	3	4					* China, Dis	China: Xizang (Tibet), Medog	中国:西藏墨脱	29.573	95.605	33	5.7	Ms	7	2		14	1	5.2	3				
2003	8	21	2	16						China, Dis	China: Sichuan, Yanyuan	中国:四川盐源	27.4	101.2	10	5	Ms	6			9	1	2.64	2	191	3		
2003	8	21	12	12	50	4	0.2			* NOAA	New Zealand: South Island, Te Anau	新西兰:南岛,蒂阿瑙湖	−45.104	167.144	28	7.5	Ms							1				
2003	8	26	21	11	36					USGS	Peru: Torata	秘鲁:塔克纳	−17.16	−70.67	31	5.7	Mw	6										
2003	8	30	10	6	40					USGS	Japan: Hokkaido	日本:北海道	41.86	142.55	51	5.5	Mw	5										
2003	9	1	23	16	35					USGS, NEIC, Dis	China: Xinjiang, Ulugqat, SW.	中国:新疆乌恰西南	38.6	75.32	10	5.7	Mw	6					1.02	2				
2003	9	14	21	42	52					* USGS	Italy: Loiano	意大利:洛亚诺	44.329	11.45	10	5.3	Mw	7				2		1			10	1

时间						海啸				资料来源	震中				深度	震级	标度	烈度	死亡人数		受伤人数		经济损失		房屋毁坏		房屋受损	
年	月	日	时	分	秒	源	浪高	级I	级S		地名(英文)	地名(中文)	纬度(°)	经度(°)					数量/人	级别	数量/人	级别	数量/$ Mill	级别	数量/间	级别	数量/间	级别
Date						Tsunami				Information	Earthquake Epicenter				Depth	Mag	Scale	MMI	Deaths		Injuries		Damage		Houses Destroyed		Houses Damaged	
Year	Mo	Dy	Hr	Mn	Sec	Sr	Wh	mI	mS		Name(English)	Name(Chinese)	Latitude	Longitude					Num	Dd	Num	Dd	$ Mill	De	Num	Dh	Num	Dh
2003	9	16	11	24	52					USGS, NEIC	Russia: Buryatiya, Chencha	俄罗斯:布里亚特州琴恰	56.06	111.25	10	5.6	Mw	5										
2003	9	17	2	59	56					USGS	Russia: Buryatiya, Khoytogol	俄罗斯:布里亚特州霍伊托戈尔村	51.74	101.43	10	4.6	mb	6										
2003	9	20	3	54	51					*	Japan: Chiba	日本:千叶	34.998	140.172	52	5.7	Mw				7	1		1				2
2003	9	21	18	16	13					*	Myanmar: Magway, E.	缅甸:马圭东部	19.917	95.672	10	6.9	Ms							1				2
2003	9	22	4	45	36					* USGS	Dominica: Puerto Plata, Santiago	多米尼加:普拉塔港,圣地亚哥	19.777	−70.673	10	6.6	Ms	10	3	1	15	1		3		3		
2003	9	25	19	50	6	4	3.9			* NOAA, USGS	Japan: Hokkaido	日本:北海道	41.815	143.91	27	8.3	Ms	8			755	3	90.0	4				
2003	9	25	21	8	0					NEIC, USGS	Japan: Hokkaido	日本:北海道	41.774	143.593	33	7.4	Mw	8										
2003	9	26	6	26	57					USGS, NEIC	Japan: Hokkaido	日本:北海道	42.16	144.67	33	5.9	Mw	5										
2003	9	27	11	33	25					* China, USGS	Russia: Altai Krai, Kosh-Agach	俄罗斯:阿尔泰边疆区科什阿加赤	50.038	87.813	16	7.9	Ms	10	3	1	5	1	10.6	3	300	3		
2003	9	29	15	27	1					*	Russia: Altai Krai, Belyashi	俄罗斯:阿尔泰边疆区别利亚希镇	50	87.89	10	5.1	mb							1				
2003	9	29	18	22	32					*	New Zealand: South Island, Christchurch	新西兰:南岛,基督城	−43.34	173.04	32	4.9	ML							1				
2003	10	1	1	3	25					* China	Russia: Altai Krai, Kosh-Agach	俄罗斯:阿尔泰边疆区科什阿加赤	50.211	87.721	10	7.3	Ms							1				1
2003	10	8	23	15	17					USGS, NEIC	Japan: Hokkaido	日本:北海道	42.21	144.69	33	5.8	Mw	5										
2003	10	13	16	30	49					USGS	Cuba: Guantanamo	古巴:关塔那摩	20.28	−75.65	10	4.6	mb	6										
2003	10	15	7	30	36					*	Japan: Chiba, S.	日本:千叶南部	35.457	139.871	78	5.2	Mw							1				
2003	10	16	3	20	55					*	Dominica: Puerto Plata	多米尼加:普拉塔港	19.761	−70.693	10	4.8	mb							1				1
2003	10	16	12	28	9					* China, Dis	China: Yunnan, Dayao	中国:云南大姚	26	101.3	5	6.1	Ms	8	3	1	57	2	50.2	4	600	3		
2003	10	25	12	41	35					* China, Dis	China: Gansu, Minle	中国:甘肃民乐	38.4	101.2	10	6.1	Ms	8	10	1	46	1	60.6	4	5082	4		
2003	10	25	12	47	59					USGS, NEIC, Dis	China: Gansu, Minle	中国:甘肃民乐	38.38	100.97	10	5.8	Mw	8					4.93	2	30	1		
2003	10	31	1	6	28	4	0.3			* NOAA	Japan Trench	日本海沟	37.812	142.619	10	7.0	Mw											
2003	11	6	13	58	44					USGS	China: Taiwan, Tainan	中国:台湾台南	23.01	120.47	33	4.8	mb	6										
2003	11	13	2	35	9					* China, Dis	China: Gansu, Minxian, NW.	中国:甘肃岷县西北	34.65	103.9	10	5.2	Ms	8	1	1	133	3	10.6	3	642	3		
2003	11	14	18	43	51					USGS, NEIC	Japan: Ibaraki, Near Coast	日本:茨城近海	36.4	141.07	41	5.7	Mw	5										
2003	11	14	18	49	43					* China, USGS, Dis	China: Yunnan, Ludian	中国:云南鲁甸	27.2	103.7	15	5.2	Ms	7	4	1	94	2	23.2	3	269	3		
2003	11	17	6	43	7	4	0.3			* NOAA	Aleutian Islands	阿留申群岛	51.146	178.65	33	7.8	Mw							1				
2003	11	18	17	14	23					*	Philippines: Samar Island	菲律宾:萨马岛	12.025	125.416	35	6.5	Ms	7	1	1	21	1		2	1	1		3
2003	11	25	5	40						China, Dis	China: Shanxi, Hongtong	中国:山西洪洞	36.17	111.63	20	4.9	Ms	6			11	1	0.07	1	3	1		
2003	11	26	13	38	58					* China, Dis	China: Yunnan, Ludian	中国:云南鲁甸	27.3	103.6	33	5	Ms	7			24	1	11.2	3	202	3		
2003	12	1	1	38	34					* China, Dis	China: Xinjiang, Zaosu	中国:新疆昭苏	42.96	80.71		6.1	Ms	8	10		44	1	21.8	3	660	3	10000	5
2003	12	5	23	41	27					* NEIC	Indonesia: Flores Islands, Ruteng	印度尼西亚:弗洛勒斯群岛,鲁滕	−8.137	120.524	33	5.4	mb							1				1
2003	12	6	0	18	55					USGS	Adriatic Sea	亚得里亚海	41.94	19.22	18	4.7	mb	6										

时间 年 Date Year	月 Mo	日 Dy	时 Hr	分 Mn	秒 Sec	海啸 Tsunami 源 Sr	浪高 Wh	级 I mI	级 S mS	资料来源 Information	震中 Earthquake Epicenter 地名(英文) Name(English)	地名(中文) Name(Chinese)	纬度(°) Latitude	经度(°) Longitude	深度 Depth	震级 Mag	标度 Scale	烈度 MMI	死亡人数 Deaths 数量/人 Num	级别 Dd	受伤人数 Injuries 数量/人 Num	级别 Dd	经济损失 Damage 数量/$ Mill $ Mill	级别 De	房屋毁坏 Houses Destroyed 数量/间 Num	级别 Dh	房屋受损 Houses Damaged 数量/间 Num	级别 Dh
2003	12	9	20	59	14					USGS	US:Virginia,Powhatan	美国:弗吉尼亚州保厄坦	37.59	-77.9	5	4.5	mb	6										
2003	12	10	4	38	12					* China,USGS	China:Taiwan,Taitung	中国:台湾台东	23.1	121.4	15	7.0	Ms	8			1	1		1				
2003	12	10	8	46	42					USGS	China:Taiwan,Taitung,Coast of E.	中国:台湾台东以东海域	22.84	121.46	10	4.9	mb	6										
2003	12	11	16	28	17					*	Iran:Ahwaz,NE.	伊朗:阿瓦士东北	31.953	49.209	33	5	mb				5	1		1	2	1		
2003	12	17	23	15	17					* CSN	Bulgaria:Provadia	保加利亚:普罗瓦迪亚	43.083	27.486	34	4.8	Ms							2	10	1	150	3
2003	12	22	19	15	56					* USGS	US:California,San Simeon	美国:加利福尼亚州圣西米恩	35.706	-121.102	8	6.6	Mw	8	2	1	40	1	300	5	40	1		
2003	12	25	7	11	12					*	Costa Rica:Puerto Armuelles	哥斯达黎加:阿摩叶斯港	8.416	-82.824	33	6.5	Mw		2	1	75	2		2				3
2003	12	26	1	56	52					* USGS	Iran:Kerman	伊朗:克尔曼	28.995	58.311	10	6.8	Ms	9	43200	5	30000	5	32.7	4		4		
2003	12	27	4	55	25	4	0.2			* NOAA	Vanuatu Islands	瓦努阿图群岛	-22.107	169.35	10	6.1	Mw											
2004	1	1	3	15	21					USGS	China:Taiwan,Hualien,Coast of E.	中国:台湾花莲以东海域	23.32	121.61	54	5.2	Mw	6										
2004	1	1	20	59	32					*	Indonesia:Bali, Lombok	印度尼西亚:巴厘岛,龙目岛	-8.31	115.788	45	5.8	Mw	6	1	1	29	1		4	6000	4		
2004	1	1	23	31	50					*	Mexico: Guerrero, Mexico City	墨西哥:格雷罗,墨西哥城	17.488	-101.303	29	6.1	Mw							1				
2004	1	10	7	25	44					USGS,NEIC	Chile:Ovalle	智利:奥瓦耶	-30.88	-71.66	55	5.7	Mw	5										
2004	1	10	7	43	18					*	Slovakia:Zvolen	斯洛伐克:兹沃伦	48.758	19.217	5	2.2	ML							1				
2004	1	10	18	38	15					* CSN	Algeria:Algiers, Boumerdes	阿尔及利亚:阿尔及尔,布米尔达斯	36.852	3.418	10	4.9	Ms				300	3		1				
2004	1	14	16	58	48					*	Iran:Bushehr,SE.	伊朗:布什尔东南	27.695	52.397	12	5.4	mb							1				
2004	1	23	5	0	31					USGS	Chile:Antofagasta,C.	智利:安托法加斯塔中部	-23.05	-69.89	71	5.9	Mw	6										
2004	1	27	16	0	38					USGS	Peru:Near Coast of S.	秘鲁:南部近海	-17.84	-71.07	56	5.8	Mw	5										
2004	1	28	22	15	31	4				* NOAA	Indonesia:Ceram Sea	印度尼西亚:塞兰海	-3.12	127.4	17	6.7	Mw											
2004	2	4	11	59	48					*	Costa Rica:Chiriqui	哥斯达黎加:奇里基	8.358	-82.877	29	6.1	Mw				4	1		1				
2004	2	5	21	5	3					*	Indonesia:Nabire	印度尼西亚:纳比雷	-3.615	135.538	17	7.1	Ms		37	1	682	3		4	2678	4		
2004	2	7	2	42	35					*	Indonesia:Nabire	印度尼西亚:纳比雷	-4.003	135.023	10	7.5	Ms							1				
2004	2	7	21	27	38					USGS,NEIC	Indonesia:Irian Jaya Barat	印度尼西亚:西巴布亚	-4.07	133.96	10	5.6	Mw	5										
2004	2	8	8	58	52					NEIC,USGS	Indonesia:Papua	印度尼西亚:巴布亚	-3.665	135.339	25.7	6.9	Mw	6										
2004	2	10	20	33	51					USGS,NEIC	Alaska Peninsula,S.	阿拉斯加半岛南部	59.37	-152.03	65	5.6	Mw	5										
2004	2	11	5	28	26					USGS,NEIC	Indonesia:Papua	印度尼西亚:巴布亚	-3.63	135.56	22	5.7	Mw	5										
2004	2	11	8	15	4	4	1			* NOAA	Israel:Jerusalem	以色列:耶路撒冷	31.675	35.551	27	5.3	Mw				4	1		2				
2004	2	14	10	30	22					* USGS	Pakistan:Balakot,Mansehra	巴基斯坦:巴拉考特,曼塞拉	34.774	73.216	11	5.4	Mw		24	1	40	1		3	1420	4	5379	4
2004	2	15	13	32	6					USGS	China:Taiwan,Nantou	中国:台湾南投	23.7	121.12	32	4.8	mb	6										
2004	2	16	14	44	40					* NEIC	Indonesia:Southern Sumatra	印度尼西亚:苏门答腊南部	-0.466	100.655	56	5.2	mb		5	1	7	1		1			100	2

年 Year	月 Mo	日 Dy	时 Hr	分 Mn	秒 Sec	源 Sr	浪高 Wh	级 I mI	级 S mS	资料来源 Information	地名(英文) Name(English)	地名(中文) Name(Chinese)	纬度(°) Latitude	经度(°) Longitude	深度 Depth	震级 Mag	标度 Scale	烈度 MMI	死亡人数 Deaths 数量/人 Num	级别 Dd	受伤人数 Injuries 数量/人 Num	级别 Dd	经济损失 Damage 数量/$ Mill	级别 De	房屋毁坏 Houses Destroyed 数量/间 Num	级别 Dh	房屋受损 Houses Damaged 数量/间 Num	级别 Dh
2004	2	22	6	46	27					*	Indonesia: Southern Sumatra	印度尼西亚:苏门答腊南部	-1.559	100.488	42	6.3	mB				1	1		1				3
2004	2	24	2	14	34					*	Burundi: Bujumbura	布隆迪:布琼布拉	-3.393	29.558	10	4.7	mb		3	1				1	24	1		
2004	2	24	2	27	46					* USGS	Morocco: Al Hoceima	摩洛哥:胡塞马	35.142	-3.997		6.4	Ms	9	628	3	926	3		4	2539	4		
2004	3	1	0	35	58					* USGS	Greece: Kalamai	希腊:卡拉玛达	37.136	22.116	9	5.6	Mw							1				1
2004	3	7	13	29	47					China, USGS, Dis	China: Xizang (Tibet), Nagqu	中国:西藏那曲	31.7	91.4	33	6.6	Ms				5	1	1.77	2				
2004	3	17	6	16	34					USGS	Philippines: Panay Island	菲律宾:班乃岛	11.15	124.71	73	5.5	Mw	5										
2004	3	17	16	49	46					USGS, NEIC	Argentina: San Luis	阿根廷:圣路易斯	-32.01	-66.7	31	5.5	Mw	5										
2004	3	20	8	53	15					USGS, NEIC	Russia: Kamchatka Peninsula	俄罗斯:堪察加半岛	53.83	160.47	52	5.6	Mw	5										
2004	3	22	4	22	58					USGS, NEIC	Argentina: Salta, N.	阿根廷:萨尔塔北部	-22.94	-64.36	16	5.8	Mw	5										
2004	3	24	1	53	46					* China, Dis	China: Inner Mongolia, West Ujimqin Banner	中国:内蒙东西乌珠穆沁旗	45.4	118.25	15	5.9	Ms	7	1		5	1	24.5	3	38000	5		
2004	3	25	19	30	49					*	Turkey: Erzurum	土耳其:埃尔佐鲁姆	39.93	40.812		5.6	Mw		10	1	46	1		1	45	1		
2004	3	28	3	51	10					*	Turkey: Askale	土耳其:阿什卡莱	39.847	40.874	5	5.6	Mw				12	1		1	50	1		
2004	4	5	21	24	4					*	Afghan: Badakhshan	阿富汗:巴达赫尚	36.512	71.029	187	6.5	Mw		3	1	5	1						
2004	4	9	1	55	51					*	Indonesia: Padang	印度尼西亚:巴东	-1.549	100.54	66	5.5	mb							1				1
2004	4	16	18	32	24					*	Indonesia: Bali Island	印度尼西亚:巴厘岛	-8.669	114.65	96	5.5	Mw							1				1
2004	4	23	1	50	30					*	Indonesia: Timor, Kupang	印度尼西亚:帝汶,古邦	-9.362	122.839	66	6.7	Mw							1				
2004	4	24	15	20	31					USGS	China: Taiwan, Hualien	中国:台湾花莲	23.9	121.64	34	4.8	mb	6										
2004	5	1	7	56	6					* China	China: Taiwan, Hualien	中国:台湾花莲	24.1	121.6	15	5.2	Ms		2	1	1	1		1				
2004	5	3	4	36	50					* USGS	Chile: Canete	智利:卡涅特	-37.695	-73.406	21	6.6	Mw	6						1				
2004	5	4	5	4	59					* China, USGS	China: Qinghai, Haixi, NW.	中国:青海海西西北	37.5	96.75	20	5.5	Ms							3			3100	4
2004	5	8	4	39	25					*	Iran: Fars	伊朗:法尔斯	29.881	51.474	67	5	mb							1	4	1	6	1
2004	5	8	8	2	54					USGS	China: Taiwan, Pingtung, Coast of E.	中国:台湾屏东以东海域	21.95	121.6	26	5.6	Mw	6										
2004	5	8	20	11	44					* CSN	Pakistan: Quetta	巴基斯坦:奎达	30.126	67.121	15	5	Ms		1	1	30	1		1				1
2004	5	10	23	27	25					USGS, Dis	China: Qinghai, Haixi	中国:青海海西	37.49	96.6	10	5.6	Mw						2.49	2	150	3		
2004	5	16	6	4	13					USGS	China: Taiwan, Taitung, Coast of E.	中国:台湾台东以东海域	23.09	121.81	34	5.6	Mw	5										
2004	5	16	11	1	15					USGS, NEIC	Philippines: Mindanao Island	菲律宾:棉兰老岛	7.63	126.17	11	5.8	Mw	5										
2004	5	19	7	4	9					China, USGS	China: Taiwan, Taitung, Coast of E.	中国:台湾台东以东海域	22.75	121.35	15	6.7	Ms	6										
2004	5	19	21	28	11					* CSN	Philippines: Bohol Island	菲律宾:保和岛	9.926	124.038	14	5.1	Ms	6						1				
2004	5	23	15	19	8					USGS	Bosnia and Herzegovina: Mostar	波斯尼亚和黑塞哥维那:莫斯塔尔	43.41	17.45	10	5	Mw	7										

时间						海啸				资料来源	震中				深度	震级	标度	烈度	死亡人数		受伤人数		经济损失		房屋毁坏		房屋受损	
年	月	日	时	分	秒	源	浪高	级 I	级 S		地名(英文)	地名(中文)	纬度(°)	经度(°)					数量/人	级别	数量/人	级别	数量/$ Mill	级别	数量/间	级别	数量/间	级别
Date						Tsunami				Information	Earthquake Epicenter				Depth	Mag	Scale	MMI	Deaths		Injuries		Damage		Houses Destroyed		Houses Damaged	
Year	Mo	Dy	Hr	Mn	Sec	Sr	Wh	mI	mS		Name(English)	Name(Chinese)	Latitude	Longitude					Num	Dd	Num	Dd	$ Mill	De	Num	Dh	Num	Dh
2004	5	28	12	38	44					*	Iran:Mazandaran, Qazvin	伊朗:马赞德兰,加兹温	36.29	51.61	17	6.3	Ms		35	1	400	3		3				3
2004	5	30	2	52	12					* USGS	Russia:Sakhalin Island	俄罗斯:库页岛(萨哈林岛)	47.31	142.12	13	4.9	mb	6						1			46	1
2004	6	6	0	9	9					USGS	China:Taiwan, Taitung, Coast of E.	中国:台湾台东以东海域	22.48	121.32	14	4.6	mb	6										
2004	6	9	11	41	17					*	Saudi Arabia:Tabuk	沙特阿拉伯:泰布克	27.836	36.905	10	4.6	ML							1				
2004	6	14	22	54	21					USGS, NEIC	Mexico:Oaxaca	墨西哥:瓦哈卡	16.34	-97.85	10	5.9	Mw	5										
2004	6	15	11	16	32					* USGS	Chile:Carahue, Temuco	智利:卡拉韦,特木科	-38.854	-73.155	38	6.1	Mw	6						1				
2004	6	16	21	25						China, Dis	China:Sichuan, Yibin	中国:四川宜宾	29.13	104.78	5	4.7	Ms	6	1		9	1	1.85	2	216	3		
2004	6	28	9	49	47					NEIC, USGS	Canada: Queen Charlotte Islands	加拿大:夏洛特皇后群岛	54.8	-134.25	20	6.8	Mw	6										
2004	6	28	14	22	47					USGS	Russia:Chita, Novaya Chara	俄罗斯:赤塔州诺瓦亚恰拉村镇	56.54	118.15	13	4.8	mb	6										
2004	7	1	22	30	9					*	Turkey:Igdir	土耳其:厄德尔	39.766	43.979	5	5.4	mb		18	1	21	1						
2004	7	6	14	37	14					USGS	Russia:Buryatiya, Tonnel'nyy	俄罗斯:布里亚特州通涅利内城	56.35	113.45	10	4.6	mb	6										
2004	7	11	23	8	44					China, Dis	China: Xizang (Tibet), Zhongba	中国:西藏仲巴	30.5	83.4	33	6.7	Ms						1.96	2	10	1	800	3
2004	7	12	13	4	7					*	Slovenia:Bovec, Kobarid	斯洛文尼亚:波维克,科巴里德	46.296	13.641	8	5.7	ML		1	1	5	1		1		1		1
2004	7	14	14	36	3					* CSN	Afghan:Herat	阿富汗:赫拉特	34.89	61.852	6	4.8	Ms							2			150	3
2004	7	17	6	10	18					USGS	Japan:Chiba, Near Coast	日本:千叶近海	34.75	140.22	46	5.6	Mw	5										
2004	7	18	4	22	23					* USGS	New Zealand: North Island, Rotorua, Tauranga	新西兰:北岛,罗托鲁瓦,陶兰加	-38	176.51	5	5.6	Mw		1	1	2	1		2			5	1
2004	7	18	8	31	46					*	Afghan:Paktia Province	阿富汗:帕克蒂亚	33.426	69.524	10	5.2	Mw		2	1	40	1		3		3		
2004	7	30	7	14	8					* CSN	Turkey:Dogubeyazit	土耳其:多乌巴亚泽特	39.634	43.966	5	5.1	Ms		1	1	5	1		1				2
2004	8	4	3	1	8					*	Turkey:Bodrum	土耳其:博德鲁姆	36.833	27.815	10	5.6	Mw				15	1						
2004	8	10	6	13	33					USGS	Japan:Miyako	日本:岩手宫古	39.63	141.96	69	5.7	Mw	6										
2004	8	10	10	26	14					* China, Dis	China:Yunnan, Ludian	中国:云南鲁甸	27.2	103.6	15	5.6	Ms	7	4	1	600	3	40.1	4	1855	4		
2004	8	11	15	48	27					*	Turkey:Elazig	土耳其:埃拉泽	38.377	39.261	7	5.7	Mw		1	1	11	1		1				
2004	8	24	10	5	34					China, USGS, NEIC, Dis	China:Xizang (Tibet), Amdo, NE.	中国:西藏安多东北	32.54	92.19	10	5.8	Ms						0.10	1			25	1
2004	8	27	0	43	55					USGS	Chile:Copiapó	智利:科皮亚波	-27.42	-70.81	30	5.9	Mw	6										
2004	8	28	13	41	26					NEIC, USGS	Chile:Curico, W.	智利:库里科西部	-35.173	-70.525	5	6.3	Mw	6										
2004	8	30	12	23	22					USGS, NEIC	Kuril Islands	千岛群岛	49.54	157.28	11	5.7	Mw	5										
2004	9	5	10	7	8	4	0.6			* NOAA, USGS	Ryukyu Trench	琉球海沟	33.07	136.618	14	7.2	Mw	6			4	1		1				
2004	9	5	14	57	16	4	0.9			* CSN, NOAA, USGS	Ryukyu Trench	琉球海沟	33.15	137.16	15	7.4	Mw	6			40	1		1				
2004	9	7	11	53	6					* USGS	Argentina:Catamarca	阿根廷:卡塔马卡	-28.573	-65.84	22	6.4	Mw	6	1	1		2		1		2		

时间 年 Year	月 Mo	日 Dy	时 Hr	分 Mn	秒 Sec	海啸 源 Sr	浪高 Wh	级 I mI	级 S mS	资料来源 Information	震中 地名(英文) Name(English)	地名(中文) Name(Chinese)	纬度(°) Latitude	经度(°) Longitude	深度 Depth	震级 Mag	标度 Scale	烈度 MMI	死亡人数 Deaths 数量/人 Num	级别 Dd	受伤人数 Injuries 数量/人 Num	级别 Dd	经济损失 Damage 数量/$ Mill	级别 De	房屋毁坏 Houses Destroyed 数量/间 Num	级别 Dh	房屋受损 Houses Damaged 数量/间 Num	级别 Dh
2004	9	7	12	15	51					* China, Dis	China: Gansu, Minxian, N.	中国:甘肃岷县北部	34. 73	103. 93	19	5	Ms	7	1		36	1	8. 0	3	600	3		
2004	9	16	18	31	21					China, Dis	China: Guangdong, Yangjiang	中国:广东阳江	21. 88	111. 59	12	4. 9	Ms	6					2. 79	2			100	2
2004	9	21	13	32	31					* CSN, USGS	Russia: Kaliningrad, Baltiysk	俄罗斯:加里宁格勒州波罗的斯克	54. 841	19. 912	10	5	Ms	6			3	1		1				
2004	9	27	22	58	25					USGS	Chile: Near Coast of C.	智利:中部近海	-32. 69	-71. 74	32	5. 5	Mw	5										
2004	9	28	17	15	24					* USGS	US: California, Parkfield	美国:加利福尼亚州帕克菲尔德	35. 819	-120. 364	9	6. 0	Mw	6						1				
2004	10	1	8	1	1					*	Nicaragua: Managua	尼加拉瓜:马纳瓜	11. 989	-86. 52	87	5. 6	Mw							1				
2004	10	6	14	40	40					USGS	Japan: Noda	日本:千叶野田	35. 95	139. 92	64	5. 8	Mw	6										
2004	10	7	21	46	20					*	Iran: Gorgan	伊朗:戈尔甘	37. 125	54. 477	35	5. 6	Mw				60	2						
2004	10	8	0	47	56					USGS	Macedonia: Bitola Municipality	马其顿:比托拉市	41. 24	21. 31	13	4. 6	Mw	6										
2004	10	15	4	8	48					* China, USGS	China: Taiwan, Hualien, Coast of E.	中国:台湾花莲以东海域	24. 4	122. 9	96	6. 3	Ms	6				2		1				
2004	10	18	22	11	41					* China, Dis	China: Yunnan, Baoshan	中国:云南保山	25. 1	99	10	5	Ms	6			16	1	26. 2	4	84	2		
2004	10	23	8	56	1					*	Japan: Niigata	日本:新潟	37. 226	138. 779	16	6. 6	Mw		40	1	3183	4		4	6000	4		
2004	10	24	5	21	35					USGS	Japan: Niigata	日本:新潟	37. 27	138. 63	10	4. 8	Mw	7										
2004	10	24	15	28	9					USGS	Japan: Niigata	日本:新潟	37. 19	138. 68	13	5. 2	Mw	6										
2004	10	24	21	4	57					NEIC, USGS	Japan: Niigata	日本:新潟	37. 308	138. 701	11	6. 0	Mw	7										
2004	10	27	1	40	50					* USGS	Japan: Niigata	日本:新潟	37. 284	138. 885	14	6	Mw	8			5	1		1	1	1		
2004	10	27	20	34	37					*	Romania: Vrancea	罗马尼亚:弗朗恰	45. 787	26. 622	96	5. 8	mb							1				
2004	11	2	10	2	13	4	0. 1			* NOAA	Canada: Off Coast of W. Vancouver	加拿大:温哥华西部海域	49. 277	-128. 772	10	6. 6	Mw											
2004	11	3	23	57	28					USGS	Japan: Niigata	日本:新潟	37. 43	138. 75	10	5. 3	Mw	7										
2004	11	4	6	22	39					*	Mediterranean Sea	地中海	35. 945	23. 115	74	5. 4	mb							1				
2004	11	4	14	3	12					USGS, NEIC	Kuril Islands	千岛群岛	43. 62	146. 81	61	5. 9	Mw	5										
2004	11	8	2	15	59					* NEIC, USGS	Japan: Niigata	日本:新潟	37. 396	138. 862	10	5. 6	mb	7			8	1		1				
2004	11	9	18	43	8					USGS	Japan: Niigata	日本:新潟	37. 37	138. 82	10	5. 1	Mw	6										
2004	11	11	2	16	45					USGS, NEIC	China: Taiwan, Hualien, Coast of E.	中国:台湾花莲以东海域	24. 41	122. 23	49	5. 7	Mw	5										
2004	11	11	21	26	41	4				* NOAA, USGS	Indonesia: Timor; Pantar	印度尼西亚:帝汶;班达岛	-8. 152	124. 868	10	7. 5	Mw	8	34	1	400	3		3	781	3		
2004	11	15	9	6	57					*	Colombia: Bajo Baudo, Buenaventura	哥伦比亚:巴霍包,布埃纳文图拉	4. 695	-77. 508	15	7. 2	Mw				10	1		3	154	3		
2004	11	19	23	49	37					*	Iran: Ahwaz	伊朗:阿瓦士	32. 023	48. 836	37	4. 8	mb							1				
2004	11	20	8	7	22					* USGS	Costa Rica: San Jose, Parrita	哥斯达黎加:圣何塞,帕利塔	9. 602	-84. 172	16	6. 4	Mw	7	8	1		2		3	526	3		
2004	11	21	11	41	8	4	0. 7			* NOAA	Guadeloupe: Basse Terre	瓜德罗普岛:巴士特尔	15. 679	-61. 706	14	6. 3	Mw		1	1	12	1		2		3		
2004	11	22	4	1	30					*	Iran: Lorestan	伊朗:洛雷斯坦	33. 297	47. 977	36	5	Mw					2		1		1		

时间 年 Year	月 Mo	日 Dy	时 Hr	分 Mn	秒 Sec	海啸 Tsunami 源 Sr	浪高 Wh	级 I mI	级 S mS	资料来源 Information	震中 Earthquake Epicenter 地名(英文) Name(English)	地名(中文) Name(Chinese)	纬度(°) Latitude	经度(°) Longitude	深度 Depth	震级 Mag	标度 Scale	烈度 MMI	死亡人数 Deaths 数量/人 Num	级别 Dd	受伤人数 Injuries 数量/人 Num	级别 Dd	经济损失 Damage 数量/$ Mill $ Mill	级别 De	房屋毁坏 Houses Destroyed 数量/间 Num	级别 Dh	房屋受损 Houses Damaged 数量/间 Num	级别 Dh
2004	11	22	20	26	24					*	New Zealand: Auckland Islands, N.	新西兰:奥克兰群岛以北	-46.676	164.721	10	7.1	Ms							1				
2004	11	24	22	59	40					* NEIC	Italy: Brescia	意大利:布雷西亚	45.626	10.559	17	5.5	ML				9	1		2		3		
2004	11	26	2	25	3					*	Indonesia: Nabire	印度尼西亚:纳比雷	-3.609	135.404	10	7.2	Ms	8	32	1	130	3	55.0	4	328	3		
2004	11	26	22	42	37					USGS	Japan: Hokkaido	日本:北海道	42.38	142.9	58	5.7	Mw	5										
2004	11	28	18	32	14	4	0.1			* NOAA	Japan: Hokkaido, Bekkai, Kushiro	日本:北海道,别海,钏路	43.006	145.119	39	7.0	Mw				24	1		1				
2004	12	1	17	42	25					* CSN	Algeria: Boumerdas	阿尔及利亚:布米尔达斯	36.848	3.448	10	4.7	Ms				15	1		1				
2004	12	2	3	45	33					USGS, NEIC	Indonesia: Papua	印度尼西亚:巴布亚	-3.35	135.45	10	5.7	Mw	5										
2004	12	2	19	16	35					*	Trinidad & Tobago: Port of Spain	特立尼达和多巴哥:西班牙港	10.49	-61.48	49	5.8	Mw							1				
2004	12	5	1	52	37					*	Germany: Emmendingen, Freiburg Im Breisgau	德国:埃门丁根,弗莱堡	48.115	8.077	10	5.5	ML	5						1				
2004	12	5	8	30	60					*	Algeria: Boumerdes	阿尔及利亚:布迈德斯	36.865	3.421	10	4.7	ML				46	1						
2004	12	6	14	15	12					* USGS	Japan: Hokkaido	日本:北海道	42.9	145.228	35	6.8	Mw	7			4	1						
2004	12	8	6	3	56					USGS, NEIC	Chile: Ovalle	智利:奥瓦耶	-30.84	-71.22	44	5.8	Mw	5										
2004	12	9	8	49	0					* NEIC	India: Cachar	印度:察查	24.757	92.539	35	5.5	mb					2		1				
2004	12	14	5	56	10					* USGS	Japan: Hokkaido, Obiro, Haboro	日本:北海道,羽幌,苫前	44.119	141.793	10	5.8	mb	7			3	1		1				
2004	12	14	23	20	13					NEIC, USGS	Cayman Islands: George Town	开曼群岛[英属]:乔治市	18.958	-81.409	10	6.8	Mw	6										
2004	12	20	23	2	12					*	Turkey: Marmaris	土耳其:马尔马里斯	37.042	28.206	5	5.4	Mw				3	1		1				
2004	12	23	14	59	4	4	0.3			* NOAA	Australia: Macquarie Island, N.	澳大利亚:麦加利岛北部	-49.312	161.345	10	8.1	Mw											
2004	12	26	0	58	53	4	51			* USGS, NOAA	Indonesia: Simeulue Island	印度尼西亚:锡默卢岛	3.295	95.982	30	9.1	Mw	10	227898	5		3	10000	5		3		
2004	12	26	7	30						China, Dis	China: Yunnan, Shuangbo	中国:云南双柏	24.7	101.5	7	5	Ms	6	1		20	1	4.92	2	38	1		
2004	12	28	9	30	40					USGS	Japan: Niigata	日本:新潟	37.24	138.79	35	4.8	Mw	6										
2005	1	2	0	24	39					USGS	Russia: Chita, Kodar	俄罗斯:赤塔州科达尔村	56.63	117.8	13	5.1	Mw	6										
2005	1	4	22	5						China, Dis	China: Sichuan, Barkam	中国:四川马尔康	32.3	101.6		4.7	Ms	6					0.81	1				
2005	1	10	18	47	30					*	Iran: Gorgan	伊朗:戈尔甘	37.103	54.574	32	5.4	Mw				110	3						
2005	1	18	14	9	6					NEIC, USGS	Japan: Hokkaido	日本:北海道	42.946	144.866	42	6.3	Mw	7										
2005	1	19	6	11	36	4	0.4			* NOAA	Japan Trench	日本海沟	34.064	141.491	28	6.6	Mw											
2005	1	20	18	56	31					*	New Zealand: North Island, Western Lake	新西兰:北岛,西莱克	-41.223	175.21	39	5.5	ML							1				
2005	1	23	20	10	12					*	Indonesia: Sulawesi	印度尼西亚:苏拉威西岛	-1.198	119.933	11	6.3	Mw		1	1	4	1		2				
2005	1	23	22	36	6					USGS	Mediterranean Sea	地中海	35.8	29.64	10	5.8	Mw	5										
2005	1	24	23	23	26					*	Ecuador: Manta	厄瓜多尔:曼塔	-1.364	-80.785	17	6.1	Mw							2		2		

时间						海啸				资料来源	震中				深度	震级	标度	烈度	死亡人数		受伤人数		经济损失		房屋毁坏		房屋受损	
年	月	日	时	分	秒	源	浪高	级 I	级 S		地名(英文)	地名(中文)	纬度(°)	经度(°)					数量/人	级别	数量/人	级别	数量/$ Mill	级别	数量/间	级别	数量/间	级别
Date						Tsunami				Information	Earthquake Epicenter				Depth	Mag	Scale	MMI	Deaths		Injuries		Damage		Houses Destroyed		Houses Damaged	
Year	Mo	Dy	Hr	Mn	Sec	Sr	Wh	mI	mS		Name(English)	Name(Chinese)	Latitude	Longitude					Num	Dd	Num	Dd	$ Mill	De	Num	Dh	Num	Dh
2005	1	25	16	30	40					* China, Dis	China: Yunnan, Pu - er	中国:云南普洱	22.9	100.8	15	5	Ms	6			5	1	6.5	3	133	3		
2005	1	25	16	44	16					*	Turkey: Hakkari	土耳其:哈卡里	37.622	43.703	41	5.9	Mw		2	1	22	1		1				
2005	1	29	7	41	31					* USGS	Spain: Lorca	西班牙:洛尔卡	37.91	-1.82	5	4.8	ML	7						2				
2005	2	2	5	55	18					* CSN	Indonesia: Java, Garut	印度尼西亚:爪哇,加鲁特	-7.037	107.819	15	5.2	Ms		1	1		2		2		2		
2005	2	5	3	34	26					NEIC, USGS	Mariana Islands	马里亚纳群岛	16.011	145.867	142.7	6.3	Mw	6										
2005	2	5	11	0	56					USGS	China: Taiwan, Hualien, Coast of E.	中国:台湾花莲以东海域	24.28	121.79	35	4.7	mb	6										
2005	2	14	18	5	59	3				* NOAA	Guadeloupe: Terre - de - Haut	瓜德罗普岛:泰尔德欧	15.775	-61.744	12	5.8	Mw											
2005	2	14	23	38	10					* China, Dis	China: Xinjiang, Uqturpan	中国:新疆乌什	41.6	79.2	33	6.2	Ms	7					19.5	3	6000	4		
2005	2	15	11	15	12					*	India: Assam: Cachar, Silchar	印度:阿萨姆邦:察查,锡尔杰尔	24.55	92.524	35	5.1	mb							1				
2005	2	15	19	46	36					USGS	Japan: Saitama	日本:埼玉	35.98	139.69	46	5.5	Mw	6										
2005	2	18	20	18	18					USGS, NEIC	China: Taiwan, Taitung, Coast of E.	中国:台湾台东以东海域	23.21	121.56	16	5.6	Mw	6										
2005	2	22	2	25	23					*	Iran: Kerman	伊朗:克尔曼	30.754	56.816	14	6.5	Ms		612	3	1411	4		4	8000	4		
2005	2	26	12	37	41					USGS, NEIC	Japan: Aomori, Near East Coast	日本:青森东部近海	40.73	142.38	68	5.7	Mw	5										
2005	3	2	11	12	15					*	Pakistan: Quetta	巴基斯坦:奎达	30.378	68.038	52	4.9	mb				1	1		1				
2005	3	5	19	7	53					China, USGS	China: Taiwan, Yilan	中国:台湾宜兰	24.9	121.85	15	6.3	Ms	6										
2005	3	7	7	17	23					USGS	Nicaragua: San Juan del Sur	尼加拉瓜:南圣胡安	11.37	-85.94	85	5.6	Mw	5										
2005	3	9	10	15	32					* NEIC	South Africa: Klerksdorp, Stilfontein	南非:克莱克斯多普,斯特芳登	-26.913	26.789	5	5	mb		2	1	58	2		2				
2005	3	11	18	47	37					USGS	Japan: Hokkaido	日本:北海道	43.08	144.67	54	5.5	Mw	5										
2005	3	12	7	36	12					*	Turkey: Bingol	土耳其:宾格尔	39.44	40.978	11	5.7	ML				16	1		2				
2005	3	13	3	2	26					USGS	Azerbaijan: Gence	阿塞拜疆:占贾	40.34	45.84	10	4.6	mb	6										
2005	3	13	3	31	23					*	Iran: Sistan And Baluchestan	伊朗:锡斯坦-俾路支斯坦	27.095	61.887	54	6.0	Mw							1				
2005	3	14	1	55	56					*	Turkey: Bingol	土耳其:宾格尔	39.354	40.89	5	5.9	ML				18	1		3		2		
2005	3	14	9	43	49					*	India: Maharashtra, Kolhapur	印度:马哈拉施特拉邦,科拉浦	17.145	73.73	10	5.1	ML				45	1		2				
2005	3	15	2	7	7					*	India: Maharashtra	印度:马哈拉施特拉邦	17.072	73.668	10	4.3	mb							1				
2005	3	20	1	53	42					* USGS	Japan: Kyushu; Fukuoka, Genkai	日本:九州;福冈,幻海	33.807	130.131	10	6.7	Ms	8	1	1	500	3		2	65	2		
2005	3	28	16	9	37	4	3			* NOAA, USGS	Indonesia: Off West Coast of N. Sumatera	印度尼西亚:北苏门答腊西部海域	2.085	97.108	30	8.7	Mw	8	1314	4	340	3		4	300	3		
2005	4	7	20	4	44					China, Dis	China: Xizang (Tibet), Zhongba	中国:西藏仲巴	30.5	83.7	33	6.5	Ms	6					1.28	2				
2005	4	10	10	29	11	4	0.4			* NOAA, CSN	Indonesia: Padang	印度尼西亚:巴东	-1.644	99.607	19	6.7	Ms	5										
2005	4	10	22	22	16					NEIC, USGS	Japan: Oamishirasato	日本:千叶大网白里	35.604	140.401	43	6.1	Mw	7										

年 Year	月 Mo	日 Dy	时 Hr	分 Mn	秒 Sec	海啸 Tsunami 源 Sr	浪高 Wh	级 I mI	级 S mS	资料来源 Information	震中 Earthquake Epicenter 地名(英文) Name(English)	地名(中文) Name(Chinese)	纬度(°) Latitude	经度(°) Longitude	深度 Depth	震级 Mag	标度 Scale	烈度 MMI	死亡人数 Deaths 数量/人 Num	级别 Dd	受伤人数 Injuries 数量/人 Num	级别 Dd	经济损失 Damage 数量/$ Mill $ Mill	级别 De	房屋毁坏 Houses Destroyed 数量/间 Num	级别 Dh	房屋受损 Houses Damaged 数量/间 Num	级别 Dh
2005	4	19	21	11	28					USGS	Japan:Fukuoka	日本:福冈	33.64	130.18	18	5.5	Mw	7										
2005	4	30	14	48	16					USGS	China:Taiwan,Hualien	中国:台湾花莲	23.96	121.64	7	5.3	Mw	6										
2005	5	3	19	11	40					USGS,NEIC	Peru:Puquio	秘鲁:普基奥	-14.92	-74.62	31	5.9	Mw	5										
2005	6	1	20	6						China,Dis	China:Xizang (Tibet),Medog	中国:西藏墨脱	29.1	94.8		5.9	Ms	6					5.2	3	68	2		
2005	6	10	9	44	36					USGS	China:Taiwan,Hualien,Coast of E.	中国:台湾花莲以东海域	23.97	121.71	9	4.7	mb	6										
2005	6	12	4	17	13					USGS,NEIC	Russia:Sakhalin Island	俄罗斯:库页岛(萨哈林岛)	52.79	143.87	10	5.6	Mw	5										
2005	6	12	15	41	47					USGS	US:California,Anza	美国:加利福尼亚州安萨	33.53	-116.57	14	5.2	Mw	6										
2005	6	13	3	58	1					USGS	Jamaica:Jacks Hill	牙买加:杰克斯山	18.32	-77.44	2	5.2	Mw	7										
2005	6	13	22	44	34					* USGS	Chile:Tarapaca	智利:达拉巴卡	-19.987	-69.197	116	7.8	Mw	7	11	1	200	3			544	3		
2005	6	15	2	50	53	4	0.1			* NOAA	US:California,Off Coast N.	美国:加利福尼亚州北部沿海	41.301	-125.97	10	7.2	Ms											
2005	6	16	20	53	26					USGS	US:California,San Bernardino	美国:加利福尼亚州圣贝纳迪诺	34.06	-117.01	11	4.9	Mw	6										
2005	6	18	9	31	6					USGS	China:Taiwan,Hualien	中国:台湾花莲	23.96	121.66	5	4.8	mb	6										
2005	6	19	16	15	15					USGS	Japan:Sanmu	日本:千叶山武	35.61	140.48	48	5.7	Mw	5										
2005	6	21	5	11	18					USGS	Chile:Iquique	智利:伊基克	-19.99	-68.81	105	5.5	Mw	5										
2005	6	30	21	26	36					USGS,NEIC	Costa Rica:Puerto Armuelles	哥斯达黎加:阿摩叶斯港	8.45	-82.87	37	5.9	Mw	5										
2005	7	5	1	52	3					*	Indonesia:Off West Coast of N. Sumatera	印度尼西亚:北苏门答腊西部海域	1.819	97.082	21	6.8	Ms							1				
2005	7	9	23	59	17					*	Indonesia:Sulawesi	印度尼西亚:苏拉威西岛	-1.174	119.963	32	5.9	Mw							1	6	1		
2005	7	10	13	10	12					* NEIC	Albania:Tropoje	阿尔巴尼亚:特罗波耶	42.389	19.812	4	5.5	ML							1		1		
2005	7	18	2	4	60					* NEIC	Indonesia:Timor	印度尼西亚:帝汶	-9.948	124.48	10	5.7	mb							1		1		
2005	7	23	7	34	57					*	Japan:Tokyo	日本:东京	35.498	139.982	61	6.1	mB				27	1		1	1	1		
2005	7	24	15	42	6					*	India:Nicobar Islands	印度:尼科巴群岛	7.92	92.19	16	7.5	Ms							1		1		
2005	7	25	15	43	33					* China,Dis	China:Heilongjiang,Lindian	中国:黑龙江林甸	46.9	125	15	5.1	Ms	6	1	1	11	1	3.39	2	312	3		
2005	7	26	4	8	37					* USGS	Mongolia:Hongor	蒙古:洪戈尔	45.365	112.615	13	5.7	mb	6						1				
2005	7	30	21	45						*	Turkey:Ankara	土耳其:安卡拉	39.437	33.089	5	5.3	Mw							1				
2005	8	5	14	14	43					* China,Dis	China:Yunnan,Huize	中国:云南会泽	26.6	103.1	20	5.3	Ms	6			44	1	21.0	3	565	3		
2005	8	5	18	7	14					* CSN	Vietnam:Ho Chi Minh City	越南:胡志明	9.985	108.383	10	5.3	Ms							1				
2005	8	9	5	9	21					*	Iran:Firuzabad	伊朗:菲鲁扎巴德	28.85	52.56	10	5.1	mb							1				
2005	8	13	3	58	44					* China,Dis	China:Yunnan,Wenshan,NW.	中国:云南文山西北	23.5	104.1	15	5.3	Ms	6			29	1	11.4	3	113	3		
2005	8	14	2	39	40					*	Chile:Tarapaca	智利:达拉巴卡	-19.78	-68.98	11	5.8	Mw							1				

年	月	日	时	分	秒	源	浪高	级 I	级 S	资料来源	地名(英文)	地名(中文)	纬度(°)	经度(°)	深度	震级	标度	烈度	死亡人数 数量/人	死亡人数 级别	受伤人数 数量/人	受伤人数 级别	经济损失 数量/$ Mill	经济损失 级别	房屋毁坏 数量/间	房屋毁坏 级别	房屋受损 数量/间	房屋受损 级别
Date						Tsunami				Information	Earthquake Epicenter				Depth	Mag	Scale	MMI	Deaths		Injuries		Damage		Houses Destroyed		Houses Damaged	
Year	Mo	Dy	Hr	Mn	Sec	Sr	Wh	mI	mS		Name(English)	Name(Chinese)	Latitude	Longitude					Num	Dd	Num	Dd	$ Mill	De	Num	Dh	Num	Dh
2005	8	14	6	33	33					* USGS	India:Maharashtra	印度:马哈拉施特拉邦	17.398	74.118	35	4.4	mb	7						2				
2005	8	16	2	46	28	4	0.1			* NOAA, USGS	Japan:Miyagi, Near Coast	日本:宫城近海	38.276	142.039	36	7.2	Mw	8			56	2		1	1	1		
2005	8	16	3	45	54					* CSN, USGS	India:Uttaranchal:Uttarkahi	印度:乌塔兰契尔邦,乌塔卡西	30.924	78.56	43	4.7	Ms	6						1		1		
2005	8	21	2	29	30					USGS	Japan:Joetsu	日本:新潟上越	37.28	138.59	13	4.8	Mw	6										
2005	8	23	19	14	7					USGS	Argentina:Mendoza	阿根廷:门多萨	-32.81	-68.77	10	4.8	Mw	6										
2005	8	25	21	8	13					NEIC, Dis	China:Xinjiang, Keriya, W.	中国:新疆和田西	36.944	79.169	17.9	5.5	Mw	6					0.80	1	57	2		
2005	8	30	8	53	17					* CSN, USGS	India:Maharashtra	印度:马哈拉施特拉邦	17.067	73.773	10	5	Ms	6						1				
2005	9	2	1	27	20					USGS	US:California, Westmorland	美国:加利福尼亚州威斯特莫兰	33.16	-115.64	9	5.1	Mw	6										
2005	9	9	11	26	7					USGS, NEIC	Argentina:San Juan	阿根廷:圣胡安	-31.68	-69.14	112	5.8	mb	5										
2005	9	23	13	48	30					USGS	Honduras:Near Coast of N.	洪都拉斯:北部近海	16.13	-87.47	23	5.9	Mw	6										
2005	9	24	19	24	3					*	Ethiopia:Dessie, NE.	埃塞俄比亚:德西东北	12.471	40.634	12	5.6	Mw							2				
2005	9	26	1	55	38					* USGS	Peru:Lamas, Chachapoyas	秘鲁:拉马斯,查查波亚斯	-5.678	-76.398	115	7.5	Mw	6	5	1	60	2		2		3		
2005	10	1	22	19	51					*	Peru:Moquegua	秘鲁:莫克瓜	-16.635	-70.794	20	5.4	ML				10	1		1	300	3		
2005	10	5	8	46	42					USGS	Indonesia:Sumatera, Aceh	印度尼西亚:苏门答腊亚齐	5.23	95.58	18	5.7	Mw	6										
2005	10	7	17	43	2					USGS	Guatemala:Near Coast	危地马拉:近海	13.3	-89.35	49	5.7	Mw	5										
2005	10	8	3	50	41					* USGS	Pakistan:Muzaffarabad	巴基斯坦:穆扎法拉巴德	34.539	73.588	26	7.7	Ms	8	86000	5	69000	5		4		3		3
2005	10	8	4	30	44					USGS, NEIC, CSN	Indonesia:Off West Coast of N. Sumatera	印度尼西亚:北苏门答腊西部海域	1.96	97.85	30	6.6	Ms	5										
2005	10	13	1	49	20					USGS	China:Taiwan, Hualien, Coast of E.	中国:台湾花莲以东海域	24.39	121.92	8	4.5	ML	6										
2005	10	15	15	51	8					NEIC, USGS	Ryukyu Islands	琉球群岛	25.309	123.351	192	6.2	Mw	7										
2005	10	17	5	45	16					USGS	Turkey:Cesme	土耳其:切什梅	38.13	26.5	8	5.5	Mw	5										
2005	10	17	9	46	54					USGS, NEIC	Turkey:Cesme	土耳其:切什梅	38.2	26.5	10	5.8	Mw	5										
2005	10	19	11	44	43					NEIC, USGS	Japan:Ibaraki, Near Coast	日本:茨城近海	36.405	140.839	32	6.5	Mw	6										
2005	10	20	21	40	4					* USGS	Turkey:Izmir	土耳其:伊兹密尔	38.152	26.751	10	5.9	Mw	6	1	1	15	1		1		2		
2005	10	22	13	12	48					USGS, NEIC	Japan:Fukushima	日本:福岛	37.15	140.93	53	5.5	Mw	5										
2005	10	24	17	35	34					* USGS	Ecuador:Baeza	厄瓜多尔:巴埃萨	-0.507	-77.745	35	4.8	mb	6						1				
2005	10	27	11	18	57					* China, Dis	China:Guangxi, Pingguo	中国:广西平果	23.604	107.798	10	4.4	Ms	6	1	1	3	1	3.13	2	10	1		
2005	10	31	2	10	29					*	Peru:Choros	秘鲁:乔罗斯	-5.852	-78.704	40	5.4	Mw								20	1		
2005	11	14	21	38	51	4	0.4			* NOAA	Japan Trench	日本海沟	38.107	144.896	11	7.0	Mw											
2005	11	17	19	26	54					NEIC, USGS	Chile:Calama	智利:卡拉马	-22.361	-67.895	147	6.8	Mw	6										
2005	11	26	0	49	36					* China, Dis	China:Jiangxi, Jiujiang	中国:江西九江	29.9	115.8	10	5.7	Ms	7	13	1	775	3	252	5	42793	5		
2005	11	26	15	56	55					* NEIC	Turkey:Malatya	土耳其:马拉蒂亚	38.26	38.814	9	5.3	mb							1				
2005	11	27	10	22	19					*	Iran:Qeshm	伊朗:格什姆	26.774	55.858	10	6.1	mB		13	1	100	2		2				

时间						海啸				资料来源	震中				深度	震级	标度	烈度	死亡人数		受伤人数		经济损失		房屋毁坏		房屋受损	
年	月	日	时	分	秒	源	浪高	级I	级S		地名(英文)	地名(中文)	纬度(°)	经度(°)					数量/人	级别	数量/人	级别	数量/$ Mill	级别	数量/间	级别	数量/间	级别
Date						Tsunami				Information	Earthquake Epicenter				Depth	Mag	Scale	MMI	Deaths		Injuries		Damage		Houses Destroyed		Houses Damaged	
Year	Mo	Dy	Hr	Mn	Sec	Sr	Wh	mI	mS		Name(English)	Name(Chinese)	Latitude	Longitude					Num	Dd	Num	Dd	$ Mill	De	Num	Dh	Num	Dh
2005	11	28	16	33	22					USGS,NEIC	Chile:Coquimbo	智利:科金博	-29.31	-70.96	48	5.5	Mw	5										
2005	12	5	12	19	57					*	Congo:Kalemie	刚果:卡莱米	-6.224	29.83	22	7.2	Ms		6	1				1	300	3		
2005	12	12	21	47	46					*	Afghan: Jalalabad, Badakhshan	阿富汗:贾拉拉巴德,巴达赫尚	36.357	71.093	225	6.5	Mw		5	1	1	1		1	100	2		
2005	12	14	7	9	54					*	India:Chamoli	印度:查莫利	30.476	79.255	44	5.3	mb		1	1	4	1		2	1	1		
2005	12	22	19	9	0					USGS	Guadeloupe:Terre-de-Haut	瓜德罗普岛:泰尔德欧	15.83	-61.71	10	4.5	mb	7										
2005	12	24	3	56	7					*	Turkey:Akhisar	土耳其:阿克希萨尔	38.139	26.761	14	4.6	ML							1				
2006	1	8	11	34	56					* USGS	Greece:Morea,Cerigo	希腊:摩里亚,察里哥	36.311	23.212	66	6.7	Mw	6			3	1		1		1		
2006	1	12	1	5	29					China,Dis	China:Yunnan,Mojiang	中国:云南墨江	23.35	101.6		5	Ms	6			1	1	13.7	3				
2006	2	14	0	55	25					* NEIC	India:Sikkim	印度:锡金邦	27.382	88.388	30	5.4	mb		2	1	2	1		1				
2006	2	20	6	56	10					USGS,NEIC	Honduras:Masaya	洪都拉斯:马萨亚	13.16	-87.56	10	5.5	Mw	5										
2006	2	20	17	20	9					* CSN	Bulgaria:Kardzali	保加利亚:克尔贾利	41.708	25.544	10	4.9	Ms				2	1				1		
2006	2	22	22	19	8					*	Mozambique:Vilankulos,NW.	莫桑比克:维兰库卢什西北	-21.324	33.583	11	7.5	Ms		4	1	36	1		2	294	3		
2006	2	23	20	4	54					*	India:Assam	印度:阿萨姆邦	26.912	91.705	10	5.8	Mw							1	126	3		
2006	2	28	7	31	3					*	Iran:Hormozgan	伊朗:荷姆兹甘	28.12	56.865	18	6.2	Ms				6	1		2		3		
2006	3	1	11	4	12					USGS,NEIC	Philippines:Mindoro Island	菲律宾:民都洛岛	13.46	120.51	22	5.8	Mw	5										
2006	3	7	18	20	46					*	India:Gujarat	印度:古吉拉特	23.777	70.899	10	5.5	Mw				7	1		1		1		
2006	3	9	4	7	29					USGS	China:Taiwan,Nantou	中国:台湾南投	23.52	120.64	18	4.7	mb	6										
2006	3	10	7	50	14					* CSN	Pakistan:Mirpur	巴基斯坦:米尔布尔	33.129	73.887	10	5.1	Ms		1	1	22	1						
2006	3	14	6	57	34	4	3.5			* NOAA, USGS	Indonesia:Ceram Sea	印度尼西亚:塞兰海	-3.595	127.214	30	6.7	Ms	6	4	1			1	2	241	3		
2006	3	20	19	44	25					* NEIC	Algeria:Bejaia	阿尔及利亚:贝贾亚	36.623	5.328	10	5	mb		4	1	9	1			62	2		
2006	3	25	7	28	58					*	Iran:Hormozgan	伊朗:荷姆兹甘	27.574	55.685	18	5.9	Mw		1	1	1	1		1				
2006	3	26	19	20	38					China,Dis	China:Gansu,Tanchang	中国:甘肃宕昌	33.91	104.38		4.8	Ms	6			1	1	0.56	1				
2006	3	27	2	50	26					USGS	Japan:Miyazzaki,Near Coast	日本:宫崎近海	32.6	132.16	34	5.5	Mw	6										
2006	3	27	23	43	39					USGS	Philippines:Panay Island	菲律宾:班乃岛	12.08	121.4	32	5.6	Mw	5										
2006	3	28	8	35	43					*	Indonesia:Sumatera,Aceh	印度尼西亚:苏门答腊亚齐	3.462	97.224	30	5	mb							1				
2006	3	31	1	17	1					* USGS	Iran:Lorestan	伊朗:洛雷斯坦	33.5	48.78	7	6.1	Mw	8	70	2	1300	4		3		3		
2006	3	31	12	23	18					* China,Dis	China:Jilin,Qian-an,S.	中国:吉林乾安南	44.7	124	10	5	Ms	6			2	1	13.7	3		2		
2006	4	1	10	2	16					* China,USGS	China:Taiwan,Taitung	中国:台湾台东	22.9	121.1	15	6.5	Ms	6			42	1		1		2		
2006	4	4	9	12	23					* CSN	Pakistan:Mingora	巴基斯坦:明戈拉	34.6	73.136	10	4.9	Ms				28	1		1		2		2
2006	4	6	17	59	16					*	India:Gujarat	印度:古吉拉特	23.322	70.477	10	5.5	Mw							1				
2006	4	11	0	2	42					*	Greece:Zakynthos	希腊:扎金索斯岛	37.64	20.92	18	5.5	Mw							1				
2006	4	15	22	40	54					USGS	China:Taiwan,Taitung,Coast of E.	中国:台湾台东以东海域	22.8	121.36	18	5.9	Mw	7										
2006	4	19	2	5	43					* China,Dis	China:Xizang (Tibet),Baingoin	中国:西藏班戈	31.5	90.3		5.6	Ms	6					0.64	1		2		

时间 Date 年 Year	月 Mo	日 Dy	时 Hr	分 Mn	秒 Sec	海啸 Tsunami 源 Sr	浪高 Wh	级 I mI	级 S mS	资料来源 Information	震中 Earthquake Epicenter 地名(英文) Name(English)	地名(中文) Name(Chinese)	纬度(°) Latitude	经度(°) Longitude	深度 Depth	震级 Mag	标度 Scale	烈度 MMI	死亡人数 Deaths 数量/人 Num	级别 Dd	受伤人数 Injuries 数量/人 Num	级别 Dd	经济损失 Damage 数量/$ Mill $ Mill	级别 De	房屋毁坏 Houses Destroyed 数量/间 Num	级别 Dh	房屋受损 Houses Damaged 数量/间 Num	级别 Dh
2006	4	20	17	50	40					USGS	Japan:Ito	日本:静冈伊东	34. 86	139. 21	22	5. 6	Mw	5										
2006	4	20	23	25	2					*	Russia:Koryakskiy,N.	俄罗斯:科里亚克区北部	60. 949	167. 089	22	7. 6	Ms				40	1	55. 0	4		3		
2006	4	28	9	5	26					USGS	China:Taiwan,Hualien	中国:台湾花莲	23. 96	121. 57	8	5. 2	Mw	6										
2006	4	30	21	40	58					NEIC,USGS	Chile:Caldera,Near Coast	智利:卡尔德拉近海	-27. 211	-71. 056	12	6. 7	Mw	6										
2006	4	30	23	4	41					USGS,NEIC	Chile:Caldera,Near Coast	智利:卡尔德拉近海	-27. 23	-71. 2	37	5. 8	Mw	5										
2006	5	2	9	24	31					USGS	Japan:Oshima	日本:东京大岛	34. 77	139. 26	26	4. 9	Mw	6										
2006	5	3	15	26	40	4	0. 3			* NOAA, USGS	Tonga Islands	汤加群岛	-20. 187	-174. 123	55	8	Mw	7			1	1		1				
2006	5	4	17	43	10					*	Panama:Boquete	巴拿马:波奎提	8. 898	-82. 543		4. 5	ML							1				
2006	5	7	6	20	54					* NEIC	Iran:Kerman,N.	伊朗:克尔曼北部	30. 79	56. 7	14	4. 8	mb				70	2		1		1		
2006	5	12	8	16	57					*	Indonesia:Southern Sumatra	印度尼西亚:苏门答腊南部	-5. 575	105. 395	17	5. 5	Mw							1		2		
2006	5	16	15	28	26					NEIC,USGS	Indonesia:Northern Sumatera	印度尼西亚:苏门答腊北部	0. 093	97. 05	12	6. 8	Mw	6										
2006	5	22	11	12	1					NEIC,USGS	Russia:Koryakskiy,N.	俄罗斯:科里亚克区北部	60. 772	165. 743	19	6. 7	Mw	7										
2006	5	24	10	11	8					USGS	Indonesia:Papua, Near North Coast	印度尼西亚:巴布亚北部近海	-2. 25	139. 15	30	5. 7	Mw	6										
2006	5	26	22	53	59					* USGS	Indonesia:Java,Bantul	印度尼西亚:爪哇,班图尔	-7. 961	110. 446	13	6. 3	Mw	9	5749	4	38568	5	3100	5	127000	5		
2006	6	3	7	15	36					* NEIC	Iran:Qeshm Island	伊朗:格什姆岛	26. 759	55. 843	12. 1	5. 4	Mw		2	1	4	1		1		2		
2006	6	3	11	7	45					*	Turkey:Hakkari	土耳其:哈卡里	37. 605	43. 787	10	4. 1	mb							1				
2006	6	3	16	34	26					*	Malawi:Salima	马拉维:萨利马	-14. 52	34. 28	10	3. 8	mb							1				
2006	6	11	20	1	26					* USGS	Japan:Kumamoto	日本:熊本	33. 129	131. 141	140	6. 3	Mw	6			8	1						
2006	6	13	14	15	38					* CSN	Albania:Tepelene	阿尔巴尼亚:德培雷恩	40. 27	19. 96	28	4. 9	Ms				1	1		1	12	1		
2006	6	17	2	4	47					USGS	China:Taiwan,Tainan	中国:台湾台南	23. 01	120. 19	10	4. 6	ML	6										
2006	6	20	16	52	58					* China,Dis	China:Gansu,Wenxian	中国:甘肃文县	33. 068	104. 95	24	5	Ms	6	1	1	19	1	9. 1	3		1		
2006	7	4	3	56	24					China,Dis	China:Hebei,Wenan	中国:河北文安	38. 9	116. 25		5. 1	Ms	6					1. 21	2				
2006	7	17	8	19	25	4	10			* NOAA	Indonesia:Java Ridge	印度尼西亚:爪哇海岭	-9. 254	107. 411	34	7. 7	Mw		664	3	6534	4		4	1623	4		
2006	7	19	9	53	8					China,Dis, USGS	China:Qinghai,Yushu	中国:青海玉树	33	96. 3		5. 6	Ms	6					5. 3	3				
2006	7	22	1	10	29					* China,Dis	China:Yunnan,Yanjin	中国:云南盐津	27. 995	104. 138		5. 1	Ms	6	22	1	114	3	29. 6	4				
2006	7	29	0	11	51					*	Afghan:Qonduz,N.	阿富汗:昆都士北部	37. 255	68. 828	34	5. 6	Mw		3	1	19	1			721	3		
2006	7	30	1	28	15					USGS	Indonesia:Sumatera, Nias Island	印度尼西亚:苏门答腊,尼亚斯岛	1. 46	97. 18	30	5. 6	Mw	6										
2006	8	5	14	3	44					* NEIC	Argentina:Mendoza	阿根廷:门多萨	-33. 131	-68. 707	22	5. 8	Mw	5						1				
2006	8	17	15	20	35					NEIC,USGS	Russia:Sakhalin Island	俄罗斯:库页岛(萨哈林岛)	46. 542	141. 908	14	6. 0	Mw	7										
2006	8	18	11	45	49					* CSN	Tadzhikistan:Khatlon	塔吉克斯坦:哈特隆州	38. 246	69. 22	10	4. 9	Ms							1				
2006	8	24	20	1	0					*	France:Angoulême	法国:昂古莱姆	45. 84	-0. 14	5	4. 3	ML							1				

年 Year	月 Mo	日 Dy	时 Hr	分 Mn	秒 Sec	源 Sr	浪高 Wh	级I mI	级S mS	资料来源 Information	地名(英文) Name(English)	地名(中文) Name(Chinese)	纬度(°) Latitude	经度(°) Longitude	深度 Depth	震级 Mag	标度 Scale	烈度 MMI	死亡人数 Deaths 数量/人 Num	死亡人数 Deaths 级别 Dd	受伤人数 Injuries 数量/人 Num	受伤人数 Injuries 级别 Dd	经济损失 Damage 数量/$ Mill	经济损失 Damage 级别 De	房屋毁坏 Houses Destroyed 数量/间 Num	房屋毁坏 Houses Destroyed 级别 Dh	房屋受损 Houses Damaged 数量/间 Num	房屋受损 Houses Damaged 级别 Dh
2006	8	24	21	50	37					NEIC, USGS	Russia: Kamchatka Peninsula	俄罗斯:堪察加半岛	51.148	157.522	43	6.5	Mw	6										
2006	8	25	5	51	43					* China, Dis	China: Yunnan, Yanjin	中国:云南盐津	28	104.2	22	5.1	Ms	6	2	1	67	2	25.1	4				
2006	9	1	10	25	17					USGS, NEIC	Aleutian Islands	阿留申群岛	53.26	159.7	51	5.7	mb	5										
2006	9	1	12	4	22					USGS, NEIC	Alaska: Unimak Island	阿拉斯加:乌尼马克岛	53.97	-166.39	75	5.9	Mw	5										
2006	9	15	20	54	36					USGS	China: Taiwan, Hualien	中国:台湾花莲	24.02	121.65	10	4.6	ML	6										
2006	9	16	9	45	24					NEIC, USGS	Indonesia: Ceram Sea	印度尼西亚:塞兰海	-3.08	129.441	17	6.3	Mw	7										
2006	9	28	6	22	10	4	0.1			* NOAA	Samoa Islands	萨摩亚群岛	-16.592	-172.033	28	6.9	Ms											
2006	9	29	13	8	26					* USGS	Trinidad & Tobago: Port of Spain	特立尼达和多巴哥:西班牙港	10.876	-61.756	53	6.1	Mw	6			3	1		1	1	1		
2006	9	29	18	23	6					* USGS	Trinidad & Tobago: Port of Spain	特立尼达和多巴哥:西班牙港	10.814	-61.758	52	5.5	Mw	6	1	1								
2006	10	15	17	7	49	4	0.1			* NOAA, USGS	Hawaiian Islands	夏威夷群岛	19.878	-155.935	39	6.7	Mw	8				3	73.0	4				
2006	10	16	1	33	36					USGS	Chile: Coquimbo	智利:科金博	-30.24	-71.32	37	5.5	Mw	5										
2006	10	17	4	2	37					USGS, NEIC	Bolivia: Potosi	玻利维亚:波托西	-21.04	-68.28	140	5.9	Mw	5										
2006	10	20	10	48	56					*	Peru: Chincha Alta, Near Coast	秘鲁:上钦查近海	-13.457	-76.677	23	6.7	Mw							1				
2006	10	20	14	31	0					USGS, NEIC	Philippines: Mindoro Island	菲律宾:民都洛岛	13.43	121.47	22	5.8	Mw	5										
2006	10	26	14	28	37					USGS, NEIC	Italy: Sicilia Island	意大利:西西里岛	38.65	15.39	212	5.8	Mw	5										
2006	10	27	10	52	6					* China	China: Hubei, Suizhou	中国:湖北随州	31.56	113.21	10	4.5	Ms							2				
2006	11	2	22	21	39					* China	China: Inner Mongolia, Chifeng, N.	中国:内蒙古赤峰北	43.469	119.558	10	4.7	Ms							3	5586	4		
2006	11	15	11	14	14	4	0.9			* NOAA	Kuril Islands	千岛群岛	46.592	153.266	10	8.3	Mw				1	1		1				
2006	11	17	18	19	52					*	France: Pyrenees	法国:比利牛斯山脉	42.99	-0.05	10	5.4	ML							1				
2006	11	20	14	38	28					USGS, NEIC	Peru: Central Tacna	秘鲁:塔克纳中部	-17.67	-70.23	38	5.6	Mw	5										
2006	11	22	11	15	10					USGS, NEIC	Kuril Islands	千岛群岛	44.15	146.78	79	5.6	Mw	5										
2006	11	23	7	15	21					* CSN	Hungary: Nyíregyháza	匈牙利:尼赖吉哈佐	48.195	22.46	10	5.1	Ms							1				
2006	11	23	11	4	42					* China, Dis	China: Xinjiang, Usu, SW.	中国:新疆乌苏西南	44.2	83.5	20	5.1	Ms						0.16	1	60	2		
2006	11	24	6	33	26					*	Indonesia: Sulawesi, Pinrang	印度尼西亚:苏拉威西岛,平朗	-3.728	119.233	31	5.2	mb							1				
2006	11	27	17	31	48					USGS	Peru: Arequipa	秘鲁:阿雷基帕	-16.05	-71.8	115	5.7	Mw	5										
2006	11	29	1	32	18					*	Indonesia: Maluku Utara	印度尼西亚:北马鲁古	2.52	128.283	39	6.2	Mw							2	50	1		
2006	12	1	14	1	48					*	Indonesia: Sumbawa	印度尼西亚:松巴哇	-8.251	118.777	43	6.3	Mw		1	1	14	1		1	20	1		
2006	12	8	16	48	39					*	Switzerland: Basel	瑞士:巴塞尔	47.58	7.6	5	3.9	ML							1				
2006	12	12	17	2	30					* CSN	Thailand: Mae Rim	泰国:湄林	18.901	98.916	10	5.1	Ms							1	5	1		
2006	12	17	13	42	12					USGS	China: Taiwan, Hualien, Coast of E.	中国:台湾花莲以东海域	23.94	121.76	18	4.5	mb	6										
2006	12	17	21	39	17					* USGS	Indonesia: Northern Sumatra	印度尼西亚:苏门答腊北部	0.626	99.859	30	5.8	Mw	6	7	1	100	2		3	680	3		

年	月	日	时	分	秒	海啸 源	浪高	级 I	级 S	资料来源	震中 地名(英文)	地名(中文)	纬度(°)	经度(°)	深度	震级	标度	烈度	死亡人数 数量/人	级别	受伤人数 数量/人	级别	经济损失 数量/$ Mill	级别	房屋毁坏 数量/间	级别	房屋受损 数量/间	级别
Date						Tsunami				Information	Earthquake Epicenter				Depth	Mag	Scale	MMI	Deaths		Injuries		Damage		Houses Destroyed		Houses Damaged	
Year	Mo	Dy	Hr	Mn	Sec	Sr	Wh	mI	mS		Name(English)	Name(Chinese)	Latitude	Longitude					Num	Dd	Num	Dd	$ Mill	De	Num	Dh	Num	Dh
2006	12	20	17	6	58					USGS	El Salvador:Santa Ana	萨尔瓦多:圣安娜	14.24	-89.5	10	5	Mw	7										
2006	12	24	22	43	27					*	India:Jaipur	印度:斋浦尔	26.88	76.15	10	4.2	mb							1				
2006	12	25	20	1	0					*	Kyrgyzstan:Kochkor	吉尔吉斯斯坦:科奇科尔	42.156	76.163	12	5.8	Ms							3	2410	4		
2006	12	26	12	26	18	4	0.1			* China, NOAA, USGS	China: Taiwan, Pingtung, Coast of W.	中国:台湾屏东西部海域	21.9	120.6	10	7.2	Ms	7	2	1	40	1		1		2		
2006	12	26	12	34	11					China, USGS	China: Taiwan, Pingtung, Coast of W.	中国:台湾屏东西部海域	21.9	120.6		6.7	Ms	7										
2006	12	27	2	30	37					USGS, NEIC	China: Taiwan, Pingtung, Coast of W.	中国:台湾屏东西部海域	22	120.48	10	5.6	Mw	5										
2006	12	31	13	39	24					*	Hungary:Budapest	匈牙利:布达佩斯	47.449	19.343	5	4.1	ML							1		1		
2007	1	8	17	21	50					*	Kyrgyzstan:Batken, W.	吉尔吉斯斯坦:巴特肯西部	39.803	70.311	18	6.0	Ms							2	187	3		
2007	1	9	6	49	49					* China	China:Gansu, Jingtai, W.	中国:甘肃景泰西	37.021	103.911	20	4.5	Ms							3	2000	4		
2007	1	9	15	49	33					USGS, NEIC	Gulf of Alaska	阿拉斯加湾	59.42	-137.12	10	5.7	Mw	5										
2007	1	10	9	18	58					* China	China:Gansu, Wudu	中国:甘肃武都	33.259	104.74	23	4.7	Ms							1		2		
2007	1	13	4	23	21	4	0.3			* NEIC, NOAA, USGS	Kuril Islands	千岛群岛	46.243	154.524	10	8.2	Ms	6										
2007	1	19	1	43	14					USGS	El Salvador:Near Coast	萨尔瓦多:近海	12.99	-89.13	55	5.4	Mw	6										
2007	1	21	7	38	57					*	Turkey:Kagizman	土耳其:卡厄兹曼	39.592	42.863	3	5.1	mb				2	1		1				
2007	1	21	11	27	45					* USGS	Molukka Sea	马鲁古海	1.065	126.282	22	7.5	Mw	6	4	1	4	1		1				
2007	1	22	4	27	8					USGS	Indonesia:Papua	印度尼西亚:巴布亚	-2.55	136.34	35	5.7	Mw	5										
2007	1	22	4	33	19					USGS, NEIC	Indonesia:Papua	印度尼西亚:巴布亚	-2.5	136.33	35	5.9	Mw	5										
2007	2	14	14	21	48					USGS	Chile:Iquique, N.	智利:伊基克北部	-19.59	-69.82	53	5.6	Mw	5										
2007	2	16	7	15	54					*	Philippines:Davao Gulf	菲律宾:达沃湾	6.614	126.24	79	4.9	mb							1				
2007	2	21	11	5	29					*	Turkey:Elazig	土耳其:埃拉泽	38.318	39.267	10	5.9	ML							1		1		1
2007	2	23	19	55	49					USGS	Chile:Aisen Region	智利:艾森区	-45.34	-72.32	25	5.7	Mw	6										
2007	3	3	20	8	29					USGS, NEIC	Molukka Sea	马鲁古海	0.01	126.81	38	5.9	Mw	5										
2007	3	6	3	49	39					* USGS	Indonesia:Southern Sumatra	印度尼西亚:苏门答腊南部	-0.493	100.498	19	6.4	Ms	8	67	2	826	3		3	43719	5		
2007	3	6	5	49	23					CSN, USGS	Indonesia:Southern Sumatra	印度尼西亚:苏门答腊南部	-0.99	100.16	35	6.8	Ms	6										
2007	3	6	13	5	12					*	Colombia:Cauca	哥伦比亚:考卡	2.082	-76.495	43	5	Ms				9	1		1	9	1		
2007	3	6	22	32	7					* CSN	Iran:Lorestan	伊朗:洛雷斯坦	33.49	48.93	16	5.2	Ms				35	1		1				
2007	3	13	2	22						China, Dis	China:Fujian, Shunchang	中国:福建顺昌	26.7	117.7		4.7	Ms	6					1.30	2				
2007	3	24	19	13	51					USGS, NEIC	Chile:Huara	智利:瓦拉	-19.72	-70.14	30	5.7	Mw	5										
2007	3	25	0	40	2	4	0.1			* NOAA	Vanuatu Islands	瓦努阿图群岛	-20.617	169.357	34	7.1	Mw											
2007	3	25	0	41	58	4	0.1			* NOAA, USGS	Japan Sea	日本海	37.336	136.588	8	6.7	Mw	9	1	1	150	3		3	513	3	455	3
2007	3	25	9	11	45					USGS	Japan Sea	日本海	37.26	136.69	14	5.2	Mw	6										

时间 年 Year	月 Mo	日 Dy	时 Hr	分 Mn	秒 Sec	海啸 源 Sr	浪高 Wh	级 I mI	级 S mS	资料来源 Information	震中 地名(英文) Name(English)	地名(中文) Name(Chinese)	纬度(°) Latitude	经度(°) Longitude	深度 Depth	震级 Mag	标度 Scale	烈度 MMI	死亡人数 数量/人 Num	死亡 级别 Dd	受伤人数 数量/人 Num	受伤 级别 Dd	经济损失 数量/$ Mill	经济损失 级别 De	房屋毁坏 数量/间 Num	房屋毁坏 级别 Dh	房屋受损 数量/间 Num	房屋受损 级别 Dh
2007	3	25	13	57	58					* USGS	Greece: Argostolion, Kefallinia	希腊:亚各斯托良,凯法利尼亚	38.34	20.42	15	5.8	Mw	6						1		1		
2007	3	27	23	8	14					USGS	Japan: Nanao	日本:石川七尾	37.09	136.81	10	4.6	Mw	6										
2007	4	1	20	39	56	4	10			* NOAA	Solomon Islands	所罗门群岛	-8.466	157.043	24	8.1	Mw		54	2				3	2500	4	500	3
2007	4	13	5	42	23					*	Mexico: Guerrero, Atoyac	墨西哥:格雷罗,阿托雅克	17.302	-100.198	34	6.0	Mw	5						1	2	1		
2007	4	15	3	19	30					* NEIC, USGS	Japan: Iga	日本:三重伊贺	34.807	136.239	16	5.4	mb	7			12	1		2	63	2		
2007	4	16	7	38	54					*	Albania: Tirana	阿尔巴尼亚:地拉那	41.172	19.897	14	5.2	ML							1		1		
2007	4	18	15	7	32					USGS	Japan: Hokkaido	日本:北海道	42.66	141.86	119	5.5	Mw	5										
2007	4	21	17	53	46	4	6			* NOAA, USGS	Chile: Aisen Region	智利:艾森区	-45.243	-72.648	37	6.3	ML	7	3	1				1				
2007	4	25	11	52	56					USGS	Philippines: Mindanao Island	菲律宾:棉兰老岛	7.4	126.44	27	5.7	Mw	6										
2007	4	28	7	18	11					* USGS	England: Folkestone	英国:福克斯通	51.085	1.009	10	5	ML	6			1	1		1				
2007	5	8	15	46	49					* CSN	US: Montana, Sheridan	美国:蒙大纳州谢立丹	45.394	-112.13	11	5.2	Ms	5						1				
2007	5	16	8	56	16					* China	Laos: Ban Kha, S.	老挝:班卡南部	20.6	101	24	6.6	Ms							1				
2007	5	18	15	59	59					USGS, NEIC	Japan: Hokkaido	日本:北海道	41.6	141.99	58	5.5	Mw	5										
2007	5	24	1	6	26					USGS, NEIC	Indonesia: Sumba Island	印度尼西亚:松巴岛	-9.55	118.8	37	5.6	Mw	5										
2007	5	29	9	36	6					*	Indonesia: Labuha	印度尼西亚:拉布哈	-1.065	127.343	24	6.1	Mw							1		2		
2007	6	2	21	34	56					* China, Dis	China: Yunnan, Pu-er	中国:云南普洱	23	101.1	5	6.4	Ms	8	3	1	419	3	247	5	18313	5		
2007	6	6	11	28	25					USGS, NEIC	Indonesia: Palau Jamdena	印度尼西亚:延德纳岛	-6.72	130.91	86	5.8	Mw	5										
2007	6	13	19	29	40					* USGS	Guatemala: Guatemala City	危地马拉:危地马拉城	13.554	-90.618	23	6.7	Mw	6						1		2		
2007	6	14	14	49	54					USGS	Philippines: Bohol Island	菲律宾:保和岛	10.38	125.31	10	5.5	Mw	6										
2007	6	18	14	29	48					*	Iran: Qom	伊朗:库姆	34.437	50.833	5	5.5	Mw							1		2		
2007	6	28	19	25	21					USGS, NEIC	Chile: Los Vilos	智利:洛斯比洛斯	-32	-71.34	68	5.7	Mw	5										
2007	6	29	18	9	11					USGS	Greece: Lefkada, Preveza	希腊:莱夫卡斯,普雷韦扎	39.27	20.26	10	5.4	Mw	6										
2007	7	1	4	12	8					USGS, NEIC	Japan: Hokkaido	日本:北海道	43.66	144.73	130	5.8	Mw	5										
2007	7	1	14	34	12					USGS, NEIC	Indonesia: Banda Sea	印度尼西亚:班达海	-5.93	130.56	134	5.9	Mw	5										
2007	7	2	18	36	3					USGS	Guatemala: Sonzacate	危地马拉:松萨卡特	13.81	-89.61	20	4.7	mb	6										
2007	7	13	0	18	11					USGS	Philippines: Panglao Island	菲律宾:彭哥鲁奥岛	9.19	123.31	35	4.9	mb	6										
2007	7	13	7	20	26					*	Ecuador: Zaruma	厄瓜多尔:萨鲁马	-3.987	-79.836	50	4.5	mb							1				
2007	7	16	1	13	22	4				* NOAA, USGS	Japan: Sado Island	日本:佐渡岛	37.57	138.478	10	6.6	Mw	9	9	1	1088	4		3	875	3		
2007	7	16	6	37	40					USGS	Japan: Sado Island	日本:佐渡岛	37.5	138.47	15	5.7	Mw	8										
2007	7	17	14	10	42					USGS, NEIC	Tanzania: Arusha	坦桑尼亚:阿鲁沙	-2.73	36.36	8	5.9	Mw	5										
2007	7	19	15	10	24					USGS	Philippines: Bohol Island	菲律宾:保和岛	10.29	125.15	63	5.3	Mw	6										
2007	7	20	10	6	53					* China, Dis	China: Xinjiang, Ili	中国:新疆伊犁	42.9	82.4	10	5.7	Ms	7					14.6	3	2120	4		
2007	7	20	11	42	22					* CSN	US: California, Montclair	美国:加利福尼亚州蒙特克莱尔	37.804	-122.193	5	4.9	Ms							1				
2007	7	21	22	44	14					* NEIC	Tajikistan: Garm	塔吉克斯坦:加尔姆	38.936	70.485	10	5.6	mb		12	1								
2007	7	22	23	2	15					* NEIC	India: Uttarkashi, Chamoli	印度:乌塔卡西,查莫利	30.881	78.239	19	5.1	mb				3	1		1		1		

年 Year	月 Mo	日 Dy	时 Hr	分 Mn	秒 Sec	海啸 Tsunami 源 Sr	浪高 Wh	级 I mI	级 S mS	资料来源 Information	震中 Earthquake Epicenter 地名(英文) Name(English)	地名(中文) Name(Chinese)	纬度(°) Latitude	经度(°) Longitude	深度 Depth	震级 Mag	标度 Scale	烈度 MMI	死亡人数 Deaths 数量/人 Num	级别 Dd	受伤人数 Injuries 数量/人 Num	级别 Dd	经济损失 Damage 数量/$ Mill	级别 De	房屋毁坏 Houses Destroyed 数量/间 Num	级别 Dh	房屋受损 Houses Damaged 数量/间 Num	级别 Dh
2007	7	23	13	40	2					USGS,NEIC	China:Taiwan,Hualien,Coast of E.	中国:台湾花莲以东海域	23.67	121.63	40	5.6	Mw	6										
2007	7	26	5	40	16					*	Molukka Sea,N.	马鲁古海北部	2.872	127.464	25	6.9	Mw					2		1		1		
2007	8	1	17	8	51					* USGS	Vanuatu Islands:Luganville	瓦努阿图群岛:卢甘维尔	-15.595	167.68	120	7.2	Mw	7						1		1		
2007	8	2	2	37	42	4	0.2			* NOAA	Russia:Sakhalin Island	俄罗斯:库页岛(萨哈林岛)	47.116	141.798	5	6.2	Ms		2	1	12	1		1	11	1	20	1
2007	8	2	3	21	43	4	0			* NOAA	Aleutian Islands	阿留申群岛	51.307	-179.971	21	6.7	Mw											
2007	8	6	8	48	40					*	US:Utah, Huntington	美国:犹他州亨廷顿	39.465	-111.237	2	4.2	mb		9	1		1						
2007	8	9	0	55	52					USGS	China:Taiwan,Taitung	中国:台湾台东	22.58	121.1	21	5.3	Ms	6										
2007	8	14	5	38	6					USGS,NEIC	Hawaiian Islands	夏威夷群岛	19.35	-155.07	9	5.6	Mw	7										
2007	8	15	23	40	58	4	1			* NOAA, USGS	Peru:Ica, Pisco, Lima	秘鲁:伊卡,皮斯科,利马	-13.386	-76.603	39	8.0	Mw	9	514	3	1090	4		4	39700	5		
2007	8	16	0	2	41					USGS,NEIC	Peru: Chincha Alta, Near Coast	秘鲁:上钦查近海	-13.26	-76.49	39	5.6	mb	5										
2007	8	16	0	19	14					USGS	Peru:Ica	秘鲁:伊卡	-14.23	-75.94	35	5.8	mb	7										
2007	8	16	1	35	38					USGS	Peru:Ica,Coast	秘鲁:伊卡近海	-14.18	-76.76	24	5.4	mb	7										
2007	8	16	2	54	20					USGS	Peru:North Ica,Coast	秘鲁:伊卡北部近海	-13.54	-76.58	41	5	mb	6										
2007	8	16	11	35	42					USGS	Peru:Ica	秘鲁:伊卡	-14.29	-76.21	35	6	Mw	6										
2007	8	17	0	38	56					*	US:Utah, Huntington	美国:犹他州亨廷顿	39.464	-111.207		1.6	ML		3	1	6	1						
2007	8	17	13	18	13					USGS,NEIC	Peru:Pisco,Near Coast	秘鲁:皮斯科近海	-13.6	-76.6	48	5.9	Mw	5										
2007	8	17	19	14	45					USGS	Japan:Ichihara	日本:千叶市原	35.36	140.18	26	5	Mw	6										
2007	8	20	19	15	54					*	India:Maharashtra,Satara	印度:马哈拉施特拉邦,萨达拉	17.2	73.7	5	4.4	mb							1				
2007	8	25	4	24	22					*	Iran:Hormozgan	伊朗:荷姆兹甘	28.154	56.652	10	5	mb				4	1						
2007	9	2	1	5	18	4	0.1			* NOAA	Solomon Islands: Santa Cruz Islands	所罗门群岛:圣克鲁斯群岛	-11.61	165.762	35	7.3	Ms											
2007	9	6	17	51	26					China,USGS	China:Taiwan,Hualien,Coast of E.	中国:台湾花莲以东海域	24.2	122.3		6.3	Ms	6										
2007	9	9	18	36	38					* CSN,USGS	Indonesia:Situbondo	印度尼西亚:诗都文罗	-7.783	114.338	35	4.9	Ms	6			13	1		1				
2007	9	10	1	49	14					*	Colombia:Narino	哥伦比亚:纳里尼奥	2.982	-77.967	31	6.8	Mw				5	1		1	35	1		
2007	9	12	11	10	27	4	1			* NOAA, USGS	Indonesia: Sumatra, Coast of SW.	印度尼西亚:苏门答腊西南海域	-4.438	101.367	34	8.5	Ms	6	25	1	161	3		3	56425	5		
2007	9	12	16	37	4					USGS,NEIC	Indonesia:Southern Sumatra	印度尼西亚:苏门答腊南部	-3.14	101.4	35	5.8	mb	5										
2007	9	12	23	49	4					* USGS	Indonesia:Southern Sumatra	印度尼西亚:苏门答腊南部	-2.625	100.841	35	8.1	Ms	6										
2007	9	13	1	26	34					USGS,NEIC	Indonesia:Southern Sumatra	印度尼西亚:苏门答腊南部	-1.9	99.82	16	5.7	mb	5										

时间 Date						海啸 Tsunami				资料来源 Information	震中 Earthquake Epicenter				深度 Depth	震级 Mag	标度 Scale	烈度 MMI	死亡人数 Deaths		受伤人数 Injuries		经济损失 Damage		房屋毁坏 Houses Destroyed		房屋受损 Houses Damaged	
年 Year	月 Mo	日 Dy	时 Hr	分 Mn	秒 Sec	源 Sr	浪高 Wh	级I mI	级S mS		地名(英文) Name(English)	地名(中文) Name(Chinese)	纬度(°) Latitude	经度(°) Longitude					数量/人 Num	级别 Dd	数量/人 Num	级别 Dd	数量/$ Mill $ Mill	级别 De	数量/间 Num	级别 Dh	数量/间 Num	级别 Dh
2007	9	13	3	35	29					NEIC,USGS	Indonesia:Southern Sumatra	印度尼西亚:苏门答腊南部	-2.13	99.627	22	7.2	Mw	6										
2007	9	15	17	59	42					USGS	Honduras:El Pedernal	洪都拉斯:埃尔佩德纳尔	14.83	-87.12	32	5.3	Mw	6										
2007	9	30	5	23	34	4	0.1			* NOAA	New Zealand:Auckland Islands,N.	新西兰:奥克兰群岛以北	-49.418	163.954	10	7.4	Mw											
2007	10	8	17	10	35					USGS,NEIC	Kuril Islands	千岛群岛	43.55	146.75	41	5.8	Mw	5										
2007	10	15	12	29	36					*	New Zealand:South Island, Milford Sound	新西兰:南岛,米尔福德桑德	-44.785	167.583	26	6.8	Ms							1				
2007	10	26	6	50	7					* NEIC	India:Kashmir	印度:克什米尔	35.304	76.753	10	5.3	mb		1	1	12	1						
2007	10	31	3	4	55					* USGS	US:California,San Jose	美国:加利福尼亚州圣何塞	37.434	-121.774	10	5.6	Mw	6						1				
2007	11	6	9	38	6					*	India:Gujarat	印度:古吉拉特	21.181	70.724	10	5.1	Mw		1	1	5	1		1		2		
2007	11	7	4	12	39					*	Philippines:Bohol Island	菲律宾:保和岛	9.721	124.647	72	5.1	mb		1	1								
2007	11	7	7	10	22					* USGS	Bangladesh:Chittagong, Bandarban	孟加拉:吉大港,班多尔班	22.15	92.388	29	5.5	Mw				10	1		1				
2007	11	14	15	40	51	4	0.3			* NOAA, USGS	Chile:Tocopilla, Maria Elena	智利:托科皮亚,玛利亚艾烈娜	-22.247	-69.89	40	7.7	Mw	8	2	1	65	2		3		4		
2007	11	16	3	13	0					*	Ecuador:Morona Santiago	厄瓜多尔:莫罗纳-圣地亚哥	-2.312	-77.838	123	6.8	Mw							1				
2007	11	20	5	20	3					*	Iran:Ahwaz,W.	伊朗:阿瓦士西部	31.68	49.93	7	4.9	ML				30	1		1		1		
2007	11	25	16	2	18					*	Indonesia:Sumbawa	印度尼西亚:松巴哇	-8.277	118.339	35	6.5	Mw		3	1		3		2		3		
2007	11	25	23	12	17					* CSN	India:Badaun, Meerut, Noida	印度:布道恩,米鲁特,诺依达	28.555	77.057	10	4.9	Ms							1		1		
2007	11	26	13	51	40					USGS,NEIC	Japan:Fukushima,Near Coast	日本:福岛近海	37.39	141.59	42	5.9	Mw	5										
2007	11	26	21	56	13					USGS,NEIC	Mexico:Uruapan	墨西哥:米却肯的乌鲁阿潘	18.65	-101.7	53	5.8	Mw	5										
2007	11	27	4	26	59					USGS	Philippines:Alaminos	菲律宾:阿拉米诺斯	16.06	119.84	35	5.9	Mw	6										
2007	11	29	19	0	20					* USGS	Martinique Island	马提尼克岛(拉丁美洲)	14.973	-61.263	148	7.4	Mw	7	1	1	102	3		1				
2007	11	29	19	34	46					USGS	Martinique Island	马提尼克岛(拉丁美洲)	15.09	-61.38	146	5.1	mb	6										
2007	12	1	1	44	32					USGS,NEIC	Indonesia:Off West Coast of N. Sumatera	印度尼西亚:北苏门答腊西部海域	1.98	97.88	44	5.9	Mw	5										
2007	12	9	2	3	29					* CSN	Brazil:Minas Gerais	巴西:米纳斯吉拉斯	-15.048	-44.231	10	5.5	Ms		1	1	6	1		2	76	2		
2007	12	9	7	28	21	4	0			* NOAA	South of Fiji Islands	斐济群岛南部	-25.996	-177.514	153	7.8	Mw											
2007	12	15	18	22	27					* USGS	Chile:Near Coast of C.	智利:中部近海	-32.689	-71.695	25	6	Mw	7			4	1		1		1		
2007	12	16	8	9	18					NEIC,USGS	Chile:Antofagasta,C.	智利:安托法加斯塔中部	-22.954	-70.182	45	6.7	Mw	6										
2007	12	17	6	29	52					USGS	Chile:Near Coast of C.	智利:中部近海	-32.71	-71.81	12	4.8	mb	6										

时间						海啸				资料来源	震中				深度	震级	标度	烈度	死亡人数		受伤人数		经济损失		房屋毁坏		房屋受损	
年	月	日	时	分	秒	源	浪高	级I	级S		地名(英文)	地名(中文)	纬度(°)	经度(°)					数量/人	级别	数量/人	级别	数量/$ Mill	级别	数量/间	级别	数量/间	级别
Date						Tsunami				Information	Earthquake Epicenter				Depth	Mag	Scale	MMI	Deaths		Injuries		Damage		Houses Destroyed		Houses Damaged	
Year	Mo	Dy	Hr	Mn	Sec	Sr	Wh	mI	mS		Name(English)	Name(Chinese)	Latitude	Longitude					Num	Dd	Num	Dd	$ Mill	De	Num	Dh	Num	Dh
2007	12	20	3	6	56					USGS	Chile:Near Coast of C.	智利:中部近海	-32.71	-71.79	30	5.5	Mw	5										
2007	12	20	7	55	16					* USGS	New Zealand: North Island, Near Coast of E.	新西兰:北岛东部近海	-39.011	178.291	20	6.9	ML	7	1	1				1	3	1		
2007	12	20	9	48	30					*	Turkey:Ankara	土耳其:安卡拉	39.417	33.212	10	5.7	ML							1		1		1
2007	12	25	16	20	53					USGS, NEIC	Chile:Iquique, N.	智利:伊基克北部	-19.44	-69.05	112	5.8	Mw	5										
2007	12	26	23	47	11					*	Turkey:Ankara	土耳其:安卡拉	39.446	33.162	8	5.6	Mw							3	2214	4		
2008	1	1	6	32	28					* NEIC	Kyrgyzstan:Osh	吉尔吉斯斯坦:奥什	40.288	72.985	6	5.8	mb							3	5385	4		
2008	1	5	1	56	45					*	Guatemala:Colomba, Flores	危地马拉:高龙巴,弗洛勒斯岛	14.129	-91.479	66	5.6	Mw							1				1
2008	1	6	5	14	20					NEIC, USGS	Greece:Arkadia	希腊:阿卡迪亚	37.216	22.693	75	6.2	Mw	6										
2008	1	7	3	12	27					*	Indonesia:Irian Jaya Barat	印度尼西亚:西巴布亚	-0.795	134.012	12	6	mB				6	1		1			22	1
2008	1	9	22	24	4					*	Algeria:Oran	阿尔及利亚:奥兰	35.616	-0.57	10	5.3	ML		1	1				2				2
2008	1	12	22	44	47					*	Bangladesh:Rangamati	孟加拉:兰加马蒂	22.761	92.333	34	5	mb							1				2
2008	1	13	12	15	36					USGS	Philippines:Tabuk	菲律宾:塔布克	17.05	120.99	10	5.7	Mw	5										
2008	1	22	9	9	28					USGS	Chile:Tarapaca	智利:达拉巴卡	-19.84	-69.95	45	5.1	mb	6										
2008	1	22	17	14	58					*	Indonesia:Sumatera, Nias Island	印度尼西亚:苏门答腊,尼亚斯岛	1.011	97.442	20	6.1	Mw		1	1	5	1		1				2
2008	1	25	19	33	25					USGS	Japan:Nanao	日本:石川七尾	37.25	136.71	11	4.6	Mw	6										
2008	1	31	21	6	47					China, Dis	China:Sichuan, Changning	中国:四川长宁	28.41	105.01	30	4.6	Ms	6			1	1	2.75	2				
2008	2	3	7	34	12					*	Congo:Bukavu	刚果:布卡武	-2.296	28.9	10	6.1	mB		38	1	717	3		3	99	2	815	3
2008	2	4	7	43	56					USGS	Puerto Rico:Mona Passage	波多黎各:莫纳海峡	19.03	-66.9	14	5.5	Mw	5										
2008	2	5	5	56	47					USGS, NEIC	Indonesia:Makassar Strait	印度尼西亚:望加锡海峡	-3.52	118.07	13	5.9	Mw	5										
2008	2	6	6	9	40					* CSN	India:Durgapur	印度:杜尔加布尔	23.433	87.111	10	4.9	Ms		1	1	50	1		2				3
2008	2	9	7	12	6					* USGS	Mexico:Mexicali	墨西哥:墨西卡利	32.456	-115.315	3	5.5	ML	6						1				
2008	2	13	20	55	32					*	Iran: Aharmahal And Bakhtiari	伊朗:恰哈马哈勒-巴赫蒂亚里	31.73	51.2	14	4.9	Ms				10	1		1			70	2
2008	2	14	2	7	47					* NEIC	Congo:Bukavu	刚果:布卡武	-2.404	28.918	10	5.4	mb		1	1	109	3		1			5	1
2008	2	15	10	36	19					*	Lebanon:Sur (Tyre)	黎巴嫩:苏尔	33.327	35.305	10	5.3	ML				10	1		1				1
2008	2	17	20	33	3					USGS	China:Taiwan, Taitung	中国:台湾台东	23.28	121.45	19	5.4	Mw	6										
2008	2	20	8	8	31					*	Indonesia:Simeulue Island	印度尼西亚:锡默卢岛	2.768	95.964	26	7.5	Ms		3	1	25	1						
2008	2	21	14	16	3					* USGS	US:Nevada, Wells	美国:内华达州韦尔斯	41.153	-114.867	7	6.0	Mw	8			3	1		2			720	3
2008	2	25	8	36	33	4	0.1			* CSN, NOAA	Indonesia:Southern Sumatra	印度尼西亚:苏门答腊南部	-2.486	99.972	25	7.7	Ms							1				2
2008	2	26	18	18	28					USGS, NEIC	Indonesia:Southern Sumatra	印度尼西亚:苏门答腊南部	-3.85	101.07	20	5.9	Mw	5										
2008	2	27	0	56	48					*	England:Lincolnshire	英国:林肯郡	53.403	-0.332	18	5.3	ML				1	1		1				1
2008	2	29	4	46						*	Brazil:Sobral	巴西:索布腊儿尔	-3.7	-40.35	10	4.3	mb							1				
2008	3	1	19	51	59					USGS, NEIC	Chile:Iquique	智利:伊基克	-20.26	-69.94	36	5.7	Mw	5										

时间						海啸				资料来源	震中				深度	震级	标度	烈度	死亡人数		受伤人数		经济损失		房屋毁坏		房屋受损	
年	月	日	时	分	秒	源	浪高	级 I	级 S		地名(英文)	地名(中文)	纬度(°)	经度(°)					数量/人	级别	数量/人	级别	数量/$ Mill	级别	数量/间	级别	数量/间	级别
Date						Tsunami				Information	Earthquake Epicenter				Depth	Mag	Scale	MMI	Deaths		Injuries		Damage		Houses Destroyed		Houses Damaged	
Year	Mo	Dy	Hr	Mn	Sec	Sr	Wh	mI	mS		Name(English)	Name(Chinese)	Latitude	Longitude					Num	Dd	Num	Dd	$ Mill	De	Num	Dh	Num	Dh
2008	3	4	17	31	47					USGS	China:Taiwan,Kaohsiung	中国:台湾高雄	23.12	120.82	11	5.2	Mw	6										
2008	3	9	11	10	41					* CSN	India:Gujarat	印度:古吉拉特	23.33	70.592	29	4.7	Ms							1				1
2008	3	20	22	33	2					* China,Dis	China:Xinjiang,Keriya	中国:新疆于田	35.6	81.6	10	7.3	Ms	7					26.7	4	2200	4		
2008	3	21	12	36	55					China,Dis	China:Yunnan,Yingjiang	中国:云南盈江	24.4	97.71	13	5	Ms	6					8.9	3	75	2		
2008	3	24	15	24	40					China,Dis	China:Hubei,Zhushan	中国:湖北竹山	32.51	110.22	10	4.2	Ms	6					0.22	1				
2008	3	24	20	39	8					USGS	Chile:Pozo Almonte,E.	智利:波索阿尔蒙特东部	-20.04	-68.96	120	6.2	Mw	6										
2008	3	26	20	6	6					USGS	Guam	关岛(西太平洋)	13.59	144.88	70	5.6	Mw	5										
2008	3	29	12	51	25					* NEIC	Peru:Lima,Near Coast	秘鲁:利马近海	-12.178	-77.164	51	5.4	mb				1	1		1	5	1		
2008	3	30	8	32	25					China,Dis	China:Gansu,Sunan	中国:甘肃肃南	37.97	101.92	11	5	Ms	6					5.4	3				
2008	4	2	8	48	50					USGS,NEIC	Indonesia:Southern Sumatra	印度尼西亚:苏门答腊南部	-4.35	102.72	67	5.7	Mw	5										
2008	4	9	12	46	13	4	0.2			* NOAA	Vanuatu Islands	瓦努阿图群岛	-20.071	168.892	33	7.3	Ms											
2008	4	15	3	3	5					*	Guatemala:Near Coast	危地马拉:近海	13.564	-90.599	33	6.1	Mw							1			8	1
2008	4	18	9	36	59					* USGS	US:Illinois,Mt Carmel	美国:伊利诺斯州芒特卡梅尔	38.452	-87.886	14	5.4	Mw	7						1				1
2008	4	20	13	14	46					China,Dis	China:Xinjiang,Yumin	中国:新疆裕民	46.09	82.81	20	5.1	Ms						12.3	3				
2008	4	20	21	42	24					China,Dis	China:Gansu,Sunan	中国:甘肃肃南	38.01	101.87	14	4.2	Ms	6					1.89	2				
2008	4	26	6	40	11					* USGS	US:Nevada,Reno	美国:内华达州雷诺	39.52	-119.93	1	5	Mw	6						1				1
2008	4	28	18	33	34	1	0			* NOAA	Vanuatu Islands	瓦努阿图群岛	-19.941	168.953	32	6.4	Mw											
2008	4	29	5	26	5					USGS,NEIC	Japan:Hokkaido	日本:北海道	41.45	142.03	46	5.8	Mw	5										
2008	4	30	3	3	7					USGS	US:California,Burnt Ranch	美国:加利福尼亚州本特兰奇	40.84	-123.5	29	5.4	Mw	6										
2008	5	1	0	15	27					* CSN	Iran:Lorestan	伊朗:洛雷斯坦	33.86	48.59	7	4.8	Ms				100	2		1				
2008	5	3	13	17	10					USGS	China:Taiwan,Hualien,Coast of E.	中国:台湾花莲以东海域	24.41	121.82	35	4.5	mb	6										
2008	5	7	16	45	20					* USGS	Japan:Ibaraki,Near Coast	日本:茨城近海	36.158	141.521	39	6.9	Mw	6			6	1		1				
2008	5	12	6	28	4					* China,Dis	China:Sichuan,Wenchuan	中国:四川汶川	30.95	103.4	19	8.0	Ms	11	87652	5	374171	5	120729	5	5360000	5	21000000	5
2008	5	13	7	7	9					China, USGS, NEIC	China:Sichuan,Dujiangyan	中国:四川都江堰	30.9	103.4	9	6.1	Ms	6										
2008	5	13	18	27	57					USGS	China:Taiwan,Taitung,Coast of E.	中国:台湾台东以东海域	22.7	121.24	20	5.2	Mw	6										
2008	5	21	19	23	57					* Song	Brazil:Alcantaras	巴西:阿尔坎塔拉斯	-3.91	-40.44	10	5.3	Mk							1				
2008	5	24	19	20	42					*	Colombia:Meta, Quetame	哥伦比亚:梅塔,奎塔美	4.33	-73.764	9	5.6	Mw		6	1				1				2
2008	5	25	8	21	47					* China	China:Sichuan,Guangyuan	中国:四川广元	32.6	105.4		6.4	Ms		8	1	927	3		4	400000	5		
2008	5	26	15	1	34					* USGS	Costa Rica:Pavones	哥斯达黎加:帕沃内斯	8.423	-82.968	13	5.6	Mw	6						1				
2008	5	27	8	37	52					* China, USGS, NEIC	China:Sichuan,Guangyuan	中国:四川广元	32.7	105.6	10	5.7	Mw							3	20000	5		
2008	5	29	15	46	0					* USGS	Iceland:Selfoss	冰岛:塞尔福斯	64.004	-21.012	10	6.3	Mw	8			30	1		1				
2008	6	6	20	2	57					* USGS	Algeria:Oran	阿尔及利亚:奥兰	35.883	-0.658	4	5.5	Mw	6	1	1	30	1		2		2		

年 Year	月 Mo	日 Dy	时 Hr	分 Mn	秒 Sec	海啸 Tsunami 源 Sr	浪高 Wh	级 I mI	级 S mS	资料来源 Information	震中 Earthquake Epicenter 地名(英文) Name(English)	地名(中文) Name(Chinese)	纬度(°) Latitude	经度(°) Longitude	深度 Depth	震级 Mag	标度 Scale	烈度 MMI	死亡人数 Deaths 数量/人 Num	级别 Dd	受伤人数 Injuries 数量/人 Num	级别 Dd	经济损失 Damage 数量/$ Mill	级别 De	房屋毁坏 Houses Destroyed 数量/间 Num	级别 Dh	房屋受损 Houses Damaged 数量/间 Num	级别 Dh
2008	6	6	21	16	34					*	India:Tekari	印度:代加里	24.702	84.964	11	3.8	mb				2	1		1				
2008	6	8	12	25	30					* USGS	Greece:Achaia	希腊:阿凯亚	37.963	21.525	16	6.4	Mw	8	2	1	240	3		3	1156	4		
2008	6	10	6	5	2					China,Dis	China: Inner Mongolia, Hulunber,E.	中国:内蒙古呼伦贝尔东部	49.03	122.72	16	5.5	Ms	6					4.60	2				
2008	6	13	23	43	45					* USGS	Japan:Oshu	日本:岩手奥州	39.03	140.881	8	7	Ms	9	13	1	357	3		3			614	3
2008	6	14	0	20	12					USGS	Japan:Miyagi	日本:宫城	38.88	140.68	6	5.5	Mw	6										
2008	6	25	23	37	12					USGS	Japan:Hokkaido	日本:北海道	41.94	142.49	55	5.5	Mw	5										
2008	7	1	0	17	33					* USGS	Peru:Pasco	秘鲁:帕斯科	-10.368	-75.512	33	5.5	Mw	6			45	1		1	60	2	25	1
2008	7	3	23	10	2					*	Iran:Mashhad	伊朗:马什哈德	35.5	58.8	10	5	Mw							1		2		
2008	7	5	7	49	3					USGS	Japan:Ibaraki,Near Coast	日本:茨城近海	36.64	140.95	49	5.1	Mw	6										
2008	7	8	7	42	11					NEIC,USGS	Ryukyu Islands	琉球群岛	27.532	128.334	43	6.0	Mw	6										
2008	7	8	9	13	7					*	Peru:Arequipa	秘鲁:阿雷基帕	-15.986	-71.748	123	6.2	Mw		1	1				1				2
2008	7	15	3	26	35					NEIC,USGS	Greece: Chalki (Dodecanese)	希腊:秋奇(萨摩斯岛)	35.8	27.86	52	6.5	Mw	7										
2008	7	19	2	39	29	4	0.2			* NOAA	Japan Trench	日本海沟	37.552	142.214	22	7	Ms											
2008	7	23	15	26	20					* USGS	Japan:Morioka	日本:岩手盛冈	39.802	141.464	108	6.8	Mw	8	1	1	200	3		2	90	2		
2008	7	24	7	9	28					* China	China:Sichuan,Guangyuan	中国:四川广元	32.8	105.5		6.0	Ms		1	1	17	1		3	1200	4		
2008	7	29	18	42	16					* NEIC,USGS	US:California,Los Angeles	美国:加利福尼亚州洛杉矶	33.953	-117.761	15	5.5	mb	6			8	1		1				1
2008	8	1	8	32	44					* China	China:Sichuan,Pingwu,SE.	中国:四川平武东南	32.1	104.7		6.1	Ms				231	3		2	540	3	2450	4
2008	8	1	10	35	24					USGS	Philippines:Mindoro Island	菲律宾:民都洛岛	13.52	120.76	135	5.6	Mw	5										
2008	8	1	18	14	11					USGS	Philippines:Iloilo	菲律宾:伊洛伊洛	10.82	122.98	14	4.6	mb	6										
2008	8	1	18	55	47					USGS	China:Taiwan,Hualien,Coast of E.	中国:台湾花莲以东海域	23.99	121.7	17	4.9	mb	6										
2008	8	5	9	49	18					* China	China:Sichuan,Guangyuan	中国:四川广元	32.8	105.5		6.1	Ms		4	1	29	1		1				1
2008	8	6	22	41	4					USGS	Indonesia:Sumbawa	印度尼西亚:松巴哇	-8.13	117.67	30	5.9	Mw	7										
2008	8	11	7	19	26					*	Venezuela:Cariaco – Cumana	委内瑞拉:卡利亚科 – 库马纳	10.514	-64.171	13	5.2	Mw							1			50	1
2008	8	15	10	25	17					* USGS	Philippines:Sorsogon	菲律宾:索索贡	12.9	124.32	10	6	Mw	6						1				
2008	8	19	21	35	9					* China,Dis	China:Yunnan,Yingjiang,N.	中国:云南盈江北部	25.1	97.9		5	Ms	6										
2008	8	21	12	24	32					* China,Dis	China:Yunnan,Yingjiang,nw.	中国:云南盈江西北	24.9	97.8		5.9	Ms	8	5	1	130	3	187	5	5	1	2420	4
2008	8	25	2	43	6					USGS,NEIC	Philippines:Leyte Island	菲律宾:莱特岛	10.31	125.25	27	5.8	Mw	5										
2008	8	25	11	25	19					* USGS	New Zealand: North Island, Pakipaki	新西兰:北岛,帕基帕基	-39.715	176.851	32	5.9	ML	6						1				
2008	8	25	13	21	59					* China	China: Xizang (Tibet), Zhongba	中国:西藏仲巴	31	83.6	12	6.8	Ms	8										
2008	8	26	8	7	8	1				NOAA	South Africa:Paternoster	南非:佩特诺斯特	-32.8	18	10	5	Ms							1				
2008	8	27	1	35	32					* USGS	Russia:Lake Baykal	俄罗斯:贝加尔湖	51.607	104.158	16	6.3	Mw	8						1				

时间 年 Year	月 Mo	日 Dy	时 Hr	分 Mn	秒 Sec	海啸 Tsunami 源 Sr	浪高 Wh	级 I mI	级 S mS	资料来源 Information	震中 Earthquake Epicenter 地名(英文) Name(English)	地名(中文) Name(Chinese)	纬度(°) Latitude	经度(°) Longitude	深度 Depth	震级 Mag	标度 Scale	烈度 MMI	死亡人数 Deaths 数量/人 Num	级别 Dd	受伤人数 Injuries 数量/人 Num	级别 Dd	经济损失 Damage 数量/$ Mill	级别 De	房屋毁坏 Houses Destroyed 数量/间 Num	级别 Dh	房屋受损 Houses Damaged 数量/间 Num	级别 Dh
2008	8	30	8	30	50					* China, Dis	China: Sichuan, Panzhihua	中国:四川攀枝花	26. 2	101. 9		6. 1	Ms	8	41	1	1010	4	637	5	39200	5		
2008	8	30	12	46	47					China, Dis	China: Xinjiang, Hejing	中国:新疆和静	42. 65	83. 95	11	5. 3	Ms	6					5. 2	3				
2008	9	3	2	22	47					* NEIC	Turkey: Adiyaman	土耳其:阿德亚曼	37. 507	38. 503	6	5. 1	ML							1				
2008	9	9	3	7	28					* USGS	Indonesia: Southern Sumatra	印度尼西亚:苏门答腊南部	-3. 935	103. 058	25	5. 4	mb	6	2	1				2			113	3
2008	9	10	11	0	34					*	Iran: Hormozgan	伊朗:荷姆兹甘	26. 743	55. 828	12	6. 1	Mw		7	1	45	1		3		3		3
2008	9	10	16	12	4					USGS	Chile: Iquique	智利:伊基克	-20. 26	-69. 22	37	5. 7	Mw	6										
2008	9	11	0	20	51	4	0. 1			* NOAA, USGS	Japan: Hokkaido	日本:北海道	41. 892	143. 754	25	7	Ms	6	6	1	77	2		3			1000	3
2008	9	13	9	32	1					USGS, NEIC	Colombia: Pereira	哥伦比亚:利萨拉尔达的佩雷拉	4. 79	-75. 52	132	5. 7	Mw	5										
2008	9	16	21	47	15					*	India: Maharashtra	印度:马哈拉施特拉邦	17. 438	73. 915	10	5	mb		1	1	20	1		3			1500	4
2008	9	27	3	4	52					USGS, NEIC	Philippines: Mindoro Island	菲律宾:民都洛岛	13. 47	120. 57	10	5. 7	Mw	5										
2008	9	27	3	9	5					USGS, NEIC	Philippines: Mindoro Island	菲律宾:民都洛岛	13. 48	120. 55	11	5. 9	Mw	5										
2008	10	5	15	52	49					* China	Kyrgyzstan: Osh, S.	吉尔吉斯斯坦:奥什南部	39. 533	73. 824	27	6. 8	Ms		74	2	140	3		2		2		
2008	10	5	15	55	24					China, USGS, NEIC, Dis	China: Xinjiang, Kashi, W.	中国:新疆喀什西部	39. 36	73. 66	35	6. 3	Ms	7					9. 6	3				
2008	10	6	7	30	46					* China, Dis	China: Xizang (Tibet), Lhasa, NW.	中国:西藏拉萨西北	29. 8	90. 3	12	6. 6	Ms	8	10	1	60	2	58. 8	4		3		
2008	10	11	9	6	11					*	Russia: Chechnya, Gudermes	俄罗斯:车臣共和国古杰尔梅斯	43. 372	46. 254	16	5. 7	Mw		13	1	100	2		3			1027	4
2008	10	28	23	9	58					*	Pakistan: Quetta	巴基斯坦:奎达	30. 639	67. 351	15	6. 6	Ms		166	3	370	3		4	3487	4	3487	4
2008	10	29	11	32	43					*	Pakistan: Ziarat	巴基斯坦:加拉特	30. 598	67. 455	14	6. 6	Ms				1	1		2		2		2
2008	11	10	1	22	3					* China, Dis	China: Qinghai, Haixi, NW.	中国:青海海西西北	37. 6	95. 9	19	6. 3	Ms	7			3	1	38. 0	4		2		2
2008	11	15	23	3	17					USGS	El Salvador: Usulutan	萨尔瓦多:乌苏卢坦	13. 05	-88. 75	48	5. 8	Mw	6										
2008	11	16	17	2	33	4	0. 1			* NOAA, USGS	Indonesia: South Sulawesi sea	印度尼西亚:苏拉威西海南部	1. 271	122. 091	30	7. 4	Mw	7	6	1	77	2		3			1000	3
2008	11	19	6	11	21					* NEIC, USGS	Panama: Puerto Armuelles	巴拿马:阿穆埃耶斯港	8. 267	-82. 967	32	6. 3	Mw	6						1				
2008	11	22	8	1	16					China, Dis	China: Hubei, Zigui	中国:湖北秭归	31. 02	110. 77	9	4. 1	Ms	6			1	1	0. 64	1				
2008	11	22	22	27	55					*	Czech Republic: Karvina	捷克:卡尔维纳	49. 914	18. 455		4. 1	ML		2	1	3	1		1				
2008	12	2	3	16	53					USGS	China: Taiwan, Taitung, Coast of E.	中国:台湾台东以东海域	23. 28	121. 6	29	5. 3	Mw	6										
2008	12	7	13	36	21					*	Iran: Qeshm	伊朗:格什姆	26. 99	55. 8	15	5. 7	mb				5	1		1				1
2008	12	9	18	53	11					*	China: Sichuan, Guangyuan	中国:四川广元	32. 518	105. 395	25	5. 5	mb		2	1	3	1						
2008	12	10	10	53	50					*	Argentina: Las Heras	阿根廷:拉斯埃拉斯	-32. 938	-69. 259	10	4. 8	ML							1				
2008	12	19	9	36	5					USGS, NEIC	Chile: Near Coast of C.	智利:中部近海	-32. 46	-71. 95	32	5. 7	Mw	5										
2008	12	23	15	24	22					USGS	Italy: Parma	意大利:帕尔马	44. 56	10. 41	28	5. 4	Mw	6										
2008	12	25	20	20	46					* China, Dis	China: Yunnan, Ruili	中国:云南瑞丽	23. 91	97. 74	10	4. 9	Ms	6			22	1	25. 7	4	30	1	5400	4

时间 年 Year	月 Mo	日 Dy	时 Hr	分 Mn	秒 Sec	海啸 源 Sr	浪高 Wh	级 I mI	级 S mS	资料来源 Information	震中 地名(英文) Name(English)	地名(中文) Name(Chinese)	纬度(°) Latitude	经度(°) Longitude	深度 Depth	震级 Mag	标度 Scale	烈度 MMI	死亡人数 Deaths 数量/人 Num	级别 Dd	受伤人数 Injuries 数量/人 Num	级别 Dd	经济损失 Damage 数量/$ Mill	级别 De	房屋毁坏 Houses Destroyed 数量/间 Num	级别 Dh	房屋受损 Houses Damaged 数量/间 Num	级别 Dh
2008	12	29	3	37	42					*	Afghan:Badakhshan	阿富汗:巴达赫尚	36.401	71.075	158	5.9	mb							1				1
2009	1	3	19	43	51	4	0.4			* NOAA	Indonesia:Irian Jaya Barat,N.	印度尼西亚:西巴布亚北部	-0.414	132.885	17	7.6	Mw		5	1	250	3		3			840	3
2009	1	3	22	33	40	3				* NOAA	Indonesia:Irian Jaya Barat	印度尼西亚:西巴布亚	-0.691	133.305	23	7.4	Ms	7										
2009	1	8	19	21	36					*	Costa Rica:La Paz	哥斯达黎加:拉巴斯	10.165	-84.197	14	6.1	Mw	7	23	1	100	2		3	518	3		
2009	1	15	17	49	39	4	0.1			* NOAA	Kuril Islands	千岛群岛	46.857	155.154	36	7.5	Ms											
2009	1	21	18	17	3					*	Peru:Paccha	秘鲁:帕克查	-11.779	-75.626	10	4.6	mb							2	50	1	500	3
2009	1	25	1	27						China,Dis	China:Xinjiang,Ili	中国:新疆伊犁	43.3	80.9		5	Ms	6					6.7	3	141	3	703	3
2009	1	29	22	43	45					USGS	Philippines:Mindanao Island	菲律宾:棉兰老岛	10.97	124.96	8	5.4	Mw	6										
2009	1	31	21	51	52					USGS,NEIC	Japan:Ibaraki,Near Coast	日本:茨城近海	36.72	141.15	34	5.7	Mw	5										
2009	2	11	17	34	51	4	0.1			* NOAA	Indonesia:Karakelong Island	印度尼西亚:卡拉克隆岛	3.884	126.397	22	7.2	Ms				64	2		2		2	597	3
2009	2	20	3	48	48					*	Pakistan:Azad Kashmir	巴基斯坦:阿萨得喀什米尔	34.204	73.899	10	5.5	mb				44	1		1				2
2009	2	20	10	2	29					* China,Dis	China:Xinjiang,Kalpin	中国:新疆柯坪	40.657	78.692	17	5.5	Ms	6					13.1	3	331	3	5613	4
2009	3	11	13	6	54					USGS,NEIC	Argentina:San Juan	阿根廷:圣胡安	-31.89	-69.19	28	5.5	Mw	6										
2009	3	11	17	24	37					USGS	Costa Rica:Pavones	哥斯达黎加:帕沃内斯	8.5	-83.22	14	5.9	Mw	6										
2009	3	19	18	17	41	4	0.1			* NOAA	Tonga Islands,S.	汤加群岛南部	-23.046	-174.659	34	7.6	Ms	6										
2009	3	26	4	44	12					*	India:Chaibasa	印度:采巴瑟	22.399	85.903	10	4.1	mb				5	1		1				1
2009	3	31	17	50	34					*	Nicaragua:San Juan Del Rio Coco	尼加拉瓜:滨河圣胡安椰	13.452	-86.06	36	4.9	ML							2	3	1	10	1
2009	4	5	9	36	26					USGS,NEIC	Japan:Miyazzaki	日本:宫崎	32.01	131.42	26	5.8	Mw	5										
2009	4	6	1	32	39					*	Italy:L'Aquila	意大利:拉奎拉	42.334	13.334	9	6.3	Mw	7	295	3	1000	3		4	15000	5		
2009	4	6	2	37	4					USGS	Italy:L'Aquila	意大利:拉奎拉	42.37	13.34	10	4.9	Mw	6										
2009	4	7	17	47	37					* USGS	Italy:L'Aquila	意大利:拉奎拉	42.275	13.464	15	5.5	Mw	6	1	1				1				1
2009	4	9	0	52	59					USGS	Italy:L'Aquila	意大利:拉奎拉	42.48	13.34	15	5.4	Mw	7										
2009	4	9	1	46	58					*	India:Jaisalmer	印度:杰伊尔梅尔	27.143	70.749	44	5.2	mb				6	1		2				2
2009	4	9	19	38	17					USGS	Italy:L'Aquila	意大利:拉奎拉	42.51	13.33	2	5.2	Mw	6										
2009	4	16	21	27	51					*	Afghan:Nangarhar	阿富汗:楠格哈尔	34.185	70.076	6	5.4	mb		19	1	51	2		2	200	3		
2009	4	19	4	8	18					China,Dis	China: Xjinjiang, Uqturpan, W.	中国:新疆乌什西部	41.27	78.27	30	5.5	Ms	6					6.7	3	76	2	398	3
2009	4	22	9	26						China,Dis	China:Xinjiang,Artux	中国:新疆阿图什	40.1	77.4		5	Ms	6					3.16	2	73	2	450	3
2009	4	27	16	46	29					USGS,NEIC	Mexico: Guerrero, Acapulco, E.	墨西哥:格雷罗州阿卡普尔科东部	17.03	-99.45	35	5.8	Mw	5										
2009	5	4	9	10	21					NEIC,USGS	Venezuela:Carabobo	委内瑞拉:卡拉沃沃	10.2	-67.01	6	5.5	Mw	6										
2009	5	17	19	50	6					*	Saudi Arabia:Umm Lajj	沙特阿拉伯:乌姆莱季	25.212	37.597	10	4.6	mb							1		2		
2009	5	19	17	35	1					*	Saudi Arabia:Umm Lajj	沙特阿拉伯:乌姆莱季	25.292	37.744	2	5.7	Mw				7	1						
2009	5	19	19	29	49					*	India:Kashmir	印度:克什米尔	33.198	75.787	21	4.9	mb							1			100	2
2009	5	22	19	24	19					USGS,NEIC	Mexico:Puebla	墨西哥:普埃布拉	18.11	-98.46	62	5.6	Mw	5										

时间						海啸				资料来源	震中				深度	震级	标度	烈度	死亡人数		受伤人数		经济损失		房屋毁坏		房屋受损	
年	月	日	时	分	秒	源	浪高	级I	级S		地名(英文)	地名(中文)	纬度(°)	经度(°)					数量/人	级别	数量/人	级别	数量/$ Mill	级别	数量/间	级别	数量/间	级别
Date						Tsunami				Information	Earthquake Epicenter				Depth	Mag	Scale	MMI	Deaths		Injuries		Damage		Houses Destroyed		Houses Damaged	
Year	Mo	Dy	Hr	Mn	Sec	Sr	Wh	mI	mS		Name(English)	Name(Chinese)	Latitude	Longitude					Num	Dd	Num	Dd	$ Mill	De	Num	Dh	Num	Dh
2009	5	24	16	17	51					*	Macedonia:Bogdanci	马其顿:博丹奇区	41.303	22.714		5.5	ML							2				3
2009	5	28	8	24	45	4	4			* NOAA	Honduras:Guanaja,Near Coast	洪都拉斯:瓜纳哈近海	16.72	-86.236	10	7.3	Mw	7	7	1	40	1		2	135	3	25	1
2009	5	29	6	20	15					*	Vanuatu Islands	瓦努阿图群岛	-17.026	168.329	13	5.7	Mw				10	1		1		2		
2009	6	2	2	17	4					*	Vanuatu Islands	瓦努阿图群岛	-17.757	167.949	15	6.3	Mw				4	1		1				2
2009	6	13	17	17	38					* USGS	Kazakhstan:Tekeli	哈萨克斯坦:铁克利	44.724	78.864	15	5.8	mb	7	1	1				1				2
2009	6	14	14	18	20					NEIC,USGS	Guatemala:Uspantán	危地马拉:乌斯潘坦	15.34	-90.58	42	5.1	Mw	6										
2009	6	22	19	28	5					USGS,NEIC	South of Alaska	阿拉斯加南部	61.94	-150.7	64	5.5	Mw	5										
2009	6	22	20	58	40					NEIC,USGS	Italy:L'Aquila	意大利:拉奎拉	42.45	13.36	14	4.7	Mw	6										
2009	6	23	7	37	18					USGS,NEIC	Japan:Miyagi,Near Coast	日本:宫城近海	38.85	142.39	37	5.6	Mw	5										
2009	7	4	6	49	36					*	Panama:Panama City	巴拿马:巴拿马城	9.59	-78.966	38	6.1	Mw	5			32	1		1			10	1
2009	7	9	11	19	16					* China,USGS,Dis	China:Yunnan,Yaoan	中国:云南姚安	25.632	101.095	7	6	Ms	8	1		372	3	312	5	10692	5	74736	5
2009	7	15	9	22	29	4	0.5			* NOAA	New Zealand:South Island,Anchor Island	新西兰:南岛,安克岛	-45.762	166.562	12	7.8	Mw	6						1				
2009	7	15	10	37	34					USGS	China:Taiwan,Hualien	中国:台湾花莲	23.76	121.57	10	4.6	mb	6										
2009	7	24	3	11	57					* CNS	China:Xizang (Tibet),Coqen	中国:西藏措勤	31.158	85.902	13	6	Ms							1	6	1		1
2009	7	26	6	10	58					USGS	China:Taiwan,Hualien,Coast of E.	中国:台湾花莲以东海域	23.43	121.51	7	5	mb	6										
2009	7	26	8	51	28					USGS	Philippines:Mindanao Island	菲律宾:棉兰老岛	11.01	124.02	102	4.6	mb	6										
2009	8	8	13	26	18					* China,Dis	China:Chongqing,Rongchang	中国:重庆荣昌	29.358	105.438	5	4.4	Ms	6	2	1	1	1	3.32	2	440	3		
2009	8	10	19	55	36	3	0			* NOAA	India:Andaman Islands	印度:安达曼群岛	14.099	92.888	5	7.6	Ms	5										
2009	8	10	20	7	9	4	0.6			* NOAA	Japan:Makinohara	日本:静冈牧之原	34.743	138.264	40	6.4	Mw	8	1	1	123	3		3	5192	4		
2009	8	12	22	48	51					NEIC	Japan Trench	日本海沟	32.82	140.4	53	6.6	Mw	6										
2009	8	16	7	38	22	4	0.2			* NOAA	Indonesia:Southern Sumatra	印度尼西亚:苏门答腊南部	-1.479	99.49	20	6.7	Ms	5			9	1						
2009	8	28	1	52	7					* China,Dis	China:Qinghai,Haixi,NW.	中国:青海海西西北	37.696	95.718	10	6.4	Ms	7					16.2	3	15	1	60	2
2009	8	30	19	27	49					*	Myanmar:Sagaing,N.	缅甸:实皆北部	25.28	95.101	82	5.2	mb							1				
2009	9	2	7	55	1					*	Indonesia:Java Island	印度尼西亚:爪哇岛	-7.782	107.297	46	7	Ms	7	81	2	1297	4		3			54000	5
2009	9	6	21	49	42					USGS,NEIC	Albania:Peshkopi	阿尔巴尼亚:佩什科比	41.48	20.39	3	5.5	Mw	5										
2009	9	6	22	41	37					*	Georgia:Kutaisi	格鲁吉亚:库塔伊西	42.66	43.443	15	6	Mw				1	1		2			1000	3
2009	9	8	18	51	23					USGS,NEIC	Indonesia:Sulawesi Utara	印度尼西亚:北苏拉威西	1.12	120.9	22	5.8	Mw	5										
2009	9	12	20	6	25					*	Venezuela:Carabobo	委内瑞拉:卡拉沃沃	10.705	-67.92	10	6.4	Ms	6			18	1		1			17	1
2009	9	13	0	13	21					USGS	Russia:Sakhalin Island	俄罗斯:库页岛(萨哈林岛)	46.89	142.23	30	4.8	mb	6										
2009	9	18	11	53	48					*	Philippines:Mindanao Island	菲律宾:棉兰老岛	6.513	124.715	10	5.7	Mw				91	2		1			76	2

时间 Date						海啸 Tsunami				资料来源 Information	震中 Earthquake Epicenter				深度 Depth	震级 Mag	标度 Scale	烈度 MMI	死亡人数 Deaths		受伤人数 Injuries		经济损失 Damage		房屋毁坏 Houses Destroyed		房屋受损 Houses Damaged	
年 Year	月 Mo	日 Dy	时 Hr	分 Mn	秒 Sec	源 Sr	浪高 Wh	级 I mI	级 S mS		地名(英文) Name(English)	地名(中文) Name(Chinese)	纬度(°) Latitude	经度(°) Longitude					数量/人 Num	级别 Dd	数量/人 Num	级别 Dd	数量/$ Mill $ Mill	级别 De	数量/间 Num	级别 Dh	数量/间 Num	级别 Dh
2009	9	18	23	6	58					* NEIC, USGS	Indonesia: Bali Island	印度尼西亚:巴厘岛	-9.138	115.593	79	6	mB	6			7	1		1				2
2009	9	21	8	53	6					*	Bhutan: Tashigang	不丹:塔希冈	27.332	91.437	14	6.1	Ms	6	11	1				3		3		3
2009	9	22	8	20	41					*	Australia: Mornington	澳大利亚:莫宁	-38.28	145.25		3.1	ML							1				
2009	9	29	17	48	11	4	16			* NEIC, NOAA	Samoa Islands	萨摩亚群岛	-15.489	-172.095	18	8.1	Ms	6	191	3	7	1	150	5				
2009	9	30	10	16	9	4	0.3			* NOAA	Indonesia: Southern Sumatra	印度尼西亚:苏门答腊南部	-0.72	99.867	81	7.5	Mw	7	1117	4	1214	4		4		3	181665	5
2009	10	1	1	52	27					*	Indonesia: Southern Sumatra	印度尼西亚:苏门答腊南部	-2.515	101.501	10	6.7	Ms		3	1			10.0	3		3		3
2009	10	3	17	36	6					NEIC	China: Taiwan, Hualien	中国:台湾花莲	23.63	121.45	28	6.1	Mw	6										
2009	10	7	22	3	14	4	0.3			* NEIC, NOAA	North Vanuatu Islands	瓦努阿图群岛北部	-13.006	166.51	45	7.7	Mw											
2009	10	9	18	11	40					* NEIC, USGS	Ecuador: Ambato	厄瓜多尔:安巴托	-0.962	-77.817	35	5.4	mb	6						1				
2009	10	22	19	51	28					* USGS	Afghan: Badakhshan	阿富汗:巴达赫尚	36.517	70.95	18	6.2	Mw		5	1				1				
2009	10	22	20	46	21					USGS	China: Taiwan, Hualien, Coast of E.	中国:台湾花莲以东海域	24.26	121.91	6	4.6	mb	6										
2009	10	29	17	0	39					*	Bhutan: Mongar, Pemagatsel, Tashigang	不丹:蒙加尔	27.262	91.417	26	5.3	mb							2	1	1	116	3
2009	11	1	21	7	23					* China, Dis	China: Yunnan, Binchuan	中国:云南宾川	25.919	100.748	25	5	Ms	6			31	1	35.9	4	1403	4	8524	4
2009	11	3	23	26	52					*	Iran: Hormozgan	伊朗:荷姆兹甘	27.334	56.202	14	5.1	mb				269	3		1				1
2009	11	5	9	32	54					CSN, USGS	China: Taiwan, Nantou	中国:台湾南投	23.84	120.7	10	6	Mw	8										
2009	11	5	11	34	19					USGS	China: Taiwan, Nantou	中国:台湾南投	23.66	120.84	10	5.5	mb	7										
2009	11	6	8	49	52					NEIC, USGS	Argentina: Jujuy	阿根廷:胡胡伊	-23.44	-64.46	5	5.5	Mw	6										
2009	11	8	19	41	43					*	Indonesia: Sumbawa	印度尼西亚:松巴哇	-8.207	118.631	18	6.6	Mw	5	2	1	200	3	2.43	2				2
2009	11	11	13	48	19					USGS	Philippines: Mindanao Island	菲律宾:棉兰老岛	9.36	125.53	23	5.7	Mw	6										
2009	11	16	19	58	60					USGS	Philippines: Mindanao Island	菲律宾:棉兰老岛	6.6	126.25	74	5.1	mb	6										
2009	11	26	19	8	11					USGS, NEIC	Guatemala: Near Coast	危地马拉:近海	13.51	-89.91	56	5.9	Mw	5										
2009	11	27	8	15	53					*	Venezuela: Lara	委内瑞拉:拉腊	10.434	-69.715	7	5.4	Mw							1				
2009	12	6	21	51	60					*	South Africa: Carletonville	南非:卡尔顿维尔	-26.414	27.494	2	3.5	ML		2	1	3	1						
2009	12	8	3	8	57					*	Malawi: Karonga	马拉维:卡朗加	-9.948	33.878	8	5.9	Ms		1	1	15	1		3			3000	4
2009	12	12	11	51	26					*	India: Maharashtra	印度:马哈拉施特拉邦	17.109	73.767	10	5.1	mb							1				2
2009	12	17	1	37	48					USGS, NEIC	Steait of Gibraltar, Coast W.	直布罗陀海峡西部海域	36.46	-9.9	19	5.6	Mw	5										
2009	12	17	23	45	36					* USGS	Japan: Ito	日本:静冈伊东	34.921	139.261	7	4.9	mb	6			7	1		1			20	1
2009	12	19	13	2	17					* CNS, NEIC	China: Taiwan, Hualien	中国:台湾花莲	23.796	121.605	57	6.6	Ms	6			14	1		1				1
2009	12	19	23	19	16					*	Malawi: Karonga	马拉维:卡朗加	-10.108	33.818	6	6	Ms		3	1	250	3		3	1111	4	3565	4
2009	12	23	1	11	58					NEIC	Indonesia: Southern Sumatra	印度尼西亚:苏门答腊南部	-1.43	99.39	19	6	Mw	6										
2009	12	24	14	1	59					USGS, NEIC	Peru: Chaparra	秘鲁:查帕拉	-15.77	-73.98	59	5.6	Mw	5										
2009	12	29	11	47	35					NEIC, USGS	Chile: Tome	智利:托梅	-36.67	-72.92	28	6.1	Mw	6										

时间						海啸				资料来源	震中				深度	震级	标度	烈度	死亡人数		受伤人数		经济损失		房屋毁坏		房屋受损	
年	月	日	时	分	秒	源	浪高	级 I	级 S		地名(英文)	地名(中文)	纬度(°)	经度(°)					数量/人	级别	数量/人	级别	数量/$ Mill	级别	数量/间	级别	数量/间	级别
Date						Tsunami				Information	Earthquake Epicenter				Depth	Mag	Scale	MMI	Deaths		Injuries		Damage		Houses Destroyed		Houses Damaged	
Year	Mo	Dy	Hr	Mn	Sec	Sr	Wh	mI	mS		Name(English)	Name(Chinese)	Latitude	Longitude					Num	Dd	Num	Dd	$ Mill	De	Num	Dh	Num	Dh
2009	12	30	18	48	58					* USGS	Mexico: Mexicali	墨西哥:墨西卡利	32. 437	-115. 165	9	5. 9	Mw	6						1				2
2009	12	31	9	57	30					* NEIC	Bhutan: Tashigang	不丹:塔希冈	27. 319	91. 51	10	5. 5	mb				2	1		2			700	3
2010	1	2	2	15	12					*	Tajikistan: Deh	塔吉克斯坦:代赫	38. 245	71. 467	47	5. 4	mb						1. 5	2	98	2	1000	3
2010	1	2	20	20	18					USGS	Chile: Purén	智利:普伦	-38. 31	-73. 27	24	7. 1	Mw	6										
2010	1	3	4	11	39					USGS	Bismarck Sea	俾斯麦海	-5. 3	145. 86	34	5. 8	Mw	5										
2010	1	3	21	48	5	4	0			* NOAA	Solomon Islands	所罗门群岛	-8. 743	157. 477	26	6. 6	Mw											
2010	1	3	22	36	28	4	3			* NOAA	Solomon Islands	所罗门群岛	-8. 799	157. 346	25	7. 1	Ms	6						1	16	1	60	2
2010	1	5	12	15	32	4	0			* NOAA	Solomon Islands	所罗门群岛	-9. 019	157. 551	15	6. 8	Mw											
2010	1	10	0	25	4					*	Indonesia: Java Island	印度尼西亚:爪哇岛	-7. 907	107. 879	65	5. 1	mb		1	1	2	1						
2010	1	10	0	27	39					* USGS	US: California, North Coast	美国:加利福尼亚州北部近海	40. 652	-124. 692	29	6. 5	Mw	7			30	1	21. 8	3				
2010	1	12	21	53	10	4	3			* NOAA	Haiti: Port - Au - Prince	海地:太子港	18. 443	-72. 571	13	7. 3	Ms	10	222570	5	300000	5	8000	5	97294	5	188383	5
2010	1	13	17	18	8					USGS	Indonesia: Irian Jaya Barat	印度尼西亚:西巴布亚	-0. 69	133. 33	10	5. 7	Mw	5										
2010	1	15	18	0	47					*	Venezuela: Cariaco	委内瑞拉:卡利亚科	10. 454	-63. 475	8	5. 5	Mw				11	1		1			3	1
2010	1	16	20	23	37					*	Iran: Khuzestan	伊朗:胡齐斯坦	32. 45	48. 3	5	5	mb							2			150	3
2010	1	17	9	37	26					* China, Dis	China: Guizhou, Anshun	中国:贵州安顺	25. 558	105. 804	27	4. 4	Ms		6	1	8	1						
2010	1	18	15	40	26					USGS	Guatemala: Near Coast	危地马拉:近海	13. 73	-90. 13	54	5. 9	Mw	6										
2010	1	25	7	15	9					USGS	Japan: Kagoshima, Near Coast of S.	日本:鹿岛南部近海	30. 96	130. 89	38	5. 5	Mw	5										
2010	1	28	16	12	52					USGS	Indonesia: Sumatera, Aceh	印度尼西亚:苏门答腊,亚齐	4. 64	96. 83	8	4. 8	mb	6										
2010	1	30	21	36	58					* China, Dis	China: Sichuan, Suining, S.	中国:四川遂宁南	30. 258	105. 726	10	5	Ms	7	1	1	16	1	43. 1	4	200	3		
2010	2	4	20	20	22					USGS	US: California, North Coast	美国:加利福尼亚州北部近海	40. 41	-124. 96	23	5. 9	Mw	5										
2010	2	9	0	47	41					USGS	Mexico: Near Coast of Oaxaca	墨西哥:瓦哈卡近海	15. 89	-96. 86	39	5. 7	Mw	5										
2010	2	22	13	32	23					China, Dis	China: Chongqing, Rongchang	中国:重庆荣昌	29. 36	105. 46	30	4. 2	Ms						2. 65	2				
2010	2	25	4	56	56					* China, Dis	China: Yunnan, Yuanmou	中国:云南元谋	25. 562	101. 93	36	5. 1	Ms	6			35	1	51. 9	4				1
2010	2	26	20	31	27	3	0. 1			* NOAA, USGS	Ryukyu Islands	琉球群岛	25. 931	128. 427	22	7	Ms	5			2	1		1				
2010	2	27	6	34	14	4	11			* NOAA, USGS	Chile: Maule	智利:马利	-35. 846	-72. 719	35	8. 8	Mw	9	521	3	12000	5	30000	5			500000	5
2010	2	27	15	45	36					* USGS	Argentina: Salta	阿根廷:萨尔塔	-24. 754	-65. 453	10	6. 3	mB	5	2	1	2	1						
2010	2	27	19	0	7					USGS	Chile: Near Coast of C.	智利:中部近海	-33. 42	-71. 83	31	6. 3	Mw	7										
2010	2	28	11	25	36					USGS	Chile: Talca	智利:塔尔卡	-34. 9	-71. 62	46	6. 2	Mw	6										
2010	3	2	2	51	21					USGS	Philippines: Santa Ana	菲律宾:圣安娜	18. 18	122. 4	17	5. 8	Mw	5										
2010	3	3	17	44	25					USGS	Chile: Near Coast of C.	智利:中部近海	-36. 61	-73. 36	20	6. 1	Mw	6										
2010	3	3	19	58	30					USGS	Chile: Near Coast of C.	智利:中部近海	-33. 41	-71. 87	38	5. 8	Mw	5										
2010	3	4	0	18	51					* USGS, Dis	China: Taiwan, Kaohsiung	中国:台湾高雄	22. 92	120. 79	21	6. 3	Mw	8			96	2	174	5			340	3
2010	3	5	3	34	29					USGS	Chile: Rancagua	智利:兰卡瓜	-34. 55	-71. 85	8	5. 7	mb	5										
2010	3	5	9	19	36					USGS	Chile: Near Coast of C.	智利:中部近海	-36. 63	-73. 22	29	6. 1	Mw	6										

时间 Date						海啸 Tsunami				资料来源 Information	震中 Earthquake Epicenter				深度 Depth	震级 Mag	标度 Scale	烈度 MMI	死亡人数 Deaths		受伤人数 Injuries		经济损失 Damage		房屋毁坏 Houses Destroyed		房屋受损 Houses Damaged	
年 Year	月 Mo	日 Dy	时 Hr	分 Mn	秒 Sec	源 Sr	浪高 Wh	级 I mI	级 S mS		地名(英文) Name(English)	地名(中文) Name(Chinese)	纬度(°) Latitude	经度(°) Longitude					数量/人 Num	级别 Dd	数量/人 Num	级别 Dd	数量/$ Mill $ Mill	级别 De	数量/间 Num	级别 Dh	数量/间 Num	级别 Dh
2010	3	5	11	47	7					USGS	Chile: Near Coast of C.	智利:中部近海	-36.67	-73.37	18	6.6	Mw	6										
2010	3	8	2	32	34					* USGS	Turkey: Elazig	土耳其:埃拉泽	38.876	39.992	12	6.1	Mw	6	51	2	100	2		2	287	3	700	3
2010	3	9	5	53	28					USGS	Chile: Lota	智利:洛塔	-37.1	-73.32	10	4.8	mb	6										
2010	3	11	14	39	44	4	0.1			* NOAA, USGS	Chile: Rancagua	智利:兰卡瓜	-34.259	-71.929	11	7	Ms	7						1				
2010	3	11	20	11	20					USGS	Chile: Rancagua	智利:兰卡瓜	-34.38	-71.98	8	5.6	Mw	5										
2010	3	12	16	50	2					USGS	Chile: Rancagua	智利:兰卡瓜	-34.23	-71.92	7	5.8	Mw	5										
2010	3	13	3	15	1					USGS	Chile: Near Coast of C.	智利:中部近海	-36.69	-73.61	15	5.1	mb	6										
2010	3	14	20	4	55					USGS	Chile: Carahue	智利:卡拉韦	-38.53	-73.53	13	5.6	Mw	5										
2010	3	16	2	21	58					USGS	Chile: Near Coast of C.	智利:中部近海	-36.22	-73.26	18	6.7	Mw	6										
2010	3	20	18	8	9					USGS	Cuba: Near Coast of S.	古巴:南部近海	19.67	-75.33	14	5.6	Mw	5										
2010	3	21	18	31	4					USGS	Chile: Near Coast of C.	智利:中部近海	-36.34	-73.16	36	5.5	Mw	5										
2010	3	22	19	58	15					USGS	Philippines: Laoag	菲律宾:佬沃	18.47	120.74	47	5.9	Mw	6										
2010	3	25	2	58	17					USGS	Chile: Talca	智利:塔尔卡	-35.11	-71.95	37	4.7	mb	6										
2010	3	26	14	52	7					USGS	Chile: Copiapo	智利:科皮亚波	-27.95	-70.82	42	6.3	Mw	6										
2010	3	29	7	35	6					USGS	Chile: Vichuquén	智利:比丘肯	-34.88	-71.93	34	5.4	Mw	6										
2010	3	30	16	54	47					* USGS	India: Andaman Islands	印度:安达曼群岛	13.667	92.831	34	6.7	Mw	5			10	1		2				3
2010	4	2	22	58	8					USGS	Chile: Concepcion	智利:康塞普西翁	-36.23	-72.88	24	6	Mw	6										
2010	4	4	13	46	45					China, Dis	China: Shanxi, Yanggao	中国:山西阳高	39.91	113.84	9	4.5	Ms						1.56	2				
2010	4	4	22	40	41					* USGS	Mexico: Mexicali	墨西哥:墨西卡利	32.128	-115.303	10	7.3	Ms	7	2	1	233	3		2				3
2010	4	5	3	15	25					USGS	US: California, El Centro	美国:加利福尼亚州埃尔森特罗	32.63	-115.78	3	4.5	mb	6										
2010	4	5	13	33	5					USGS	US: California, El Centro	美国:加利福尼亚州埃尔森特罗	32.64	-115.8	0	4.7	mb	6										
2010	4	5	22	36	57					USGS	Chile: Iquique	智利:伊基克	-19.86	-68.84	94	5.8	Mw	5										
2010	4	6	22	15	2	4	0.4			* NOAA, USGS	Indonesia: Off West Coast of N. Sumatera	印度尼西亚:北苏门答腊西部海域	2.36	97.132	31	7.9	Ms	5										
2010	4	9	22	23	3					USGS	Argentina: San Juan	阿根廷:圣胡安	-28.56	-68.12	117	5.8	Mw	5										
2010	4	10	15	6	34					USGS	Chile: Taltal	智利:塔尔塔尔	-25.68	-70.67	49	5.5	Mw	5										
2010	4	13	20	49	7					USGS	China: Taiwan, Taitung	中国:台湾台东	23.12	121.44	1	4.9	mb	6										
2010	4	13	23	49	37					* China, Dis	China: Qinghai, Yushu	中国:青海玉树	33.271	96.629	10	7.1	Ms	9	2968	4	11000	5	3347	5	15000	5		
2010	4	15	23	59	38					USGS	US: Utah, Randolph	美国:犹他州兰道夫	41.7	-111.09	7	4.6	Mw	6										
2010	4	18	1	49	39					USGS	Chile: Near Coast of C.	智利:中部近海	-37.16	-73.75	29	5.6	Mw	5										
2010	4	18	20	28	50					*	Afghan: Bamyan	阿富汗:巴米扬	35.697	67.654	10	5.7	mb		11	1	70	2		4	2000	4		
2010	4	20	0	17	8					*	Australia: Kalgoorlie	澳大利亚:卡尔古利	-30.53	121.653	10	5.2	mb				3	1		1				1
2010	4	23	10	3	6					USGS	Chile: Nacimiento	智利:纳西缅托	-37.53	-72.97	32	6	Mw	6										
2010	5	1	22	36	29					*	India: Chamoli	印度:查谟利	30.099	80.026	36	4.5	mb							1				
2010	5	2	14	52	40					USGS	Chile: Rancagua	智利:兰卡瓜	-34.23	-71.88	10	5.9	Mw	6										
2010	5	6	2	42	48					* USGS	Peru: Tacna	秘鲁:塔克纳	-18.058	-70.547	37	6.2	Mw	5			11	1		2				2
2010	5	8	5	39	28					USGS	Indonesia: Gulf of Tomini	印度尼西亚:托米尼湾	-0.73	122.49	20	5.7	Mw	6										

时间 Date 年 Year	月 Mo	日 Dy	时 Hr	分 Mn	秒 Sec	海啸 Tsunami 源 Sr	浪高 Wh	级 I mI	级 S mS	资料来源 Information	震中 Earthquake Epicenter 地名(英文) Name(English)	地名(中文) Name(Chinese)	纬度(°) Latitude	经度(°) Longitude	深度 Depth	震级 Mag	标度 Scale	烈度 MMI	死亡人数 Deaths 数量/人 Num	级别 Dd	受伤人数 Injuries 数量/人 Num	级别 Dd	经济损失 Damage 数量/$ Mill	级别 De	房屋毁坏 Houses Destroyed 数量/间 Num	级别 Dh	房屋受损 Houses Damaged 数量/间 Num	级别 Dh
2010	5	9	5	59	42					* USGS	Indonesia: Off West Coast of N. Sumatera	印度尼西亚:北苏门答腊西部海域	3.748	96.018	38	7.3	Ms	5						1				
2010	5	14	12	29	22					*	Algeria: Alger	阿尔及利亚:阿尔及尔	35.9	4.12	2	5.2	mb		2	1	43	1						
2010	5	16	5	16	10					*	Puerto Rico: Vega Baja	波多黎各:下维加	18.4	-67.07	113	5.8	Mw							1				1
2010	5	20	22	16	31					USGS	Costa Rica: Off Coast	哥斯达黎加:沿海	9.25	-84.3	21	5.9	Mw	5										
2010	5	29	11	46	50	5	0			* NOAA	Mariana Islands	马里亚纳群岛	16.49	145.72	10	4.4	Mw											
2010	5	31	10	16	2					USGS	Philippines: Mindanao Island	菲律宾:棉兰老岛	6.95	124	35	5.9	Mw	5										
2010	6	1	16	5	30					USGS	Chile: Near Coast of C.	智利:中部近海	-36.82	-73.5	14	5.6	Mw	5										
2010	6	2	9	28	53					USGS	Papua New Guinea: West New Britain	巴布亚新几内亚:西新不列颠	-6.16	149.41	34	5.9	Mw	5										
2010	6	5	12	58	11					China, Dis	China: Shanxi, Yangqu	中国:山西阳曲	38.19	112.64	6	4.6	Ms						0.63	1				
2010	6	10	6	38	2					China, Dis	China: Xinjiang, Ulugqat	中国:新疆乌恰	39.89	74.7	9	5.1	Ms	6					3.53	2				
2010	6	10	9	46	54					USGS	Argentina: San Juan, N.	阿根廷:圣胡安北部	-29.19	-68.16	43	4.8	mb	6										
2010	6	12	19	26	50	4				* NOAA, USGS	India: Andaman - Nicobar Islands	印度:安达曼-尼科巴群岛	7.748	91.938	35	7.5	Mw	6										
2010	6	15	4	26	58					* USGS	US: California, Seeley	美国:加利福尼亚州西利	32.7	-115.92	5	5.8	Mw	7						1				1
2010	6	16	3	16	29					* USGS	Indonesia: Pulau Japen	印度尼西亚:亚彭岛	-2.141	136.46	29	7	Mw	6	17	1				3	2556	4		
2010	6	18	23	9	31					* USGS	India: Andaman Islands	印度:安达曼群岛	13.2	93.09	20	5.9	Mw	6						1				
2010	6	22	23	14	11					*	India: Haldwani	印度:赫尔德瓦	29.872	80.428	16	5.2	Ms							1		1		1
2010	6	23	17	41	41					* USGS	Canada: Ottawa	加拿大:渥太华	45.904	-75.497	16	5.2	Mw	6						1				
2010	6	29	1	40	1					USGS	Chile: Canete	智利:卡涅特	-37.84	-73.28	17	5.5	Mw	6										
2010	6	30	7	22	28					* USGS	Mexico: Qaxaca	墨西哥:瓦哈卡	16.4	-97.78	20	6.3	Mw	7	1	1								
2010	7	7	23	53	34					USGS	US: California, Thermal	美国:加利福尼亚州瑟默尔	33.42	-116.49	14	5.5	Mw	6										
2010	7	8	19	43	38					USGS	China: Taiwan, Hualien, Coast of E.	中国:台湾花莲以东海域	24.42	122.11	24	5.3	mb	6										
2010	7	14	8	32	21					USGS	Chile: Contulmo	智利:孔图尔莫	-38.07	-73.31	22	6.6	Mw	6										
2010	7	14	15	5	50					USGS	Chile: Contulmo	智利:孔图尔莫	-38.22	-73.23	35	5.8	Mw	6										
2010	7	17	6	7	43					USGS	Chile: Antofagasta, S.	智利:安托法加斯塔南部	-24.72	-69.84	49	5.5	Mw	5										
2010	7	18	13	34	59					USGS	Papua New Guinea: West New Britain	巴布亚新几内亚:西新不列颠	-5.93	150.59	35	7.3	Mw	7										
2010	7	20	19	38	9					*	Iran: Janah	伊朗:焦纳赫	27.009	53.855	10	5.8	Mw		1	1	32	1		2				3
2010	7	25	3	52	12					USGS	China: Taiwan, Pingtung	中国:台湾屏东	22.76	120.84	32	5.4	mb	6										
2010	7	30	13	50	13					*	Iran: Mashhad	伊朗:马什哈德	35.217	59.308	24	5.4	Mw				274	3		3				
2010	8	5	6	1	47					USGS	Chile: Curanilahue	智利:库拉尼拉韦	-37.44	-73.28	18	5.9	Mw	6										
2010	8	10	5	23	46	4				* NOAA, USGS	Vanuatu Islands	瓦努阿图群岛	-17.561	168.028	35	7.3	Mw	7										
2010	8	12	11	54	16					* USGS	Ecuador: Pastaza	厄瓜多尔:帕斯塔萨	-1.27	-77.31	206	7.1	Mw							1				

时间						海啸				资料来源	震中				深度	震级	标度	烈度	死亡人数		受伤人数		经济损失		房屋毁坏		房屋受损	
年	月	日	时	分	秒	源	浪高	级I	级S		地名(英文)	地名(中文)	纬度(°)	经度(°)					数量/人	级别	数量/人	级别	数量/$ Mill	级别	数量/间	级别	数量/间	级别
Date						Tsunami				Information	Earthquake Epicenter				Depth	Mag	Scale	MMI	Deaths		Injuries		Damage		Houses Destroyed		Houses Damaged	
Year	Mo	Dy	Hr	Mn	Sec	Sr	Wh	mI	mS		Name(English)	Name(Chinese)	Latitude	Longitude					Num	Dd	Num	Dd	$ Mill	De	Num	Dh	Num	Dh
2010	8	13	21	19	33	4	0.1			* NOAA, USGS	Guam, SW.	关岛(西太平洋)西南	12.503	141.474	10	6.9	Mw											
2010	8	27	19	23	48					*	Iran: Damghan	伊朗:达姆甘	35.457	54.55	10	5.7	Mw		3	1	200	3		2	700	3		
2010	8	29	0	53	27					China, Dis	China: Yunnan, Qiaojia	中国:云南巧家	27.13	103.02	10	4.8	Ms				17	1						
2010	9	3	16	35	44	1				* USGS	New Zealand: South Island, Christchurch	新西兰:南岛,基督城	-43.332	172.438	16	7	Mw	9						3				3
2010	9	3	17	6	51					USGS	Indonesia: Sumatera, Near West Coast	印度尼西亚:苏门答腊西部近海	-3.65	101.96	73	5.6	mb	5										
2010	9	4	4	55	56					USGS	New Zealand: South Island, Christchurch	新西兰:南岛,基督城	-43.57	171.97	5	5	mb	6										
2010	9	6	11	24	2					*	New Zealand: South Island, Christchurch	新西兰:南岛,基督城	-43.57	172.388	9	5	Mw	5						1				
2010	9	6	22	48	33					* USGS	New Zealand: North Island, Porangahau	新西兰:北岛,波朗阿豪	-40.433	176.818	21	5.1	Mw	6						1				
2010	9	7	19	49	57					* USGS	New Zealand: South Island, Christchurch	新西兰:南岛,基督城	-43.598	172.69	6	5	Mw	7						1				
2010	9	10	17	24	17					*	Bangladesh: Chandpur	孟加拉:坚德布尔	23.407	90.648	10	4.8	Mw	5						1				
2010	9	13	5	47	49					USGS	Japan: Hokkaido	日本:北海道	41.49	141.99	60	5.8	Mw	5										
2010	9	23	16	36	18					USGS	Chile: Hualane	智利:瓦拉涅	-34.91	-71.62	49	5.3	mb	6										
2010	9	27	11	22	44					*	Iran: Shiraz	伊朗:设拉子	29.651	51.69	18	5.5	Mw		1	1	3	1		1		1		
2010	9	28	17	33	52					USGS	China: Taiwan, Hualien, Coast of E.	中国:台湾花莲以东海域	24.09	121.74	5	4.7	Mw	6										
2010	9	29	8	0	1					USGS	Japan: Fukushima	日本:福岛	37.26	139.88	33	5.5	Mw	5										
2010	9	29	17	11	26					USGS	Indonesia: Banda Sea	印度尼西亚:班达海	-4.96	133.76	26	7	Mw	8										
2010	10	2	19	23	12					USGS	China: Taiwan, Yilan	中国:台湾宜兰	24.33	121.76	16	4.8	mb	6										
2010	10	3	0	26	54					USGS	Japan: Joetsu	日本:新潟上越	37.08	138.18	28	5	mb	6										
2010	10	9	1	54	5					USGS	Costa Rica: La Paz	哥斯达黎加:拉巴斯	10.21	-84.29	91	5.8	Mw	5										
2010	10	10	21	44	26					*	Pakistan: Haripur	巴基斯坦:赫里布尔	33.869	72.887	33	5.2	Mw		1	1	15	1		2			100	2
2010	10	21	2	49	56					USGS	Chile: Off Coast of C.	智利:中部沿海	-34.74	-73.72	10	5.9	Mw	5										
2010	10	22	19	31	38					USGS	Bolivia: Potosi, W.	玻利维亚:波托西西部	-20.85	-68.35	132	5.8	Mw	5										
2010	10	23	5	58	28					USGS	Chile: Canete	智利:卡涅特	-37.74	-73.36	15	5.5	Mw	5										
2010	10	24	8	58	55					China, Dis	China: Henan, Taikang	中国:河南太康	34.07	114.65	6	4.7	Ms				12	1	2.12	2				
2010	10	25	14	42	22	4	7			* NOAA, USGS	Indonesia: Southern Sumatra	印度尼西亚:苏门答腊南部	-3.484	100.114	21	7.8	Mw		431	3					700	3		
2010	11	2	10	38	25					USGS	Chile: San Carlos	智利:圣卡洛斯	-36.41	-71.78	75	4.5	mb	6										
2010	11	3	0	56	56					* USGS	Serbia: Kraljevo	塞尔维亚:克拉列沃	43.718	20.624	10	5.5	Mw	6	2	1	100	2		2				3
2010	11	6	3	52	20					*	Iran: Dorud	伊朗:道鲁德	33.37	48.94	5	4.9	Ms				104	3		1				2
2010	11	16	1	39	43					USGS	Indonesia: Papua	印度尼西亚:巴布亚	-1.99	139.02	13	5.9	Mw	5										
2010	11	21	12	31	45					USGS	China: Taiwan, Hualien	中国:台湾花莲	23.83	121.66	47	5.6	Mw	5										
2010	12	2	3	12	10					USGS	Papua New Guinea: West New Britain	巴布亚新几内亚:西新不列颠	-6	149.98	33	6.6	Mw	6										

年 Year	月 Mo	日 Dy	时 Hr	分 Mn	秒 Sec	海啸 Tsunami 源 Sr	浪高 Wh	级 I mI	级 S mS	资料来源 Information	震中 Earthquake Epicenter 地名(英文) Name(English)	地名(中文) Name(Chinese)	纬度(°) Latitude	经度(°) Longitude	深度 Depth	震级 Mag	标度 Scale	烈度 MMI	死亡人数 Deaths 数量/人 Num	级别 Dd	受伤人数 Injuries 数量/人 Num	级别 Dd	经济损失 Damage 数量/$ Mill $ Mill	级别 De	房屋毁坏 Houses Destroyed 数量/间 Num	级别 Dh	房屋受损 Houses Damaged 数量/间 Num	级别 Dh
2010	12	20	18	41	29					* USGS	Iran:Kerman	伊朗:克尔曼	28.491	59.117	12	6.7	Mw		11	1	40	1		3		3	1800	4
2010	12	21	17	19	10	4				* NOAA, USGS	Japan Trench	日本海沟	26.892	143.726	14	7.4	Mw											
2010	12	25	13	16	37	4				* NOAA, USGS	Vanuatu Islands	瓦努阿图群岛	-19.775	167.895	12	7.3	Mw											
2011	1	1	9	56	58					USGS,CSN	Argentina: Monte Quemado, S.	阿根廷:蒙特克马多南部	-26.79	-63.09	576	7	Mw	5										
2011	1	2	20	20	18					USGS,CSN	Chile:Concepcion,Near Coast	智利:康塞普西翁近海	-38.37	-73.35	24	7.1	Mw	7										
2011	1	5	16	32	25					* USGS	Iran:Fars,Shiraz	伊朗:法尔斯省设拉子	30.155	51.658	32	4.5	mb				16	1		2				
2011	1	9	10	3	44	4				* USGS, CSN, NOAA	Vanuatu Region	瓦努阿图地区	-19.16	168.31	24	6.6	Mw											
2011	1	10	6	2	52					USGS,CSN	Chile: Concepcion, Near Coast	智利:康塞普西翁近海	-35.59	-73.06	24	5.9	Mw	5										
2011	1	17	23	29	49					USGS,CSN	Chile:Coquimbo,S.	智利:科金博南部	-30.32	-71.51	65	5.6	Ms	5										
2011	1	18	20	23	23					* USGS,CSN	Pakistan:Quetta,SW.	巴基斯坦:奎达西南	28.732	63.928	68	7.2	Mw		1	1				2	200	3	200	3
2011	1	18	21	30	47					USGS,CSN	Chile:Tarapaca,N.	智利:塔拉帕卡北部	-19.2	-69.4	102	6	mb	5										
2011	1	21	15	36	9					USGS,CSN	Chile: San Antonio, Near Coast	智利:圣安东尼奥近海	-33.97	-72.24	11	5.5	Ms	5										
2011	1	29	17	41	37					* USGS	Hungary:Oroszlany	匈牙利:俄罗斯拉妮	47.561	18.317	1	4.3	Mw	5						1				1
2011	2	1	8	16	32					USGS,CSN	China:Taiwan,Hualien,Coast of E.	中国:台湾花莲以东海域	24.17	121.83	21	5.6	Ms	5										
2011	2	4	13	53	44					USGS,CSN	Myanmar:Sagaing,N.	缅甸:实皆北部	24.64	94.68	66	6.3	Mw	5										
2011	2	5	1	56	14					USGS	Japan:Yokohama,Near Coast	日本:神奈川横滨近海	34.77	140.35	65	5.2	mb	5										
2011	2	5	16	11	40					USGS,CSN	Chile:Concepcion,Near Coast	智利:康塞普西翁近海	-37.62	-73.45	28	5.7	Mw	5										
2011	2	8	13	3	31					USGS	Chile:Copiapo,SE.	智利:科皮亚波东南	-27.62	-69.52	94	5.4	Mw	5										
2011	2	10	2	12	25					USGS,CSN	Chile:Copiapo	智利:科皮亚波	-27.62	-70.32	61	5.5	Ms	5										
2011	2	10	13	3	3					USGS	Japan:Iwaki,Near Coast	日本:福岛磐城近海	37.14	141.28	33	5.3	Mw	5										
2011	2	11	20	5	30	4	0.2			* USGS,CSN	Chile: Concepcion, Near Coast	智利:康塞普西翁近海	-36.344	-72.959	18	6.8	Mw	6										
2011	2	11	23	39	21					USGS,CSN	Chile: Concepcion, Near Coast	智利:康塞普西翁近海	-37.2	-73.2	15	6	Mw	5										
2011	2	12	1	17	1					USGS,CSN	Chile:Concepcion	智利:康塞普西翁	-37.02	-72.95	16	6.1	Mw	6										
2011	2	13	8	51	34					USGS,CSN	Chile:Concepcion,Near Coast	智利:康塞普西翁近海	-36.56	-73.18	20	5.9	Mw	5										
2011	2	13	10	35	7					USGS,CSN	Chile:Concepcion,Near Coast	智利:康塞普西翁近海	-36.65	-73.18	17	6	Mw	6										
2011	2	13	13	44	36					USGS,CSN	Chile:Concepcion,Near Coast	智利:康塞普西翁近海	-36.56	-73.28	18	5.6	Mw	6										
2011	2	14	3	40	10					USGS,CSN	Chile:Talca,Near Coast	智利:塔尔卡近海	-35.38	-72.83	21	6.6	Mw	5										

时间 Date 年 Year	月 Mo	日 Dy	时 Hr	分 Mn	秒 Sec	海啸 Tsunami 源 Sr	浪高 Wh	级 I mI	级 S mS	资料来源 Information	震中 Earthquake Epicenter 地名(英文) Name(English)	地名(中文) Name(Chinese)	纬度(°) Latitude	经度(°) Longitude	深度 Depth	震级 Mag	标度 Scale	烈度 MMI	死亡人数 Deaths 数量/人 Num	级别 Dd	受伤人数 Injuries 数量/人 Num	级别 Dd	经济损失 Damage 数量/$ Mill	级别 De	房屋毁坏 Houses Destroyed 数量/间 Num	级别 Dh	房屋受损 Houses Damaged 数量/间 Num	级别 Dh
2011	2	14	21	56	45					USGS,CSN	Chile:Pica,NE.	智利:皮卡东北	-19.97	-68.83	105	5.5	mb	5										
2011	2	15	13	33	53					USGS,CSN	Indonesia:Lembo	印度尼西亚:伦博	-2.5	121.48	16	6.1	Mw	5										
2011	2	21	23	51	43					* USGS,CSN	New Zealand: South Island, Christchurch	新西兰:南岛,基督城	-43.6	172.71	5	6.3	Mw		140	3				3				
2011	2	26	20	38	2					USGS	Japan:Takayama	日本:岐阜高山	36.12	137.35	3	5.2	mb	5										
2011	2	28	1	29	25					USGS,CSN	Chile:Concepcion,Near Coast	智利:康塞普西翁近海	-37.36	-73.69	31	5.8	Mw	6										
2011	2	28	20	45	43					USGS	Chile:Pica,NE.	智利:皮卡东北	-20.39	-68.9	104	5.2	Mw	5										
2011	3	3	15	12	2					USGS	Philippines:Cantilan	菲律宾:坎蒂兰	9.46	125.94	52	5.5	Mw	6										
2011	3	6	12	31	60					USGS	Chile:Putre,NE.	智利:普特雷东北	-18.04	-69.34	118	6.3	Mw	6										
2011	3	9	2	45	18	4	0.6			* USGS	Japan:Miyagi,Coast of E.	日本:宫城东部海域	38.51	142.792	14	7.3	Mw	5										
2011	3	11	5	46	23	4	24			* USGS	Japan:Miyagi,Coast of E.	日本:宫城东部海域	38.322	142.369	32	9	Mw	12	27759	5	3006	4						
2011	3	11	6	15	40					USGS,CSN	Japan:Hitachi,Near Coast	日本:茨城日立近海	36.27	141.15	35	7.3	Mw	5										
2011	3	15	13	31	46					USGS	Japan:Fujinomiya	日本:静冈富士宫	35.3	138.54	9	6	Mw	5										
2011	3	19	9	56	48					USGS	Japan:Daigo	日本:茨城大子町	36.79	140.3	6	5.8	Mw	5										
2011	3	24	13	55	12					* USGS	Myanmar:Mong Hpayak	缅甸:孟帕亚	20.705	99.949	10	6.8	Mw		74	2	111	3		2			413	3
2011	4	1	10	49	49					USGS	Japan:Akita	日本:秋田	40.3	140.21	40	5	mb	7										
2011	4	1	11	57	54					USGS	Japan:Iwate,Kamaishi	日本:岩手釜石	39.32	141.95	41	6	Mw	5										
2011	4	1	13	29	11					USGS	Greece:Crete Island	希腊:克里特岛	35.66	26.56	59	6.1	Mw	6										
2011	4	2	10	59	37					USGS	Chile:Iquique,N.	智利:伊基克北部	-19.58	-69.07	83	6	Mw	6										
2011	4	3	7	38	46					USGS	Japan:Fukushima,Near Coast	日本:福岛近海	37.63	141.45	59	5.4	mb	5										
2011	4	3	20	6	41					USGS	Indonesia:Java Ridge	印度尼西亚:爪哇海岭	-9.83	107.73	14	6.8	Mw	5										
2011	4	7	13	11	23					USGS	Mexico:Coatzacoalcos	墨西哥:夸察夸尔科斯	17.38	-93.95	159	6.7	Mw	5										
2011	4	7	14	32	41					* USGS	Japan:Miyagi,Coast of E.	日本:宫城东部海域	38.253	141.64	49	7.1	Mw	7	3	1	93	2						
2011	4	9	9	42	22					USGS	Japan:Miyagi,Coast of E.	日本:宫城东部海域	38.28	141.7	65	5.4	mb	6										
2011	4	11	4	51	47					USGS	Japan:Fukushima,Near Coast	日本:福岛近海	37.5	141.22	40	5	mb	5										
2011	4	13	15	14	43					USGS	Chile:Near Coast of C.	智利:中部近海	-33.75	-71.84	34	5.1	mb	5										
2011	4	16	5	49	22					USGS	New Zealand: South Island, Christchurch	新西兰:南岛,基督城	-43.61	172.79	10	5	Mw	5										
2011	5	5	16	57	38					USGS	Aleutian Islands	阿留申群岛	55.08	-160.44	47	5.8	Mw	5										
2011	5	8	6	50	23					USGS	Greece:Kos Island	希腊:科斯岛	36.62	27.25	13	5.2	Mw	5										
2011	5	9	15	4	23					USGS	New Zealand: South Island, Christchurch	新西兰:南岛,基督城	-43.59	172.49	16	5	Mw	5										
2011	5	11	16	47	26					*	Spain: Lorca	西班牙:洛尔卡	37.7	-1.67	1	5.1	Ms		10	1				1		1		1
2011	5	13	22	47	57					USGS	Costa Rica:La Paz	哥斯达黎加:拉巴斯	10.06	-84.32	87	6	Mw	6										
2011	6	2	17	7	54					USGS	China:Taiwan,Taitung,Coast of E.	中国:台湾台东以东海域	22.28	121.38	41	5	mb	5										
2011	6	5	10	25	15					USGS	Chile:Talca	智利:塔尔卡	-35	-72.19	32	5.5	mb	7										
2011	6	5	21	9	55					USGS	New Zealand: South Island, Christchurch	新西兰:南岛,基督城	-43.58	172.39	8	5	Mw	5										

时间 年 Year	月 Mo	日 Dy	时 Hr	分 Mn	秒 Sec	海啸 Tsunami 源 Sr	浪高 Wh	级 I mI	级 S mS	资料来源 Information	震中 Earthquake Epicenter 地名(英文) Name(English)	地名(中文) Name(Chinese)	纬度(°) Latitude	经度(°) Longitude	深度 Depth	震级 Mag	标度 Scale	烈度 MMI	死亡人数 Deaths 数量/人 Num	级别 Dd	受伤人数 Injuries 数量/人 Num	级别 Dd	经济损失 Damage 数量/$ Mill $ Mill	级别 De	房屋毁坏 Houses Destroyed 数量/间 Num	级别 Dh	房屋受损 Houses Damaged 数量/间 Num	级别 Dh
2011	6	13	1	1	0					USGS	New Zealand: South Island, Christchurch	新西兰:南岛,基督城	-43.58	172.76	9	5.2	Mw	5										
2011	6	13	2	20	49					USGS	New Zealand: South Island, Christchurch	新西兰:南岛,基督城	-43.56	172.74	6	5.9	Mw	7										
2011	6	24	3	9	40					USGS	Andreanof Islands, Aleutian Is.	阿留申群岛,安德烈亚诺夫群岛	52.1	-171.87	58	7.2	Mw	6										
2011	6	26	12	16	39					USGS	Indonesia: Pulau Japen	印度尼西亚:亚彭岛	-2.39	136.64	17	6.3	Mw	5										

第二部分

全球巨大地震灾害(巨灾)信息目录

全球地震灾害中死亡人数超过1万人或经济损失超过$ 100 million(即1亿美元)的灾害信息目录

时间 Date 年 Year	月 Mo	日 Dy	时 Hr	分 Mn	秒 Sec	海啸 Tsunami 源 Sr	浪高 Wh	级 I mI	级 S mS	资料来源 Information	震中 Earthquake Epicenter 地名(英文) Name(English)	地名(中文) Name(Chinese)	纬度(°) Latitude	经度(°) Longitude	深度 Depth	震级 Mag	标度 Scale	烈度 MMI	死亡人数 Deaths 数量/人 Num	级别 Dd	受伤人数 Injuries 数量/人 Num	级别 Dd	经济损失 Damage 数量/$ Mill $ Mill	级别 De	房屋毁坏 Houses Destroyed 数量/间 Num	级别 Dh	房屋受损 Houses Damaged 数量/间 Num	级别 Dh
-33										* Song	Egypt:Yamit	埃及:耶米特	31.2	34.2		7.7	Mk	9	30000	5								
115	12	13				2				* NOAA	Turkey:Hatay	土耳其:哈塔伊	36.1	36.1		7.5	Ms	11	260000	5				4				
342										* Song	Turkey:Hatay	土耳其:哈塔伊	36.2	36.1		7.7	Mk		40000	5				4				
458	9									* GSHAP	Turkey:Hatay	土耳其:哈塔伊	36.2	36.4	20	7.7	Ms	10	80000	5				3				
525	5	29								* GSHAP	Turkey:Antakya, Samandag	土耳其:哈塔伊,沙满列	36.25	36.1	40	7.9	Ms	9.5	250000	5				4				
533	11	29								* Song	Syria:Halab (Aleppo)	叙利亚:阿勒颇	36.1	37.1		7.7	Mk		130000	5								
565										* Song	Turkey:Hatay	土耳其:哈塔伊	36.2	36.1		7.7	Mk		30000	5								
587	9	30								* Song	Turkey:Hatay	土耳其:哈塔伊	36.1	36.1		7.7	Mk	9	60000	5				4				
662	4	26								* Song	Iran:Semnan, Damghan	伊朗:塞姆南,达木罕	35.3	54		7.7	Mk		40000	5				3				
838	11	23								* Song	Uzbekistan:Fergana	乌兹别克斯坦:费尔干纳	40.4	71.3		7.7	Mk		15000	5				4				
844	9	18								* Song	Syria:Dimashq (Damascus)	叙利亚:大马士革	33.5	36.3		7.7	Mk	8	50000	5				4				
845	9	6								* Song	Iraq:Al – Mawsil (Mosul)	伊拉克:勿斯离(摩苏尔)	36.2	43.1		7.7	Mk		50000	5								
847										* Song	Iraq:Al – Mawsil(Mosul)	伊拉克:勿斯离(摩苏尔)	36.21	42.08		7.7	Mk	10	70000	5				3				
850	7	15								* Song	Iran:Tehran, Mahmudabad	伊朗:德黑兰,马哈茂达巴德	35.3	51.2		7.7	Mk		45000	5				3				
851										*	Armenia:Yerevan(Erivan)	亚美尼亚:耶烈万(叶里温)	40	44.6	10	5.2	Ms	8	12000	5				3				
856	12	3								* Song	Tunisia:Tunis	突尼斯:突尼斯	36.8	10.2		7.7	Mk	10	45000	5				4				
856	12	22								* Iran	Iran:Semnan, Dāmghān	伊朗:塞姆南,达姆甘	35.9	54		7.9	Ms	10	200000	5				4		4		
856	12									* Song	Greece:Korinthos, Patrai (Patras)	希腊:科林斯,帕特雷	37.9	22.9		7.7	Mk		45000	5								
858	1									*	Armenia:Yerevan	亚美尼亚:叶里温	40	44.6	10	5.2	Muk		12000	5				3				
871	11	18								*	Iran:Kermānshāh	伊朗:克尔曼沙赫	33.2	47.2		6.8	Ms	7	20000	5				4		4		
893	12	24								* Song	Armenia:Yerevan(Erivan)	亚美尼亚:耶烈万(叶里温)	40	44.6	10	7.7	Mk	10	180000	5				4		4		
1007	9	17								* Song	Iraq:Dinavar, Baghdad	伊拉克:迪娜,巴格达	33.2	44.2		7.7	Mk	8	16000	5				3				
1008	4	11				2				* NOAA, Song	Iran:Persian Gulf	伊朗:波斯湾	27.665	52.348		7.7	Mk		16000	5				4				
1033	12	10								* Song	Israel:Jerusalem	以色列:耶路撒冷	32	35		7.7	Mk	10	70000	5				3		3		
1038	1	15								* China	China:Shanxi, Dingxiang	中国:山西定襄	38.4	112.9		7.25	Ms	10	32300	5				4				
1042	8	21								* Song	Iran:Tabriz	伊朗:大不里士	38	46.2		7.7	Mk		40000	5				4				
1042	11	4	13	30						*	Iran:Tabriz	伊朗:大不里士	38.1	46.3	15	7.6	Muk	9	50000	5				4				
1057	3	30								* China	China:Beijing, Daxing	中国:北京大兴	39.7	116.3		6.75	Ms	9	25000	5				4				
1067	4	20								* *	Jordan:Aqaba	约旦:亚喀巴	29.5	35		6.5	Ms		25000	5				3				
1068	3	18				3			4	* NOAA, Song	Israel:Ramla	以色列:拉姆拉	31.92	34.85		7.2	Mk	9	25000	5				4		4		
1101										*	Iran:Neyshabur	伊朗:内沙布尔	36	59	10	6.5	Muk	10	60000	5				3				

时间 Date						海啸 Tsunami				资料来源	震中 Earthquake Epicenter				深度	震级	标度	烈度	死亡人数 Deaths		受伤人数 Injuries		经济损失 Damage		房屋毁坏 Houses Destroyed		房屋受损 Houses Damaged	
年	月	日	时	分	秒	源	浪高	级 I	级 S		地名(英文)	地名(中文)	纬度(°)	经度(°)					数量/人	级别	数量/人	级别	数量/$ Mill	级别	数量/间	级别	数量/间	级别
Year	Mo	Dy	Hr	Mn	Sec	Sr	Wh	mI	mS	Information	Name(English)	Name(Chinese)	Latitude	Longitude	Depth	Mag	Scale	MMI	Num	Dd	Num	Dd	$ Mill	De	Num	Dh	Num	Dh
1137										* Song	Italy:Sicily,Catania	意大利:西西里岛,卡塔尼亚	37.3	15.1		6.8	Mk		15000	5								
1139	9	30								* GSHAP	Azerbaijan:Gəncə	阿塞拜疆:占贾	40.3	46.3	16	7.3	Ms	11	230000	5				4				
1143	4									* China	China:Ningxia,Yinchuan	中国:宁夏银川	38.5	106.3		6.5	Ms	8	10000	5				3		3		
1158										* Song	Syria:Malatya,Dimashq	叙利亚:马拉蒂亚,大马士革	34.5	36.5		7.7	Mk		20000	5				4		4		
1169	2	4				5			4	* Italy,NOAA	Italy:Sicily,Siracusa (Syracuse)	意大利:西西里岛,锡拉库萨	37.32	15.03		7	Ms	11	16000	5				4				
1169										* Song	Syria:Halab (Aleppo),Dimashq	叙利亚:阿勒颇,大马士革	36.3	37.3		7.7	Mk	10	80000	5				3				
1183										* GSHAP	Syria:Aleppo	叙利亚:阿勒颇	36	36.3	12	6.3	Ms	9	20000	5				3				
1202	5	20				4			5	* NOAA	Syria:Dimashq (Damascus)	叙利亚:大马士革	33.5	36		7.6	Ms	11	1100000	5				4		4		
1219	6	9								* China	China:Ningxia,Guyuan,S.	中国:宁夏固原南	35.6	106.2		6.5	Ms	9	10000	5				4				
1222	12	25	11							* Italy	Italy:Brescia	意大利:布雷西亚	45.48	10.68		6.05	Ms	10	12000	5				4		4		
1268	9	10								* GSHAP	Turkey:Seyhan	土耳其:杰伊汗	37.5	35.5	12	6.2	Ms	9	50000	5								
1290	10	4								* China	China:Inner Mongolia,Ningcheng,W.	中国:内蒙古宁城西	41.6	119.3		6.75	Ms	9	100000	5				4				
1293	5	26	21			4		1	1	* Japan,NOAA	Japan:Kamakura	日本:神奈川镰仓	35.2	139.4		7.1	Ms		23024	5				3		3		
1299	6	4								Japan,Song	Japan:Osaka,Kinai	日本:大阪畿内	32	132		8	Mk		10000	5								
1336	10	21	1	30						*	Iran:Razavi Khorasan	伊朗:呼罗珊	34.7	59.7		7.6	Muk		20000	5				3				
1367										China	China:Shanxi,Taiyuan	中国:山西太原	37.9	112.5		5.5	Ms	7	10000	5								
1444										* Song	Turkey:Nemrut Mtns	土耳其:尼姆鲁特山	38.7	42.2		7.7	Mk		30000	5								
1455	12	5								* Song	Italy:Napoli (Naples)	意大利:那不勒斯(拿坡里)	40.4	14.1		6.8	Mk		40000	5								
1456	12	5	4	30		2			4	* Italy,NOAA	Italy:Benevento,Campobasso	意大利:贝内文托,坎布巴索	41.15	14.867		6.96	Ms	11	30000	5				4				
1457										* Song	Egypt:Yamit	埃及:耶米特	31.2	34.2		7.7	Mk		32000	5								
1458										* Turkey	Turkey:Erzincan	土耳其:埃尔津占	39.9	40.4		7.5	Ms	10	32000	5				3				
1481	5	3				2	1.8	1.8	3	* NOAA	Greece:Dodecanese Islands	希腊:多德卡尼斯群岛	36	28		7.1	Ms	10	30000	5				4				
1482										*	Turkey:Erzincan,Erzurum	土耳其:埃尔津占,埃尔佐鲁姆	39.9	40.4		7.5	Muk	10	30000	5				3				
1498	9	20				4	10	3	4	* Japan, Usami,NOAA	Japan:Shizuoka,Near Coast	日本:静冈近海	34	138.1		8.6	Ms	11	26000	5				4	5000	4		
1500	1	13								* China	China:Yunnan,Yiliang	中国:云南宜良	24.9	103.1		7	Ms	9	10000	5								
1509	9	14				3			3	* NOAA,GSHAP	Turkey:Istanbul	土耳其:伊斯坦布尔	40.7	29.3		7.7	Ms	11	13000	5				4	1700	4		
1522										* * Song	Iran:Tabriz	伊朗:大不里士	38	46.2		7.7	Mk		70000	5				3				
1531	1	26				1				* NOAA,Song	Portugal:Lisbon	葡萄牙:里斯本	38.7	−9.1		8	Mk	10	30000	5				3	1500	4		
1556	2	2								* China	China:Shaanxi,Huaxian	中国:陕西华县	34.5	109.7		8.25	Ms	11	830000	5				4				
1622	10	25								* China	China:Ningxia,Haiyuan,N.	中国:宁夏固原北	36.5	106.3		7	Ms	10	12000	5				4	11800	5		

时间 年 Year	月 Mo	日 Dy	时 Hr	分 Mn	秒 Sec	海啸 源 Sr	浪高 Wh	级 I mI	级 S mS	资料来源 Information	震中 地名(英文) Name(English)	地名(中文) Name(Chinese)	纬度(°) Latitude	经度(°) Longitude	深度 Depth	震级 Mag	标度 Scale	烈度 MMI	死亡人数 数量/人 Num	级别 Dd	受伤人数 数量/人 Num	级别 Dd	经济损失 数量/$ Mill	级别 De	房屋毁坏 数量/间 Num	级别 Dh	房屋受损 数量/间 Num	级别 Dh
1626	7	30								* Italy	Italy:Napoli (Naples)	意大利:那不勒斯	41.73	15.35		6.73	Ms		70000	5				3				
1638	3	27	15			2			5	* Italy, NOAA	Italy:Calabria, Cosenza	意大利:卡拉布里亚,科森扎	39.3	16.2		7	Ms	11	19000	5				4				
1639	5	4								* Song	Iran:Qazvin	伊朗:加兹温	36.2	50		7.7	Mk		12000	5				3				
1641	2	5								* Iran	Iran:Tabriz	伊朗:大不里士	37.9	46.1		6.8	Ms	9	30000	5				3				
1654	7	21								* China	China:Gansu, Tianshui, S.	中国:甘肃天水南	34.3	105.5		8	Ms	11	10400	5				4		4		
1654										* Song	Peru:Lima	秘鲁:利马	-12.1	-76.6		7.7	Mk		11000	5								
1656										* Song	Peru:Lima, Near Coast	秘鲁:利马近海	-12.5	-77		7.7	Mk		11000	5				2				
1657										* Song	Peru:Lima	秘鲁:利马	-12.4	-76.8		7.7	Mk		11000	5								
1667	11	18								* Song	Iran:Bojnurd	伊朗:博季努尔德	37.2	57.5		7.7	Mk		12000	5				3				
1667	12	17								* GSHAP	Azerbaijan:Samaxi	阿塞拜疆:沙马基区	40.6	48.6	12	6.9	Ms	10	80000	5				4		4		
1668	7	10				3			2	* NOAA	Turkey:Izmir	土耳其:伊兹密尔	38.4	26.9		6.6	Ms	10	17500	5				3				
1668	7	25				3				* China, NOAA	China:Shandong, Tancheng	中国:山东郯城	34.8	118.5		8.5	Ms	12	42578	5				4		4		
1679	9	2								* China	China:Hebei, Shanhe - Pinggu	中国:河北三河平谷	40	117		8	Ms	11	13162	5				4		4		
1688	7	5								* Song	Turkey:Izmir	土耳其:伊兹密尔	38.3	27.1		7.7	Mk		15000	5								
1688	7	10	11	45		2			2	* NOAA	Turkey:Izmir	土耳其:伊兹密尔	38.4	26.9		7	Ms	10	16000	5				3		3		3
1693	1	11	13	30		5			4	* Italy, NOAA	Italy:Sicily, Calabria, Catania	意大利:西西里岛,卡拉布里亚,卡塔尼亚	37.13	15.02		7.41	Ms	11	93000	5				4	972	3		
1695	5	18								* China	China:Shanxi, Linfen	中国:山西临汾	36	111.5		7.75	Ms	10	20000	5				4		4		
1703	1	14	18							* Italy, GSHAP	Italy:Norcia, L'Aquila	意大利:诺尔恰,拉奎拉	42.68	13.12		6.81	Ms	11	40000	5				4				
1707	10	28	5			5	25.7	3.5	4	* Usami, Japan, NOAA	Japan:Tokushima, Near Coast	日本:德岛近海	33.2	134.8		8.4	Muk	11	30000	5				4	29000	5		
1716	5									* Song	Algeria:Algiers	阿尔及利亚:阿尔及尔	36.8	3		7.7	Mk		20000	5				4				
1718	6	19								* China	China:Gansu, Tongwei, S.	中国:甘肃通渭南	35	105.2		7.5	Ms	10	73000	5				4		4		
1721	4	26	3							* GSHAP	Iran:Tabriz	伊朗:大不里士	37.9	46.7	15	7.7	Ms		40000	5				4		4		
1727	11	18								* Song	Iran:Tabriz	伊朗:大不里士	38	46.2		7.7	Mk	8	77000	5				4				
1730	12	30								* * Song	Japan:Hokkaido	日本:北海道	43.3	142.5		7.7	Mk		137000	5								
1737	10	11				4				* GSHAP	Myanmar:Sagaing	缅甸:实皆	24.4	95.2		7.5	Ms		300000	5								
1739	1	3								* China	China:Ningxia, Pingluo	中国:宁夏平罗	38.8	106.5		8	Ms	10	50000	5				4		4		
1752	6	21				2			3	* GSHAP, NOAA	Syria:Hamah (Hama)	叙利亚:哈马	35	36		7	Ms	9	20000	5								
1752										* Song	Egypt:Yamit	埃及:耶米特	31.2	34.2		7.7	Mk	8	20000	5								
1754	9	2	21	30		2				* GSHAP, NOAA	Egypt:Al - Qahirah (Cairo)	埃及:开罗	30.8	31		7.2	Ms		40000	5				3				
1755	6	7								* Iran	Iran:Kashan	伊朗:卡尚	34	51.4		5.9	Ms		40000	5				3				
1755	11	1	8	50		4	30	3.6		* NOAA	Steait Of Gibraltar, W.	直布罗陀海峡西部	36	-11		8.5	Ms	11	60000	5				4				
1757	8	6								* Song	Italy:Siracusa (Syracuse)	意大利:锡拉库萨(锡拉丘兹)	37	15		6.6	Mk	10	10000	5				3				
1759	11	25								* Song	Lebanon:Sur (Tyre)	黎巴嫩:苏尔	33.3	35.7		7.7	Mk		30000	5								
1771	4	24				4	85	6.4	6	* Usami, Japan, NOAA	Ryukyu Islands	琉球群岛	24	124.3		7.4	Ms	10	13486	5				4	3237	4		

年 Year	月 Mo	日 Dy	时 Hr	分 Mn	秒 Sec	源 Sr	浪高 Wh	级I mI	级S mS	资料来源 Information	地名(英文) Name(English)	地名(中文) Name(Chinese)	纬度(°) Latitude	经度(°) Longitude	深度 Depth	震级 Mag	标度 Scale	烈度 MMI	死亡人数 Deaths 数量/人 Num	死亡人数 Deaths 级别 Dd	受伤人数 Injuries 数量/人 Num	受伤人数 Injuries 级别 Dd	经济损失 Damage 数量/$ Mill	经济损失 Damage 级别 De	房屋毁坏 Houses Destroyed 数量/间 Num	房屋毁坏 Houses Destroyed 级别 Dh	房屋受损 Houses Damaged 数量/间 Num	房屋受损 Houses Damaged 级别 Dh
1778	1	30								* Song	Iran:Esfahan	伊朗:伊斯法罕	33.6	51.3		7.7	Mk		30000	5				3				
1779	12	27								*	Iran:Tabriz	伊朗:大不里士	38	46.7		6.5	Muk	7	10000	5				3				
1780	1	8	19	30						*	Iran:Tabriz	伊朗:大不里士	38	46.2	20	7.7	Muk	9	200000	5				4		4		
1783	2	5	12			4			4	* Italy, NOAA	Italy:Sicily, Messina	意大利:西西里岛,墨西拿	38.3	15.97	13	6.91	Ms	11	30000	5				4		4		
1792	5	21	9			5	55	3.5	3	* Usami, Japan, NOAA	Japan:Nagasaki	日本:长崎	32.8	130.3		6.4	Ms		15030	5		3		3	6200	4		
1797	2	4	12	30						* GSHAP	Ecuador:Chimborazo, N.	厄瓜多尔:钦博腊索山北部	-1.7	-78.7		8.3	Muk	11	40000	5				4				
1797	12	4								* Song	Venezuela:Cumana, Cariaco	委内瑞拉:库马纳,卡利亚科	10.5	-64.2		7.7	Mk		16000	5								
1812	3	26	20	7		2				* NOAA	Venezuela:La Guaira	委内瑞拉:拉瓜伊拉	10.6	-66.9	33	7.7	Muk	10	26000	5				3				
1815	10	23								* China	China:Shanxi, Pinglu	中国:山西平陆	34.8	111.2		6.75	Ms	9	13000	5				4	20000	5		
1815	11	22				3		1	1.5	* NOAA	Indonesia:Bali Island	印度尼西亚:巴厘岛	-8	115.2	122	7	Ms		11453	5								
1822	9	5								* Song	Turkey:Hatay; Syria:Aleppo	土耳其:哈塔伊;叙利亚:阿勒颇	36	36		7.7	Mk	11	20000	5				4				
1847	5	8	13							* Usami	Japan:Naganoi	日本:长野	37	138		7.4	Ms	10	12000	5				4	34000	5		
1850	9	12								* China	China:Sichuan, Xichang, SE.	中国:四川西昌东南	27.7	102.4		7.5	Ms	10	20650	5				4				
1853	4	22								* Song	Iran:Fars, Shiraz	伊朗:法尔斯,设拉子	29.6	52.5		7.7	Mk	9	13000	5				4		4		
1857	9	16								* Song	Italy:Calabria, Montemurro	意大利:卡拉布里亚,蒙特穆罗	39.4	16.4		6.8	Mk		10000	5				3				
1857	12	16	21	18						* Italy	Italy:Campania, Montemurro	意大利:坎佩尼亚,蒙特穆罗	40.3	16		6.96	Muk	10	13488	5				4				
1859	6	2	8							*	Turkey:Erzurum	土耳其:埃尔佐鲁姆	39.9	41.3		6.1	Muk		15000	5				3				
1861	3	21	0	16		4				* NOAA, Song	Argentina:Mendoza	阿根廷:门多萨	-32.8	-68.8		8	Mk		14000	5				4		4		4
1868	8	13	21	30		4	18	4.2	3.5	* GSHAP, NOAA	Chile:Arica, Near Coast	智利:阿里卡近海	-18.6	-71	25	8.5	Ms	11	25000	5			300	5				
1868	8	16	6	30						*	Ecuador:Imbabura	厄瓜多尔:因巴布拉	0.31	-78.18	20	7.7	Ms	10	70000	5				4		4		
1875	5	18	16	25						*	Colombia:Cucuta, San Cayetano	哥伦比亚:库库塔,圣卡耶塔诺	7.9	-72.5	20	7.5	Muk	10	10000	5				3				
1876										* * India	India:Andaman Islands	印度:安达曼群岛	12	92.8		8.5	Ms		215000	5			0.25	1				
1879	7	1								* China	China:Gansu, Wudu, S.	中国:甘肃武都南	33.2	104.7		8	Ms	11	22000	5		4		4		4		
1883	10	15	13	30						*	Greece:Chios	希腊:希俄斯岛	38.4	26.1		7.3	Ms	10	15000	5				4	3600	4		
1893	11	17	15	6						* Iran	Iran:Qūchān	伊朗:古昌	37	58.4		7.1	Ms	10	18000	5				4		4		
1895	1	17	8	30						*	Iran:Qūchān	伊朗:古昌	37.1	58.4		6.8	Ms		11000	5				4		4		
1896	6	15	10	33		4	38	5.2	3.8	* GSHAP, NOAA	Japan Trench	日本海沟	39.5	144		8.4	Muk		31122	5	13247	5		4	11000	5		
1898	11	17	15	6						*	Iran:Qūchān	伊朗:古昌	37.2	58.4	11	6.6	Muk	10	18000	5				3				
1905	4	4	0	50						* Engdahl	India:Kangra	印度:坎格拉	33	76	60	7.8	Mw	10	20000	5				4				
1906	4	18	13	12	21	4	0.1	-3.3	-2	* Engdahl, NOAA	US:California, San Francisco	美国:加利福尼亚州旧金山	37.67	-122.48	20	7.8	M	11	700	3			400	5				

时间						海啸				资料来源	震中				深度	震级	标度	烈度	死亡人数		受伤人数		经济损失		房屋毁坏		房屋受损	
年	月	日	时	分	秒	源	浪高	级 I	级 S		地名(英文)	地名(中文)	纬度(°)	经度(°)					数量/人	级别	数量/人	级别	数量/$ Mill	级别	数量/间	级别	数量/间	级别
Date						Tsunami				Information	Earthquake Epicenter				Depth	Mag	Scale	MMI	Deaths		Injuries		Damage		Houses Destroyed		Houses Damaged	
Year	Mo	Dy	Hr	Mn	Sec	Sr	Wh	mI	mS		Name(English)	Name(Chinese)	Latitude	Longitude					Num	Dd	Num	Dd	$ Mill	De	Num	Dh	Num	Dh
1906	8	17	0	40		4	3.6	1.8	2	* Shi Z., Engdahl, NOAA	Chile:Valparaíso, Near Coast	智利:瓦尔帕莱索近海	-33	-72	25	8.2	M	11	1500	4			100	5				
1907	10	21	4	23	36					*GSHAP, Engdahl	Tadzhikistan:Khatlon	塔吉克斯坦:哈特隆州	38	69	33	7.2	Mw	9	12000	5				3		3		
1908	12	28	4	20	24	4	13		5	* Italy, Engdahl, NOAA, GSHAP	Italy:Messina, Sicily	意大利:墨西拿,西西里岛	38.15	15.68	10	7.24	Ms	11	82220	5			116	5		4		
1915	1	13	6	52	42					* Italy, Engdahl	Italy:Marsica, Avezzano	意大利:马尔西卡山,阿韦扎偌	42.013	13.53	10	6.9	Ms	11	29978	5			60.0	4				
1920	12	16	12	5	55					* China, Engdahl, Dis	China:Ningxia, Haiyuan	中国:宁夏海原	36.7	104.9	25	8.5	Ms	12	200000	5			25.0	4				
1923	9	1	2	58	37	4	13	3.6	3	* Usami, Engdahl, NOAA	Japan:Tokyo, Yokohama	日本:东京,横滨	35.1	139.5	35	7.9	M		142807	5	103733	5	600	5	128266	5	574299	5
1927	5	22	22	32	48					* China, Engdahl	China:Gansu, Gulang, W.	中国:甘肃古浪西	37.7	102.2	25	8	Ms	11	40912	5	524	3		4	26674	5		
1931	8	10	21	18	48					* China, Engdahl	China:Xinjiang, Fuyun	中国:新疆富蕴	47.1	89.8	35	8	Mw	11	10000	5				4		4		
1934	1	15	8	43	25					* India, Engdahl	India:Bihar; Nepal:Kathmandu	印度:比哈尔;尼泊尔:加德满都	26.5	86.5	35	8.1	M	11	10600	5				4		4		4
1935	5	30	21	32	57	1				* Engdahl	Pakistan:Quetta	巴基斯坦:奎达	28.894	66.176	35	8.1	Mw	10	60000	5			25.0	4		4		4
1939	1	25	3	32	14	2				* Engdahl, NOAA	Chile:Chillan	智利:奇廉	-36.2	-72.2	60	7.7	Mw	10	30000	5			920	5		4		
1939	12	26	23	57	23	4	0.5		4	* Engdahl, NOAA	Turkey:Erzincan	土耳其:埃尔津占	39.77	39.533	35	7.8	Ms	12	32700	5			20.0	3		4		
1940	1	15								* Song	Argentina:San Juan	阿根廷:圣胡安	-31	-69		7	Mk		10000	5								
1944	1	15	23	49	30					* Engdahl	Argentina:San Juan	阿根廷:圣胡安	-31.5	-68.5	50	7.1	Mw		8000	4			100	5				
1948	10	5	20	12	5					* Engdahl	Turkmenistan:Asgabat	土库曼斯坦:阿什哈巴德	37.9	58.6	18	7.2	Mw	10	19800	5		4	25.0	4		4		
1953	5	6	17	16	48	2				* Engdahl, NOAA	Chile:Coelemu	智利:科埃莱穆	-37.254	-72.92	68.4	7.5	mB	10	9	1	26	1	500	5				
1953	8	12	9	23	55	2				* Engdahl, NOAA	Greece:Lixouri – Argostoli	希腊:利克苏里 – 阿尔戈斯托利	38.046	20.766	15	7.2	Mw	10	476	3	2412	4	100	5	27773	5		
1960	2	29	23	40	12	1				* NOAA	Morocco:Agadir	摩洛哥:阿加迪尔	30.5	-9.5		6.8	Ms	10	13100	5	25000	5	120	5		3		
1960	5	22	19	11	18	4	25	4.6	4	* Engdahl, NOAA	Chile:Puerto Montt, Valdivia	智利:蒙特港,巴尔迪维亚	-38.235	-73.047	35	9.5	M	12	2223	4	3000	4	1000	5	58622	5		
1962	9	1	19	20	41					* Engdahl	Iran:Qazvin	伊朗:加兹温	35.556	49.81	17.6	6.9	Ms	9	12225	5	2776	4	30.0	4	21310	5		
1963	7	26	4	17	13					* Turkey	Macedonia:Skopje	马其顿:斯科普里	42.1	21.5	5	6	Ms	10	1070	4	3300	4	1000	5		4		
1964	3	28	3	36	13	4	67	6.1	5	* Engdahl, NOAA	Gulf of Alaska	阿拉斯加湾	61.017	-147.648	6.6	9.2	M	10	139	3			430	5		3		
1964	6	16	4	1	41	4	5.8	2.7	2	* ISC, Usami, Engdahl, NOAA	Japan Sea	日本海	38.434	139.226	13.1	7.5	M	5	26	1	450	3	800	5	2250	4		
1965	3	28	16	33	17					* Shi Z., Engdahl	Chile:Valparaiso	智利:瓦尔帕莱索	-32.492	-71.212	69.9	7.4	mb		400	3			125	5				
1966	3	22	7	19	27					* China, Dis	China:Hebei, Ningjin, SE.	中国:河北宁晋东南	37.5	115.1	9	7.2	Ms	10	8064	3	38451	5	1637	5	5000000	5		
1966	4	26								* Song	Uzbekistan:Tashkent	乌兹别克斯坦:塔什干	41.2	69.1		7.7	Mk		10	1			300	5				
1967	7	29	0	0	3	4	0.1			* Engdahl, NOAA	Venezuela:El Tocuyo	委内瑞拉:托丘约	10.555	-67.31	23.7	6.5	Mw	8	300	3	1536	4	140	5				
1968	1	15	2	1	9					* Italy	Italy:Sicily, Belice Valley	意大利:西西里岛,贝利切谷	37.77	12.98	33	6.12	Ms		216	3	563	3	320	5				
1968	5	16	0	49	0	4	6	2.3	-0.5	* ISC, Engdahl, NOAA	Japan Trench	日本海沟	40.903	143.346	25.8	8.3	Mw	6	52	2	329	3	131	5	1218	4		

时间 Date 年 Year	月 Mo	日 Dy	时 Hr	分 Mn	秒 Sec	海啸 Tsunami 源 Sr	浪高 Wh	级 I mI	级 S mS	资料来源 Information	震中 Earthquake Epicenter 地名(英文) Name(English)	地名(中文) Name(Chinese)	纬度(°) Latitude	经度(°) Longitude	深度 Depth	震级 Mag	标度 Scale	烈度 MMI	死亡人数 Deaths 数量/人 Num	级别 Dd	受伤人数 Injuries 数量/人 Num	级别 Dd	经济损失 Damage 数量/$ Mill $ Mill	级别 De	房屋毁坏 Houses Destroyed 数量/间 Num	级别 Dh	房屋受损 Houses Damaged 数量/间 Num	级别 Dh
1968	8	31	10	47	40					* ISC, Engdahl	Iran: Razavi Khorasan	伊朗:呼罗珊	34.045	58.96	12.3	7.2	Mw	10	12100	5	17000	5	35.0	4	12000	5		
1970	1	4	17	0	40					* China, Engdahl, Dis	China: Yunnan, Tonghai	中国:云南通海	24.147	102.462	14	7.8	Ms	10	15621	4	26783	5	411	5	166117	5	172339	5
1970	5	31	20	23	32	4	0.4	0.8		* Engdahl, Shi Z., NOAA	Peru: Casma, Near Coast	秘鲁:卡斯马近海	-9.248	-78.84	73	7.9	M	10	66794	5	50000	5	530	5		3		
1971	2	9	14	0	42					* Shi Z., Engdahl	US: California, San Fernando	美国:加利福尼亚州圣费尔南多	34.401	-118.392	6.4	6.7	M	11	65	2	2000	4	505	5				
1971	7	9	3	3	20	4	1.2	0.3	0	* Shi Z., Engdahl, NOAA	Chile: Valparaiso	智利:瓦尔帕莱索	-32.558	-71.085	59	7.8	Mw	9	83	2	447	3	236	5		3		
1972	4	10	2	6	51					* Engdahl	Iran: Fars, Qir, Karzin	伊朗:法尔斯,吉尔,卡尔津	28.408	52.789	11	6.9	Ms	9	30000	5	1700	4		4		4		
1972	6	21	15	6	53					*	Italy: Ancona	意大利:安科纳	43.8	13.3	4	4.4	mb		2	1			300	5				
1972	12	23	6	29	45					* Engdahl	Nicaragua: Managua	尼加拉瓜:马拉瓜	12.347	-86.128	7.3	6.2	Ms		10000	5	20000	5	800	5				
1974	4	22	0	29	17					* China, Dis	China: Jiangsu, Liyang	中国:江苏溧阳	31.6	119.1	16	5.5	Ms	7	8		214	3	144	5	11081	5	77700	5
1975	2	4	11	36	5					* China, Engdahl, Dis	China: Liaoning, Haicheng	中国:辽宁海城	40.717	122.734	8	7.3	Ms	10	1328	3	16980	5	1001	5		4		
1976	2	4	9	1	46	4	0.1			* Shi Z., CSN, ISC, Engdahl, NOAA	Guatemala: Chimaltenango, Guatemala City	危地马拉:奇马尔特南戈,危地马拉城	15.297	-89.145	12.1	7.5	M	9	23000	5	76000	5	2147	5				
1976	5	6	20	0	15					* Italy, Engdahl	Italy: Udine	意大利:乌迪内	46.385	13.266	20.9	6.5	Mw	10	978	3	1700	4	3600	5				
1976	5	29	12	23	21					* China, Engdahl, Dis	China: Yunnan, Longling, E.	中国:云南龙陵东	24.514	98.915	6	7.3	Ms	9	98	2	2442	4	171	5	420000	5		
1976	7	14	7	13	24					* Engdahl	Indonesia: Bali Island	印度尼西亚:巴厘岛	-8.227	114.775	25.4	6.5	Mw		563	3			195	5				
1976	7	27	19	42	56					* China, Engdahl, Dis	China: Hebei, Tangshan	中国:河北唐山	39.606	117.888	16.6	7.8	Ms	11	242000	5	164000	5	12232	5				
1976	8	16	16	11	12	4	8.5	2.3	2.5	* Bautista, Engdahl, NOAA	Philippines: Mindanao, Lebak	菲律宾:棉兰老岛,莱巴克	6.292	124.09	57.7	8	Mw	6	5066	4	10000	5	130	5				
1977	3	4	19	21	56					* Engdahl, USGS	Romania: Paltin	罗马尼亚:帕尔廷	45.777	26.703	88.9	7.5	Mw	9	1581	4	10500	5	800	5				
1978	6	12	8	14	29	4	0.6		0.5	* Engdahl, NOAA	Japan: Miyagi, Near Coast	日本:宫城近海	38.224	142.009	53.3	7.7	Mw	8	28	1	10000	5	800	5		3		
1978	6	20	20	3	24	4	0.5			* Engdahl, NOAA	Greece: Thessaloniki	希腊:塞萨洛尼基	40.765	23.304	7.7	6.3	Mw		50	1		3	1000	5				
1978	9	3	5	8	30					* ISC, USGS	Germany: Bisingen	德国:毕森根市	48.29	9.01	8	5.9	ML	8				3	150	5				
1978	9	16	15	35	55					* Engdahl	Iran: Razavi Khorasan	伊朗:呼罗珊	33.268	57.387	15	7.4	Mw		20000	5			50.0	4		4		
1979	4	15	6	19	45	4	0.6		1	* Engdahl, NOAA	Adriatic Sea	亚得里亚海	42.001	19.154	15	7	Mw	9	131	3	1001	4	2700	5		4		
1979	7	9	10	57	23					* China, Dis, USGS, ISC	China: Jiangsu, Liyang, SW.	中国:江苏溧阳西南	31.45	119.25	12	6	Ms	8	41	1	2954	4	164	5	113909	5	229750	5
1980	5	18	15	32	18					* Engdahl	US: Washington, Mt St Helens	美国:华盛顿州圣海伦山	46.36	-121.993	15	5.7	Mw	5	57	2			2000	5				
1980	7	29	14	58	42					* ISC, Engdahl	Nepal: Seti	尼泊尔:塞蒂	29.616	81.1	13.8	6.6	Mw		200	3		3	245	5				
1980	10	10	12	25	26	4	0.7		2	* Engdahl, NOAA	Algeria: Bordj Abou El Hasen, Dahra	阿尔及利亚:阿布哈桑堡,赫尔	36.154	1.417	15	7.7	Mw	10	5000	4	9000	4	5200	5	25000	5		

时间						海啸				资料来源	震中				深度	震级	标度	烈度	死亡人数		受伤人数		经济损失		房屋毁坏		房屋受损	
年	月	日	时	分	秒	源	浪高	级 I	级 S		地名(英文)	地名(中文)	纬度(°)	经度(°)					数量/人	级别	数量/人	级别	数量/$ Mill	级别	数量/间	级别	数量/间	级别
Date						Tsunami				Information	Earthquake Epicenter				Depth	Mag	Scale	MMI	Deaths		Injuries		Damage		Houses Destroyed		Houses Damaged	
Year	Mo	Dy	Hr	Mn	Sec	Sr	Wh	mI	mS		Name(English)	Name(Chinese)	Latitude	Longitude					Num	Dd	Num	Dd	$ Mill	De	Num	Dh	Num	Dh
1980	11	23	18	34	55					* Engdahl	Italy:Avellino, Potenza, Caserta	意大利:艾维连奴,波坦察,卡塞塔	40.794	15.312	6.8	6.9	Mw	10	4689	4	7700	4	20000	5				
1981	2	24	20	53	38	4			3	* ISC, Engdahl, NOAA	Greece:Gulf of Corinth	希腊:科林斯海湾	38.16	22.974	16.9	6.6	Mw	8	22	1	400	3	900	5				
1981	7	28	17	22	24					* Engdahl	Iran:Kerman	伊朗:克尔曼	29.964	57.766	13.8	7.3	Mw		3000	4	1000	3	1000	5				
1982	12	13	9	12	51					* ISC, Engdahl	Yemen:Dhamar	也门:扎马尔	14.669	44.246	7	6.2	Mw	8	2800	4	1500	4	2000	5		4		
1983	3	31	13	12	53					* GSHAP	Colombia:Popayan	哥伦比亚:波帕扬	2.461	-76.686	22	7.0	Mw	9	350	3	1200	4	411	5				
1983	5	26	3	0	1	4	15	3.9	2	* ISC, Engdahl, NOAA	Japan:Akita, Near West Coast	日本:秋田西部近海	40.468	139.08	20	7.7	Mw	8	104	3	324	3	800	5	3513	4		
1983	11	6	21	9	43					* China, Dis	China:Shandong, Heze	中国:山东菏泽	35.17	115.25	15	6.0	Ms	7	46	1	5138	4	162	5	61208	5	280171	5
1985	3	3	22	47	10	4	3.5	1.6		* Chile, Engdahl, NOAA	Chile:San Antonio, Valparaiso	智利:圣安东尼奥,瓦尔帕莱索	-33.132	-71.708	40	8	Mw	8	200	3	2575	4	1500	5		3		
1985	9	19	13	17	49	4	3	1.6		* Engdahl, NOAA	Mexico:Michoacan, Mexico City	墨西哥:米却肯,墨西哥城	18.437	-102.358	15	8	M	9	9500	4	30000	5	4000	5		4		
1985	10	13	15	59	53					* Engdahl, USGS	Tajikistan:Khudzhand	塔吉克斯坦:苦盏	40.338	69.814	16.2	5.8	Mw	9	29	1	80	2	200	5		3		
1986	8	30	21	28	37					* Engdahl	Romania: Bucharest, Kishinev	罗马尼亚:布加勒斯特,基希讷乌	45.525	26.272	135.9	7.2	Mw	8	2	1	558	3	730	5	55000	5		
1986	10	10	17	49	26					* Engdahl	El Salvador:San Salvador	萨尔瓦多:圣萨尔瓦多	13.796	-89.155	10.9	5.7	Mw		1100	4	10000	5	1030	5				
1987	3	2	1	42	34					* Engdahl, USGS	New Zealand:North Island, Whakatane	新西兰:北岛,瓦卡塔尼	-38.015	176.921	15	6.5	Mw	10	1	1	25	1	210	5				
1987	3	6	4	10	44					* GSHAP, Engdahl	Ecuador:Napo, Quito	厄瓜多尔:纳波,基多	0.083	-77.785	16.4	7.2	Mw	9	1000	3			700	5				
1987	10	1	14	42	20					* USGS, ISC, Engdahl	US:California, Whittier	美国:加利福尼亚州惠提尔	34.061	-118.134	14.4	6.0	Mw	8	8	1	200	3	358	5				
1988	8	20	23	9	11					* Engdahl	Nepal:Sagarmatha	尼泊尔:萨加玛塔	26.758	86.624	57	6.9	Mw	8	1091	4			132	5				
1988	11	6	13	3	21					* China, Engdahl, Dis	China:Yunnan, Ximeng, N.	中国:云南临沧东北	22.814	99.605	18	7.4	Ms	10	748	3	7700	4	606	5	412000	5		
1988	12	7	7	41	26					* Engdahl	Armenia:Leninakan, Spitak	亚美尼亚:列宁纳坎,斯皮塔克	40.928	44.114	5	6.8	M	10	25000	5			16200	5		4		
1989	4	15	20	34	11					* China, Engdahl, Dis	China:Sichuan, Batang, SE.	中国:四川巴塘东南	30.007	99.237	13	6.6	Ms	8	9	1	121	3	112	5	75604	5	267594	5
1989	10	18	14	57	22					* China, Dis	China:Shanxi, Datong, E.	中国:山西大同东	39.92	113.91	13	6.0	Ms	8	15	1	145	3	102	5	39000	5	76000	5
1990	4	26	9	37	13					* China, Engdahl, USGS, Dis	China:Qinghai, Gonghe, SW.	中国:青海共和西南	36.04	100.279	8	7.0	Ms	9	119	3	2149	4	564	5	6000	4		
1990	6	20	21	0	14					* Iran, Engdahl	Iran:Rasht, Qazvin, Zanjan	伊朗:拉什特,加兹温,赞詹	37.001	49.186	19	7.9	Ms	7	40000	5	105000	5	8000	5		4		
1990	7	16	7	26	36					* Bautista, Engdahl	Philippines:Baguio, Cabanatuan, Dagupan	菲律宾:碧瑶,卡巴纳端,达古潘	15.721	121.181	24.9	7.7	Mw	9	2412	4			370	5				
1990	11	6	18	45	54					* Engdahl	Iran: Darab	伊朗:达拉卜	28.266	55.484	11	6.6	Mw		22	1			232	5				
1990	12	13	0	24	26	4	0.1			* Italy, NOAA	Italy:Sicily, Carlentini	意大利:西西里岛,卡抡蒂尼	37.266	15.121	11	5.68	Ms	7	19	1	200	3	500	5				

年 Year	月 Mo	日 Dy	时 Hr	分 Mn	秒 Sec	源 Sr	浪高 Wh	级 I mI	级 S mS	资料来源 Information	地名(英文) Name(English)	地名(中文) Name(Chinese)	纬度(°) Latitude	经度(°) Longitude	深度 Depth	震级 Mag	标度 Scale	烈度 MMI	死亡人数 Deaths 数量/人 Num	死亡人数 Deaths 级别 Dd	受伤人数 Injuries 数量/人 Num	受伤人数 Injuries 级别 Dd	经济损失 Damage 数量/$ Mill $ Mill	经济损失 Damage 级别 De	房屋毁坏 Houses Destroyed 数量/间 Num	房屋毁坏 Houses Destroyed 级别 Dh	房屋受损 Houses Damaged 数量/间 Num	房屋受损 Houses Damaged 级别 Dh
1991	4	22	21	56	54	4	3	1		* ISC, Engdahl, NOAA	Costa Rica: Limon, Pandora	哥斯达黎加:利蒙,潘多拉	9.675	-83.072	12.3	7.6	Mw	10	87	2			510	5				
1991	4	29	9	12	50					* Engdahl	Georgia: Kutaisi	格鲁吉亚:库塔伊西	42.448	43.669	17	7.3	Mw	9	270	3			1700	5		4		
1992	4	13	1	20	1					* USGS	Netherlands: Roermond	荷兰:鲁尔蒙德	51.153	5.798	21	5.9	ML	8	1	1			100	5				
1992	8	19	2	4	39					* Engdahl	Kyrgyzstan: Chui, SW.	吉尔吉斯斯坦:楚河州西南	42.122	73.621	27	7.5	Mw	9	54	2			130	5				
1992	10	12	13	9	57					* Engdahl	Egypt: Cairo	埃及:开罗	29.729	31.158	22	5.8	Mw		545	3	6512	4	1200	5	9350	4		
1992	12	12	5	29	28	4	26	4.7	2.7	* Engdahl, NOAA	Indonesia: Flores Islands	印度尼西亚:弗洛勒斯岛	-8.482	121.844	28	7.8	Mw		2500	4	500	3	100	5	31785	5		
1993	1	15	11	6	8					* Engdahl, USGS	Japan: Hokkadio, Kushiro, Hachinohe	日本:北海道,钏路,八户	43.022	144.124	102	6.1	mb	9	2	1			358	5				
1993	7	12	13	17	14	4	54	5	3.1	* ISC, Engdahl, NOAA	Japan Sea, N.	日本海北部	42.883	139.225	20.4	7.7	Mw	8	230	3	233	3	1207	5	2374	4		
1993	8	8	8	34	27	4	2.1	-1		* Engdahl, NOAA	Guam: Tuman Bay, Apra Harbor	关岛(西太平洋):图曼湾,阿普拉港	12.983	144.838	62.1	7.8	Mw	9			48	1	250	5				
1993	9	29	22	25	50					* India, ISC, Engdahl	India: Latur - Osmanabad	印度:拉土尔-奥斯马纳巴德	18.079	76.516	7	6.2	M	8	9748	4	30000	5	1300	5		4		
1994	1	17	12	30	57	3	0.1	-3.3	-3	* ISC, Engdahl, NOAA	US: California, Northridge	美国:加利福尼亚州北岭	34.185	-118.563	19	6.7	M	9	60	2	7000	4	40000	5	40000	5		
1994	2	15	17	7	46					* ISC, Engdahl	Indonesia: Southern Sumatra	印度尼西亚:苏门答腊南部	-4.976	104.286	23	6.9	Mw		207	3	2000	4	169	5	6000	4		
1994	10	4	13	22	58	4	10	2.3	2.6	* Engdahl, NOAA, USGS	Japan: Hokkaido, Near Coast of E.	日本:北海道东部海域	43.945	147.224	14	8.3	Mw	9	11	1	242	3	11700	5				
1994	12	28	12	19	26	4	0.5			* Engdahl, NOAA, USGS	Japan Trench	日本海沟	40.53	143.403	29.2	7.8	Mw	10	3	1	200	3	170	5				
1995	1	16	20	46	54	4	0.2	-2.3	-2	* ISC, Engdahl, NOAA	Japan: Kobe	日本:神户	34.572	135.03	22	7.3	Mw	11	5502	4	36896	5	131500	5	200000	5		
1995	5	13	8	47	14					* ISC, Engdahl	Greece: Grevena - Kozani	希腊:格莱维纳-科札尼	40.151	21.713	14	6.6	Mw	8			25	1	450	5	12000	5		
1995	5	27	13	3	54	4	0.1	-2.3	-2	* ISC, Engdahl, NOAA	Russia: Sakhalin Island	俄罗斯:库页岛(萨哈林岛)	52.597	142.827	11	7.5	Mw	9	1989	4	750	3	300	5				
1995	6	15	0	15	51	4	1	-1		* Engdahl, NOAA	Greece: Patrai	希腊:帕特雷	38.448	22.31	14	6.5	Mw	7	26	1	60	2	660	5				
1995	10	1	15	57	18					* Engdahl	Turkey: Evciler, Dinar	土耳其:艾布西雷尔,第纳尔	38.077	30.143	31.2	6.4	Mw	8	101	3	348	3	206	5	5100	4		
1996	2	3	11	14	22					* China, Engdahl, Dis	China: Yunnan, Lijiang	中国:云南丽江	27.317	100.333	11	7.0	Ms	9	309	3	17057	5	367	5	959000	5		
1996	5	3	3	32	49					* China, Engdahl, Dis	China: Inner Mongolia, Baotou	中国:内蒙包头	40.778	109.714	24.5	6.4	Ms	8	26	1	453	3	323	5				
1997	5	10	7	57	32					* ISC, Engdahl	Iran: Birjand	伊朗:比尔詹德	33.833	59.796	12.8	7.5	Mw	10	1728	4	2300	4	100	5	10533	5		
1997	5	21	22	51	31					* India, Engdahl	India: Jabalpur	印度:贾巴尔普尔	23.066	80.121	36	5.8	M	8	56	2	1000	3	143	5	8546	4	52690	5

年 Year	月 Mo	日 Dy	时 Hr	分 Mn	秒 Sec	海啸 Tsunami 源 Sr	浪高 Wh	级 I mI	级 S mS	资料来源 Information	震中 Earthquake Epicenter 地名(英文) Name(English)	地名(中文) Name(Chinese)	纬度(°) Latitude	经度(°) Longitude	深度 Depth	震级 Mag	标度 Scale	烈度 MMI	死亡人数 Deaths 数量/人 Num	级别 Dd	受伤人数 Injuries 数量/人 Num	级别 Dd	经济损失 Damage 数量/$ Mill	级别 De	房屋毁坏 Houses Destroyed 数量/间 Num	级别 Dh	房屋受损 Houses Damaged 数量/间 Num	级别 Dh
1997	9	26	9	40	28					*ISC,Engdahl,USGS	Italy:Romagna	意大利:弗里	43.078	12.79	10	6	Mw	10	14	1	100	2	4525	5	80000	5		
1998	1	10	3	50	40					*China,Engdahl,Dis	China:Hebei,Shangyi,E.	中国:河北尚义东	41.133	114.532	5	6.2	Ms	8	49	2	656	3	101	5	169150	5		
1999	1	25	18	19	18					*Engdahl	Colombia:Armenia, Calarca	哥伦比亚:亚美尼亚,卡拉卡	4.449	-75.652	17	6.2	Mw		1185	4	4750	4	2900	5		4		
1999	6	15	20	42	7					*Engdahl,USGS	Mexico:Puebla,Veracruz	墨西哥:普埃布拉,韦拉克鲁斯	18.374	-97.457	63	7	Mw	8	20	1	200	3	227	5			2000	4
1999	8	17	0	1	40	4	2.5			*Engdahl,NOAA	Turkey:Istanbul, Kocaeli	土耳其:伊斯坦布尔,科贾埃利	40.773	30.002	13.3	7.6	M	10	17118	5	50000	5	20000	5			73342	5
1999	9	7	11	56	51					*Engdahl	Greece:Athens	希腊:雅典	38.13	23.613	10	6	Mw	9	143	3	1600		655	5	53000	5		
1999	9	20	17	47	19					*China,Engdahl,Dis	China:Taiwan,Nantou	中国:台湾南投	23.819	120.863	21	7.7	M	10	2297	4	8700	4	14000	5	82000	5		
1999	9	30	16	31	15					*Engdahl,USGS	Mexico:Oaxaca	墨西哥:瓦哈卡	16.046	-96.912	40	7.5	Mw	8	33	1	215	3	165	5			2000	4
1999	11	12	16	57	21					*Engdahl	Turkey: Adapazari, Zongul-dak	土耳其:阿达帕札勒,松古达克	40.821	31.227	11	7.5	Ms	9	834	3	4948	4	10000	5				
2000	1	14	23	37	8					*China,Dis	China:Yunnan,Yaoan	中国:云南姚安	25.624	101.051	17.4	6.5	Ms	8	7	1	2591	4	129	5	41000	5		
2000	10	6	4	30	21					*Engdahl	Japan:Okayama, Tottori	日本:冈山,鸟取	35.454	133.107	9	6.7	Mw	9			130	3	150	5	104	3	2230	4
2001	1	13	17	33	32					*Engdahl	El Salvador:Near Coast	萨尔瓦多:近海	13.038	-88.661	38	7.7	M	8	844	3	4723	4	753	5	108226	5	169632	5
2001	1	26	3	16	42					*India,Engdahl	India:Gujarat,Bhuj	印度:古吉拉特,普杰	23.394	70.234	16	7.7	M	10	20005	5	166836	5	2623	5	339000	5		
2001	2	13	14	22	8					*Engdahl	El Salvador:La Paz	萨尔瓦多:拉巴斯	13.627	-89.021	11	6.6	Mw	6	315	3	3399	4	349	5	41302	5	15706	5
2001	2	28	18	54	33					*Engdahl	US:Washington, Olympia, Seattle	美国:华盛顿州奥林匹亚,西雅图	47.112	-122.603	54	6.8	M	8	1	1	400	3	2000	5				
2001	3	24	6	27	54					*Engdahl	Japan:Hiroshima, Okayama	日本:广岛冈山	34.074	132.496	42	6.8	Mw	9	2	1			500	5			3700	4
2001	6	23	20	33	15	4	7			*Engdahl,NOAA	Peru:Arequipa, Moquegua, Tacna	秘鲁:阿雷基帕,莫克瓜,塔克纳	-16.305	-73.55	29.8	8.4	M	8	103	3	2713	4	200	5	22399	5		
2002	6	22	2	58	21					*USGS	Iran:Qazvin,W.	伊朗:加兹温西部	35.626	49.047	10	6.5	Mw	8	261	3	1300	4	300	5		4		
2002	9	6	1	21	29					*	Italy:Sicily,Palermo	意大利:西西里岛,巴勒莫	38.381	13.701	5	6.0	Mw		2	1	20	1	500	5				2
2002	10	31	10	32	59					*Italy,USGS	Italy:San Guiliano Di Puglia, Campobasso	意大利:圣安诺迪普利亚,坎布巴索	41.694	14.925	10	5.9	Mw	8	29	1	135	3	796	5				4
2003	2	24	1	3	41					*China,Dis	China:Xinjiang,Maralbishi,W.	中国:新疆巴楚西	39.5	77.2	11	6.8	Ms	9	268	3	4853	4	169	5	71000	5		
2003	5	21	18	44	20	4	3	1	1.5	*NOAA	Algeria:Algiers, Cherchell	阿尔及利亚:阿尔及尔,舍尔沙勒	36.964	3.634	12	6.9	Ms	10	2266	4	10261	5	5000	5	43000	5	43000	5
2003	5	26	9	24	33					*USGS	Japan:Iwate, Miyagi	日本:岩手宫城	38.849	141.568	68	7.0	Mw	8			143	3	233	5			720	3
2003	7	25	15	13	8					*NEIC,USGS	Japan:Miyagi, Iwate	日本:宫城岩手	38.432	141.003	10	5.6	Mw	8			569	3	411	5			1025	4
2003	12	22	19	15	56					*USGS	US:California,San Simeon	美国:加利福尼亚州圣西米恩	35.706	-121.102	8	6.6	Mw	8	2	1	40	1	300	5	40	1		
2003	12	26	1	56	52					*USGS	Iran:Kerman	伊朗:克尔曼	28.995	58.311	10	6.8	Ms	9	43200	5	30000	5	32.7	4		4		

时间 年 Year	月 Mo	日 Dy	时 Hr	分 Mn	秒 Sec	海啸 Tsunami 源 Sr	浪高 Wh	级 I mI	级 S mS	资料来源 Information	震中 Earthquake Epicenter 地名(英文) Name(English)	地名(中文) Name(Chinese)	纬度(°) Latitude	经度(°) Longitude	深度 Depth	震级 Mag	标度 Scale	烈度 MMI	死亡人数 Deaths 数量/人 Num	级别 Dd	受伤人数 Injuries 数量/人 Num	级别 Dd	经济损失 Damage 数量/$ Mill $ Mill	级别 De	房屋毁坏 Houses Destroyed 数量/间 Num	级别 Dh	房屋受损 Houses Damaged 数量/间 Num	级别 Dh
2004	12	26	0	58	53	4	51			* USGS, NOAA	Indonesia: Simeulue Island	印度尼西亚:锡默卢岛	3.295	95.982	30	9.1	Mw	10	227898	5		3	10000	5		3		
2005	10	8	3	50	41					* USGS	Pakistan: Muzaffarabad	巴基斯坦:穆扎法拉巴德	34.539	73.588	26	7.7	Ms	8	86000	5	69000	5		4		3		3
2005	11	26	0	49	36					* China, Dis	China: Jiangxi, Jiujiang	中国:江西九江	29.9	115.8	10	5.7	Ms	7	13	1	775	3	252	5	42793	5		
2006	5	26	22	53	59					* USGS	Indonesia: Java, Bantul	印度尼西亚:爪哇,班图尔	-7.961	110.446	13	6.3	Mw	9	5749	4	38568	5	3100	5	127000	5		
2007	6	2	21	34	56					* China, Dis	China: Yunnan, Pu-er	中国:云南普洱	23	101.1	5	6.4	Ms	8	3	1	419	3	247	5	18313	5		
2008	5	12	6	28	4					* China, Dis	China: Sichuan, Wenchuan	中国:四川汶川	30.95	103.4	19	8.0	Ms	11	87652	5	374171	5	120729	5	5360000	5	21000000	5
2008	8	21	12	24	32					* China, Dis	China: Yunnan, Yingjiang, NW.	中国:云南盈江西北	24.9	97.8		5.9	Ms	8	5	1	130	3	187	5	5	1	2420	4
2008	8	30	8	30	50					* China, Dis	China: Sichuan, Panzhihua	中国:四川攀枝花	26.2	101.9		6.1	Ms	8	41	1	1010	4	637	5	39200	5		
2009	7	9	11	19	16					* China, USGS, Dis	China: Yunnan, Yaoan	中国:云南姚安	25.632	101.095	7	6	Ms	8	1		372	3	312	5	10692	5	74736	5
2009	9	29	17	48	11	4	16			* NEIC, NOAA	Samoa Islands	萨摩亚群岛	-15.489	-172.095	18	8.1	Ms	6	191	3	7	1	150	5				
2010	1	12	21	53	10	4	3			* NOAA	Haiti: Port-Au-Prince	海地:太子港	18.443	-72.571	13	7.3	Ms	10	222570	5	300000	5	8000	5	97294	5	188383	5
2010	2	27	6	34	14	4	11			* NOAA, USGS	Chile: Maule	智利:马利	-35.846	-72.719	35	8.8	Mw	9	521	3	12000	5	30000	5			500000	5
2010	3	4	0	18	51					* USGS, Dis	China: Taiwan, Kaohsiung	中国:台湾高雄	22.92	120.79	21	6.3	Mw	8			96	2	174	5			340	3
2010	4	13	23	49	37					* China, Dis	China: Qinghai, Yushu	中国:青海玉树	33.271	96.629	10	7.1	Ms	9	2968	4	11000	5	3347	5	15000	5		
2011	3	11	5	46	23	4	24			* USGS	Japan: Miyagi, Coast of E.	日本:宫城东部海域	38.322	142.369	32	9	Mw	12	27759	5	3006	4						

第三部分

全球无震级地震事件的震级确定方法与灾害信息目录修订

1　研究思路与方法

《全球重大灾害性地震目录(2150B. C. ~1991A. D.)》(Paula K. Dunbar, et al. ,1992；罗伟等编译, 1996)收集了自公元前2150年至公元1991年的全球重大灾害性地震目录。美国地质调查局(USGS, United States Geological Survey)的国家地震信息中心(NEIC, National Earthquake Information Center)增加了1992年至今的全球重大灾害性地震目录，并统一在USGS网站(http://neic. usgs. gov/neis/epic/epic_global. html)。该网站收集了自公元前2150年至公元2011年6月全球重大灾害性地震5700多条，包括地震时间、地点、震级、深度、烈度、死亡人数(或死亡级别)、经济损失数量(或经济损失级别)、受伤人数(或受伤级别)、房屋毁坏数目(或房屋毁坏级别)、房屋受损数目(或房屋受损级别)以及海啸等信息。这些信息中，地震时间、地点以及灾害信息比较完整，而地震震级却非常不完整。统计表明，全球灾害性地震目录中，公元前2150年至公元1899年无震级地震事件占69.2%；公元1900年至公元2009年占14.4%。因此如何确定无震级地震事件的震级是本书的研究重点，在此基础上编辑、修订全球地震灾害信息目录和全球地震目录，这对全球地震及其灾害研究是一项重要的基础工作。

1.1　有震级地震事件的灾害信息特点

对地震烈度与震级的关系研究表明(图1-1)，烈度与震级分布的离散性非常大，线性拟合相关系数也较低。也就是说，不能采用简单的线性拟合对无震级地震进行赋值。对于发生在陆地的地震，烈度值一般为震中烈度；如果地震发生海域，烈度值一般为震中距最近的陆地记录的烈度最大值，因此烈度与震级的关系离散非常大。

对灾害性地震的死亡级别 Dd 的震级分布的分析表明(图1-2)，死亡级别 $Dd=1\sim4$ 与震级两者之间的线性关系不明显，且离散性非常大，而死亡人数与震级的分布也非常离散，因此不能简单从死亡级别或死亡人数确定震级。

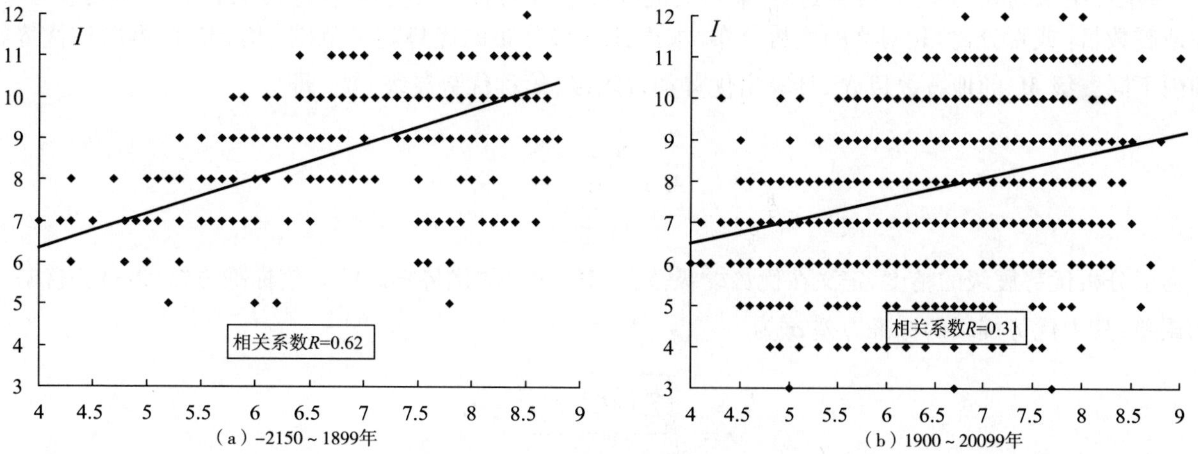

(a) -2150~1899年　　(b) 1900~20099年

图1-1　灾害性地震烈度的震级分布

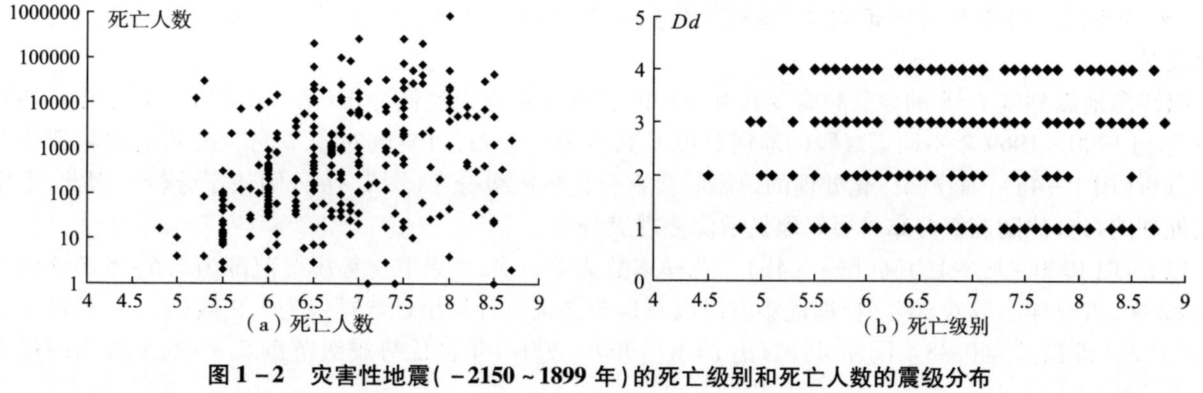

(a) 死亡人数　　(b) 死亡级别

图1-2　灾害性地震(-2150~1899年)的死亡级别和死亡人数的震级分布

灾害性地震的经济损失数量和级别 De 的震级分布表明（图 1－3），4 级以上地震的经济损失级别 De 均有可能为 1～4，而经济损失数量与震级的分布也非常离散，因此也不能简单从经济损失级别或经济损失数量确定震级。

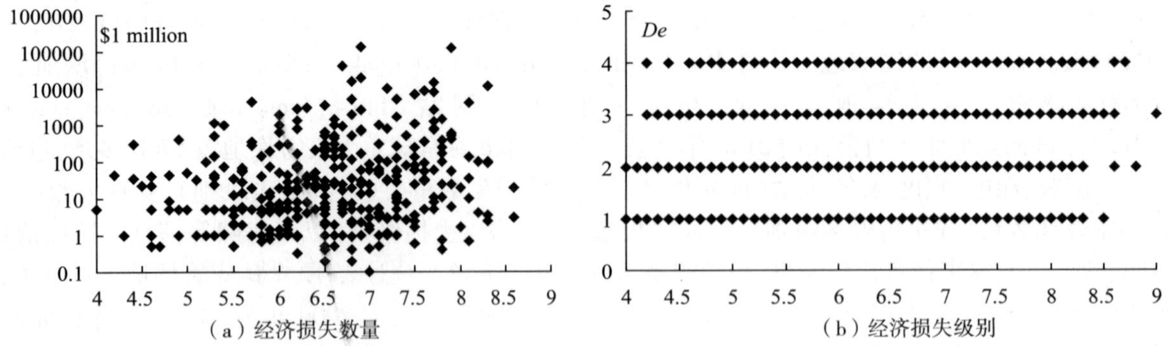

图 1－3　灾害性地震（1900～2009 年）的经济损失数量和级别的震级分布

图中 $ **1**million 为百万美元

综上所述，我们不能简单利用统计灾害地震信息与震级的线性关系确定无震级地震的震级，而是提出一种确定不同灾害信息的优势震级的方法研究灾害信息与震级的关系。

1.2　优势震级及其误差的定义

针对某一类地震灾害信息的某个级别，如浅源地震烈度 $I=8$，统计所有烈度为 8 度的浅源地震事件的震级分布，即统计给出 8 度地震在不同震级范围内的地震数目（即地震频度）N_i，再求出这些地震之和 $\sum_i N_i$。为了便于分析，可对地震数目进一步作归一化处理，计算出不同震级范围内的地震数目的百分比（$N_i/\sum_i N_i$）。对统计结果列表和作图，可看到，对某一类地震灾害信息的某一级别，在地震数目随不同震级分布中，存在地震数目（或百分比）相对高的优势分布，求出该优势分布的优势震级范围［M_a，M_b］，再取该优势震级范围内不同震级 M_i 的地震数目 N_i，计算出优势加权震级（简称优势震级）$\bar{M}$。即

$$\bar{M}=\frac{\sum_{i=a}^{b} M_i \cdot N_i}{\sum_{i=a}^{b} N_i}$$

为了分析优势震级的精度，定义在优势震级范围［M_a，M_b］的优势震级的 2 倍标准方差（2σ）为优势震级 $\bar{M}$ 的误差，其中优势震级的标准方差 σ 为

$$\sigma=\sqrt{\frac{\sum_{i=a}^{b}(M_i-\bar{M})^2 \cdot N_i}{\sum_{i=a}^{b} N_i}}$$

式中，N_i 为不同震级段 M_i 的统计样本（地震次数）；$\bar{M}$ 为优势震级，M_a 和 M_b 分别为优势震级范围的开始和结束震级。

以浅源地震烈度 $I=8$ 的地震频度及其百分比的震级分布作为实例分析（表 1），图 1－4 给出了 1900～2009 年与 1900～1969 年不同震级段的地震频度及其百分比分布，可看到对于不同时段的地震频度分布不便于分析（图 1－4a），而作归一化处理的地震频度百分比随震级分布（图 1－4b）则便于分析。因此，采用归一化处理的百分比随震级分布可更好地显示优势震级分布。

以 $I=8$（1900～1969）为例（图 1－4b），总样本数为 103 次，如果取优势震级范围为 5.5～6.5 级内样本数为 82 次，占总样本数的 80%，根据优势震级以及误差定义可计算出优势震级为 5.9 级（表 2），标准方差为 0.24（表 3），即误差为 0.48。同样可计算出 $I=8$（1900～2009）年在优势震级范围 5.5～6.5 级内的优势震

级 $\bar{M}$ 均为 5.9 级，标准方差为 0.36，误差为 0.72。

表 1　烈度 $I=8$ 的地震事件（频度及其百分比）的震级分布

震级段	$I=8$（1900~2009）		$I=8$（1900~1969）	
M_i	N_i	$N_i/\sum_i N_i$	N_i	$N_i/\sum_i N_i$
4.5	9	4.57%	4	3.88%
5.0	24	12.18%	10	9.71%
5.5	48	24.37%	26	25.24%
6.0	66	33.50%	42	40.78%
6.5	29	14.72%	14	13.59%
7.0	14	7.11%	4	3.88%
7.5	5	2.54%	1	0.97%
8.0	2	1.02%	2	1.94%
$\sum_i N_i$	197	100%	103	100%

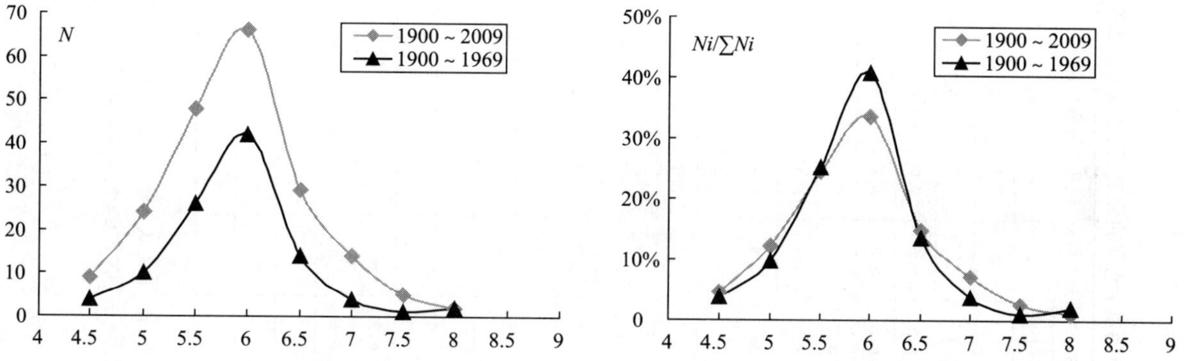

（a）地震频度的震级分布　　（b）地震频度百分比的震级分布

图 1-4　烈度 $I=8$ 浅源地震的频度及其百分比的震级分布

1.3　不同地震灾害的分类

一般天然地震分为构造地震、火山地震、塌陷地震。而构造地震分为浅源地震、中源地震、深源地震。浅源地震又分为剪切型、逆冲型、正断型地震，而发生在海洋中浅源逆冲型大地震才可能产生海啸。因此同震级的浅源、中源、深源地震以及伴有海啸（火山）的地震所造成的地震烈度、死亡人数（或死亡级别）、经济损失数量（或经济损失级别）存在较大差异。另外，不同年代和不同地区的地震灾害也存在差异。

所以在分析地震灾害信息的优势震级时，首先分辨有海啸（火山）的地震[简称为海啸（火山）地震]；排除有海啸灾害的地震又分浅源地震、中源地震、深源地震；然后再分不同年代、不同地区（如意大利、美国、南美洲、日本、希腊等地区）。

1.4　无震级地震事件的震级确定思路

在分析 -2150~2010 年的全球灾害性地震目录中已有震级的地震烈度、死亡级别、经济损失级别等参数的优势震级时，综合考虑地震发生的不同地区、不同年代、不同地震灾害类型（伴有海啸）、不同震源深度（浅源、中源、深源）地震以及典型地区等因素，建立了一个不同情况下的地震灾害信息的优势震级参数（表 2）及其标准方差（表 3）。

对于同一地震事件，由地震烈度、经济损失级别、死亡级别信息分别给出的不同震级，究竟选择哪一种震级作为该次地震事件的震级？通过数学统计分析，设计三种不同震级赋值方案（最大震级法、平均震级法、加权系数法），通过检验研究表明，最大震级法是最佳的震级赋值方法。

由各种灾害信息的优势震级和确定地震事件震级的方法，确定出无震级的地震事件的震级，然后再通过全球不同地区的网站和出版物收集的地震灾害信息，编辑、修订全球地震目录和地震灾害信息目录。

表 2　全球不同地区、不同年代、不同地震灾害类型(浅源、中源、深源、伴有海啸)地震的烈度、死亡级别、经济损失级别等参数的优势震级参数

参数名称		时间段(年)	烈度(I)										有死亡级别(或死亡人数)(Dd)					有经济损失级别(或经济损失数量)(De)					无灾害信息
级别			3	4	5	6	7	8	9	10	11	12	1	2	3	4	5	1	2	3	4	5	
海啸地震	全球(除地中海地区外)海啸(火山)地震	-2150 ~ 1899	7			7.2	7.3	7.3	7.5	7.9	8	8.5	7	7	7.5	7.9	8	7	7.1	7.7	8	8	7
		1900 ~ 2009	7			7.2	7.3	7.3	7.5	7.7	8.1	8.5	7	7	7.3	7.8	8	7.2	7.2	7.7	7.7	8	
	地中海地区海啸(火山)地震	-2150 ~ 1899					5.7	5.7	6.7	6.7	7.1		6.5	6.6	7.0	7.0	7.2	6.2	6.6	6.8	7.2	7.2	
		1900 ~ 2010				5.8	5.8	6.4	6.8	6.9	7.3		6.6	6.8	6.8	7.3	7.6	6.5	6.5	6.7	6.9	6.9	
不同震源深度	浅源地震($H<70$km)	-2150 ~ 1899	5			5	5.5	6.1	6.5	7.3	8	8.5	5.8	6	6.2	7	7.7	5.5	5.9	6.3	7.1	7.7	5
		1900 ~ 1969	5			5	5.5	5.9	6.5	7	7.8	8.5	5.8	6.1	6.4	7	7.7	5.5	5.9	6.2	6.7	7.7	
		1970 ~ 2009	5			5	5.5	5.9	6.5	7	7.8	8.5	5.7	6.4	6.4	7	7.7	5.3	5.7	5.8	6.4	7.7	
	中源地震($70 \leq H<300$km)	-2150 ~ 1969	6			7.4							7.4					7.4					6
		1970 ~ 2009	6			6.4							6.5					6.5					
	深源地震($H \geq 300$km)	-2150 ~ 2009	7.5																				
特殊地区	意大利地区	-217 ~ 2009					5.3	5.3	5.7	6.0	6.5		5.7	5.7	6.0	6.6	6.8	5.4	5.5	6.0	6.2	6.3	5
	美国地区	1568 ~ 1899	4.6	4.6	5.0	5.5	5.7	6.4	6.6	7.6	8.2												4.6
		1900 ~ 1962	4.6	4.6	4.9	5.1	5.6	6.1	6.4	7.2	7.8												4.6
	南美洲地区	1541 ~ 1959	4.5	4.5	4.5	5	6	6.2	6.7	7													4.5
		1960 ~ 1991	4.5	4.5	4.5	5	5.1	6.2	6.7	7													4.5
	日本地区	144 ~ 1899					6.2	6.4	6.9	7.2	8		6.5	6.5	7	7.3		6.6	6.7	7.2	7.4		6.1
		1900 ~ 2009											6.6	7	7	7.7		6.4	6.4	6.9	7.2		
	希腊地区	-330 ~ 2009				4.7	5.1	5.7	6.1	7.0													
	阿尔巴尼亚地区	57 ~ 2009							5.8	6.2	6.7												
	巴尔干山脉西北地区	361 ~ 2009				4.7	4.8	5.8	6.3	6.3													

注:①烈度 I:数字 3 ~ 12 表示烈度值;

②死亡级别 Dd: 数字 1 表示死亡人数 1 ~ 50 人; 数字 2 表示死亡人数 51 ~ 100 人; 数字 3 表示死亡人数 101 ~ 1000 人; 数字 4 表示死亡人数 1001 ~ 9999 人; 数字 5 表示死亡人数≥10000 人。

③经济级别 De: 数字 1 表示经济损失数量 < $ 1 million;数字 2 表示经济损失数量 $ 1 ~ 4.9 million;数字 3 表示经济损失数量 $ 5 ~ 24 million;数字 4 表示经济损失数量 $ 25 ~ 99 million;数字 5 表示经济损失数量≥ $ 100 million。

④无灾害信息:表示无烈度信息、无死亡信息、无经济损失信息。

表 3　全球不同地区、不同年代、不同地震灾害类型(浅源、中源、深源、伴有海啸)地震烈度、死亡级别、经济损失级别等的优势震级的标准方差 σ

参数名称		时间段(年)	烈度(I)										有死亡级别(或死亡人数)(Dd)					有经济损失级别(或经济损失数量)(De)					无灾害信息
级别			3	4	5	6	7	8	9	10	11	12	1	2	3	4	5	1	2	3	4	5	
海啸地震	全球(除地中海地区外)海啸(火山)地震	-2150~1899		0.45		0.44	0.38	0.35	0.36	0.61	0.37	0.35	0.73	0.22	0.25	0.32	0.58	0.45	0.65	0.70	0.35	0.43	0.37
		1900~2009		0.44		0.39	0.37	0.36	0.37	0.48	0.44	0.35	0.36	0.46	0.30	0.51	0.58	0.41	0.25	0.62	0.37	0.43	0.42
	地中海地区海啸(火山)地震	-2150~1899					0.20	0.20	0.24	0.40	0.37		0.20	0.10	0.58	0.32	0.20	0.25	0.26	0.26	0.39		
		1900~2010				0.3	0.30	0.39	0.23	0.42	0.60		0.41	0.20	0.24	0.54	0.76	0.50	0.35	0.51	0.31	0.31	
不同震源深度	浅源地震($H<70$km)	-2150~1899		0.20		0.20	0.20	0.29	0.34	0.43	0.24	0.35	0.46	0.49	0.56	0.45	0.76	0.37	0.37	0.45	0.56	0.72	0.25
		1900~1969		0.20		0.20	0.36	0.24	0.35	0.36	0.28	0.35	0.47	0.35	0.58	0.39	0.76	0.55	0.39	0.49	0.51	0.72	0.24
		1970~2009		0.42		0.42	0.40	0.39	0.40	0.35	0.20	0.35	0.51	0.49	0.32	0.42	0.76	0.66	0.51	0.65	0.60	0.72	0.40
	中源地震($7\leq H<300$km)	-2150~1969				0.25	0.25	0.29	0.50	0.43	0.35		0.37					0.36					0.15
		1970~2009		0.60		0.59	0.43	0.55	0.50	0.5	0.5		0.67					0.64					1.16
	深源地震($H\geq300$km)	-2150~2009	0.25										0.5					0.29					0.18
特殊地区	意大利地区	-217~2009					0.36	0.33	0.37	0.54	0.50		0.36	0.47	0.29	0.46	0.29	0.56	0.37	0.54	0.61	0.44	0.23
	美国地区	1568~1899			0.59	0.40	0.41	0.55	0.29	0.47	0.25												
		1900~1962	0.20	0.20	0.50	0.74	0.46	0.70	0.44	0.24	0.26												
	南美洲地区	1541~1959	0.56	0.46	0.42	0.75	0.47	0.39	0.34	0.00													
		1960~1991	0.60	0.54	0.39	0.35	0.36	0.44	0.70														
	日本地区	144~1899				0.23	0.24	0.22	0.24	0.34			0.38	0.33	0.48	0.60	0.30	0.43	0.26	0.59	0.50		0.38
		1900~2009											043	0.35	0.35	0.20	0.70	0.47	041	0.31	0.26		
	希腊地区	-330~2009				0.22	0.61	0.54	0.67	0.86													
	阿尔巴尼亚地区	57~2009							0.62	0.33	0.49												
	巴尔干山脉西北地区	361~2009				0.22	0.31	0.48	0.29	0.42													

注:①烈度 I:数字 3~12 表示烈度值;

②死亡级别 Dd: 数字 1 表示死亡人数 1~50 人; 数字 2 表示死亡人数 51~100 人; 数字 3 表示死亡人数 101~1000 人; 数字 4 表示死亡人数 1001~9999 人; 数字 5 表示死亡人数≥10000 人。

③经济级别 De: 数字 1 表示经济损失数量 < \$ 1 million;数字 2 表示经济损失数量 \$ 1~4.9 million;数字 3 表示经济损失数量 \$ 5~24 million;数字 4 表示经济损失数量 \$ 25~99 million;数字 5 表示经济损失数量≥ \$ 100 million。

④无灾害信息:表示无烈度信息、无死亡信息、无经济损失信息。

2　浅源地震灾害信息的优势震级

由于震源深度超过 70km 的中、深源地震与震源深度小于 70km 的浅源地震（排除伴有海啸的地震）的震

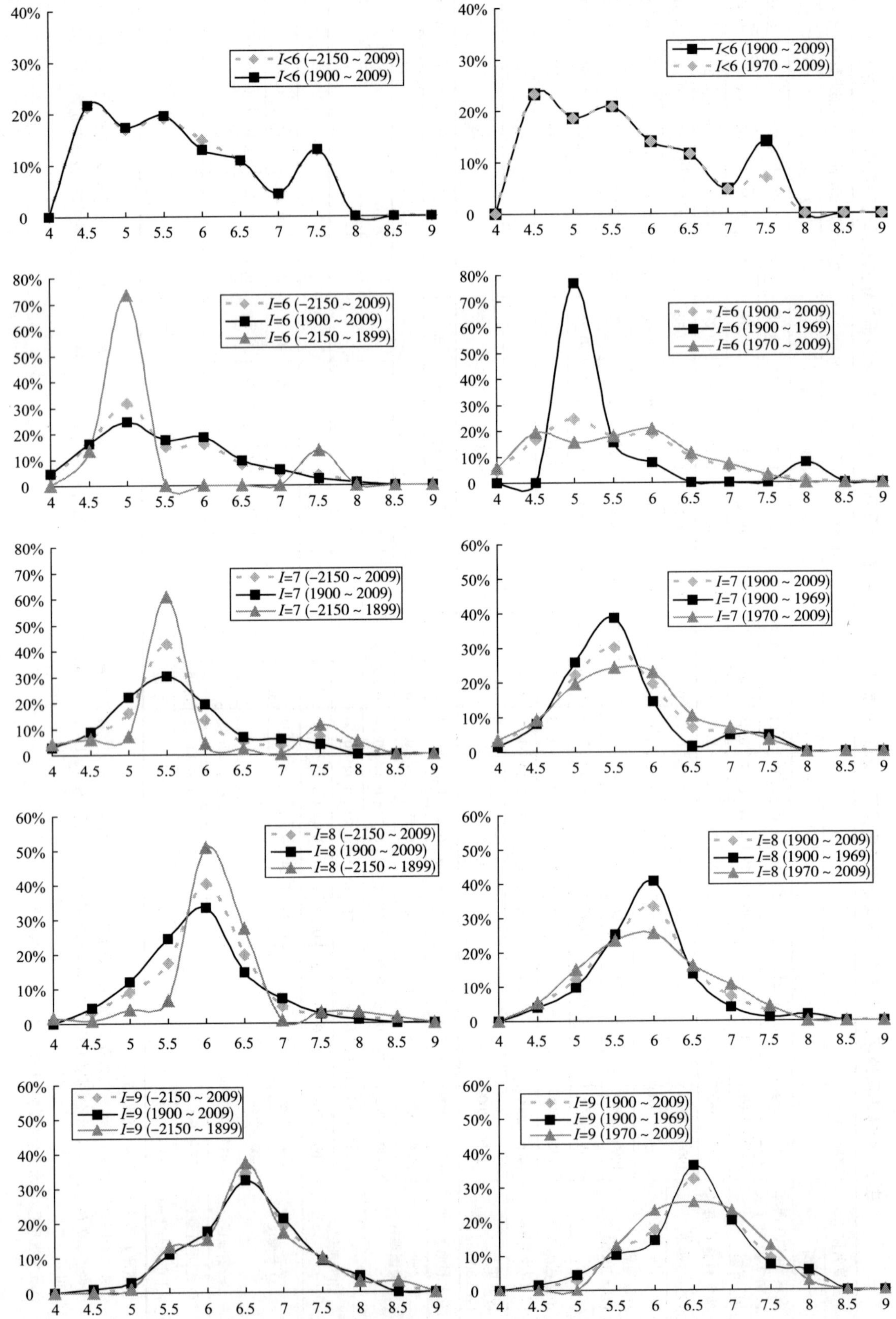

图 2－1　全球浅源地震不同烈度（I）的优势震级分布

中烈度（地震造成的最大烈度）、死亡人数和经济损失存在差别，因此首先分析浅源地震（震源深度小于70km 并无海啸灾害）的灾害信息的优势震级。

2.1　浅源地震烈度的优势震级

分析 –2150 ~ 1899 年、1900 ~ 1969 年、1970 ~ 2009 年不同时间段的浅源地震的烈度与震级关系。图 2 –1 给出了全球地震烈度低于 10 度的地震频度与震级分布。

由于烈度为 10 度的地震的优势震级段在 6.5 ~ 8 级和 5.5 ~ 6.5 级两个优势震级段。仔细分析表明 1900 ~ 1969 年震级范围 5.5 ~ 6.5 级内的 28 次地震分布国家主要是希腊、阿尔巴尼亚、巴尔干山脉西北、南美洲等地区，因此剔除这些地区的地震后再计算不同时段烈度 10 度的优势震级分布（图 2 –2），可见其优势震级范围为 6.5 ~ 8.0 级。考虑到烈度为 10 度的优势震级应大于烈度为 9 度的优势震级 6.5，因此在计算烈度 $I=10$ 度的优势时，取震级 6.5 ~ 8.0 级内地震进行计算。

全球地震烈度 $I=11$ 的优势震级范围除 7 ~ 8.5 级外还有 5.5 ~ 7 级。仔细分析了优势震级范围 5.5 ~ 7 级 15 次地震分布国家主要是希腊、南美洲、阿尔及利亚。图 2 –3 给出了排除希腊和南美洲等地区的全球地震再计算不同时段烈度 11 度的优势震级分布，可见其优势震级范围为 7 ~ 8.5 级。考虑到烈度为 11 度的优势震级应大于烈度为 10 度的优势震级 7.0，因此在计算烈度 $I=11$ 度的优势时，取震级 7 ~ 8.5 级内地震进行计算。

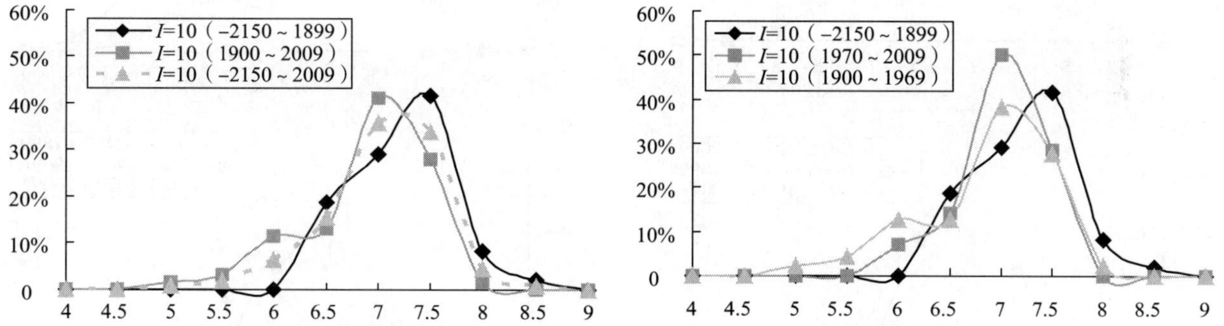

图 2 –2　全球（排除希腊、阿尔巴尼亚、亚贝尔肯斯和南美洲）浅源地震烈度 $I=10$ 的优势震级分布

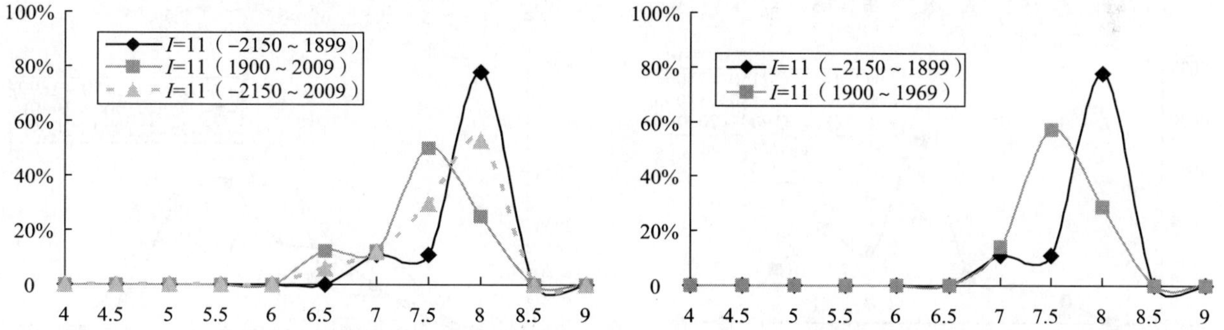

图 2 –3　全球（排除希腊和南美洲）浅源地震的烈度 $I=11$ 的优势震级分布

在全球烈度为 12 度的 6 次浅源地震（包括伴有海啸）中，除美国的 2 次 12 度地震的震级偏低外，其他 4 次地震的震级平均为 8.5。考虑到地震烈度达到 12 度的地震一般均为毁灭性地震，因此无论地震是否造成海啸，除专门分析的特殊地区（如意大利、希腊、阿尔巴尼亚、巴尔干山脉西北、南美洲等）外，只要达到烈度 12 度，其震级均取 8.5 级。

通过以上分析可得全球浅源地震不同时段烈度信息的优势震级（表 2）及其标准方差（表 3）。

2.2　浅源地震的死亡人数（或死亡级别）的优势震级

首先分析了 –2150 ~ 2009 年、–2150 ~ 1899 年、1900 ~ 2009 年 3 个时段浅源地震的死亡级别信息地震频度的震级分布，1900 ~ 1969 年与 1970 年之后地震的死亡级别地震频度的优势分布存在差异，图 2 –4 给出不同时段的浅源地震的死亡级别 *Dd* 的优势震级分布。不同时段的浅源地震的死亡级别 *Dd*(或死亡人数)的优势震级见表 2 及其标准方差见表 3。

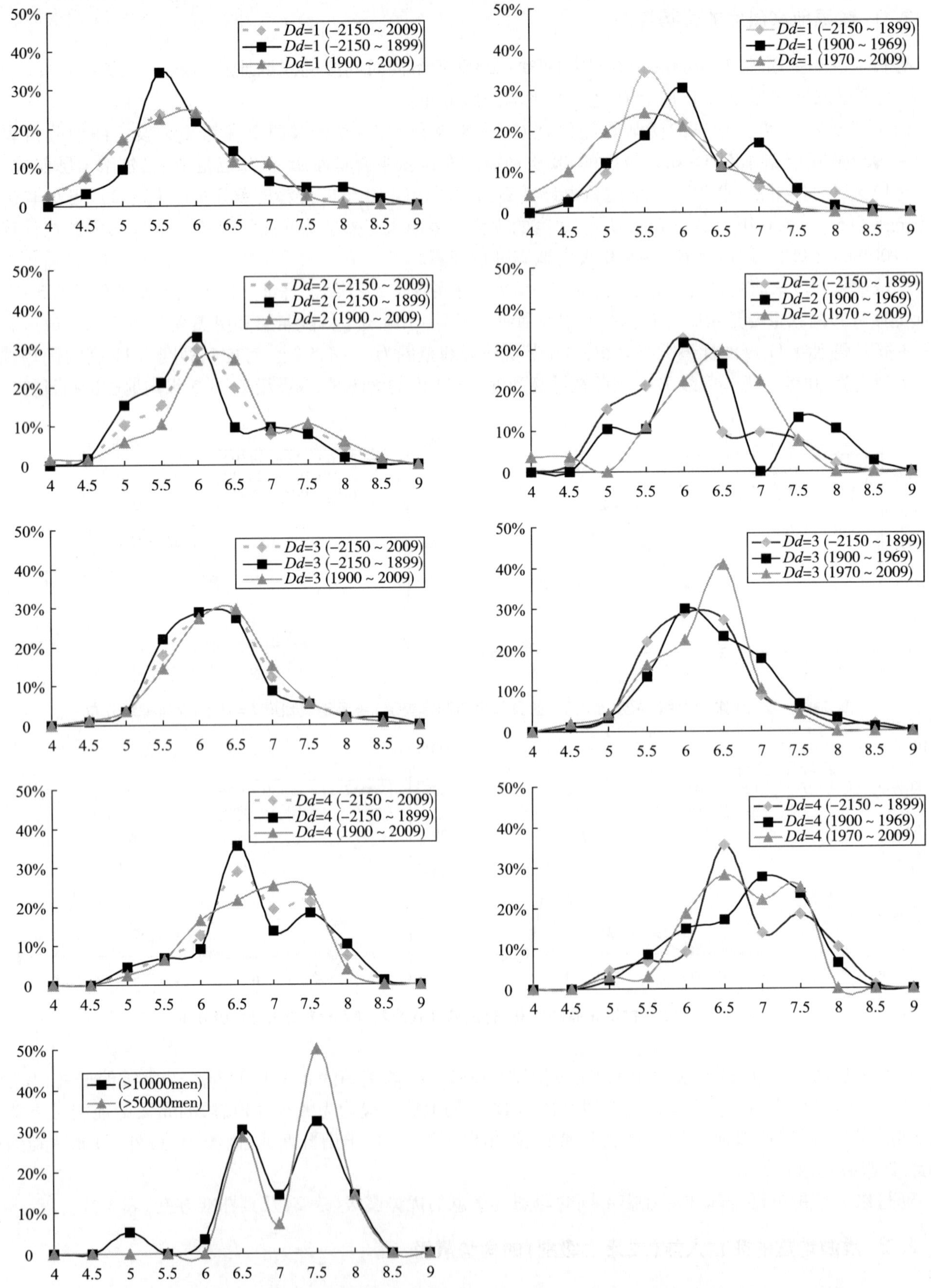

图 2－4　浅源地震的死亡级别 *Dd*(或死亡人数)的优势震级分布

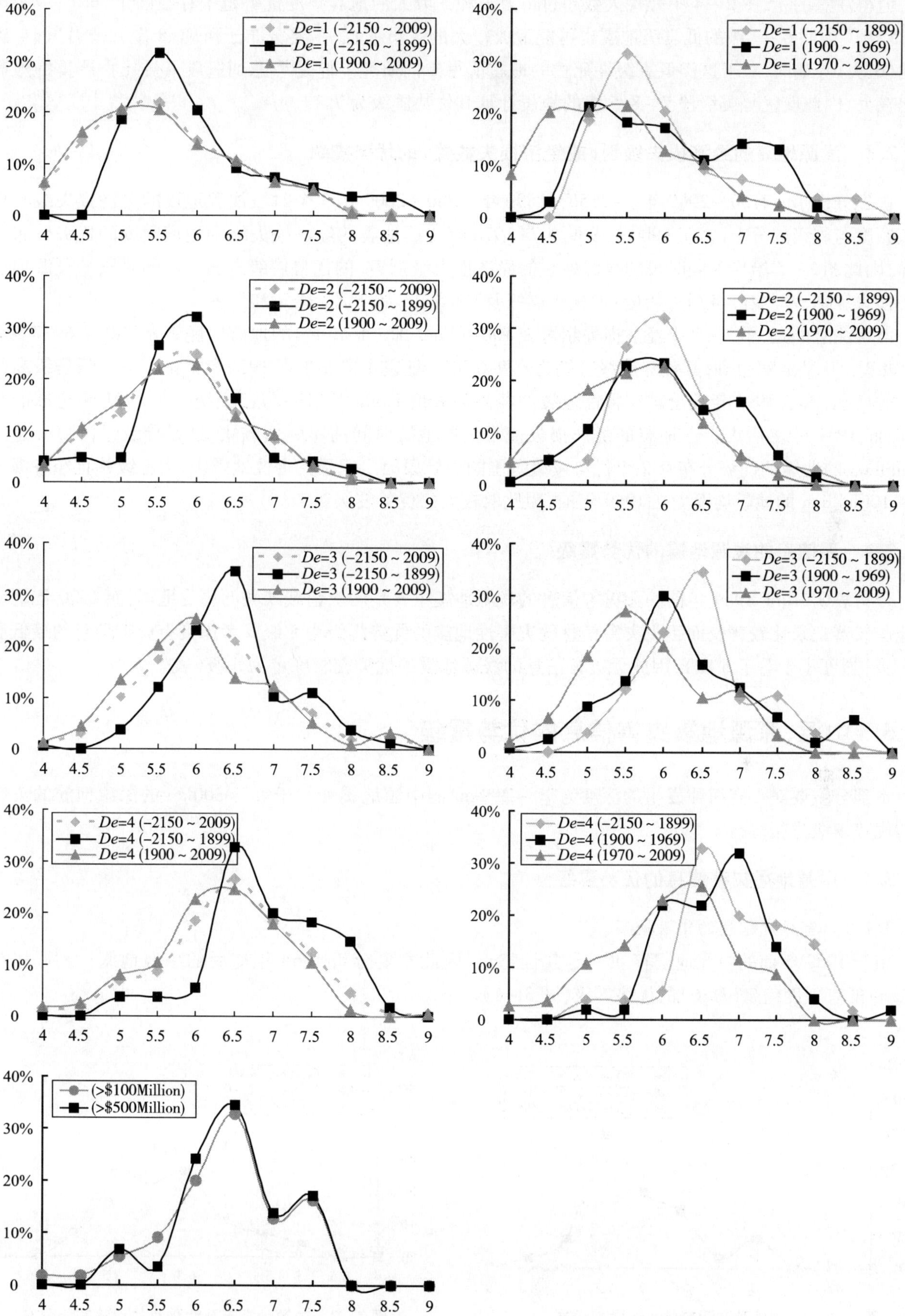

图 2－5　浅源地震的经济损失级别 *De*(或经济损失数量)的优势震级分布

值得注意的是，图 2－4 中死亡人数超过 1 万人和 5 万人的地震频度优势范围存在两个，即 6～7 级和 7～8.5 级。说明 6～7 级的低震级地震也可能造成较大的人员死亡，主要分布于伊朗（8 次）、土耳其（4 次）、中国（6 次）等地区，对于这类低震级高死亡的地震值得专门研究。但是考虑到造成人员死亡严重的地震一般比较大，因此取优势震级段 7～8.5 级的地震计算其优势震级为 7.7。

2.3　浅源地震的经济损失级别（或经济损失数量）的优势震级

首先分析了－2150～2009 年、－2150～1899 年、1900～2009 年 3 个时段浅源地震的经济损失级别信息地震频度与震级的分布，由于 1900～1969 年与 1970 年之后地震的经济损失级别地震频度的优势分布存在差异，因此图 2－5 给出不同时段的浅源地震的经济损失级别 *De* 的优势震级分布。不同时段的浅源地震的经济损失级别 *Dd*（或经济损失数量）的优势震级及其标准方差分别见表 2 和见表 3。

值得注意的是，图 2－5 中经济损失超过 $ 100million（即 1 亿美元）的地震的优势分布存在 6～7 级和 7～8 级 2 个优势震级范围，其优势震级分别为 6.5 和 7.7，地震主要发生在 1970 年之后。对于低震级高经济损失的情况，由于 1991 年前全球灾害性地震的经济损失值 Paula 等（1992）已经统一为 1991 年全球的经济标准，而 1991 年之后灾害性地震的经济损失值是按照地震时间的实际值收集，这是导致经济损失超过 $ 100million 的地震的优势分布存 2 个优势震级范围的主要原因。但是灾害性地震中，无震级并且经济损失超过 $ 100million 的地震均发生在 1969 年前，因此取较大的优势震级 7.7。

2.4　无信息的浅源地震的优势震级

分析表明，由于 1969 年前的无灾害信息的浅源地震主要是历史记载缺失的历史地震，而 1970 年之后全球地震仪器记录比较普及而仍无灾害信息的灾害性地震的优势震级为 5 级。考虑到有灾害信息的最低震级为 5 级（烈度小于等于 6 度），因此无灾害信息的浅源地震的优势震级确定为 5 级（表 2）。

3　中源、深源地震灾害信息的优势震级

本部分主要对没有海啸发生的深度为 70～299km 的中源地震和大于等于 300km 的深源地震的灾害信息的优势震级进行分析。

3.1　中源地震灾害信息的优势震级

3.1.1　*有烈度信息的中源地震*

由于 1969 年前的中源地震存在一定共性特点，因此主要分析 1969 年前后的中源地震（深度为 70～299km）的有烈度信息（$I \geqslant 6$）的优势震级（图 3－1）。

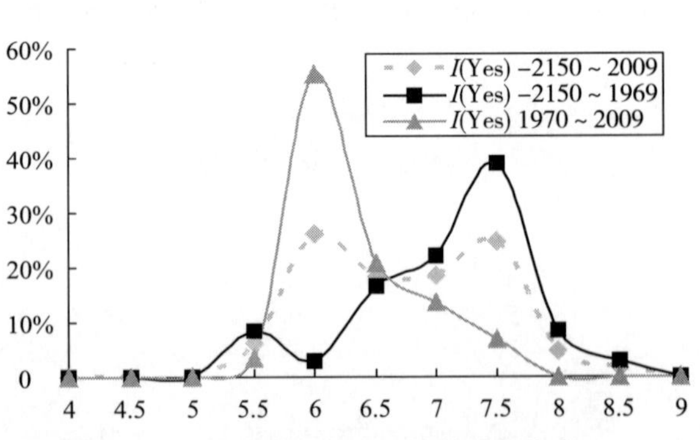

图 3－1　中源地震有烈度的优势震级分布

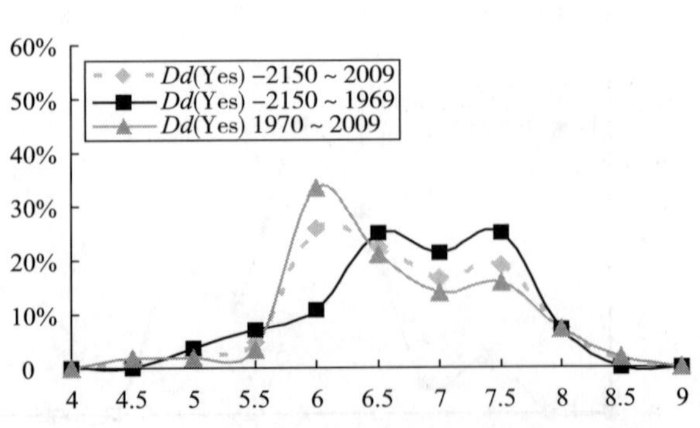

图 3－2　中源地震有死亡信息的优势震级分布

图中 *I*（Yes）表示有烈度（$I \geqslant 6$）信息；*Dd*（Yes）表示有死亡信息

1969 年前有烈度信息（$I \geq 6$）的中源地震的优势震级范围在 6.5～8.0 级，优势震级为 7.4 级；而 1969 年后的有信息（$I \geq 6$）的中源地震的优势震级范围为 5.5～7.5 级，优势震级为 6.4。

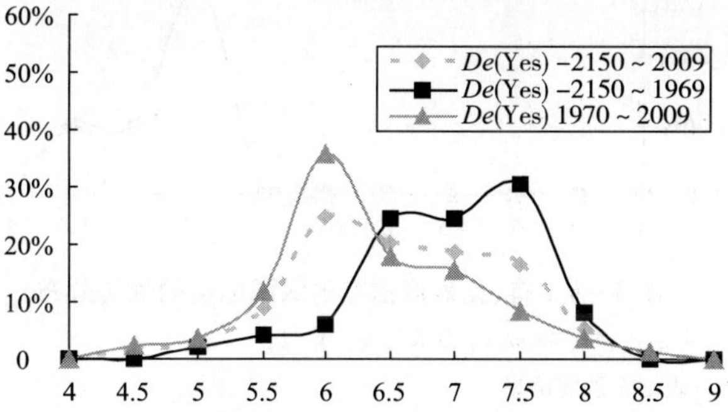

图 3－3　中源地震有经济损失信息的优势震级分布

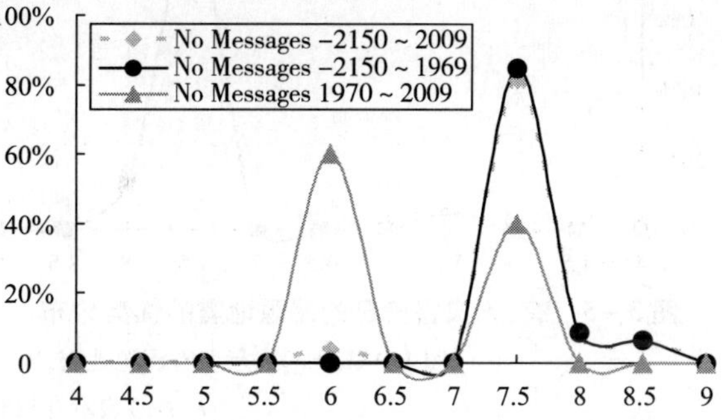

图 3－4　无灾害信息的中源地震的优势震级分布

图中 *De*（Yes）表示有死亡信息；　图中"NO Messages"表示无灾害信息

3.1.2　有死亡级别（或死亡人数）信息的中源地震

中源地震中死亡级别为 $Dd = 1$ 与 $Dd = 2 \sim 4$ 的优势分布存在差异，但是考虑到样本数的问题，计算优势震级时，只要有死亡信息的中源地震作为整体考虑（图 3－2）。因此，1969 年前有死亡级别信息的中源地震的优势震级为 7.4；而 1969 年后的中源地震的优势震级为 6.5。

3.1.3　有经济损失级别（或经济损失数量）信息的中源地震

考虑到样本数的问题，计算优势震级时，只要有经济损失（或经济损失数量）信息的中源地震作为整体考虑（图 3－3），分析表明，1969 年前有经济损失级别信息的中源地震的优势震级为 7.4；而 1969 年后的中源地震的优势震级为 6.5。

3.1.4　无灾害信息的中源地震

对无信息的中源地震的优势分布分析表明（图 3－4），1969 年前无信息的中源地震的优势震级为 7.5；而 1969 年后的中源地震的优势震级为 6.0 级和 7.5 级。

综上所述，对于 1969 年前的中源地震，有烈度信息（$I \geq 6$）的优势震级为 7.4 级，有死亡和经济损失信息的优势震级均为 7.4 级，因此 1969 年前有灾害信息的中源地震的优势震级均取 7.4 级。对于 1970 年之后的中源地震，有烈度（$I \geq 6$）、死亡、经济损失信息的优势震级分别为 6.4 级、6.5 级、6.5 级（表 2），相应标准方差见表 3。

对于无灾害信息的中源地震有 6.0 级和 7.5 级两个优势震级，考虑到无信息地震一般应小于有信息的地震，因此无灾害信息（包括烈度 $I < 6$）的中源地震取优势震级为 6.0 级（表 2）。

3.2　深源地震灾害信息的优势震级

深源地震（深度≥300km）中最大震源深度为 651km。图 3－5 给出了有、无灾害信息的深源地震的优势震级分布，其优势震级均为 7.5 级。仔细分析深源地震有、无烈度信息（图 3－6）；有、无死亡信息（图 3－7）；有、无经济损失信息（图 3－8）的优势震级分布表明，无论有无灾害信息的深源地震的优势震级均为 7.5 级（表 2），相应标准方差却有所不同（表 3）。

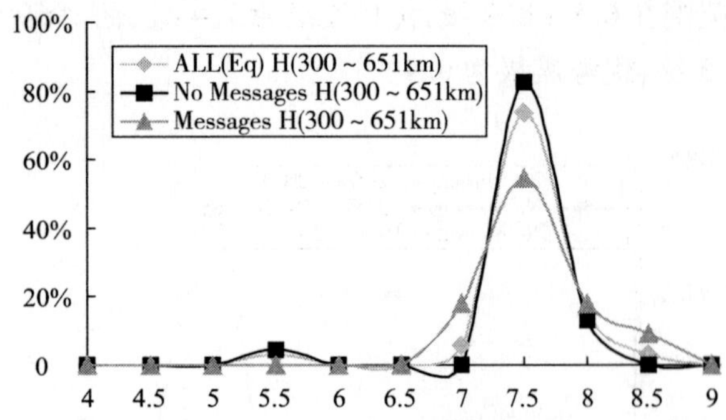

图 3-5　有、无灾害信息的深源地震的优势分布

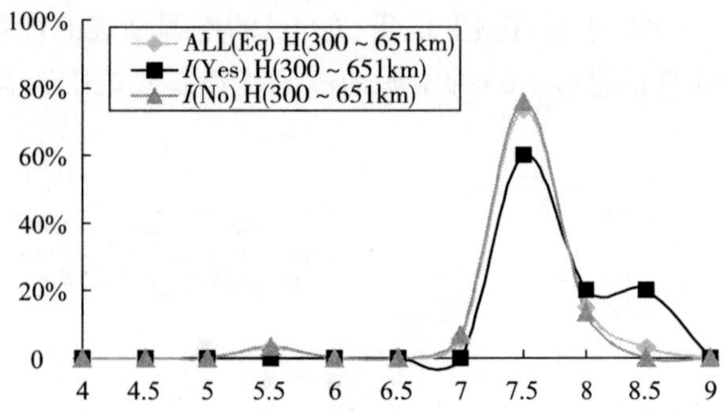

图 3-6　有、无烈度信息的深源地震的优势分布

图中 ALL(Eq)表示所有深源地震，Messages 表示灾害信息；No Messages 表示无灾害信息；*I*(Yes)表示有烈度信息；*I*(No)表示无烈度信息

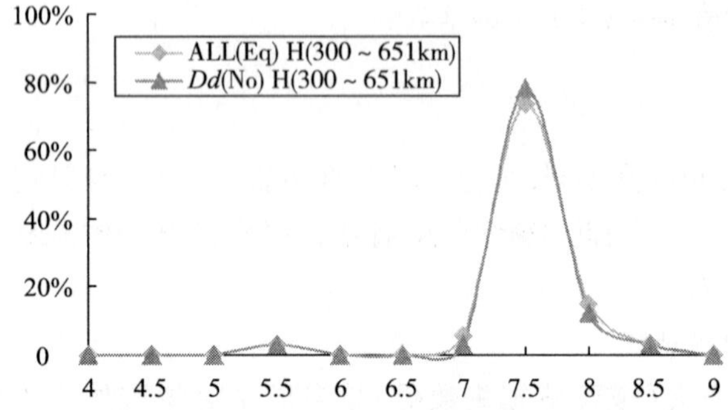

图 3-7　有、无死亡信息的深源地震的优势分布

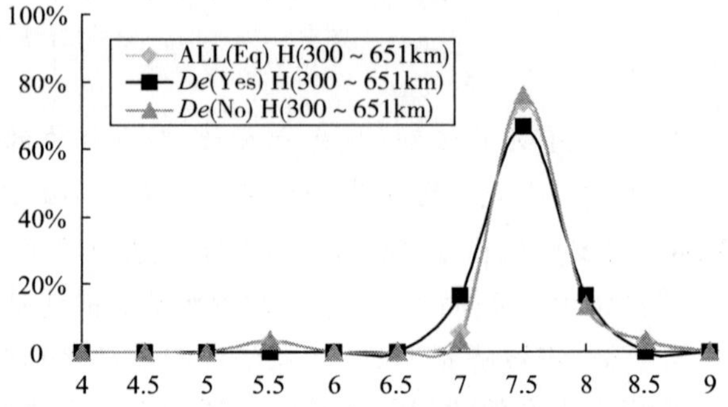

图 3-8　有、无经济损失的深源地震的优势分布

图中 ALL(Eq)表示所有深源地震，*Dd*(No)表示无死亡信息；*De*(Yes)表示有经济信息；*De*(No)表示无经济信息

4　海啸(火山)地震分析

伴有海啸(或火山)信息的地震称为海啸(火山)地震或海啸地震。由于海啸(火山)地震与非海啸地震的不同灾害信息的优势震级范围差别较大，如烈度 $I=6$ 时，海啸(火山)地震的优势震级范围为 7～7.5 级，而非海啸地震的优势震级范围为 5～6 级。另外，烈度 $I=11$ 时，海啸地震的优势震级 8 级左右，但是非海啸地震存在 6.5 级和 7.5～8.0 级 2 个优势震级，分析表明，优势震级为 6.5 级的地震主要分布在地中海附近地区。

因此本部分主要分析除地中海地区外的全球海啸(火山)地震的灾害信息的优势震级，而地中海地区的海啸(火山)地震的灾害信息的优势震级将专门研究。

4.1　全球(除地中海地区外)海啸(火山)地震烈度的优势震级

分析 -2150～1899 年和 1900～2009 年两个时间段的海啸(火山)地震的烈度信息的优势震级分布。图 4-1 给出了海啸(火山)地震的不同烈度的优势震级分布，并计算出不同烈度的优势震级及其标准方差(表 2 和表 3)。在海啸(火山)地震烈度为 12 度的地震中，平均震级为 8.5 级，只要烈度到达 12 度，一般为毁灭性地震，因此，烈度为 12 度的海啸(火山)地震的优势震级为 8.5 级。

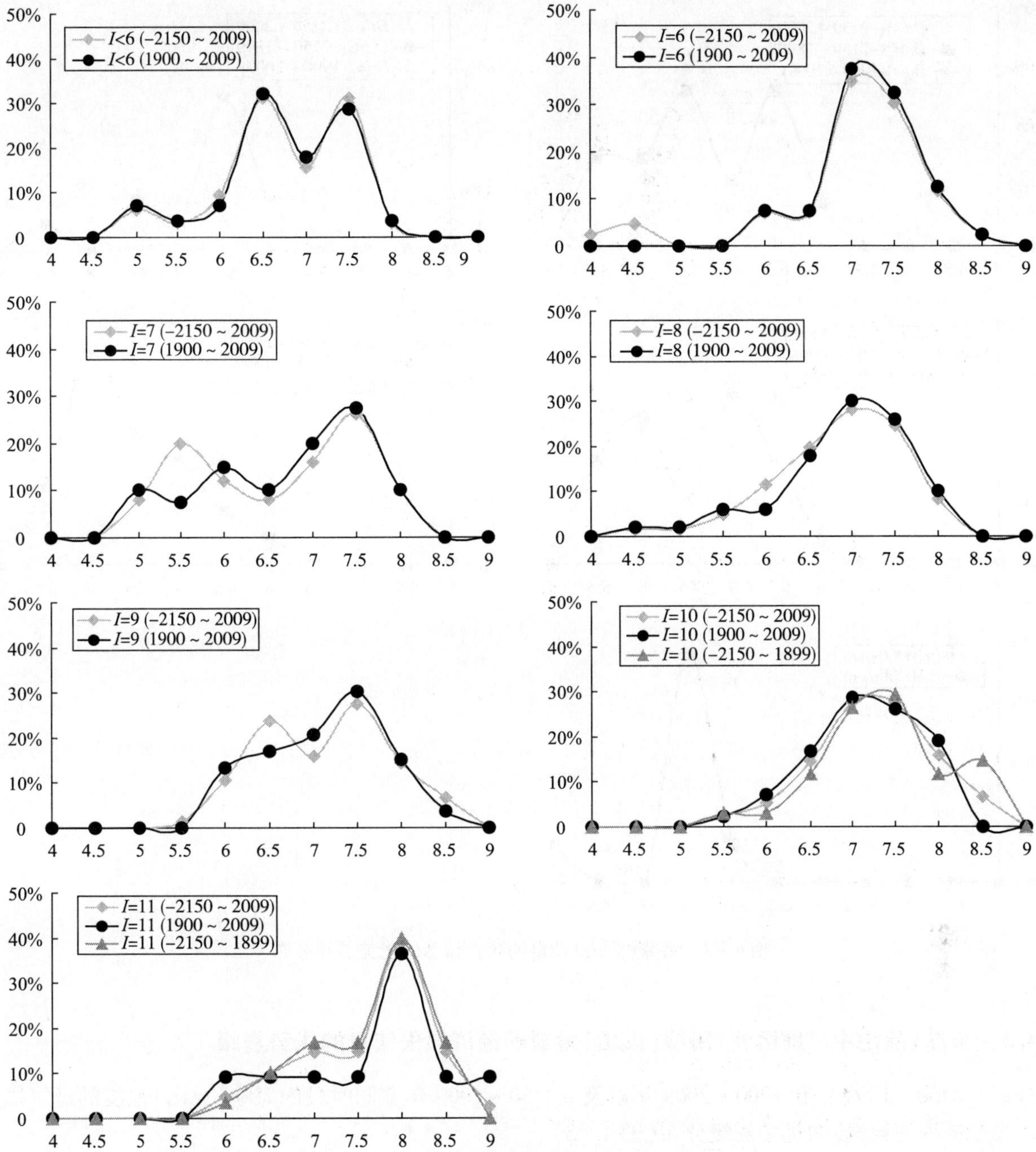

图 4－1　海啸(火山)地震的不同烈度的优势震级分布

4.2　全球(除地中海地区外)海啸(火山)地震的死亡信息的优势震级

分析－2150～1899 年和 1900～2009 年以及－2150～2009 年不同时段的海啸(火山)地震的死亡级别 *Dd*(或死亡人数)的优势震级分布(图 4－2)，并计算出各时段不同死亡级别的优势震级及其标准方差(表 2 和表 3)。

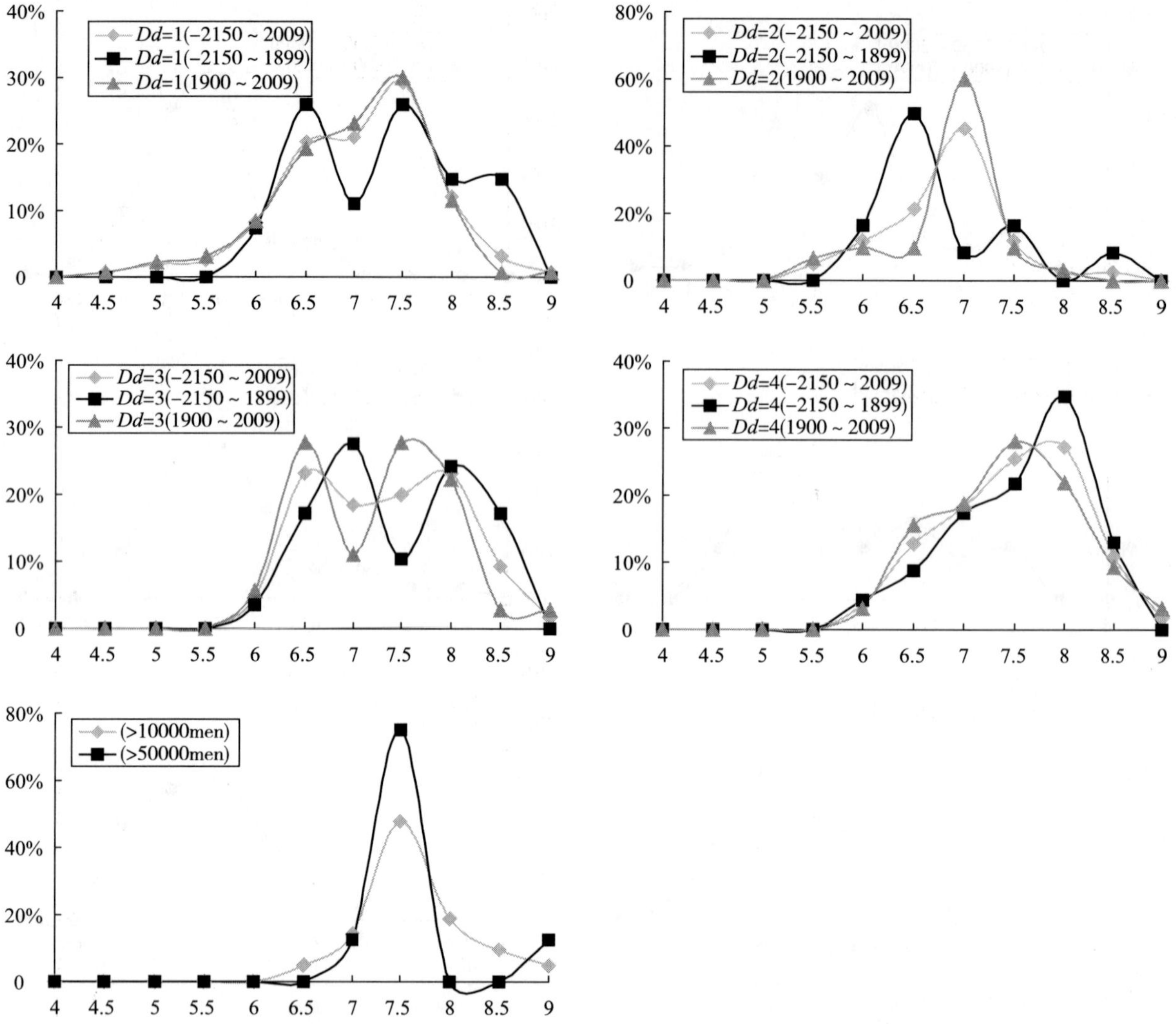

图 4－2　海啸（火山）地震的死亡信息的优势震级分布

4.3　全球（除地中海地区外）海啸（火山）地震的经济损失信息的优势震级

分析－2150～1899 年和 1900～2009 年以及－2150～2009 年不同时段的海啸（火山）地震的经济损失级别 *De*（或经济损失数量）的优势震级分布（图 4－3）。

在海啸地震中，经济损失超过＄100Million（即 1 亿美元）的地震的优势震级有 6.5 级和 7.5 级，分析显示，低震级主要为意大利和希腊地区的少数地震，因此在计算优势震级时，主要取 7.5 级以上地震进行计算。不同时段不同经济损失级别的优势震级及其标准方差见表 2 和表 3。

4.4　全球（除地中海地区外）无灾害信息的海啸（火山）地震的优势震级

分别分析－2150～1899 年、1900～1969 年和 1970～2009 年无灾害信息的海啸（火山）地震的优势震级分布（图 4－4），可得其优势震级分别为 6.98、7.11 和 6.68。可见地震形成海啸的而无海啸灾害记录的地震震级为 7 级左右，因此，所有无灾害信息的海啸（火山）地震的优势震级取 7.0 级（表 2），其标准方差见表 3。

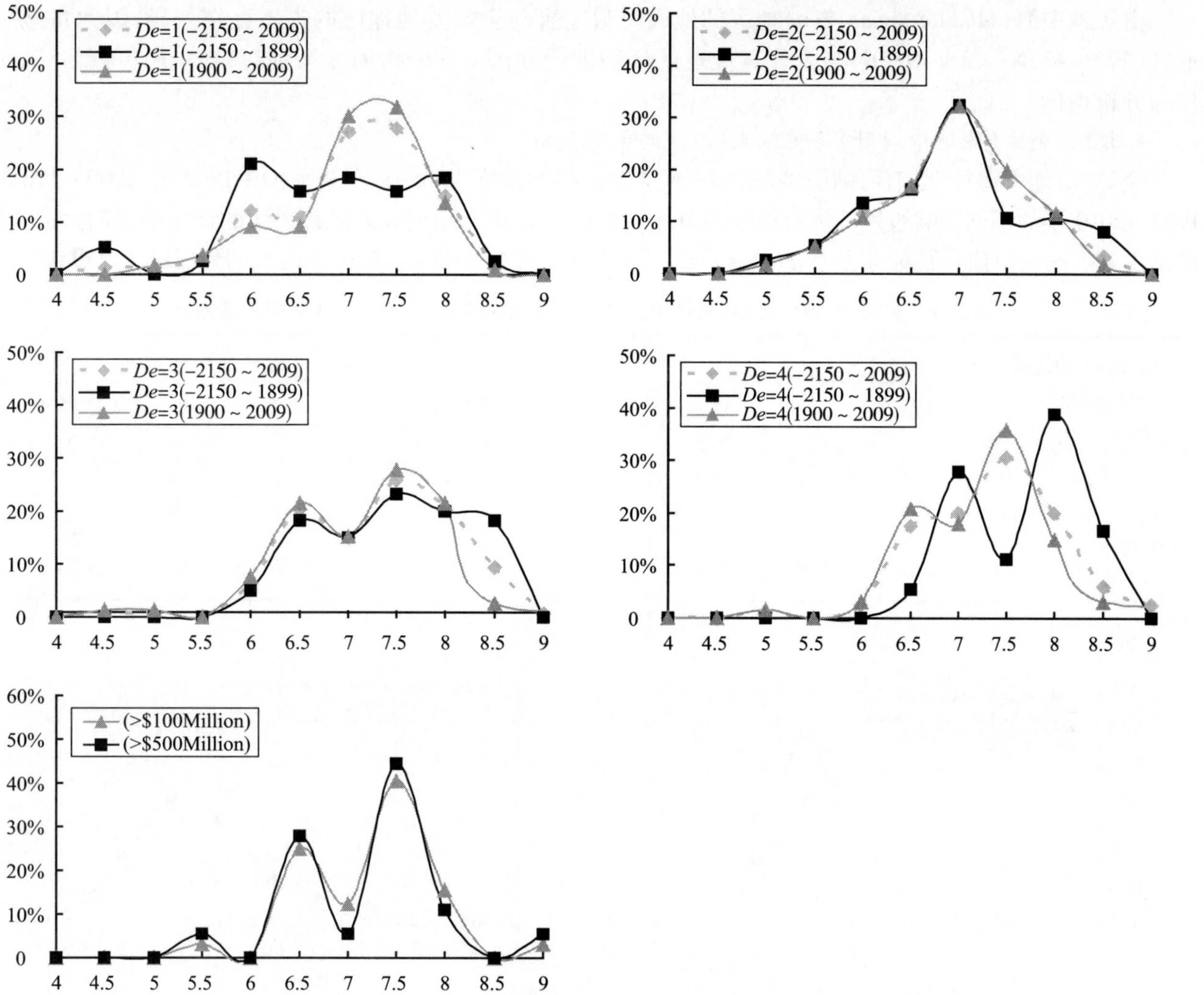

图 4-3　海啸(火山)地震的经济损失信息的优势震级分布

图 4-4　无灾害信息的海啸(火山)地震的优势震级分布

4.5　全球地震海啸信息的优势震级

通过美国国家海洋和大气管理局(NOAA)网站(http://www. nesdis. noaa. gov/)收集到全球海啸灾害资料 2434 条,挑选出地震(伴有火山)造成的海啸灾害信息。

对于海啸级别(简称为啸级)有两种定义,其一是根据 Iida 等(1967)定义的海啸级别 $m = \log_2 h$,其中 h 为最大浪高,单位为米,海啸级别范围为 -5 ~ 10。在地震灾害信息目录中,根据该方法计算的海啸级别(即啸级)用"啸级 I"(mI)表示。其二是根据 Soloviev 等(1974)定义的海啸级别 $m = \log_2(2^{1/2} * h)$,其中 h 为最大浪高,单位为米,海啸级别范围为 -5 ~ 10。在地震灾害信息目录中,根据该方法计算的海啸级别(即啸级)用"啸级 S"(mS)表示。

由于地中海(Mediterranean Sea)地区的地震海啸灾害与全球其他地区的灾害存在差异,因此将地中海地区(27°~45°N; -1°~55°E)与全球其他地区分别进行分析。在分析海啸级别时,均采用"啸级 S"(mS)作为分析指标。

4.5.1　全球(除地中海外)海啸级别(mS)的优势震级

全球(除地中海外)既有海啸级别(mS)又有地震震级的地震 1342 条,分析 -60~1899 年、1900~1963 年、1964~2010 年的不同海啸级别的优势震级的分布(图 4-5),并统计相应的优势震级的计算值,综合多方面考虑给出最后的确定值及其标准方差 σ(表 4),依据该表可对有海啸级别信息的无震级的地震赋予其震级。

表 4　全球(除地中海外)与地中海地区不同海啸级别(mS)的优势震级及误差

啸级 mS 的优势震级及误差		$mS<1$		$mS=1$		$mS=2$		$mS=3$		$mS\geq4$	
		优势震级	σ	优势震级	σ	优势震级	σ	优势震级	σ	优势震级	σ
全球(除地中海外)	-60~1899	7.0	0.27	7.0	0.31	7.5	0.44	7.7	0.53	7.9	0.40
	1900~1963	7.0	0.32	7.3	0.40	7.7	0.26	7.8	0.51	8.1	0.29
	1964~2004	7.1	0.39	7.4	0.29	7.6	0.26	7.9	0.28	8.2	0.30
地中海地区	-1356~2010	6.6	0.39	6.7	0.25	6.7	0.25	6.7	0.25	6.7	0.43

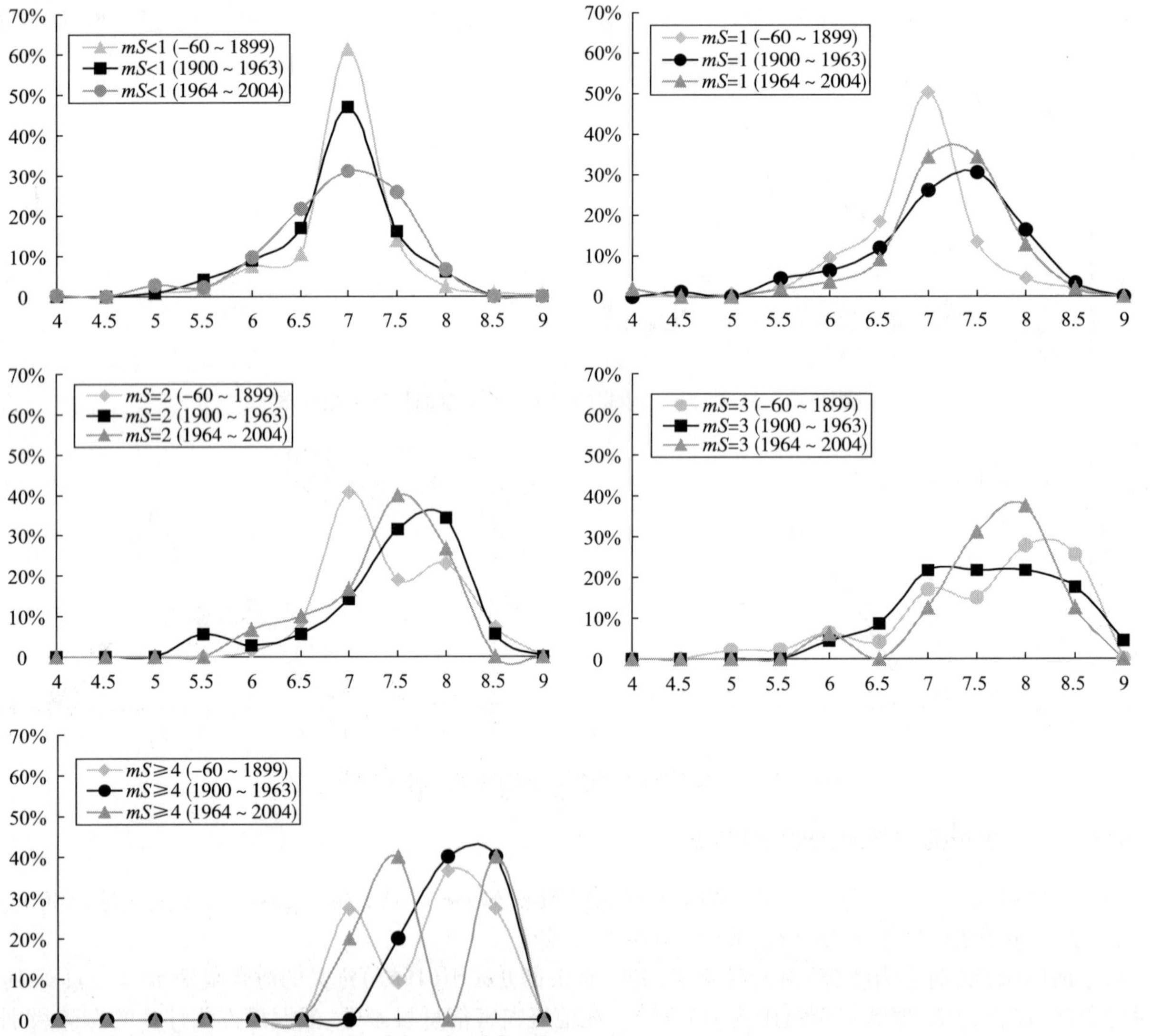

图 4-5　全球(除地中海外)不同海啸级别(mS)的优势震级分布

4.5.2　地中海地区的海啸级别的优势震级分析

地中海地区(27°～45°N；-1°～55°E)既有海啸级别(mS)又有地震震级的地震268条,其中-1356～1899年194条,1900～2010年74条。通过分析表明,1900年前后有海啸级别的地震的优势震级分布基本一致(图4-6a),并且考虑到样本数的问题,因此不对时间段进行区分,只对不同海啸级别的优势震级分布进行分析(图4-6b),并统计相应的优势震级计算值(表4),综合考虑给出最后的确定值。依据该表可对地中海地区有海啸级别信息的无震级的地震赋予其震级。

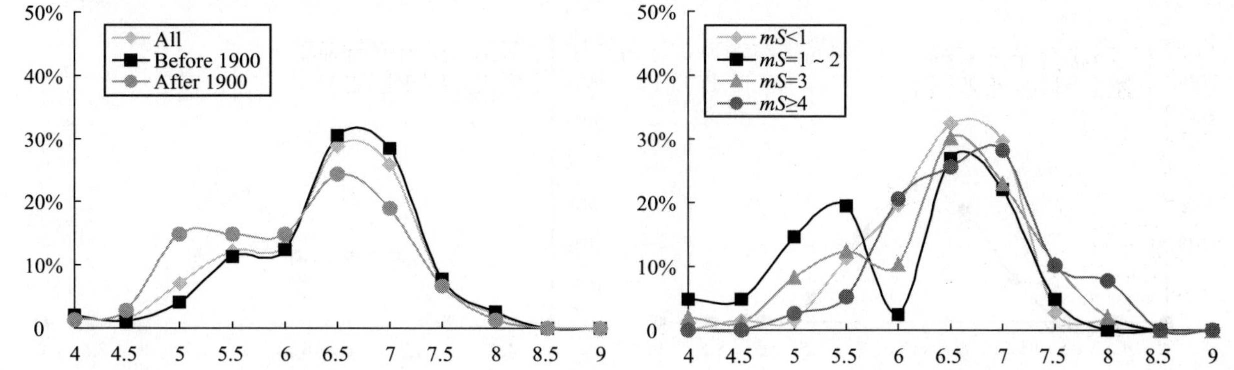

（a）不同时段　　（b）不同海啸级别

图4-6　地中海地区不同海啸级别的优势地震震级分布

4.6　地中海地区海啸(火山)地震灾害信息的优势震级

4.6.1　地中海地区海啸(火山)地震烈度的优势震级

地中海地区(27°～45°N；-1°～55°E)有海啸信息的地震既有烈度信息又有地震震级的地震145条,其中1899年前100条,1900年后45条。通过分析两个时段不同烈度的优势震级分布(图4-7),并计算相应的优势震级及其标准方差(表2和表3)。如果震级优势震级分布存在两个优势震级段,如$I=9$(1900～2010)、$I\geq 11$(1900～2010),则计算两个优势震级段内的平均震级作为优势震级。

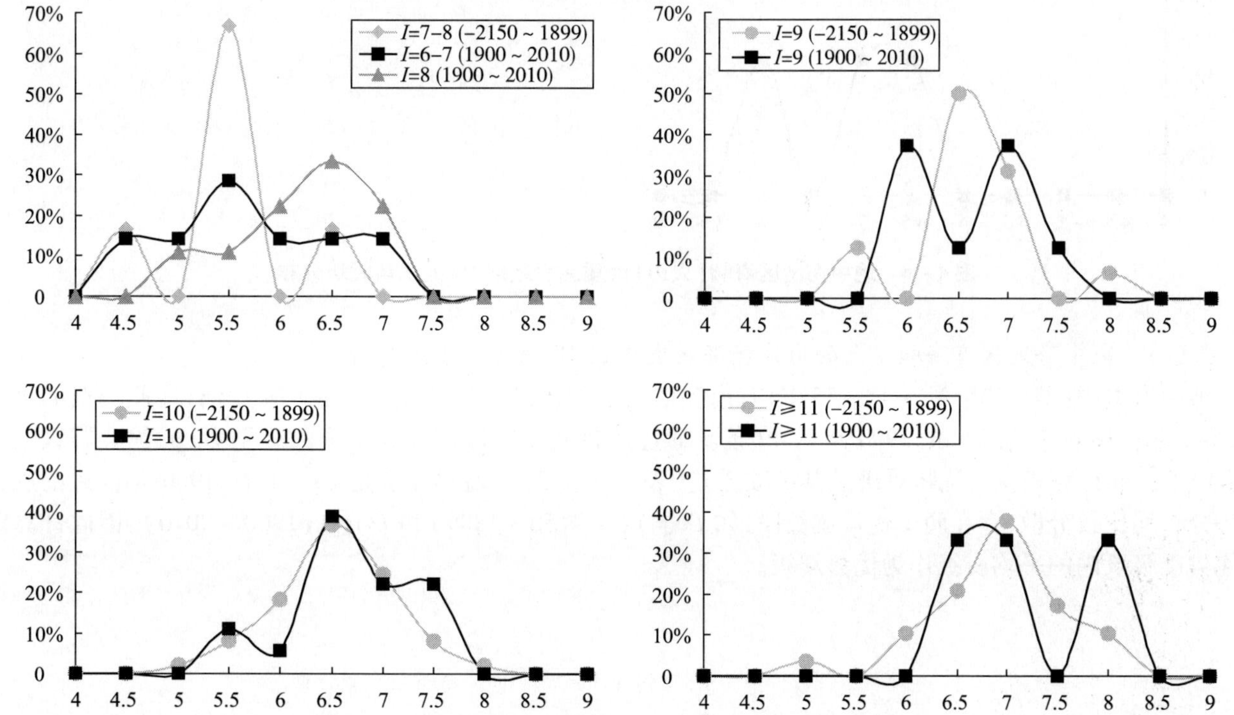

图4-7　地中海地区有海啸(火山)地震烈度的优势震级分布

4.6.2　地中海地区海啸（火山）地震的死亡级别 *Dd* 的优势震级

地中海地区（27°～45°N；−1°～55°E）有海啸信息的地震既有死亡人数级别（*Dd*）又有地震震级的地震 120 条，其中 1899 年前 79 条，1900 年后 41 条。通过分析两个时段不同死亡级别 *Dd* 的优势震级分布（图 4－8），统计相应的优势震级及其标准方差（表 2 和表 3）。如果震级优势震级分布存在两个优势震级段，如 *Dd*≥4（1900～2010）、*Dd*＝5（1900～2010），则计算两个优势震级段内的平均震级作为优势震级。

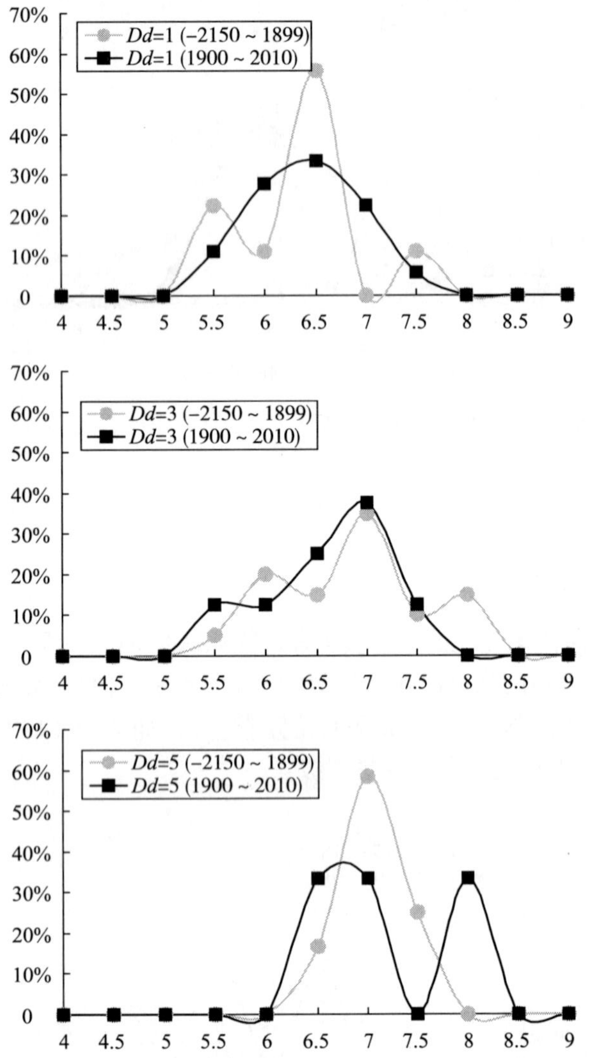

图 4－8　地中海地区海啸（火山）地震死亡级别 *Dd* 的优势震级分布

4.6.3　地中海地区有海啸信息的地震经济损失级别 *De* 的优势震级分析

地中海地区（27°～45°N；−1°～55°E）有海啸信息的地震既有经济损失级别（*De*）又有地震震级的地震 122 条，其中 1899 年前 73 条，1900 年后 49 条。通过分析两个时段不同经济损失级别 *De* 的优势震级分布（图 4－9），并计算相应的优势震级及其标准方差（表 2 和表 3）。值得注意是 *De*＝1 时，1900 年前后的震级优势分布均比较分散，存在两个优势震级段，如 *De*＝1（－2150～1899）和 *De*＝1（1900～2010），因此计算两个优势震级段内的平均震级作为优势震级。

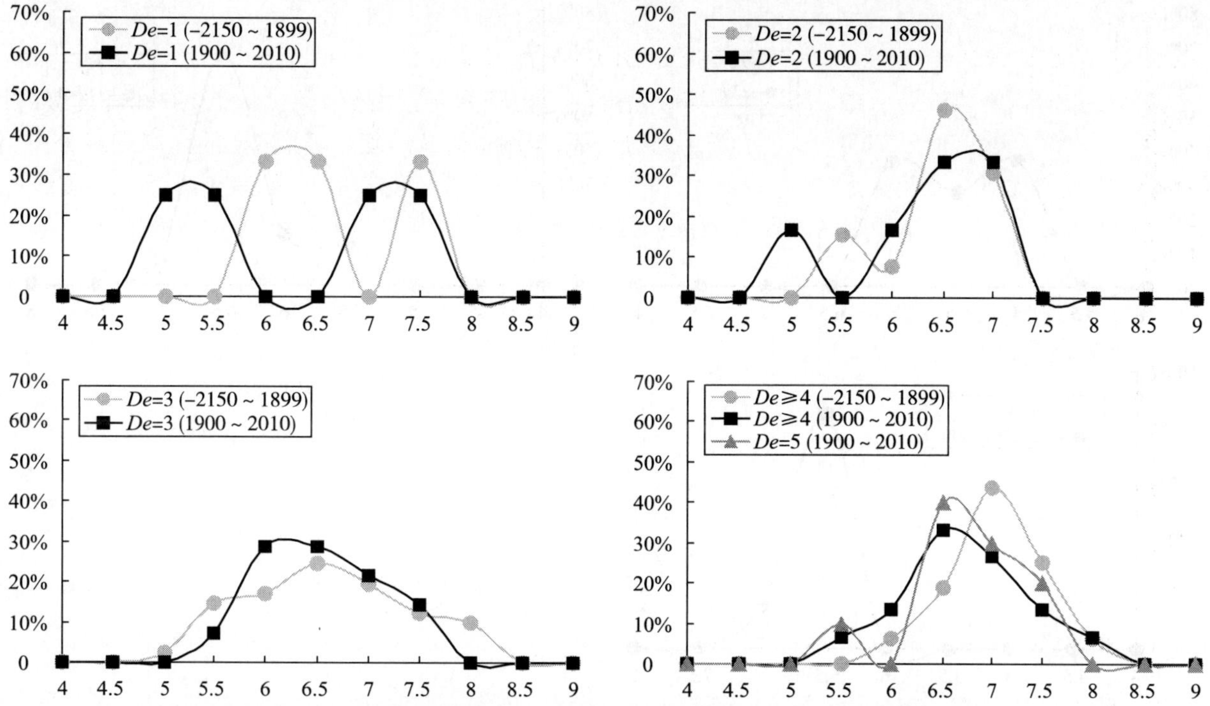

图 4－9　地中海地区海啸(火山)地震的经济损失级别 *De* 的优势震级分布

5　典型地区的地震灾害信息的优势震级

5.1　意大利地区地震灾害信息的优势震级

在所有没有震级的烈度为 12 度的地震中，意大利就有 68 次。但分析意大利地区既有震级又有烈度的地震表明，该地区的烈度与震级关系与全球地震烈度与震级关系偏差较大。因此从网页(http://emidius.mi.ingv.it/CPTI04/)下载的意大利地震目录 2447 次，基于该地震目录对灾害性地震目录进行校对，整理出意大利地区有灾害信息的地震目录 361 次。

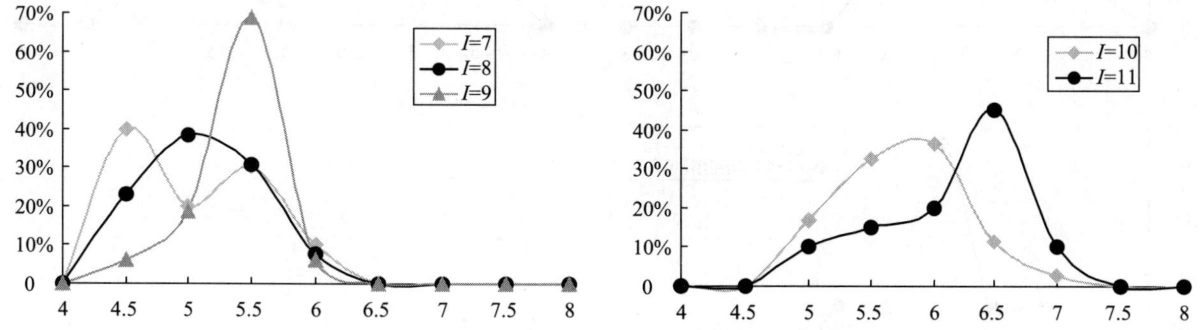

图 5－1　意大利地区地震的不同烈度的优势震级分布

5.1.1　意大利地区地震烈度的优势震级

针对既有烈度又有震级的 131 次地震的烈度优势震级分布(图 5－1)，计算出意大利地区不同地震烈度的优势震级及其标准方差(表 2 和表 3)。

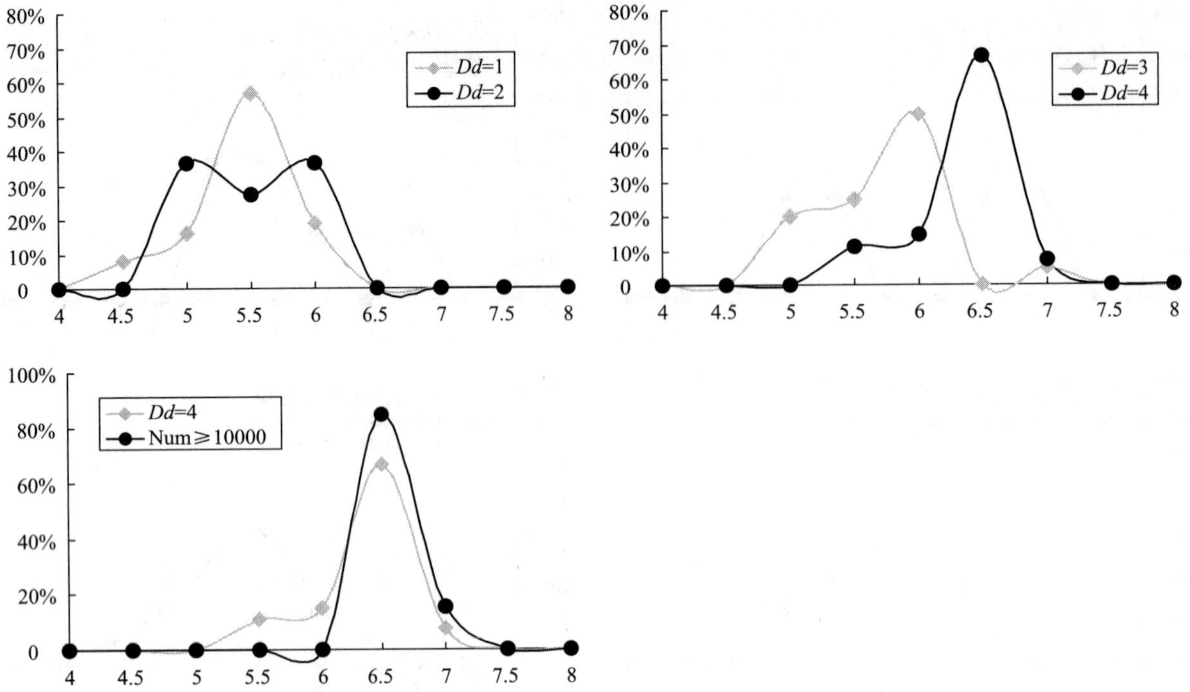

图 5－2　意大利地区的地震不同死亡级别 *Dd* 的优势震级分布

5.1.2　意大利地区死亡级别的优势震级

通过意大利地区既有死亡级别又有震级的 95 次地震的死亡级别的优势震级分布(图 5－2),计算出不同死亡级别 *Dd*(或死亡人数)的优势震级及其标准方差(表 2 和表 3)。

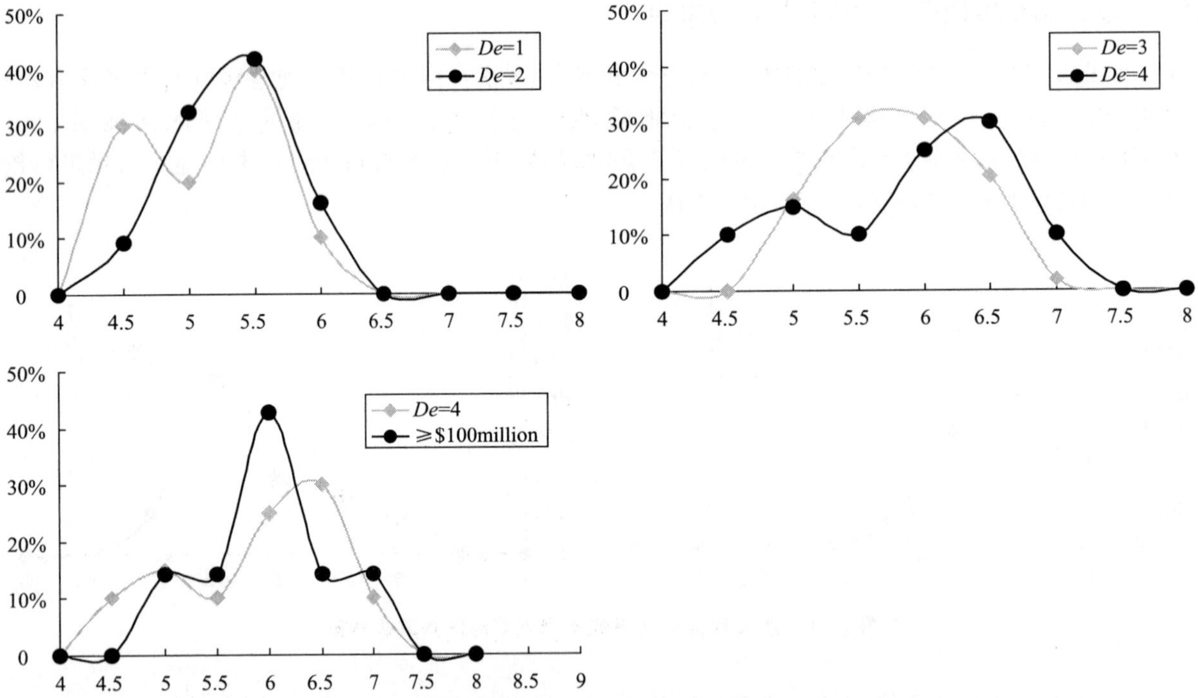

图 5－3　意大利地区地震的不同经济损失级别的优势震级分布

5.1.3　意大利地区地震的经济损失级别的优势震级

意大利地区既有经济损失级别又有震级的 122 次地震,通过意大利地区地震经济损失级别 *De* 的优势震级分布(图 5－3)计算出不同经济损失级别的优势震级及其标准方差(表 2 和表 3)。

5.1.4　意大利地区无灾害信息地震的优势震级

意大利地区无烈度、无死亡级别、无经济损失级别的灾害性地震只有2次，其平均震级为4.99，因此意大利地区的无信息的灾害性地震的优势震级确定为5.0级（表2）。

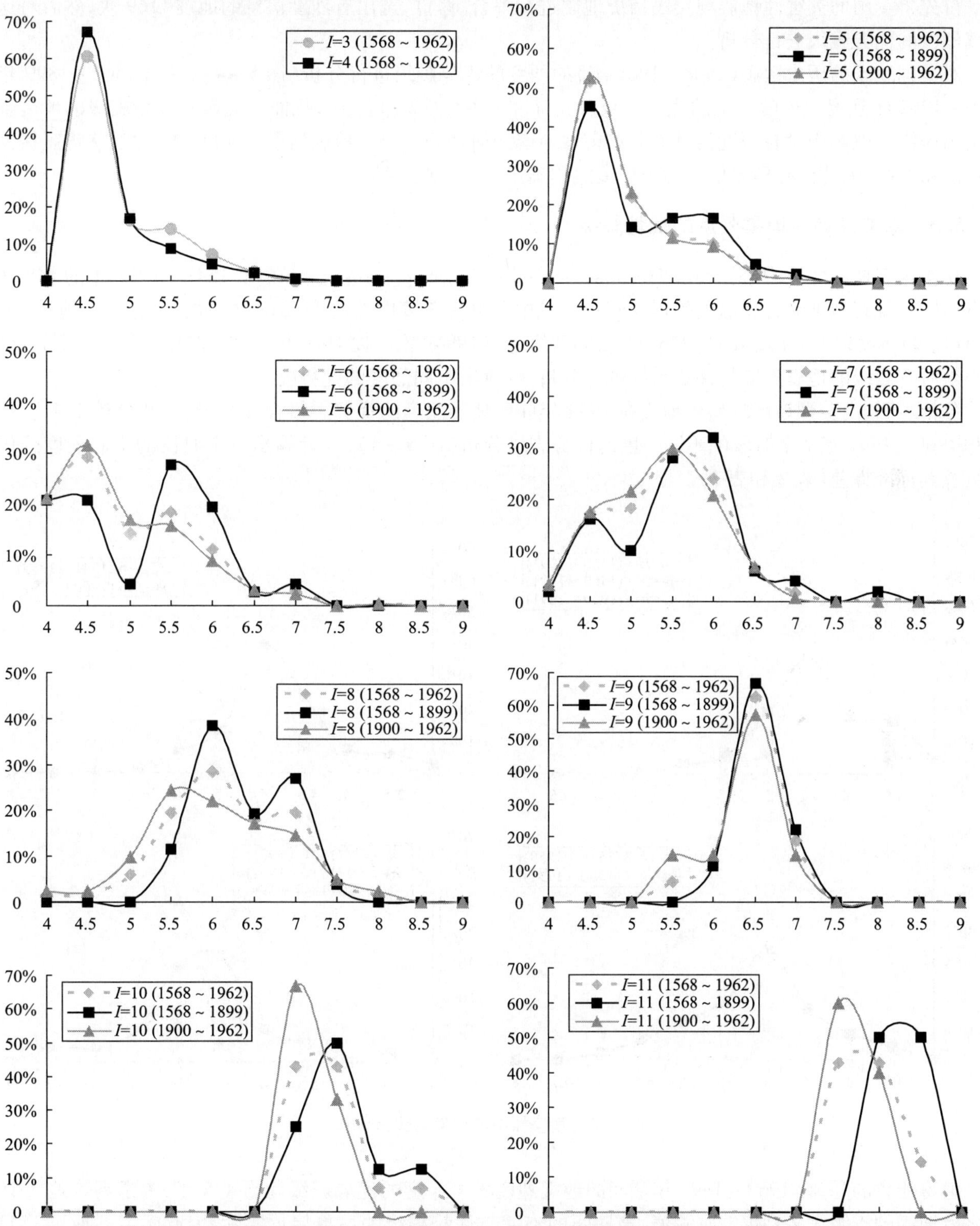

图5-4　美国地区地震烈度的优势震级分布

5.2　美国地区地震烈度的优势震级

从美国地质调查局USGS(United States Geological Survey)的地震数据库(http://neic.usgs.gov/neis/epic/epic_global. html)下载到1568年至1962年的历史地震4203次,其中621次地震没有震级,在621次地震中有烈度信息的地震有340次,281次无烈度信息。为了更合理确定美国历史地震中无震级地震事件的震级,因此必须开展对美国地区地震烈度的优势震级分析。

首先将美国的灾害性地震与美国历史地震进行整合、修订,选出有烈度信息的地震1169次,然后对这些地震烈度的优势震级进行分析。

对美国地区的历史地震(1568～1962年)的烈度的优势震级进行分析(图5－4),求出1562～1899年和1900～1962年烈度在3度以上的优势震级及其标准方差(表2和表3),从而可对有烈度无震级的地震事件确定出震级。但对于没有烈度信息的非灾害性地震如何处理?由于地震烈度为3度和4度的优势震级处于稳定值4.6级,因此没有烈度信息的历史地震均确定为4.6级(表2)。

5.3　南美洲地区地震烈度的优势震级

从南美洲地震区域中心(http://www.seismo.ethz.ch/gshap/ceresis/)下载了1541～1991年的44840次地震,其中,既有烈度又有震级的地震4007次,其中烈度为3度以上地震3313次。但是,无震级地震23185次,有烈度(3度以上)无震级的3236次,无信息的地震19949次。要对这些无震级的地震事件确定其震级,就必须对有震级的地震烈度的优势震级进行分析,计算出不同烈度的优势震级。

分析表明,南美洲地区的历史地震在1959年前后地震烈度的优势震级存在差异,因此分析1541～1959年和1960～1991年2个时段的不同烈度的优势震级分布(图5－5),并计算出2个时段的不同烈度的优势震级及其标准方差(表2和表3)。

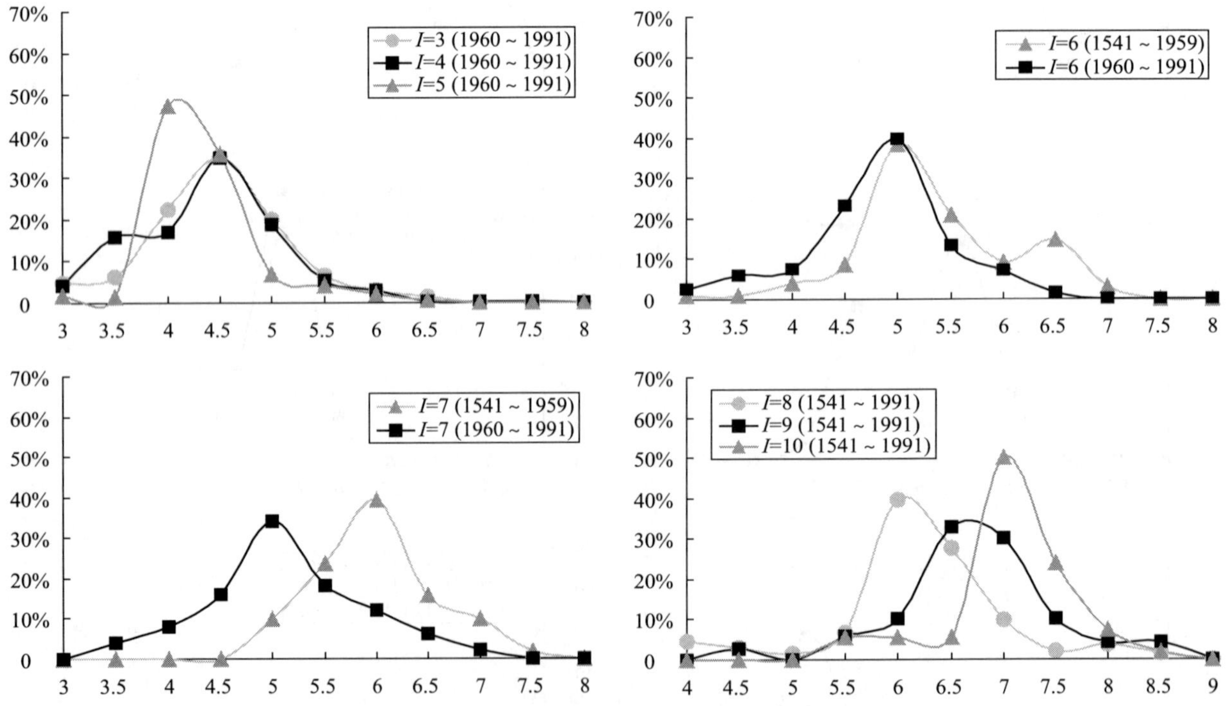

图5－5　南美洲地震烈度的优势分布

值得注意的是,在1960～1991年期间的地震烈度3、4、5度的优势震级均为4.5级,考虑到该地区1960年之后地震的震级大多是仪器观测值,该期间的烈度与优势震级关系更接近实际,因此南美洲地区1541～1959年地震烈度3～5度的优势震级均取4.5级。对于无灾害信息的灾害性地震的优势震级也取4.5级。

5.4　欧亚地震带中段部分地区的地震烈度分析

首先从网站(http://www.seismo.ethz.ch/gshap/cirpan/)下载中欧地区地震目录与灾害性地震目录(http://earthquake. usgs. gov/earthquakes/eqarchives/epic/)进行修订，然后再进行如下地区地震灾害信息的优势震级分析。

5.4.1　希腊地区地震烈度的优势震级

选出希腊地区有烈度 6 度以上信息的灾害性地震 75 次，分析这些地震的烈度的优势震级分布(图 5 - 6)，并计算各烈度值的优势震级及其标准方差(表2 和表3)。烈度 $I=6$ 的优势震级为4.7；$I=7$ 的优势震级为5.1；$I=8$ 的优势震级为5.7；$I=9$ 的优势震级为6.1；$I=10$ 存在5.5 ~6.5 级和6.5 ~7.5 级2 个优势震级范围，由于 $I=9$ 的优势震级范围也为5.5 ~6.5 级，因此计算 $I=10$ 的优势震级范围取6.5 ~7.5 级，计算优势震级为7.0 级。而 $I=11$ 的样本较少无法计算，因此 $I=11$ 的优势震级取 $I=10$ 的优势震级7.0 级。

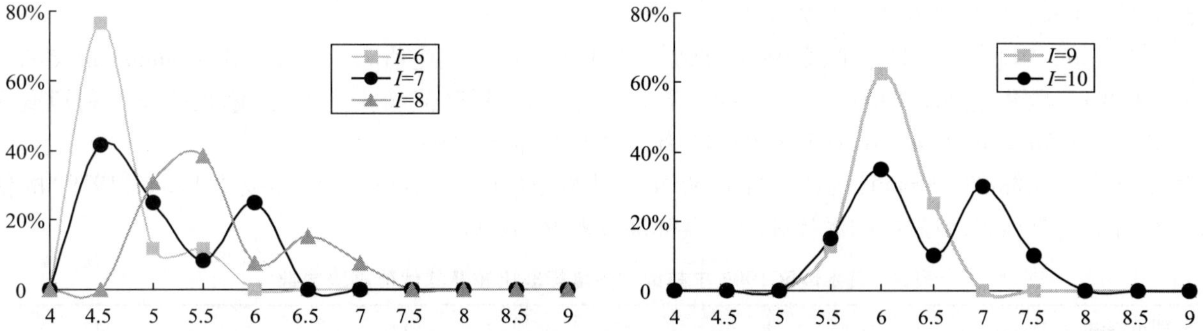

图 5 -6　希腊地区地震烈度的优势震级分布

5.4.2　阿尔巴尼亚地区地震烈度的优势震级

灾害性地震目录中阿尔巴尼亚地区无震级但有烈度信息的地震25 次，最低烈度为9 度，最高烈度为11 度。而该地区的烈度与震级关系与全球地震的统计存在差异，为了该地区无震级的地震事件的震级确定更合理，因此必须对该地区地震烈度信息的优势震级进行分析。

灾害性地震目录与中欧地区地震目录共同修订了50 次地震，有烈度信息的地震只有 17 次，内含烈度 $I=10$ 的地震9 次，其优势震级为6.2 级(图 5 -7)；烈度 $I=11$ 的地震3 次，其平均震级为6.7 级；烈度 $I=9$ 的地震3 次，其平均震级为5.8 级。具体参数见表2 和表3。

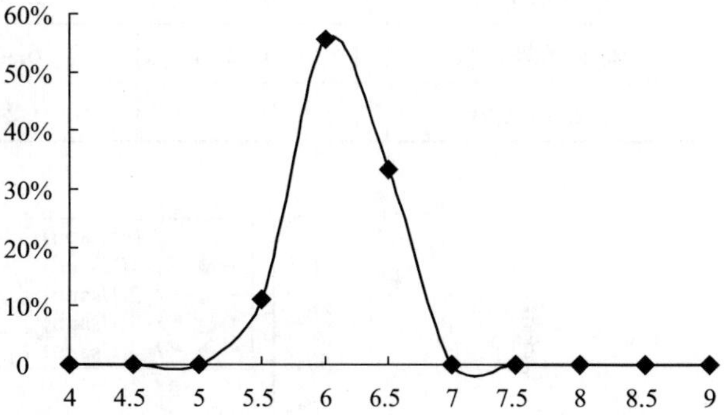

图 5 -7　阿尔巴尼亚地区烈度 $I=10$ 的优势震级分布

5.4.3　巴尔干山脉西北地区地震烈度的优势震级

灾害性地震目录中巴尔干山脉西北地区(40.0° ~46.5°N；14.0° ~22.5°E)(在灾害性地震目录中，地名为"BALKANS NW"的地震)无震级但有灾害信息的地震69 次，由灾害性地震与中欧地区地震目录共同修订的地震 146 次，其中有烈度信息地震 90 次。

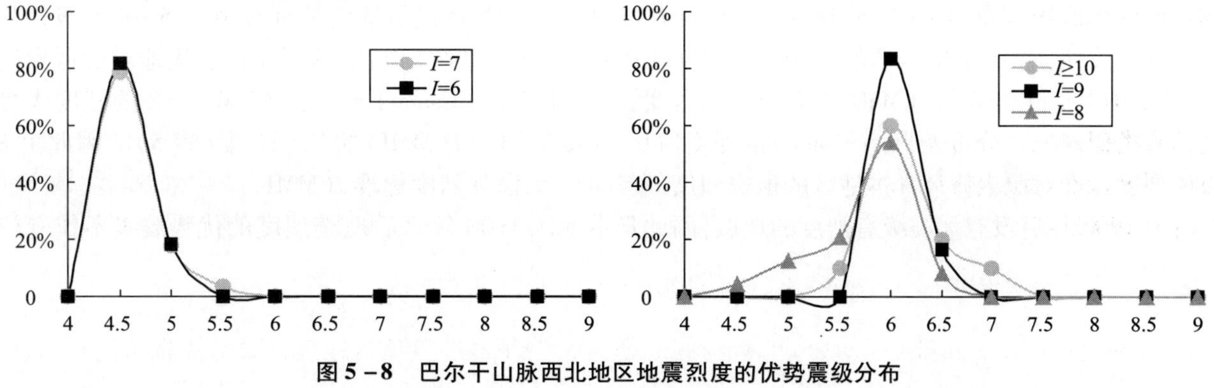

图 5 -8　巴尔干山脉西北地区地震烈度的优势震级分布

由于该地区地震的烈度与震级关系与全球地震的统计存在差异，因此必须对该地区地震烈度信息的优势震级进行分析。图 5 - 8 给出了巴尔干山脉西北地区不同烈度的优势震级分布，并计算出不同烈度的优势震级及其标准方差（表 2 和表 3）。

5.5　日本地区的地震分析

通过对日本地区历史地震的收集（Usami，1979；卢振恒，1991），整理出近 2000 条地震目录，其中近 1750 条有震级的地震目录中，509 条有地震灾害信息（烈度、死亡人数或级别、经济损失数量或级别、房屋毁坏数量或级别、海啸等）。另外，有近 250 条地震有灾害信息但无震级参数。为了通过地震灾害信息更合理确定日本地区无震级地震事件的震级，则需要对日本地区的历史地震灾害信息的优势震级进行分析。

5.5.1　日本地区地震烈度的优势震级

文献（Usami，1979）给出日本地区 599 ~ 1899 年 191 条地震的烈度值 *I*（Usami）（由 Imamura 定义的烈度值从 0 ~ 4 度）。收集整理出 1900 年之后的 47 条地震的烈度（烈度值从 5 ~ 11 度，修正的麦卡利烈度标准（MMI，Modified Mercalli Intensity，1931）即国际统一烈度标准 *I*（MMI）。

根据日本烈度标准 *I*（Usami）统计分析 1900 年前日本地区的历史地震不同烈度 *I*（Usami，1979）的优势震级分布（图 5 - 9）以及该烈度的优势震级及其标准方差 σ（表 5）。

表 5　日本地区 1900 年前地震烈度标准比较及其优势震级参数

日本烈度标准 *I*（Usami）	0	1	2	3	4
国际烈度标准 *I*（MMI）	7	8	9	10	11
计算的优势震级	6.17	6.38	6.91	7.21	8.0
确定优势震级	6.2	6.4	6.9	7.2	8
标准方差 σ	0.23	0.24	0.22	0.24	0.34

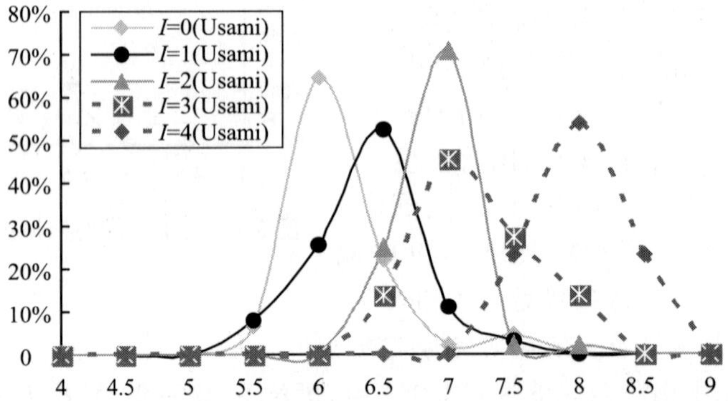

图 5 - 9　日本地区 599 ~ 1899 年地震的不同烈度（由 Imamura 定义）的优势震级分布

图 5 - 10 给出了 1900 年前日本地震烈度标准 *I*（Usami）（Usami，1979）与 1900 年后国际烈度标准 *I*（MMI）的优势震级分布的比较。*I*（Usami）= 0 与 *I*（MMI）= 7 的烈度的震级优势分布中，5.5 ~ 6.5 级优势震级段具有一致性，而 *I*（MMI）= 7 的烈度分布还存在 7 ~ 7.5 级的优势震级段，这属于高震级地震的低烈度现象，因此取 *I*（Usami）= 0 和 *I*（MMI）= 7 为同一烈度级别。同样，*I*（Usami）= 1 与 *I*（MMI）= 8 的烈度优势分布也具有类似现象。分析表明，*I*（Usami）的烈度值 0 ~ 4 度等同于 *I*（MMI）的 7 ~ 11 度（表 5）。因此由表 5 中两种烈度标准对照表修订日本地区的地震烈度 *I*（Usami）为国际烈度标准 *I*（MMI）。

由于 1900 年后没有无震级有烈度的地震，因此日本地区 1900 年之后地震烈度的优势震级不作专门分析。

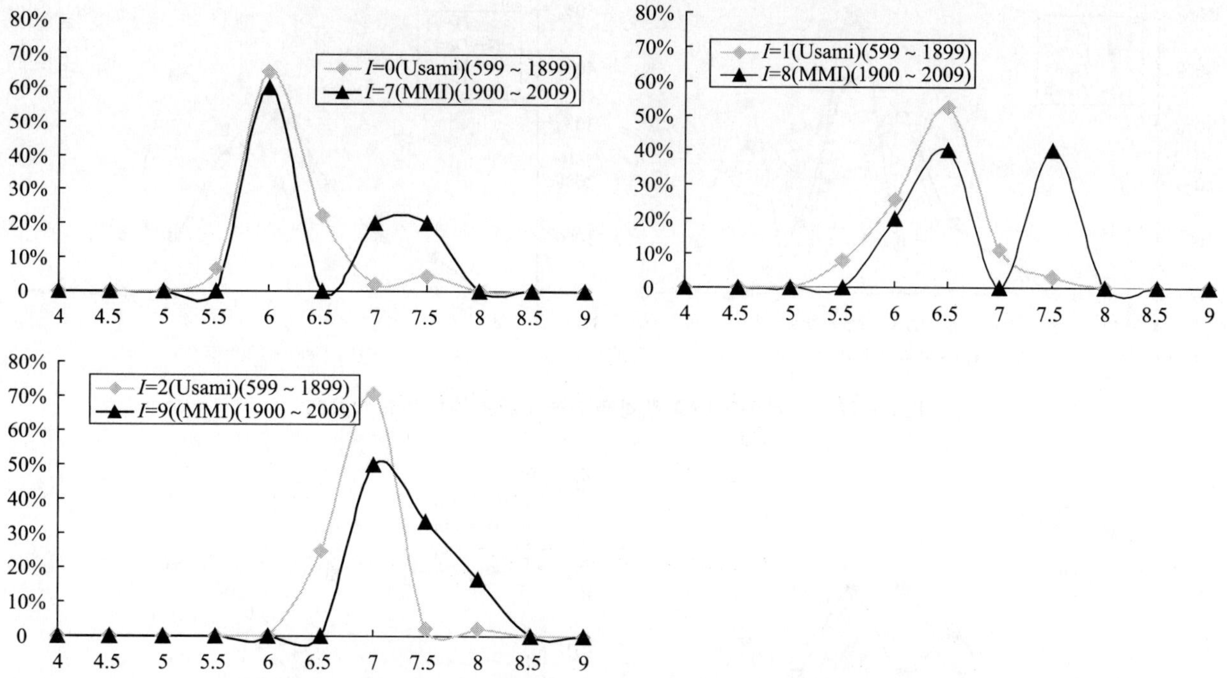

图 5－10　日本地区 1900 年前后两种地震烈度标准的优势震级分布的比较

5.5.2　日本地区地震死亡级别的优势震级

通过对日本地区历史地震的收集(Usami,1979;卢振恒,1991),整理出 231 条既有震级又有死亡人数或死亡级别的地震。图 5－11 给出了日本地区 144～1899 年和 1900～2009 年死亡级别 Dd 的优势震级分布,并计算出不同死亡级别 *Dd* 的优势震级及其标准方差(表 2 和表 3)。

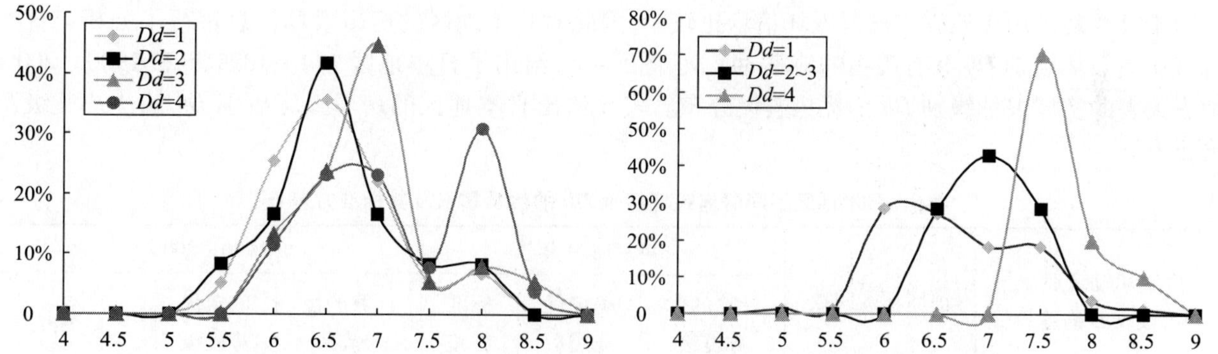

(a) 144～1899年　　(b) 1900～2009年

图 5－11　日本地区 1900 年前、后的死亡级别的优势震级分布

5.5.3　日本地区地震经济损失级别 *De* 的优势震级

日本地区既有经济损失级别又有震级的 157 次地震,图 5－12 给出了日本地区 144～1899 年和 1900～2009 年的地震经济损失级别 *De* 的优势震级分布,并计算出不同经济损失级别 *De* 的优势震级及其标准方差(表 2 和表 3)。

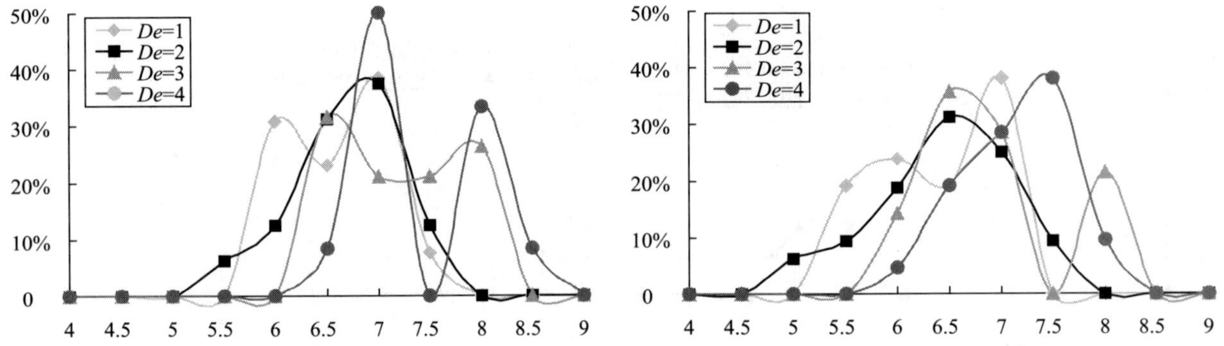

(a) 144 ~ 1899年　　(b) 1900～2009年

图 5 - 12　日本地区地震不同经济损失级别的优势震级分布

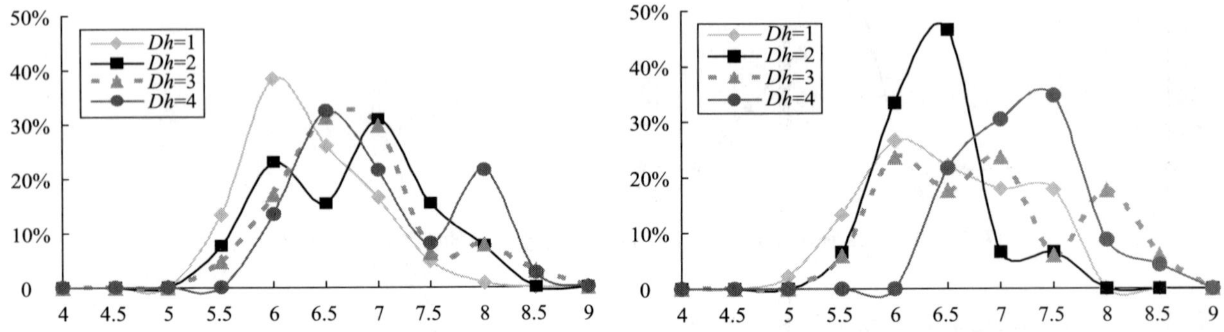

(a) 144 ~ 1899年　　(b) 1900～2009年

图 5 - 13　日本地区地震的不同房屋毁坏级别 *Dh* 的优势震级分布

5.5.4　日本地区房屋毁坏级别 *Dh* 的优势震级

由于日本地区历史地震中房屋毁坏信息比较全，因此对日本地区的房屋毁坏信息进行了分析。日本地区既有房屋毁坏级别 *Dh* 又有震级的地震 341 次，图 5 - 13 给出了日本地区 144 ~ 1899 年和 1900 ~ 2009 年的地震灾害的房屋毁坏级别 *Dh* 的优势震级分布。表 6 给出日本地区的房屋毁坏级别 *Dh* 的优势震级及其标准方差 σ。

表 6　日本地区不同房屋毁坏级别 *Dh* 的优势震级及其标准方差 σ

房屋坏毁级别 *Dh* 及文字描述	房屋坏毁间数	144 ~ 1899 年			1900 ~ 2009 年		
		计算的优势震级	确定优势震级	标准方差	计算的优势震级	确定优势震级	标准方差
1(Few)少数	1 ~ 50 间	6.31	6.3	0.39	6.46	6.4	0.30
2(Some)一些	51 ~ 100 间	6.73	6.7	0.46	6.37	6.4	0.27
3(Many)许多	101 ~ 1000 间	6.76	6.8	0.44	6.96	7.0	0.66
4(Very Many)非常多	≥1001 间	7.0	7.0	0.39	7.22	7.2	0.42

5.5.5　日本地区只有房屋受损信息而无其他灾害信息地震的优势震级

日本地区历史地震记载中，有数量不少只有房屋受损信息而无其他灾害信息的历史记录，这类地震 33 次，其优势震级为 6.1（图 5 - 14）。

日本地区无烈度、无死亡信息、无经济损失信息以及无房屋损毁信息的灾害性地震有 28 次，其优势震级为 6.1（图 5 - 14）。因此日本地区只有房屋受损记录而无其他灾害信息的地震与无灾害信息的灾害性地震的优势震级均为 6.1 级（表 2），其标准方差为 0.38（表 3）。

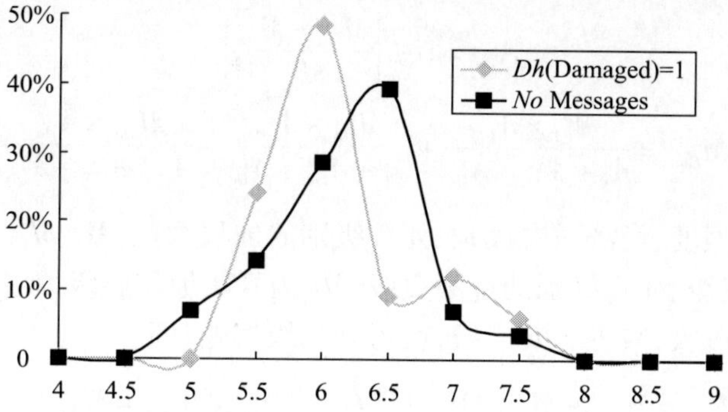

图 5-14　日本地区只有房屋受损信息和无灾害信息地震的优势震级分布

Dh(Damaged)=1 表示只有房屋受损信息的地震；No Messages 表示无灾害信息的灾害性地震。

6　震级的赋值方法及检验

综合考虑地震发生的不同地区、不同年代、地震类别(海啸或非海啸)、震源深度(浅源、中源、深源)以及特殊地区，分析了不同情况的地震烈度、死亡级别、经济损失级别、海啸级别等灾害信息的优势震级，得到不同情况的优势震级参数及其标准方差 σ(表 2、表 3、表 4、表 5、表 6)。基于这些结果，通过检验寻求震级的赋值方法。

首先考虑特殊地区、然后考虑海啸(火山)地震，最后考虑不同震源深度等情况下既有灾害信息又有震级的地震事件的烈度 *I*、死亡级别 *Dd*、经济损失级别 *De* 等参数分别给出的三种震级，通过数学统计分析，给出所赋震级与原有震级之差，选择确定最后震级的最佳方法。

为了验证所用方法的稳定性和可行性，结合实例分析，选择出最佳的震级赋值方法。

6.1　三种震级赋值方法

设计了三种震级赋值方法，分别为最大震级法、平均震级法、加权系数法。利用已有震级的地震目录加以检验，分别统计三种方法的计算结果和真实地震震级的误差值和误差率，最后选出最佳的震级赋值方法。

最大震级法是指选择地震烈度的优势震级、死亡级别的优势震级、经济损失级别的优势震级中最大的震级作为震级赋值结果，即

$$M_{max} = MAX(M_I, M_{De}, M_{Dd}) \tag{6-1}$$

式中，M_{max} 为最大震级，M_I、M_{De}、M_{Dd} 分别为地震烈度的优势震级、经济损失级别的优势震级、死亡级别的优势震级。考虑到这三种指标都是通过宏观调查所得，因此取烈度、经济损失级别、死亡级别信息确定的震级中的最大值可能更符合真实震级。

平均震级法是指取三者的平均值为震级赋值结果，即

$$M_{Ave} = \frac{M_I + M_{Dd} + M_{De}}{N_i} \qquad N_i = 1,2,3 \tag{6-2}$$

式中，M_{Ave} 为平均震级，M_I、M_{De}、M_{Dd} 分别为地震烈度的优势震级、经济损失级别的优势震级、死亡级别的优势震级。$N_i = 1$ 时表示只有一种信息的震级；$N_i = 2$ 时表示有两种信息的震级；$N_i = 3$ 时表示有三种信息的震级。

加权系数法是指对这三组震级所得的结果和真实震级的差异大小为加权系数，三组震级分别乘以它们的加权系数，再相加就得加权后的震级。公式如下：

$$A_I = 1 - \left| \frac{M_I - M_{ag}}{M_{ag}} \right| \tag{6-3}$$

$$A_{Dd} = 1 - \left| \frac{M_{Dd} - M_{ag}}{M_{ag}} \right| \tag{6-4}$$

$$A_{De} = 1 - \left| \frac{M_{De} - M_{ag}}{M_{ag}} \right| \tag{6-5}$$

$$M_{Corr} = \frac{M_I \times A_I}{A_I + A_{Dd} + A_{De}} + \frac{M_{Dd} \times A_{Dd}}{A_I + A_{Dd} + A_{De}} + \frac{M_{De} \times A_{De}}{A_I + A_{Dd} + A_{De}} \tag{6-6}$$

式中，A_I、A_{De}、A_{Dd}分别为地震烈度、经济损失级别、死亡级别的加权系数，M_I、M_{De}、M_{Dd}分别为地震烈度的优势震级、经济损失级别的优势震级、死亡级别的优势震级，M_{ag}为真实地震震级，M_{Corr}为加权系数震级。

将上述方案得到的最后震级，减去真实震级，就得到震级偏差，即

$$dM_{max} = M_{max} - M_{ag};dM_{Ave} = M_{Ave} - M_{ag};dM_{Corr} = M_{Ave} - M_{ag} \tag{6-7}$$

式中，dM_{max}、dM_{Ave}、dM_{Corr}分别为最大震级、平均震级、加权系数震级与真实震级的偏差。

最后，根据震级偏差进行统计，得到最佳的震级赋值方法。

6.2　三种震级赋值方法的检验与比较分析

根据上述的三种震级赋值方法，选择全球海啸（火山）地震、浅源地震、中源地震、深源地震、意大利地区地震、美国地区地震以及南美洲灾害性地震中既有震级又有灾害信息的地震 3352 次，其中 -2150 ~ 1989 年 908 次；1900 ~ 1969 年 1187 次，1970 ~ 2009 年 1257 次，依据全球不同情况下地震灾害信息的优势震级参数（表 2）对灾害性地震中的震级进行检验。图 6 - 1 分别为 -2150 ~ 1989 年、1900 ~ 1969 年、1970 ~ 2009 年以及 -2150 ~ 2009 年最大震级、平均震级、加权系数震级偏差样本统计，分析表明三种方案得到的结果非常一致，都有以下的特点：(1) 偏差值的分布以 0 为对称轴呈对称分布，基本符合均值为 0 的正态分布。(2) 样本的偏差值主要集中在 ±0.5 这个区间内，超过这个区间，迅速衰减。

表 7　-2150 ~ 2009 年全球有震级的灾害性地震的震级偏差检验统计百分比

时间段	-2150 ~ 1899 年			1900 ~ 1969 年			1970 ~ 2009 年		
偏差	dM_{Max}	dM_{Ave}	dM_{Corr}	dM_{Max}	dM_{Ave}	dM_{Corr}	dM_{Max}	dM_{Ave}	dM_{Corr}
$-0.5 \leqslant x \leqslant 0.5$	61.56%	63.88%	63.55%	59.90%	57.88%	57.46%	59.90%	58.15%	58.23%
$-1 \leqslant x \leqslant 1$	85.57%	86.56%	86.56%	84.16%	83.82%	83.40%	85.36%	84.49%	84.33%
$-1.5 \leqslant x \leqslant 1.5$	93.61%	93.61%	93.61%	95.11%	94.61%	94.19%	95.70%	94.75%	94.59%

为了进一步对比三种取值方案的优劣，分别列出了 -2150 ~ 1989 年、1900 ~ 1969 年、1970 ~ 2009 年最大震级、平均震级、加权系数震级偏差值在 ±0.5、±1.0、±1.5 之间样本统计，具体数据见表 7。

从表 7 可见，在 -2150 ~ 1899 年时间段内，偏差在 ±0.5 以内效果最好的是平均震级法（占 63.88%）。偏差在 ±1.0 和 ±1.5 精度以内三种方法效果基本一致。

在 1900 ~ 1969 年，效果最好的为最大震级法所定的震级偏差。在 ±0.5 以内为 59.90%、±1.0 以内为 84.16%、±1.5 以内的为 95.11%。

在 1970 ~ 2009 年，效果最好的为最大震级所定的地震。在 ±0.5 以内为 59.90%、±1.0 以内为 85.36%、±1.5 以内的为 95.70%。

总之，在 -2150 ~ 1899 年，震级确定方法效果最好的虽然是平均震级法，但是该时间段内，没有地震仪器观测，地震震级是通过灾害记载情况通过统计分析估计而得，震级不如 1900 年之后有地震仪器观测结果可靠。在 1900 ~ 1969 年和 1970 ~ 2009 年，效果最好的是最大震级法，该时间段内的地震震级基本上是地震仪器观测结果，采用最大震级法所得的震级偏差效果最好。所以采用最大震级法作为震级的最后赋值方法是最佳的。

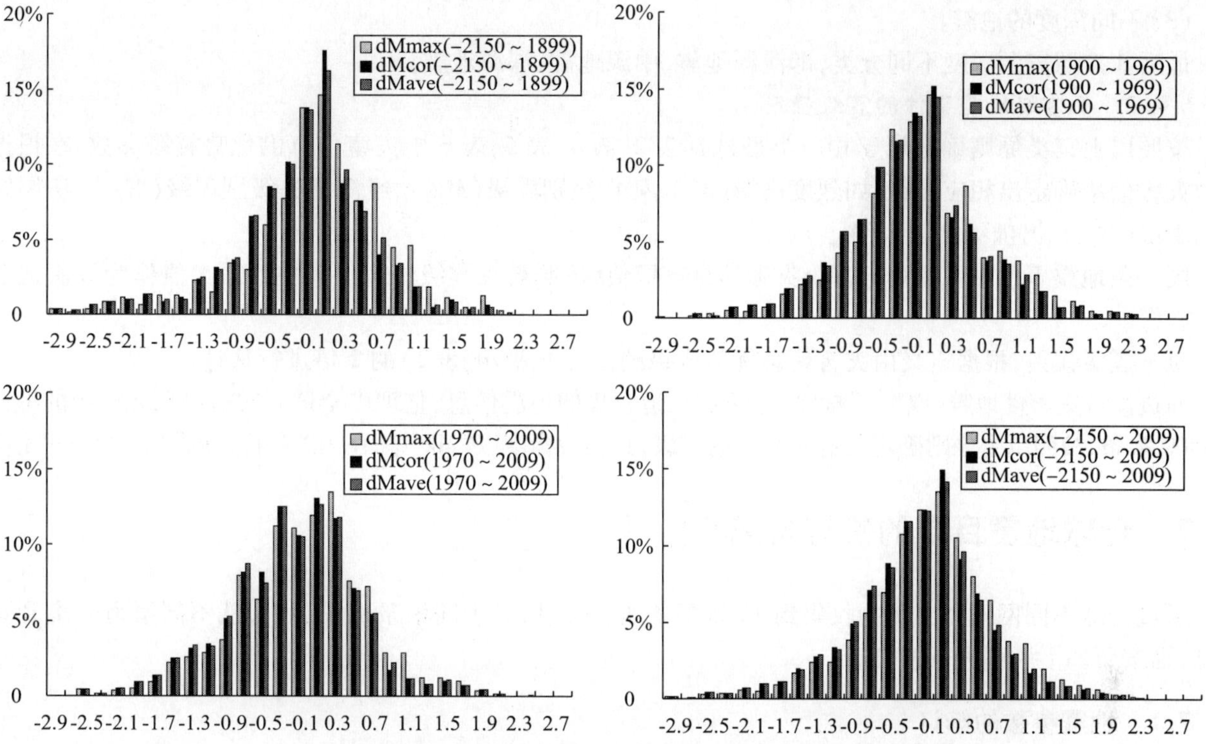

图6－1　全球不同时段的最大震级、平均震级、加权系数震级偏差检验统计百分比

6.3　修正后的全球灾害性地震的检验

为验证最大震级法的稳定性和可行性，收集全世界各网站和相关地震资料中的灾害信息，对灾害性地震进行修订后的地震目录1186条作为检验对象。利用全球不同情况下灾害性地震信息的优势震级（表2）作为赋值参数，并采用最大震级法，对所赋震级与真实震级的偏差进行比较分析。

分析表明，偏差值基本符合均值为0的正态分布，且绝大多数震级偏差集中在±0.5这个区间内。其中，偏差比值在±0.5内的地震为61.51%，在±1.0内的地震为83.74%，在±1.5内的地震为94.38%。这一结果与全球灾害性地震的检验结果基本一致，表明采用最大震级法作为震级赋值方法是具有较好的稳定性和可靠的赋值结果。

综上所述，根据不同地区、不同年代、不同地震灾害类型、不同震源深度的地震的烈度 I、死亡级别 Dd、经济损失级别 De 等信息的优势震级作为震级赋值参数，并由地震烈度、经济损失级别、死亡级别分别给出的三种震级，通过数学统计分析，设计三种震级赋值方法，通过检验分析表明，选择最大震级法是最佳的震级赋值方法。为验证最大震级法的稳定性和可行性，又分析了修订后的全球灾害性地震目录，结果表明最大震级法作为震级赋值方法是可行的。

6.4　全球无震级的灾害性地震事件的震级确定

根据无震级地震事件的灾害信息的优势震级（表2）赋震级时，遵循如下原则：

6.4.1　*优势震级选择的优先权*

（1）伴有海啸发生的地震。

确定是否发生在地中海地区（27°～45°N；－1°～55°E）并伴有海啸发生的地震，然后才是全球其他地区发生的伴有海啸（火山）的地震。

（2）特殊地区的地震。

确定地震是否发生在特殊地区，如美国、南美洲、美国、日本、意大利、希腊、阿尔巴尼亚、巴尔干山脉西北地区。

(3)不同深度的地震。

最后才按照震源深度不同分类,即浅源地震、中源地震、深源地震。

6.4.2 无震级地震事件的震级确定

按照以上三类原则确定属于相应类型选择表2、表4、表5、表6中灾害信息的优势震级参数,在根据地震的灾害信息确定出相应震级,如烈度震级(M_I)、死亡级别震级(M_{Dd})、经济损失级别震级(M_{De})、房屋毁坏级别震级(M_{Dh})、海啸级别震级(M_{mS})。

同一条地震事件中可能列出多个灾害信息震级值,按照最大震级法选择其中的最大值作为该次地震事件的震级。

对于震级误差,根据定义由灾害信息优势震级的标准方差σ(表2)的2倍进行估计。

通过修订灾害性地震(以"*"标注)与不同渠道收集的地震信息,整理出全球有灾害信息无震级的地震事件4400多条,按照以上原则确定出这些地震的震级,其震级标度以"Mk"表示,在"资料来源"列入"Song"信息。

7 全球地震目录的修订与编辑

通过全球不同网站和出版物收集到45万多条地震目录,对于同一条地震事件,从不同渠道收集到不同信息,则按照如下原则进行修订。

7.1 地震参数的修订

在地震参数的修订过程中,以信息来源可信度高的地震参数为准的原则。地震发生时间统一为国际标准时间(格林威治时间),并标注选择震级的震级标度。

首先考虑Engdahl给出的地震参数,然后再考虑各国家(或地区)以及全球资料中的信息作参考。如资料来源中标注"Engdahl,GSHAP"表示由两个渠道(Engdahl和GSHAP)收集资料共同修订结果;"Turkey"表示由土耳其(Turkey)单个信息渠道的资料结果。

7.2 地震灾害信息

在修订过程中,以灾害性地震(以"*"标注)的基本信息为主。在灾害信息修订过程中,以各国和各地区的灾害信息进行修订,并标注相应的资料来源,如中国的地震灾害信息以收集到的信息为准,并在"资料来源"中标注"Dis"。

7.3 地震海啸灾害信息

通过美国国家海洋和大气管理局(NOAA)网站(http://www.nesdis.noaa.gov/)收集全球海啸灾害信息,挑选出地震(包括伴有火山)造成的海啸灾害信息,并修订灾害性地震中的灾害信息,并在"资料来源"中标注"NOAA"。

7.4 震中参考地名的修订

1900年之前的地震事件没有仪器记录,因此震中位置一般是地震破坏最严重城市的经度和纬度。1900年之后的地震震中一般是通过仪器测算的震中经度和纬度。因此统一按照震中经度和纬度在Google Earth上修订地震震中参考英文地名,并翻译为中文。原则上震中参考地名为"国名:州名或县级地名"。

7.5 全球地震灾害信息目录及地震目录修订

7.5.1 地震目录修订

修订、编辑了全球公元前9999年至公元1963年3级以上地震和1964年至公元2011年6月4级以上地震目录15万余条。

为了研究全球地震活动性的需要，修订、编辑了全球公元前9999年至公元1963年4.5级以上地震和1964年至2011年6月5.5级以上地震59000多条，包括地震时间、震中(经度、纬度、英文地名、中文地名)、深度、震级、震级标度以及资料来源。

7.5.2 地震灾害信息修订

修订、编辑了从公元前9999年至2011年6月全球有灾害信息的地震灾害信息目录13580多条。每一条地震灾害信息目录中包括地震参数、海啸信息、灾害信息以及资料来源信息，其中，地震参数包括地震时间、震中(经度、纬度、英文地名、中文地名)、深度、震级和震级标度。海啸灾害信息包括海啸源、最大浪高、啸级 $I(mI)$(Iida 等，1967)、啸级 $S(mS)$(Soloviev 等，1974)。地震灾害信息包括烈度 I(修订的麦卡利烈度，MMI)、死亡人员和级别 Dd、受伤人数和级别 Dd、经济损失数量和经济损失级别(De)、房屋毁坏数量和级别(Dh)，房屋受损数量和级别(Dh)。

7.6 全球地震目录的完整性

7.6.1 应用震级分段频度与累积频度粗略分析

为了分析地震目录完整性的最低震级，基于震级分段频度与累积频度统计粗略分析地震目录的完整性。在震级分段频度统计中，一般低震级段频度应大于该高震级段频度。如果出现低震级段的频度低于高震级段频度，则此拐点可视为完整地震目录的最低震级。

由震级分段频度与累积频度统计分析表明，全球1699年前7级以下地震严重缺失。1700～1899年7级以下地震存在缺失。1900～1930年7级以上地震基本完整。1931～1956年6.5级以上地震基本完整。1956～1963年6级以上地震基本完整。1964～1999年5.5级以上地震基本完整。2000年之后5级以上地震完整。

7.6.2 震级与频度关系估计地震目录完整性

应用震级与频度关系 $\lg\Sigma\bar{N}=\mathrm{b}M+\mathrm{a}$，式中，$\Sigma\bar{N}$ 为年平均频度；M 为震级；a、b 为常数，震级每隔0.5级为一个级别。

全球1900～2008年6.5级以上完整性地震目录的年平均频度的对数 $\lg\Sigma\bar{N}$ 与震级 M 拟合关系 $\lg\Sigma\bar{N}=-1.1464M+9.2242$，相关系数 $R=0.9960$。

全球1990～2008年5级以上完整性地震目录的年平均频度的对数 $\lg\Sigma\bar{N}$ 与震级 M 拟合关系 $\lg\Sigma\bar{N}=-1.1077M+8.9697$，相关系数 $R=0.9988$。

表8 全球年平均频度与震级的标准拟合关系

方案	1900～2008年	1990～2008年	平均
a	9.2242	8.9697	
b	-1.1464	-1.1077	
R	0.9960	0.9988	
$\bar{N}(M\geq5.0)$	3106	2699	2902
$\bar{N}(M\geq5.5)$	830	754	792
$\bar{N}(M\geq6.0)$	222	211	216
$\bar{N}(M\geq6.5)$	59	59	59
$\bar{N}(M\geq7.0)$	16	16	16
$\bar{N}(M\geq7.5)$	4	5	4.5
$\bar{N}(M\geq8.0)$	1	1	1

通过以上两种地震年平均频度对数与震级关系计算出的不同震级范围的年平均数(表8)，再求出两者平均值作为全球标准的年平均频度数 $\bar{N}_{标准}$。

地震目录完整率 W 定义为(魏富胜、许忠怀等,2009):

$$W = \frac{\overline{N}}{\overline{N}_{标准}}$$

式中,$\overline{N}$ 为一定时间段内统计得到的年平均地震频度,$\overline{N}_{标准}$ 为根据线性拟合关系式得到的年平均频度(表8)。

根据全球地震目录分析表明,1800 年之前地震目录完整性较差,7.5 级以上地震的完整率均不足 30%,表明 7.5 级以上地震的缺失都较严重。

1800 ~ 1899 年 7 级以上地震的完整率近 50%;7.5 级以上的地震完整率为 64.03%,也就是说,7 级以上地震只有正常水平的一半左右。

1900 ~ 1956 年 6.5 级以上地震完整性较好。1957 ~ 1969 年为 6 级以上地震完整性达到 71.29%。1970 ~ 2009 年 5 级以上地震目录较完整。

根据全球地震目录不同时期在不同震级范围的完整率分布(表 9),定义完整率大于 70.7% 的震级为地震目录基本完整的最低震级(魏富胜,许忠怀等,2009),完整率在 50% 左右的震级为参考震级。

表 9　全球不同时期地震目录基本完整的最低震级和参考震级

时间段(年)	1800 ~ 1899	1900 ~ 1930	1931 ~ 1956	1957 ~ 1969	1970 ~ 1989	1990 ~ 1999	2000 ~ 2008
最低震级(W≥70.7%)	≈7.5	6.5	6.2	6.0	5.0	5.0	5.0
参考震级(W≥50%)	7.0	6.3	6.0	5.5	4.7	4.7	4.5

修订后的全球地震目录的完整性分析表明(表 9),1799 年前的地震目录完整率均不足 30%,表明地震缺失严重。1800 ~ 1899 年地震目录基本完整的最低震级为 7.5 级,参考震级为 7 级。1900 ~ 1930 年地震目录基本完整的最低震级为 6.5 级,参考震级为 6.3 级。1931 ~ 1956 年地震目录基本完整的最低震级为 6.2 级,参考震级为 6 级。1957 ~ 1969 年地震目录基本完整的最低震级为 6 级,参考震级为 5.5 级。1970 ~ 1999 年地震目录基本完整为 5 级以上地震,参考震级为 4.7 级。2000 年之后 5 级以上地震目录为基本完整,参考震级为 4.5 级。

参 考 文 献

陈棋福、郑大林、车时等编，2002，中国震例（1992～1994），北京：地震出版社。

陈棋福、郑大林、刘桂萍等编，2002，中国震例（1995～1996），北京：地震出版社。

陈棋福、郑大林、高荣胜等编，2003，中国震例（1997～1999），北京：地震出版社。

陈棋福、郑大林、车时等编，2008，中国震例（2000～2002），北京：地震出版社。

刁守中等编、2008，中国历史有感地震目录，北京：地震出版社。

傅征祥、刘桂萍、邵志刚等，2009，板块构造和地震活动性，北京：地震出版社。

高建国，1990，地震损失简表，北京：地震出版社。

顾功叙等编，1983，中国地震目录（公元前1831年至公元1969年），北京：科学出版社。

国家地震局震害防御司编，1995，中国历史强震目录（公元前23世纪至公元1911年），北京：地震出版社。

郭增建、陈鑫连主编，1986，地震对策，北京：地震出版社。

李裕澈编译，2001，朝鲜·韩国地震目录（公元27～1985年），北京：地震出版社。

卢振恒编，1991，日本破坏地震概观，北京：地震出版社。

罗伟等编译，1996，全球重大灾害性地震目录（2150B. C. ～1991A. D.），北京：地震出版社。

时振梁等编，1986，世界地震目录（1900～1980 $M\geqslant6$），北京：地图出版社。

宋治平、张国民、刘杰等编著，2011，全球地震目录（9999B. C. ～1963A. D. M≥5. 0；1964 A. D. ～2010A. D. $M\geqslant$ 6. 0），北京：地震出版社。

汪素云等编，1999，中国近代地震目录（公元1912～1990年），北京：中国科学技术出版社。

魏富胜、许忠怀、王淑辉等，2009，中国大陆地区的地震检测能力，地震地磁观测与研究，30（5）：26～33。

谢毓寿、蔡美彪主编，1983，中国地震历史资料汇编（第五卷），北京：科学出版社。

张肇诚、罗兰格、李海华等编，1988，中国震例（1966～1975），北京：地震出版社。

张肇诚、罗兰格、李海华等编，1990，中国震例（1976～1980），北京：地震出版社。

张肇诚、罗兰格、李海华等编，1990，中国震例（1981～1985），北京：地震出版社。

张肇诚、郑大林、徐京华等编，1999，中国震例（1986～1988），北京：地震出版社。

张肇诚、郑大林、徐京华等编，2000，中国震例（1989～1991），北京：地震出版社。

《中国地震年鉴》编纂委员会，1990，中国地震年鉴（1949～1981），北京：地震出版社。

Choy G. L. and J. L. Boatwright, 1995, Global patterns of radiated seismic energy and apparent stress. J. Geophys. Res. 100, 18205－18228.

Bautista, M. L. P. and K. Oike, 2000, Estimation of the magnitudes and epicenters of Philippine historical earthquakes, Tectonophys., 317, 137－169.

Engdahl, E. R., and A. Villasenor, 2002, Global Seismicity: 1900－1999, in W. H. K. Lee, H. Kanamori, P. C. Jennings, and C. Kisslinger (editors), International Handbook of Earthquake and Engineering Seismology, Part A, Chapter 41, Academic Press. p 665－690.

Gutenberg B. and C. F. Richter, 1956, Magnitude and energy of earthquakes. Ann. Geofis. 9, 1－15.

Hanks, T. C. and H. Kanamori, 1979, A moment magnitude scale. J. Geophys. Res. 84, 2348－2350.

Harry O. Wood and Frank Neumann, 1931, Modified Mercalli intensity scale of 1931, Bulletin of the Seismological Society of America, Vol. 21, No. 4, p 277－283.

Iida, Kumizi, Doak C. Cox, and George Pararas－Carayannis, 1967, Preliminary catalog of tsunamis occurring in the Pacific Ocean. University of Hawaii, Honolulu. p 274.

Miguel Saderra Maso, S. J., 1910, Catalogue of Violent and Destructive Earthquakes in the Philippines (1599－1909), Manila Bureau of Printing.

Paula K. Dunbar, Patricia A. Lockridge, and Lowell S. Whiteside, 1992, Catalog of significant earthquakes 2150 B. C. － 1991

A. D. , U. S. Dept. of Commerce, National Oceanic and Atmospheric Administration.
Shigehisa Nakamura, 1978, On Statistical Tsunami Risk of the Philippine, South East Asian Studies, 15 (4): 581 - 590.
Soloviev, S. L. , and Ch. N. Go. 1974, A Catalogue of Tsunamis on the Western Shore of the Pacific Ocean (173 - 1968). Nauka Publishing House, Moscow, USSR, p310.
Tatsuo Usami, 1979, Study of Historical Earthquakes in Japan, Bulletin of the Earthquake Research Institute, Vol. 54, p399 - 439.

致　谢

在本书的编辑和修订过程中，得到了丁国瑜院士、马宗晋院士、许绍燮院士、梅世蓉研究员、时振梁研究员、任金卫研究员、朱元清研究员、傅征祥研究员、赵俊猛研究员、汪素云研究员、金学申研究员、刁守中研究员、郑大林研究员、武宦英高级工程师等专家学者的真诚指导；在本项研究工作中，得到上海市地震局张骏局长、王建军副局长、李红芳副局长、王绍博副局长以及金胜处长的支持和帮助；在目录校对过程中，得到杨光亮博士、孙礼建硕士、董菲菲硕士、温燕林硕士、王俊非硕士、解昭娣博士等的支持，在此一并表示真诚的感谢！